May 18–22, 2015
Florence, Italy

Association for
Computing Machinery

*Advancing Computing as a Science & Profession*

# MobiSys'15

## Proceedings of the 13th Annual International Conference on
## Mobile Systems, Applications, and Services

*Sponsored by:*

**ACM SIGMobile**

*Incooperation with:*

**ACM SIGOPS**

*Supported by:*

**Hewlett-Packard, Google, IBM, Microsoft Research, & NSF**

Association for
Computing Machinery

*Advancing Computing as a Science & Profession*

**The Association for Computing Machinery**
**2 Penn Plaza, Suite 701**
**New York, New York 10121-0701**



**Notice to Past Authors of ACM-Published Articles**
ACM intends to create a complete electronic archive of all articles and/or other material previously published by ACM. If you have written a work that has been previously published by ACM in any journal or conference proceedings prior to 1978, or any SIG Newsletter at any time, and you do NOT want this work to appear in the ACM Digital Library, please inform permissions@acm.org, stating the title of the work, the author(s), and where and when published.

**ISBN:** 978-1-4503-3494-5 (Digital)

**ISBN:** 978-1-4503-3443-3 (Print)

Additional copies may be ordered prepaid from:

**ACM Order Department**
PO Box 30777
New York, NY 10087-0777, USA

Phone: 1-800-342-6626 (USA and Canada)
+1-212-626-0500 (Global)
Fax: +1-212-944-1318
E-mail: acmhelp@acm.org
Hours of Operation: 8:30 am – 4:30 pm ET

Printed in the USA

# General Chairs' Welcome

On behalf of the entire organizing committee, it is a great pleasure to welcome you to the 13th International Conference on Mobile Systems, Applications and Services – MobiSys 2015 in Florence, Italy.

The Program Chairs, Marco Gruteser and Jason Hong, have an excellent technical program lined up for you. I thank them, their Program Committee, and the external review committee for doing the heavy lifting on this front. We hope that you will enjoy the talks and have many stimulating discussions during your three days at this conference. The scientific program is enriched by our keynote presentations from Krishan Sabnani (Research VP at Bell Labs), and Deborah Estrin (Professor of Computer Science at Cornell Tech in New York City); which will outline the vision for the future of clouds and mobile data science.

In addition to the regular program, this year's MobiSys also includes a high quality program of videos, demos, posters and workshops. The video presentations are integrated with the technical presentations of the main track, and posters and demos will be presented at the end of the first day.

The workshop program consists of 5 workshops that will cover exciting topics in mobile Physical Analytics, mobile gaming, wearable computing, drone networks, mobile internet of things, mobile user interfaces, and mobile technologies applied to social sciences. The workshop program also includes a Ph.D. Forum that provides a friendly and supportive environment for doctoral students to present and discuss their dissertation work.

Last but not least, this year's MobiSys is co-located with WWW to enable community cross-pollination. I wish to thank Stefan Saroiu, Stefano Leonardi, the MobiSys Program Chairs, and the WWW Program Chairs for organizing a joint session and a joint keynote, which are open to attendees of both events.

We wish to thank the Organizing Committee members and the SigMobile leadership who have helped a lot during the conference preparation. Thank you all!

Finally, I wish to honor the memory of ACM MobiSys 2015 Co-Chair Gaetano Borriello, a dear friend and a leading member of our community. He will be greatly missed.

I sincerely hope that you will find your curiosity – as well as all of your senses – satisfied this week in Florence!

**Giovanni Pau**
*ACM MobiSys 2015 General Co-Chair*
*UPMC-LIP6*

# Program Chairs' Welcome

Welcome to MobiSys 2015, the 13th Conference on Mobile Systems, Applications, and Services. This year's technical program covers a wide and rich range of topics in mobile systems. The research themes include wearable computing, privacy and security, gaming, wireless networks, and more.

We are delighted to anchor the technical program with keynote talks by Dr. Krishan Sabnani and Dr. Deborah Estrin. Drs. Sabnani and Estrin have been leading researchers in Internet design, wireless networks, and sensing for over twenty years. In addition to the keynotes, we have an exciting technical program that includes 29 full-length technical papers chosen by the technical program committee (TPC).

This year, we had a record number of 219 submissions. To reduce the number of reviews each TPC member had to write, we augmented the TPC with an external review committee (ERC) of 30 experts. Most ERC members reviewed seven papers during the initial round of the review process.

Our review process consisted of three rounds. In the first round, all submissions received three reviews, each written by a member of the TPC or ERC. If a reviewer recommended that a paper be accepted, the paper advanced to the second round. In the second round, papers received two or more additional reviews. At the end of the second round, reviewers discussed each remaining paper online to determine whether it should advance to the third round of decisions. The third round of decisions occurred during an all-day face-to-face meeting of the TPC. By the conclusion of this meeting, the TPC had identified the 29 papers in the program. Finally, all accepted papers were shepherded by a TPC member to ensure that the final manuscripts met the standards of the committee. We also took strict precautions throughout the review process to avoid conflicts of interest.

Creating the technical program for MobiSys 2015 was a team effort, and we would like to thank the TPC members, ERC members, and shepherds who worked extremely hard reading papers and providing feedback to paper authors. We would also like to thank the authors for sending us a pool of very high-quality submissions.

We are also grateful to our colleagues who helped organize the conference, including the steering committee, the poster and demo chairs (Liqun Li, Ilias Leontiadis, Justin Manweiler, Andreas Terzis), the publicity chairs (Ling-Jyh Chen, Christos Efstratiou, Robert LiKamWa), the publication chair (Marco Levorato), the workshop co-chairs (Rajesh Balan, Andrea Passarella, Xia Zhou), the travel grants co-chairs (Jun Bi, Tamer Nadeem), the industrial liaison chair (Marco Magnarosa), and the web chair (Francesco Bronzino).

We would especially like to thank the general chairs, Gaetano Borriello and Giovanni Pau, and the local arrangements chair Gustavo Marfia. Their handling of the conference logistics was invaluable. We are also indebted to Justin Manweiler, who, in his role has Hotmobile general chair, handled the logistics of the co-located MobiSys technical program committee meeting. Finally, we thank our sponsors, ACM SIGMOBILE, and our supporters, HP, Google, Microsoft Research, IBM, and the National Science Foundation. We hope that you will find the technical program exciting and thought provoking, and that the conference will provide you with a valuable opportunity to share experiences and ideas with others from around the world.

Lastly, we would like to dedicate this year's Mobisys program in remembrance of Gaetano Borriello. Gaetano was not only an active member of our community, but also a mentor and friend to many of us. We will remember him for his warmth, his humor, his pioneering work, his leadership, and his kindness. He will be greatly missed.

**Marco Gruteser**
*MobiSys '15 Program Co-Chair*
*Rutgers University, USA*

**Jason Hong**
*MobiSys '15 Program Co-Chair*
*Carnegie Mellon University, USA*

# Table of Contents


## MobiSys'15 Organization ........ xiii

## MobiSys'15 Sponsors & Supporters ........ xv

## Session 1: Sensing and Applications

- **Invisible Sensing of Vehicle Steering with Smartphones** ........ 1
  Dongyao Chen, Kyong-Tak Cho, Sihui Han, Zhizhuo Jin, Kang G. Shin *(University of Michigan)*
- **Turning a Mobile Device into a Mouse in the Air** ........ 15
  Sangki Yun, Yi-Chao Chen, Lili Qiu *(The University of Texas at Austin)*
- **Tracking Keystrokes Using Wireless Signals** ........ 31
  Bo Chen, Vivek Yenamandra, Kannan Srinivasan *(The Ohio State University)*
- **Contactless Sleep Apnea Detection on Smartphones** ........ 45
  Rajalakshmi Nandakumar, Shyamnath Gollakota, Nathaniel Watson *(University of Washington)*

## Session 2: Mobile Advertising

- **MDdScope: Characterizing Mobile In-App Targeted Ads** ........ 59
  Suman Nath *(Microsoft Research)*
- **AdAttester: Secure Online Mobile Advertisement Attestation Using TrustZone** ........ 75
  Wenhao Li, Haibo Li, Haibo Chen, Yubin Xia *(Shanghai Jiao Tong University)*
- **Efficient Privilege De-Escalation for Ad Libraries in Mobile Apps** ........ 89
  Bin Liu *(Samsung Research America)*, Bin Liu *(Carnegie Mellon University)*,
  Hongxia Jin *(Samsung Research America)*, Ramesh Govindan *(University of Southern California)*

## Session 3: Mobility, Gaming, and Performance

- **GameOn: p2p Gaming on Public Transport** ........ 105
  Nairan Zhang *(University of Wisconsin-Madison)*,
  Youngki Lee, Meera Radhakrishnan, Rajesh Krishna Balan *(Singapore Management University)*
- **Kahawai: High-Quality Mobile Gaming Using GPU Offload** ........ 121
  Eduardo Cuervo, Alec Wolman *(Microsoft Research)*, Landon P. Cox *(Duke University)*,
  Kiron Lebeck *(University of Washington)*, Ali Razeen *(Duke University)*,
  Stefan Saroiu, Madanlal Musuvathi *(Microsoft Research)*
- **Accelerating Mobile Applications through Flip-Flop Replication** ........ 137
  Mark S. Gordon, David Ke Hong, Peter M. Chen, Jason Flinn,
  Scott Mahlke, Zhuoqing Morley Mao *(University of Michigan)*
- **Outatime: Using Speculation to Enable Low-Latency Continuous Interaction for Mobile Cloud Gaming** ........ 151
  Kyungmin Lee *(University of Michigan)*,
  David Chu, Eduardo Cuervo, Johannes Kopf *(Microsoft Research)*,
  Yury Degtyarev *(St. Petersburg Polytechnic University)*,
  Sergey Grizan *(Siberian Federal University)*,
  Alec Wolman *(Microsoft Research)*, Jason Flinn *(University of Michigan)*

## Session 4: Cameras

- **RollingLight: Enabling Line-of-Sight Light-to-Camera Communications** ........ 167
  Hui-Yu Lee, Hao-Min Lin, Yu-Lin Wei, Hsin-I Wu,
  Hsin-Mu Tsai *(National Taiwan University & Intel-NTU Connected Context Computing Center, Taiwan)*,
  Kate Ching-Ju Lin *(Academia Sinica & Intel-NTU Connected Context Computing Center, Taiwan)*

- **InFrame++: Achieve Simultaneous Screen-Human Viewing and Hidden Screen-Camera Communication** .......... 181
  Anran Wang *(Beihang University)*, Zhuoran Li, Chunyi Peng *(The Ohio State University)*, Guobin Shen *(Microsoft Research, China)*, Gan Fang *(The Ohio State University)*, Bing Zeng *(University of Electronic Science and Technology of China)*
- **Real-Time Screen-Camera Communication Behind Any Scene** .......... 197
  Tianxing Li, Chuankai An, Xinran Xiao, Andrew T. Campbell, Xia Zhou *(Dartmouth College)*
- **Starfish: Efficient Concurrency Support for Computer Vision Applications** .......... 213
  Robert LiKamWa, Lin Zhong *(Rice University)*

## Session 5: Wearables

- **Typingring: A Wearable Ring Platform for Text Input** .......... 227
  Shahriar Nirjon, Jeremy Gummeson, Dan Gelb, Kyu-Han Kim *(Hewlett-Packard Labs)*
- **U-Wear: Software-Defined Ultrasonic Networking for Wearable Devices** .......... 241
  G. Enrico Santagati, Tommaso Melodia *(Northeastern University, Boston)*
- **LookUp: Enabling Pedestrian Safety Services via Shoe Sensing** .......... 257
  Shubham Jain *(Rutgers University)*, Carlo Borgiattino *(Politecnico di Torino)*, Yanzhi Ren *(Stevens Institute of Technology, Hoboken, NJ)*, Marco Gruteser *(Rutgers University)*, Yingying Chen *(Stevens Institute of Technology, Hoboken, NJ)*, Carla-Fabiana Chiasserini *(Politecnico di Torino)*
- **ZOE: A Cloud-less Dialog-enabled Continuous Sensing Wearable Exploiting Heterogeneous Computation** .......... 273
  Nicholas D. Lane *(Bell Labs)*, Petko Georgiev, Cecilia Mascolo *(University of Cambridge)*, Ying Gao *(Intel Research)*

## Session 6: Understanding and Improving Mobile App Capabilities

- **Reducing Smartphone Application Delay through Read/Write Isolation** .......... 287
  David T. Nguyen,Gang Zhou *(College of William and Mary)*, Guoliang Xing *(Michigan State University)*, Xin Qi, Zijiang Hao, Ge Peng, Qing Yang *(College of William and Mary)*
- **AccelWord: Energy Efficient Hotword Detection through Accelerometer** .......... 301
  Li Zhang, Parth H. Pathak, Muchen Wu, Yixin Zhao, Prasant Mohapatra *(University of California, Davis)*
- **Wearables Can Afford: Light-weight Indoor Positioning with Visible Light** .......... 317
  Zhice Yang, Zeyu Wang *(Hong Kong University of Science and Technology)*, Jiansong Zhang *(Microsoft Research Asia)*, Chenyu Huang *(Wuhan University)*, Qian Zhang *(Hong Kong University of Science and Technology)*
- **OverLay: Practical Mobile Augmented Reality** .......... 331
  Puneet Jain *(Duke University)*, Justin Manweiler *(IBM Research)*, Romit Roy Choudhury *(University of Illinois)*

## Session 7: Joint WWW-MobiSys Session

- **Visually Fingerprinting Humans without Face Recognition** .......... 345
  He Wang *(University of Illinois at Urbana-Champaign)*, Xuan Bao *(Samsung Research America)*, Romit Roy Choudhury *(University of Illinois at Urbana-Champaign)*, Srihari Nelakuditi *(University of South Carolina)*
- **Analyzing the Use of Quick Response Codes in the Wild** .......... 359
  Adam Lerner *(University of Washington)*, Alisha Saxena *(Massachusetts Institute of Technology)*, Kirk Ouimet, Ben Turley *(Scan, Inc.)*, Anthony Vance *(Brigham Young University)*, Tadayoshi Kohno, Franziska Roesner *(University of Washington)*

## Session 8: Mobility and Networking


- **Beyond the Radio: Illuminating the Higher Layers of Mobile Networks** .................................. 375
  Narseo Vallina-Rodriguez, Srikanth Sundaresan *(ICSI)*, Christian Kreibich *(ICSI & Lastline)*,
  Nicholas Weaver, Vern Paxson *(ICSI & UC Berkeley)*
- **Mobilyzer: An Open Platform for Controllable Mobile Network Measurements** .................. 389
  Ashkan Nikravesh, Hongyi Yao, Shichang Xu *(University of Michigan)*,
  David Choffnes *(Northeastern University)*, Z. Morley Mao *(University of Michigan)*
- **Energy Efficient WiFi Display** .................................................................................................. 405
  Chi Zhang, Xinyu Zhang *(University of Wisconsin-Madison)*, Ranveer Chandra *(Microsoft Research)*
- **Practicalizing Delay-Tolerant Mobile Apps with Cedos** .............................................................. 419
  YoungGyoun Moon, Donghwi Kim, Younghwan Go, Yeongjin Kim, Yung Yi, Song Chong,
  KyoungSoo Park *(Korea Advanced Institute of Science and Technology)*


## Video Presentations


- **Video: Lookup!: Enabling Pedestrian Safety Services via Shoe Sensing** ............................. 435
  Shubham Jain *(Rutgers University)*, Carlo Borgiattino *(Politecnico di Torino)*,
  Yanzhi Ren *(Stevens Institute of Technology)*, Marco Gruteser *(Rutgers University)*,
  Yingying Chen *(Stevens Institute of Technology)*, Carla Fabiana Chiasserini *(Politecnico di Torino)*
- **Video: Lightweight Visible Light Communication for Indoor Positioning** ............................. 437
  Zeyu Wang, *n*Zhice Yang *(Hong Kong University of Science and Technology)*,
  Jiansong Zhang *(Microsoft Research Asia)*, Chenyu Huang *(Wuhan Univeristy)*,
  Qian Zhang *(Hong Kong University of Science and Technology)*


## Demo Presentations


- **Demo: Mobile Crowdsensing of Road Surface Roughness** ...................................................... 439
  Giacomo Alessandroni, Alessandro Bogliolo, Alberto Carini, Saverio Delpriori, Valerio Freschi,
  Lorenz Klopfenstein, Emanuele Lattanzi, Gioele Luchetti, Brendan Paolini,
  Andrea Seraghiti *(DiSBeF - University of Urbino)*
- **Demo: D2D Rescue of Overloaded Cellular Channels** ............................................................... 441
  Farid Benbadis *(Thales Communications & Security)*,
  Filippo Rebecchi *(Thales Communications & Security and LIP6/CNRS – UPMC Sorbonne Universités)*,
  Florian Cosnier *(Thales Communications & Security)*,
  Matteo Sammarco, Marcelo Dias de Amorim *(LIP6/CNRS – UPMC Sorbonne Universités)*,
  Vania Conana *(Thales Communications & Security)*
- **Demo: Irides: Attaining Quality, Responsiveness and Mobility for Virtual Reality Head-mounted Displays** ........................................................... 443
  Yury Degtyarev *(St. Petersburg Polytechnic University)*,
  Eduardo Cuervo, David Chu *(Microsoft Research)*
- **Demo: Using Wearables to Learn from Human Dynamics** ....................................................... 445
  Sébastien Faye, Raphael Frank *(University of Luxembourg)*
- **Demo: Breathing-Based Text Input for Mobile Phones** .............................................................. 447
  Jackson Feijó Filho, Thiago Valle, Wilson Prata *(Nokia Technology Institute)*
- **Demo: Continuous Emotional Status in Mobile-Mediated Communications** ........................ 449
  Jackson Feijó Filho, Wilson Prata, Thiago Valle *(Nokia Technology Institute)*
- **Demo: Mobile Software Emotions Logging: Towards an Automatic Usability Evaluation** .................................................................... 451
  Jackson Feijó Filho, Wilson Prata, Thiago Valle *(Nokia Technology Institute)*
- **Demo: TouchCom - Creating Real Excalibur Experience with Body Touch Communication** ............................................................................ 453
  Yawhuei Lam *(ETH Zurich)*, Virag Varga *(Disney Research Zurich & ETH Zurich)*,
  Lito Kriara *(Disney Research Zurich)*, Thomas Gross *(ETH Zurich)*,
  Stefan Mangold *(Disney Research Zurich)*

- **Demo: Real-Time Screen-Camera Communication Behind Any Scene** ................................ 455
  Tianxing Li, Chuankai An, Xinran Xiao, Andrew T. Campbell, Xia Zhou *(Dartmouth College)*
- **Demo: Energy Harvesting Using Everyday Objects** ................................ 457
  Adiyan Mujibiya, Junji Torii *(Rakuten, Inc.)*
- **Demo: NOMAD: An Edge Cloud Platform for Hyper-Responsive Mobile Apps** ................................ 459
  Andreas Pamboris *(Imperial College London)*, Miguel Báguena *(Universitat Politècnica de València)*, Alexander L. Wolf *(Imperial College London)*, Pietro Manzoni *(Universitat Politècnica de València)*, Peter Pietzuch *(Imperial College London)*
- **Demo: Bringing the Internet of Toys to Life** ................................ 461
  Virag Varga *(Disney Research Zurich & ETH Zurich)*, Lito Kriara, Vladimir Vukadinovic *(Disney Research Zurich)*, Thomas Gross *(ETH Zurich)*, Stefan Mangold *(Disney Research Zurich)*
- **Demo: Achieving Simultaneous Screen-Human Viewing and Hidden Screen-Camera Communication** ................................ 463
  Anran Wang *(Beihang University)*, Zhuoran Li, Gan Fang, Chunyi Peng *(The Ohio State University)*, Guobin Shen *(Miscrosoft Research, China)*, Bing Zeng *(University of Electronic Science and Technology of China)*
- **Demo: Lightweight Visible Light Communication for Indoor Positioning** ................................ 465
  Zeyu Wang, Zhice Yang *(Hong Kong University of Science and Technology)*, Jiansong Zhang *(Microsoft Research Asia)*, Chenyu Huang *(Wuhan University)*, Qian Zhang *(Hong Kong University of Science and Technology)*
- **Demo: Mobilyzer: Mobile Network Measurement Made Easy** ................................ 467
  Shichang Xu, Ashkan Nikravesh, Hongyi Yao *(University of Michigan)*, David Choffnes *(Northeastern University)*, Z. Morley Mao *(University of Michigan)*
- **Demo: Turning a Mobile Device into a Mouse in the Air** ................................ 469
  Sangki Yun, Yi-Chao Chen, Wenguang Mao, Lili Qiu *(The University of Texas at Austin)*
- **Demo: Finger and Hand Gesture Recognition Using Smartwatch** ................................ 471
  Yixin Zhao, Parth H. Pathak, Chao Xu, Prasant Mohapatra *(University of California, Davis)*


## Poster Presentations


- **Poster: bPart - A Small and Versatile Bluetooth Low Energy Sensor Platform for Mobile Sensing** ................................ 473
  Matthias Berning, Matthias Budde, Till Riedel, Michael Beigl *(Karlsruhe Institute of Technology)*
- **Poster: Detecting if a Smartphone is Indoors or Outdoors with Ultrasounds** ................................ 475
  Igor Bisio, Alessandro Delfino, Fabio Lavagetto *(University of Genoa)*
- **Poster: Swarming Drones Can Connect You to the Network** ................................ 477
  Albert Y. Chung, Jongtack Jung, Kangho Kim, Hyung Kyu Lee, Jiyeon Lee, Suk Kyu Lee, Seungho Yoo, Hwangnam Kim *(Korea University)*
- **Poster: Constructing a Unique Profile for Mobile User Identification in Location Recommendation Systems** ................................ 479
  Muawya H. Sarnoub Eldaw, Mark Levene, George Roussos *(Birkbeck, University of London)*
- **Poster: Detection of Cyberbullying in a Mobile Social Network: Systems Issues** ................................ 481
  Homa Hosseinmardi, Sabrina Arredondo Mattson, Rahat Ibn Rafiq, Richard Han, Qin Lv, Shivakant Mishra *(University of Colorado Boulder)*
- **Poster: A Hybrid Indoor Audio Localization System** ................................ 483
  Lito Kriara, Giorgio Corbellini, Vladimir Vukadinovic *(Disney Research Zurich)*, Ruben Kaelin, Roman Frigg *(Disney Research Zurich & ETH Zurich)*, Stefan Mangold *(Disney Research Zurich)*
- **Poster: TVisor – A Practical and Lightweight Mobile Red-Green Dual-OS Architecture** ................................ 485
  Wenhao Li, Liang Liang, Mingyang Ma, Yubin Xia, Haibo Chen *(Shanghai Jiao Tong University)*

- **Poster: A Continuous and Noninvasive User Authentication System for Google Glass** ........ 487
  Ge Peng, David T. Nguyen, Gang Zhou *(College of William and Mary),*
  Shuangquan Wang *(Institute of Computing Technology, Chinese Academy of Sciences)*
- **Poster: A Context Simulation Harness for Realistic Mobile App Testing** ........ 489
  Manoj R. Rege, Vlado Handziski, Adam Wolisz *(Technische Universität Berlin)*
- **Poster: Localized Content for Village Schools** ........ 491
  Morgan Vigil *(University of California, Santa Barbara),*
  David Johnson *(Center for Scientific and Industrial Research, South Africa),*
  Elizabeth Belding *(University of California, Santa Barbara)*
- **Poster: Context-Triggered Mobile Network Measurement** ........ 493
  Shichang Xu, Ashkan Nikravesh, Hongyi Yao *(University of Michigan),*
  David R. Choffnes *(Northeastern University),* Z. Morley Mao *(University of Michigan)*
- **Poster: Emergency Management Using SHERLOCK** ........ 495
  Roberto Yus, Eduardo Mena *(University of Zaragoza)*
- **Poster: Location Verification and Recovery for Mobile In-Vehicle Applications** ........ 497
  Kexiong (Curtis) Zeng, Yanzhi Dou, Yaling Yang *(Virginia Tech),* Ranveer Chandra *(Microsoft Research)*

**Author Index** ........ 499

# MobiSys 2015 – The Thirteenth International Conference on Mobile Systems, Applications, & Services Organization

| | |
|---|---|
| **General Co-chairs** | Gaetano Borriello *(University of Washington, USA)*<br>Giovanni Pau *(UPMC-LIP6, France / UCLA, USA)* |
| **Technical Program Co-chairs** | Marco Gruteser *(Rutgers University, USA)*<br>Jason Hong *(Carnegie Mellon University, USA)* |
| **Local Arrangements Chair** | Gustavo Marfia *(Università di Bologna, Italy)* |
| **Workshop Co-chairs** | Rajesh Balan *(SMU, Singapore)*<br>Andrea Passarella *(CNR, Italy)*<br>Xia Zhou *(Dartmouth College, USA)* |
| **Posters/Demos/Video Co-Chairs** | Liqun Li *(Microsoft Research Asia, China)*<br>Ilias Leontiadis *(Telefonica Research, Spain)*<br>Justin Manweiler *(IBM Research, USA)*<br>Andreas Terzis *(Google, USA)* |
| **Publication Chair** | Marco Levorato *(University of California, Irvine, USA)* |
| **Publicity Co-Chairs** | Ling-Jyh Chen *(Academia Sinica, Taiwan)*<br>Christos Efstratiou *(University of Kent, UK)*<br>Robert LiKamWa *(Rice University, USA)* |
| **Industrial Liaison Chair** | Marco Magnarosa *(Cubit Innovation Labs, Italy)* |
| **Travel Grants Co-Chairs** | Jun Bi *(Tsinghua University, China)*<br>Tamer Nadeem *(Old Dominion University, USA)* |
| **Web Chair** | Francesco Bronzino *(Rutgers University, USA)* |
| **Technical Program Committee** | Yuvraj Agarwal *(Carnegie Mellon University, USA)*<br>Mary Baker *(HP Labs, USA)*<br>Rajesh Balan *(Singapore Management University, Singapore)*<br>Ramon Caceres *(Google, USA)*<br>Hao Chen *(University of California, Davis, USA)*<br>Yingying (Jennifer) Chen *(Stevens Institute of Technology, USA)*<br>Romit Roy Choudhury *(University of Illinois at Urbana-Champaign, USA)*<br>David Chu *(Microsoft Research, USA)*<br>Landon Cox *(Duke University, USA)* |

**Technical Program Committee (continued)**

Peter Druschel *(MPI-SWS, Germany)*
Prabal Dutta *(University of Michigan, USA)*
Deepak Ganesan *(University of Massachusetts at Amherst, USA)*
Shyam Gollakota *(University of Washington, USA)*
Ben Greenstein *(Google, USA)*
Robin Kravets *(University of Illinois at Urbana-Champaign, USA)*
Anthony LaMarca *(Intel Labs, USA)*
Janne Lindqvist *(Rutgers University, USA)*
Yunxin Liu *(Microsoft Research Asia, China)*
Z. Morley Mao *(University of Michigan, USA)*
Margaret Martonosi *(Princeton University, USA)*
Cecilia Mascolo *(University of Cambridge, USA)*
Suman Nath *(Microsoft Research, USA)*
Chunyi Peng *(The Ohio State University, USA)*
Bodhi Priyantha *(Microsoft Research, USA)*
Mahadev Satyanarayanan *(Carnegie Mellon University, USA)*
James Scott *(Microsoft Research, UK)*
Junehwa Song *(KAIST, South Korea)*
Tam Vu *(University of Colorado, Denver, USA)*
Lin Zhong *(Rice University, USA)*

**External Review Committee**

Ashwin Ashok
Fan Bai
Alastair Beresford
Octav Chipara
Eduardo Cuervo Laffaye
Samir Das
Nigel Davies
Jeremy Gummeson
Charlie Hu
Wenjun Hu
Minkyong Kim
Nic Lane
Youngki Lee
Mo Li
Qin (Christine) Lv
Justin Manweiler
Tamer Nadeem
Vishnu Navda
Srihari Nelakuditi
Lenin Ravindranath Sivalingam
Souvik Sen
Kannan Srinivasan
Andreas Terzis
Michael Tsai
Kamin Whitehouse
Guoliang Xing
Chenren Xu
Wenyuan Xu
Jie Yang
Pei Zhang

# MobiSys 2015 Sponsors and Supporters

**Sponsor**

sigmobile

**In cooperation with**

acm SIGOPS
ACM SIG on Operating Systems

**Silver Supporter**

hp

**Bronze Supporters**

Google

IBM

Microsoft Research

**Travel Grant Support**

NSF

# Invisible Sensing of Vehicle Steering with Smartphones

Dongyao Chen, Kyong-Tak Cho, Sihui Han, Zhizhuo Jin, and Kang G. Shin
Real-Time Computing Laboratory
Department of Electrical Engineering and Computer Science
University of Michigan – Ann Arbor, U.S.A
{chendy, ktcho, sihuihan, jzzfrank, kgshin}@umich.edu

## ABSTRACT

Detecting how a vehicle is steered and then alarming drivers in real time is of utmost importance to the vehicle and the driver's safety, since fatal accidents are often caused by dangerous steering. Existing solutions for detecting dangerous maneuvers are implemented either in only high-end vehicles or on smartphones as mobile applications. However, most of them rely on the use of cameras, the performance of which is seriously constrained by their high visibility requirement. Moreover, such an over/sole-reliance on the use of cameras can be a distraction to the driver.

To alleviate these problems, we develop a vehicle steering detection middleware called `V-Sense` which can run on commodity smartphones without additional sensors or infrastructure support. Instead of using cameras, the core of `V-Sense` senses a vehicle's steering by only utilizing non-vision sensors on the smartphone. We design and evaluate algorithms for detecting and differentiating various vehicle maneuvers, including lane-changes, turns, and driving on curvy roads. Since `V-Sense` does not rely on use of cameras, its detection of vehicle steering is not affected by the (in)visibility of road objects or other vehicles. We first detail the design, implementation and evaluation of `V-Sense` and then demonstrate its practicality with two prevalent use cases: camera-free steering detection and fine-grained lane guidance. Our extensive evaluation results show that `V-Sense` is accurate in determining and differentiating various steering maneuvers, and is thus useful for a wide range of safety-assistance applications without additional sensors or infrastructure.

## Categories and Subject Descriptors

H.4 [**Information Systems Applications**]: :Miscellaneous

## Keywords

Camera-free sensing, vehicle steering detection, driving assistant application, smartphone


*MobiSys'15*, May 18–22, 2015, Florence, Italy.

http://dx.doi.org/10.1145/2742647.2742659.

(a) Lighting (b) Weather (c) Pavement (d) Placement

Figure 1: Visibility distortion under different conditions

## 1. INTRODUCTION

Automobiles bring a wide range of conveniences as well as fatalities. In 2012, the reported number of fatalities from road accidents was 30,800 in the U.S. alone [4]. Of these fatalities, 23.1% involved lane control — i.e., merging or changing lanes or driving on curvy roads — and 7.7% involved turning maneuvers, i.e., turning left/right or making U-turns. In total, 30.8% of the fatalities were related to vehicle steering maneuvers.[1]

As most of these fatalities had resulted from the driver's careless or erroneous steering, those accidents could have been minimized or prevented if effective safety mechanisms had been deployed in the vehicles. There has been an ongoing push for incorporating electronic safety features in the vehicles to assist drivers' steering.

Steering-assistance systems, such as lane-departure warning or lane-keeping assistance, are the typical examples. They all exploit the advanced built-in sensors (e.g., cameras, radars, and infrared sensors) to detect the lane for driving assistance [13]. However, since they require special sensors which are only available on recent high-end cars, such safety solutions cannot be applied to a wide range of type/year models of cars.

[1] We refer to *steering maneuvers* as either changing lanes, turning left/right, or driving on curvy roads.

To overcome such limitations, instead of using built-in vehicle sensors, efforts are being made to exploit the sensors in smartphones to assist drivers in their steering maneuvers. At one end of the spectrum of such applications, cameras have been used widely. The front/rear cameras of a smartphone are exploited to capture the images of road objects (e.g., traffic lanes, curb, and the preceding vehicle) which are then analyzed with image processing [8, 20, 29]. Although such systems claim that smartphone cameras are sufficient in assisting the driver, they have limitations in terms of computational overhead and inaccuracy. The accuracy of camera-based approaches depends on *visibility* and can thus be infeasible, depending on the conditions listed below and shown in Fig. 1.

- **Lighting**: The functionality of camera-based approaches cannot be guaranteed in case of insufficient light, especially at night time.
- **Weather**: Rainy or snowy weather will make roads waterly or icy, and will thus distort the light reflection, rendering it difficult to identify road objects.
- **Pavement**: Bad pavement conditions will distort the shape of road objects and will thus cause false or miss detections.
- **Camera placement**: Placing the phone at a location where the camera cannot capture the road objects (e.g., in the driver's pocket), will diminish the feasibility of the camera-based approach.

The other end of the spectrum is to not use cameras. Smartphone sensors, such as gyroscope, accelerometer, magnetometer, etc., can be exploited to detect the vehicle steering maneuvers and thus perform the same steering-assistance functionalities that would have been achieved with use of cameras [25, 28]. These approaches have advantages of requiring much less computational resources and power, and also being immune to visibility distortions. However, it is known to be very difficult to differentiate the steering maneuvers, which is one of the main reasons for camera-based approaches being most prevalent.

In this paper, we propose `V-Sense`, a novel vehicle steering sensing middleware on smartphones, which overcomes the limitations and difficulties inherent in the existing camera-based and camera-free approaches. `V-Sense` is a camera-free middleware that can be utilized for various applications. It utilizes built-in Inertial Measurement Units (IMUs) on smartphones to detect various steering maneuvers of a vehicle. Specifically, `V-Sense` determines the changes in the angle of vehicle heading (i.e., steering) and the corresponding displacement during a steering maneuver. `V-Sense` classifies steering maneuvers into different types, such as turn, lane change, driving on curvy roads, etc., and exploits the classified results for various applications. We will elaborate on these applications in the following sections.

The contributions of this paper are three-fold:

- Design of `V-Sense`, an all-time vehicle steering sensing middleware which does not rely on use of cameras;
- Detection and differentiation of various steering maneuvers by only utilizing a smartphone's built-in sensors; and
- Proposal of two driving-assistance applications — i.e., careless steering detection and fine-grained lane guidance — which are based on `V-Sense` functionalities.

The remainder of this paper is organized as follows. Section 2 describes the motivation behind the design of `V-Sense`. Section 3 details the overall system and functionalities of `V-Sense`. We first evaluate the performance of `V-Sense` in Section 4 and then show two different applications of `V-Sense` in Sections 5 and 6. After reviewing the related work in Section 7, we finally conclude the paper in Section 8.

## 2. MOTIVATION

Without relying on use of cameras and by only utilizing non-vision sensors on commodity smartphones, `V-Sense` can detect various steering maneuvers, such as left/right turns, changing lanes, or driving on curvy roads. How could such functionalities of `V-Sense` without using cameras at all, assist the driver in terms of both convenience and safety? Can it actually help in reducing fatalities from road accidents? Given below are two proof-of-concept applications of `V-Sense` that enhance safety and convenience of the driver's steering.

### *Careless steering detection.*

Careless steering — changing lanes or making turns *without* using the turn signal on the car — is one of the main reasons for steering-related fatalities. A study from the Society of Automotive Engineers (SAE) unveiled that people in the U.S. forget to use their turn signals 2 billion times each day in total, or roughly 750 billion times per year. Based on such figures, SAE argued that about 2 millions of accidents can be prevented by eliminating turn signal neglects or careless steering [27]. In this application, `V-Sense` provides the functionalities required for detecting such careless maneuver. By combining lane-change detection via `V-Sense` and turn signal sound detection — which is designed based on a matched filter — the application determines whether the steering maneuver was accompanied with a turn signal, i.e., detecting whether the steering was careless or not.

### *Fine-grained lane guidance.*

Existing navigation applications (e.g., Google map) provide information on *which* lane to stay on for preparing the next maneuver, i.e., indicating the correct lane. However, they lack functionalities of telling *whether* the vehicle is actually on that lane. If the driver fails to stay on the correct lane before its next maneuver, s/he would have to reroute or, in the worst case, take abrupt and thus dangerous lane changes to that lane. In order to provide assist the driver to determine whether the vehicle is on the correct lane, `V-Sense` provides the functionalities for fine-grained lane guidance. By integrating `V-Sense` and existing navigation systems, one can determine which lane the driver is currently on, and whether the lane is correct or not, without using cameras.

## 3. SYSTEM DESIGN

This section details the design and functionalities of `V-Sense`. First, we describe how IMUs on smartphones are utilized to determine whether the vehicle is making turn, changing lane, or driving on a curvy road. Then, we show

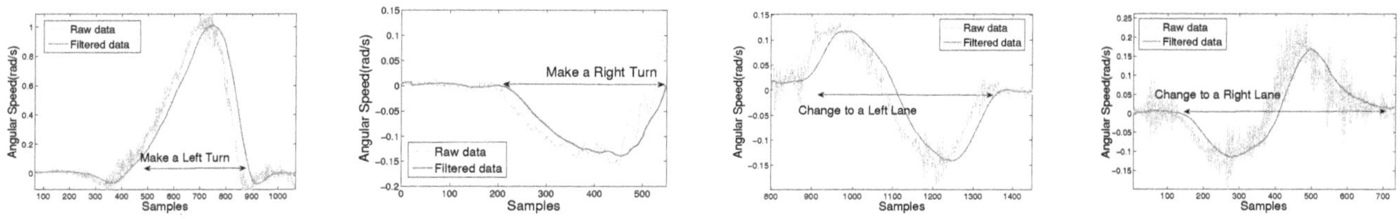


(a) Make a left turn (b) Make a right turn (c) Change to a left lane (d) Change to a right lane

Figure 3: Gyroscope readings when the vehicle makes a left/right turn or left/right lane changing.

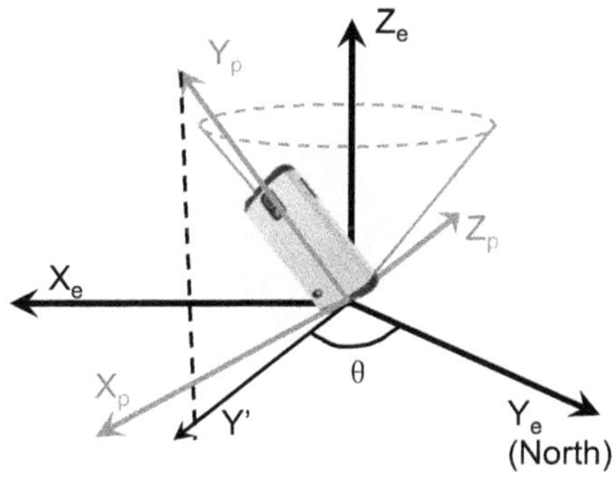


Figure 2: Align the phone coordinate system with the geo-frame coordinate system. This figure was borrowed from [30].

how V-Sense classifies such different vehicle steering maneuvers based on the detection results.

## 3.1 Coordinate Alignment

Since the phone's coordinate changes over time, in order to maintain the consistency of analysis, we align the smartphone coordinate ($\{X_p, Y_p, Z_p\}$) with the geo-frame coordinate ($\{X_e, Y_e, Z_e\}$), as shown in Fig. 2. This allows us to simplify the change of the readings from 3 degrees of freedom (DoFs) to 1 DoF. The key idea is that with the measurements of the direction of the applied gravity to the smartphone ($Y$), the smartphone coordinate can be fixed within a cone. Then, combining the result with the angle ($\theta$) derived from the magnetometer readings and the thus-determined rotation matrix, the smartphone coordinate can be aligned with the geo-frame coordinate. We refer interested readers to [30] for detailed formulation of the rotation matrix.

## 3.2 Bump Detection

When a car changes its direction via steering (e.g., changing lanes, making turns, and driving on curvy roads), the Z-axis gyroscope reading (i.e., yaw rate reading) on the phone can be utilized to represent the vehicle angular speed of that change of direction. Fig. 3 illustrates the Z-axis gyroscope measurements from the phone during a right/left turn, and changing to a right/left lane, respectively. During a left turn, a counter-clockwise rotation around the Z-axis occurs and thus generates positive readings (i.e., a positive bump), whereas during a right turn, a clockwise rotation occurs and thus generates negative readings (i.e., a negative bump).[2] Similarly, during a left lane change, a positive bump is followed by a negative bump, whereas during a right lane change, the opposite occurs.

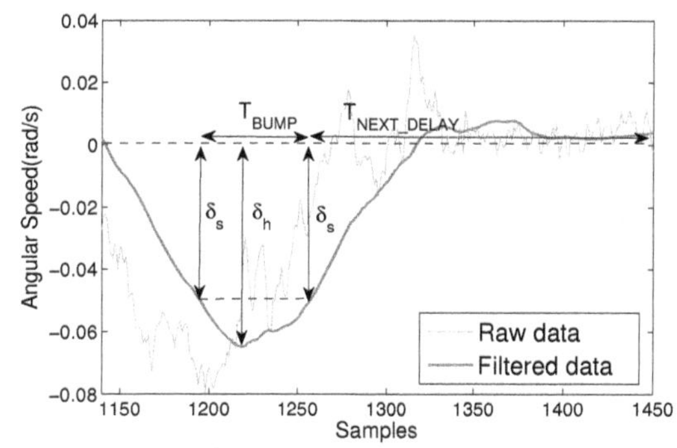


(a) One bump: a turn

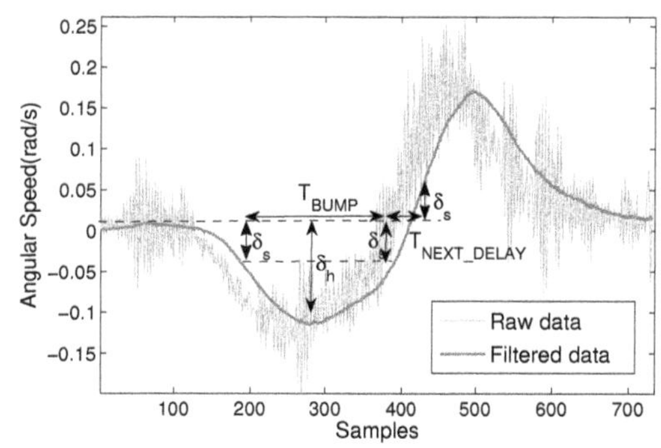


(b) Two consecutive bumps: lane change

Figure 4: Statistical features of bumps in gyroscope reading during different steering maneuvers

Based on this observation, we can infer that by detecting *bumps* in the Z-axis gyroscope readings, we can determine whether the vehicle has made a turn or has changed a lane. The other steering maneuver, i.e., driving on a curvy road, will show a similar *shape* but with a different *size* in terms of width and height of the bumps. We will elaborate on how V-Sense differentiates such steering maneuvers in Section 3.3.

We adopt a moving average filter to remove noise from the raw gyroscope readings. The delay parameter of the filter is set to 60 samples which correspond to 0.05 second in the time domain. Such a decision was made based on

[2] We refer to such a temporal rise/drop, or vice versa, of the yaw rate as *bumps*.

**Algorithm 1** Algorithm for Detecting Bumps

**Inputs:**
  State, $Y$ (Yaw rate), System parameters
**if** State = *No-Bump* and $|Y| > \delta_s$ **then**
  (Start of 1st bump)
  State ← *One-Bump*
  Record the start point of a possible bump
**else if** State = *One-Bump* and $|Y| < \delta_s$ **then**
  Record the end point of a possible bump
  **if** bump is valid **then**
    State ← *Waiting-for-Bump*
  **else**
    State ← *No-Bump*
  **end if**
**else if** State = *Waiting-for-Bump* **then**
  $T_{dwell}$ ← State dwell duration
  **if** $T_{dwell} < T_{NEXT\_DELAY}$ and $|Y| > \delta_s$ **then**
    (Start of 2nd bump)
    **if** 2nd bump is valid **then**
      Two valid bumps → **"Lane change"**
    **else**
      One valid bump → **"Turn"**
    **end if**
    State ← *No-Bump*
  **else if** $T_{dwell} > T_{NEXT\_DELAY}$ **then**
    One valid bump → Turn
    State ← *No-Bump*
  **else**
    Continue in *Waiting-for-Bump* state
  **end if**
**else**
  Continue in current state
**end if**

our experimental observation: it is short but good enough to extract the waveform of the bumps.

As shown in Fig. 4, we define four system parameters: $\delta_s, \delta_h$, $T_{BUMP}$, and $T_{NEXT\_DELAY}$. To reduce false positives and differentiate the bumps from jitters, a bump should satisfy the following three constraints for its validity: (1) all the readings during a bump should be larger than $\delta_s$, (2) the largest value of a bump should be no less than $\delta_h$, and (3) the duration of a bump should be no less than $T_{BUMP}$.

Based on these constraints of a valid bump, we designed an algorithm as shown in Algorithm 1, which keeps running when `V-Sense` operates. There are three states in the bump detection algorithm: *No-Bump*, *One-Bump*, and *Waiting-for-Bump*.

In *No-Bump* state, we continuously monitor the Z-axis gyroscope readings, i.e., yaw rate. When the absolute value of the measured yaw rate reaches $\delta_s$, we interpret this as the start of a possible bump and the algorithm enters *One-Bump* state.

The *One-Bump* state terminates when the yaw rate drops back to a value below $\delta_s$. If the sojourn/dwell time in *One-Bump* state was larger than $T_{BUMP}$ and the largest measured yaw rate was larger than $\delta_h$, hence satisfying the three constraints, we consider the first detected bump to be valid. In such a case, the algorithm enters *Waiting-for-Bump* state, Otherwise, it returns to *No-Bump*.

In *Waiting-for-Bump* state, it further monitors the yaw rate readings for a maximum dwell time $T_{NEXT\_DELAY}$. In the meanwhile, if another bump starts, i.e., the yaw rate reaching $\delta_s$ with a sign opposite to the first bump's is detected, it goes through the same procedure as before in validating it. If determined as valid, this would mean that two consecutive bumps with opposite signs have been detected. Thus, the algorithm determines the maneuver to be a *lane change*. Otherwise, if the second bump turns out to be invalid, then it would mean that only a single valid bump was detected and thus the algorithm determines the maneuver to be a *turn*. After making all decisions, the algorithm goes back to the initial *No-Bump* state.

The bump-detection algorithm is executed iteratively for each collected sample, and goes through a different procedure depending on the current state.

## 3.3 Differentiating Steering Maneuvers

When the vehicle is steered, bumps in the yaw rate readings are constructed. Based on the bump detection algorithm, `V-Sense` detects such bumps and differentiates between maneuvers of a lane change and a turn.

One possible problem in using this would be when driving on a curvy road. As illustrated in Fig. 5, when driving on a curvy road, it might have the same *shape* of trajectory as in lane change or a turn, and hence construct the same number and shape of bumps. In such a case, `V-Sense` might misinterpret the drive on a curvy road as a lane change or turn, thus yielding false positives/negatives. Therefore, it is imperative for `V-Sense` to differentiate between lane changes, turns, and also driving on curvy roads.

We achieve this by classifying the maneuvers based on not only the number and shape of the bumps as in Algorithm 1, but also with their horizontal displacement.[3] Let $W_{LANE}$ denote the horizontal displacement after a lane change. Since the average lane width is around 3.65 meters [14], $W_{LANE}$ is expected to be around that value after a lane change. In contrast, while driving on a curvy road, the horizontal displacement, denoted as $W_{CURVY}$, is usually much larger than $W_{LANE}$. Based on this observation, if `V-Sense` has detected two bumps — which means a possible lane change — it then derives the horizontal displacement during that steering maneuver. If the derived value is larger than 3.65 meters, `V-Sense` determines the vehicle to be driving on a curvy road, rather than making a lane change.

Also, to differentiate between turns at the intersection (i.e., a sharp turn) and driving on a curvy road, we exploit the fact that the horizontal displacement during a turn is much smaller than that during driving on a curvy road. Figs. 5(c) and 5(d) illustrate this, where $W_{TURN}$ and $W_{CURVY}$ represent the horizontal displacements during a turn and driving on a curvy road, respectively. If `V-Sense` detects only one bump, it further examines the horizontal displacement to distinguish between turning and driving on a curvy road.

Note that to differentiate turns from lane changes, only the number and shape of the bumps are required, which can be met by the bump-detection algorithm.

## 3.4 Horizontal Displacement

In order to correctly distinguish between lane change, turn, and driving on a curvy road, we must determine the horizontal displacement, in addition to the detection of bumps.

[3] *Horizontal displacement* is a value that represents the change of position in the X-axis after the steering maneuver.

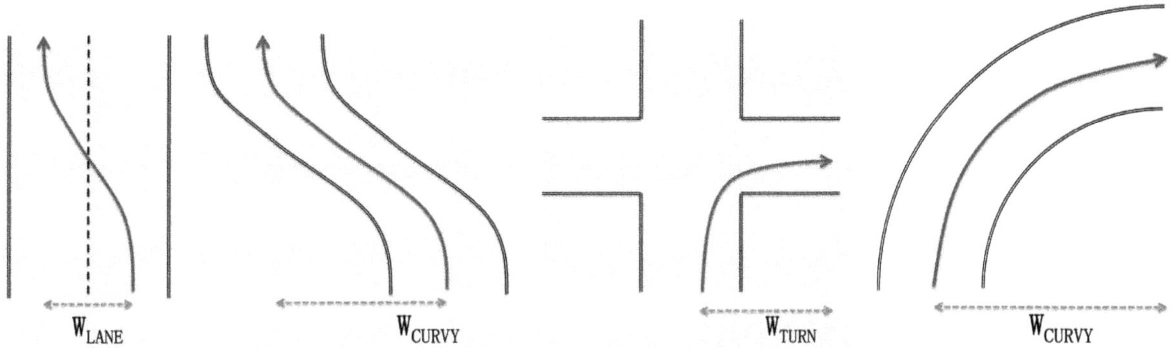


(a) Lane change (b) A S-shaped curvy road (c) Turning (d) A L-shaped curvy road

Figure 5: The same vehicle trajectory shape for four different scenarios: (a) lane change, (b) driving on an S-shaped curvy road, (c) turning, and (d) driving on an L-shaped curvy road.

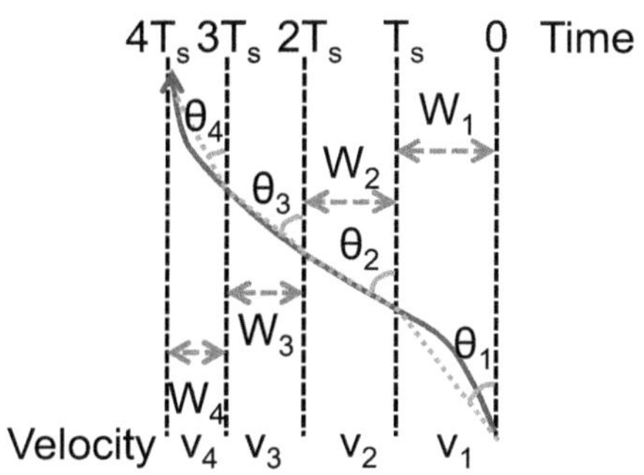


Figure 6: Deriving the horizontal displacement based on gyroscope readings and estimated velocity

We derive the horizontal displacement from the readings of a smartphone's gyroscope and accelerometer.

Fig. 6 shows an example vehicle trajectory during a left lane change or maneuver on a curvy road as illustrated in Figs. 5(a) and 5(b). The dotted vertical line represents the time when the sensors are sampled with frequency of $1/T_s$. Here $\theta_n$ denotes the angle of the vehicle's heading, whereas $v_n$ represents the average velocity during the sampling period. During each sampling period $T_s$, the vehicle's horizontal displacement can be expressed as:

$$W_n = v_n T_s sin(\theta_n). \tag{1}$$

Since the yaw-rate readings from the gyroscope represent the vehicle's angular velocity around the Z-axis, $\theta_n$ can be expressed as:

$$\begin{aligned}\theta_n &= \theta_{n-1} + Y_{avg}T_s \\ &\approx \theta_{n-1} + Y_n T_s,\end{aligned} \tag{2}$$

where $Y_{avg}$ represents the average yaw rate during the sampling period, and $Y_n$ the instantaneous yaw rate measured at the end of the sampling period. Note that the above approximation holds since the sampling period on smartphones can be significantly reduced. Thus, the total horizontal displacement from time 0 to $NT_s$ can be derived as:

$$\begin{aligned}W_{final} &= \sum_{n=1}^{N} W_n \\ &= \sum_{n=1}^{N} v_n T_s sin(\theta_n) \\ &= \sum_{n=1}^{N} v_n T_s sin(\sum_{k=1}^{n} Y_k T_s)\end{aligned} \tag{3}$$

where $T_s$ is a predefined parameter denoting the sampling period of the application. The third equality comes from the fact that the initial angle of the vehicle's heading, $\theta_0 = 0$, since this is the reference point. $Y_k$ can be acquired from the gyroscope readings, while $v_n$ can be derived from the accelerometer and GPS readings. We further elaborate on how to obtain an accurate value of $v_n$ in Section 3.6.

We exploit the gyroscope and accelerometer readings to determine $W_{final}$. Then, by analyzing the thus-determined value, `V-Sense` distinguishes between the cases of lane change or turn and driving on curvy roads. Using in-depth evaluations, we will later show that the derivation of horizontal displacement is accurate for various cases (e.g., lane change, left/right turn, U-turn).

## 3.5 Change in Vehicle's Heading Angle

Based on bump detection and horizontal displacement, `V-Sense` classifies various steering maneuvers into three classes: lane change, turn, and driving on a curvy road. To further classify different turning maneuvers (e.g., left/right turn at the intersections, U-turn), `V-Sense` derives the change in the vehicle's heading angle, i.e., the difference in the heading angle between the start and the end of a steering maneuver.

As in Eq. (2), the angle of vehicle's heading at sampling time $nT_s$ can be derived by accumulating the $n$ yaw-rate measurements. As an example, consider Fig. 6; at sampling time $3T_s$, the angle of the vehicle's heading would be $\theta_3 = \sum_{n=1}^{3} Y_n T_s$. In other words, the change in the vehicle's heading from time 0 to $NT_s$ can be expressed as:

$$\theta_{final} = \sum_{n=1}^{N} Y_n T_s. \tag{4}$$

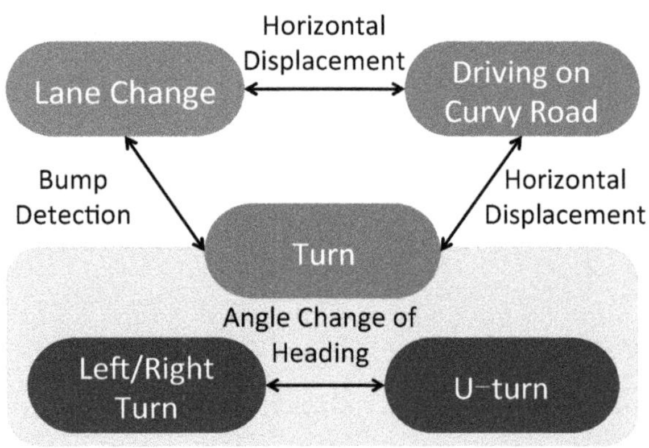


Figure 7: State diagram of maneuver classification in V-Sense.

For example, after making a left/right turn at the intersection, $\theta_{final} \approx \pm 90^{\circ}$, whereas after making a U-turn, $\theta_{final} \approx \pm 180^{\circ}$. Thus, by exploiting the derived values, V-Sense can further classify the turns into a left/right turn or a U-turn.

Fig. 7 summarizes the overall maneuver classification in V-Sense as a state diagram. V-Sense first determines whether the steering maneuver is a turn or a lane change by calculating the number of bumps. If it is a turn, V-Sense will calculate the angle change to determine whether the turn is a regular left/right turn or a sharp U-turn. Second, V-Sense calculates the horizontal displacement to determine whether it is an curvy road or not.

## 3.6 Velocity Estimation

In order to derive the horizontal displacement and set $T_{BUMP}$ and $T_{NEXT\_DELAY}$, we need accurate measurement of the vehicle's instantaneous velocity.

There are two ways of acquiring the velocity with a smartphone: reading the Speed Over Ground (SOG) output from the GPS module inside the smartphone, or exploiting the IMU. The GPS does provide measurements of the velocity, whereas the acceleration can be derived from IMU readings. However, the GPS output rate is very low, e.g., 1Hz on Samsung Galaxy S4, as shown in Fig. 8, and hence cannot properly capture velocity changes within a sampling period. On the other hand, the IMU has a much higher output rate but contains lots of noise as well as some biases as shown in Fig. 8. Thus, just simply using either the velocity measurement from GPS or taking an integral of the accelerator IMU output is not sufficient. Hence, in order to exploit the distinct advantages of GPS and IMU, we fuse the data by using a Kalman filter [19] to estimate the velocity.

We first construct a model for estimating the velocity:

$$v(k|k-1) = v(k-1|k-1) + (a(k) - b(k-1|k-1))T_s \quad (5)$$

where $v(k|k-1)$ is the estimated velocity at time $k$ based on the optimized velocity at time $k-1$; $v(k-1|k-1)$ is the optimized velocity at time $k-1$; $a(k)$ is the acceleration output at time $k$; $b(k-1|k-1)$ is the optimized bias of the accelerometer at time $k-1$; $T_s$ is the sampling period of the accelerometer.

Here we treat $b$ as a constant bias [22]:

$$b(k|k-1) = b(k-1|k-1). \quad (6)$$

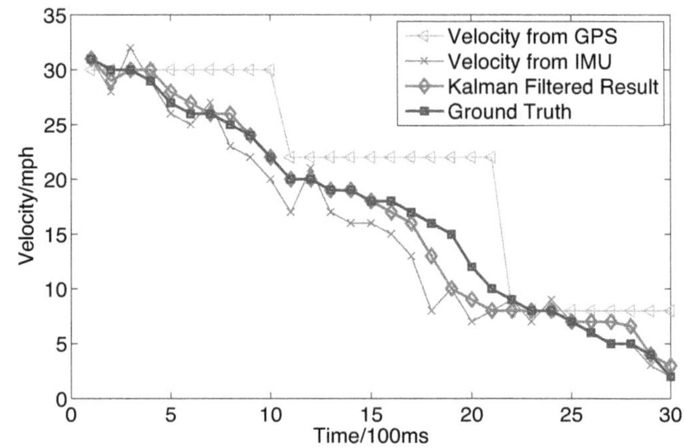


Figure 8: The accuracy of velocity estimation by fusing sensor readings

Thus, we have a matrix representation of the model as:

$$X(k|k-1) = AX(k-1|k-1) + BU(k) \quad (7)$$

where $X = \begin{bmatrix} v \\ b \end{bmatrix}$, $A = \begin{bmatrix} 1 & -T_s \\ 0 & 1 \end{bmatrix}$, $B = \begin{bmatrix} T_s \\ 0 \end{bmatrix}$, and $U$ is the output from accelerometer. So, the covariance matrix is estimated by:

$$P(k|k-1) = APA^T + Q, \quad Q = \begin{bmatrix} q_v & 0 \\ 0 & q_a \end{bmatrix} \quad (8)$$

where $P$ is the covariance matrix, and $Q$ is the covariance of the process noise which can be regarded as the Gaussian white noise. Thus, the state can be estimated as:

$$X(k|k) = X(k|k-1) + g(k)(S(k) - HX(k|k-1)) \quad (9)$$

where $g(k)$ is the matrix of Kalman gain and $S(k)$ is the speed relative to the ground measured by the GPS, and $H = [1 \quad 0]$. We refer the interested readers to [19] for more details.

Fig. 8 shows velocity estimation by using such a model based on Kalman Filter. Here we get the ground truth velocity by directly reading it from the OBD-II port, and compare it with our estimation results. Fig. 8 shows that the velocity can be accurately estimated in real time, thus yielding accurate horizontal displacements.

## 3.7 Parameter Setting

The bump-detection algorithm uses four main parameters: $\delta_s$, $\delta_h$, $T_{BUMP}$ and $T_{NEXT\_DELAY}$. $\delta_s$ determines the start/end point of a bump and thus is the smallest reading value, whereas $\delta_h$ determines the largest reading value of the bump, and hence represents its height. Based on the constraints of a *valid* bump, its minimum and maximum should be larger than $\delta_s$ and $\delta_h$, respectively.

With large values of $\delta_h$ and $\delta_s$, small bumps — which may be caused by background noise or sensing errors — can be ignored and thus reduce the false-positive rate, whereas the false-negative rate might increase. On the other hand, with small values of $\delta_h$ and $\delta_s$, the false-negative rate can be reduced but will become susceptible to background noise, thus increasing the false-positive rate. From extensive road tests, we found that parameters of $\delta_s = 0.05$ and $\delta_h = 0.07$ represent a good tradeoff, and are thus used as default values

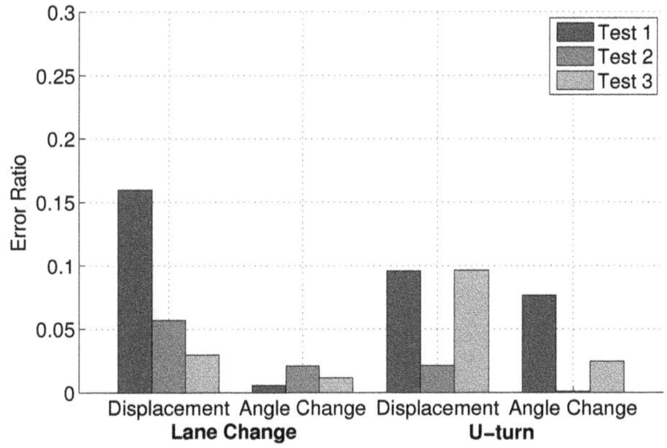


Figure 9: Error of the determined values compared with the ground truth.

for simplicity. However, the optimal parameter setting may slightly vary with the driving habit. Developing an adaptive parameter selection mechanism is part of our future work.

As for the other two parameters, $T_{BUMP}$ represents the time duration of a valid bump, whereas $T_{NEXT\_DELAY}$ represents the maximum waiting time for the following bump, in case of a lane change. Since the time duration of a turn or lane change is usually several seconds [24], we set $T_{BUMP}$ = 1.5 seconds and $T_{NEXT\_DELAY}$ = 3 seconds as their default values.

# 4. EVALUATION

To evaluate the performance of `V-Sense`, we implemented `V-Sense` on a Samsung Galaxy S4 with a 1.6GHz quad-core processor running Android 4.4.1 KitKat OS. We have conducted a total of 40 hours of test, and tried to cover different environments both in a parking lot and real roads. First, we evaluated the accuracy of `V-Sense` in determining the change of heading angle and the horizontal displacement in a short road test. Then, we evaluate the performance of `V-Sense`'s classification with a longer road test containing various road features. The cars we used for the test were a 2010 Mitsubishi Lancer and a 2006 Mazda 6. During these experiments, the smartphones were either mounted on the windshield, or kept in the driver's pocket.

## 4.1 Accuracy of Estimating Angle Change and Displacement

By making several lane changes, turns, and U-turns during a short road test, we evaluated the accuracy of `V-Sense` in estimating the change of heading angle and the horizontal displacement. During the road test, we made three lane changes, one to the left lane and the other two to the right lane, and three U-turns. We collected the horizontal displacements and changes of heading angle from `V-Sense` to check whether the estimated values are close to their ground truth. The results of the two separate tests are summarized in Table 1. For consistency, we present all numbers as their absolute values.

During a lane change, the ground truth horizontal displacement is expected to be equal to the actual lane width, which was around 3.7m for our experiment. However, for the change of heading angle, it is expected to be 0°, since

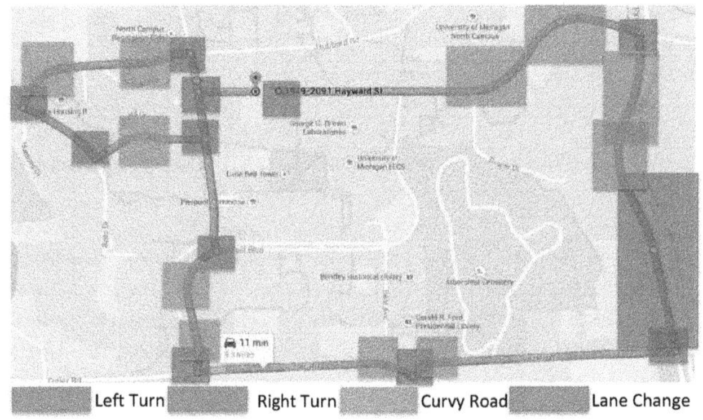


(a) Testing route #1, around campus, 3.3 miles

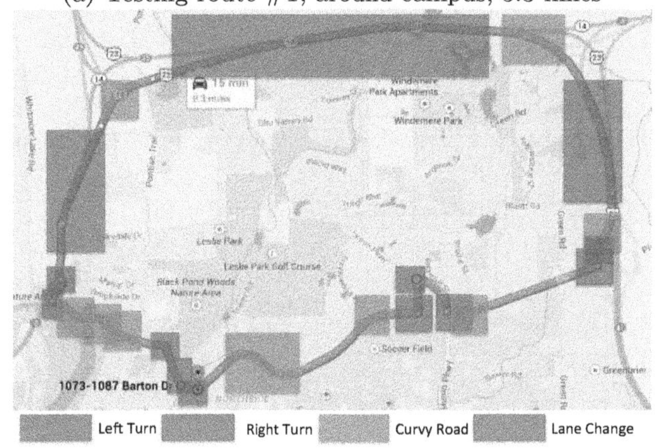


(b) Testing route #2, freeway included, 8.3 miles

Figure 10: Real road testing routes used for evaluation in Ann Arbor, MI

this is a measure of the difference between the initial and the final heading angles.

On the other hand, during a U-turn, the ground truth of horizontal displacement and the change of heading angle are the road width for U-turns, which was approximately 16m in our case, and 180°, respectively.

Fig. 9 shows the error ratio — which is the ratio of the absolute deviation to the ground truth value — in the two experiments. For all cases, the estimated horizontal displacement and change of heading angle have a very low error ratio, i.e., `V-Sense` is very accurate.

The high accuracy of `V-Sense` in determining the two values means that it can correctly classify various steering maneuvers, which is validated in the following subsection by conducting long road tests.

## 4.2 Accuracy of Maneuver Classification

To evaluate how well `V-Sense` classifies different steering maneuvers, we performed two long road tests. To guarantee the generality of our experiment, we carefully chose two different test routes as shown in Figs. 10 (a) and (b) near our campus. The routes run through typical urban areas and freeways, the former including residential, downtown, and school areas. The road features are highlighted in both figures with detailed information as follows.

- Left/right turn (LT/RT): Each turn at an intersection exemplifies a left/right turn.

| | Lane Change | | | | U-turn | | | |
|---|---|---|---|---|---|---|---|---|
| | #1 | #2 | #3 | Average | #1 | #2 | #3 | Average |
| **Displacement [m]** | 4.29 | 3.49 | 3.59 | 3.79 | 14.47 | 15.66 | 14.46 | 14.86 |
| **Angle Change [deg]** | 2.03 | 7.49 | 4.12 | 4.54 | 193.73 | 179.85 | 184.41 | 185.99 |

Table 1: Determined horizontal displacement and angle change of heading for lane changes/U-turns.

- Curvy road (CR): There are several curvy roads in the chosen routes. Among them, there are two long L-shaped curvy roads on the US#23 freeway, which are challenging for our bump detection scheme alone to determine.
- Multiple traffic lanes (LC): A lane change is possible in both urban areas and on the US#23 freeway. Specifically, there are 2 lanes in each direction in the urban road, and 4 lanes in each direction on the US#23 freeway.

The number of features in the examined routes is summarized in Table 2.

| Route | Distance [miles] | RT | LT | LC | CR |
|---|---|---|---|---|---|
| #1 | 3.4 | 6 | 5 | 4 | 11 |
| #2 | 8.3 | 5 | 5 | 15 | 9 |

Table 2: Summary of different road features in testing routes.

To validate the independence of `V-Sense` from driving habits, we had 5 volunteers participating in our test, three male drivers and two female drivers. Each of them drove twice on both route #1 and #2. In the first test, they mounted the phone on the windshield, whereas in the second test, the phone was kept inside the driver's pocket.

The on-road experimental results are plotted in Fig. 11, and can be highlighted as follows.

- `V-Sense` achieves 100% accuracy in detecting both right and left turns, regardless of the phone's placement and road condition. This is because when turning, the heights of the bumps in the readings tend to be high enough to be accurately detected and classified.
- For lane changes, `V-Sense` achieves 93% accuracy when the phone is mounted on the windshield, and 85% accuracy when the phone is in the driver's pocket. The false-negative results are mostly due to the fact that `V-Sense` occasionally misinterprets a lane change as driving on a curvy road, because a few of the lane changes in our test took longer than expected, especially on the freeway where drivers tend to take extra caution, thus making slower lane changes. The accumulated error in the gyroscope reading can also degrade the performance in such a case [30]. However, its occurrence is expected to be rare considering the average elapsed time for lane changing, i.e., less than 6 seconds.
- `V-Sense` achieves nearly 97% accuracy in detecting curvy roads with the phone mounted on the windshield, and nearly 92% accuracy with the phone kept in the driver's pocket. These results also reflect the accuracy of the coordinate alignment mentioned in Section 3.1. Also, note that `V-Sense` was able to detect the two long L-shaped curvy roads on the US#23 freeway using bump detection and horizontal displacement derivation.

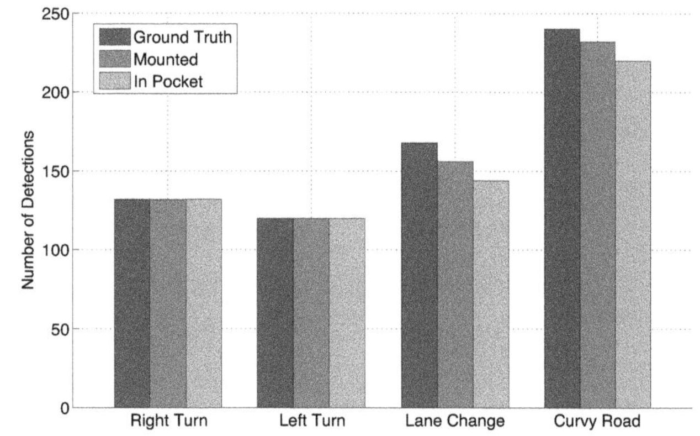


Figure 11: Performance of recognizing different steering patterns on both route #1 and #2

### 4.3 `V-Sense` vs. Camera-Based Approach

We also compare the performance of `V-Sense`, a camera-free approach, with existing camera-based approaches. Since most of the existing driving assistant applications can only detect lane changes, not turns or driving on curvy roads, we do this comparison with only the results of lane-change detection. The evaluation is based on tests of both route #1 and route #2. We choose iOnRoad [8], BlackSensor [2], Drivea [3], and Augmented Driving [1] for comparison with `V-Sense`. All of these four apps have the capability of detecting lane departures. Of these apps, iOnRoad is the most popular one with more than 1,000,000 downloads from Google Play, and it is still under active maintenance, whereas Drivea is the least popular, still with more than 10,000 downloads.

Since the use of cameras is almost 100% ineffective at night or under a bad weather, we compared the performance of `V-Sense` with difference apps based on the camera approach, during daytime and under a perfect weather condition. Here we used two Samsung Galaxy S4 smartphones: phone $A$ runs `V-Sense` while phone $B$ is running either iOnRoad, BlackSensor, Drivea, or Augemented Driving. In all experiments, phone $A$ was placed next to the driver's seat, while phone $B$ was mounted on the car's windshield to have a clear view of the road.

As shown in Fig. 12, `V-Sense` achieves about 3× better accuracy than iOnRoad, 5× better than BlackSensor and Augmented Driving, and 11× better than Drivea. According to our experiments conducted even under a perfect weather condition, the performances of all the compared apps were still seriously constrained by the environment, while `V-Sense` worked well, irrespective of the environment. In particular, the performance of camera-based lane detection degraded severely in at least four cases: heavy shadow on the road, broken road, strong sunlight, and sharp turns as shown in Fig. 13.

(a) Heavy Shadow (b) Broken Road (c) Strong Sun Light (d) Sharp Turns

Figure 13: Non-functional environments for the camera-based driving assistant application in the experiment.

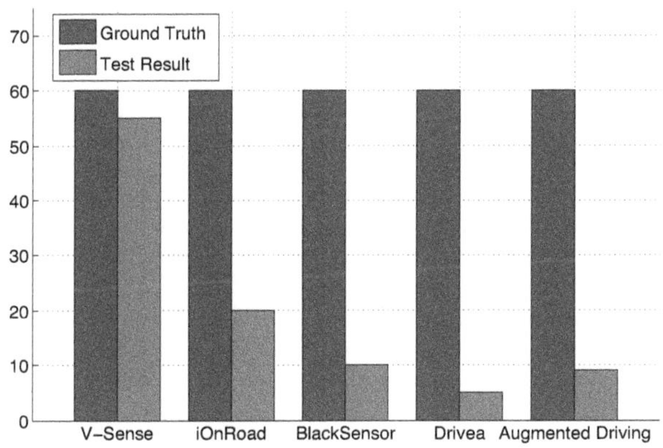


Figure 12: Comparison of `V-Sense`, iOnRoad, BlackSensor, Drivea, and Augmented Driving in lane-change detection.

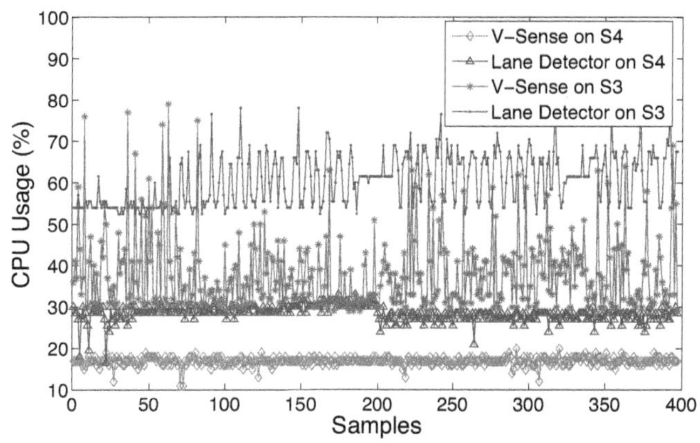


Figure 14: Comparison of CPU usage between `V-Sense` and lane detector

## 4.4 Computational Cost of V-Sense

The high computational requirement is always the problem for existing driver assistant applications. For example, CarSafe [29] indicates its CPU utilization to be 64% when run on Samsung Galaxy S3. We evaluated the computational cost of `V-Sense` on smartphones, including Samsung Galaxy S3 (with 1.4GHz quad-core Cortex-A9 CPU), and Samsung Galaxy S4 (with 1.6GHz quad-core Cortex-A15 CPU). The CPU utilization was monitored by using `adb top` provided by Android SDK.

For a fair comparison with the camera-based approach, we extracted the lane change detection functionality and implemented a simple application only with the lane-change detection function. The techniques used in this application exploit the phone's rear camera to acquire the road's image, and implement a popular lane-detection algorithm [17] to extract the lane.

Our experimental results are plotted in Fig. 14. We found that, on Galaxy S4, the average CPU utilization of `V-Sense` was 16.9%, whereas for the lane detector, it was 28.4%. On Galaxy S3, the average CPU utilization of `V-Sense` was 38.1%, whereas for the lane detector, it was 60.6%. These results show that `V-Sense` uses 50% less CPU than the camera-based approach. In other words, `V-Sense` not only achieves higher accuracy but also lower computational overhead than camera-based approaches.

# 5. APPLICATION I: DETECTION OF CARELESS STEERING

`V-Sense` can be used to detect careless steering: changing lanes or making turns without turning on the turn signal. Detecting a driver's careless steering is important, since it would enhance the safety of not only the driver but also people/vehicles around him. Moreover, it can also be used by insurance companies in monitoring the driver's driving habit and thus determining the insurance premium accordingly, which would then motivate the drivers to avoid careless steering.

In this section, we present and evaluate a simple proof-of-concept of careless steering detection. We use `V-Sense` to detect and differentiate various steering maneuvers, such as making turns, changing lanes, and driving on curvy roads. Furthermore, we present a scheme to detect whether the driver has actually used the turn signal during each steering maneuver.

## 5.1 Overview

Fig. 15 shows the information flow of careless steering detection using data collected from the gyroscope, GPS, accelerometer, and microphone on a smartphone. This application is comprised of `V-Sense` and sound detection module. `V-Sense` detects possible lane changes or turns using the gyroscope readings. Upon detecting the start point of a lane change or turn, i.e. bump, the sound detection module activates the microphone and starts to detect the turn signal sound. If a lane change or turn is detected without the detection of signal sound, the application declares the driver is driving carelessly, and triggers alarm to notify the driver. Otherwise, the application declares it as attentive driving.

## 5.2 Detection of Turn Signal

In order to detect whether the driver has used the turn signal, `V-Sense` uses the following three steps: (i) collect

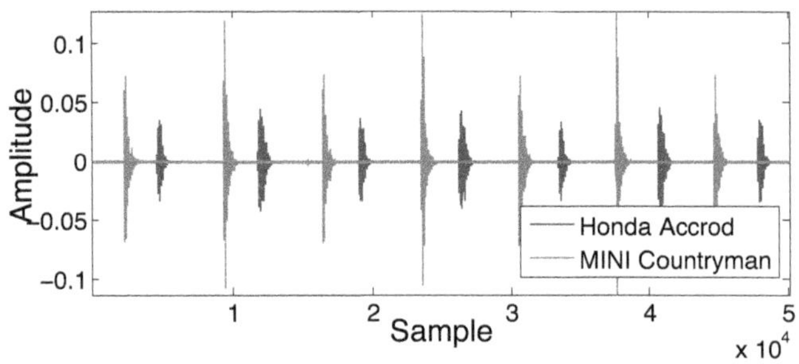


(a) Signal sample

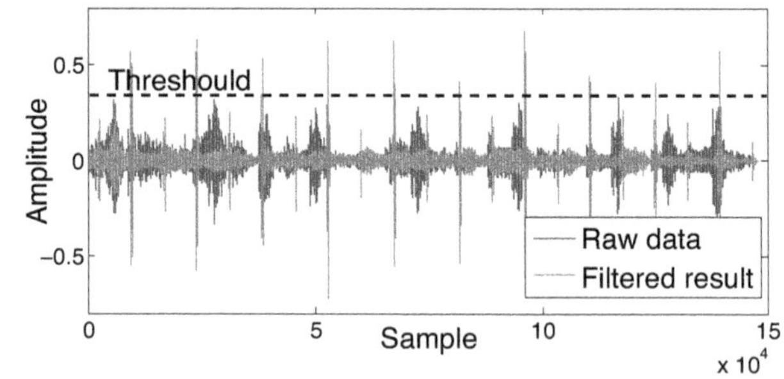


(b) Matched filter result

Figure 16: Turn signal samples and the filtered result by using a matched filter, (a) turn signal sample from a 2006 HONDA Accord and MINI Countryman; (b) matched result from the filter with the existence of background noises inside the car.

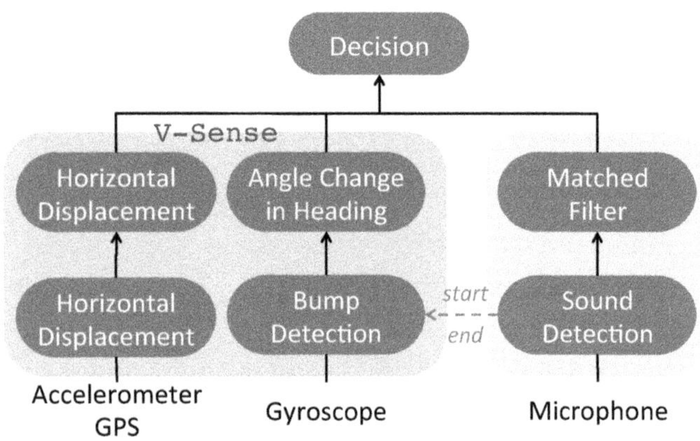


Figure 15: Information flow of careless steering detection by combining **V-Sense** and sound detection module.

training samples of the turn signal sound; (ii) eliminate background noise with a matched filter; (iii) make a decision on whether the turn signal was used during the turn or lane change.

### 5.2.1 *Collection of Training Sample Data Set*

We first collected the turn signal sounds from two different cars, 2006 Honda Accord and MINI Countryman, which are used as sample data sets as shown in Fig. 16(a). The measured steady rates of the turn signal in the 2006 Honda Accord and MINI Countryman were 161 and 163 ticks per second (shown in Fig. 16), respectively.

As the turn signal sounds acquired from the 2006 Honda Accord has lower amplitude, and would thus be more difficult to detect, we studied the sound detection module using this data set. To test the performance of our turn signal detection module in real driving scenario, we turned on the engine and played music which acts the background noise inside the car.

### 5.2.2 *Elimination of Noise with a Matched Filter*

To detect the sound emitted from the turn signals, the detection module has to overcome two challenges: (i) it must be resilient to the variation of SNR due to unpredictable detection conditions; (ii) the delay in detecting a single turn signal must be low in order to be ready for detecting the subsequent signal. We utilized a matched filter to meet these challenges.

The matched filter is used to detect the presence of a known signal in the unknown signals [23]. The key idea behind the matched filter is to design an impulse response that maximizes the output SNR. Due to unpredictable driving conditions, the noise inside the car cannot be easily modeled. Thus, we model the turn signal and extract the signal sound by using one convolution with the matched filter kernel. Since the turn (sound) signal can be modeled as series of discrete signals, we use the discrete version of matched filter, in which the output, $y[n]$, can be expressed as:

$$y[n] = \sum_{k=-\infty}^{\infty} h[n-k]h[k], \tag{10}$$

where the impulse response, $h[n]$, of the matched filter is

$$h[n] = g[n] \otimes v[n_0 - n], \tag{11}$$

where $g[n]$ denotes the power spectral density of background noise. We can thus acquire the matched signal *Matched* by applying

$$Result[n] = Signal[n] \otimes h[n], \tag{12}$$

where $signal[n]$ is the sound recorded by the smartphone's microphone inside the car and $Result[n]$ is the output of the matched filter.

### 5.2.3 *Making a Decision*

If the amplitude of the matched filter output is larger than $T$, a pre-defined threshold set to 0.35 by default, **V-Sense** declares the detection of a turn signal sound. If the detected turn signal is accompanied by a lane change or turn detected by **V-Sense**, then the application declares the steering maneuver as being attentive. On the other hand, if no such turn signal sound was detected, the application declares the steering to be careless, and then alarms the driver.

## 5.3 Performance of Sound Detection

Fig. 16(b) shows the performance of our sound detection module which extract signal sound from background noise. We conducted experiments in a regular driving setting, where music played inside the car and the passengers were talking occasionally. The matched filter was able to extract and identify the sound of the turn signals from the background noise, even when the amplitude of the noise was very high (radio played music at the max volume).

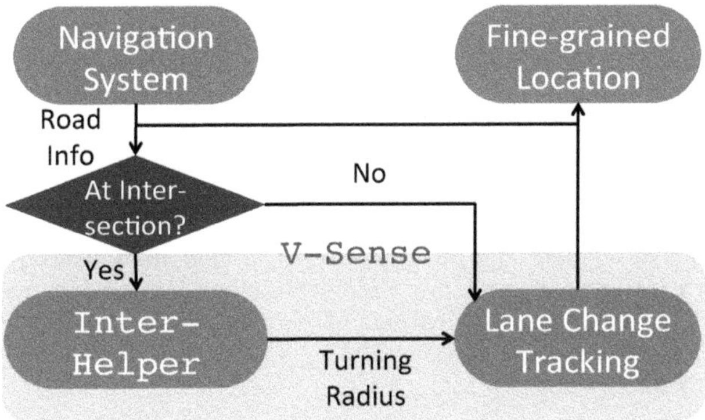


Figure 17: Information flow of fine-grained lane guidance by incorporating navigation system and V-Sense.

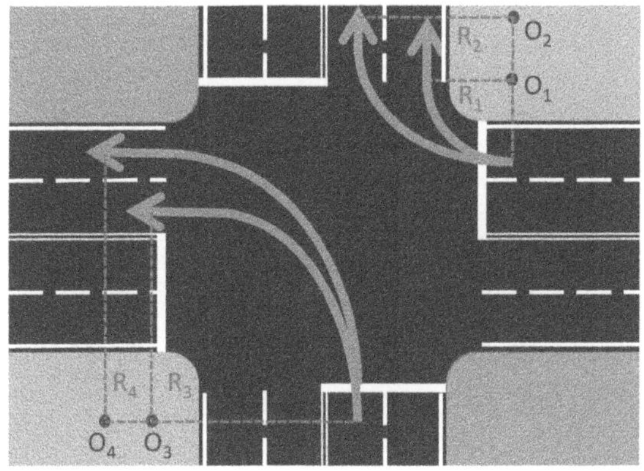


Figure 18: Turns and the corresponding turning radius at a 4-lane single carriageway intersection.

By integrating this accurate sound detection module with V-Sense, the application detects careless steering and thus enhances driving safety significantly.

# 6. APPLICATION II: FINE-GRAINED LANE GUIDANCE

In this section, we demonstrate a proof-of-concept fine-grained lane guidance application using V-Sense. Fine-grained lane guidance allows existing navigation systems provide higher guidance accuracy. Specifically, fine-grained lane guidance detects whether the driver is in the correct lane and alarms the driver if not.

Existing navigation systems on smartphones are constrained by the accuracy of the built-in GPS sensor, which is at best 5~10m [26]. When the line-of-sight transmission between the satellite and the phone is blocked by obstacles, such as tunnels, bridges, and tall buildings, the accuracy quickly drops to 20~100m [18]. Such limitations make it impossible for legacy navigation systems to recognize the exact traffic lane that the vehicle is on. The latest update of Google Maps does include a lane guidance function [5], but in a rather limited way: it can only provide information on which lane the vehicle should stay, not whether it is actually on that lane.

We incorporate V-Sense in an existing navigation system to provide a true fine-grained lane guidance. Fine-grained lane guidance is important, since it can reduce abrupt lane changes, and also very helpful for drivers who have lack driving experience.

## 6.1 Achieving Fine-Grained Lane Guidance

Based on information from an on-line map, the correct lane for the next maneuver can be easily determined, which is a function already provided by existing navigation systems. Hence, the main challenge of realizing the fine-grained lane guidance application is the determination of the current lane that the vehicle is running on. To meet this challenge, we need to determine the vehicle's current lane via lane change detection. The current lane can be determined based on whether and how the vehicle has changed its lane. Thus, by detecting and analyzing the lane changes made by the vehicle, we can determine the vehicle's current lane.

Lane changes may take place in two situations: (i) middle of a road or; (ii) at intersections.[4] For the first case, V-Sense can reliably detect lane changes on the road using techniques in Section 3. To implement accurate lane tracking for the second case, we develop an add-on module of V-Sense called InterHelper. In Fig. 17, we show how the navigation system and V-Sense cooperate to determine the fine-grained location. The navigation system is capable for determining whether the vehicle is at the intersection. Once the vehicle reaches an intersection, InterHelper is triggered and starts to estimate the turning radius, $R_i$. Note that $R_i$ is equivalent to the horizontal displacement during the turn, which can be derived by using the techniques described in Section 3.4. This information enable V-Sense to finally determine the fine-grained location.

As shown in Fig. 18, there are four possibilities of lane change at a typical 4-lane single carriageway intersection. That is, each car has two choices of making either right or left turn. Here, we assume the turning trajectory is an arc, which is a common assumption in intersection design [7]. $O_1$, $O_2$, $O_3$ and $O_4$ are centers of turning circles. InterHelper classifies each case by differentiating the turning radius, i.e., $R_1$, $R_2$, $R_3$ and $R_4$.

For a typical intersection, the right turn radius, $R_1$ is 10.8m [15], the left turn radius, $R_3$ is 20.7m, and the width of a typical intersection is 19.2m [12]. Moreover, the lane width is around 3.65m [24]. Based on these facts and extensive road experiments, we set the threshold of differentiating $R_1$ and $R_2$ as 13.1m, and the threshold of differentiating $R_3$ and $R_4$ as 21.64m. Using such thresholds and the horizontal displacement obtained from V-Sense, the application determines whether the vehicle has changed its lane during a turn at the intersection.

## 6.2 Performance of InterHelper

In order to evaluate the performance of the fine-grained lane guidance application, we conducted 80 left and right turns at different intersections in Ann Arbor, Michigan, U.S., and the results are shown in Fig. 19.

The application is shown to be able to detect 95% of right turns with $R_1$, 90% with $R_2$, 90% of left turns with $R_3$ and

[4]Although it is illegal to change lane at intersections in some U.S. states (e.g., California [16]), we still consider such a case for generality.

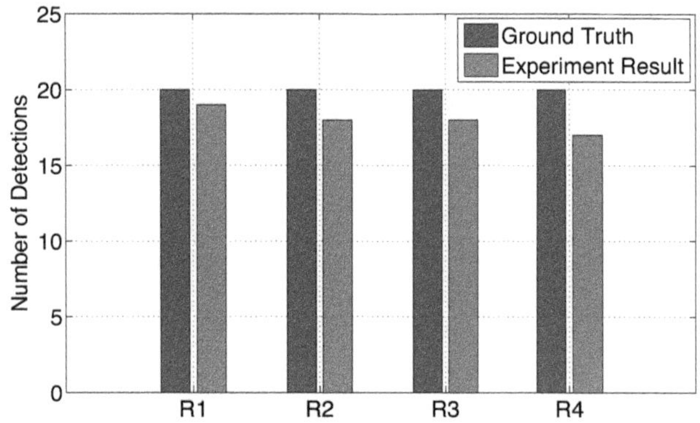


Figure 19: Performance of `InterHelper`.

85% with $R_4$. We can therefore conclude that by integrating `InterHelper` into `V-Sense`, the application is capable of detecting lane changes in all cases, thus determining the vehicle's current lane.

# 7. RELATED WORK

Detecting vehicle dynamics is critical for driving assistant systems and has also been an active research area. The related efforts can be categorized into two main approaches: camera-based or camera-free. For the camera-based approach, the vehicle or a stand-alone device detects the vehicle's maneuver by using its position (determined by the captured images) with respect to the lane boundaries [6, 10, 9]. Some commercial applications, such as iOnRoad [8] and Blacksensor [2], are capable of detecting lane departures by processing the images taken by cameras on smartphones, and thereby recognizes turns. However, all these methods require a mounted or built-in camera and also a clear view of the road. So, their performance can be seriously undermined if the visibility of the road is poor.

Camera-free systems achieve comparable (to camera-based systems) results regardless of the visibility of the road. The authors of [28] utilized the gyroscope, accelerometer readings of the smartphone and other direct readings from the OBD-II port to detect left/right turns and also the vehicle's real-time velocity. MIROAD [25] also utilized the gyroscope and accelerometer of the smartphone to acquire necessary data to detect vehicle motions via dynamic time wrapping (DTW). The authors of [21] utilized the orientation sensor and accelerometer to detect the driving pattern, thus determining if the driver is intoxicated. In contrast to [28], `V-Sense` is infrastructure-free, i.e., no additional hardware is required. It combines the GPS and IMU readings to acquire accurate and real-time velocity estimation. More importantly, in contrast with the existing work, `V-Sense` differentiates not only between left and right turns but also between lane change, U-turn, and driving on curvy roads. These in turn enable `V-Sense` to accurately handle various scenarios, such as fine-grained lane navigation in Section 6.

Furthermore, recent research and industrial efforts have been focusing on building driving assistant applications on smartphones. CarSafe [29] detects drowsiness by observing the driver's eye movement with the phone's front camera. Commercial applications [8, 2, 3, 1] utilized the phone's front camera to detect the front car and traffic lane, alerting the driver if any dangerous scenario is detected. Most of these applications require the user to mount the phone and use the camera to collect necessary information. This mount-before-go feature could limit the users' willingness, and eventually undermine the application's usability.

In contrast, `V-Sense` is a mount-free design for detecting steering maneuvers regardless of the position of the smartphone. Besides, without image processing, `V-Sense` incurs relatively lower computational cost. This mount-free design could pave s way for the development of many various driving assistant applications. For example, a recent study shows steering patterns could be utilized as a drowsiness indicator [11].

# 8. CONCLUSION

As an important and emerging subject in both research and industry communities, several driving assistant systems have been proposed. However, the capability of many existing work is limited by its reliance on the visibility of the road objects. Such an approach is only effective when the phone is carefully mounted and also has good visibility, i.e., its performance is undermined by its environment.

In this paper, we proposed `V-Sense`, a camera-free middleware for driving assistant systems. `V-Sense` can accurately and inexpensively detect and differentiate vehicle steering by only utilizing built-in sensors on smartphones. By leveraging an effective bump detection algorithm and studying the nature of steering, `V-Sense` is capable of differentiating various steering patterns, such as lane change, turn, and driving on curvy roads. Based on the camera-free feature of `V-Sense`, we presented two proof-of-concept applications: careless steering detection and fine-grained lane guidance. `V-Sense` provides new functionalities without relying on cameras to provide a broader range of driving assistance.

# 9. ACKNOWLEDGEMENTS

We would like to thank Morley Mao and Yuanchao Shu of University of Michigan for discussions of this project. We are also grateful to our shepherd Janne Lindqvist and the anonymous reviewers for their helpful suggestions and comments.

# 10. REFERENCES

[1] Augmented driving. https://itunes.apple.com/us/app/augmented-driving/id366841514?mt=8.

[2] Blacksensor on google play. https://play.google.com/store/apps/details?id=com.chahoo.bsdrive&hl=en.

[3] Drivea app. http://www.drivea.info/.

[4] Fatality analysis reporting system (fars) encyclopedia. http://www-fars.nhtsa.dot.gov/Main/index.aspx.

[5] Google map enable lane guidance. https://support.google.com/gmm/answer/3273406?hl=en.

[6] Honda, advanced driver-assistive system. http://world.honda.com/news/2014/4141024Honda-SENSING-Driver-Assistive-System/.

[7] Intersection design. http://www.deldot.gov/information/pubs_forms/manuals/road_design/pdf/revisions062811/07_Intersections.pdf?100411.

[8] ionroad app. http://www.ionroad.com/.

[9] Mobileye. http://www.mobileye.com/.

[10] Road edge and barrier detection with steer assist. https://www.youtube.com/watch?v=xrLVaWnJmMI.

[11] Steering patterns as drowsy indicator. http://www.sae.org/events/gim/presentations/2012/sgambati.pdf.

[12] Turning radius and intersection size. http://articles.latimes.com/2005/apr/20/autos/hy-wheel20.

[13] Volvo xc90. http://www.volvocars.com/us/cars/new-models/all-new-xc90.

[14] Traffic lane. http://en.wikipedia.org/wiki/Lane.

[15] Turning radius. http://en.wikipedia.org/wiki/Turning_radius.

[16] Lane change at intersection in california. http://articles.latimes.com/2005/apr/20/autos/hy-wheel20.

[17] M. Aly. Real time detection of lane markers in urban streets. In *Intelligent Vehicles Symposium, 2008 IEEE*, pages 7–12, June 2008.

[18] C. Bo, X.-Y. Li, T. Jung, X. Mao, Y. Tao, and L. Yao. Smartloc: Push the limit of the inertial sensor based metropolitan localization using smartphone. In *Proc. of ACM Mobicom*, pages 195–198, 2013.

[19] F. Caron, E. Duflos, D. Pomorski, and P. Vanheeghe. Gps/imu data fusion using multisensor kalman filtering: introduction of contextual aspects. *Information Fusion*, 7(2):221 – 230, 2006.

[20] H. Dahlkamp, A. Kaehler, D. Stavens, S. Thrun, and G. Bradski. Self-supervised monocular road detection in desert terrain. In *Proceedings of Robotics: Science and Systems*, Philadelphia, USA, August 2006.

[21] J. Dai, J. Teng, X. Bai, Z. Shen, and D. Xuan. Mobile phone based drunk driving detection. In *International Conference on Pervasive Computing Technologies for Healthcare (PervasiveHealth)*, pages 1–8, March 2010.

[22] B. Friedland. Treatment of bias in recursive filtering. *IEEE Transactions on Automatic Control*, 14(4):359–367, Aug 1969.

[23] J. A. Gubner. *Probability and random processes for electrical and computer engineers*. Cambridge University Press, 2006.

[24] S. Hetrick. Examination of driver lane change behavior and the potential effectiveness of warning onset rules for lane change or "side" crash avoidance systems, 1997.

[25] D. Johnson and M. Trivedi. Driving style recognition using a smartphone as a sensor platform. In *International IEEE Conference on Intelligent Transportation Systems (ITSC)*, pages 1609–1615, Oct 2011.

[26] T. Menard, J. Miller, M. Nowak, and D. Norris. Comparing the gps capabilities of the samsung galaxy s, motorola droid x, and the apple iphone for vehicle tracking using freesim mobile. In *IEEE Intelligent Transportation Systems (ITSC)*, pages 985–990, 2011.

[27] R. Ponziani. Turn signal usage rate results: A comprehensive field study of 12,000 observed turning vehicles. *SAE International Paper, 2012-01-0261*, 2012.

[28] Y. Wang, J. Yang, H. Liu, Y. Chen, M. Gruteser, and R. P. Martin. Sensing vehicle dynamics for determining driver phone use. In *Proc. of ACM MobiSys*. ACM, 2013.

[29] C.-W. You, N. D. Lane, F. Chen, R. Wang, Z. Chen, T. J. Bao, M. Montes-de Oca, Y. Cheng, M. Lin, L. Torresani, and A. T. Campbell. Carsafe app: Alerting drowsy and distracted drivers using dual cameras on smartphones. In *Proc. of ACM MobiSys*. ACM, 2013.

[30] P. Zhou, M. Li, and G. Shen. Use it free: Instantly knowing your phone attitude. In *Proc. of ACM Mobicom*. ACM, 2014.

# Turning a Mobile Device into a Mouse in the Air

Sangki Yun, Yi-Chao Chen, Lili Qiu
The University of Texas at Austin
{sangki,yichao,lili}@cs.utexas.edu

## ABSTRACT

A mouse has been one of the most successful user interfaces due to its intuitive use. As more devices are equipped with displays and offer rich options for users to choose from, a traditional mouse that requires a surface to operate is no longer sufficient. While different types of air mice are available in the market, they rely on accelerometers and gyroscopes, which significantly limit the accuracy and ease of use.

In this paper, we develop a system that can accurately track hand movement to realize a mouse. A unique advantage of our scheme is that it achieves high tracking accuracy using the existing hardware already available in the mobile devices (*e.g.*, smart phones and smart watches) and equipment to be controlled (*e.g.*, smart TVs). More specifically, our approach sends inaudible sound pulses at a few selected frequencies, and uses the frequency shifts to estimate the speed and distance traveled. We then develop techniques to quickly calibrate the distance between speakers and narrow down the device's initial position using its movement trajectory. Based on the information, we continuously track the device's new position in real time. This is feasible because many devices, such as smart TVs, PCs, and laptops, already have multiple speakers. When only one speaker is available, we can leverage the frequency shift of sound along with the phase of received WiFi signal to enable tracking. Our evaluation and user study demonstrate that our system achieves high tracking accuracy (*e.g.*, median error of around 1.4 cm) and ease of use.

## Categories and Subject Descriptors

C.2.m [**Computer-Communication Networks**]: Miscellaneous

## General Terms

Algorithms, Measurement, Performance

## Keywords

Doppler Effect; Tracking; Accelerometer; Gyroscope

## 1. INTRODUCTION

**Motivation:** A mouse has been one of the most successful technologies for controlling the graphic user interface due to its ease of use. Its attraction will soon penetrate well beyond just computers. There already have been mice designed for game consoles and smart TVs. A smart TV allows a user to run popular computer programs and smartphone applications. For example, a smart TV user may want to use a Web browser and click on a certain URL or some part of a map using a mouse. A traditional remote controller, which uses buttons for user input, is no longer sufficient to exploit full functionalities offered by the smart TV. More and more devices in the future, such as Google Glasses, baby monitors, and new generation of home appliances, will all desire mouse functionalities, which allow users to choose from a wide variety of options and easily click on different parts of the view.

On the other hand, a traditional mouse, which requires a flat and smooth surface to operate, cannot satisfy many new usage scenarios. A user may want to interact with the remote device while on the move. For example, a speaker wants to freely move around and click on different objects in his slide; a smart TV user wants to watch TV in any part of a room; a Google Glass user wants to query about objects while he is touring around. Wouldn't it be nice if a user can simply turn his smartphone or smart watch into a mouse by moving it in the air?

**Challenges:** In order to enable the air mouse capability, the device movement should be tracked very accurately, within a few centimeters. Existing indoor localization that provides meter-level accuracy cannot achieve this goal. Many smart TV and set-top box manufacturers provide advanced remote controllers [37]. Some of them even provides motion control and gesture recognition using inertial sensors, such as accelerometers and gyroscopes [34, 35]. Existing accelerometers are well known for their significant measurement errors, and cannot provide accurate tracking. We further confirm this using our measurement studies. Gyroscopes achieve better accuracy in tracking rotation. However, a user has to learn to how to rotate in order to control the displacement in a 2-D space. This is not intuitive, and is especially hard for moving in a diagonal direction, thereby degrading user experience and speed of control.

A few recent works track RFID tags in centimeter-level [40, 41, 46], but they require multiple special RFID readers, each with 4 antennas. Using external devices, such as depth sensor (*e.g.*, Kinect [1]) and IR sensor (*e.g.*, Wii [2]), incurs significant additional cost and limits the types of devices that can be controlled.

**Our approach:** In this paper, we propose Accurate Air Mouse (AAMouse) that accurately tracks device movement in real time. It enables any mobile device with a microphone, such as a smart phone and smart watch, to serve as a mouse to control an electronic device with speakers. A unique feature of our approach is that it uses existing hardware in mobile and electronic devices.

Figure 1 shows an example of our system, where a mobile device with a microphone serves as a mouse for a smart TV with two


*MobiSys'15,* May 18–22, 2015, Florence, Italy.

http://dx.doi.org/10.1145/2742647.2742662.

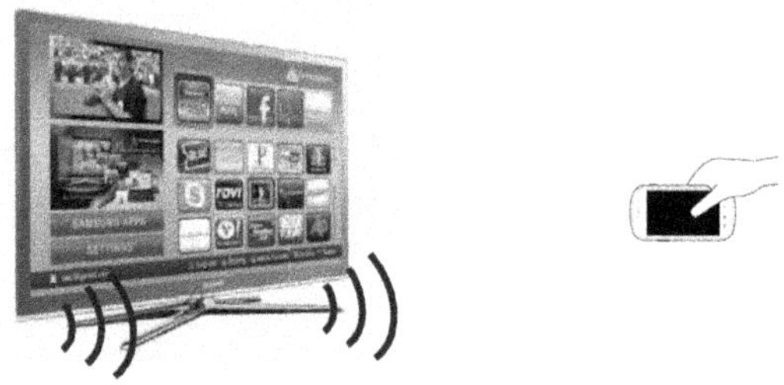

**Figure 1: Enabling accurate device tracking using the Doppler effect of the acoustic signal.**

speakers. The smart TV emits inaudible acoustic signals, and the mobile device records and feeds it back to the smart TV, which estimates the device position based on the Doppler shift.

While there are some existing work that leverages the Doppler shift for gesture recognition, tracking is more challenging since gesture recognition only requires matching against one of the training patterns whereas tracking requires accurate positioning of the device. This not only requires accurate estimation of frequency shift, but also translating the frequency shift into a position involves significant additional research issues, such as how to estimate the distance between the speakers, the device's initial device position, and its new position based on the frequency shift.

We address these challenging issues in the following way. We first estimate frequency shift and use it to position the device assuming that the distance between the speakers and the device's initial position are both known. Then we develop techniques to quickly calibrate the distance between the speakers using the Doppler shift. To address the device's unknown initial position, we employ particle filter, which generates many particles corresponding to the device's possible positions and filters the particles whose locations are inconsistent with the measured frequency shifts. The device's position is estimated as the centroid of the remaining particles. To further enhance robustness, we transmit signals at multiple frequencies, perform outlier removal, and combine the remaining estimations. Finally, we generalize our approach to handle the equipment that has only one speaker along with another wireless device (*e.g.*, WiFi). In this case, we use the frequency shift from the inaudible acoustic signal and the phase of received WiFi signal to derive the distance of the mobile device from the speaker and WiFi transmitter. We apply the same framework to continuously track the device in real time as before.

We implement a prototype on a smart phone and a desktop PC. We perform detailed experiments and user studies to demonstrate the feasibility and effectiveness of real-time tracking. Our evaluation reveals the limitations of accelerometer based tracking. Meanwhile, we show AAMouse can track the trajectory of the device movement with a median trajectory error of 1.4 cm. This is comparable to RF-IDraw [41] that requires an array of 4 antennas. Compared to Tagoram [46] with unknown track, AAMouse is 7 times more accurate. In addition, we show that AAMouse also provides better user experience than Gyroscope based approach, which is widely used in commercial air mouse and smart TV remote controllers, due to its more intuitive use.

**Paper outline:** The rest of this paper is organized as follows. Section 2 uses measurement to show accelerometers are not sufficient to provide accurate position information. We describe our approach in Section 3, and present implementation details in Section 4. We evaluate its performance in Section 5. We review related work in Section 6, and conclude in Section 7.

# 2. MOTIVATION

Most recent smart phones are equipped with MEMS accelerometer sensors to measure the movement of the device. A natural thought is to use the accelerometer for device tracking. In this section, we show that existing accelerometers do not provide high enough accuracy for tracking or enabling mouse functionalities. We describe fundamental reasons behind the limited accuracy.

An accelerometer typically gives 3-axis output that allows us to calculate both the direction and speed of the movement. In theory, we can integrate acceleration to get velocity and integrate velocity to get the distance traveled. However, it is well known that the accelerometer based positioning offers limited accuracy [18, 26]. Here are a few fundamental issues with using acceleration for device tracking.

1. The measurement result is easily affected by gravity. While there have been some techniques to remove the effect of gravity, their accuracy is still limited.

2. Computing velocity based on acceleration is hard (*e.g.*, the acceleration is close to zero as the device movement speed approaches a constant speed, and the acceleration is large as the device suddenly stops).

3. Estimating distance traveled based on acceleration requires double integration, and small measurement error can easily get exploded during double integration.

In this section, we conduct measurement studies and confirm that existing acceleration based tracking is error-prone. We will show more user study on accelerometer based tracking in Section 5.

To demonstrate these issues, we observe that the acceleration measured by the accelerometer inherently includes gravity, which is approximately 9.8 $m/s^2$ on earth. When the device lies perfectly flat, gravity only affects the acceleration of Z-axis, so X and Y-axis have zero accelerations. However, while holding the device, one cannot avoid natural hand vibration, which generates gravity induced acceleration in all axes. This acceleration is much larger than that caused by intentional movement (*e.g.*, which is around 0.12 $m/s^2$ on average in our experiments). This makes the acceleration based tracking unreliable.

One way to remove gravity from the measured acceleration is to apply a high-pass filter [11]. As the frequency of gravity is low, it is considered that filtering low frequency acceleration is effective in reducing the impact of gravity. Google Android SDK provides a linear accelerometer API, which gives acceleration after a high-pass filter. This is helpful in removing gravity in a coarse scale, but it still does not provide sufficient accuracy to track the device position. This is due to two reasons: (i) filtering always incurs additional delay and (ii) residual acceleration after filtering is still large enough to result in significant positioning errors.

Next we perform the measurement of linear acceleration in Android devices. We use Google NEXUS 4 and Samsung Galaxy 3. Their accelerometers come from InvenSense [15], which is one of the few accelerometer manufacturers that provides accelerometers for latest iPhones and many android phones, since InvenSense MEMS sensors are considered the most accurate.

Our experiments have 3 users. The sampling rate of the accelerometer was set to the highest (*i.e.*, 200Hz). To get the ground-truth, we attach a camera on the ceiling, and run an object tracking program to track the mobile phone movement precisely.

Figure 2(a) shows a snapshot of the acceleration while a user is holding the device. We only plot Y-axis acceleration for ease of viewing. While a user is holding the device, the average magnitude

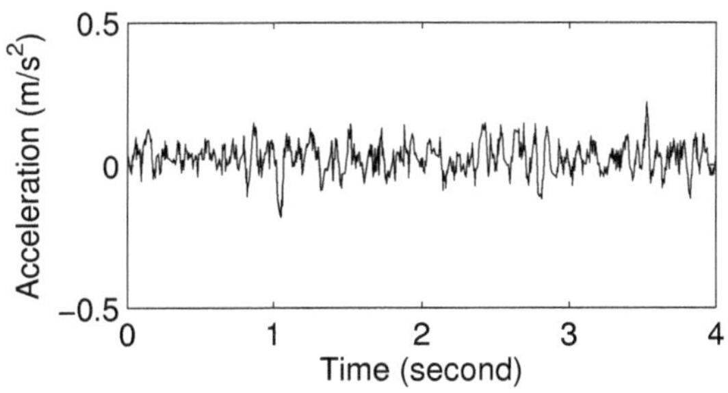


(a) Acceleration while the device is not moving

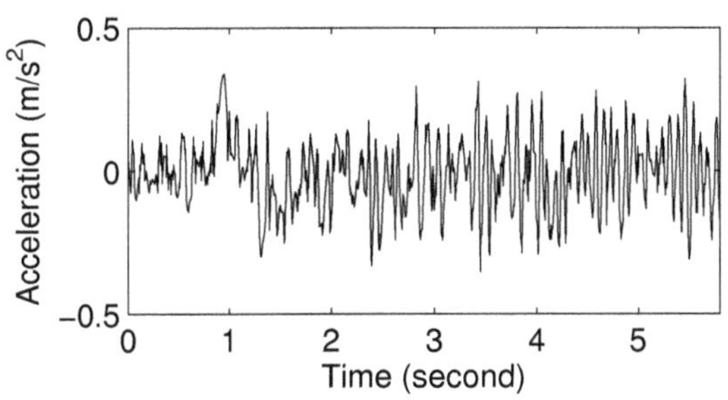


(b) Acceleration while the device is moving

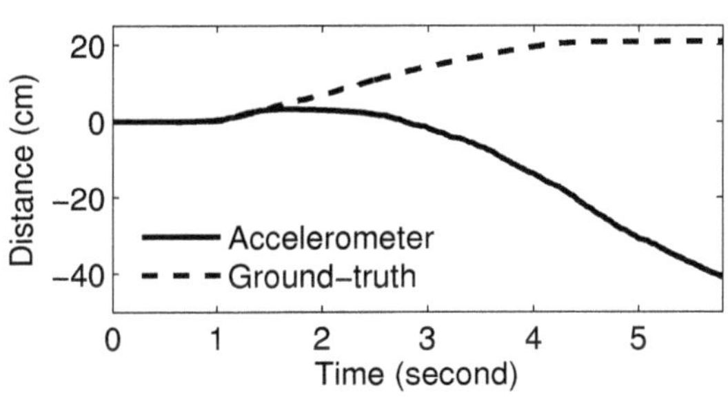


(c) Moving distance tracked by accelerometer

**Figure 2: Comparison of acceleration while device is moving and not moving. The device's position tracked by an accelerometer significantly deviates from the ground truth.**

is 0.05 $m/s^2$ across all users and devices. This can be regarded as measurement noise because it is generated while the device is not moving.

Figure 2(b) shows the acceleration while the user is moving the device in one direction. In this experiment, users are asked to mimic the speed of controlling a mouse. The device starts to move at 1 second, and stops at 4.3 second. Comparing Figure 2(a) and (b), it is hard to tell exactly when the device starts moving and when it stops. At the beginning of the movement, it gives high enough acceleration to calculate the initial velocity, but as the device velocity approaches close to a constant, the acceleration decreases, which makes the position tracking unreliable. In addition, even after the movement has stopped, the acceleration remains high due to deacceleration and filtering noise.

Figure 2(c) shows the distance calculated by double integration of the acceleration. We can observe the tracking error is significant, and the direction is completely off. While this is just one run, it is common to see such a significant error in other runs. The average acceleration while the device is moving is 0.12 $m/s^2$, which is not very different from the measurement noise. Using double integration to get the distance causes small measurement error to get accumulated quickly. Figure 2(c) shows that the distance increases even after the device has stopped due to the accumulated error. This shows that the existing accelerometers do not provide high enough accuracy to track small-scale movements.

# 3. OUR APPROACH

This section presents our approach to device tracking.

## 3.1 Doppler Effect Based Tracking

The Doppler effect is a well known phenomenon where the frequency of a signal changes as a sender or receiver moves [24]. Without loss of generality, we consider that only the receiver moves while the sender remains static. Let $F$ denote the original frequency of the signal, $F^s$ denote the amount of frequency shift, and $v$ and $c$ denote the receiver's speed towards the sender and the propagation speed of wave, respectively. They have the following relationship:

$$v = \frac{F^s}{F}c. \tag{1}$$

So if we know $F$ and $c$ and can measure $F^s$, we can use the above relationship to estimate the speed of movement. Compared to the acceleration that requires double integration to get the distance, the Doppler shift allows us to get distance using a single integration, which is more reliable.

The Doppler effect is observed in any wave, including RF and acoustic signal. We use acoustic signal to achieve high accuracy due to its (i) narrower bandwidth and (ii) slower propagation speed. Its narrower bandwidth makes it easy to detect 1 Hz frequency shift than that in RF signals (*i.e.*, 44.1 KHz in acoustic signals versus 20 MHz in WiFi). In order to improve the accuracy of detecting frequency shift in WiFi signals, WiSee [30] proposes to reduce the bandwidth of the received signal by first decoding the data to get the channel estimate and then re-encoding repeated data using the estimated channel. Even with significant computational overhead, WiSee detects only 2 Hz frequency shift. In comparison, we can easily detect 1 Hz frequency shift in real-time using acoustic signal. Even assuming that we can detect 1 Hz frequency shift in both WiFi and acoustic signals, the accuracy in speed estimation is still higher in acoustic signal due to its slower speed. The acoustic signal travels at 346. $m/s$ in dry air at 26 °C. If we use sound frequency of 17 KHz, the speed resolution is $\frac{1 \times 346.6}{17000} \approx 0.02m/s = 2cm/s$. In comparison, when the RF center frequency is 2.4 GHz, the resolution is $\frac{1 \times 3 \times 10^8}{2.4 \times 10^9} = 0.125m/s = 12.5cm/s$, which is around 6 times as large. This implies that for the same movement, the Doppler shift of the acoustic signal is 6× that of RF signal, which allows us to more accurately measure the movement speed.

Moreover, acoustic signal can be easily generated and received using speakers and microphones, which are widely available on TVs, Google Glasses, smartphones, and smart watches. To avoid disturbance to other people, we can generate inaudible acoustic signals. While in theory some people may hear up to 20 KHz, we find sound above 17 KHz is typically inaudible. We can easily emit inaudible sound using any device that can play audio files with a sampling rate of at least 44.1 KHz.

We perform a simple experiment to see how accurately we can track the device movement using the Doppler shift. Using MATLAB, we generate a 17 KHz sinusoid audio file that takes 1 Hz in the frequency domain, and play it using a normal PC speaker, and record it using a microphone on Google NEXUS 4. We measure the Doppler shift while the device is moving towards the speaker. The details on how to accurately calculate the Doppler shift will be explained in Section 3.2. Figure 3 shows the Doppler shift and the moving distance over time estimated by Equation 1. The device starts moving at 1 second and stops at 2.8 second. Unlike acceler-

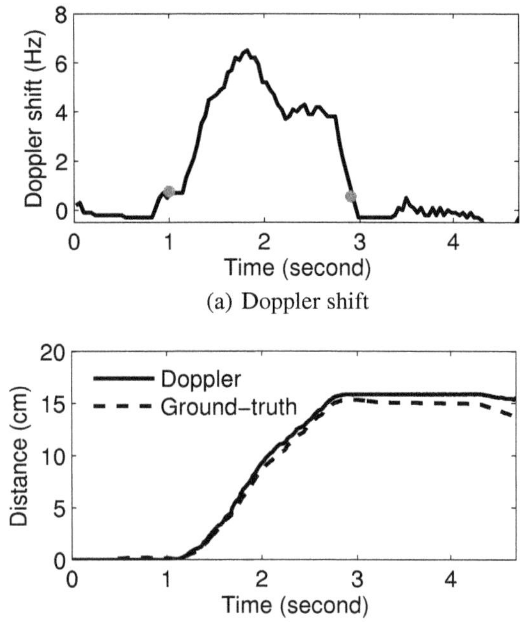


(a) Doppler shift

(b) Moving distance

**Figure 3: The Doppler shift and the moving distance estimated based on it. The tracking error is less than 1 cm. The red dots in Figure 3(a) represent the start and end of the movement.**

ation measurement in Figure 2, it is easy to tell the start and stop time of the device movement (*e.g.*, the Doppler shift is well above 1 Hz during movement and well below 1 Hz when it stops). Moreover, since we get speed from the Doppler shift and can calculate the distance traveled using a single integration rather than double integrations in accelerometer, the accuracy improves significantly. As shown in Figure 3(b), the maximum tracking error is only 0.7 cm.

Based on the above concept, we develop the following system, as illustrated in Figure 1, where a sender with two speakers sends inaudible sound pulses to a mobile device to be tracked. The mobile device can be any device with a microphone, such as a smart phone and smart watch. To distinguish which speaker generates the signal, the two speakers emit different frequencies. The device initiates tracking using a simple gesture or tapping the screen, and starts recording the audio signal from the microphone. The mobile device can either locally process the received signal to compute its location, or send the received audio file via a wireless interface (*e.g.*, WiFi or bluetooth) back to the sender for it to process the data and track the device. The audio signal is simply a sequence of pulse-coded modulation (PCM) bits, which is typically 16 bits per sample. Assuming 44.1 KHz sampling rate, the amount of the audio data per second is 705.6 Kb, which is lower than the bit-rate of classic Bluetooth (*i.e.*, 2.1 Mbps) [13]. Depending on the application, it can be translated into the cursor position or used to track the trajectory of the user's movement.

There are several important research issues we should address to realize the above system:

- How to estimate the Doppler shift?
- How to estimate the position based on the Doppler shift?
- How to improve robustness?
- How to determine the distance between speakers?
- How to determine the mobile device's initial position?
- How to extend this approach to control devices without multiple speakers?

Below we address each of these challenges in turn. Note that we focus on tracking in a 2-D space for mouse applications. Other applications may require tracking in a 3-D space. Our approach supports 3-D tracking when there are 3 or more anchor points (*e.g.*, 3 speakers).

## 3.2 Estimating the Doppler Shift

To record sound in inaudible range (*i.e.*, between 17KHz and 22KHz) without aliasing, we should use the audio sampling rate at least 44 KHz [27]. We use 44.1 KHz sampling rate since most android devices support it by default. To achieve high tracking accuracy, we aim to estimate frequency shift with a resolution of 1 Hz. This implies we need to perform 44100-point FFT to analyze the signal in the frequency domain in 1 Hz-level. This poses a challenge: a long FFT does not allow us to continuously track a device in real time. For 44100-point FFT, we need to store 44100 samples, which takes one second. During that time, the device's position might already have changed several times, which significantly degrades the reliability and responsiveness of tracking.

To address this issue, we use Short-term Fourier Transform (STFT), which is used to analyze the change of spectrum over time [42]. It uses fewer data samples than that required by FFT. The missing values of the input is filled with zeros. Then the FFT output has desired resolution. However, this alone may cause aliasing due to under-sampling. To minimize the distortion, windowing is applied in time domain and each window contains all the audio samples during the current sampling interval. We use Hamming window for that purpose [16].

In our design, we set input length to 44100 and use 1764 audio samples (*i.e.*, the total number of audio samples in 40 ms) as the input, which gives FFT output with 1 Hz resolution every 40 ms. From it, we measure the Doppler shift by finding the peak frequency (*i.e.*, the frequency with the highest value) and subtracting it from the original signal frequency. The complexity is determined by the width of spectrum to be scanned in order to detect the peak frequency. We set it to 100 Hz assuming that the maximum possible Doppler shift is 50 Hz, which corresponds to 1 m/s. According to our experiment, when a person moves a mobile device with a hand, its speed does not exceed 1 $m/s$. Figure 4(a) and (b) show an example of the received audio signal in the frequency domain and the estimated Doppler shift, respectively, while the device is moving around a circle.

## 3.3 Tracking the Position

Next we use the estimated frequency shift to derive the position of the mobile device. In this section, we assume the distance between the speakers and the initial position of the mobile device are both known. We will relax these assumptions in Section 3.5 and 3.6.

We estimate the frequency shift from the two speakers to get the distance change from the speakers. More specifically, let $D$ denote the distance between the speakers. We construct a virtual two-dimensional coordinate where the origin is the left speaker and the X-axis is aligned with the line between speakers. In this coordinate, the left and right speakers are located at $(0,0)$ and $(D,0)$, respectively. Let $(x_0, y_0)$ denote the device's initial position in this coordinate. The distances from the device to the speakers 1 and 2 are denoted by $D_{0,1}$ and $D_{0,2}$, respectively. Let $t_s$ be the sampling interval in which we estimate the frequency shift. Our evaluation

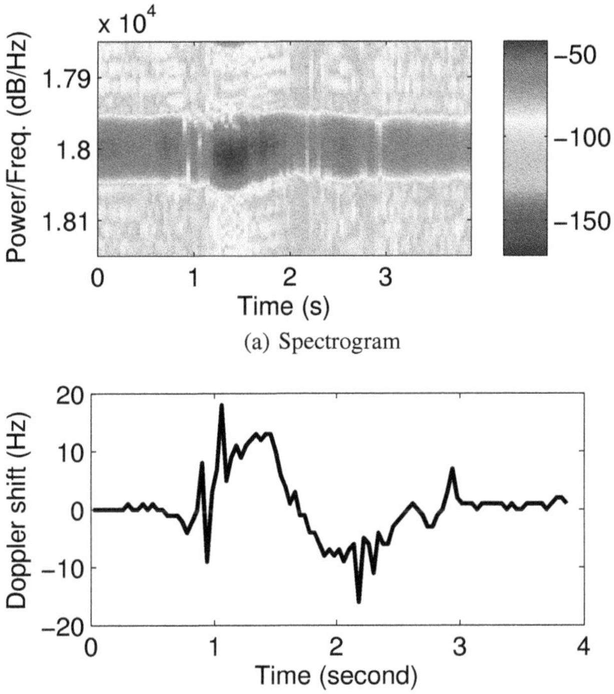


(a) Spectrogram

(b) Doppler shift

**Figure 4: Frequency domain analysis of the recorded audio and the Doppler shift.**

uses 40 ms, which means the cursor's position is updated every 40 ms, which corresponds to popular video frame rates of 24-25 frames per second [10]. After $t_s$, we can get the new distance from the two speakers $D_{1,1}$ and $D_{1,2}$ using the Doppler shift. From the measured Doppler shift and Equation 1, we get:

$$
\begin{aligned}
D_{1,1} = & \quad D_{0,1} + \left(\frac{F_{1,1}^s}{F_1}c\right) t_s, \\
D_{1,2} = & \quad D_{0,2} + \left(\frac{F_{1,2}^s}{F_2}c\right) t_s,
\end{aligned}
$$

where $F_k$ and $F_{i,k}^s$ are the sound frequency and Doppler shift from speaker $k$ during the $i$-th sampling interval, respectively.

Given the updated distance from the speakers, the remaining question is how to get the new position. As illustrated in Figure 5, the new position should be the intersection of the two circles whose center points are $(0, 0)$ and $(D, 0)$, and radii are $D_{1,1}$ and $D_{1,2}$, respectively. We can calculate the intersection of the two circles efficiently as follows [3]:

$$
\begin{aligned}
\theta_1 &= cos^{-1}\left(\frac{D_{1,1}^2 + D^2 - D_{1,2}^2}{2DD_{1,1}}\right), \\
(x^1, y^1) &= (D_{1,1}\cos(\theta_1), D_{1,1}sin(\theta_1)), \\
(x^2, y^2) &= (D_{1,1}cos(-\theta_1), D_{1,1}sin(-\theta_1)),
\end{aligned}
$$

where $(x^1, y^1)$ and $(x^2, y^2)$ are two intersection points of the circles. Note that if $D_{1,1}+D_{1,2} < D$, there is no intersection between the two circles. If $D_{1,1} + D_{1,2} = D$, there is one intersection. In the other cases, there are two intersection points. In the last case, we choose the point closer to $(x_0, y_0)$ as the next position, denoted as $(x_1, y_1)$, since the movement is continuous and our sampling interval is small.

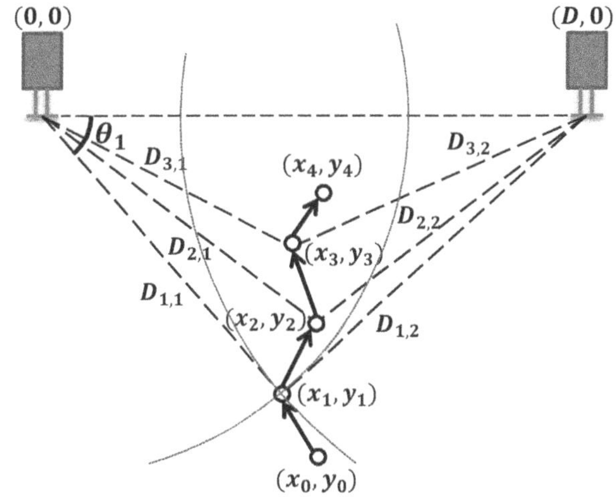


**Figure 5: Tracking the position based on the Doppler shift. Whenever a new Doppler sample arrives, we calculate the distance from the speakers, and estimate the new position by finding the intersection of the two circles.**

In the next Doppler sampling interval, we measure $F_{2,1}^s$ and $F_{2,2}^s$, calculate $D_{2,1}$ and $D_{2,2}$, and derive $(x_2, y_2)$ from it. This process is repeated until the device stops moving. To minimize the impact of errors in the frequency shift estimation, we filter out the frequency shift below 1 Hz and use the remaining frequency shifts to estimate the speeds and distance.

## 3.4 Improving the Accuracy

To achieve high accuracy in device tracking, it is crucial to accurately estimate the Doppler shift. However, measuring it from a single sound wave may not be reliable. The accuracy of estimating the Doppler shift in part depends on SNR of the received signal. Due to frequency selective fading, SNR varies across frequencies. To enhance robustness, we send 1-Hz sound tones at different center frequencies, and use all of them to measure the Doppler shift.

In order to leverage multiple frequencies, the first question is which center frequencies should be used. If the different center frequencies are too close, they will interfere with each other especially under movement. As mentioned earlier, the hand movement speed for mouse applications is typically within 1 $m/s$, which corresponds to 50 Hz Doppler shift. To be conservative, we set adjacent sound tones to be 200 Hz apart. Based on our evaluation result in Section 5.1, we allocate 10 sound tones for each speaker.

The next question is how to take advantage of the measurements at multiple frequencies to improve the accuracy. One approach is to apply Maximal Ratio Combining (MRC) technique used in the receiver antenna diversity, which averages the received signal weighted by the inverse of the noise variance. It is known to be optimal when the noise follows a Gaussian distribution [44]. However, we find some frequencies may incur significantly higher noise than others, and it is important to remove such outliers before combining them using a weighted average. In our system, the Doppler sampling interval is 40 $ms$. 10 Hz difference from the previous measurement implies the velocity has changed 0.2 $m/s$ during 40 $ms$, which translates into an acceleration of 5 $m/s^2$. Such a large acceleration is unlikely to be caused by the device movement. So whenever the change in frequency shifts during two consecutive sampling intervals (*i.e.*, $|F_{i+1,k}^s - F_{i,k}^s|$) is larger than 10 Hz, we consider it as an error and remove it before performing MRC. In an

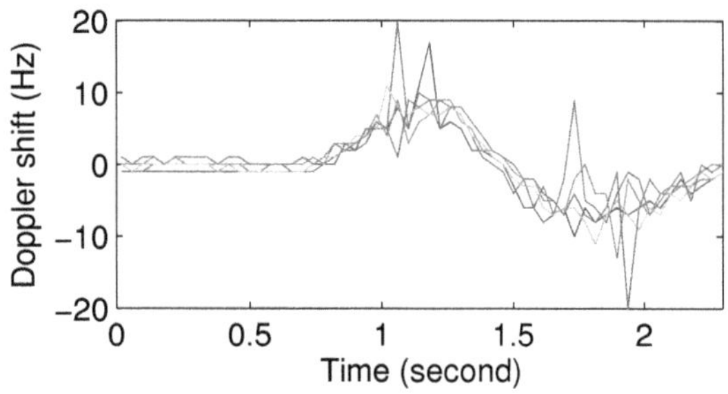


(a) Doppler shift measured from 5 tones

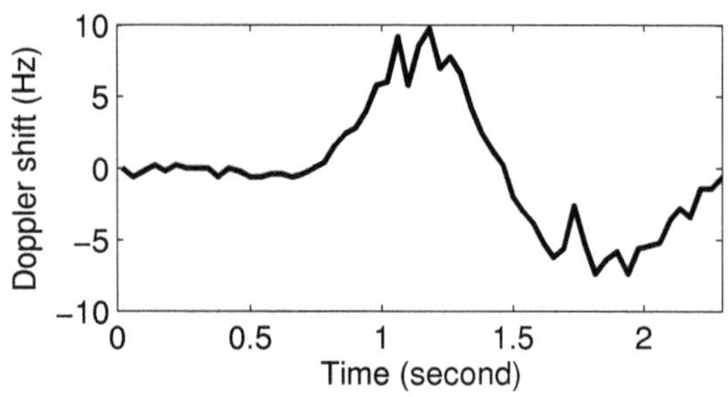


(b) Doppler shift after MRC without outlier removal

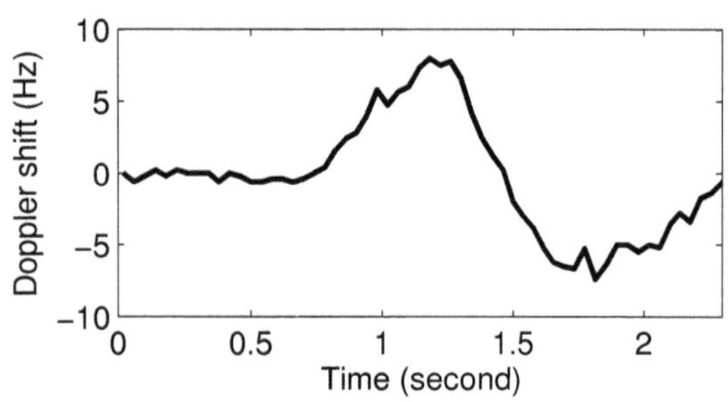


(c) Doppler shift after MRC with outlier removal

**Figure 6: Improving the accuracy of the Doppler shift estimation using MRC and outlier removal.**

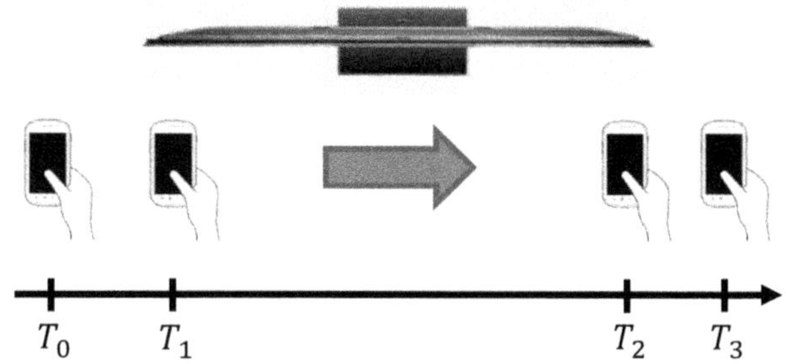


(a) Calibration process.

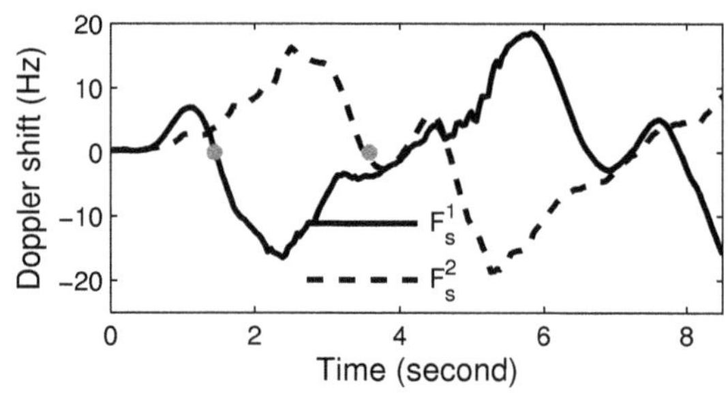


(b) Doppler shift while scanning the TV (round trip).

**Figure 7: Illustration of the calibration process. We measure the distance between two speakers by estimating $T_1$ and $T_2$ (*i.e.*, the time it gets closest to the left and right speakers, respectively) and the speed during $T_1$ and $T_2$ using the Doppler shift. The red dots in Figure 7(b) represent $T_1$ and $T_2$, where $T_1 = 1.48$ and $T_2 = 3.58$.**

exceptional case where all measurement differences exceed 10 Hz, we select the one closest to the previous measurement. After MRC, the Kalman filtering is applied to smooth the estimation. We set the process noise covariance $Q$ and measurement noise covariance $R$ in the Kalman filter both to 0.00001.

Figure 6 shows the raw Doppler shift measurements and the result after MRC with and without outlier removal. It shows that the Doppler estimation after outlier removal yields more smooth output and likely contains smaller errors. In Section 5.1, we show that the outlier removal improves the accuracy by 26% when 5 sound tones are used.

## 3.5 Finding the Distance between the Speakers

So far, we assume the distance between the speakers is known a priori. In practice, this information may not be available in advance. One solution is to ask the user to measure the distance between the speakers using a ruler and report it. This is troublesome. Moreover, sometimes users do not know the exact location of the speakers. Therefore, it is desirable to provide a simple yet effective calibration mechanism that measures the speaker distance whenever the speakers' positions change.

We propose a Doppler based calibration method. It only takes a few seconds for a user to conduct calibration. As shown in Figure 7(a), during the calibration, the TV emits inaudible sound and the device records it using its microphone. The user scans the TV with his hand holding the device. The user starts from the left end of the TV, and move towards the right end of the TV in a straight line. The user stops after it moves beyond the right end, and comes back to the left end. The user can repeat this procedure a few times to improve the accuracy.

Figure 7(b) shows the change of the Doppler shift while a user is performing the calibration. We can easily detect the time when the device moves past the left and right speakers, and measure the distance by calculating the movement speed based on the Doppler shift. As mentioned in Section 3.1, the Doppler shift is positive as the receiver moves towards the sender. When the device is at the left side of both speakers, both $F_1^s$ and $F_2^s$ are positive as it moves towards the right. As it passes the left speaker at 1.48 second (as shown in Figure 7), $F_1^s$ changes to negative while $F_2^s$ stays positive. Similarly, as the device passes the right speaker, $F_2^s$ changes from positive to negative. By finding these points, we find the amount of time user spends moving between the two speakers, and measure the distance using the Doppler shift. To improve the accuracy, we obtain one distance estimate in each direction, and average the estimated distances in both directions.

One question is how many repetitions are required to achieve reasonable accuracy. It depends on the distance error and its impact on device tracking. To better understand the impact, we inject error to the distance estimation. As shown in Section 5, when users repeat the calibration three times (*i.e.*, moving the mobile device back and forth for three times), the 95 percentile error is 5 cm. The experiment also shows the impact of 5 cm speaker distance error on device tracking is negligible. Therefore, three repetitions is generally sufficient.

## 3.6 Finding the Initial Device Position

Next we consider how to handle the issue that the device's initial position is unknown. To address this, we use particle filter. Particle filter has been successfully used in localization to address the uncertainty of the location [33, 9]. We use it in the following way. Initially, we generate many particles uniformly distributed in an area where each particle corresponds to a possible initial position of the device. In the next Doppler sampling interval, it determines the device movement from the current particles. If the device movement is not feasible, the particle is filtered out. In Section 3.3, we mentioned that the position of the device is determined by finding the intersection of the two circles. If $D_1 + D_2 \geq D$, we can find one or more intersections; otherwise, there is no intersection. In this case, we regard the current particle is infeasible and filters it out. The device movement is determined by averaging the movement of the all remaining particles.

More specifically, let $\mathbf{P}$ be the set of particles, which is initialized as $\mathbf{P} = \{(x_o^1, y_o^1), ..., (x_o^N, y_o^N)\}$, where $(x_o^k, y_o^k)$ is the initial position of the $k^{th}$ particle and $N$ is the number of particles. During a new Doppler sampling interval, the particles that give infeasible movement are filtered out from $\mathbf{P}$. After the $i^{th}$ movement, the position at the $(i+1)^{th}$ sample is tracked by averaging the difference between the $(i+1)^{th}$ and $i^{th}$ particle positions. That is,

$$(x_{i+1}, y_{i+1}) = (x_i + \frac{\sum_{k \in \mathbf{P}} (x_{i+1}^k - x_i^k)}{|\mathbf{P}|}, y_i + \frac{\sum_{k \in \mathbf{P}} (y_{i+1}^k - y_i^k)}{|\mathbf{P}|}),$$

where $|\mathbf{P}|$ is the number of remaining particles in $\mathbf{P}$.

The question remains how many particles to allocate. There is a trade off between complexity and accuracy. Increasing the number of particles is likely to increase the accuracy of initial position estimation. We use 625 particles to balance the trade off. 625 particles take 3.63 ms to process, well below 40 ms sampling interval. Refer to Section 4 for further details of this choice.

In Section 5.1, we evaluate the impact of the initial position error on the tracking accuracy. It shows the tracking accuracy is not sensitive to the initial position error. Even with 20 cm error, the median tracking error increases by only 0.2 $cm$. Note that we determine the initial position not because we want to know the exact initial location of the device, but because we need it to track the next position. Regardless of the physical position of the device, the cursor always starts from the center of the screen. So the initial position error does not directly translate into the tracking error.

## 3.7 Controlling a Device with One Speaker

So far we have assumed the equipment to be controlled has two speakers so that we can estimate the distance from these speakers to track the mobile device. All Smart TVs have two speakers. Most laptops (*e.g.*, Lenovo X series, Acer Aspire S3, Dell XPS 13) have two speakers. Some recent laptops (*e.g.*, Dell Studio 17) have 3 speakers to offer better multimedia experience. Three speakers provide more anchor points and allow us to track in a 3-D space or further improve tracking accuracy in a 2-D space.

In this section, we further extend our approach to handle the devices that have only one speaker. We assume it has another wireless device (*e.g.*, WiFi or bluetooth). Then we use the Doppler effect of acoustic signal from the speaker along with the RF signal from the wireless device to enable tracking.

We use the same framework as described above for tracking. The new issue is how to estimate the distance between the mobile device and the wireless device on the equipment. We use the following known relationship from the phase rotation of the received RF signal to compute the distance:

$$\phi_{t1} = -mod(\frac{2\pi}{\lambda} d_{t1}, 2\pi)$$
$$\phi_{t2} = -mod(\frac{2\pi}{\lambda} d_{t2}, 2\pi)$$

where $\phi_{t1}$ and $\phi_{t2}$ denote the phase of the received signal at the mobile device at time $t1$ and $t2$, respectively, and $d_{t1}$ and $d_{t2}$ are their respective distances. This enables us to track the new distance from the RF source by

$$d_{t2} = (\frac{\phi_{t2} - \phi_{t1}}{2\pi} + k)\lambda + d_{t1}. \quad (2)$$

$k$ is an integer and set to 0 here, since our sampling interval of RF phase is 10 ms and it is safe to assume we move less than one wavelength during a sampling interval.

One of the challenges in RF phase based tracking is accurate measurement of the received signal phase. In particular, the carrier frequency offset (CFO) between the sender and the receiver causes the phase to change over time even if the receiver is not moving. A few recent works, such as MegaMIMO [32, 47], show that it is feasible to track the phase change over time with precise CFO estimation. To simplify our implementation, we connect a sender and a receiver with the same external clock in our experiment to guarantee that they have no frequency offset. We estimate the phase of the receiver while the sender is continuously sending 1 MHz wide OFDM symbols.

As in Section 3.3, if we know the device's initial location and the distance between the speaker and RF source, we can track the position by finding the intersections of the two circles whose radii are the distance measured by the Doppler shift and RF phase tracking, respectively. We can again apply particle filter to address the issue that the device's initial position is unknown. We can adopt similar calibration to measure the distance between the speaker and RF source by detecting the speaker's position based on the change in the sign of the Doppler shift (*i.e.*, going from positive to negative) and detecting the RF source's position based on the change in the phase of the received RF signal (*i.e.*, going from decreasing phase to increasing phase).

# 4. IMPLEMENTATION

We implement our system and validate the feasibility of the real-time device tracking. The mobile program is implemented on Android, which collects the inertial sensor data or audio signal and sends it to the tracking processor through Android debug bridge. Tracking is implemented in JAVA, which tracks the position of the device using the audio signal in real-time, as described in Section 3. For comparison, we also implement other tracking methods based on an accelerometer, gyroscope, and camera.

**AAMouse:** Unless otherwise specified, we use the Doppler based tracking. Since tracking requires non-negligible amount of computation, all tracking algorithms are handled by the tracking processor while the mobile device is only responsible for delivering the recorded audio samples to the processor. To support real-time processing, we observe the main processing overhead is FFT. During each Doppler sampling interval (*i.e.*, 40ms), we 1) perform 44100-point FFT, 2) find peak frequency in each band, 3) combine them after removing outliers, and 4) calculate the position for each particle. Except FFT, the complexity is $O(WN + P)$, where $W$ is the width of spectrum to scan for each tone, $N$ is the number of

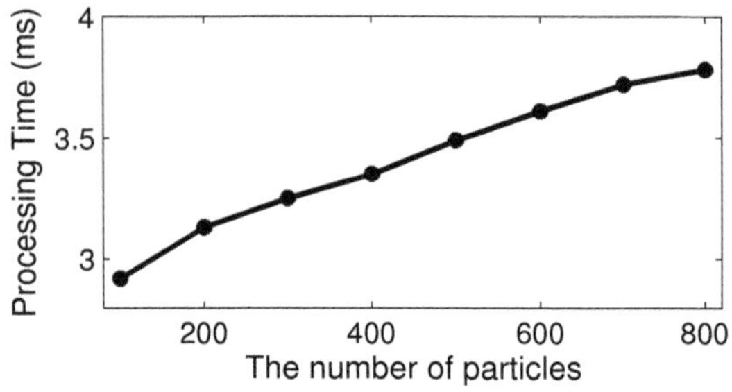


**Figure 8: Processing time with a varying number of particles.**

tones, and $P$ is the number of particles. To minimize the computational overhead, we set $W$ and $N$ to 100 and 10, respectively. To determine how many particles to use, we measured the processing time of tracking that is performed every Doppler sampling interval (*i.e.*, 40 ms) while varying the number of particles from 100 to 800. We used a PC with Intel i7 2GHz processor and 4GB memory as our testbed. As shown in Figure 8, there is a constant overhead of 2.8 ms on average, which does not depend on the number of particles. The additional overhead incurred by particle filtering is relatively small, and linearly increases with $P$. Therefore, we allocate $25 \times 25 = 625$ particles every 20 cm to cover $5m \times 5m$ space. In this case, it takes 3.63 ms to process the data, well below 40 ms sampling interval. The computation overhead is reduced further because the particles are filtered out during the tracking.

We also evaluate the Doppler and phase based tracking for an object that has only one speaker. We use USRP nodes as a sender and receiver to get the phase information, and attach the USRP receiver antenna to the smartphone with a microphone so that the WiFi and audio signals are received at the same location. We implement a UHD program that records the phase of the received RF signal at USRP and feeds it to the tracking program, which tracks the device location using the phase change of the RF signal as well as Doppler shift of the acoustic signal. While we use USRP to generate RF signals, one can also use commodity WiFi cards to get the phase information and remove CFO [17, 18].

**Accelerometer based tracking:** For comparison, we also implement accelerometer based tracking, which uses double integration of acceleration to estimate distance. We follow the instruction in [36]. One of the difficulties in accelerometer based positioning is to determine the threshold used for detecting device movement. It is difficult to find a proper threshold that achieves both low false positive and low false negative. So we set a low threshold (*i.e.*, 0.07 $m/s^2$) to avoid treating device movement as $stop$ by mistake.

**Gyroscope based tracking:** This mimics the gyroscope based tracking used in commercial air mouse products [5] and smart TV motion controllers [34, 35]. The gyroscope measures the angular velocity, and translates it into a 2-D displacement of a cursor.

**Camera based tracking:** The goal of camera based tracking is to get the ground-truth of the device movement. Using a camera attached to the ceiling of our laboratory, we track the position of the device very precisely. We implement a simple vision based object tracking program using OpenCV [7]. To improve the accuracy, we attach a label with a distinct color (blue in our setup) to the device and implement a program to track that color. Camera based tracking is suitable for providing the ground truth in our setting, but is not a practical solution in general, since it requires not only lines of sight to the object at all time but also computational intensive and error-prone object recognition and tracking (especially for a general object and background).

# 5. EVALUATION

**Experimental setup:** We evaluate the tracking performance of AAMouse and compare its usability with the other tracking methods. We use a DELL XPS desktop with Intel i7 CPU and 4GB memory as a main processor, and use Google NEXUS 4 as our main mobile device for user study. The audio source is Logitech S120 2.0 speaker. The volume of the speaker is set to 30 out of 100 to make sure it works in a normal volume range. By default, the distance between the two speakers is 0.9 m, and the distance between the speakers and the mobile device is around 2 m. We also vary these values to understand their impacts.

For our experiment, we implement a program that displays a pointer and the trajectory of the device movement in real-time so that users can see how well the pointer moves as they intend. To emit sound tones in inaudible frequency range, we play a wave format audio file with specific frequency tones that we generate using MATLAB. The left and right speakers use 17 - 19 KHz and 19 - 21 KHz spectrum, respectively. Each speaker emits 10 1-Hz sound tones with 200 Hz spacing in between. The best 5 tones are selected to estimate the Doppler shift as described in Section 5.1.

**Evaluation methodology:** We conduct user study with 8 students (5 male and 3 female students). They use all four schemes: AAMouse, accelerometer, gyroscope, and camera based tracking. Each user has 10-minute training for each scheme. When using AAMouse, the users are asked to hold the device in such a way to avoid their hands blocking the microphone. When evaluating the accelerometer and gyroscope based approaches, the users hold the device so that the phone is parallel to the line defined by the two speaker so that the coordinates of the accelerometer or gyroscope are consistent with the coordinates defined by the speakers. To quantify the accuracy and usability, we perform two kinds of experiments. The first experiment is to validate if the mobile device can be used as a pointing device like a mouse. We show a target on the screen, and ask the user to touch it. Each user repeats for 40 times. In the second experiment, we show simple shapes, such as a circle, triangle, diamond, and heart on the screen, and ask the users to use a mobile device to trace the shapes on the screen as closely as possible so that we can quantify how accurately they can control the pointer. Each user draws a shape for 5 times. The overall experiment lasts about one hour for each user excluding the training time. The average distance of the trajectory in the pointing and drawing experiments are 21.1 cm and 65.4 cm, respectively. The average tracking times for the pointing and the drawing are 3.2 and 8.4 seconds, respectively. The tracking and visualization are both done online in real-time. Meanwhile, we also store the complete traces to compute various performance metrics offline. The error is measured by comparing the actual pointer trajectory with that from the camera based tracking. We also compare the distance traveled in order to touch a target, which reflects the amount of user effort.

## 5.1 Micro benchmark

Before presenting user study results, we first show a few micro benchmarks.

**Trajectory Accuracy:** To quantify the accuracy of trajectory tracking, we compare the trajectory a user traverses when trying to touch a target or draw a shape using AAMouse with the trajectories tracked by the camera, which serves as the ground truth. We sample the trajectory tracked by AAMouse at the camera sampling rate (*i.e.*, every 50 ms). For each sampled point, we compute the distance to the closest point on the trajectory tracked by the camera. We use the average distance across all sampled points as the error metric.

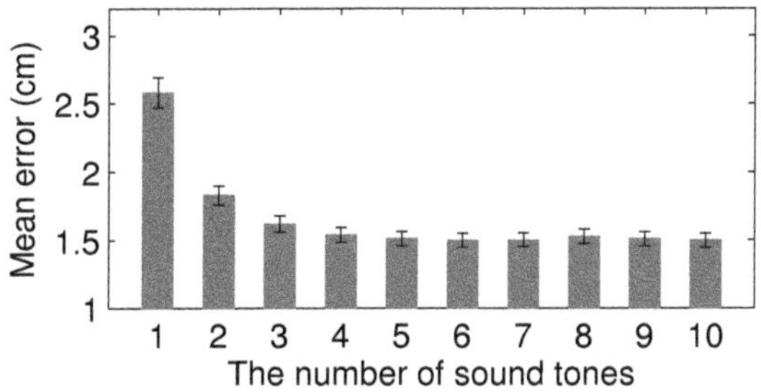


(a) With outlier removal.

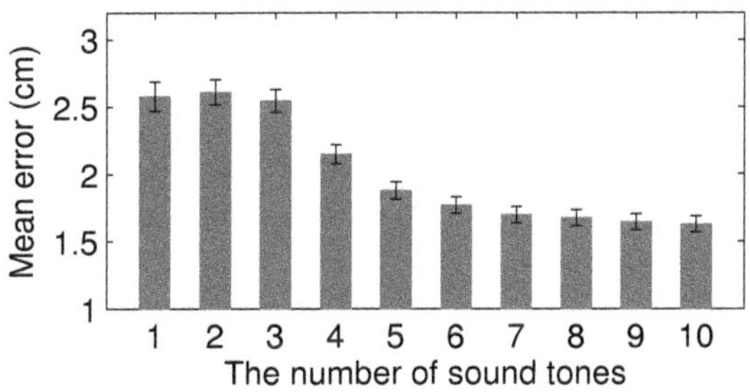


(b) Without outlier removal.

**Figure 9: AAMouse trajectory error with different numbers of sound tones. The numbers of sound tones in both figures are the numbers before outlier removal.**

Figure 9(a) shows the mean trajectory error as we vary the number of sound tones used to estimate the Doppler shift, where the error bars represent 90% confidence interval. We observe that the mean trajectory error decreases from 2.7 cm to 1.9 cm by increasing the number of sound tones from 1 to 2. The error decreases further as we use more sound tones, but the improvement is marginal. Therefore, we decide to use 5 tones in the remaining evaluation to balance the tradeoff between accuracy and computation overhead.

Figure 9(b) is the mean trajectory error without the outlier removal introduced in Section 3.4. The results show that the outlier removal is crucial. If outliers are not removed, the benefit of using more tones is smaller and it requires more sound tones to achieve the same accuracy. This is because we need many samples to mitigate the significant error introduced by the outliers. With 5 sound tones, the mean trajectory error with outliers is 26% higher than that without outliers; even with 10 sound tones, the mean trajectory error with outliers is still around 6% higher.

**Speaker distance error:** In this experiment, a user moves the mobile device across the sender's left and right speakers to estimate the distance between its two speakers, as described in Section 3.5. The actual distance between the speakers is 0.9 m.

Figure 10 shows the CDF of distance error as we vary the number of scannings, where a scan means that a user moves the device from the left end to the right end, passing both speakers, and then comes back (*i.e.*, one round-trip). As we would expect, increasing the number of scannings reduces the measurement error. When the user scans three times, 95% and 99% of the experiments have measurement errors within 5 and 10 cm, respectively. Further increasing the number of scannings yields marginal improvement in the accuracy.

Next we examine how the error in the speaker distance estimation affects the tracking accuracy. We inject varying amount of error to the speak distance estimation. As shown in Figure 11, the tracking error increases slightly with the increasing error in the

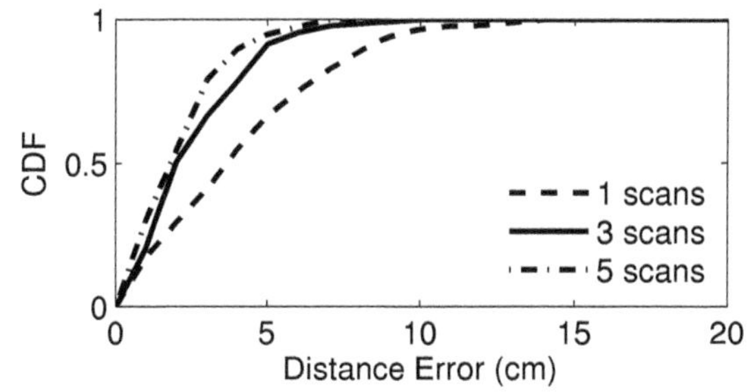


**Figure 10: CDF of the speaker distance measurement result with different numbers of scannings.**

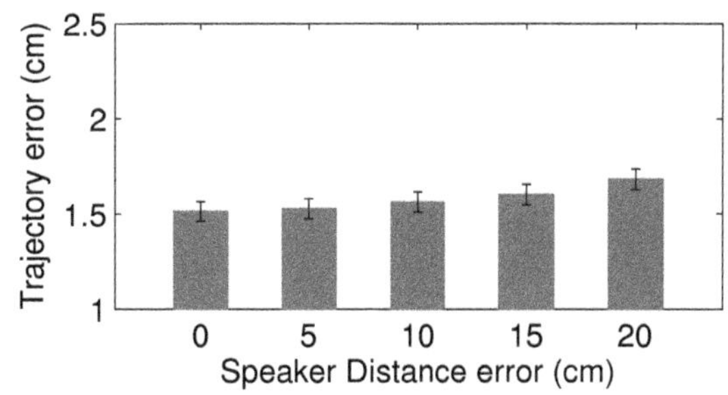


**Figure 11: Trajectory error as the error of the speaker distance varies.**

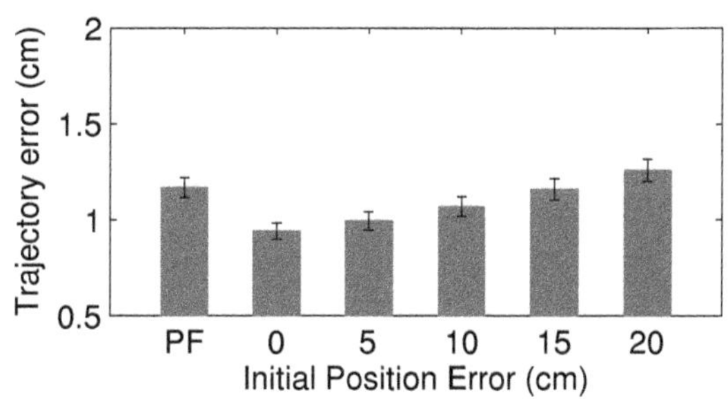


**Figure 12: Trajectory error as the error of the device initial position varies.**

speaker distance estimation. The speaker distance estimation error of 10 cm increases the mean error by 0.05 cm (*i.e.*, from 1.51 to 1.56 cm). In Section 3.3, we explain that the position is tracked by finding the intersections of two circles whose center points are the speaker locations. Erroneous estimation of speaker positions degrades tracking accuracy, but the degradation is not significant, as shown in Figure 11.

**Impact of initial position error:** Finally, we show the impact of the initial position estimation error on the tracking accuracy. As it is difficult to know the initial position of the device in advance, we use particle filter as described in Section 3.6. For this experiment, the users start moving the device from a fixed initial position and perform the same experiments of pointing and drawing. We compare the tracking error when (i) the initial position is known, (ii) the initial position is known with a fixed amount of error, and (iii) using particle filter to estimate the initial position. Note that this is the only experiment where users start from the fixed initial position, while in all the other experiments users all start from an arbitrary initial position, which is more realistic.

Figure 12 presents the mean tracking error where *PF* is our particle filter approach. If the initial position is known, the accuracy can be further improved, but this is often infeasible. With particle filter, we can limit the impact of the initial position error. The result shows that the tracking error with particle filter is quite small: 1.4 cm, which is slightly larger than the case when there is 15 cm error in the initial position estimation, but smaller than that of 20 cm error in the initial position estimation.

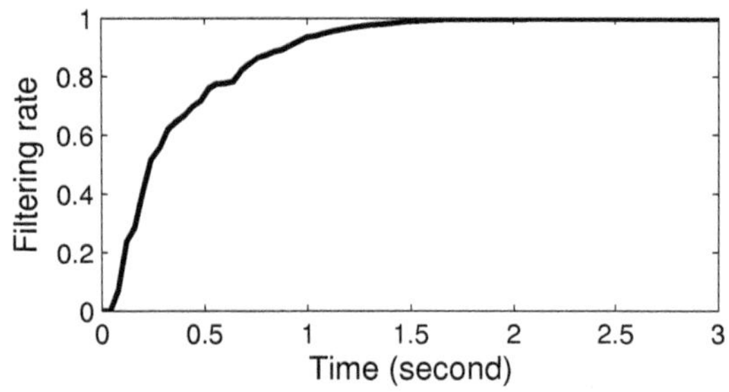


**Figure 13: Particle filter convergence time.**

**Particle filter convergence:** Figure 13 shows the particle filter convergence. Using the user experiment data, we plot the average fraction of the particles that are filtered over time. The result shows that after one second since the tracking starts, 93% of particles are filtered out. This demonstrates that particle filter converges fast.

## 5.2 AAMouse evaluation

**Tracking accuracy:** Next we compare the accuracy of AAMouse with the accelerometer based tracking. Their errors are measured in the same way as described in Section 5.1. Figure 14 shows the cumulative distribution of the trajectory errors for AAMouse and the accelerometer based tracking. The median error for AAMouse is 1.4 cm while that for the accelerometer is 17.9 cm. The 90th percentile errors of AAMouse and accelerometer are 3.4 cm and 37.7 cm, respectively. AAMouse has 10 times lower error than accelerometer in terms of both the median and 90th percentile errors.

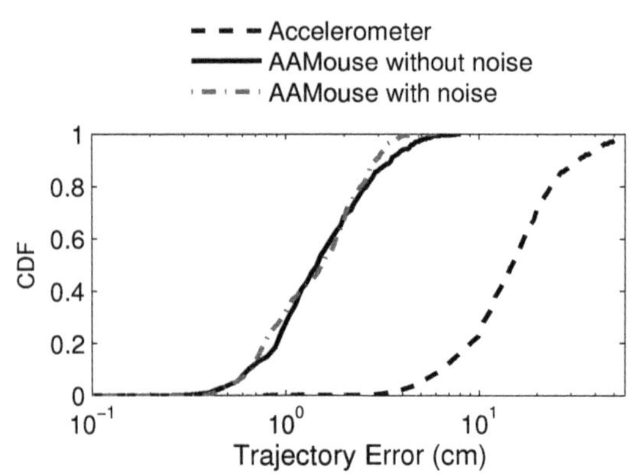


**Figure 14: CDF of trajectory error.**

**Tracking accuracy under background noise:** In order to evaluate the robustness of AAMouse against background noise, we perform additional experiments on AAMouse while the speakers generate both music and inaudible sound tones for tracking. This emulates the scenarios where smart TVs play background sound while sending inaudible acoustic signals for device tracking. According to [20], electronic music tend to generate noise at higher frequencies than other music genres. Therefore we use a few music clips in YouTube and select "Top EDM 2014 Music Playlist Tracklist" [25]

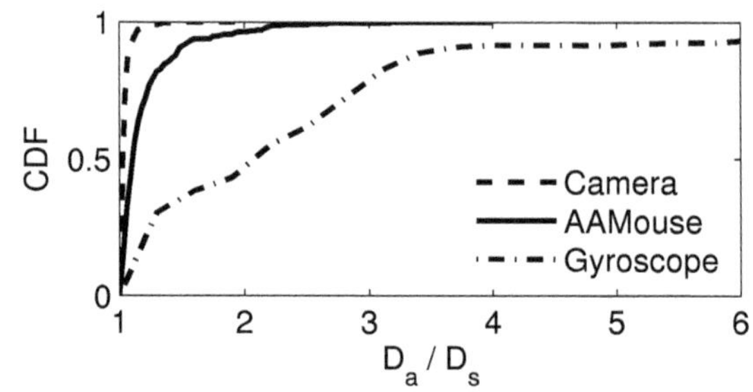


**Figure 15: CDF of unnecessary movement to reach the target.**

as the background noise. As shown in Figure 14, the accuracy remains the same. This is because the frequency of human voice and many music genres, such as Jazz, Pop and Classic, do not exceed 10 KHz. Even for some music with clangs and artificial sounds, such as rock and electronic music, their frequency hardly exceeds 15 KHz. Therefore they do not affect AAMouse, which uses higher than 17 KHz frequency band. This is also consistent with the findings reported in Spartacus [39], which uses inaudible sound for device pairing.

**Target pointing evaluation:** To evaluate the usability of AAMouse as a pointing device, we measure the distance that the pointer travels in order to touch a specific target. The main purpose of this experiment is to evaluate how easily one can control the pointer. If the device tracking is inaccurate, the pointer movement will be erroneous, which will increase the distance traveled. Similarly, if the tracking mechanism is not intuitive, the pointer might not move as the user intends, which will also increase the distance. We use $R = D_a/D_s$ to quantify the accuracy, where $D_a$ and $D_s$ are the actual distance traveled and the shortest path distance, respectively. When the metric is 1, it means that the movement follows the shortest path and has no tracking error. A larger value indicates a higher tracking error or harder to use.

We compare AAMouse, gyroscope, and camera-based tracking, which all succeed in touching the target every time since the users are required to change the pointer position until the target is reached. We do not compare with the accelerometer based scheme since its error is too large: despite significant time and effort users spend, they still fail to touch the target in over 90% cases.

Figure 15 shows the CDF of $R = D_a/D_s$ for the three schemes. In terms of the median error, camera based tracking and AAMouse yields almost the same performance (*i.e.*, 1.03 versus 1.05), but Gyroscope based tracking yields 1.4, considerably higher than the other two. The performance gap grows even larger in worse cases. The 80th percentile $R$ for the camera, AAMouse and gyroscope based tracking are 1.06, 1.17 and 2.98, respectively. In the case of AAMouse, the pointer travel distance increases mostly due to the tracking error. When the users try to touch the target, they move the device towards the direction of the target. If there is tracking error, the pointer deviates from the direction intended by the user, which extends the moving distance. As it is shown in Figure 14 and 15, the tracking accuracy of AAMouse is acceptable, so it does not significantly increase $R$. On the other hand, the moving distance of the gyroscope based tracking increases mainly due to unintuitive use rather than tracking error. According to our observation, the gyroscope itself is quite accurate in measuring the amount of rotation. However, it is not intuitive to users how much they have to rotate their wrists in order to move the pointers in an intended direction, which makes them fail to reach the target. In particular, users have trouble moving a pointer in a diagonal direction, as it requires them to rotate their wrist in two axes simultaneously. The users have to make several attempts before finally touching the pointer, which increases $R$.

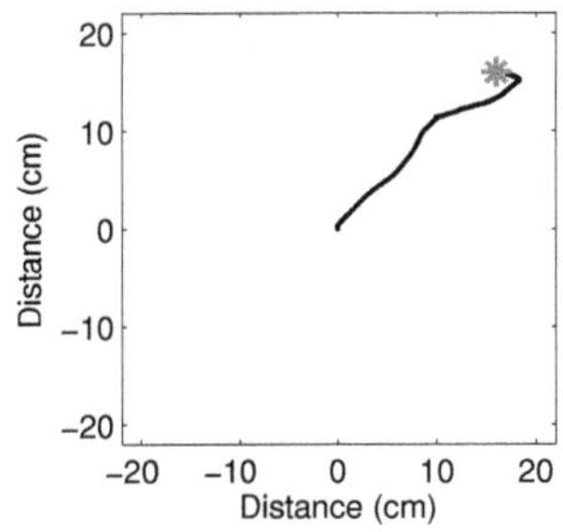


(a) AAMouse.

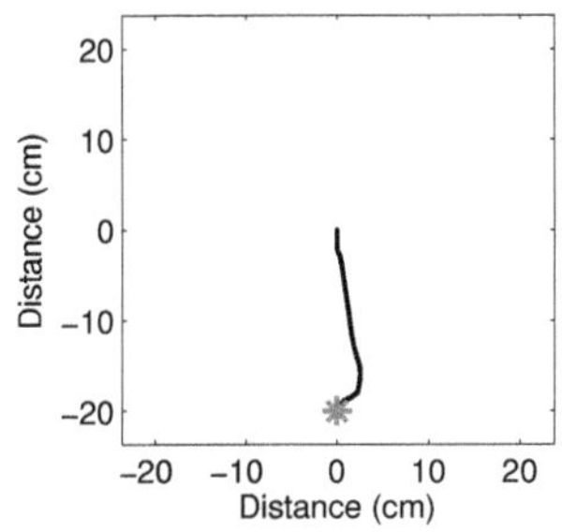


(b) Camera based tracking.

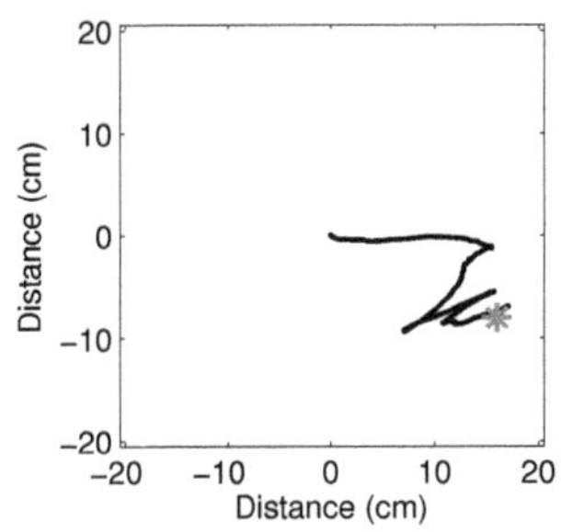


(c) Gyroscope based tracking.

**Figure 16: Trajectory of AAMouse, camera and gyroscope based tracking while the users are trying to reach the target point. $R$ of each scheme corresponds to the 80th percentile.**

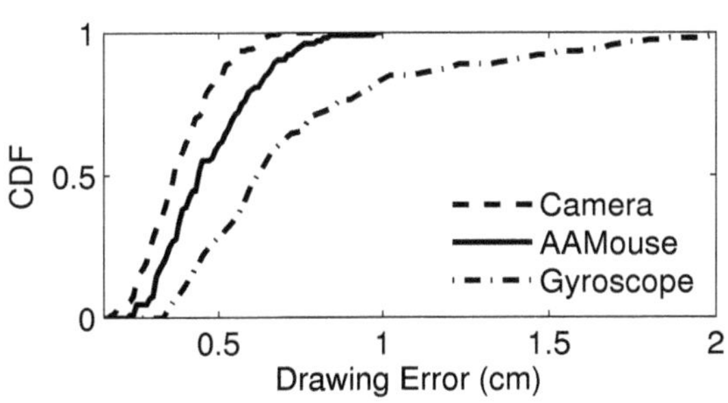


**Figure 17: CDF of drawing error.**

Figure 16 shows example trajectories when the user is trying to reach the target under the 80th percentile $R$. As we can see,

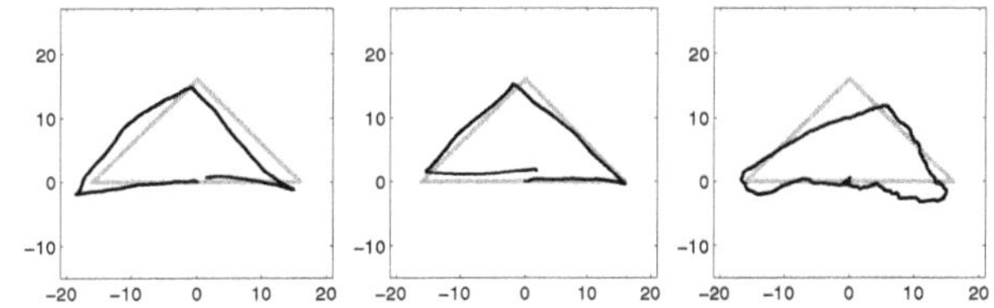

(a) AAMouse (b) Camera (c) Gyro

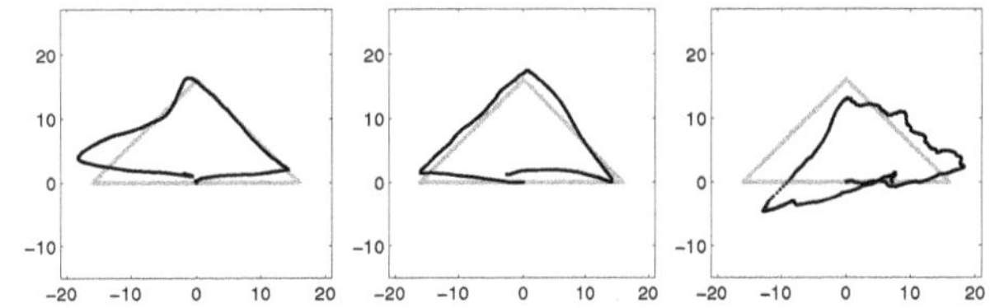

(d) AAMouse (e) Camera (f) Gyro

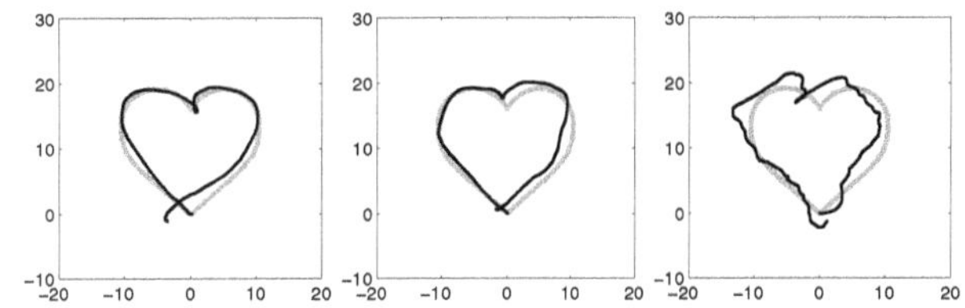

(g) AAMouse (h) Camera (i) Gyro

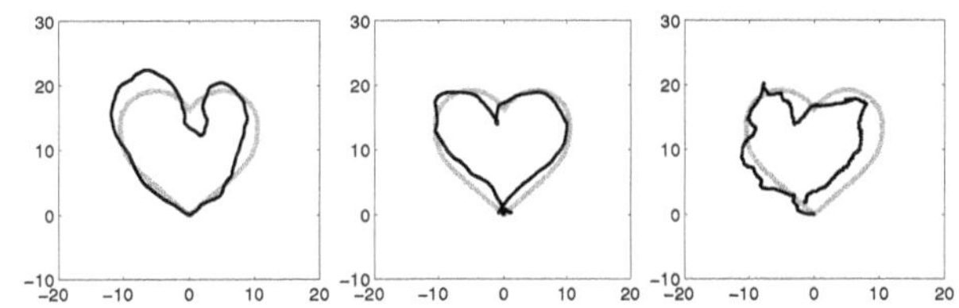

(j) AAMouse (k) Camera (l) Gyro

**Figure 18: Figures drawn by AAMouse, camera and gyroscope based tracking. (a),(b),(c), (g), (h), (i) and (d),(e),(f), (j), (k), (l) correspond to the median and 80th percentile errors of each scheme, respectively. The units of both the x-axis and y-axis are centimeters.**

AAMouse and camera users spend similar amount of effort to reach the target, but the gyroscope user spends considerable more efforts to reach the target.

**Drawing evaluation:** Another way of evaluating the usability is to ask a user to draw simple shapes: a triangle, diamond, circle, and heart. The user follows the boundaries of the shapes shown on the screen using the pointer controlled by AAMouse, gyroscope, or camera. Due to the tracking error and imprecise user control, the user cannot draw perfect shapes. We measure the quality of the drawings by calculating the distance between the drawn figure and the original shape. For each point in the figure, we calculate its distance to the closest point in the original shape, and average across all points. While this does not perfectly capture the quality of the drawing, it provides reasonable distinction between well-drawn and poorly-drawn figures.

Figure 17 shows the CDF of the drawing error. The median drawing errors for camera, AAMouse and gyroscope based tracking are 0.39, 0.47, and 0.61 cm, respectively, and the 80th percentile errors are 0.51, 0.63, and 0.99 cm, respectively. Figure 18 shows the sample drawings with the corresponding errors. In the interest of space, we omit the results of circle and diamond. The shapes drawn by AAMouse and camera are similar, and do not significantly deviate from the original shapes, whereas the figures from the gyroscope have visibly larger error. In case of larger drawing error shown in Figure 18 (d),(e),(f), (j), (k) and (l), the quality difference is even more significant. With the camera, the user is able to draw close to the original shape. The figure from AAMouse is less accurate, but still follows the original shape. On the other hand, the gyroscope based figure contains significant errors, and hardly resembles the original shape.

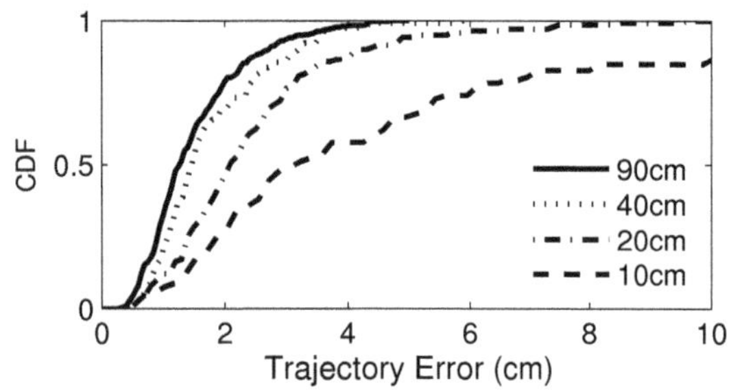


**Figure 19: CDF of trajectory error as the speaker distance varies.**

**Impact of the speaker distance:** Next we evaluate the impact of the speaker distance on the accuracy of AAMouse. In Section 3.3, we explain that we track the position by finding the intersection of two circles whose radii are the distances from the speakers. As the distance between the speakers gets closer, the overlap between the two circles increases, which causes a small distance error to result in a larger tracking error. Figure 19 shows the CDF of AAMouse trajectory error as we vary the distance between speakers from 10, 20, 40, to 90 cm while keeping the distance between the speakers and mobile device to be around 2 m. Reducing the spacing to 40 cm slightly decreases the accuracy. Reducing the spacing to 20 cm increases the median error from 1.4 cm to 2 cm, which is still acceptable. However, the error under 10 cm spacing is significant. These results suggest when the mobile device is around 2 m from the speakers, AAMouse requires at least 20 cm separation between the two speakers to achieve high accuracy. All smart TVs and most laptops have more than 20 cm distance between speakers, and can support AAMouse well. For example, even a small 13-inch laptop like Apple 13-inch MacBook Pro is 32 cm wide, and its two speakers are at the left and right ends and separated by around 32 cm [23].

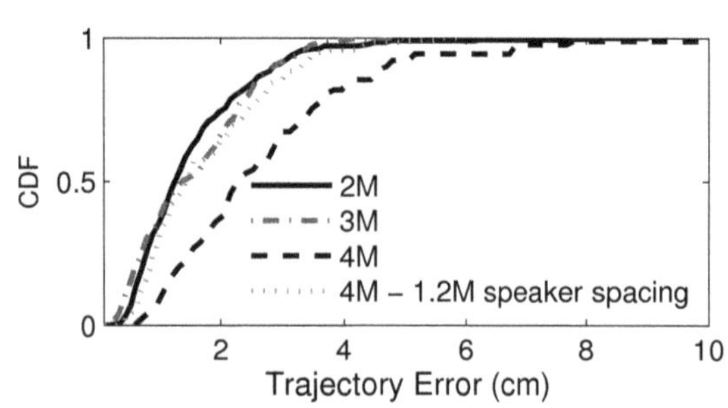


**Figure 20: CDF of trajectory error as the distances between the speakers and the microphone varies.**

**Range experiment:** Figure 20 shows CDF of the trajectory as we vary the distances between the speaker and the microphone. It shows the accuracy degradation is negligible when we increase the distance from 2 m to 3 m. When the distance increases to 4 m, the degradation increases. The degradation is due to weaker sound signals, and more importantly, reduced relative distance between the speakers versus the distance from the speaker to the mobile device. If the distance from the speaker to the microphone increases while the speaker spacing remains the same, the circles from two speakers have larger overlap, which produces a higher tracking error as we see in Figure 19. To confirm this, we extend the speaker spacing from 90 cm to 120 cm. The result shows that increasing the speakers' distance avoids accuracy degradation, and the error is similar to that in 2 m case. As bigger TVs are getting more popular, AAMouse can achieve high accuracy beyond 4 m range. For example, TVs bigger than 60-inch are widely available in market. The distance between the two speakers on such TVs is larger than 130 cm, and can easily support accurate tracking beyond 4 m.

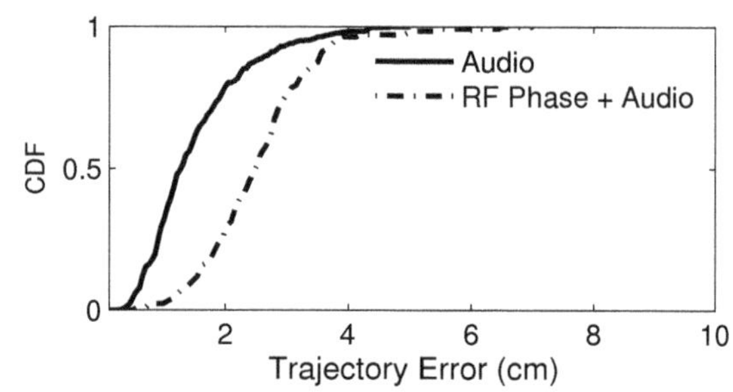


**Figure 21: CDF of trajectory error while RF phase is used for tracking as well as Doppler.**

**Using RF signal phase:** We evaluate the tracking accuracy when RF signal phase is used for tracking along with the Doppler shift estimation from one speaker. We use a USRP node with an antenna to replace a right speaker, and keep the distance between the left speaker and the USRP transmitter at 90 cm. While our implementation uses USRP to derive distance estimation, it is possible to apply the approach on the commodity WiFi card [17]. Figure 21 shows CDF of the trajectory error, and confirms the feasibility of tracking using the Doppler shift and the phase of RF signal. The median error increases from 1.4 cm to 2.5 cm because RF phase is more easily affected by multi-path fading and environmental change such as human movement. Even while the device is not moving, the phase may change due to movement of other human bodies (besides hand movement). In comparison, while the Doppler shift is also affected by other human body movement, we use the peak frequency and ignore the other frequency shifts, which enhances its robustness.

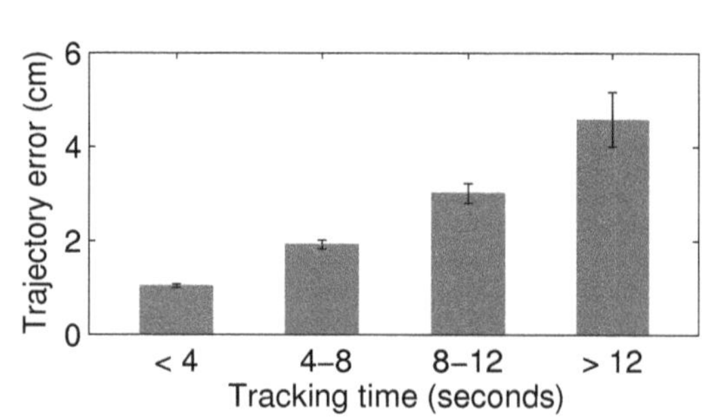


**Figure 22: Trajectory error with different tracking time.**

**Impact of the tracking error accumulation:** AAMouse tracks the device by estimating the movement from the previous position based on the velocity derived from Doppler shift. The estimation error of the previous position will increase the estimation error of the next position. Therefore, the error tends to increase over time. To evaluate the impact of tracking time on the accuracy, we classify the traces according to the tracking time. In our user study data, the tracking time of each individual experiment depends on the user and the tracking goal (*i.e.*, pointing or drawing), and the minimum, maximum, and mean tracking times are 1.8, 13.5, and 4.9 seconds, respectively. Figure 22 shows the mean tracking error for four different ranges of tracking time. As we can see, longer tracking time leads to larger tracking error. When the tracking time is between 8 and 12 seconds, the mean error is 2.9 cm; but when tracking time is longer than 12 seconds, the error increases to 4.5 cm. This suggests that AAMouse is most effective for short-term tracking (*e.g.*, less than 10 seconds). To support short-term tracking, a user can initiate tracking using a simple gesture or tapping the screen.

Even for longer-term tracking, users are generally not sensitive to the position error slowly accumulated over time. This is especially so for drawing applications, where users are mainly interested in whether the pointer is moving in the way as they intend, and the error in absolute device position is not obvious to the user. To demonstrate it, we ask a user to repeatedly draw circles using AAMouse and track it over 25 seconds. Figure 23 shows the circles drawn by AAMouse (black) as well as the ground-truth device movement (green) at the beginning of the tracking and after 20 seconds, where the trajectory errors are 1.2 and 7.9 cm, respectively. As shown in Figure 23 (b), after 20 seconds, the absolute position error increases due to error accumulation, but the shape is still preserved.

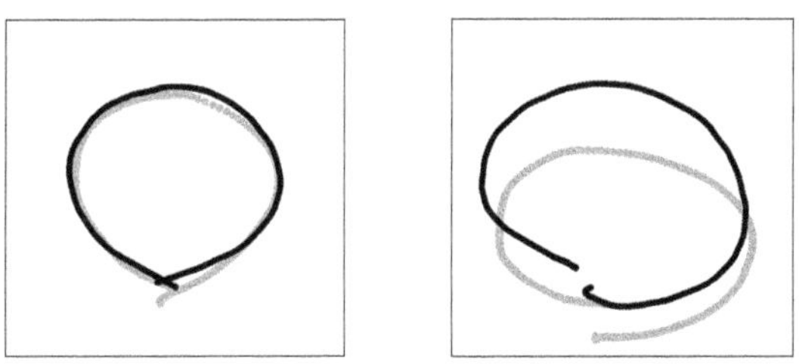

(a) In the beginning. (b) After 20 seconds.

**Figure 23: Compare the circles drawn by AAMouse (black) and the ground-truth (green).**

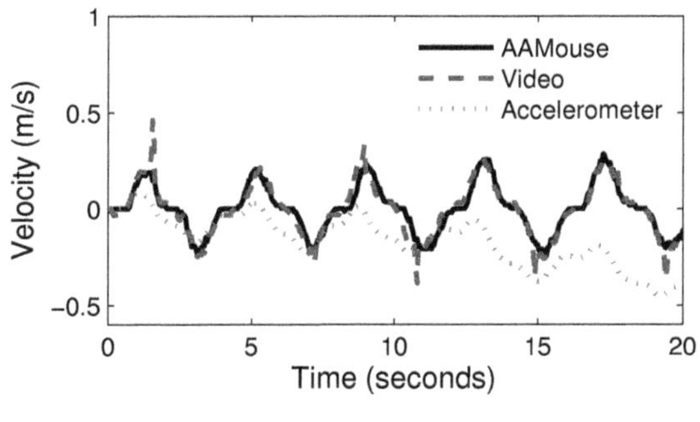


**Figure 24: Velocity while moving the device backward and forward.**

From our experience, we find the user is mainly concerned about instantaneous tracking error because it moves the pointer differently from what the user intends. This can happen in accelerometer based tracking due to double integration of the acceleration, which causes speed estimation error. In comparison, AAMouse estimates the velocity using the measured Doppler shift every time, so the error of speed estimation does not accumulate over time. To confirm the intuition, we perform the following experiment, where we repeatedly move the mobile device back and forth, and measure the velocity using AAMouse, camera, and accelerometer. As shown in Figure 24, the error is accumulated with the accelerometer: the difference between accelerometer and video based velocity estimation increases over time. In comparison, the difference between the video and Doppler based velocity estimation is small and remains constant over time.

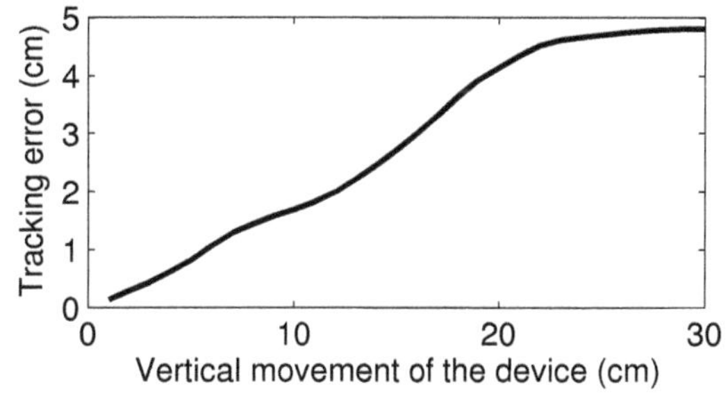


**Figure 25: Tracking error as the device is moving vertically.**

**Impact of vertical movements:** So far, we focus on tracking in a 2-D space by using either 2 speakers or one speaker and one wireless device as anchors. Using more anchors allows us to track in a 3-D space. If we are limited to two anchors, we can track the device movement in the horizontal plane (assuming the speakers are placed horizontally next to each other); and vertical movement cannot be tracked. To understand the impact how vertical movements affect the tracking accuracy, we vertically move the device while fixing its position in the horizontal plane. Since the device does not have horizontal movement, any movement tracked is an error. Figure 25 shows the tracking error when we vertically move the device up to 30 cm. We repeat 30 times, and get the average tracking distance of AAMouse. Like the other experiments, the distance between 2 speakers is 0.9 m and the distance between the speaker and the device is approximately 2 m. The result shows that the tracking error generated by 30 cm vertical movement is less than 5 cm. With the Doppler shift measurement, AAMouse tracks the device by observing the change in the distance between the two speakers and the device. Given the distance between the speaker and the device, the distance change by the vertical movement is much smaller than that by the horizontal movement. Moreover, as a mouse application, a user is typically aware that vertical movement may incur tracking error and avoids large vertical movement. If they limit their vertical movement to 10 cm, the tracking error reduces to 1.7 cm. Therefore, the error introduced by vertical movement is likely to be small.

## 6. RELATED WORK

**Localization and device tracking:** Localization has received significant research attention over the last few decades. However, most of the previous works achieve coarse grained localization, and do not satisfy our goal of achieving centimeter-level accuracy. There are a few ranging-based localization papers that use acoustic signals to estimate the distance based on time-of-arrival (*e.g.*, [29, 48,

31]). Different from these ranging based works, we focus on continuous trajectory tracking to enable mouse functionalities. [38] uses 6 beacon nodes as transmitters to achieve a median error of 12 cm under the line-of-sight. To achieve such an accuracy, it requires special hardware, dense deployment, and line-of-sight, which may not be feasible in many cases. Another fine grained indoor localizations is ArrayTrack [45], but its median error is still 23 cm. Recently, there have been a few works that track the trajectory of RFID tags in centimeter-level [40, 41, 46]. They require special RFID readers with many antennas. RF-IDraw [41] uses two RFID readers, each with 4 antennas, and Tagoram [46] uses four readers, each equipped with 4 antennas. In home environment, it is difficult to imagine that people deploy RFID readers to track their devices. We achieve comparable accuracy by exploiting two speakers that are available in most TVs, PCs, and laptops. Moreover, although Tagoram achieves millimeter-level accuracy when the target moves along a known track, in an unknown track their median error is 12 cm, well above our error (*i.e.*, 1.4 cm).

**Using inertial sensors:** [22] uses the acceleration measured from the accelerometer of the smart phone for localization. Due to significant error from the acceleration measurement, it uses dead reckoning approach that finds the position by estimating the number of steps and the heading direction instead of double integration. Zee [33] uses a similar approach to fill in the gap between the locations estimated using WiFi. Both of them achieve sub-meter level accuracy. Such an approach is suitable for tracking walking, but not hand movement, which is our focus.

Inertial sensors are also used for gesture recognition and device tracking [28, 4]. E-gesture [28] uses gyroscope and accelerometer for gesture recognition, but it is not applicable to device tracking. [4] tracks the device movement and recognizes the alphabet the user writes. Their tracking algorithm is similar to the acceleration based tracking used as a baseline comparison in Section 5. Our evaluation result shows that AAMouse achieves much higher accuracy than the accelerometer based tracking.

**Using Doppler for motion and device tracking:** WiSee [30] is a novel method for device-free gesture recognition using the Doppler shift of the WiFi RF signal. Its main benefit is that users do not need to carry any device. Its focus is gesture recognition, which distinguishes one gesture from another, instead of estimating the exact position, so it is not sufficient for our purpose. A few other works [12, 8, 6, 39] use the Doppler shift of the audio signal for gesture recognition rather than device tracking. DopLink [6] enables the interaction among devices using the Doppler shift, and Spartacus [39] finds the direction of the device movement using the Doppler shift and pairs it with another device that moves in the same direction. Swadloon [14] exploits the Doppler shift of audio signal for fine-grained indoor localization. It assumes the position of the anchor nodes (*i.e.*, speakers) are known, and its error is around 50 $cm$, well below our accuracy requirement. [19] proposes acoustic signal based localization, but it uses chirp ranging instead of the Doppler effect. Its localization accuracy is close to 1 $m$, and its tracking accuracy during device movement has not been evaluated.

**Infrastructure based tracking:** Microsoft X-box Kinect [1] and Nintendo Wii [2] have been widely successful as gaming controllers. They augment the game reality by using motion tracking and gesture recognition. Kinect recognizes the gesture of the user using the depth sensing camera. Wii uses Infrared (IR) signal to track the movement of the controller. The sensor bar on the top of TV emits IR signal and the IR camera attached to the Wii controller determines its position relative to the sensor bar by detecting the change in IR blobs [43]. Different from these devices, our approach enables mouse functionalities using the speakers and microphones that are already available in most TV and mobile devices and does not require line-of-sight.

**Gyroscope based Air mouse:** One of our main applications is to let a user point at a specific target using a mobile device as a mouse. There have been a few types of *Air mice* [5] in the market. These are usually used as remote controllers for laptops and PCs. Advanced remote controllers for smart TVs, such as Roku 3 [34], Samsung Smart Remote [35], and LG magic motion controller [21], provide similar functionality. They all use gyroscopes, which measure the angular velocity to track motion, where a user rotates his wrist to control the pointer position in a 2-D space. Rotating the device yields the change of the angular velocity, which is translated into the pointer movement. Such a movement is not intuitive to users. We performed user study to compare gyroscope based device control with our scheme. As shown in Section 5, users traverse 40% more distance to touch a target. When asked to draw simple shapes using the gyroscope, the outputs are rather different from the original shapes.

## 7. CONCLUSION

In this paper, we develop a novel system that can accurately track hand movement and apply it to realize a mouse. A unique advantage of our scheme is that it achieves high tracking accuracy (*e.g.*, median error of around 1.4 cm) using the existing hardware already available in the mobile devices and equipment to be controlled (*e.g.*, smart TVs). Our evaluation and user study demonstrate the feasibility and effectiveness of our approach. Moving forward, we are interested in further enhancing the accuracy and robustness of tracking. Moreover, we would like to conduct larger-scale user study and develop interesting applications that benefit from accurate tracking.

## Acknowledgements

We are grateful to Shyam Gollakota and anonymous reviewers' insightful comments.

## 8. REFERENCES

[1] Microsoft X-box Kinect. http://xbox.com.
[2] Nintendo Wii. http://www.nintendo.com/wii.
[3] Circle-circle intersection. http://mathworld.wolfram.com/Circle-CircleIntersection.html.
[4] S. Agrawal, I. Constandache, S. Gaonkar, R. Roy Choudhury, K. Caves, and F. DeRuyter. Using mobile phones to write in air. In *Proc. of ACM MobiSys*, pages 15–28, 2011.
[5] Logitech air mouse. http://www.logitech.com.
[6] M. T. I. Aumi, S. Gupta, M. Goel, E. Larson, and S. Patel. Doplink: Using the doppler effect for multi-device interaction. In *Proc. of ACM UbiComp*, pages 583–586, 2013.
[7] G. Bradski. The OpenCV library. *Doctor Dobbs Journal*, 25(11):120–126, 2000.
[8] K.-Y. Chen, D. Ashbrook, M. Goel, S.-H. Lee, and S. Patel. Airlink: Sharing files between multiple devices using in-air gestures. In *Proc. of ACM Ubicomp*, 2014.
[9] F. Dellaert, D. Fox, W. Burgard, and S. Thrun. Monte carlo localization for mobile robots. In *Proc. of Robotics and Automation*, volume 2, pages 1322–1328, 1999.
[10] Frame rate. http://en.wikipedia.org/wiki/Frame_rate.

[11] D. Goehl and D. Sachs. Motion sensors gaining inertia with popular consumer electronics. *White Paper, IvenSense Inc*, 2007.

[12] S. Gupta, D. Morris, S. Patel, and D. Tan. Soundwave: using the doppler effect to sense gestures. In *Proc. of the SIGCHI*, pages 1911–1914, 2012.

[13] R. Heydon and N. Hunn. Bluetooth low energy. *CSR Presentation, Bluetooth SIG https://www. bluetooth. org/DocMan/handlers/DownloadDoc. ashx*, 2012.

[14] W. Huang, Y. Xiong, X.-Y. Li, H. Lin, X. Mao, P. Yang, and Y. Liu. Shake and walk: Acoustic direction finding and fine-grained indoor localization using smartphones. In *Proc. of IEEE INFOCOM*, 2014.

[15] InvenSense. `http://www.invensense.com`.

[16] E. Jacobsen and R. Lyons. The sliding DFT. *IEEE Signal Processing Magazine*, 20(2):74–80, 2003.

[17] S. Kumar, D. Cifuentes, S. Gollakota, and D. Katabi. Bringing cross-layer MIMO to today's wireless lans. In *In Proc. of ACM SIGCOMM*, August 2013.

[18] S. Kumar, S. Gil, D. Katabi, and D. Rus. Accurate indoor localization with zero start-up cost. In *Proc. of ACM MobiCom*, pages 483–494, 2014.

[19] P. Lazik and A. Rowe. Indoor pseudo-ranging of mobile devices using ultrasonic chirps. In *Proc. of ACM SenSys*, pages 99–112, 2012.

[20] C.-H. Lee, J.-L. Shih, K.-M. Yu, and H.-S. Lin. Automatic music genre classification based on modulation spectral analysis of spectral and cepstral features. *IEEE Transactions on Multimedia*, 11(4):670–682, 2009.

[21] LG magic motion remote. `http://www.lg.com/us/tv-accessories/lg-AN-MR200-motion-remote`.

[22] F. Li, C. Zhao, G. Ding, J. Gong, C. Liu, and F. Zhao. A reliable and accurate indoor localization method using phone inertial sensors. In *Proc. of UbiComp*, pages 421–430, 2012.

[23] Apple 13-inch MacBook Pro technical specifications. `https://www.apple.com/macbook-pro/specs/`.

[24] R. A. Meyers. Encyclopedia of physical science and technology. *Facts on File*, 1987.

[25] Top EDM 2014 music playlist tracklist. `https://www.youtube.com/watch?v=PHIRcu3Ero0`.

[26] H. Nyqvist and F. Gustafsson. A high-performance tracking system based on camera and IMU. In *Proc. of 16th IEEE International Conference on Information Fusion (FUSION)*, pages 2065–2072, 2013.

[27] A. V. Oppenheim, R. W. Schafer, J. R. Buck, et al. *Discrete-time signal processing*, volume 2. Prentice-hall Englewood Cliffs, 1989.

[28] T. Park, J. Lee, I. Hwang, C. Yoo, L. Nachman, and J. Song. E-gesture: a collaborative architecture for energy-efficient gesture recognition with hand-worn sensor and mobile devices. In *Proc. of ACM SenSys*, pages 260–273, 2011.

[29] C. Peng, G. Shen, Y. Zhang, Y. Li, and K. Tan. BeepBeep: a high accuracy acoustic ranging system using COTS mobile devices. In *Proc. of ACM SenSys*, 2007.

[30] Q. Pu, S. Gupta, S. Gollakota, and S. Patel. Whole-home gesture recognition using wireless signals. In *Proc. of ACM MobiCom*, 2013.

[31] J. Qiu, D. Chu, X. Meng, and T. Moscibroda. On the feasibility of real-time phone-to-phone 3D localization. In *Proc. of ACM MobiSys*, 2011.

[32] H. S. Rahul, S. Kumar, and D. Katabi. MegaMIMO: scaling wireless capacity with user demands. In *Proc. of ACM SIGCOMM*, pages 235–246, 2012.

[33] A. Rai, K. K. Chintalapudi, V. N. Padmanabhan, and R. Sen. Zee: zero-effort crowdsourcing for indoor localization. In *Proc. of ACM MobiCom*, 2012.

[34] Roku 3 streaming player. `https://www.roku.com/products/roku-3`.

[35] CES 2014: Samsung shows off new gyroscopic remote control. `http://www.digitalversus.com/tv-television/ces-2014-samsung-shows-off-n%ew-gyroscopic-remote-control-n32491.html`.

[36] K. Seifert and O. Camacho. Implementing positioning algorithms using accelerometers. *Freescale Semiconductor*, 2007.

[37] CES 2014 trends: New remotes and interfaces to make smart TVs actually usable. `http://spectrum.ieee.org/tech-talk/consumer-electronics/audiovideo/ces-%2014-trends-getting-smart-tv-under-control`.

[38] A. Smith, H. Balakrishnan, M. Goraczko, and N. Priyantha. Tracking moving devices with the cricket location system. In *Proc. of ACM MobiSys*, 2005.

[39] Z. Sun, A. Purohit, R. Bose, and P. Zhang. Spartacus: spatially-aware interaction for mobile devices through energy-efficient audio sensing. In *Proc. of ACM Mobisys*, pages 263–276, 2013.

[40] J. Wang and D. Katabi. Dude, where's my card? RFID positioning that works with multipath and non-line of sight. In *Proc. of the ACM SIGCOMM*, pages 51–62, 2013.

[41] J. Wang, D. Vasisht, and D. Katabi. RF-IDraw: virtual touch screen in the air using rf signals. In *Proc. of ACM SIGCOMM*, 2014.

[42] P. D. Welch. The use of fast fourier transform for the estimation of power spectra: a method based on time averaging over short, modified periodograms. *IEEE Transactions on audio and electroacoustics*, 15(2):70–73, 1967.

[43] C. A. Wingrave, B. Williamson, P. D. Varcholik, J. Rose, A. Miller, E. Charbonneau, J. Bott, and J. LaViola. The wiimote and beyond: Spatially convenient devices for 3d user interfaces. *IEEE Computer Graphics and Applications*, 30(2):71–85, 2010.

[44] G. Woo, P. Kheradpour, D. Shen, and D. Katabi. Beyond the bits: Cooperative packet recovery using physical layer information. In *Proc. of ACM MobiCom*, 2007.

[45] J. Xiong and K. Jamieson. Arraytrack: A fine-grained indoor location system. In *Proc. of NSDI*, pages 71–84, 2013.

[46] L. Yang, Y. Chen, X.-Y. Li, C. Xiao, M. Li, and Y. Liu. Tagoram: Real-time tracking of mobile RFID tags to high precision using cots devices. In *Proc. of ACM MobiCom*, 2014.

[47] S. Yun, L. Qiu, and A. Bhartia. Multi-point to multi-point MIMO in wireless LANs. In *Proc. of INFOCOM Mini-Conference*, April 2013.

[48] Z. Zhang, D. Chu, X. Chen, and T. Moscibroda. Swordfight: Enabling a new class of phone-to-phone action games on commodity phones. In *Proc. of ACM MobiSys*, 2012.

# Tracking Keystrokes Using Wireless Signals

Bo Chen†, Vivek Yenamandra† and Kannan Srinivasan
Department of Computer Science and Engineering
The Ohio State University, Columbus, OH 43210
{chebo, yenamand, kannan}@cse.ohio-state.edu
†Co-primary Authors

## Abstract

We implement a passive remote keystroke detection mechanism using only changes in the wireless channel. The detection algorithm does not require the user to wear any active devices nor does it require a change in the user's wireless transmission technique. The receiver system is implemented with five antennas.We cancel the signals received on multiple antennas. The key insight to realizing a fine-grained localization system is to exploit the extremely high sensitivity of cancellation performance (interference cancellation in full-duplex for example) to exact amplitude and phase matching. The receiver design introduces a delay mismatch between the received signal streams to guarantee imperfect cancellation across the transmission bandwidth except at one in-band frequency resulting in a trough in the cancellation spectrum. We detect keystrokes by forming an array of observed trough frequency across different antenna pairs.

We implement our receiver system on the NI-based SDR platform. With full-training the receiver detects a keystroke within one key offset with an accuracy of 91.8%. With a short $\approx 10$ character training input, this accuracy drops to 85%.

## 1. INTRODUCTION

The objective of this paper is to determine if it is feasible for a nearby receiver to detect and identify the keystrokes of a user typing on a wireless device by simply observing the resultant variations in the wireless channel. We assume a continuously transmitting wireless user device with a keyboard interface and place our receiver (hacker) in the vicinity of the user's device. The key challenge is that the hacker placed in the vicinity of the user's mobile device (say 5 meters), must still be capable of detecting keystrokes separated by only 2 cms. This accuracy is an order of magnitude higher than existing state-of-the-art systems [18]. Unlike fine-grained RFID tag localization, we assume the user does not wear any active tag/device to assist with localization of the finger presses [14]. Further, we consider a scenario where the hacker has to deal with limited training data since the user does not actively type anything to assist with keystroke detection [16]. Finally, we assume that the hacker is equipped with fundamental hardware capabilities comparable to existing wireless systems proposed in literature. The goal of this paper is to investigate the possibility of a constrained fine-grained wireless localization/detection system and its potential implications on issues of security/privacy. We present the design of a multi-antenna receiver system that enables the hacker to detect keystrokes by simply observing its effect on the wireless channel between the user and the hacker. We hope the findings of this work will serve as a catalyst to re-evaluate user interface designs for passing sensitive data considering the availability of increasingly sophisticated passive localization and gesture recognition wireless systems.

We have the user type on a keyboard interface of a device that is continuously transmitting wireless signals. We *cancel* the signals received on multiple antennas at the receiver. Consider two such antennas. We cancel the signal received on one antenna with the copy of it observed on the second antenna. In order to perfectly cancel the signals received on two antennas, we need to match both the amplitude and the phase of the signals. The cancellation performance is highly sensitive to matching the signals accurately in both amplitude and phase. To achieve uniform cancellation across the entire transmission bandwidth we need to match these signals across all transmission frequencies. We exploit this sensitivity of cancellation performance to map variation in cancellation performance across frequency to detecting and localizing keystrokes.

First, the receiver compensates for the difference in the channel between the user and each antenna. Second, we introduce a delay difference between the two receiver channels (from each antenna) to *introduce* a phase mismatch between the two signals. This phase mismatch causes degradation of cancellation performance across the transmission bandwidth except at specific frequencies where the phase mismatch between the two paths is an integral multiple of $2\pi$ radians. At these frequencies, the signal cancels *perfectly* while the cancellation performance at adjacent frequencies is still degraded because of phase mismatch. This results in *troughs* at specific frequencies when observing the power spectrum of the cancelled signal. We envision the user's finger when typing as the source of one multipath. When the user presses a different key, the source of this multipath changes resulting in the change of the delay difference between the two channels. This change in delay difference and the corresponding change in phase mismatch causes a change in frequency at


*MobiSys'15,* May 18–22, 2015, Florence, Italy.

http://dx.doi.org/10.1145/2742647.2742673.

which the cancellation is perfect and the resultant trough is observed. We map different keystrokes to the variation in the trough of the cancelled signal's power spectrum.

Ideally, a hacker system is constrained by limited-to-no training information. One can imagine getting short, limited training information by providing a hotspot high quality connection to the user and having the user type a set of keys to gain access. Thus, we assume such limited training data may be available at the beginning. However, since in our setting, the user is not assisting with detection, the user is not obligated to repeat key presses to provide large training data to assist with subsequent classification. Therefore, we use techniques that extrapolate key press identification beyond the keys used for training.

To our knowledge, this is the first RF keystroke detection and identification system. We develop new techniques to push the state-of-the-art gesture recognition and localization techniques to enable fine-grained keystroke detection with limited "training." The experiments in this paper rely on continuous wireless transmissions from the user device to enable keystroke detection and identification at the receiver. However, as discussed in Sec. 8, we believe with some implementation changes, the proposed receiver design itself should fundamentally be able to detect and identify keystrokes even in the presence of typical packetized Wi-Fi transmissions from the user device. We believe the findings of this paper presents the feasibility of potentially spying on keystrokes on a wireless device by an anonymous receiver, thus, exposing a potential threat.

We prototype our receiver on the NI based SDR platform. The two receive chains use NI-5791 radio front-ends, Virtex-5 based FPGAs for baseband signal processing and PXIe-8133 controller for real-time detection of keystrokes. Our receiver design only relies on the receive chains receiving the same signal from the transmitter and is agnostic to the underlying PHY layer design of the wireless transmission. With full-training the receiver detects a keystroke within one key offset with an accuracy of 91.8%. With a short $\approx$ 10 character training input, this accuracy drops to 85%.

The rest of this paper is organized as follows. In Sec. 2 we survey prior work and elucidate their shortcomings for our scenario, Sec. 4 details the design decisions of our receiver system from the physical signal perspective, Sec. 5 discusses the training and clustering algorithms we adopt for our system, Sec. 7 discusses the details of prototype implementation and system evaluation, Sec.8 discusses the current implementation limitations and finally Sec. 9 concludes the paper.

## 2. RELATED WORK

Researchers have been developing systems for indoor localization and gesture recognition. This section elaborates on the shortcomings of existing work to our setting.

**Indoor Localization:** Most of the work in the field of indoor localization involved adapting principles of RADAR based target finding to the RF based approach in indoor environments. RADAR [4] was one of the pioneering works in the field of indoor wireless localization. In this work, the authors aimed at localizing users inside buildings based on RSSI measurements at multiple access points and propagation models. Since then researchers have studied localization problems based on different types of wireless systems for various applications. A stream of work aimed at localizing transmitting nodes such as PinIt [14], PinPoint [9] etc. These systems rely on transmissions from nodes for localizing them. These techniques are referred to as active localization techniques where the readers perform signal processing techniques on the signals transmitted by the targeted device. Alternatively, researchers have studied using WiFi transmissions for localization and activity/gesture recognition. Arraytrack [18] is an example of an active localization system that uses a multi-antenna receiver to detect the angle-of-arrival (AoA) of the targeted device by observing the signal from that device on the multiple antennas at the receiver. Our work differs from this line of work. We seek to localize the finger and detect the key press where the user is not wearing any active tags. Our system is a passive localization and gesture recognition system.

An alternative line of work has considered passive localization and activity/gesture recognition systems. These systems observe the effect of the targeted device on the established wireless channel. Most of these designs require both a transmitter and a receiver. As part of the design, these techniques establish a channel between the transmitter and the receiver. The design typically involves changes in the transmitter to assist the receiver with localizing the passive targeted device. For example, in Wi-Vi [3], two transmit antennas beamform such that they null their signal at the receive antenna. This nulling phenomena relies on the channel. Changes in the channel due to movement of the passive targeted device causes change in the nulling performance which is mapped to the location of the target. 3D Body tracking [2] uses a continuous wave transmitter to help with tracking using time difference of arrival approaches. In Wi-Hear [13], the authors beamform the transmitter towards the mouth of the user to detect changes in channel caused by movement of the mouth at the receiver. Our system differs from this line of work since we use a single node to detect wireless keystrokes. We do not use an additional transmitter to beamform the signal in the direction of the targeted device. The rationale behind such a constraint is we envision the hacker to be stealth and not have a discernible placement of multiple nodes or antennas around the targeted user to detect their keystrokes. More recent works exploit synchronization between multiple far-apart nodes to achieve fine-grained localization [19] using triangulation techniques. Our system, however, operates by itself since having a spatially-extravagant setup itself could trigger suspicion.

Some researchers have observed changes in wireless channel between commodity radios due to the presence and movement of humans. For instance, E-eyes [17] localizes a person to a room in a house by measuring the change in the channel between a fixed WiFi device (say a TV) and the AP. The authors study temporal variations of the channel to provide broad activity classification. This approach would seem obvious for our setting. The user is on a wireless mobile device that is transmitting. The hacker device can in theory, be a receiver that continuously measures the channel between itself and the user and employ signal processing techniques on the observed channel measurements to detect and differentiate different keystrokes by measuring changes in the phase and/or magnitude of the channel. We implemented a receiver system with this objective. We continuously measure the phase of the channel and seek to find a pattern in phase variation for the same repeated action (example: pressing the same key.) However, as illustrated in Fig. 1, the variation in absolute phase and magnitude of the channel is so small that these changes are buried within the noise. The finite resolution of off-the-shelf ADCs limits the efficacy of this procedure. Thus, existing signal processing techniques on absolute channel measurements does not provide information specific to our setting.

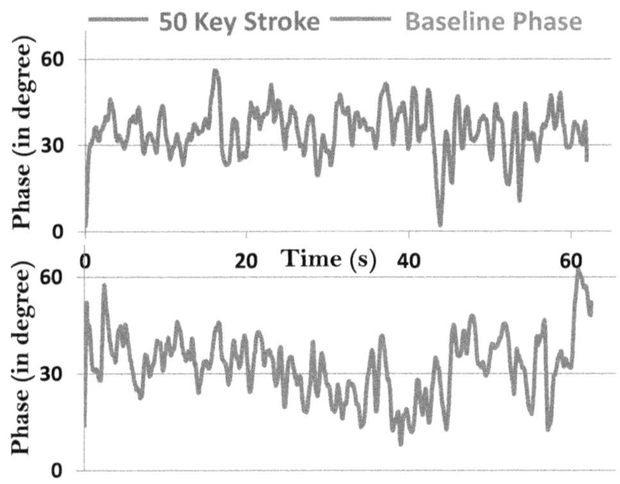


**Figure 1: Phase Variation in Channel: In the presence and absence of repeated key stroke, 'A'. The absolute phase variation is minimal causing the signal to be buried within noise**

**Gesture recognition:** In addition to indoor localization, researchers have also studied the problem of gesture recognition. The problem of detecting keystrokes is not merely a localization problem. The hacker must be capable of differentiating between a user simply moving his fingers along the keyboard and actually pressing a particular key. Here, the act of key press itself is the activity that the hacker must be capable of detecting. While E-eyes [17] classifies between different activities while providing some location information, the classification and localization is very coarse-grained for our application. There are finer gesture recognition systems such as WiSee [11], AllSee [10] etc. WiSee detects a gesture using the phenomena of Doppler shift. The movement of a hand to and from a receiver changes the relative frequency of the wireless signal observed at the receiver. The authors present signal processing techniques to detect small Doppler shifts resulting from simple hand gestures. While this is a fine-grained gesture detection system, it does not provide any information about the location of the target and these principles do not directly extend to our scenario. RF-Idraw [15] is a wireless system to detect a user writing in the air. RF-Idraw has a user wear an active RFID tag to help with tracking the movement of the finger. The technique deployed does not extend to a scenario where the target is passive. Further, the system is concerned with tracking motion of a finger and not precise location of the finger. The requirement for our considered setting is more stringent.

Finally, a recent system [16] enables a mobile device to detect keystrokes pressed on a nearby hard surface (For ex: Enabling a user a larger paper keyboard interface for a small-screen mobile device.) This paper requires the mobile device to be placed in the immediate vicinity of this paper keyboard. The system observes the acoustic channel using the microphone input on the mobile system and harnesses the multipath sound profile to detect between different keystrokes. This solution requires the reader to be placed really close to the user and requires an extensive training period for key detection and classification. In contrast, our work does not have the luxury of user cooperation to have extensive training. Furthermore, proximity is also not possible in our setup. This makes our system susceptible to more external channel variations. However, as Section 5 shows, our system can identify and filter out external variations.

**Spying Keystrokes:** There has been recent work focused on detecting keystrokes anonymously. In [12], the authors observe the effect of keystrokes on the electromagnetic radiation emanating from the keyboard to detect the keystroke pressed. The authors exploit the fact that keyboards are typically cheap devices with poor electromagnetic shielding. The receiver observes the electromagnetic radiation effect of the clock and data signals for different keystrokes. These signals are digital signals of the order of 10s of MHz (up to about 150 MHz after accounting for observable harmonics of the on-board clock signals). Thus, to observe these signals the receiver requires large antennas. In [12], the authors use a 1m copper wire antenna for the receiver, which can be prohibitively large to maintain discreetness as a hacker. More recently, in [1], the author employs an anonymous wireless USB device to spy on keystrokes from a wireless keyboard. However, this work relies on the information of the data-transmission protocol of the wireless keyboard and its weak security features. Our design only observes the changes in the wireless channel between the user and the hacker due to the movement of the finger because of a keystroke to detect the keystroke. Our design is agnostic to the underlying PHY and MAC protocols.

**Full Duplex Systems:** Thus far, we have listed the shortcomings of existing literature for the discreet hacker scenario considered in this paper. In order to be able to detect and distinguish between small changes in the phase of the wireless channel, we exploit the sensitivity of self-interference cancellation of full-duplex systems to exact phase matching. Small changes in phase of the channel causes change in the frequency at which we observe the cancellation trough. In recent times, there has been a large drive in developing full-duplex systems, [5–8]. There is a subtle difference between our cancellation and typical full-duplex self-interference cancellation.

These systems have a training phase to estimate the channel between the transmitter and the receiver. The receiver then cancels the observed signal with the internally generated copy of the received signal. In our implementation we do not have an explicit training signal for cancellation. Instead, we make use of the fact that the two receive streams receive the same signal. We model the difference in the channel between the transmitter and these two receivers to subsequently subtract the receive stream.

# 3. DESIGN PRINCIPLES

This section presents the core design of our system, its tuning knobs and the sensitivity of the system.

## 3.1 2-Receiver Setup

Fig. 2 illustrates the scenario considered in this paper. A user on a wireless device types on a keyboard interface. The wireless device has a transmitting antenna. For now, we assume the keyboard interface is at a fixed distance and orientation with respect to the user's antenna as would be the case in laptops. The hacker places his wireless device close (< 5m) to the user to detect the keystrokes. The hacker's wireless receiver contains two antennas that are fixed in distance and orientation relative to each other. The receiver then cancels the signal received on one antenna with that received on the other antenna. This cancellation performance is sensitive to the phase mismatch between the transmitter and the two receive antennas caused by movement of the finger in the act of a key press.

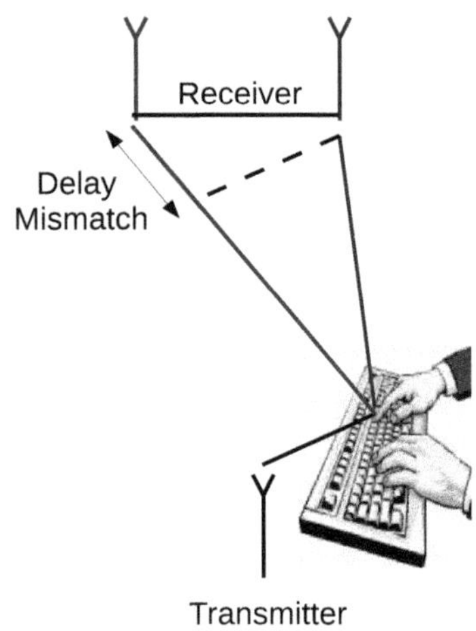


**Figure 2: Delay mismatch due to keystroke $\delta_t$.**

## 3.2 Intuition

Initially, the receiver estimates the difference in the wireless channels between the transmitting antenna and the two receive antennas. Once the receiver matches the amplitude and phase of the channel from the transmitter to each receive antenna, it can, in theory, cancel the signals on the two receive antennas to achieve perfect cancellation across the entire transmission bandwidth, $B$. Let the two signals received on the two receive antennas, after this matching, be $y_1$ and $y_2$, which are functions of both frequency (in radians), $\omega$, and time, $t$.

$$y_1(\omega, t) = A(\omega, t)e^{j\omega t} \quad (1a)$$
$$y_2(\omega, t) = A(\omega, t)e^{j\omega t} \quad (1b)$$

Note that if we subtract (cancel) $y_1$ from $y_2$ then the cancellation will be near-perfect and will be so across the entire bandwidth, a desired property in full duplex designs. We deviate from this goal and artificially introduce a delay of $\Delta_t$ to one of the two received signals as indicated in Eq. 2.

$$y_{2delay}(\omega, t) = A(t)e^{j\omega t - \omega\Delta_t} \quad (2)$$

Now, while the two signals are still matched in amplitude, the introduced delay causes a phase mismatch across frequencies: Each signal experiences a phase shift proportional to $\omega \times \Delta_t$ radians. Clearly, subtracting $y_1$ from $y_2$ will not yield perfect cancellation anymore (Eq. 3b). In these equations, we drop the parameters $\omega$ and $t$ for notation simplicity.

$$y_{cancel} = y_{2delay} - y_1 \quad (3a)$$
$$= A(t)\left\{e^{j\omega t - \omega\Delta_t} - e^{j\omega t}\right\} \quad (3b)$$
$$y_{cancel} = 0 \iff \omega\Delta_t = \pm 2n\pi, n \in 0, 1, 2, \cdots \quad (3c)$$

While the cancellation of the two streams does not reduce to 0 across all frequencies, there exist specific frequencies at where this cancellation is perfect. We introduce the delay, $\Delta_t$ such that we find $\omega \in B$ where $y_{cancel} = 0$. We refer to this frequency as $\omega_t$. This leads to observing a sharp trough at $\omega_t$ within the transmission bandwidth, $B$.

Now, the system is bootstrapped. As the user types different keys, however, the two received signals observe varying delays between the two receive antennas. This variation introduces significant phase changes across the bandwidth. This causes the location of the trough to change.

Assume the receiver estimates the channel between itself and the user when the user has placed his hands in a resting position on the keyboard. After introducing a delay, the receiver observes a cancellation spectrum with a trough at frequency $\omega_t$. When the user now moves his finger to press a different key, the difference in delay between the two receive streams changes. This can be easily understood by visualizing the finger as a source of transmission. When the position of the finger changes, the delay between the finger and each receive antenna changes. This causes a change in the initial delay difference between the two receive streams from $\Delta_t$. Let us denote this delay change due to change in finger position by $\delta_t$. This additional delay again introduces different phase shifts at different frequencies. This causes the cancellation trough to move to a different frequency, say $\omega_{new}$. In other words, at $\omega_{new}$, the phase mismatch between the two streams is an integer multiple of $2\pi$ radians as indicated in Eq. 4. Fig. 3 gives a sense of how sensitive this cancellation is on the delay variations introduced by $\delta_t$.

$$\omega_{new}\{\Delta_t + \delta_t\} = \pm 2n\pi, n \in 0, 1, 2, \cdots \quad (4)$$

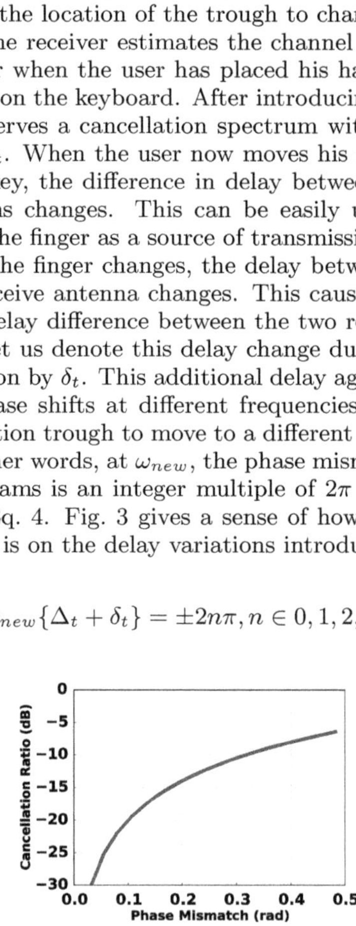


**Figure 3: Cancellation Ratio vs Phase Mismatch introduced by $\delta_t$. Cancellation Ratio is the ratio between signal power after and before cancellation: Lower the ratio, better the cancellation. A small increase in phase mismatch adversely affects cancellation quality.**

Thus, by tracking $\omega_{new}$, we can track the location of the finger over the keyboard interface. This is the core principle of our design.

## 3.3 System Sensitivity

In this section, we identify the variables that affect the sensitivity of our system. These variables are the tuning knobs in our design.

### *3.3.1 Sensitivity to $\Delta_t$*

As discussed in Sec. 3.2, we introduce a delay between the two receive streams to ensure we do *not* observe a flat cancellation spectrum. Once the receiver estimates the channel between the user to each of its receive antennas, we can ensure phase matches only at a particular in-band frequency by carefully selecting $\Delta_t$. Subsequent key presses can be identified by observing the shift in frequency at which the trough is observed.

However, the selection of $\Delta_t$ serves another purpose. As indicated in Eq. 3b, the phase mismatch between the two receive streams at a particular frequency is $\omega.\Delta_t$. Thus, for a given frequency the phase mismatch increases as $\Delta_t$ increases. This makes the *width* of the observed trough narrower. Suppose the receiver observes a trough at frequency $\omega_t$, where the phase mismatch between the two streams is $2\pi$ radians. The phase mismatch at an adjacent frequency $\omega$ is then $2\pi + |\omega - \omega_t|\Delta_t$ radians. Thus, for the same frequency offset from the frequency at which the trough is observed, $\omega_t$, the phase mismatch increases with an increase in $\Delta_t$. As indicated in Fig. 3 this increased phase mismatch causes a larger degradation of cancellation performance at frequencies adjacent to $\omega_t$, causing the observed trough in the cancellation spectrum to become narrower. This is indicated in Fig. 4.

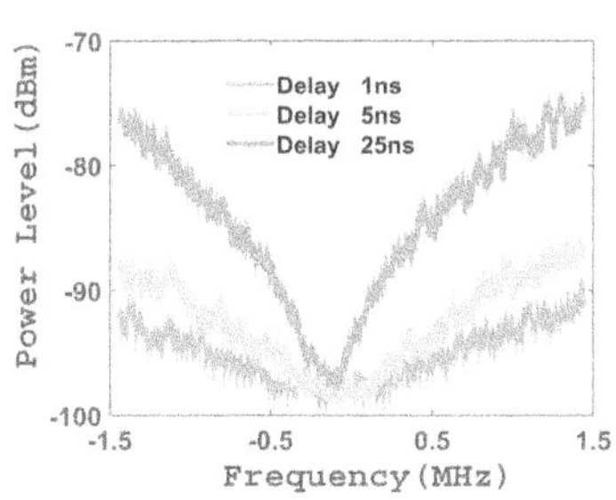


**Figure 4: The width of observed trough in Cancellation Spectrum vs $\Delta_t$. Larger $\Delta_t$ gives narrower trough.**

In addition to making the trough deeper, the selection of $\Delta_t$ also affects the sensitivity of the receiver. For instance, let us assume a user presses key 4 and then, presses key 5 (on a typical keyboard interface). For this key press sequence, Fig. 4 shows the difference in the frequencies where the trough appears (marked as sensitivity in the figure) against $\Delta_t$. It shows that reducing $\Delta_t$ increases sensitivity. This means that simply pressing adjacent keys can push the trough beyond the observable bandwidth ($B$). On the other hand, choosing a very large $\Delta_t$ will not noticeably move the trough. Thus, $\Delta_t$ should be chosen carefully as shown in the next section.

The following section will detail our design algorithms and present convergence times for the trough generation part of our design.

# 4. SYSTEM DESIGN

Thus far, we have detailed the setup of our system and the intuition behind some of the design parameters of the design. Further, we illustrated the cancellation performance's sensitivity. This section discusses the design of our system in detail.

As stated before, the first bootstrapping step is to cancel the two signals from the two receive antennas such that a trough appears within the observed bandwidth. To do this, we need to match the amplitude of the two received signals in addition to introducing a delay of $\Delta_t$, iteratively. Fig. 5 illustrates this process.

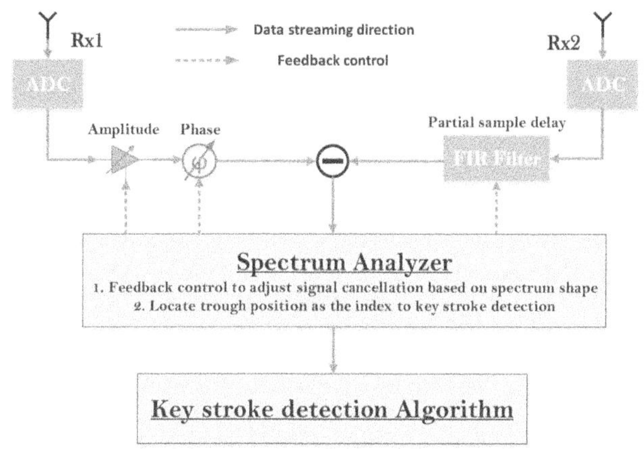


**Figure 5: Block Diagram illustrating the design principles of our receiver.**

## 4.1 Matching Amplitude

As Fig. 2 shows, we have a receiver with multiple antennas at fixed distances relative to each other. We place the receiver at a certain distance with respect to the user. The distance between the user and the receiver ($\approx 5m$) is significantly higher than the distance between the antennas ($\approx 6cms$). We initially assume that the two receive antennas receive the signal with comparable power. Thus, initially, we observe a trough in the cancellation spectrum. We are guaranteed the presence of a trough since we introduce a delay in one of the receive streams as indicated in Fig. 5. After subtracting the two receive streams, we send the cancellation signal through a spectrum analyzer block as indicated in Fig. 5. The spectrum analyzer block computes the spectrum of the cancellation signal. On the computed spectrum, we run a trough detection algorithm to accurately detect the trough frequency. Since the initial assumption of equal amplitudes on both receive streams is only an approximation, the cancellation at the detected trough is not *perfect*. In other words, the trough observed in the cancellation spectrum is not deep. Thus, in addition to a trough detection algorithm, the spectrum analyzer block also runs an amplitude matching algorithm. The amplitude matching algorithm continuously seeks to match the amplitudes of the two receive streams to result in perfect cancellation at the trough frequency. This results in a deep trough in the observed spectrum as well as increases the accuracy of the detection of the trough.

To match the amplitudes of the two streams, we define *correction ratio*. The correction ratio settles to a ratio that

**Algorithm 1:** Pseudo-code for Magnitude Matching Algorithm

```
// Parameter Initialization:
ratio = 1
scale = 1.003
case = 1

// Keep running Loop:
while true do
    if pre_Ptrough > curr_Ptrough then
        case = 1 − case
    endif
    switch case do
        1: ratio = ratio × scale
        0: ratio = ratio ÷ scale
    endswitch
    // delay to guarantee the new ratio takes effect
    delay()
endwhile
```

would match the amplitude of the two streams, specifically at the trough frequency. To match the amplitude of the two streams, we multiply the weaker receive stream (in terms of signal strength) with the computed *correction ratio*. The receiver subtracts one of the receive streams with the receive stream updated with the new correction ratio. The spectrum analyzer block then computes the spectrum of the updated cancellation signal. The amplitude matching algorithm observes the effect of the previous correction ratio on the cancellation spectrum.

Initially, we assume the correction ratio to be 1. The amplitude matching algorithm adjusts the correction ratio with the objective of minimizing the power at the trough frequency. The algorithm to settle on the correction ratio is given in Algorithm 1. The correction ratio is multiplied in each iteration with *scale* depending on the effect of the previous value of the correction ratio. Thus, a smaller *scale* factor makes the steady-state correction ratio more stable resulting a deeper trough. However, a smaller *scale* factor also causes the correction ratio to take longer to reach that steady-state. We evaluate this trade-off in greater detail in Sec. 7.

**Convergence Time:** As indicated in the algorithm listed above, we use a scale factor of 1.003 in our design. This implies that, in each iteration, we change the value of the correction ratio by 0.3% of its current value. At a first glance, this might suggest that the correction ratio might take a long time to reach steady state and the latency might be intolerable. However, in our experiments we observe the contrary. We measure the time it takes for the correction ratio to settle to a value to match the amplitude of the two receive streams. Initially, the trough detection algorithm locates the frequency at which the trough occurs. The amplitude matching algorithm then alters the correction ratio to match the amplitudes of the two receive streams. As suggested in Fig. 3 the cancellation performance is highly sensitive to phase and amplitude matching. When the amplitudes of the two streams are close to each other then a small change in the amplitude can potentially change the cancellation performance significantly. We measure the time taken by amplitude matching algorithm for different orientations of the user relative to the hacker device and under different environment conditions (with respect to objects in the environment and their corresponding multipath profiles). Fig. 6 plots the time taken for one such experiment run. In addition, it also contains the ratio of the change in amplitude of one of the streams from its initial amplitude to its matched amplitude. The time taken is quite insignificant (of the order of 10s of milliseconds) compared to the typical cadence of typing on a keyboard. Further, the amplitude matching algorithm is only instantiated periodically. Typically, once the amplitudes converge, the relative ratio of amplitudes on the two receive streams only changes in the presence of significant environment changes. We believe we can decrease the convergence time further by implementing the algorithm on the FPGA itself.

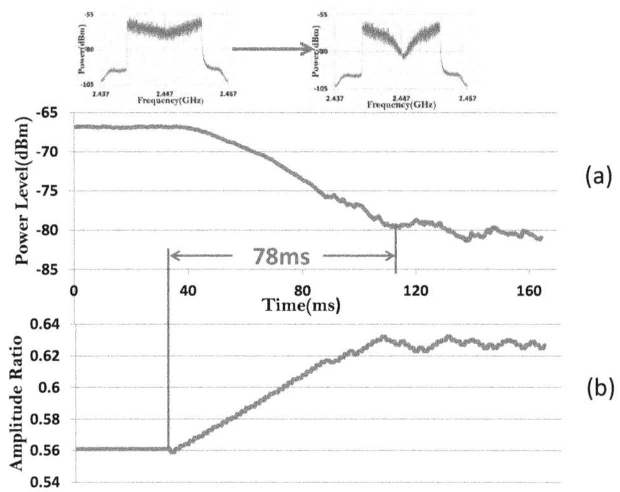


**Figure 6: Amplitude Matching Algorithm: The correction ratio converges to match the amplitudes of the two RX streams in about 78ms. The resultant drop in the power at the trough frequency is also indicated. To give a qualitative feel of the effect of amplitude matching algorithm we present a snapshot of the power spectrum before and after the onset of the algorithm.**

## 4.2 Designing $\Delta_t$

Sec. 3.2 discussed the impact of $\Delta_t$ on the system's performance. As indicated in Fig. 5, we introduce this delay in one of the receive streams to cause a phase mismatch between the two receive streams. We add this delay mismatch between the two receive streams in the digital domain by adding it after ADC sampling. The two receive RF-chains have identical specifications. The delay of the signal from the receive antenna to the input of the ADC in each of the receive stream is deterministic and consistent. However, since each receive stream has its own independent ADC, initially we noticed a sampling offset between the two ADCs. While this sampling offset is consistent for the duration of each run, on each power cycle, this sampling offset can change to a different value. However, the NI-based platform used to implement the receiver system is equipped with control lines in the backplane shared across different FPGAs of the receiver. We use these control lines to synchronize the ADCs on each power cycle. The implementation system is explained in greater detail in Sec. 7. Synchronizing the ADCs resulted in a consistent delay between the receive antenna and the baseband in each receive stream. This consistency enables us to add deterministic delay mismatch between the two receive streams.

We introduce the delay mismatch between the two streams using the *partial sample delay* block as indicated in Fig. 5. We implement the partial sample delay block using an FIR filter. The FIR filter has a linear phase characteristic across its passband frequency to introduce the desired delay. The delay introduced by this filter can be configured to sub sample periods. For the desired delay, the receiver computes the FIR filter coefficients (by performing an IFFT of the delayed channel) and loads them into the filter.

One would expect the optimal delay mismatch introduced between the two streams to be dependent on the distance between the receiver and the user and the orientation of the user with respect to the receiver. As discussed in Sec. 3.2, the delay mismatch affects the depth of the observed trough in the cancellation spectrum as well as location sensitivity. Also, assume for a given keystroke, say A, the trough in the spectrum is observed at frequency $\omega_A$. For a given orientation and distance between the user and the receiver, we would expect that for each repeated key press of A, we observe a trough at $\omega_A$. However, due to noise in phase measurement, we observe that the trough is observed at a distribution of frequencies centered around $\omega_A$. The variance of this distribution tends to zero as we increase the delay mismatch. We elaborate on this in Sec. 7. Considering the influence of delay mismatch on the performance of the receiver, we observe that for majority of the scenarios considered in this paper, a fixed delay mismatch provides *sufficient* performance. Thus, in our implementation, we fix the delay of this partial sample delay block and thus the delay mismatch between the two streams.

**Determining Delay Mismatch:**

We seek to determine the impact of delay mismatch on the performance of the system. We fix the position of the transmitter and the position of the keyboard relative to the transmitting antenna. We place the keyboard close to the transmitting antenna and at a lower plane to mimic the setting of a typical laptop. We place the hacker device at a distance of 3m from the transmitter. The two receive antennas of the hacker are spaced apart by 6cms. We fix the orientation of the hacker with respect to the transmitter and the keyboard. We have a subject repeatedly type two adjacent keys, '4' and '5' respectively. For each delay input to the partial sample delay block, we measure the sensitivity of the hacker device. We define sensitivity as the difference in the observed trough frequency, $F_4 - F_5$, where $F_k$ is the frequency of the observed trough when key 'k' is pressed. We vary the delay in the partial sample delay from 0.01 to the time period of one sample in fractional steps (as indicated in Fig. 7(a)). For each delay setting we have the user type the keys '4' and '5' repeatedly 50 times.

For each key press, we record the location of the detected trough. We observe that the average sensitivity decreases as we increase the delay mismatch. However, while the sensitivity decreases we observe that even for a delay mismatch of one sample duration, the two keys can be reliably distinguished. The sampling rate of our system is 20 Msps. Specifically, for a delay mismatch of 0.01 $\times$ sample period, the sensitivity of adjacent keystrokes is $\approx$ 6 MHz. Increasing the delay mismatch to 0.1 $\times$ sample period reduces the sensitivity to $\approx$ 3 MHz.

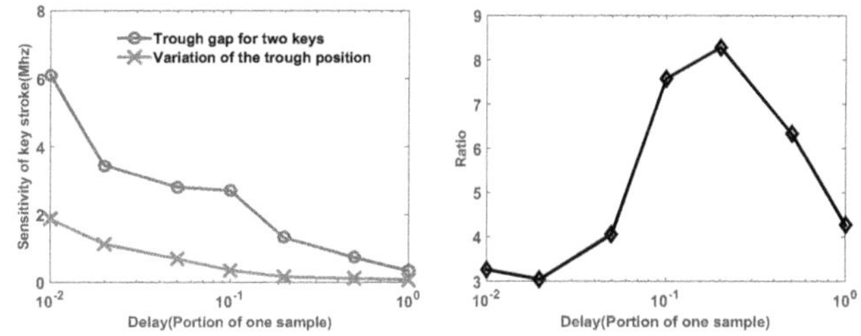


(a) Sensitivity and Variance. (b) Ratio of Sensitivity to Variance.

**Figure 7: Influence of delay mismatch on the sensitivity of key detection. As expected from the discussion in Sec. 3.2 the sensitivity decreases as the delay increases. However, the lack of sensitivity assists in reducing the variation of the trough location due to measurement noise. We observe introducing delay mismatch of 0.1$\times$ sample period is an acceptable value to achieve a workable trade-off in most scenarios.**

In addition to computing the average sensitivity, we also measured the repeatability of the trough location for a given key stroke. For each repeated key press, we record its trough location and compute the variance in the trough location. As indicated in Fig. 7(a), we observe that for small delay offset, the variance in the trough location is $\approx$ 2 MHz. A small delay offset implies that the phase mismatch between the two receive streams is small. Thus a small change in the observed phase in either of the receive streams causes the frequency at which the phase matches to change. This causes high variation in the trough location for a small delay offset. Measurement noise and multipath can cause variation in the observed phase of the two streams which in turn causes variation in the observed trough location for the same key press in the case of small delay mismatch. However, as we increase the delay mismatch, we decrease the sensitivity of the hacker and the trough location for a given keystroke is more robust to measurement noise.

To quantify the trade-off between sensitivity and accuracy of a given trough location we define a ratio between sensitivity and trough accuracy. We plot this ratio for different delay mismatch inputs in Fig. 7(b). We observe that a delay mismatch of 0.1 $\times$ sampling period provides sufficient sensitivity with acceptable trough location robustness. We observe that this delay is acceptable for majority of the orientations between the hacker and the user. Thus, in our system, we preconfigure the partial sample delay block to provide 0.1$\times$sample period delay mismatch between the receive streams.

Finally, for the selected delay mismatch, it is possible that in the cancellation spectrum, we do not observe a trough. This is because, it is possible for the frequency at which the phase matches can fall outside the transmission bandwidth. This can occur due to changes in the environment or orientation of the user with respect to the hacker. While changes in environment can push the trough outside the transmission bandwidth we are guaranteed the existence of a frequency itself at which a trough exists since we introduce the delay mismatch between the two streams. Thus, when we do not observe a trough in the cancellation spectrum, we examine the shape of the spectrum. For example, if the trough occurs at a frequency to the *right* of the transmission bandwidth, then the observed spectrum appears *tilted down* in the direction of the trough frequency. This is illustrated in Fig. 8. We then sweep the phase of one stream between $[-\pi, \pi]$ to match its phase with the other stream at a frequency that falls within the transmission bandwidth. Similar to the amplitude matching algorithm, the spectrum analyzer block also contains a spectrum shape sensing algorithm that is responsible for observing the shape of the spectrum and updating the value in the phase block indicated in Fig. 5.

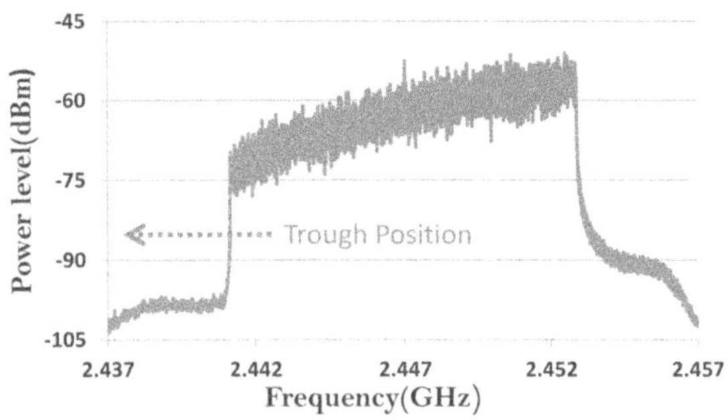


**Figure 8: Spectrum shape sensing block observes the shape of the spectrum to control change in the phase block (Fig.5) to retrieve trough to an in-band frequency.**

Further, this enables us to control the initial location of the trough at frequency, say $\omega_{initial}$. We re-initialize the trough location to this frequency at designed intervals. This operation only determines the location of the trough and does not vary the width or robustness of the trough location. Thus, in this operation we are not changing the delay of the signal but simply changing the phase to ensure location of the trough.

# 5. KEYSTROKE DETECTION

Thus far, we have discussed the design principles and decisions of all parameters until the spectrum analyzer block of the design process illustrated in Fig. 5. This section details the keystroke detection algorithm block in our system.

The design decisions discussed thus far, determine the sensitivity of the hacker system. The desired sensitivity enables the hacker to distinguish between the location of the user's finger on one key from its adjacent key. However, it does not provide any information regarding whether the key was actually pressed. Second, assume that for a given keystroke, the hacker observes a trough at frequency $\omega$. In a relatively stable environment, the same keystroke should cause a trough in the cancellation spectrum at the same frequency as indicated in Fig. 7(a). However, when there are changes in the environment, such as a person walking in the vicinity of the user-hacker setup can cause the location of the trough in the spectrum to change. Thus, it is important for the keystroke detection algorithm to differentiate the cause of movement of the trough location in the cancellation spectrum due to an actual keystroke from that caused due to channel variations.

To overcome the above concerns, our keystroke detection algorithm tracks the change in trough frequency over time. This temporal information enables the hacker to distinguish a keystroke from other changes in the environment that affect the cancellation spectrum in a similar manner. The algorithm computes the rate of change in the trough frequency. Using an empirically selected threshold, the algorithm then classifies a given change in trough location as either a keystroke or not a keystroke. The temporal variation of the trough frequency when a keystroke is repeated is given in Fig. 9.

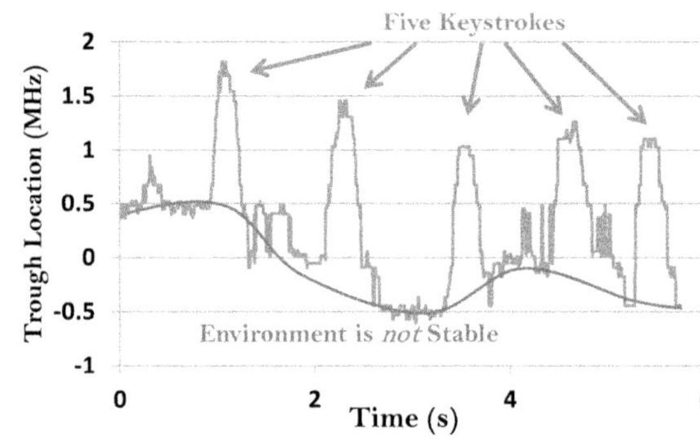


**Figure 9: Tracking time variations in trough frequency due to changing environment conditions introduced by moving people near the user.**

We measured this temporal information of the change in trough frequency locations by having a user repeat a keystroke repeatedly. While the user is repeatedly pressing a key, we ask another person to walk in the vicinity of the user-hacker setup. As indicated in the above figure the absolute trough location varies over time due to change in the channel caused by the movement of a person in the channel. However, the rate of change of the keystroke is significantly higher than typical changes encountered in environment. This is because a keystroke is typically a short 'impulse' like movement of the finger. It must be noted that while the trough location itself in the cancellation spectrum can change, the rate of change in the trough location for a keystroke remains reliably steady for a given orientation between the hacker and the user. We perform repeated experiments to arrive at an empirical threshold for rate of change of the trough frequency. Similar to selection of $\Delta_t$ parameter we find that a single threshold selection suffices for detecting keystrokes with high probability in most envisioned user-hacker scenarios considered in this paper.

Finally, in some cases it is possible that the change in environment is large enough to force the observed trough in the cancellation spectrum outside the transmission bandwidth. Once the trough detection algorithm in the spectrum analyzer block detects the absence of the spectrum it triggers the spectrum shape sensing block which subsequently changes the phase of one of the receive streams to force the trough back inside the transmission bandwidth. We repeat the previous experiment where the user repeatedly enters the same keystroke sequence. Unlike the previous experiment, here the user is asked to type two keys. We ask the user to introduce large variation in the channel (for example: using the free hand to mimic the action of swatting a fly). We use the keystroke detection algorithm discussed above to detect the keystroke. Fig. 10 plots the change in trough frequency location over time. The sudden variation in the absolute trough frequency is caused by a large change

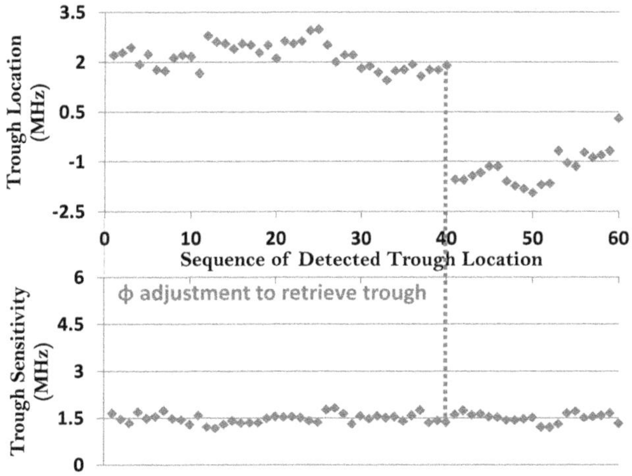


**Figure 10: Tracking trough sensitivity and absolute trough frequency sequences. While large channel variations (introduced by user moving his hand) can vary absolute trough frequency, trough sensitivity remains the same for a given receiver location, orientation and given set of user keystrokes.**

in the environment which causes the hacker to adjust the phase to reinforce the trough frequency to within the transmission bandwidth. However, as indicated in the figure, this operation does not change the observed sensitivity. The key takeaway from this experiment is the following: Even in the case of large channel variations, the sensitivity of the hacker for a given pair of keystrokes remains reliably stable as long as the orientation of the hacker relative to the user remains the same. We exploit this observation to increase the confidence of relative keystroke detection given knowledge of an initial reference keystroke. This is explained in greater detail in Sec. 7.

# 6. IMPLEMENTATION

We implement the hacker's receiver system on the NI-based SDR platform. We implement an initial receive system with two antennas. We later extend this design to five receive antennas for preliminary results. In this section we present the implementation details of a two-antenna receiver to detect keystrokes.

We equip our SDR platform with two antennas and two independent receive RF chains. Each RF chain uses the NI-5791 radio front-end and a Virtex-5 based FPGAs for baseband processing. We operate the receivers in the 2.4 GHz ISM band. The ADC of each receive chain samples at 130 MSps. The ADC resolution is 14 bits. We sample data into the FIFO itself at 20MSps. We establish a DMA (Direct Memory Access) channel between the two receive FPGAs to transfer samples from the RX2's ADC (indicated in Fig. 5), to RX1. In the FPGA of the second receive chain we cancel the two received streams of samples. We implement the partial sample delay block indicated in Fig. 5 and the amplitude correction block also on the same FPGAs. The subsequent cancellation samples are processed into a FIFO that are transferred to a central controller. The central controller is implemented on the RTOS based PXIe-8133 to enable deterministic processing and data transporting delays between the central controller and the FIFOs in the FPGA of the receive chains. The central controller is responsible for synchronizing the independent RF oscillators as well as the sampling clocks of the ADCs of each receive chain. In addition, the central controller reads the cancellation samples from the second FPGA. We implement the Spectrum Analyzer block along with the trough detection, spectrum shape sensing and amplitude matching algorithms on the central controller. The computed correction ratio is continuously fed back to the second FPGA using the control lines between the central controller and the FPGAs. The keystroke detection algorithm is implemented on the central controller as well.

The central controller synchronizes the baseband and RF clocks of the two receive RF chains. The SDR platform provides a backplane of 8 wires to interface each FPGA to the central controller. These wires are used for both the purpose of data transfer as well as for providing control signals. We share the internal reference clock of the SDR platform on one of the lines in the backplane. Each receive chain synchronize their RF and baseband clocks to this reference. We also implement timing synchronization between the two FPGAs to render consistency to the sample offset between the two ADCs.

Finally, we implement the transmitter using the same hardware configuration i.e. Virtex-5 based FPGA for baseband processing and an NI-5791 front-end. We operate the transmitter in the 2.4 GHz ISM band with a transmission bandwidth of 20 MHz. The receiver hacker is agnostic to the underlying PHY design of the transmitter. None the less, we implement an OFDM based PHY to mimic WiFi transmissions.

# 7. EVALUATION

This section presents a thorough evaluation of our receiver system. In the first half of this section, we evaluate the various design decisions that affect the performance of the system. In the second half, we present a holistic evaluation of the system performance.

## 7.1 Microbenchmark Evaluation

In this section, we evaluate the design decisions of all parameters that affect key differentiation. Specifically, the design of algorithms to detect specific keystrokes is discussed in the next subsection. Here we evaluate the design of only those parameters that influence the ability to observe distinct signals for different closely spaced keys.

### *7.1.1 Orientation Effect*

We set out to measure the sensitivity of the hacker for different positions of the hacker relative to the user, in a given environment. For this exercise, we equip our hacker with two antennas. We place the hacker 3m from the user and move the device to different positions along a circle centered around the user. We sweep the circle in eight equi-angular steps. For each position of the hacker, we have the user type adjacent keys '4' and '5'. We measure the difference in the respective observed frequency troughs at the hacker. We plot the measured sensitivity for each position of the hacker in Fig. 11(a). As indicated in the figure, while in the initial position, we observed a sensitivity of $\approx 6$ MHz, as we moved around the user we noticed that the sensitivity significantly depreciates for the same keystrokes. Specifically, when the hacker is placed diametrically opposite to the initial position

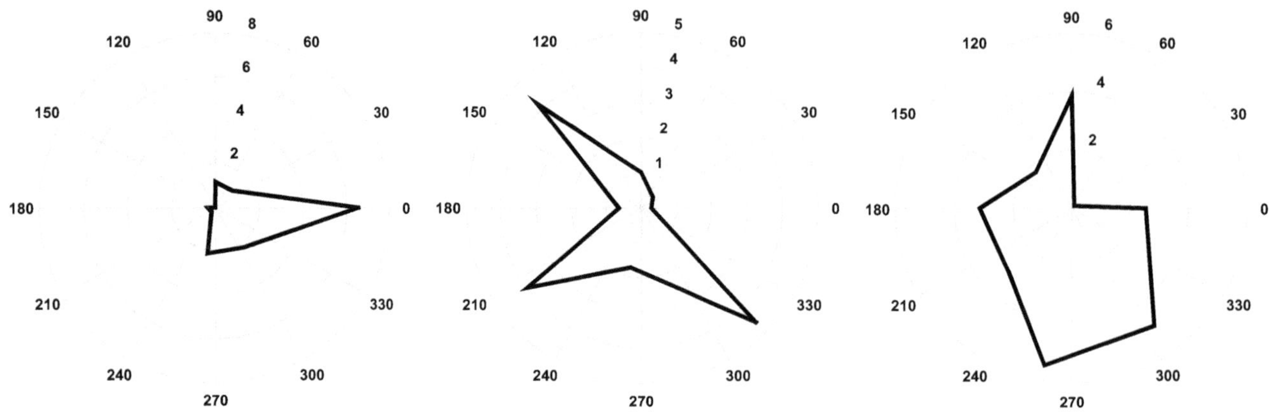


(a) Moves aroud the user. (b) Rotates across different orientations at a given location. (c) Moves Around User For Different Orientations.

**Figure 11: Effect of Orientation on Receiver Sensitivity: The receiver is moved around the user as described. For each receiver location the sensitivity for given keystrokes is measured. Figs. 11(a),11(b),11(c) plot the sensitivity at the receiver for different locations and orientations relative to the user. The units of sensitivity is MHz.**

(at an angle of 180 degrees), we observe that the hacker can barely distinguish between the two key strokes and that the sensitivity is orders of magnitude below 1 MHz.

To investigate the significant sensitivity degradation, we placed the hacker device at the 180 degree position again. This time, we rotated the hacker device at this position through $2\pi$ radians, again in eight equi-angular steps. This changes the orientation of the hacker's antennas relative to the user. For each position we again have the user repeat the same keystrokes, namely '4' and '5'. We measure the sensitivity at each of these orientations and plot the sensitivity in Fig. 11(b). The significance of the orientation between the hacker and the user is evident. While at our initial orientation the sensitivity is very poor when we rotate the hacker by 45 degrees in the clock wise direction, we notice a sensitivity of $\approx$ 4 MHz. Further, we discover two more orientations at which we measure decent sensitivity.

Finally, we repeat the experiment we initially set out to do i.e. measure the hacker's sensitivity for different positions around the user. This time, however, we increase the distance between the hacker and user to 4m. We again move the hacker around the user in a circle. At each position we rotate the hacker across four orientations. We plot the maximum sensitivity observed at each position in Fig. 11(c). We note that at except one position, we observe appreciable sensitivity of the order of $\approx$ 3 MHz for at least one of the four orientations around the user. The increase in distance between the user and the hacker does *not* significantly degrade the sensitivity.

The main takeaway from the above set of experiments is that the orientation between the hacker and user is more critical to the hacker's performance than the absolute distance between them. The orientation is a function of the placement of the hacker's antennas and the location of successive key presses. For a given pair of receive antennas at the hacker, the orientation of the user's keystrokes relative to the hacker can change depending on the keystrokes pressed by the user. For instance, if the orientation between the hacker and the user is consistent when the user presses key 'A' and then key 'S', then the hacker's orientation rotates by $\approx$ 90 degrees when the user presses key 'A' and then key 'Z'. This can cause the hacker to have different sensitivity performance between differentiating key 'A' from key 'S' and key 'A' from key 'Z'. To make our hacker less sensitive to the orientation of the hacker relative to the user, we can increase the number of antennas at the hacker. We study the increase in reliability of key detection in the presence of additional antennas later in this section.

### *7.1.2 Multiple Antennas*

The previous experiments established the sensitivity of the hacker system's performance to the orientation between the hacker and the user. To make the hacker robust to different orientations, we require multiple antennas at the hacker. As described in the previous section, for a given location of the hacker, the orientation of the hacker relative to the user can change depending on the keystrokes pressed by the user. Thus, for a given pair of antennas at the hacker, while they might show high sensitivity for a pair of keys pressed by the user, the same pair can demonstrate poor sensitivity for another set of keys at a different orientation.

In a hacker with just two antennas, different keystrokes are distinguished by the difference in sensitivity. For example, say the hacker detects a trough at frequency $F_A$ when key A is pressed and at frequency $F_S$ when key S is pressed. To make the example extreme, assume the hacker detects a trough at frequency $F_A$ even when key Z is pressed. Now assume the hacker is aware that the current key press is A. If the hacker observes the trough at the next keystroke detection at frequency $F_S$ then the hacker can detect the keystroke as S. With reference to A, the keystroke S can then be mapped to the number $F_S - F_A$. However, if at the next keystroke detection the trough is located again at frequency $F_A$ then the hacker cannot decide between keys A and Z since relative to $F_A$ both these keys are mapped to 0.

Now assume we add a third antenna to this hacker device. The third antenna is placed such that the three antennas are not co-linear. The design process of the hacker system with three antennas is simply an extension of the design process illustrated in Fig. 5 for a two antenna hacker system. We simply add an additional DMA channel between the third FPGA and the first FPGA to transfer the samples from the ADC of the third antenna to the first FPGA. This stream of samples is subjected to the same delay and correction ratio as the samples from the second antenna. Since the orientation of the first and third antenna pair relative to the user is different from that of the first and second antenna pair, the sensitivity observed on this pair of antennas is different for the same set of keystrokes. Say, for this pair of antennas, the relative mapping of key S relative to key A is $F'_S - F'_A$ and that of key Z relative to key A is $F'_Z - F'_A$. Combining the mapping from both antenna pairs the cumulative mapping of key S relative to key A is an array $[F_S - F_A, F'_S - F'_A]$ and key Z relative to key A is $[0, F'_Z - F'_A]$. Intuitively, one would expect that the probability that relative to a given keystroke the inability of distinguishing different keystrokes significantly reduces as the number of antennas increase.

Extending the discussion to a hacker with N antennas, each keystroke can be mapped relative to a given keystroke with an array of N-1 elements $[F^1_{Diff}, F^2_{Diff}, \cdots, F^{N-1}_{Diff}]$ where $F^k_{Diff}$ is the sensitivity of that keystroke relative to the given keystroke observed on the pair of antennas $1, K+1$. Finally, following the observations in Fig. 10, we must note that given the trough frequency array of a particular keystroke, the mapping of other keystrokes relative to this keystroke remains constant under all channel conditions. However, the absolute trough frequency of the reference keystroke itself may change over time.

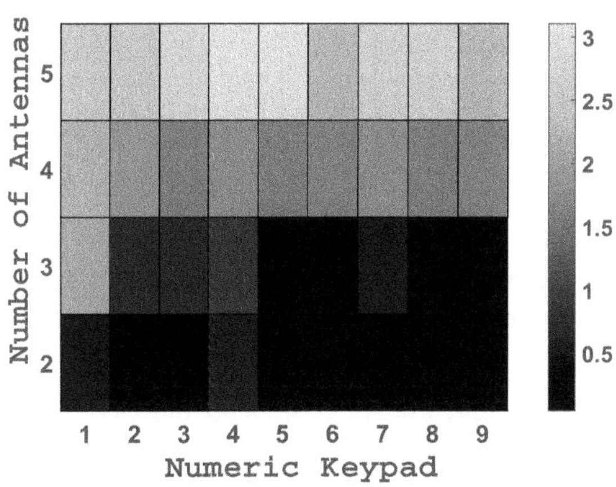


**Figure 12: Minimum Sensitivity (MHz) of numeric keypad relative to each key on the numeric keypad as a function of the number of antennas.**

We seek to evaluate the ability of the hacker to distinguish between different keystrokes relative to a given keystroke as a function of the number of antennas on the hacker. For this experiment we limit the key presses to the number pad on the right side of a typical keyboard. We have a user type an initial number (between 1-9). Using that key as a reference we ask the user to type the remaining number keys between 1-9 in a random order alternating each number key press with a key press of the selected initial reference number key. We ask the user to repeat with this process by selecting a different initial reference key. We repeat the experiment with five users for a fixed location and orientation of the hacker relative to the user device. We compute the sensitivity between the selected reference key and each number key. We compute the minimum sensitivity for a given reference key and record it. For a generic N antenna hacker device, we define the sensitivity between a given keystroke and the reference keystroke by the Euclidean distance between the mapping of the given keystroke and that of the reference keystroke. By the definition of our mapping, the reference keystroke always maps to an array with $N-1$ zeros. The sensitivity then is simply $\sqrt{F_1^2 + F_2^2 + \cdots F_{N-1}^2}$ where $F_i$ is the measured sensitivity between the antenna pair $1, i+1$.

For each user, we repeat the experiment by equipping the hacker with the effect of 2,3,4 and 5 antennas respectively. For each setup of the hacker we place the antennas at a distance of approximately 6 cm from each other in a compact configuration. The results are indicated in Fig. 12. We observe that once the receiver is equipped with 4 or more antennas, then the minimum sensitivity is at least 2 MHz to all the number pad keys independent of the initial reference key selection. This affirms our intuition that additional antennas makes the hacker robust to different orientations. Further, increasing the number of antennas also increases the sensitivity of the hacker thus increasing its ability to distinguish between closely spaced keys. As stated before, the sensitivity between a pair of keys is independent of channel variations for given location and orientation of the hacker relative to the user.

## 7.2 System Evaluation

This section evaluates the performance of the hacker system. Following the observations from the multi-antenna experiment recorded in Fig. 12, we imlpement our hacker system with five antennas. We fix the location of the user and the hacker. For all experiments in this section, we fix the location of the hacker at a distance of 5m from the user. All experiments are performed inside our lab furnished with metal furniture and other strong sources of multipath. We repeat all the experiments in this section with five users. Each user types one key at a time using a single finger at slower than average typing speeds.

**Robustness to Channel Variation:** In the first experiment, we seek to evaluate the key detection capability of our hacker system under varying channel conditions. In this experiment, we have the user repeatedly press the number pad key 5. While the user is typing, we introduce variation in the channel by having people walk in the lab in the vicinity of the user-hacker system. We must note that we have the people move outside the line-of-sight of the user-hacker channel. However, it still effects the multipath profile of the channel. The user himself is in a *rest* position while typing. Here, by rest position we mean that while the user can move intermittently (say his hand or head), the user is not constantly in motion. Initially, we train the hacker with the sensitivity of the number pad keys from 1-9 relative to 5 by having the user type keys sequentially from 1 to 9. Further, we train the receiver with an initial absolute mapping of key 5. In other words, the hacker has an initial reference of trough locations observed on each pair of antennas when it is aware that the key being pressed is 5. Let us denote this initial absolute mapping of key 5 with $V_5$. Since we have five antennas, each mapping of the number pad keys relative to key 5 is an array of length 4. Let us denote the mapping of number pad key K relative to 5 with $V_{K,5}$. We have the user repeat this sequence twice to train the receiver.

Because of the change in the channel between the user and the hacker, the mapping of the key recorded by the hacker can change each time. This can potentially cause the repeated key press 5 sometimes be interpreted as key press of an adjacent key. Further, since key 5 is in the middle of the number pad, the probability of detecting a 5 with one of its neighbors is highest among the keys in the number pad. Let us assume the current mapping recorded by the hacker is $V'$. Let $V'$ be different from $V_5$. We measure the Euclidian distance between $V'$ and $V_5$. For majority of the key presses, we notice that this distance is close to 0 and significantly lower than the sensitivity between key 5 and any other key on the number pad. This results in the hacker decoding that the received mapping is for key 5. Once the hacker detects the key press as key 5, it attributes the difference in the observed mapping from the reference mapping to variation in the channel. The hacker subsequently updates its reference mapping after accounting for channel variation. With each user we repeat the experiment for fifty runs and observe that we detect the key press as 5 correctly on 90% of the runs. In the few instances where the channel change is large, key press 5 can be misinterpreted as one of the adjacent keys. This result is illustrated in Fig. 13.

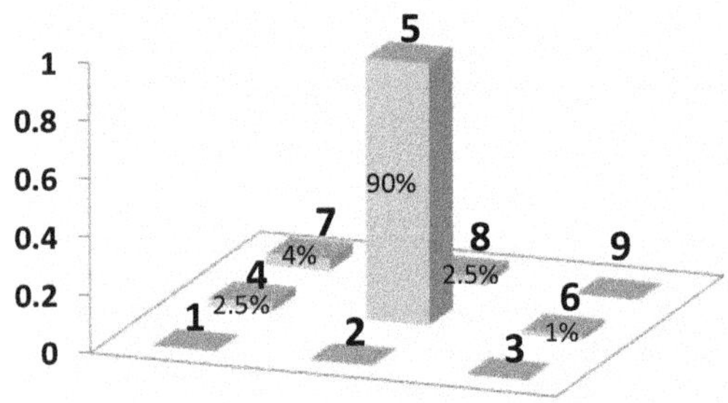


**Figure 13: Detecting repeated keystroke '5' in a changing channel.**

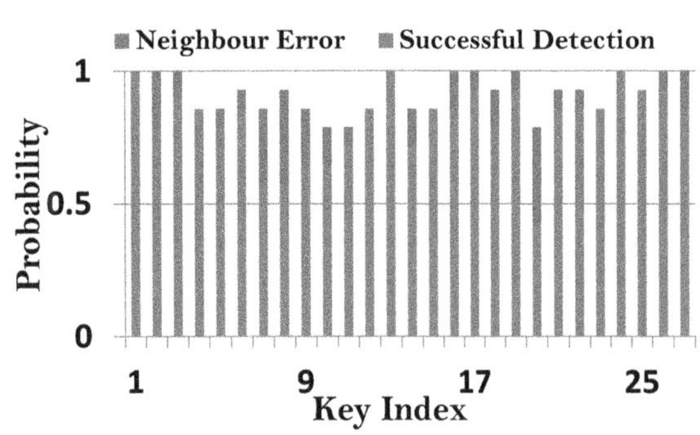


**Figure 14: Keystroke detection accuracy given full training.**

**Complete Training:** Next, we evaluate the effectiveness of the hacker to detect different keystrokes spread across the keyboard. We perform this experiment under the same conditions as before. Like before, for the partial and complete training experiments, we have people move in the lab during the experiment. Specifically, on a typical QWERTY keyboard, the hacker intends to detect all the letter keys as well as the ',' key adjacent to key 'M'. First, to evaluate the feasibility of a wireless keystroke detection technique, we assume the hacker device is trained for each of the 27 keys. We have the user type each of these keys *once* to train the hacker. For each of these key presses the hacker constructs an array to map the observed trough locations to the key press. Once trained, the user types from these keys randomly one key at a time. Each user types 270 keys such that he types each key ten times. However, the keys are typed in a random order. The hacker estimates the keystroke by mapping the readings to the key for which the Euclidian distance between the observed trough locations and the reference readings of the key is minimum. Similar to the previous experiment, in the presence of a perfectly static channel, one would expect the Euclidian distance between the estimated key and the reference key to be 0. We attribute change in the Euclidian distance to noise and changes in the environment. Once we assign the key, we update the reference readings of all the keys such that the Euclidian distance between the observed reading and the new reference of the assigned key is zero. The hacker's performance in estimating each of the 27 keys given full, short training is given in Fig. 14. The hacker has an average detection accuracy of 81.48%. In most instances where the key was misinterpreted, it was estimated to be one of its horizontally adjacent keys. The hacker estimates either the key or its neighbor with an accuracy of 91.8%.

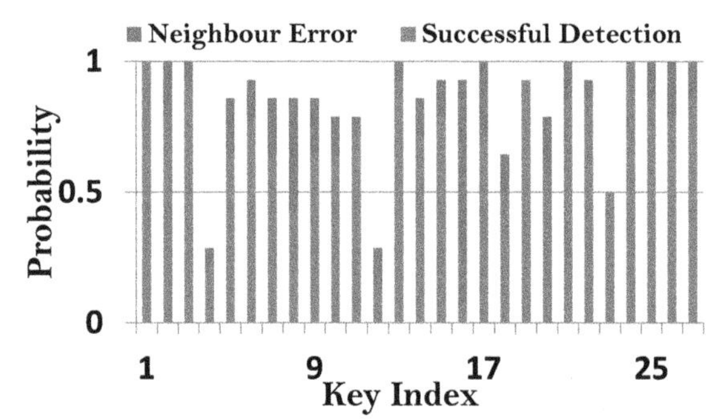


**Figure 15: Keystroke detection accuracy given partial training data. 13 equally spaced keys are input once to provide initial training data.**

**Partial Training:** Finally, we evaluate the hacker's keystroke detection ability in the event of limited training inforamtion. In this experiment, the user types 13 of the 27 keys (leaving every alternate key) *once* to provide initial training information to the hacker. Then, the user proceeds to type from the 27 keys in a random order. Like the previous experiment, each user types 270 keys in total. The hacker estimates a reference for those keystrokes that do not have a direct training input by extrapolation across neighboring keys with training input. Fig. 15 indicates the key detection accuracy in this scenario. The average detection accuracy is $\approx 70\%$ and the detection accuracy of either the intended keystroke or its neighbor is 85%. Although majority of the keystrokes are detected with reasonable accuracy, some of the keystrokes are almost always misinterpreted due to a noisy training input either at that key or its neighbor. While the detection accuracy at first glance might seem a little underwhelming, the word detection accuracy can potentially be significantly higher with simply an initial short training keystroke input of $\approx 10$ characters.

## 8. DISCUSSION AND LIMITATIONS

In this section we discuss the limitations of our implementation.

1. **Typing at faster speeds:** In our experiments, the users type at a slow and lower than average speed as indicated in Fig. 9. In our setup, we have the algorithms for keystroke detection and locating the trough in the cancellation spectrum on the central controller. The samples from different ADCs are transferred across FPGAs and the subtracted samples at one of these FPGAs are then forwarded to the central controller. The central controller then computes the power spectrum on these samples and performs subsequent keystroke detection algorithms. In our implementation, the central controller loads samples over multiple symbols for each power spectrum computation. The speed is limited by our implementation time which includes the time to move the samples in addition to the processing delay of our power spectrum computation and keystroke detection algorithms on the central controller. This limits our implementation from detecting typing at faster speeds reliably. The implementation speed of our algorithm can be significantly improved by moving its execution to the FPGA. This should enable the receiver to detect faster keystrokes.

2. **Packetized WiFi Transmissions:** Fundamentally, our technique requires the user's device to transmit a wireless signal in order to facilitate keystroke identification. Thus, if the user is not transmitting a wireless signal, the receiver cannot decode the keystrokes. The experiments in Sec. 7 were carried out using *continuous* transmissions from a SDR transmitter. However, WiFi transmissions are packetized and not continuous. Our trough identification and location algorithm works on the cancellation spectrum. As the transmission becomes increasingly discontinuous and packetized the observed cancellation spectrum fluctuation increases. We observe negligible spectrum fluctuations for UDP transmissions with an inter packet latency of up to 10ms. As the packets become less continuous and the spectrum fluctuation increases, our implementation will not detect the keystrokes reliably due to its implementation speed for reasons discussed above. However, if the packet transmission is extremely scarce, for example at rates of 1 packet/second, then our receiver will be fundamentally not be able to detect the user keystrokes.

3. **Typing with two hands:** In our experiments, the users type one key at a time with the index finger with just one hand. We have this restriction to ensure consistency in the way a user types a certain key over both the training phase and the random key input phase. As observed in our experiments, this setting ensures that as long as the user in a rest position, the recording of each keystroke is repeatable even in environments where there is movement around the user. However, with longer training sequences and/or more sophisticated self-learning classifiers and algorithms, we believe there is no fundamental limit in preventing the system from decoding users that type with both hands.

4. **User Movement:** In the experiments in Sec. 7, each user maintains a rest position while typing. As illustrated in Fig. 10, when the user introduces movement (say a movement of the hand or the head), the sensitivity of the receiver is retained as long as the position of the user device and the hacker remains the same. For this reason the training information recorded in the experiments is the sensitivity between pairs of antennas for each keystroke. Thus, while user movements can change the absolute trough locations, the keystroke is still reliably identified by our algorithm since the *relative* trough location does not change.

5. **Change in keyboard orientation:** Currently, our system does not support a scenario wherein the user changes the position of the keyboard after the training phase. Changing the position causes the observed recordings to change from the associated trained readings. In our implementation, this will cause the observed recording to be wrongly interpreted as a different key. However, using simple algorithms to examine a series of keystrokes (which can be interpreted as letters forming a word), we can detect persistent unusual patterns and discard the available training information. This will prevent the receiver from misinterpreting the detected keystrokes. With more sophisticated self-learning algorithms, we can potentially refine the training information with the observed recordings of known keys. (For example: keys such as the space bar and the vowels are used more frequently while typing and the frequency of similar observations can be used to determine the key and update its training information.)

6. **Impact of User Antenna Placement:** If the user's antenna was directional such that *none* of the radiation power is directed towards the keyboard and the user's hands then our receiver can fundamentally not detect the keystrokes. Thus, we require some wireless energy transmitted by the user to the receiver to be reflected off the user's keyboard/fingers and hand. We carry out our experiments using a single omni-directional antenna to transmit the continuous wireless signals for the user. We placed the antenna above the user keyboard at an angle typical of a laptop (Laptops typically have the Wi-Fi antennas on the top edge of the screen). For different positions of the antenna relative to the keyboard (within the constraint of typical laptop settings) we did not observe a dependency between the antenna placement and the keystroke detection of our receiver.

7. **Multi-antenna transmitter:** Our experiments used a single antenna transmitter. As 802.11 evolves, portable devices will have more antennas. If multiple antennas transmit the same symbol (for diversity gain) then our existing receiver system should still be able to detect the keystrokes by treating the multiple antennas as an effective single antenna. However, if the antennas transmit independent data streams, then our current receiver system design as is will not support keystroke detection. We can deploy receive beamforming techniques to isolate the individual streams to perform keystroke detection but this will sacrifice the PHY-agnostic characteristic of our current design.

## 9. CONCLUSION

In this paper, our goal was to demonstrate keystroke identification using wireless transmissions. We believe that this exposes a serious security threat even for current commodity wireless users. As described before, we envision such an attack to happen in public venues where the attacker can be far enough to look unsuspicious and close enough (within 5m) to decipher key strokes. Our system can be scaled in many ways to improve the accuracy of key detection and improve distance range. We highlight these possible improvements in this section.

**Spectra other than 2.4G:** Wi-Fi also operates in 5.8GHz ISM band. Higher center frequency will allow more antennas to be easily mounted on current nodes. This will improve our accuracy. In fact, Wi-Fi can operate in wider bandwidths than 20MHz; 40MHz, 80MHz and even more. As Section 3 showed, wider bandwidth will allow more control over sensitivity. Thus, higher precision in keystroke detection will be possible.

**Keystroke identification ⇒ hacking:** This paper demonstrated the feasibility of identifying keystrokes and also identifying which key was pressed. Clearly, the next step is to use this attack to hack username/password, credit card details and so on. There exist immense machine learning algorithms that can assist with this step. Such techniques can also deal with intermittent keystroke data from a given user, similar to auto-correct on smart phones. However, autofill options can make it more difficult for such techniques to carryout a fully successful hack. We leave this as future work.

Moving forward, we should rethink ways to protect against such security and privacy issues in the future. One possible research is to look for new user interfaces that allow users to input data into the system reliably. Clearly, biometric scans are not prone to our attack, while traditional username/password-type inputs are.

## Acknowledgments

We would like to thank our shepherd, Shyamnath Gollakota, and the anonymous reviewers for their comments and suggestions to improve our paper.

## 10. REFERENCES

[1] http://samy.pl/keysweeper/.

[2] Adib, F., Kabelac, Z., Katabi, D., and Miller, R. C. 3d tracking via body radio reflections. In *Usenix NSDI* (2013), vol. 14.

[3] Adib, F., and Katabi, D. See through walls with wifi! In *Proceedings of the ACM SIGCOMM 2013 conference on SIGCOMM* (2013), ACM, pp. 75–86.

[4] Bahl, P., and Padmanabhan, V. N. Radar: An in-building rf-based user location and tracking system. In *INFOCOM 2000. Nineteenth Annual Joint Conference of the IEEE Computer and Communications Societies. Proceedings. IEEE* (2000), vol. 2, Ieee, pp. 775–784.

[5] Bharadia, D., and Katti, S. Full duplex mimo radios. *Self 1*, A2 (2014), A3.

[6] Bharadia, D., McMilin, E., and Katti, S. Full duplex radios. In *Proceedings of the ACM SIGCOMM 2013 conference on SIGCOMM* (2013), ACM, pp. 375–386.

[7] Choi, J. I., Jain, M., Srinivasan, K., Levis, P., and Katti, S. Achieving single channel, full duplex wireless communication. In *Proceedings of the sixteenth annual international conference on Mobile computing and networking* (2010), ACM, pp. 1–12.

[8] Jain, M., Choi, J. I., Kim, T., Bharadia, D., Seth, S., Srinivasan, K., Levis, P., Katti, S., and Sinha, P. Practical, real-time, full duplex wireless. In *Proceedings of the 17th annual international conference on Mobile computing and networking* (2011), ACM, pp. 301–312.

[9] Joshi, K. R., Hong, S. S., and Katti, S. Pinpoint: Localizing interfering radios. In *NSDI* (2013), pp. 241–253.

[10] Kellogg, B., Talla, V., and Gollakota, S. Bringing gesture recognition to all devices. In *Usenix NSDI* (2014), vol. 14.

[11] Pu, Q., Gupta, S., Gollakota, S., and Patel, S. Whole-home gesture recognition using wireless signals. In *Proceedings of the 19th annual international conference on Mobile computing & networking* (2013), ACM, pp. 27–38.

[12] Vuagnoux, M., and Pasini, S. Compromising electromagnetic emanations of wired and wireless keyboards. In *USENIX security symposium* (2009), pp. 1–16.

[13] Wang, G., Zou, Y., Zhou, Z., Wu, K., and Ni, L. M. We can hear you with wi-fi! In *Proceedings of the 20th annual international conference on Mobile computing and networking* (2014), ACM, pp. 593–604.

[14] Wang, J., and Katabi, D. Dude, where's my card?: Rfid positioning that works with multipath and non-line of sight. In *Proceedings of the ACM SIGCOMM 2013 conference on SIGCOMM* (2013), ACM, pp. 51–62.

[15] Wang, J., Vasisht, D., and Katabi, D. Rf-idraw: virtual touch screen in the air using rf signals. In *Proceedings of the 2014 ACM conference on SIGCOMM* (2014), ACM, pp. 235–246.

[16] Wang, J., Zhao, K., Zhang, X., and Peng, C. Ubiquitous keyboard for small mobile devices: harnessing multipath fading for fine-grained keystroke localization. In *Proceedings of the 12th annual international conference on Mobile systems, applications, and services* (2014), ACM, pp. 14–27.

[17] Wang, Y., Liu, J., Chen, Y., Gruteser, M., Yang, J., and Liu, H. E-eyes: device-free location-oriented activity identification using fine-grained wifi signatures. In *Proceedings of the 20th annual international conference on Mobile computing and networking* (2014), ACM, pp. 617–628.

[18] Xiong, J., and Jamieson, K. Arraytrack: A fine-grained indoor location system. In *NSDI* (2013), pp. 71–84.

[19] Xiong, J., Jamieson, K., and Sundaresan, K. Synchronicity: Pushing the envelope of fine-grained localization with distributed mimo. In *Proceedings of the 1st ACM Workshop on Hot Topics in Wireless* (2014), HotWireless '14.

# Contactless Sleep Apnea Detection on Smartphones

Rajalakshmi Nandakumar
Computer Science and Engineering
University of Washington
rajaln@uw.edu

Shyamnath Gollakota
Computer Science and Engineering
University of Washington
gshyam@uw.edu

Nathaniel Watson M.D.
UW Medicine Sleep Center
University of Washington
nwatson@uw.edu

**Abstract –** We present a contactless solution for detecting sleep apnea events on smartphones. To achieve this, we introduce a novel system that monitors the minute chest and abdomen movements caused by breathing on smartphones. Our system works with the phone away from the subject and can simultaneously identify and track the fine-grained breathing movements from multiple subjects. We do this by transforming the phone into an active sonar system that emits frequency-modulated sound signals and listens to their reflections; our design monitors the minute changes to these reflections to extract the chest movements. Results from a home bedroom environment shows that our design operates efficiently at distances of up to a meter and works even with the subject under a blanket.

Building on the above system, we develop algorithms that identify various sleep apnea events including obstructive apnea, central apnea, and hypopnea from the sonar reflections. We deploy our system at the UW Medicine Sleep Center at Harborview and perform a clinical study with 37 patients for a total of 296 hours. Our study demonstrates that the number of respiratory events identified by our system is highly correlated with the ground truth and has a correlation coefficient of 0.9957, 0.9860, and 0.9533 for central apnea, obstructive apnea and hypopnea respectively. Furthermore, the average error in computing of rate of apnea and hypopnea events is as low as 1.9 events/hr.

## Categories and Subject Descriptors

J.3 [**Computer Applications**]: Life and Medical Sciences

## General Terms

Design; Human Factors; Algorithms

## Keywords

Mobile Health; Sleep Apnea; Phone Sonar; Contactless Breathing Monitoring

## 1. Introduction

Sleep apnea is a common medical disorder that occurs when breathing is disrupted during sleep. It is estimated to affect more than 18 million American adults [9, 41] and is linked to attention deficit/hyperactivity disorder, high blood pressure, diabetes, heart attack, stroke, and increased motor vehicle accidents [6, 39]. Diagnosing sleep apnea in the clinic requires the polysomnography test which is an expensive, time-consuming and labor-intensive process. It requires a trained technician to attach and monitor various sensors on the patient for the sleep duration and is typically associated with long waiting lists [21]. While portable recording systems are being developed for use in home settings, they require instrumenting either the patient [25, 20, 20] or the bed [30] with various sensors and most still require a trained technician to setup the recording system [30].


*MobiSys'15,* May 18–22, 2015, Florence, Italy.

ACM 978-1-4503-3494-5/15/05 ...$15.00.
http://dx.doi.org/10.1145/2742647.2742674 .

**Figure 1—Sensors used in the polysomnography test.** The figure shows all the sensors used in the test along with the data collection unit. Polysomnography is used to diagnose various sleep disorders including sleep apnea. Our goal is to use a smartphone to detect sleep apnea events without any sensors on the human body.

In this paper we ask the following question: Can we leverage smartphones to detect sleep apnea events without the need for sensor instrumentation? The key challenge is that detecting sleep apnea events requires tracking the fine-grained abdomen and chest movements due to breathing [18]. While the iPhone Respiratory app [4] can track the breathing movements, it requires placing the phone on the body between the ribcage and the stomach and hence is intrusive. Vision-based solutions [43] can track these movements without instrumenting users, but are limited to line-of-sight and good lighting conditions and hence are not applicable to the sleep environment, i.e., in the dark or under a blanket.

We introduce a novel contactless system that tracks the chest and abdomen movements on smartphones and works in the sleep environment. It operates with the phone away from the user and can concurrently track the breathing movements from multiple users. Using this design, we build *ApneaApp*, a smartphone-based solution for detecting sleep-related respiratory events reported in a clinical polysomnography test including hypopnea (when the subject's breathing becomes shallow), obstructive apnea (a complete or partial blockage of the subject's airway) and central apnea (when the subject holds his or her breath).

Our key insight is to transform the phone into an active sonar system. At a high level, we transmit 18-20 kHz sound waves from the phone speaker and listen to their reflections at the microphone. The chest and abdomen motion due to breathing creates changes to the reflected sound waves. These changes, however, are minute and extracting them reliably from other environmental reflections is challenging. To overcome this, we employ FMCW (frequency modulated continuous wave) transmissions that allow us to separate reflections arriving at different times by mapping time differences to shifts in the carrier frequency. Specifically, the reflections from the human body arrive at a specific time depending on the distance from the phone speaker. Thus, focusing on the corresponding frequency allows us to reliably extract the amplitude changes due to breathing, in the presence of all other environmental reflections. Further, since reflections from multiple subjects would arrive at different times, the corresponding frequencies provide us with the ability to simultaneously track multiple breathing signals. Finally, non-breathing body motion creates reflection patterns distinct from breathing, enabling us to distinguish between them.

We implement our design on off-the-shelf smartphones and run benchmark experiments with five healthy participants in a bedroom environment using the Vernier respiratory belt as a baseline. Our results show the following:

- Our system estimates the coarse-grained breathing frequency[1] to within 99.2% of the baseline at distances of up to a meter from the subject. This translated to an error of less than 0.11 breaths/min. These accuracies remain this high even when the subjects use blankets.
- The above accuracies remain unaffected by audible noise in the environment from vehicles on a nearby street as well as human conversations. This is because, we use a high-pass filter to filter out audible signals below 18 kHz.
- It can separate and concurrently track the breathing movements of two subjects on the bed separated by 20 cm.

Building on the above system, we design algorithms to compute the number of central, obstructive and hypopnea events as well as the apnea-hypopnea index which is the average rate of apnea and hypopnea events during the sleep duration. We achieve this by processing both the fine- and coarse- grained changes due to the chest and abdomen movements as well as non-breathing body motion. We deploy ApneaApp at the UW Medicine Sleep Center at Harborview and perform a clinical study with 37 patients for a total of 296 hours. The patients in our study were ordered by their physicians to undergo the polysomnography (PSG) test. Our study was done concurrently with the PSG test and we consider the sensor data and diagnosis from the latter as the ground truth for evaluating our system. Our study shows the following:

- Across patients, the number of central apnea, hypopnea and obstructive apnea events detected by our system is highly correlated with the ground truth. Specifically, the intra-class correlation coefficient between PSG and ApneaApp, is 0.9957, 0.9533 and 0.9860 for central apnea, hypopnea and obstructive apnea respectively.

[1]Detecting sleep apnea events requires tracking the fine-grained abdomen and chest motion variations in addition to the coarse-grained breathing frequency. We evaluate ApneaApp's ability to track these variations in our clinical study.

**Respiratory Summary:**

**Types of Respiratory Events / Respiratory Effort Related Arousal (RERA) Events**

| Respiratory Events | Number | Index | RERA | Parameter | Total | Index |
|---|---|---|---|---|---|---|
| Obstructive Apneas | 123 | 15.7 /hr | | Total: | 129 | 16.4 |
| Mixed Apneas | 0 | 0.0 /hr | | Non-REM: | 105 | 16.5 |
| Central Apneas | 1 | 0.1 /hr | | REM: | 24 | 16.1 |
| **Total Apneas** | **124** | **15.8 /hr** | | Supine: | 129 | 16.4 |
| **Total Hypopneas*** | **371** | **47.2 /hr** | | Lateral: | N/A | N/A |
| **Apneas + Hypopneas*** | **495** | **63.0 /hr** | | Prone: | N/A | N/A |

**Figure 2—Snapshot of a Clinical PSG Report.** It summarizes the number of obstructive, central and hypopnea events along with the apneas-hypopneas index (AHI). An AHI value between 0–5 is classified as no-apnea, values between 5–15 are classified as mild-apnea, AHI values between 15–30 are classified as moderate-apnea, and higher AHIs are severe apnea conditions.

- The average error in computing the rate of apnea and hypopnea events is 1.9 events/hr; this is a clinically acceptable value [30].
- Our system accurately classifies 32 out of 37 patients between four sleep apnea levels (no apnea, mild, moderate, and severe apnea). The five misclassifications occur between no-apnea and mild-apnea; four of them happen right at the boundary between the two levels with an error less than 1 event/hr. These boundary cases are handled separately by physicians depending on the patient preferences, symptoms, and insurance; thus, effectively reducing the number of misclassifications to one.
- We ran an audibility test with 87 sleep apnea patients (ages between 23 and 93 with a mean age of 50) and 57 healthy undergraduate students at UW CSE. None of the 87 sleep apnea patients reported any audible sounds from ApneaApp. Only two of the 57 undergraduates reported hearing audible sounds. This demonstrates that ApneaApp is inaudible for most of the adult population.

**Contributions:** We make four key contributions: (1) We introduce a novel contactless technique for tracking chest and abdomen movements due to breathing on smartphones. We achieve this by analyzing the reflections from FMCW sonar transmissions. (2) We design algorithms to detect central apnea, obstructive apnea, and hypopnea as well as estimate the apnea-hypopnea index from the sonar reflections. (3) We implement our design on off-the-shelf smartphones and demonstrate the ability to concurrently track breathing movements from multiple subjects. (4) We perform a clinical study with 37 patients demonstrating the feasibility of using our system to accurately compute the number of central, obstructive, and hypopnea events as well as the apnea-hypopnea index.

## 2. POLYSOMNOGRAPHY OVERVIEW

The clinical polysomnography test (PSG) is traditionally used to diagnose sleep apnea and other sleep disorders. It is conducted overnight in a sleep laboratory where a trained technician monitors the patient's sleeping patterns. To do this, the technician attaches the patient with a number of sensors including a chest and abdomen belt to measure breathing movements, a nasal pressure transducer, a snore microphone, a pulse oximeter to measure oxygen saturation, a movement sensor on each leg to detect movements and five EEG sensors to measure brain activity. The sensors are all connected using wires and the technician monitors the live data stream from the sensors, throughout the sleep duration.

Fig. 2 shows a snapshot of a PSG report. The key metric used for sleep apnea diagnosis is the AHI — the Apnea-Hypopnea Index — that represents the rate at which apnea and hypopnea events occur during the sleep period. Physicians classify the sleep apnea level using these AHI values. Specifically, AHI values between 0–5 are classified as no-apnea, those between 5–15 are classified as mild-

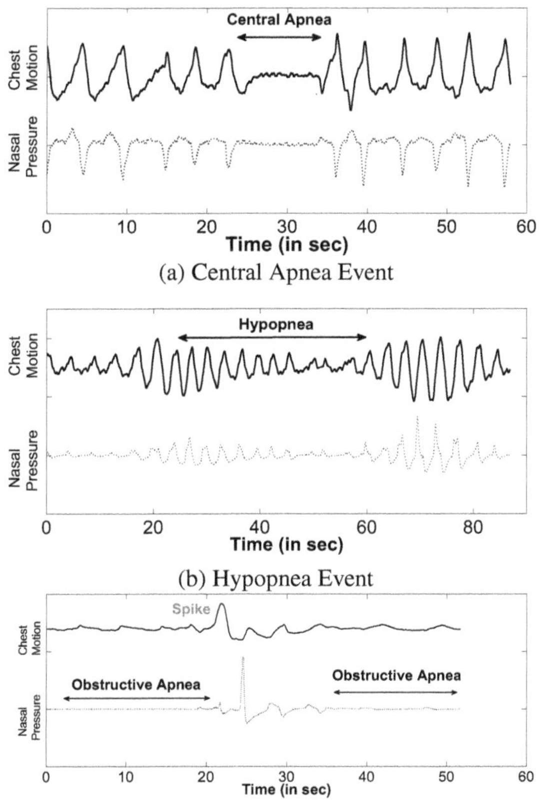


(a) Central Apnea Event



(b) Hypopnea Event



(c) Obstructive Apnea Event

**Figure 3—American Academy of Sleep Medicine (AASM) Signal Characterization of the Apnea Events.** The figures show the chest motion and nasal pressure signals for the three apneas. A central apnea event occurs when the subject holds her breath for a non-negligible duration. A hypopnea event occurs when the subject's chest motion drops by more than 30% with an accompanying 3–4% oxygen desaturation. Finally, an obstructive apnea event occurs when the subject makes an increased effort to pull air into the lungs but air does not reach the lungs due to blockage.

apnea, AHI values between 15–30 are classified as moderate-apnea, and higher AHIs are severe apnea.

The apnea-hypopnea index is computed as follows:

$$AHI = \frac{\#central\ apnea + \#hypopnea + \#obstructive\ apnea}{total\ sleep\ time}$$

In the above equation, central apnea, hypopnea, and obstructive apnea denote the various apnea conditions that are tracked during the study. Mixed apneas are another class of apneas that are sometimes included in the above equation. However, none of our PSG reports showed non-zero mixed apneas and so we ignore them in our computation.

To compute the above parameters, the eight-hour sensor data is split into 30-second intervals called epochs. The scoring process of analyzing these epochs involves two main steps. The first step is staging, which identifies whether the patient is awake or asleep in each epoch. This is achieved by examining the brain activity obtained from the five EEG sensors. At the end of this step, each epoch is marked as being in either a wake or sleep stage. The second step involves identifying the number of central apnea, hypopnea, and obstructive apnea events, using the AASM guidelines [18] outlined below.

**Identifying central apnea events.** A central apnea event occurs when the subject holds her breath for a non-negligible duration. Fig. 3(a) shows the nasal pressure and chest motion signals during a central apnea event. The figure shows that the chest movements are flat indicating the absence of breathing effort; consequentially the nasal pressure is also flat. If this persists for more than ten seconds, it is marked as a central apnea event.

**Identifying hypopnea events.** A hypopnea event occurs when the subject's breathing becomes shallow. Fig. 3(b) plots the nasal pressure and chest motion signals during a hypopnea event. The figure shows that during a hypopnea event, the chest movements reduce in amplitude. In particular, if this amplitude drops by more than 30% and has an accompanying 3–4% oxygen desaturation, then the corresponding epoch is marked as hypopnea. We note that recent clinical research [30] has shown that the 30% reduction alone can be used for detecting hypopneas without a significant loss of accuracies.

**Identifying obstructive apnea events.** Obstructive apnea occurs when there is a complete or partial blockage of the upper airway during sleep. During an obstructive apnea event, the subject makes an effort to pull air into the lungs, however air does not reach the lungs because of blockage. Fig. 3(c) shows the signals where the breathing effort can be seen in the chest band signals and the air flow is flat in the nasal pressure sensor.

We note the following three points about PSG:

- The current procedure for sensor data collection and processing is both labor and time intensive. Specifically, it takes about an hour for the technician to fit each patient with these sensors. Throughout a sleep duration of eight hours, the technician monitors the sensors and ensures that they remain properly attached to the patient's body. The sensor data is then processed manually to tag every epoch with the sleep apnea events.
- While portable sleep apnea testing is performed in the home, it still require setting up the patient with chest and abdomen belts, nasal pressure sensors, transducer and thermistors, EKG and pulse oximetry. Home testing has a high failure rate of up to 33% due to the loss of signal resulting from detachment of wires and cables [33].
- A PSG test is also used to diagnosis other sleep-related conditions including upper airway resistance syndrome which involve respiratory effort related arousals (RERA) that are shown in Fig. 2. RERAs are sleep arousals that do not meet the above definitions of apneas and hypopneas. While these are respiratory-related and could be detected using our sonar-based system, exploring them in detail is not in the scope of this paper.

## 3. APNEAAPP

ApneaApp is a contactless system that enables detection of sleep apnea events using smartphones. To understand how ApneaApp operates, we first describe how we transform the phone into an active sonar system that tracks the chest and abdomen movements due to breathing. We then describe our algorithms to detect sleep apnea events from these movements.

### 3.1 Transforming the Phone into an Active Sonar

An FMCW waveform is a chirp signal, as shown in Fig. 4, where the transmitted frequency increases linearly with time between 18 kHz and 20 kHz. These signals reflect off the reflector (e.g., human body) and arrive at the microphone after a time delay. To determine this delay, at a high level, an FMCW receiver com-

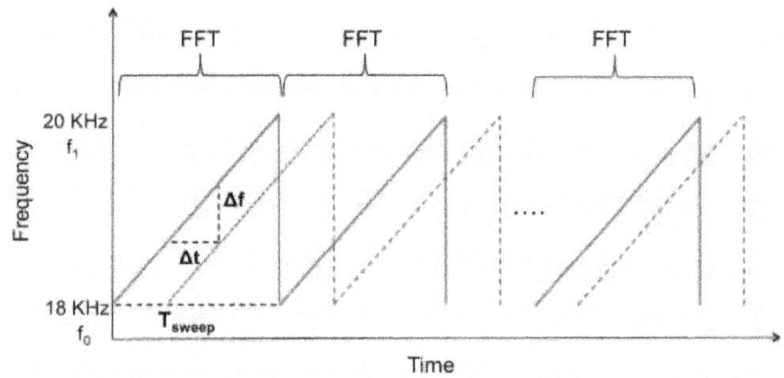


**Figure 4—Traditional FMCW Processing.** The transmitter continuously transmits signals where the frequency increases linearly with time between $f_0$ and $f_1$. The reflections that arrive with a time delay $\Delta t$ create a frequency shift $\Delta f$. The receiver extracts this frequency shift by performing an FFT over the chirp duration.

pares the frequencies of the transmitted and reflected signals. Since the transmitted frequency increases linearly in time, time delays in the reflected signals translate to frequency shifts in comparison to the transmitted signals.

For instance, the red line is the transmitted signal from the phone speaker and the green line is the reflected signal from a human body that arrives with a time delay $\Delta t$. This delay is given by $\frac{2d}{v_{sound}}$, where $d$ is the distance from the human body and $v_{sound}$ is the speed of sound. Now, the frequency shift $\Delta f$ between the transmitted and reflected signal is:

$$\Delta f = \frac{f_1 - f_0}{T_{sweep}} \Delta t$$

When we have multiple reflectors that are at different distances from the receiver, their reflections translate to different frequency shifts in the signal. An FMCW receiver can extract all these frequency shifts by performing an Fourier transform over a chirp duration as shown in Fig. 4. The chirp duration, $T_{sweep}$, in practice is picked so that the reflections from all points within the desired operational distance would start arriving before the chirp ends. Since our operational distance is a meter we pick a chirp duration of 10.75 ms in our implementation.

*Challenge:* The act of breathing creates minute chest and abdomen motion that can be captured by monitoring the corresponding bin in the Fourier transform as a function of time. The challenge however is that breathing movements are minute and create a very small frequency shift. Specifically, a 2 cm breathing displacement creates a 11.7 Hz shift.[2] This is problematic because given our sampling rate and chirp duration, the width of each FFT bin is 93.75 Hz which is much greater than the frequency shifts created due to breathing.

To address this problem, as shown in Fig. 5, the ApneaApp receiver performs a Fourier transform over $N$ FMCW chirps. This is in contrast to a traditional FMCW receiver that computes a Fourier transform over the duration of a single FMCW chirp. Such an operation, decreases the width of each FFT bin by a factor of $N$. In our implementation we set N to ten which results in an FFT bin width of 9.37 Hz. This allows us to capture the minute frequency shifts resulting from the breathing movements. We note that performing an

[2]Given the speed of sound, a 48 kHz sampling rate translates to a resolution of 0.71 cm per sample. Further, a 10.7 ms chirp duration corresponds to 512 samples. With 18–20 kHz FMCW chirps, each sample corresponds to a 3.9 Hz frequency shift. Thus, a displacement of 0.71 cm translates to a 3.9 Hz change in the frequency domain. Consequentially, a 2 cm breathing movement creates a 11.7 Hz frequency shift.

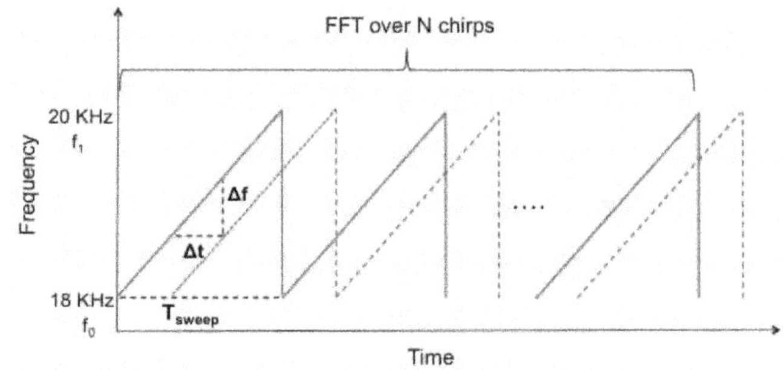


**Figure 5—FMCW Processing in ApneaApp.** To extract the minute frequency shifts created by breathing motion, ApneaApp performs an FFT over an integer number of chirp durations.

FFT over multiple chirp durations reduces our ability to track high-frequency movements that occur during these chirps. However, in our implementation, ten chirps correspond to a very short 107 ms, a duration within which significant breathing movements are unlikely to occur.

The final question is: *how do we compute the distance of the subject from the phone?* At a high level, we start at a distance of zero and search for breathing movements at increasing distance values up to the maximum distance of one meter. Specifically, we search for breathing movements in the 58 Fourier bin corresponding to 18 kHz to 18.546 kHz.[3] In our implementation we reduce the computation by searching in every alternate FFT bin. To search for these breathing movements in each FFT bin, we perform another FFT over a 30s duration and search for peaks in the typical breathing frequencies of 0.2-0.3 Hz.

To summarize, the phone transmits FMCW signals in the 18-20 kHz range with a chirp duration of 10.7 ms from its speaker. The microphones receive the reflected signals and process them to track the breathing movements. Specifically, we first find the distance to the human by searching for a periodic breathing signal starting from the closed distance value to the maximum range of one meter. Once we find this distance, we track the breathing movements by performing in a shorter FFT over ten chirp durations and monitor the reflected signals corresponding to the estimated distance value. Note that the above procedure is repeated every time the user moves their position, which we identify using the algorithm in §3.2.2. This prevents the need for manually calibrating the distance between the user and the phone.

We note the following points about our algorithm.

*Computational Complexity.* Our algorithm requires one 5120-point FFT and between one to twenty nine 24000-point FFTs to successfully extract the breathing motion. We stop our search at the first FFT bin that has the breathing movements.

*Tracking breathing from multiple subjects.* Reflections corresponding to subjects at different distances arrive with different time delays. Thus they create different frequency shifts with the FMCW signal. Therefore, to track breathing from two subjects, we modify the above algorithm to continue its search until it finds two FFT bins with the breathing motion.

*Leveraging angle-of-arrival algorithms.* One could track breathing movements from equidistant subjects who are at different angles, by using multiple microphones and implementing angle-of-arrival

[3]For 18-20 kHz FMCW transmissions, a distance of zero corresponds to the FFT bin for 18-kHz. The operational distance of 1 m corresponds to a frequency shift of 18.546 Hz.

algorithms. Evaluating this, however, is not in the scope of this paper.

*FMCW versus pulse-modulated transmissions.* Pulse-modulated transmissions use high-amplitude short pulses and are an alternative to continue-wave FMCW signals. In our experiment, however, they created low frequency components in the 0-18 kHz range that made them noticeably audible. FMCW transmissions, on the other hand, have lower-amplitudes and are limited to 18-20 kHz, making them inaudible for most of the adult population.

## 3.2 Sleep Apnea Detection Algorithm

As described in §2, diagnosing sleep apnea requires estimating the Apnea-Hypopnea Index (AHI) which is the average rate of apnea events during the sleep duration. This requires computing the number of central, obstructive, and hypopneas as well the total sleep time. In this section, we first describe our algorithms to compute the number of apneas and then the total sleep time.

### *3.2.1 Estimating the Number of Apneas*

ApneaApp detects a hypopnea event when the chest motion reduces below a threshold (30%).[4] A central apnea event is detected when the subject holds her breath and as a result the amplitude of the chest motion signal reduces to zero. Thus, ApneaApp identifies hypopnea when the amplitude of the breathing motion decreases below the threshold but the periodicity that is expected in a breathing signal still exists. But to identify central apnea, we couple an amplitude reduction in the chest motion signal with an absence of the breathing periodicity.

An obstructive apnea event, on the other hand, occurs when there is an obstruction in the airflow, i.e., the subject makes a breathing effort but the airflow is obstructed by a tissue overgrowth in the neck. In a clinical PSG study, obstructive apnea is detected using the nasal pressure sensor that directly measures the airflow; this, however, is not available in our system. We instead perform an analysis of the chest motion data that reveals that the subject usually tends to increase her breathing effort in these scenarios. This results in a clear spike in the amplitude of the chest motion, as shown in Fig. 3(c).

Thus, measuring the amplitude and periodicity in the chest motion signal is critical to detecting obstructive, central and hypopneas. Note that as shown in Fig. 3, the chest motion signal can be approximated as a periodic sinusoidal wave. Hence the magnitude of the peaks of these sinusoidal waves represents the amplitude and their peak locations determine their periodicity. Thus, we design a peak detection algorithm to compute the amplitude and periodicity of the chest motion signal.

**ApneaApp's peak detection algorithm.** Standard peak detection algorithms identify the transition point at which the signal changes from an increasing to a decreasing trend. In other words, for every set of three points, if the middle point is the maximum, then it is labeled as a peak. Such an algorithm, however, would result in a number of erroneous peaks with our chest motion signal. As an example, Fig. 6 plots a typical chest motion signal. Running the standard peak detection algorithm on this signal results in a number of unintended peaks as shown in the figure. To reduce the number of such peaks, we introduce two key heuristics.

[4]AASM and Medicare guidelines require the 30% reduction to be accompanied with a 3% and 4% oxygen saturation respectively. However, recent clinical research [30] has shown that the 30% reduction alone can be used for detecting hypopneas.

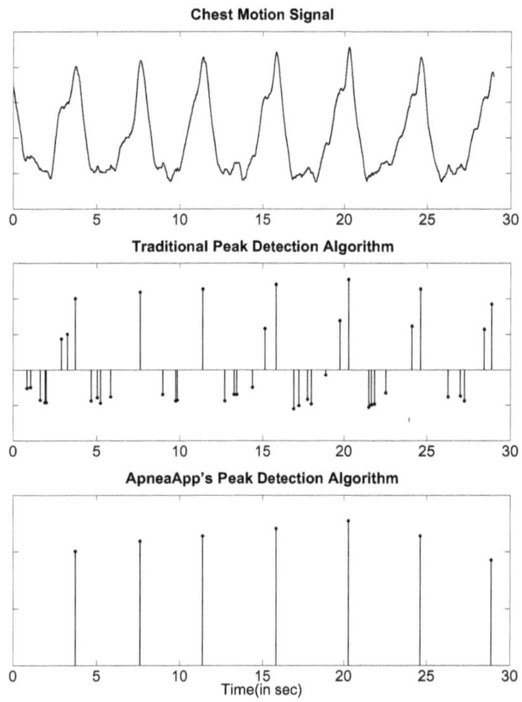


**Figure 6—Understanding ApneaApp's peak detection algorithm.** Standard peak detection algorithms identify the transition point at which the signal changes from an increasing trend to a decreasing trend. Thus, they identify a number of unintended peaks in our chest motion signal. ApneaApp's peak detection algorithm, in contrast, uses minimum peak distance and amplitude heuristics to reduce these unintended peaks.

The first heuristic is to set a threshold on the minimum distance between two consecutive peaks. In particular, the breathing frequency in an adult human typically varies between 12-18 breaths/min. Thus each breath takes 3.3 s at the maximum frequency of 18 breaths/min. We set a conservative threshold of three seconds in our implementation.

The second heuristic is to set a threshold on the minimum amplitude at which a peak is detected. To do this, we first run the above peak detection algorithm with the minimum distance heuristic on the chest motion data for the first hour to obtain an initial set of peaks. We then compute the minimum amplitude threshold as $\mu_{peaks} - 2\sigma_{peaks}$, where $\mu_{peaks}$ and $\sigma_{peaks}$ are the mean and standard deviation of the peak amplitudes. Finally, we go back and apply both the amplitude as well as the minimum distance thresholds on the entire chest motion data for the eight-hour sleep duration to obtain the actual set of peaks. Fig. 6 shows that our peak detection algorithm identifies the correct peaks.

**Central apnea estimation algorithm.** We run the peak detection algorithm to identify the locations of the peaks in the chest motion signal. We then compute the distance between these consecutive peaks. If this distance is greater than ten seconds, it means that the subject holds her breath for a non-negligible period of time and hence we declare it as a central apnea event.

**Hypopnea estimation algorithm.** We again use the peak detection algorithm to detect the peaks. When the peak values reduce beyond a threshold and still maintain their periodicity, we declare it as a hypopnea event. To compute this threshold for our sonar data, we perform a linear regression on the data from a single patient to max-

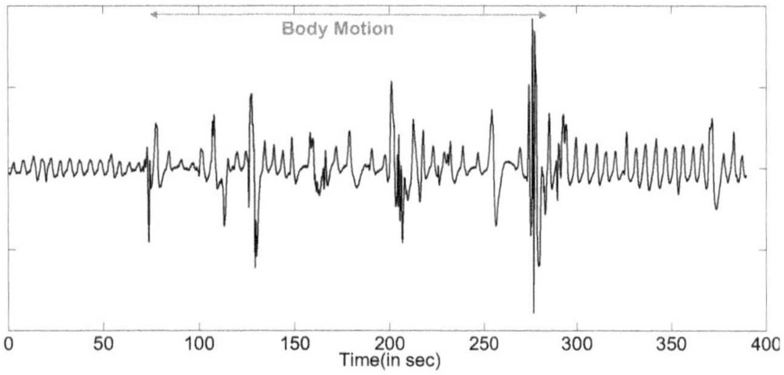


**Figure 7—Differentiating body movements from breathing.** ApneaApp leverages that when the subject moves her body, the sonar reflections experience large variations that do not have the periodicity of the breathing motion.

imize the hypopnea detection accuracy and identify a threshold of 38%. We use this threshold for all the patients in our clinical study.

**Obstructive apnea estimation algorithm.** As described earlier we detect obstructive apnea using sudden spikes in the chest motion signal. We identify the spikes from the peaks in the signal when the amplitude in these peaks increases by 50%. Further, if multiple spikes occur within a second we consider them to be part of a single obstructive apnea event. We note that some of the patients with periodic limb movement disorder periodically move their limbs. To avoid confusing them with obstructive apnea, we ignore periodic spikes in the chest motion signal.

### *3.2.2 Estimating the total sleep time*

In a polysomnography test, the EEG sensors are used to measure the brain activity to determine whether the subject is asleep or awake; this is then used to measure the total sleep time of a subject. Recent work [30] has shown that one can use body movements to compute the total sleep time and the resulting accuracies are acceptable for the purposes of estimating the apnea-hypopnea index. Thus, ApneaApp measures the total sleep time by identifying the non-breathing body movements and subtracting their duration from the total experiment time.

To identify these movements, we leverage that when the subject's body moves, the sonar reflections experience large variations that do not have the periodicity of the breathing motion. By identifying these aperiodic signals that are shown in Fig. 7, ApneaApp detects body movements. Specifically, we run our peak detection algorithm after disabling the minimum distance heuristic. We then check if the resulting peaks are aperiodic. To do this, we perform a second order derivative (difference of the difference) over the peak locations. For periodic breathing motion, this derivative is close to zero but is higher for aperiodic signals. We use a threshold of five to detect such aperiodic signals and compute the corresponding body motion durations.

Now, we compute the total sleep time by subtracting the body motion durations from the total experiment time. We note that if a patient moves twice within a short period, it is likely that she was awake for the whole duration between the movements. Thus, for the purposes of computing the sleep time, we combine any body movements that occur within a ten-minute period into a single awake duration.

## 4. IMPLEMENTATION

We implement ApneaApp as a third party Android app that does not require rooting the smartphone. ApneaApp plays frequency-

| | Samsung S4 | S5 | Galaxy Nexus | HTC One |
|---|---|---|---|---|
| 18-20 kHz Mic | Yes | Yes | Yes | Yes |
| 18-20 kHz Speaker | Yes | Yes | Yes | Yes |
| Separated Speaker/Mic | Yes | Yes | No | Yes |
| Apnea Detection | Yes | Yes | No | Yes |
| Breathing Frequency | Yes | Yes | Yes | Yes |

**Table 1—Smartphone requirements for ApneaApp.** The table shows that accurate apnea detection requires a phone that has a speaker-microphone pair that is not co-located. This is because a co-located speaker-microphone pair results in unpredictable variations in the amplitude of the microphone signal. However, monitoring breathing frequency does not require stable amplitude and hence can work even with co-located speakers and microphones.

modulated samples on the phone speaker and continuously record the raw samples from the microphone.

To understand the smartphone capabilities necessary to accurately assess sleep apnea, we experiment with four different Android phones: Samsung Galaxy S4, Samsung Galaxy S5, HTC One, and Galaxy Nexus. To operate ApneaApp the phone requires the ability to transmit and receive audio signals in the 18-20 kHz range from the speaker and microphone respectively. Table. 1 shows that all the tested smartphones satisfy this requirement.

Another critical requirement is a stable amplitude at the microphone. This is important since our algorithm leverages amplitude changes to detect sleep apnea events. Our experiments reveal that, across all the tested smartphones, when the co-located microphone-speaker pair concurrently transmit and receive signals, the amplitude at the microphone experiences unpredictable variations. This happens because of a feedback loop between the co-located microphone and speaker and can result in sleep apnea misclassifications.

To address this issue, we leverage that many smartphones today come with an additional microphone that is not co-located with the speaker. Our results show that using this microphone eliminates any unintended interaction with the phone speaker. This means that smartphones that do not have this additional microphone, such as the Galaxy Nexus, cannot be used to accurately detect sleep apnea events with ApneaApp. Note, however, that the measurement of breathing frequency is not affected by this feedback loop and hence ApneaApp can still be used to track the breathing frequency on Galaxy Nexus phones.

## 5. CLINICAL STUDY

We conducted a clinical sleep study with 37 patients (17 female and 20 male) between ages of 23-93 (mean: 50) for a total of 296 hours and compare the results from ApneaApp with the PSG study reports. The study was conducted at the sleep laboratory in the UW Medicine Sleep Center at Harborview.

**Participants.** The patients who participated in our study were examined by a sleep physician for common sleep disorders like excessive snoring or daytime fatigue and prescribed to undergo the in-laboratory polysomnography (PSG) study. The sleep lab is equipped to conduct PSG studies for a maximum of eleven patients per night; we randomly choose up to five subjects per night for our study. We do not screen patients based on their gender, race or national origin, but only consider adults. The patients who participated in our study were not provided any monetary benefits. We note two key points: First, our participant group included both patients undergoing the regular PSG study to diagnose sleep apnea as well as those undergoing the CPAP treatment [27] after being diagnosed positive for sleep apnea. Second, out of the 38 patients we approached, 37 consented to participate in our sleep study. Further, there was significant interest amongst them in using a smartphone instead of the existing PSG procedure to diagnose their sleep illness.

**Protocols.** In clinical PSG studies, the sleep lab technician assigns each patient to a separate room furnished with an adjustable king size bed. Each room is also fitted with a camera to get a visual log of the patient. Polysomnography was performed as follows according to American Academy of Sleep Medicine criteria: Lectro-encephalographic electrodes were positioned at two frontal (F7, F8), two central (C3, C4), and two occipital (O1, O2) locations (International 10-20 system of measurement) and were referenced to the contralateral mastoids. Chin electromyogram and right and left electroculogram electrodes were also applied. Airflow was measured using a nasal pressure cannula placed in the nose and a thermistor placed in the nose and over the mouth, allowing differentiation between nasal and oral breathing. Chest and abdominal respiratory effort were assessed by piezo respiratory-effort bands placed around the chest and abdomen, and snoring with a small microphone sensor placed on the throat just lateral to the trachea (Pro-Tech Services, Inc., Mukilteo, WA). Oxygen saturation was measured from the index finger via pulse oximetry (Nellcor, Pleasanton, CA). Bilateral electromyogram electrodes were placed on the anterior tibialis muscle to monitor leg movements. After fitting the sensors, the technician performs bio-calibrations by asking the patient to do specific activities like leg motion, snoring and breathing exercises and ensure that the sensors are properly attached.

The procedures for our ApneaApp study occur concurrently with existing PSG protocols. Specifically, as the sleep technician attaches sensors to the patient, the first author places a Samsung Galaxy S4 smartphone running ApneaApp at the other end of the bed. The position and the orientation of the phone vary across patients depending on their sleep habits. For example, some patients prefer to surround themselves with pillows in which case the phone is placed behind the pillows at a farther distance. The distance of the phone from the patient varies between 0.3 and 0.7 meters. We leave the room and return in the morning to collect the smartphones from the sleep lab. The phone is plugged in throughout the study.[5] The above procedures were reviewed and approved by the UW Human Subjects Division.

**Data Processing.** The data from the clinical PSG study is sent to a third-party entity that scores the sensor data and provides the number of central and obstructive apneas, and hypopneas. Currently, a trained sleep technician manually performs the above scoring process resulting in a minimum delay of three days to obtain the scored data. Specifically, obstructive apneas, hypopneas, and central apneas were scored by the technician as follows: Obstructive apneas were defined by at least a 90% reduction in the pressure-flow signal with corresponding respiratory effort; central apneas were defined by at least a 90% reduction in pressure-flow signal without respiratory effort; and hypopneas were defined as a greater than 30% reduction in amplitude in pressure-flow signal lasting at least 10 seconds with an associated 4% oxygen desaturation.

To process the sonar data collected using ApneaApp, we run the algorithm described in §3.2. The scored ground truth data per patient from the PSG study is more than 1 GB. Thus, we compare it with ApneaApp's signals using Matlab.

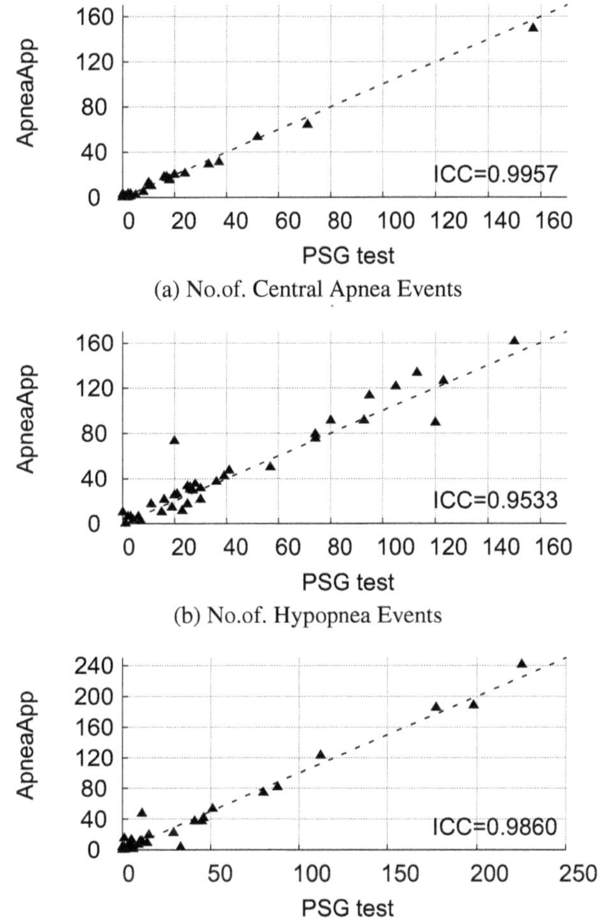


(a) No.of. Central Apnea Events

(b) No.of. Hypopnea Events

(c) No.of. Obstructive Apnea Events

**Figure 8—Scatter-plots of the Number of Apnea Events.** The x-axis and the y-axis show the number of apnea events estimating by PSG and ApneaApp respectively. The plots show that there is a high correlation between the number of central, obstructive and hypopnea events identified by PSG and ApneaApp.

## 5.1 Sleep Apnea Detection Accuracy

The key metric used for sleep apnea diagnosis is the Apnea-Hypopnea Index (AHI), which represents the average rate at which apnea and hypopnea events occur during the sleep duration. To compute this, as described in §2, we need to estimate the number of central, obstructive and hypopnea events as well as the total sleep time. In this section, we evaluate ApneaApp's effectiveness in estimating these parameters.

**Accuracy of apnea events.** First we examine ApneaApp's effectiveness in computing the number of central apnea, hypopnea, and obstructive apnea events. We compare the number of apnea events computed by our algorithm described in §3.2 with the baseline numbers provided by the PSG study. Figs. 8 (a)-(c) show the scatter plots for central, obstructive and hypopnea events. The 45-degree line denotes the ideal scenario when our estimates match the baseline.

The plots show that the number of apnea events detected by ApneaApp is highly correlated with the PSG test. Specifically, the in-

[5]A full-charged Samsung Galaxy S4 running ApneaApp lasts around four hours. When plugged in, however, the phone can simultaneously run ApneaApp and go from a no-charge state to being full-charged in four and a half hours. Since phones are often left charging during the night, we believe that the latter would be a typical ApneaApp use case.

| False Positives | False Negatives |
|---|---|
| 0.0023% ($\frac{59}{26070}$) | 0.0336% ($\frac{43}{1281}$) |

**Table 2—Detecting Body Motion.** ApneaApp detects body motion using abrupt changes to the periodicity of breathing movements. We use the body motion sensors from the PSG study as our ground truth. The table shows that we can accurately detect body movements without any sensor instrumentation of the human body.

terclass correlation coefficient (ICC)[6] between ApneaApp and PSG is 0.9957, 0.9533 and 0.9860 for central apnea, hypopnea and obstructive apnea respectively. We further note the following.

- Amongst the apneas, the number of central apnea events computed by ApneaApp has the highest correlation (ICC=0.9957). This is because a central apnea event is detected as the absence of chest motion; this can be done accurately using the algorithm in §3.2.
- The number of hypopneas has a lower correlation coefficient (ICC=0.9533). The key reason for this is that hypopneas are detected when the amplitude of the breathing motion reduces by more than a threshold. Thus, small errors near this threshold can result in misclassifications. We note that in the PSG study, the technicians mark the hypopnea events manually by ball parking the 30% threshold; this introduces a number of misclassified hypopnea events in the ground truth data itself. We also note that the error due to the lack of oxygen desaturation information in the case of ApneaApp was negligible.
- ApneaApp can accurately compute the number of obstructive apneas by monitoring the chest movements alone (ICC =0.9860), without a nasal pressure transducer that can directly monitor air flow. Analyzing the misclassifications further reveals that ApneaApp misses obstructive apnea events where the airflow is obstructed for a very small duration (10-15s). This is expected because such events might result in less noticeable changes in the breathing effort/movements but would be noticeable at the nasal pressure transducer signal used in the PSG test.

**Body Movements and sleep time estimation.** To compute AHI, we need to measure the total sleep time. In the clinical PSG study, the staging step in the scoring process calculates the total sleep time using the brain activity (EEG) information. Since ApneaApp does not have the brain activity data, it measures the sleep time indirectly using body movements: the absence of body movements is used as an indicator that the patient is asleep. We evaluate ApneaApp's accuracy first in detecting non-breathing body movements and then in estimating the sleep time.

*(i) Body Motion Detection Accuracy.* ApneaApp detects non-breathing body movements using abrupt changes in the periodicity of the breathing movements (see §3.2.2). To evaluate this, we use the body motion sensor data from the PSG study as the ground truth. Every 30 second epoch in the PSG data is annotated with the movement information; we consider each of these epochs as an event. We count a false positive when a body movement is detected by ApneaApp in the absence of one and a false negative when ApneaApp does not detect a body movement that is present in the PSG data.

Table. 2 shows the number of false positive and false negatives across the 37 patients. The results show that ApneaApp can accurately detect 1238 of the 1281 body movement epochs. Further, ApneaApp misclassifies only 59 epochs as body movements across all the 37 patients. This is expected because body movements create significant changes to the reflected signal and hence can be easily distinguished from breathing movements. Thus we conclude that ApneaApp can accurately detect body movements without the need for placing sensors on the human body.

*(ii) Sleep Time Estimation Accuracy.* ApneaApp computes sleep time by subtracting the total duration of body movements from the total experiment time. Next, we evaluate how well this correlates with the sleep time computed in the PSG study using the brain activity (EEG sensors). Fig. 9 plots the total sleep time computed from both ApneaApp and the EEG sensor data across the 37 subjects. The plot shows that the mean and median sleep time error is 36 and 27 mins respectively. Further, ApneaApp overestimates the sleep time by an hour for six patients. This happens because these patients woke up in the middle of the night and lie on the bed without frequent movements, while trying to fall asleep. The brain activity during this period is high but there is little to no frequent motion. This is a fundamental limitation of estimating the total sleep time without access to the brain activity data. However, as we will see next, ApneaApp's sleep time accuracies are acceptable for diagnosing sleep apnea.

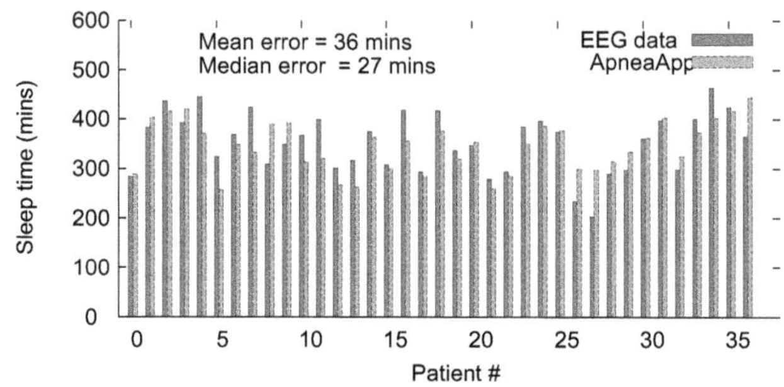


**Figure 9—Sleep time Estimation Error.** We compare the sleep time estimated using body movements (ApneaApp) and brain activity (EEG data). The mean and median error is 36 and 27 mins. ApneaApp tends to overestimate the sleep time for patients who wake up and lie on the bed without any movements while trying to fall asleep. ApneaApp's sleep time accuracies are however sufficient for the purposes of diagnosing sleep apnea. We also note that in practice patients could provide direct feedback about these unusually long awake periods to improve our estimation further.

**Accuracy of AHI estimation.** Finally, we evaluate how well ApneaApp can compute the apnea-hypopnea index and diagnose sleep apnea. The results are as follows:

- Fig. 10 plots a scatter plot of the AHI values computed by ApneaApp versus PSG for the 37 patients. The figure shows that the AHI values are highly correlated between ApneaApp and PSG with an interclass correlation coefficient of 0.9816. Further, the average error in computing AHI is 1.9 events/hr. Larger errors tend to happen at higher AHI values where the diagnosis is fortunately more tolerant to large errors, i.e., the diagnosis is the same whether the AHI is 40 or 50.
- Fig. 11 shows the confusion matrix of the sleep apnea levels diagnosed by ApneaApp with thresholds of 5, 15, and 30. The ta-

[6]ICC is a standard statistic used in the sleep literature for quantifying the effectiveness of two procedures (in our case, PSG and ApneaApp) to produce correlated observations across a range of values [30]. ICC is also a more appropriate metric for us compared to recall accuracy: missing one of four apnea events results in a low recall accuracy of 75%. This however does not capture the system-level performance since for a eight-hour duration, the resulting AHI error is only 0.125.

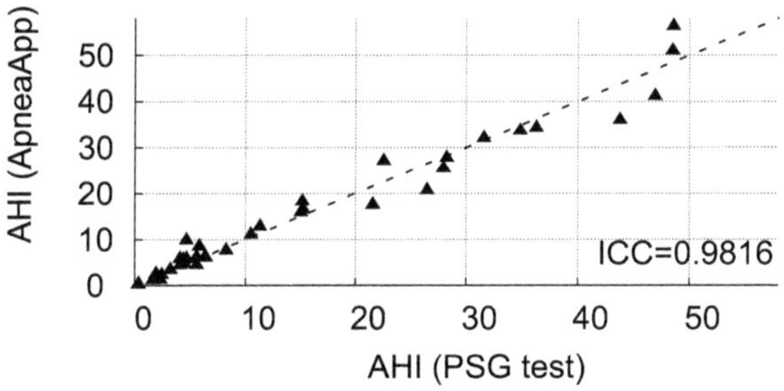


**Figure 10—Scatter-plot of the AHI Values.** The mean error in the AHI values computed between PSG and ApneaApp is 1.9. Larger errors typically happen at higher AHIs where the diagnosis is fortunately more tolerant to large error, i.e., the diagnosis is the same whether the AHI is 40 or 50.

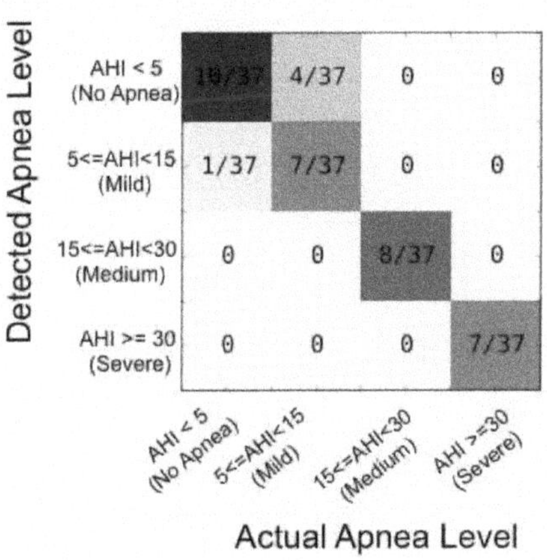


**Figure 11—Confusion Matrix of the Sleep Apnea Levels.** We accurately classifies 32 out of 37 patients between four sleep apnea levels. The five misclassifications occur between no-apnea and mild-apnea; four of them happen right at the boundary between the two levels with an error less than 1 event/hr. These boundary cases are handled separately by physicians depending on the patient preferences, symptoms, and insurance, effectively reducing the number of misclassifications to one.

ble shows that ApneaApp diagnoses the sleep apnea level accurately for 32 out of 37 patients. The five misclassifications are between the no-apnea and mild-apnea diagnosis. Specifically, four patients who have mild-apnea are diagnosed by ApneaApp as having no apnea while one patient with no-apnea is diagnosed as having mild sleep apnea.

- For four of the five misclassified patients, the AHI values are in the 4.5-5.5 range centered at the threshold between no-apnea and mild-apnea. These boundary cases are handled separately by physicians depending on the patient preferences, symptoms, and insurance, effectively reducing the number of misclassifications to one.

## 6. MICROBENCHMARKS

We run experiments with five participants (ages 24–25) in a home bedroom environment to evaluate the effects of various parameters such as orientation, position and distance. The bedroom is next to a major street with significant foot and vehicular traffic. Since we cannot imitate the sleep apnea events where the chest motion experiences amplitude variations, in these set of experiments we use the coarse-grained breathing frequency as a proxy to understand the effects of the various parameters. To obtain the ground truth data for the breathing frequency, we use a Vernier respiratory belt worn at the abdomen level.

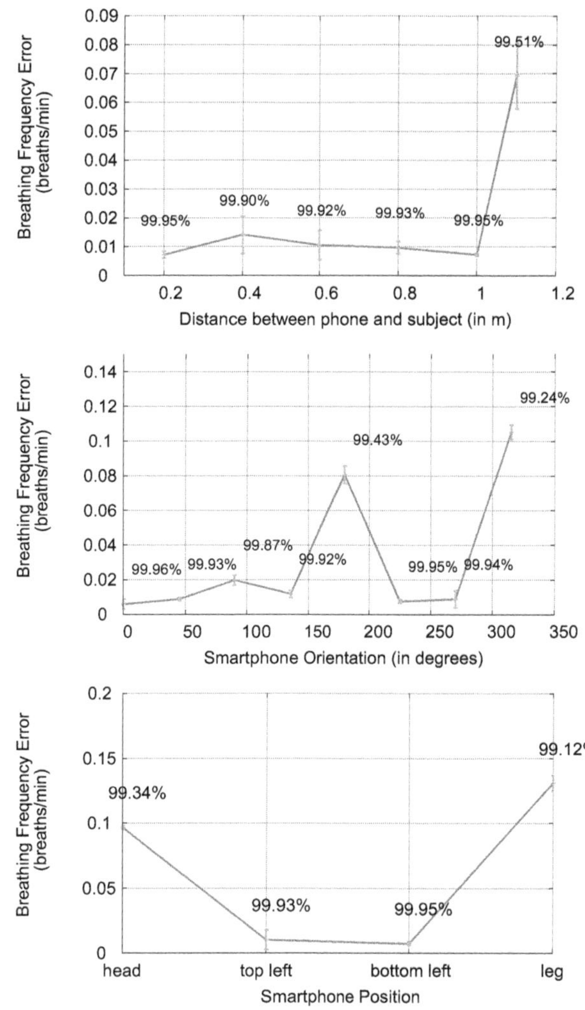


**Figure 12—Effects of phone distance, orientation and position.** The plots show the results for a subject sleeping in the supine position.

### 6.1 Effect of Phone Distance, Orientation and Position

We first evaluate the effect of the phone distance, orientation and position on the breathing frequency accuracies.

*Effect of the phone's distance.* We place the phone on the left side of the subject sleeping in the supine position. In each trial, we monitor the breathing frequency over a three-minute duration after which the subject is asked to get out of the bed. For each distance value, we perform five trials for a total of ten minutes per location. We measure the accuracy of the breathing frequency estimated by ApneaApp versus the Vernier respiratory belt and plot the results in Fig. 12. The figure shows that:

- The breathing frequency accuracy is as high as 99.90% at distances up to one meter. We note that these accuracies are much higher than those observed for sleep apnea. This is because, as

**Figure 13—The various phone positions used for the results in Fig. 12.** We experiment with four different positions along a semicircle centered at the subject.

described in §4, the breathing frequency on the phone is relatively stable compared to the amplitude variations that are necessary for detecting sleep apnea events.

- As the distance increases beyond a meter the accuracies decrease. This is because the strength of the reflections due to breathing reduces with distance, making the breathing signal noisy. The one-meter range is, however large enough to enable contactless breath monitoring that is non-intrusive, as demonstrated in our clinical study. It also limits the negative effects of environmental changes farther away than a meter on ApneaApp's accuracies.
- The accuracies are unaffected by audible noise in the environment from the vehicular and foot traffic on the street. Introducing human conversations in the vicinity of the experiments also does not affect these accuracies. This is because, we use a high-pass filter to filter out audible signals below 18 kHz.

*Effect of the phone's orientation.* We place the phone 20 cm away and to the left of the subject. We then rotate the phone and compute the accuracies for each phone orientation. As before, for each trial, we perform five experiments for a total of 10 minutes per phone orientation. Fig. 12 plots the results as a function of the phone's orientation. We observe that the accuracies remain high, demonstrating that during ApneaApp's operation we do not need to fix the phone orientation.

*Effect of the phone's position.* Next, we experiment with the phone at different positions around the subject. Specifically we place the phone is four different positions — near the head, near the legs, and two positions to the left — along a semicircle of radius 40 cm centered at the subject as shown in Fig. 13. Fig. 12 shows that the accuracies are high when the phone is in the left positions and slightly lower when placed near the head and the feet. This is because in the latter positions, the head and the leg effectively block the chest/abdomen motion. We however note that the maximum error is less than 0.13 breaths per minute across all the phone positions.

## 6.2 Effect of Sleeping Position and Blankets

Next, we evaluate the accuracies for different sleeping positions and in the presence of blankets.

*Effect of the subject's sleeping position.* We consider four different sleeping positions: supine (on the back), prone (on the abdomen), lying on the left, and the right. We place the smartphone at a distance of 20 cm to the left of the subjects and measure the breathing rate accuracies. As before, for each sleep position we monitor the breathing rate over chunks of two minutes for a total of ten minutes. Fig. 14 shows that the average residual error is below 0.16 breaths per minute across all the sleeping positions. We note that the accuracy is lower when the patient is lying with her face down (prone). In this position, we noticed that both the signals from the Vernier belt and ApneaApp experience a larger variation. We however note that our clinical study tracks the chest movements throughout the sleep duration where the patient's sleeping position was not controlled.

*Effect of Blankets.* We measure the breathing frequency accuracy for various blanket thicknesses. The subjects are asked to sleep in the supine position and the phone is placed left of the subject at a distance of 40 cm. We use four blankets with thicknesses varying from 2-5 cm. Fig. 15 shows that the accuracies are not noticeably degraded by the use of blankets. This demonstrates that ApneaApp is well suited for the sleep environment, which is further validated by our clinical study where all the patients used blankets.

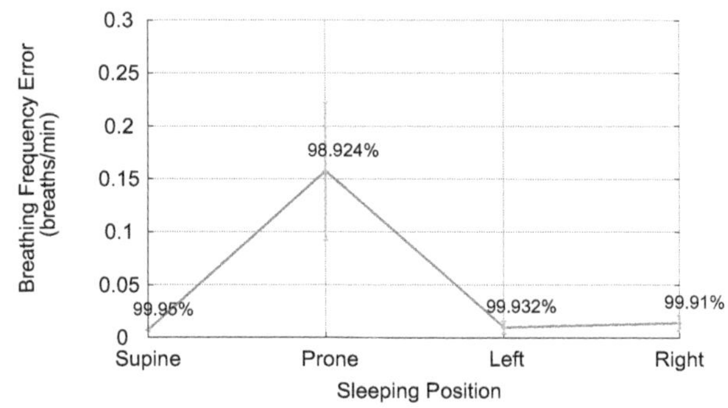


**Figure 14—Effect of sleeping position.** The accuracy is lower when the patient is lying with her face down (prone). In this position, both the signals from the Vernier belt and ApneaApp experience larger variations. We however note that in our clinical study we track the chest movements throughout the sleep duration where the patient's sleeping position was not controlled.

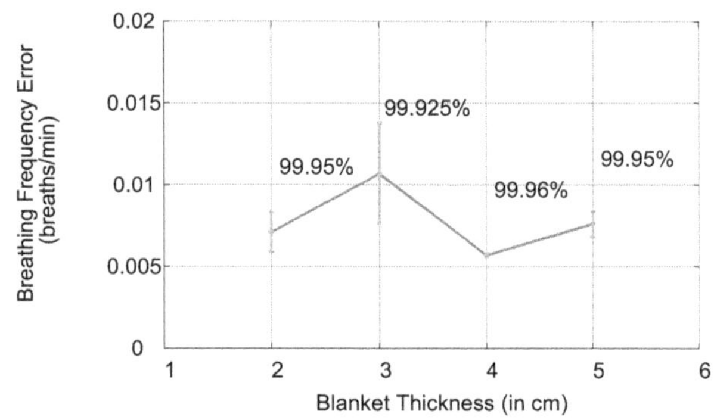


**Figure 15—Effect of blankets.** We use four blankets with thicknesses varying from 2-5 cm. The plot shows that the accuracies are high even when blankets separate the subject from the phone.

## 6.3 Breathing Signals from Multiple Subjects

As discussed in §3.1, the sonar reflections from multiple subject arrive at different times at the microphone. Thus, ApneaApp can simultaneously track breathing movements from more than one sub-

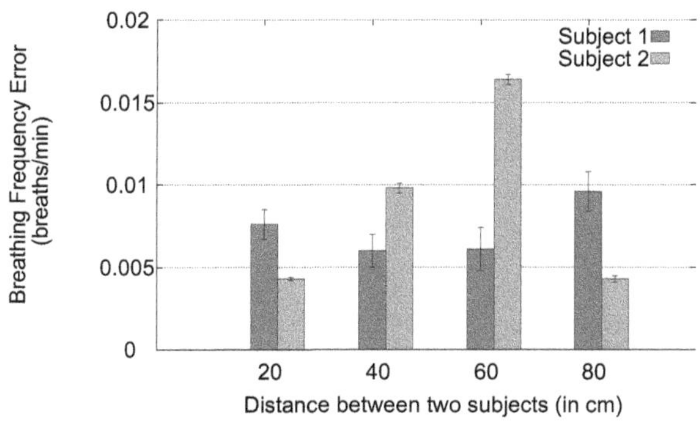


**Figure 16—Extracting breathing from two subjects.** The plot shows that ApneaApp can simultaneously track and monitor the breathing signals from two subjects on the bed.

ject. To evaluate this, we monitor the breathing rate from two subjects sleeping in the supine position on the bed. Both the subjects where fitted with the Vernier respiratory strap to record the ground truth. The phone was placed at one side of the bed at a distance of 20 cm from the first subject. We increase the distance between the two subjects at intervals of 20 cm starting at the minimum distance of 20 cm where the two subjects could sleep without overlapping. As before, we repeat the experiments over five trials for a total of 15 minutes at each distance value.

Fig. 16 plots the accuracies for the two subjects as a function of the distance between them. The plots show that ApneaApp can accurately distinguish between breathing signals of subjects even when they are as close as 20 cm from each other. This is expected, because as described in §3.1, our FMCW transmissions can be used to resolve reflections with a greater resolution than 20 cm. The key point, however, is that we can identify and track the breathing signals from more than one subject — a capability that is important for use in the home environment.

### 6.4 Evaluating ApneaApp's Audibility

ApneaApp transmits FMCW audio signals in the 18-20 kHz range. To evaluate the audibility of these signals, we ran ApneaApp with 144 subjects: 37 of whom were sleep apnea patients who took part in our clinical study, 50 additional sleep apnea patients not part of our clinical study, and 57 healthy undergraduate subjects who are seniors in the UW CSE department.

None of the 87 sleep patients reported any audible sounds from the phone. Further, the 37 patients who took part in our clinical study had no audibility issues for the eight-hour sleep duration. One of the undergraduates could hear faint sounds when the phone was placed next to his ear and a second undergraduate reported hearing a sound similar to TV static at distances of up to one meter. However 55 of the 57 undergraduate students reported no audible sounds from the phone even when placed right next to the ear. This shows that ApneaApp is inaudible for most adults, which is the target population for ApneaApp.

## 7. RELATED WORK

Our work is related to prior art in three domains.

**(a) Mobile Health and Wellness Systems:** There has been recent interest in the mobile health and wellness community to better understand sleep quality. Wearable sleep sensors such as FitBit [2], WakeMate [14], and Jawbone [5] capture the movements from an accelerometer to sense basic sleep patterns such as hours slept and the number of wakings. Lullaby [26] leverages sensors deployed in the bedroom to understand the effect of environmental factors (e.g., ambient noise and lighting conditions) on sleep quality. More recent work including Toss-N-Turn and iSleep leverage smartphone sensors as sleep quality detectors [29, 19, 24]. Specifically, they use accelerometers to detect coarse non-breathing body movements [29, 24] and microphones for cough [24] and snoring [24, 11]. ApneaApp builds on this foundational work but is complementary to it. We introduce a novel contactless system for smartphones that can track fine-grained chest and abdomen movements due to breathing. We then demonstrate the ability to detect sleep apnea events on smartphones.

Our work is also related to prior work on monitoring physiological signals using wearable sensors [12] including mouthpieces and chest bands [13, 7]. Designs such as BodyBeat [34] use custom-built piezoelectric microphones on the body surface to monitor body sounds such as respiration, food intake and laughter. More recent work [36] leverages audible breathing sounds from an ear bud to infer the breathing frequency. The Android app, iBreath [23], combines the audible breathing sounds from a Bluetooth headset with the accelerometer on the phone to infer the breathing frequency while running. These systems are very promising for their application domains. For diagnosing sleep apnea, however, we are unaware of clinical-validated research that demonstrates the ability to compute AHI values and detect sleep apnea events using only audible breathing sounds/frequency. In contrast, we propose a novel contactless solution that can monitor the chest movements by actively transmitting FMCW audio signals. We then demonstrate the ability to detect various sleep apnea conditions including obstructive, central, and hypopnea as well as compute the AHI values.

**(b) RF-based Breathing Rate Monitors:** Prior RF-based approaches [44, 37, 22] leverage changes in radio signals to estimate the breathing frequency. This includes using a network of 2.4 GHz wireless sensors in the bedroom [31, 32] as well as expensive ultra-wideband RF radar systems with 500 MHz to 2 GHz of bandwidth [35, 45]. While promising, none of these approaches have been demonstrated to work on off-the-shelf smartphones. We also believe that the sonar approach introduced in this paper is more attractive for two main reasons. First, a microphone that samples at 48 kHz gives a range resolution of 0.7 cm; RF based approaches need Gigahertz of bandwidth to get a similar resolution. Second, the one-meter operational range of our sonar system reduces the effect of environmental movements making it more robust in real world sleep scenarios.

**(c) Sleep Apnea Research and Systems:** Polysomnography [18] is the standard clinical test for diagnosing sleep apnea in the medical setting. This however is an expensive test that requires attaching various sensors to the patient for the sleep duration. While portable recording systems [25, 20] are being developed for use in home settings, they require the attachment of various sensors and most still require a trained technician to setup the system [30].

Mobile phone app developers have also designed questionnaires (e.g., Home Sleep Apnea A-Z [3], Sleep Access [8]) to screen patients for the PSG test. Sleep Apnea Monitor app [10] help users diagnosed with sleep apnea to sleep on their side instead of their back by buzzing when the user moves to their back. It does so by attaching the phone to the person's leg. Prior research has also explored the feasibility of leveraging snoring and movement information [15, 17] to perform screening for PSG. While correlation existing between sleep apnea and snoring, such an approach does not monitor breathing movements and hence cannot identify sleep apnea events [42, 30]. To address this issue, commercial systems such as Sonomat [30] use embedded sensors in a mattress pad to track the breathing movements and sounds [1, 30]. Our work instead focuses on detecting sleep apnea events by tracking breathing movements on smartphones, without the need for any other sensors.

Finally, medical research has proposed the use of ultrasound imaging, instead of MRI, to measure the tongue volume and width of upper airway [16, 38]. This information has been demonstrated to be helpful in diagnosing obstructive apnea [28]. In contrast to this work, we transform a smartphone into an active sonar system and develop algorithms to extract hypopnea, obstructive apnea, and central apnea information from the sonar signal changes.

## 8. LIMITATIONS AND FUTURE DIRECTIONS

We discuss the limitations of our system as well as various opportunities to improve it.

*Increasing the AHI estimation accuracies.* We design ApneaApp to operate in a home setting without the need for instrumenting the users with sensors. We note however that a clinical PSG test uses a number of sensors that provide physiological information that is not available in our current design. For example, EEG sensors provide the brain activity data that helps accurately find different sleep stages (REM, non-REM, and awake). One could imagine analyzing fine-grained changes in the sonar reflections to find correlations with the sleep stages. Specifically, we plan to explore correlations between physiological parameters such as breathing rate and motion with the various sleep stages.

Similarly, since the PSG test uses cameras to produce a visual log of the patient, the report also summarizes the patient's sleeping position and the corresponding number of sleep apnea events. We plan to explore the feasibility of using accelerometers to predict these sleeping positions. Another direction is to augment the chest movements from our system with audible audio signals including snoring and evaluate the resulting accuracy improvements. Supplementing our system with these capabilities can improve our accuracies and also provide additional diagnostic information.

*Detecting other respiratory-related events.* In addition to diagnosing sleep apnea, a PSG test is also used to detect other events such as the respiratory-effort related-arousals (RERAs). These are arousals in the sleep that do not meet the definition of apnea and hypopnea events. A direction worth exploring is to leverage our sonar design with other smartphone sensors to detect these non-sleep apnea conditions.

*Extracting other physiological information.* In this paper, we focus on extracting the minute chest and abdomen movements due to breathing. We note however that in principle our sonar design can also be used to extract the heart rate without requiring contact with the human body. Prior RF-based radar systems have demonstrated the feasibility of extracting heart rate from radio signals with Gigahertz of bandwidth. While heart rate is not necessary for sleep apnea diagnosis, we plan to use narrowband sonar transmissions on a smartphone and enable contactless heart rate detection, with the goal of better understanding the sleep architecture [40].

## 9. CONCLUSION

We present a contactless solution that detects sleep apnea events on smartphones. To achieve this, we introduce a novel technique that can track chest and abdomen movements due to breathing on smartphones using FMCW sonar transmissions. We design algorithms to detect central apnea, obstructive apnea, and hypopnea as well as estimate the total sleep time by analyzing the FMCW reflections from the human body. We implement our design on off-the-shelf smartphones and demonstrate the ability to concurrently track breathing movements from multiple subjects. Finally, we present results from a clinical study with 37 patients that demonstrate the feasibility of using our system to accurately compute the number of central, obstructive, and hypopnea events as well as the apnea-hypopnea index.

**Acknowledgements.** We would like to thank Ben Ransford, Vamsi Talla, Bryce Kellogg, and Donny Huang for their feedback on the paper. We also thank our shepherd Bodhi Priyantha and the anonymous MobiSys reviewers for their helpful comments. We are grateful to Heather Beseler for managing the administrative process at the UW Medicine Sleep Center at Harborview that made our sleep study possible. We also thank Nong Tang for helping us better understand the mechanics of the polysomonography tests conducted at the sleep center as well as the scoring process performed by the technicians. Finally, we thank all the sleep technicians at the center for their support during our study. This research is funded in part by NSF and University of Washington.

## 10. REFERENCES

[1] Bam labs, sleep iq only from sleep number. http://bamlabs.com.
[2] Fitbit. www.fitbit.com.
[3] Home sleep apnea a-z. https://play.google.com/store/apps/details?id=com.app_aviisha123.layout&hl=en.
[4] Iphone app: Respiratory rate. https://itunes.apple.com/us/app/respiratory-rate/id538726900?mt=8.
[5] Jawbone. https://jawbone.com/.
[6] Morbidity and mortality weekly report,centers for disease control and prevention. In Weekly, Vol.60, No. 8, 2011.
[7] Nose breathe mouthpiece. http://www.nosebreathe.com/.
[8] Sleep access. http://sleepaccess.com/.
[9] Sleep apnea: Epidemiology. http://www.sleepdex.org/epidemiologyapnea.htm.
[10] Sleep apnea monitor. https://itunes.apple.com/gb/app/sleep-apnea-monitor/id464587229?
[11] Sleep as android: Snoring detection. https://sites.google.com/site/sleepasandroid/.
[12] Snuza - portable baby monitors. http://www.snuza.com/.
[13] Vernier respiration monitor belt. http://www.vernier.com/products/sensors/rmb/.
[14] Wakemate. https://play.google.com/store/apps/details?id=com.wakemate.android.
[15] U. Abeyratne, S. Silva, C. Hukins, and B. Duce. Obstructive sleep apnea screening by integrating snore feature classes. In Physiological Measurement, 2013.
[16] M. Al-Abed, P. Antich, D. Watenpaugh, and K. Behbehani. Detection of airway occlusion in simulated obstructive sleep apnea/hypopnea using ultrasound: An in vitro study. In Engineering in Medicine and Biology Society (EMBC), 2013.
[17] S. Alqassim, M. Ganesh, S. Khoja, M. Zaidi, F. Aloul, and A. Sagahyroon. Sleep apnea monitoring using mobile phones. In e-Health Networking, Applications and Services (Healthcom), 2012.

[18] I. C, A.-I. S, C. A. Jr., and Q. SF. The aasm manual for the scoring of sleep and associated events. In 1st ed. Westchester IL: American Academy of Sleep Medicine, 2007.

[19] Z. Chen, M. Lin, F. Chen, N. D. Lane, G. Cardone, R. Wang, T. Li, Y. Chen, T. Choudhury, and A. T. Campbell. Unobtrusive sleep monitoring using smartphones. In PervasiveHealth 2013.

[20] W. J. Deutsch PA, Simmons MS. Cost-effectiveness of split-night polysomnography and home studies in the evaluation of obstructive sleep apnea syndrome. In J Clin Sleep Med 2006;2:145-53.

[21] W. W. Flemons, N. J. Douglas, S. T. Kuna, D. O. Rodenstein, and J. Wheatley. Access to diagnosis and treatment of patients with suspected sleep apnea. In American Journal of Respiratory and Critical Care Medicine, Vol. 169, No. 6 (2004).

[22] N. Fox, C. Heneghan, M. Gonzalez, R. Shouldice, and P. de Chazal. An evaluation of a non-contact biomotion sensor with actimetry. In Engineering in Medicine and Biology Society, 2007.

[23] T. Hao, G. Xing, and G. Zhou. ibreath: A convenient mobile app that tracks breathing during running.

[24] T. Hao, G. Xing, and G. Zhou. isleep: Unobtrusive sleep quality monitoring using smartphones. In SenSys '13.

[25] M. JF, C. J, and e. a. Pereira R. Effectiveness of home respiratory polygraphy for the diagnosis of sleep apnoea and hypopnoea syndrome. In Thorax 2011;66:567-73.

[26] M. Kay, E. K. Choe, J. Shepherd, B. Greenstein, N. Watson, S. Consolvo, and J. A. Kientz. Lullaby: A capture & access system for understanding the sleep environment. In UbiComp '12.

[27] C. A. Kushida, A. Chediak, R. B. Berry, L. K. Brown, D. Gozal, C. Iber, S. Parthasarathy, S. F. Quan, and J. A. Rowley. Clinical guidelines for the manual titration of positive airway pressure in patients with obstructive sleep apnea. Journal of Clinical Sleep Medicine.

[28] Y. Lahav, E. Rosenzweig, Z. Heyman, J. Doljansky, A. Green, and Y. Dagan. Tongue base ultrasound: a diagnostic tool for predicting obstructive sleep apnea. In Ann Otol Rhinol Laryngol, 2009.

[29] J.-K. Min, A. Doryab, J. Wiese, S. Amini, J. Zimmerman, and J. I. Hong. Toss 'n' turn: Smartphone as sleep and sleep quality detector. In CHI '14.

[30] M. Norman, S. Middleton, O. Erskin, P. Middleton, J. Wheatley, and C. Sullivan. Validation of the sonomat: a contactless monitoring system used for the diagnosis of sleep disordered breathing. In Sleep, Sep 2014.

[31] N. Patwari, L. Brewer, Q. Tate, O. Kaltiokallio, and M. Bocca. Breathfinding: A wireless network that monitors and locates breathing in a home. Selected Topics in Signal Processing, IEEE Journal of, 2014.

[32] N. Patwari, J. Wilson, S. Ananthanarayanan, S. Kasera, and D. Westenskow. Monitoring breathing via signal strength in wireless networks. Mobile Computing, IEEE Transactions on, 2014.

[33] Rafael Golpe and Antonio JimÃl'nez and Rosario Carpizo. Home sleep studies in the assessment of sleep apnea/ hypopnea syndrome. In CHEST, 2002.

[34] T. Rahman, A. T. Adams, M. Zhang, E. Cherry, B. Zhou, H. Peng, and T. Choudhury. Bodybeat: A mobile system for sensing non-speech body sounds. In MobiSys '14.

[35] T. Ralston, G. Charvat, and J. Peabody. Real-time through-wall imaging using an ultrawideband multiple-input multiple-output (mimo) phased array radar system. In Phased Array Systems and Technology (ARRAY), 2010.

[36] Ren, Yanzh and Wang, Chen and Chen, Yingying and Yang, Jie. Poster: Hearing your breathing: fine-grained sleep monitoring using smartphones. In MOBICOM Posters, 2014.

[37] R. Shouldice, C. Heneghan, G. Petres, A. Zaffaroni, P. Boyle, W. McNicholas, and P. de Chazal. Real time breathing rate estimation from a non contact biosensor. In Engineering in Medicine and Biology Society (EMBC), 2010.

[38] C.-C. Shu, P. Lee, J.-W. Lin, C.-T. Huang, Y.-C. Chang, C.-J. Yu, and H.-C. Wang. The use of sub-mental ultrasonography for identifying patients with severe obstructive sleep apnea. PLoS ONE, 2013.

[39] K. Strohl, S. Merritt, J. Blatt, A. Pack, F. Council, S. Rogus, K. Georges, T. Roth, J. Kiley, j Stutts, R. Kurrus, P. Waller, A. McCartt, and Willis. Ncsr/nhtsa epert panel on driver fatigue and sleepiness. In Drowsy Driving and Automobile Crashes.

[40] K. Tanida, M. Shibata, and M. Heitkemper. Sleep stage assessment using power spectral indices of heart rate variability with a simple algorithm: limitations clarified from preliminary study. Biol Res Nurs, 2013.

[41] Terry Young and Mari Palta and Jerome Dempsey and James Skatrud and Steven Weber and Safwan Badr. The occurrence of sleep-disordered breathing among middle-aged adults. In The New England Journal of Medicine, 1993.

[42] A. Visvanathan, A. Gibb, and R. Brady. Increasing clinical presence of mobile communication technology: avoiding the pitfalls. In Telemed J E Health, 2011.

[43] H.-Y. Wu, M. Rubinstein, E. Shih, J. Guttag, F. Durand, and W. Freeman. Eulerian video magnification for revealing subtle changes in the world. ACM Trans. Graph., 2012.

[44] A. Zaffaroni, P. de Chazal, C. Heneghan, P. Boyle, P. Mppm, and W. McNicholas. Sleepminder: an innovative contact-free device for the estimation of the apnoea-hypopnoea index. In Proc. IEEE Engineering Medical biology Society, 2009.

[45] D. Zito, D. Pepe, M. Mincica, and F. Zito. A 90nm cmos soc uwb pulse radar for respiratory rate monitoring. In Solid-State Circuits Conference Digest of Technical Papers (ISSCC), 2011.

# MAdScope: Characterizing Mobile In-App Targeted Ads

Suman Nath
Microsoft Research
suman.nath@microsoft.com

## ABSTRACT

Advertising is the primary source of revenue for many mobile apps. One important goal of the ad delivery process is targeting users, based on criteria like users' geolocation, context, demographics, long-term behavior, etc. In this paper we report an in-depth study that broadly characterizes what targeting information mobile apps send to ad networks and how effectively, if at all, ad networks utilize the information for targeting users. Our study is based on a novel tool, called MAdScope, that can (1) quickly harvest ads from a large collection of apps, (2) systematically probe an ad network to characterize its targeting mechanism, and (3) emulate user profiles of specific preferences and interests to study behavioral targeting. Our analysis of 500K ad requests from 150K Android apps and 101 ad networks indicates that apps do not yet exploit the full potential of targeting: even though ad controls provide APIs to send a lot of information to ad networks, much key targeting information is optional and is often not provided by app developers. We also use MAdScope to systematically probe top 10 in-app ad networks to harvest over 1 million ads and find that while targeting is used by many of the top networks, there remain many instances where targeting information or behavioral profile does not have a statistically significant impact on how ads are chosen. We also contrast our findings with a recent study of targeted in-browser ads.

## Categories and Subject Descriptors

C.4 [**Performance Of Systems** ]: [Measurement techniques]

## Keywords

In-app Advertising; Mobile Advertising; Targeted Advertising; User Profiles; Measurement


*MobiSys'15*, May 18–22, 2015, Florence, Italy.

http://dx.doi.org/10.1145/2742647.2742653 .

## 1. INTRODUCTION

In-app advertising is a key economic driver in mobile app ecosystem, funding a wide variety of free apps. Gartner predicts the mobile ad market to grow to $13.5 billion in 2015 [9]. The growth is primarily due to increasing engagement of users with apps—users are reported to spend significantly more time on mobile apps than on traditional web, and the gap is increasing [6].

Of central importance in the ad delivery process is *targeting*—the process of selecting specific ads to display to a given user of an app. In-app *ad controls*, which fetch ads from backend ad networks and display them to users, target users based on criteria such as app type, device attributes (e.g., screen size), user's long-term behavior, demographic, and geolocation. The presumption is that targeting benefits all parties in the ad ecosystem: users, app developers, ad networks, and advertisers. Note that targeting is not unique to in-app ads; it has been successfully used for in-browser ads as well [1,8,11,30].

Despite its importance, in-app ad targeting is relatively ill-explored (compared to its in-browser counterpart). Existing results on in-browser ads (e.g., [1,3,7,8,11,23,30]) cannot be directly generalized to in-app ads for several reasons. First, unlike in-browser ads that cannot easily access user information because of the same origin policy [29], in-app ads run with the same permission as the app itself, making it easier for ad controls to exfiltrate user information. Therefore some targeting information (e.g., user's geolocation) is likely to be used more commonly by in-app ads than by in-browser ads, while some information (e.g., all or frequently used apps on the device) is unique to in-app ads. Second, ad controls often leave much targeting information optional to be provided by apps, and hence targeting behavior of even the same ad control may vary across apps depending on whether apps actually provide the optional targeting information. Third, some ad networks and advertisers such as mobile marketplaces are unique or more common in in-app ads and their characteristics have not been investigated before. Finally, the methodology for harvesting in-app ads is significantly different from that for harvesting in-browser ads.

In this paper, we present a first-of-its-kind study of targeted display ads delivered to mobile apps. Our objectives are to broadly characterize in-app display advertisement and to understand targeting mechanisms employed by apps and ad networks from an empirical perspective. The study seeks to understand several key questions including the following: *What targeting information do apps choose to send to ad networks? How effectively, if at all, do different ad networks utilize such information to target users? Do ad networks differentiate between different apps or different users using the same app, and if so by how much? What impact does targeting have on ad delivery process?*

Answers to the above questions are important not just for a general audience inquisitive into in-app ad ecosystem, but also for two important constituents of the ad ecosystem: app developers and ad networks. An app developer can use the answers to guide his decisions on what ad networks to choose to effectively target users. He can also reduce the targeting information that the app needs to send to only the ones that influence targeting decisions, thereby reducing bandwidth and exfiltrated user data. An ad network can use the answers to find how often app developers provide a specific optional targeting information to other ad networks and how much targeting opportunity it currently misses by not supporting the targeting information.

An empirical study of in-app ad ecosystem is challenging for various reasons: The vast number of mobile apps that show display ads, the large number of ad networks that serve ads to mobile apps, the diversity and dynamics of targeting mechanisms across ad networks and users all present significant challenges. Our first contribution in this paper is a novel tool called MAdScope that can address these challenges. Central to MAdScope are three key mechanisms to (1) quickly harvest ads from a large collection of apps, (2) systematically probe an ad network to characterize its targeting mechanism, and (3) emulate user profiles, i.e., interact with the ad ecosystem as if interactions were by users of specific preferences and interests, in order to understand if an ad network does behavioral targeting. Various aspects of these mechanisms are inspired by recent works on profile-based ad crawling [1], differential correlation [16], and ad classification [27], but adapted to in-app ads. All these capabilities are essential for understanding the full spectrum of targeting behavior of in-app ad ecosystem. We believe that MAdScope and its mechanisms will be valuable for future studies of in-app ad ecosystem as well.

Our second contribution is to characterize targeting behavior of in-app ad ecosystem by using MAdScope. We first study what targeting information apps send to ad networks. Our analysis of 500K unique ad requests harvested from 150K apps and 101 ad networks shows that apps do not yet exploit the full potential of targeting. Ad networks are aggressive in terms of allowing apps to provide targeting information of various categories: device, geolocation, demographic, keywords, and child flag—at least 76 of the 101 ad networks we studied can collect some of these information. However, much of the targeting information (41% on average per ad network) is left optional to developers, who do not often (in > 90% of the apps) provide them. For 17% of the apps, ad networks receive no targeting information since they leave all targeting information as optional and apps/developers do not provide any of them.

We next investigate how effectively top 10 ad networks utilize various targeting information to target users. We consider both *attribute-based targeting* that targets users based on various attributes encoded in ad requests, and *behavioral targeting* that targets based on user's historical activities. By analyzing over a million ad impressions, we found many instances where ad networks effectively utilize targeting information and behavioral profiles to target users, although the degree of utilization varies widely across networks. Our results show that in-app ads differ from in-browser ads in multiple ways—in-app advertising employs significantly less behavioral and demographic-based targeting but more location-based targeting, and it shows more entertainment-related ads.

Surprisingly, our study points out many instances where targeting information or behavioral profile does not have a statistically significant impact on how ads are chosen (within our observation window of one day). We are not certain why ad networks collect targeting information if not for selecting ads. Three plausible explanations for an ad network to collect such data could be: (1) forward-compatibility—the ad network wants keep the option open to select ads based on the information in future, and still be compatible to current or old versions of its ad controls used by existing apps, (2) backward-incompatibility—the targeting information is no longer used by the ad network but is still provided by old versions of its ad control, and (3) information brokerage—the ad network sells the information to other parties.

We would like to contrast our work with existing works on in-app ads. Most of the prior work has demonstrated the large extent to which apps are capable of collecting user's personal information and the potential implications to user's privacy [12,17,20,24,26] and device resources [4,15,19,28]. These works do not investigate user targeting. A recent work [27] investigates targeting, but in a limited scale and scope—it shows various categories of targeted ads shown to 100 apps by one ad network, but does not characterize how apps use optional targeting information and how effectively ad networks utilize targeting information and behavioral profile. To the best of our knowledge, no prior work investigates the key questions we investigate in the context of in-app ads.

In the rest of the paper, we first discuss backgrounds and challenges of measuring in-app ads in Section 2. We then describe MAdScope's mechanisms and our results characterizing apps (Section 3) and ad networks (Section 4) from targeting point of view. We also contrast our findings with a recent study on in-browser ads in Section 5). Finally we discuss related works in Section 6) and conclude in Section 7.

## 2. BACKGROUND AND GOALS

### 2.1 In-app Ads

To display ads from a third-party mobile ad network such as AdMob[1] and MobClix[2] in an app, the app developer first registers with the ad network. The ad network provides the developer with an ad control (i.e. a library with some visual elements embedded within) that he includes in his app and assigns some screen "real estate". When a user runs the app, the ad control fetches ads from the ad network and displays it to the user. As mentioned in Section 1, unlike in-browser ads, in-app ads run with the same permission as the app itself.

The ad ecosystem consists of multiple entities including advertisers, ad agencies and brokers, ad networks, apps, and app users. Figure 1 shows a generic workflow of a mobile app requesting an ad and actions resulting from a click on the ad. First, ad control in the app requests for an ad from

[1] http://www.google.com/ads/admob
[2] https://developer.mobclix.com

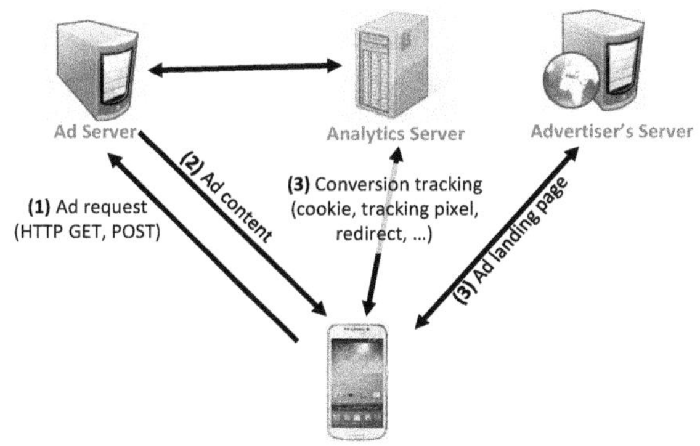


**Figure 1: In-app ad serving workflow.**

ad network. Second, the ad server serves an ad with associated contents, which the ad control displays in the app. The ad server may collect the ad offline from various brokers and ad agencies, or in real time from ad auction networks. Third, a click on the ad initiates connections to an ad analytics server, which tracks ad conversions, and to advertiser's server, which serves the landing page of the ad. Depending on the ad control, the click may generate only one connection to the analytics server, which can redirect the connection to the landing page.

► **Targeting.** An ad request, which is typically an HTTP GET or POST method, may include various targeting attributes such as app name, device properties, user's location, demographic, etc. An ad network can use these information to select targeted ads for the user. While some targeting information is automatically collected and sent by the ad control, some others are optionally provided by apps/developers (through ad control APIs). Targeting can also be based on a user's long-term behavior such as the types of apps he uses and the types of ads he clicks on. The ad server can obtain such statistics from analytics servers and maintain it for each user as his *profile*.

## 2.2 Goals

Our goal is to broadly characterize behavior of two important parties in mobile in-app ad ecosystem: apps and ad networks, and to understand their targeting mechanisms from empirical perspective. There are two key aspects of such understanding.

► **Client-side behavior.** *What various targeting information do mobile apps send to ad networks?* The goal is different from that in prior work [12, 26] that demonstrated, by analyzing ad controls, the large extent to which ad controls are *capable of* collecting user's personal information. Actually sending some of the information to ad networks, however, is often left optional to apps— depending on how app developers customize their use of ad controls within apps, some of the personal information the ad controls are capable of collecting may or may not actually be sent to ad networks. For example, AdMob, the most popular ad control in our datasets, allows apps to optionally send user's current location and demographic information such as his age and gender. How often apps actually send such information require analyzing ad requests made by apps—mere examination of individual ad controls is not sufficient.

Answer to the above question will illustrate the actual usage of these optional targeting information—whether developers really care about targeting users, whether they take additional efforts to provide these optional targeting information despite runtime overhead and privacy implications [12, 26], and if they do, what type of targeting information apps actually send to ad networks.

► **Ad network behavior.** Even if specific targeting information, such as a user's geolocation, is sent to ad networks, do the networks actually use the information for targeting users? If they do, how much do they rely on specific targeting information in selecting ads for a user? Answers to these questions can be useful for developers in choosing the right ad network and understanding whether it is worth providing optional targeting information. For example, as our results in Section 4 show, not all ad networks that collect geolocation actually use it to target users. Based on the results, a developer who wishes to show location-based ads in his app can choose an ad network that actually utilizes geolocation to target users. On the other hand, if the developer decides to use an ad network that can accept user's geolocation as an optional attribute but does not utilize the information for targeting users, he can choose not to provide the information to reduce exfiltrated user data, access permissions, and development and runtime overhead.

To the best of our knowledge, no previous works try to answer the above questions for mobile in-app ads. Answering the questions is challenging due to the following reasons.

## 2.3 Challenges

► **Scalability.** To understand what targeting information apps send to ad networks, we need to analyze a large enough sample of ad requests from real apps. One obvious way to collect such data is to capture app traffic in large network providers [28], but this requires access to such network providers. Another option is to recruit real users and to capture their ad traffic [27], but this is hard to scale to a large number of apps. Another option, which we explore in this paper, is to use an automation tool to automatically execute apps and to capture their ad traffic [18, 22]. Correctness and scalability of this approach, however, hinge upon answering several non-obvious questions: *Does poor coverage of existing automation tools introduce any bias to collected sample of ads requests? How long do we need to run an app to capture all its ad requests?*

► **Black-box ad networks.** Without knowing internal targeting algorithm of an ad network, we need to characterize its targeting mechanism only from its externally observable behaviors. Passively monitoring ad requests and fetched ads from existing apps may not be sufficient for this purpose. For example, to determine if an ad network targets users based on their locations, we need to compare ads from requests (1) with and without location information, (2) without any other optional targeting information (to isolate the impact of location), and (3) with the same mandatory information (e.g., IMEI number). The available sample of ad requests may not contain requests satisfying all these criteria. For instance, if all available ad requests to an ad network contain location information, we cannot know how the network would behave with a request without location information. Moreover, there are many variabilities such as available ad inventory and time of day that can affect targeting behavior of ad networks. One must use sound statistical tools to derive meaningful conclusions in the presence of such variability.

► **Profile-based targeting.** Behavioral targeting of display ads on the Web utilizes user's long term behavioral profiles [1] such as the sites he visits and the ads he clicks on. To study such targeting for in-app ads, we need to mimic multiple user profiles and study how ad networks target different profiles. For scalability, the profiles need to be built automatically. This can be tricky due to a *click-contamination problem* discussed in Section 4. For instance, to automatically build a profile of a "sports-loving" user, we need to automatically click on all and only sports-related ads. To automatically determine if an ad is about sports, we often need to analyze its landing page, which may be determined only after clicking the ad. If the ad is not about sports, this click can contaminate the "sports-loving" profile.

In this paper we address these challenges with a novel tool called MAdScope and use it later in the paper to understand targeted ads within mobile apps. At a high level, MAdScope has two functionalities (Figure 2): (1) passively harvesting ads from existing apps; we use this to understand what targeting information is sent to ad networks, and (2) actively probing ad networks; we use this to characterize targeting behavior of ad networks. We describe them in more detail in next two sections.

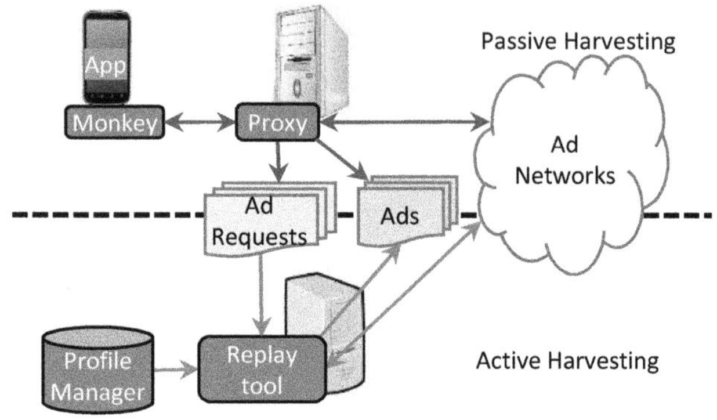


**Figure 2: MAdScope architecture. Top half involves passive ad harvesting (Section 3), while the bottom half involves active ad harvesting (Section 4).**

# 3. CHARACTERIZING CLIENT BEHAVIOR WITH PASSIVE AD HARVESTING

## 3.1 Passive Ad Harvesting in MAdScope

MAdScope harvests ad requests and impressions by running unmodified apps on a mobile device. To harvest ads (ad requests and corresponding responses) from an app, it launches the app on a mobile device, navigates to its pages, and captures ads shown in those pages with a network sniffer that runs on the same device or at a proxy sitting between the device and the Internet. The sniffer or the proxy captures all network traffic to and from the device, from which ad requests/responses are identified by looking for specific ad signatures (See MadFraud [5] for a principled approach of identifying ad requests from apps).

A recent work [27] used a similar methodology to harvest ads shown in 100 apps, but relied on humans to run the apps. Using human is not scalable. Since our goal involves ads from a large number of apps, MAdScope avoids the above scalability bottleneck by using a *Monkey*: a UI automation tool that can automatically launch an app in a real device and navigate through its pages by interacting with it, e.g., by clicking buttons, filling out text fields, swiping panels, etc. Previous work used Monkeys for various applications including app testing [22], ad frauds detection [5, 18], security bug detection [2], etc.

As mentioned before, one of our goals is to study what targeting information are sent to ad networks via ad requests. For our results to be sound, they need to be based on *all* or *an unbiased sample* of ad requests issued by a large sample of apps. All unique ad requests of an app can be collected by an ideal Monkey capable of visiting all runtime states (e.g., pages) of the app and thus triggering all ad requests the app can make. In practice, however, Monkeys have poor coverage. For instance, a Monkey may fail to visit some pages that can only be accessed by providing a correct user-name/password combination not known to the Monkey and hence miss the ad requests issued in those pages. (See [2] for a list of other reasons why a Monkey can have poor coverage.) If the missed ad requests are significantly different from the harvested ones, in terms of what targeting information is being sent out, the harvested sample can be a biased one. The amount of time a Monkey is given to explore an app can also affect the quality of harvested ad request sample: a longer exploration time may yield more ad requests, but at the cost of fewer explored apps within a given time. Therefore, before we analyze the ad requests collected by a Monkey, we need to first understand whether the ad request samples we collect are biased due to (a) poor coverage of the Monkey and (b) limited exploration time. We now investigate them empirically.

### *3.1.1 Understanding Ad Harvesting*

To understand how apps make ad requests, we run top 3,000 ad-supported free Android apps in the Google Play market with a combination of human and an existing Monkey tool called PUMA [14]. We configured PUMA to launch each app on a Nexus 5 smartphone and to navigate through various app pages for at most 20 minutes per app. For around 700 apps, PUMA had low coverage—it explored fewer then 10 unique pages per app as the apps required login passwords and/or had custom controls that PUMA failed to interact with. We manually ran those apps (e.g., by supplying user name and password) to make sure that at least 10 or all unique pages are explored for each app. All network traffic to/from the device was captured with a proxy, where we identified ad requests by using techniques described in [5]. We harvested ad requests from a total of 31,203 unique app pages.

► **Observation 1.** *Most apps make the first ad request during launch time.*

Figure 3 shows the CDF of apps and the number of interactions PUMA made before an app issued its first ad request. As shown, for 81% of the apps, PUMA had to simply launch the app and make no interactions at all. These apps make ad requests during launch time so that the ads can be displayed on the first app page as soon as possible. Moreover, only 5 interactions were sufficient to harvest ad requests from > 95% of the apps, suggesting that even a basic Monkey that can interact with an app in a limited way

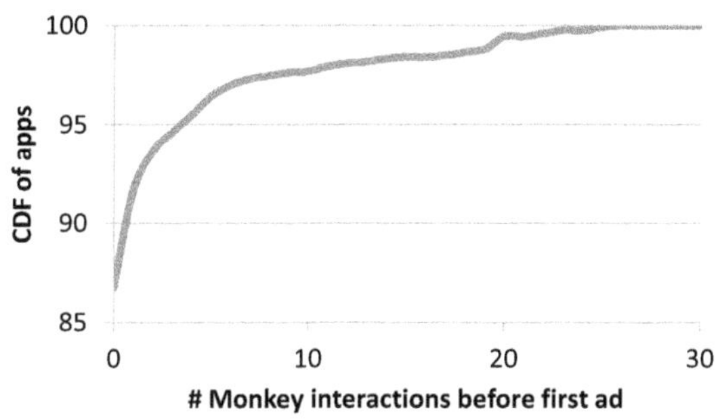


**Figure 3: CDF of app count and number of Monkey interactions required to observe the first ad. No interaction is needed for 81% of the apps.**

is able to capture first ad requests from a large fraction of apps.

► **Observation 2.** *For most apps, the first ad request is similar to all its ad requests.*

Let us first explain how we define two ad requests to be similar. A typical ad request is an HTTP GET or POST method call, consisting of a request page address (a host name and a path) and a query string with multiple attribute-value pairs separated by the '&' symbol. Attributes in a query string are either *variable* or *invariant*, depending on whether their values change or remain constant in two back-to-back ad requests from the same app page, over all apps.[3] For example, a timestamp attribute and a sequence number attribute are variable, while an IMEI number and a publisher ID are invariant. We consider two ad requests to be similar if they have the same request page address and the same values of invariant attributes. Intuitively, two similar ad requests convey the same or very similar targeting information.

Our results show that for 94.7% of the apps, the first ad request an app makes is similar to its subsequent requests.[4] Note that many of these apps required login and password and we had to manually run them to explore them well. We did not observe any instance where ad requests differ before and after user login. For 4.2% apps, subsequent ad requests differ from their first requests by only one attribute (e.g., `FirstPage=true` in first request and `false` in subsequent ones) and hence can be constructed from their first requests. Only ≈ 1% apps issue multiple different ad requests in different pages. Manual inspection reveals that these apps use keyword-based targeting and send different targeting keywords in different pages based on their contents.

### 3.1.2 *Passive Harvesting in MAdScope*

Insights from the above results guide us to the following scalable ad harvesting strategy in MAdScope: it launches an app and explores it with PUMA only until the app issues the first ad request or PUMA fails to explore further. We claim that the strategy yields:

[3]Note that attribute-value pairs encrypted with random salts look random. The above definition would treat such attributes as non-invariant, even if their unencrypted values are the same.

[4]Ad impressions returned by these similar requests, however, can be different.

| Ad domain | Frequency |
|---|---|
| doubleclick.net | 36% |
| mobclix.com | 22% |
| appsgeyser.com | 12% |
| adsmogo.com | 12% |
| wapx.cn | 3.8% |
| nend.net | 1.1% |
| mopub.com | 0.9% |
| mobfox.com | 0.8% |
| applovin.com | 0.7% |
| airpush.com | 0.7% |

**Table 1: Top ten ad domains in the datasets.**

- **Unbiased sample of ads:** Poor coverage or limited exploration time of PUMA does not introduce any significant bias on the harvested sample of ad requests. As Observation 1 shows, even if it explores zero or very small number of app pages, it still can harvest ad requests from most apps. Moreover, as Observation 2 shows, collecting only one ad request per app is sufficient, since that represents *all* ad requests made by 99% of the apps (i.e., not many unique ad requests are missed from unexplored pages).
- **Scalable harvesting:** As Observation 1 shows, MAdScope needs to make a small number of interactions to harvest its ad, enabling it to quickly harvest ads from a large number of apps. In our experiments, we could harvest ads from around 4000 apps per device per day.

## 3.2 Empirical Results

### 3.2.1 *Datasets and Basic Statistics*

We use the following two datasets:

**Dataset 1.** This dataset contains 211,231 unique ad requests collected by MAdScope from 22,324 most popular free apps in Google Play market.

**Dataset 2.** The dataset is shared by the authors of the MadFraud system [5]. It consists of ad requests from 130,339 Android apps, selected randomly from a pool of 669,591 apps authors crawled from 19 markets including Google Play. Unlike Dataset 1, this dataset contains only ad requests that apps made during launch time: each app is launched, kept running for 60 seconds without any user interaction, and ads are captured. It consists of 353,181 unique ad requests. Note that, due to our Observation 1 and Observation 2, this dataset represents an almost unbiased sample of ad requests.

Overall, both the datasets contain ~500K unique ad requests from ~150K apps. They contain 143 unique ad request pages from 101 unique top level ad network domains. Table 1 shows ten most frequent top level domains appearing in the ad requests.

### 3.2.2 *How much information is sent to ad networks?*

To approximate the magnitude of information sent by apps to ad networks, we count the number of attribute-value pairs in each ad request. Figure 4(a) shows the cumulative distributions of the number of attribute-value pairs in all ad requests. As shown, ad requests contain a large number of attribute-value pairs: 26.3 pairs on average per re-

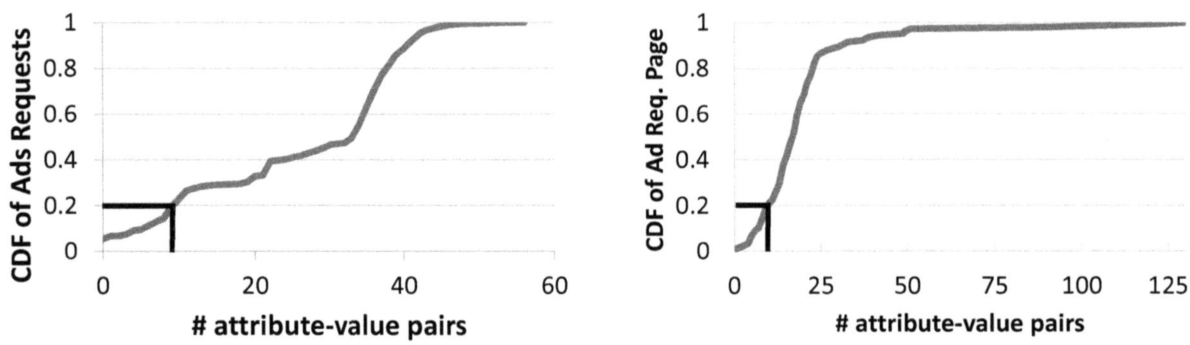


(a) Attr-value pairs in ad requests

(b) Attr-value pairs in request pages

**Figure 4: CDF of the number of attribute-value pairs appearing (a) in all ad requests and (b) in all ad request pages.** $> 80\%$ ***of ad requests and*** $> 80\%$ ***of ad request pages contain*** $> 10$ ***attribute-value pairs.***

quest. More than 80% of all ad requests contain more than 10 attribute-value pairs.

We also aggregate the counts per ad request page address: for each address, we take union of all attribute-value pairs that appear in any ad request to that address and count them. Figure 4(b) shows the CDF of the number of attribute-value pairs of all 143 ad request pages in our datasets. Overall, ad networks are aggressive in collecting various attributes. The average number of attribute-value pairs per ad request page address is 20.4, with $> 80\%$ of the ad request pages supporting $> 10$ attribute-value pairs.

The results above demonstrate that ad networks are aggressive in collecting a large number of attributes via ad requests. Note that many of the attributes are automatically collected by ad controls (and hence are transparent to developers), while others are left optional to developers who need to explicitly provide their values. Moreover, not all these attributes are relevant to targeting users. We characterize these aspects next.

| Category | Example values |
|---|---|
| Location | Latitude and Longitude, City, Zipcode |
| Keywords | Keywords |
| Device | IMEI number, MAC address, Android ID, IP address, CPU speed, RAM size, Screen size, Device model, Carrier name |
| Demographic | Age, Gender, Language |
| Child flag | True/False |

**Table 2: Targeting attribute categories and values.**

### *3.2.3 Mandatory and Optional Attributes*

We define an attribute to be mandatory for a request page address if it appears in *all* ad requests to that page address from all apps; otherwise, the attribute is optional. The intuition is that if an attribute is optional, then it is highly likely for *some* developers to not use it and hence ad requests from their apps to not include the attribute. For example, the ad control requesting ads from googleads.g.doubleclick.com/mads/gma allows developers to explicitly provide value of the optional attribute `cust_age`; however, only a subset of the developers actually provide the attribute value. One limitation of this classification is that a mandatory attribute will deem optional if it does not appear in *all* versions of the ad control. For instance, if a mandatory attribute is introduced in a later version of the ad control, all ad requests from the latest version of the ad control will have the attribute, while none from an earlier version will have it.

We observed that, surprisingly, a large fraction (55%) of attributes are optional. On average, each ad request page address has 9.1 mandatory attributes and 11.3 optional attributes.

The result highlights the significance of our data-driven analysis of ad clients. By manually examining the usage of an ad client (as in previous works [12,26]), one could identify extent to which ad clients are capable of collecting user's personal information. But since a large fraction of such information is optional, this gives only the upper bound, not the actual magnitude, of information leak. In contrast, examining ad requests from real apps gives the true magnitude of the information being sent to ad networks.

### *3.2.4 Identifying Targeting Attributes*

To analyze targeting behavior, we must first identify various targeting information that are sent from apps to ad networks in ad requests. In other words, we need to identify which attributes in an ad request contain targeting information. Since there are many ad providers for Android (101 in our datasets), it would be prohibitive to manually reverse engineer each ad provider's ad serving protocol to determine which attributes in an ad request correspond to what targeting information. Instead, we develop a semi-automated method for such identification purely based on ad requests appearing in our datasets.

Our method consists of two steps. First, we keep only the attributes that satisfy either of the two criteria (and discard the others): (1) the attribute contains a relatively small number (we used a threshold of five) of distinct values in the entire datasets, or (2) its values are English words. Intuitively, since the ad requests in our datasets are harvested from a small set of similarly configured identical devices from the same location, a targeting attribute should contain one or a very small number of values across all requests. For example, if the apps are all run from the same location, a location attribute should always have the same value. Attributes containing English words include target-

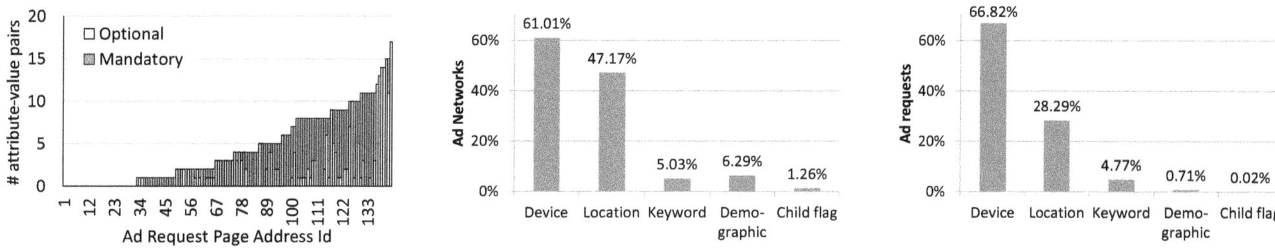


(a) Targeting attributes (b) Categories in ad networks (c) Categories in ad requests

**Figure 5: (a) shows distribution of identified mandatory and optional targeting attributes in all ad networks. *A significant number of targeting attributes are optional* (b) and (c) show frequencies of various categories of targeting attributes in all ad networks and in all ad requests, respectively.**

ing keywords. The process discards attributes with arbitrary values such as timestamps or hashed values.

Second, for each of the remaining attributes, we manually inspect its name and values in our datasets and identify if the name and values are semantically meaningful (for example, `cust_gender=male` has a semantically meaningful interpretation but `q3=5` does not). We select all attributes with meaningful interpretation. Note that the first step discards attributes that are unlikely to have meaningful interpretation, and thus reduces laborious manual effort. Finally the selected attributes for each request page are categorizes into five different categories: Location, Keywords, Device, Demograhic, and Child Flag. Example values of attributes of these categories are shown in Table 2.

► **Targeting Dictionary.** The targeting attributes, their categories, and whether they are mandatory or optional are encoded in MAdScope as a *Targeting Dictionary*. This is a static dictionary that maps each ad request page address to a set of targeting attributes that may appear in corresponding query strings and whose semantics are known. For instance, for the ad request page address googleads.g.doubleclick.com/mads/gma, the dictionary contains the information that the attribute `cust_age` is optional and its value is age of the user in plain text. MAdScope uses this dictionary for systematically probing various ad networks to learn their targeting behavior (Section 4).

Our datasets contain 143 unique request page addresses and 2921 unique attributes for these requests. By using the above methodology, we could recognize 626 targeting attributes (21% of the unique attributes). Note that the above methodology may miss some targeting information sent by an app, e.g., when they are sent as hashed or encrypted values or codes (e.g., "v=1" instead of "gender=male"). Therefore our results on extent of targeting is actually a lower bound.

### 3.2.5 Targeting Attribute Counts

Figure 5(a) shows the distribution of identified targeting attributes in all ad request page addresses. (Page addresses are sorted based on increasing order of the number of identified targeting attributes.) 112 of total 143 ad request page addresses contain at least one targeting attributes. On average, each address contains 4.4 targeting attributes.

Figure 5(a) also distinguishes between mandatory and optional targeting attributes. On average, 41% of targeting attributes are optional—there are 1.8 optional and 2.6 mandatory targeting attributes per ad request page address. The

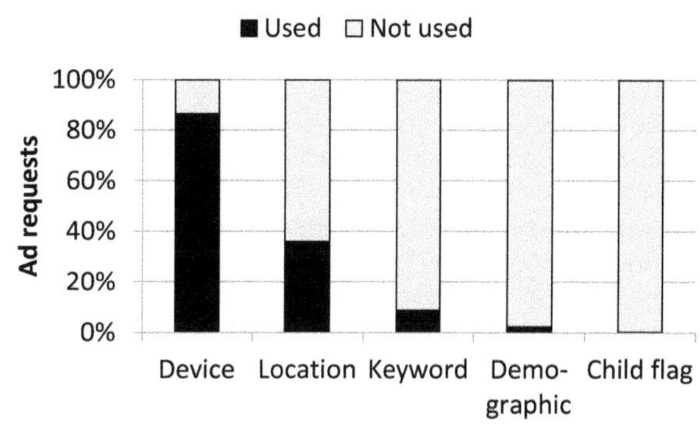


**Figure 6: Frequencies of ad requests that do not use a category of targeting attributes even though the ad network support that category.**

high fraction of optional targeting attributes, again, highlights the importance of data-driven analysis of ad clients.

We also categorize targeting attributes into various categories shown in Table 2. Figure 5(b) and (c) show distributions of various categories of targeting attributes in all ad request page addresses and in all ad requests, respectively. As shown, two most common categories of attributes are device-related attributes such as IMEI number or device Android ID and location attributes such as latitude and longitude. Keyword-based (also known as contextual) and demographics-based targeting is less common. Few ad networks collect a child flag, to serve child-appropriate ads.

### 3.2.6 Omission of Optional Attributes

Figure 6 shows how often apps/developers actually provide the optional targeting attributes of various categories. As shown, a large fraction of the ad requests do not include attributes of a targeting category even though their ad networks support that category. For instance, 65% of the ad requests do not provide location attributes even though their ad networks allow location attributes. The fractions of ad requests not utilizing the opportunity of providing targeting attributes are higher (> 90%) for other categories, except for the Device category that is often automatically collected by ad controls. A developer may omit providing an optional attribute for many reasons: to reduce exfiltrated user information, to avoid asking for additional permission (e.g., for location attribute), to avoid additional programming efforts to include the attribute, to avoid runtime overhead of sending additional attributes over the network, or even due to his lack of awareness of the targeting attribute.

A few ad networks leave all targeting information optional. For 17% of ad requests in our datasets, corresponding ad networks do not receive any targeting information since they leave all targeting information as optional and apps/developers do not provide any of them.

### 3.2.7 *Static Targeting Attributes*

Some targeting attributes such as location are usually specified dynamically, e.g., based on user's current geolocation. Interestingly, we observed that some developers specify some of the attributes statically. For example, the app **`Virtual Table Tennis 3D`** requests ads from ad.where.com, with **`city=ADELAIDE`** irrespective of the user's current location. Similarly, we observed a few apps requesting ads from doubleclick.net by setting **`Age=10`** and **`Gender=female`**. We suspect that most users of these apps are kids and girls, and without an easy way to determine the true age/gender of the users, app developers statically target the dominant user group.

To quantify such static targeting attributes, we counted all ad requests that specify location or demographics different from the Monkey's profile. We found that at least 3.3% of all ad requests contain one or more such statically defined attribute values.

# 4. CHARACTERIZING AD NETWORKS WITH ACTIVE AD HARVESTING

The goal of active probing in MAdScope is to issue ad requests to a target ad network, with carefully chosen combinations of targeting attributes and values, in order to facilitate understanding of targeting mechanism of the ad network. For instance, to understand how much an ad network targets users based on their locations or whether its ad serving rate changes when targeting is enabled, we would like to compare responses from many ad requests without location and with various locations. MAdScope's active probing can issue such customized ad requests. Similarly, to understand if an ad network does behavioral targeting, we would need to build long term behavioral profiles and compare ads received by various profiles. MAdScope can build such profiles and issue ad requests from them.

One way to issue customized ad requests is to build a custom app with the desired ad control and to customize it with various optional attributes (such as location). However, this allows only to customize the parameters that ad controls allow developers to set; other parameters that ad controls collect automatically (such as Android ID or IMEI number, or location for some ad controls) cannot be customized.

To address this, MAdScope relies on modifying and replaying passively harvested ad requests. This is supported by the following two observations.

► **Observation 3.** *A passively harvested ad request can be replayed later to harvest more ads.*

► **Observation 4.** *Targeting attributes in ad requests can be modified before replaying.*

To validate Observation 3, we selected a sample of 50 random apps. For each app, we performed the following three tasks until we got 100 ads from each: (1) launched the app on a mobile device and kept it running while it made periodic ad requests; (2) issued the first ad request of the app (passively harvested as described before) each time the app requested an ad in task 1, from a replay tool running on a desktop PC; (3) replayed the ad request 100 times after a week. We also wrote parsers for the ads returned by these requests, to determine if responses from the ad requests were valid.

We observed that all replay requests (including the ones replayed a week later) returned valid ads and on average, the overlap between ads received by apps and real-time replay was $> 82\%$. This implies that ad networks treat requests from the app and from the replay tool in a similar way. This also suggests that passively harvested ad requests can be quickly replayed from multiple desktops to harvest a large number of ads.

Observation 4 is motivated by the fact that most targeting attributes appear in plain text in ad requests. Ad providers do not typically encrypt ad requests because of the extra overhead that is required on the ad server to support a large number of SSL connections [26]. To validate Observation 4, we took ad requests from the previous experiment. For each ad request, we created a modified request by changing the value of one random targeting attribute, or dropping it if the attribute is optional. For example, if the original request contains **`gender=male`**, the modified request contained **`gender=female`**. We then replayed both versions of the requests 50 times each and observed that ad networks responded to the modified requests with valid ads (i.e., they could be successfully parsed), validating Observation 4.

## 4.1 Active Probing in MAdScope

Figure 2 shows the overall architecture of MAdScope and its active probing components. The key component is a replay tool that uses insights from the above results to actively probe an ad network: It starts with ad requests passively harvested from real apps, selectively modifies various targeting attributes in the HTTP GET/POST requests, replays the modified HTTP requests with the same request header as the original ad request, and analyzes the responses (i.e., ads). What attributes in ad requests are modified depends on what targeting behavior to emulate.

Other than these basic components, MAdScope has several additional components that are crucial for understanding ad targeting. They involve how ad networks are probed, how targeted ads are identified, and how ads are classified. We describe them next, starting with the probing mechanism to understand targeting.

### 4.1.1 *Probing for Attribute-based Targeting*

From MAdScope's perspective, there are two broad categories of targeting. *Attribute-based* targeting is stateless where ad networks select ads solely based on various attribute-values within ad requests. Examples include targeting based on keywords (contextual ads), location, demographic information encoded in ad requests. *Behavioral targeting*, on the other hand, is stateful where ad networks select ads based on historical behavior of the user, e.g., what types of ads he clicked on and what types of apps he used in the recent past. We start with attribute-based targeting.

To construct ad requests with targeting enabled for category $C$ to an ad network $N$, MAdScope samples an ad request to $N$ from its passively harvested pool of ad requests. It then consults its targeting dictionary to identify targeting attributes of category $C$ in the request and discards any other optional targeting attributes from it (to isolate the impact of $C$ from other targeting categories). Finally it enumerates a few values of $C$, possibly sampled from passively harvested ad requests, and for each value, it produces one modified ad request by setting the attribute of category $C$ to that value (other attributes keep the same value across all requests). The ad requests are then replayed by MAdScope. To avoid any potential impact of behavioural targeting based on device ID, different ad requests are issued with different device IDs.

For instance, to construct ad requests to adfonic.net with location-based targeting enabled, MAdScope samples an ad request with hostname adfonic.net from its passively harvested pool of ad requests. Using the targeting dictionary described in Section 3.2.4, it identifies location attributes `u.latitude`, `u.longitude`, and `u.postalCode` and discards other optional targeting attributes such as `u.gender`, `u.ageLow`, and `u.ageHigh` from the request. It then produces multiple requests by setting values of location attributes to latitude/longitude and postal codes of top US cities.

In a very small number of cases, however, we found that targeting values (e.g., location in ad requests to googleads.g.doubleclick.net) appear encrypted or hashed. For them, MAdScope uses encrypted/hashed targeting values from its passively harvested request pool. For example, to harvest encrypted location values for googleads.g.doubleclick.net, MAdScope uses the *mock location* feature of popular mobile OS such as Android, iOS, and Windows Phone that allows MAdScope to set the location of the device to a target location before harvesting ad requests. MAdScope then identifies encrypted location attributes in those harvested ads and uses them in ad requests to be replayed.

Note that the above procedure tries to identify the effect of one category of targeting attribute at a time, in isolation from other optional attributes. In practice, it is possible for an ad network to take targeting decisions based on multiple, rather than a single, categories of attributes. For example, an ad network may target women in a specific city, but such targeting would not be revealed by probing with only gender or with only location attributes. Identifying impact of combinations of attributes is challenging due to an exponential number of combinations. Recent work has shown how to explore such combinations in a scalable way [16]; incorporating such techniques to MAdScope is part of our future work.

### 4.1.2 Probing for Behavioral Targeting

Unlike attribute-based targeting, behavioral targeting is done based on a user's profile, representing his historical behavior such as types of apps he uses or ads he clicks on. MAdScope can automatically build profiles of specific interests and preferences and can issue ad requests with those profiles.

There are several ways to create user profiles. One can mimic actions of a particular user (e.g., [3]). Characteristics of profiles built in this fashion can be arbitrary close to the profiles observed in reality. However, the approach is not scalable. MAdScope instead generates user location- and interest-based profiles by mimicking actions that reflect the target location and interest. (A similar approach was used in [1] to create profiles for in-browser ads.) The strategy enables MAdScope to generate profiles for virtually *any* location and interest.

Given a target location $L$ and interest $I$, we would like MAdScope to mimic various user actions that are related to $L$ and $I$ and that an ad network may observe, e.g., through targeting attribute values in ad requests or by correlating app and web usage data. More specifically, given $L$ and $I$, we would like MAdScope to emulate the following tasks for an extended period of time.

1. Set the user's mobile device's location to $L$ before making any ad request.
2. Use various apps related to interest $I$ only. Apps related to interest $I$ are chosen by matching $I$ with Google Play app category [27].
3. Browse various web sites related to interest $I$. Web sites related to interest $I$ are chosen by matching $I$ to website categorization service such as Alexa[5] [1]. An ad network may correlate web and app usage to deliver ads to app based on the type of web page visited [21].
4. Click on ads of category $I$. Category of an ad is determined by a classifier we describe later.

By emulating the above tasks, MAdScope lets ad networks observe (a subset of) the activities and build a user's profile related to $L$ and $I$. Step (1) is needed to make sure that an ad network can infer $L$ as a significant location of the user and show location-based ad for $L$ even when he is not at $L$. Steps (2), (3), and (4) are needed because they reflect user's interest, which an ad network can use to target ad. Among them (4) is particularly important since a click is a strong signal for a user's need or interest.

Interestingly, MAdScope can perform actions (1), (2), and (3) easily with its replay tool, without using any real device. Since we only care about the interactions between apps and ad networks, instead of actually launching and using the target apps, MAdScope can simply replay ad requests made by those apps. To enforce location $L$ and interest $I$, MAdScope replays ad requests harvested from apps of category $I$ with location attributes set to $L$. Finally, it repeatedly visits top Alexa web sites of category $I$.

However, it is challenging to faithfully emulate clicks only on ads relevant to the profile category due to the following *click contamination* problem.

▶ **Click Contamination.** While building a user's profile of interest category $I$, MAdScope receives a sequence of ads, of which it must click on all and only ads of category $I$. Clicking on ads not related to $I$ may contaminate the profile (i.e., confuse the ad networks about user's true interest).

Category of an ad may be determined based on its textual content. However, many ads display images and videos and contain no or very little texts and hence cannot be classified with sufficient confidence. A more foolproof strategy is to classify based on content or Alexa category of the landing page of the ad (the page that a click on the ad leads to). Unfortunately, landing pages are not often mentioned in the ad itself; rather the ad contains a redirection URL, a click on which is redirected through an analytics server, typically used for accounting purpose, to a final landing page. Thus, to determine landing page of an ad, we need to click on it

[5] http://www.alexa.com

$$\underbrace{\texttt{http://ads.lfstmedia.com/click}}_{RedirectionServer}\underbrace{\texttt{/cmp10183}}_{AdId}\underbrace{\texttt{/XXX/2?\_ads}=\texttt{XXX\&adkey}=\texttt{XXX\&\_androididsha1}=\texttt{XXX\&slot}=\texttt{XXX\&impts}=\texttt{XXX\&}\ldots}_{DeviceParams}$$

**Figure 7: Anatomy of a click URL of a MobClix ad. XXX denotes encrypted and numeric values.**

even if we later find that its category does not match the profile category. This can contaminate the profile.

To address this, we use the following mechanism.

► **Profile isolation via a dummy profile.** MAdScope uses a dummy profile whose only purpose is to click on ads in order to determine their landing page. A redirecting click url consists of three components shown in Figure 7: a Redirection Server that receives the click and eventually redirects it to advertiser's landing page, Ad Id that maps the ad to landing page and that the redirection server uses to decide which landing page to redirect to, and Device Params that contains various device-specific information that redirection server uses to identify the source of the click. The same ad shown in two different devices have the same redirection server and ad id, but different device attributes.

We utilize the above structure of click urls to click an ad without contaminating the profile. Given an ad request $r$, we issue it twice, once with the original profile and again with the dummy profile, to receive ads $a$ and $a'$ respectively. By parsing the ads, we identify their click urls $u$ and $u'$. We then generate a click url $u''$ by concatenating the Redirection Server and the Ad Id from $u$ but Device Params from $u'$ and click (i.e., issue an HTTP GET request to) it. The effect is a click on the ad $a$, but pretending the source of the click to be the dummy profile, which gives us the landing page without any click from the original profile.

### 4.1.3 Ad Classifier

MAdScope provides a classifier that given an ad can determine its Alexa category[6]. This classifier is useful for various analysis and for building behavioral profile.

Category of an ad can be determined based on its landing page or its content. To determine category based on the ad's landing page, we rely on multiple sources, since we did not find an authoritative source that would assign a category to all of the landing pages in our data set. We used site categorization services from Alexa and WebPulse[7] from Blue Coat. However, as we show later, a significant number of the advertisers do not appear in Alexa (or WebPulse), and hence we train a machine learning classifier that predicts the category of a web page based on its content. The same classifier can be used for content-based classification if an ad contains enough textual contents.

► **Classification features.** For each top-level Alexa category, we consider top 1000 web sites. For each site, we take English words appearing in its title and keyword metadata in its HTML document header and discard frequent words such as 'the' and 'and'. We then normalize each word by stemming it[8]. Finally, for each category, we construct a "bag of words" with all stemmed words and their 2-grams in all 1000 web sites of that category. The bag is used as features for the category.

► **Classification algorithm.** Given the feature sets for all categories, we train a multi-class logistic regression classifier [25], which is commonly used for text classification. We use a min-max normalizer for normalizing features, 20 random sweeps with L1 and L2 weights of 0, 0, 1, and 1 (for a linear combination of L1 and L2 regularization), and optimization tolerances of $10^{-4}$ and $10^{-7}$.

► **Classification accuracy.** To evaluate the performance of the classifier, we apply cross validation to the ground truth. We split the ground truth into 3 folds, train a classifier on 2 of those folds and then evaluate its performance on the remaining fold. Overall, the classifier has an average accuracy of 0.76 across all categories. The Log-loss reduction or the Reduction in Information Gain (RIG) is 78%, which can be interpreted as the advantage of the classifier—the probability of a correct prediction is 78% better than random guessing.

### 4.1.4 Identifying Targeted Ads

To identify whether an ad is targeted, we use the intuition that a targeted ad is shown more frequently to some specific value of a targeting attribute than others. For each ad, we count how many times it is been shown to different values of a targeting attribute. This gives us empirical distribution of the ad over all targeting values. If the ad is not targeted to specific values, it is fair to assume that the observed distribution should be close to uniform. To compare the observed distribution with uniform distribution, we use Pearson's $\chi^2$ test with the null hypothesis being "observed distribution is uniform". The test involves computing $p$-value, whose value is small (less than 0.05) if the null hypothesis is rejected and close to 1 if the hypothesis is accepted. We say that an ad is targeted if the $p$-value of its observed distribution is less than 0.05.

The statistical analysis is meaningful only for ads that are shown at least a few times; we use a threshold of 10.

## 4.2 Limitations

Before we present our results, we would like to point out a few limitations of our methodology to set the expectation right. Targeting behaviour of an ad network may depend on many variabilities such as its available ad inventory, demands of ads, its targeting algorithm which may evolve over time, time of the day, etc. Although our attribute-based targeting results are based on a week long probe, the window may not be sufficiently large to capture all variabilities. Our results are based on a small number of targeting values (e.g., locations of five big US cities); it is possible that an ad network employs custom targeting strategies for specific values which we might miss. For example, if an ad network used a different location-based targeting algorithms for USA and China, we would miss its behavior for China since we used USA locations only.

[6] http://www.alexa.com/topsites/category

[7] http://sitereview.bluecoat.com/sitereview.jsp

[8] Stemming is the process for reducing inflected (or sometimes derived) words to their base or root form; e.g., "photos" to "photo".

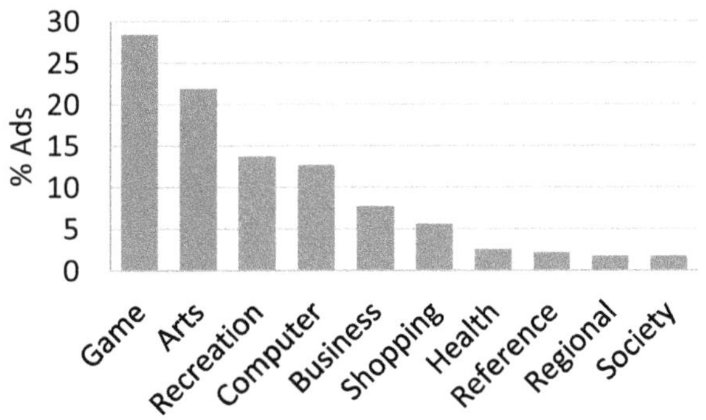


**Figure 8: Distribution of ads over top ten Alexa categories**

It is also possible that we failed to identify behavioral targeting of some ad network. This can happen for a few reasons. First, we use a window of one day to build profiles, after which we test for behavioral targeting. It is possible that our profile-building window of one day is too small to capture behavioral targeting of the network (although it is unlikely based on results from [1]). Second, the ad network may rely on other actions than what MAdScope emulates (Section 4.1.2) to build behavioral profiles. Third, MAdScope's ad classifier is not perfect, and hence it can click on unrelated ads to contaminate profiles. The ad network under study may be sensitive to such contaminated profiles.

## 4.3 Empirical Results

### *4.3.1 Ads and Advertisers*

We start with some results about ads and advertisers, which are based on ad impressions received by replaying 100,000 randomly selected ad requests from our datasets.

► **Ad serving rate.** Ad serving rate indicates the fraction of ad requests returning valid ads. We say an ad network fails to return an ad when in response to an ad request, it returns an unsuccessful HTTP response (e.g., error 503: Service Unavailable) or an empty ad (likely due to lack of enough ads to serve).

We observed various degrees of ad serving rates for different ad networks. While most of the ad networks we tried had good (> 95%) ad serving rate, we experienced poor serving rates for two ad networks: adsmogo.com and mobclix.com. Ad serving rates for these two networks were 43% and 81% respectively. Such a poor ad serving rate is bad for app developers since they waste opportunities to show ads to users.

► **Advertiser rank analysis.** We observed a total of 4037 unique advertisers. We determined their ranks by using Alexa's top 1 million web sites. About 55% of the advertisers appear in Alexa's top 1 million web sites, with an average ranking of 217K. Remaining 45% of the advertisers do not appear in Alexa's top 1 million web sites and hence we could not determine their global web rank. Ads from these unranked constitute 75% of the total ads in our corpus. This shows that most of the mobile ads come from obscure advertisers who are not among the top 1 million web sites listed by Alexa.

► **Ad categories.** We categorized 1734 of 4037 advertisers using Alexa, 836 using WebPulse, and the rest with our classifier. Figure 8 shows ad distribution for the top 20 root level Alexa categories. The top advertiser category is Game, where the landing page is a Google Play page for downloading Android games. Some other major categories are Arts, Recreation, Computer, Business, and Shopping.

### *4.3.2 Attribute-based Targeting Analysis*

To characterize attribute-based targeting of ad networks, we use MAdScope to actively probe top ten ad networks in our dataset. To capture temporal variability, each ad network was probed once every two hours, over a period of a week starting from October 10, 2014. To probe an ad network $N$, MAdScope first uses the targeting dictionary to identify categories of targeting information collected by $N$. The top ad network, doubleclick.net, allows targeting based on six different categories of attributes: location, keywords, device, demographics, child flag, and app name. Other networks allow a subset of these categories. We identified a total of 26 {ad network, targeting category} combinations. For each network $N$ and category $C$, MAdScope then creates up to 5 ad requests, with different values of targeting attributes of category $C$ plus one request without any optional attribute of category $C$. (Note that MAdScope isolates $C$ by omitting targeting attributes of other categories in ad requests.) Each ad request is then issued 100 times and the responses are captured. The overall process generated slightly over a million ad impressions over a week.

► **Utilization of targeting attributes.** Our key results on attribute-based targeting are shown in Table 3 that shows how effectively ad networks utilize various targeting information for targeting users. We compare ads received with different targeting values. For each {ad network, targeting category} combination, we calculate the fraction of ads whose distribution across targeting values does not follow a uniform distribution with any statistical significance (i.e., $p$-value of the $\chi^2$ test is less than 0.05). The closer the value to 1, the more targeted the ad. A value of 1 means 100% of the ads are distributed in a non-uniform way (i.e., they are targeted) across all targeting values. The same metric was used in [1] and [27] to quantify targeted ads.

We observed many instances where targeting information has statistically significant impact on how an ad network selects ads (shown by cells with values close to 1 in Table 3). For example, we found doubleclick.net to select ads based on targeting keywords every time such keywords are available, while it targets users based on their locations 80% of the cases when location information is available.

We also observed many instances where ad networks collect many different types of targeting information, but do not use the information to target users. This is shown as cells in Table 3 with a zero values. For example, even though appsgeyser.com allows apps to send location information, the information does not have a statistically significant impact on how the network selects ads.

- **Location.** We expected location-based ads to be common and location information to be utilized by all top ad networks. Surprisingly, three of the seven ad networks that collect location information do not utilize it for targeting user. The fourth network, applovin.com, utilizes location information only marginally.

- **Keywords.** We found three networks to accept targeting keywords and two of them to actually use them.

| Ad network | Location | Keywords | Device | Demographics | App | Child flag |
|---|---|---|---|---|---|---|
| doubleclick.net | 0.80 | 1.00 | 0 | 0.17 | 1.00 | 0 |
| mobclix.com | × | 0 | 0.10 | × | × | × |
| appsgeyser.com | 0 | × | × | × | 1.00 | × |
| adsmogo.com | 0 | × | × | × | 0 | × |
| wapx.cn | 0.08 | × | 0 | × | 0 | × |
| nend.net | 1.00 | × | 0 | × | 0.23 | × |
| mopub.com | × | 1.00 | 0 | × | × | × |
| mobfox.com | × | × | 0 | × | 0 | × |
| applovin.com | 0.25 | × | 0.3 | × | 1.00 | × |
| airpush.com | 0 | × | × | × | 0.75 | × |

**Table 3: Ratio of ads shown by different (ad network, targeting category) combinations whose distribution across profiles does not follow uniform distribution with statistical significance. A cell marked with × indicates that the ad network does not collect targeting information of that category.**

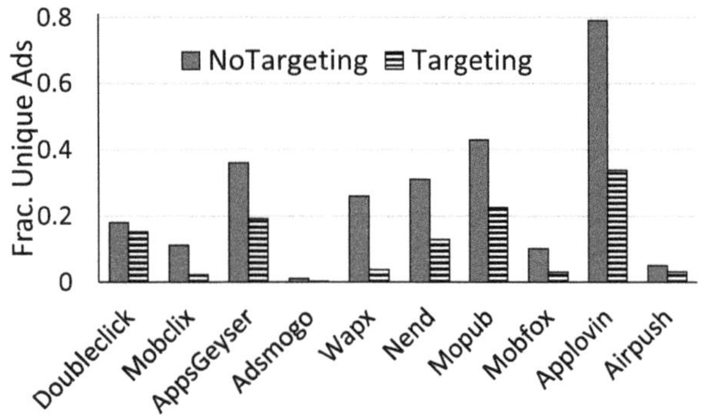


**Figure 9: Arrival rate of unique ads. Without targeting, average rate for all top ten ad networks is 26%, with targeting it is 11%.**

• **Device.** Most (7 out of 10) ad networks collect device-specific information, but most ignore it for targeting purpose.

• **Demographics and Child flag.** Only one top ad network collects these information, but use them only marginally.

• **App name/ID.** Eight of the top ten ad networks collect app names and only half of them use the information to select ads.

Note that we identified targeting information from ad requests made by real apps and some of the targeting information is optional, which implies that app developers explicitly provide these optional targeting information without getting any perceived targeting benefit. As mentioned in Section 1, ad networks most likely collect such targeting information for forward-compatibility and for information brokerage.

Also note that the results in Table 3 should not be interpreted as a way to decide whether one ad network is necessarily "better" than another. An ad network may not collect or effectively use targeting information, but yet it can be lucrative to developers in terms of payouts and to advertisers in terms of conversion rates (and vice versa). Evaluating ad networks in terms of these metrics is part of our future work.

► **Impact of targeting on average distinct ad arrival rate.** Figure 9 shows the fraction of distinct ads of all ads harvested from each of the top ten ad providers. Two ads are considered distinct if they have the same text or image content and have the same click url. For each ad network, we report the fraction of distinct ads for two scenarios: when targeting is enabled and when targeting is disabled (i.e., when ad requests do not contain any targeting attributes).

Figure 9 shows several key points. First, all ad networks serve a large fraction of duplicate ads. On average, only 26% of the ads were distinct, suggesting that ad networks could benefit from caching ads on the client, as suggested by prior works [15, 19, 27]. The fraction of distinct ads vary widely across ad networks, ranging from 1% to 80%.

Second, targeting reduces the fraction of distinct ads. We observed this for all ad networks. When averaged over all ten top ad networks, the average fractions of distinct ads reduces from 26% to 11% when targeting is enabled. This is most likely because the pool of distinct ads applicable to specific targeting scenario is substantially smaller than those applicable to any or no targeting. This suggests that developers are likely to see more distinct ads when they do not overly target their ad requests. This might be one reason of why many developers do not provide optional targeting attributes even if ad networks allow them (Figure 6).

### *4.3.3 Behavioral Targeting Analysis*

We use the following two-step methodology to detect if top ten ad networks use behavioral targeting. In the training step, we let MAdScope create five profiles with (1) different device ids, (2) different locations $L$: New York, Los Angeles, Houston, Atlanta, and Seattle (five big cities in USA), and (3) different interests $I$: Game, Arts, Recreation, Computer, and Business (top five ad categories shown in Figure 8). We then use MAdScope to issue 5000 ad requests for each profile, over a period of one day. Then in the testing step, we use MAdScope to issue 1000 ad requests for each profile, with the ad requests containing only device information but no location or specific interest information (i.e., we select ad requests from a set of 100 apps from all categories, remove their optional targeting attributes, and replay them for each profile). Intuitively, if the ad network has learnt about the users' interests and locations from the training step and if it does behavioral targeting, it should show different ads to different profiles even though the attributes in ad requests do not indicate any specific location or interest. We use the same $\chi^2$ test to decide if the ads received by different profiles are distributed uniformly across profiles.

We found that doubleclick.net, used by 36% ad requests in our datasets, differentiates between profiles in a statistically significant way while serving ads. We did not observe any statistically significant impact of profiles for other networks, but that could well be due to the limitations mentioned in Section 4.2. For doubleclick.net, the impact of profiles is significant—we found that 80% of the ads were targeted towards specific profiles (e.g., distributed non-uniformly).

Note that in building profiles, MAdScope used four different types of activities mentioned in Section 4.1.2 (e.g., using a specific location $L$, using apps of a specific category $I$, etc.) We now investigate which of these tasks affect the profiles actually used by ad networks. To do that, we repeat the previous experiment four times, with MAdScope configured to build profiles based on only one task in each experiment. For example, in the first experiment, MAdScope builds profiles with location $L$ only, but uses apps, ads, and web pages of many different categories. In the second experiment, it uses apps on category $I$ only, but uses many different locations and categories of ads and web pages, and so on.

We observed that for doubleclick.net, only two types of actions impact targeting: types of used apps and types of clicked ads. Historical locations and web browser usage information do not seem to play any role on targeting.

## 5. COMPARISON OF WEB AND APP

We here contrast our findings for in-app ads with that from a recent study on in-browser ads [1].

▶ **Advertiser category.** Top categories of advertiser seem to be different for in-app ads than for in-browser ads. In [1], authors report that top three advertiser categories for in-browser ads are Financial Services, Shopping, and Computers. In contrast, our study shows that top thee categories for in-app ads are Games (mostly games in app stores), Arts (e.g., wallpapers), Recreation (e.g., ring tones). This probably aligns with general usage of browser and apps: financial services and shopping are mostly browser-based activities, while apps are used mostly for entertainment purposes.

▶ **Behavioral targeting.** As authors in [1] reports, behavioral targeting is common in in-browser ads. We used a conceptually similar methodology, but observed such targeting for only one of the top ten in-app ad networks.

▶ **Demographics.** Demographic information is a common targeting attribute in in-browser ads [1]. In contrast, it is not commonly used in in-app ads. Only one of top ten ad networks supports targeting based on demographic information; but this it an optional attribute and many app developers omit the attribute. Even if app developers provide demographic information of the user, the top ad network use it only marginally to target users.

▶ **Location.** Authors in [1] did not report location as a major targeting attribute in in-browser ads. In contrast, most (seven out of top ten) in-app ad networks collect location information, and many use the information to target users.

## 6. RELATED WORK

▶ **In-app ads.** A few studies characterize various aspects of in-app ad traffic. In [28], authors analyzed a data set corresponding to one day of traffic for a major European mobile carrier with more than 3 million subscribers and characterize mobile ad traffic along a number of dimensions, such as overall traffic, frequency, as well as possible implications in terms of benefits of well-known techniques, such as pre-fetching and caching, to limit the energy and network signalling overhead caused by current systems. CAMEO [15] analyzed AdMob ads collected from 100+ PlanetLab nodes and 20 phones and showed feasibility of caching and prefetching of ads. Mohan et al. [19] also show a similar result. (A recent study [4], however, showed that the power savings due to ad prefetching is small.) Unlike our work, these works do not characterize targeted ads. The only work we are aware of that aims to characterize user targeting in in-app ads is a study by Ullah et al. [27], which shows various categories of targeted ads shown to 100 apps by one ad network. Our study is more comprehensive and it differs from this previous study in its (1) scale (we analyze ad requests from 150K apps and 101 ad networks, while Ullah et al. analyze requests from 100 apps and mostly from one ad network, AdMob), (2) analysis of targeting attributes in ad requests, and (3) active probing (we probe top ten ad networks to understand what targeting attribute they actually use for targeting).

Most prior work on in-app ads focus primarily on security and privacy. Grace et al. [12] use their automated tool called AdRisk to analyze 100 ad libraries and investigate potential privacy and security risks of these libraries involving their resource permissions, dynamic code loading, permission probing and JavaScript linkages. Concurrent to this work, Stevens et al. [26] also investigate various privacy vulnerabilities in the most popular Android advertising libraries. They point out whether permissions required by various ad libraries are required, optional, or undocumented and investigate privacy concerns such as how UDIDs are handled and what user data is sent in ad requests. Several other works acknowledged the dangers of the lack privilege separation between Android application and and ad code and propose methods of separating them [20,24]. Leontiadis et al. [17] analyze an impressive number of 250K Android apps and show that current privacy protection mechanisms are not effective as developers and advert companies are not deterred and propose a market-aware privacy protection framework that aims to achieve an equilibrium between the developer's revenue and the user's privacy. The primary focus of all these papers is privacy and security issues of in-app ads, while ours is on characterization of user targeting in in-app ad landscape.

▶ **In-browser ads.** Previous work on online advertising has focused primarily on in-browser advertising and most work has considered the problems associated with privacy [7,11]. The study by Guha et al. [13] describes challenges in measuring online advertising systems. Roesner et al. [23] present a taxonomy of different trackers i.e., in-site, cross site, cookie sharing, and social media trackers, demonstrate how prevalent tracking is, and propose an extension that helps to protect user privacy. Castelluccia et al. [3] demonstrate that it is possible to reverse engineer a user's profiles and interests by analyzing ads targeted to her. Another thread of previous work investigated ad fraud, which hurts the advertisers who are paying for the ads [10]. XRay [16] is a differential correlation technique to identify how various tracking information are being used by targeted ads. MAdScope's overall goal is similar, but for in-app ads. More relevant to our study is a recent study of online in-browser display advertising by Barford et al. [1], where authors provided a general understanding of the characteristics and dynamics of online display advertising and insights on the targeting mechanisms that are used by ad serving entities. Our goal is similar, but for in-app advertising. As mentioned before, in-app advertising works differently from in-browser advertising and our results indicate that they significantly differ in important characteristics.

▶ **Dynamic analysis of apps.** MAdScope uses a Monkey to passively harvest ads. Similar Monkeys have been used recently for other applications such as app testing [22], ad frauds detection [5, 18], but none of these work studies user targeting by in-app ads.

# 7. CONCLUSION

We reported an in-depth study that seeks to broadly understand what targeting information mobile apps send to ad networks and how effectively, if at all, ad networks utilize the information for targeting purpose. Using a novel tool, called MAdScope, we analyzed 500K ad requests from 150K Android apps and showed that targeting is limited in in-app ads: even though ad controls provide APIs to send a lot of information to ad networks, much key targeting information is optional and is often not provided by apps. We also used MAdScope to systematically probe top 10 in-app ad networks to harvest over 1 million ads and found that while targeting is used by many of the top networks, there remain many instances where targeting information or behavioral profile does not have a statistically significant impact on how ads are chosen. We also contrasted our findings with a recent study of targeted in-browser ads.

In-app ad ecosystem is evolving and this study represents an important snapshot. It will be interesting to see how in-app targeting evolves in a few years. MAdScope can be a valuable tool for such future studies.

## Acknowledgements

The author would like to thank the shepherd, Ben Greenstein, and anonymous reviewers of ACM MobiSys 2015 for their feedback, Shuai Hao for developing the PUMA tool; Hao Chen and Jon Crussell for sharing the MadFraud dataset.

# 8. REFERENCES

[1] P. Barford, I. Canadi, D. Krushevskaja, Q. Ma, and S. Muthukrishnan. AdScape: harvesting and analyzing online display ads. In *Int. conf. on WWW*, 2014.

[2] R. Bhoraskar, S. Han, J. Jeon, T. Azim, S. Chen, J. Jung, S. Nath, R. Wang, and D. Wetherall. Brahmastra: Driving apps to test the security of third-party components. In *USENIX Security*, 2014.

[3] C. Castelluccia, M. A. Kaafar, and T. Minh-Dung. Betrayed by Your Ads! In *PETS- Privacy Enhancing Tools Symposium*, 2012.

[4] X. Chen, A. Jindal, and Y. C. Hu. How much energy can we save from prefetching ads?: energy drain analysis of top 100 apps. In *Proceedings of the Workshop on Power-Aware Computing and Systems (HotPower)*. ACM, 2013.

[5] J. Crussell, R. Stevens, and H. Chen. MAdFraud: Investigating ad fraud in android applications. In *ACM MobiSys*, 2014.

[6] T. Danny. Flurry releases newest app use stats. http://tech.co/flurry-app-stats-2014-09.

[7] D. S. Evans. The online advertising industry: Economics, evolution, and privacy. In *Journal of Economic Perspectives*, 2009.

[8] A. Farahat and M. C. Bailey. How effective is targeted advertising? In *Int. conf. on WWW*, 2012.

[9] GameHouse. Mobile advertising statistics—5 big trends you need to know! http://partners.gamehouse.com/mobile-advertising-statistics-5-big-trends-need-know/.

[10] M. Gandhi, M. Jakobsson, and J. Ratkiewicz. Badvertisements: Stealthy click-fraud with unwitting accessories. *Online Fraud, Part I Journal of Digital Forensic Practice*, 1(2), 2006.

[11] A. Goldfarb and C. Tucker. Online display advertising: Targeting and obtrusiveness. In *Marketing Science*, 2010.

[12] M. Grace, W. Zhou, X. Jiang, and A. Sadeghi. Unsafe exposure analysis of mobile in-app advertisements. In *Conference on Security and Privacy in Wireless and Mobile Networks (WiSEC)*, 2012.

[13] S. Guha, B. Cheng, and P. Francis. Challenges in measuring online advertising systems. In *ACM SIGCOMM Internet Measurement Conference*, 2010.

[14] S. Hao, B. Liu, S. Nath, W. G. Halfond, and R. Govindan. PUMA: Programmable ui-automation for large scale dynamic analysis of mobile apps. In *ACM MobiSys*, 2014.

[15] A. J. Khan, K. Jayarajah, D. Han, A. Misra, R. Balan, and S. Seshan. CAMEO: A middleware for mobile advertisement delivery. In *ACM MobiSys*, 2013.

[16] M. Lécuyer, G. Ducoffe, F. Lan, A. Papancea, T. Petsios, R. Spahn, A. Chaintreau, and R. Geambasu. Xray: Enhancing the web's transparency with differential correlation. In *USENIX Security*, 2014.

[17] I. Leontiadis, C. Efstratiou, M. Picone, and C. Mascolo. Don't kill my ads!: balancing privacy in an ad-supported mobile application market. In *Workshop on Mobile Computing Systems & Applications*, page 2. ACM, 2012.

[18] B. Liu, S. Nath, R. Govindan, and J. Liu. DECAF: Detecting and characterizing ad fraud in mobile apps. In *USENIX NSDI*, 2014.

[19] P. Mohan, S. Nath, and O. Riva. Prefetching mobile ads: Can advertising systems afford it? In *ACM EuroSys*, 2013.

[20] P. Pearce, A. Felt, G. Nunez, and D. Wagner. AdDroid: Privilege separation for applications and advertisers in android. In *Symposium on Information, Computer and Communications Security*, 2012.

[21] T. Peterson. Google tests way to track consumers from mobile browsers to the apps they use. http://adage.com/article/digital/google-tie-mobile-web-app-trackers-ad-targeting/294502/.

[22] L. Ravindranath, S. Nath, J. Padhye, and H. Balakrishnan. Automatic and scalable fault detection for mobile applications. In *ACM MobiSys*, 2014.

[23] F. Roesner, T. Kohno, and D. Wetherall. Betrayed by Your Ads! In *USENIX NSDI*, 2012.

[24] S. Shekhar, M. Dietz, and D. S. Wallach. Adsplit: Separating smartphone advertising from applications. In *USENIX Security Symposium*, 2012.

[25] A. N. Srivastava and M. Sahami. *Text mining: classification, clustering, and applications.* CRC Press, 2010.

[26] R. Stevens, C. Gibler, J. Crussell, , J. Erickson, and H. Chen. Investigating user privacy in android ad libraries. In *IEEE Mobile Security Technologies (MoST)*, 2012.

[27] I. Ullah, R. Boreli, D. Kaafar, and S. Kanhere. Characterising user targeting for in-app mobile ads. In *INFOCOM International Workshop on Security and Privacy in Big Data (BigSecurity 2014)*, 2014.

[28] N. Vallina-Rodriguez, J. Shah, A. Finamore, Y. Grunenberger, H. Haddadi, K. Papagiannaki, and J. Crowcroft. Breaking for commercials: Characterizing mobile advertising. In *ACM SIGCOMM Internet Measurement Conference*, 2012.

[29] W3C. Same origin policy. http://www.w3.org/Security/wiki/Same_Origin_Policy.

[30] J. Yan, N. Liu, G. Wang, W. Zhang, Y. Jiang, and Z. Chen. How much can behavioral targeting help online advertising? In *Int. conf. on WWW*, 2009.

# AdAttester: Secure Online Mobile Advertisement Attestation Using TrustZone

Wenhao Li, Haibo Li, Haibo Chen, Yubin Xia
Institute of Parallel and Distributed Systems
Shanghai Jiao Tong University

## ABSTRACT

Mobile advertisement (ad for short) is a major financial pillar for developers to provide free mobile apps. However, it is frequently thwarted by ad fraud, where rogue code tricks *ad providers* by forging ad display or user clicks, or both. With the mobile ad market growing drastically (e.g., from \$8.76 billion in 2012 to \$17.96 billion in 2013), it is vitally important to provide a verifiable mobile ad framework to detect and prevent ad frauds. Unfortunately, this is notoriously hard as mobile ads usually run in an execution environment with a huge TCB.

This paper proposes a verifiable mobile ad framework called AdAttester, based on ARM's TrustZone technology. AdAttester provides two novel security primitives, namely *unforgeable clicks* and *verifiable display*. The two primitives attest that ad-related operations (e.g., user clicks) are initiated by the end user (instead of a bot) and that the ad is displayed intact and timely. AdAttester leverages the secure world of TrustZone to implement these two primitives to collect proofs, which are piggybacked on ad requests to ad providers for attestation. AdAttester is non-intrusive to mobile users and can be incrementally deployed in existing ad ecosystem. A prototype of AdAttester is implemented for Android running on a Samsung Exynos 4412 board. Evaluation using 182 typical mobile apps with ad frauds shows that AdAttester can accurately distinguish ad fraud from legitimate ad operations, yet incurs small performance overhead and little impact on user experience.

## 1. INTRODUCTION

Mobile ad is a key pillar to the mobile app ecosystem: developers provide free mobile apps with embedded ad libraries from *ad providers* to users and get paid by the ad provider for the ads displayed and/or clicked. A recent report shows that the mobile ad market revenue increases from \$8.76 billion to \$17.96 billion and is predicted to reach \$31.45 billion in 2014 [19].

Unfortunately, this huge-revenue ecosystem is severely thwarted by ad frauds, where rouge code tricks the ad provider with forged display (also called *impression* [26]) or clicks. For example, recent studies pointed out that ads in mobile apps are plagued by various types of frauds: mobile ad providers are estimated to lose nearly 1 billion dollars in 2013 due to these frauds and around one third of mobile ad clicks may constitute click-spam [18]. The most recent research study [33] shows that, one of the largest click fraud botnets, called ZeroAccess, induces advertising losses on the order of \$100,000 per day. Ad frauds can typically be characterized into two types [26]: (1) *Bot-driven frauds* employ bot networks to initiate forged ad impressions and clicks; (2) *Interaction frauds* manipulate visual layouts of ads to trigger ad impressions and unaware clicks from the end users.

Because of the urgent need to detecting mobile ad frauds, prior approaches have made important first steps by using an offline-based approach [16, 26]. Specifically, they trigger the execution of mobile apps in a controlled environment to observe deviated behavior to detect ad frauds. However, such approaches are limited to *interaction frauds* whose behavior can be triggered by automatic testing; it is hard for them to detect *bot-driven frauds* because botnets are compromised bots (thus real devices) that have been installed with the ad fraudulent applications, which could be instructed to make arbitrary network requests stealthily to users (such as ZeroAccess [33]). Further, such approaches suffer from both relatively high false positives and false negatives because the lack of reliable proofs to ad providers for attestation.

Reliably and securely detecting ad fraud raises two important questions: 1) *display integrity*: how could the ad providers know that their ads are displayed in the users' screen without their advertising policies being violated? 2) *user action authenticity*: how do the ad providers know that an ad request is from a user click but not a bot? Unfortunately, answering the two questions in current mobile platforms are notoriously hard due to the complex software stack that is potentially controlled by malicious botnets and/or rouge app code, which can forge arbitrary actions on mobile ads without users' awareness, making it hard (if not impossible) for ad providers to distinguish such forged actions from legitimate ones in a reliable way.

In this paper, we propose AdAttester, a system that reliably detects and prevents well-known ad frauds. The key insight of AdAttester is to provide attestable proofs to ad providers. To achieve this, we provide two novel security primitives:

- *Unforgeable clicks*: A user action, such as an ad click, could not be forged by malicious code that sends ad click network requests silently without users' awareness. Thus, ad providers can reliably detect the forged ad clicks.

- *Verifiable display*: If an ad's content is displayed on the mobile screen, a verifiable proof of the display content and the displaying duration will be generated and sent to the ad provider for verification.


*MobiSys'15*, May 18–22, 2015, Florence, Italy.

http://dx.doi.org/10.1145/2742647.2742676.

AdAttester uses a trusted extension of hardware, namely ARM TrustZone [10], to implement these two primitives, which avoids the need to trust the mobile software stack. AdAttester leverages the split execution mode in TrustZone and assigns specific peripheral devices to be accessible by the secure world only. Specifically, AdAttester puts the touch device driver and display device manipulation logic to the secure world, so as to securely get the ad click event and read the display content. To ensure that the user actions are unforgeable, AdAttester will sign each touch input whenever the touch positions lies within the ad view area, then send the signed touch inputs and the *eigenvalue* of the clicked ad area in the display screen to the ad provider (i.e., ad server) together with the ad request. Providing verifiable display is done by checking the ad display content periodically and calculating the *eigenvalue* of the display content. These eigenvalues will also be sent to the ad server together with the ad request; the ad providers will compare the requested eigenvalues with the correct ones that are calculated at the time of releasing the ads.

With these two security primitives, the bot-driven frauds and interaction frauds can be detected reliably. The ad providers may define some policies to determine whether a sequence of ad requests conform the predefined policies and whether such ad requests should be paid.

To deploy AdAttester, mobile users need to install a small trusted ad attestation application in secure world and AdAttester provides a list of ad attestation APIs in normal world OS for ad providers to adopt to their ad SDKs. Note that the trusted ad attestation application needs to be certified by trusted parties and unauthorized code such as code provided by ad providers could not run in secure world, and the TCB of AdAttester is small: only the hardware and software running in secure world of TrustZone.

We have implemented AdAttester in a Samsung Exynos 4412 board. We show that AdAttester can effectively detect all types of mobile ad frauds found in [16]. Evaluation shows that AdAttester incurs small performance overhead and little impact on user experience.

In summary, we make the following contributions:

- Two novel security primitives: *unforgeable clicks* and *verifiable display*, which provide attestable proofs of user interaction and can be deployed to effectively detect and prevent mobile ad frauds.

- The design and implementation of a verifiable mobile advertising framework named AdAttester, the first system to detect and prevent well-known mobile ad frauds online on the real hardware with small overhead.

- A comprehensive evaluation on performance and using a set of mobile apps with ad frauds to confirm the effectiveness and efficiency.

The rest of this paper is organized as follows. The next section describes some background information on mobile ads, ad frauds and ARM TrustZone. Section 3 describes the threat model, design goal and an overview of AdAttester. Section 4 presents the two primitives, followed by how they are leveraged for detecting ad frauds (section 5). Section 6 describes the security and deployment analysis. Section 7 describes some implementation issues using ARM TrustZone. Section 8 and 9 evaluate the effectiveness, performance and disruption of AdAttester. Section 10 discusses potential limitations of AdAttester and possible future work. Finally, section 11 relates AdAttester to state-of-the-art and section 12 concludes this paper.

# 2. BACKGROUND AND MOTIVATION

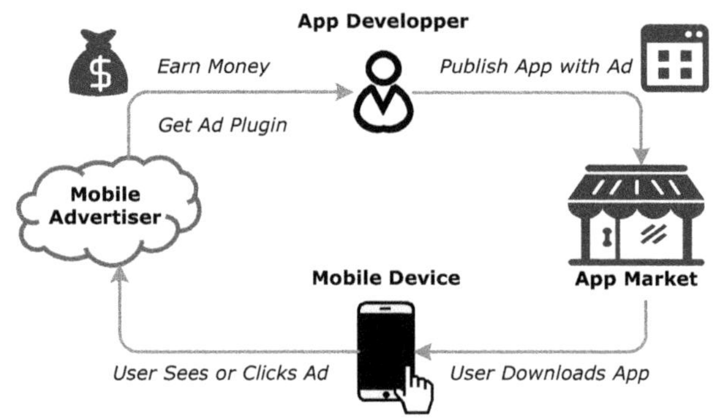


Figure 1: The ecosystem of mobile advertising

## 2.1 Mobile App Advertising and Ad Frauds

Mobile ads are the key to the ecosystem of mobile app development: developers design and implement mobile apps and distribute them to users for free; instead they get paid when users click or view ads, which are fetched from ad providers through the ad libraries embedded in mobile apps, as shown in Figure 1. Specifically, to embed ads in an app, an app publisher (developer) first registers with an ad provider, who provides the developer with a publisher ID and an ad library which will be embedded in her apps. Then the developer includes this ad library in her apps and allocates some screen real estate to the ads. The ad library is responsible for fetching, displaying and handling ads when the app is running. The app developer then uploads the apps to some app markets (e.g., Google Play) for users to download and use. App developer is paid by the ad provider based on the number of ad clicks or impressions, or both.

To make sure ads are delivered and displayed non-intrusively, ad providers usually have strict guidelines on how ads should be used and displayed in apps; otherwise the ad providers may refuse to pay for the ads. For example, AdMob's guidelines and policies clearly state that developers are strictly prohibited from using any means to inflate impressions or clicks artificially, and the number of visible ads per page must not exceed one [7].

App developers, however, have the incentives to violate those policies in order to earn more money, which are called violation frauds. Such frauds could be intentional or unintentional. In general, the types of ad frauds can be characterized into two categories [26]:

*Bot-driven frauds:* These frauds employ bot networks to initiate forged ad impressions and clicks. The bot networks could be compromised mobile devices, PCs or desktops, similar to the traditional web advertising bot networks. Violators may first carefully analyze the correct sequence of how a paid ad could be made successfully, and then distribute an automated tool to the bot network to process the ad requests secretly. Bot-driven frauds widely exist; a conservative estimation concludes that 2% to 40% of ad traffics are botnet traffic and the accumulated monthly figure could be $6.2 billion in web advertising [3, 5]. These frauds are now targeting at mobile ads [4].

*Interaction-driven frauds:* These frauds include *placement fraud* that ads are placed in violation of the ad guidelines or even use a display view to cover the ad view so as to receive impression fee while not affecting user experience. In general, this can be done in multiple ways, including resizing ads to too small to read, hiding them behind other display elements or placing them outside the display screen. There could also be *unaware fraud* that an app sends ad requests in the background or forges ad click requests without user's consciousness. Evaluation by Crussell et al. [16] over 130,339 apps shows that 12,421 apps have background impressions and 21 apps fabricate user clicks. Liu et al. [26] show that 2% to 54% apps have certain types of placement frauds.

Although ad providers have guidelines to restrict the behavior of developers, there are few technical ways to guarantee that the guidelines are not violated. Currently, an ad server will analyze all the received clicks to identify suspicious ones that might be forged click, using some heuristic methods such as pattern matching or anomaly detection. However, these methods are known to have high false positives as well as false negatives, since they are based on inferring, which is intrinsically not accurate.

## 2.2 ARM TrustZone

**Split CPU Mode Execution:** The lack of a secure execution environment in mobile devices motivated the design of ARM TrustZone. Though TrustZone was designed more than 10 years ago, it is manufactured for the mass market only until recent years, due to the urgent need of a foundation for mobile security. Briefly speaking, ARM TrustZone is a security extension introduced to achieve strong isolation between a security-sensitive execution environment (secure world) and a commodity environment (normal world). This is done by dividing access permissions of the processor, memory and peripherals between the two worlds. The secure world can access all states of normal world but not vice-versa. As shown in Figure 2, there is a higher privileged mode called TrustZone secure monitor mode that is responsible for switching between the two worlds by either executing the *SMC* instruction or receiving interrupts.

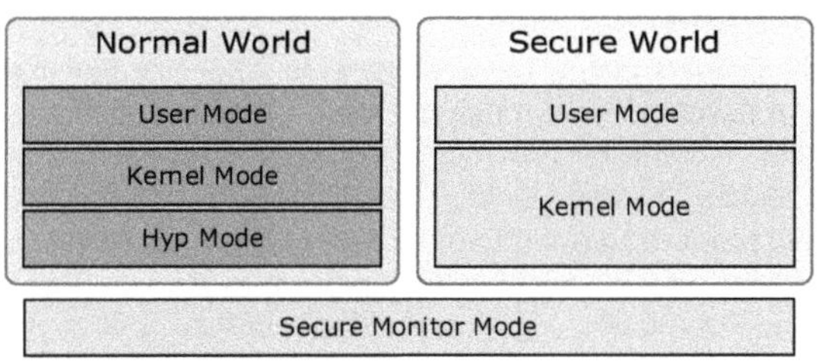


Figure 2: Split CPU mode with TrustZone support

**Memory and Peripheral Protection:** TrustZone supports memory partitioning between the two worlds. The DRAM could be partitioned into several memory regions by TrustZone Address Space Controller (TZASC), each of which can be configured to be used in either worlds or both. By default, secure world applications can access normal world memory but not vice-versa. System peripherals such as touch input or display controller could be configured as secure by TrustZone Protection Controller (TZPC) to ensure these peripherals could only be accessed in the secure world. Currently most of mobile phones run their OSes in the normal world, designate touch input and display controller as non-secure peripherals. By setting the touch input and display controller as secure peripherals using TZPC, we can have a secure input and display that are isolated from the normal world OS. Besides, DMA is also world-awareness and a normal world DMA that transfers data to or from secure memory will be denied.

**Secure OS and Trusted Application**: To leverage the benefits from ARM TrustZone, many mobile vendors nowadays, including Samsung, Apple and Huawei, deploy a secure OS (i.e., Trusted Execution Environment [2] ) in the secure world, which runs in parallel with the commodity OS such as Android and iOS in the normal world in their mobile devices. They also provide some SDKs for some trustworthy third-parties to deploy their secure services called Trusted Applications (TA) running in the secure world. Typical Trusted Application in today's mobile devices are Digital Rights Management (DRM) and mobile secure payment. Note that TAs running in secure world are certified by trusted parties and unauthorized code such as code provided by ad providers will not be permitted to run in the secure world of TrustZone.

With this trend of deploying secure OS and TA on mobile devices in industry, we observe that it is practical to run an ad service as a TA to provide more secure and verifiable information about the validity of ad operations. Hence, AdAttester mainly runs as a TA in the secure world.

# 3. THREAT MODEL AND OVERVIEW

## 3.1 Goals

The main goal of AdAttester is to provide secure online ad attestation to effectively detect mobile ad frauds. Unlike prior offline-based analysis, AdAttester aims to provide a framework to enhance the mobile ad ecosystem by making mobile ad related operations attestable, even facing the challenges that the commodity mobile software stack is not trustworthy. Further, AdAttester is designed to provide verifiable attestation to detect both *bot-driven* and *interaction-driven* frauds. These two types of frauds constitute the most common ways by ad frauds nowadays and there is still no effective way to reliably detect them on-the-fly. Note that AdAttester is currently not designed with the capability to detect some app-specific policies like how many ads may be placed in a single page.

Besides providing secure online attestation to detect ad frauds, there are four extra requirements to make AdAttester practical.

- *Non-intrusiveness:* AdAttester must attest the requests on behalf of user's actions automatically without users' involvement and awareness. Thus, ad providers, developers and users have the incentives to use and deploy AdAttester.
- *Incremental deployable:* For a new ad fraud detection framework to be deployable, AdAttester should be compatible to existing ad deployment ecosystem such that existing ad delivery and accounting framework can still run under AdAttester.
- *Privacy-preserving:* AdAttester should preserve the existing properties of privacy semantics and should not leak out more privacy information than existing ad solutions.
- *Small TCB:* To make the process of ad attestation secure, the TCB of AdAttester must be small enough.

## 3.2 Threat Model and Assumptions

AdAttester assumes the mobile device is equipped with ARM TrustZone (TrustZone is already widely deployed in mobile devices) and the device manufacturer implements TrustZone features correctly without hardware security flaws. Further, AdAttester assumes that the device contains a persistent per-device public key pair, which constitutes a unique device identity. This identity is used to uniquely identify the ad proofs from a mobile device.

AdAttester trusts the hardware of mobile devices including the TrustZone extension and thus precludes physical attacks that may read the protected memory and tamper with TrustZone. Like other systems leveraging TrustZone, AdAttester trusts the software stack running inside the secure world. AdAttester strives to keep the TCB of the code running in the secure world small, which makes it reasonable to trust the secure world as a whole. In contrast, the entire OS and its applications in the normal world are not trusted and are susceptible to be compromised. This is because the software stack for the normal world, which usually contains a full-fledged Linux, an application framework and/or a Java virtual machine, comprises millions of lines of code. Attackers who compromise the OS could launch various software attacks and modify any code of the OS or even the mobile ad apps. Since software running in secure world may leak some side-channel traces to attackers controlling the normal world, we will discuss how to mitigate the potential risk of leaking device private key through side-channels attacks in section 6, though there are no such kind of attacks yet.

In the current scheme, AdAttester assumes the ad provider (mobile advertiser) is trustworthy and will not be compromised by attackers. This assumption can be relaxed by requiring a secure processor or a trusted hypervisor [41, 42, 45] in the ad server (like ObliviAd [11]).

## 3.3 Overview

Figure 3 illustrates an overview of how AdAttester works. On the client side, when a user clicks an ad, AdAttester will generate a proof, which contains eigenvalues of the displayed ad view that the user clicks and a nonce that comes from ad server to avoid replay attack. For show-ad, instead of sending messages per click, the mobile device will collect proofs in a random interval, e.g., every five seconds, which also contains eigenvalues of ad image and nonce. The proof will be signed using the private key of the mobile device and sent to the ad server for attestation.

The ad server maintains a per-ad repository, which contains the related ad information, like eigenvalues of some image or video ads, and valid ad positions and sizes. A new module, named AdVerifier, is introduced to check the proof of each click and impression. Once receiving a message, the AdVerifier first checks its signature, nonce and proofs. If all checks pass, the AdVerifier will deliver the click message to the ad server for further processing.

To make the proof reliable, AdAttester must ensure the following conditions. First, the click is actually from user, instead of being forged. Second, the eigenvalues are actually calculated from the screen data, instead of some data not shown to users. This is guaranteed by two primitives, namely *verifiable display* and *unforgeable clicks*, which are enabled by AdAttester's non-bypassable use of TrustZone (section 4).

Figure 4 further shows the overall architecture of AdAttester. Commodity operating system (e.g., Android) runs in the normal world and a secure OS runs in the secure world. In AdAttester, the touch screen and display devices are only controlled by the secure OS to provide a reliable source of user input and display information. The trusted TZAttester, which runs in the secure world as a Trusted Application, is deployed to generate attestation blob. An untrusted AdAttester Service runs as a system service in the untrusted OS framework. The AdAttester Service cooperates with the TZAttester and provides ad libraries in applications with interfaces of getting attestation data whenever the ad libraries need to send ad requests and the application runs in the foreground. The TrustZone driver (TZ Driver in the figure) in the normal world provides APIs for AdAttester Service to call the TZAttester in the secure world.

# 4. AdAttester PRIMITIVES

This section first describes the necessary information to be collected for the two primitives and then describe how such information is collected securely.

Figure 3: An overview of how AdAttester works. When a user viewing and/or clicking a mobile ad, AdAttester will generate a signed proof describing the impressions and/or user clicks. The Ad server managed by the ad provider will attest this ad operation by comparing the proof with a per-ad repository

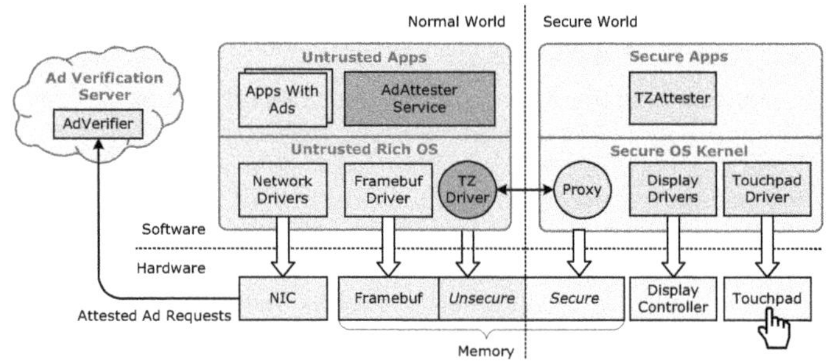


Figure 4: AdAttester architecture. AdAttester consists of three parts, two in the local mobile device and one in the remote ad server. The local mobile side consists of (1) a trusted TZAttester running in secure world and (2) an AdAttester Service running in the OS framework in normal world. The remote ad server has (3) a trusted AdVerifier that verifies the ad requests

## 4.1 Primitives

As the primary means for an ad provider to decide how much to pay for a developer is through counting the times of impressions and clicks, AdAttester provides two primitives, namely *verifiable display* and *unforgeable clicks*. The *verifiable display* ensures that a verifiable proof of ad impression (i.e., display) in the mobile screen and its duration will be generated and sent to the ad provider for attestation. Similarly, *unforgeable clicks* ensures that a proof is generated to attest that a click to a specific ad is initiated by a user, instead of malware such as a bot. These two primitives serve as the key building blocks to build a secure online ad attestation.

The message format of these two primitives is shown in Figure 5. A signed proof message for ad impression contains a sequence of hash values of the displayed ad, a nonce which is used to defend

**Attested Message Format**

```
impression_blob = {
        displayed ad hashes, nonce, interval,
        duration, ad_info, device_info
}
signed_ad_impression = {
        K_priv{SHA(impression_blob)},
        impression_blob, certified K_pub, meta_data
}

click_blob = {
        clicked ad hash, nonce, ad_info, device_info
}
signed_ad_click = {
        K_priv{SHA(click_blob)}, click_blob,
        certified K_pub, meta_data
}
```

Figure 5: AdAttester primitives message format

message reuse attack (called replay attack), display timestamps describing the duration of ad display and interval of sampling, ad information including ad ID, displayed ad size and position in the screen, device information such as screen size and resolution, some other ad library-specific metadata and a certified public key. Similarly, a signed proof message for an ad click contains the hash value of the displayed ad around the click point, a nonce, ad information, device information, metadata and certified public key.

## 4.2 Obtaining Verifiable Ad Proofs

Generating verifiable ad proofs means that AdAttester must have a way to determine the origin of a user's click and what was displayed on the mobile screen. AdAttester achieves this by leveraging the secure OS in the secure world to control the input and display devices. This is achieved by assigning the input and display devices to be only accessible by the secure world. The secure OS provides touch input driver and secure configuration of display controller handler so that TZAttester in the secure world can get reliable information of input and display. AdAttester uses both the trusted TZAttester in the secure world and the untrusted AdAttester Service in the normal world to cooperatively collect necessary proofs for attestation. Note that the developers may control the untrusted part of AdAttester to refuse to cooperate with TZAttester, which, however, may cause a valid ad impression/click not to be attested correctly.

The first proof can be reliably obtained by collecting a user click from the secure input and signing it with a private key. A straightforward way to obtain display information is to get a snapshot of the displayed ad and send it to the ad server for attestation. This method, however, may leak user's privacy and violate our privacy-preserving requirement. To preserve user's privacy while providing verifiable display, we do not directly send the raw display data to ad server, but calculate and send the eigenvalue of the display data (i.e., data hash), which is a one-way operation and server can hardly reverse it to get the original data.

The display device driver puts the framebuffer region to the untrusted memory used by the normal world software. Hence, existing display libraries can still write display data directly to the framebuffer without trapping to the secure world, which will not greatly decrease performance. As TZAttester in the secure world could control the framebuffer, it can also get reliable display information, for example, the framebuffer region address. This is important because if the display controller is controlled by the normal world software, the normal world software could deceive TZAttester into getting a wrong framebuffer region and thus attesting on an incorrect display region.

The touch input is only accessible in the secure world, and the touch input driver is implemented in the secure world. Hence, whenever an input interrupt arrives, the touch input driver will first get the input data (i.e., input position on the screen), then the input data will be saved by TZAttester before being sent to the untrusted OS in the normal world. On getting the input data, TZAttester will check whether: (1) an ad is currently displayed; (2) the touch position locates within the ad display. If both conditions are satisfied, TZAttester will calculate the eigenvalue of the ad view region from the framebuffer. The information for checking whether an ad is currently displayed and its exact display region is provided by AdAttester Service in the untrusted OS. Note that if the information is incorrect, then the signed advertising information could be easily detected by the remote AdVerifier. The eigenvalue of the clicked ad view together with some other information such as a message nonce and device resolution, will be signed using the device private key and thus a piece of verifiable advertising information is generated. Besides, to attest ads (such as video ads) that need to attest for a period, a secure timer is used to periodically attest the display data. One possibly bypassable case is that an adversary knowing the interval can display the ad only when AdAttester is about to attest the displayed ad. The ad may be displayed short enough so that a user will not even notice it, yet from AdAttester's point of view, the ad was displayed continuously. To defend against this case, AdAttester chooses a random start time to attest with a random interval check or attest consecutively for several times in one interval period.

To retain good performance, AdAttester Service works cooperatively with TZAttester to provide necessary information so that TZAttester could decide whether an attestation proof should be generated. AdAttester Service tracks the view system of the untrusted OS and will notify TZAttester with some necessary information, including the position of the ad view whenever an ad view is displayed, hidden or resized.

### 4.2.1 *Tracking Ad View*

As a mobile ad will change it views during the execution of mobile apps, AdAttester needs to track the ad views to correctly generate proofs.

AdAttester instruments the view system of the untrusted OS to track the status of ad views. This step is necessary to reduce performance impact incurred by AdAttester; otherwise, TZAttester needs to attest the display view every time a touch input event generates. To identify ad views, ad libraries need to register ad view elements to the view system and AdAttester Service. If an ad view is shown on screen, updated or hidden from screen, the view system will invoke the notification method of AdAttester Service, which in turn will notify TZAttester in the secure world.

### 4.2.2 *Identifying Ad Display Region*

To calculate the eigenvalue of the ad view, TZAttester needs to identify and read the display content. Directly reading this data from framebuffer is feasible because the secure display driver sets the address of the framebuffer, which could not be forged by attackers in our threat model. To get the correct display data, the untrusted AdAttester Service must tell TZAttester the exact position in the display screen, otherwise an incorrect eigenvalue will be calculated, which will be detected by the remote AdVerifier.

In the hardware abstraction layer, the display device driver in secure OS allocates twice the screen size of memory and uses one as a back buffer while other as the primary surface. The drawing is done on the back buffer while the content of the primary surface is used to display the current screen content. Page flipping is used so that when the drawing is complete on the back buffer, the back buffer becomes the primary surface and the old primary surface becomes the back buffer. Since the driver is controlled by the secure world, TZAttester could get the currently primary surface and retrieve the ad content using the provided ad position information.

### 4.2.3 *Calculating Eigenvalue*

There are many algorithms to calculate eigenvalues for an image (and video). Example include SIFT [29] and SURF [12], which can tolerate complex transformations like rotation and scale down and have also recently been parallelized [15, 20]. Basically, they represent an image as a set of 64-bit or 128-bit vectors and compare their similarities by comparing the bit vectors. Originally, we used SIFT to calculate eigenvalue for attestation. However, the generated eigenvalue is sometimes too big (may even exceed the original image size), which may consume too much network bandwidth. We observed that for images in mobile ad views, it is unlikely that an image would be rotated (though it may be scaled up/down). Hence, a scale-resistant algorithm is enough for our purpose. Hence, we use the perceptual hash algorithm [24] to reduce the eigenvalue size to 64 bit. This significantly reduce the size compared to SIFT, but can still accurately calculate the similarity of images.

# 5. SECURE ONLINE AD ATTESTATION

This section describes how the two primitives are used to construct the secure online ad attestation by slightly adjusting the ad libraries using APIs provided by AdAttester. Note that AdAttester is completely transparent to mobile apps.

## 5.1 Attesting Ads

Mobile ads have several types, including *banner ad, rectangle ad* and *interstitial ad.* Banner ads use a small portion of the screen to tempt users to "click through" to a richer, full-screen experience such as a website or app store page. They can have a variety of file formats, from static JPEG and GIF banners to simple text and in-banner video ads. Rectangle ads are similar to banner ads, except that they usually have a larger height than banner ads occupying a larger portion of screen. Interstitial ads, on the other hand, immediately present rich HTML5 experiences or "web apps" at natural app transition points such as launch, video pre-roll or game level load. Besides directly showing ads on screen, some ads are displayed on the notification bar to tempt users into a higher click rate.

We classify these kinds of ads into two categories: image ads (i.e., text and static image) and video ads (i.e., video media). Table 1 shows the overall APIs provided by AdAttester to ad libraries. In the following, we describe how to attest such ads using these APIs.

**Adopt AdAttester to Ad SDK.** Adopting AdAttester to existing ad SDKs requires minor changes on impression and click tracking. The first change is to notify the trusted TZAttester when an impression ad is shown and hidden by calling one of the APIs: *adattester_track_videoad, adattester_track_imagead* and *adattester_track_update.* The second change is to call the trusted TZAttester to generate attestation when a click is triggered or an impression is finished by calling one of the two APIs: *adattester_attest_impression* and *adattester_click* and add the attested blob to ad request. When an app comes to background, AdAttester Service will not accept any ad attestation requests from that app because in that case, a malicious app or ad could forge a faked ad attestation request on behalf of the foreground app, which in turn, may leak out some sensitive information such as the area a user clicks.

**Ad Impression Attestation:** To attest impression-based paid ads (e.g., the video ads), the *adattester_track_videoad, adattester_track_imagead* and *adattester_track_update* APIs are provided to keep tracking of the giving ad views. TZAttester keeps a secure timer and will calculate the signature (i.e., the eigenvalue) of the displayed ad view at a random interval. These APIs will return a track ID so that subsequent calls (namely the *adattester_track_update* that updates an ad which is being tracked, *adattester_attest_impression* that generates impression attestation and *atttester_attest_click* that generates click attestation) could find the right tracked ad. When the impression time expires and an attestation is needed, the normal world software will call function *adattester_attest_impression* and provide necessary ad information to do an attestation.

**Ad Click Attestation:** Click-based paid ads, on the other hand, are slightly different from impression-based ones. TZAttester tracks status of currently visible ad views with the help of the untrusted AdAttester Service in the normal world, which will in turn notify TZAttester by invoking the create, update and delete ads API. When a user click triggers ad events, the normal world AdAttester Service will call function *adattester_attest_click* to attest the user click. When the API *adattester_attest_click* is invoked, it will check whether the attested ad is currently being tracked and will put the tracked data into the attested blob to handle the situation when a user clicks an impression ad (i.e., a video ad) if so.

## 5.2 Ad Attestation Proofs

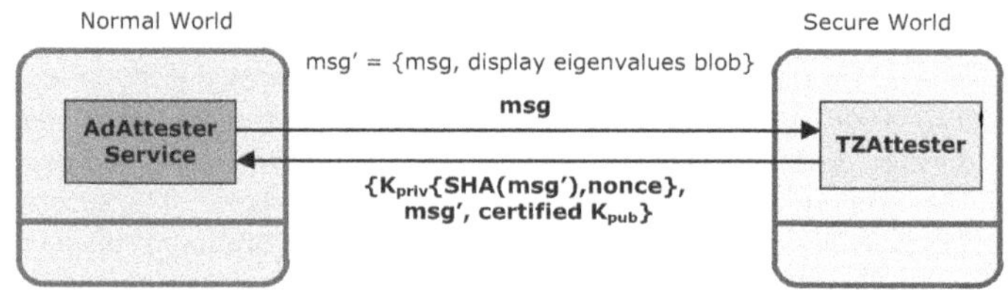


Figure 7: The attestation process of AdAttester

**Device Keys.** An AdAttester-enabled device contains a persistent per-device public key pair, which constitutes a unique device identity. The per-device public key pair widely exists in TrustZone-enabled mobile devices nowadays. At manufacturing time, the key pair is flashed into secure fuses (write-once persistent memory) using eFuse technology and is accessible only in the secure world. For privacy, the device generates an attestation public key pair (called attestation identity keys or AIKs), which is used to sign data inside attestation blob and will be certified by the trusted private CAs after confirming that the key is generated by TrustZone-enabled devices. Another alternative design is to use group signatures [13] to improve anonymity.

**Attestation Structure.** Figure 7 shows message format of the attestation proofs. An attestation message contains several parts: a hash of the attested message which is the combination of an application-specific data blob and the blob of the corresponding display data, a nonce that is used to check freshness of the request to protect against replay attacks, a certificate of the device attestation identity key. The nonce is stored in the ad server, increased and synchronized between the ad server and a mobile device when an ad session starts.

## 5.3 Detecting Fraud Behavior

Detecting ad frauds consists of three phases (Figure 6): a *feature extraction phase*, in which an ad preprocessing tool generates and saves an ad signature database; an *online checking phase*, which extracts and checks the legality of ad requests which may be signed; a *log analysis phase*, which uses existing advertising analytics tools to further detect frauds.

**Feature Extraction.** The feature extraction phase takes a set of ad images or videos as input source and splits the input source into a list of images. For each image, we calculate the eigenvalue (section 4.2.3). For a video, we generate a list of images and their corresponding eigenvalues to be used for proof.

**Online Checking.** When an ad request comes, the ad server will first check whether the request is attested. If the request not is attested, the legacy fraud detection and request processing modules will process that request, otherwise the AdVerifier will check the attested request. The AdVerifier will verify the certificate of the AIK to assure that the AIK comes from a TrustZone-enabled device by traversing the public-key chain enclosed in the attestation blob and use the certified public key to decrypt the nonce and the

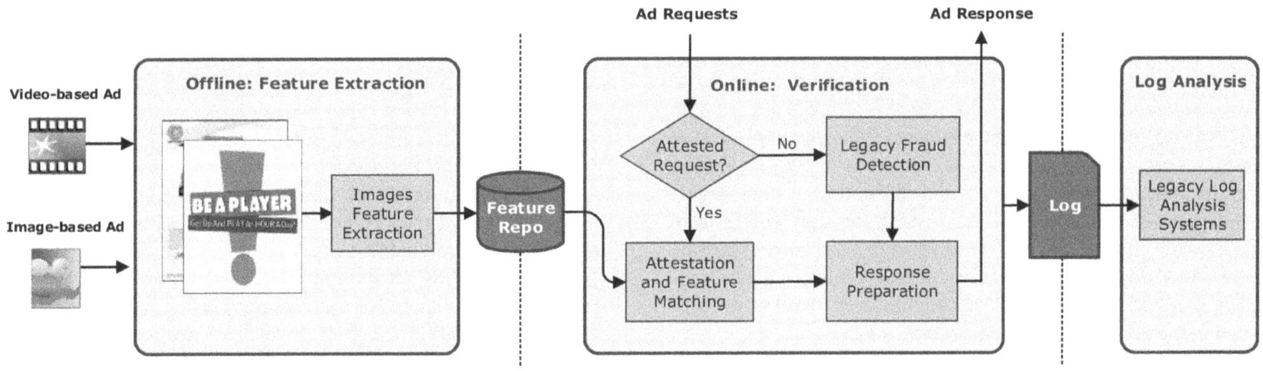


Figure 6: The ad fraud checking framework of AdAttester

Table 1: APIs provided by AdAttester to ad libraries

| Command and parameters | Description |
|---|---|
| *adattester_register_adview(ad_view)* | Register an ad view to AdAttester Service for view tracking |
| *adattester_create_ad(ad_info)* | Notification to AdAttester Service when an ad view is created |
| *adattester_update_ad(ad_info)* | Notification to AdAttester Service when an ad view is updated |
| *adattester_delete_ad(ad_info)* | Notification to AdAttester Service when an ad view is destroyed or hidden |
| *adattester_track_videoad(ad_info, seconds)* | Tell AdAttester Service to attest a video ad for a period of time |
| *adattester_track_imagead(ad_info, seconds)* | Tell AdAttester Service to attest an image ad for a period of time |
| *adattester_track_update(track_id, ad_info, new_seconds)* | Update tracking of a tracking ad |
| *adattester_attest_impression(track_id, ad_info, device_info, metadata)* | Call AdAttester Service to attest an impression-triggered ad packet |
| *adattester_attest_click(ad_info, device_info, metadata)* | Call AdAttester Service to attest a click-triggered ad packet |

payload hash value. Since the certified public key will consume a relatively large portion of ad network traffic, the ad server will maintain an ID to certified public key mapping so that client only needs to transfer its public key for the first time and uses the ID got from ad server for the rest of requests. The integrity of the message payload is checked by recalculating the hash value of the payload and comparing it with the decrypted one. The AdVerifier will retrieve the image feature data according to the ad ID from the ad request and compare the data with the ad request one. If the difference between the pre-stored image feature and the ad request one is within a predefined deviation (currently we set the maximum similarity distance value to 10 using perceptual hash algorithm), we could confirm the ad request comes from a legitimate user action from a real device. At last, the ad request will be processed by the request processing module and an ad response will be returned to the client.

**Log Analysis.** During the *online checking phase*, the necessary information (i.e., ad request payload and client IP) will be logged for further analysis. This phase is necessary even for the attested ad requests because some fraudsters may employ teams of people to click on ads using TrustZone-enabled devices, which could not be directly detected by AdAttester and AdAttester relies on existing fraud checking approaches to detecting this kind of frauds.

# 6. SECURITY ANALYSIS AND DEPLOYMENT

**Attacks On Untrusted AdAttester Service:** Though AdAttester relies on untrusted AdAttester Service running on the normal world to collect necessary information for proofs, AdAttester still ensures that the ad impressions and clicks cannot be forged. If AdAttester Service refuses to corporate with AdAttester, such as DOS attacks, the generated proofs will not be attested by AdVerifier. This essentially violates the sole purpose of mobile ad developers and attackers, who would try their best to avoid this.

**Side-channel Attacks on Device Keys:** Side-channel attacks that target on device keys is a potential threat to the security of AdAttester and even the whole TrustZone platform. Existing approaches such as Prime-and-probe [40], Flush-and-reload [43] may be also feasible to stealing the device keys, though to our best knowledge, there are no such successful attacks on TrustZone. Defensive methods against such attacks include: using lock-down cache lines for key calculation in secure world, using hardware encrypt/decrypt engines on the SoC (most of mobile devices are equipped with this feature), flushes sensitive cache on world-switch or using cache or SoC internal RAM for private key computation [21,32].

**Potential Abuses:** Given the capabilities AdAttester could peek the device input and screen through TrustZone's eyes, AdAttester needs to mitigate the potentially possible abuses that could be gained by either malicious ads or applications. For screen display data, since AdAttester calculates the eigenvalue of the displayed ads and transfers the 64-bit-long eigenvalue to normal world AdAttester Service upon an attested call, this eigenvalue could be leaked to attackers. However, the algorithm for generating the eigenvalue is a one-way operation and attackers could get little valuable information from it. For input data, although AdAttester does not send the touch position outside the secure world, there are two scenarios to be discussed based on different threat model: one is that the normal world is completely compromised and the other is that only the ads or applications are malicious.

In the first scenario, because the touch input data will eventually be delivered to the normal world, attackers could easily get the input data even without AdAttester. In the second scenario, a malicious ad or app may ask TZAttester to attest non-existent ads so that after requesting for attesting ads, the malicious ad or app could know the regions where a user clicks. However, this is not feasible because AdAttester Service in the untrusted OS will keep track of ad view states and if an ad asks for tracking a non-display ad or asks for tracking when the application is not in the foreground, AdAttester Service will refuse to serve it. AdAttester may suffer from deputy or mediation attacks [14] which also exist in current mobile ads, AdAttester doesn't make it easier or leak out more privacy information than existing solutions and this kind of attacks could be prevented using ad separation (see Section 11).

**Deployability and Incentives:** Although AdAttester requires slight modification to existing mobile OS and ad libraries, ad providers and users as well as vendors could have the incentives to use and deploy, and the deployment effort of AdAttester for each party is small, the solution, on the other hand, could benefit the whole ecosystem of mobile advertising. (1) For ad providers, they have the incentives to deploy AdVerifier in their ad server on top of their existing ad infrastructures and adopt the APIs for attesting ads to their mobile ad SDKs which only requires several lines of code modification because it could significant prevent mobile ad frauds and thus reduce their loss. (2) Although mobile vendors are required to modify normal world OS to track ad views, the modification is largely independent and only requires adding hundreds of Java code. Besides, mobile vendors today are always optimistic to provide new features in their products, especially giving that mobile advertisement is now a major income for application developers. (3) For mobile users, they are required to install TZAttester as a trusted application in the secure OS, which is easy to deploy. By deploying TZAttester, mobile users benefit from costing network consumption due to stealthy ad requests reduction and from potential risks when a bot steals ad requests on behalf of the user. Besides, AdAttester could bring some new business scenarios where mobile users could benefit directly. For example, content providers could pay for the traffic generated by mobile users watching their ads, promotions or visiting their websites and AdAttester could provide trusted proofs to content providers.

# 7. IMPLEMENTATION

We have implemented the mobile side of AdAttester on a TrustZone-enabled development board called Samsung Exynos 4412, which is equipped ARM Cortex-A9 processor at the frequency of 1.4GHz. The system running in the normal world is Android Ice Cream Sandwich (Android 4.0 version), with Linux kernel version 3.0.2. The secure OS running in the secure world is T6 [9], a secure OS for ARM with TrustZone support. The trusted TZAttester runs as a Trusted Application in T6. We implemented the server side (the AdVerifier of AdAttester) on a 2-core machine equipped with Intel Xeon CPU E3-1230 V2 at 3.30GHz, which runs Ubuntu 12.04.

**Device Configuration** We use a development board instead of a mobile phone to implement and evaluate AdAttester as we need to get the authority from the phone manufactures to sign the TZAttester as a Trusted Application. Through the development board, we have full control of the secure world and thus can deploy our own secure OS and the TZAttester. One limitation with our board is that it does not have fused a public key pair and disallows us from flashing one into the secure fuses. We address this problem by hard-coding the public key pair in the secure OS image and envision a future in which device key is certified by trusted CAs instead of the vendors themselves.

**System Boot** Devices with TrustZone support will start in the secure world and run a secure world firmware after executing a vender-specific bootloader. Originally, in Samsung SoC, the secure world firmware (called *tzsw*) is proprietary and close-sourced. We replace it with a secure bootloader to control the secure world software. The secure bootloader will load the secure OS image and check the signature of the image using its embedded public key to ensure the integrity before executing T6. T6 will setup the secure environment, including partitioning the secure and non-secure memory in TZASC (reserving 16MB for the secure world used by T6 and leaving others for the normal world), setting the touch input and display controller peripheral as secure peripherals in TZPC. Note that interrupts that belongs to the touch input and display controller will be set as secure interrupt and thus will be handled by T6. After configuration, T6 will switch to the normal world to execute the normal world bootloader and boot Android.

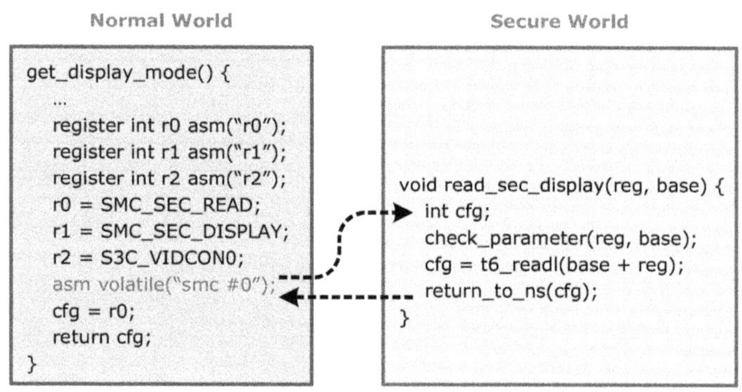


Figure 8: World switch when accessing display controller. A read or write operation on secure registers is changed to a crossing world call

**Secure Input and Reliable Display** Touch screen peripheral is protected from the normal world by setting the TZPC at startup and its driver is implemented in the secure world. A shared memory region between worlds is created for exchanging input data. We created a kernel workqueue, which waits on a variable and copies the input data in the shared memory region to the input buffer (using linked list) of the Linux input core (input subsystem). When the touch input driver in the secure world receives a completed sequence of input data (ABS_X, ABS_Y, ABS_PRESSURE, etc.), it will copy the data to the shared buffer and notify the normal world kernel workqueue by setting its waited variable.

Display controller is also set to be a secure peripheral in TZPC at system startup. Because the purpose of setting the display controller as secure is to get a reliable display content, which could not be faked by the normal world software. Specifically, TZAttester needs to get the exact display data from display framebuffer and if the display controller is controlled by untrusted software, TZAttester may get a faked framebuffer. To achieve this while keeping the modification of original code as small as possible, we modify the display controller driver in the normal world explicitly by changing the access of the peripheral registers to an SMC call (see Figure 8). To determine the exact address of the framebuffer, TZAttester could directly read the corresponding registers of the display controller in the secure world. The data format read from the framebuffer is RGB and TZAttester will convert it into jpeg format and use average hash algorithm [24] to calculate the eigenvalue of the displayed data.

**TZAttester Execution** AdAttester tracks all ad views in the Android view system layer and will notify the trusted TZAttester in secure world when an ad view is shown, resized and hidden. To omit some unnecessary crossing world notifications, changes of those ad views that are covered at least half of their size, either unintentional or on purpose (e.g., placement fraud), will not be notified to trusted TZAttester.

AdAttester Service is implemented as a privileged system service of Android that passively waits for attestation requests from ad libraries in applications. Ad libraries need to be modified to use attestation interface, but their modifications are quite small. The only change is to call AdAttester Service using the provided APIs to obtain an attestation blob when tracking ad actions and sending ad requests.

**AdVerifier Implementation** The AdVerifier of AdAttester locates at the ad server to process ad requests. The feature extraction phase module is a separated program implemented in Python. It takes images or videos as inputs, splits the images or videos into separated image frames and uses an image feature extraction algorithm to generate ad image features. Note that the image feature extraction algorithm is the same as the one implemented in mobile trusted TZAttester.

The online checking phase module is implemented in PHP code and we use nginx as its HTTP server. When an ad request comes, it will first check whether the request is signed. If so, it will decrypt the packet and check the validity of the nonce value. Here is the validating process on nonce value: each ad response from ad server contains a server timestamp (i.e., 2014-12-05-23-18-18), the mobile client incrementally generates the nonce value based on this timestamp. The server checks the nonce value assuring it is strictly larger than the old one it previously receives which is stored in the server but does not exceed the one based on current timestamp. If the nonce is valid, it will get the ad view display image feature from the packet, then retrieve the image feature data according to the ad ID from the ad request and compare the data with the ad request one.

# 8. AD FRAUD DETECTION EVALUATION

This section evaluates the effectiveness of AdAttester by the ad fraud apps from MAdFraud [16], which were crawled from several major app markets and filtered from 130,339 apps. As some of the ads in the fraudulent apps cannot be executed in our phones and we only instrument one version of each Ad SDK, we only use 182 out of 1,000 typical ad fraud apps from MAdFraud, as shown in Table 2

## 8.1 Dataset and Evaluation Methods

### *8.1.1 Ad SDK Instrumentation*

Since the ad libraries need to be modified to use AdAttester, we need to instrument those ad libraries to invoke the APIs provided by AdAttester. Table 2 shows the ad SDKs we instrumented and their corresponding number of tested ad fraud apps. Admob and Doubleclick are grouped into 'Admob' as they appear together at most of time and apps that contain more than one ad SDKs are counted several times. Ad SDKs are either close-sourced or open-sourced. For the open-sourced ones, we instrument the source code by calling AdAttester Service and adding the attested blob to the ad request before the SDK wants to send ad request and then generate a jar package. Then we replace the existing ad package with our new one and repackage the apps. For the close-sourced ones, we manually decompile and analyze ad SDKs to instrument the necessary code. Here we show how we instrument the SDKs by explaining a close-sourced ad SDK named Admob and an open-sourced ad SDK named Mopub.

Table 2: Top instrumented ad SDKs. *Total*: number of fraud apps in total, *Version*: instrumented SDK version, *Tested Num*: number of tested apps

| *SDK Name* | *Total* | *Percentage* | *Version* | *Tested Num* |
|---|---|---|---|---|
| Google Ads | 791 | 79.1% | 6.0.1 | 48 |
| Millennialmedia | 155 | 15.5% | 4.2.6 | 21 |
| Inmobi | 95 | 9.5% | 3.6.x | 23 |
| Airpush | 64 | 6.4% | 4.0.2 | 33 |
| Mobfox | 60 | 6.0% | 1.4 | 12 |
| Mobclix | 46 | 4.6% | 4.0.x | 10 |
| Cauly | 40 | 4.0% | 1.2.5 | 8 |
| Smaato | 38 | 3.8% | 2.5.2 | 13 |
| Mdotm | 29 | 2.9% | 2.0.2 | 3 |
| Waps | 28 | 2.8% | 1.5.x | 14 |
| Inneractive | 27 | 2.7% | 3.1.7 | 9 |
| Adlantis | 26 | 2.6% | 1.3.7 | 5 |
| Domob | 24 | 2.4% | 1.5 | 12 |
| Adwo | 19 | 1.9% | 2.5.1 | 5 |
| Youmi | 18 | 1.8% | 3.0 | 10 |
| Mopub | 17 | 1.7% | 1.9.x | 5 |
| Nend | 15 | 1.5% | 1.2.1 | 7 |
| Vpon | 14 | 1.4% | 3.0.3 | 5 |
| Wiyun | 13 | 1.3% | 1.2.3 | 2 |
| Chartboost | 10 | 1.0% | 3.1.5 | 2 |
| Guohead | 8 | 0.8% | 1.6.8 | 3 |
| Applovin | 8 | 0.8% | 5.0.0 | 4 |
| Appmedia | 7 | 0.7% | 1.1.0 | 3 |
| Wooboo | 7 | 0.7% | 1.2 | 3 |
| Casee | 5 | 0.5% | 2.7 | 3 |
| Adsmogo | 2 | 0.2% | 1.2.8 | 1 |

**Admob**: Admob SDK is a closed-source ad library owned by Google and is now offered through Google Play services. Google uses code obfuscation techniques to protect its SDK library, which increases the difficulty of analysis tremendously. By careful instrumentations, we locate the exact location (i.e., *AdActivity.smali*) where an URL is opened as a response to the click event. We insert code there to call the system service to get attested blob and append it to the URL as parameter. Impression tracking, however, is more complex because we need to instrument several methods distributed in different files, namely internal/d.smali, internal/c.smali and internal/g.smali.

**MoPub**: MoPub SDK [6] is an open-source ad library owned by MoPub Inc. and is used as an ad mediation network provider. It is easy to instrument with the availability of source code and official documents. We download version v3.2 from Github and modify the following files. First, we add a function getAttesterBlob() in MoPubView to get attesterBlob by calling AdAttester Service. Then, we modify adClicked() in MoPubView to call getAttesterBlob() and store the attesterBlob value in AdConfiguration, which contains the configuration information of MoPub SDK. Finally, in registerClick(), which is located in AdViewController.java and starts a new thread to handle the click event(naming starting a new Activity, such as browser or APP market), we update the mClickThroughUrl using the attesterBlob in AdConfiguration. Thus, the attesterBlob is added to the requesting URL. The impression tracking is easy because there is an isolated file called *ImpressionTrackingManager.java* that manages the impression tracking and we just need to instrument this file.

For each ad SDK, we only instrumented one version of it. Among the instrumented ones, some ad fraud apps are useless and discarded due to at least one of the three problems: (1) they cannot display ad views in our board, probably because their fraud behavior has already been discovered by ad providers; (2) they can-

Table 3: Fraudulent behavior among the tested apps

| Fraud Type | Fraud Apps |
|---|---|
| Frequent Ad Requests | 154 |
| Ads Outside Screen | 23 |
| Ads Covered/Hidden | 63 |
| Ads Too Small | 9 |
| Unaware Click | 0 |

not run due to incompatibility in Android SDK version; (3) some apps have self-integrity check and refuses to start after being instrumented. The right two columns of Table 2 show the SDK versions we instrumented and the number of fraud apps we successfully ran.

We discarded a few ad SDKs including Madhouse, Adhub and Energysource because most of apps that embedded these SDKs also include some other ad SDKs which we have instrumented. We manually double checked that the instrumentation for each app worked correctly.

### *8.1.2 Online And Offline Analysis through Proxy*

Since we do not have the original ad data, we set up a proxy server to redirect all ad network packets of our device so that we could get the ad data for testing the effectiveness of AdAttester. Our requirement is that this test environment should not require any modification to our ad framework AdAttester and existing ad ecosystem. To meet this requirement, we use *iptables* to configure network of target ad apps in our test device and redirect all ad network packets to our own server for analysis by creating a daemon with root privileged to execute the *iptables* scripts. The remote AdVerifier components are deployed in the proxy server. The proxy server will receive all the ad network packets and send them to the AdVerifier, which will validate ad frauds of those requests and write the result and behavior into a file for further analysis. Then it will modify the ad packets by removing the attestation blob that added by TZAttester in the mobile client and send them to the real ad server.

Each fraudulent app was run twice, each for around 90 seconds to 2 minutes. In the first run, we open the app and traverse all pages to find pages that contain ads without clicking them. In the second run, we reopen the app and click every visible ad we could see. In both runs, we use an Android tool called *hierarchyviewer* to see detail structure of hierarchy view of the app and manually find any placement frauds and/or unaware user click frauds. After the two rounds, we analyze the ad request log in our proxy server. Together with the potential placement frauds, we compare the results derived from AdVerifier with our manual analysis to determine if they were accurately detected.

We also simulated a bot-like ad fraud by writing a script in the test board to simulate clicks. Not surprisingly, as these bot-driven clicks are not signed by AdAttester and thus can by easily identified by the AdVerifier in the ad server.

## 8.2 Ad Fraud Findings

**Fraudulent Behavior:** Table 3 shows the fraudulent behavior among our tested apps. Most of the apps send ad requests frequently (at an interval of 3s to 20s), even when there are no ads visible on the screen. However, most of these frequent ad requests are not signed by TZAttester and thus will not be paid. We then carefully read the developer manual of several ad SDKs and find many of them provide an API to periodically fetch ads from ad server. We conclude that most of these frequent fetching ad requests are not intentional frauds, probably due to the carelessness of misusing the provided API or app developers want to have different ad content displayed to users to have a higher click rate. Besides the frequent ad requests, a large portion of ad requests contain impression frauds. The fraudulent behavior includes: using a floating and user-friendly element (such as an image) to cover displayed ad, putting an ad outside of the screen and a user needs to scroll up to see the ad, setting the height of an ad to zero to hide the ad from the user. These impression requests are signed by our TZAttester and considered fraudulent by our AdVerifier.

Table 4: Benchmark scores using AnTuTu

| AuTuTu Test | Original Android | AdAttester Android | Overhead |
|---|---|---|---|
| Total Score | 16322 | 16191 | 0.80% |
| 2D Graphic | 2280 | 2268 | 0.53% |
| 3D Graphic | 4580 | 4561 | 0.41% |

Interestingly, we find some apps put several ad views from different ad SDKs to the same position and these ad libraries send impression almost simultaneously but at most one of them is treated legal by our AdVerifier. We also find several apps resize ad views to too small to be recognized (since we don't know how small a view will be considered fraudulent by ad providers, we treat any ad views smaller than 32*32 as illegal in our test). However, in our tested applications we did not find apps that have unaware click frauds and all clicks the ad AdVerifier has checked are triggered by our clicks and legally signed by TZAttester.

**False Positives:** Among over 600 legal ad clicks, 13 of them are considered illegal by the ad AdVerifier. Further analysis shows all the 13 clicks are banner ad clicks and happened when banner ads are changing their image content to another ad content with animation. When the content of an ad region is changing from one ad image to another in progress with animation, the eigenvalue of the ad region is quite different with all possible values we have in our database and thus is considered invalid ad request. To eliminate this kind of false positives, we suggest ad SDK providers to disable click event dispatching when a banner ad is changing its ad image with animation or more aggressively, they could disable ad animation directly during changing content to another ad image. It should be noted that all these false positives occurred only when an ad view is changing its content from one ad to another and video ads (i.e., video media and GIF image) will not have any false positive because all the possible eigenvalues of video ads are already calculated and included during offline feature extraction phase.

There is also another possible source of false positive. If a user happens to click an ad during the ad's self-animation, a wrong eigenvalue might be generated. A trivial solution is to simply disable self-animation, which is not general enough. We propose another solution called *Double-Snapshot* to detect and handle such rare cases. During offline feature extraction phase, we calculate eigenvalue of all the possible animating frame that an ad image may have and discard some eigenvalues that could violate the ad guidelines (i.e., 80% of ad image is hidden). When a user clicks the ad, TZAttester will get two snapshots: the first one on the touch-down event and the second on the touch-up event. TZAttester then detects "click in the middle of self-animation" by the two snapshots. If that is the case, TZAttester will use the eigenvalues of animation set in AdVerifier to verify the legality of the ad click.

# 9. PERFORMANCE EVALUATION

## 9.1 Ad View Tracking Overhead

We evaluate the performance impact of tracking ad views on applications. We use a popular Android benchmarking tool named AnTuTu [8], which runs a series of tests and provides a score re-

Table 5: Input latency comparison

| Original Android | Android with AdAttester |
|---|---|
| 66.92 ms | 66.94 ms |

port. We run the benchmark 10 times, each time with a reboot to eliminate impact caused by other factors (i.e., different system workload), then calculate the average score. Table 4 shows the performance data (higher score is better). Most of the impact from AdAttester is in the view system of Android graphics and other parts such as SDCard, memory access, float operation and integer operation are not affected by AdAttester. Thus, we omit those scores from the final results. From the result, it can be seen that AdAttester imposes almost no overhead on 2D graphics (0.53%) and 3D graphics (0.41%). This is because the access of display controller (read and write operation) is mostly done at system starts and will not be frequently updated in latter usage.

## 9.2 Input Event Handling Latency

The input latency is calculated by the execution time from the moment an input interrupt comes to the point that the input data is received by applications. Specifically, the input latency is the interval between an input interrupt which is generated by a user's touch input arrives at the interrupt handler in *ft5x0x_ts_interrupt()* and the touch input data is received by the applications through touch handler called *onTouchEvent()* in Android app. The extra input latency introduced by AdAttester includes two world switches, some ad states checking and shared data copy. World switch from secure world to normal world costs 1858 cycles and switches from normal world to secure world costs 2041 cycles. We measured the input latency of AdAttester and the latency running in the original Android for 50 times separately and calculated the averaged value. Evaluation result in Table 5 shows that there is almost no overhead incurred by putting input device driver to secure world.

## 9.3 Ad Network Traffic

We evaluate the increase on ad network traffic using 20 apps embedded with different ad SDKs from the top list in Google Play. First, we run these apps for 2 minutes normally without clicking ads. Second, we run them for 2 minutes and click every ad the app holds. Table 6 shows the results. The network traffic increase is less than 3.3%, which is very small compared to the original ad network traffic because the only traffic increase is from tracking impressions and clicks, which is quite small comparing to the overall traffic. During tracking ad impressions and clicks, the additional network traffic for one attested packet is never larger than 35% and mostly less than 20%.

## 9.4 AdVerifier Response Latency

AdVerifier processes ad attestation requests and we measured the introduced performance slowdown by simulating 100 to 1,500 concurrent user requests using Apache Benchmark [1]. The test was done in a local network environment and we used SHA1 hash algorithm to calculate the hash of message blob and 1024-bit modulus for RSA signature. The number of public keys stored in the server is 500,00. Figure 9 shows the service latency (in ms) results with and without AdVerifier. The average latency increased is 0.04 ms, which should be an acceptable overhead.

## 9.5 Other Evaluation

**Time Cost to Generate Attestation Blob in AdAttester:** Generating an attestation blob is computing-intensive and we used

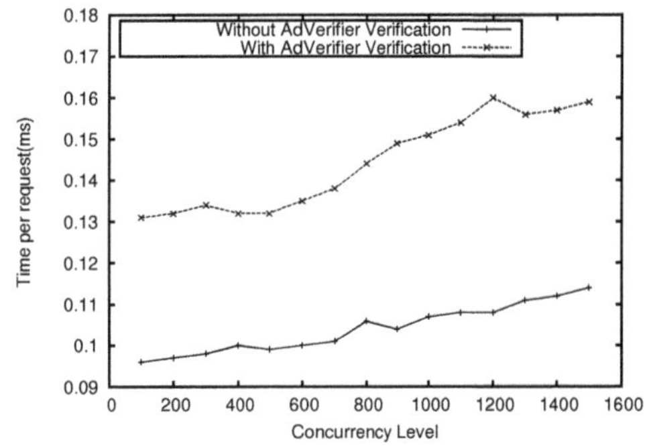


Figure 9: AdVerifier response latency compared with ad service without AdVerifier in a 2-core server. We used SHA1 for hashing and 1024-bit modulus for RSA signature

Table 7: Duration for getting an attestation blob

| RSA Key Size (byte) | Duration (ms) |
|---|---|
| 512 | 0.68 |
| 1024 | 3.73 |
| 2048 | 25.56 |

SHA1 hashing algorithm and RSA signing with different size of keys for generating attestation blob. The hashing time is negligible compared with RSA signing. Table 7 shows the evaluation result. AdAttester uses an asynchronous notification for generating attestation blob and ad libraries could use batching to attest ad requests if this overhead matters. The above results were got using software-only encryptions and this duration could be further reduced using hardware accelerated RSA encryption available in SoC, which will be our future improvement work.

**Implementation Complexity and TCB Size:** The TCB of AdAttester in the mobile client is the software running in the secure world. The secure OS, T6, contains about 6,000 LoC. TZAttester is less than 600 LoC. The secure input driver and display peripheral operation handling contain about 800 LoC. The TCB size in total is less than 7,400 LoC, which is very small. In the normal world, the implementation of tracking ad views in Android view system contains 164 source lines of java code distributed in two files and AdAttester Service has 325 source lines of Java code. In the remote AdVerifier, the feature extraction program contains 234 source lines of Python code and AdVerifier online checking contains 467 source lines of PHP code in our prototype.

# 10. DISCUSSIONS AND FUTURE WORK

**Relaxing Threat Model of AdAttester by Trusting OS:** While AdAttester could securely fight against malicious application developers and botnets, it requires the availability of per-device key, which may prevent AdAttester from being widely adopted. The main purpose of using device key is to prove that the request comes from a real mobile device which is hard to be compromised (using TrustZone) instead of a rogue device. Directly relaxing our threat model by trusting the OS and putting the secure TZAttester to normal OS could solve this problem, but comes at cost: it may become a little hard to defect frauds from botnets. This problem could be mitigated by using software-based attestation [36] [38], which will be our future work to explore.

**Attest Ads to Developers:** Currently, AdAttester mainly consider the case of mobile ad frauds by the developers and botnets. One interesting question is how to attest ad impressions and clicks

Table 6: Network traffic increase

| App Name | Ad SDK | Total /bytes | Impression /bytes | Click /bytes | Impression Increase /bytes, percentage | Click Increase /bytes, percentage | Overall Increase /bytes, percentage |
|---|---|---|---|---|---|---|---|
| Jumper | Inmobi<br>Mobclix<br>Smaato | 63277 | 3728 | 1991 | 1280, 34.3% | 128, 6.4% | 1408, 2.2% |
| English Norwegian | Google Ads | 17245 | 1314 | 6071 | 320, 24.4% | 256, 42.8% | 576, 3.3% |
| Solitaire | Inmobi<br>Google Ads<br>Millennialmedia | 42495 | 3989 | 4378 | 960, 24.1% | 128, 19.7% | 1088, 2.6% |
| Big Snake | Mopub<br>Airpush<br>Google Ads<br>Millennialmedia | 25398 | 2760 | 876 | 640, 23.2% | 128, 14.3% | 768, 3.0% |
| Despicable Me Skills | Google Ads | 11957 | 1235 | 1573 | 160, 13.0% | 128, 14.3% | 288, 2.4% |
| Electric Bliss Wallpapers | Inneractive<br>Google Ads<br>Millennialmedia | 49220 | 2357 | 1140 | 480, 13.0% | 128, 14.3% | 608, 1.2% |
| Zimane Kurdi | Google Ads | 37144 | 2357 | 4024 | 480, 20.4% | 128, 7.1% | 608, 1.6% |
| Alien Destroyer | Google Ads<br>Airpush | 35188 | 2358 | 6343 | 480, 20.4% | 256, 17.2% | 736, 2.1% |
| Indian Newspapers | Inneractive<br>Google Ads<br>Millennialmedia | 97292 | 7973 | 1137 | 1600, 20.1% | 128, 9.4% | 1728, 1.8% |
| Quiz des Communestet | Google Ads | 59806 | 4829 | 2111 | 960, 19.9% | 128, 11.6% | 1088, 1.8% |

to the developers. Though many ad providers are relatively reputed, this research question is still relevant since the ad providers may also have the incentives to deceive the developers in order to pay less. Considering mutual distrust between ad providers and developers, AdAttester could be further extended to send collected proofs (could be summary stats) to developers such that they can use the proofs to attest the ad providers if developers found significant deviation in their revenues. We leave this as our future work.

**Multiple Ads on One Page:** Currently, as AdAttester relies on the commodity software stack to know which ad is current on screen, AdAttester cannot detect mobile ads that violate the ad policy of the ad provider, which usually only allow one ad on one page to minimize impact on users' experiences. Fortunately, this may still be distinguished by the ad providers though statistical analysis, which we will study in our future work.

# 11. RELATED WORK

AdAttester is motivated by the urgent need of a verifiable approach for ad impression and clicks; it differs from prior work in that it is the first to provide verifiable mobile ad attestation to reliably detect mobile ad frauds online.

**Mobile Ad Separation** There are several systems focusing on restricting the privilege of advertising code in the mobile client. AdSplit [37] puts the advertisement into a separate activity and passes all requests from the activity onto a newly introduced advertisement service. AdDroid [34] encapsulates the ad libraries into Android framework and introduces a new advertising API to allow applications to show ads without requesting privacy-sensitive permissions. AFrame [46] isolates ad libraries by covering not only the process and permission isolation, but also the display and input isolation.

**Ad Privacy Preserving.** Another line of research on advertisement is to protect users' private information. Privad [22] provides a faster and more private advertising framework by using a client to locally serve ad and introducing a dealer server to separate ad requests in web advertising. Adnostic [39] proposes client-side software that provides target ads to a user without compromising user privacy. ObliviAd [11] uses secure hardware (i.e., secure processor) in the ad server for private information retrieval aiming at providing two privacy goals: profile privacy and profile unlinkability. These systems are complementary to AdAttester and may further improve the privacy of AdAttester.

**Web Advertising Fraud.** Ad fraud has been studied extensively for years in online web advertising. Daswani [17] gives an overview on techniques of web ad frauds; Miller et al. [31] summarize techniques and innovations of today's clickbots. Prior work on detecting bot-driven click frauds mainly analyzes query logs [44] in search engine to aggregate ad traffic across IP addresses [30], or through complex analysis from peer-to-peer measurements and command-and-control telemetry [33]. NAB [23] uses TPM to attest user actions by analyzing mouse and keyboard activity to identify and certify human-generated activity, thus filter out bot-driven clicks and spam. However, NAB doesn't address the problem of ad verification and the approach they took to deal with bot-driven clicks isn't feasible for mobile devices.

**Mobile Advertising Fraud.** Though ad frauds have been relatively well-studied in desktop environments, there are very few research studies on mobile ad frauds. Existing approaches mainly focus on offline testing to detect ad frauds. DECAF [26] characterizes ad fraud in mobile apps and proposes offline techniques to detect display fraud on Windows-based mobile platforms by using automated testing. The techniques they used are analyzing the status of ad UI offline to determine whether ads are hidden, obfuscated or stacked. MAdFraud [16] studies mobile ad fraud perpetrated by Android apps and identifies two kinds of fraudulent behavior: requesting ads in the background and clicking on ads without user interaction. They further developed an analysis tool to automatically trigger and expose ad fraud in Android emulators. However, the intrinsic limitation of offline testing on coverage and the lack of a reliable way to distinguish benign from fraud ads make it hard for such approaches to detecting sophisticated means of doing frauds, especially bot-driven frauds. In contrast, the verifiable nature of AdAttester makes it cryptographically reliable to identify ad frauds.

**Attestation Using TrustZone.** There are several systems that use TrustZone to provide attested data or actions. VeriUI [27] runs a Linux in TrustZone secure world to provide an attested login for users, which demonstrates that a responsive UI could be provided with a small attack surface. The attested login augments user credentials with a certificate describing the software and hardware that handled the credentials. TrustedSensors [28] uses TrustZone to attest sensors data and provides two sensor abstractions, namely sensor attestation and sensor seal. SIMlets [35] splits the bill for mobile data using TrustZone and allows content providers to pay for the traffic generated by mobile users visiting their websites or using their services. TrustUI [25] uses TrustZone to provde trusted paths between mobile user and mobile device as well as between mobile device and remote service without trusting the device drivers.

## 12. CONCLUSION

This paper argued that the lack of verifiable ad attestation proofs is a key obstacle to defend against mobile ad frauds. To this end, this paper described AdAttester, a system that effectively detects and prevents well-known ad frauds. AdAttester is enabled by two primitives, namely *verifiable display* and *unforgeable clicks*, which securely attests to the ad sever whether an impression or a click is actually delivered to or conducted by a real user. The two primitives have been implemented using ARM TrustZone to exclude the commodity software stack out of the TCB. Based on these two primitives, AdAttester successfully checked the legality of every ad click and impression request by determining whether the ad request violates predefined rules. We have implemented AdAttester on a Samsung Exynos 4412 board, which runs Android as the mobile operating systems. Evaluations with a set of mobile ad frauds that use all well-known ad SDKs confirmed that AdAttester can reliably detect ad frauds, while incurring small performance overhead and little impact on user experience.

## Acknowledgments

We thank our shepherd Landon Cox and the anonymous reviewers for their insightful comments, Prof. Hao Chen for making their mobile ad fraud dataset available to us, our group member Liang Liang for helping us evaluate the performance impact of AdAttester. This work is supported in part by a research grant from Huawei Technologies, Inc., the National Natural Science Foundation of China (No. 61303011), the Program for New Century Excellent Talents in University, Ministry of Education of China (No. ZXZY037003), a foundation for the Author of National Excellent Doctoral Dissertation of PR China (No. TS0220103006), the Shanghai Science and Technology Development Fund for high-tech achievement translation (No. 14511100902), a research grant from Intel and the Singapore NRF (CREATE E2S2).

## 13. REFERENCES

[1] Apache http server benchmarking tool. `http://httpd.apache.org/docs/2.2/programs/ab.html`.

[2] Trusted execution environment of globalplatform. `http://www.globalplatform.org/specificationsdevice.asp`.

[3] Bots are hot, but publishers and advertisers are cold to combating the situation. `http://www.adexchanger.com/online-advertising/bots-are-hot-but-publishers-and-advertisers-are-cold-to-combating-the-situation/`, 2013.

[4] Bots mobilize. `http://www.dmnews.com/bots-mobilize/article/291566/`, 2013.

[5] Bots win! nonhuman ad impressions still selling like hotcakes. `http://www.adexchanger.com/online-advertising/bots-win-non-human-ads-still-selling-like-hotcakes/`, 2013.

[6] Mopub android sdk. `https://github.com/mopub/mopub-android-sdk`, 2013.

[7] Admob publisher guidelines and policies. `https://support.google.com/admob/answer/2753860?hl=en`, 2014.

[8] Antutu benchmark. `https://play.google.com/store/apps/details?id=com.google.android.stardroid&hl=en`, 2014.

[9] T6, a secure os and tee for mobile devices. `http://trustkernel.org/`, 2015.

[10] T. Alves and D. Felton. Trustzone: Integrated hardware and software security. *ARM white paper*, 3(4), 2004.

[11] M. Backes, A. Kate, M. Maffei, and K. Pecina. Obliviad: Provably secure and practical online behavioral advertising. In *Security and Privacy (SP), 2012 IEEE Symposium on*, pages 257–271. IEEE, 2012.

[12] H. Bay, T. Tuytelaars, and L. Van Gool. Surf: Speeded up robust features. In *Computer Vision–ECCV 2006*, pages 404–417. Springer, 2006.

[13] E. Brickell, J. Camenisch, and L. Chen. Direct anonymous attestation. In *Proceedings of the 11th ACM conference on Computer and communications security*, pages 132–145. ACM, 2004.

[14] S. Bugiel, L. Davi, A. Dmitrienko, T. Fischer, A.-R. Sadeghi, and B. Shastry. Towards taming privilege-escalation attacks on android. In *NDSS*, 2012.

[15] P. Chen, D. Yang, W. Zhang, Y. Li, B. Zang, and H. Chen. Adaptive pipeline parallelism for image feature extraction algorithms. In *Parallel Processing (ICPP), 2012 41st International Conference on*, pages 299–308. IEEE, 2012.

[16] J. Crussell, R. Stevens, and H. Chen. Madfraud: investigating ad fraud in android applications. In *Proceedings of the 12th*

*annual international conference on Mobile systems, applications, and services*, pages 123–134. ACM, 2014.

[17] N. Daswani, C. Mysen, V. Rao, S. Weis, K. Gharachorloo, and S. Ghosemajumder. Online advertising fraud. *Crimeware: understanding new attacks and defenses*, 2008.

[18] V. Dave, S. Guha, and Y. Zhang. Measuring and fingerprinting click-spam in ad networks. In *Proceedings of the ACM SIGCOMM 2012 conference on Applications, technologies, architectures, and protocols for computer communication*, pages 175–186. ACM, 2012.

[19] emakerter. Driven by facebook and google, mobile ad market soars 105http://www.emarketer.com/Article/Driven-by-Facebook-Google-Mobile-Ad-Market-Soars-10537-2013/1010690, 2014.

[20] Z. Fang, D. Yang, W. Zhang, H. Chen, and B. Zang. A comprehensive analysis and parallelization of an image retrieval algorithm. In *Performance Analysis of Systems and Software (ISPASS), 2011 IEEE International Symposium on*, pages 154–164. IEEE, 2011.

[21] L. Guan, J. Lin, B. Luo, and J. Jing. Copker: Computing with private keys without ram. 2014.

[22] S. Guha, B. Cheng, and P. Francis. Privad: Practical privacy in online advertising. In *NSDI*, 2011.

[23] R. Gummadi, H. Balakrishnan, P. Maniatis, and S. Ratnasamy. Not-a-bot (nab): Improving service availability in the face of botnet attacks. 2009.

[24] N. Krawetz. Perceptual hash algorithm: the average hash algorithm. http://www.hackerfactor.com/blog/?/archives/432-Looks-Like-It.html.

[25] W. Li, M. Ma, J. Han, Y. Xia, B. Zang, C.-K. Chu, and T. Li. Building trusted path on untrusted device drivers for mobile devices. In *Proceedings of 5th Asia-Pacific Workshop on Systems*, page 8. ACM, 2014.

[26] B. Liu, S. Nath, R. Govindan, and J. Liu. Decaf: detecting and characterizing ad fraud in mobile apps. In *Proceedings of the 11th USENIX Conference on Networked Systems Design and Implementation*, pages 57–70. USENIX Association, 2014.

[27] D. Liu and L. P. Cox. Veriui: Attested login for mobile devices. In *Proceedings of the 15th Workshop on Mobile Computing Systems and Applications*, page 7. ACM, 2014.

[28] H. Liu, S. Saroiu, A. Wolman, and H. Raj. Software abstractions for trusted sensors. In *Proceedings of the 10th international conference on Mobile systems, applications, and services*, pages 365–378. ACM, 2012.

[29] D. G. Lowe. Distinctive image features from scale-invariant keypoints. *International journal of computer vision*, 60(2):91–110, 2004.

[30] A. Metwally, D. Agrawal, and A. El Abbadi. Detectives: detecting coalition hit inflation attacks in advertising networks streams. In *Proceedings of the 16th international conference on World Wide Web*, pages 241–250. ACM, 2007.

[31] B. Miller, P. Pearce, C. Grier, C. Kreibich, and V. Paxson. Whatąŕs clicking what? techniques and innovations of todayąŕs clickbots. In *Detection of Intrusions and Malware, and Vulnerability Assessment*, pages 164–183. Springer, 2011.

[32] T. Müller, F. C. Freiling, and A. Dewald. Tresor runs encryption securely outside ram. In *USENIX Security Symposium*, pages 17–17, 2011.

[33] P. Pearce, V. Dave, C. Grier, K. Levchenko, S. Guha, D. McCoy, V. Paxson, S. Savage, and G. M. Voelker. Characterizing large-scale click fraud in zeroaccess. In *Proceedings of the 2014 ACM SIGSAC Conference on Computer and Communications Security*, CCS '14, pages 141–152, New York, NY, USA, 2014. ACM.

[34] P. Pearce, A. P. Felt, G. Nunez, and D. Wagner. Addroid: Privilege separation for applications and advertisers in android. In *Proceedings of the 7th ACM Symposium on Information, Computer and Communications Security*, pages 71–72. ACM, 2012.

[35] H. Raj, S. Saroiu, A. Wolman, and J. Padhye. Splitting the bill for mobile data with simlets. In *Proceedings of the 14th Workshop on Mobile Computing Systems and Applications*, page 1. ACM, 2013.

[36] A. Seshadri, A. Perrig, L. Van Doorn, and P. Khosla. Swatt: Software-based attestation for embedded devices. In *Security and Privacy, 2004. Proceedings. 2004 IEEE Symposium on*, pages 272–282. IEEE, 2004.

[37] S. Shekhar, M. Dietz, and D. S. Wallach. Adsplit: Separating smartphone advertising from applications. In *USENIX Security Symposium*, pages 553–567, 2012.

[38] E. G. Sirer, W. de Bruijn, P. Reynolds, A. Shieh, K. Walsh, D. Williams, and F. B. Schneider. Logical attestation: an authorization architecture for trustworthy computing. In *Proceedings of the Twenty-Third ACM Symposium on Operating Systems Principles*, pages 249–264. ACM, 2011.

[39] V. Toubiana, A. Narayanan, D. Boneh, H. Nissenbaum, and S. Barocas. Adnostic: Privacy preserving targeted advertising. In *NDSS*, 2010.

[40] E. Tromer, D. A. Osvik, and A. Shamir. Efficient cache attacks on aes, and countermeasures. *Journal of Cryptology*, 23(1):37–71, 2010.

[41] A. Vasudevan, S. Chaki, L. Jia, J. McCune, J. Newsome, and A. Datta. Design, implementation and verification of an extensible and modular hypervisor framework. In *Security and Privacy (SP), 2013 IEEE Symposium on*, pages 430–444. IEEE, 2013.

[42] Y. Xia, Y. Liu, and H. Chen. Architecture support for guest-transparent vm protection from untrusted hypervisor and physical attacks. In *High Performance Computer Architecture (HPCA2013), 2013 IEEE 19th International Symposium on*, pages 246–257. IEEE, 2013.

[43] Y. Yarom and K. Falkner. Flush+reload: A high resolution, low noise, l3 cache side-channel attack. In *23rd USENIX Security Symposium (USENIX Security 14)*, pages 719–732, San Diego, CA, Aug. 2014. USENIX Association.

[44] F. Yu, Y. Xie, and Q. Ke. Sbotminer: large scale search bot detection. In *Proceedings of the third ACM international conference on Web search and data mining*, pages 421–430. ACM, 2010.

[45] F. Zhang, J. Chen, H. Chen, and B. Zang. Cloudvisor: retrofitting protection of virtual machines in multi-tenant cloud with nested virtualization. In *Proceedings of the Twenty-Third ACM Symposium on Operating Systems Principles*, pages 203–216. ACM, 2011.

[46] X. Zhang, A. Ahlawat, and W. Du. Aframe: isolating advertisements from mobile applications in android. In *Proceedings of the 29th Annual Computer Security Applications Conference*, pages 9–18. ACM, 2013.

# Efficient Privilege De-Escalation for Ad Libraries in Mobile Apps

Bin Liu[*], Bin Liu[†], Hongxia Jin[*], Ramesh Govindan[‡]
[*]Samsung Research America, Mountain View, CA
[†]School of Computer Science, Carnegie Mellon University, Pittsburgh, PA
[‡]Department of Computer Science, University of Southern California, Los Angeles, CA
{bin2.liu, hongxia.jin}@samsung.com bliu1@cs.cmu.edu ramesh@usc.edu

## ABSTRACT

The proliferation of mobile apps is due in part to the advertising ecosystem which enables developers to earn revenue while providing free apps. Ad-supported apps can be developed rapidly with the availability of ad libraries. However, today's ad libraries essentially have access to the same resources as the parent app, and this has caused significant privacy concerns. In this paper, we explore efficient methods to de-escalate privileges for ad libraries where the resource access privileges for ad libraries can be different from that of the app logic. Our system, PEDAL, contains a novel machine classifier for detecting ad libraries even in the presence of obfuscated code, and techniques for automatically instrumenting bytecode to effect privilege de-escalation even in the presence of privilege inheritance. We evaluate PEDAL on a large set of apps from the Google Play store and demonstrate that it has a 98% accuracy in detecting ad libraries and imposes less than 1% runtime overhead on apps.

## Categories and Subject Descriptors

D.3.3 [**Programming Languages**]: Language Constructs and Features—*Modules, packages*; K.4.1 [**Computers and Society**]: Public Policy Issues—*Privacy*

## General Terms

Design, Experimentation, Languages, Measurement, Security

## Keywords

Previlege De-Escalation; Ad Libraries; Mobile Apps; Static Analysis; App Instrumentation

## 1. INTRODUCTION

Mobile device usage has reached astronomical levels in recent years. According to a recent report from Gartner Forecasts [12], Android device shipments alone are predicted to hit 1.17 billion by the end of 2014. Much of this growth has been fueled by two factors: the ease of app development, and the availability of free apps.


*MobiSys'15*, May 18–22, 2015, Florence, Italy.
Copyright © 2015 ACM 978-1-4503-3494-5/15/05 ...$15.00.
http://dx.doi.org/10.1145/2742647.2742668.

The ease of app development has been enabled in part by system support for component-oriented development [10], in which app developers can easily integrate libraries (sometimes from third-parties) as components of their app. In the Android ecosystem, libraries are used for various purposes. Social SDKs, like Facebook, Twitter4j and WeChat, allow developers to integrate popular social elements to their apps. Development tools, such as ActionbarSherlock, HoloEverywhere and GeocoderPlus, provide developers with feature-rich and relatively well-maintained plugins for enhancing, say the utility, UI, and image processing capabilities of their apps.

The availability of free apps has been enabled by an ad ecosystem in which app publishers incorporate ad delivery software in their apps. This software is provided by ad networks who contract with advertisers to deliver ads to end users. App developers are paid by ad networks either by the number of times ads are seen by users, or the number of times they are clicked, or some combination thereof. More than 83% of apps [11] in Google Play are free and developers of free apps mostly rely on advertising for revenue [58].

To facilitate ad delivery, ad networks provide *ad libraries* to app developers. Ad libraries, like AdMob, InMobi and Vungle, offer developers solutions for monetizing their apps by showing ads to app users. To show ads in their apps, developers need to bundle ad SDKs in their app code to display ads to users through corresponding ad widgets. These ad widgets can communicate with their ad networks to fetch and show proper ads, according to apps' context or users' information, such as location.

In this ecosystem, incentives are skewed against the user. Developers have the incentive to deliver the most relevant apps to maximize their revenue, as do ad networks. This results in ad libraries taking unwarranted liberties with personal data on devices in order to more efficiently target ads. As a result, although users seem to understand the privacy risks with using mobile apps in general [19], they are especially concerned about privacy risks posed by ad libraries [54]. An extensive user study [43] points out that "mobile advertising services were a consistent privacy concern for the most participants" and users "felt the least comfortable when private resources were used for advertising." In another previous study [41] on location privacy of mobile advertising, users stated that they would "feel more comfortable" with advanced privacy controls than "with a simple opt-in/out-out mechanism".

One approach to this problem is to selectively *de-escalate privileges* to each component of an app. In this way, an ad library can have fewer privileges than the app logic itself. The Android access control model, which governs access to sensitive data such as location, identifiers, and contacts, and which has not evolved significantly over many releases, is also too coarse-grained to permit such privilege de-escalation. The current access control model allows users to specify *permissions* at app install time, and these permissions apply to all components of the app. In response to this, there is a large literature that has explored finer-grained access control methods (Section 8). In general, these methods are effective but require significant changes to the underlying OS, or, when they do not require such changes, can sometimes be ineffective in enforcing access to sensitive data. Moreover, simple solutions that deny privileges to ad libraries that are not needed by the app logic are likely to be ineffective: our measurements show that in a majority of apps in a large corpus of over 60,000 apps, the permissions requested by the ad are a subset of the permissions needed by the app logic (Section 5).

In this paper, we propose a pragmatic approach to selective privilege de-escalation for ad libraries. In our approach, a user can allow the app logic access to location and the contacts database, but, if she chooses, deny these privileges to the ad library. Our system, called PEDAL, has several desirable properties: it *does not require OS or VM modifications*, is *resistant to obfuscated code*, *prevents privileges inherited by the ad library* from app code, and *is highly efficient*.

The design of PEDAL poses two challenges: how to identify ad library code in an app, and how to effect selective privilege de-escalation.

The first challenge is non-trivial because, in a compiled binary, there is no annotation that preserves the separation between bytecode from app logic and bytecode from an ad library. More important, library bytecode can often be obfuscated to prevent reverse engineering. In this paper, PEDAL surmounts these challenges by observing that, even in the presence of obfuscation, ad libraries have several features that can be used to identify them. These features arise from the functionality of ad libraries (ad delivery) and from their modularity (they have to expose well-defined interfaces to apps). Based on this observation, PEDAL includes a highly effective, obfuscation-resistant, machine classifier that can *separate* ad library from app logic code (Section 4).

Effecting privilege de-escalation is non-trivial also, since a pragmatic solution must not require changes to the OS or the VM, or must not require rooting[1] a phone, since these can adversely affect deployability. Moreover, any solution must be highly efficient; significant slowdowns in app execution time can affect usability. Most importantly, in a substantial fraction (25%, Section 6) of apps, ad libraries *inherit* privileges from the app logic — they access sensitive resources like location etc. by invoking callbacks to app code. Any solution for privilege de-escalation must prevent this kind of privilege inheritance. PEDAL uses efficient binary rewriting and information flow analysis to overcome these challenges (Section 4).

Figure 1 and Figure 2 show two examples of PEDAL in action. The first example shows how a user can, in the AccuWeather app, disable Internet access permissions for ad libraries but keep it enabled for this app's main logic. Figure 1 shows that while the app can still function (can download breaking news), the ad space is empty because the ad library cannot download ads. In the second example, in the AroundMe app, the ad library inherits location privileges from the app logic. In this case, the user can choose to use PEDAL's controller app, which allows users to specify de-escalation policies (see Figure 8 for details), to feed obscured location data. In the example shown, PEDAL feeds the correct location (San Jose) to the app, but feeds Sunnyvale (a city close to San Jose) to the ad library. Figure 2(b) shows the result: while the app lists hotels near the real location, the ad library recommends hotels around the obscured location.

[1]http://betanews.com/2013/10/01/5-reasons-not-to-root-android/

(a) Normal version (b) Controlled version

Figure 1: Disable Internet access for ad libraries.

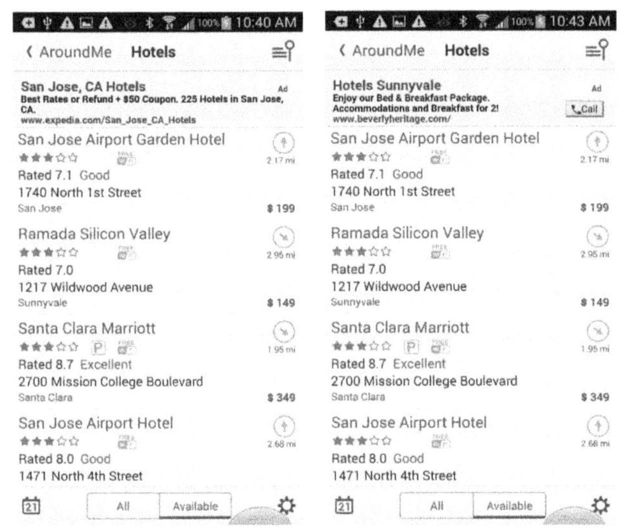


(a) Normal version (b) Controlled version

Figure 2: Return obscured location for ad libraries.

PEDAL can be used both by end-users and app markets. Individual Android users may use this system to enable self-defined resource access control for ad libraries of apps on their phones. App markets may also apply PEDAL to enforce their policies on ad libraries. For example, an app market may provide *plausible-obscured-location* options to users to enjoy apps with obscured but plausible location targeted ads. For example, instead of feeding accurate location, say San Jose, to ad libraries, PEDAL may still feed plausible nearby locations, such as Santa Clara or Sunnyvale to them to require useful ads. In this scenario, the ad widgets cannot collect accurate location information but the ads can still be relevant to the user's current location.

As an aside, there is a fundamental difference between PEDAL and existing ad blockers such as AdBlock Plus [14]: Ad blockers attempt to completely prevent ad delivery, while PEDAL allows the option of only blocking access of certain resource types to ad modules but still allowing ads to be delivered. In addition, ad blockers usually require rooted phones to enable full functionality while PEDAL does not.

Overall, this paper makes four contributions:

- The design and implementation of a system, PEDAL, for selective privilege de-escalation for ad libraries.
- An efficient, accurate, automatic and obfuscation-resistant method for identifying ad libraries embedded in app binaries. Our method uses a machine classifier based on features extracted using static analysis of bytecode.
- An efficient and flexible privilege de-escalation method that prevents privilege inheritance. This method uses binary rewriting, so does not require changing the Android OS or rooting the phone.
- Extensive experiments on a large set of real apps to show that PEDAL is both effective and efficient. Our prototype of PEDAL has 98.9% precision and 97.7% recall on identifying ad libraries and requires only 0.57 seconds per app for identification and rewriting. Apps incur less than 1% additional running time and can very effectively de-escalate privileges for ad libraries.

The rest of the paper is organized as follows: Section 2 provides background and motivates the design of PEDAL. Sections 3 and 4 discuss the architecture, and the design and implementation of PEDAL. Sections 5 and 6 evaluate the efficacy of ad library identification, and of privilege de-escalation, respectively. Section 7 discusses PEDAL usage scenarios and future refinements. Related work is described in Section 8, and the paper is summarized in Section 9.

# 2. BACKGROUND AND MOTIVATION

Before describing PEDAL, we provide some background on app execution, code obfuscation, and the app privilege model in Android.

## 2.1 Background

**Libraries in Android.** Android apps are written in a dialect of Java, and compiled down into a bytecode that is executed by the Dalvik Virtual Machine (DVM). Apps may include library code either for special purpose uses (such as image or video processing), or for analytics or ad delivery. In this paper, we focus on libraries for ad delivery: some apps can include more than one such library.

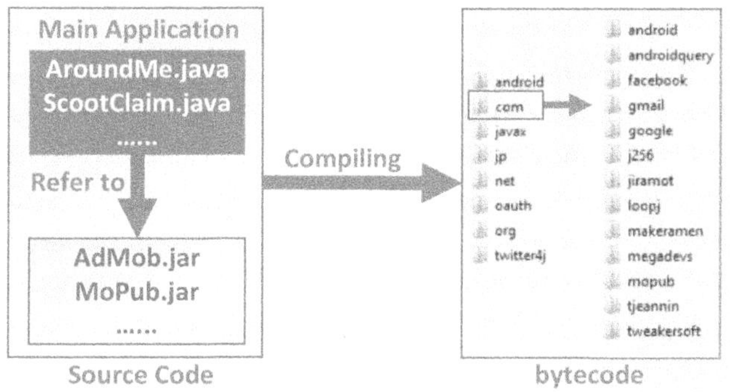


Figure 3: Source code to bytecode.

When developing an Android app, the developer sees clear boundaries between the app's source code and every other library. For example, as shown in Figure 3, the developers of the AroundMe app maintain their own source code. The app source also includes multiple libraries[2] provided by various third parties. However, when this app source is compiled to bytecode, the boundaries between the developers' code and libraries become unclear: compilation does not preserve all syntactic distinctions. Thus, it is sometime difficult to tell whether two classes belong to the app code or belong the a same library. One syntactic distinction that is preserved after compilation is the folder path for each class file. The folder path uniquely names a class file in a hierarchical namespace, and often, the upper levels of the hierarchy name the library that the class file belongs to.

**Obfuscation.** To prevent reverse engineering of source code from bytecode, app developers and library developers sometimes obfuscate the bytecode in two ways: at the package level and at the code-level. Package level obfuscation is motivated by prior work that has used folder path names to *statically* analyze app binaries to characterize potential risks [35], compute permission usage statistics [56], understand longitudinal code changes [26], extract usage patterns [57], and characterize apps [58] and so on. All of these pieces of work perform these analyses by matching bytecode paths against a manually-maintained blacklist of ad library names. For example, a path `/com/millennialmedia/android` indicates the presence of the ad library "Millennial Media". To foil this detection, some ad libraries, like AirPush, LeadBolt and AdsMogo, perform package name obfuscation and generate random package names for different developers.

Source code level obfuscation renames classes, methods and fields to semantically obscure names to prevent from reverse engineering the source code. Figure 4 shows a simple example of using package name obfuscation and source code obfuscation. Clearly, source code level obfuscation makes it harder to reverse engineer the original source from bytecode.

A nontrivial fraction of Android apps contain obfuscated code. We manually examined 200 randomly chosen apps from a corpus of about 60,000 (Section 5), and found that 107 of them contained ad libraries with source-code level obfuscation, and 37 of them obfuscated app code.

**The Android Permissions Model.** The Android permissions model governs app access to *resources*. A resource is an abstraction for data generated either by a hardware device (GPS or camera), data unique to a device (phone number, device ID, MAC address), or data generated by users and generally considered private (contact information). The Android permissions model requires an app developer 1) to notify users of which resources are required for the app, and 2) to explicitly ask the user's permission, at app install time, for access to these resources. Once the app is installed, the app and all its included libraries are granted access to these resources as long as the app is installed on the phone.

This model is at once too permissive and too coarse-grained, and there have been many examples of instances where permissions have been misused to breach privacy, often by ad libraries [26, 35, 55]. In response to this, recent versions of Android include a hidden permission manager called "App Ops" [1] that allows users to manage app permissions after installation. Moreover, several pieces of research have proposed finer-grained and restrictive access control for resources; we cover these in Section 8.

[2]Not included in this example are native libraries [6] that are written in native-code languages such as C/C++. The purpose of introducing native libraries is mainly for reusing existing code libraries written in C/C++. We discuss native libraries later.

```java
package com.somecompany.ads.sdk
public class AdRequest {
    private final int requestId;
    private final String requestMessage;

    public AdRequest(int id,
                     String message) {
        requestId = id;
        requestMessage = message;
    }
    public int getId() {
        return requestId;
    }
    public String getMessage() {
        return message;
    }
}
```

(a) Source code

```java
package com.ylzr.btpl187440
public class a {
    private final int a;
    private final String b;

    public a(int paramInt,
             String paramString) {
        this.a = paramInt;
        this.b = paramString;
    }
    public int a() {
        return this.a;
    }
    public String b() {
        return this.b;
    }
}
```

(b) Obfuscated code

Figure 4: Perform package name obfuscation and source code obfuscation on the source code

## 2.2 Privilege De-Escalation

Motivated by the shortcomings of the current permission model, we focus on a specific problem: how to selectively de-escalate the privileges given to ad libraries? In other words, even though a user may grant an app permissions to several resources, we would like to restrict access by ad libraries to some of these resources. Our position is that ad libraries may, in general need a different set of resources than the apps they are included in, so users should be able to selectively control privileges for these libraries separately from the main app logic.

Why focus on ad libraries? In Figure 5(a), a measurement of more than 60,000 apps shows that nearly 57% of apps use ad libraries. This indicates the magnitude of the problem: more than 1 of every 2 apps may be susceptible to privacy leakage. Furthermore, in roughly half of the ad-included apps, the ad libraries requested permission for a resource that was not required by the app logic itself!

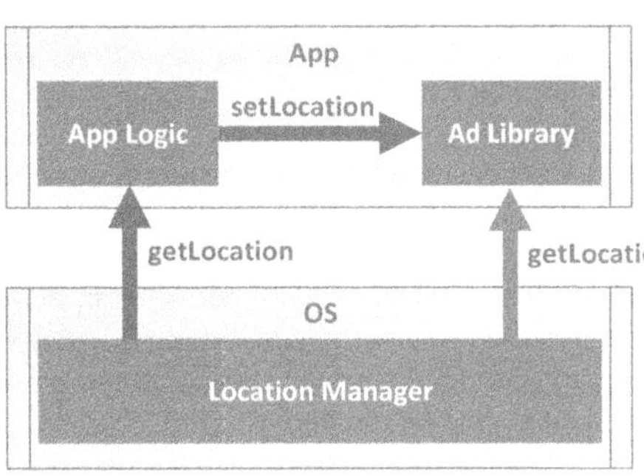


Figure 6: Two ways of resource access. Taking Location as an example, ad libraries can directly get the location information by calling system calls, or provide interfaces for the app logic to transfer the location information to it.

There are several ways in which to address this problem, but we consider a part of the design space that has not been explored before. We focus on a solution that has the following properties:

- It permits users to *selectively de-escalate* the privileges associated with ad libraries, without affecting privileges granted to other libraries or to the app itself.
- It is *obfuscation-resistant*: it has a high likelihood of success even in the presence of source-code obfuscation. This is motivated by the finding above that non-trivial amounts of obfuscation exist in today's apps.
- It must *not require changes to the operating system or the API*, or require special forms of modification (like rooting the phone). These assumptions enhance the deployability of the solution.
- It must be *efficient* and only minimally impact the execution time of the app.
- Finally, it must guard against *privilege inheritance* by ad libraries. In many apps, ad libraries, rather than access resources directly, invoke methods in the app logic that provide access to resources (Figure 6). Effectively, ad libraries inherit privileges granted to the app itself, and any privilege de-escalation must prevent this. In our corpus of 60,000 apps, we have found substantial numbers of apps that inherit access to location, the phone ID, and, to a lesser extent, the contact information and the account profile, as shown in Figure 5(b).

# 3. EFFICIENT PRIVILEGE DE-ESCALATION

In this paper, we describe the design and evaluation of a system for efficient privilege de-escalation. The system, named PEDAL, contains two parts: a Separator and a Rewriter (Figure 7). The input to PEDAL is a packaged app, and the output is a repacked app with de-escalated privileges for any (obfuscated) ad libraries in the app. In this section, we describe the overall architecture of PEDAL, leaving the detailed design and implementation to the next section.

The input app is first unpacked and transformed to Java bytecode, then sent to the Separator for feature extraction and classification. Feature extraction and classification is designed to separate the bytecodes to two different sets. The Separator scans and collects statistics on bytecodes[3] to generate feature vectors. Those feature vectors are input to a classifier which outputs two bytecode sets: the ad library set and the app logic set.

The Rewriter then performs binary rewriting on the bytecode sets. Specifically, the goal of the Rewriter is to interpose on 1) direct access to resources from both sets, and 2) calls from the app logic code to the ad library set that accesses resources (to prevent privilege inheritance, Section 2). Rewriter maintains a list denoting

[3]Note that we do not consider native code when performing classification because the usage of native code in ad libraries is minimal. (Section 6).

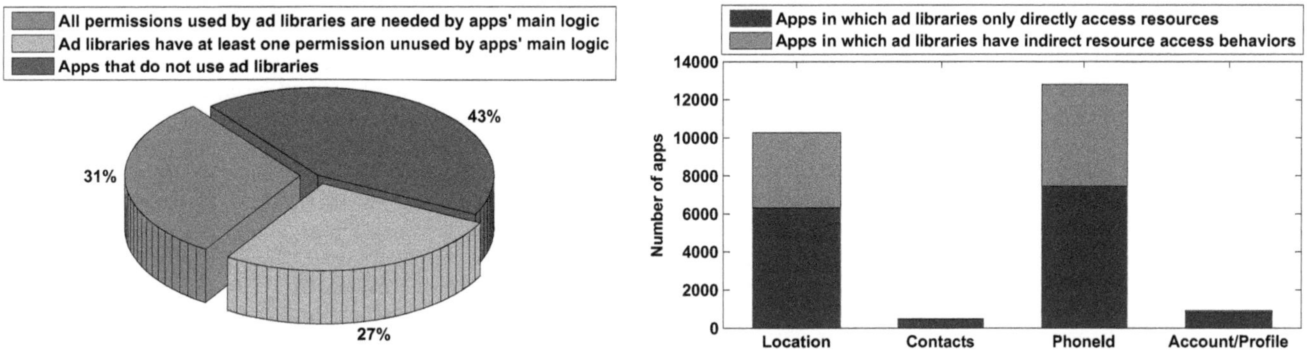


(a) Classify apps by ad libraries and permissions (b) Direct and indirect resource access of ad libraries

Figure 5: A measurement of 63,105 apps

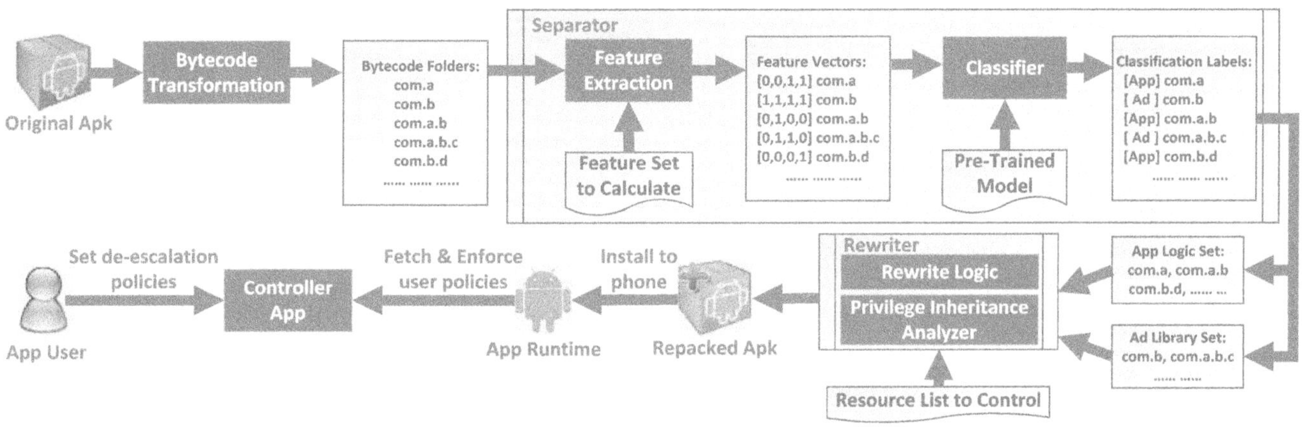


Figure 7: System Architecture

what private resources to control, such as Internet, location, contacts, phone ID and so on, takes both bytecode folder sets as inputs, and outputs the controllable versions (with respect to the resource types to control) of the two sets. As we describe later, the Rewriter does not attempt to interpose on all functions that lead to resource access, but 1) identifies a small set of *core resource access functions* and rewrites these functions which are used for *directly* accessing the concerned private resources, and 2) uses information flow analysis techniques to identify and rewrite another small set of functions which are used for ad libraries to *indirectly* access resources. The two rewritten bytecode sets, with other necessary files, are then repackaged back to a new app.

Finally, PEDAL contains a *Controller* app (Figure 7) for users to specify de-escalation policies for ad libraries.

This design achieves the requirements listed in Section 2 as follows. Classification and binary-rewriting achieve selective de-escalation on ad libraries. As we show later (and this is a major contribution of our work), the Separator is obfuscation-resistant. By using binary rewriting, our approach does not require OS level changes, and also achieves significant efficiency. Finally, the Rewriter, by analyzing information flow across bytecode sets, can prevent privilege inheritance.

# 4. PEDAL DESIGN AND IMPLEMENTATION

In this section, we present the detailed design and implementation of PEDAL.

## 4.1 The Separator

The goal of the Separator is to identify potentially obfuscated ad libraries packaged within an app. Before we explain the Separator, we observe that Java class files are usually named hierarchically. This naming hierarchy enables unique names for classes, permitting flexible inclusion of software from different sources into an application. Each bytecode corresponding to each Java class is then conceptually in a "folder" whose path name specifies the part of the hierarchy that class name is in. For example, the folder whose path is `/com/millennialmedia/android` would contain the ad library distributed by Millenial Media.

At a high-level, Separator marks each bytecode within an app as belonging to an ad library or not (i.e., it *separates* bytecodes, hence the name). Specifically, Separator identifies one or more folders that contain ad libraries. Folders can be nested, so a folder marked as containing an ad library implies that all bytecodes in subfolders are also part of the ad library.

As an aside, since Separator identifies ad libraries at the granularity of a folder, a potential approach to foil the Separator is to inter-mingle app logic and library code within a single folder. In practice, this is hard to do: the hierarchical class namespace, such as /com/google/android/gms/ads, /com/mopub/mobileads, /com/mobfox, /com/airpush/android, /com/mobclix/android/sdk, /com/applovin, and so on, is designed to enable separable development of code by different vendors, so that the folder hierarchy is used to distinguish code from different vendors. In this way, a developer can easily incorporate class files from different vendors. Even within a given vendor, hierarchical naming is used to ensure modularity: for example, Google uses different hierarchical names for its analytics library and its ad library. Finally, we emphasize that while Separator relies on class hierarchies, it is robust to folder path name obfuscation, as described below.

The key idea behind Separator is to use a binary machine classifier trained to identify ad libraries, even in the presence of obfuscation. The classifier accepts a feature vector of a bytecode folder (described below) and predicts whether the folder belongs to an ad library. We have manually extracted labeled training data from several hundred ad libraries and apps to train the classifier, and the details are presented in Section 5. The main challenge in our work is selecting features for the classifier that would enable accurate classification in the presence of obfuscation.

**Bytecode Extraction.** Our approach does not require source code; rather it extracts semantic features from bytecode. For this, we convert Dalvik bytecode to Java bytecode using well known techniques [36], then perform feature extraction on the Java bytecode.

**Feature Extraction.** The most important aspect of Separator design is to choose the set of features that ensure high classification accuracy. The features need to be: 1) effective and accurate, correctly separating ad libraries from apps; 2) easy and fast, requiring few complex operations to calculate; 3) general enough to support a variety of ad libraries from different vendors; and 4) robust enough to support both obfuscated and non-obfuscated ad libraries. After examining and analyzing the bytecodes of popular ad library SDKs, we chose 128 features that meet the above goals and are informative to ad library classification. These features can be categorized into the following groups.

*Usage of Android basic components:* These are binary features of whether a bytecode folder contains the usage of Android basic components[4]: activity, service, content provider and broadcast receiver. Compared to other software libraries, ad libraries are usually implemented as an independent module. For example, they may contain activities for displaying ads, may hold background services for periodically requesting ads, may use content providers for storing and retrieving informational data, and may register broadcast receivers for better reacting to system events (e.g., disabled screen or low battery).

*Usage of selective Android permissions:* These are binary features of whether a bytecode folder uses the following Android permissions: *INTERNET*, *ACCESS_NETWORK_STATE/_WIFI_STATE*, *ACCESS_FINE/_COARSE_LOCATION*, and *WRITE_EXTERNAL_STORAGE*. These permissions are most likely to be used by ad libraries (they may, of course, be used by the app logic or by other components, so permissions usage is only one of the many features we consider). *INTERNET* is necessary for communicating with ad networks. *NETWORK_STATE* and *WIFI_STATE* are for checking the availability and status of network connections. *LOCATION* is for better ad targeting, and *WRITE_EXTERNAL_STORAGE*, which implicitly allows *READ_EXTERNAL_STORAGE*, is for saving and serving cached ads when the device is offline.

To determine this feature vector, we first extract API calls and content provider URIs from the bytecode, then map that information to permissions using PScout [21]. Note that we have also tried taking all Android permissions and treated each one as an individual feature. However, in practice, this causes model overfitting and degrades the classifier performance.

*Usage of visual elements:* These are binary features of whether a bytecode folder has implemented instances of visual elements. Ad libraries provide user interfaces (UI) for showing ads. For example, interstitial ads prefer to implement their own activities for displaying full-screen ads, and banner ads usually extend webview or imageview to show ads inside small rectangles. Features in this group check whether there are customized classes that are derived from the commonly used UI widgets, such as activity, webview and videoview. We identified 12 classes from *android.app*, *android.widget* or *android.webkit* that can be used for implementing ad UI components.

*Usage of information sources and sinks:* Information sources refer to system calls that read non-constant information from a shared resource, and information sinks refer to system calls that write a piece of information to a shared resource [51]. Ad libraries prefer certain types of information. For example, they often use account and phone state information to uniquely identify user devices. We extract features in this group by using SuSi [51], a machine-learning approach to classify Android system calls to 12 information source categories and 15 information sink categories. These source and sink categories form 27 features. Each binary feature indicates whether any API call belonging to a category is observed in a bytecode folder.

*Usage of APIs for runtime permission check:* One interesting observation, which was first pointed out in [56], is that sometimes ad libraries may try to dynamically check certain permissions and take advantage of these permissions if they are available to apps. This check can be performed through a cluster of API calls like android.content.Context.check*Permission (where "*" denotes a collection of API call names such as "checkCallingOrSelfPermission"). Thus, one feature is added to indicate whether a bytecode folder has called any functions for runtime permissions checks.

*Keyword matching for class, method and field names:* In practice, we have found that the combination of these features accurately recognizes most ad libraries. However, these features can sometimes wrongly classify social-network or e-business plugins into ad libraries, such as Facebook or Amazon. These plugins have very similar behaviors as ad libraries and do, indeed, have many of these features. Therefore, the added binary features in this group show, in a bytecode folder, whether the names of classes, methods or fields contain specific keywords that are often used in ad libraries but rarely used in social-network and e-business plugins, such as "ads," "adsdk," "interstitial," "campaign," "impression," "mraid (Mobile Rich Media Ad Interface Definitions)," and so on. We use a dictionary of 26 such keywords, and 78 (26×3) features for keywords defined for classes, methods and fields, respectively.

**Obfuscation-Resistance.** The features we have chosen for classification are robust to code obfuscation. First, code obfuscation is used to protect developer code from reverse engineering, and it does not obscure API calls, content provider URI or class names of the Android system. For example, ProGuard [15], an official Android obfuscation tool, explicitly confirms this in its manual. Obviously, except for the last group of features (keyword matches), all the features are only related to Android system entities and will not be affected by code obfuscation. Second, code obfuscation can foil keyword matching by obscuring most names in an ad library; however, it still needs to preserve some interface names so that can be easily understood by developers and simplify integration with applications. For instance, Chartboost [9], a popular ad library that uses obfuscation, still preserves some methods and classes with explicit and in-

[4]We refer interested readers to [5] for more Android application fundamentals.

formative names, such as *showInterstitial*, *requestMorePromotion* and *ImpressionActivity*, for ease of integration. Thus, in most cases, we can still capture features for the last feature group even with an obfuscated ad library. Actually, as shown in the evaluation, even without keyword matching features, the classifier can still make reasonable decisions based on other feature groups.

Finally, our features *will not be affected by package name obfuscation* because the Separator does not rely on the path or package name or components thereof, only on the class hierarchy itself. For example, if `/com/millenialmedia/android` is obfuscated to `/a/b/e`, Separator's features do not change and it will be able to identify all bytecodes in folder `/a/b/e` as belonging to an ad library. Path name obfuscation makes it harder to associate the ad library with its developer, but that association is not necessary for PEDAL's functionality.

**An Optimization.** Each Android app has a main bytecode package that usually carries the implementation of the most important part of the app logic. The name of the bytecode folder that contains this is globally unique across an app store, and is defined in the app's manifest. Instead of attempting to classify this main bytecode package, we directly mark this folder as *not* being an ad library. This optimization has two advantages: 1) it can prevent the potential influence of wrongly classifying this major functional folder as an ad library; and 2) it can speed up the total classification time by skipping feature vector generation for these folders – classification time matters because it can impact how quickly an app store can process a batch of apps.

**Augmenting Separator with call-graph information.** The classifier itself focuses on finding the key functional components of ad libraries such as components for fetching/displaying ads or sending user data to ad networks, so it may miss some auxiliary libraries referenced by the key functional components. These libraries are still logically part of the ad library, but may not contain any of the signatures of these libraries. We applied call-graph information to attempt to ascertain these auxiliary libraries. However, as we show in Section 5, doing this incurred significant cost without additional benefit: intuitively, if these auxiliary libraries do not have signatures similar to ad libraries and perform some auxiliary function (e.g., parsing JSON objects), it is probably not necessary to instrument them to perform privilege de-escalation. So our PEDAL prototype does not use this technique.

## 4.2 The Rewriter

The output of the Separator is input to the Rewriter, which effects efficient privilege de-escalation by binary re-writing based on user-specified privacy policies. We begin by first describing user-specified policies permitted in PEDAL, then describe the Rewriter design.

**User-Specified Policies.** In PEDAL, users specify policies using a Controller app (Figure 8). This controller app is accessed through a unique URI, and a special provider permission is set up to prevent unauthorized apps from accessing it. This provider permission is granted to every rewritten app by adding a permission claim entry to their AndroidManifest.xml files using the AXML library [8]. At runtime, a rewritten app can access the content provider by using *queryController* (details are explained below), to read the user's configuration and effect user-specified policies. Conceptually, each policy entry is a quadruple:

$(AppName, ResourceType, ComponentType, Policy)$

where *AppName* is an app's identifier, *ResourceType* is one of the five resources listed in Table 1, *ComponentType* takes the values $\{AD, APP\}$, and dictates whether the policy is specified for the ad library or the app logic, and finally, *Policy* takes the value from $\{ALLOW, OBSCURE, BLOCK\}$. Our current instantiation of PEDAL supports the five resource types listed in Table 1, and users may thus selectively permit or deny an ad library access to each of these resource types. These five resource categories cover the types of resources accessed by ad libraries. It is easy to extend PEDAL to support other resource types.

```
// the original function is:
// Location LocationManager.getLastKnownLocation(
//                    String provider)
public static Location PEDAL.getLastKnownLocation(
            LocationManager manager, String provider) {
    Policy currentPolicy = queryController("AccuWeather",
                "Location", "AD");
    if (currentPolicy == Policy.BLOCK) {
        return null;
    }
    else if (currentPolicy == Policy.OBSCURE) {
        Location obscuredLocation = new Location(provider);
        // set obscuredLocation to Sunnyvale
        obscuredLocation.setLatitude(37.369);
        obscuredLocation.setLongitude(-122.036);
        return obscuredLocation
    }
    // queryController returns Policy.ALLOW
    return manager.getLastKnownLocation(provider);
}

private static Policy PEDAL.queryController(appName,
            resourceType, componentType) {
    // query user's configuration
    // resourceType is:
    // Internet, Location, a content provider URI, etc.
    // componentType is: "AD" or "APP"
}
```

Figure 9: Example of rewriting a normal system call (This figure and Figure 10 use Java-style pseudo-code to describe the instrumentation technique for ease of understanding. PEDAL rewrites byte-code, and does not require access to Java or Dalvik source.)

In addition, users may choose to obscure the returned results for specific resource types. App developers may derive revenue from some of these resources. For example, when an ad library can obtain a user's location and deliver targeted ads, the developer might get more revenue than when no location is available. So, PEDAL permits users to specify policies that enable some form of obscured result to be returned. We discuss this below in some detail.

Finally, users can change policy settings at any time, and policy changes take immediate effect (even while an app is running). The Rewriter accesses these policies at run-time through a *queryController* interface, as discussed below.

**Rewriting for Privilege De-Escalation.** Conceptually, re-writing for privilege de-escalation is straightforward: Rewriter can interpose on resource accesses by the ad library or the app logic, and permit access only if the user-specified policies grant access. In the example in Figure 9, the call to *queryController* permits access to the Location resource if the policy permits, otherwise it returns null or an obscured location. However, there are several subtleties in the design, as described below.

*Interposing on content providers.* Rewriting content provider[5] based resource access is slightly more involved. Figure 10 shows another

[5]Content providers are basic Android components, and are actually databases addressable by their application-defined URIs. One use of content providers is to share information between apps.

Figure 8: Controller App Design

Table 1: Core Functions for Different Resource Types

| Resource Type | Related Permissions | Number of Core Functions | Core Function Examples |
|---|---|---|---|
| Internet | INTERNET<br>ACCCESS_NETWORK_STATE | 15 | java.net.URLConnection.openConnection<br>org.apache.http.HttpResponse.execute |
| Location | ACCESS_COARSE_LOCATION<br>ACCESS_FINE_LOCATION | 12 | android.location.LocationListener.onLocationChanged<br>android.location.LocationManager.getLastKnownLocation |
| Contacts | READ_CONTACTS | 8 | android.content.ContentProvider.query<br>android.content.CursorLoader.<init> |
| Phone ID | READ_PHONE_STATE<br>ACCESS_WIFI_STATE | 6 | android.telephony.TelephonyManager.getDeviceId<br>android.net.wifi.WifiInfo.getMacAddress |
| Account/Profile | GET_ACCOUNTS<br>READ_PROFILE | 5 | android.accounts.AccountManager.getAccounts<br>android.accounts.AccountManager.getAccountsByType |

```
// the original function is:
// Cursor ContentResolver.query(Uri uri,
//             String[] projection, String selection,
//             String[] selectionArgs, String sortOrder)
public static Cursor PEDAL.query(
            ContentResolver resolver, Uri uri,
            String[] projectin, String selection,
            String[] selectionArgs, String sortOrder){
    // uri.toString() is something like:
    // content://com.android.contacts, content://call_log
    Policy currentPolicy = queryController("Facebook",
                uri.toString(), "APP");
    if (currentPolicy == Policy.BLOCK) {
        return null;
    }
    else if (currentPolicy == Policy.OBSCURE) {
        // Uri for obscured content provider
        Uri obscuredUri = PEDAL.getObscuredUri(uri);
        return resolver.query(obscuredUri,
                    projection, selection,
                    selectionArg, sortOrder);
    }
    // queryController returns Policy.ALLOW
    return resolver.query(uri, projection,
                selection, selectionArg, sortOrder);
}
```

Figure 10: Example of rewriting a system call for operating a content provider

example for rewriting the API call *query*. This function can be used to access all types of resources that are implemented through content providers, and the *uri* parameter is used to differentiate which resource type is actually queried. For example, if *uri* is "content://com.android.contacts" or "content://contacts," then the resource type is contacts; if it is "content://call_log," then the resource type is call logs; and if it is "content://com.android.calendar," then the resource type is calendar. When *queryController* receives a content provider URI as the *resourceType* parameter, it first maps the URI (using PScout [21]) to the resource type the URI pertains to, and then follows the same procedure as when it directly receives a resource type string, like "Location" above.

*Obscuring Results.* Our current prototype permits users to obscure contacts, location, phone ID, and profile information. Specifically, for location, phone ID, and profile information, PEDAL initiates a new object with pre-defined fake values, and returns this new instance to the app logic or the ad library. However, as discussed above, access to contacts is through a special URI, and the return is a cursor pointer to the actual database. Therefore, it is a little tricky to *OBSCURE* contacts. We have implemented a fake content provider (essentially, an app) that contains all the fields that have been defined in the real contacts content provider tables. To *OBSCURE* contacts, PEDAL simply replaces the real provider URI with the URI of the fake content provider, and returns the usable cursor pointing to the fake database. We have left to future work to determine how best to obscure results that preserve user privacy without affecting the app developer's revenue stream.

*Optimizing the Rewriter.* The API for accessing a resource, like the Internet or Location, may have many calls, not all of which need to be interposed. For example, there are a total of 95 calls [4] for the Internet resource, but only about 15 of them (called *core resource access functions*, or core functions for short) need to be interposed on to enforce policy. The other calls provide either higher-level abstractions that ultimately call one of these core functions, or provide utility functionality (for example, for parsing headers, etc.). Avoiding interposing on the non core functions can reduce overhead (Section 5) by avoiding calls to *queryController* for dynamic policy checking. Table 1 lists the number of core functions for each of the 5 resource types we support.

**Preventing Privilege Inheritance.** As we have discussed, ad libraries may also access resources indirectly through the app logic. To prevent this, we use an information flow analysis tool, FlowDroid [20] with a reported accuracy of over 90%. Our usage of flow analysis is constrained: we are interested in code paths from calls to resource access core functions in the app logic to Internet access calls in the ad library. Such code paths indicate the potential for privilege inheritance misuse. Note that our approach only focuses on

```
// the original sharing function is:
// void AdRequest.setLocation(Location location)
public static void PEDAL.setLocation(
            AdRequest ad, Location location) {
    Policy currentPolicy = queryController("AroundMe",
            "Location", "AD");
    if (currentPolicy == Policy.BLOCK) {
        // do nothing
        return;
    }
    else if (currentPolicy == Policy.OBSCURE) {
        // set obscuredLocation to Sunnyvale
                ......
        ad.setLocation(obscuredLocation);
        return;
    }
    // queryController returns Policy.ALLOW
    ad.setLocation(location)
}
```

Figure 11: Example of rewriting a resource sharing function for location sharing to an ad library.

Table 2: Feature Selection and Classifier Performance

| Feature Selection | Category | Recall | Precision |
|---|---|---|---|
| All Features | Ad Library | 0.991 | 0.988 |
| | Non-Ad Module | 0.976 | 0.982 |
| | Weighted Average | 0.984 | 0.985 |
| No Keyword-Matching Features | Ad Library | 0.857 | 0.866 |
| | Non-Ad Module | 0.827 | 0.815 |
| | Weighted Average | 0.842 | 0.841 |
| Only Keyword-Matching Features | Ad Library | 0.746 | 0.716 |
| | Non-Ad Module | 0.925 | 0.919 |
| | Weighted Average | 0.836 | 0.818 |
| No Basic-Component Features | Ad Library | 0.908 | 0.905 |
| | Non-Ad Module | 0.913 | 0.916 |
| | Weighted Average | 0.911 | 0.911 |
| No Permission Features | Ad Library | 0.899 | 0.899 |
| | Non-Ad Module | 0.887 | 0.902 |
| | Weighted Average | 0.893 | 0.901 |
| No Visual-Element Features | Ad Library | 0.937 | 0.928 |
| | Non-Ad Module | 0.928 | 0.925 |
| | Weighted Average | 0.933 | 0.927 |
| No Sources-and-Sinks Features | Ad Library | 0.922 | 0.91 |
| | Non-Ad Module | 0.902 | 0.884 |
| | Weighted Average | 0.912 | 0.897 |
| No Permission-Check Feature | Ad Library | 0.97 | 0.973 |
| | Non-Ad Module | 0.955 | 0.949 |
| | Weighted Average | 0.963 | 0.961 |

those kinds of privilege inheritance that can lead to misuse (actual leakage of data).

Once these potential leakage paths have been identified, Rewriter performs the same kind of interposition as above. Consider the "Location" resource. For this, we first find the core resource access functions that the app logic uses to fetch location information (information flow sources), and then find the places within the ad library part where the Internet core functions are called (information flow sinks). Then, we apply FlowDroid to search for all paths between the defined flow sources and sinks, and further find and interpose on all unique sharing functions that cross the boundary between the app logic and the ad library, as shown in Figure 11. However, in some cases, we cannot fake a resource type in a sharing function if the resource value has been transformed somewhere along the path. For example, it is possible that, a piece of "Location" information, say latitude 40.714 and longitude -74.006, is accessed in the app logic, and then transformed into a string "New York", and finally what is returned to the ad library part is the string instead of the actual location object. In these cases, because we do not have enough knowledge to analyze the semantics of the transfer between the original object type and the transferred object type, we conservatively block or return a null object for these sharing functions regardless of users' policy setting.

**Other Details.** Java reflection can foil our interposition technique, since reflection can invoke any method of an object at runtime without explicitly exposing the actual function signatures. To deal with this, PEDAL intercepts function calls to *reflect.Method.invoke* to decide the actual function signatures during runtime using the function call *reflect.Method.toGenericString*, and then distributes the *invoke* call to the actual control logic if core functions are dynamically detected. A similar technique can be used if reflection is used to achieve privilege inheritance. However, PEDAL cannot handle native libraries; in Section 5, we show that ad libraries rarely use native code.

After replacing all core functions and sharing functions with their rewritten versions, the modified bytecode together with other app files are then repacked to a modified package file. The repacking tool we have implemented strictly preserves and follows the procedure and parameters of the original packing process. Finally, the app is signed; we use the strategy introduced in [62] to re-sign apps using a parallel set of randomly generated keys.

## 5. EVALUATION: THE SEPARATOR

In this section, we systematically evaluate the PEDAL classifier. The highlights of our evaluation are:

- PEDAL is highly accurate (98.9% precision, 97.7% recall) in separating ad libraries from apps. The system is robust to obfuscation: it can identify obfuscated ad libraries with 97.4% accuracy.
- PEDAL can discover nearly 5× more ad library sources than the number of ad libraries in blacklists prepared by prior work [26,27,35,44,49,55,57,58].

**The Dataset.** We crawled the Google Play Store [13] and downloaded 63,105 free apps between June 2nd, 2014 and August 1st, 2014. About 5% of these apps failed the Dalvik to Java bytecode conversion step, so our analysis uses the remaining 59,759 apps.

**Classifier Training.** We use LibSVM [29], a state-of-the-art SVM library, to build our classifier. We obtained training samples of the classifier, which are ad and non-ad modules, from two sources. First, we collected 100 JAR files of popular ad SDKs listed in [7,35]. From the JAR files we extracted 335 ad modules as positive training data points, among which 117 use code obfuscation and 26 use package name obfuscation. Second, we collected the top 500 free apps in Google Play on August 1st, 2014, and extracted non-ad bytecode modules from these APK files. We randomly sampled 335 non-ad modules among them as negative training data points. The kernel (sigmoid) and parameters ($\gamma$=0.125, $d$=3, $cost$=8) of the SVM model were chosen according to a grid search of parameters in exponential scale. After a 10-fold cross validation, our classifier performed with accuracy of 98.5% on classifying ad and non-ad modules. To demonstrate that our classifier is not biased by including popular examples in the training set, we intentionally omitted Google AdMob, the most popular ad library, from the training set.

**Feature Efficacy.** We now quantify the accuracy loss when omitting each feature selectively (Table 2).

First, keyword-matching features which represent the occurrences of key phrases, such as "ads," "promotion," in class, function, or field names, play an important role in boosting the accuracy of our classifier. If we exclude these features, the classifier would perform with an accuracy of 84%, which is lower than using the full feature set. Ad libraries appear to preserve such human readable names even in obfuscated library code, since this simplifies integrating the library into the app.

We then explored classifier accuracy if the classifier were to use only keyword-matching features. Compared to only using the remaining feature set (i.e., without keyword matching), these two approaches appear to have comparable accuracy. However, the accuracy of detecting ad libraries using only keyword-matching is very low. Taking these two results together, our results show that using keyword matching is necessary, but not sufficient (in the sense that other features are also necessary), to ensure high-accuracy.

Finally, omitting other groups of features selectively resulted in accuracy losses of between 2%~9%, suggesting that every feature group is important for the classification. As an aside, we have explored many other feature sets related to function argument types, function return types, class inheritance, full permission list and so on. These additional sets only marginally increase accuracy, and can sometimes reduce accuracy due to classifier overfitting. Thus, the finally chosen features reflect the best tradeoff between the classification accuracy and the complexity of the feature space.

**Classifier Evaluation on Real-world Apps.** To further evaluate our classifier on real-world usage scenarios, we tested the classifier on a subset of real apps. We randomly chose 200 apps from our corpus of free Android apps. For each app, we applied the classifier to automatically identify the ad libraries in it, and examined the results by manually checking the bytecode to see whether the classifier can accurately and completely find the ad libraries within the app. Specifically, we checked ad-related behaviors by scanning through string elements, data format for URL requests and sensitive API calls in the bytecode of these apps, since this information cannot be obfuscated. Of the 200 apps, the classifier accurately and completely identified ad libraries in 186 apps (93.0%). From the 200 apps, we found 357 ad library occurrence from 174 unique ad libraries, of which the classifier identified 347. Note that among these 357 ones, 173 of them (48.5%) did not appear in the classifier training set (AdMob takes the largest number of 78). Among these apps, we found obfuscated bytecode in 120 of them (107 of them have obfuscated codes in ad library modules). Our classifier can still automatically capture 97.4% of the ad library appearances in these obfuscated bytecode blocks. In total, considering the performance on each individual app, the average precision of the classifier is 98.9% (median=100%, sd=6.0%), and the average recall is 97.7% (median=100%, sd=9.7%).

**New Ad Libraries.** We then applied PEDAL to our entire collection of 59,759 apps. Among all these apps, our system found 34,167 apps (57.17%) that contain at least one ad library. Moreover, our classifier discovered many ad libraries previously unknown to us.

PEDAL discovered 2,598 unique ad library modules, such as the popular "com.millennialmedia.android," and "com.google.ads", as well as the unpopular "com.linxad" and "com.aarki." Note that this count is only based on folder names, and obfuscation might cause this estimate to be off. For example, two essentially different ad libraries can have the same folder name "com.a.b" after obfuscation. Conversely, a single ad library may be obfuscated differently in different apps.

Table 3: Top-10 Frequently Occurring Ad Libraries by Ad Network Names

| Name of ad library source | Frequency in the 34,167-app corpus |
|---|---|
| Google AdMob | 21,772 |
| Millennial Media | 3,871 |
| Flurry | 3,215 |
| InMobi | 1,929 |
| MoPub | 1,777 |
| Mobclix | 1,581 |
| Airpush | 1,316 |
| MobFox | 1,092 |
| Leadbolt | 926 |
| Tapjoy | 899 |

Among these 2,598 ad library modules, we identified 546 unique ad library sources[6] by: 1) retaining modules that are used by at least three different app publishers and 2) grouping modules that are known to be with a same ad network or have the same package prefix. The average occurrence of ad library sources (among the collection of 546 identified sources) in each app is 2.12 (max=35, min=1, median=1, sd=2.18). Table 3 presents the most frequently occurring ad libraries in our collection of apps with respect to the 546 unique sources.

Compared to the initial 100 ad library sources we applied in classifier training, our system discovered many more new ad libraries. This number is at least 5× more than the reported numbers in other static code analysis based papers that maintain blacklists of ad library package names [26,27,35,44,49,55,57,58]. These findings suggest that a blacklist-based approach may be ineffective in identifying ad libraries. To quantify this, Figure 12 measures the (a) the percentage of apps that contain at least one library in the Top-*N* most popular ad sources (a single ad source may contain multiple ad libraries) and (b) the percentage of apps whose ad libraries are entirely contained in the Top-*N* most popular ad sources. When *N* is 100 (respectively, 200), these two values are 88.84% and 85.78% (respectively, 93.37% and 90.50%). Indeed, even if we used all the 546 ad library sources we discovered in a blacklist, these two percentages are 97.23% and 95.69%. This is because there are some highly obfuscated ad library package names that cannot be used in the blacklist: for example, an obfuscated package name "a.b.c" cannot be added to the blacklist because in different apps it may represent different functional modules after obfuscation.

**The Efficacy of Call Graph Information.** As discussed in Section 4, our classifier is designed to capture core functional modules of ad libraries, and may miss some auxiliary modules. Therefore, we explored whether it would be beneficial to detect these auxiliary modules using call-graph analysis. To do this, we used Soot [17] to generate the class-level call graph of an app, then marked any auxiliary module as an ad library module if it was transitively called from a known ad library and was not a Android system library. We tested the efficacy of this approach on a random subset of 8,693 apps using ad libraries.

Call graph generation failed on 730 (8.4%) apps due to code obfuscation. For the remaining 7,963 apps, call graph analysis increases the classification cost by *over two orders of magnitude*, a factor of 143.12 on average (max=7,690.0, min=1.47, median=106, sd=347.5). On the other hand, this approach identified 684 new ad module occurrences (7.07% of all 9,676 occurrences), of which only 55 (0.8%) have requested new permissions, compared to ad libraries identified using the non-call-graph method. Thus, in general, this

[6]Modules that have obfuscated or randomized package names are excluded from grouping. Thus, the actual number of unique sources may be more than this number.

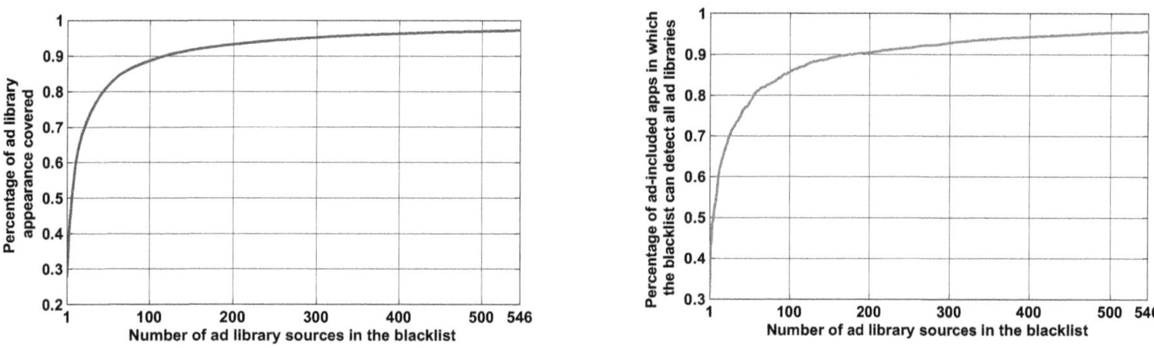


(a) Percentage of ad library occurrences covered

(b) Percentage of ad-included apps in which the blacklist can detect all ad libraries

Figure 12: CDF comparing with the blacklist approach

Table 4: Top-10 Frequently-Used Permissions

| Used by apps' main logic (among 59,759 apps) | | Used by Ad Libraries (among 546 Ad Sources) | | | |
|---|---|---|---|---|---|
| | | Actually Used by Ads | | Checked for Availability by Ads | |
| Permission | Frequency | Permission | Frequency | Permission | Frequency |
| INTERNET | 43,498 | INTERNET | 546 | ACCESS_FINE_LOCATION | 104 |
| ACCESS_NETWORK_STATE | 36,485 | ACCESS_NETWORK_STATE | 413 | ACCESS_COARSE_LOCATION | 101 |
| READ_PHONE_STATE | 15,265 | READ_PHONE_STATE | 264 | ACCESS_NETWORK_STATE | 86 |
| VIBRATE | 14,299 | RECEIVE_BOOT_COMPLETED | 246 | INTERNET | 81 |
| WAKE_LOCK | 13,656 | WAKE_LOCK | 208 | READ_PHONE_STATE | 81 |
| ACCESS_FINE_LOCATION | 13,205 | ACCESS_COARSE_LOCATION | 190 | WRITE_EXTERNAL_STORAGE | 71 |
| ACCESS_COARSE_LOCATION | 11,153 | ACCESS_FINE_LOCATION | 173 | ACCESS_WIFI_STATE | 70 |
| ACCESS_WIFI_STATE | 6,987 | ACCESS_WIFI_STATE | 137 | CALL_PHONE | 39 |
| RECEIVE_BOOT_COMPLETED | 5,984 | GET_ACCOUNTS | 111 | READ_CONTACTS | 35 |
| READ_CONTACTS | 4,943 | READ_CONTACTS | 49 | GET_ACCOUNTS | 32 |

approach increases cost significantly while providing diminishing returns.

**Is privilege de-escalation necessary?** If the permissions used by ad libraries are disjoint from the ones used by the apps' main logic, we can simply apply tools such as App Ops [2] to disable those permissions requested by the ad library. Table 4 shows the statistics of the most frequently used permissions by both the ad libraries[7] and the app logic. There is significant overlap in the permissions requested by apps and by the ad library; of our nearly 60,000 apps, 29,926 apps have at least one permission common to both app logic and ad library. Of these, we found 15,988 apps (53.43%) in which the permissions used by ad libraries are *ALL* used by its app function. This motivates PEDAL's design, which enables finer-grained permissions than the underlying Android model.

PEDAL's design also foils ad libraries that access resources without explicitly requesting permissions. These libraries check available permissions at runtime, and sometimes use permissions granted to the app that includes the library. We analyzed both the bytecode and the documentation of 30 randomly selected ad library SDKs, and found that 5 of them have undocumented usage of important privacy-related permissions. For example, neither "com.appflood" nor "com.applovin" claims any dependency on permissions ACCESS_FINE_LOCATION or ACCESS_COARSE_LOCATION in their documentation. However, in the bytecode of these two libraries, we found that they both check and have API calls that rely on the location-related permissions. Similarly, "com.greystripe" claims to only use Internet-related permissions, but we found that this library checks and makes API calls to permissions CAMERA and READ_PROFILE.

[7]Note that each ad library source may have multiple versions, and we dated every versions of a same source using the heuristic introduced in [26], Therefore, the permission usage of an individual ad library source is based on its latest version found in our app corpus.

## 6. EVALUATION: THE REWRITER

In this section, we evaluate the overhead introduced by the Rewriter on 34,167 apps with at least one ad library. Our main results are:

- PEDAL processes an app in about a minute on a single thread. This task is trivially parallelizable.
- PEDAL introduces negligible runtime overhead (less than 1% on time cost), but can still effectively achieve privilege de-escalation.

**The robustness of the Rewriter.** The process of binary rewriting and re-packaging an app can sometimes be fragile: the resulting app may sometimes not install or run on a phone. To quantify this, we took the 34,167 apps that contained an ad library and re-packaged them. This step generated no failures. Then, we tested how many of these re-packaged apps would install correctly on an Android device (Galaxy S3). Of these, 32,965 (96.48%) apps installed perfectly; the ones that failed to install were due to dexopt failures. Finally, we used the PUMA [37] Android UI-automation framework to run each repacked app for 3 minutes or until all UI states were explored (whichever is shorter). In each app, the ad libraries' privilege was restricted: access to a resource either generated an exception or returned obscured or null data. In total, 10 Android emulators were created on a server running Ubuntu 14.04 with 20-core 2.8GHz CPU and 200GB memory and the corpus of 32,965 apps was equally partitioned across these emulators. Of these apps, 3,287 apps could not function properly and crashed mainly because of unhandled exceptions. For example, some apps call *HttpClient.execute* but fail to deal with the cases in which

Table 5: Micro-Benchmark: Running Time Cost of Each Step

| Processing Step | Time Cost (in seconds, on 29,678 ad-included apks) | | | | |
|---|---|---|---|---|---|
| | Average | Median | Max | Min | Stdev |
| Apk to Java Bytecode | 5.81 | 4.52 | 52.24 | 0.48 | 5.01 |
| Module Classification | 0.57 | 0.24 | 11.95 | 0.00 | 0.81 |
| Indirect Flow Analysis | 28.93 | 8.58 | 455.44 | 0.34 | 49.99 |
| Java Bytecode Rewriting | 3.43 | 1.67 | 72.70 | 0.04 | 4.93 |
| Repacking to Apk | 17.82 | 10.54 | 617.86 | 1.99 | 27.77 |
| Total time | 56.63 | 25.98 | 1075.85 | 2.73 | 93.25 |

Table 6: Top-10 Frequency of Native Function Names

| Used by apps' main logic | | Used by Ad Libraries | |
|---|---|---|---|
| Function Name | App Freq | Function Name | App Freq |
| nativeInit | 1266 | UnitySendMessage | 195 |
| nativeRender | 1115 | getAsString | 113 |
| nativeResize | 930 | getAsBool | 108 |
| nativePause | 905 | getAsInt | 108 |
| nativeResume | 872 | newObject | 98 |
| nativeDone | 852 | getActivity | 74 |
| init | 710 | getLength | 52 |
| installNdk | 609 | getObjectAt | 52 |
| checkLibraryVersion | 599 | dispatchStatusEventAsync | 46 |
| newPolygonShape | 571 | getAsDouble | 13 |

*IOExceptions* are thrown, although these exceptions are supposed to be properly handled according to API specs. In summary, PEDAL is reasonably robust end-to-end: out of the 34,167 apps, 29,678 (86.86%) were crash-free and successfully reported PEDAL debug tags. In the rest of this section, we report results on this set of apps.

**Rewriting overhead.** Table 5 shows statistics for all steps discussed in Section 4. Classification and rewriting incur, on average, 0.57s and 3.43s for each app respectively. Flow analysis for detecting privilege inheritance is as expensive as repacking in some cases when multimedia resources need to be re-packed. Overall, the mean per-app processing time is 56.62s, which is acceptable, especially for app stores, since apps can be processed in parallel.

**Execution overhead.** The runtime overhead of an app is the cost of invoking *queryController*. Our micro-benchmarks for this call revealed an average running time of 13.09 ms (sd=22.87 ms) for a normal resource, and 13.45 ms (sd=23.34 ms) for the URI resource. Other invocations (e.g., those dealing with invocations) cost less than 1ms.

To quantify the overhead end-to-end, we selected 100 apps which used the most number of ad libraries and also accessed the location resources. Executing these 100 apps on PUMA [37] showed a total increase in runtime of 0.89% (min=0.02%, max=1.81%, sd=0.51%) relative to unmodified versions of these apps[8]. This suggests that PEDAL introduces negligible overhead, so is eminently practical.

**How often do ad libraries inherit privileges?** With our experimental infrastructure, we are also able to quantify instances where ad libraries inherit privilege. We find that there are 7,499 apps out of the 29,678 (more than 25%) that access at least one of the five resource types through the app logic; this motivates Rewriter's careful information flow based analysis. Phone ID is the most commonly inherited resource, in 5,348 apps, and Location is next in 3,934 apps. Other resources are rarely inherited (about 0.5% in total).

**Does PEDAL need to handle native code?** We performed static analysis on the apps to search for calls on native code functions and found there are 5,381 apps (18.13%) that use native calls[9]. However, out of the 5,381 apps, only 314 apps (1.06% of the total 29,678 apps) use native calls in ad libraries. Table 6 lists the names of the top-10 used native function calls, generated by disassembling app binaries using `objdump`[10] and `IDA Pro`[11]. None of these appear to access resources. Finally, we did not find any instance of app logic invoking native code defined in ad libraries, suggesting privilege inheritance is unlikely. For this reason, PEDAL does not perform native code analysis.

**How effective is PEDAL's privilege de-escalation?** To quantify this, we ran 3 versions of the experiments on the 100 apps discussed above. Our UI automation tool replayed the same click stream to each version, and collected screenshots of each app page visited. In the first experiment, we analyzed the original apps without rewriting them. The 100 apps generated 1000 pages, and the unmodified app showed 843 ads. We manually checked and found that 304 of these ads were targeted at San Jose, the phone's location. In the second experiment, we disabled Internet access for the ad libraries. The apps after rewriting generated only 9 ads, indicating that selective network de-escalation was effective. (These 9 ads were generated by an ad library that used an HTTP client which invoked a core function for network access that was not in our set). In the third experiment, we obscured location data by feeding a fake location in New York, NY for a phone located in San Jose, CA. Among the 806 ads shown, 249 were New York based, while only 23 targeted the real location San Jose, CA. It is not trivial to determine how many ads should have been location targeted because the targeting strategies are hard to reverse engineer. However, in the unmodified app set, we observed that 304/843 or about 36% of the ads were targeted. In this set, if the same proportion were to hold, we would expect to see about 290 targeted ads, and our manual analysis uncovered about 272, which is close to the expected number. Thus, we feel confident that PEDAL's miss rate (the rate at which it fails to catch resource accesses) is relatively low (approximate 23/272). The 23 ads that targeted the San Jose location were attributed to two causes: the failure of the classifier to identify ad libraries, and the failure of the information flow analysis to detect privilege inheritance. Overall, these results suggest that obscuring location is generally effective; our corpus of 100 apps includes apps with the most ad library sources, so PEDAL's efficacy is likely to be higher for other apps than reported here.

**PEDAL & ART.** Android 4.4 introduced a new runtime, ART[12], which has officially replaced Dalvik in the newly released Android 5.0. Other proposed fine-grained control systems, such as the popular XPrivacy [18], cannot work with ART[13] because they are tightly coupled with the Dalvik environment or the old OS architecture. However, we have verified that PEDAL modified apps work with ART without any noticeable changes, since PEDAL does not require OS or runtime support.

## 7. DISCUSSION

**Failures in Privilege De-Escalation.** PEDAL's privilege de-escalation is not perfect: as shown in the evaluation, the Separator can introduce both false positives and false negatives, which can lead to wrongly classifying a social plugin as an ad library, or to an unstable app. However, these infrequent situations, users can choose to revoke and turn off privilege de-escalation for an app by using the *Controller* (Figure 8).

Another mechanism that may make the de-escalation more robust and efficient is that the app store can include developers in the loop, so that they can test the instrumented apps throughly and

[8]In running these experiments, we carefully ensured that both versions of the app were fed identical click streams by the "monkey".

[9]This number is slightly higher than the number of 17.41% reported by a recent large-scale study [58].

[10]http://en.wikipedia.org/wiki/Objdump

[11]https://www.hex-rays.com/products/ida/

[12]http://source.android.com/devices/tech/dalvik/art.html

[13]https://github.com/M66B/XPrivacy#FAQ75

understand the de-escalation effects before publishing the rewritten apps. However, developers may not always have the incentive or be willing to cooperate for fear of losing advertising revenue.

**Resigning Apps.** The last step of PEDAL is to resign a repacked app using a randomly generated developer key. This approach has two problems. First, automatic app updates can no longer be delivered because the signature of the app does not match the one from the original developer. However, in this case, the app store can actively monitor the app's update and prepare repacked versions for each update. Second, some features of the original app may break. For example, a repacked app may show a blank map if this app uses Google Maps API because the API certificate is tied to the original developer key used to sign the app which has been replaced during repacking. We have not found more effective solutions for this problem other than involving the developer.

**Future Improvements.** PEDAL can be improved along several dimensions:

Its classifier accuracy can be improved by designing better features or using more advanced classifiers. Specifically, the current selected features only reflect the most general characteristics of existing ad libraries, and we may need to re-design some of these features as ad libraries evolve. Moreover, although the designed features are resistant to package-level and code-level obfuscation, it is unclear whether they also work for other advanced obfuscation techniques, such as flow obfuscation/logic structural obfuscation, incremental obfuscation and so on. While we have not discovered uses of these advanced obfuscation techniques in today's ad libraries, in future work we plan to explore how effective our features are for such techniques.

In addition, although our core function list is fairly comprehensive, future work might wish to extend this set as the Android API evolves. Fortunately, PEDAL is designed to be extensible, and adding new core functions is simply a matter of adding some signatures. Improved information flow analysis tools can also improve the accuracy of PEDAL; for example, the tool we use, FlowDroid [20] has known limitations with respect to reflection.

Finally, PEDAL cannot detect the use of native code for resource access. Native code cannot bypass resource permissions since these are enforced by the kernel, but can bypass PEDAL's privilege de-escalation. As we show above, today's ad libraries do not appear to use native code for resource access. This is primarily because native code cannot access Android abstractions such as services and content providers [6]; these provide apps with access to location, the contact database, call logs, account/profile, etc. Also, recently, Android terms for ad networks enforce user tracking through a unique Google Advertising ID [3] assigned to each user, which also cannot be accessed by native code. Native code can use lower-level APIs for Internet access (sockets). In this case, PEDAL can effect privilege de-escalation by collaborating with a transparent Web proxy, such as Sandrop [16], an approach we have left to future work. Thus, most of the resources protected by PEDAL cannot be accessed natively, and for the Internet resource, a plausible solution exists. In the future, PEDAL can protect other resources (if any) that might be accessible by native code, by extending binary rewriting to native code, perhaps using Dynamic Binary Translation techniques [42, 50, 63], and we have left this to future work.

**Extensions and Generalizations.** PEDAL's contributions go beyond privilege de-escalation. Our classifier-based approach can be used to identify bytecode sets with different properties, such as social network or e-business plugins, or to train classifiers to recognize multiple categories. Moreover, PEDAL's privilege de-escalation can be combined with methods that implement other forms of fine-grained access control to support advanced privacy policies such as "allow location data access for ad libraries only during daytime," "block Internet access to http://www.hotads.com for ad libraries."

More generally, the strategy we have investigated in the paper is to first *separate and distribute code fragments to different functional sets*, and then *control each separated component individually*. This strategy should be generally applicable to other mobile platforms, though the details of the approach will differ for different platforms. For example, Windows Mobile platform uses C# (and C# bytecode), so it should be quite straightforward to extend our technique to support it by using bytecode analysis and rewriting frameworks for C#, such as CCI (Common Compiler Infrastructure)[14]. iOS uses Objective C, and other work has used binary rewriting for iOS apps as well [60], so we believe PEDAL's approach can be extended to iOS apps as well.

**Reconciling Controllability and Usability.** PEDAL can be treated as an extension to the default model of Android resource access control. However, while providing finer-grained options, it also increases the information workload for users to manage the settings, and, thus, may be preferred only by experienced or expert users. One way to address this extra workload is to use the technique of Privacy Revelations [61] to provide more details about how users' private data are spread among the app logic part and the ad library part so that app users can better understand and manage these settings. Another possible solution is to apply profile-based methods [44, 45] to reconcile privacy and usability to reduce users' burden of managing the settings by learning users' general preferences and providing smart default settings for users.

**Possible Countermeasures.** Ad libraries or app developers could foil PEDAL by: (1) Performing code obfuscation even for public APIs; in this case, developers may need to use some confusing APIs, such as "a.b" or "b.c.d" to integrate and call ad libraries, and this can reduce the accuracy of our Separator to around 84% according to Table 2; (2) Instead of using third-party ad libraries, developers can implement their own ad libraries (and may have to set up their own ad networks) and mix the implementation together with app logic, in which case, it could be very difficult to make any meaningful separation. While these countermeasures are feasible, they require significantly more development efforts.

## 8. RELATED WORK

Our work is inspired by two strands of work: one on selective privileges and fine-grained access control in mobile systems, and the other on analyzing malicious behaviors within the ad ecosystem.

**Selective Privileges.** Most closely related to PEDAL is prior work that has considered the precise form of selective privilege assignment for ad libraries. AdSplit [55] achieves this goal by extending the Android OS so that the application logic and the ad library run in different processes with different user IDs. AdDroid [49] instead suggests introducing a new set of API calls and permissions for ad libraries to Android system. LayerCake [53] modifies Android to permit ad libraries to embed UI elements in the main logic, without exposing data or privileges of the main app. Finally, Compac [59] modifies the Android OS to enable component level privileges, and developers need to manually distinguish components. Unlike these systems, PEDAL does not require modifications to the underlying operating system or its APIs, and does not require developer intervention.

**Fine-grained Access Control.** A complementary set of systems has considered fine-grained access control to resources. One line of

[14]https://ccimetadata.codeplex.com

work in this area has explored access control and information flow control techniques and associated expressive policy specification languages. Starting with TaintDroid [33], a long line of work has explored these techniques and languages: AppFence [38], MockDroid [25], Apex [48], TISSA [64], FlaskDroid [28], ASM [47] and ASF [22]. Another line of work has explored library re-writing [62] or loader modifications [18] to achieve the same goal. A third line of work has used binary rewriting (using techniques discussed in [31,36]) to achieve fine-grained access control [23,24,32,39,40,52] and derived and enforced sub-permissions in popular permission groups. None of these pieces of work attempt to enforce per-component access control; PEDAL is complementary and separates privileges per component, and PEDAL can be combined with some of these to provide finer-grained per component access control.

**Ad Analysis.** We have also been inspired by another line of work that explores the static or dynamic behavior of ad libraries. For example, several pieces of work have used static analysis to explore ad library security and privacy [35], the evolution of ad libraries [26], statistics of ad library usage on Google Play [58], characteristics of ad library APIs [27], users' common privacy preferences on ad libraries [44], and usage of ad-supported apps [57]. Our component separation technique builds upon the blacklisting techniques employed by these pieces of work: for example, [58] maintained a list of 21 ad libraries, [26] used a list of 68 ad libraries, and [35] generated a list of 100 ad libraries. In contrast, PEDAL is able to identify over 5× more ad library sources than prior work.

Finally, PEDAL is complementary to prior work that has used dynamic analysis to identify ad fraud [30, 46], or to estimate the impact of app plagiarism on ad revenue [34].

# 9. CONCLUSION

In this paper, we have described PEDAL, a system to achieve selective privilege de-escalation for ad libraries. PEDAL performs automated classification to identify ad library code, and rewrites core resource access functions and resource sharing functions of these bytecode sets to achieve de-escalation. PEDAL is robust, by design, to both package name obfuscations and source code obfuscation. Despite this, PEDAL shows remarkable classification accuracy and efficacy, yet requires reasonable computing power to process apps. Finally, PEDAL is effective and imposes negligible runtime overhead for apps.

## Acknowledgements

We would like to thank our shepherd, Landon Cox, and the anonymous referees, for their insightful suggestions for improving the technical content and presentation of the paper.

# 10. REFERENCES


[1] Android 4.3 Includes Hidden App Permissions Manager That Could Bolster Privacy & Security. `http://techcrunch.com/2013/07/26/android-app-ops/`, 2013.

[2] How to Restore Access to App Ops in Android 4.4.2+. `http://www.howtogeek.com/177915/how-to-restore-access-to-app-ops.....-in-android-4.4.2/`, 2013.

[3] Advertising ID. `https://developer.android.com/google/play-services/id.html`, 2014.

[4] Android API Guides. `https://developer.android.com/guide/index.html`, 2014.

[5] Android Application Fundamentals. `http://developer.android.com/guide/components/fundamentals.html`, 2014.

[6] Android NDK. `http://developer.android.com/tools/sdk/ndk/index.html`, 2014.

[7] AppBrain Statistics on Android Libraries: Ad Networks. `http://www.appbrain.com/stats/libraries/ad`, 2014.

[8] AXML: Read Write Android Binary XML and resources.arsc Files. `https://code.google.com/p/axml/`, 2014.

[9] Chartboost. `http://www.chartboost.com/`, 2014.

[10] Component-based Software Engineering. `http://en.wikipedia.org/wiki/Component-based_software_engineering`, 2014.

[11] Distribution of Free vs. Paid Android Apps. `http://www.appbrain.com/stats/free-and-paid-android-applications`, 2014.

[12] Gartner Says Worldwide Traditional PC, Tablet, Ultramobile and Mobile Phone Shipments to Grow 4.2 Percent in 2014. `http://www.gartner.com/newsroom/id/2791017`, 2014.

[13] Google Play. `https://play.google.com/store`, 2014.

[14] Install Adblock Plus for Android. `https://adblockplus.org/en/android-install`, 2014.

[15] ProGuard. `http://developer.android.com/tools/help/proguard.html`, 2014.

[16] Sandrop: Secure Android Proxy. `https://code.google.com/p/sandrop/`, 2014.

[17] Soot: a Java Optimization Framework. `http://www.sable.mcgill.ca/soot/`, 2014.

[18] XPricacy. `https://github.com/M66B/XPrivacy#xprivacy`, 2014.

[19] P. Aditya, B. Bhattacharjee, P. Druschel, V. Erdélyi, and M. Lentz. Brave New World: Privacy Risks for Mobile Users. In *Proc. ACM SPME*, 2014.

[20] S. Arzt, S. Rasthofer, C. Fritz, E. Bodden, A. Bartel, J. Klein, Y. L. Traon, D. Octeau, and P. McDaniel. FlowDroid: Precise Context, Flow, Field, Object-sensitive and Lifecycle-aware Taint Analysis for Android Apps. In *Proc. ACM PLDI*, 2014.

[21] K. Au, B. Zhou, J. Huang, and D. Lie. PScout: Analyzing the Android Permission Specification. In *Proc. ACM CCS*, 2012.

[22] M. Backes, S. Bugiel, S. Gerling, and P. Styp-Rekowsky. Android Security Framework: Enabling Generic and Extensible Access Control on Android. *arXiv preprint arXiv:1404.1395*, 2014.

[23] M. Backes, S. Gerling, C. Hammer, M. Maffei, and von P. Styp-Rekowsky. AppGuard: Enforcing User Requirements on Android Apps. In *Proc. ETAPS TACAS*. 2013.

[24] A. Bartel, J. Klein, M. Monperrus, K. Allix, and Y. Traon. Improving privacy on android smartphones through in-vivo bytecode instrumentation. *arXiv preprint arXiv:1208.4536*, 2012.

[25] A. R. Beresfordand, A. Rice, N. Skehin, and R. Sohan. MockDroid: Trading Privacy for Application Functionality on Smartphones. In *ACM HotMobile*, 2011.

[26] T. Book, A. Pridgen, and D. Wallach. Longitudinal Analysis of Android Ad Library Permissions. In *Proc. IEEE MoST*, 2013.

[27] T. Book and D. Wallach. A Case of Collusion: A Study of the Interface between Ad Libraries and Their Apps. In *Proc. ACM SPSM*, 2013.

[28] S. Bugiel, S. Heuser, and A. Sadeghi. Flexible and Fine-grained Mandatory Access Control on Android for Diverse Security and Privacy Policies. In *Proc. USENIX security*, 2013.

[29] C. Chang and C. Lin. LIBSVM: A Library for Support Vector Machines. *ACM Transactions on Intelligent Systems and Technology*, 2:27:1–27:27, 2011. Software available at `http://www.csie.ntu.edu.tw/~cjlin/libsvm`.

[30] J. Crussell, R. Stevens, and H. Chen. MAdFraud: Investigating Ad Fraud in Android Applications. In *Proc. ACM MobiSys*, 2014.

[31] B. Davis and H. Chen. Retroskeleton: Retrofitting Android apps. In *Proc. ACM MobiSys*, 2013.

[32] B. Davis, B. Sanders, A. Khodaverdian, and H. Chen. I-ARM-Droid: A Rewriting Framework for In-app Reference Monitors for Android Applications. In *Proc. IEEE MoST*, 2012.

[33] W. Enck, P. Gilbert, B. Chun, L. Cox, J. Jung, P. McDaniel, and A. Sheth. TaintDroid: An Information-flow Tracking System for Realtime Privacy Monitoring on Smartphones. In *Proc. OSDI*, 2010.

[34] C. Gibler, R. Stevens, J. Crussell, H. Chen, H. Zang, and H. Choi. AdRob: Examining the Landscape and Impact of Android Application Plagiarism. In *Proc. ACM MobiSys*, 2013.

[35] M. Grace, W. Zhou, X. Jiang, and A. Sadeghi. Unsafe Exposure Analysis of Mobile In-app Advertisements. In *Proc. ACM WiSec*, 2012.

[36] S. Hao, D. Li, W. Halfond, and R. Govindan. Sif: A selective instrumentation framework for mobile applications. In *Proc. ACM MobiSys*, 2013.

[37] S. Hao, B. Liu, S. Nath, W. Halfond, and R. Govindan. PUMA: Programmable UI-automation for Large Scale Dynamic Analysis of Mobile Apps. In *Proc. MobiSys*, 2014.

[38] P. Hornyack, S. Han, J. Jung, S. Schechter, and D. Wetherall. These Aren't the Droids You're Looking for: Retrofitting Android to Protect Data from Imperious Applications. In *Proc. ACM CCS*, 2011.

[39] J. Jeon, K. Micinski, and J. Vaughan. Application-Centric Security Policies on Unmodified Android. *University of Maryland Computer Science Department Technical Report*, 2011.

[40] J. Jeon, K. Micinski, J. Vaughan, A. Fogel, N. Reddy, J. Foster, and T. Millstein. Dr. Android and Mr. Hide: Fine-grained Permissions in Android Applications. In *Proc. SPSM*, 2012.

[41] P. G. Kelley, M. Benisch, L. F. Cranor, and N. Sadeh. When are users comfortable sharing locations with advertisers? In *Proceedings of the SIGCHI Conference on Human Factors in Computing Systems*, CHI '11, pages 2449–2452, New York, NY, USA, 2011. ACM.

[42] V. Kiriansky, D. Bruening, and S. Amarasinghe. Secure execution via program shepherding. In *Proc. USENIX Security*, 2002.

[43] J. Lin, S. Amini, J. Hong, N. Sadeh, J. Lindqvist, and J. Zhang. Expectation and Purpose: Understanding Users' Mental Models of Mobile App Privacy through Crowdsourcing. In *Proc. ACM UbiComp*, 2012.

[44] J. Lin, B. Liu, J. Hong, and N. Sadeh. Modeling Users' Mobile App Privacy Preferences: Restoring Usability in a Sea of Permission Settings. In *Proc. SOUPS*, 2014.

[45] B. Liu, J. Lin, and N. Sadeh. Reconciling Mobile App Privacy and Usability on Smartphones: Could User Privacy Profiles Help? In *Proc. WWW*, 2014.

[46] B. Liu, S. Nath, R. Govindan, and J. Liu. DECAF: Detecting and Characterizing Ad Fraud in Mobile Apps. In *USENIX NSDI*, 2014.

[47] A. Nadkarni and W. Enck. ASM: A Programmable Interface for Extending Android Security. In *Proc. USENIX security*, 2014.

[48] M. Nauman, S. Khan, and X. Zhang. Apex: Extending Android Permission Model and Enforcement with User-defined Runtime Constraints. In *Proc. ASIACCS*, 2010.

[49] P. Pearce, A. Felt, G. Nunez, and D. Wagner. AdDroid: Privilege Separation for Applications and Advertisers in Android. In *Proc. ACM ASIACCS*, 2012.

[50] M. Probst. Dynamic Binary Translation. In *Proc. UKUUG Linux DeveloperâĂŹs Conference*, 2002.

[51] S. Rasthofer, S. Arzt, and E. Bodden. A Machine-learning Approach for Classifying and Categorizing Android Sources and Sinks. In *Proc. NDSS*, 2014.

[52] N. Reddy, J. Jeon, J. Vaughan, T. Millstein, and J. Foster. Application-Centric Security Policies on Unmodified Android. *UCLA Computer Science Department Technical Report*, 2011.

[53] F. Roesner and T. Kohno. Securing embedded user interfaces: Android and beyond. In *Proc. USENIX Security*, 2013.

[54] S. Rosen, Z. Qian, and Z. Mao. AppProfiler: a Flexible Method of Exposing Privacy-related Behavior in Android Applications to End Users. In *Proc. ACM CODASPY*, 2013.

[55] S. Shekhar, M. Dietz, and D. Wallach. AdSplit: Separating Smartphone Advertising from Applications. In *Proc. USENIX Security*, 2012.

[56] R. Stevens, C. Gibler, J. Crussell, J. Erickson, and H. Chen. Investigating User Privacy in Android Ad Libraries. In *Proc. IEEE MoST*, 2012.

[57] A. Tongaonkar, S. Dai, A. Nucci, and D. Song. Understanding Mobile App Usage Patterns Using in-App Advertisements. In *Proc. Passive and Active Measurement*, 2013.

[58] N. Viennot, E. Garcia, and J. Nieh. A Measurement Study of Google Play. In *Proc. ACM SIGMETRICS*, 2014.

[59] Y. Wang, S. Hariharan, C. Zhao, J. Liu, and W. Du. Compac: Enforce Component-level Access Control in Android. In *ACM CODASPY*, 2014.

[60] T. Werthmann, R. Hund, L. Davi, A. Sadeghi, and T. Holz. PSiOS: Bring Your Own Privacy & Security to iOS Devices. In *ACM ASIACCS*, 2013.

[61] D. Wetherall, D. Choffnes, B. Greenstein, S. Han, P. Hornyack, J. Jung, S. Schechter, and X. Wang. Privacy Revelations for Web and Mobile Apps.

[62] R. Xu, H. Saidi, and R. Anderson. Aurasium: Practical Policy Enforcement for Android Applications. In *Proc. USENIX Security*, 2012.

[63] B. Yee, D. Sehr, G. Dardyk, J. Chen, R. Muth, T. Ormandy, S. Okasaka, N. Narula, and N. Fullagar. Native client: A sandbox for portable, untrusted x86 native code. In *Proc. IEEE Security and Privacy*, 2009.

[64] Y. Zhou, X. Zhang, X. Jiang, and V. Freeh. Taming Information-stealing Smartphone Applications (on Android). In *Proc. TRUST*, 2011.

# GameOn: p2p Gaming On Public Transport

Nairan Zhang‡*, Youngki Lee†, Meera Radhakrishnan†, and Rajesh Krishna Balan†
‡Department of Electrical and Computer Engineering, University of Wisconsin-Madison,
†School of Information Systems, Singapore Management University

## ABSTRACT

Mobile games, and especially multiplayer games are a very popular daily distraction for many users. We hypothesise that commuters travelling on public buses or trains would enjoy being able to play multiplayer games with their fellow commuters to alleviate the commute burden and boredom. We present quantitative data to show that the typical one-way commute time is fairly long (at least 25 minutes on average) as well as survey results indicating that commuters are willing to play multiplayer games with other random commuters. In this paper, we present *GameOn*, a system that allows commuters to participate in multiplayer games with each other using p2p networking techniques that reduces the need to use high latency and possibly expensive cellular data connections. We show how *GameOn* uses a cloud-based matchmaking server to eliminate the overheads of discovery as well as show why *GameOn* uses Wi-Fi Direct over Bluetooth as the p2p networking medium. We describe the various system components of *GameOn* and their implementation. Finally, we present numerous results collected by using *GameOn*, with three real games, on many different public trains and buses with up to four human players in each game play.

## Categories and Subject Descriptors

C.2.1 [**Network Architecture and Design**]: Wireless communication; C.3 [**Special-Purpose and Application-based Systems**]: Real-time and embedded systems; C.5.3 [**Microcomputers**]: Portable devices

## General Terms

Design, Experimentation, Performance, Measurement

## Keywords

p2p Games; Mobile Gaming; Public Transportation

*This work was done when he was a Ph.D. intern at Singapore Management University.


*MobiSys'15*, May 18–22, 2015, Florence, Italy.

ACM 978-1-4503-3494-5/15/05 ...$15.00.
http://dx.doi.org/10.1145/2742647.2742660.

## 1. INTRODUCTION

Games remain the most popular application category on both the iOS and Android ecosystems [14] in terms of downloads, usage, and revenue earned. In particular, multiplayer games are becoming increasingly popular to both game players and developers. Players find that the unpredictability that arises from playing against human opponents keeps them engaged for much longer periods while game developers find that more engaged users generate a lot more ads and in-game sales revenues than players who play for a few minutes and then leave. Indeed some of the most lucrative and popular games on both the mobile [11] and console markets [37] tend to be multiplayer-focused games such as Brave Frontier, Clash of Clans, and Pirate Kings on mobile devices and FIFA 15, Destiny, and Call of Duty: Advanced Warfare on consoles. In these games, players usually play against random strangers either individually or in groups where each group is made up of friends or even random strangers.

Multiplayer games encourage players to spend tens of minutes or longer for every game session (especially for games where the other human players are also interacting in real time) unlike casual single player games such as Candy Crush or Angry Birds that are optimised for one to five minutes of short game sessions. As such, these types of longer multiplayer games tend to be played during lunch breaks or after work/school is over.

However, there is also another opportunity to play longer multiplayer games. In many dense crowded urban cities (which are common in Asia and Europe, and include some US cities like New York City and San Francisco), the cost of driving tends to be quite high in terms of traffic, time taken, aggravation, and parking availability, etc. As such, a significant fraction of the population in these cities take public transport for their daily commute. These commutes also tend to be long – for example, as we show in Section 3, the average one-way commute time in Singapore is about 26 minutes with larger times reported for other urban cities (e.g., 40 minutes for New York City, 66 minutes for Tokyo, and 97 minutes for Beijing).

This commute period is a natural "down time" where the commuter can be engaged. Currently, many commuters spend the time by sleeping, reading something, or using their phones to check email, browse the web, chat with friends, watch videos, listen to music, or play games. We also observed that an increasingly large fraction has access to smartphones (87% smartphone penetration in Singapore and Hong Kong and rapidly rising in other Asian cities [28]) that have the performance and networking capabilities required for mobile game playing. We thus hypothesise that these commuters could benefit from playing spontaneous multiplayer games, to ease the commute boredom, if the functionality was available.

Thus, we present *GameOn*, a system for allowing public transport commuters to engage in multiplayer games with fellow commuters travelling on the same bus or train. The key technical challenges we overcame were:

**High 3G/LTE latencies**. This causes serious lag and playability issues in multiplayer games (especially in the near real-time games like shooting or racing games). We overcame this by using p2p networking solutions for the actual game plays.

**Identifying the appropriate p2p networking mechanisms**. As we show in Section 4.4, Bluetooth [6] does not work well for this use case. Instead, we used Wi-Fi Direct [39], a relatively new Wi-Fi mode optimised for p2p communications, which is now a standard feature on new smartphones, as our communication medium. We showed performance characteristics of both Bluetooth and Wi-Fi Direct in various p2p game scenarios.

**Matching game players in an efficient way**. A drawback of pure p2p solutions is that neighbour discovery can take a long time. We overcame this by using the insight that all the passengers still have Internet connectivity via cellular connections — albeit with high latency and low bandwidth. We leveraged this and used a central server to perform the matchmaking of players. This also allowed us to match players based on various pre-collected player information such as skill levels, travel times, and other preferences.

**Working with minimal modifications to existing systems**. For *GameOn* to be successful, it should be as backward compatible as possible. As such, we designed it to run as a normal application (root access is not needed) with minimal changes needed to existing applications. For instance, we retained the existing client-server models used by most existing games to minimise code changes. Thus, one smartphone will have to serve as both the master server as well as a client — we show that the energy overhead for the server phone is still quite acceptable. We also intentionally kept *GameOn* as simple as possible to make it easier to deploy, debug, and explain to end users.

Overall, we make the following contributions:

- A detailed analysis of the public transport travel times in Singapore. In particular, we show how long passengers are co-located on the same train or bus (which is the shared time when they can play a game together). We also present summary results for 11 other cities.
- A detailed comparison of the efficacy of Bluetooth and Wi-Fi Direct as a communication medium for playing multiplayer games. We show results from both in-lab synthetic experiments as well as real-world experiments conducted by playing games on actual public trains at various times of the day.
- A detailed description of the design and implementation of *GameOn*. This includes a discussion of how the *GameOn* matchmaker can be extended to support many more metrics (such as co-location times and connection stability) to enable spontaneous p2p games, beyond ping times commonly used by existing matchmakers.
- An in-depth evaluation of *GameOn* that comprises of both micro benchmarks involving synthetic evaluations of various system components as well as real-world tests involving actual game play, using three different popular games, on a public train (at various times of the day). The games chosen were *OpenArena* [34], *Racer* [27], and *2048* [30], which represent the shooter, car racing, and casual game genres, respectively. We have posted videos of *GameOn* being used with these games on commuter trains and buses at **http://tinyurl.com/gameon-videos**.

## 2. MOTIVATING SCENARIOS

*Jill is heading to school and her regular commute involves a 25 minute train ride. She boards the train and settles in for the somewhat long journey. She starts using her smartphone to do her regular routine — check emails, browse news articles, facebook posts, and videos tagged by friends. However, she quickly finishes all of these and realises that she is still 20 minutes away from her station and she is getting bored.*

*Fortunately, she remembers about that new application, called* GameOn*, that her friend asked her to install. She starts* GameOn *and sees that 3 people around her are interested in playing Quake III multiplayer (which is setup to require at least 4 people). She expresses her interest in playing the game. Within seconds,* GameOn *starts a server on one of the 4 phones, and automatically connects all the 4 game players (using their anonymous in-game IDs) to the server using Wi-Fi Direct and the game starts. 10 minutes later, the game concludes as some of the participants get off the train. Jill is happy with her performance and wonders who she was playing with (that info is not revealed).*

*She realises that she still has ≈ 10 minutes left and she decides to see if a quick round of 2048 (a puzzle game) is possible. She re-starts* GameOn *and specifies that she is looking for one other person to play 2048 with. Within seconds, she is connected with another anonymous player (on the same train) and the game starts. This continues until Jill reaches her train stop at which point she ends the game, gets off, and goes to her classes happily.*

The above scenario motivates the entire design of *GameOn*. In Section 3, we first show that passengers spend sufficient shared time on public buses and trains. We then present the design, implementation, and evaluation of *GameOn* in the remaining sections.

## 3. IS GAMEON EVEN PRACTICAL?

To support the above scenarios, we require a number of preconditions to be true as follows:

1 First and most importantly, commuters must be on the same train or bus long enough for a shared game session to be feasible. Prior work [29] has published the minimum game length at about 10 minutes. Accounting for the overheads of settling onto the bus/train and allowing for time to finish reading emails, news sites, etc., we pessimistically need commuters to be co-located with a large number of other commuters on the same train or bus for at least 20 to 25 minutes for a *GameOn*-like system to be plausible.
We present rigorous analysis of Singapore's transportation system data (Section 3.1) along with summary data from other countries (Section 3.2), and show that these shared commute times are very achievable in practice.

2 Second, commuters need to have a smartphone that is capable of supporting a wide range of multiplayer games. Fortunately, industry progress has solved this issues and modern smartphones (any smartphone bought from 2013 onwards) have the CPU, GPU, memory, and networking capabilities to support many different types of multiplayer games. Indeed the ability to play many types of games is a key selling point for smartphones in some countries.
Note: It is possible for our solution to be adapted to work on feature phones (using Bluetooth instead of Wi-Fi Direct – albeit with worse performance in some cases). However, we did not do that as a) the number of games available on feature phones is limited and, b) the smartphone penetration rate has been growing rapidly even in developing countries

(such as Indonesia, Thailand, and India) due to decreasing phone costs and increasing prosperity [12].

3 Third and finally, commuters must have the interest to play games while on buses and trains with others, probably random commuters. Fortunately, statistics [14] show that games are the most popular applications downloaded from any app store and this popularity increases as the population gets younger. In addition, multiplayer games tend to be the most engaging of all game types. Thus, we believe that the desire to play multiplayer games is present in a large fraction of the commuting population. We also present results from a self-reported survey in Section 3.1, showing that a majority of commuters are interested in playing mobile multiplayer games even with random commuters.

## 3.1 Public Commute Times in Singapore

In this section, we present a detailed analysis of the commute times observed in Singapore.

### 3.1.1 *Singapore's Public Transportation Network*

Singapore is a small country of about 715 square kilometres (≈60% the size of New York City) with about 5.3 million inhabitants. It has a modern integrated public transportation network of trains, buses, and taxis (not considered for this analysis). The bus network uses about about 360 bus routes to serve over 4,800 bus stops while the train network comprises of over 120 stations across 5 main lines. In total, the buses and trains handle over 6 million trips per day [18].

Singapore uses a NFC-based store value card system to pay for bus and train rides that requires every commuter to tap their NFC cards at both entry and exit before the actual fare is computed based on the distance travelled. This is different from fixed rate systems used elsewhere, such as the New York City and Paris subways, which only require a tap on entry. This requirement to tap in and out makes it possible for data analysts to know exactly when a particular NFC card has entered or exited a bus or train station (even though the owner of the card is unknown).

### 3.1.2 *Singapore Transportation Data Set*

We used three months of bus and train entry and exit data (from November 2011 to January 2012) obtained from the Land Transport Authority of Singapore [16]. For every public bus, we had the time and location (bus stop number) where every passenger boarded and alighted. For trains, we have, for every train station, the exact time when a commuter entered and left that train station. With these two sets of data along with the publicly available train/bus timings and route maps, we can quantitatively determine the average commute time needed to reach any destination in Singapore. Table 1 summarises the data used for this analysis.

For the purpose of this analysis, we used our university campus as the final destination and calculate the commute time statistics needed to reach our campus from any location in Singapore. Note 1: because our university campus is located down town, it is very well connected and served by 3 different train stations and 43 different bus routes across 7 different bus stops. Note 2: when performing our analysis, we only considered the most direct routes to our campus that did not require switching between trains to buses and vice versa.

### 3.1.3 *Quantitative Analysis Results*

Table 2 shows the results of our data-driven analysis for both trains and buses across all 5 weekdays for both peak hours (7.30 a.m. - 9.30 a.m.) and off-peak hours (9.31 a.m. - 5.59 p.m.). Note that we only consider the morning peak period as the evening peak period will not have too many people coming to campus.

| Bus Data | Nov. 2011 | Dec. 2011 | Jan. 2012 |
|---|---|---|---|
| Total # of Records | 100,521,633 | 100,732,193 | 105,449,970 |
| Unique Bus Routes | 353 | 353 | 353 |
| Unique Bus Stops | 4873 | 4873 | 4873 |
| Unique Commuters | 3,910,636 | 4,364,309 | 4,202,792 |

| Train Data | Nov. 2011 | Dec. 2011 | Jan. 2012 |
|---|---|---|---|
| Total # of Records | 62,272,880 | 63,655,069 | 63,092,608 |
| Unique Train Stations | 127 | 127 | 127 |
| Unique Commuters | 4,210,625 | 4,051,357 | 4,384,240 |

**Table 1: Summary of Public Transportation Data**

| | Commute Time (mins) | | | |
|---|---|---|---|---|
| | Bus | | Train | |
| | Peak | Off-Peak | Peak | Off-Peak |
| Mon | 17.4 (9.2) | 18.5 (10.6) | 24.1 (11.1) | 23.3 (13.4) |
| Tue | 16.5 (11.8) | 17.1 (9.8) | 27.5 (12.9) | 21.1 (13.7) |
| Wed | 17.0 (10.4) | 17.9 (10.1) | 25.6 (11.2) | 20.5 (13.3) |
| Thu | 16.9 (11.0) | 17.1 (10.3) | 27.9 (12.9) | 20.9 (13.6) |
| Fri | 17.1 (10.7) | 17.4 (10.2) | 25.6 (11.2) | 21.1 (13.6) |
| All | 16.9 (10.8) | 17.6 (10.2) | 26.5 (12.1) | 21.4 (13.5) |

Numbers in parenthesis are the standard deviations

**Table 2: Average Commute Times for Buses and Trains**

The data shows that the average time spent on a bus is about 17 minutes with a fairly high standard deviation (numbers in parenthesis). For trains, the average time is about 26 minutes with a reasonably large standard deviation as well. This matches well with reported data [18] that states that trains are the preferred option for longer routes. However, even though these numbers look low, many commuters experience higher commute times as they need to take more indirect routes that involve multiple trains/buses for their commute. We show this through a survey in the following section where the majority of respondents reported high commute times with more than one transfer.

### 3.1.4 *Qualitative Survey Results*

In addition to the data driven analysis presented above, which is completely game agnostic, we also surveyed a large number of undergraduates along with a few working professionals to obtained their self-reported commute times and willingness to play multiplayer games while commuting.

We send out an online survey (with 20 questions) to various school mailing lists, and 118 participants voluntarily responded to the survey. To avoid biasing the answers, we did not provide any details about *GameOn* in the survey, and participants had no idea what the purpose of the survey was (except that it was a public transportation survey). All user-centric experiments reported in this paper were conducted after obtaining an appropriate IRB approval. We did not provide any form of compensation for doing the survey.

Out of 118 participants, 85 (72%) were males and 33 (28%) were females, across various age groups: 18-20 - 15 (13%), 21-25 - 69 (58%), 26-30 - 20 (17%), 31+ - 4 (4%). 91 (77%) were students with 24 (20%) working professionals and 3 (3%) others. 69 (58%) participants used an Android smartphone, 41 (35%) an iPhone, with just 8 (7%) others. The full set of survey responses can be obtained at **http://tinyurl.com/gameon-responses** with the raw data at **http://tinyurl.com/gameon-responses-raw**.

| City | Average One-Way Commute Time (minutes) |
|---|---|
| London | 39.5 [36] |
| New York | 40.0 [1] |
| Montreal | 38.0 [25] |
| Toronto | 39.5 [25] |
| Tokyo | 66.0 [4] |
| Seoul | 53.0 [33] |
| Hong Kong | 46.0 [8] |
| Taipei | 37.5 [26] |
| Beijing | 97.0 [7] |
| Delhi | 42.3 [38] |
| Mumbai | 47.3 [38] |

**Table 3: Average Commute Times for Other Cities**

The key survey results were the following: 90% (106 participants) used public transport daily with 67 (57%) taking buses and 86 (73%) taking trains (note: some participants take both trains and buses). The average one-way commute time for the participants (time spent only on buses/trains/cars going from home to work/school excluding any walking time) was "Less than 10 minutes" - 4 (3%), "10-20 minutes" - 17 (14%), "20-30 minutes" - 27 (23%), "30-40 minutes" - 27 (23%), "40-50 minutes" - 15 (13%), "50-60 minutes" - 13 (11%), "Other" - 15 (13%). In particular, 83% of the participants had commute times $> 20$ minutes. In addition, 61% of the participants took more than one bus/train during commuting.

In addition, 90 participants (76%) stated that they played mobile games on their phones with 67 (57%) saying that they played mobile games while commuting. The most popular type of game played were Casual games (56 responses (47%)), with Puzzle Games (37 (31%)), and Strategy Games (30 (25%)) close behind.

Finally, 64 participants (54%) answered yes to the question "Are you interested in playing multiplayer games with other commuters travelling in the same bus/train/car?". When asked why they wanted to play these games, the answers provided were "Ease the boredom during the commute" - 44 (37%), "Potential to meet more people who share similar interests" - 34 (28%), "Thrill of competitive challenge inherent in multiplayer gaming" - 33 (28%), "Other" - 2 (2%).

For the 54 participants (46%) who were against the idea, the most common reason offered (via a free form text box) was the unwillingness to pay for 3G/LTE bandwidth just to play a game on the train – "Dataplan consumption and slow / connectivity issue when in train". They also felt that the 3G/LTE speeds were not good enough for gaming – "You need a solid connection when playing such games during commuting. Singapore's telco isn't able to provide that solid connection underground". Another strong opinion raised was the fear that playing with nearby strangers would impact their real world comfort levels – "Do you really think we are that open to play with strangers standing right next to us? Its okay when we do it over the internet because we don't know who that is". Finally, some participants feared that the game experience would be bad due to poor player quality or players leaving abruptly.

Overall, the survey results indicate that there is potential for *GameOn* to be successful. However, to become even more accepted, *GameOn* must reduce the use of 3G/LTE bandwidth that a) may have high usage charges in some countries, and b) might have connectivity issues in certain parts of the transport network. *GameOn* overcomes this by using completely local bandwidth provided by Wi-Fi Direct to support the various games. Thus, it does not incur any charges and is much less likely to have connectivity issues. In addition, the survey shows that the matchmaking component also needs to take into account the physical proximity of people when making a match – we might want to avoid matching people who are physically too close to each other and also take into account the expected trip length for each person to avoid game interruptions caused by people leaving.

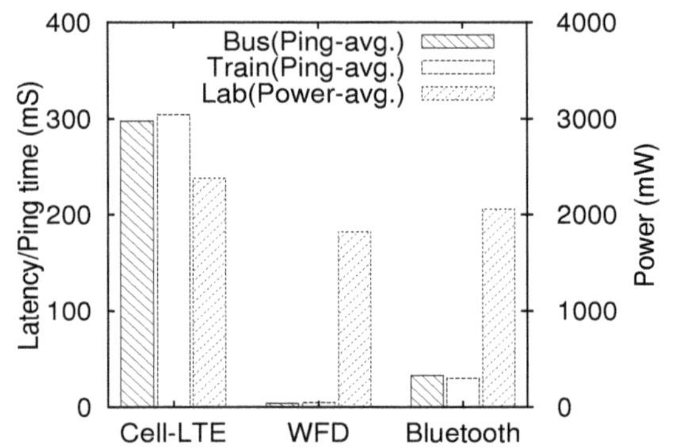


All experiments were conducted with a Galaxy S3 & S5 Android smartphones. The latencies were computed by pinging a common in-lab server. The power consumption was measured in our lab using a Monsoon power monitor [24]. WFD == Wi-Fi Direct.

**Figure 1: Latency & Power Consumption Comparison**

## 3.2 Commute Times in Other Major Cities

We additionally describe analysis of the commute times observed in other urban cities (from prior work and online sources). Table 3 shows our findings. What we observe is that commute times in other cities tends to be higher (some quite significantly!) than those in Singapore (which were computed using raw data). Hence, *GameOn* might also prove to be useful in other cities.

# 4. DESIGN GOALS & ASSUMPTIONS

In this section, we present the design goals for *GameOn* along with our assumptions.

## 4.1 Design Goals

The main design goals for *GameOn* were:

- **Provide a smooth gameplay experience**: This is the most important design goal and it permeates all the other goals below. In a nutshell, *GameOn* should add as little overhead as possible to both game players and game developers.
- **Low latency networking with sufficient bandwidth**: A key cause of discontent in multiplayer games is lag caused by network issues. Thus, *GameOn* should not introduce any user noticeable lag or bandwidth artefacts when games are being played. We compared the client to server latencies and energy consumption of LTE, Bluetooth, and Wi-Fi Direct (results shown in Figure 1) and found Wi-Fi Direct to have the lowest latencies and the lowest energy consumption. *GameOn* thus uses Wi-Fi Direct for the actual game plays while using the cellular Internet connectivity only for the matchmaking process (a low bandwidth latency tolerant task that requires history tracking)
- **Easy and effective matchmaking**: Commuters should be able to easily express their game interests and also easily find games that they can join. The matchmaker should also ensure that the players in the game do not leave abruptly and that any skill, demographics, or other factors are also factored in, where necessary, when performing the matchmaking. For example, even though *GameOn* enables playing multiplayer games with fellow passengers in close proximity, some players may not want to be matched with players located next

to them on the bus/train as they may not want their physical identities to be easily discovered. To support this, we use a centralised matchmaking service, that can track historical performance etc., located in the cloud.

- **Use simple user-space mechanisms**: For *GameOn* to be easily deployable, it has to be a user space component (i.e., no rooting of the phone is required) and it should be as simple as possible (making it easier to explain to end users and more robust overall). In addition, we retain the existing client-server models used by almost all multiplayer games. However, this requires us to dynamically host the server on one of the smartphones of the commuters playing that game. The game and player statistics are then uploaded to the matchmaking service after the game ends.
- **Low energy usage**: *GameOn* should not add any significant energy cost beyond the cost of playing the game itself. In particular, the smartphone that has to host the game should not see a large increase in energy usage.

## 4.2 Assumptions

The assumptions we made when devising a solution that addressed our design goals were the following: 1) We assume that every commuter had access to a smartphone with cellular Internet connectivity. The smartphone was necessary for gameplay while the connectivity was necessary to use a central matchmaker. 2) Some changes to the game interfaces may be needed for *GameOn* to be fully operational. In particular, the game will a) have to report game statistics (in game scores etc.) to *GameOn* so that it can be used during matchmaking and b) have to use the *GameOn* APIs to send data to/from other p2p clients. Indeed, to demonstrate how easy our APIs are to use, for our evaluation, we converted, with minimal effort, an open source *single player version* of a popular game, *2048*, to work as a multiplayer game using *GameOn*. Finally, 3) we assume that the multiplayer games will only be played by a small number of players – 2 to 6 players at most. This system is not designed by larger games that involve 10s or 100s simultaneous players. However, there can be multiple games being played simultaneously in the same area.

## 4.3 Overall Architecture

To satisfy the design requirements stated in Section 4, *GameOn* was designed to use a hybrid p2p architecture composed of *GameOn* clients interacting with each other using local networking capabilities coupled with a matchmaking service located in the cloud. Figure 2 shows the architecture overview of *GameOn*. We focus our discussion on only a few core modules (the shaded blocks in Figure 2). Overall, *GameOn* comprises of two components:

**1. *GameOn* clients**: A *GameOn* client supports various multiplayer games that can be played by peers co-located on a train or bus. It has a UI component that allows players to login, specify grouping preferences, and discover co-located peers. When a user starts *GameOn*, peer discovery is started and any discovered peers (along with their performance metrics) is passed to the matchmaker. Upon request, the matchmaker provides the *GameOn* client with the list of playable games and corresponding game hosts. When a peer is already hosting a user's desirable game, the *GameOn* client makes a new game client connection to the peer. Otherwise, it serves as a game host for the user's specified game and waits for other players to join.

The game play is automatically initiated when the required number of players join. During game play, *GameOn* clients form a star topology by default, and all the game packets are relayed through

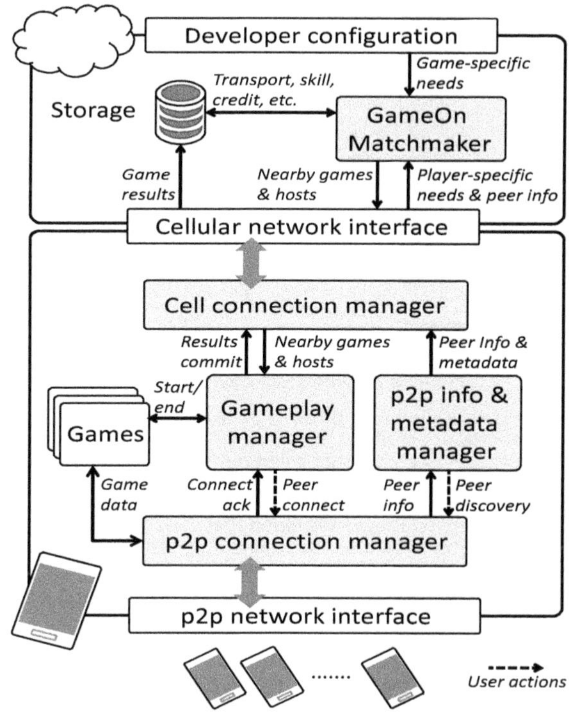


**Figure 2: The *GameOn* Architecture**

the host device; *GameOn* also supports a multi-hop topology when a host cannot be connected to a client directly due to distance (located on the other side of the train for example). The *Gameplay Manager* component configures the *p2p connection manager* component by specifying the role of the player in a group and the topology of collocated peers. Note: We do not require any changes to the existing game logic to support this type of p2p game play. *GameOn* wraps around the original networking APIs (Section 4.5) used by the multiplayer games and automatically re-routes packets to p2p hosts using either Wi-Fi Direct or Bluetooth. When the game ends, the game results and performance data are reported to the matchmaking server to update its records.

**2. The *GameOn* matchmaking server**: This server allows *GameOn* clients to find a set of players that are co-located and who will stay on the same bus/train long enough for a satisfying game session. It collects various information required for p2p matchmaking from *GameOn* clients such as the observed signal strength and ping times between peers, as well as the mobility patterns (how long they spend on a specific train etc.) and skill levels (how well they did in previous sessions of a game etc.) of each user (as represented by their mobile phones). We show how the matchmaker can use all available data (mobility history, user preferences, game-specific skill levels, and performance measures) to match the best set of people together for any game request.

## 4.4 Which p2p Protocol is Best on Trains?

The success of *GameOn* depends on having reliable p2p networking connectivity between peers on a bus or train. However, these are particularly challenging environments due to their movement, layouts, and frequent passenger movements. In this subsection, we present detailed performance results to understand the performance of wireless protocols in these environments.

The first key question we addressed was the choice of network protocol. The two main options were Bluetooth and Wi-Fi Direct. Eventually, we chose Wi-Fi Direct as its overall performance, beyond just the better latencies and power consumption (Figure 1), was better as explained below.

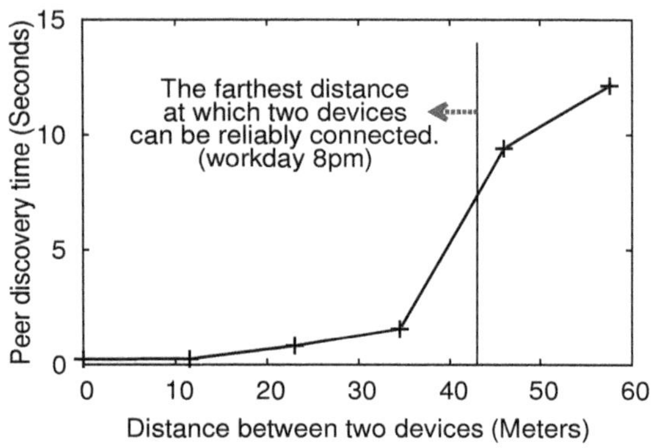


We found that discovery times > 10 seconds, corresponding to a peer distance of about 46 meters (2 carriages away) was a good indicator of a peer that could not be reliably connected to. We then shortened the inter-device distance by a meter at a time (roughly) and were able to reliably connect two devices at a 38 to 43 meter range. We found that even very far devices (70 meters away) could be eventually discovered (taking 108 seconds). We omit these long tail numbers from the plot.

**Figure 3: Discovery Time vs. Distance (Wi-Fi Direct)**

### 4.4.1 *Experiment Setup*

To understand how the protocols behave in realistic environments, we conducted experiments using Galaxy S3 and S5 smartphones on a train during three time periods – when the train was extremely full (6 p.m.), normal load (8 p.m.), and empty (midnight). We used the Galaxy S3 (running Android 4.3) as the stationary peer and moved the S5 (running Android 4.4.2) to different adjacent train carriages (up to 3 carriages away) and measured (on the S3), using both Bluetooth and Wi-Fi Direct, the RSSI signal strengths of the S5 and the ping times to the S5. Each train consisted of 3 carriages [17]. Each carriage was filled with numerous metallic objects (seats, hand rails, guard rails etc.) and was 23 meters in length, 3.2 meters in width, and 2.1 meters in height with a very small (negligible) inter-carriage gap. We repeated each experiment multiple times over different days. We do not report any results for buses as the public buses are shorter in length (each bus is about 12 meters long [32]) than a train carriage. Thus, the train is a more demanding environment.

### 4.4.2 *Peer Discovery, Connectivity & Density*

The first step in connecting phones together in a p2p fashion is to discover them. In our preliminary measurements, we also discovered that just because a device can be discovered does not mean that a successful connection can be made to it. A typical Wi-Fi Direct connection starts with scanning, then group owner negotiation, then provisioning, and finally DHCP. When peers are side-by-side, these steps can be done quickly without packet loss. However, as peers are further away and/or in "noisy" environments, these steps can become harder to complete.

To include the effect of people density in this experiment, we performed it during normal hours (when the train was normally crowded). With this level of crowd, we can assume that the density of people increases linearly as we move further away from the discovery node. To perform this experiment, we used one device as the stationary node and moved another device further and further away (in increments of half a train carriage every time). Both devices then tried to discover the other device. In addition to discovering the device, we also tried to connect to the device after it was discovered. We found that even though both devices could eventually discover each other (taking about 10 seconds) even at a two train carriage distance (about 46 meters), they were unable to actually connect to each other. However, at shorter distances, the two devices could discover and connect to each other. Our experiment results are shown in Figure 3.

The *GameOn* matchmaker has to make decisions about peering without being able to actually check the connectivity between those hosts – at best it knows something about inter-peer ping times. As such, a naive host assignment might pair hosts together who can discover each other but cannot actually connect (because one of the steps involved (probably DHCP) fails). What we discovered, for Wi-Fi Direct, was that the discovery time turned out to be a good predictor of connectivity. In particular, as shown in Figure 3, peers that could be discovered within 10 seconds (i.e., before the discovery time shoots up) can be successfully connected to.

However, even a 10 second discovery time can be too long as every scan is costly in terms of battery usage. Thus we reduced the scan time to 5 seconds to strike a balance between power consumption and finding enough nearby connectable peers. Each peer performs a scan every time it requests a peer match list from the matchmaker. This allows the matchmaker to gradually build a client map for a bus / train without needing aggressive client scanning.

The discussion above is solely for Wi-Fi Direct. We also repeated this discovery and connectivity tests for Bluetooth and achieved very disappointing results. We found that Bluetooth was unreliable beyond 20 to 25 meters. We show the difference between Bluetooth and Wi-Fi Direct in terms of RSSI and ping times in Figure 4.

### 4.4.3 *Effect of Density on Network Latency*

We now investigate the effect of people density on wireless performance – in particular the latency of the connection. This is important as games require low latency network connections. To do this, we picked three different times of the day (corresponding to light, normal, and heavy train/bus use) and four different inter-client distances. We measured the inter-client ping times and also measured the RSSI values. Note: the ping times changed when we repeated this experiment across different days. In the rest of this section, we present the ping times for the worst day.

Figure 4 shows how the signal strength and ping times changed as the distance to the peer phone varied. We observe that in all cases, Wi-Fi Direct performs better than Bluetooth. In particular, the second row of results shows the RSSI observed when the stationary phone connects to the moving peer using various protocols. The actual RSSI values are not important (as they fluctuate due to noise etc.). What matters is the pattern and trends.

For Wi-Fi Direct, we could connect using both the 5Ghz and 2.4Ghz spectrums with no clear winner in spectrum choice emerging. We found that, when the train was normally occupied, the maximum distance that a peer could be connected to was 2 carriages away using Wi-Fi Direct. For Bluetooth, the range was just 1 carriage away. When the train was busy, the range of Wi-Fi Direct decreased to just the same train carriage while Bluetooth could only usefully connect to clients very close by (distances greater than 20 meters had very high ping times).

The last row shows the ping times achievable to the connected peer using Wi-Fi Direct and Bluetooth. In all cases, the ping times for Wi-Fi Direct are much lower than Bluetooth. In addition, Bluetooth stops working (the line for the ping graphs stops) at much lower distances than Wi-Fi Direct. For example, on a normal occupancy train, Bluetooth stops receiving pings at about 20 meters while Wi-Fi Direct continues until about 60 meters.

### 4.4.4 *Connectivity Issues at Train Stations*

Unfortunately, even with Wi-Fi Direct, we found that if peers were 2 or more carriages apart, on entering a station, the process of

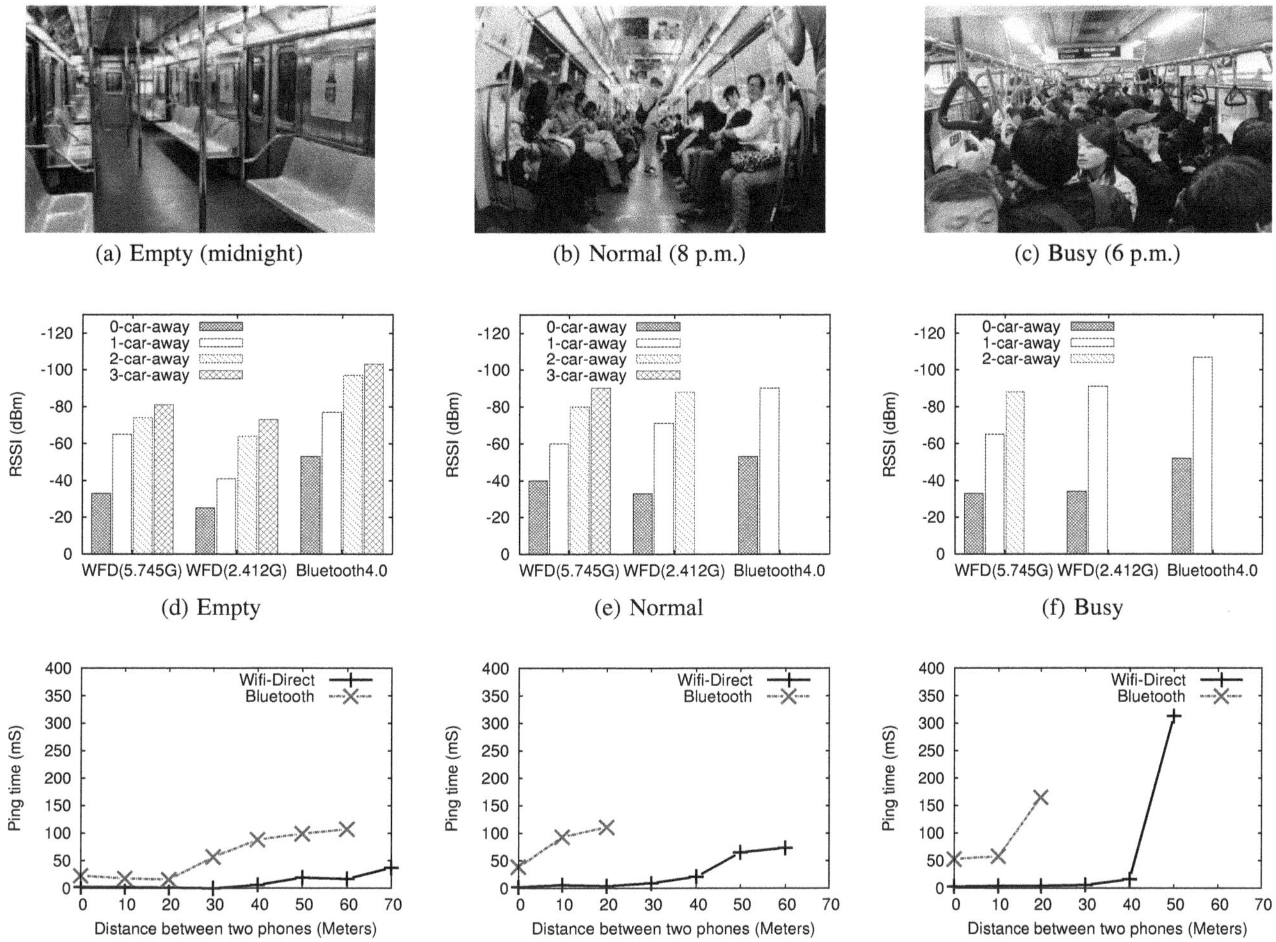


(a) Empty (midnight) (b) Normal (8 p.m.) (c) Busy (6 p.m.)

(d) Empty (e) Normal (f) Busy

(g) Empty (h) Normal (i) Busy

The top row shows the state of the train (empty, normal, busy) at the time of the measurement, the middle row shows the observed RSSI values of a peer device by a stationary phone (after connecting to that peer) when the peer device was placed further and further away (by up to 3 train carriages). The bottom row shows the observed ping times on one device (to the other) as the other device moved further away. Missing data in the figures indicates that the other phone was not connectable to or pingable at that distance using that protocol. Each result was repeated multiple times over different days and the averages are shown. We omit the error bars to improve readability as these results are presenting trends (actual values are not important).

**Figure 4: Comparison of Observed RSSI & Ping Times at Different Times on a Public Train**

| Games | Multiplayer already? | Language | Lines of code added |
|---|---|---|---|
| OpenArena [34] | Y | C / C++ | 8 |
| Racer [27] | N | Java | 86 |
| 2048 [30] | N | Java / JavaScript | 14 |

**Table 4: Three Games Modified to Use *GameOn***

opening the doors to let passengers embark and disembark resulted in high latency spikes. Figure 5 shows this where a peer (located 1 carriage away) experiences constant good ping times while another peer (located 2 carriages away) experiences consistent latency spikes which corresponded directly with the train entering a station, stopping, opening its door, and then leaving (the high latency goes away at this point). We have no current solution other than adding a matchmaking heuristic to not match peers more than one carriage away for games that cannot handle brief latency spikes.

## 4.5 Modifying Games to Work with GameOn

In this section, we describe how *GameOn* support can be added to existing games by making two different modification; 1) support local client-server multiplayer, and b) interface with *GameOn's* networking, matchmaking, and reporting APIs.

### *4.5.1 Games Used for Evaluation*

The first requirement for any game to work with *GameOn* is for the game to support client-server multiplayer. To make a game multiplayer compatible, it requires creating a server component for the game along with changing the UI, where necessary, to display any multiplayer-specific information. In this work, we decided to use both existing multiplayer games as well as support single-player games to understand the complexity inherent in making different types of games work with *GameOn*.

The three games we used are described in Table 4. *OpenArena* was the only game that already multiplayer-enabled with separate client and server components. Even in this case, as shown in Figure 6, we need to modify the game to use a local server (that is running on a peer phone and accessed via Wi-Fi Direct) instead of a server sitting in the cloud that is accessed via a cellular link.

Unlike OpenArena, *Racer* and *2048* were single player games that had no server component. For both games, we created a simple server that basically stored and forwarded packets to other clients. To help developers to extend existing singleplayer games to communicate with a game server, we provide two functions to share game state: *sendCommand(String jsonObjectInString)* is used to

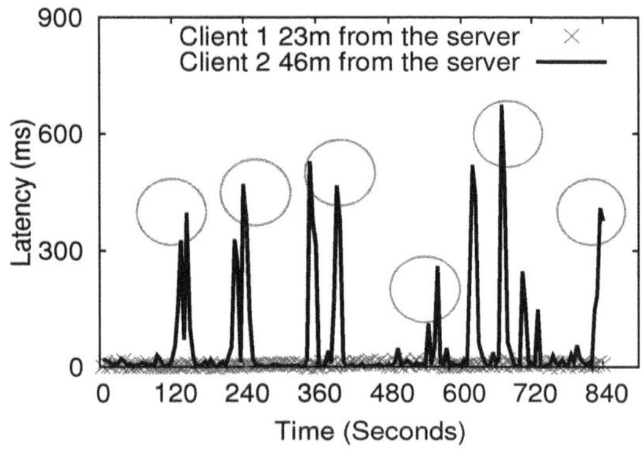


During a 15-minute experiment, the train stopped at 6 stations (times at each station are circled). We conducted this experiment during peak hours.

**Figure 5: Latency Spikes at Stations**

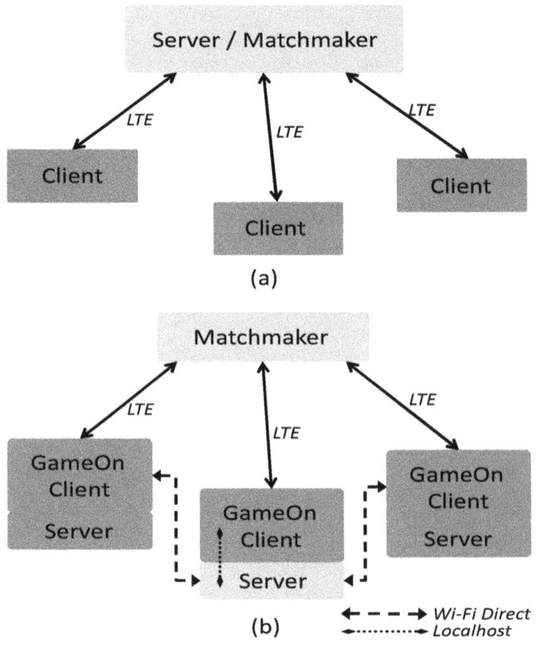


Unlike traditional approaches, in *GameOn*, each peer can serve as a client and also as a server. *GameOn* selects only one peer to serve as the game server. Game traffic is exchanged with peers using p2p connections (usually Wi-Fi Direct).

**Figure 6: Traditional Approach (a) vs. *GameOn* Approach (b)**

send client moves periodically, and *updateSnapshot()* is used to receive global game states from the game server.

In all cases, the amount of additional code we had to write was minimal (86 lines for *Racer* and 14 for *2048*). For both games, we did not modify the UI component and just leveraged the existing game code that could already display the output of a secondary player. Currently *GameOn* does not provide any UI modules as these components are very game specific. Instead, *GameOn* focuses on the networking components and provides enough infrastructure (and APIs) to allow game developers to concentrate on the UI and gameplay portions of the game and let *GameOn* handle all the networking bits.

### *4.5.2 Using GameOn Libraries*

Next, we had to modify all three games to use the *GameOn* APIs. This required 1) using the *GameOn* matchmaking service, 2) using the *GameOn* networking libraries, and 3) using the *GameOn* game statistics reporting libraries.

The matchmaking service is initiated by the player (in our prototype, the player presses a UI button). This is a single API call in *GameOn* and it sends a request to the matchmaker, using JSON objects, along with the performance measurements from the current client (neighbours discovered, ping times to neighbours etc.). The matchmaker responds with a list of games and hosts. The developer can then use *GameOn's* p2p APIs to initiate a game request with discovered clients. Once the game starts, the state sharing APIs described earlier are used to play the game. Finally, the developer has to use the *GameOn* reporting libraries to commit the game results back to the matchmaker (for use in global statistics and future matchmaking sessions). Note: games don't communicate with the matchmaker directly. That functionality is handled transparently by *GameOn* .

The *GameOn* networking libraries handle most networking requests. Internally, the *GameOn* networking logic uses two layers: a physical Wi-Fi Direct group, and a logical game group. In our current implementation, the physical group is built using legacy Android APIs (for backward compatibility), while the logical group is built using TCP/UDP sockets. All status sharing information is exchanged via the TCP/UDP sockets. For simplicity reasons, when a player initiates a new game, our current implementation makes him or her the game server and owner of the logical group. All subsequent players are clients in the group. This logic can be changed, if necessary, to share the server load among other all players.

Overall, all these changes were easy to implement. A single grad student, with no game development experience, managed to modify all three games in less than 2 days each. Most of the time was spent understanding how each of the games maintained its game state (to find the right places to insert the networking and statistics reporting APIs). As shown in Table 4, the amount of code that needed to be created was minimal. *OpenArena*, in particular, needed very little code as it already had discrete client-server components.

The goal of the *GameOn* matchmaker is to find groups of commuters on the same bus / train who can play a game together. In such dynamic environments, these formed groups should be chosen so that they are stable – i.e., members don't abruptly leave. For example, a group is not considered to be stable if the elected game host alights (thus ending the game) very soon after a game session is started.

## 4.6 Data Used For Matchmaking

To make these matchmaking decisions, the matchmaker can use data from three information sources as shown in Table 5.

### *4.6.1 Performance Data*

The first is performance data such as RSSI values and ping times of various nodes (as observed by other nodes). The *GameOn* client periodically updates its discovery results to the matchmaker. With this data, the matchmaker can create a logical map of where each player is situated relative to other players. It can then use the heuristics shown earlier (peers more than 1 carriage apart can experience variable ping times etc.) to match clients together.

In addition to network measurements, we can also use historical predictions about how long a particular client will remain on the train/bus as a key input. These values can be computed using historical data (using techniques similar to Balan et. al [5]). We show in Section 6.3.4 how using predicted trip times can improve the matchmaking performance.

| Data | Reason To Use It |
|---|---|
| | **Performance** |
| Detection time | Hint for a robust connection |
| RSSI | Hint for a robust connection |
| Ping time | Hint for distance and crowdedness |
| Pred. Trip time | Games don't end abruptly |
| | **Game-specific** |
| Player Level | Ensure a fair/engaging game |
| Player Credibility | Ensure no cheating |
| Min. Player No. | Ensure game is interesting |
| | **User-specified** |
| Only with friends | Guarantee game experience |
| Nobody close by | Reduce real-world detection probability |
| Similar interests | Find future friends |

**Table 5: Data that can be used by the Matchmaker**

### *4.6.2 Game-Specific Data*

The next category of matchmaking data is game specific data. This is data that categorises players into different buckets – based on their skill levels, probability of cheating, and other game-specific data. In addition, games can specify minimum and maximum game player numbers to ensure a high game experience. Grouping players according to the skill level is a well-known matchmaking metric. There are a few algorithms that have been employed by commercial video gaming platforms. For example, Xbox Live [23] uses the TrueSkill ranking system [13] that computes the skills of gamers. Unfortunately, our current prototype does not use any of this data or these algorithms as we do not have the game-specific player information to generate this data historical data. However, adding this data into the matchmaking decision process, when the information does become available, is fairly straightforward.

### *4.6.3 User-Specific Data*

The last category of data that can help the matchmaker is user-specific data. This is data that encapsulates a specific user's preferences and interests. For example, a player may not want to play games with nearby people as they are afraid it might lead to a confrontation. On the other hand, another player might want to meet nearby game players – but only if their interests match. Unfortunately, similar to game-specific data, our current prototype does not use this type of data as we have no historical or player records to generate the data from. However, once the data is available, integrating it into the matchmaker is easy.

## 4.7 Matchmaking Algorithm

In this work, we do not propose any new matchmaking algorithms. Instead, we leverage existing techniques to build a reasonable matchmaking solver. Our current prototype uses a weighted sum of components to determine the final match score of each player relative to every other player. The matchmaker then clusters these matched scores together to group players together who have similar scores. Currently, we use equally weighted normalised forms of co-location time, detection time, and ping time as the data sources for the match. In future work, we plan to investigate more sophisticated algorithms (including dynamic matchers that change their match goals (i.e., weights) based on the current situation) as well as add more data sources to the matching process.

# 5. IMPLEMENTATION

The *GameOn* Android client was implemented using Android 14 APIs (Android 4.0) as a user space application. It implements two background services that do the following; 1) *Cell connection manager* (225 lines of code) that uses *WebSockets* to communicate with the cloud-based matchmaker using JSON objects, and 2) *p2p connection manager* (1,027 lines of code) that implements the functions required to support multiple communication mediums (Wi-Fi Direct, Bluetooth, and etc.) as well as support multiple roles (client, server, relay node, and etc.). The *GameOn* client also provides a simple UI (201 lines of code) for the player to sign in, configure which games are available, configure their in-game names (handle), and to select games to play, and accept game requests. All the components are wrapped around a central control core (539 lines of code) that runs in separate threads.

We implemented the matchmaker in Java (188 lines of code) using the Play Framework [31] version 2.3.7. The matchmaker uses *WebSocket* and multiple threads to support multiple *GameOn* clients. All client generated data is stored in a MySQL database. The server also has a web interface for game developers to configure their game requirements and access game and credit records. The code size is small as the matchmaker currently uses "Performance" data only to make its decisions. However, as discussed earlier, the matchmaking logic can be easily modified to support use other data sources as and when they become available.

# 6. EVALUATION

In this section, we present performance evaluation of *GameOn*. We first experimented *GameOn* 's performance under various real-world use cases. In addition, we present detailed results from micro-benchmark experiments conducted under controlled settings, including overheads of matchmaking and hosting games as a server, performance impacts by various underlying network topologies (star topology vs. multi-hop topology), and impact of co-location time to game plays.

## 6.1 Experimental Setup

We performed all the experiments using Samsung Galaxy S3 (running Android 4.3) and S5 (running Android 4.4.2) phone. We used the three benchmark games described in Section 4.5 for all our real-world usage results as well as some of our micro-benchmarks. The matchmaker was run on an Ubuntu server with a 3.4GHz 4-core CPU with 32 GB of memory. All power consumption values were measured using a Monsoon power monitor [24].

## 6.2 GameOn Working in Real Environments

We evaluated the end-to-end real-world performance of *GameOn* by playing three games on real public transports. The main goal was to compare *GameOn*'s performance with that of the game played with *GameOn*. Each experiment was a 10 minute game session conducted by a four person group. After each gameplay session, all group members were asked to report their current phone battery level (which was compared to the reading just before the session started). [1]

Figure 7 shows the latencies observed when playing the three games under five scenarios across three different times. In the first scenario, the games were hosted on an Internet server that was accessed using a cellular LTE connection. All four players in this scenario played solely as clients. The remaining four scenarios use *GameOn* where one peer device is selected to be the server with all the other peers connecting to it via Wi-Fi Direct. The four scenarios were "All players in the same train carriage, but spread throughout the carriage" (Train-23m), "All players spread across two train carriages (Train-46m), "All players spread across the same single deck

[1] **http://tinyurl.com/gameon-videos** has videos of *GameOn* being used by commuters to play real games on a commuter train

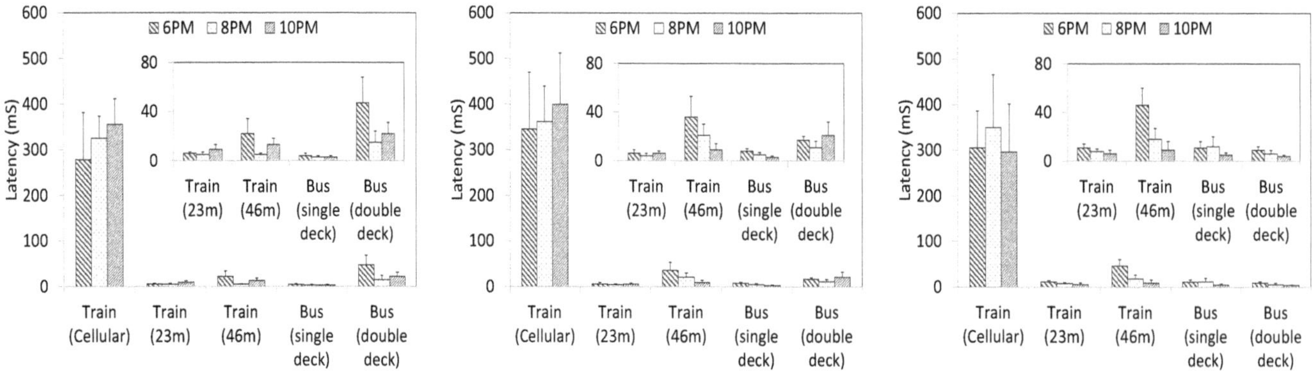


(a) Quake 3 (OpenArena) (b) Racer (c) 2048

**Figure 7: Game Latencies across 5 Scenarios and 3 Test Times**

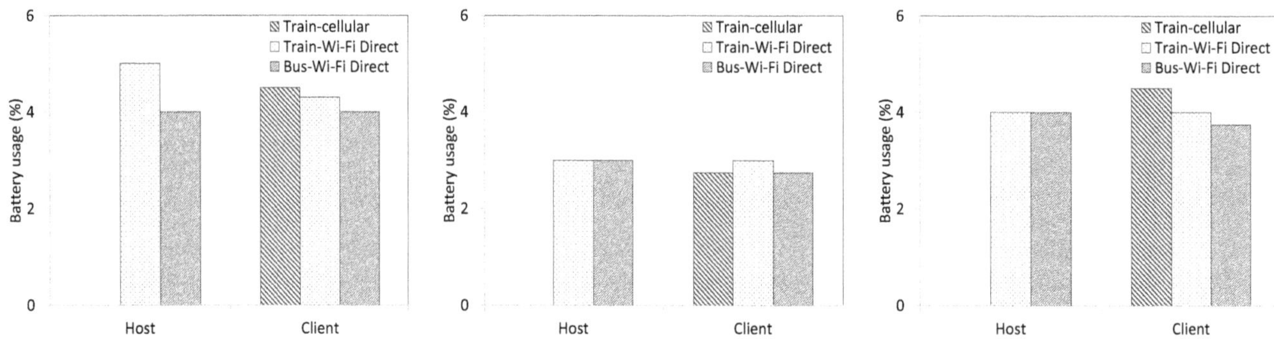


(a) Quake 3 (OpenArena) (b) Racer (c) 2048

**Figure 8: Battery Usage after 10 Minutes of Game Play**

bus" (Bus-Single-Deck), and "All players spread across the same double deck bus with the server on the lower deck" (Bus-Double-Deck). During game play, we periodically logged the ping latencies to the server on each client phone.

From the figure, we observe that LTE latencies are about 10 times longer latencies than *GameOn* and that *GameOn* has very low latencies even across different types of transport and at different times (peak hours, normal etc.)

Figure 8 shows the battery usage of the phone when playing those three games. Since these experiments were done on buses and trains, we could not connect a hardware power monitor to the phones. Instead, we just used the Android battery levels as a gauge. The "Host" values is the power consumption of the phone that was chosen to host the server while "Client" values are the power consumption of the other client-only phones. Note: the "Host" phone serves as both a server *and* a client.

From the figure, we observe that hosting a server is not that expensive – power wise. Indeed, the power consumption for Hosts and Clients are quite similar and within the margin of error. Across the protocols, the power consumption is also somewhat similar.

The measured latency and energy values show that *GameOn* is capable of providing good local multiplayer game experience even in different types of train and bus environments. However, does it impact the user experience in some subtle way? To verify this, we asked each of the 4 game players to answer two self-reported questions on whether they felt the game was playable. To calibrate each member, they were asked, before doing the experiment, to play each game in a lab setting with no *GameOn* modifications to understand what the unmodified game felt like under perfect conditions. The two self reported questions were 1) "The game experience is the same as the one in the lab" and 2) "The phone feels hotter than it did in the lab". For both questions, the members had to answer using a 5-point Likert scale (1 – Strongly Agree to 5 – Strongly Disagree).

**Figure 9: *GameOn* Being Used on a Real Public Train**

The final score was that all 4 game players strongly agreed that the modified game had the same experience as the in-lab unmodified version. In addition, all 4 players also strongly disagreed that the phone felt hotter than it did in the lab. However, they also mentioned that one of the games, *2048*, was not the easiest to play in a multiplayer fashion due to some UI limitations. However, this bug was not introduced by *GameOn* and was beyond our ability to fix.

Figure 9 demonstrates two players playing a game on the same train using *GameOn*. In this use case, the two players are a half-carriage away from each other – one sitting and one standing. Figure 10 shows the matchmaking process to start the game session. At step (a), the player 1 starts a new game session using the *GameOn*

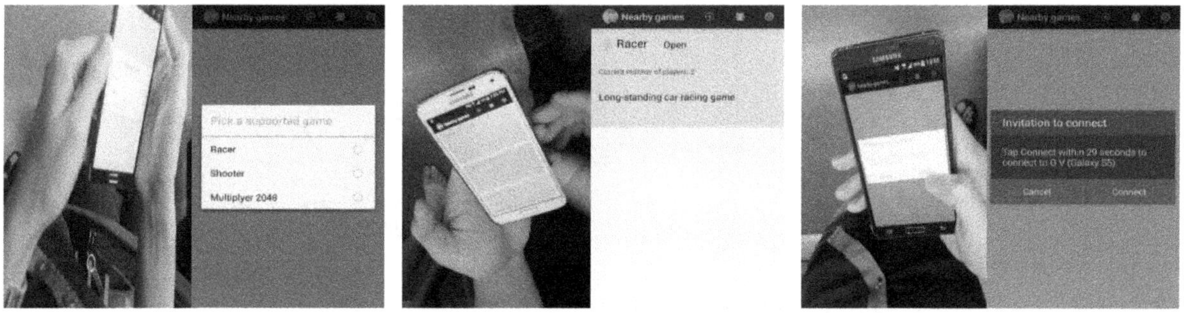


(a) Player 1 Starts a New Game (b) Player 2 Searches for a Game to Play (c) Player 2 Joins Player 1's Game

**Figure 10: The Demonstration of the Bootstrap of a *GameOn* Game Play**

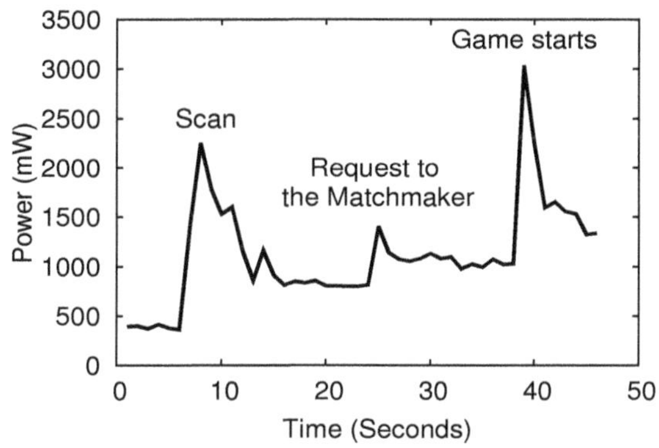


**Figure 11: Energy Overhead of Scanning**

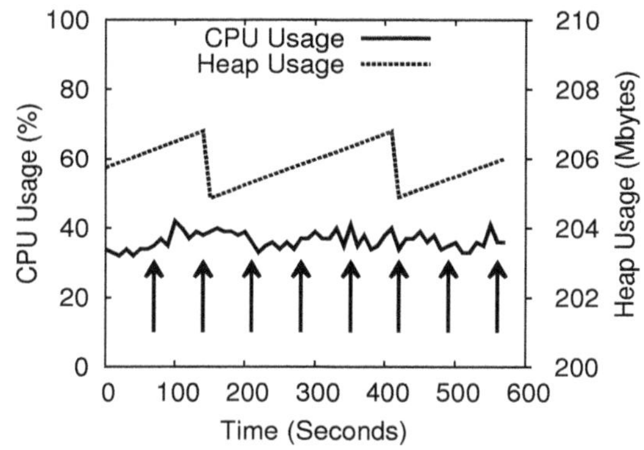


Up to 8 clients join the group gradually. The arrows represent the time at which one more client joins. The saw tooth decrease in heap size is when the Java garbage collector activates.

**Figure 12: CPU & Memory Overhead**

UI, by selecting a game to host. At step (b), player 2 starts *GameOn* and queries the *GameOn* matchmaker to find the available games in their vicinity. Player 2 then picks one of the available games through the *GameOn* UI – he can only host a game if there are no suitable games available. Finally, at step (c), player 1 accepts the join request from player 2, and the game starts.

## 6.3 Micro-benchmarks

We now present micro-benchmarks results:

### 6.3.1 *GameOn Overheads*

We evaluated the overheads of two key operations: peer discovery and requesting a suitable game group from the matchmaker. Figure 11 shows the energy cost of scanning for nearby players via Wi-Fi Direct and that of sending a request for a game group. By themselves, both actions cause reasonably high spikes in the power consumption. However, compared with the power spike when the game itself starts, the scanning and requesting costs are acceptable.

### 6.3.2 *Resource Usage and Group Scalability*

*GameOn* selects a player to host the game server and all the other players will connect to this server. As shown earlier, this does not increase the energy cost of the server device. However, what about the scalability of the device? Can it support multiple game clients without any performance degradation?

To understand this, we scheduled 8 clients to join a particular server one after the other at fixed intervals over a 10-minute period. On the server device, we logged its resource usage, including CPU utilisation, heap usage, and network traffic using Wi-Fi Direct, every 10 seconds. Figure 12 shows the CPU and heap usage plots. Each plot starts from a single client case where the server phone is connected to itself with new clients (up to a max of 8) periodically connecting. The heap usage shows a zigzag curve due to memory being reclaimed by the Android garbage collector at regular intervals. From the figure, we observe that the CPU and heap usage do not substantially increase even when the server device is hosting all 8 client players.

We next investigate how large p2p groups can become before performance (in terms of server ping times) and server energy consumption become factors. Figure 13 shows the ping times and power consumption when the group size scales up. When connected to 8 players, the power consumption of the server increases 23.7% compared to hosting just 1 player. Thus, hosting a game does not add a very large overhead to the phone's energy usage. However, we found that the ping latencies increase quite fast as more and more clients are added. In particular, we observed a large latency rise when the 7th client was connected. Thus, we find that a current modern smartphone can comfortably serve as the server for up to 6 clients. After this point, the ping latencies start to increase significantly which could result in gameplay issues.

Figure 14 shows the network usage of the server in terms of the number of bytes exchanged over the Wi-Fi Direct link. We observe that both the received and transmitted traffic grows quadratically as the group size increases. A transmitted packet from the server usually includes a snapshot of the whole group state, while a received packet usually includes only a single client command or update. Thus, on the server, the amount of data received is usually much lower than the amount sent.

### 6.3.3 *Support for Other Topologies*

In all previous experiments, we have used a star topology where every client is connected directly to the server. However, in some cases, a client may not be able to connect directly to the server (when the client is at the other end of a crowded train for example). For example, Figure 15 shows a scenario where the four players are

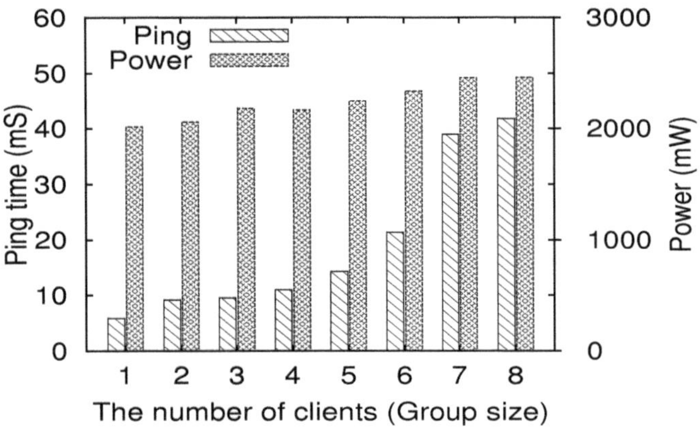


The ping latencies and power consumption of the server device when hosting a game. The ping time at the client side increases quickly while the power consumption at the host side rises linearly. The result proves a modern smartphone can modestly support a group of 1-8 players.

**Figure 13: Power & Latency Overhead**

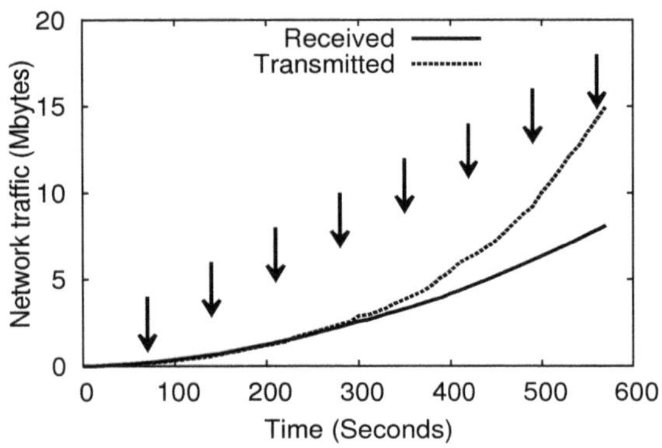


Up to 8 clients join the group gradually. The arrows represent the time at which one more client joins. As the group size becomes larger, both the transmitted and received traffic increases quadratically.

**Figure 14: Network Overhead**

spread out linearly so that the rightmost player does not have a reliable connection with the server client. In these cases, is it possible to leverage intermediate clients as relay nodes to form a multi-hop *linked-list* topology where a node is connected to an intermediate node that connects it to the server? *GameOn* supports multi-hop networks but with some limitations. In particular, joining two Wi-Fi Direct groups (to create a multi-hop network) at the same time is not allowed, even in the latest version of Android. This joining of groups feature is an optional feature in the Wi-Fi Direct standard that has not been implemented in Android. Thus, to create a relay node for a multi-hop environment, we have to use two different networking technologies / radios. In this case, we will have to use Bluetooth together with Wi-Fi Direct with one side of the linked-list using Bluetooth and the other side using Wi-Fi Direct. However, as stated earlier, Bluetooth is not the best protocol for the scenarios *GameOn* is tackling. We re-visit these claims using a three-node scenario as shown in Figure 15.

Figure 16 shows the energy consumption when using three nodes with a star and a linked-list topology. We instrumented the *Racer* game so that it automatically looped the same track to create a repeatable trace. For each experiment, we turned off all background processes and measured the power consumption using the Monsoon power monitor. It should be noted that the absolute numbers

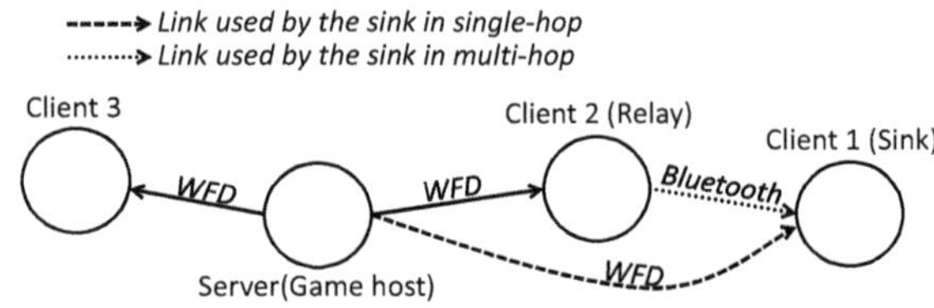


The arrows indicate the server information flow direction. Dotted Wi-Fi Direct link indicates poor connectivity.

**Figure 15: Single-hop vs. Multi-hop Topologies**

Power consumption of three nodes using different topologies. In the linked-list topology, the relay node (client 2) connects to the source node via a Wi-Fi Direct link, and is connected by the sink node via a Bluetooth link.

**Figure 16: Power Consumption under Various Topologies**

are not that interesting as they are device-specific. Instead we focus on the difference between the two topologies.

We observed that in the star topology, the server node (the one sending most of the data) consumes the most power followed by the other two nodes (client 2 and client 1). When using the linked-list topology, the host (server) and sink (client 1) nodes consume similar power to the star topology. However, the relay node (client 2) uses 13% more power in the linked-list case. This is because it has to use two radios (Wi-Fi Direct and Bluetooth) simultaneously to bridge the two sides of the relay.

We now evaluate the effectiveness of the linked-list topology at reducing latency spikes caused by nodes being too far away from each other. To do this, we placed two node (a source and a sink) two train carriages apart from each other on a public train (that was moving and picking up passengers etc.). We then placed a relay node in between the two nodes (i.e., the relay node was 1 carriage away from both the source and the sink). The source and the sink were then connected to each other using Wi-Fi Direct. The source was also connected to the relay node via Wi-Fi Direct while the sink connected to the relay node via Bluetooth. The sink then started pinging the source across both the direct Wi-Fi Direct connection as well as the multi-hop (via the relay) Bluetooth connection.

Figure 17 shows the latency results. We observe that the direct link between the source and the sink (i.e., the star topology) showed variable ping times as the distance was far and the link quality was thus affected by passenger movements etc. However, the link via the relay node showed much more predictable and stable performance. However, the ping times for the Bluetooth link are still high (yet stable) as Bluetooth is not the best protocol (as shown earlier) for this type of environment.

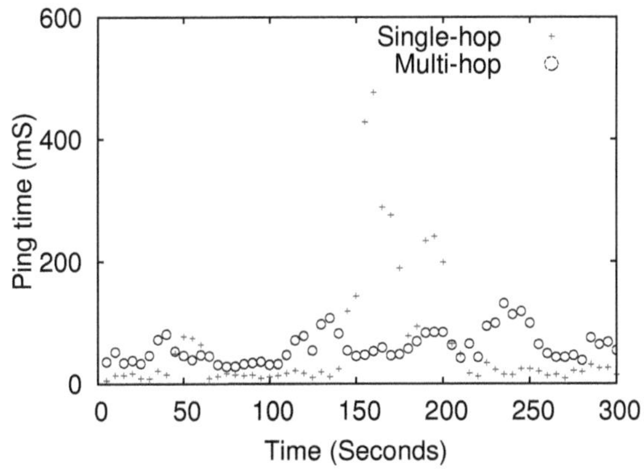


Client-side latencies under two topologies. A client (sink) is connected to the group owner via two different routes at the same time. One is a direct connection via a Wi-Fi Direct link. And the other one is a connection to the relay node via a Bluetooth link.

**Figure 17: Latency of Various Topologies**

### 6.3.4 *Improving Matchmaking With Time Predictions*

In this final test, we show that using predictions of how long a particular trip will last for a given individual can have big positive effects on the matchmaking performance. To perform this test, we selected only the trips that started from one of the starting train stations (called *k*) to a specific train station at our university. The starting train station was chosen because the trains start off empty there (so everyone on that train when it leaves got on at station *k*) and it was not an interchange station. I.e., everyone had to swipe their NFC cards at that station itself to get into it. It was not possible for them to enter at some other station and take another train to this station. 2) We picked a specific time (8 a.m.) and day (1st Monday of Nov.) and extracted all the commuters who entered station *k* at that time and day. 3) We then exhaustively created all possible 2, 3, 4, 5, 6 person groups that could be created from the set of people who entered that station. 4) We then computed how long each of these groups actually stayed together (i.e., the minimum co-location time until someone in that group left the train). This result represents a naive matchmaker that just selects people randomly and hopes that they will be together long enough.

Figure 18 shows the results of this test. We observe that the time the entire group was together is quite low and with a very high standard deviation (indicating that some groups were together for much less time). In addition, as the group size increased, the time spent together decreased significantly as the probability of any one person in the group leaving increased. This result shows that just randomly grouping people together can lead to bad outcomes.

However, we found that using predicted individual trip times can result in better estimates. First, we created historical buckets for each user (similar to Balan et. al [5]) that was station, day, and time specific. We then used this history to calculate, for each user, a predicted trip start time (with stdev.) for any station at any time and day. This prediction lets us increase the minimum co-location time for all group sizes as we can cluster passengers by their predicted trip times. For example, our standard deviation for any given trip time and group size dropped to a few % compared to 60-70% with the naive approach. However, this approach can lead to data sparsity issues. For example, only 3,500 of the 15,948 passengers (22%) used to generate Figure 18 had multiple trips from that station from which we could calculate a history. We plan to look at techniques to improve this yield in future work.

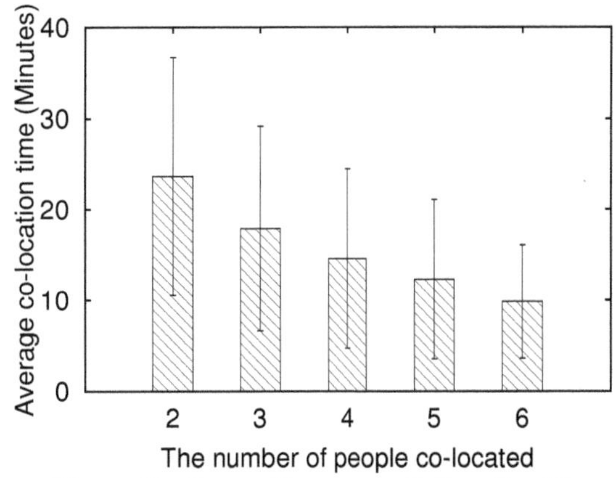


**Figure 18: Group Size versus Collocation Time**

## 6.4 Summary

In this section, we showed that *GameOn* works well in the real world with good latencies and end-user experiences with up to 4 players in a variety of bus and train environments. We then showed that the energy, CPU, ping latencies, and memory overheads of hosting a game server are minimal if the number of game clients is kept low (under 8). Next, we should that we could support multi-hop p2p methodologies in addition to he base star topology. Finally, we showed that naively predicting the co-location time can result in very sub-optimal matches.

# 7. DISCUSSION

The idea of commuters playing games with fellow commuters raises a number of interesting questions. In particular, why would commuters play games on their phones as they drain a lot of energy. Even though, as we showed earlier, *GameOn* itself does not have a large energy overhead, the base energy consumption of a game is already huge – on the order of few Watts in some cases! Thus playing a game for about 20 to 40 minutes will significantly reduce your phone's battery lifetime. So why would people do that?

One reason why might be that they are commuting either to work / school or back home. In both cases, there is an opportunity to charge their phone at the other side (at their work desk, classroom, home). Thus, playing a game with whatever "residual energy" is left in the phone might be okay as a recharge point is available immediately afterwards. However, we have not investigated this willingness in more depth beyond the survey presented earlier (Section 3.1.4).

Another concern raised is that multiplayer games usually result in someone losing. What happens if that person gets angry and starts looking for the person(s) they lost to? Would it be a form of "game-rage" (similar to road rage)? Identifying the people you are playing with will be hard in crowded trains where everyone is awake and using their phone. But what about on longer train journeys where a majority of commuters are sleeping? These types of social phenomena and implications need to be investigated in more details.

## 7.1 Limitations

The main limitations of the current *GameOn* prototype are: 1) The matchmaker, while supporting many attributes well (as far as we can tell), cannot be completely validated as we do not have data for many of the skill and player-centric attributes. 2) We have built *GameOn* to handle only the system aspects of multiplayer games. Unfortunately, we have no control over the game itself which has a larger say on user satisfaction. For example, *GameOn* can handle cases where users join and leave a game in the middle (as long as the player hosting the server does not leave) and *GameOn* can handle alternate game modes such as "spectator mode" if those modes use standard networking APIs. However, *GameOn*, by itself, can do very little to make a game "fun" which is ultimately the most important criteria. And 3), the multi-hop support needs to use Bluetooth and Wi-Fi Direct for multi-hop settings (thus lowering its range to what Bluetooth supports) as Android does not currently allow multiple Wi-Fi Direct connections. Finally, the survey presented in Section 3.1.4 was conducted mostly with undergraduate students and thus may not be generalisable. In addition, our performance experiments were conducted using only two different models of phones. Thus results may vary with other phone types.

# 8. RELATED WORK

**p2p game matchmaking:** Switchboard [22] proposed techniques to predict latencies during a game play using quick pre-game measurements. Htrae [2] predicts inter-player latencies using geolocation data. Ly et al. [21] developed an approach to select the best detour route for game packets. However, these systems and techniques were targeting game consoles or devices connected to the Internet. Our goal is to use p2p networking to connect players on public transport.

**Mobile p2p applications:** Collaborative smartphone applications have emerged in diverse application domains such as media sharing [15] and context sensing [19][20]. Like *GameOn*, they propose several core techniques to enable in-situ collaboration among co-located smartphones. McNamara et al. [15] devised a scheme to predict remaining co-location duration for stable exchange of multimedia files. CoMon [19] proposed a resource planning mechanism to maximise benefit while achieving fairness. However, building a system for collaborative mobile gaming imposes a set of unique challenges due to the strict gaming latency and power requirements. To address these, we developed a new end-to-end system, *GameOn*, with careful attention to various system components such as network protocols, peer discovery, matchmaking, and low latency game play. Some airlines offer multi-player games among passengers during long-haul flights [35]. However, only a few limited games can be supported through wired entertainment systems embedded in passenger seats whereas *GameOn* can support commodity mobile games on smartphones without any infrastructure support in buses or trains.

**Mobile p2p framework:** There have been efforts to develop generic platforms to facilitate development of various mobile p2p applications [10]. For example, the well-known open source project Alljoyn [3], aims to provide a set of APIs and runtime to easily build network connections among multiple mobile devices. *GameOn* opens a new application domain of multiplayer gaming by supporting game-specific requirements that Alljoyn does not support. It will be an interesting to test if Alljoyn can work with *GameOn*. There have also been prior work to re-write binaries without source code access. RetroSkeleton [9] presents an app rewriting framework that allows developers to integrate new features into existing apps. *GameOn* did not use re-writing methods initially as we wanted to understand the challenges required to port existing games to use *GameOn*.

# 9. CONCLUSION

In this paper, we presented *GameOn*, a system for allowing commuters on public transportation to play multiplayer games with each other using Wi-Fi Direct as a p2p communication medium. We motivated the reasons why *GameOn* is useful (long commute times) and then described the various components of *GameOn*. Finally, we presented extensive evaluation results showing that *GameOn* works. Even though *GameOn* is a proof-of-concept idea, it has been implemented and works quite well with the modified games (videos available at **http://tinyurl.com/gameon-videos** ). However, this is just step one. Our broader goal is to use *GameOn* as a platform for providing many different types of commuter friendly engagement channels. For example, we plan to extend *GameOn* to allow users who share similar interests (that are discovered through specific types of games) to meet up with each other in the physical world. We are also considering system-level support for spectator-mode; where commuters can join existing games as passive observers instead of active players. Both of these planned extensions should increase the adoption rate of *GameOn*.


# 10. ACKNOWLEDGEMENTS

We sincerely thank David Chu for shepherding our paper, and the anonymous reviewers for their valuable feedback. We also thank Lixuan Zhai, Xiaonan Guo, Nguyen Minh, Shriguru Nayak, Kazae Quek, Huynh Nguyen, Hai Le Gia, Kasthuri Jayarajah and Kartik Muralidharan for their helps to perform the in-bus and in-train measurements and evaluations. Finally, this work was supported partially by the Singapore Ministry of Education's Academic Research Fund Tier 2 under research grant MOE2011-T2-1001, and partially by the National Research Foundation, Prime Minister's Office, Singapore, under the IDM Futures Funding Initiative. Any opinions, findings, conclusions or recommendations expressed in this material are those of the authors and do not necessarily reflect the views of the granting agencies or Singapore Management University.


# 11. REFERENCES


[1] Aaron M. Renn, New Geography. *Commuting In New York City, 2000-2010*. http://www.newgeography.com/content/002691-commuting-new-york-city-2000-2010/, 2012. Accessed on 25th March 2015.

[2] Agarwal, S. and Lorch, J. R. Matchmaking for online games and other latency-sensitive p2p systems. *Proceedings of the ACM SIGCOMM conference on Data communication (SIGCOMM)*, 2009.

[3] The Allseen Alliance. https://allseenalliance.org/. Accessed on 25th March 2015.

[4] Bakki, N. *Commuting time of workers in Japan, 2011*. http://nbakki.hatenablog.com/entry/2014/02/20/124942/ , 2014. Accessed on 25th March 2015.

[5] Balan, R. K., Nguyen, K. X., and Jiang, L. Real-time trip information service for a large taxi fleet. *Proceedings of the 9th International Conference on Mobile Systems, Applications, and Services (MobiSys)*, 2011.

[6] Bluetooth SIG. *Learn the Bluetooth(R) technology basics*. http://www.bluetooth.com/Pages/what-is-bluetooth-technology.aspx, 2014. Accessed on 25th March 2015.

[7] chinadaily.com.cn. *Commuting time in capital averages 97 minutes*. http://www.chinadaily.com.cn/china/2014-11/24/content_18967891.htm/, 2014. Accessed on 25th March 2015.

[8] Cox, W. *Hong Kong's Decentralizing Commuting Patterns*. http://www.newgeography.com/content/003300-hong-kong-s-decentralizing-commuting-patterns/, 2012. Accessed on 25th March 2015.

[9] Davis, B. and Chen, H. Retroskeleton: Retrofitting android apps. *Proceeding of the 11th annual international conference on Mobile systems, applications, and services (MobiSys)*, 2013.
[10] Fitzek, F. H. P. and Charaf, H. *Mobile Peer to Peer (P2P): A Tutorial Guide*. Wiley, 2009.
[11] Google. *Top Grossing Games on the Android Marketplace*. https://play.google.com/store/apps/collection/topgrossing?hl=en. Accessed on 3rd December 2014.
[12] GSMA Intelligence. *The Mobile Economy Asia Pacific 2014*. http://asiapacific.gsmamobileeconomy.com/GSMA_ME_APAC_2014.pdf, 2014. Accessed on 6th December 2014.
[13] Herbrich, R., Minka, T., and Graepel, T. Trueskill(tm): A bayesian skill rating system. *Advances in Neural Information Processing Systems 20 (NIPS)*, 2007.
[14] Khalaf, S. *Flurry Five-Year Report: Its an App World. The Web Just Lives in It*. http://www.flurry.com/bid/95723/Flurry-Five-Year-Report-It-s-an-App-World-The-Web-Just-Lives-in-It, 2013. Accessed on 6th December 2014.
[15] L. McNamara, C. M. and Capra, L. Media sharing based on colocation prediction in urban transport. *Proceedings of ACM 14th International Conference on Mobile Computing and Networking (MobiCom)*, 2008.
[16] Land Transport Authority of Singapore. http://www.lta.gov.sg. Accessed on 25th March 2015.
[17] Land Transport Authority of Singapore. *Fast Facts*. http://www.lta.gov.sg/content/ltaweb/en/public-transport/projects/circle-line/fast-facts.html. Accessed on 25th March 2015.
[18] Land Transport Authority of Singapore. *Singapore Land Transport: Statistics In Brief*. http://www.lta.gov.sg/content/ltaweb/en/publications-and-research.html. Accessed on 25th March 2015.
[19] Lee, Y., Ju, Y., Min, C., Kang, S., Hwang, I., and Song, J. Comon: cooperative ambience monitoring platform with continuity and benefit awareness. *Proceedings of the 9th International Conference on Mobile Systems, Applications, and Services (MobiSys)*, 2012.
[20] Lee, Y., Min, C., Hwang, C., Lee, J., Hwang, I., Ju, Y., Yoo, C., Moon, M., Lee, U., and Song, J. Sociophone: Everyday face-to-face interaction monitoring platform using multi-phone sensor fusion. *Proceeding of the 11th Annual International Conference on Mobile Systems, Applications, and Services (MobiSys)*, 2013.
[21] Ly, C., Hsu, C.-H., and Hefeeda, M. Improving online gaming quality using detour paths. *Proceedings of the international conference on Multimedia (MM)*, 2010.
[22] Manweiler, J., Agarwal, S., Zhang, M., Choudhury, R. R., and Bahl, P. Switchboard: a matchmaking system for multiplayer mobile games. *Proceedings of the 9th International Conference on Mobile Systems, Applications, and Services (MobiSys)*, 2011.
[23] Microsoft. *Xbox Live*. http://www.xbox.com/en-US/live.
[24] Monsoon Solutions Inc. *Monsoon Power Moniter*. http://www.msoon.com/LabEquipment/PowerMonitor/.
[25] National Post. *Travel times prove transit's a non-starter*. http://www.financialpost.com/story.html?id=0f49732a-b9d9-477d-828b-01a727147219/. Accessed on 25th March 2015.
[26] National Statistics, Republic of China (Taiwan). *2000 Taiwan Social Development Trends Survey Results*. http://eng.stat.gov.tw/ct.asp?xItem=9378&ctNode=1647, 2000. Accessed on 25th March 2015.
[27] Nicolas Gramlich. *AndEngine game engine*. https://github.com/nicolasgramlich/AndEngine. Accessed on 3rd December 2014.
[28] Nielsen. *The Asian Mobile Consumer Decoded*. http://www.nielsen.com/ph/en/insights/news/2014/asian-mobile-consumers.html, 2014. Accessed on 25th March 2015.
[29] Patro, A., Rayanchu, S., Griepentrog, M., Ma, Y., and Banerjee, S. The anatomy of a large mobile massively multiplayer online game. *Proceedings of the First ACM International Workshop on Mobile Gaming (MobiGames)*, 2012.
[30] Paul Sarbinowski. *2048 Android port*. https://github.com/uberspot/2048-android. Accessed on 3rd December 2014.
[31] Play Framework. https://www.playframework.com/. Accessed on 25th March 2015.
[32] SBS Transit. *Bus Memory Lane*. http://www.sbstransit.com.sg/about/memorylane.aspx. Accessed on 25th March 2015.
[33] Seoul Metropolitan Government. *Seoul Public Transportation*. http://english.seoul.go.kr/wp-content/uploads/2014/06/Seoul-Public-Transportation-English.pdf, 2014. Accessed on 25th March 2015.
[34] Sergii Pylypenko. *Openarena Android port site*. https://play.google.com/store/apps/details?id=ws.openarena.sdl&hl=en. Accessed on 3rd December 2014.
[35] Singapore Airlines. *Flying with us - Games and applications*. http://www.singaporeair.com/en_UK/flying-with-us/games-applicationslanding/games/. Accessed on 25th March 2015.
[36] Trade Union Congress (TUC), UK. *Commute times increase as the UK's transport system gets more crowded*. http://www.tuc.org.uk/economic-issues/labour-market-and-economic-reports/industrial-issues/transport-policy/commute-times/, 2014. Accessed on 25th March 2015.
[37] VGChartz. *Top Selling Console Games for 2014*. http://www.vgchartz.com/yearly/2014/Global/. Accessed on 3rd December 2014.
[38] Vinita Dawra Nangia, The Times of India. *Travel times prove transit's a non-starter*. http://timesofindia.indiatimes.com/life-style/Is-commute-time-taking-over-your-life/articleshow/3508745.cms/, 2008. Accessed on 25th March 2015.
[39] Wi-Fi Alliance. *Portable Wi-Fi(R) that goes with you anywhere*. http://www.wi-fi.org/discover-wi-fi/wi-fi-direct, 2014. Accessed on 25th March 2015.

# Kahawai: High-Quality Mobile Gaming Using GPU Offload

Eduardo Cuervo†, Alec Wolman†, Landon P. Cox‡, Kiron Lebeck*, Ali Razeen‡,
Stefan Saroiu†, Madanlal Musuvathi†

†Microsoft Research, ‡Duke University, *University of Washington

## ABSTRACT

This paper presents Kahawai[1], a system that provides high-quality gaming on mobile devices, such as tablets and smartphones, by offloading a portion of the GPU computation to server-side infrastructure. In contrast with previous thin-client approaches that require a server-side GPU to render the entire content, Kahawai uses collaborative rendering to combine the output of a mobile GPU and a server-side GPU into the displayed output. Compared to a thin client, collaborative rendering requires significantly less network bandwidth between the mobile device and the server to achieve the same visual quality and, unlike a thin client, collaborative rendering supports disconnected operation, allowing a user to play offline – albeit with reduced visual quality.

Kahawai implements two separate techniques for collaborative rendering: (1) a mobile device can render each frame with reduced detail while a server sends a stream of per-frame differences to transform each frame into a high detail version, or (2) a mobile device can render a subset of the frames while a server provides the missing frames. Both techniques are compatible with the hardware-accelerated H.264 video decoders found on most modern mobile devices. We implemented a Kahawai prototype and integrated it with the idTech 4 open-source game engine, an advanced engine used by many commercial games. In our evaluation, we show that Kahawai can deliver gameplay at an acceptable frame rate, and achieve high visual quality using as little as one-sixth of the bandwidth of the conventional thin-client approach. Furthermore, a 50-person user study with our prototype shows that Kahawai can deliver the same gaming experience as a thin client under excellent network conditions.

## Categories and Subject Descriptors

C.2.4 [**Computer-Communication Networks**]: Distributed Systems—*Client/server*

## Keywords

code offload; GPU; computer games; mobile devices

[1]Kahawai is the Hawaiian word for stream.


*MobiSys'15,* May 18–22, 2015, Florence, Italy.

ACM 978-1-4503-3494-5/15/05 ...$15.00.
http://dx.doi.org/10.1145/2742647.2742657 .

## 1. INTRODUCTION

Since the advent of consumer mobile devices equipped with high resolution touchscreens along with powerful CPUs and GPUs, gaming has been one of the most popular activities on smartphones and tablets. Recent studies estimate that 46% of mobile users play games, and out of the total time spent using their devices, users play games 49% of the time [15]. As mobile device screens grow larger and screen resolutions increase, finer graphical detail and advanced graphical effects are becoming more important for mobile applications, especially games.

To provide richer visual experiences, mobile devices have seen rapid improvements in their GPU processing capabilities, but today's devices cannot duplicate the sophisticated graphical detail provided by gaming consoles and high-end desktop GPUs. The primary reason for this performance gap is power consumption. A high-end desktop GPU may consume 500 Watts of power, whereas a high-end mobile GPU will consume less than 10 Watts. As a result, mobile GPUs will lag behind their desktop contemporaries for the foreseeable future. The battery capacity of mobile devices is limited and growing slowly, and high power consumption requires sophisticated and bulky thermal dissipation systems that are incompatible with mobile form factors.

Prior research efforts sought to close the performance and energy gaps between mobile devices and server-side infrastructure through remote execution and code offload [3, 7, 9, 14]. However, that work has focused on general purpose workloads running on a mobile device's CPU. Although there has been previous work on remote rendering [28, 37], we are unaware of any prior systems that support GPU offloading from mobile devices to server infrastructure.

Thin-client architectures are another widely explored area of previous work [24, 35], and commercial systems such as OnLive, Playstation Now, and Nvidia Shield take a thin-client approach to mobile gaming. Here, a cloud server with a powerful CPU and GPU execute the game and render its output. The mobile device forwards the user's input to a server, and receives the game's audio-visual output encoded as compressed video. Though popular, thin-client gaming has two drawbacks. First, transmitting game content that meets gamers' expectations with regards to screen resolution, frame rate, and video quality results in high bandwidth requirements. This is particularly worrisome for players connecting over data-capped connections. Second, thin-clients cannot support offline gaming since all game code executes on a remote server.

In this paper, we present *Kahawai*, a GPU offload system that overcomes the drawbacks of thin-client gaming. The main technique used by Kahawai is *collaborative rendering*. Collaborative rendering relies on a mobile GPU to generate low-fidelity output, which when combined with server-side GPU output allows a mobile device to display a high-fidelity result.

The key insight behind collaborative rendering is that while fine-grained details are prohibitively expensive for mobile GPUs to render at an acceptable frame rate, these details represent a small portion of the total information encoded within the displayed output. Thus, collaborative rendering relies on the mobile GPU to render low-fidelity content containing most of the displayed output, and relies on the server infrastructure to fill in the details.

Collaborative rendering in Kahawai addresses thin-client gaming's main shortcomings. First, when the mobile device is connected to a server, Kahawai provides high-quality gaming at significant network bandwidth savings relative to a thin-client. Second, disconnected Kahawai clients can play games offline using their own GPU, albeit with reduced visual quality. To enable collaborative rendering, Kahawai requires careful synchronization between two instances of the same game: one executing on the mobile device and the other on the server. To support this, we integrated partial deterministic replay into a popular open-source game engine, the idTech 4 game engine used by many commercial games.

We have developed two separate collaborative rendering techniques as part of Kahawai, with each targeting a different aspect of the game stream's fidelity (i.e., per-frame detail and frame rate). In our first technique, *delta encoding*, the mobile device produces reduced-fidelity output by generating every frame at a lower level of detail. The server-side GPU concurrently renders two versions of the game output: a high-fidelity, finely detailed version, and a low-fidelity version that matches the mobile device's output. The server uses these two outputs to calculate delta frames representing the visual differences between the high-fidelity and low-fidelity frames. The server then sends a compressed video stream of delta frames to the client, and the mobile device decompresses the stream and applies the deltas to the frames that it rendered locally.

In our second technique, *client-side I-frame rendering*, the mobile device produces reduced-fidelity output by rendering highly detailed frames at a lower rate. The server renders the missing frames at a higher rate, and sends the missing frames as compressed video. The mobile device decodes the video, combines the frames in the correct order, and displays the results. Both of our techniques are compatible with the hardware-accelerated H.264 video decoders built in to many of today's mobile devices.

Our Kahawai prototype is integrated into the idTech 4 game engine, and demonstrates the benefits of collaborative rendering using a commercial game, Doom 3, built on this engine. We show that compared with a thin client using H.264, delta encoding provides far superior visual quality when bandwidth is constrained to less than 0.5 Mbps. Even more impressive, we show that a thin client requires six times as much bandwidth as client-side I-frame rendering to achieve comparable visual quality. Finally, a 50-person user study demonstrates that Kahawai delivers a high-quality gaming experience equivalent to the thin client approach.

# 2. BACKGROUND

Kahawai relies on concepts and principles from the following related topics: cloud gaming [39, 25, 26]; game structure and performance [20, 12, 16]; video compression [34]; and image quality comparisons [38, 22]. In [8], we present extensive background on the above topics.

Many modern games are built on top of a *game engine*. These engines provide a general platform that greatly simplifies game development. Engines typically separate game-specific content, such as artwork, levels, characters, and weapons, from core functionality such as rendering, physics, sound, and input handling. Some of the most popular game engines for fast-action games are Unreal [12], Unity [36], idTech [20], and the MT Framework. We implemented Kahawai by modifying version 4 of the idTech engine. Fully integrating Kahawai into an engine requires access to the engine's source code, but this does not limit the generality of our approach. Even without access to source code, we successfully applied collaborative rendering to the game Street Fighter 4 [5] by intercepting calls to the custom Capcom engine on which it runs. When adopting a particular game engine, game developers typically obtain a license that includes access to game-engine source code.

In addition to access to the game-engine source code, delta encoding also requires a way to generate a high-detail and low-detail version of each output frame. Desktop PC games commonly provide a large number of settings that control the performance and visual quality of the rendered graphics. Game designers provide these settings so that players with more powerful GPUs can experience a higher-quality version of the game, while those with less powerful GPUs can play at an acceptable frame rate. Game settings control a wide variety of graphical details within the game, including lighting, shadows, fog, texture compression, bump mapping, anti-aliasing, anisotropic filtering, and even the complexity of the 3D models given to the rendering pipeline.

OpenGL [33] and Direct3D [30] are industry standard rendering APIs for programming modern GPUs. These frameworks describe how a given 3D scene should be rendered and abstract away the hardware details of a GPU's implementation. Hardware manufacturers implement support for these APIs in a way that best exploits the characteristics of their hardware. Each API implementation is provided as a binary device driver from the GPU manufacturer [4]. Kahawai does not require access to these driver internals.

It is important to note that given the exact same scene description, rendering APIs do *not* guarantee pixel-exact outputs for different GPUs. In fact, we observe pixel-level differences even for different GPUs produced by the same manufacturer and using the same device driver. These differences are usually imperceptible to the human eye, and in Section 6, we quantify the extent of these differences. We also demonstrate that these differences have a negligible effect on the quality of Kahawai's output.

Finally, to provide the appearance of consistent and smooth motion, most real-time rendering applications like games attempt to render between 30 and 60 frames per second. In practice it is hard to define the exact point when a frame rate is high enough to avoid flicker. However, even at high illumination perceived quality plateaus around 60 Hz [17].

# 3. Kahawai ARCHITECTURE

This section provides a high-level overview of the two collaborative rendering techniques we have developed for Kahawai.

## 3.1 Overview

Kahawai supports collaborative rendering by reducing client-side output fidelity along two dimensions: under *delta encoding* the mobile GPU renders low-detail frames at a high rate, while under *client-side I-Frame rendering* the mobile GPU renders high-detail frames at a low rate.

Figure 1 shows the architecture for delta encoding. The basic idea is to utilize game settings to generate two versions of the game output: a high-detail version and a low-detail version. Kahawai exploits graphical similarities between these two versions to compute a highly compressed video of the differences.

The mobile device uses its mobile GPU to render a low-detail stream. The server executes two instances of the game, one for each level of detail, and generates a delta frame by computing the pixel-by-pixel visual difference between its high-detail and low-detail frames. We use *partial deterministic replay*, described in Section 5,

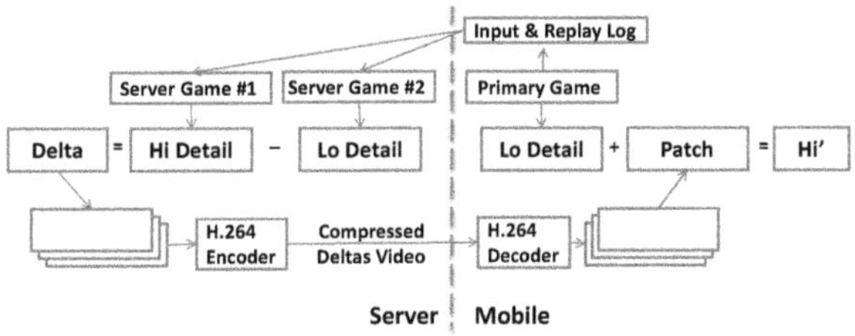


**Figure 1:** *Architecture of Delta Encoding. The server renders both high-detail and low-detail versions of each frame, calculates the visual difference into a delta frame, and then encodes an H.264 video of the delta frames. The mobile device decodes the video, and uses it to patch the low-detail frames rendered by the mobile GPU. The mobile device sends a log to the server to enable the server-side game instances to correctly follow the mobile client.*

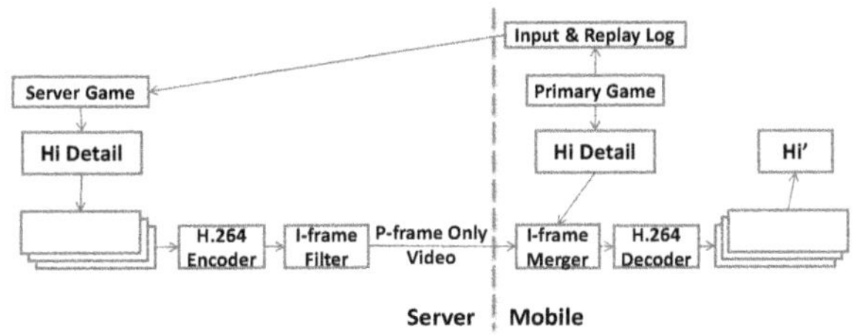


**Figure 2:** *Architecture of Client-Side I-Frame Rendering. The server renders a hi-detail version of each frame, and encodes the frames as H.264 video. A filter discards the I-Frames from the encoded video, then sends the video back to the client. The client uses the mobile GPU to render I-Frames, and merges them back into the video stream before invoking the H.264 decoder.*

to control concurrent instances of the game running on the server. The server sends a compressed H.264 video of delta frames to the client, which decompresses the video and applies each frame from the received video as a patch to each low-detail frame it renders with its mobile GPU. The end result is an image stream that almost perfectly matches the high-detail output rendered on the server.

Figure 2, shows the architecture for our second technique, client-side I-frame rendering. For this technique, the client generates high-detail game output at a low frame rate, and the server generates high-detail game output at a high rate.

Compressed video is composed of three types of frames: Intra-coded I-frames, Predicted P-frames, and Bi-directional Predicted B-frames. For our purposes, it is only necessary to understand the high-level differences between I-Frames and P-frames. In particular, an I-frame is relatively large and self-contained; an I-frame encodes all of the visual information needed to display its content. On the other hand, P-frames are smaller and contain references to prior frames in the stream. To display a P-frame, a machine must have the P-frame and any other frames it references.

Under client-side I-frame rendering, the server generates an H.264 video of its high-detail, high-rate game output, but drops the I-frames before sending the video to the client. The client receives the video containing only P-frames, recreates the missing I-frames by inserting output from its mobile GPU, and then uses its H.264 decoder to display the final, merged output. The end result, as with delta encoding, is graphical output that almost perfectly matches the high-detail, full frame-rate version rendered by the server GPU. It may be possible to combine these two techniques, but we leave this for future work.

## 3.2 Requirements

Both collaborative rendering techniques require servers to send H.264-compliant video to clients. H.264 is the de-facto standard for compressed mobile video, and nearly all modern mobile devices have dedicated hardware to accelerate H.264-encoding and -decoding. This hardware improves performance and energy consumption, and frees the mobile CPU and GPU to execute the game instead of encoding and decoding video.

Hardware-accelerated video decoding does not eliminate the need to move video through the memory system, but this overhead is modest compared to the total memory bandwidth of most devices. For example, decoding a 1080p HD video at 60 FPS only requires 400 MB/sec, whereas the memory bus bandwidth on a modern smartphone such as the iPhone 6 is 9 GB/sec.

Both techniques also require frame-by-frame synchronization. Specifically, because we run multiple instances of the game, each rendered object must be in the same position within a given frame for all executions. Low-detail versions may have missing objects found in a high-detail version, but the positions of objects common to both versions must match exactly. We describe in Section 5 how our implementation supports this requirement.

Delta encoding places two specific requirements on the game itself (as opposed to requirements on the game engine). First, the game must provide configuration settings that allow the mobile device to render a low-detail version of the game output at an acceptable frame rate. We view 30 FPS as the minimum acceptable frame rate, and 60 FPS as the maximum. Second, an H.264 video composed of delta frames must be smaller than an H.264 video of high-detail output. The size of the difference represents delta-encoding's bandwidth savings over standard thin-client gaming.

For client-side I-frame rendering, the mobile device must render high-detail frames fast enough and without impacting the game's responsiveness. For example, consider a mobile device that can generate four FPS of high-detail frames. Even if the server GPU is fast enough to generate the missing 56 FPS, the latency of generating each of those four frames on the client will be about 250 ms per frame. Studies of fast-action games have shown that users can tolerate end-to-end latencies on the order of 100 to 200 milliseconds [39, 25], and we estimate that a mobile device must generate at least six FPS of high-detail output for client-side I-frame rendering to be worthwhile.

# 4. COLLABORATIVE RENDERING

In this section, we describe the design details of Kahawai's two collaborative rendering techniques and characterize when they are most effective.

## 4.1 Delta encoding

Delta encoding relies on adjusting a game's settings to produce both high-detail and low-detail versions of the game's graphics output. The high-detail version should contain all of the game's visual effects at their maximum level of detail. The low-detail version should allow the mobile GPU to reach an acceptable frame rate, i.e., between 30 and 60 FPS.

The key observation underlying delta encoding is that the high-detail and the low-detail versions of most games' output share the same *visual structure*. That is, games frequently create high- and low-quality versions of a scene using the same logical objects (e.g., enemies, characters, and other items) in the same positions on the screen. Figure 3 shows the high- and low-quality versions of a scene from Street Fighter 4. Such outputs may differ in their level of detail, texture quality, or polygon count, but they convey most of the same information. As a result, encoding the difference between

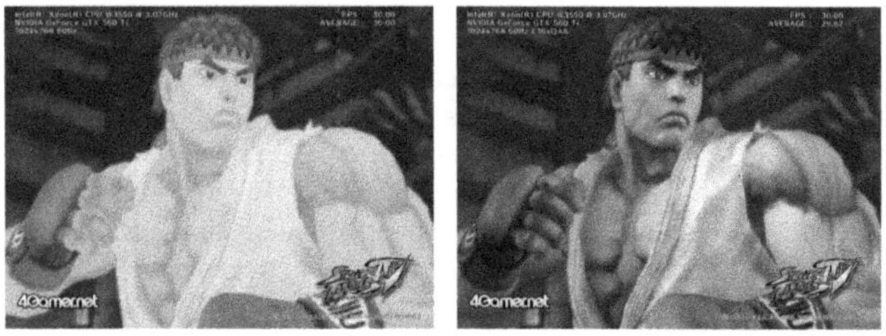

**Figure 3:** *Same visual structure. Lo(Left) and Hi(Right)*

**Figure 4:** *Extra objects at high detail. Lo(Left) and Hi(Right)*

high- and low-quality versions of a frame frequently requires far fewer bits than encoding the high-quality frame itself.

Section 3 outlines the basic steps involved in delta encoding. Delta encoding requires less bandwidth than the conventional thin-client approach as long as the H.264 stream of delta frames is smaller than the H.264 stream of high-detail game output. In the common case, the bandwidth savings of delta encoding will be significant, although there are circumstances in which delta encoding will generate more traffic than a thin-client approach.

It is not obvious that H.264 will effectively compress a video of delta frames, but we have found that delta frames exhibit the same strong temporal locality as the original video frames. As long as this holds, H.264 will deliver high compression ratios for streams of delta frames.

H.264 also provides lossy compression and is designed to hide lost information from the human eye. Information loss is a result of the transformation and quantization (compression) processes in the encoder, which round individual pixel values to improve compression ratios. These losses introduce two challenges when transmitting a video of delta frames: (1) quantization of the delta values introduces visible visual artifacts when the delta is patched into low-detail frames on the mobile device, and (2) the encoded delta does not provide a pixel-exact representation of the difference between a high-detail and low-detail frame.

The challenge of visual artifacts is due to the extended value range that deltas encode. For each pixel, the delta represents the difference between the high-detail value and the low-detail value. The difference can be positive or negative, requiring an extra bit to encode the sign information. Without quantization, one could use modular arithmetic as a simple workaround. Consider an example: if the maximum channel value is 255, high = 10, and low = 253, then delta = -243, which means one could also represent the delta as +12.

However, quantization on the deltas introduces a problem. Consider another example: suppose high = 2 and low = 253, so that the delta = 4 with modular arithmetic. During quantization, the delta could be rounded from 4 to 2. When applying the patch later, low (253) + delta (2) = 255 which means that high is now 255. Quantization of this delta value essentially converts a very dark pixel value into a very bright pixel value, creating a visible artifact.

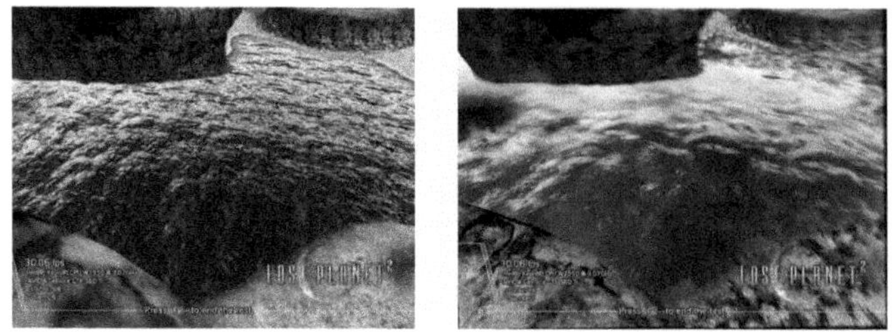

**Figure 5:** *Higher entropy at low quality. Lo(Left) and Hi(Right)*

We solve this problem by applying a solution proposed by Levoy [28]. Before invoking the H.264 encoder, we apply the transformation in Equation 1.

$$\Delta = \frac{Hi - Lo}{2} + 127 \tag{1}$$

This has the effect of dropping the least significant bit in favor of the sign bit. After H.264 decoding, we apply Equation 2 before applying the patch.

$$Hi = Min(2(\Delta - 127) + Lo, 255) \tag{2}$$

Unfortunately, deltas lose one bit of information as a result of this technique. However, this information loss is small and comparable to the loss normally induced by quantization noise in H.264.

The second challenge we faced with delta encoding is that encoded deltas do not perfectly capture the difference between high-detail and low-detail frames. This is primarily due to lossy compression and, to a lesser degree, to subtle pixel differences between frames generated by different GPU hardware and drivers. Loss due to compression is inversely proportional to how similar the high and lo definition frames are. A delta between two relatively similar frames will result in a smaller distribution of delta values, and will therefore suffer from less quantization noise than a delta from dissimilar frames. In our experiments, we have found that when high- and low-detail frames are sufficiently dissimilar, delta encoding can require more bandwidth or induce worse output quality than simply sending an H.264 encoding of the high-detail output.

To see why, consider the scenes in Figures 4 and 5. First, sometimes games introduce *extra* objects to the high-quality version of a scene. For example, in Figure 4 the high-quality version of a Lost Planet 2 scene includes extra clouds, blades of grass, and other background objects. When this happens, the delta is unlikely to be much smaller than the original high-quality frame.

Similarly, the high-quality version of a frame may be easier to compress than a delta due to how a game generates frames of different qualities. Figure 5 shows how Lost Planet 2 uses a more computationally demanding visual effect to generate smoothly waving water in the high-quality version of a scene, and creates water by statically applying a high-entropy texture to a surface in the low-quality version. Because the high-entropy, low-quality scene has more randomness than the smooth water surface of the high-quality scene, it is harder to compress. As a result, the delta between the high- and low-quality versions is also high entropy and does not compress as well as the original high-quality frame.

These scenes from for Lost Planet 2 show that delta encoding may not always be effective for all games. However, for games such as Doom 3 and Street Fighter 4 at any configuration, delta encoding can be a powerful way to reduce the amount of data sent from a cloud-gaming server to a client.

## 4.2 Client-side I-frame rendering

Our second collaborative rendering technique is client-side I-frame rendering. For this technique, the client uses its mobile GPU to render high-detail frames at a low rate, and the server renders high-detail frames at a high rate. The server compresses the high-detail frames into a video, replaces the I-frames in the video with empty place-holders, and sends the remaining P-frames to the mobile device. The mobile device then fills in the missing I-frames with the high-detail frames it renders locally.

The bandwidth savings of this technique compared to a thin-client is proportional to the rate at which a client can generate I-frames. This is partially because I-frames are relatively large and suppressing them saves bandwidth. However, more subtly, the faster a client can generate I-frames, the smaller server-generated P-frames become.

The reason P-frames are smaller under client-side I-frame rendering is that as quantization (compression) in H.264 increases, frames become less similar to their original sources. P-frames based on compressed reference frames must encode changes in the current frame as well as make up for loss accumulated over previously compressed frames.

If the encoder is configured to output a low-bandwidth stream, frames will be encoded using heavier quantization and will incur more information loss. This loss accumulates across P-frames until another I-frame arrives in the sequence. This phenomenon is similar to temporal error propagation [6], in which frames dropped from a streaming video affect contiguous frames in the sequence.

In a normal H.264 stream, loss accumulation cannot be solved by inserting I-frames more frequently. More frequent I-frames would lead to higher-quality P-frames under the same level of quantization, but the encoder would exceed its bandwidth budget because I-frames are usually much larger than P-frames. However, with Kahawai's client-side I-frame rendering there is no bandwidth penalty for increasing the frequency of I-frames in the stream because the client generates these frames locally. Thus, by increasing the I-frame rate, Kahawai reduces P-frame loss accumulation.

An additional benefit of client-side I-frame rendering is that client-rendered I-frames are perfect reference frames because they are not quantized. Thus, these I-frames are more similar to subsequent frames in the stream than they would be under a normal H.264 video. This allows an encoder to use fewer bits to generate P-frames referring to previous client-rendered I-frames at the same level of quality.

Finally, it is also possible to achieve a desired I-frame rate on the mobile device, at the expense of a moderate reduction in quality, by decreasing the game settings used to render high-detail frames. This allows the mobile device to render I-frames at a higher rate. If this is not enough to meet the delay and bandwidth constraints of the game, then we consider the game to be unsuitable for Kahawai's client-side I-frame rendering.

# 5. Kahawai IMPLEMENTATION

To evaluate collaborative rendering, we built two Kahawai prototypes. One is integrated with the open-source version of the idTech 4 Engine, which is also known as the Doom 3 engine. The idTech 4 engine is implemented in C++ and uses OpenGL for graphics. In addition to Doom 3, commercial games like Quake 4, Wolfenstein, Prey, and Brink have also been built on top of the idTech 4 engine.

Our second prototype uses binary interception to implement Kahawai on a closed-source game, Street Fighter 4. Street Fighter 4 is a fighting game with very different gameplay and design than Doom 3. Street Fighter 4 is built on top of the DirectX based Capcom engine that preceded the MT Framework engine used in games like Resident Evil 5, Devil May Cry 4, and Lost Planet 2.

We implemented deterministic graphical output, codec support, and full delta encoding for Street Fighter 4, but we were unable to implement features that required access to source code, such as the client-side portion of I-frame rendering and handling network disconnections. Without access to the game's source code, we could not prevent the client from rendering P-frames. Access to the engine's source would have allowed us to fully implement both collaborative rendering techniques and all other features of Kahawai.

In the rest of this section, we focus on three key challenges: (1) supporting deterministic graphical output, (2) handling input, and (3) implementing the codec support for our two collaborative rendering techniques.

## 5.1 Deterministic graphical output

Collaborative rendering requires two concurrently executing game instances to produce the same graphical output. For delta encoding, the client game's output must match the output of the low-detail game executing on the server. For client-side I-frame rendering, the client game's I-frames must match the server's I-frames. For game output to match, inputs originating on the mobile client must be deterministically replayed by server-side game instances.

Previous work has proposed combining deterministic replay with computational offload [14], but implementing replay at too low a level can cause high overhead, especially on multi-processor machines. Games are computationally demanding, and slowing down a game will lead to a poor user experience. On the other hand, entangling replay with a game's internal logic would be impractical.

Instead, Kahawai takes a middle ground by integrating *partial* deterministic replay with the idTech 4 engine and the Capcom Engine. The approach relies on the observation that Kahawai does not need to faithfully recreate all aspects of a game's execution as long as replays produce the same graphical output as the original. For example, collaborative rendering can work even if a server-side game instance produces different file writes and thread schedules than those in the original client execution.

We define the graphical output of a game as the sequence of OpenGL or DirectX calls it emits. For example, the idTech engine interacts with the OpenGL graphics subsystem within a single thread, which we call the *render thread*. At a high-level, the main loop for the render thread looks like:

```
while (1) {
    SampleInput();      // process input buffered during
                        // rendering of previous frame
    Frame();            // update the game state
    UpdateScreen();     // make calls to OpenGL, then
                        // glFinish() and SwapBuffer()
}
```

The call to *Frame* is used to update internal game state, and the call to *UpdateScreen* is used to render the new state on the screen. For example, for objects in motion, the game engine uses calls to *GetSystemTime* inside *Frame* to determine how much time has elapsed since the last loop iteration. This elapsed time is used to determine how far to move objects within the scene.

Our goal for partial deterministic replay is to ensure that, for a particular loop iteration rendering frame N, the sequence of OpenGL calls (and their parameters) made within UpdateScreen for frame N is identical across executions. To verify that partial replay executes correctly, we run a game multiple times using a specific input log and a specific configuration of the game settings. We then use *glReadBuffer* to grab the rendered output of each frame for each execution and confirm that there are no pixel differences. Note that we run these tests on the *same* GPU and driver.

Interestingly, Street Fighter 4 appears to rely solely on an internal logical clock. This is evidenced by the fact that the game-play responsiveness scales proportionally with the frame rate, and that user actions (e.g., punching and kicking) take a constant number of frames to execute regardless of frame rate. As a result, Street Fighter 4 only required intercepting requests for the system time and the DirectX equivalent of SwapBuffers (Present) using Detours [19]. Unlike Street Fighter 4, Doom 3 and the idTech engine presented more sources of non-deterministic behavior that required access to the source code to address.

There are three sources of non-determinism that can affect the visual output of the idTech engine's rendering thread. The first source is system time: Kahawai intercepts all calls to *GetSystemTime* from the render and audio threads and ensures that replayed executions receive the same time values. The second source of non-determinism is the pseudo random number generator. Interestingly, we did not need to intercept these calls because correctly replaying keyboard and mouse inputs ensures that random-number generation is deterministic. The last source of non-determinism is the game's music. The rendering thread changes a scene's illumination by directly reading data from the sound buffer. For example, when a game's music gets louder, lights in a game may become brighter. Rather than attempting to make the audio thread deterministic, Kahawai includes a configuration flag to tell the engine to use system time instead of reading from the sound buffer. As far as we can tell, this change did not impact gameplay in any other way.

Finally, our current Kahawai prototype handles mid-game disconnections from the server by falling back to low-detail rendering using only the mobile GPU. When the network allows the mobile device to reconnect to the server, we leverage the idTech 4 game engine's support for game-state checkpoint and restore (many other modern game engines also support game checkpoint and restore). The idTech *save game* mechanism allows players to persist the current game state and to resume at a later time. When the client reconnects, it performs the following steps: (1) it executes until the game can be saved; (2) it pauses execution; (3) it sends the saved state to the server; and (4) it resumes execution after the server confirms it has finished restoring the game state. From that point on, offloaded execution behaves normally with the client and server synchronized. In the future, we plan to implement a background restore mechanism that does not pause game play.

## 5.2 Input handling

The key challenge for handling game inputs can be seen by looking at the rendering loop shown in the previous section. The thread executing this loop sequentially processes buffered inputs, updates the game state, and renders the scene. While the loop is executing the *Frame* and *UpdateScreen* calls for frame N, the system is buffering input events for frame N+1. To keep the client and server games in sync, Kahawai must ensure that when the client processes an input event at frame N, the server must also process that event at the exact same frame number N. To accomplish this, the client's render thread timestamps inputs with the appropriate frame number before sending them to the server, and the server pauses until it receives inputs for its next frame.

A naive approach to input handling in Kahawai would leave the input sampling as part of the rendering loop, but this creates performance problems. Suppose the one-way delay from a client to a server is 20ms. After the client finishes rendering frame N, it must send all buffered inputs for frame N+1 to the server. The server cannot render the next frame N+1 until at least 20ms after the client has finished rendering frame N and sampled the input for frame N+1. As a result, the game's frame rate becomes inversely proportional

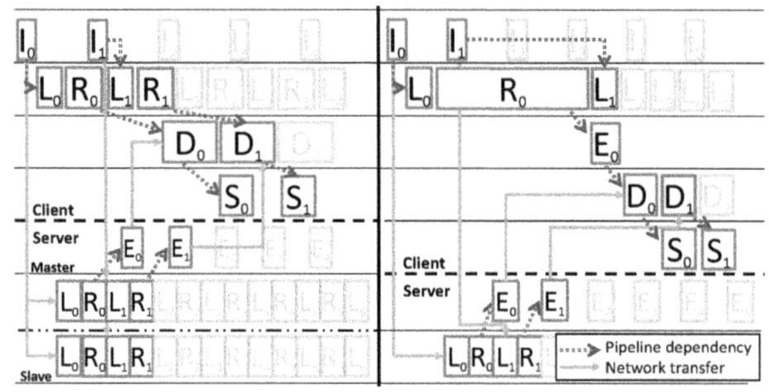


**Figure 6:** *Pipeline overview and network dependencies for both Delta (left) and I-frame (right). The subscripts indicate the frame number. Green arrows indicate local pipeline dependencies, and purple arrows show network pipeline dependencies.*

to the network latency between the client and server, which is unacceptable for game play.

Kahawai solves this problem with pipelining by decoupling input processing from the main game loop. In fact many of Kahawai's tasks are run asynchronously in a pipelined fashion. This pipeline allows Kahawai to asynchronously process and display frames rather than waiting on the network to make progress. The next section describes the Kahawai input and output pipelines in greater detail.

### 5.2.1 Pipeline summary

Kahawai executes tasks in parallel whenever possible to reduce their impact on frame rate and input-to-display latency (i.e., the time from when a user generates an input to when the result of the input appears on the screen). Figure 6 shows the pipeline for both collaborative rendering techniques. The main tasks of rendering, encoding, decoding, and showing form the stages of a pipeline. Each stage executes in a different thread and depends on the output of the previous stage. Parallelism emerges from overlapping the stages operating on data from different frames. In Kahawai we have the following asynchronous stages:

- Input (I): In this brief stage, Kahawai queries the keyboard, mouse, and joystick for user input, and queues the results.
- Logic (L): In this stage the CPU executes the game logic using a set of inputs obtained from the input queue, and updates the game state.
- Render (R): In this stage the GPU generates frames using the updated game state. In addition Kahawai captures the rendered output to memory. Client-side I-frame rendering skips the render stage for P-frames on the client.
- Decode (D): This stage transforms an H.264 stream into decoded frames. For delta encoding, the decode stage also requires the incoming delta to be decoded and then applied to the rendered frames.
- Encode (E): For delta encoding, this stage is only performed on the server. For client-side I-frame rendering, the client encodes a locally rendered I-frame by packing the full I-frame into a lossless (I-PCM) H.264 frame through a very cheap transformation.
- Show (S): In the client, this stage presents the game content to the user at the desired frame rate.

The cost of each individual stage is highly variable, depending on the logical (e.g. physics) and graphical (e.g. polygon count) complexity of the frame being processed.

#### 5.2.2 *Input sampling interval*

In a pipelined implementation of Kahawai, sampling the input is the first stage. Figuring out the correct sample rate is critical to overall game performance. If Kahawai samples inputs too often, input-to-display latency will increase and gameplay will suffer. This is because the sampled inputs are placed on a queue, and the thread that executes the logic and render stages dequeues an entry when it has finished its work on the previous frame. If the inputs are being generated faster than the rate of the bottleneck stage in the pipeline, then the length of the input queue will grow and so will the input-to-display latency. If Kahawai samples too infrequently, pipeline throughput will suffer. This is because when the input queue is empty, the logic and render thread will block waiting for the input sampling thread to enqueue a new sampled input.

To ensure that Kahawai samples inputs correctly, we designed an adaptive clocking mechanism that determines how often the input thread samples buffered inputs. Adaptive clocking is needed because network delay and the time to complete each stage in the pipeline are highly variable.

Client-side I-frame creates another complication. Here, the set of stages that make up the pipeline varies depending on the frame type. For each I-frame, there are additional Render and Encode stages on the client that are not required for P-frames. In particular, for I-frames the Render stage will often be the bottleneck stage of the pipeline. Thus, Kahawai must compute the average pipeline performance over a sequence of frames that includes at least one I-frame and the set of dependent P-frames that follow it.

In a pipelined and multi-threaded system with predictable performance, system throughput should be inversely proportional to the time to complete the slowest stage in the pipeline. Our goal for the adaptive clock is to estimate this value over a time window to improve user experience. We found that in practice too short of a time window leads to burstiness that creates jittery gameplay, and too long of a window artificially limits system throughput. Our current implementation uses a window of 50 frames for Delta, and 10 frames for I-frame.

There are three additional complexities that affect our calculation of the adaptive clock. First, part of the time executing the Logic pipeline stage is spent blocking waiting for input from the input queue. Any time spent blocking waiting for input must be subtracted from our estimate of the cost of the Logic stage. Second, we must adjust the clock to compensate for the one-way network delay between the client and server. This affects the system throughput – if input is not sampled early enough, the server will block waiting for input and that will in turn cause the client stages that depend on server output to be delayed. Finally, to compensate for inaccurate timing measurements, we monitor the length of queued inputs, and slow the adaptive clock if the number of queued inputs exceeds a constant threshold.

### 5.3 Codec support

Both collaborative rendering techniques require capturing GPU output on a frame-by-frame basis. Once we have captured frames from the GPU or received frames over the network, we send them to our collaborative video codec. For delta encoding, two simultaneous instances on the server intercept frames, and share the frames through memory mapped files. The server computes a delta from the two frames, transforms it as described in Section 4.1, and then encodes it using x264 [40] as our H.264 encoder. On the mobile client side, we use ffmpeg [13] as our H.264 decoder, apply the correction as described in Section 4.1 and then apply patches to captured frames from the mobile GPU.

We experimented with the Intel QuickSync [21] hardware H.264 decoder on our tablet, and found that even though it reduced CPU load, it also imposed a substantial latency penalty over using a software decoder. We use software for H.264 encoding as well, due to the lack of flexibility of the hardware encoding APIs to produce streams like those needed by I-frame rendering in which every nth frame is lossless. We expect these APIs will improve over time as real-time hardware encoding and decoding becomes more pervasive. The use of software encoding and decoding limited the resolutions we could support to 720p, hardware support should easily allow full HD (1080p).

For client-side I-frame rendering, we configure x264 to generate I-frames at predictable intervals. We then filter the encoded video to discard the I-frames, while sending the compressed P-frames along with placeholders for the missing I-frames. On the mobile side, we use frame capture to extract the locally rendered I-frames and insert them into the video stream, and finally we send the video to ffmpeg for decoding.

In total we only had to modify 70 lines out of the 600K lines of the idTech 4 engine to enable the functionality of Kahawai. The rest of the Kahawai implementation is in a separate module that we link with the game engine. These modifications introduce determinism, allow the engine to skip the rendering of P-frames, and add mid-game disconnection support. Because these changes are done only to the engine, and not to the actual Doom 3 game, then any other game that runs on idTech 4, such as the upcoming Quadrilateral Cowboy, will work with Kahawai without further modification.

To support Street Fighter 4, where we did not have source code, we created a Detours hook and linked it to the original game binary and our Kahawai module. Implementing this hook required 450 lines of code. It ensures determinism and intercepts the DirectX rendering call *Present*.

## 6. EVALUATION

To evaluate Kahawai, we explore the following questions:

- How does collaborative rendering affect users' gaming experience compared to a thin-client approach?
- How does the bandwidth, input-to-output latency, and visual quality of the collaborative rendering approach compare to a thin-client approach?
- How do variations in GPU and driver impact image quality?

To answer the first question, we conducted a user study with 50 participants and our Kahawai prototype. To answer the next two questions, we measured the performance of our Kahawai prototype under trace-driven, emulated gameplay.

### 6.1 User study

To better understand how collaborative rendering affects users' gaming experience, we conducted a user study in which 50 participants were asked to play a small portion of Doom 3 under one of seven system configurations: unmodified Doom 3, thin client (under low and high network latency), delta encoding (under low and high network latency), and client-side I-frame rendering (under low and high network latency). In our results, we refer to the configuration where participants played unmodified Doom on a PC with a high-end GPU as the thick-client configuration, or "thick". The study was performed between December 1st and 3rd, 2014 in an office inside Microsoft's building 112 in Redmond, Washington.

### 6.1.1 Study design

We asked each participant to complete a portion of the Doom 3 "Central Processing" level. Players begin in a hallway with one monster, continue through a lava-filled room, and end in a room full of monsters. Prior to playing the game, players were given detailed instructions about their goals and the game controls. Each player began the task with full armor and health, as well as a fully loaded plasma gun and a flashlight. All other weapons were disabled.

Participants controlled their on-screen avatars via keyboard and mouse inputs. For example, players could change their avatar's view, make their avatar move, and shoot their avatar's gun. The game screen displayed an avatar's armor, health, stamina, clip-ammunition, and reserve-ammunition levels. After each kill we displayed the number of monsters killed and the number remaining.

Each participant's goal was to kill all 12 monsters, and after completing the task we recorded their remaining health, armor, ammunition, and how long they played. The game stopped as soon as a player has killed all 12 monsters. If a player died before they completed the task, we recorded how many monsters they killed and how long they survived. Players lost health primarily due to attacks by monsters.

Note that players who fell into the lava died instantly, but we allowed them to restart the game once. We included only their post-fall data in our results. Only three of our 50 participants fell into the lava, and interestingly all were self-described gaming experts who often play first-person-shooter (FPS) games. One of these players even brought their own mouse to the study. These participants admitted that because of over-confidence they initially skipped our instructions and rushed straight into the lava.

The tablet used by participants in our thin-client, delta, and I-frame configurations was a Microsoft Surface Pro 3 with a dual core Intel i5-4300U CPU, 8GB of RAM, and 256GB of SSD storage connected by a LAN to a Dell XPS 8700 PC with a quad-core 3.2Ghz Intel i7-4770 CPU, 24GB of RAM, and an Nvidia GTX 780 Ti GPU. Thick-client participants played directly on the PC. Both machines were plugged into identical Dell 24-inch monitors with external mice and keyboards. This prevented participants from knowing which device they were using. For all configurations the game resolution was set to 720p (1280 x 720).

For low-latency configurations, we used an unmodified LAN with approximately 2 ms of round-trip latency between the tablet and server, which corresponds to a typical round-trip time (RTT) over a home LAN. For high-latency configurations, we introduced a 70 ms RTT which corresponds real-world observations over an LTE connection [18].

We asked all participants to complete two surveys (pre-study and post-study). The pre-study survey contained a consent form, asked for basic demographic information, and assessed their interest in and use of technology and gaming. Participants were asked to rate their gaming expertise on a scale of one ("Novice") to three ("Beginner") to four ("Competent") to five ("Proficient") to seven ("Expert"). We used these expertise ratings to create similar player pools for each of our seven system configurations. This survey also asked participants to select their level of agreement with five statements on a scale from one ("Strongly disagree") to seven ("Strongly agree"), including *"I consider myself a gamer."* and *"I often play first-person shooter games (e.g., Halo)."* The pre-study survey also included the following three questions: *"Please list any games that you play regularly."*, *"Please list your all-time favorite games (if any)."*, *"Have you ever played Doom 3?"*.

Participants completed the post-study survey after completing the game. This survey was designed to gauge participants' qualitative evaluation of their game-play experience. It consisted of

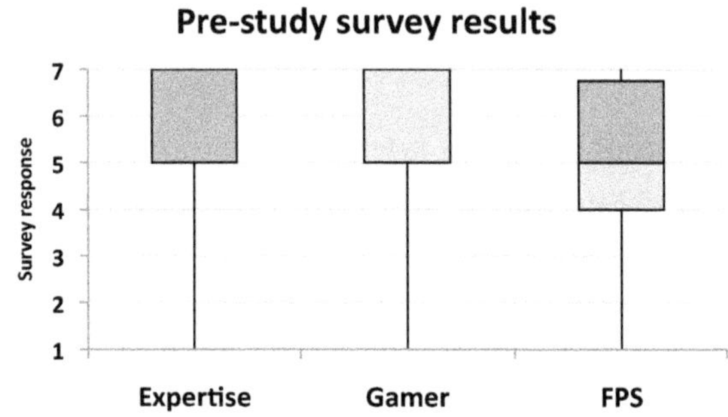


**Figure 7:** *Results from the pre-study survey in which participants rated themselves on gaming expertise and their agreement with statements "I consider myself a gamer" and "I often play first-person-shooter (FPS) games". For "Expertise", the max and 75th percentile responses were both seven, and the 50th and 25th percentile responses were five. For "Gamer", the max, 75th, and 50th percentile responses were all seven.*

four statements, and participants were asked to rate their level of agreement with those statements on a scale from one ("Strongly disagree") to seven ("Strongly agree"). In particular, we wanted to know whether the game was fun (i.e., *"The level of Doom 3 I just played was fun."*), was easy, looked good, and ran smoothly.

### 6.1.2 Recruitment and training

After receiving study approval from the Microsoft Research Global Privacy Manager, we recruited potential participants through several gaming-related and general-purpose mailing lists (e.g., Microsoft Computer Gamers, MS Fighting Gamers, MSR Redmond, and Mexicans in Redmond). Our solicitation instructed employees to complete the pre-study survey and promised a $5 meal card as an incentive for participation.

We recruited 67 employees who completed the pre-study survey. We did not tell participants about our research or which system configuration they were assigned. After cancellations, we ended up with 50 of the selected respondents who participated in the study in early December of 2014.

From the pre-study survey, our 50 participants spend an average of two hours per day playing video games, 10 hours per day on a PC, and three hours per day using a smartphone or tablet. 38 participants frequently played games on their PC, and the most commonly owned gaming consoles were the Xbox 360 (owned by 30 participants) and the Xbox One (owned by 27 participants).

Figure 7 shows box plots summarizing answers to three of our pre-study survey questions. For all box plots in the user study, the top and bottom edges of each dark-gray box represent the 75th and 50th percentile responses, whereas the top and bottom edges of each light-gray box represent the 50th and 25th percentile responses. The top and bottom whiskers extend to the max and min responses. Nearly 40% of our participants rated themselves as a gaming "Expert" (i.e., seven, the highest possible response), though the median expertise rating was "Proficient" (i.e., five). Over 50% of participants strongly agreed with the statement that they were a gamer, and over 25% strongly agreed with the statement that they often played FPS games. Overall, the pre-study survey results indicate that our participant pool was both enthusiastic about and familiar with computer games, which was not surprising given the

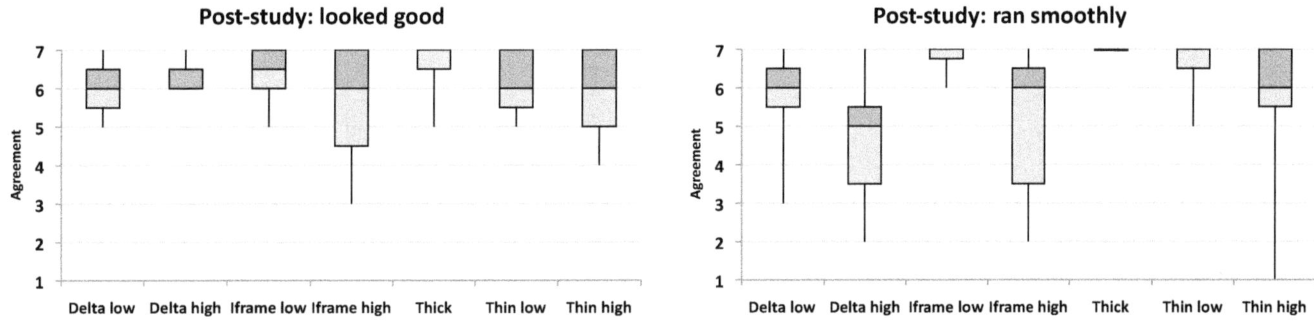


**Figure 8:** *Results from the post-study survey rating participants agreement with statements that the game looked good and ran smoothly. A one rating corresponds to strong disagreement and seven corresponds to strong agreement. For "thick", all thick-client participants strongly agreed that the game ran smoothly.*

email lists we used to recruit participants. Finally, only five of the 50 participants were female.

### *6.1.3 Results and analysis*

Of the 50 participants, eight played under the I-frame configuration with low latency, while every other configuration had seven players. As mentioned previously, we used the expertise ratings from our pre-study survey to create player groups for each of our seven system configurations that were as similar as possible. Despite our efforts, we could not create groups with identical expertise profiles. However, the delta (high latency), I-frame (low latency), thick-client, thin-client (low latency), and thin-client (high latency) groups all had a median expertise of "Proficient." The delta (low latency) group had a median expertise of "Expert," and I-frame (high latency) group had a median expertise of "Competent."

Our hypothesis at the onset of the study was that collaborative rendering (i.e., delta and I-frame) would provide the equivalent of a thin-client gaming experience under the same network latency. We also suspected that network latency would degrade the gaming experiences experience (i.e., that thick client with zero network latency would provide the best experience and that offloading systems under high latency would provide the worst). We measured gaming experience qualitatively using post-study survey responses and quantitatively using players' game performances.

#### *Perceived quality*

Figure 8 shows the results of our post-study surveys, broken down by system configuration. There was strong agreement across all system configurations that Doom 3 "looked good." Not surprisingly, participants who played the thick-client configuration had the highest median response with seven. I-frame with low latency had a median response of 6.5, and all other configurations had median responses of six. These responses indicate that collaborative rendering delivers a gaming experience that users find to look as good as a thin-client approach.

There was more variation in participants' responses to how smoothly the game ran. Thick client, I-frame under low latency, and thin client under low latency all had median responses of seven. Responses for both I-frame and thin client under high latency dropped to six. Delta players provided a median response of six under low latency and a median response of five under high latency. Overall, higher latency appears to have led to worse perceived smoothness. However, both collaborative rendering configurations provided comparable smoothness to thin client: I-frame performed on par with thin client, and delta performed only slightly worse.

#### *Player performance*

We were also interested in metrics that measured how collaborative rendering affects participants ability to play the game. Even if collaborative rendering is visually equivalent to a thin-client approach, it should not make games harder to play. To see if system configuration had any noticeable impact on game difficulty, we looked at the time players took to complete their task and their health at the end of the game. Figure 9 shows these results for each configuration.

The median completion time for all configurations was between 58 seconds (I-frame with low latency) and 78 seconds (delta with low latency). For I-frame and thin client, lower latency led to faster completion times. Completion times for both delta configurations were higher than the low-latency I-frame and thin-client configurations. However, overall there is no obvious difference between the completion times on collaborative-rendering configurations and thin-client configurations. Our intuition is that while latency did have a small effect in performance, the actual rendering technique did not. Instead the performance variations were likely caused by individual skills variations among people reporting the same level of expertise, lack of custom input device / keyboard configuration, time of day and luck among others. This can explains why 'thick', our baseline, did not get the lowest completion times.

The median health for all configurations was between 78 (thin client with high latency) and 42 (I-frame with high latency). For final health, there appears to be little correlation between health and latency. For delta and thin client, median health suffered when latency was lower, whereas for I-frame, median health improved when latency was lower. Furthermore, thick client had a worse median health (56) than all offloading configurations except I-frame with high latency. Similar to completion time, other factors appear to have influenced health other than latency and overall, system configuration did not appear to have any obvious impact on a player's final health.

In summary, our user study indicates that collaborative rendering does not make the game harder to play than a thin-client approach.

**Public Deployment**. We deployed Kahawai publicly at MobiSys 2014 demo session [10]. Around thirty participants played the system. The response was positive.

## 6.2 Trace-driven experiments

Our user study indicates that collaborative rendering provides the same gaming experience as a thin-client approach. In this section, we use trace-driven inputs to our Kahawai prototype to characterize the bandwidth consumption, input-to-display latency, and visual

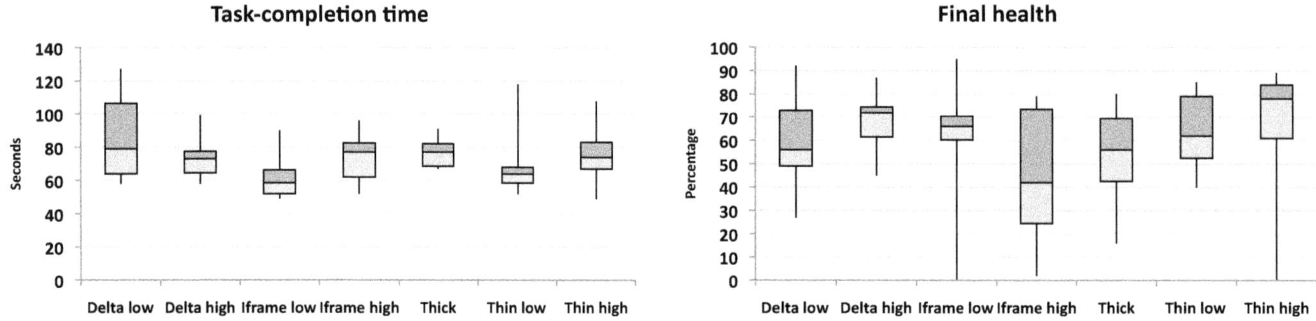


**Figure 9:** *We recorded the time each participant took to complete a portion of Doom 3 and their health levels after they completed the task.*

| Mean Opinion Score | SSIM Score | SSIM (dB) Score |
|---|---|---|
| 1 (Bad) | 0 to .5 | 0 to 3 |
| 2 (Poor) | .5 to .86 | 3 to 8.53 |
| 3 (Fair) | .86 to .9 | 8.53 to 10 |
| 4 (Good) | .9 to .97 | 10 to 15.22 |
| 5 (Excellent, Identical) | .98 to 1 | Above 15.23 |

**Table 1:** *Comparison between mean opinion scores and values in the SSIM scale.*

quality of the collaborative rendering approach, and we use those same metrics to compare directly with a thin client approach.

### 6.2.1 *Methodology*

We used the same client and server in our user study and trace-driven experiments. For consistent output in our video quality experiments, we generated Doom 3 sequences using idTech 4's demo recording feature. For our client-side I-frame experiments, our mobile client generates I-frames at 12 FPS.

To assess Kahawai's image quality. we use structural similarity (SSIM) [38] to measure image quality. SSIM allows us to determine how similar a frame generated by Kahawai is to the highest quality version of that frame. Unlike other image quality metrics like peak signal-to-noise ratio (PSNR) and mean-squared error (MSE), SSIM was designed to model the human eye's perception [23]. A raw SSIM score of greater than 0.9 indicates a strong level of similarity between two images, matching a PSNR of above 50 according to Hore [1]. An SSIM score of one indicates no difference between two images. Table 1 shows the SSIM scale ranges.

The workload we use to evaluate our Kahawai prototype consists of three different scenes in the Doom 3 game. We use the "Demo1" script, consisting of a player moving through a dimly lit environment (*Demo1*), a script of a player moving slowly through a brightly lit and subtly textured environment (*light room*), and a battle scene against the final boss featuring varied lighting conditions and a complex composition (*CyberDemon*). We chose these scenes to expose Kahawai to a range of graphical content. Each scene contains 500 frames at 720p. We used the pre-recorded demo sequences to test video quality, and we played emulating those sequences to test the performance and input latency of our prototype.

For our Doom 3 experiments, we compare three approaches to mobile gaming: delta-encoding (*Delta*), client-side I-frame rendering (*I-Frame*), H.264 streaming (*Thin-client*), and running the game locally in the server (*Thick-client*).

We configure the idTech 4 game engine using two graphics configurations. For our high-detail settings, we used the "Ultra" quality

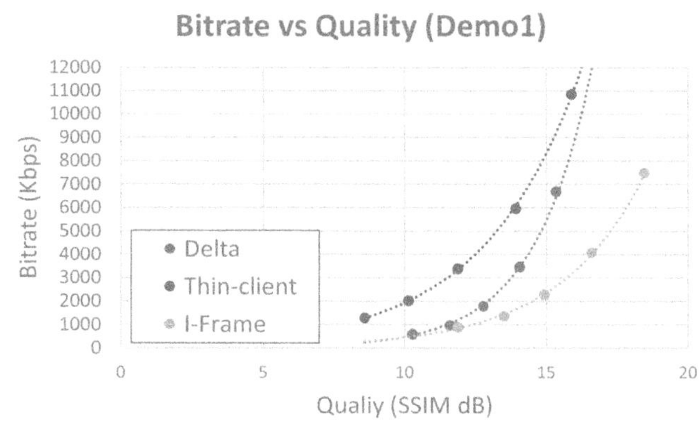


**Figure 10:** *Bitrate vs quality for the* Demo1 *scene.*

preset, and for our low quality settings we use a modified version of the "Low" quality preset, with bump mapping disabled. X264, our H.264 video encoder, can be configured using a wide range of parameters. We choose a single typical configuration for our experiments, based on the medium preset and the zero latency tune. For our latency and performance evaluation we used the faster preset to compensate for the current lack of low latency hardware encoding support and added 4x multisampling to the highest definition settings to stress the client's hardware. Our client can render locally an average of 15 FPS under this configuration, making it unplayable.

We only encoded video without audio and compared the size of the video streams alone. As we mentioned in Section 5, for Delta and I-Frame we don't need to send the audio stream. The client handles sound locally. In a real world deployment, adding sound would require 128 Kbps or more for thin client on top of the bitrate used for the video stream.

### 6.2.2 *Doom 3 experiments*

Given this setup, we sought to answer the following questions:

- For each of Kahawai's collaborative-rendering techniques, how do the bandwidth requirements and visual quality compare to a thin-client approach?
- For delta encoding, how does increasing the client GPU power, as represented by improving the quality of rendering, affect the bandwidth requirements?
- For client-side I-Frame rendering, how does increasing the client GPU power, as represented by increasing the FPS of I-frames, affect the bandwidth requirements?

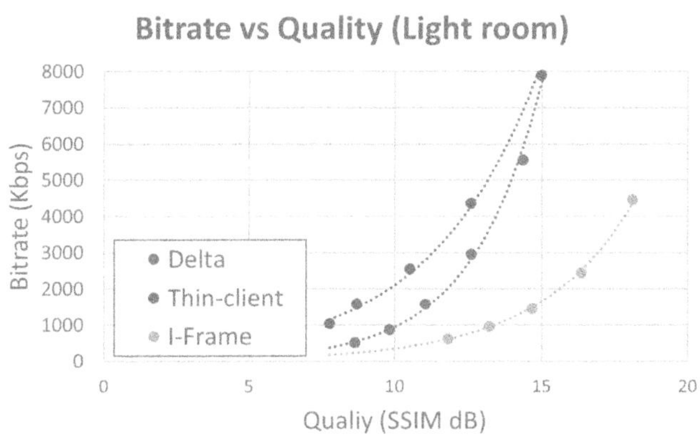


**Figure 11:** *Bitrate vs quality for the* light room *scene.*

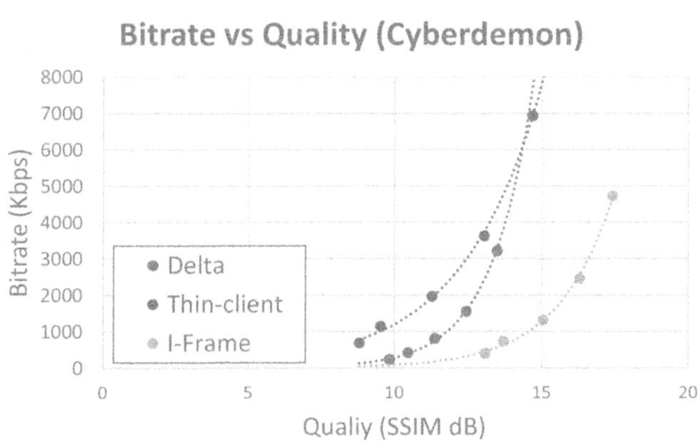


**Figure 12:** *Bitrate vs quality for the* CyberDemon *scene.*

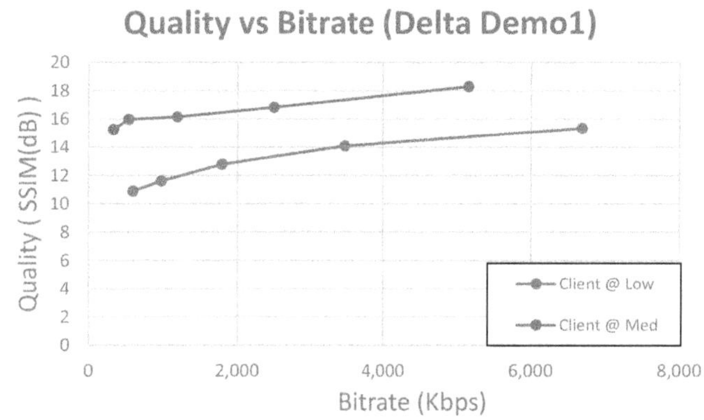


**Figure 13:** *Quality versus Bitrate for different quality fidelities.*

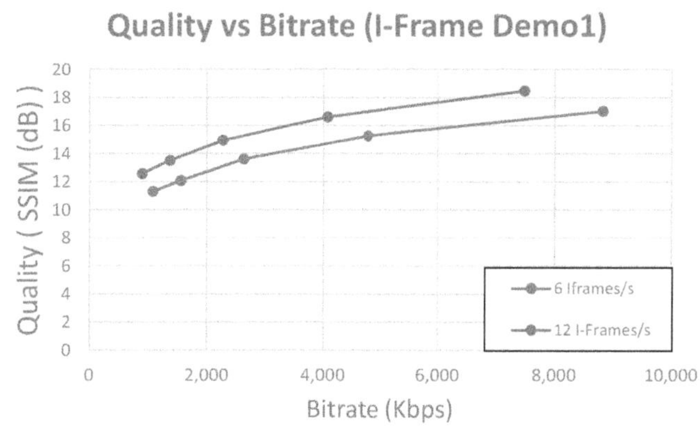


**Figure 14:** *Quality versus Bitrate for different temporal fidelities.*

- Can Kahawai's collaborative-rendering techniques provide full framerate while keeping latency similar to that of the thin-client approach.

To answer these questions, we play each of our scenes using three approaches (deltas, I-frames, and thin-client) while varying the H.264 constant rate-factor (CRF). Specifying a particular CRF value sets the target quality for a video stream, which the encoder tries to achieve using the lowest possible bitrate (i.e., the required bandwidth). Lower CRF values correlate with higher target quality, and higher CRF values correlate with lower target quality. For our experiments, we use CRF values of 20 (highest target quality), 25, 30 (middle high target quality), 35 (middle low) and 40 (lowest target quality). We use the SSIM (dB) logarithmic scale to measure the actual quality of each frame by comparing the frame the client displays with the lossless original frame that the server generates. See Table 1 for a summary of how to interpret SSIM (dB) scores.

To achieve a target quality, the encoder reduces the required bandwidth by opportunistically dropping information from fast-moving frames. The idea is that when frames change quickly, losing information will be less noticeable to the human eye. The higher the CRF, the more aggressively the encoder will drop information. Thus, CRF impacts both the measured quality of each frame (i.e., SSIM) and the size of the video stream (i.e, required bandwidth). This motivates our choice to use multiple CRF values when evaluating each technique.

Figures 10, 11 and 12 show our bitrate and SSIM results for each technique in the demo1, light room and CyberDemon scenes, respectively. Each line represents a different technique, and each data point on each line represents a different CRF value (from right to left, the points correspond to CRF values of 20, 25, 30, 35 and 40). It is important to notice that using a higher CRF does not mean that any stream encoded with it will have a lower bitrate, it just means that the compression factor is higher. For example, in Figure 12, the bitrate of the Delta stream with a CRF of 20 is lower than the bitrate for the thin-client with a CRF of 25.

Our results are impressive, especially for client-side I-frame rendering. For the Demo1 scene, client-side I-frame rendering can achieve a high video quality, averaging a good SSIM (dB) score of 11.894 using under 900 Kbps (CRF of 40), and an excellent score of 16.593 using only 4 Mbps. In comparison, the thin client approach needs almost three times the bandwidth (around 6 Mbps more) to achieve a similar, but lower score of 15.88 SSIM (dB). Similarly, the CyberDemon scene shows that client-side I-frame rendering can achieve similar quality to the thin-client approach using less than one-fifth of the bandwidth, looking at the data points for a CRF of 30 client-side I-frame rendering versus a CRF of 20 for the thin-client. Finally, the light room scene behaves similarly to the other two scenes, but shows even higher savings due to the strong temporal locality present in the slow moving scene. Here, client-side I-frame rendering achieves similar quality (14.67) using slightly over one-sixth of the bandwidth used by thin-client (14.98).

Delta encoding thrives at the lower end of the bitrate spectrum, providing much better quality than the thin-client approach when bandwidth is constrained. For example, it can be seen in Demo1 that we can achieve good video quality (SSIM of 10.31) using only

| Scene | Metric | AMD 6450 | | Intel HD 3000 | | Nvidia 8200 | | H.264 CRF=25 | |
|---|---|---|---|---|---|---|---|---|---|
| High Detail | % of changed pixels / stdev | 34.1 | 4.9 | 32.9 | 4.6 | 0.2 | 0.2 | 91.2 | 2.7 |
| | SSIM (dB) / stdev | 26.0 | 2.2 | 25.8 | 2.3 | 47.0 | 4.7 | 12.6 | 1.6 |
| Low Detail | % of changed pixels / stdev | 40.3 | 4.6 | 38.0 | 4.2 | 0.1 | 0.1 | 92.2 | 2.8 |
| | SSIM (dB) / stdev | 27.3 | 0.5 | 27.7 | 0.5 | 47.0 | 5.1 | 16.0 | 1.8 |

**Table 2:** *Pixel and Quality Differences Between GPU Types.*

590 Kbps. Similarly, in the other two scenes, still produces good quality video for less than 1 Mbps.

It is important to notice that as the bitrate increases, the savings that delta encoding provides over thin-client decrease. For a very high bitrate, thin-client should actually outperform delta encoding, due to the information that is lost during delta encoding (Section 4.1). However, because the purpose of delta encoding is to work at low bitrates, this should not be cause for concern.

We show the impact of the client's output fidelity in the resulting bitrate. For delta encoding, the client's fidelity is measured as how much detail can the client include in its "'low"' quality setting. Figure 13 shows a comparison using delta encoding on the Demo1 scene. One line shows the client rendering the game using our modified low settings *Delta-Low*, while the other shows the client rendering the game using the built-in medium settings. Our results show that generating a delta from two scenes that are more similar to each other will result in more compressible deltas. In this scenario, delta encoding can achieve an excellent video quality (an average SSIM (dB) of 15.986) using as little as 528 Kbps, placing it slightly above the operating range of widely adopted high-quality music streaming services.

Increasing the client's temporal fidelity (the number of I-frames rendered per second), when using client-side I-frame rendering also reduces the required bitrate. Figure 14 shows a comparison using client-side I-frame rendering on the demo1 scene. One line shows the client rendering at 12 I-frames per second, as we use in all our other experiments, while the other line shows the client rendering only 6 I-frames per second. In this scenario, I-Frame with a client rendering 12 FPS settings can achieve an excellent SSIM (dB) of 16.59 using only 4 Mbps while it takes almost 9 Mbps to do it with a client rendering at 6 FPS.

## 6.3 GPU and driver variation

Rendering APIs such as OpenGL do *not* guarantee pixel-exact outputs even when the input scene descriptions are identical. In Table 2, we characterize the extent of this effect in terms of both the pixel differences and the image quality as measured by SSIM (dB). For this experiment, we render a scene on our server using the Nvidia GTX 580 GPU. We then compare the rendered scene on a frame-by-frame basis with the same scene rendered on three other GPUs: the AMD 6450, the Intel HD3000, and the Nvidia 8200 GTS. We perform this experiment twice: once using the scene rendered at high detail, and again using the scene rendered at low detail. We also compare the original scene with an H.264 compressed version using a CRF of 25.

Table 2 shows the results of this experiment. We see that the absolute percentage of pixels that are different is quite large: GPUs from other manufacturers show pixel differences of 33% to 40%, whereas a different GPU model from the same manufacturer shows very small pixel differences of .11% to .22%. Even across manufacturers, where the absolute percentage of changed pixels is large, the impact of those pixel differences on image quality is extremely small. We see that the SSIM (dB) values for the GPU from the same manufacturer are above 45, and for GPUs from different manufacturers are still above 25. Comparing these results to the effects of H.264 compression on image quality, we see that the impact of GPU and driver variation on image quality appears to be substantially less than the effects of H.264 compression on image quality.

## 6.4 Latency and performance tests

A major concern with offloading rendering to a server is the impact on latency and throughput, and most importantly how that affects gameplay. The key measure for throughput is FPS, and for latency is the time from when a user performs an input to when the effect of that input becomes visible. To determine whether Kahawai provides good frame rates with modest latency overhead above either the network RTT (for delta encoding) or the time to render a high quality I-frame (for client-side I-frame), we perform the following experiment.

We run Doom 3 interactively in four different scenes. These scenes correspond to the same three scripted scenes we used in our trace-driven evaluation, plus the scene we used for our user study. We play each scene for a total of 60 seconds. For throughput, we measure the average framerate across each scene as well as the standard deviation. To characterize latency, we measure the time elapsed between when Kahawai samples an input event and when Kahawai shows the frame reflecting the effect of that input event. For latency we also report the mean and the standard deviation. The results are shown in Figures 15, 16, 17 and 18.

First, these figures show that Kahawai performs well over a low-latency network connection, as shown by the blue bars in Figure 15 through Figure 18. These results are consistent with our user study, in which players rated low-latency configurations higher. The average framerates for delta-encoding are just above 40 FPS, and for I-frame they exceed 80 FPS. Figure 16 and Figure 18 show that I-frame's latency and throughput vary more than than delta-encoding's. This is not surprising since the work needed to process P-frames on the client is much less than the time to process I-frames. Figure 17 and Figure 18 show that the additional latency imposed by delta-encoding is higher than that imposed by I-frame, but that both are modest when the underlying network RTT is low.

The higher latency for delta-encoding is caused by our implementation, but is not fundamental. Delta-encoding requires the client GPU to capture each rendered frame, and perform RGB to YUV color conversion on it. We need the image in YUV format for input to the delta-patching algorithm described in Section 4.1. We implement RGB to YUV in OpenCL on the tablet GPU, but the Intel OpenCL runtime has a bug that causes us to perform an extra GPU to GPU memory copy for each frame. In addition, we have not yet implemented delta-patching in OpenCL on the GPU. This change would eliminate the additional memory copy from GPU to host memory and back.

Finally, Figure 17 and Figure 18 show that when the network RTT is high, the input-to-display latency exceeds 100ms. These latency values are high enough that users can perceive a loss in quality. This is consistent with players' rating the visual quality and smoothness of the thick client as better than any of the offloading systems in our user study. However, our user study also found that players perceived the visual quality and smoothness of collaborative rendering to be equivalent to a thin client. Figure 9 shows

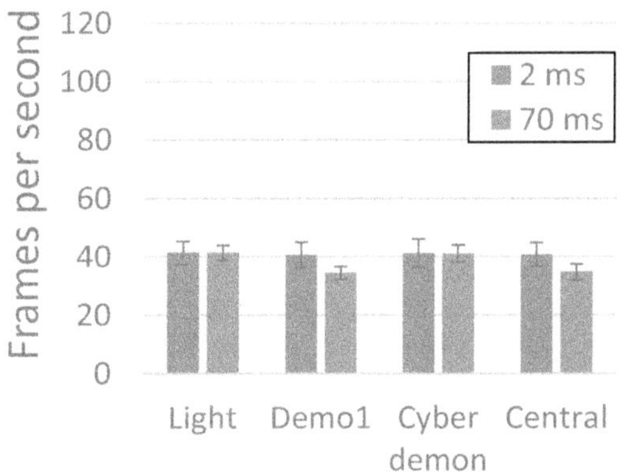


**Figure 15:** *Delta throughput*

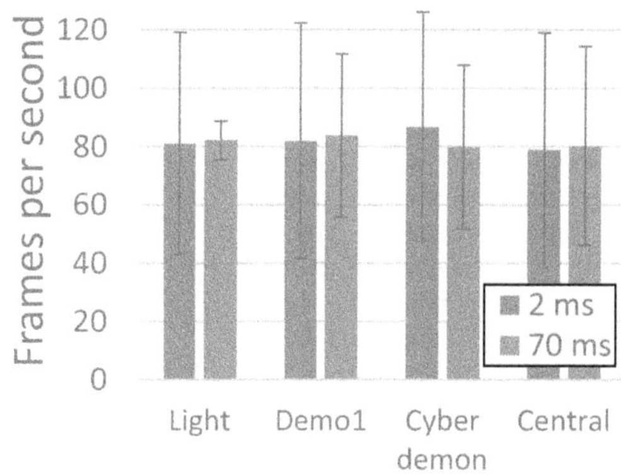


**Figure 16:** *I-Frame throughput*

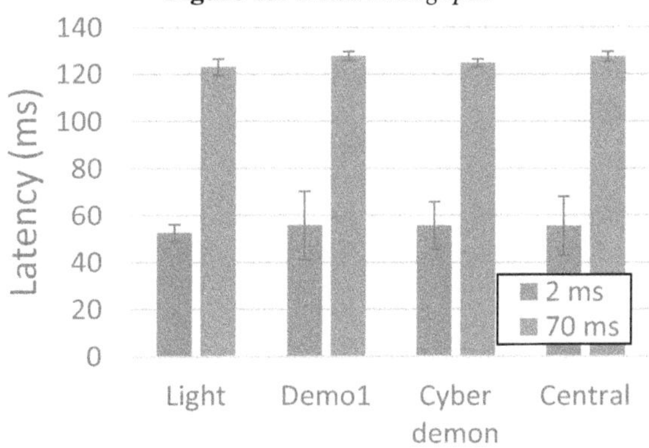


**Figure 17:** *Delta latency*

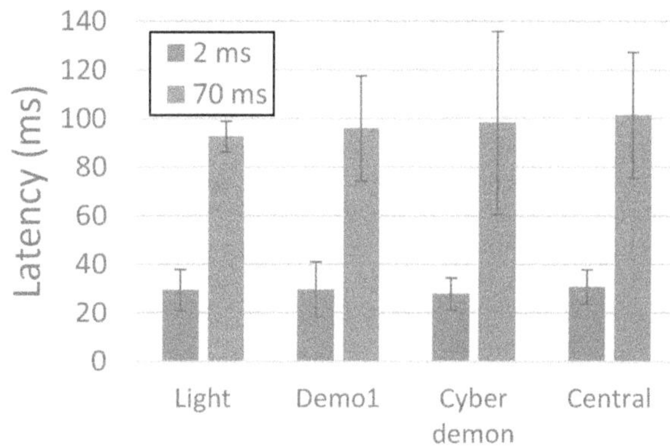


**Figure 18:** *I-Frame latency*

that collaborative rendering also did not impact players' game performance during our user study. Nonetheless, these results suggest that Kahawai will perform best when offloading over a LAN or to a server within a nearby CDN.

# 7. RELATED WORK

Adjusting data fidelity to match the quality of a mobile client's connectivity is a well-studied technique in mobile computing. For example, in Odyssey [32] depending on the network conditions, a mobile client can specify the fidelity at which a server should send it data items. Narayanan et al.[31] previously observed that different fidelities of the same 3D rendering expose the same visual structure, allowing a low fidelity rendering to be useful enough under resource constraints. Collaborative rendering also relies on low-fidelity data representations to reduce network usage, but combines locally-computed low-fidelity data with information from a server to give mobile clients access to high-fidelity data.

Overcoming the resource constraints of mobile devices by partitioning programs between a device and more powerful server infrastructure is also a well-studied area. Chroma [3] allows programmers to specify program partitions and conditions under which to adopt those partitions. CloneCloud [7] and MAUI [9] leverage features of managed-language runtimes to automatically partition a program depending on runtime prediction of the partition's energy and performance benefits. Unfortunately, both of these systems are designed for general-purpose CPU workloads and are inappropriate for applications like fast-action games that heavily rely on a GPU.

Thin-client computing is an extreme form of code offload in which all of a program's computation runs on a remote server [35, 24]. This approach has been embraced by companies like OnLive, Playstation Now, and Nvidia Shield as a way to deliver high-fidelity gaming experiences on mobile devices. Collaborative rendering has two advantages over thin-client gaming: (1) it offers substantial bandwidth savings, and (2) it allows mobile clients to use their own GPU to provide low-fidelity game play when a device is poorly connected or completely disconnected.

We have also worked on Outatime [27], a cloud-gaming system designed to address another important problem: network latency. Outatime produces speculative frames of possible outcomes and delivers them to the client ahead of time. Outatime predicts inputs and compensates for misprediction errors in the client through a graphics technique called view interpolation. While Kahawai greatly reduces the bandwidth required for cloud gaming by moderately increasing input latency, Outatime masks a substantial amount of network latency at the cost of extra bandwidth consumption. In the future, we may integrate the two system into a single low-bandwidth, latency-resilient cloud-gaming system.

Delta-encoding's use of synchronized, duplicate processes is similar to techniques developed for primary/backup fault tolerance[2] and deterministic replay [11, 14]. However, the work that most closely resembles delta-encoding is that of Levoy[28]. In Polygon-assisted compression of images, Levoy proposed selectively disabling detail and effects that are complex to render in clients and sending them as compressed deltas. Delta encoding takes a similar approach, and we have borrowed some of this work's calculations. The primary difference between our work and Levoy's is our efficient use of H.264. In particular, delta-encoding is well suited to H.264 because of the temporal locality among delta frames exhibited by fast-action games.

Mann's work on Selective Pixel Transmission[29] also tries to reduce network communication by extrapolating frames through locally rendered, textureless models and frequent reference frame deltas. A high frequency of the reference frame deltas is necessary to limit the temporal error propagation caused by extrapolating frames from the basic model. Furthermore, in order to obtain a better balance between bandwidth and image quality, only a subset of the pixels in the delta are transmitted.

This approach resembles some of the techniques used in client-side I-frame rendering. However, instead of extrapolating frames, we constantly transfer progressive differences between each reference frame. We use the deltas to make up for limitations in the mobile GPU instead of limiting the amount of error. The high frequency of I-frames in our approach is used to reduce the size of the P-frames rather than to sync the images in the server and client.

## 8. CONCLUSIONS

This paper presents Kahawai, an approach to GPU offload for mobile games that relies on collaborative rendering. To implement collaborative rendering, a mobile device renders low-fidelity graphics output and combines it with high-fidelity information sent by the server to create a high-fidelity result. In Kahawai, we have developed two collaborative rendering techniques: delta encoding and client-side I-frame rendering.

Experiments with our Kahawai prototype demonstrate its potential to provide high visual quality with modest bandwidth requirements. We show that with access to the source code of only the game engine and with minimal changes, we can enable Kahawai for any game. Furthermore, we show that even without any access to source code, it is possible to enable Kahawai for some games. We show that our delta encoding technique, when compared with an H.264 thin client, provides much better visual quality when bandwidth is low – less than 0.6 Mbps. Even more impressive, we show that an H.264 thin client requires up to six times as much bandwidth as client-side I-frame rendering to achieve high visual quality. Finally, a 50-person user study with our Kahawai prototype demonstrates that collaborative rendering provides the same user experience as a thin client.

## 9. ACKNOWLEDGMENTS

We would like to thank the anonymous reviewers and our shepherd, Mahadev Satyanarayanan, for their insightful feedback as well as our colleague Dinei Florencio for sharing his expertise on video compression. This work was partially funded by the National Science Foundation under award CNS-0747283.

## 10. REFERENCES

[1] H. Alain and D. Ziou. Image quality metrics: PSNR vs. SSIM. In *Proc. of ICPR*, 2010.

[2] P. A. Alsberg and J. D. Day. A Principle for Resilient Sharing of Distributed Resources. In *Proc. of ICSE*, 1976.

[3] R. K. Balan, D. Gergle, M. Satyanarayanan, and J. Herbsleb. Simplifying Cyber Foraging for Mobile Devices. In *Proc. of MobiSys*, 2007.

[4] H. Bao. Real-time Graphics Rendering Engine. *Most*, pages 1–6, 2011.

[5] Capcom. Street Fighter IV, 2004. `http://www.streetfighter.com/us/usfiv`.

[6] L. Cheng, A. Bhushan, R. Pajarola, and M. El Zarki. Real-time 3D Graphics Streaming using MPEG-4. In *BroadWISE*, July 2004.

[7] B. Chun, S. Ihm, P. Maniatis, M. Naik, and A. Patti. CloneCloud: Elastic Execution between Mobile Device and Cloud. In *Proc. of EuroSys*, 2011.

[8] E. Cuervo. *Enhancing Mobile Devices through Code Offload*. PhD thesis, Duke University, 2012.

[9] E. Cuervo, A. Balasubramanian, D.-k. Cho, A. Wolman, S. Saroiu, R. Chandra, and P. Bahl. MAUI: Making Smartphones Last Longer with Code Offload. In *Proc. of MobiSys*, 2010.

[10] E. Cuervo, A. Wolman, L. Cox, S. Saroiu, M. Musuvathi, and A. Razeen. Demo: Kahawai: High-Quality Mobile Gaming Using GPU. *MobiSys*, 2014.

[11] G. W. Dunlap, S. T. King, S. Cinar, M. A. Basrai, and P. M. Chen. ReVirt: Enabling Intrusion Analysis through Virtual-Machine Logging and Replay. In *Proc. of OSDI*, 2002.

[12] Epic Games. Unreal game engine. `http://unrealengine.com/`.

[13] Ffmpeg. `http://ffmpeg.org/`.

[14] J. Flinn and Z. M. Mao. Can deterministic replay be an enabling tool for mobile computing? In *Proc. of HotMobile*, 2011.

[15] Flurry. `http://blog.flurry.com/`, Jan 2012.

[16] J. Gregory. *Game Engine Architecture, Second Edition*. A K Peters, 2014.

[17] S. Hecht. Intermittent stimulation by light. *The Journal of general physiology*, 1935:965–977, 1936.

[18] J. Huang, F. Qian, A. Gerber, Z. M. Mao, S. Sen, and O. Spatscheck. A Close Examination of Performance and Power Characteristics of 4G LTE Networks. In *Proc. of MobiSys*, 2012.

[19] G. Hunt and D. Brubacher. Detours: Binary Interception of Win32 Functions. In *Proc. of the 3rd USENIX Windows NT Symposium*, July 1999.

[20] IDSoftware. Doom 3 source, 2011. `https://github.com/TTimo/doom3.gpl`.

[21] Intel QuickSync. `http://www.intel.com/content/www/us/en/architecture-and-technology/quick-sync-video/quick-sync-video-general.html`.

[22] ITU-T Recommendation J.247. *Objective Perceptual Multimedia Video Quality Measurement in the Presence of a Full Reference*. ITU-T, Aug. 2008.

[23] Z. Kotevski and P. Mitrevski. Experimental Comparison of PSNR and SSIM Metrics for Video Quality Estimation. In *ICT Innovations 2009*, pages 357–366. Springer, 2010.

[24] A. Lai and J. Nieh. Limits of Wide-Area Thin-Client Computing. In *Proc. of SIGMETRICS*, 2002.

[25] R. Leadbetter. Console Gaming: The Lag Factor, Sept. 2009. `http://www.eurogamer.net`.

[26] R. Leadbetter. OnLive Latency: The Reckoning, July 2010. `http://www.eurogamer.net/articles/digitalfoundry-onlive-lag-analysis`.

[27] K. Lee, D. Chu, E. Cuervo, Y. Degtyarev, S. Grizan, J. Kopf, A. Wolman, and J. Flinn. Outatime: Using Speculation to Enable Low-Latency Continuous Interaction for Mobile Cloud Gaming. In *Proc. of MobiSys*, 2015.

[28] M. Levoy. Polygon-assisted JPEG and MPEG compression of synthetic images. *Proc. of SIGGRAPH*, 1995.

[29] Y. Mann and D. Cohen-Or. Selective Pixel Transmission for Navigating in Remote Virtual Environments. *Computer Graphics Forum*, 16(3), Sept. 1997.

[30] Microsoft. DirectX Developer Center, 2012. `http://msdn.microsoft.com/en-us/directx`.

[31] D. Narayanan and M. Satyanarayanan. Predictive Resource Management for Wearable Computing. In *Proc. of MobiSys*, 2003.

[32] B. Noble, M. Satyanarayanan, D. Narayanan, J. E. Tilton, J. Flinn, and K. R. Walker. Agile Application-Aware Adaptation for Mobility. In *Proc. of SOSP*, 1997.

[33] OpenGL. OpenGL - The Industry Standard for High Performance Graphics. `http://www.opengl.org/`.

[34] I. Richardson. *The H.264 Advanced Video Compression Standard*. John Wiley & Sons, 2010.

[35] N. Tolia, D. G. Andersen, and M. Satyanarayanan. Quantifying Interactive User Experience on Thin Clients. *IEEE Computer*, 39(3), Mar. 2006.

[36] Unity. Unity 3D Engine 5. `http://unity3d.com/5`.

[37] VirtualGL. `http://www.virtualgl.org/`.

[38] Z. Wang, A. C. Bovik, H. R. Sheikh, and E. P. Simoncelli. Image Quality Assessment: From Error Visibility to Structural Similarity. *IEEE Transactions on Image Processing*, 13(4):600–612, 2004.

[39] M. West. Measuring Responsiveness in Video Games, July 2008. `http://www.gamasutra.com`.

[40] x264. `http://www.videolan.org/developers/x264.html`.

# Accelerating Mobile Applications through Flip-Flop Replication

Mark S. Gordon David Ke Hong
Peter M. Chen Jason Flinn Scott Mahlke Zhuoqing Morley Mao
EECS Department, University of Michigan
Ann Arbor, MI, USA
{msgsss,kehong,pmchen,jflinn,mahlke,zmao}@umich.edu

## ABSTRACT

Mobile devices have less computational power and poorer Internet connections than other computers. Computation offload, in which some portions of an application are migrated to a server, has been proposed as one way to remedy this deficiency. Yet, partition-based offload is challenging because it requires applications to accurately predict whether mobile or remote computation will be faster, and it requires that the computation be large enough to overcome the cost of shipping state to and from the server. Further, offload does not currently benefit network-intensive applications.

In this paper, we introduce Tango, a new method for using a remote server to accelerate mobile applications. Tango *replicates* the application and executes it on both the client and the server. Since either the client or the server execution may be faster during different phases of the application, Tango allows either replica to lead the execution. Tango attempts to reduces user-perceived application latency by predicting which replica will be faster and allowing it to lead execution and display output, leveraging the better network and computation resources of the server when the application can benefit from it. It uses techniques inspired by deterministic replay to keep the two replicas in sync, and it uses *flip-flop replication* to allow leadership to float between replicas. Tango currently works for several unmodified Android applications. In our results, two computation-heavy applications obtain up to 2–3x speedup, and five network applications obtain from 0 to 2.6x speedup.

## 1. INTRODUCTION

Mobile devices have less computational power and poorer Internet connections than desktop and server computers. Size, power, and wireless networking constraints make it likely that this relationship will continue for the foreseeable future.

One way to increase the apparent computational power of a mobile device is to partition computation and *offload* some to a remote server [1, 6, 7, 13, 16]. However, offloading is not a panacea. Finding the optimal partition can be difficult, and the right partitioning strategy may change with environmental conditions such as network latency. Using a suboptimal partitioning strategy may increase network traffic and lower performance, and switching between local and offloaded computation may incur significant overhead due to the need to transfer state (e.g., all inputs and outputs of the offloaded computation) between computers.

One way to mitigate poor wireless network quality (e.g., high latency) is to reduce the number of network round-trips required to complete a user action. However, multiple network round-trips usually arise from data dependencies between consecutive requests to remote services. Costly reengineering of the application and/or service may be necessary to either eliminate such dependencies or hoist them into the cloud service.

The fundamental problem is that the right place to run a program depends on many factors. For example, code that interacts frequently with the user will often run best on the mobile device, while code that performs heavy computation or communicates frequently with other computers will often run best on a cloud server. Dynamically varying resource constraints, such as network quality and pre-existing load on the remote server, play a large role in determining where best to run code; for example, if the network is congested, it may be better to run more computation on a slower mobile device to avoid waiting for data to arrive at a remote server.

In this paper, we propose an alternative approach for improving user-perceived performance on mobile devices. Our approach is based on *replication* rather than partitioning. Instead of predicting which parts of the code should run on the mobile device and which parts should run in the cloud, our system, called Tango, runs the code on both devices and attempts to achieve the user-perceived performance of the faster replica.

Tango uses five main techniques to achieve this goal. First, Tango allows *either* replica to send output to the user. This is the fundamental property that reduces user-perceived latency: to the user, a Tango application will ideally appear to be running the faster replica—whichever replica that happens to be at the moment. For example, output from the remote server can be displayed on the mobile screen, even before the mobile computation reaches the point in its execution where the output is produced.

Second, Tango uses *deterministic replay* to ensure the replicas perform the same computation and (importantly) produce the same output [3]. This guarantee is what lets Tango safely use the output of the first replica: the trailing replica will *always* produce the same result, so it does not matter which replica's output is externalized. Deterministic replay typically designates one replica as the *leader*. The leader logs all non-deterministic events (e.g., network input, user input, and thread scheduling). The other replica is the *follower*—it supplies non-deterministic results from the log rather than re-executing such operations. Since the vast majority of operations performed by an application are deterministic, logging


*MobiSys'15,* May 18–22, 2015, Florence, Italy.

http://dx.doi.org/10.1145/2742647.2742649.

and replaying a (relatively) small amount of information ensures replica equivalency.

Third, in contrast to traditional deterministic replay, Tango shares the role of logging non-deterministic inputs from external sources between computers. Tango also shares the role of externalizing outputs from the replicated computation. For example, in the domain of mobile computing, some input sources are inherently tied to the mobile device (e.g., user input), while others are best tied to a remote server (e.g., network input, since the remote server usually has a better connection). Tango splits roles according to the type of I/O. The mobile device logs user input and sensor data, and it externalizes screen output. The remote server logs network input and externalizes network output.

Fourth, Tango replicates some I/O sources to reduce the amount of non-determinism that needs to be logged and to improve performance. Tango replicates data storage functionality such as the file system and databases. It also replicates substantial portions of the user interface stack.

Fifth, Tango allows either replica to log *internal* sources of non-determinism, which include thread scheduling, time queries, and asynchronous event scheduling. Unfortunately, prior uses of deterministic replay forced one computer (the follower) to always lag behind the other (the leader) to log such events. This a-priori designation limits performance in instances where the leader replica runs slower than the follower. Thus, Tango allows the role of leader to float between the two replicas: a technique we call *flip-flop replication*. When Tango predicts that the follower would be the faster replica, it flips the leader and follower roles. The role of leader may change many times during the execution of an application, e.g., due to alternation between periods of user interaction and periods of computation and/or network communication.

The Tango approach has many benefits. First, Tango achieves interactive performance that is very close to a system that always chooses the fastest location for execution. It does so without needing to predict resource availability, profile applications, or predict user behavior. Second, Tango supports low-overhead control transfer. In contrast to offloading, it does not need to ship all data used in offloaded computations because such data is automatically produced by the remote replica. This is particularly important because the amount of state reachable by offloaded computation can often be quite large. Third, Tango can provide fault tolerance by running multiple replicas. Importantly, by persisting its deterministic log within the cloud, Tango allows remote components to safely communicate over the network, so it hides the latency of multiple round trips over high-latency mobile networks. Finally, Tango can achieve these properties without modifying applications or profiling their executions. In practice, however, our prototype does not fully support the complexity of the Android platform, as discussed in Section 5, and this limits the set of applications that can be run with Tango at present. In addition, some applications may not be able to benefit from Tango due to more fundamental design limitations discussed in Section 8.

We show results from seven applications running Tango. Two computation-heavy applications obtain up to 2–3x speedup, and five network applications obtain from 0 to 2.6x speedup.

# 2. ARCHITECTURAL OVERVIEW

Tango targets interactive applications that run in the Dalvik VM on the Android platform (this includes the vast majority of Android applications). Tango harnesses a trusted remote server to accelerate an application running on a mobile Android device. The server could be managed, for example, by a trusted cloud service provider and be located in a data center.

Tango splits an application into a replicated portion and a non-replicated portion. The entirety of the replicated portion runs on *both* the mobile computer and remote server. In contrast, different components of the non-replicated portion run on *either* the mobile computer or the remote server. The high-level view of Tango's architecture is depicted in Figures 1 and 2. Each of four high level components can be thought of us as existing in their own address space; communicating over unidirectional channels shown by the arrows. In each diagram the left two components exist on the server while the right two exist on the client. The two diagrams demonstrate how communication patterns change when the leader is switched. Differences are highlighted as dotted lines.

## 2.1 Replicated Portion

The bulk of the replicated portion consists of the application code running in the Dalvik VM. The entire Dalvik execution of the application within the VM is replicated; Tango deterministic co-execution guarantees that both replicas execute the exact same Dalvik instructions on the same data. Since these instructions are deterministic, they produce the same result.

Our choice of enforcing determinism at the level of the Dalvik VM was driven by the desire to be processor-agnostic. The diversity in mobile phone and server hardware means that different platforms run a diverse set of processors with different ISAs (e.g., an x86 server and an ARM phone). It would be exceedingly difficult to guarantee determinism for binaries across ISAs (e.g., through deterministic binary-to-binary translation). We could emulate a different architecture on the server [21] but only at a significant performance cost. However, by implementing determinism in a VM such as Dalvik, we can simply guarantee determinism at the level of the Dalvik virtual ISA; this is sufficient for deterministic execution as long as the VM on each platform correctly implements the language ISA specification.

A second advantage of replicating at the level of the Dalvik VM is flexibility: a user can choose to run some applications with Tango and some without Tango. Since each application has its own instance of the Dalvik VM, we can replicate only the VMs for the chosen applications. The required isolation of application data in Android also enables this design choice.

In addition to the Dalvik VM, Tango also replicates many of the native methods that are invoked by the Dalvik VM. First, many native methods in standard libraries are deterministic and have no external side effects. We have identified and flagged many such methods, such as Java's math, compression, and locale implementations. Each Tango replica simply executes such flagged methods as though it were part of the Dalvik VM itself. Second, Dalvik applications have frequent interactions with the UI stack; these interactions are low-level and much more frequent than displaying user output or receiving user input. Tango therefore replicates the UI stack on the server; it simply omits any externalization of data to an I/O device. Third, storage (file system and database) interactions are very deterministic, so Tango replicates the storage subsystem.

We note, however, that our original decision assumed that applications are mostly composed of managed code, and native code execution would be a rare exception. As we discuss in Section 5, this assumption appears to be growing less true over time. Therefore, future systems may wish to revisit this decision and consider alternative replication strategies.

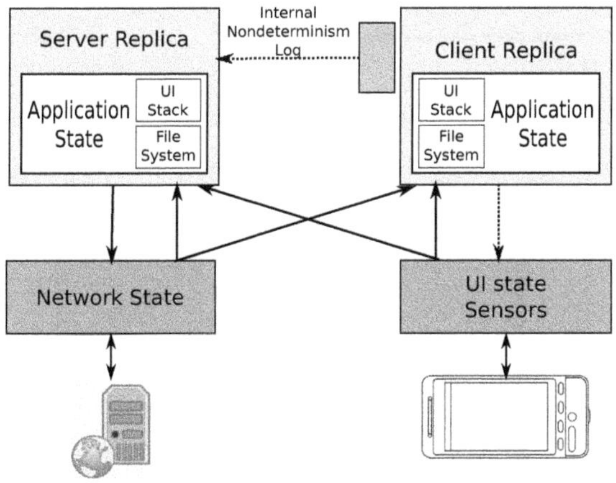


**Figure 1: Tango's architecture: client is the leader. (Note that Client Replica externalizes the UI.)**

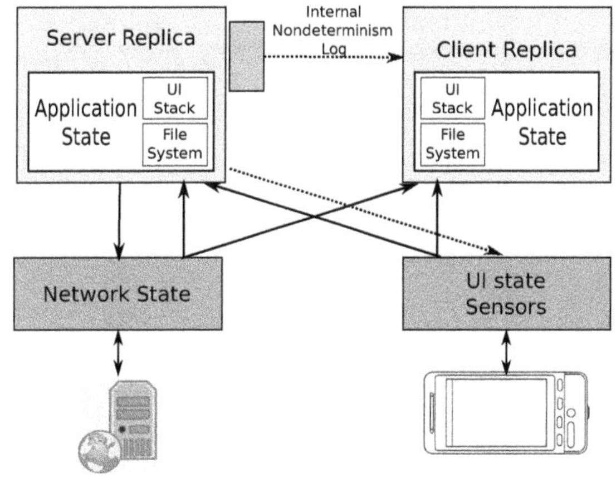


**Figure 2: Tango's architecture: server is the leader. (Note that Server Replica externalizes the UI.)**

## 2.2 Non-Replicated Portion

Some components of the system are nondeterministic (e.g., those that receive input from the user). These components cannot be executed independently on both replicas, lest the results differ and the replicas' executions diverge. Instead, Tango executes these methods only once, on behalf of the leading replica that reaches the native method first. Tango logs the result (return code and any modified Dalvik state). When the following replica arrives at the native method, Tango does not execute the method—instead, it replicates the effects on the Dalvik state and returns the same result. Figures 1 and 2 show the separation between these non replicated components (the darker boxes) and the application replicas, depending on which endpoint is leading.

Many of these non-replicated methods perform I/O. Such methods are sources of *external nondeterminism*. Data received from the user, the network, inter-process communication (IPC), sensors, and other sources must be logged and replayed so that each replica receives the same inputs. We observe that many of these data sources have natural affinity with one particular replica, and we pin each to its natural replica. For example, user input, IPC, and sensor data must come from the mobile client. In contrast, the cloud server almost always has a better network connection (e.g., lower latency and higher bandwidth) than the mobile device, so network communication should be done on the server. This is why network state is kept on the server while UI state and sensors are tied to the client in Figures 1 and 2.

Tango partitions execution so that these pinned methods run in a separate thread of control, called the *native thread*. Because they are deterministic, both replicas will execute the same methods with the same data in the same order. To call such a method, each replica sends a message to the *native thread*; for the replica on the local computer, this is a memory operation, but for the other replica, this is a network message. The native thread executes the method and sends the results to *both* replicas, as shown in Figures 1 and 2. The trailing replica may not have reached this point in its execution, so it logs the result until it is needed. Note that the follower need not send a request to the native thread.

There exists a final class of nondeterminism that is not inherently tied to any computer, which we call *internal nondeterminism*. This includes thread scheduling decisions, the timing of the delivery of asynchronous events, time queries, and entropy queries (e.g. reading `/dev/random`). Because Dalvik thread scheduling decisions are frequent, Tango implements a deterministic thread scheduler so that each replica independently makes the same scheduling choices—this avoids the need to communicate such choices between replicas. For asynchronous events and time queries, a single replica, called the leader, is responsible for executing such operations and sending the result to the other replica, called the follower. For example, in Figure 1, the client is the leader and thus handles the internal non-determinism. The follower generates the same asynchronous events at the same point in its execution and supplies the same time values to ensure replica equivalence. Because asynchronous events can be scheduled at any point in execution, the follower is prevented from surpassing the leader.

Tango implements a mechanism we call *flip-flop replication* to allow leadership to switch between replicas. Using a set of simple heuristics, this mechanism attempts to have the replica that can execute faster be the leader at any moment. Since different computers have different strengths, it is common for leadership to switch back and forth between computers; for instance, the mobile phone typically leads during periods of user interaction, and the server typically leads during compute-intensive periods or periods with network communication. The differences in Figures 1 and 2 illustrate that when the server is the leader, it can externalize the UI state on behalf of the client. In contrast, when the client is the leader, only the client will generate UI output.

# 3. EXAMPLE SCENARIO

In this section, we illustrate how Tango works by describing how it would accelerate an example application.

The scenario begins with the user interacting intensively with the application user interface. Events such as button and screen presses are broadcast to both replicas, but the client replica receives them first because communication with the server replica is subject to a network round trip. Thus, the client replica is the leader and decides when these events are scheduled into the application execution. The application may execute many synchronous native methods that query UI state; the leading client replica receives a quick response because of its co-location with the UI.

In a standard thin client solution, the server replica would lag far behind during this stage since it would initiate many synchronous UI requests and each would be subject to a full round-trip delay over a high-latency mobile network. In Tango, however, the UI events, the asynchronous scheduling decisions, and the result of synchronous native methods are all *pushed* to the server before the

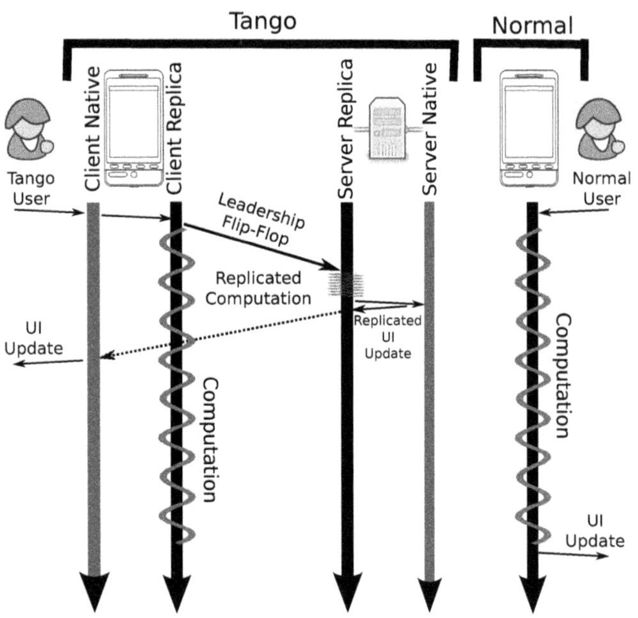


**Figure 3: Compute-intensive phase: comparing Tango's speedup from faster server execution with normal execution.**

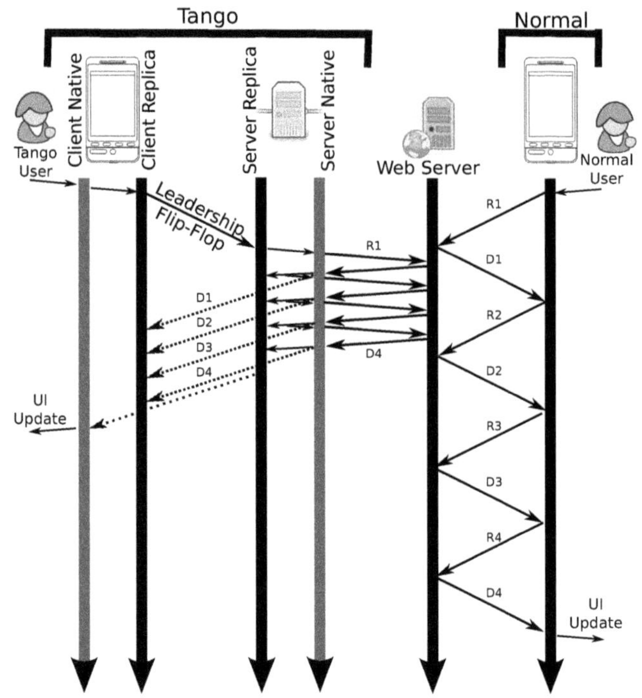


**Figure 4: Network-intensive phase: comparing Tango's speedup from faster network response times from the server replica with a normal interaction with a Web server.**

server asks for the results. Thus, all the information the server will need for its execution is sent in pipeline fashion, *before the server even asks for the data*, and the server replica lags only a one-way network delay behind the client replica at the end of this phase.

The application next enters a compute-intensive phase of execution triggered by the user's input, as illustrated in Figure 3. Since the server has a faster processor than the client, the server replica quickly catches up and Tango switches leadership to the server. Note that because the server replica has followed the same execution as the client, it has the same state as the client replica and no state needs to be sent during the leader switch.

During the compute-intensive phase of execution, the server replica calls UI methods that send output directly to the client native thread. The client displays this output even though the local replica on the mobile computer is lagging behind the server because it is still working through the computation that was just externalized by the client native thread. This allows the user to experience the faster responsiveness of the server replica during this phase.

After receiving the output, the user spends some time thinking about his/her response to this output. While the user is thinking, the client replica catches up to the current state of the server. When the user interacts with the UI, the client again becomes the leader. In the event that the client does not have time to catch up before the next user interaction, the server will continue to operate as leader until the client does catch up. During this time Tango will be operating like a thin client, with all user interactions being routed through the server.

The next phase of the application involves frequent network communication with an external computer, as shown in Figure 4. The network operations are best done on the server, since it has a lower latency connection to the network. The server therefore assumes leadership.

The network communication involves several rounds of synchronous message exchanges with the external computer. Each round involves sending a message to the external computer, waiting for its response, then computing the next step in the message exchange (e.g., an SSL handshake followed by several database queries with data dependencies). In an unmodified client, this phase is slow since it involves many round trips over the high-latency wireless network. However, the server replica interacts with the external computer much faster because it runs in a data center and has an excellent Internet connection. In a mirror image of the first phase, network input, asynchronous scheduling decisions from the leading server replica, and responses to network methods are all sent to the client in pipeline fashion. Even with a slower processor, the client remains only a one-way network delay behind the server. Although the client takes longer to perform the small amount of computation in this phase, it catches up during network communication. The server waits for the remote computer to respond to each message, while the slightly-lagging client replica already has the response in its log. Thus, either the server or the client replica can quickly display output at the end of this phase.

This multi-phase execution may repeat indefinitely. For example, the application may next interact heavily with the user, and so on. In each phase, Tango allows external components (i.e., the user and other computers) to experience the faster responsiveness of the replica that executes most quickly during that phase, while the slower replica can catch up to the faster replica during idle periods (e.g., when the application waits for the user and other computers). These two phases, compute-intensive and network-intensive, can be combined to get further benefits from Tango.

This scenario helps identify the specific instances in which we expect Tango to show the most benefit. First, to benefit from use of a remote server, the application should include at least one computation-heavy phase or network phase with multiple communication round-trips. Second, for Tango to outperform a thin-client solution, the application should have a phase that interacts with the user or other I/O on the client. Finally, if the application has compute-heavy phases, there should also be phases with user think time or I/O during which the client computation can catch up with the server. We believe that many mobile applications share these exact characteristics, in other words they combine user interaction with computation and/or network communication.

# 4. IMPLEMENTATION

To build our prototype, we modified the Dalvik Virtual Machine used in the Android operating system. Our modifications are built on top of version 10.1 of the CyanogenMod open source project [8] (based on Android's Jellybean branch).

Conceptually, an application running within the Dalvik VM can be thought of as consisting of two components: the Java state managed by the Dalvik VM and the native state managed by native code external to the Dalvik VM. The Dalvik VM's behavior is mostly deterministic, while interactions with many sources of nondeterminism such as user input, the network, the file system, and device sensors go through the native code. Therefore, it is most natural to deterministically replicate the Dalvik code, but not (by default) the native code.

## 4.1 Thread Scheduling

In order to make the behavior of the Dalvik VM fully deterministic, each replica must make the same thread scheduling decisions. Potentially, Tango could require the leader to record all thread scheduling decisions and send them to the follower, which would then replay those decisions. However, that strategy would add considerable network traffic to communicate those decisions. Instead, Tango uses a *deterministic* thread scheduling algorithm so that each replica independently makes the same decisions.

Tango allows a single *managed* thread to execute at a time. A thread is managed any time it is directly interacting with Dalvik VM state. As will be discussed in the next section, a thread interacting with native state can be *unmanaged* and can execute concurrently with a managed thread or other unmanaged threads.

Tango performs deterministic round-robin scheduling among the managed threads. The pre-existing Dalvik VM garbage collection mechanism intercepts all backwards jumps, method invocations, and exceptions raised—an executing Java thread must occasionally execute some of these *GC points* in order to continue to run. If a thread executes a pre-defined number of GC points without blocking, the Tango deterministic scheduler preempts it and runs the next runnable managed thread in the round-robin queue.

The Tango scheduler also provides deterministic implementations of synchronization primitives such as locks and condition variables. For instance, a thread requesting a lock simply checks if the lock is already owned. If so, it adds itself to a wait list for the lock and yields execution to the next runnable managed thread. Otherwise, it acquires the lock and continues executing.

## 4.2 Native Methods

A Java thread invokes native methods (which are usually written in C/C++) by using the Java Native Interface (JNI). Native methods do not interact directly with Dalvik VM state; instead, they use the JNI to do things like create objects, invoke Java methods, and access/modify object data. Tango records which calls are made by native code and what parameters are provided, so that it can faithfully replicate interactions between the Dalvik VM and the native code on both replicas. Since Tango records and deterministically reproduces *all* interactions between native methods and Dalvik state, it is able to run a native thread concurrently with another managed thread without leading to replica divergence (The reason it cannot run two managed threads concurrently is that it does not observe interactions via shared memory).

Thus, when a Java thread invokes a native method, Tango's default behavior is to move it from managed to unmanaged execution. This process requires no logging; the thread simply allows the next managed thread to execute and continues executing itself (although it may no longer access Dalvik VM state).

When the native method finishes, the unmanaged thread that invoked it must transition back to managed mode. At this point, the thread is inserted back on the round-robin scheduling queue of the Tango scheduler. However, to prevent replica divergence, both replicas must insert the thread at the exact same point in the execution of the managed threads. Essentially, the two replicas must agree on when an *asynchronous event*, in this case the completion of the native method, happens in relation to the execution stream of the Dalvik VM.

Tango uses the number of context switches as a convenient counter that denotes particular points in the application's execution. Asynchronous events are allowed to occur only at context switches. The leader has sole authority over determining when an asynchronous event happens. It logs the counter value and sends it to the follower. The follower schedules the identical event at the same point in its execution stream, ensuring replica determinism. Note that this implies that the follower should never execute ahead of the leader; otherwise, it may learn too late that it should have inserted an asynchronous event at a context switch that it has already executed.

In summary, when a native method finishes, the leader transitions the invoking thread from unmanaged to managed mode at the next context switch among managed threads. The follower will execute the same transition at the same point. Tango uses this technique for all asynchronous events. For instance, when a Java thread performs a timed wait on a condition variable, the replicas must agree on when the thread wakes up. Tango casts the wakeup as an asynchronous event to ensure determinism.

Finally, there can be long periods of execution where the leader does not need to record any asynchronous scheduling decisions. To allow the follower to make progress, the leader occasionally sends a negative acknowledgment confirming that no asynchronous events were inserted up to the current point in its execution. This allows the follower to continue execution up to that point.

## 4.3 Native Method Invocation

We next describe the invocation of a generic native method; the following section describes specific optimizations that Tango employs for certain classes of native methods.

A generic native method is not called directly by the unmanaged thread; instead the native method is run on the client in another thread context, called the *native thread*. Thus, if the client is the leader, its unmanaged thread performs an IPC to invoke the method. If the server is the leader, its unmanaged thread performs a remote procedure call.

The use of native threads allows the progress of the native code to be decoupled from the progress of the replica. For instance, if the server is the leader, it can update the screen via a native method running on the client, even though the corresponding thread on the client replica may still be working through the proceeding computation.

In our implementation, there are actually many native threads. Each native thread corresponds to a Java thread within the Dalvik VM. A native thread operates by running an event loop waiting for invocations from the corresponding Java thread on the leader replica. After finishing, it sends its response, containing the return values and/or modified Dalvik state, to both replicas. Tango synchronizes the native threads so that they do not perform concurrent conflicting operations.

The following replica may actually receive the response before it reaches the point in its execution where it invokes the native method. In this case, it logs the response and simply uses the logged values rather than invoking the method again. If the response has not yet arrived by the time it reaches the method invocation, the unmanaged thread on the follower blocks until it receives the response.

#### 4.3.1 *Native Method Annotations*

Handling every native method in a totally generic way is impractical given the overhead of the generic approach and the large number of native methods called during an application's execution. Fortunately, there are several optimizations we can make for many native methods that have known behavior. We have annotated the most commonly used methods in the Android runtime to identify which optimizations can be used.

The possible annotations are as follows:

- *Deterministic:* the native method always produces the same results given the same inputs and has no external side effects. Such a method may be natively deterministic, or we may have added sufficient logging and replay of logged values to make it deterministic. Each replica executes a deterministic method locally; there is no divergence because both executions produce the same result.
- *Sync:* a method with the deterministic annotation that is also guaranteed never to block. For such methods, the calling Dalvik thread remains in managed mode rather than switching to unmanaged mode. This avoids the overhead of scheduling an asynchronous event to transition back to managed mode.
- *Inlineable:* a method with the sync annotation that is also guaranteed to be of short duration and which can run in any thread context. Calls to this method may be performed directly on the invoking thread within the replica as a performance optimization. Section 4.3.3 has additional details about these methods.
- *Ideal:* an inlineable method that also relies on no state from other native methods and does not externalize output. For Tango's purposes, these methods are considered part of the Dalvik VM itself. For example, java.lang.Math.log() is ideal.

#### 4.3.2 *Pointer Derandomization*

Many methods that we would like to annotate as deterministic are not actually deterministic from Tango's perspective because they write a pointer to some native resource (as an int or long) into the Dalvik VM's state. If both replicas run such a method locally, then they would write different values to the VM state, leading to divergence. To address this issue, Tango implements pointer aliases. Pointer aliases map the native pointers to a deterministic index in a table. The alias can then be stored in the Dalvik VM without leading to state divergence. When the resource is accessed, it must be dealiased by the native code.

To implement this correctly, any thread that attempts to create a pointer alias should operate independently and draw from a different set of aliases. Otherwise it would be necessary to communicate the order in which the aliases were created. Tango accomplishes this by using the high bits of the alias to represent the thread context that created it and the low bits to represent the index into a pointer alias table for that context.

#### 4.3.3 *Inlining*

The primary overhead when invoking native methods with Tango is that all data must be communicated between the Java thread and the corresponding native thread. Moving this data and switching thread contexts is substantially more expensive than simply invoking the native method directly on the Java thread. The *Inlineable* annotation provides a hint that a method can be run in the context of the calling Java thread to avoid this overhead.

However inlining works against one of the goals of Tango; namely, that the native state should be able to progress beyond the replica state. When a method is inlined, it gets its inputs from the calling replica, which prevents the desired decoupling. Therefore, a method is only inlined by the leading replica.

Additionally, the decision to inline a method cannot easily be undone. If a method was inlined and then did not return quickly, it could keep the replica and native state coupled for an extended period of time. It is for this reason that we use the inlineable annotation only for short-lived methods.

Finally, allowing a method to be inlined means that it may be executed in different thread contexts (the Java thread or the corresponding native thread). Some native methods make use of thread-local storage or are otherwise sensitive to the thread context, and they will not function correctly when inlined. Therefore, a native method must be agnostic to its executing thread in order to be marked inlineable.

### 4.4 External Nondeterminism

*External nondeterminism* refers to nondeterminism that has its source outside of the Dalvik VM and can be generated by only one device. Examples include user input, interprocess communication, network communication, and querying device sensors. Most of these sources of nondeterminism must be provided by the client device. However, some sources, like network communication, are better provided by the replay server.

#### 4.4.1 *External Inputs*

The client and server run proxy threads that receive input from external sources such as the user interface and network. When such input is received, the proxy thread pushes the data to both the client and server replicas. This avoids the need for the leader to ask for input data when the data is not received by the computer that is currently leading (for example, network data when the client is leading).

Although both replicas receive the same data, the leader decides *when* the data arrives within the replicated execution stream. The arrival of external data is an asynchronous event that is scheduled using the methods described in Section 4.2.

Next, we describe how Tango handles each source of external nondeterminism.

#### 4.4.2 *Network Communication*

One of the main ways that Tango improves user-perceived performance is by moving network communication to the server. Data received from the network is pushed to both replicas as soon as it arrives. The leader decides when the data arrives in the execution stream. This means that it decides the *number* of bytes returned by a `read` socket call (though the content of those bytes is pushed to both replicas). If the following replica has not yet received the data, it blocks until it arrives and delivers the specified amount of bytes. The leader also decides the timing and results of `poll` and `select`.

#### 4.4.3 User Interface

User input is handled similarly to network input, except that it is the client that receives and broadcasts the input to both replicas.

User output is more complicated because Java threads invoke many native methods to perform even the simplest UI output operations. We originally found these interactions to be a significant source of performance overhead. However, we observed that almost the entirety of the Android UI stack is in fact deterministic, or can be made to behave deterministically with minor modifications including the use of pointer aliases described in Section 4.3.2. Therefore, Tango replicates the UI stack and runs separate copies on the client and server.

When the server is the leader, it broadcasts invocations of native methods in the UI stack to both of the replicated stacks. The server stack does not update the screen, but it provides immediate responses to the server replica to each of the numerous method invocations without intervening round-trip network delays. This lets the server execute quickly and continue to generate UI updates. *Critically, the server knows what information the client user interface stack will need because it has its own stack requesting the same data.* This allows all of the needed data to be sent to the client in pipelined fashion.

#### 4.4.4 File System

Tango replicates portions of the client file system on the server. A significant percentage of the file system on Android phones is normally mounted as read only; this portion is simply replicated on the server.

Additionally, the Android file system implements strong partitioning separating different applications. Tango replicates the application-specific portion of the file system by having each replica update its local copy. Since each replica deterministically performs the same operations and the file system is itself deterministic, this ensures that the state of the file system remains consistent.

The remaining portion of the file system (e.g., the SD card) can be updated by many applications, some of which may run under Tango and some of which may not. Therefore, reads and writes to these files are not deterministic and instead must be performed by a native thread running only on the client.

This strategy makes all file system operations deterministic. Most operations require no extra communication, since they are performed deterministically on both the client and server. For instance, a newly installed application will start with the initial application-specific file system portion on both the client and server. Since the same file system operations are performed in both locations, the application-specific portion remains in sync throughout multiple executions of the application. Our implementation also provides deterministic access to Dalvik's SQLite interface, which is the standard database implementation on Android.

#### 4.4.5 Time

Android applications frequently query the time. In Tango, the leader produces the timestamp and the follower uses the same value in response to the time query. During a leader switch, the previous leader sends the new leader its current timer values. The new leader adjusts time values that it subsequently returns to the application by an appropriate delta. To reduce the amount of data sent from the leader to the follower, we could potentially adopt a semi-deterministic clock, such as the one used in Arnold [9].

## 4.5 Leader Switching

Switching leadership is implemented by having the current leader send a message to the follower requesting a switch. This message includes the point where the current leader is in the execution of the program, and the current leader pauses its execution at this point until it receives a reply. If the follower accepts leadership, it will act as leader once it reaches the designated point in the program's execution. If the follower rejects leadership, it sends a rejection message to the current leader; that replica resumes execution and acts as leader. Thus, for any given point in the execution of the program, there is exactly one leader. A leadership switch incurs at least a one-way message delay in program execution (and possibly more if the follower has not fully caught up when it receives the message). A rejected leadership switch incurs a RTT delay.

The last challenge of Tango is then to determine when to switch leaders, using the above mechanism. Intuitively, the server should become the leader when there is a significant amount of computation to perform, or when there is network communication. Similarly, we want the client to lead when there is user interaction or other activities that are pinned to the client.

Because switching leadership is cheap, it always makes sense to switch when there is a dependency that will require an RTT to satisfy by the current leader. Therefore, if the leader needs data from the follower and the follower replica is not too far behind, the leader switches leadership to the follower. This heuristic is how switches due to UI input, network communication, and pinned native methods are informed. In the case of network communication, switches are triggered during a call to connect or when data is sent. This could degrade performance only in the case that no data is received in response to a request or when another dependency forces leadership back to the client before a response is received. Otherwise, this heuristic does not degrade performance compared to normal application execution.

Deciding to switch leadership due to computation is significantly more difficult. Tango must predict that there will be enough computation before the next dependency pinned to the client to at least make up for the RTT penalty incurred by switching leaders back and forth. Tango uses a technique similar to COMET [16] in which it tracks how much computation has been done since the last invocation of a native method that was pinned on the client. Currently, we switch after 200 ms of computation. Empirically, this value seems to set a good balance between not triggering superfluous leader switches and not forcing the client to lead for large amounts of computation. A more sophisticated approach would also factor in RTT and relative computation performance.

However, in all cases, a switch does not occur until Tango believes that the execution of the follower has "caught up" to the execution of the leader. This property is somewhat tricky to determine in a distributed system where there can be substantial latency between the two replicas.

To address this problem, we use a simple heuristic based on the following replica's *lag*. When the follower receives an asynchronous event or negative acknowledgment, it tags the event or negative acknowledgment with a timestamp indicating when the event was received. When the follower reaches the corresponding point in its execution, it compares the current time with the tagged timestamp to determine the lag for that event. If the lag exceeds a pre-defined threshold (500 ms), the follower transitions into a *lagging* state, pushing a notification of this change to the leader. While the follower is in this state, it rejects all leadership switches, and (upon receipt of the notification) the leader will no longer offer to switch, even if one of the triggering events above occurs.

To switch out of the lagging state the follower must observe an event lag of under 100 ms. This transition causes a notification to be pushed to the leader, and the leader may again offer to switch leadership if a triggering event occurs.

## 4.6 Server faults

Tango is designed to tolerate server faults. Consider the following potential problem. If the remote server is the leader, it may fail after sending several messages to remote computers. The content of these messages may depend on non-deterministic operations that the server has previously executed (e.g., random number generation, thread scheduling, or data received from a remote computer in a previous decision). The following replica on the client does not know these non-deterministic values, so it cannot produce the same application state that led to the messages already seen by external computers. Thus, there is no way to continue application execution. This scenario is why current offloading solutions such as Maui [7] and CloneCloud [6] do not allow methods that involve external communication to execute on the server.

In Tango, we solve this problem by sending the log of non-determinism to a backup server located near the remote replica, a standard log-based, rollback-recovery technique [11]. The non-deterministic events are sent to the backup server asynchronously as they are recorded. Prior to externalizing any output (e.g., network messages and UI updates), the remote server waits for the backup server to acknowledge the receipt of all non-deterministic events that precede the output.

When the client detects that the server has failed, it can fetch the logged non-deterministic events from the backup server. The client replica simply replays these events in the same manner as if they had come directly from the remote server. Once the client replica is caught up to the last operation performed by the remote server, it continues alone as a non-replicated execution. In principal, it could also start a new remote replica and resume Tango replication.

Tango currently tolerates a single server stop fault, but it could tolerate up to $n$ simultaneous stop faults by persisting the log to $n$ backup servers. Our measurements show that the overhead of persisting the log is negligible for $n = 2$. Note that it would be much harder to provide this fault tolerance in a standard offload system; one would either need to save an entire checkpoint of application state on the backup server prior to externalizing any output, or one would have to reproduce much of the Tango functionality to add log-based rollback-recovery to an existing offload system.

# 5. LESSONS LEARNED

We learned two major lessons in the course of this project; one was painful and the other was a pleasant surprise. We discuss both lessons in this section.

## 5.1 Engineering complexities

Retrofitting an established platform like Android that was not created with Tango's goals in mind proved to be considerably more challenging than we originally expected. Our expectation, outlined in our original position paper [14], was that using the Dalvik VM as the unit of application replication would lead to a clean partitioning, with the vast majority of the application executing within the replicated portion and there being only a few narrow interfaces between the replicated VM and the non-replicated system infrastructure. Unfortunately, as evidenced by the long time we have worked on this idea since publishing the original position paper, that expectation proved to be overly optimistic.

The complexity of the Android platform had two effects. First, it greatly increased the work required to support the unmodified applications reported in this paper. Second, even after significant implementation effort, many applications are still unable to reap the benefits of Tango that they probably should. Broadly speaking, there are three common reasons that applications that could benefit from Tango do not: implementation errors in our code, inter-process communication, and use of extensive native libraries such as WebKit.

Tango operates on top of the large Android code base, significant portions of which we have retrofitted to behave deterministically (or to which have added sufficient logging to compensate for nondeterminism). Ensuring correctness with a small developer team has been very challenging. Many applications that should benefit from Tango crash due to the resulting instability.

The interface between Dalvik applications and the rest of the Android system has proven to be broad rather than narrow. For instance, interaction with the UI stack was so frequent that we were forced to replicate the UI stack itself. A current source of pain for us is that Android IPC calls are common—all applications must communicate with the system server (itself a Dalvik VM instance). For many of these IPC calls, nothing is returned so Tango can faithfully replay them without logging. However, many other calls that are inherently deterministic may return values that are dependent on state within the system server. A potential solution to this problem is to replay the system server alongside the application. However, this is a substantial engineering challenge because the system server makes use of many native methods not available within normal applications.

Most Android applications execute a large number of native methods, and the percentage of such methods appears to be growing over time. This is challenging for Tango because we must identify, categorize, and possibly make deterministic each such method. Additionally, some applications make heavy use of native libraries, notably the WebKit browser engine. While it should be technically possible to make most elements of WebKit and similar libraries behave deterministically, the engineering effort is again substantial. So, Tango currently does not work effectively with applications that use these libraries. In particular this means that Tango does not work with Web browsers that use WebKit.

Tango is designed to work with any conformant implementation of the Dalvik Virtual Machine. Therefore Tango should work just as well in the presence of a JIT or within Android's new Ahead-of-Time compilation system, ART. However, the current prototype does not support the JIT and was built on the traditional Dalvik virtual machine. Supporting the JIT would require more engineering effort. Switching over to ART would require a significant porting effort.

Given these limitations, it is clear that Tango should be regarded as a research prototype for demonstrating the potential of replication. We believe it has been successful in this regard. Were we to start afresh, we might consider other methods of replicating execution: for example, requiring that the ISA be the same between client and server and enforcing determinism at the process level inside the OS.

## 5.2 Benefit to network applications

Originally, we envisioned Tango solely as a way to accelerate applications with computation-heavy phases. The pleasant surprise during the course of this project was discovering that Tango could also benefit applications with network-intensive phases. The key insight is that the log of non-determinism simultaneously provides a method to keep the client and server executions in sync *and* a log for rollback-recovery that allows the server to safely externalize network output after committing the log to another server.

Indeed, we expect that the number of network-intensive applications that could benefit from Tango currently far exceeds the number of compute-intensive applications that could benefit. Mobile application developers currently go to considerable effort

| Benchmark | Package Name | Description | Interaction | Network RTTs |
|---|---|---|---|---|
| Sudoku | de.georgwiese.sudokusolver | Game aid, solves Sudoku puzzles given known values | Finish solving a Sudoku grid given a single cell. | N/A |
| Poker | com.leslie.cjpokeroddscalculator | Game aid, uses Monte Carlo simulation to find odds of winning a poker game | Compute the probability of winning from initial poker state. | N/A |
| Hoot | com.hootsuite.droid.full | Manages posts to/from multiple social networks including Twitter, Facebook, LinkedIn, and Foursquare. | Search Twitter given a keyword (queries api.twitter.com) | 5 |
| TapTu | com.taptu.streams | A social news reader that supports Facebook, Twitter, and LinkedIn | Update Facebook feed (queries api.facebook.com) | 4 |
| Email | com.android.email | A built-in email application for Android platforms | Update Email's inbox | 4 |
| Instagram | com.instagram.android | A social network application for sharing photos and videos | Update Instagram posts | 3 |
| Pinterest | com.pinterest | A social network application for creating and sharing visual bookmarks | Update Pinterest boards | 2-8 |

**Table 1: Description of applications used in macrobenchmarks.**

to reduce the number of round-trips between the client and the cloud, adding considerable development cost and complexity. With Tango's form of replication, this application complexity is not necessary; the cost of multiple round-trips are automatically hidden by execution on the server replica.

# 6. EVALUATION

To evaluate Tango, we ran it both against small microbenchmarks and whole applications from Google Play. The macrobenchmarks in Section 6.2 show how Tango performs on unmodified, real-world applications, demonstrating that performance gains can be obtained for both compute-intensive and network-intensive applications. The microbenchmarks in Section 6.3 quantify the overhead of preemption and the overhead added to the Java Native Interface.

## 6.1 Methodology

We tested Tango on a Samsung Galaxy S3 smartphone running the Android 4.2.2 (Jellybean) operating system. To provide support for a variety of mobile platforms we implemented Tango on top of the CyanogenMod [8] 10.1 code base. The replay server used for all experiments has a 3.40 GHz i5 processor (i5-3570) with 4 GB of RAM. For repeatability of results, the mobile client and replay server were connected via USB. Network latency was emulated during experiments by setting netem [19] rules on the client. To further investigate Tango in real world environments, we also evaluated Tango's performance when the mobile client and replay server are connected over a campus WiFi network.

Tango does not currently support the Just-In-Time compiler. All *baseline* builds of the Dalvik VM are therefore built without a JIT for a fair comparison.

## 6.2 Macrobenchmarks

We used seven applications available on Google Play to evaluate the performance benefits of Tango. Two of these applications, *Sudoku* and *Poker*, are compute-intensive, and the other five, *Hoot*, *TapTu*, *Email*, *Instagram* and *Pinterest* are network-intensive. For each application, we configured Tango to connect its mobile client and replay server over either USB or WiFi and selected a representative latency-sensitive interaction to measure user-perceived latency. Table 1 details the applications and the recorded user interactions. For the emulated configuration, we added from 0 ms to 500 ms of network delay to both the baseline and Tango configurations.

The compute-intensive applications were selected from the applications used in COMET [16]. The network-intensive applications were selected by looking for popular or mash-up applications that contained some repeatable user interaction for testing. From this set, due to the challenges described in Section 5.1, we dropped applications that do not currently work with Tango.

While investigating applications suitable for measurement, we found approximately 10 applications that function properly with Tango but cannot currently achieve performance improvements due to the limitations discussed in Section 5.1. These applications have several client-pinned dependencies due to either IPC or use of WebKit that force leadership back to the client after a compute chunk but before the externalization of output, or, alternatively, before a network transaction completes. In the case of computation-based applications, this results in an RTT performance degradation. In the case of network applications, there is typically no degradation. We did not evaluate one additional application, Gmail, because we saw that it completed its network operation in a single RTT and therefore would not benefit from Tango.

### 6.2.1 *Compute-intensive Macrobenchmarks*

For the compute-intensive benchmarks, we recorded the time difference between the user input that triggered the interaction and the externalization of the final screen update as their user-perceived latency. We repeated this experiment ten times for each configuration. Figures 5 and 6 show average latencies and 95% confidence intervals for Sudoku and Poker, respectively. For 100 ms round-trip network latency, which is the typical delay for current LTE networks, Tango reduced user-perceived latency for *Sudoku* by 0.6 seconds (50%). For *Poker* at 100 ms network latency, Tango reduced the user-perceived latency by 1.9 seconds (68%). Over WiFi, Tango decreased user-perceived latency for *Sudoku* and *Poker* by 0.6 seconds (53%) and 1.9 seconds (68%), respectively.

To better understand where the performance benefits are coming from and how much further Tango could be improved, we took

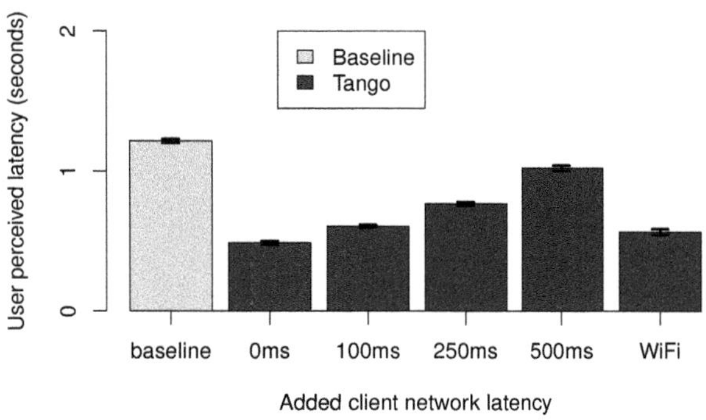


**Figure 5:** **Sudoku performance**

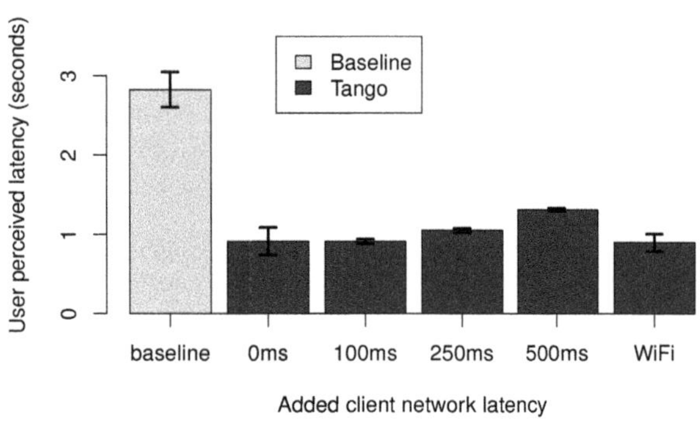


**Figure 6:** **Poker performance**

a closer look at the Sudoku application. Tango took on average 485 ms when performing the Sudoku interaction with no latency. The first 268 ms after user interaction were spent with the client leading execution. This corresponds to approximately 68 ms of UI interaction, followed by 200 ms of computation before the leadership switch is triggered. After the leadership switch, the server finishes the computation and executes the screen updates on its local UI stack in another 100 ms. The remaining 117 ms are spent by the client to display the screen output created by the server. This overhead is exacerbated by CPU contention with the client replica still performing the replicated computation. By momentarily stopping the replica execution on the client this overhead can be brought down to 45 ms. This indicates that more sophisticated scheduling could yield further performance benefits.

### 6.2.2 *Network-intensive Macrobenchmarks*

We evaluated *Hoot*, *TapTu*, *Email*, *Instagram* and *Pinterest* to investigate Tango's performance gain in network-intensive applications. *Hoot* and *TapTu* use social network APIs to allow users to interact with multiple sites such as Facebook and Twitter. *Email* is the built-in Email application in Android systems that retrieves email update from remote servers. *Instagram* is a social network application for users to share images and videos. *Pinterest* allows users to bookmark image based posts on their pin boards.

In these network applications, we focus on the user-perceived latency for a network update by refreshing the screen, a common

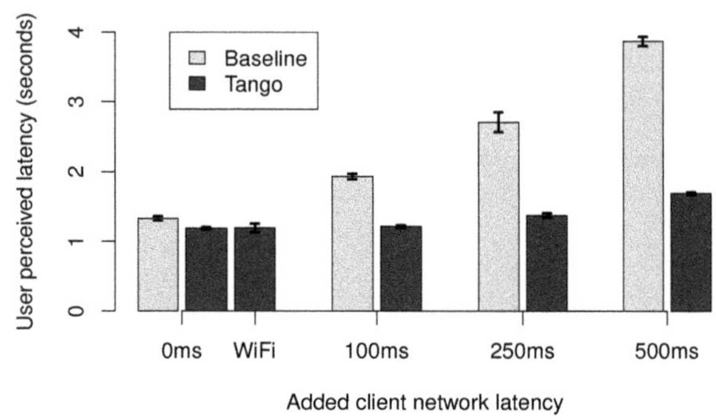


**Figure 7:** **Hoot performance**

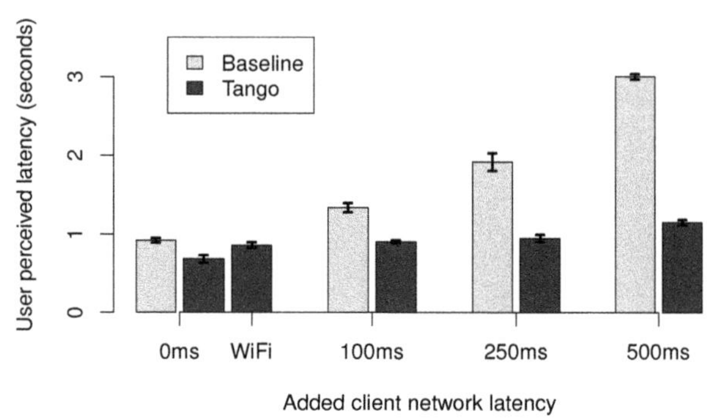


**Figure 8:** **TapTu performance**

action in many network-based mobile applications. Similar to the computation benchmarks, we recorded the time difference between the first user input and the final display output as the user-perceived latency. We repeated these experiments 14 times for each configuration (we ran more trials because of the added variance inherent in accessing external sites). The average latencies and 95% confidence intervals are presented in Figures 7, 8, 9, 10 and 11. The results show that Tango achieves speedup of 1.6–2.3x, 1.5–2.6x, 1.5–2.2x and 1.3–2.2x under different network latencies for *Hoot*, *TapTu*, *Email* and *Instagram*, respectively. The user-perceived delay for *Pinterest* was similar in all scenarios except that there was a 17% improvement in user-perceived latency at 500 ms network latency.

Compared to the compute-intensive applications, the relationship between performance gains and network latency is inverted. The user-perceived latency under different network RTT values follows a relatively simple model of $\alpha_x + \beta_x \times RTT$. For *baseline* and Tango, $\alpha_x$ is approximately the same. However, $\beta_{baseline}$ is proportional to the number of request/response pairs in the interaction while $\beta_{Tango}$ is fixed at approximately 1, reflecting only two leadership switches. Using a least squares linear regression, we calculate $\beta_{baseline} = 5.05$ for *Hoot*, $\beta_{baseline} = 4.16$ for *TapTu*, $\beta_{baseline} = 3.87$ for *Email* and $\beta_{baseline} = 3.60$ for *Instagram*. These numbers indicate that *Hoot*, *TapTu*, *Email* and *Instagram* do approximately 5, 4, 4 and 3 requests in serial,

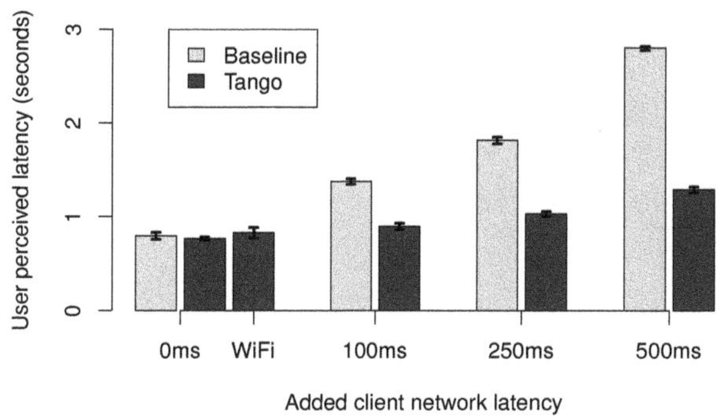


**Figure 9:** **Email performance**

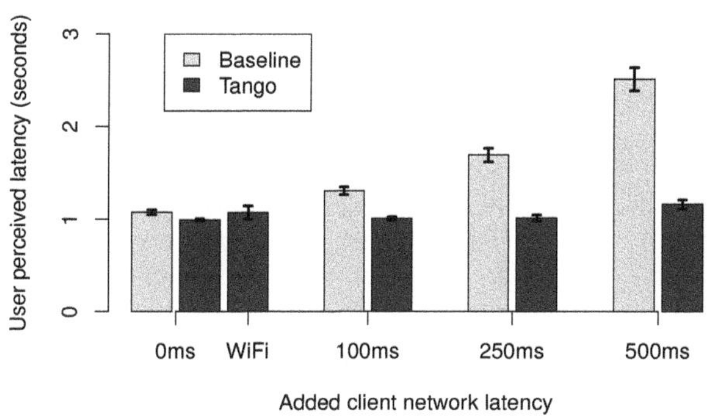


**Figure 10:** **Instagram performance**

respectively. The same linear regression computes $\beta_{Tango} = 1.05$, $\beta_{Tango} = 0.85$, $\beta_{Tango} = 1.03$ and $\beta_{Tango} = 0.34$ for *Hoot*, *TapTu*, *Email* and *Instagram*, respectively. The coefficient of determination for *Hoot*, *TapTu*, *Email* are over 0.94 in the baseline case and range between 0.7 and 0.93 in the Tango case, indicating that the linear regression model is a good fit for characterizing their latency. *Instagram* and *Pinterest* are exceptions. Applying the same regression on them yields coefficient of determinations of 0.48 and 0.52, respectively. We believe that this mismatch is due to these applications overlapping computation and network interaction in a sophisticated manner.

We verified the regression models using *tcpdump*. *Hoot* updates its Twitter feed by making an HTTPS query to api.facebook.com during the first RTT. An HTTPS request from a new connection takes one RTT to establish a TCP connection, two RTTs to complete an SSL handshake, and a final RTT to request an object over HTTPS and receive a response. In total, 5 RTTs are spent in refreshing the Twitter feed in *Hoot*. Similarly, *Email* makes an HTTPS request from a new connection, taking 4 RTTs. The other applications had similar behavior. *Pinterest*, however, was an outlier in that it appeared to vary the number of serial network requests it made and it also seemed to have enough computation to overlap with network activity so that only one round-trip was on the critical path at low latencies.

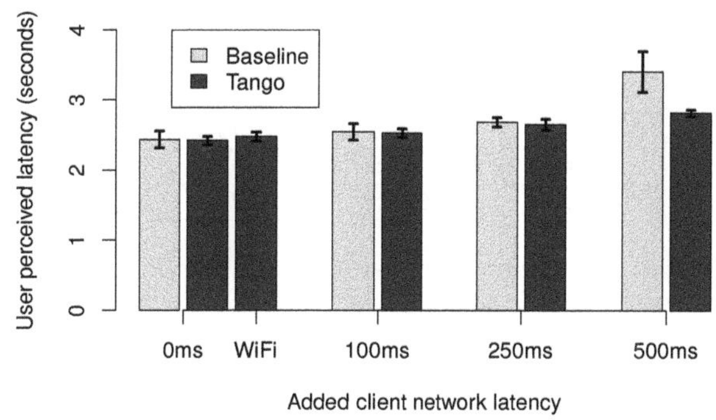


**Figure 11:** **Pinterest performance**

| App. | Baseline | Tango | Percentage |
|---|---|---|---|
| Sudoku | 2.47±.18 J | 2.43±.17 J | -1.62% |
| Poker | 7.14±.41 J | 5.43±.22 J | -23.9% |
| Hoot | 2.77±.15 J | 2.46±.21 J | -11.2% |
| Taptu | 2.14±.23 J | 1.74±.21 J | -18.7% |
| Email | 1.74±.12 J | 1.78±.18 J | +2.30% |
| Instagram | 2.26±.16 J | 2.35±.20 J | +3.98% |
| Pinterest | 4.16±.49 J | 4.06±.30 J | -2.40% |

**Table 2:** **System energy consumption on the smartphone**

### *6.2.3 Energy Consumption*

We also measured the difference in energy consumption caused by using Tango with each application. To measure energy, we assume that a user will pause for a fixed think-time after seeing each screen update before beginning the next iteration of the benchmark. We used a user think time of 3 seconds for *Poker* and 1 second for all other applications (in the case of *Poker*, this ensures that the client catches up during the designated user think time). The energy measurements are collected using a *Monsoon Power Monitor* with WiFi used for communication and cellular data disabled on the smartphone. Each energy measurement includes the time to finish all computation on both the client and server, as well as the fixed user think-time after displaying the result. Energy measurements on each application benchmark are repeated 10 times. Table 2 shows the average values and 95% confidence intervals for the amount of energy consumed by the smartphone for each application.

Compared to the baseline, Tango uses less energy for most, but not all, benchmarks. It uses 2–4% more energy for *Email* and *Instagram*, but reduces energy usage by up to 19% for the other network-intensive applications. For compute-intensive applications, Tango reduces energy usage by up to 24% (in *Poker*). There are two factors at work. First, Tango introduces some overhead through extra computation and communication, increasing energy usage. However, Tango also reduces the time to display a result, decreasing energy usage because activities take less time.

For the compute-intensive benchmarks, Tango must finish the computation on the client after displaying the result; however, the finish of the computation can be overlapped with user think-time for interactive applications. In the future, we could further reduce energy usage by shipping a checkpoint of application state from the

| App. | Received Data | Sent Data |
|---|---|---|
| Sudoku | 115 KB | 25 KB |
| Poker | 49 KB | 25 KB |
| Hoot | 195 KB | 133 KB |
| TapTu | 74 KB | 14 KB |
| Email | 98 KB | 49 KB |
| Instagram | 25 KB | 45 KB |
| Pinterest | 461 KB | 39 KB |

**Table 3: Size of log being communicated during replay. *Received data* refers to data being received by the client. *Sent data* refers to data being sent by the client.**

server to the client to avoid the need to finish the computation on the client.

### 6.2.4 *Log Sizes*

Of course, Tango has to communicate log data between the client and server to operate. Table 3 shows the amount of (compressed) data being transmitted over the network between client and server for Tango. The log sizes recorded in the table include application initialization and *three* user interactions. Each run takes approximately 30 seconds, putting the required average client upload bandwidth at 3.7–35 kbps and the average client download speed at 6.7–125 kbps, which is very small compared to typical bandwidth in modern cellular networks.

## 6.3 Microbenchmarks

There are two primary sources of overhead that Tango introduces into the system; the code to implement preemptions (see Section 4.1) and the handling of native calls made by an application. Therefore, we measure overhead with two different benchmarks; one tests the overhead of pure computation (no native calls) and the other tests the overhead of a tight loop of native calls with varying policies. In these tests, we replaced the replay server with a dummy terminal that records all transmitted data (so leader switching is disabled).

### 6.3.1 *Pure Computation*

We tested Tango on two pure computation applications and measured their relative overhead compared to the *baseline* build. The first test, which simply calculates Fibonacci numbers recursively, had an overhead of 8.48%. This test runs entirely in the interpreter which should maximize the cost of preemption. The second test, which allocated objects in a tight loop, had a lower overhead of -2.01%. We expect this test to have a lower overhead than the Fibonacci test because it spends more time doing allocations and garbage collection where no overheads have been added. It is unclear why Tango outperforms the *baseline* build for this test, but the result is reproducible. The most likely cause is our changes to the default Dalvik thread scheduler, which may favor this benchmark.

### 6.3.2 *Native Methods*

Next we measured the performance overhead of invoking native methods with different annotations. Table 4 shows the overhead of making native calls with the *Deterministic*, *Sync*, *Inlineable*, and *Ideal* annotations. The definitions of these annotations are given in Section 4.3.1.

Each of these test scenarios calls a native method that performs the same operation; a simple hash computation on a 10 character string passed from Java. It is clear that executing an unannotated

| Annotation | Baseline | Tango | |
|---|---|---|---|
| | Calls/ms | Calls/ms | Bytes/Call |
| None | 729 | 9.18 | 2.87 |
| Deterministic | N/A | 9.97 | 0.565 |
| Sync | N/A | 13.1 | ~0 |
| Inlineable | N/A | 196 | ~0 |
| Ideal | N/A | 456 | ~0 |

**Table 4: The throughput and logging overhead during a tight loop around a native method with various flags.**

| App. | None | Deter. | Sync | Inlineable | Ideal | Estimated Overhead |
|---|---|---|---|---|---|---|
| Sudoku | 20 | 880 | 1280 | 57271 | 3149 | 401 ms |
| Poker | 17 | 935 | 788 | 26944 | 516 | 254 ms |
| Hoot | 36 | 11106 | 3093 | 46001 | 9864 | 1510 ms |
| TapTu | 31 | 6555 | 6054 | 22698 | 1662 | 1190 ms |
| Email | 40 | 1448 | 3246 | 22011 | 655 | 474 ms |
| Instagram | 2684 | 1676 | 851 | 43666 | 3721 | 684 ms |
| Pinterest | 2638 | 3836 | 2126 | 189156 | 22642 | 1550 ms |

**Table 5: Number of different categories of native calls during initialization and three user interactions.**

native method can be very expensive, with a reduction in throughput of nearly 80X. The *Deterministic*, *Sync*, and *Inlineable* tests each show the reduction in overhead when the output of the native method no longer needs to be logged, when no scheduling decisions need to be logged, and when the native method can be executed directly on the calling Java thread respectively. The most dramatic difference is when the *Inlineable* flag is applied; revealing that the overhead of invoking a native method on a native thread is significant.

The *Ideal* annotation is used when the native method can be passed a completely uninstrumented JNI function table, which allows it to achieve the lowest overhead. The remaining overhead comes from Tango-related code that touches all native functions (i.e., the code that decides how to invoke a native function based on these flags).

While these overheads are fairly high for this microbenchmark, in practice, the number of native functions invoked during an application's execution is much lower. Table 5 shows how many times native functions with different flags are called during a sample run of three apps we used for testing. The overheads were estimated using the data from Table 4. Each of these runs represents about 30 seconds to a minute worth of execution, putting the overhead in the 1–6% range.

# 7. RELATED WORK

Tango is the first method to deterministically replicate a computation on the mobile client and a remote server to improve performance.

Using cloud resources to improve the performance of mobile applications is a tantalizing goal, so many prior systems have focused on offloading computation from the mobile computer to the server [13]. Prior systems such as Maui [7], CloneCloud [6], Odessa [22], Comet [16], and Spectra [15] all *partition* functionality by executing a given piece of the computation on either a mobile device or a server, but not on both. Partitioning of a mobile application is a specific instance of partitioning distributed applications in general [18]. Partitioning is usually subject to some constraints related to functionality or privacy. For example, some functionality is tied to a specific device (e.g., sensors on the mobile device), and some state may be considered too sensitive to allow it or data derived from it to migrate off the mobile device [4].

Partitioning of an application may take place at units of various granularity, such as function calls or threads. None of these partition-based offloading systems allow code that externalizes network output to be offloaded because of the fault-tolerance issues discussed in Section 4.6; thus, a major benefit of Tango is that it can offload network-intensive phases that prior systems cannot.

Chroma [2] and Slingshot [24] replicate a computation on multiple servers, but they do not enforce determinism at all. Similarly, Higgins et al. [17] replicate a simple speech recognition service on a client and server, but rely on the service to be stateless and deterministic. Unlike Tango, their replicas will diverge and yield different results for more complex services.

Other systems deterministically replicate a mobile application and execute it with additional instrumentation on the server to debug the execution or add security checks [5, 21]. The goal of such systems is not to improve performance; in fact, the server replica always trails the mobile replica and so cannot offer faster response time.

Replication has long been used to provide fault tolerance [11]. Some systems use deterministic record and replay to keep replicas synchronized [3]. However, prior systems only switch the role of leader on failure (because their goal is fault-tolerance, not improving interactive performance). Tango targets a heterogeneous environment in which different replicas have different strengths and weaknesses. Therefore, it is often beneficial to switch the role of leader as the application enters different phases of execution, and Tango is designed to identify such opportunities and switch appropriately.

Tango uses many techniques developed for deterministic record and replay [10, 12, 23, 25] but applies them to replicate computation on multiple computers. It differs from these prior systems in that different types of external nondeterminism are intercepted on different computers for the same logical computation, then broadcast to all computers. Further, some forms of nondeterminism are mitigated by replicating additional software components such as the file system and UI stack on multiple computers.

# 8. LIMITATIONS

Many of the limitations of Tango from an implementation perspective have been discussed in Section 5.1. The remaining limitations are related to the actual design of Tango.

One of the most significant limitations of Tango is dealing with false dependencies among threads. Suppose that an application has a thread that does network communication and another that is reading sensor information. The former thread would perform better if the server is the leader, while the latter thread would perform better if the client is the leader. With Tango, only one endpoint can lead at any given time.

The other key limitations of Tango primarily affect computation-heavy applications. First, Tango forces serialization of all managed threads within an application. Modern phones usually have more than one CPU core, meaning that applications running within Tango cannot make use of all resources available to them. To remedy this problem, we would need to adopt a deterministic multicore scheduling algorithm such as Kendo [20].

Second, even when Tango correctly predicts a large amount of upcoming computation, it is still possible to see a loss in performance. This is because any time that the server must return leadership to the client (e.g., due to a series of client-pinned native methods) prior to externalizing output, then user-perceived latency does not improve. Effectively, we have simply added an RTT to the user perceived latency. We could potentially overcome this with better prediction, or we could use checkpoint and restore to transfer the server's application state to the client. In the case of checkpoint and restore, the amount of state transferred would have to be small enough to make this practical.

Third, deciding when to switch leaders remains a difficult task. This work provides a simple solution that appears to work well in practice. However, on some applications, an oracle could do significantly better. In the case of especially poor decisions, Tango may even degrade user-perceived latency.

# 9. CONCLUSION

We have presented a system called Tango, which accelerates mobile applications by replicating their execution on a remote server. By displaying output to the user from the replica that is currently leading the execution, Tango reduces the latency seen by users. To accomplish this speedup, we developed a technique called flip-flop replication, in which the leadership role floats to the replica that is currently faster, with the other replica following the execution through deterministic replay. Tango works for unmodified applications that run on the Dalvik VM on Android devices. We demonstrated speedups of 2–3x for two compute-intensive applications and speedups of up to 2.6x for five network-intensive applications.

## Acknowledgments

We thank the reviewers and our shepherd, Lin Zhong, for their thoughtful comments. This material is based upon work supported by the National Science Foundation under grant numbers CNS-0905149, CNS-1059372, CNS-1345226, and CNS-1039657. Any opinions, findings, conclusions, or recommendations expressed in this material are those of the authors and do not necessarily reflect the views of the University of Michigan or the National Science Foundation.

# 10. REFERENCES

[1] R. Balan, J. Flinn, M. Satyanarayanan, S. Sinnamohideen, and H.-I. Yang. The case for cyber foraging. In *the 10th ACM SIGOPS European Workshop*, Saint-Emilion, France, September 2002.

[2] R. K. Balan, M. Satyanarayanan, S. Park, and T. Okoshi. Tactics-based remote execution for mobile computing. In *Proceedings of the 1st International Conference on Mobile Systems, Applications and Services*, pages 273–286, San Francisco, CA, May 2003.

[3] T. C. Bressoud and F. B. Schneider. Hypervisor-based fault tolerance. *ACM Trans. on Computer Systems*, 14(1):80–107, February 1996.

[4] S. Chong, J. Liu, A. C. Myers, X. Qi, K. Vikram, L. Zheng, and X. Zheng. Secure web applications via automatic partitioning . In *Proceedings of the 2007 Symposium on Operating System Principles (SOSP)*, October 2007.

[5] J. Chow, T. Garfinkel, and P. M. Chen. Decoupling dynamic program analysis from execution in virtual environments. In *Proceedings of the 2008 USENIX Annual Technical Conference*, pages 1–14, June 2008.

[6] B.-G. Chun, S. Ihm, P. Maniatis, M. Naik, and A. Patti. CloneCloud: Elastic execution between mobile device and cloud. In *Proceedings of the 6th ACM European Conference on Computer Systems*, Salzburg, Austria, April 2011.

[7] E. Cuervo, A. Balasubramanian, D. ki Cho, A. Wolman, S. Saroiu, R. Chandra, and P. Bahl. MAUI: Making smartphones last longer with code offload. In *Proceedings of*

*the 8th International Conference on Mobile Systems, Applications and Services*, pages 49–62, San Francisco, CA, June 2010.

[8] CyanogenMod Community. CyanogenMod – Android community operating system. `http://www.cyanogenmod.com/`.

[9] D. Devecsery, M. Chow, X. Dou, J. Flinn, and P. M. Chen. Eidetic systems. In *Proceedings of the 11th USENIX Symposium on Operating Systems Design and Implementation (OSDI)*, Broomfield, CO, October 2014.

[10] G. W. Dunlap, S. T. King, S. Cinar, M. A. Basrai, and P. M. Chen. ReVirt: Enabling intrusion analysis through virtual-machine logging and replay. In *Proceedings of the 5th Symposium on Operating Systems Design and Implementation*, pages 211–224, Boston, MA, December 2002.

[11] E. N. Elnozahy, L. Alvisi, Y.-M. Wang, and D. B. Johnson. A survey of rollback-recovery protocols in message-passing systems. *ACM Computing Surveys*, 34(3):375–408, September 2002.

[12] S. I. Feldman and C. B. Brown. Igor: a system for program debugging via reversible execution. In *PADD '88: Proceedings of the 1988 ACM SIGPLAN and SIGOPS workshop on Parallel and distributed debugging*, pages 112–123, 1988.

[13] J. Flinn. *Cyber Foraging: Bridging Mobile and Cloud Computing*. Morgan and Claypool Publishers, September 2012.

[14] J. Flinn and Z. M. Mao. Can deterministic replay be an enabling tool for mobile computing? In *Proceedings of the 12th Workshop on Mobile Computing Systems and Applications (HotMobile)*, March 2011.

[15] J. Flinn, S. Park, and M. Satyanarayanan. Balancing Performance, Energy, and Quality in Pervasive Computing. In *Proceedings of the 22nd International Conference on. Distributed Computing Systems*, Vienna, Austria, July 2002.

[16] M. S. Gordon, D. A. Jamshidi, S. Mahlke, Z. M. Mao, and X. Chen. Comet: Code offload by migrating execution transparently. In *Proceedings of the 10th Symposium on Operating Systems Design and Implementation*, 2012.

[17] B. D. Higgins, K. Lee, J. Flinn, T. J. Giuli, B. Noble, and C. Peplin. The future is cloudy: Reflecting prediction error in mobile applications. In *Proceedings of the 6th International Conference on Mobile Computing, Applications, and Services*, Austin, TX, November 2014.

[18] G. C. Hunt and M. L. Scott. The Coign automatic distributed partitioning system. In *Proceedings of the 3rd Symposium on Operating Systems Design and Implementation*, pages 187–200, New Orleans, LA, February 1999.

[19] The Linux Foundation, `http://www.linuxfoundation.org/collaborate/workgroups/networking/netem`. *netem*.

[20] M. Olszewski, J. Ansel, and S. Amarasinghe. Kendo: efficient deterministic multithreading in software. In *Proceedings of the 14th International Conference on Architectural Support for Programming Languages and Operating Systems*, pages 97–108, March 2009.

[21] G. Portokalidis, P. Homburg, K. Anagnostakis, and H. Bos. Paranoid android: Versatile protection for smartphones. In *Proceedings of the Annual Computer Security Applications Conference*, December 2010.

[22] M.-R. Ra, A. Sheth, L. Mummert, P. Pillai, D. Wetherall, and R. Govidan. Odessa: Enabling interactive perception applications on mobile devices. In *Proceedings of the 9th International Conference on Mobile Systems, Applications and Services*, Washington, DC, June 2011.

[23] S. Srinivasan, C. Andrews, S. Kandula, and Y. Zhou. Flashback: A light-weight extension for rollback and deterministic replay for software debugging. In *Proceedings of the 2004 USENIX Technical Conference*, pages 29–44, Boston, MA, June 2004.

[24] Y.-Y. Su and J. Flinn. Slingshot: Deploying stateful services in wireless hotspots. In *Proceedings of the 3rd International Conference on Mobile Systems, Applications and Services*, pages 79–92, Seattle, WA, June 2005.

[25] M. Xu, V. Malyugin, J. Sheldon, G. Venkitachalam, and B. Weissman. Retrace: Collecting execution trace with virtual machine deterministic replay. In *Proceedings of the 2007 Workshop on Modeling, Benchmarking and Simulation (MoBS)*, June 2007.

# Outatime: Using Speculation to Enable Low-Latency Continuous Interaction for Mobile Cloud Gaming

Kyungmin Lee[†] David Chu[‡] Eduardo Cuervo[‡] Johannes Kopf[‡]
Yury Degtyarev[◦] Sergey Grizan[⋄] Alec Wolman[‡] Jason Flinn[†]
[†]University of Michigan [‡]Microsoft Research
[◦]St. Petersburg Polytechnic University [⋄]Siberian Federal University

## ABSTRACT

Gaming on phones, tablets and laptops is very popular. Cloud gaming — where remote servers perform game execution and rendering on behalf of thin clients that simply send input and display output frames — promises any device the ability to play any game any time. Unfortunately, the reality is that wide-area network latencies are often prohibitive; cellular, Wi-Fi and even wired residential end host round trip times (RTTs) can exceed 100ms, a threshold above which many gamers tend to deem responsiveness unacceptable.

In this paper, we present Outatime, a speculative execution system for mobile cloud gaming that is able to mask up to 120ms of network latency. Outatime renders speculative frames of future possible outcomes, delivering them to the client one entire RTT ahead of time, and recovers quickly from mis-speculations when they occur. Clients perceive little latency. To achieve this, Outatime combines: 1) future state prediction; 2) state approximation with image-based rendering and event time-shifting; 3) fast state checkpoint and rollback; and 4) state compression for bandwidth savings.

To evaluate the Outatime speculation system, we use two high quality, commercially-released games: a twitch-based first person shooter, Doom 3, and an action role playing game, Fable 3. Through user studies and performance benchmarks, we find that players strongly prefer Outatime to traditional thin-client gaming where the network RTT is fully visible, and that Outatime successfully mimics playing across a low-latency network.

## Categories and Subject Descriptors

C.2.4 [**Computer-Communication Networks**]: Distributed Systems—*Distributed Applications*; I.6.8 [**Simulation and Modeling**]: Types of Simulation—*Gaming*

## Keywords

Cloud gaming; Speculation; Network latency


*MobiSys'15,* May 18–22, 2015, Florence, Italy.

http://dx.doi.org/10.1145/2742647.2742656.

## 1. INTRODUCTION

Gaming is the most popular mobile activity, accounting for nearly a third of the time spent on mobile devices [18]. Recently, cloud gaming — where datacenter servers execute the games on behalf of thin clients that merely transmit UI input events and display output rendered by the servers — has emerged as an interesting alternative to traditional client-side execution. Cloud gaming offers several advantages. First, every client can enjoy the high-end graphics provided by powerful server GPUs. This is especially appealing for mobile devices such as basic laptops, phones, tablets, TVs and other displays lacking high-end GPUs. Second, cloud gaming eases developer pain. Platform compatibility headaches and vexing per-platform performance tuning — sources of much developer frustration [32, 40, 44] — are eliminated. Third, cloud gaming simplifies software deployment and management. Server management (e.g., for bug fixes, software updates, hardware upgrades, content additions, etc.) is far easier than modifying clients. Finally, players can select from a vast library of titles and instantly play any of them. Sony, Nvidia, Amazon and OnLive are among the providers that currently offer cloud gaming services [1–3, 10].

However, cloud gaming faces a key technical dilemma: how can players attain *real-time interactivity* in the face of wide-area latency? Real-time interactivity means client input events should be quickly reflected on the client display. User studies have shown that players are sensitive to as little as 60 ms latency, and are aggravated at latencies in excess of 100ms [6,12,33]. A further delay degradation from 150ms to 250ms lowers user engagement by 75% [9].

One way to address latency is to move servers closer to clients. Unfortunately, not only are decentralized edge servers more expensive to build and maintain, local spikes in demand cannot be routed to remote servers which further magnifies costs. Most importantly, high latencies are often attributed to the networks's last mile. Recent studies have found that the 95th percentile of network latencies for 3G, Wi-Fi and LTE are over 600ms, 300ms and 400ms, respectively [21, 22, 35]. In fact, even well-established residential wired last mile links tend to suffer from latencies in excess of 100ms when under load [5,37]. Unlike non-interactive video streaming, buffering is not possible for interactive gaming.

Instead, we propose to mitigate wide-area latency via speculative execution. Our system, *Outatime*,[1] delivers real-time gaming interactivity as fast as — and in some cases, even

[1] *Outatime* : License plates of a car capable of time travel.

faster than — traditional local client-side execution, despite latencies up to 120ms.

Outatime's basic approach is to employ speculative execution to render multiple possible frame outputs which could occur RTT milliseconds in the future. While the fundamentals of speculative execution are well-understood, the *dynamism* and *sensitivity* of graphically intensive twitch-based interaction makes for stringent demands on speculation. Dynamism leads to rapid state space explosion. Sensitivity means users are able to (visually) identify incorrect states. Outatime employs the following techniques to manage speculative state in the face of dynamism and sensitivity.

**Future State Prediction:** Given the user's historical tendencies and recent behavior, we show that some categories of user actions are highly predictable. We develop a Markov-based prediction model that examines recent user input to forecast expected future input. We use two techniques to improve prediction quality: supersampling of input events, and Kalman filtering to improve users' perception of smoothness.

**State Approximation:** For some types of mispredictions, Outatime approximates the correct state by applying *error compensation* on the (mis)predicted frame. The resulting frame is very close to what the client ought to see. Our misprediction compensation uses *image-based rendering (IBR)*, a technique that transforms pre-rendered images from one viewpoint to a different viewpoint using only a small amount of additional 3D metadata.

Certain user inputs (*e.g.,* firing a gun) cannot be easily predicted. For these, we use parallel speculative executions to explore multiple outcomes. However, the set of all possible states over long RTTs can be very large. To address this, we approximate the state space by subsampling it, and time shifting actual event streams to match event streams that are "close enough" *i.e.,* below players' sensitivity thresholds. These techniques greatly reduces the state space with minimal impact on the quality of interaction, thereby permitting speculation within a reasonable deadline.

**State Checkpoint and Rollback:** Core to Outatime is a real-time process checkpoint and rollback service. Checkpoint and rollback prevents mispredictions from propagating forward. We develop a hybrid memory-page based and object-based checkpoint mechanism that is fast and well-suited for graphically-intensive real-time simulations like games.

**State Compression for Saving Bandwidth:** Speculation's latency reduction benefits come at the cost of higher bandwidth utilization. To reduce this overhead, we develop a video encoding scheme which provides a 40% bitrate reduction over standard encoding by taking advantage of the visual coherence of speculated frames. The final bitrate overhead of speculation depends on the RTT. It is 1.9× for 120ms.

To illustrate Outatime in the context of fast interaction, we evaluate Outatime's prediction techniques using two action games where even small latencies are disadvantageous. Doom 3 is a twitch-based first person shooter where responsiveness is paramount. Fable 3 is a role playing game with frequent fast action combat. Both are high-quality, commercially-released games, and are very similar to phone and tablet games in the first person shooter and role playing genres, respectively.

Through interactive gamer testing, we found that even experienced players perceived only minor differences in responsiveness on Outatime when operating at up to 120ms RTT when compared head-to-head to a system with no latency. Latencies up to 250ms RTT were even acceptable for less experienced players. Moreover, unlike in standard cloud gaming systems, Outatime players' in-game skills performance did not drop off as RTT increased up to 120ms. Overall, player surveys scored Outatime gameplay highly. We have also deployed Outatime to the general public on limited occasions and received positive reception [14, 19, 27, 39]. While we have focused our evaluation on desktop and laptop clients experiencing high network latency, our techniques are broadly applicable to phone and tablet clients as well. Outatime's only client prerequisites are video decode and modest GPU capabilities which are standard in today's devices.

The remainder of the paper is organized as follows. §2 reviews game architectures and the impact of latency. §3 presents an overview of the Outatime architecture. §4 and §5 detail our two main methods of speculation. §6 and §7 discusses how we save, load and compress state. §8 introduces application to multiplayer. §9 covers the implementation. §10 evaluates Outatime via user study and performance benchmarks. §11 covers related work and §13 discusses implications of the work.

## 2. BACKGROUND & IMPACT OF LATENCY

The vast majority of game applications are structured around the *game loop,* a repetitive execution of the following stages: 1) read user input; 2) update game state; and 3) render and display frame. Each iteration of this loop is a logical tick of the game clock and corresponds to 32ms of wall-clock time for an effective frame rate of 30 frames per second (fps).[2] The time taken for one iteration of the game loop is the *frame time.* Frame time is a key metric for assessing interactivity since it corresponds to the delay between a user's input and observed output.

Network latency has an acute effect on interaction for cloud gaming. In standard cloud gaming, the frame time must include the additional overhead of the network RTT, as illustrated in Figure 1a. Let time be discretized into 32ms clock ticks, and let the RTT be 4 ticks (128ms). At $t_5$, the client reads user input $i_5$ and transmits it to the server. At $t_7$, the server receives the input, updates the game state, and renders the frame, $f_5$. At $t_8$, the server transmits the output frame to the client, which receives it at $t_{10}$. Note that the frame time incurs the full RTT overhead. In this example, an RTT of 128ms results in a frame time of 160 ms.

## 3. GOALS AND SYSTEM ARCHITECTURE

For Outatime, responsiveness is paramount; Outatime's goal is to consistently deliver low frame times (< 32ms) at high frame rate (> 30fps) even in the face of long RTTs. In exchange, we are willing to transmit a higher volume of data and potentially even introduce (small and ephemeral) visual artifacts, ideally sufficiently minor that most players rarely notice.

The basic principle underlying Outatime is to speculatively generate possible output frames and transmit them to the client a full RTT ahead of the client's actual corresponding input. As shown in Figure 1b, the client sends input as

[2] $\frac{1}{30fps} \approx$ 32ms for mathematical convenience.

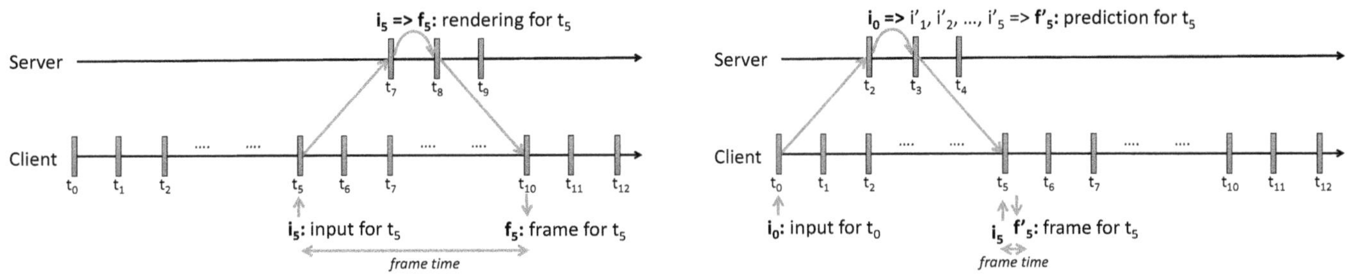


(a) Standard cloud gaming: Frame time depends on net latency.

(b) Outatime: Frame time is negligible.

Figure 1: Comparison of frame delivery time lines. RTT= 4 ticks, server processing time = 1 tick.

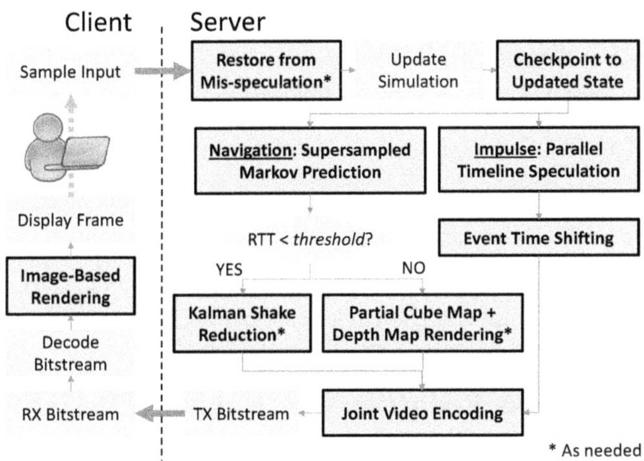


Figure 2: The Outatime Architecture. Bold boxes represent the main areas of this paper's technical focus.

before; at $t_0$, the client sends the input $i_0$ which happens to be the input generated more than one RTT interval prior to $t_5$. The server receives $i_0$ at $t_2$, computes a sequence of probable future input up to one RTT later as $i'_1, i'_2, ..., i'_5$ (we use $'$ to denote speculation), renders its respective frame $f'_5$, and sends these to the client. Upon reception at the client at time $t_5$, the client verifies that its actual input sequence recorded during the elapsed interval matches the server's predicted sequence: $i_1 = i'_1, i_2 = i'_2, ..., i_5 = i'_5$. If the input sequences match, then the client can safely display $f'_5$ without modification because we ensure that the game output is deterministic for a given input [11]. If the input sequence differs, the client approximates the actual state by applying *error compensation* to $f'_5$ and displays a corrected frame. We describe error compensation in detail in §4.5. Unlike in standard cloud gaming where clients wait more than one RTT for a response, Outatime immediately delivers response frames to the client after the corresponding input.

Speculation performance in Outatime depends upon being able to accurately predict future input and generate its corresponding output frames. Outatime does this by identifying two main classes of game input, and building speculation mechanisms for each, as illustrated in Figure 2. The first class, *navigation*, consists of input events that control view (rotation) and movement (translation) and modify the player's field of view. Navigation inputs tend to exhibit continuity over short time windows, and therefore Outatime makes effective predictions for navigation. The second class, *impulse*, consists of events that are inherently sporadic such as firing a weapon or activating an object, yet are fundamental to the player's perception of responsiveness. For example, in first person shooters, instantaneous weapon firing is core to gameplay. Unlike navigation inputs, the sporadic nature of impulse events makes them less amenable to prediction. Instead, Outatime generates parallel speculations for multiple possible future impulse time lines. To tame state space explosion, Outatime subsamples the state space and time shifts impulse events to the closest speculated timeline. This enables Outatime to provide the player the perception that impulse is handled instantaneously. Besides navigation and impulse, we classify other input that is slow relative to RTT as *delay tolerant.* One typical example of delay tolerant input is activating the heads-up display. Delay tolerant input is not subject to speculation, and we discuss how it is handled in §5.

Figure 2 also shows how Outatime's server and client are equipped to deal with speculations that are occasionally wrong. The server continually checkpoints valid state and restores from (mis-)speculated state at 30 fps. The client executes IBR — a very basic graphics procedure — to compensate for navigation mispredictions when they occur. Otherwise, Outatime, like standard cloud gaming systems, makes minimal assumptions about client capabilities. Namely, the client should be able to perform standard operations such as decode a bitstream, display frames and transmit standard input such as button, mouse, keyboard and touch events. In contrast, high-end games that run solely on a client device can demand much more powerful CPU and GPU processing, as we show in §10.

## 4. SPECULATION FOR NAVIGATION

Navigation speculation entails predicting a sequence of future navigation input events at discrete time steps. Hence, we use a discrete time Markov chain for navigation inference. We first describe how we applied the Markov model to input prediction, and our use of supersampling to improve the inference accuracy. Next, we refine our prediction in one of two ways, depending on the severity of the expected error. We determine the expected error as a function of RTT from offline training. When errors are sufficiently low (typically corresponding to RTT< 40ms), we apply an additional Kalman filter to reduce video "shake"). Otherwise, we use misprediction compensation on the client to post-process the frame rendered by the server.

## 4.1 Basic Markov Prediction

We construct a Markov model for navigation. Time is quantized, with each discrete interval representing a game tick. Let the random variable navigation vector $N_t$ represent the change in 3-D translation and rotation at time $t$:

$$N_t = \{\delta_{x,t}, \delta_{y,t}, \delta_{z,t}, \theta_{x,t}, \theta_{y,t}, \theta_{z,t}\}$$

Each component above is quantized. Let $n_t$ represent an actual empirical navigation vector received from the client. Our state estimation problem is to find the maximum likelihood estimator $\hat{N}_{t+\lambda}$ where $\lambda$ is the RTT.

Using the Markov model, the probability distribution of the navigation vector at the next time step is dependent only upon the navigation vector from the current time step: $p(N_{t+1}|N_t)$. We predict the most likely navigation vector $\hat{N}_{t+1}$ at the next time step as:

$$\begin{aligned}\hat{N}_{t+1} &= \mathrm{E}[p(N_{t+1}|N_t = n_t)] \\ &= \operatorname*{argmax}_{N_{t+1}} p(N_{t+1}|N_t = n_t)\end{aligned}$$

where $N_t = n_t$ indicates that the current time step has been assigned a fixed value by sampling the actual user input $n_t$. In many cases, the RTT is longer than a single time step (32ms). To handle this case, we predict the most likely value after one RTT as:

$$\hat{N}_{t+\lambda} = \operatorname*{argmax}_{N_{t+\lambda}} p(N_{t+1}|N_t = n_t) \prod_{i=1..\lambda-1} p(N_{t+i+1}|N_{t+i})$$

where $\lambda$ represents the RTT latency expressed in units of clock ticks.

Our results indicate that the Markov assumption holds up well in practice: namely, $N_{t+1}$ is memoryless (i.e., independent of the past given $N_t$). In fact, additional history in the form of longer Markov chains did not show a measurable benefit in terms of prediction accuracy. Rather than constructing a single model for the entire navigation vector, instead we treat each component of the vector $N$ independently, and construct six separate models. The benefit of this approach is that less training is required when estimating $\hat{N}$, and we observed that this assumption of treating the vector components independently does not hurt prediction accuracy. Below in §4.3, we discuss the issue of training in more detail.

## 4.2 Supersampling

We further refine our navigation predictions by *supersampling*: sampling input at a rate that is faster than the game's usage of the input. Supersampling helps with prediction accuracy because it lowers sampling noise. To construct a supersampled Markov model, we first poll the input device at the fastest rate possible. This rate is dependent on the specific input device. It is at least 100Hz for touch digitizers and at least 125Hz for standard mice. With a 32ms clock tick, we can often capture at least four samples per tick. We then build the Markov model as before. The inference is similar to the equation above, with the main difference being the production operator incrementing by $i \stackrel{+}{=} 0.25$. A summary of navigation prediction accuracy from the user study described in §10 is shown in Figure 3. Most dimensions of rotational and translational displacement exhibit little performance degradation with longer RTTs. Yaw ($\theta_x$), player's horizontal view angle, exhibits the most error, and we show its performance in detail in Figure 4 for user traces collected from both Doom 3 and Fable 3 at various RTTs from 40ms to 240ms. Doom 3 exhibits greater error than Fable 3 due to its more frenetic gameplay. Based on subjective assessment, prediction error below 4° is under the threshold at which output frame differences are perceivable.

Based on these results, we make two observations. First, for RTT $\leq$ 40ms (where 98% and 93% of errors are less than 4° for Doom 3 and Fable 3 respectively), errors are sufficiently minor and infrequent. Note that the client can detect the magnitude of the error (because it knows the ground truth), and drop any frames with excessive error. A frame rate drop from 30fps to $30 \times 0.95 = 28.5$fps is unlikely to affect most players' perceptions. For RTT > 40ms, we require additional misprediction compensation mechanisms. Before discussing both of these cases in turn, we first address the question of how much training is needed for successful application of the predictive model.

## 4.3 Bootstrap Time

Construction of a reasonable Markov Model requires sufficient training data collected during an observation period. Figure 5 shows that prediction error improves as observation time increases from 30 seconds to 300 seconds, after which the prediction error distribution remains stable. Somewhat surprisingly, having test players different from training players only marginally impacts prediction performance as long as test and train players are of similar skill level. Therefore, we chose to use a single model per coarse-grained skill level (novice or experienced) which is agnostic of the player.

## 4.4 Shake Reduction with Kalman Filtering

While the Markov model yields high prediction accuracy for RTT< 40ms, minor mispredictions can introduce a distracting visual effect that we describe as video shake. As a simple example, consider a single dimension of input such as yaw. The ground truth over three frames may be that the yaw remains unchanged, but the prediction error might be $+2°, -3°, +3°$. Unfortunately, the user would perceive a shaking effect because the frames would jump by 5° in one direction, and then 6° in another. From our experience with early prototypes, the manifested shakiness was sufficiently noticeable so as to reduce playability.

We apply a Kalman filter [25] in order to compensate for video shake. The filter's advantage is that it weighs estimates in proportion to sample noise and prediction error. Conceptually, when errors in past predictions are low relative to sample noise, predictions are given greater weight for state update. Conversely, when measurement noise is low, samples make greater contribution to the new state. For space, we omit technical development of the filter for our problem. One interesting filter modification we make is that we extend the filter to support error accumulation over variable RTT time steps; samples are weighed against an RTT's worth of prediction error.

Using the Kalman formulation, we assume a linear model with Gaussian noise, that is:

$$N_{t+1} = AN_t + \omega \tag{1}$$

$$n_t = N_t + \nu \tag{2}$$

for some state transition matrix $A$ and white Gaussian noise $\omega$. We assign $A = \{a_{ij}\}$ as a matrix which encodes the maximum likelihood Markov transitions where $a_{ij} = 1$ if $i = n_t$ and $j = \hat{N}_{t+\lambda}$, and zero otherwise; $\omega = \mathcal{N}(0, Q_\omega)$ is a normal distribution where $Q_\omega$ is the covariance matrix of the dynamic noise; $\nu = \mathcal{N}(0, Q_\nu)$ is a normal distribution where

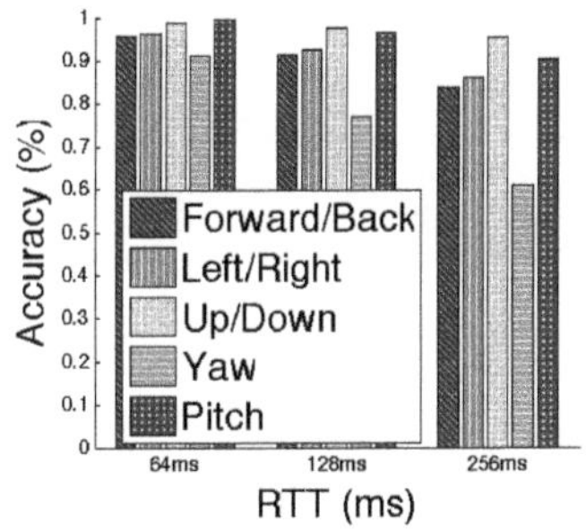


Figure 3: Doom 3 Navigation Prediction Summary. Roll ($\theta_z$) is not an input in Doom 3 and need not be predicted.

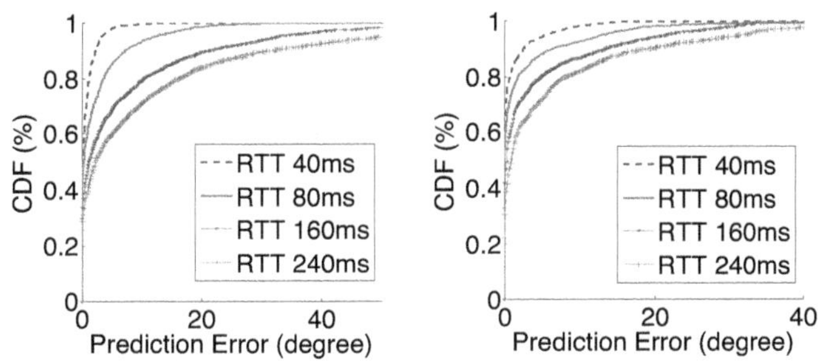


(a) Doom 3

(b) Fable 3

Figure 4: Prediction for Yaw ($\theta_x$), the navigation component with the highest variance. Error under 4° is imperceptible.

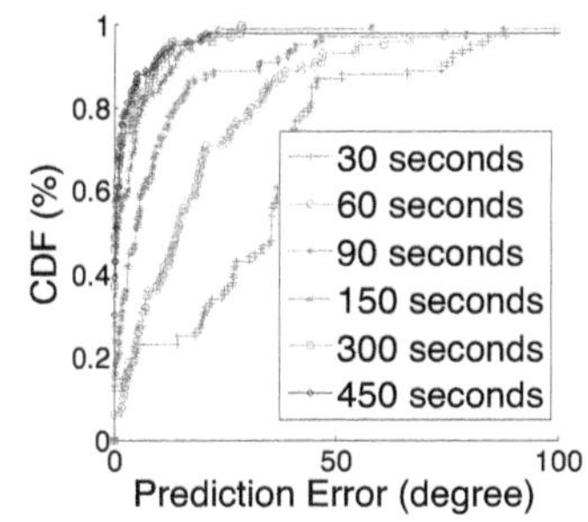


Figure 5: Error Decreases with More Observation Time. Data is for Fable 3 at RTT= 160ms.

$Q_\nu$ is the covariance matrix of the sampling noise. We assign covariances $Q_\omega$ and $Q_\nu$ based on *a priori* observations.

For the base case where the RTT is one clock tick, we generate navigation predictions $\hat{N}_{t+1|t}$ for time $t+1$ given observations up to and including $t$ as follows:

$$\hat{N}_{t+1|t} = A\hat{N}_{t|t} \tag{3}$$

Similarly, navigation error covariance predictions $P_{t+1|t}$ are computed as follows.

$$P_{t+1|t} = AP_{t|t}A^T + Q_\omega \tag{4}$$

When a new measurement $n_t$ arrives, we update the estimate of both the navigation prediction and its error covariance at the current time step as:

$$\hat{N}_{t|t} = \hat{N}_{t|t-1} + G_t(n_t - \hat{N}_{t|t-1}) \tag{5}$$

$$P_{t|t} = P_{t|t-1} - G_t P_{t|t-1} \tag{6}$$

where $G_t$ is the Kalman gain, which is:

$$G_t = P_{t|t-1}[P_{t|t-1} + Q_v]^{-1} \tag{7}$$

Lastly, we initialize the Kalman filter based on the *a priori* distribution: $\hat{N}_{1|0} = E[N_1]$.

Note the feedback loop between the error covariance and Kalman gain weighting favors the measurement $n_t$ when the prediction error is high and favors the prediction $\hat{N}_{t|t-1}$ when error is low. Moreover, the weighting naturally smooths shaking caused by inaccurate prediction by favoring the existing value of $\hat{N}$.

To extend $\lambda$ timesteps for predictions of $\hat{N}_{t+\lambda|t}$, we compute $\lambda$ intermediate iterations of Equation (3),(4), (6) and (7). When a new measurement $n_{t+\lambda}$ is received, the accumulation of prediction error $P_{t+\lambda|t}$ will have increased the gain $G_{t+\lambda}$. The large gain then favors the observation when adjusting the estimate in Equation (5).

## 4.5 Misprediction Compensation with Image-based Rendering

When RTT > 40ms, a noticeable fraction of navigation input is mispredicted, resulting in users perceiving lack of motor control. Our goal in misprediction compensation is for the server to generate auxiliary view data $f^\Delta$ alongside its predicted frame $f'$ such that the client can reconstruct a frame $f''$ that is a much better approximation of the desired frame $f$ than $f'$.

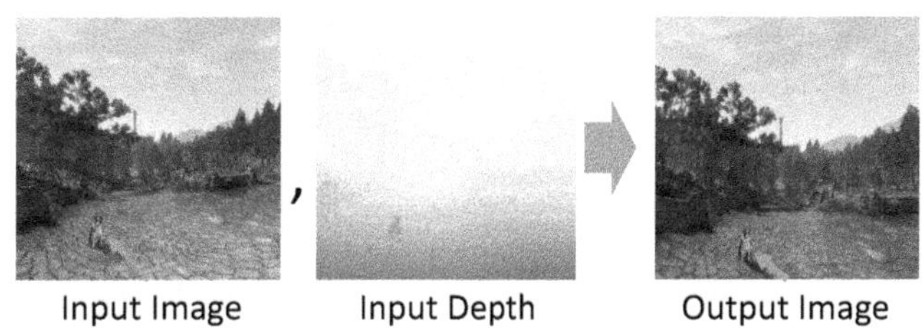


Figure 6: Image-based Rendering Example w/ Fable 3. Forward translation and leftward rotation is applied. The dog (indicated by green arrow) is closer and toward the center after IBR.

### 4.5.1 Image-based Rendering

We compensate for mispredictions with *image-based rendering (IBR)*. IBR is a means to derive novel camera viewpoints from fixed initial camera viewpoints. The specific implementation of IBR that we use operates by having initial cameras capture depth information ($f^\Delta$) in addition to 2D RGB color information ($f'$). It then applies a warp to create a new 2D image ($f''$) from $f'$ and $f^\Delta$ [38]. Figure 6 illustrates an example whereby an original image and its depth information is used to generate a new image from a novel viewpoint. Note that the new image is both translated and rotated with respect to the original, and contains some visual artifacts in the form of blurred pixels and low resolution areas when IBR is inaccurate.

To enable IBR, two requirements must be satisfied. First, the depth information must accurately reflect the 3D scene. Fortunately, the graphics pipeline's z-buffer precisely contains per-pixel depth information and is already a byproduct of standard rendering. Second, the original 2D scene must be sufficiently large so as to ensure that any new view is bounded within the original. To handle this case, instead of rendering a normal 2D image by default, we render a cube map [17] centered at the player's position. As shown in Figure 7, the cube map draws a panoramic 360° image on the six sides of a cube. In this way, the cube map ensures that any IBR image is within its bounds.

Unfortunately, naïve use of the depth map and cube map can lead to significant overhead. The cube map's six faces are approximately[3] six times the size of the original image.

[3]The original image is not square but rather 16:9 or 4:3.

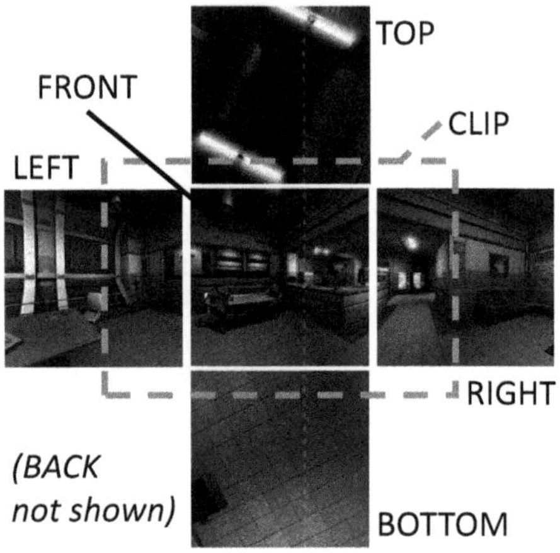


Figure 7: Cube Map Example w/ Doom 3. Clip region shown.

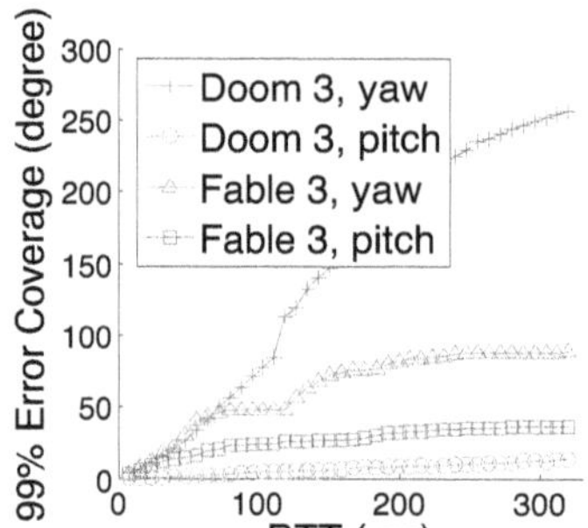


Figure 8: Angular coverage of 99% of prediction errors is much less than 360° even for high RTT.

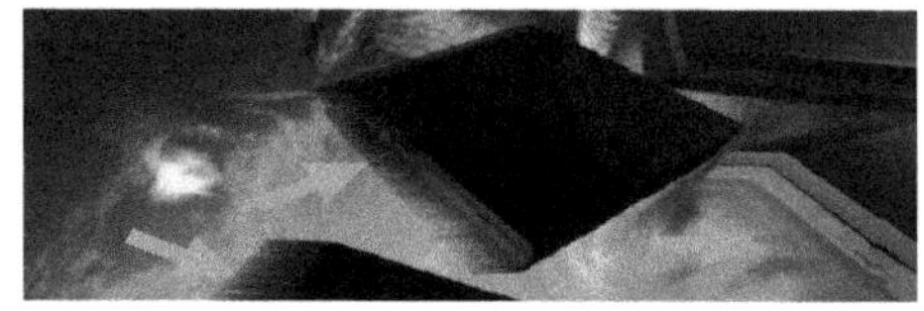

(a) Visible Smears

(b) Patched Smears

Figure 9: Misprediction's visual artifacts appear as smears which we mitigate.

The z-buffer is the same resolution as the original image, and depth information is needed for every cube face. Taken together, the total overhead is nominally 12×. This cost is incurred at multiple points in the system where data size is the main determinant of resource utilization, such as server rendering, encoding, bandwidth and decoding. We use the following technique to reduce this overhead.

### 4.5.2 Clipped Cube Map

We observe that it is unlikely that the player's true view will diverge egregiously from the most likely predicted view; transmitting a cube map that can compensate for errors in 360° is gratuitous. Therefore, we render a *clipped cube map* rather than a full cube map. The percentage of clipping depends on the expected variance of the prediction error. If the variance is high, then we render more of the cube. On the other hand, if the prediction variance is low, we render less of the cube. The dotted line in Figure 7 marks the clip region for an example rendering.

In order to size the clip, we define a cut plane $c$ such that the clipped cube bounds the output image with probability $1-\epsilon$. The cut plane then is a function of the variance of the prediction, and hence the partial cube map approaches a full cube when player movement exhibits high variance over the subject RTT horizon. To calculate $c$, we choose not a single predicted Markov state, but rather a set $\mathcal{N}$ of $k$ states such that the set covers $1-\epsilon$ of the expected probability density:

$$\mathcal{N} = \{n_{t+1}^i | \sum_{i=1..k} p(N_{t+1} = n_{t+1}^i | N_t = n_t) \geq 1-\epsilon\}$$

The clipped cube map then only needs to cover the range represented by the states in $\mathcal{N}$. For a single dimension such as yaw, the range is then simply the largest distance difference, and the cut plane along the yaw axis is defined as follows:

$$c_{yaw} = \max_{n_{t+1}^i \in \mathcal{N}} yaw(n_{t+1}^i) - \min_{n_{t+1}^j \in \mathcal{N}} yaw(n_{t+1}^j)$$

This suffices to cover $1-\epsilon$ of the probable yaw states.

In practice, error ranges are significantly less than 360° and therefore the size of the cube map can be substantially reduced. Figure 8 shows the distribution of $c_{yaw}$ and $c_{pitch}$ in Fable 3 and Doom 3 for $\epsilon = 0.01$, meaning that 99% of mispredictions are compensated. Doom 3's pitch range, player's vertical view angle, is very narrow (because players hardly look up or down), and both Fable 3's yaw and pitch ranges are modest at under 80° even for RTT $\geq 300ms$. Even for Doom 3's pronounced yaw range, only 225° of coverage is needed at 250 ms. The clip parameters are also applied to the depth map in order to similarly reduce its size.

In theory, compounding translation error on top of rotation error can further expand the clip region. It turns out that translation accuracy (see Figure 3) is sufficiently high to obviate consideration of accumulated translation error for the purposes of clipping.

### 4.5.3 Patching Visual Artifacts

Lastly, we add a technique to mitigate visual artifacts. These occasionally appear when the navigation prediction is wrong and there is significant depth disparity between foreground and background objects. For example, in Figure 9a, the floating stones are much closer to the camera than the lava in the background. As a result, IBR reveals "blind spots" behind the stones as indicated by the green arrows, which are manifest as visual "smears".

Our blind spot patching technique mitigates this problem, as seen in Figure 9b. As part of IBR, we extrude the object borders in the depth map with lightweight image processing which propagates depth values from foreground borders onto the background. However, we keep the color buffer the same. This way blind spots will exhibit less depth disparity and will share adjacent colors with the background, appearing as more reasonable extensions of the background. The results are more pleasing scenes especially when near and far objects are intermingled.

## 5. SPECULATION FOR IMPULSE EVENTS

The prototypical impulse events are FIRE for first person shooters, and INTERACT (with other characters or objects) for role playing games. We define an impulse event as being *registered* when its corresponding user input is *activated*. For example, a user's button activation may register a FIRE event.

The objective for impulse speculation is to respond quickly to player's impulse input while avoiding any visual inconsis-

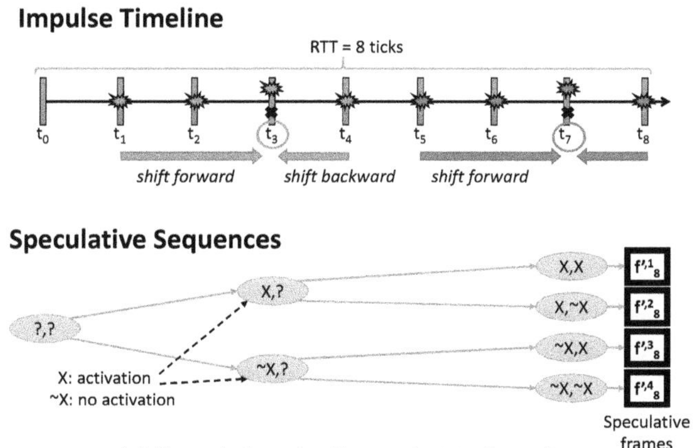


(a) Speculative timeline and state branches

(b) ~X, ~X (c) ~X, X (d) X,~X (e) X,X

Figure 10: Subsampling and time-shifting impulse events allows the server to bound speculation to a maximum of four sequences even for RTT= 256ms. Screenshots (b) – (e) show speculative frames corresponding to four activation sequences of weapon fire and no fire.

tencies. For example, in a first person shooter, weapons should fire quickly when triggered, and enemies should not reappear shortly after dying. The latter type of visual (and semantic) inconsistency is disconcerting to players, yet may occur when mispredictions occur in a prediction-based approach. Therefore, we employ a speculation technique for impulse that differs substantially from navigation speculation. Rather than attempt to predict impulse events, instead we explore multiple outcomes in parallel.

An overview of Outatime's impulse speculation is as follows. The server creates a *speculative input sequence* for all possible event sequences that may occur within one RTT, executes each sequence, renders the final frame of each sequence, and sends the set of speculative input sequences and frame pairs to the client. Upon reception, the client chooses the event sequence that matches the events that actually transpired, and displays its corresponding frame.

As RTT increases, the number of possible sequences grows exponentially. Consider an RTT of 256ms, which is 8 clock ticks. An activation may lead to an event registration at any of the 8 ticks, leading to an overwhelming $2^8$ possible sequences. In general, $2^\lambda$ sequences are possible for an RTT of $\lambda$ ticks. We use two state approximations to tame state space explosion: subsampling and time-shifting.

## 5.1 Subsampling

We reduce the number of possible sequences by only permitting activations at the subsampling periodicity $\sigma$ which is a periodicity greater than one clock tick. The benefit is that the state space is reduced to $2^{\frac{\lambda}{\sigma}}$. The drawback is that subsampling alone would cause activations not falling on the sampling periodicity to be lost, which would appear counter-intuitive to users.

## 5.2 Time-Shifting

To address the shortcomings of subsampling, *time-shifting* causes activations to be registered either earlier or later in time in order to align them with the nearest subsampled tick. Time shifting to an earlier time is feasible using speculation because the shift occurs on a speculative sequence at the server — not an actual sequence that has already been committed by the client. Put another way, as long as the client has not yet displayed the output frame at a particular tick, it is always safe to shift an event backwards to that tick.

Specifically, for any integer $k$, an activation issued between $t_{\sigma*k-\frac{\sigma}{2}}$ and $t_{\sigma*k-1}$ is deferred until $t_{\sigma*k}$. An activation issued between $t_{\sigma*k+1}$ and $t_{\sigma*k+\frac{\sigma}{2}-1}$ is treated as if it had arrived earlier in time at $t_{\sigma*k}$. Figure 10a illustrates combined subsampling and time-shifting, where the activations that occur at $t_1$ through $t_2$ are shifted later to $t_3$ and activations that occur at $t_4$ are shifted earlier to $t_3$. The corresponding state tree in Figure 10a shows the possible event sequences and four resulting speculative frames, $f_8'^1$, $f_8'^2$, $f_8'^3$ and $f_8'^4$. Note that it is not necessary to handle activations at $t_0$ within the illustrated 8 tick window because speculations that started at earlier clock ticks (e.g. at $t_{-1}$) would have covered them.

The ability to time-shift both forward and backward allows us to further halve the subsampling rate to double $\sigma$ without impacting player perception. Using 60ms as the threshold of player perception [6, 33], we note that time-shifting forward alone permits a subsampling period of $\sigma = 2$ (64ms) with an average shift of 32ms. With the added ability to time-shift backward as well, we can support a subsampling period of $\sigma = 4$ (128ms) yet still maintain an average shift of only 32ms. For $\sigma = 4$ and RTT$\leq$ 256ms, we generate a maximum of four speculative sequences as shown in Figure 10a. When RTT $>$ 256ms, we further lower the subsampling frequency sufficiently to ensure that we bound speculation to a maximum of four sequences. Specifically, $\sigma = \frac{\lambda}{2}$. While this can potentially result in users noticing the lowered sample rate, it allows us to cap the overhead of speculation.

## 5.3 Advanced Impulse Events

While binary impulse events are the most common, some games provide more options. For example, a Fable 3 player may cast a magic spell either directionally or unidirectionally which is a ternary impulse event due to mutual exclusion. Some first person shooters support primary and secondary fire modes (Doom 3 does not) which is also a ternary impulse event. With a ternary (or quaternary) impulse event, the state branching factor is three (or four) rather than two at every subsampling tick. With four parallel speculative sequences and a subsampling interval of $\sigma$ = 128ms, Outatime is able to support RTT $\leq$ 128ms for ternary and quaternary impulse events without lowering the subsampling frequency.

## 5.4 Delay Tolerant Events

We classify any input event that is slow relative to RTT as *delay tolerant*. We use a practical observation to simplify handling of delay tolerant events. According to our measurements on Fable 3 and Doom 3, delay tolerant events exhibited very high *cool down times* that exceeded 256ms. The cool down time is the period after an event is registered during which no other impulse events can be registered. For example, in Doom 3, weapon reloading takes anywhere from 1000ms to 2500ms during which time the weapon reload animation is shown. Weapon switching takes even longer. Fable 3 delay tolerant events have even higher cool down times. We take the approach that whenever a delay tolerant input is activated at the client, it is permissible to miss one full RTT of the event's consequences, as long as we can *compress time* after the RTT. The time compression procedure works as follows: for a delay tolerant event which displays $\tau$ frames worth of animation during its cool down (e.g. a weapon reload animation which takes $\tau$ frames), we may miss $\lambda$ frames due to the RTT. During the remaining $\tau - \lambda$ frames, we choose to compress time by sampling $\tau - \lambda$ frames uniformly from the original animation sequence $\tau$. The net effect is that delay tolerant event animations appear to play at fast speed. In return, we are assured that all events are properly processed because the delay tolerant event's cool down is greater than the RTT. For example, weapon switching or reloading immediately followed by firing is handled correctly.

# 6. FAST CHECKPOINT AND ROLLBACK

As with other systems that perform speculation [30, 42], Outatime uses checkpoint and restore to play forward a speculative sequence, and roll back the sequence if it turns out to be incorrect. In contrast to these previous systems, our continuous 30fps interactivity performance constraints are qualitatively much more demanding, and we highlight how we have managed these requirements.

Unique among speculation systems, we use a hybrid of page-level checkpointing and object-level checkpointing. This is because we need very fast checkpointing and restore; whereas page-level checkpointing is efficient when most objects need checkpointing, object-level checkpointing is higher performance when few objects need checkpointing. In general, it is only necessary to checkpoint *Simulation State Objects (SSOs)*: those objects which reproduce the world state. Checkpointing objects which have no bearing on the simulation, such as buffer contents, only increase runtime overhead. Therefore, we choose either object-level or page-level checkpointing based on the density of SSOs among co-located objects. We currently make the choice between page-level or object-level manually at the granularity of the binaries (executables and libraries), though it is also conceivable to do so automatically at the level of the compilation units.

For page-level checkpointing, we intercept calls to the default `libc` memory allocator with a version that implements page-level copy-on-write. At the start of a speculation (at every clock tick for navigation and at each $\sigma$ clock ticks for impulse), the allocator marks all pages read-only. When a page fault occurs, the allocator makes a copy of the original page and sets the protection level of the faulted page to read-write. When new input arrives, the allocator invalidates and discards some speculative sequences which do not match the new input. For example in Figure 10a, if no event activation occurs at $t_3$, then the sequences corresponding to $f_8'^1$ and $f_8'^2$ are invalid. State changes of the other speculative sequences up until $t_3$ are committed. In order to correctly roll back a speculation, the allocator copies back the original content of the dirty pages using the copies that it created. The allocator also tracks any pages created as a result of `new` object allocations since the last checkpoint. Any such pages are discarded. During speculation, the allocator also defers page deallocation resulting from object `delete` until commit because deleted objects may need to be restored if the speculation is later invalidated.

For object-level checkpointing, we track lifetimes of objects rather than pages for any object the developer has marked for tracking. To rollback a speculation, we delete any object that did not exist at the checkpoint, and restore any objects that were deleted during speculation. Moreover, we take advantage of *inverse functions* when available to quickly undo object state changes. Many SSOs in games expose custom inverse functions that undo the actions of previous state change. For example, for geometry objects that speculatively execute a $move(\Delta x)$ function, a suitable inverse is $move(-\Delta x)$. Identifying and tracking invertible functions is a trade-off in developer effort; we found the savings in checkpoint and rollback time to be very significant in certain cases (§10).

# 7. BANDWIDTH COMPRESSION

Navigation and impulse speculation generate additional frames to transmit from server to client. As an example, consider impulse speculation which for RTT of 256ms transmits four speculative frames for four possible worlds. Nominally, this bandwidth overhead is four times that of transmitting a single frame.

We can achieve a large reduction in bandwidth by observing that frames from different speculations share significant spatial and temporal coherence. Using Figure 10a as an example, $f_8'^1$ and $f_8'^2$ are likely to look very similar, with the only difference being two frames' worth of a weapon discharge animation in $f_8'^1$. Corresponding screenshots Figure 10b–10e show that the surrounding environment is largely unchanged, and therefore the spatial coherence is often high. In addition, when Outatime speculates for the next four frames, $f_9'^1$-$f_9'^1$, $f_9'^1$ is likely to look similar not only to $f_8'^1$, but also to $f_8'^2$, and therefore the temporal coherence is also often high. Similarly, navigation speculation's clipped cube map faces often exhibit both temporal and spatial coherence.

Outatime takes advantage of temporal and spatial coherence to reduce bandwidth by *joint encoding* of speculative frames. Encoding is the server-side process of compressing raw RGB frames into a compact bitstream which are then transmitted to the client where they are decoded and displayed. A key step of standard codecs such as H.264 is to divide each frame into macroblocks (e.g., $64 \times 64$ bit). A search process then identifies macroblocks that are equivalent (in some lossy domain) both intra-frame and inter-frame. In Outatime, we perform joint encoding by extending the search process to be inter-speculation; macroblocks across streams of different speculations are compared for equivalence. When an equivalency is found, we need only transmit the data for the first macroblock, and use pointers to it for the other macroblocks.

The addition of inter-speculation search does not change the client's decoding complexity but does introduce more encoding complexity on the server. Fortunately, modern GPUs are equipped with very fast hardware accelerated encoders [23, 31]. We have reprogrammed these otherwise idle hardware accelerated capabilities for our speculation's joint encoding.

# 8. MULTIPLAYER

Thus far, we have described Outatime from the perspective of a single user. Outatime works in a straightforward manner for multiplayer as well, though it is useful to clarify some nuances. As a matter of background, we briefly review distributed consistency in multiplayer systems. The standard architecture of a multiplayer gaming system is composed of traditional thick clients at the end hosts and a game *state coordination server* which reconciles distributed state updates to produce an eventually consistent view of events. For responsiveness, each client may perform local dead reckoning [8,16]. As an example, player one locally computes the position of player two based off of last reported trajectory. If player one should fire at player two who deviates from the dead-reckoned path, whether a hit is actually scored depends on the coordination server's reconciliation choice. Reconciliation can be crude and disconcerting when local dead-reckoned results are overridden; users perceive *glitches* such as: 1) an opponent's avatar appears to teleport if the opponent does not follow the dead-reckoned path, 2) a player in a firefight fires first yet still suffers a fatality, 3) "sponging" occurs — a phenomenon whereby a player sees an opponent soak up lots of damage without getting hurt [4].

With multiplayer, Outatime applies the architecture of Figure 2 to clients without altering the coordination server: end hosts run thin clients and servers run end hosts' corresponding Outatime server processes. The coordination server — which need not be co-located with the Outatime server processes — runs as in standard multiplayer. Outatime's multiplayer consistency is equivalent to standard multiplayer's because dead-reckoning is still used for opponents' positions; glitches can occur, but they are no more or less frequent than in standard multiplayer. As future work, we are interested in extending Outatime's speculative approach in conjunction with AI-led state approximations [7] to better remedy glitches that appear generally in any multiplayer game.

# 9. IMPLEMENTATION

To prototype Outatime, we modified Doom 3 (originally 366,000 lines of code) and Fable 3 (originally 959,000 lines of code). Doom 3 was released in 2004 and open sourced in 2011. Fable 3 was released in 2011. While both games are several years old, we note that the core gameplay of first person shooters and role playing games upon which Outatime relies has not fundamentally changed in newer games. The following section's discussion is with respect to Doom 3. Our experience with Fable 3 was similar

We have made the following key modifications to Doom 3. To enable deterministic speculation, we made changes according to [11] such as de-randomizing the random number generator, enforcing deterministic thread scheduling, and replacing timer interrupts with non-time-based function callbacks. To support impulse speculation, we spawn up to four Doom 3 *slaves*, each of which is a modified instance of the original game. Each slave accepts the following commands: `advance` consumes an input sequence and simulates game logic accordingly; `render` produces a frame corresponding to the current simulation state; `undo` discards any uncommitted state; `commit` makes any input applied thus far permanent. Each slave receives instructions from our *master* process regarding the speculation (i.e., input sequence) it should be executing, and returns framebuffers as encoded bitstream packets to the master using shared memory. To support navigation speculation, we add an additional slave command: `rendercube`, which produces the cubemap and depth maps necessary for IBR. The number of slaves spawned depends on the network latency. When RTT exceeds 128 ms, four slaves can cover four speculative state branches. Otherwise, three slaves suffice. The client is a simple thin client with the ability to perform IBR.

We implemented bandwidth compression with hardware-accelerated video encode and decode. The server-side joint video encode pipeline and client-side decode pipeline used the Nvidia NVENC hardware encoder and Nvidia Video Processor decoder, respectively [31]. The encode pipeline consists of raw frame capture, color space conversion and H.264 bitstream encoding. The decode pipeline consists of H.264 bitstream decoding and color space conversion to raw frames. We implemented the client-side IBR function as an OpenGL GLSL shader which consumes decoded raw frames and produces a compensated final frame for display.

Lastly, we also examined the source code for Unreal Engine [16], one of several widely used commercial game engines upon which many games are built, and verified that the modifications described above are general and feasible there as well. Specifically, support exists for rendering multiple views, the key primitive of `rendercube` [15]. Other key operations such as checkpoint, rollback and determinism can be implemented at the level of the C++ library linker. Therefore, we suggest speculative execution is broadly applicable across commercial titles, and can be systematized with additional work.

# 10. EVALUATION

We use both user studies and performance benchmarking to characterize the cost and benefits of Outatime. User studies are useful to assess perceived responsiveness and visual quality degradation, and to learn how macro-level system behavior impacts gameplay. Our primary tests are on Doom 3 because twitch-based gaming is very sensitive to latency. We confirm the results with limited secondary tests on Fable 3. A summary of our findings are as follows.

- Based on subjective assessment, players — including seasoned gamers — rate Outatime playable with only minor impairment noticeable up to 128ms.
- Users demonstrate very little drop off of in-game skills with Outatime as compared to a standard cloud gaming system.
- Our real-time checkpointing and rollback service is a key enabler for speculation, taking less than 1ms for checkpointing app state.
- Speculation imposes increased demands on resource. At 128ms, bandwidth consumption is 1.97× higher than standard cloud gaming. However, frame rates are still satisfactorily fast at 52fps at 95th percentile.

## 10.1 Experimental Setup

We tested Outatime against the following baselines. *Standard Thick Client* consists of out-of-the-box Doom 3, which is a traditional client-only application. *Standard Thin Client* emulates the traditional cloud gaming architecture shown in

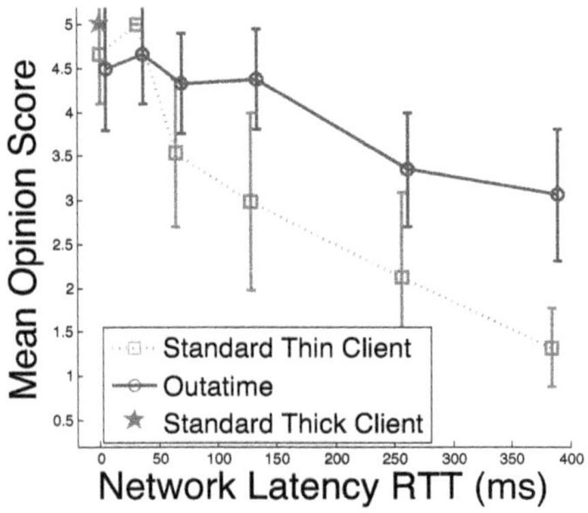


Figure 11: Impact of Latency on User Experience

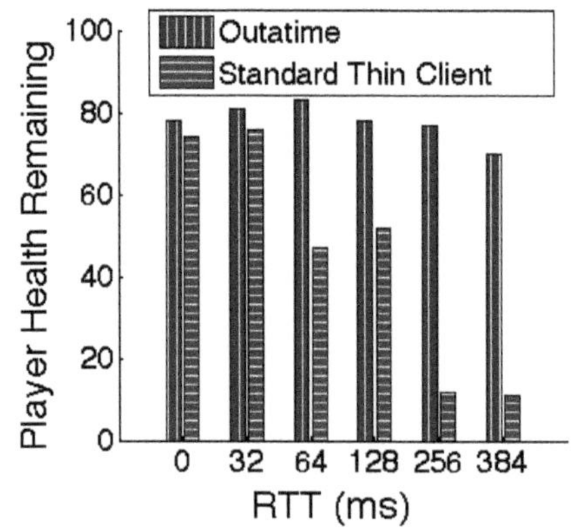


Figure 12: Remaining Health

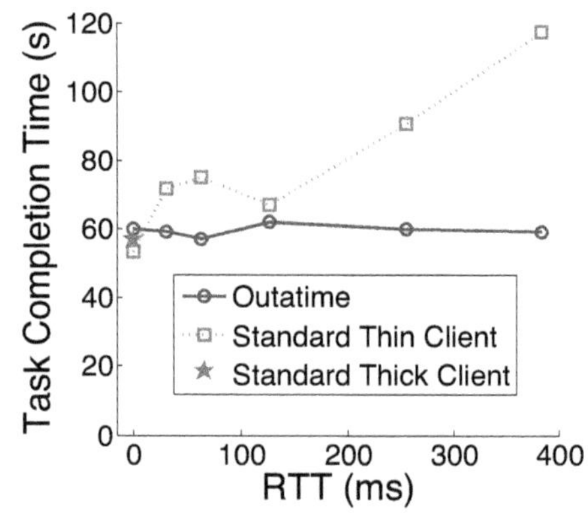


Figure 13: Task Completion Time

Figure 1a, where Doom 3 is executed on a server without speculation, and the player submits input and views output frames on a client. The server consists of an HP z420 machine with quad core Intel i7, 16GB memory, and an Nvidia GTX 680 GPU w/4GB memory. For Thin Client and Outatime, we emulated a network with a defined RTT. The emulation consisted of delaying input processing and output frames to and from the server and client by a fixed RTT. The client process was hosted on the same machine as the server in order to finely control network RTT. We also used the same machine to run the Thick Client. User input was issued via mouse and keyboard. We configured Doom 3 for a $1024 \times 1024$ output resolution. We conducted formal user studies with sixty-four participants overall over three separate study sessions. Two studies were for Doom 3 and consisted of twenty-three participants (Study A) and eighteen participants (Study B). The third was for Fable 3 (Study C) and is described in more detail later in this section. Both Study A and Study B consisted of coworkers and colleagues who were recruited based on their voluntary response to a call for participation in a gaming study. The self-reported age range was 24–42 (39 male, 2 female). The main difference between the studies was that Study B's participants were drawn primarily from a local gaming interest group and were compensated with a $5 gift card, whereas Study A's participants were not. Prior to engagement, all participants were provided an overview of the study, and consented to participate in accordance with institutional ethics and privacy policies. They also made a self-assessment regarding their own video game skill at three granularities: 1) overall video game experience, 2) experience with the first person shooter genre, and 3) experience with Doom 3 specifically. While all Study A's participants reported either Beginner (score=2) or No Experience (score=1) for Doom 3, Study B's participants self-reported as being "gamers" much more frequently, with 72% having previously played Doom 3. For both Study A and B, participants first played the unmodified game to gain familiarity. They then played the same map at various network latency settings with and without Outatime enabled. Participants were blind as to the network latency and whether Outatime was enabled.

## 10.2 User Perception of Gameplay

The user study centered around three criteria.

- *Mean Opinion Score (MOS):* Participants assign a subjective 1–5 score on their experience where 5 indicates no difference from reference, 4 indicates minor differences, 3 indicates acceptable differences, 2 indicates annoying differences and 1 indicates unplayable. MOS is a standard metric in the evaluation of video and audio communication services.

- *Skill Impact:* We use the decrease in players' in-game health as a proxy for the skill degradation resulting from higher latency.

- *Task Completion Time:* Participants are asked to finish an in-game task in the shortest possible time under varying latency conditions.

Each participant first played a reference level on the Thick Client system, during which time they had an opportunity to familiarize themselves with game controls, as well as experience best-case responsiveness and visual quality. Next, they re-played the level three to ten times with either Outatime or Thin Client and an RTT selected randomly from $\{0ms, 64ms, 128ms, 256ms, 384ms\}$. Among the multiple replays, they also played once on Thick Client as a control. Participants and the experimenter were blind to the system configuration during re-plays. Some of the participants repeated the entire process for a second level. We configured the level so that participants only had access to the fastest firing weapon so that any degradations in responsiveness would be more readily apparent.

After each re-play, participants were asked to rank their experience relative to the reference on an MOS scale according to three questions: (1) How was your overall user experience? (2) How was the responsiveness of the controls? (3) How was the graphical visual quality? We also solicited free-form comments and recorded in-game vocal exclamations which turned out to be illuminating. Lastly, we recorded general player statistics during play, such as remaining player health and time to finish the level.

### 10.2.1 *Mean Opinion Score*

Figure 11 summarizes overall MOS across participants from Study A and Study B when playing on Outatime, Thin Client and Thick Client at various RTTs. Thick client is not MOS= 5 due to a placebo effect. Thin Client MOS follows a sharp downward trend, indicating that the game becomes increasingly frustrating to play as early as 128ms. Free form participant comments from those self-identified as experts strongly reinforced this assessment.

- Thin Client @ 64ms: *"OK, can play. Not acceptable for expert."*
- Thin Client @ 128ms: *"Felt slow. Needed to guess actions to play."*
- Thin Client @ 128ms: *"Controls were extremely delayed."*

For Outatime, the MOS stays relatively high with scores between 4 to 4.5 up through 128ms. Comments from those self-assessed as experts are shown below.

- Outatime @ 128ms: *"Controls were fluid, animations worked as expected, no rendering issues on movement and no transition issues with textures."*
- Outatime @ 128ms: *"Shooting was a bit glitchy, but you don't notice too much. Controls were about the same, good responsiveness and all."*
- Outatime @ 128ms: *"Frame rate comfortable; liked the smoothness."*

Participants with high prior experience tended to assign lower MOS scores to both Thin and Outatime, especially at high latencies. This was evident with participants in Study B who ranked latencies at 256ms merely acceptable or annoying. However, Study B participants still ranked Outatime well at 128ms with a score of 4.4. This compares favorably to their corresponding Thin Client at 128ms score of 3.3. On the other hand, even at 256ms, Study A users ranked Outatime as still acceptable at 4.5. This is likely the result of Study A users' less frenetic gameplay, which results in fewer mispredictions. Therefore, we suggest that Outatime is appropriate for novice players up to 256ms, and more advanced players up to 128ms.

Responsiveness MOS ratings were overall very high (above 4 for all RTTs) for Outatime indicating that Outatime does well at masking latency. Visual quality MOS ratings for Outatime followed the same trends as Overall MOS ratings. The results are elided for space.

### 10.2.2 *Skill Impact*

We found that longer latencies also hurt performance on in-game skills such as avoiding enemy attacks. For Study A, we instructed participants to eliminate all enemies in a level while preserving as much health as possible. Figure 12 shows the participants' remaining health after finishing the level. Interestingly, even though participants playing on Thin Client reported only modest degradation in MOS at 64ms, participant health dropped off sharply from over 70/100 to under 50/100, suggesting that in-game skills were impaired. Outatime exhibited no significant drop off for RTT$\leq$ 256ms.

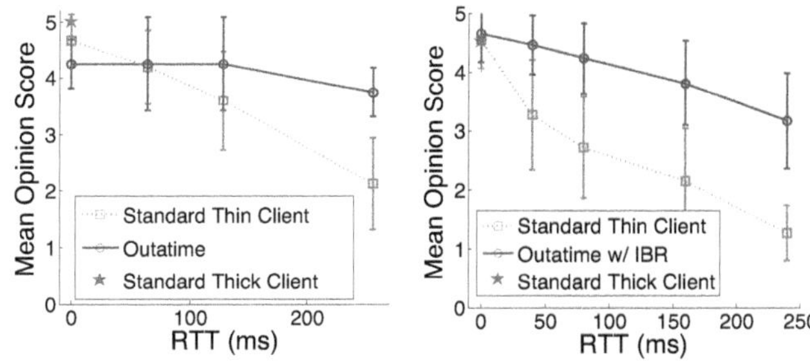


(a) Impulse Speculation (b) Navigation Speculation

Figure 14: Fable 3 MOS

| | Checkpoint Restore | App Logic | Render | Encode | Total (ms) |
|---|---|---|---|---|---|
| Thin Client | N/A | $0.5 \pm 0.1$ | $1.6 \pm 0.3$ | $7.3 \pm 0.6$ | $9.4 \pm 1.0$ |
| **Outatime** | | | | | |
| Kalman@64ms | $1.9 \pm 0.6$ | $4.6 \pm 1.9$ | $1.9 \pm 0.3$ | $6.9 \pm 1.8$ | $15.2 \pm 4.6$ |
| IBR @128ms | $2.2 \pm 0.8$ | $6.7 \pm 4.0$ | $2.9 \pm 2.1$ | $20.7 \pm 7.4$ | $32.4 \pm 14.3$ |
| IBR @256ms | $2.3 \pm 1.1$ | $8.8 \pm 5.3$ | $3.9 \pm 3.2$ | $32.5 \pm 12.2$ | $47.5 \pm 21.9$ |

Table 1: Server Processing Time Per-Frame ± StdDev. Note that Outatime's server processing time is masked by speculation whereas Thin Client's is not.

In the free form comments, several participants mentioned that they consciously changed their style of play to cope with higher Thin Client latencies. For example, they remained in defensive positions more often, and did not explore as aggressively as they would have otherwise. Outatime elicited no such comments.

### 10.2.3 *Task Completion Time*

Lastly, we measured participants' level completion time. Participants were instructed to eliminate all enemies from a level as quickly as possible. Figure 13 shows that RTT $\geq$ 256ms lowered Thin Client completion times, but had little impact on Outatime completion times.

## 10.3 Fable 3 Verification

We setup Fable 3 for similar testing to Doom 3. We recruited twenty-three additional subjects (age 20–34, 4 females, 19 males) who were unfamiliar with the Doom 3 experiments. In this study, we separated the testing of Impule and Navigation speculation in order to isolate their component effects. Figure 14a and Figure 14b show that the MOS impact of impulse speculation and navigation speculation for Fable 3. Impulse speculation tends to hold up better than Navigation speculation to longer RTTs. This supports our anecdotal observation that visual artifacts from IBR can be noticeable especially over longer time horizons, whereas Outatime's parallel timeline speculation works well to cover all possible impulse events.

## 10.4 System Performance and Overhead

We report a variety of client, server and bandwidth metrics. During server testing, we use a trace-driven client. Similarly, we use a trace-driven server during client tests.

### 10.4.1 *Client Performance*

Figure 15 shows that Outatime and Thick Client both achieve the target frame time of 32ms, which is directly

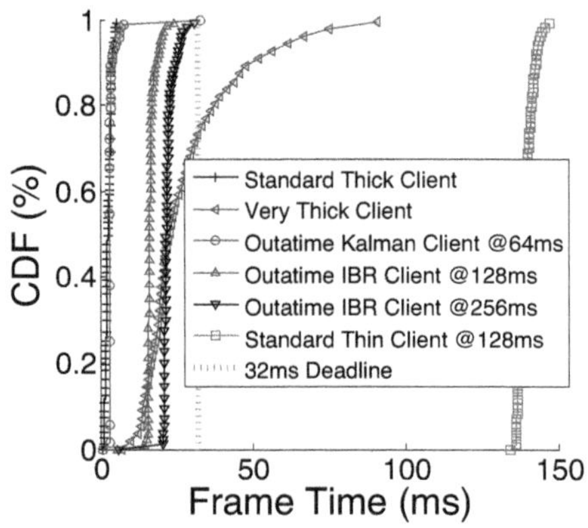


Figure 15: Client Frame Time

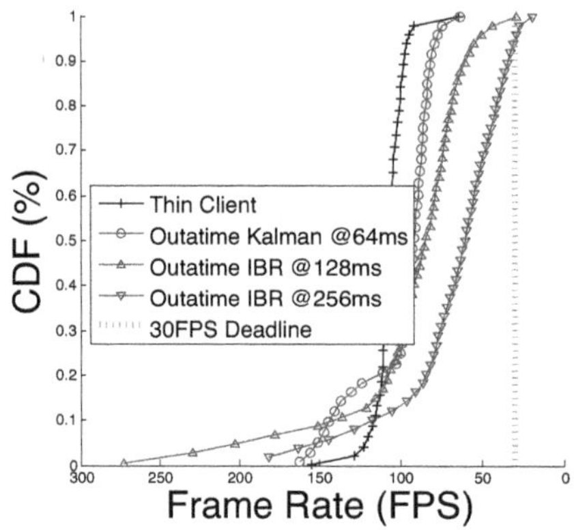


Figure 16: Frame Throughput Measured at Server

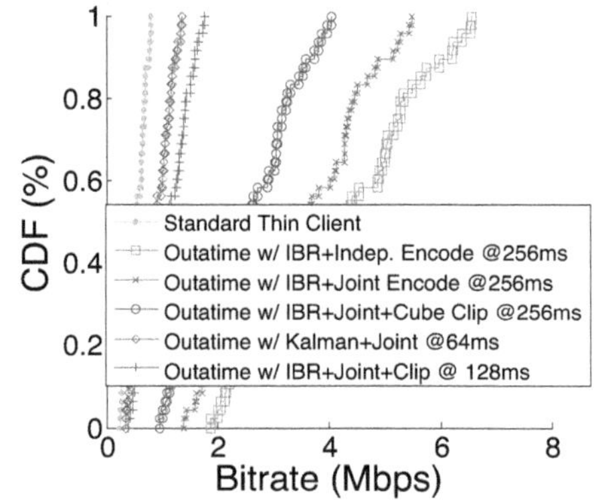


Figure 17: Bandwidth Overhead

| Method | Time (ms) |
|---|---|
| Built-in Save Game | 333000 |
| Baseline Object-only | 45.55 |
| Outatime's Hybrid | 0.076 |

Table 2: Fast Hybrid Checkpoint vs. Alternatives

linked to players' perceptions of low latency. The bulk of Outatime's time is spent on decoding, which is dependent solely upon the system's hardware decoder and is not the focus of optimization in this paper. Non-decoding time, primarily IBR, accounts for less than 2ms, even when run on a 2010-year notebook's Nvidia GT 320M, which is 21× less powerful than the server's GTX 680 according to PassMark GPU benchmarks. In contrast, Thin Client's frame time is clearly vulnerable to RTT.

We also tested a configuration that is more representative of a modern high-end game to assess whether it is possible for Outatime to in fact run faster than a Thick Client implementation. Specifically, we modified Doom 3 to run the *Perfected Doom* mod, an enhancement to Doom 3 that increases graphics quality significantly, and more closely matches a modern game.[4]. As shown by Very Thick Client in Figure 15, this causes huge spikes in frame time up to 76ms at the 95th percentile, which is unplayable. On the other hand, cloud gaming client performance such as in Outatime is not tied to the game's complexity. Therefore, the Outatime client can actually outperform the Thick Client in the case of graphically- or computationally-demanding modern games.

### 10.4.2 *Server Throughput and Processing Time*

We next quantify the server load in two ways. The first is frame rate where we target at least 30fps throughput. The second is the server's per frame processing time. This is the time it takes for input received at the server to be converted into an output frame. Importantly, processing time is not the inverse of throughput because our server implementation is highly parallelized.

[4]`http://www.moddb.com/mods/perfected-doom-3-version-500`

Figure 16 shows the server's frame rate. Outatime is able to operate at above 30fps for every supported latency. In the case of 128ms, the frame rate is 52fps or better 95th percent of the time. Table 1 shows the server's processing time. Outatime with Kalman takes longer than Thin Client due to impulse speculation, checkpoint, restore and rollback. Outatime with IBR adds cube and depth map rendering and frame transfer. Processing time is higher at 256ms than at 128ms due to the need to run extra slaves to service more speculative branches. Note that for Outatime, processing time has no bearing on the client's frame time because of Outatime's use of speculation. However, for Thin Client, server processing time (9ms in this case) further increases overall frame time.

### 10.4.3 *Checkpoint and Rollback*

We perform a comparative benchmark of our fast checkpoint/rollback implementation to two other possible implementations in Table 2. The setup is a standalone stress test on Doom 3 where checkpoint speed is isolated from other system effects. Our implementation using hybrid object- and page-level checkpointing is approximately 7000× faster than Doom's built-in state-saving Load/Save game feature, and 300× faster than an object-only checkpointing implementation. A similar advantage would exist against page-only checkpointing as well. In absolute terms, tens of milliseconds is simply too costly for continuous real-time checkpointing, whereas sub-millisecond speed makes speculation feasible.

### 10.4.4 *Bitrate*

While our prototype performs cube clipping directly on rendered frames and uses a hardware accelerated codec pipeline for efficiency, we conducted compression testing offline using **`ffmpeg`** and **`libx264`**, two publicly available codec libraries, for easier repeatability. Figure 17 shows the bitrate of Thin Client and various Outatime configurations. The baseline Thin Client median bitrate is 0.53Mbps. When running Outatime with IBR Navigation Speculation and Impulse Speculation with RTT= 256ms, transmission of all speculative frames (cube map faces, depth map faces and speculative impulse frames) with independent encoding consumes a median of 4.01Mbps. After joint encoding, transmission drops to 3.33Mbps. Outatime's use of clipped cube map with joint encoding consumes 2.41Mbps, which is 4.54× the bitrate of Thin Client and a 40% reduction from independent. Finally, when RTT≤ 128ms, joint encoding and clipping consumes only 1.04Mbps, which is only 1.97× more than Thin Client. The savings are due to lower prediction error over a shorter time horizon (Figure 8) and transmitting half as many speculative branch frames. When running Outatime with Kalman-based Navigation Speculation and Impulse, the bitrate is further lowered to 0.8Mbps, or 1.51× Thin Client.

## 10.5 Public Deployment

We deployed Outatime publicly at MobiSys 2014's demo session [27]. Around fifty participants played the system. The response was positive with best demo recognition received.

# 11. RELATED WORK

Speculative execution is a general technique for reducing perceived latency. In the domain of distributed systems, Crom [29] allows Web browsers to speculatively execute javascript event handlers (which can prefetch server content, for example) in temporary shadow contexts of the browser. Mosh provides a more responsive remote terminal experience by permitting the client to speculate on the terminal screen's future content, by leveraging the observation that most keystrokes for a terminal application are echoed verbatim to the screen [43]. The authors of [26] show that by speculating on remote desktop and VNC server responses, clients can achieve lower perceived response latency, albeit at the cost of occasional visual artifacts on misprediction. A common theme of this prior work is to build core speculation (e.g. state prediction, state generation) into the client. In contrast, Outatime performs speculation at the server. This is because client vs. server graphical rendering capabilities can differ by orders of magnitude, and clients cannot be reliably counted on to render (regular or speculative) frames. Time Warp [24] improved distributed simulation performance by speculatively executing computation on distributed nodes. However, to support speculation, it made many assumptions that would be inappropriate for game development, e.g., processes cannot use heap storage. Outatime is a specific instance of application-specific speculation, defined by Wester et al. [42] and applied to the Speculator system. According to the taxonomy of Wester et al., Outatime implements novel application-specific policies for creating speculations, speculative output, and rollback.

Alternatives to cloud streaming such as HTML5 are intriguing, though interactive games have had stronger performance demands than what browsers tend to offer. Even with native client execution [13, 20], the benefits of cloud-hosting and Outatime (instant start, easier management, etc.) still apply. For mitigating network latency stemming in multiplayer gaming, see §8.

Outatime's use of IBR to compensate for navigation events is inspired by work in the graphics community. Early efforts focused on reducing (non-network) latency of virtual reality simulations using basic movement prediction and primitive image warping [34]. The authors of [41] apply hardware-supported IBR to reduce local scene rendering latency. The authors of [28] investigated the use of IBR for network latency compensation of thin clients. IBR alone is well-suited for rendering novel views of static scenes (*e.g.,* museums) but fails to cope with dynamic scenes (*e.g.,* moving entities) with heavy user interaction (impulse events), as is standard in games. In contrast, Outatime's speculative execution handles dynamic scenes and user interaction.

# 12. DISCUSSION

Outatime is currently unable to cope with some types of game events. For example, teleportation via wormholes do not map well to IBR's inherent assumption of movement in Euclidian space. One possibility is to extend impulse-like parallel speculation even for navigation events in limited cases. Another interesting avenue of investigation is harnessing additional in-game predictive signals to improve on such speculation. Example signals include player status and visible scene object *e.g.,* presence of wormholes. In addition, applying more powerful predictive time-series models altogether might yield significant gains, especially over longer RTTs. Also, large numbers of simultaneous impulse events over short time horizons limit Outatime's ability to meet high frame rate performance targets. Certain genres of games (e.g., fighting, real-time strategy) exhibit this vulnerability more so than others, so additional state space approximation mechanisms may be needed in such cases [36]. Lastly, support for audio is an area of future work.

Another interesting direction is to explore optimization of parallel speculations. Currently, each speculative branch incurs the full cost of a normal execution. Instead, it may be possible to perform only the "diff" operations between branches (such as rendering only differing objects and inexpensively recompositing the scene at the client), thereby saving significant compute, rendering and bandwidth costs.

We have not focused on client power consumption in this work, but it is potentially a very ripe area for savings. This is because Outatime's thin client approach essentially converts the client's work from an arbitrary app-dependent rendering cost to a fixed IBR cost (see Figure 15) since IBR cost is only dependent upon the client screen resolution. The potential for implementing IBR as a highly optimized silicon accelerator is very intriguing.

# 13. CONCLUSION

Games, by their very nature of being virtual environments, are well-suited for speculation, roll back and replay. We demonstrated Outatime on Doom 3, a twitch-based first person shooter, and Fable 3, an action role-playing game because they belong to popular game genres with demanding response times. This leads us to be optimistic about Outatime's applicability across genres, with potentially bigger savings for slower-paced games. We found that players overwhelmingly favor Outatime's masking of high RTT times over naked exposure to long latency. In turn, this enables cloud gaming providers to reach much larger mobile community while maintaining a high level of user experience.

# 14. REFERENCES


[1] Amazon appstream. `http://aws.amazon.com/appstream`.

[2] Nvidia grid cloud gaming. `http://shield.nvidia.com/grid`.

[3] Sony playstation now streaming. `http://us.playstation.com/playstationnow`.

[4] Sponging is no longer a myth. http://youtu.be/Bt433RepDwM.

[5] M. Allman. Comments on bufferbloat. *SIGCOMM Comput. Commun. Rev.*, 43(1):30–37, Jan. 2012.

[6] T. Beigbeder, R. Coughlan, C. Lusher, J. Plunkett, E. Agu, and M. Claypool. The effects of loss and latency on user performance in unreal tournament 2003. In *NetGames'04*, pages 144–151, New York, NY, USA, 2004. ACM.

[7] A. Bharambe, J. R. Douceur, J. R. Lorch, T. Moscibroda, J. Pang, S. Seshan, and X. Zhuang. Donnybrook: Enabling large-scale, high-speed, peer-to-peer games. In *SIGCOMM'08*, pages 389–400, New York, NY, USA, 2008. ACM.

[8] A. Bharambe, J. Pang, and S. Seshan. Colyseus: A distributed architecture for online multiplayer games. In *NSDI'06*, pages 12–12, Berkeley, CA, USA, 2006. USENIX Association.

[9] K.-T. Chen, P. Huang, and C.-L. Lei. How sensitive are online gamers to network quality? *Commun. ACM*, 49(11):34–38, Nov. 2006.

[10] M. Claypool, D. Finkel, A. Grant, and M. Solano. Thin to win?: network performance analysis of the onlive thin client game system. In *Proceedings of the 11th Annual Workshop on Network and Systems Support for Games*, NetGames '12, pages 1:1–1:6, Piscataway, NJ, USA, 2012. IEEE Press.

[11] E. Cuervo. *Enhancing Mobile Devices through Code Offload*. PhD thesis, Duke University, 2012.

[12] M. Dick, O. Wellnitz, and L. Wolf. Analysis of factors affecting players' performance and perception in multiplayer games. In *NetGames'05*, pages 1–7, New York, NY, USA, 2005. ACM.

[13] J. R. Douceur, J. Elson, J. Howell, and J. R. Lorch. Leveraging legacy code to deploy desktop applications on the web. In *Proceedings of the 8th USENIX Conference on Operating Systems Design and Implementation*, OSDI'08, pages 339–354, Berkeley, CA, USA, 2008. USENIX Association.

[14] Engadget. Microsoft's delorean is a cloud gaming system that knows what you'll do next. http://www.engadget.com/2014/08/23/microsoft-delorean/.

[15] Epic Games. Unreal graphics programming. https://docs.unrealengine.com/latest/INT/Programming/Rendering/index.html.

[16] Epic Games. Unreal networking architecture. http://udn.epicgames.com/Three/NetworkingOverview.html.

[17] R. Fernando. *GPU Gems: Programming Techniques, Tips and Tricks for Real-Time Graphics*. Addison-Wesley Professional, 2007.

[18] Flurry. Apps solidify leadership six years into the mobile revolution. http://www.flurry.com/bid/109749/Apps-Solidify-Leadership-Six-Years-into-the-Mobile-Revolution, 2014.

[19] Gamespot. Microsoft researching cloud gaming solution that hides latency by predicting your actions. http://www.gamespot.com/articles/microsoft-researching-cloud-gaming-solution-that-h/1100-6421896/, 8 2014.

[20] Google. Native client. http://youtu.be/Bt433RepDwM.

[21] J. Huang, F. Qian, A. Gerber, Z. M. Mao, S. Sen, and O. Spatscheck. A close examination of performance and power characteristics of 4g lte networks. In *MobiSys'12*, pages 225–238, New York, NY, USA, 2012. ACM.

[22] J. Huang, F. Qian, Y. Guo, Y. Zhou, Q. Xu, Z. M. Mao, S. Sen, and O. Spatscheck. An in-depth study of lte: effect of network protocol and application behavior on performance. In *SIGCOMM'13*, pages 363–374, New York, NY, USA, 2013. ACM.

[23] Intel. QuickSync Programmable Video Processor. http://www.intel.com/content/www/us/en/architecture-and-technology/quick-sync-video/quick-sync-video-general.html.

[24] D. Jefferson, B. Beckman, F. Wieland, L. Blume, M. DiLoreto, P.Hontalas, P. Laroche, K. Sturdevant, J. Tupman, V. Warren, J. Weidel, H. Younger, and S. Bellenot. Time Warp operating system. In *SOSP'87*, pages 77–93, Austin, TX, November 1987.

[25] R. E. Kalman. A new approach to linear filtering and prediction problems. *Transactions of the ASME–Journal of Basic Engineering*, 82(Series D):35–45, 1960.

[26] J. R. Lange, P. A. Dinda, and S. Rossoff. Experiences with client-based speculative remote display. In *ATC'08*, pages 419–432, Berkeley, CA, USA, 2008. USENIX Association.

[27] K. Lee, D. Chu, E. Cuervo, J. Kopf, A. Wolman, and J. Flinn. Demo: Delorean: Using speculation to enable low-latency continuous interaction for mobile cloud gaming. MobiSys '14, 2014.

[28] W. R. Mark, L. McMillan, and G. Bishop. Post-rendering 3d warping. In *Proceedings of the 1997 Symposium on Interactive 3D Graphics*, I3D '97, pages 7–ff., New York, NY, USA, 1997. ACM.

[29] J. Mickens, J. Elson, J. Howell, and J. Lorch. Crom: Faster web browsing using speculative execution. In *NSDI'10*, pages 9–9, Berkeley, CA, USA, 2010. USENIX Association.

[30] E. B. Nightingale, P. M. Chen, and J. Flinn. Speculative execution in a distributed file system. *ACM Trans. Comput. Syst.*, 24(4):361–392, Nov. 2006.

[31] Nvidia. Video codec sdk. https://developer.nvidia.com/nvidia-video-codec-sdk.

[32] PCWorld. Popcap games ceo: Android still too fragmented. http://bit.ly/1hQv8Mn, Mar 2012.

[33] P. Quax, P. Monsieurs, W. Lamotte, D. D. Vleeschauwer, and N. Degrande. Objective and subjective evaluation of the influence of small amounts of delay and jitter on a recent first person shooter game. In W. chang Feng, editor, *NETGAMES*, pages 152–156. ACM, 2004.

[34] R. H. So and M. J. Griffin. Compensating lags in head-coupled displays using head position prediction and image deflection. *Journal of Aircraft*, 29(6):1064–1068, 1992.

[35] J. Sommers and P. Barford. Cell vs. wifi: on the performance of metro area mobile connections. In *IMC'12*, pages 301–314, New York, NY, USA, 2012. ACM.

[36] M. Stanton, B. Humberston, B. Kase, J. F. O'Brien, K. Fatahalian, and A. Treuille. Self-refining games

using player analytics. *ACM Trans. Graph.*, 33(4):73:1–73:9, July 2014.

[37] S. Sundaresan, W. de Donato, N. Feamster, R. Teixeira, S. Crawford, and A. Pescapè. Broadband internet performance: A view from the gateway. In *Proceedings of the ACM SIGCOMM 2011 Conference*, SIGCOMM '11, pages 134–145, New York, NY, USA, 2011. ACM.

[38] R. Szeliski. *Computer Vision: Algorithms and Applications.* Springer, 2011.

[39] TechCrunch. Microsoft research shows off delorean, its tech for building a lag-free cloud gaming service. `http://techcrunch.com/2014/08/22/microsoft-research-shows-off-delorean-its-tech-for-building-a-lag-free-cloud-gaming-service/`.

[40] TechHive. Game developers still not sold on android. `http://www.techhive.com/article/2032740/game-developers-still-not-sold-on-android.html`, Apr 2013.

[41] J. Torborg and J. T. Kajiya. Talisman: Commodity realtime 3d graphics for the pc. In *Proceedings of the 23rd Annual Conference on Computer Graphics and Interactive Techniques*, SIGGRAPH '96, pages 353–363, New York, NY, USA, 1996. ACM.

[42] B. Wester, P. M. Chen, and J. Flinn. Operating system support for application-specific speculation. In *EuroSys'11*, pages 229–242. ACM, April 2011.

[43] K. Winstein and H. Balakrishnan. Mosh: An Interactive Remote Shell for Mobile Clients. In *USENIX Annual Technical Conference*, Boston, MA, June 2012.

[44] Wired. As android rises, app makers tumble into google's matrix of pain. `http://www.wired.com/business/2013/08/android-matrix-of-pain/`, Aug 2013.

# RollingLight: Enabling Line-of-Sight Light-to-Camera Communications

Hui-Yu Lee[†§], Hao-Min Lin[†§], Yu-Lin Wei[†§], Hsin-I Wu[†§], Hsin-Mu Tsai[†§] and Kate Ching-Ju Lin[‡§]
[†]Department of Computer Science and Information Engineering, National Taiwan University, Taipei, Taiwan
[‡]Research Center for Information Technology Innovation, Academia Sinica, Taipei, Taiwan
[§]Intel-NTU Connected Context Computing Center, Taipei, Taiwan
{r01922028, d00922003, r03922027, r02944020, hsinmu}@csie.ntu.edu.tw, katelin@citi.sinica.edu.tw

## ABSTRACT

Recent literatures have demonstrated the feasibility and applicability of light-to-camera communications. They either use this new technology to realize specific applications, e.g., localization, by sending repetitive signal patterns, or consider non-line-of-sight scenarios. We however notice that line-of-sight light-to-camera communications has a great potential because it provides a natural way to enable *visual association*, i.e., visually associating the received information with the transmitter's identity. Such capability benefits broader applications, such as augmented reality, advertising, and driver assistance systems. Hence, this paper designs, implements, and evaluates RollingLight, a line-of-sight light-to-camera communication system that enables a light to talk to diverse off-the-shelf rolling shutter cameras. To boost the data rate and enhance reliability, RollingLight addresses the following practical challenges. First, its demodulation algorithm allows cameras with heterogeneous sampling rates to accurately decode high-order frequency modulation in real-time. Second, it incorporates a number of designs to resolve the issues caused by inherently unsynchronized light-to-camera channels. We have built a prototype of RollingLight with USRP-N200, and also implemented a real system with Arduino Mega 2560, both tested with a range of different camera receivers. We also implement a real iOS application to examine our real-time decoding capability. The experimental results show that, even to serve commodity cameras with a large variety of frame rates, RollingLight can still deliver a throughput of 11.32 bytes per second.

## Categories and Subject Descriptors

C.2.1 [**Network Architecture and Design**]: Wireless Communication; B.4.1 [**Data Communications Devices**]; C.3 [**Special-Purpose and Application-Based Systems**]

## Keywords

Visible Light Communications, Camera Communications, Rolling Shutter, Frequency Shift Keying, Smartphones


*MobiSys'15,* May 18–22, 2015, Florence, Italy.

ACM 978-1-4503-3494-5/15/05 ...$15.00.
http://dx.doi.org/10.1145/2742647.2742651 .

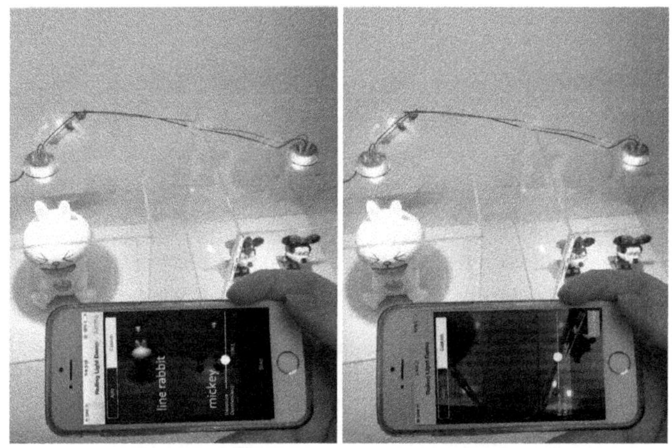


(a) LOS light-to-camera (b) NLOS light-to-camera

**Figure 1—Comparison between LOS and NLOS light-to-camera communications.** Unlike non-line-of-sight light-to-camera systems, where a camera can only observe the mixed reflected light signals, as in Fig. 1(b), line-of-sight systems allow a camera to naturally associate the received information with each transmitting light, as in (a).

## 1. INTRODUCTION

Information received via conventional radio frequency (RF) wireless communication such as WiFi or Bluetooth is often hard to be visually associated with the transmitter's identity, especially when multiple transmitters are located in close proximity. The ability to visually identify which object transmits the received information can enable a number of augmented reality applications, in which the received information associated with different transmitting objects can be combined with the perceived view and rendered at correct locations. For example, as shown in Fig. 1(a), when multiple products are exhibited together, if the information received by a smartphone can be correctly associated with the transmitting objects (or their nearby objects), then the information can be presented to the user in an intuitive way. Near-Field Communication (NFC), though can also identify the transmitter in proximity, does not have the ability to receive information from multiple objects simultaneously due to the limited operational range of a few centimeters.

This paper presents RollingLight, a light-to-camera communication system that enables line-of-sight (LOS) data transmission for a wide range of commodity cameras. Unlike non-line-of-sight light-to-camera systems, where a camera can only observe the mixed reflected light signals, as shown in Fig. 1(b), line-of-sight systems allow a camera to naturally associate the received information with each transmitting light. In particular, when a camera observes a light in LOS, in the image, the group of pixels occupied by the light displays the appearance of the light or the object illuminated by the light, which can be recognized by either human or computer vision techniques. The very same group of pixels also carries the extra information transmitted by that light, as shown in Fig. 1(a). Hence, those pixels combine the two types of information, i.e., visual information and transmitted information, providing a very natural way to *visually associate* the received information with the transmitter's identity. For example, in a museum or exhibition, the light on top of each exhibited object can deliver a brief introduction of that object or an URL link connecting to the detailed guide information.

RollingLight exploits the *rolling shutter* mechanism that exists in most commodity cameras today. Rolling shutter allows a camera to sample the received optical signal multiple times in a single captured image. When a rolling shutter camera receives square waves of different frequencies, the captured images contain bright and dark strips in widths proportional to the inverse of the frequency. As a result, we can use different signal frequencies to represent different data symbols. Although there have been a number of existing light-to-camera systems, they are either designed for non-LOS (NLOS) communications [19] or specific applications (e.g., localization [15]) that only require repetitive and short transmissions. LOS light-to-camera communications however present several new practical challenges that have not yet been investigated.

First, camera sensors have diverse specifications. Even if a transmitter sends a signal of the same frequency, different cameras would observe different strip widths. Existing systems that either have low data rate or support only repetitive transmission can ignore this problem since small error in strip width estimation would not affect the bit error rate. However, to boost the throughput, a high order frequency modulation is needed, in which case small error in strip width estimation would result in a high bit error rate. To address this problem, we modified a pitch detection algorithm (PDA) [8] to accurately estimate the signal frequency, and borrowed the idea of channel estimation from RF-based systems to accurately determine the camera's rolling shutter sampling rate. These designs allow RollingLight to correctly map the observed strip width to the transmitted signal frequency.

In addition, different cameras typically have different frame rates, and thus the transmitter cannot tune its symbol duration to match the frame duration of every camera. As a result, a camera could receive multiple symbols in an image or have symbol losses. Even worse, unlike NLOS links where the stripe pattern is observed in the entire image, as shown in Fig. 1(b), LOS links could capture a light that occupies only a portion of the image, and might experience a higher symbol loss probability. More importantly, while loss probability could be quite stable for NLOS scenarios, it however would be very dynamic for LOS scenarios, depending on the camera's frame rate, image size, exposure duration, and read-out duration. We hence derived the expressions to estimate the loss probabilities of different cameras and various link conditions. This allows an application developer to prevent losses by adding an appropriate level of redundancy for the target devices and environments it wants to serve.

We have implemented RollingLight on the Arduino Mega 2560 board, and developed an iOS decoding application. These are used to evaluate the real-time decoding capability of our design. We have further built a flexible experimental prototype using the USRP N200 radio platform, connected with a special front-end to drive the LED light. This is used to characterize and understand the limitations of the LOS light-to-camera channels with a variety of devices and environments. Our implementation uses high-order frequency-shift-keying-based (FSK-based) modulation and XOR-based parity

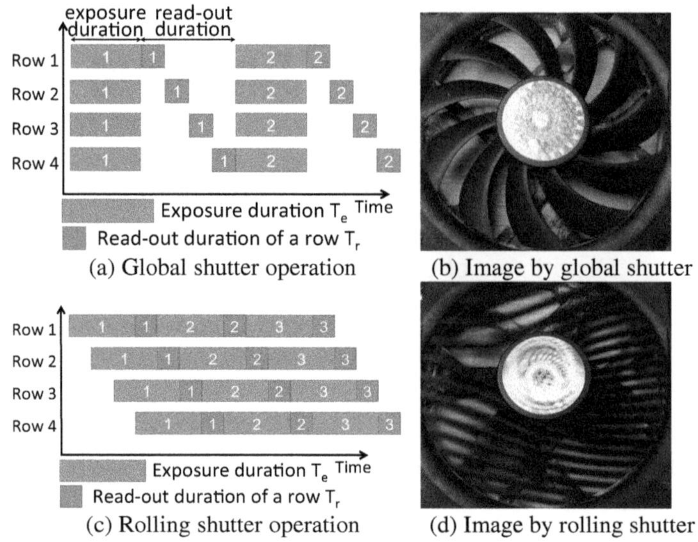


**Figure 2—Comparison between global shutter and rolling shutter.** A rolling-shutter camera exposes right before the read-out. The exposure duration is hence shifted by a fixed amount of *read-out* duration, as shown in (c), resulting in the so-called rolling shutter effect, as shown in (d).

coding. The key findings from our measurements and experiments are as follows:

- Existing rolling shutter cameras have very different sampling rates, ranging from 39.2 to 52.4 read-out's per millisecond among our tested devices. This heterogeneity is closely related to a proper choice of usable frequencies for FSK-based modulation and, hence, the achievable data rate.
- Unlike other demodulation schemes, which either only work in the high or low frequency region, RollingLight's demodulation algorithm is consistently reliable in a wide range of frequencies.
- Even with the overhead of dealing with mixed-symbol frames and symbol losses to ensure reliability for diverse forms of cameras, RollingLight can still achieve a throughput of 11.32 bytes per second. This rate is sufficient to support several indoor applications, such as localization, augmented reality and navigation in museum, exhibition or shopping center.
- The average per image processing time of RollingLight's real-time decoder is 18.15 milliseconds, which is much smaller than the frame duration of most smartphones on today's market.

# 2. PRIMER & CHARACTERISTICS

Before describing our RollingLight design, we give some background about rolling shutter cameras, and use measurements to show some important characteristics.

## 2.1 Rolling Shutter Cameras

There are two types of cameras: 1) global shutter and 2) rolling shutter. Global shutter is commonly implemented on CCD sensors. It exposes all pixels on the sensor simultaneously, as shown in Fig. 2(a), and gathers incoming light over all pixels during the exposure duration. An example image is shown in Fig. 2(b)[1]. Although some CMOS sensors use a global shutter, the majority of

[1] Fig. 2(b) is in fact taken by an iPhone 5 when the fan is not moving, micmicking an image taken by the global shutter.

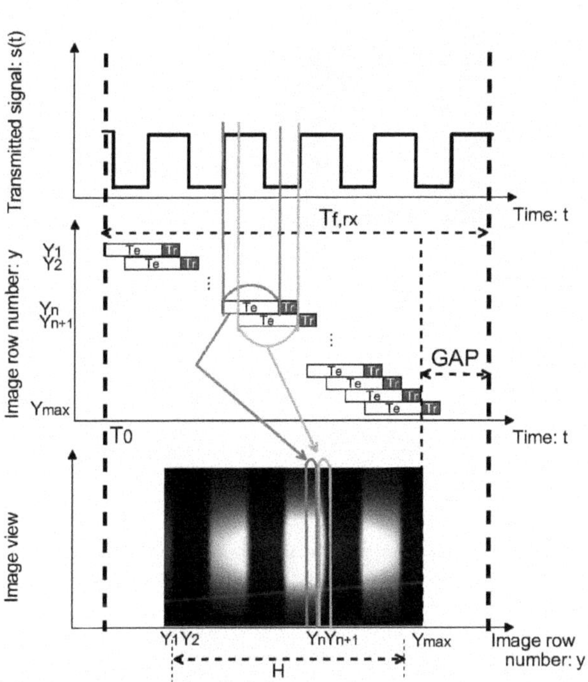


**Figure 3—Receiving operation of a rolling shutter camera.** The top figure shows the transmitted square wave. The middle figure illustrates the exposure and read-out processes. The bottom figure demonstrates the resulting image after 90 degrees counterclockwise rotation.

them found on the market utilize a rolling shutter. One of the key properties of a rolling shutter is its *sequential read-out architecture*. Since rolling shutters do not have storage to cache the accumulated charge during exposure operation, each row of pixels has to be exposed right before the read-out, as shown in Fig. 2(c). Since the read-out procedure of different rows cannot overlap, the exposure duration of a row of pixels is hence shifted by a fixed amount of *read-out duration*, denoted by $T_r$, resulting in the so-called rolling shutter effect. An example image is shown in Fig. 2(d).

Fig. 3(a) illustrates a square wave transmitted by an LED light. For each pixel of a particular row, the incoming intensity modulated signal is integrated for a period of exposure duration, denoted by $T_e$. Let $r(t)$ denote the received signal at time $t$, which includes the signal from the transmitted light and other ambient interference. The intensity of a pixel in the $y$-th row of the image, $I[y]$, is then equal to the total amount of photons received during exposure, which can be expressed as follows:

$$I[y] = \int_{T_0+(y-1)T_r}^{T_0+(y-1)T_r+T_e} r(t)dt, \; 1 \leq y \leq Y_{\max}, \quad (1)$$

where $T_0$ is a reference time corresponding to the start of the exposure duration of the first row in the image, and $Y_{\max}$ is the number of rows in the image. Since the intensity of the accumulated charge changes row by row, the light will appear as bright and dark strips in the image.[2] Note that, for LOS reception, the transmitting light might only illuminate a partial area of the image. For example, in Fig. 3(b), the transmitted signal is only observed in rows $[Y_n, Y_n + H - 1]$, where $H$ represents the height of the image area illuminated by the transmitting light. The corresponding re-

[2]For a special case where the exposure duration happens to be the multiple of the signal period, a rolling shutter camera would not observe strips.

(a) 8000 Hz (b) 4000 Hz (c) 2000 Hz

**Figure 4—Stripe pattern.** Different transmitting frequencies correspond to different strip widths in the received images.

ceived image, after 90-degree counterclockwise rotation, is plotted in Fig. 3(c).

A camera does not expose at all time in a frame duration $T_{f,rx}$, i.e., the inverse of its frame rate. There exists a *time gap* between the end time of the exposure of the last row, $T_0+(Y_{\max}-1)T_r+T_e$, and the start time of the next image frame, $T_0 + T_{f,rx}$. Namely, during this idle time gap of length $T_{f,rx} - (Y_{\max} - 1)T_r - T_e$, the camera is not performing exposure, i.e., not receiving, and hence the transmitted signal during this time is lost. This gap is especially significant when the exposure duration $T_e$ is short. In addition, if the transmitting light only occupies part of the image, a larger portion of the transmitted signal would be lost.[3] Specifically, if a light only occupies rows $[Y_n, Y_n + H - 1]$ in the image, then the signals sent during the exposure of rows $[Y_1, Y_{n-1}]$ and $[Y_n + H, Y_{\max}]$ are missed. This is very different from the NLOS case, where the camera receives the reflected light signals and then the strips are always observed in the whole image. Signal losses in a NLOS link hence only occur during the aforementioned idle time gap. That is, a NLOS link experiences relatively constant losses, while a LOS link might suffer from dynamic losses, depending on not only the idle time gap but also the size and the location of the captured light in the image. Therefore, RollingLight needs to cope with those dynamic signal losses in order to ensure reliable reception for different cameras and various link conditions.

## 2.2 Rolling Shutter Frequency-Shift Keying (RS-FSK) Modulation

RollingLight uses square wave in its modulation. One of the nice properties of square wave is that it only needs two output levels, which avoids complex driving circuitry and reduces the overall system cost. With rolling shutter sampling, a square wave of a certain frequency transmitted by the light would result in a stripe pattern in the image. In addition, different frequencies correspond to different widths of strips, as shown in Fig. 4, and, most importantly, this strip width does not change with the location and the orientation of a camera and how large the light is in an image. In other words, the captured stripe pattern is not distorted due to either perspective distortion or physical light shapes. RollingLight uses different frequencies of square wave to represent different symbols if their corresponding strip widths are distinguishable. This is the common FSK modulation used in many communication systems. Let $\mathcal{F}$ denote the set of frequencies used for modulation. Then, each symbol can represent $\lfloor \log_2 |\mathcal{F}| \rfloor$ data bits. By increasing the number of frequencies, we can increase the order of modulation, and hence the data rate.

The receiving camera can demodulate the signal if it can measure the strip width of the received image and convert it back to the trans-

[3]Note that digital zoom in does not help with this symbol loss problem. This is because it gets a closer view of a particular area without adjusting a camera's lens. Thus, the rows of pixels occupied by the light and the duration of signal reception are both unchanged.

(a) iPhone 5c (width: 108 pixels) (b) iPhone 5s (width: 164 pixels) (c) iPhone 6Plus (width: 158 pixels)

**Figure 5—Devices receive different stripe patterns.** Different devices observe different strip widths even when the transmitted frequency is the same, 250 Hz.

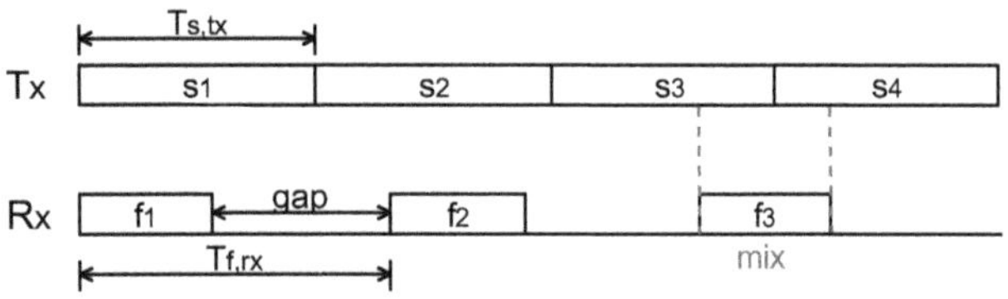


(a) Case 1: frame duration $T_{f,rx}$ > symbol duration $T_{s,tx}$

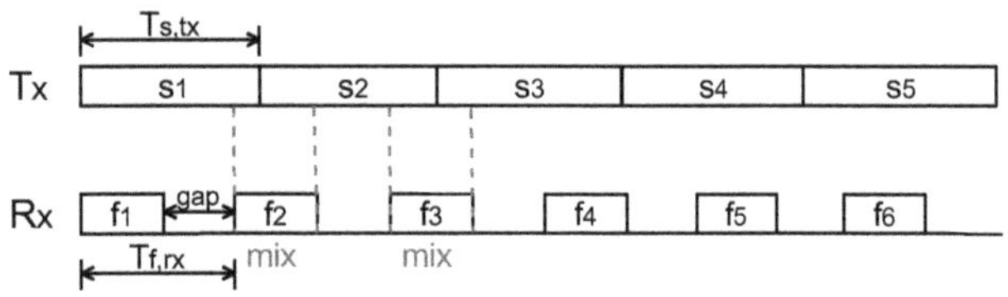


(b) Case 2: frame duration $T_{f,rx}$ < symbol duration $T_{s,tx}$

**Figure 6—Mixed-symbol due to unsynchronization.** In unsynchronized light-to-camera channels, a received frame might contain a mixture of multiple symbols.

mitted frequency. While the basic idea is simple, there are however a number of practical challenges needed to be solved. First, for a given transmitting light, different cameras might observe different strip widths because each camera has a different read-out duration $T_r$. To verify this, we use different smartphones with the same resolution (2,448 rows) to detect the stripe pattern of a light transmitting a 250-Hz square wave. For fair comparison, we adjust the location of the smartphones such that the light occupies the whole image, i.e., it occupies the same number of rows. Fig. 5 shows that the number of strips observed by different cameras is not constant, which indicates that the strip width changes with different devices. Second, the strip width in an image is always an integer, while the corresponding signal period is a real number. This difference introduces error in strip width estimation. We will discuss in §3.2 how RollingLight's demodulation copes with device diversity and enhances the accuracy in strip width estimation.

## 2.3 Unsynchronized Communications

Cameras on the market usually have different frame rates. Not only this, the frame rate of a camera could even fluctuate. For example, as mentioned by [11], the frame rate of the camera on Samsung Galaxy S3 fluctuates between 21 and 29 fps with a mean of 25 fps. Thus, it is especially difficult for a light-to-camera system to synchronize the transmitting light with a wide variety of cameras. That is, the transmitting symbol rate, i.e., the inverse of the symbol duration $T_{s,tx}$, might not be equal to a camera's frame rate, i.e., the inverse of the frame duration $T_{f,rx}$. Such an unsynchronized communication channel is very likely to experience the *mixed-symbol frame* and *symbol loss* problems. To understand the causes of these problems, we classify the unsynchronized scenarios into two cases.

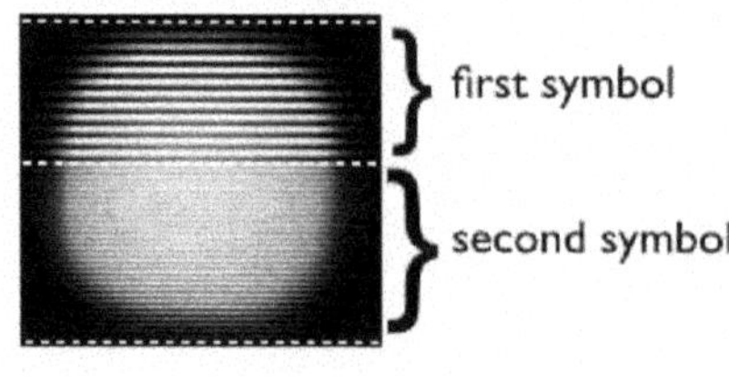


**Figure 7—Example of a mixed-symbol frame.** Different strip widths observed in a frame that contains two partial symbols.

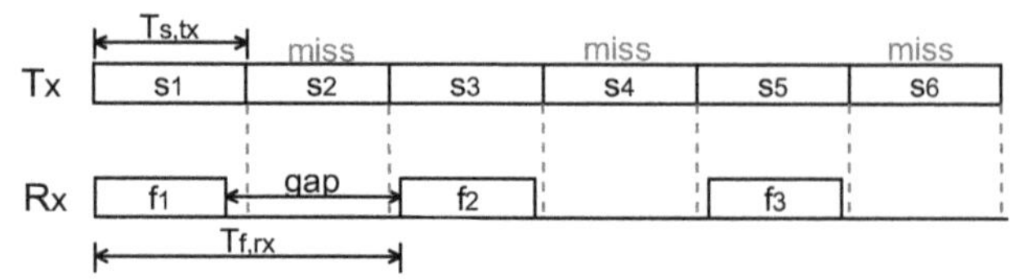


**Figure 8—Symbol loss due to unsynchronization.** Some symbols are lost during the idle time of discontinuous receiving. (Only occurs in Case 1.)

- *Case 1: When the frame duration is longer than the symbol duration, i.e.,* $T_{f,rx} > T_{s,tx}$.
- *Case 2: When the frame duration is shorter than the symbol duration, i.e.,* $T_{f,rx} < T_{s,tx}$.

The *mixed-symbol frame* problem refers to the scenario of receiving a mixture of two or more consecutive transmitted symbols in the same image frame. This problem occurs in both unsynchronized cases. As shown in Fig. 6(a), an example of case 1, frame $f_3$ contains two transmitted symbols $s_3$ and $s_4$. Similarly, as shown in Fig. 6(b), an example of case 2, frame $f_3$ contains two transmitted symbols $s_2$ and $s_3$. For an image with mixed symbols, the receiver will observe different strip widths in different parts of the image, as shown in Fig. 7. Even when the transmitting symbol rate is exactly the same with the receiving frame rate, the mixed-symbol frame problem can still occur if the boundaries of the transmitted symbols and the captured frames are not perfectly aligned.

On the other hand, the *symbol loss* problem means that some transmitted symbols are not detected in any received frames. This problem only occurs in case 1, i.e., $T_{f,rx} > T_{s,tx}$. The root of this problem is the characteristic of a camera's discontinuous receiving, as mentioned in §2.1. Recall that there exists a time gap between the end of exposure in this frame and the start of exposure in the next frame. Then, when the length of this gap is longer than a symbol duration, some symbols could entirely be dropped. For example, as shown in Fig. 8, symbols $s_2$, $s_4$ and $s_6$ are lost.

To check how severe the above problems could be in unsynchronized light-to-camera channels, we mimic the measurements performed in [11]. Specifically, we configure the light to transmit square wave with several different symbol rates, each of which is used to send 100 symbols. PointGrey Flea3 camera [2] is used to receive the signal and record 30-fps video. We then use our demodulation scheme, which will be introduced in §3.2, to offline decode the frames. Fig. 9 maps the frame index shown in y-axis to the corresponding detected symbol indices in x-axis. In each figure, we use blue and red circles to represent the first and second symbol detected in a frame, respectively. We can see from the figures that mixed-symbol frames exist in most of the cases, even when the frame rate is the same as the symbol rate, as shown in Fig. 9(c). In addition, different levels of unsynchronization lead to different symbol loss ratios, as shown in Fig. 9(e) and Fig. 9(f). We

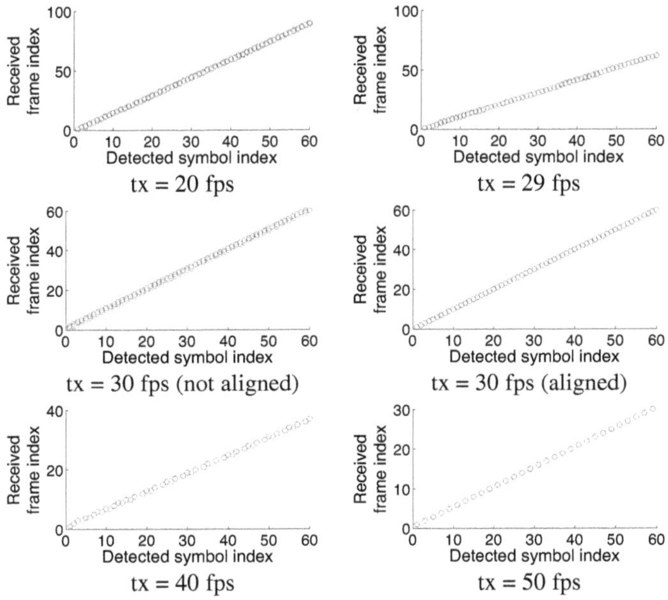


**Figure 9—Symbol losses and mixed symbols caused by different frame rates.** Frame patterns received by a camera with a 30 fps frame rate under different transmitting symbol rates. Blue circles represent the first symbol detected in a frame, while red circles represent the second symbol detected in a frame.

will hence describe in §3.3 how RollingLight addresses the mixed-symbol frame problem. We will also derive the loss probability of cameras with heterogeneous settings. The derivation enables RollingLight to determine a proper amount of redundancy that ensures successful decoding in most of commodity cameras.

# 3. ROLLINGLIGHT DESIGN

## 3.1 Overview

RollingLight's transmitting light first maps data bits into symbols, each of which represents a number of bits. Each symbol is then represented by square wave of one of the frequencies in $\mathcal{F}$ and of duration $T_{s,tx}$. Every $n$ data symbols are used to generate a parity symbol, which is appended to the end of these $n$ data symbols. The value $n$ is picked based on the estimation of the symbol loss probability (see §3.3). We then add a symbol splitter (SS) to the beginning of each symbol in order to address the mixed-symbol frame problem (see §3.3). Finally, a group of symbols are formed as a packet, which is preceded by a preamble used for estimating the read-out duration and performing demodulation. The light then transmits the resultant square wave, as shown in Fig. 10.

RollingLight's receiving camera captures a series of images. It first utilizes a number of image processing techniques to crop the areas occupied by different transmitting lights from each image (see §3.4). It then detects the splitters in order to find the symbol boundary. Each transmitted symbol might only present in a single image or across multiple consecutive images. Hence, for each symbol, we find the image that contains the longest segment of that symbol. Finally, the longest segment of all the transmitted symbols are demodulated into codeword bits (see §3.2), which are then decoded into data bits.

## 3.2 RollingLight's Demodulation

In order to demodulate the symbols, we first need to know the relationship between the transmitted frequency $f$ and the strip width

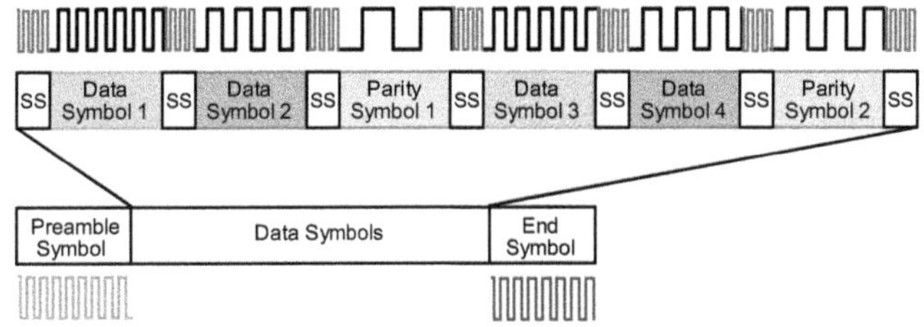


**Figure 10—Packet Format of RollingLight.** A preamble symbol is used to learn the read-out duration. Symbols are separated by a symbol splitter (SS). This example adds one parity symbol for every two data symbols. Green, red and blue symbols represent the symbols with a sequence number 1, 2 and 3, respectively.

$W$. Here, the strip width is defined as the number of pixels occupied by a bright or dark strip in a received image. Note that, for a square wave of frequency $f$, the duration of a complete cycle is $1/f$ seconds. Therefore, for every $1/f$ seconds a camera exposes, it should be able to read out a pair of bright and dark strips in the received image. On the other hand, recall that the time a camera spends to read out a row of pixels is its read-out duration $T_r$. Therefore, in theory, the strip width can be found by

$$W_{real} = \frac{\frac{1}{2f}}{T_r} = \frac{1}{2fT_r}. \quad (2)$$

Note that the strip width derived from the above theoretical equation is a real number. However, in practice, a receiver can only measure the number of rows occupied by a strip $W$ as an integer estimate of $W_{real}$, and demodulate the symbol by

$$f' = \frac{1}{2WT_r}. \quad (3)$$

Unfortunately, knowing the above relationship is still insufficient for a receiver to demodulate the signals. The reason is that the read-out duration of each camera $T_r$ is usually an unknown parameter. To address this issue, we exploit an idea analogue to *channel estimation* used in many RF-based communication systems. In particular, $T_r$ can be considered as the *channel* of a light-to-camera link in our system. To estimate this *channel*, we let the transmitting light send a *known preamble* at the beginning of a packet. This preamble can be used to estimate the read-out duration $T_r$.[4] Let $f_p$ be the frequency of the preamble; the read-out duration can be estimated by

$$T_r' = \frac{1}{2f_pW_p}. \quad (4)$$

Then, any camera can use its learned read-out duration $T_r'$ to demodulate a transmitted symbol by first estimating the transmitted frequency $f'$ based on Eq. 3 and mapping $f'$ to the closest one in the frequency set $\mathcal{F}$. Another thing worth noting is that this preamble can also be used to determine a proper exposure duration. Specifically, to avoid overexposure, we can start from the smallest exposure duration setting, and gradually increase the value until a successful detection.

We can also observe from Eq. 2 that the set of usable frequencies $\mathcal{F}$ should be carefully selected according to two factors: 1) the estimation error of the strip width, and 2) the maximal and the minimal

[4]We let the light transmit with a frequency that is higher than cameras' Nyquist sampling rate when the light is idle, i.e., sending nothing. As a result, cameras do not see any strip when the light is idle, and hence can use image processing techniques to locate the start of a preamble. In addition, to prevent from missing a preamble, we send the preamble for 3 symbol durations.

strip width that can be detected by most of commodity cameras. Say a camera can detect the strip width from $W_{\min}$ to $W_{\max}$ with a maximal estimation error $\omega$, i.e., $|W_{real} - W| \le \omega$. Then, we can select the frequency set as

$$\mathcal{F}=\{\frac{1}{2(W_{\min}+2k\omega)T_r} : \forall k=0,1,\cdots,\lfloor\frac{W_{\max}-W_{\min}}{2\omega}\rfloor-1\}. \tag{5}$$

By doing this, the difference between the strip widths of two consecutive frequencies is a constant $2\omega$. This hence allows us to tolerate an error in strip width estimation between $\pm\omega$.

To improve the probability of correct demodulation, we need to enhance the accuracy of the estimated strip width $W$. To do so, we adopt a well-known pitch detection algorithm, YIN [8], to find the period of the periodical signals in the received image. YIN is commonly used to find the fundamental period of audio signal in speech or music. Note that RollingLight modulates data by frequencies with a constant gap of different time-domain signal periods (i.e., constant strip width difference). Therefore, YIN, which performs *time-domain auto-correlation*, is especially suitable for our application, as compared to FFT transformation that identifies the peak frequency. Another advantage of the YIN-based algorithm is that it naturally addresses the non-uniform brightness issue of a captured light. In particular, previous work [18, 11] has observed that the center of the light received in the image is usually brighter than the corners. The YIN-based algorithm [8] already incorporates several tricks to handle the waveform with slowly changing DC, i.e., surface with non-uniform brightness.

**YIN-based strip width estimation:** We start by summing up all the pixels in each row to obtain an one-dimensional signal.

$$I[y] = \sum_{x=1}^{X_{\max}} I[x][y], \tag{6}$$

where $I[x][y]$ is the intensity (luminance)[5] of the pixel at location $(x, y)$ in the received image. This operation averages out the noises in different columns of pixels. We can then use the following difference function $d_\Delta(\delta)$ to find the period of the periodical signal $I[y]$, i.e., twice of the strip width $2W$.

$$d_\Delta(\delta) = \sum_{y=1}^{H/2-1} (I[y] - I[y+\delta])^2. \tag{7}$$

Ideally, if $I[y]$ is a clean square wave without noise, $d_\Delta(\delta) = 0$ when $\delta$ is a multiple of the signal period, i.e., $\delta = 2kW$ for all $k = 1, 2, 3, \cdots$ in our considered problem. Intuitively, to find the signal period, we can search for the smallest integer value $\delta$ from $[1, H/2]$ such that $d_\Delta(\delta) = 0$. However, the received signals are usually disturbed by noise, and hence the difference function is very unlikely to be exactly zero at the period. This makes the task of searching the first period in the disturbed signal more challenging. To cope with this, we adopt the tricks proposed in [8] to find the first period $\delta^*$, and estimate the strip width by $W = \delta^*/2$.

The above searching procedure only considers the integer values of $\delta$. However, as derived in Eq. 2, the actual signal period of the signal $2W_{real}$ is typically a real number, which is proportional to the inverse of the read-out duration, i.e., the sampling rate. Hence, we further use parabolic interpolation to improve accuracy of the strip width estimation as follows.

$$W = \hat{\delta}'/2 = \frac{\delta^*}{2} + \frac{y_{+1} - y_{-1}}{4(2y_0 - y_{+1} - y_{-1})} \tag{8}$$

, where $y_{-1} = d_\Delta(\delta^* - 1)$, $y_0 = d_\Delta(\delta^*)$, and $y_{+1} = d_\Delta(\delta^* + 1)$.

[5]If the obtained image is in RGB instead of grayscale, it needs to be converted to obtain the luminance information.

## 3.3 Dealing with Unsynchronized Channels

As mentioned in §2.3, unsynchronized light-to-camera channels cause *mixed-symbol* frames and *symbol losses*. We now describe how RollingLight addresses these two issues.

**Separating mixed symbols in an image:** Receiving a frame with mixed symbols is a very frequent event, which cannot be neglected. An image that contains a mixture of symbols with different frequencies could cause YIN-based strip width estimation to fail. In order for a receiver to separate those mixed symbols in an image, RollingLight inserts a short *symbol splitter* before the beginning of each data symbol, as shown in Fig. 10. A splitter is sent with a given time period $T_s$ and a known frequency $f_s$, which is not used by the preamble and data symbols. To detect the location of the splitter in an image, the receiver first uses its read-out duration $T_r$, which is learned from the preamble, and the known frequency $f_s$ to calculate the expected strip width of the splitter, $W_s = 1/2f_sT_r$. The receiver can further estimate the number of pixels occupied by a splitter as $H_s = T_s/T_r$. Given the information about the expected strip width $W_s$ and the size of a splitter $H_s$, we can locate the splitter by an approach similar to our YIN-based algorithm. Specifically, we calculate the difference function of the period $2W_s$ for a group of $H_s$ pixels starting from the $i$-th row as follows.

$$d_\Delta(2W_s, i) = \sum_{y=i}^{i+H_s/2-1} (I[y] - I[y+2W_s])^2.$$

The difference value $d_\Delta(2W_s, i)$ would approximate to zero if the splitter locates in the $i$-th row. Therefore, the most possible location of the splitter in an image can be found by

$$i^* = \arg\min_i d_\Delta(2W_s, i),$$

and we determine that the $i^*$-th row is a splitter if $d_\Delta(2W_s, i^*)$ is smaller than a threshold. In our measurements, we found that the splitter can be detected with a fairly high probability when it contains 6 pairs of strips. We hence use this as the default setting in our experiments.

**Recovering from symbol losses:** To ensure that a receiver can recover from symbol losses, we append a parity symbol after every $n$ data symbols by XOR-ing those $n$ data symbols. Then, if any of those $n$ data symbol is lost, it can be recovered by XOR-ing the remaining $(n-1)$ data symbols with the parity symbol. However, there are still two open problems: *i)* How much redundancy is required to serve most commodity devices? and *ii)* How do we determine the location of the lost symbol so that we can put the recovered symbol in right location?

To answer question *i)*, we need to first understand how many losses would be observed by different devices. We note that a symbol loss event occurs if the whole symbol is sent during the receiver's idle gap, implying that the symbol duration is shorter than the duration of the idle gap, as shown in Fig. 8. Therefore, if the symbol duration $T_{s,tx}$ is fixed, the symbol loss probability that a receiver observes can be estimated by

$$\begin{aligned} P_{\text{loss}} &= \max\left(\frac{T_{gap} - T_{s,tx}}{T_{f,rx}}, 0\right) \\ &= \max\left(\frac{T_{f,rx} - (H-1)T_r - T_e - T_{s,tx}}{T_{f,rx}}, 0\right). \end{aligned} \tag{9}$$

We can see from the above equation that different cameras could experience quite different loss rates due to their heterogeneous parameters, e.g., $T_r$ and $T_e$, and the uncertain size of the light cap-

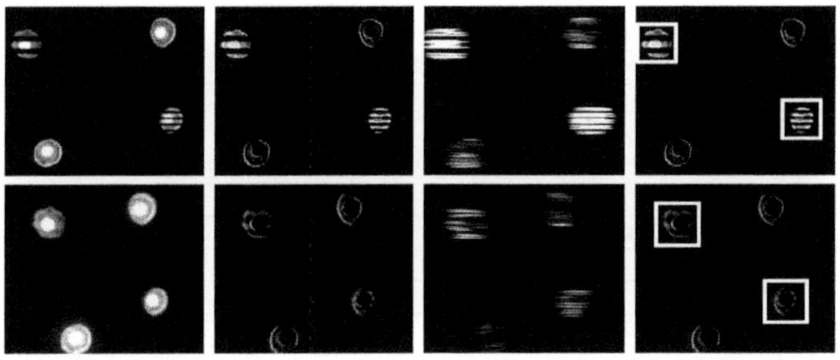

(a) Original (b) Denoise (c) Haar-like (d) Result

**Figure 11—Image processing for locating RollingLight's transmitting lights.** The top row shows the images taken with exposure duration 1/5000 sec, while the bottom row shows the images taken with exposure duration 1/400 sec.

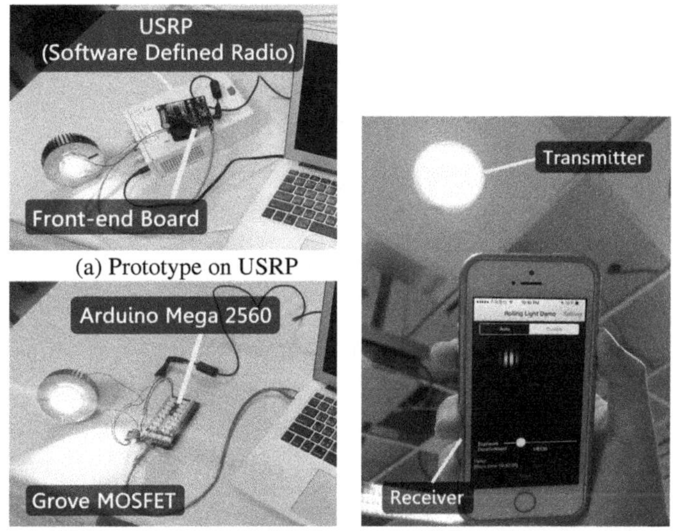


(a) Prototype on USRP

(b) Real system on Arduino (c) Experiment scenario

**Figure 12—Experimental setup.** We implemented RollingLight's transmitter on both USRP and Arduino systems, and experimented using different receiving cameras. We also implement an iOS decoding application to check real-time decoding capability.

tured in the image, $H$. Note that light-to-camera communication is an one-way communication link, via which the transmitter cannot get any information from the receivers. As a result, it is very hard for a light to dynamically adapt the level of redundancy required by a specific receiver. To trade-off between compatibility and achievable data rate, a system designer can find the maximal loss rate $P_{loss}$ observed by a finite set of devices that the system targets to serve. To ensure that this set of devices can be resilient to symbol losses, we can add one parity symbol for every $\lfloor 1/P_{loss} \rfloor$ data symbols.

To solve the second problem, we label each data symbol, including those parity symbols, with one of the sequence numbers $\{0, 1, 2\}$, as shown in Fig. 10, where three different colors of symbols represent three different sequence numbers. That is, the sequence number of the $k$-th symbol is $\mod(k, 3)$. Three sequence numbers are already sufficient for RollingLight because of the following reasons. First, since the loss pattern in light-to-camera channels is quite regular, instead of random loss. Second, from our measurements performed on diverse devices (see §5.2), the maximum loss probability is about 0.5. The two reasons together imply that we do not need to worry about consecutive losses.

The three sequence numbers, in theory, can be represented by 1.5 bits. However, if we simply add digital bits as a sequence number right before a data symbol, it would require a 2-bit overhead, which is a waste. To efficiently utilize the available bandwidth, we exploit the following trick. We partition the set of available modulation frequencies into three equal-sized groups, $\mathcal{F}_1$, $\mathcal{F}_2$ and $\mathcal{F}_3$. If the sequence number of a symbol is $i$, we modulate the symbol using one of the frequencies in $\mathcal{F}_i$. Then, the receiver can easily detect the sequence number by checking which group the demodulated frequency belongs to. By doing this, we can improve the number of bits per symbol from $\log_2(|\mathcal{F}|) - 2 = \log_2(|\mathcal{F}|/4)$ to $\log_2(|\mathcal{F}|/3)$.

So far, we only discuss the case when a symbol is entirely dropped. There exists another case that a symbol is received, but is demodulated incorrectly since the number of received strips is not enough to get an accurate strip width estimation. In this case, we can also try to utilize the parity symbol to correct the erroneous data symbol. However, theoretically, the parity can only be used to "detect" error, instead of "correcting" error, because we have no idea which data symbol is in error. Hence, when we detect an error in a chunk of data symbols, we guess that the symbol in a chuck with the smallest number of strips is in error, and use the parity symbol to correct it. Given that the parity symbols could also be used to correct low-confidence symbols, we can slightly increase the amount of redundancy by adding one parity symbol for every $\lfloor 1/(P_{loss} + P_{err} - P_{loss}P_{err}) \rfloor$ data symbols, where $P_{err}$ is a symbol error probability we want to protect.

## 3.4 Image Pre-processing

Before measuring the strip width for demodulation, RollingLight's receiver performs a number of image processing techniques to denoise the received images and find the boundary of the target transmitting lights. For example, the images taken with a larger exposure duration might have background noise. In addition, the appearance of the light (e.g., repeated lamp pattern) might also interfere the stripe pattern in the captured image. Therefore, we first apply a noise subtraction technique to reduce the noise. In particular, we generate a background image by averaging the latest few received images, and then subtract the background from the current image to obtain the denoised image (Fig. 11(b)). To identify the lights that display the stripe pattern, we apply the haar-like filter [23] on the denoised image. After haar-like filtering, the pixel values of the areas occupied by conventional lights will decrease, as shown in Fig. 11(c). We can finally apply Luxapose's boundary detection mechanisms [15] on the resulting image to locate the boundary of RollingLight's transmitting lights. We refer the readers to [15] for the detailed boundary detection techniques. Fig. 11(d) illustrates the final denoised images overlaid with the boundary of the detected transmitting lights.

More sophisticated detection and tracking algorithms based on computer vision techniques can be utilized if necessary. Note that only denoising needs to be performed per frame. We will show in §5.3 that denoising can be done in real-time. All the other pre-processing is an one-time job in the beginning of transmissions. Their complexity hence does not affect real-time decoding.

# 4. IMPLEMENTATION

We implemented two RollingLight prototypes: The first one is a flexible experimental prototype, built with USRP N200 [1] software defined radio, as shown in Fig. 12(a). The flexibility allows us to examine RollingLight's performance in a variety of scenarios. The other one is built with the Arduino Mega 2560 board [13], as shown

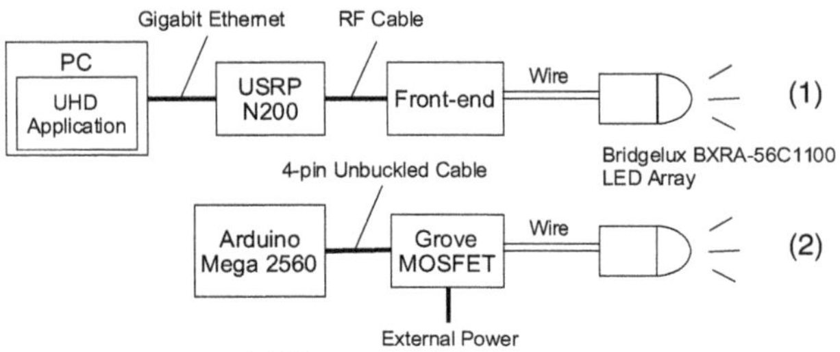


(a) Transmitter components

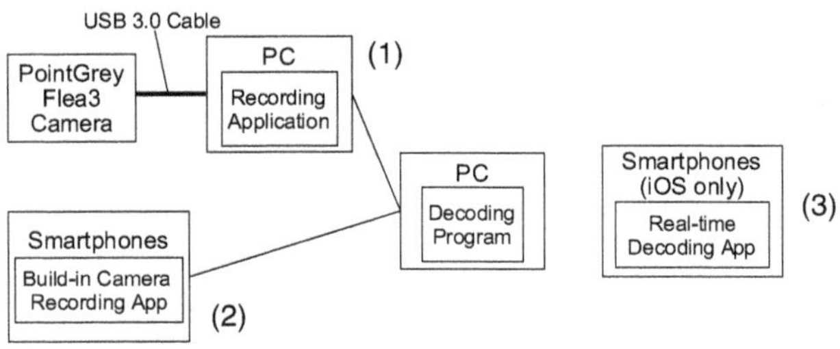


(b) Receiver components

**Figure 13—System components of the transmitter and receiver.**

in Fig. 12(b). This is close to a real system and is used to verify RollingLight's real-time decoding ability. In the flexible prototype, the transmitting light is connected to a USRP N200 via a special front-end board, as shown in Fig. 13(a). We implement in USRP all the transmission components of RollingLight, including modulation, preamble/splitter insertion, and parity coding. The USRP generates voltage varying signals with a sampling rate of 1 MHz, which is then converted to current varying signals by the front-end and used to drive the LED light. On the other hand, we also implement all the components in an Arduino Mega 2560 board, which is connected to a MOSFET component that amplifies the signal to a proper voltage level for an LED light. The Mega 2560's microcontroller has hardware support to generate pulse width modulation (PWM), and thus can be used to generate square waves of different frequencies. Unless otherwise specified, we set the default symbol rate to 30 symbols per second. We test our design using different types of LEDs, such as Bridgelux bxra-56c1100 LED Array.

On the receiver side, we experiment using a number of devices, including an experimental USB camera, PointGrey Flea3 camera [2], and different smartphones, such as Apple iPhone 5s, HTC New One, and Samsung Galaxy S4, as shown in Fig. 13(b). The experimental USB camera allows us to check the performance for various settings, such as different exposure durations and frame rates. To check RollingLight's real-time decoding capability, we develop all the decoding components, including image pre-processing, splitter detection, demodulation and loss recovery, as a real application on iOS devices. For all the other devices, we record video and perform offline decoding. To speed up the decoding process in the iOS application, we implement the application using multiple threads. One thread reads the images captured by the camera, and puts them into a pending queue. The other thread pulls the buffered images from the pending queue, and performs demodulation and decoding.

# 5. RESULTS

In this section, we first perform extensive measurements that help us to understand the characteristics and limitations of LOS light-to-camera channels. We then experimentally evaluate the performance of RollingLight. The measurements and experiments are carried out in the indoor testbed environments shown in Fig. 12(c), and are designed to answer the following questions:

- How large is the strip width estimation error, and how does it affect the achievable throughput?
- How does RollingLight's demodulation perform, compared to other schemes?
- What is RollingLight's achievable throughput in different environments for a variety of cameras?
- Can RollingLight's decoding be done in real-time?

**Table 1—Timing Parameters of Different Devices**

| | Image Resolution ($X_{\max}$ x $Y_{\max}$) | Frame Rate (fps) | Measured Read-out Duration ($\mu$s) | Time Gap (ms) (Percentage of Frame Duration) |
|---|---|---|---|---|
| Point Grey Flea3 | 2048x1080 | 30 | 14.73 | 17.42 (52.27%) |
| Apple iPhone 6 Plus | 1920x1080 | 30 | 21.42 | 10.20 (30.60%) |
| Apple iPhone 5s | 1920x1080 | 29.98 | 20.65 | 11.03 (33.10%) |
| HTC New One | 1920x1080 | 29.94 | 19.08 | 12.79 (38.30%) |
| Samsung Galaxy S4 | 1920x1080 | 29.93 | 25.53 | 5.84 (17.48%) |

## 5.1 Characterizing LOS Light-to-Camera Links

### *5.1.1 Estimated Timing Parameters*

We first measure the timing parameters of different devices on the market, including the frame rate, the read-out duration and the idle gap.

*Measurement Setting:* We let the light repetitively send the preamble, i.e., the square wave of frequency 5,600 Hz, and, hence, there is no need to worry about the symbol duration here. We record the video captured by each device, and find the frame rate of each device outputted by the ffmpeg video decoder. Each device then uses the received signals to learn its read-out duration based on Eq. 4. To improve the accuracy of read-out duration estimation, we try to decrease the exposure duration of a device, as a result increasing the intensity difference between bright and dark strips. To do so, we manually set the exposure duration of the Flea camera to the minimum value. However, the exposure duration of the tested smartphones cannot be configured manually. Thus, we reduce the distance of the light-to-camera link so that the camera can automatically pick a low exposure duration.

*Results:* Table 1 summarizes the timing parameters of the tested devices. Our key findings are as follows.

- The frame rates of different cameras are slightly different, but are all close to 30 fps. We hence use the symbol rate 30 symbols per second in all the later measurements and experiments.
- The read-out duration of different devices ranges from 19 $\mu$s to 25.5 $\mu$s, which verifies the need for each device to learn its "channel" in order to accurately detect the frequency-modulated signals.
- Due to heterogeneity in devices' read-out duration, devices could experience very different idle gaps, and could lose different amounts of information. In addition, in the case that the transmitting light does not illuminate all the rows in the image, this time gap could further increase. Even if the transmitter sets the symbol rate similar to most of the devices, some devices might still see symbol loss when the size of the captured size is small and the exposure duration is short. Hence, a transmitting light should add a redundancy reliable enough for all the devices and target scenarios it wants to serve. For example, say we hope that

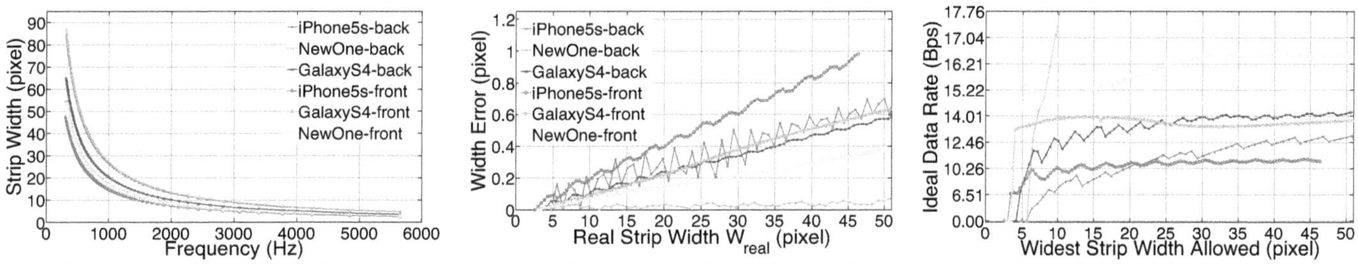


(a) Strip widths observed by different cameras (b) Error in strip width detection (c) Ideal achievable data rate

**Figure 14—Available frequencies.** Measurement results of different devices for frequency set selection. The set of usable frequencies is chosen according to both the received strip widths and the width detection error of diverse devices.

any camera can reliably receive the information if it captures the light with at least $H$ rows of pixels. Then, we need to use $H$ and the measured timing parameters of different cameras to estimate $P_{loss}$ in the worst case and add redundancy accordingly.

### 5.1.2 Required Frequency Spacing

Recall that the set of usable frequencies should be determined based on 1) the strip widths that can be detected by cameras, and 2) the spacing required by two consecutive frequencies, as mentioned in Sec. 3.2. Therefore, we next use measurements to identify the suitable set of frequencies that can be detected by most commodity devices on the market.

*Measurement settings:* The light modulates the symbols using a series of frequencies between 300 Hz and 5,600 Hz, and continuously sends the modulated signals with a symbol duration 1/30 seconds. Each device captures the light with a size of around 1,000 rows of pixels, and uses the preamble to learn its read-out duration.

*Results:* Fig. 14(a) plots the strip width detected by each different camera for various frequencies of the signal. The figures show that, for a given frequency, different cameras have a distinct read-out duration, and hence could observe a very different strip width. The difference is especially large in the low frequency region, which corresponds to a wide strip. This implies that, without knowing the read-out duration, a device cannot decode the frequency-modulated signals, and channel estimation becomes necessary for realizing high-order frequency modulation. In addition, we should apply the following strategy to pick the lowest and highest frequencies.

- In short, to pick the lowest frequency $f_{\min}$, we need to know the minimal detectable frequency of a device $i$, denoted by $f^i_{\min}$, and select the most conservative one, $f_{\min} = \max_i f^i_{\min}$. Given a fixed LED size in the image, the number of strips observed by different cameras will be different. Because any camera requires at least a few pairs of dark and bright strips to detect their period, the lowest detectable frequency for each camera is hence also different. For example, if we need at least 6 strips (i.e., 3 pairs) in a captured light occupying 300 rows of pixels, the widest strip we allow is 50 pixel. We should pick $1/100T_r^{\min}$ as the lowest frequency, where $T_r^{\min}$ is the shortest possible read-out duration in the target devices.

- On the other hand, to pick the highest frequency $f_{\max}$, we need to know the maximal detectable frequency of a device $i$, denoted by $f^i_{\max}$, and select the most conservative one, $f_{\max} = \min_i f^i_{\max}$. Say we expect that a camera should capture the light with a strip width of at least 6 pixels. Then, we should pick $1/12T_r^{\max}$ as the highest frequency, where $T_r^{\max}$ is the longest possible read-out duration in the target devices.

We next check what is the frequency spacing resilient to the error in strip width estimation. Fig. 14(b) plots the estimation error for various strip widths. Since, in this measurement, the frequencies of the transmitted symbols are known by each device, we can use the learned channel $T_r$ to calculate the real strip width by $W_{real} = 1/2fT_r$. The estimation error is defined as $|W_{real} - W|$, where $W$ is the width measured from the received images based on the YIN algorithm. The results show that the error of some devices fluctuates as the frequency changes, since the error due to discretization is periodic with respect to the signal period and hence the frequency. In addition, a wider strip suffers from a larger error. This is because, when the LED size in an image is fixed, a wider strip leads to a fewer number of strips, as a result decreasing the accuracy of the YIN algorithm. However, the estimation error is bounded by one pixel for the entire range of the tested frequencies. We can hence set the gap between the strip widths of two consecutive frequencies to two pixel, and determine the frequency set based on Eq. 5.

We finally want to check the ideal achievable data rate of each camera when we customize the optimal frequency set $\mathcal{F}$ for that camera. In particular, for each camera with a read-out duration $T_r$, $f_{\min}$ is set to $1/2T_r$ and $f_{\max}$ is set to $1/2W_{\max}T_r$, where $W_{max}$ is the widest width allowed. The optimal frequency set of each camera can be chosen based on Eq. 5 by setting $\omega$ to the maximal estimation error it experiences. The achievable data rate is then computed by $\log_2(|\mathcal{F}|/3)$ because we use three sequence numbers. Fig. 14(c) shows that the ideal achievable rate of different devices when the widest strip width we allow varies from 1 pixel to 100 pixels. A camera with a smaller error in strip width estimation can achieve a higher rate. In general, the achievable rate increases when we allow a wider strip. It however has a limit because the allowed strip width is eventually constrained by the resolution of an image. Fortunately, we can observe from the figure that the data rate converges quickly when the allowed strip width increases. Hence, in our system implementation, we set the narrowest and widest strip width to 5 pixels and 100 pixels, respectively, with a spacing of 2 pixels, which corresponds to a set of 48 available frequencies.

### 5.1.3 Demodulation Error Probability

We next compare the performance of our YIN width estimation algorithm with two baseline approaches: *i)* DIP-based scheme, and *ii)* FFT-based scheme. All the schemes sum up all the pixels in each row, and generate an one-dimensional signal as shown in Eq. 6. The DIP-based scheme uses the average value as a threshold to partition the signals into two parts, dark strips and bright strips, and output the average width of all the strips. The FFT-based scheme uses Fourier Transform to find the frequency of the stripe pattern (i.e.,

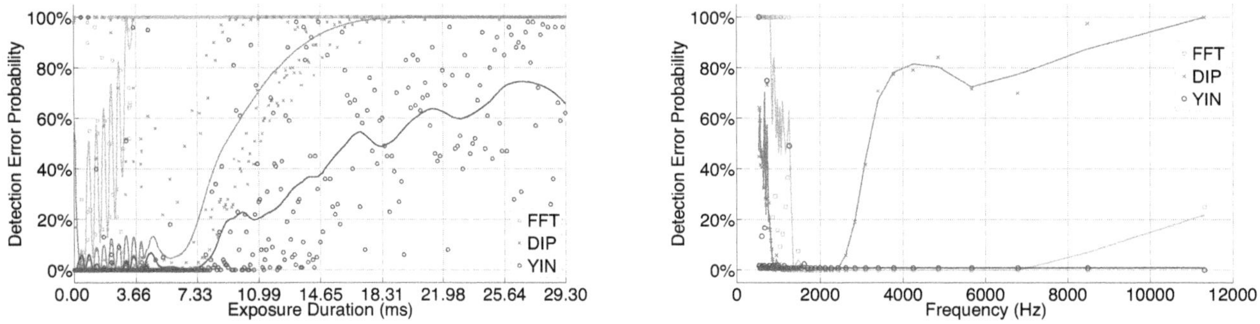


(a) Error for different exposure duration (frequency: 3,400 Hz) (b) Error for different frequencies (exposure duration: 29.28 ms)

**Figure 15—Detection error of different width detection algorithms.** The YIN-based algorithm can support a relatively high exposure duration and a wide range of frequencies.

1/2W), which actually equals to the frequency of the transmitted signal $f$ multiplied by the read-out duration $T_r$.

*Experimental setting:* We compare the error in strip width estimation of three schemes in various scenarios, e.g., different exposure duration and different transmitted frequencies. Since smartphones do not allow us to fine tune the parameters, we use the Flea camera in this experiment. The camera captures the light occupying the entire image. The estimated width is deemed incorrect if the estimation error exceeds one pixel, i.e., $|W_{real} - W| > 1$.

*Results:* Fig. 15(a) plots the estimation error probability for different settings of exposure duration, ranging from 0.01473 ms to 29.28 ms. The transmitted frequency is fixed to 3,400 Hz in this experiment. There exist some periodical jumps because the camera can hardly observe the stripe pattern when the exposure duration happens to be a multiple of the period of the square wave. In general, the estimation error increases when the exposure duration increases because the difference between the intensity of bright strips and that of dark strips becomes smaller when the camera accumulates charge longer. The figure shows that both FFT-based and DIP-based schemes fail to operate when the exposure duration exceeds 18 ms. In contrast, our YIN-based algorithm can still maintain a certain level of estimation probability, and hence can be applied in more environments.

Fig. 15(b) plots the estimation error probability for different modulation frequencies. The tested frequencies vary from 300 Hz to 5,600 Hz, and the exposure duration is fixed to 0.01473 ms. The results show that the performance of YIN estimation is consistently reliable in a wide range of frequencies. The FFT-based approach however experiences a much higher error probability in the low frequency band. This is because a unit of error in frequency domain, i.e., $|f - \tilde{f}| = 1$, corresponds to a larger error in strip width estimation, i.e., $|W_{real} - W| = |1/f - 1/f'|/T_r \approx 1/f^2 T_r$, when the frequency $f$ is small. On the other hand, the DIP-based approach performs worse in the high frequency band. When the strip width becomes narrow, any pair of the bright and dark strips disturbed by noise would contribute a significant error to the average width. In contrast, both the YIN-based and FFT-based schemes are capable of filtering out the effect of burst noise, and hence perform well even when the strip is narrow.

### 5.1.4 SNR of LOS and NLOS Links

We next check how ambient lights affect the LOS and NLOS light-to-camera links.

*Measurement setting:* We measure the SNR of a link with different distances, ranging from 1 meter to 5 meters. The SNR of a link is measured in two steps. A camera first receives a number of images when the light is turned off, and then receives a number of images when the light uses RollingLight to send a pure 2,000 Hz sine wave. To check the impact of ambient lights, we further deploy different numbers of interfering light sources (1170 lm per light source) nearby the transmitting light. The transmitting light and all interfering lights point to the same direction. We calculate the received power of the captured stripe pattern in an image by finding the average power at the transmitted frequency. The SNR is then calculated by the average received power calculated from the images received in the second step divided by the noise power, i.e., the power calculated from images received in the first step. We report the average results of the measurements collected from the Flea camera.

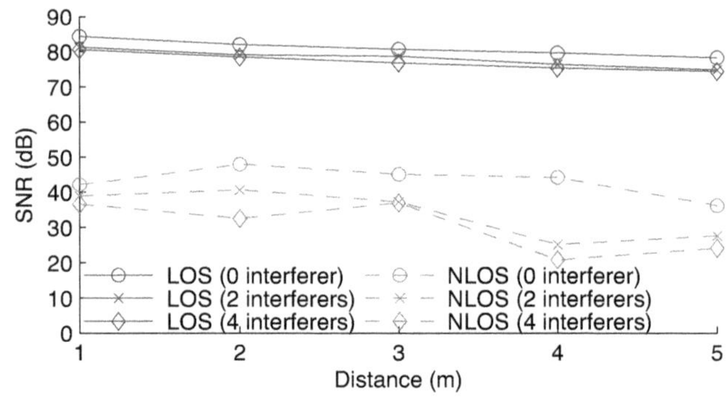


**Figure 16—Impact of ambient noise on SNR of LOS and NLOS links.** LOS links achieve a higher SNR than NLOS links. In addition, LOS links receive direct light signals, and are hence more resilient to ambient noise.

*Result:* Fig. 16 shows that LOS links allow the receiving camera to receive direct light signals, and achieve a much stronger SNR as compared to NLOS links, which receive reflected light signals. This reveals that our LOS design is not only useful for realizing visual association applications, but can also improve the capacity of a light-to-camera link. Moreover, the results also demonstrate that LOS links are more resilient to ambient noise because other light sources would only interfere with the camera when they reflect off the surface of the transmitting light. As a result, ambient lights are less likely to interfere the limited reflecting area, i.e., light surface, and thus has very little impact on the performance of a LOS link. In contrast, NLOS links receive the reflected signals in the entire im-

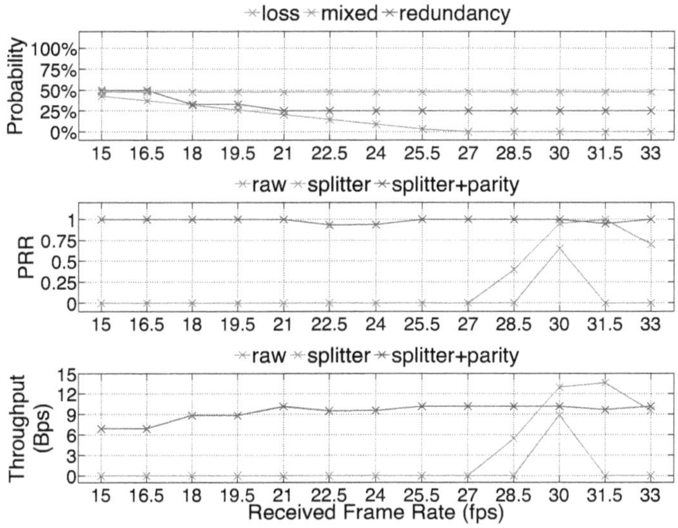


**Figure 17—Results for various frame rates.** Impact of the frame rate on (a) probabilities of symbol loss and mixed-symbol frames, (b) packet reception rate, and (c) throughput.

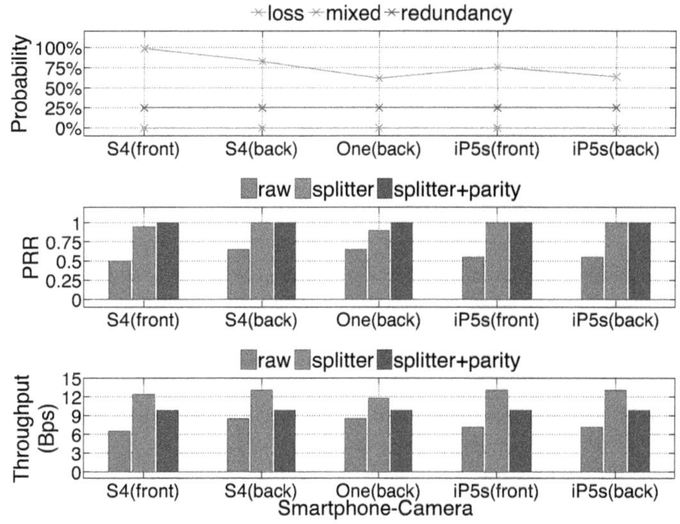


**Figure 18—Performance of different smartphones.** All the devices experience symbol losses and mixed-symbol frames, as shown in (a). RollingLight's sequence number and parity symbols address the two issues, and hence improve packet reception ratio, as shown in (b) and achieve a throughput of 11.32 bytes per second for a wide range of cameras, as shown in (c).

age, which could be easily mixed with the interfering light reflected from any surface. Any area that contains a higher noise power contributed by strong interference reflection could degrade the SNR of the received signal extracted from the entire image.

*Discussion:* A NLOS link typically experiences fewer symbol losses because a receiving camera captures the reflected light signals in the whole image and hence only misses symbols sent during the idle time gap. However, the receiving signal power of a NLOS link is also attenuated significantly due to reflection, which increases the error probability of strip width estimation, i.e., demodulation. A camera hence needs to be very close to the reflection surface to be able to receive. Moreover, signals from multiple transmitting lights are mixed by the reflection surface and would create significant interference to one another, and additional multiple access techniques are required to resolve the issue. When applications can work around these limitations, NLOS communications allow a wider service area as the receiving camera does not have to point at the transmitter as long as strong optical reflections present. For example, NLOS is a good fit to support room area communications, where a transmitting light needs to deliver the same information to most clients in a room. The applicability and limitations of NLOS communications are worth investigated in future studies.

## 5.2 Throughput Performance

In this section, we check the throughput of our RollingLight for various camera frame rates, different smartphones, and different image sizes. We use 48 modulation frequencies from 520 Hz to 4,000 Hz, and hence each symbol represents $\log_2(48/3) = 4$ data bits.

### 5.2.1 Impact of the Frame Rate

We first check the impact of the camera frame rate on the throughput. Since the frame rate of a smartphone usually cannot be manually adjusted, we use a Flea3 camera in this experiment.

*Experimental setting:* The frame rate is set ranging from 15fps to 33fps, and the symbol rate is fixed to 30 symbols per second. The exposure duration of the receiver is set to 14.73 ms. In this experiment, we place the receiver at a location where the light can occupy the whole image. The transmitting light repetitively sends 20 randomly-generated 20-bytes packets, and we output the average performance of 20 packets. For each setting, we compare the throughput of three schemes: *i)* raw symbols, *ii)* symbols with the splitter, and *iii)* symbols with the splitter and parity. To add proper redundancy (the ratio of parity to data), we estimate $P_{loss}$ for each different frame rate setting based on Eq. 9, and add redundancy, $\max(1/4, 1/\lfloor 1/P_{loss} \rfloor)$, in the third scheme.

*Results:* Fig. 17(a) plots the percentage of symbols that are lost and the percentage of images that contains mixed symbols. The results verify that the ratio of mixed-symbol frames is fairly high. Hence, if we do not add the symbol splitter, the packet reception ratio (PRR) is very low even if the frame rate is the same with the symbol rate, as shown in Fig. 17(b). This is because the symbol might be miss-aligned with the image frame. On the other hand, the symbol loss ratio increases when the frame rate decreases. This trend matches our derived loss probability in Eq. 9 because the other parameters, including the size $H$, exposure duration $T_e$ and the read-out duration $T_r$, are now fixed. Therefore, even if we have added the splitter, the packet reception rate still drops to zero when the frame rate is lower than 27 fps. After adding redundancy tagged in Fig. 17(a), we can see from Fig. 17(b) that the resulting packet reception ratio can be improved to almost 100%. The final throughput with consideration of the overhead is plotted in Fig. 17(c). Though the throughput decreases slightly after adding parity symbols, the reliability is significantly improved for a wide range of frame rates.

### 5.2.2 Throughput of Different Smartphones

We next check the decoding performance of different commodity smartphones.

*Experimental setting:* The frame rate of our tested devices ranges from 29.6fps to 30fps. In addition, the read-out duration and the resolution of different cameras could also be different. This will affect the probabilities of symbol loss and mixed-symbol frame. We again place the receiver at a location where the light can occupy the whole image. The light repetitively sends 20 different 20-bytes packets, and add redundancy 1/4, i.e., one parity for four data symbols. We perform real-time decoding on iPhone, and offline decode the recorded video for the rest of devices.

*Results:* Fig. 18(a) shows that all the devices consistently see a high probability of mixed-symbol frames. However, the average loss probability is close to zero. This is because the frame rate of these devices is only slightly different from the symbol rate. Therefore, when the light occupies the whole image, the receiving idle gap is small enough to avoid missing any symbols. However, we will show in the next experiment that the situation becomes very different when the size of a captured light in the image decreases. The packet reception ratio of different devices is plotted in Fig. 18(b). We can see that, even though different cameras have different read-out duration and observe different strip widths for the same transmitted frequency, our demodulation scheme enables them to accurately learn their channels and correctly decode most of the packets. After considering the overhead, RollingLight can achieve a throughput of 11.32 bytes per second, as shown in Fig. 18(c). We note that the throughput of the scheme without parity is higher that of RollingLight because the symbol loss rate is pretty low in this experimental setting. The story however will be different when the size of the captured light decreases.

### 5.2.3 Impact of the Size of the Captured Light

In a line-of-sight light-to-camera link, the size of the captured light (in number of pixels) is typically related to the resolution of a camera or the distance of a light-to-camera link. Hence, in practical scenarios, it is very unlikely that a device can always capture the light occupying the whole image. Hence, in this experiment, we examine how does the LED size in the image affect our performance.

*Experimental setting:* We change the location of a camera so that the size of the captured light in the image varies from 200 pixels to 1,000 pixels. In this experiment, we use our iOS application to perform real-time decoding on several iPhone5s, which have an average frame rate of 29.98 fps. Again, the light repetitively sends 20 different 20-bytes packets, and adds redundancy $\max(1/8, 1/\lfloor 1/P_{loss} \rfloor)$ based on $P_{loss}$ estimated by Eq. 9.

*Results:* Fig. 19 plots the results for various sizes of the captured light in an image. A smaller LED size implies a longer idle gap of signal receiving because, for the duration of read-out rows of pixels that do not capture the light, the camera does not get any information sent by the light. Hence, as shown in Fig. 19(a), even though the frame rate is very close to the symbol rate, the symbol loss ratio starts to increase when the LED size is smaller than 600 pixels. Fig. 19(b) and (c) plots the corresponding packet reception ratio and throughput. The results show that the reception ratio still drops when the size of the LED image decreases, even after we add parity symbols. The main reason is that, even if we can completely avoid symbol loss, an image might only capture part of a symbol, which might not be demodulated correctly when it does not contain a sufficient number of strips. This problem is especially critical when the symbol is modulated using a lower frequency, which corresponds to a wider strip width. Therefore, without adding redundancy, the achievable throughput might be slightly higher than that with redundancy when the LED size is large, but drops to zero when the image size is smaller than 600 pixels. The 600-pixel light corresponds to an 1.6m light-to-camera link for a 60cm×60cm transmitting light, which is a common setting for most of indoor applications, such as museum, exhibition, or shopping center. The results demonstrate that RollingLight can reliably deliver a throughput of 11.32 bytes per second for typical indoor environments.

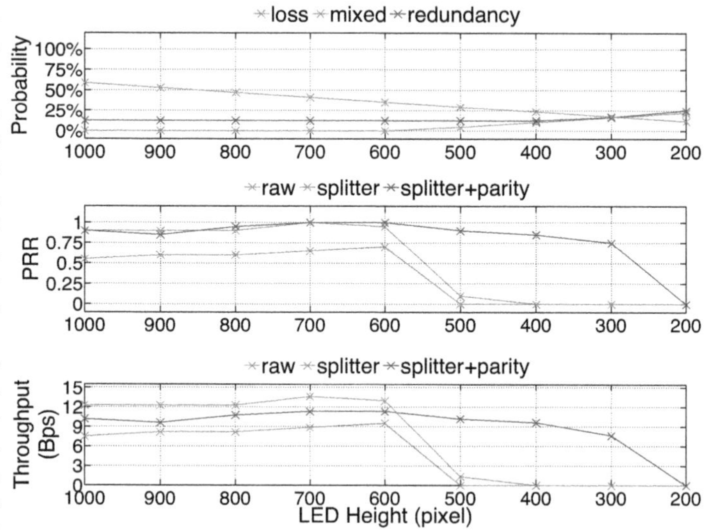


**Figure 19—Impact of LED size in the image.** The smaller the captured light in the image, the higher the loss probability, as shown in (a). RollingLight delivers an acceptable PRR (b) and throughput (c) for indoor applications, corresponding to about a 600-pixel light size.

**Table 2**—Processing time of each component

| Component | Time (ms) |
|---|---|
| Image Buffer to OpenCV Mat | 0.0281 |
| Denoise | 12.8583 |
| Symbol Splitter Detection | 2.1547 |
| YIN Strip Width Detection and Demodulation | 3.1054 |
| Total | 18.1465 |

## 5.3 Decoding Time

We finally measure the time required to process each 1920×1080 image frame in our iOS decoding application. We experiment on an Apple iPhone 5S with A7 dual-core 1.3 GHz Cyclone (ARM v8-based) processor and 1 GB DDR3 RAM. The execution time of all the receiver components is listed in Table 2. We assume that the receiver does not significantly move the device, and only perform light boundary detection in the initial of packet reception. In addition, parity decoding is performed in the end of a packet, instead of per image frame. Thus, the costs of locating the light and parity decoding are excluded here. We ask the camera to output the YUV images, and hence eliminate the cost of image format conversion. This significantly reduces the time of image reading to 0.03 milliseconds. The total processing time of each frame is about 18.15 milliseconds, which is smaller than the frame duration of most existing smartphones. This means RollingLight's decoding can be done in real-time. This experiment considers a scenario with a single transmitting light. For some scenarios where multiple transmitting lights are captured in an image, the size of each light also becomes smaller and requires less processing time. Given a fixed image size, the decoding time for various numbers of light sources should be comparable.

## 6. RELATED WORK

The related works fall in the following categories.

**Screen-to-camera communications:** A number of prior works [5, 18, 10, 11, 24, 4] exploits a display to deliver information bits to cameras. PixNet [18] modulates the large quantity of pixels on a LCD display as OFDM symbols, and designs a OFDM-based receiver algorithm for cameras. COBRA [10] further utilizes the color information of pixels to improve the SNR of a screen-to-camera link. It however does not address the unsynchronized problem, but simply avoids information loss by repeating every packet twice. Strata [12] adds layered coding to QR codes so that different cameras with heterogeneous channel conditions can observe different amount of information. LightSync [11] then deals with unsynchronized screen-to-camera channels by introducing inter-frame erasure coding and adding sequence numbers. To deal with channel variation, e.g., due to perspective distortion, the work [4] proposes a rate adaptation scheme for camera-based communications. VR-Codes (NewsFlash) [24] and HiLight [16] then leverage the property that a camera sees something different from the human to embed extra information in an image. VRCodes [24] is one of the designs that leverage the rolling-shutter effect to realize display-to-camera communications. It demonstrates the potential of sending intensity-modulated signals from a display. However, similar to other existing light-to-camera designs, it does not address the practical challenges, including signal losses due to dynamic time gaps and high-order FSK demodulation. Compared to the above screen-to-camera works, our RollingLight considers light-to-camera communication channels, which introduce additional practical issues imposed by the optical transmitting sources.

**Light-to-camera communications:** Several recent works investigate how to realize light-to-camera communications. In [21], the author proposes to modulate bits by undersampled frequency shift OOK (UFSOOK). While this scheme can ensure decoding in an extremely low SNR link, it can only support a data rate of 0.5 bits per image frame. Some other works [7, 19] then exploit the rolling shutter effect to increase the data rate of a light-to-camera link. The one in [7] tries to increase the data rate by reducing the symbol duration. However, as we mentioned in Sec. 2.1, a camera typically receives signal discontinuously. Those short symbols sent during a camera's idle gap will all be dropped. Even worse, when the idle gap is long, due to short exposure duration or the small size of the captured light, the symbol loss rate could be fairly high. This loss issue however stays unsolved in [7]. The other [19] focuses on non-line-of-sight light-to-camera communications, which allow a camera to see the indirect light sources and capture the stripe pattern in the whole image. In the non-line-of-sight scenarios, the gap of discontinuous receiving is constant, and, hence, the impact of the unsychronization problem is not as significant as that in the LOS scenarios. While this work neglects the impact of unsynchronized channels, its performance could degrade for LOS links. In contrast, we tackle the unsynchronization problem particularly for line-of-sight light-to-camera channels, and further propose a demodulation algorithm that operates in a wide range of frequency band and fits a variety of devices on the market. Finally, light-to-camera communication is also applied in special applications, e.g., localization [15], where each light only sends repetitive information. It however does not cope with signal losses due to dynamic time gaps, and hence overestimates the practical achievable rate of a light-to-camera link. Our work instead focuses on improving the rate and reliability of data transmissions in a line-of-sight light-to-camera link.

**Other visible light communication (VLC) designs:** Some other visible light communication schemes use special devices, e.g., photodiode [22, 20, 9, 6] or high-speed cameras [3, 14, 17], to receive signal sent by a light. Those receiving devices have a much higher sampling rate than a rolling shutter camera, and their characteristics are very different from built-in cameras of smartphones. Their approaches hence cannot be directly applied in our targeted applications.

# 7. CONCLUSION

This paper presents RollingLight, a line-of-sight light-to-camera communication system. We design a demodulation scheme that enables each of diverse cameras to learn its read-out duration and accurately convert the received strip width to the transmitted frequency. This accuracy allows us to use the high-order FSK modulation, and hence push the achievable throughput of a LOS light-to-camera link. We also develop a number of techniques, including symbol splitter insertion and parity coding, to address the problem of unsynchronized light-to-camera channels, which is especially critical for the LOS scenario. We perform extensive measurements to characterize the LOS light-to-camera channels, and find a proper set of modulation frequencies detectable by most of today's devices. Our prototyping and real system implementation show that RollingLight can achieve a throughput of 12 bytes per second. In addition, RollingLight's decoding can be done in about 18 milliseconds per frame, which is much shorter than the frame duration of most commodity cameras. We believe that RollingLight's reliable and real-time LOS communication capability will create a great potential of realizing a variety of mobile applications that require visual-association-enabled communications.

# 8. ACKNOWLEDGEMENTS

We thank Polly Huang, Richard. D. Roberts, the reviewers, and our shepherd, Chunyi Peng, for their insightful comments and suggestions. This work is supported in part by Ministry of Science and Technology, National Taiwan University, and Intel Corporation under grants MOST-103-2911-I-002-001, NSC-102-2221-E-002-093-MY2, MOST-103-2221-E-001 -017 -MY2, NSC-102-2221-E-001 -012 -MY2 and NTU-ICRP-104R7501.

# 9. REFERENCES

[1] Ettus Inc., universal software radio peripheral. http://ettus.com.

[2] PointGrey Flea3 Product Datasheet. http://www.ptgrey.com/products/flea3/Flea3_Datasheet.pdf.

[3] S. Arai, S. Mase, T. Yamazato, T. Endo, T. Fujii, M. Tanimoto, K. Kidono, Y. Kimura, and Y. Ninomiya. Experimental on hierarchical transmission scheme for visible light communication using led traffic light and high-speed camera. In *IEEE VTC*, 2007.

[4] A. Ashok, M. Gruteser, N. Mandayam, T. Kwon, W. Yuan, M. Varga, and K. Dana. Rate adaptation in visual MIMO. In *IEEE SECON*, 2011.

[5] A. Ashok, M. Gruteser, N. Mandayam, J. Silva, M. Varga, and K. Dana. Challenge: Mobile optical networks through visual MIMO. In *ACM MobiCom*, 2010.

[6] G. Cossu, A. M. Khalid, P. Choudhury, R. Corsini, and E. Ciaramella. 3.4 Gbit/s visible optical wireless transmission based on RGB LED. *Opt. Express*, 20(26):B501–B506, Dec 2012.

[7] C. Danakis, M. Afgani, G. Povey, I. Underwood, and H. Haas. Using a CMOS camera sensor for visible light communication. In *IEEE Globecom*, 2012.

[8] A. De Cheveigné and H. Kawahara. YIN, a fundamental frequency estimator for speech and music. *The Journal of the Acoustical Society of America*, 111(4):1917–1930, 2002.

[9] L. Grobe, A. Paraskevopoulos, J. Hilt, D. Schulz, F. Lassak, F. Hartlieb, C. Kottke, V. Jungnickel, and K.-D. Langer.

High-speed visible light communication systems. *Communications Magazine, IEEE*, 51(12):60–66, December 2013.

[10] T. Hao, R. Zhou, and G. Xing. COBRA: color barcode streaming for smartphone systems. In *ACM MobiSys*, 2012.

[11] W. Hu, H. Gu, and Q. Pu. LightSync: unsynchronized visual communication over screen-camera links. In *ACM MobiCom*, 2013.

[12] W. Hu, J. Mao, Z. Huang, Y. Xue, J. She, K. Bian, and G. Shen. Strata: Layered coding for scalable visual communication. In *ACM MobiCom*, 2014.

[13] A. Inc. Arduino Mega 2560.

[14] S. Iwasaki, C. Premachandra, T. Endo, T. Fujii, M. Tanimoto, and Y. Kimura. Visible light road-to-vehicle communication using high-speed camera. In *IEEE Intelligent Vehicles Symposium*, 2008.

[15] Y.-S. Kuo, P. Pannuto, K.-J. Hsiao, and P. Dutta. Luxapose: Indoor positioning with mobile phones and visible light. In *ACM MobiCom*, 2014.

[16] T. Li, C. An, A. T. Campbell, and X. Zhou. HiLight: Hiding bits in pixel translucency changes. In *ACM Workshop on Visible Light Communication Systems (VLCS)*, 2014.

[17] T. Nagura, T. Yamazato, M. Katayama, T. Yendo, T. Fujii, and H. Okada. Improved decoding methods of visible light communication system for its using led array and high-speed camera. In *IEEE VTC*, 2010.

[18] S. D. Perli, N. Ahmed, and D. Katabi. Pixnet: interference-free wireless links using LCD-camera pairs. In *ACM MobiCom*, 2010.

[19] N. Rajagopal, P. Lazik, and A. Rowe. Visual light landmarks for mobile devices. In *IEEE IPSN*, 2014.

[20] S. Rajagopal, R. D. Roberts, and S.-K. Lim. IEEE 802.15.7 Visible Light Communication: Modulation Schemes and Dimming Support. *IEEE Communications Magazine*, 50:72 – 82, March 2012.

[21] R. D. Roberts. Undersampled frequency shift ON-OFF keying (UFSOOK) for camera communications (CamCom). In *IEEE Wireless and Optical Communication Conference*, 2013.

[22] S. Schmid, G. Corbellini, S. Mangold, and T. R. Gross. LED-to-LED visible light communication networks. In *ACM MobiHoc*, 2013.

[23] P. Viola and M. Jones. Rapid object detection using a boosted cascade of simple features. In *IEEE CVPR*, 2001.

[24] G. Woo, A. Lippman, and R. Raskar. Vrcodes: Unobtrusive and active visual codes for interaction by exploiting rolling shutter. In *IEEE International Symposium on Mixed and Augmented Reality (ISMAR)*, 2012.

# InFrame++: Achieve Simultaneous Screen-Human Viewing and Hidden Screen-Camera Communication

Anran Wang *
Beihang University
wangar@act.buaa.edu.cn

Zhuoran Li *
The Ohio State University
li.5233 @osu.edu

Chunyi Peng
The Ohio State University
chunyi@cse.ohio-state.edu

Guobin Shen
Microsoft Research, China
jackysh@microsoft.com

Gan Fang
The Ohio State University
fang.254@osu.edu

Bing Zeng
University of Electronic Science and Technology of China
eezeng@uestc.edu.cn

## ABSTRACT

Recent efforts in visible light communication over screen-camera links have exploited the display for data communication. Such practices, albeit convenient, have led to contention between space allocated for users and content reserved for devices, in addition to their visual anti-aesthetics and distractedness. In this paper, we propose INFRAME++, a system that enables concurrent, *dual-mode*, *f*ull-frame communication for both users and devices. INFRAME++ leverages the spatial-temporal flicker-fusion property of human vision system and the fast frame rate of modern display. It multiplexes data onto full-frame video contents through novel complementary frame composition, hierarchical frame structure, and CDMA-like modulation. It thus ensures opportunistic and unobtrusive screen-camera data communication without affecting the primary video-viewing experience for human users. Our prototype and experiments have confirmed its effectiveness of delivering data to devices in its visual communication with imperceptible video artifacts for viewers. INFRAME++ is able to achieve 150-240 kbps at 120FPS over a 24' LCD monitor with one data frame per 12 display frames. It supports up to 360kbps while data:video is 1:6.

## Categories and Subject Descriptors

C.2.0 [**Computer-Communication Networks**]: General—*Data communications*; H.5.1 [**Information Interface and Presentation**]: Multimedia Information Systems—*Video*; H.5.2 [**Information Interface and Presentation**]: User Interfaces—*Screen design*

## Keywords

Screen-camera communication; Hidden visible communication; Dual-mode visible communication; Full-frame video; InFrame++

*The first two authors are co-primary student authors. The correspondence faculty author is C. Peng.


*MobiSys'15*, May 18–22, 2015, Florence, Italy.

http://dx.doi.org/10.1145/2742647.2742652 .

## 1. INTRODUCTION

Recent years have been witnessing the rapid growth of electronic visual displays deployed in the emerging cyber-physical world. Indeed, we are surrounded by such devices in various form factors, ranging from a phone screen, a tablet display, a computer monitor, to a TV, an advertising electronic board and even larger multi-screen displays. These visual displays have become a primary source for information from the user's standpoint. For example, video playback has contributed to 79% of Internet traffic [1]. Under such common usage scenarios, the main role of a screen is to convey information to human eyes. The display thus establishes the *screen-to-eye* communication.

It is often highly desirable to further convey certain side information to a user while she watches the display. A real-life example is to refer the viewer to a movie webpage for additional information. Another popular case is for vendors to present additional information (*e.g.*, product specification and sales) in the TV commercials. With the growing prevalence of cameras, *screen-to-camera* visible communication has rapidly emerged as a convenient, impromptu communication channel [11, 14, 15, 22, 30]. Information is encoded into visual patterns and shown on the screen. Camera-equipped devices subsequently capture the screen and retrieve the data information thereafter.

Unfortunately, such special visual patterns (*e.g.*, Quick Response (QR) codes) are not quite consumable, if at all, by humans who are more comfortable with human-friendly contents such as texts, images and videos. When a display becomes the same source concurrently for both human-friendly primary content and camera-friendly side information, the two contend for the display. Recognizing such contention and the fact that delivering human-consumable content is more primary purpose, current practices have all resorted to some kind of compromise, either spatially or temporally. In the QR code case, the code would take a small area and resides at a corner of the entire screen (Figure 1a), or occupy the whole screen in turn after human-friendly contents (Figure 1b). The former spatial compromise, however, not only limits its information-carrying capability, but also incurs extra work to properly capture codes (*e.g.*, being close enough to QR codes). Albeit small, the appearance of the QR code is still deemed distractive, thus impairing user-viewing experiences. The latter temporal compromise indeed yield a larger display size and makes it less effort demanding in capture and also possible to carry more bits. However, such practice is viable only for interactive scenarios and on interactive devices.

(a) Spatial compromise (b) Temporal compromise

**Figure 1: Current practices of compromising the screen-to-eye and screen-to-camera communications. (a) Small QR code located at the corner (in the case of an ice hockey game); (b) Two consecutive frames, one for each channel (while scanning QR code at WeChat [3]).**

In this work, we address the key challenge in visual communication systems: Can we completely eliminate the tension between the screen-to-eye and screen-to-camera channels? If succeeded, we can afford the users to enjoy normal full-frame viewing experience (as though the side channel would not exist), while still being able to simultaneously convey side information over the visual screen-to-camera channel. The solution calls for a novel paradigm of *dual-mode, full-frame communication*, which enables concurrent delivery of primary video content to users and additional information to devices over screen-to-camera visual links without impairing user-viewing experiences.

In this paper, we present the design and implementation of INFRAME++, which offers a promising and definite solution to the above challenge. Figure 2 illustrates the concept of INFRAME++. In INFRAME++, composite contents are produced (in frames) for the display by multiplexing the video content frames (intended for human viewers) and the data (intended for devices, also in frames). These composite frames can be rendered to human eyes without affecting the viewing experience. The user thus watches the video as usual without sensing the embedded data frames. In the meantime, the data carried by the composite frames can be captured and decoded by the camera to retrieve the embedded side information. To enable the above functions, INFRAME++ leverages the capability discrepancy and distinctive features of the human vision system and devices (display and camera), *e.g.*, screens can display content faster than human eyes perceive; cameras have shutter but human eyes do not, etc.. Video and data carried by the composite frames thus operate at different time scales. Video contents are perceived at the slow pace due to physical limits of human eyes, whereas data frames are displayed at the fast speed, which can be captured and decoded only by the camera. In essence, INFRAME++ establishes two concurrent visual communication channels – the *primary* screen-to-eye channel for humans and the *secondary* screen-to-camera channel for devices. Both channels originate from the same screen, coexisting and counteracting against each other.

Specifically, we have two concrete goals for INFRAME++. First, the information-carrying data stream over the screen-to-camera channel should not affect the user perception of the content delivered over the primary channel. Second, we seek to achieve high data rate over the secondary screen-to-camera channel, which is vital to enabling new application scenarios for visual data communication in the future. To this end, we have to effectively manage the interference from the primary screen-to-eye channel. Note that the visual content of the primary channel will inevitably interfere the secondary channel. Even worse than the results disclosed in early work, the screen-to-camera channel may suffer from severe distortions such as frame rate mismatch, rolling shutter effect, poor capture quality, *etc.*.

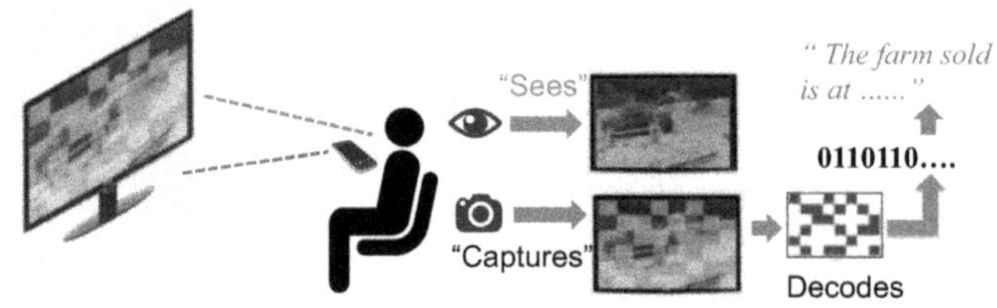


**Figure 2: Concept of INFRAME++: screen-to-eye for videos and screen-to-camera for data communication over the full-frame same visible channel simultaneously.**

For the first goal, we propose the novel concept of *spatial-temporal complementary frames* (STCFs). STCFs fully exploit the spatial and temporal low-pass filtering properties of human vision system. Each of the complementary frames in STCFs contains a pair of data frames, which have complementary contents and are displayed back-to-back [31]. Every data frame is further constructed from spatially complementary visual patterns that possess alternating complementary cells (*i.e.*, group of pixels). When data frames are multiplexed to the original screen content and displayed at fast frame rate, we can effectively suppress the visibility of data frames and preserve normal viewing experiences. On the other hand, a camera takes (temporal) snapshots of the multiplexed stream with high spatial resolution. The snapshots exhibit obvious artifacts introduced by complementary visual patterns, which can be processed to extract the information bits. We further design smoothing transitional frames so that STCFs can be morphed into data frames.

For the second goal, we devise a hierarchical data frame structure (consisting of Cells, Blocks and Segments) and a CDMA-like modulation scheme. A Cell is the minimum logical unit making up from neighboring pixels with the same value. A Block, consisting of multiple Cells, is the basic coding unit. Information bits are modulated in Blocks. A Segment is a group of Blocks, over which certain error protection is exerted. These hierarchical units allow for robust data extraction from the captured artifacts. To handle other screen-to-camera channel distortions, we further design special preambles that consist of regularly distributed special locators and alignment blocks, as well as reference symbols in special visual patterns that help to learn dynamic channels.

We have implemented the INFRAME++ prototype and conducted thorough evaluation including user studies. Our experiments confirm that INFRAME++ enables dual-mode full-frame visible communication to both humans and devices simultaneously. Without noticeable artifacts or flickers, INFRAME++ is able to yield up to 360 kbps (150-240kpbs in most test cases) of data rates for the screen-to-camera communication, up to 30–60x improvement, compared with our prior work [31].

In summary, we have made three main contributions in this work:

- We propose a novel dual-mode full-frame visible communication paradigm, in which the same display can stream high-rate data to a user device while retaining normal viewing experiences.
- We introduce the spatial-temporal complementary frame concept and verify its the feasibility through user studies. We further address several practical challenges, and prototype and assess a complete working system.
- We demonstrate its promise for high-rate data delivery by achieving 150-240 kbps rate (up to 360 kpbs), an order of magnitude higher than early proposals.

We believe that, as more display devices are deployed in the emerging cyber-physical world, the new visual communication paradigm of INFRAME++ will become more appealing for its superior user experience and its high rate for the embedded data.

The rest of the paper is organized as follows. §2 introduces the background on human vision system and modern cameras. §3 gives an overview of INFRAME++. §4 and §5 describe our detailed design in screen-to-eye and screen-to-camera channels. §6 presents the implementation and evaluation of INFRAME++. §7 discusses the potential applications and open issues. §8 compares with related work, followed by the conclusion in §9.

# 2. BACKGROUND

Vision is the primary information acquisition means for human beings. Human vision system (HVS) is highly advanced and complicated. In this section, we present some related basic properties of HVS, and for comparison purpose, also capabilities of displays and cameras.

## 2.1 Human Vision System (HVS)

Human eyes are the core instrument in human vision system, which reacts to light and thus obtains the perception of object shapes, colors, depth and motion, *etc.*. The structure of an eye is similar to that of a camera [4], in the sense that an eye also has a lens (crystalline lens) and a sensor plate (retina). The sensor units (receptor cells) on the retina are greater at the center and lowest at the edges, thereby creating central (also called foveal) and peripheral vision. Central vision accounts for the high visual acuity capability, essential to capturing major visual details. The larger peripheral area is dominated by highly-sensitive light sensors (rod cells) and thus it is good at detecting motion, and becomes more effective in the dark.

While offering rich information from the physical world, our naked eyes have inherent physical limits in resolution, both spatial and temporal. In particular, our visual perception possesses three optical features, namely *center-surround response*, *low-pass flicker fusion*, and *phantom array effect*, that relate to the spatial resolution, temporal resolution and motion sensitivity, respectively.

**Center-surround response.** Human eyes cannot discriminate overly fine details, due to the physical limit of the minimum distance between adjacent sensing cells on the central retina. Typically, the excellent spatial resolution of human eyes is $0.07^o$, corresponding at 1.2mm at 1 meter watching distance [28]. The spatial resolution is also affected by the spatial contrast. The receptive field of human eyes has different responses at center and surrounding. Small (or large) receptive fields are stimulated by high (or low) spatial frequencies. Typically, our spatial perception follows a bandpass (close to low-pass) characteristics: the largest frequency is about 2-4 cycles per visual angle (equivalent to one cycle contrast within 5mm at 1m watching distance) [28]. In short, human eyes can not distinguish too tiny things, and finer details fuse and appear as some kind of average. One example is the eyesight check: when the fine details exceeds that of the eye, one will only see the rough shape.

**Low-pass flicker fusion.** Time-variant fluctuations of light intensity are not perceptible to human eyes when it is beyond a certain frequency, termed *critical flicker frequency* (CFF for short hereafter) [18, 27]. Instead, human eyes only perceive the average luminance. The temporal behavior of human vision system can be approximated as a *linear low-pass filter* at a high frequency exceeding the CFF. A common example is the viewing of a rotating car wheel. When it rotates fast enough, semi-transparent perception will result in. Note but the CFF is affected by many factors including color contrasts, motion, luminance waveforms, and to name a few. In typical scenarios, the CFF of human eyes is believed to be about 40-50Hz according to vast vision research results [6, 10, 18]. For instance, flickers presented by a 60Hz CRT monitor are not perceptible.

**Phantom array effect.** This describes another special property of human eyes – sensitive to motion. While fast-moving objects zoom across view (either by object motion, or by eye motion such as rolling eyes), flicker can be noticed even when the display frequency is much higher [13]. For example, we can observe the flashing of an LED flashing at a frequency far exceeding typical CFF if the LED is moving in a dark environment, but we only see a constantly lit LED if it is still. Unlike flicker fusion, the origin of phantom array effect is not fully understood. Recent studies uncover that lower flicker amplitude, larger duty cycle and larger beam size make it less visible [25, 29].

## 2.2 Modern Display and Camera

With rapid technology advancement in recent years, displays and cameras are thriving rapidly. Most of off-the-shelf LCD displays, especially those 3D capable ones, supports 120Hz or higher refresh rate. For example, Eizo FG2421 24' LCD monitor, which is used in our work, supports 120 frames per second (FPS) and even 240FPS (in turbo mode). Other monitors like LG 47LH55 even physically supports 240 FPS. Moreover, with emergence of organic light-emitting diode (OLED) based displays, a much lower response time (less than 0.01 ms) is supported compared with LCD, indicating its ability to support a rather high refresh rate.

Cameras are also evolving dramatically. Special purpose high resolution cameras can yield giga-pixel images and reach over 2000 FPS video capture frame rate. Even commodity smartphone cameras can support high resolution images at a fast capture rate, which exceeds what the retina is looking for. For example, Samsung Galaxy S5 supports 16-mega pixel resolution and 120FPS capture rate, while iPhone 6 accommodates 8-mega pixel resolution and up to 240FPS capture rate.

## 2.3 A Comparison

One particular difference between an eye and a camera is that the eye does not contain a shutter. As a result, there is no exposure process while we see things, nor we see things in frames (or snapshots). It also accounts for the flicker fusion property. In contrast, camera takes discrete snapshots, every detail on the snapshot can be examined. Moreover, while human vision system is still far advanced than a camera, per the specific metric of spatial and temporal resolution, it is already well exceeded by the camera.

The distinctive properties of HVS and cameras, and their capability gap provide potential design room we can explore. Considering the fact that HVS has largely remained constant over long time whereas display and camera technologies continue advancing at fast paces, the capability gap, hence the design room, will grow larger in future.

# 3. INFRAME++ OVERVIEW

Our goal is to enable full-frame, dual-mode visible communication that allows users to enjoy normal full-frame viewing experiences while, at the same time, allowing side information being streamed to camera-equipped devices. Compared with alternative ways to deliver side information (*e.g.* using WiFi for receiving the audio), it enjoys intrinsic synchronization between primary content and side information, and the convenience of impromptus communication (*i.e.* avoidance of device pairing), among others.

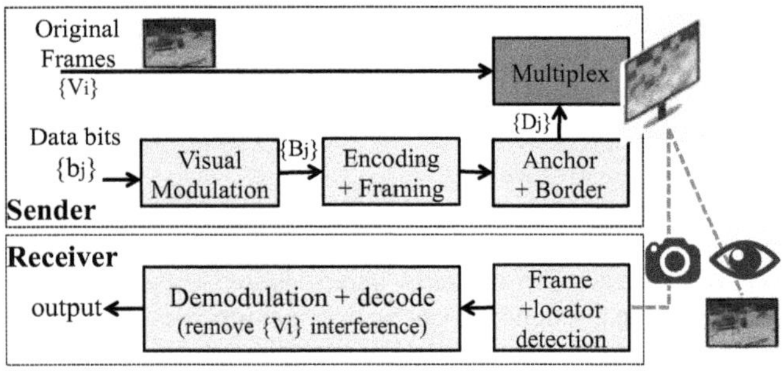


**Figure 3: INFRAME++ architecture and operations.**

**Requirements and Basic Idea.** To achieve the goal, we need to establish concurrent screen-to-eye and screen-to-camera communication channels. Given that the fundamental purpose of a screen is to show content to users, the screen-to-eye channel is more primary. Thus, a *first* requirement is to ensure *unimpaired* viewing experience, that is, full-frame viewing without any perceivable quality degradation. To serve as an effective side channel, a *second* requirement is to achieve high data rate at the existence of the primary video content.

The two visible communication channels share the same source – the screen, whereas to achieve the goal, we need to establish two distinctive channels, one for human and one for device. Thus the only possibility is to exploit the different capabilities of human vision system and the camera. As mentioned in previous section, human vision system has the low-pass filtering property in both spatial and temporal domain but a camera can take discrete snapshots of the screen content, we may come up with the design that embeds high frequency artifacts. If these artifacts can be low-pass filtered out but remain catchable by the camera, we can convey information using the artifacts.

**Challenges.** Despite the ever increasing capability gap between human vision system and the dispaly/camera, it is non-trivial to realize the idea. There are two main challenges arisen from inherently conflicting screen-to-eye and screen-to-camera channels.

∘ *Retaining normal viewing with side channel.* The requirement not to affect the primary screen-to-eye channel imposes a rigid constraint on the secondary screen-to-camera channel. Although human eyes have a low temporal resolution, they are very sensitive to flickers. We thus need to find an appropriate frame multiplexing scheme to combine a data stream and arbitrary screen content, and ensure multiplexing will not introduce any perceivable color distortion, artifacts and flickers. It is especially challenging when the content in the screen-to-camera channel is dynamic.

∘ *Enabling data communication with primary content.* To serve the primary video watching goal, the perceived luminance level is mainly dominated by the original frames whereas the injected data patterns only contribute to small "noise". Since the original luminance level is distinct at different pixels in one frame, its dynamic range usually overwhelm the noise made for data delivery. This is a critical issue to design a data frame structure so that they can be retrieved from the multiplexed frames without loss of its carrying data. In the meanwhile, we have to address the constraints in the traditional screen-to-camera communication, such as blurring and rolling shutter effects in [11, 14, 30].

**INFRAME++ design.** As will be elaborated in subsequent sections, we overcome the first challenge through the key concept of *spatial-temporal complementary frames* and the superior frame rate of displays (§4). Information bits are carried with spatial complementary visual patterns that are assembled into temporal complementary frames. The resulting complementary frames are multiplexed with the original screen contents. When displayed at high frame rate (*e.g.* 120FPS), complementary frames perceptually cancel each out and original screen contents retain. It thus ensures normal viewing experiences. On the contrary, a camera takes (temporal) snapshots and with high spatial resolution. The captured multiplexed frame will have obvious artifacts, which can be processed to extract information bits.

We address the second challenge through the design of a hierarchical data frame structure made up from Cells, Blocks and Segments, and a CDMA-like modulation scheme. Information bits are modulated in Blocks that exhibit spatial complementary visual patterns. Error protection is applied among Blocks in a Segment. These designs allow robust extraction of data from captured artifacts. To handle other screen-to-camera channel distortions, we also design special preambles that consists of regularly distributed special locators, and further design synchronization symbols in special visual patterns to help realign Cells and Blocks.

**Architecture and Operations.** Figure 3 illustrates the architecture of INFRAME++. It consists of encoding logic at the sender and decoding logic at the receiver.

Given the original frames $\{V_i\}$ and the input data bit stream $\{b_j\}$, INFRAME++ works as follows. Information bits $\{b_j\}$ are first embedded into certain visual patterns $\{B_j\}$ by the visual modulation module. In the subsequent encoding and frame module, error protection is exerted and similarly modulated. The generated visual patterns are grouped into Segments and further formed them into full-size data frames. Preambles and specially designed borders are added subsequently. Finally, the data frames are multiplexed to the origin frames in some way and display them on the screen.

At the receiver side, the process is essentially reversed. It first detects the preamble and restores locator positions, via the locator detection module. It proceeds to detect the existence of visual patterns, and demodulate them if exist, through a correlation-based matching process. The extracted bits then go through the error correction process and give the original information bits. With great efforts to hide data communication, INFRAME++ also ensures unobstructive human viewing experience as anticipated.

# 4. RESPECT USER VIEWING OVER PRIMARY SCREEN-TO-EYE CHANNEL

This central problem is how to embed information-carrying visual patterns into the original frames so that such changes remain invisible to naked human eyes. Our solution is to use the spatial-temporal complementary frames. In this section, we elaborate its concept and design, and also present the handling of sharp switch between dynamic data frames.

## 4.1 Spatial-temporal Complementary Frames

Spatial-temporal complementary frames (STCF) are a new development from the (temporal) complementary frames we originally proposed in [31]. For presentation integrity, we also include the basic definition of complementary frames here.

Let us first define *complementary pixels*. Two pixels $p$ and $p^*$ complement each other with respect to the luminance level $v$ if their pixel values sum up to $2v$, *i.e.*, $v_p + v_{p^*} = 2v$. Note that, in actual data frame, the average luminance level is set to zero ($v = 0$) and we have $v_{p^*} = -v_p$, whereas in the illustrations we have set the luminance value to mid-gray ($v = 128$) as it is not possible to show a pixel with negative value.

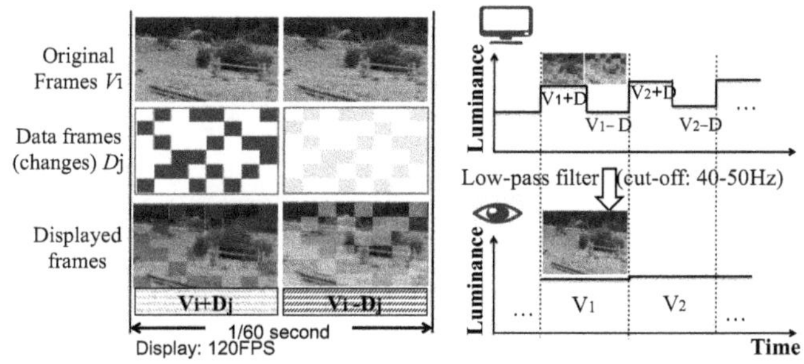


(a) TCF structure (b) Perception effects

**Figure 4: Illustration of temporal complementary frames (TCFs) (a) and their visual effects perceived by eyes (b) through a low-pass filtering flicker fusion.**

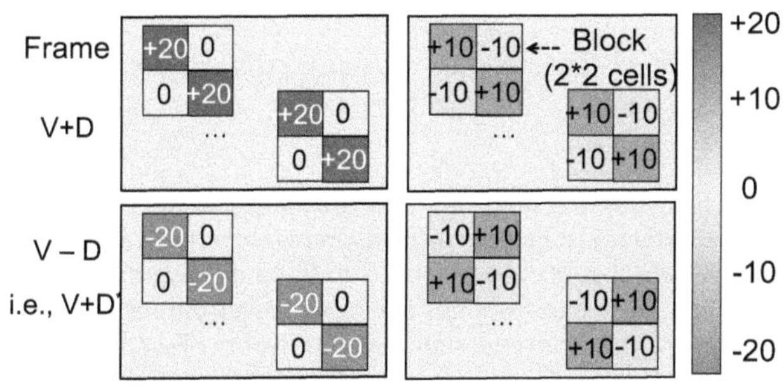


(a) Without spatial complements (b) With spatial complements

**Figure 5: Illustration of spatial complementary frames (SCFs): (a) no spatial complements (only TCF is applied) and (b) spatial complements is used with TCF (that is, STCF).**

**Temporal complementary frames (TCF).** A pair of data frames $D$ and $D^*$ are called temporal complementary frames (complementary frames for short) with respect to the luminance level $v$ if all their pixels are complementary w.r.t $v$. It is easy to see that, after the temporal low-pass flicker fusion of human vision system, two complementary frames will yield average frames with luminance level $v$. (Again, in practice, we will set $v = 0$ when multiplexing with video content.) Note that, complementary frames always appear in pairs and take effect with temporal fusion. Given one data frame, it is easy to obtain its complementary frame. Figure 4 illustrates the basic idea of a complementary pattern design over consecutive frames.

**Spatial complementary frame (SCF).** Based on the complementary pixel concept, a frame consisting of spatially alternating complementary pixels (*i.e.* neighboring pixels are always complementary to each other) are called a spatial complementary frame. Figure 5b illustrates one spatially complementary pattern, where two neighboring pixels meet $v_p + v_p^* = 0$. Due to the spatial low-pass filtering property of human eyes, a spatial complementary frame will be perceived as a grey frame with average luminance. We realize it is actually the exact principle of dithering used in printing that can produce mid-tones with only black ink. When adding a zero-mean spatial complementary frame to a video frame, we will hardly see the difference.

**Spatial-temporal complementary frames (STCF).** Combining the two concepts above, we define spatial-temporal complementary frames as a pair of complementary frames each of which is a spatial complementary frame itself. Clearly, STCFs can leverage both the spatial and temporal low-pass filtering properties of human vision system. Compared with TCF, STCF would also be able to mitigate the phantom array effect. Hence, STCFs are more effective in suppressing the visibility of data frames when multiplexed to video content, as confirmed in the following feasibility study.

(a) Frame $V + D$ using STCF (b) Zoom-in view

**Figure 6: Examples of STCF frame (a) and its zoom-in view (b) using a normal sunset video frame.**

## 4.2 STCF Frame Structure Design

Recall the very purpose of design STCF is to convey data to a camera, therefore, we need to make sure enough artifacts (under the assertion of unnoticeable to humans) can be captured by the camera. Considering the possible blurring and geometric distortions (either the display or the camera) of the screen-to-camera channel, in INFRAME++, we make two changes.

First, we use a *Cell* as the basic operation unit (instead of the raw physical pixel of the display or camera). A Cell consists of $p * p$ physical pixels. All the element pixels of a Cell have (or assumed to have) the same luminance value when forming (at the sender) or handling (at the receiver) spatial-temporal complementary frames. Clearly, the cell size defines the minimum spatial resolution in use.

Second, we introduce a *Block* as the basic information-carrying unit. A Block consists $c * c$ ($c$ is an even number) neighboring complementary Cells, and exhibits certain visual pattern. In a simplest case, we may use existence of element cells of a Block area to convey one bit, as done in [31]. To pursue higher throughput, in INFRAME++, we allow flexible composition of Blocks from Cells while ensure Cell-level complementary within a Block (see §5). Thus, Blocks will exhibit multiple visual patterns, and one Block can carry multiple bits.

Figure 5a and 5b illustrate two consecutive frames of the original complementary frame scheme in [31] and the proposed STCF. For frame $V + D$, in the original scheme, some Blocks may contain Cells organized in a chessboard pattern, with values $\delta = 20$ and 0; and other Blocks may contain all zero Cells. In contrast, in STCF, Blocks may contain Cells organized in different pattern, but with values $\delta = \pm 10$, and Cells are all complementary to their neighbors in a Block, even without a temporarily complementary frame. For the temporially complementary frame $V - D$, all the adjustment values are reversed.

Figure 6 illustrates the visual effect of multiplexed frames when SCTFs are adopted. Due to spatially complementary patterns, SCTFs are less noticeable even when being presented in the static form of an image, compared with our prior work [31]. One may argue that the original scheme uses patterns of $\delta$/0 Cells, and it is actually a mean-shifted version of a spatial complementary pattern. We point out that such a mean-shift (of STCF) has profound impact. Without it, the average luminance of a chessboard-patterned Block will have a non-zero change, whereas a zero Block have a zero average. When multiplexed to video content, they will cause unequal

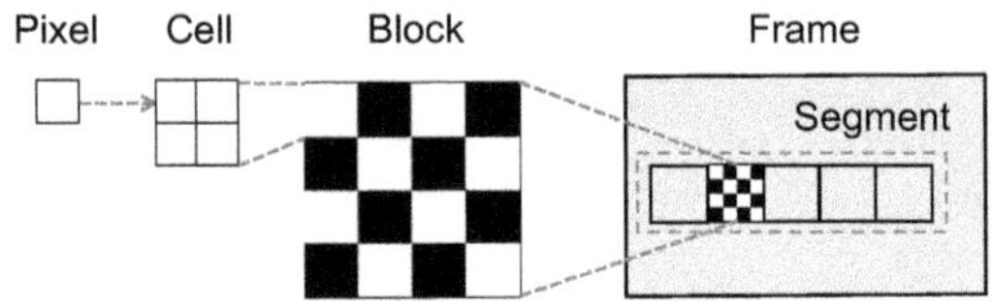


(a) Spatial structure

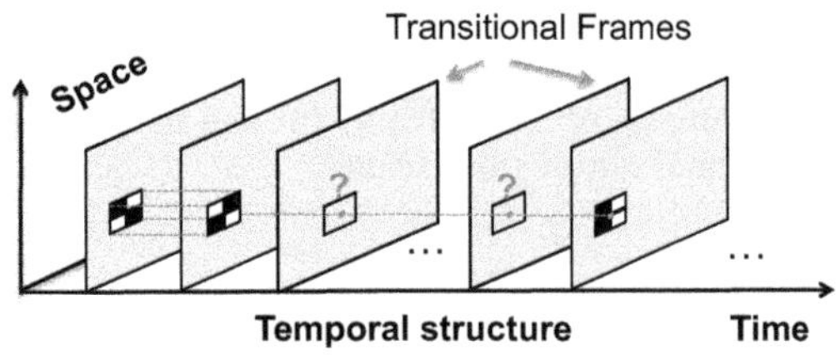


(b) Temporal structure

**Figure 7: Structure of STCF in space and over time.**

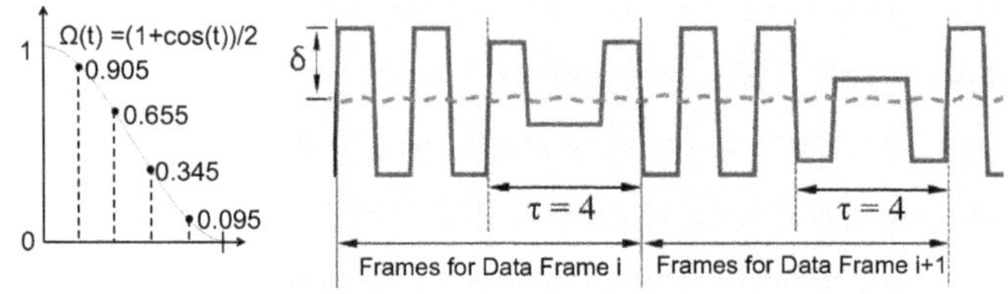


(a) $\Omega(t)$ (b) Amplitude transition waveforms

**Figure 8: An example of transition waveform when data frame amplitude varies from $\delta$ to $-\delta$ (green and blue solid curve) and its perception effect (purple dotted curve) after applying an electronic low-pass filter. Here, $\tau = 4$ and $\Omega(t)$ is half of the square-root raised Cosine waveform. For simplicity, the primary video frame $V$ is not displayed, but the delta part for data frames.**

luminance changes that can only rely on the complementary frame to mitigate. Worse even, the actual impact on human perception will be dependent on the actual video content. For example, adding the same delta to a bright or dark area will lead to different visual changes. On the contrary, the average of a Block in STCF is always zero. Multiplexing STCF with video content will have minimum visual impact. An alternative way to read this benefit is that we can use much larger $\delta$ in STCF if to achieve the same level of invisibility of the original scheme. This is also helpful as it allows more effective capture and detection of artifacts at the receiver.

Note that the introduction of Cells and Blocks makes it possible that the resulting data frame is not spatially complementary in the strict sense as neighboring pixels may be of identical values. Nevertheless, the resulting STCFs are still effective. They are significantly better than the scheme of [31]. Such improvements and the effectiveness of STCF have been validated through an extensive study in § 6.

Figure 7 shows the overall frame structure of formal STCF. Figure 7a decomposes the hierarchical spatial structure. A frame is made from intermediate logic units of Segments (for error protection purpose, see §5.3), Blocks, Cells, and the actual physical pixels. Figure 7b shows the temporal structure. Each data frame is rendered as a pair complementary frames. However, it encounters with a sharp change due to the transition between different data frames. To alleviate that, in addition to the complementary frames (the first two frames), we propose the transitional frames to ensure smooth switch to a different data frame, as described below.

## 4.3 Smoothing Transitional Frames

STCF can transmit a data frame invisibly. Different data frames will end up with different STCFs. We thus face with a critical challenge when transmitting dynamic data frames. This is concerning how to switch between consecutive STCF pairs. If it sharply switches from one to another (*e.g.*, from $V_1 - D_1$ to $V_1 + D_2$), strong flickers are noticed due to the low-pass filter property of human eyes. The abrupt switching is equivalent to a quick motion and imposes severe vision interference.

To mitigate the effect, we propose *smoothing transitional frames* to ensure gradual switch. We introduce a transition function $\Omega(t)$ to gradually change the amplitude of one data frame in a transition cycle $\tau$. When their luminance amplitude needs to switch from $\delta_j$ to $\delta_{j+1}$ between two successive data frames $D_j$ and $D_{j+1}$, the luminance of each Cell (*i.e.* all physical pixels in the Cell) in the $t$-th transition frame ($t = 0, 1, \ldots, \tau - 1$) turns into

$$v + \begin{cases} (-1)^t[(\delta_j - \delta_{j+1}) \cdot \Omega(t) + \delta_{j+1}], & \delta_j > \delta_{j+1} \\ (-1)^t[(\delta_{j+1} - \delta_j) \cdot \Omega(t) + \delta_j], & \delta_j < \delta_{j+1} \\ (-1)^t \delta_j, & \delta_j = \delta_{j+1} \end{cases} \quad (1)$$

Note that, if a Cell does not need to change, the amplitude will remain constant, just like the original complementary frames. $\Omega(t)$ is a waveform that decreases from 1 to 0. In our experiments, we use the half the square-root raised Cosine waveform for $\Omega(t)$ after comparing with linear and stair function forms. Parameters $\tau$ is also critical to data communication. Through our user study, we find that a small $\tau$ ($\leq 4$) is needed when STCF is adopted. This greatly reduces the count of transition frames when the temporary scheme is used where a minimum value is 10-14 in [31].

Figure 8 gives an illustrative example of a switch from $\delta$ to $-\delta$. That is, when $\tau = 4$, $\Omega(t) = [0.905, 0.655, 0.345, 0.095]$. By applying the above equation, the amplitude coefficients for each frame (including complementary frame pairs) are $0.81\delta$, $-0.31\delta$, $-0.31\delta$, $0.81\delta$, in turn. Notice that there have adopted multiple replica complementary frames out of one single data frame. Such repeated transmissions are to cope with possible mismatches between the display refresh rate (*e.g.* 120FPS) and camera capture rate (*e.g.* 30FPS). For example, a public display may send data over a variety of cameras.

In essence, we generate multiple intermediate data frames, which are multiplexed with video frames, to ensure imperceptible transition between two different data frames. Spatially, each data frame adopts special patterns to alleviate their visual effects. Temporally, we take two forms of smoothing. One is over two consecutive frames that complement to each other, and the other is over multiple transition frames which gradually switches between different data frames. Note that, the above temporal smoothing also helps to mitigate the rolling shutter effect [24] as the corrupted data can be recovered from other frames. We will address this problem in next section.

# 5. BOOST DATA COMMUNICATION OVER SCREEN-TO-CAMERA CHANNEL

With the presence of the primary screen-to-eye content, what available at the receiver is some artifacts – a mixture of the original video content plus the added data frame that have undergone various screen-to-camera channel distortions such as blurring, geometrical distortion, imprecise positioning, frame rate mismatch, rolling shutter effects, *etc.*. Despite the STCF design, the requirement not to affect the normal viewing experience dictates the amplitude of the data frame to be relatively small when compared to the dynamic range of video content. This is in sharp comparison with other screen-to-camera work where the "background" of their codes are clean and large amplitude (*e.g.* black or white) is allowed [11, 14, 22, 30]. It is also different from those work that hide codes in static images [19, 34, 36] where the background does not change, and those video/image watermarking and steganography work [5, 9, 12, 17, 20, 26, 35] where the altered video/images assumed available at the receiver without any errors (no screen-to-camera channels). To achieve high throughput, it is imperative to make good use of these artifacts. In this section, we present our designs and special measures to achieve the goal.

## 5.1 CDMA-like Modulation

As aforementioned, Blocks can be formed from complementary Cells in different ways and exhibit as different visual patterns. Thus, a Block may carry multiple bits. Assume $K$ bits are mapped into certain Block $D_k[c, c]$, $k \in \{1, 2, \ldots 2^K\}$, and $2^K$ is the number of unique Block type. Each Block has a size of $c * c$ Cells ($c$ is an even number). Modulation is concerning how to select (or form) these Blocks. After multiplexing, the screen area corresponding to the Block is displayed in the form of $V[c, c] \pm D_k[c, c]$. On the receiver side, it is captured as $V'[c, c] \pm D'_k[c, c]$. Demodulation is to infer which Block (*i.e.* visual pattern) is used at the specific position of the captured frame.

With the interference of video content and possible channel distortions in mind, we devise a Code Division Multiple Access (CDMA)-like modulation scheme to facilitate accurate and robust demodulation at the receiver. For simplicity, we assume $D_k[c, c]$ is an $c * c$ matrix which is arranged by a code vector $\phi_k$ (each element is 1 or -1), multiplied by $\delta$. These codes satisfies two properties: the orthogonality between any two codes and the zero sum of each code. That is, $\langle \phi_k, \phi_j \rangle = 0, k \neq j$ and $\sum(\phi_k) = 0$, where $\langle , \rangle$ is an operator of inner product.

By exploiting their orthogonality and the zero sum, we infer the block type with the maximum inner product with the received block. That is,

$$\hat{k} = \arg\max_k \langle D_k[c, c], V'[c, c] + D'_k[c, c] \rangle. \tag{2}$$

This is because

$$\begin{aligned} & \langle D_j[c, c], V'[c, c] + D'_k[c, c] \rangle \\ = & \langle D_j[c, c], V'[c, c] \rangle + \langle D_j[c, c], D'_k[c, c] \\ = & \sum_r \sum_l (\delta_j(r, l) \cdot v'(r, l)) + \sum_r \sum_l (\delta_j(r, l) \cdot \delta'_k(r, l)) \\ \approx & \; v' \cdot \delta \cdot \sum(\phi_j) + \delta^2 \cdot \langle \phi_j, \phi_k \rangle \\ = & \begin{cases} 0, & \text{if } k \neq j \\ c^2 \delta^2, & \text{if } k = j \end{cases} \end{aligned} \tag{3}$$

The first part assumes that the luminance level of original video is almost invariant in a small block[1] and thus our demodulation can work regardless of unknown $V$. The second part reaches its maximum only when $j = k$, otherwise it approximates to zero.

Note our design is different from the typical use of CDMA, where each bit is spread with one specific code (vector). Instead, we select a set of orthogonal codes (the selection criteria given as below) and map them into a bit sequence. For convenience, we assume the Cell size $c = 2^n$. We generate a set of orthogonal vectors of size $2^{n+1}$ using Walsh functions [2] and arrange each into a matrix. We then choose a subset as desired CDMA code that satisfies the following constraints:

1. The length of contiguous 1 or -1 vertically or horizontally is no more than a given number $\eta$.
2. Each matrix is unique subject to circular shifts. That is, a code cannot be identical to a circular shift of any other matrices in the subset.
3. Each matrix is unique subject to reverse operation (*i.e.* interchange 1 and $-1$). That is, a code cannot be the exact element-wise opposite of any other matrices in the subset.
4. The absolute Hamming distance of any two different matrices in the subset is $2^{2n-1}$.

We define the *absolute Hamming distance* of matrix $A$ and $B$ as follows.

DEFINITION 1. *Let $d(r, l) = h(\texttt{cshift}(A, r, l), B)$, where $h$ is the Hamming distance function, and* `cshift` *is the circular shift matrix of A by $r$ rows and $l$ columns. The absolute Hamming distance is the minimum value,* $\min_{r,l}\{N/2 - |N/2 - d(r, l)|\}$, *where $N$ is the matrix size.*

Each of above constraints has certain implications. The first constraint is to ensure invisibility. A code/matrix represents a visual pattern. We discover that we will not perceive flickers if the continuous cell is small enough (see §6.1). So $\eta$ should be set to an appropriate number. The second constraint is to tolerate possible imprecise Block locating (*e.g.* Block position shift) at the receiver, which may cause a detected Block to contain partial contents from two neighboring actual Blocks. The third constraint is due to the complementary frame design, and it is not possible to know which frame (*e.g.* $V+D$ or $V-D$) is captured. We thus need to avoid opposite patterns within a frame. The last constraint ensures that the chosen matrices are *optimal* in a sense that they are most different from each other, since the value $2^{2k-1}$ is the maximum absolute Hamming distance of any two $2^k * 2^k$ binary matrices. Hence, this modulation scheme is resilient to errors caused by blurs or distortions.

**Modulation operation.** In INFRAME++, we modulate each block by the above scheme. Generally, we map $K$ bits to a block containing $2^n * 2^n$ cells. We set $\eta = 2$ and write a program to search for the subset. Table 1 visualizes the qualified matrices when $n$ and $K$ both are chosen from 1, 2 and 3, where black and white color corresponding to element '1' and '-1', respectively. The matrices (*i.e.* codes) governs the modulation and its element indicates the modifications we will apply to a Cell. If the matrix element is 1,

| Matrix size | Subset |
|---|---|
| 2*2 |  |
| 4*4 | 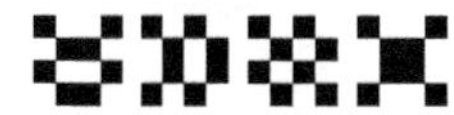 |
| 8*8 |  |

**Table 1: Examples of the matrices used in INFRAME++. Black indicates 1 while white indicates -1.**

[1]This assumption holds for most cases as Block size is small (*e.g.* 12×12 in our implementation) especially on HD videos. If the video indeed contains rich texture, error detection may result. This is confirmed in our experiments and we handle such cases with error protection.

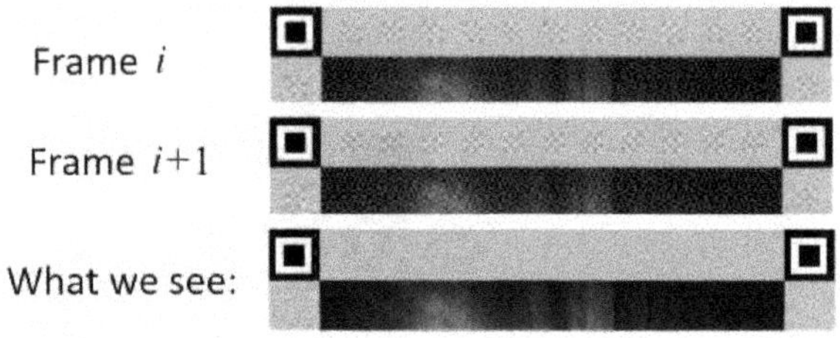


**Figure 9: Illustration of frame locators and alignment Blocks along border.**

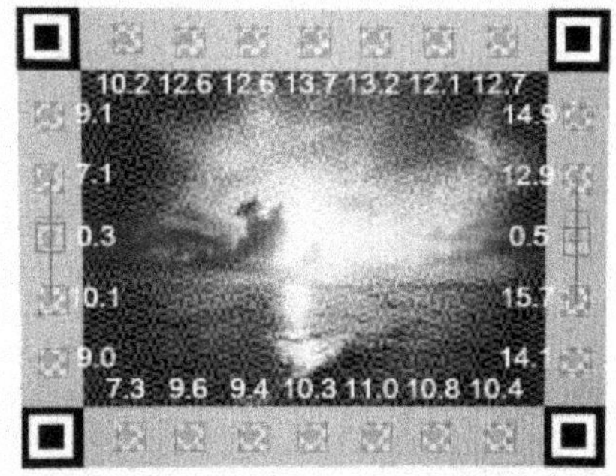


**Figure 10: The locating procedure of alignment Blocks. Green points are estimated positions of alignment Blocks, and red rectangles are final determined positions. White numbers are variances of correlation values. The third Block in the left border and corresponding one in the right border are not clear due to rolling shutter effect, thus leading to a low variance (0.3 and 0.5). Their positions are re-calculated by interpolation. Note that locators and Blocks are enlarged for clearer visual.**

then the luminance level of the Cell (all the $p * p$ physical pixels) increases by $\delta$. Otherwise, it decreases by $\delta$. The spatial coding efficiency – *i.e.*, how many bits are carried per Cell or pixel – can be computed as $K/c^2$ (per cell) or $K/(cp)^2$ (per pixel). To ensure high throughput, it should be tuned high while keeping the error rate low.

**Demodulation in INFRAME++.** Basically, demodulation works by comparing, and selecting the maximum, the inner-product of the received Block and all the possible codes, as given in Equ(2). However, the absolute value of the cross-correlation has to be used to cater for the (temporal) complementary frames. In addition, we take the extra measures to address some practical issues. First, the captured Block size may be different from code matrices, we need to match their sizes via down-sampling (mostly) or up-sampling. Assume original Block size is $cp * cp$ (in physical pixels). For an $M * M$ captured Block, we need to resample it and restore a $cp * cp$ Block for correlation matching. In practice, we may use the nearest mapping strategy for computation efficiency. The $(i, j)$-th element will take value of the $([\frac{i*M}{cp}], [\frac{j*M}{cp}])$-th element of the captured Block. Second, we perform a local search in a window of [-2,2] pixels in both X and Y dimension around the predicted Block position to counteract possible block shifting caused by inaccurate Block locating (see next). We thus obtain multiple inner products and will pick the maximum one.

## 5.2 Robust Block Localization

Despite the CDMA-like modulation and the search process adopted in correlation-based demodulation process, to achieve good performance, a prerequisite condition is to accurately locate the Blocks, as the search process only does local refinement. The Block locating method also needs to be robust to possible channel distortions.

**Locator and alignment patterns.** In INFRAME++, we follow the practice of a standard QR code [16] design but adapt the design to serve our needs. In particular, we adopt the standard *locator* of a QR code for its proven robustness and ease of detection. A locator is a regular square with each border is arranged with 1:1:3:1:1 for black, white, black, white and black in turn, as shown at corners in Figure 9. We use four locators, one at each frame corner, whereas the QR code needs only three [16]. While we can make locators invisible in principle, we deliberately make them visible in INFRAME++, for several considerations: 1) robust detection of locators is crucial; 2) we need to make user aware of the existence of the side screen-to-camera channel; 3) we can achieve fast locating by avoiding correlation-based detection; and 4) putting them at corners is not distractive anyway.

We also adopt *alignment patterns* along the four borders of the screen (whereas the QR code applies on the top and left borders only). Unlike locators, the border alignment patterns are made invisible. We use the regular chessboard pattern that contains $6 \times 6$ alternating Cells ($\pm\delta$), using the double width and height of a regular cell. For sake of clear presentation, we term them as *alignment Blocks*. Clearly, alignment Blocks are also spatial complementary patterns. In our design, alignment Blocks are evenly distributed along the borders and take half of space, as shown in Figure 9.

Alignment Blocks are designated to handle potential geometrical distortions, such as radial distortion of display, pincushion distortion of camera, and perspective distortion from imperfect capture, *etc.*.Since they serve as references to real data Blocks, special care is taken to ensure accurate identification of alignment Blocks. Note that, like normal data Blocks, alignment Blocks are detected using correlation matching and a local search process is also exerted. We thus design the following logic to infer their positions. First, we calculate their theoretical positions from the positions of frame locators. We then try to detect the alignment Block and record the intermediate correlation values obtained in the search process. If the variance of those correlation values exceeds a threshold, we treat the one with maximum correlation as the actual alignment Block; otherwise, we treat it as a miss detection. Finally, the positions of missing alignment Blocks are re-calculated through interpolation using nearest successful neighbors. Figure 10 shows an example. The rationale is that, if an alignment Block is indeed corrupted, the search process will result in similar correlation values, hence no clear winner and small variances.

**Block locating.** Ideally we can readily locate the data Blocks using the positions of alignment Blocks. However, channel distortions can be non-linear and non-uniform, *e.g.*, pincushion distortion from a camera. Simple linear locating method can thus lead to erroneous locating results. The locating schemes introduced in [30] are also not applicable since it is difficult to differentiate locators from the original video content. In INFRAME++, we locate a data Block using the following algorithm (for Y coordinate), taking as input the coordinates of frame locators and alignment Blocks on the borders. The key idea is to consider possibly different distortion ratio of the left border ($left$) and the right border ($right$). The algorithm for determine the X coordinate is similar.

$$left = \frac{border_{left}[j].Y - corner_{left-top}.Y}{corner_{left-bottom}.Y - corner_{left-top}.Y}$$

$$right = \frac{border_{left}[j].Y - corner_{right-top}.Y}{corner_{right-bottom}.Y - corner_{right-top}.Y}$$

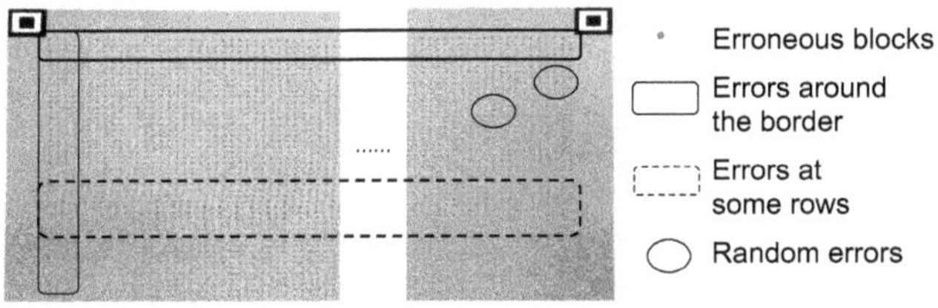


**Figure 11: Illustration of the error distribution without error protection mechanism where a CDMA-like modulation is applied only. The red points represent wrong blocks and the green marks the correct blocks after demodulation. Note that the middle parts of both are removed to save space.**

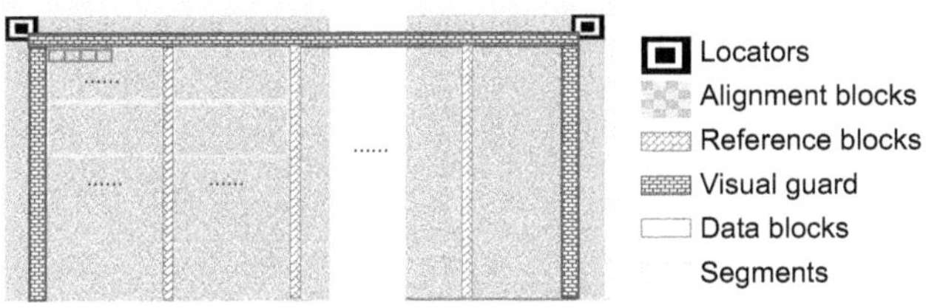


**Figure 12: Illustration of one INFRAME++ data frame layout.**

$$r_X = \frac{border_{top}[i].X - corner_{left-top}.X}{corner_{right-top}.X - corner_{left-top}.X}$$
$$r_Y = left * (1 - r_X) + right * r_X$$
$$Y = border_{top}[i].Y * (1 - r_Y) + border_{bottom}[i] * r_Y$$

## 5.3 Error Resilience

We analyze the error distribution (see Figure 11 for an illustrative example) and identify three common types of errors: 1) errors around borders; 2) errors at specific rows; and 3) random errors. They match well with observations in other related work. The first is mainly caused by more severe blurring and distortion at borders [11]; the second results from the rolling shutter effect [14]; and the last can arise from the interference from primary video content and many other factors [15, 30]. We propose several techniques to make INFRAME++ more resilient to errors. They induce extra overhead or redundancy, which is a trade-off for reliability.

**Visual guard.** Instead of taking big efforts to recover data at highly erroneous areas, we choose not to send data there. We thus devise visual guard by leaving blank area around borders, as shown in Figure 12. At the guard areas, the original video content is untouched. This provides a natural isolation (guard interval) between data Blocks, border alignment Blocks and even background (out of the screen). This measure wastes some resources (guard areas do not carry bits) but the overhead is comparably small for the full-screen data delivery.

**Channel reference Blocks.** Due to inherent rolling shutter effects, the screen-to-camera channel are selectively lossy. It is critical for us to self-learn and respond to the varying channel quality. Borrowing the concept of reference symbol in wireless communications, we place channel reference Blocks (with known patterns) at specific known positions. We insert them evenly into data Blocks (for example, every $x$ rows and $y$ columns, as shown in Figure 12). This allows us to estimate the error rate at specific rows (or areas) from these reference Blocks. Once the error rate ($\frac{|error(Ref)|}{|Ref|}$) is larger than some threshold (say, 0.3), we discard those rows (or areas) and treat them as an erasure. As data frames are repeatedly sent with multiple complementary frames, we can fill up erasures from subsequent frames, or through error protection coding. Note that techniques [14] to combat rolling shutter effects complements our design.

**Error detection and coding.** We apply channel coding to enhance its resilience to random errors. To this end, we introduce one additional structural unit – *Segment*. A Segment consists of a group of neighboring Blocks (see Figure 7(a)) and is the minimum unit for error coding. Within a Segment, we apply simple but common error detection and/or correction code such as parity-check, forward error coding (FEC) [33], and RS code [32]. Further framing optimizations [30] are permitted, *e.g.*, to handle erasure. They complement our design.

## 5.4 Lessons and Discussion

We have tried several techniques proposed in conventional screen-to-camera communication to boost throughput of INFRAME++. Some failed or offered limited help. We summarize several lessons we have learned and discuss potential improvement.

First, individual color channels are hardly useful for INFRAME++. It was expected to double or even triple data throughput if each R,G,B color channel could carry data independently, as demonstrated in [11]. We found three-fold reasons: 1) energy leakage and cross-corruption among channels when being captured by a camera; 2) impact of the primary video; and 3) only very small delta amplitude can be used. The latter two become more an issue due to the former phenomenon.

Second, we noticed that the data-carrying ability depends on the video content. Certain dark and slow-moving portions are able to carry more bits. This shows room for potential improvements through video content adaptation. However, due to heavy computation overhead to analyze the video, this technique is not appealing to real-time rendering. But it is possible to do it offline, especially when the data is pre-defined and paired with the video. In this work, we focus on a generic scheme. We leave the adaptive design for future work.

Third, we admitted that the above scheme for resilience, including visual guard, channel reference blocks, and error coding, indeed lowers the achieved throughput (as shown in §6). The parameters used serve as knotting points between the throughput and the error rate. They should be adapt to dynamic environments (camera capability, visible channel quality, distance) and different communication requirements (tolerance to errors) as well. However, in this work, we used a set of pre-configured parameters and they may not achieve the best performance in all the test environment. We leave the adaptive design as future work.

Fourth, INFRAME++ has two trigger manners during video watching. The first uses an automatic trigger where the video processing will detect whether INFRAME++ is adopted in the video through detecting of four locators. The second is a manual one where the user clicks a button or opens an INFRAME++ receiver app after knowing a INFRAME++-enabled video in advance. In this work, we use the latter and all the videos are INFRAME++ enabled. The automatic discovery yields better usability (free of human efforts) but requires more resource for continuous processing. Energy efficiency and detection error handling are other questions that we need to address in more practical scenarios.

# 6. IMPLEMENTATION & EVALUATION

We implement the prototype of INFRAME++ with about 5000 lines of code. It consists of a sender and a receiver. The sender takes an original video stream and a data bitstream as its input, generates the multiplexed stream, and then plays back the video stream at precisely controlled frame rate. The receiver takes the captured

| Pure color (ex: gray) | Football | Golf | Beach | Sunset |
|---|---|---|---|---|
|  |  |  |  |  |

**Table 2: The screenshots of major test video clips.**

frames as its input, detects the existence of visual patterns, and decodes the recovered, possible corrupted frames into the output data. For real-time rendering, the sender is mainly implemented in GPU. Specifically, we use C# to write most logical part of the program, but also use the *DirectCompute* [21] techniques in DirectX 11 to realize the multiplexing and rendering in parallel in GPU. As a result, it supports real-time playback under 120FPS frame rate in all of our experimental settings. Currently, the receiver works in an offline mode. We use the smartphone camera to capture the video frames and run processing afterwards.

We evaluate INFRAME++ in two aspects. First, we conduct a user study to validate whether our design ensures normal screen-to-human viewing without quality degradation or interference. Second, we assess its data communication performance (*i.e.*, throughput, bit error rate and processing speed).

**Experimental Settings.** We use an Eizo FG2421 24' LCD monitor, which supports $1920\times1080$ spatial resolution and 120FPS frame rate. In our experiments, we set the brightness as 100%. On the receiver side, we use three phone models (Lumia 1020, Samsung Galaxy S5 and Note 3) to capture the display. The video-capturing resolution and frame rate are set to be $1920\times1080$ and 30FPS, respectively. We use a pseudo-random data generator with a pre-set seed to generate the input data stream. All experiments are conducted in typical indoor office settings, at the default watching distance 60cm (a desktop width). We have conducted an extensive study to assess the impacts of various design choices and environments conditions, including luminance contrast range $\delta$, cell size $c$, count of transitional frames $\tau$, CDMA block scheme, and data frame rate, as well as scenario settings such as video sources and watching distance.

## 6.1 Subjective Perception Assessment

We conduct a user study to evaluate the subjective perception quality and identify a good set of design parameters for INFRAME++. We invited 15 volunteering participants (college students and company employees) in USA and China, 6 female and 9 male, aged between 21 to 36, with half of them wearing glasses. Among the participants, there were a designer and a video expert, who are more sensitive to video quality. We showed original and revised videos side by side, and asked them to rate the flicker (video quality change) with scores 0 to 4, where 0 indicates "*no difference at all*," and 1 to 4 signifies "*almost unnoticeable*," "*merely noticeable*," "*evident flicker*," and "*strong flicker or artifact*," respectively. In our user study, 0 and 1 denote satisfactory scores. In some tests where the observation is highly consistent among testers and anticipated (*e.g.*, testing with a smaller $\delta = 10$ when invisibility at a larger $\delta > 20$ is validated), the participant scale varies from 6 to 15.

**Video sources.** We first test with a variety of video sources to examine whether our scheme can be widely applicable. We select 12 video clips with different characteristics on brightness, contrast, texture and motion. Table 2 shows the screenshots of five representative video clips. We employ the pure colored video with different brightness where their RGBs vary from (50, 50, 50) to (200, 200, 200) (from dark to light). The pure colored video is adopted for its ease to detect any visual artifact. Other clips are manually classified into several categories: (1) contrast: strong (sunset, sunrise, beach), mild (golf, car race, elephant) and weak/no (football, lattice); (2) motion: fast (football, golf, car race), mild (beach, sunset), slow/static(elephant, lattice); and (3) regular texture (lattice).

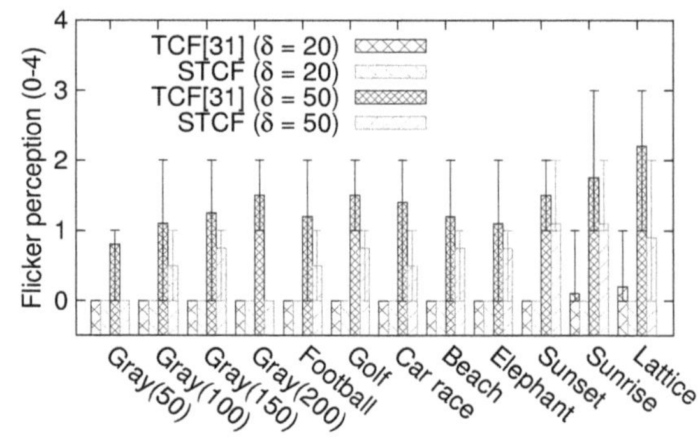


**Figure 13: Flicker perception (avg, min, max) in tests with various background videos/images.**

Figure 13 show the perceived flicker scores using STCF, compared with TCF [31]. We use a Cell of $3 * 3$ pixels and a Block of $4 * 4$ Cells, that is, $12 * 12$ pixels. We test with two luminance adjustment ranges ($\delta = 20, 50$). That is, the amplitude in STCF is $\pm\delta/2$ whereas the one in TCF is $\delta$ or 0. More options are evaluated in the following tests. We make three observations. First, it is viable to alter different video frames without noticeable flickers. When STCF is adopted, most scores are 0 even when $\delta$ is as large as 50. Second, the visual perception slightly changes under different brightness, motion and contrast characteristics. Generally speaking, it is easier to notice flickers in a brighter, faster-moving video with stronger contrast. Third, the adoption of spatial complementary patterns greatly alleviates flickers than the pure temporal one. This allows INFRAME++ a larger choice room to chase for good data communication performance. By default, we choose gray and sunset as the source videos.

**Luminance adjustment range $\delta$.** Figure 14a present the averaged flicker scores as $\delta$ varies from 10 to 70. For clarity, we provide the max-min score in the STCF (gray) case. As expected, the smaller the adjustment, the fewer flickers. Even when $\delta$ goes up to 50, the resulting visual quality change is still mostly imperceivable for both schemes. However, STCF is much more robust, with fewer flickers under the same condition. Considering invisibility is a subtle and subjective perception (the score is split when $\delta \geq 40$), and the changes should be significant enough to be captured. We believe that $\delta \in (20, 40)$ is a safe choice.

**Cell size and distance.** Figure 14b shows the perceived flicker with regards to various cell sizes when $\delta = 20$, at a watching dis-

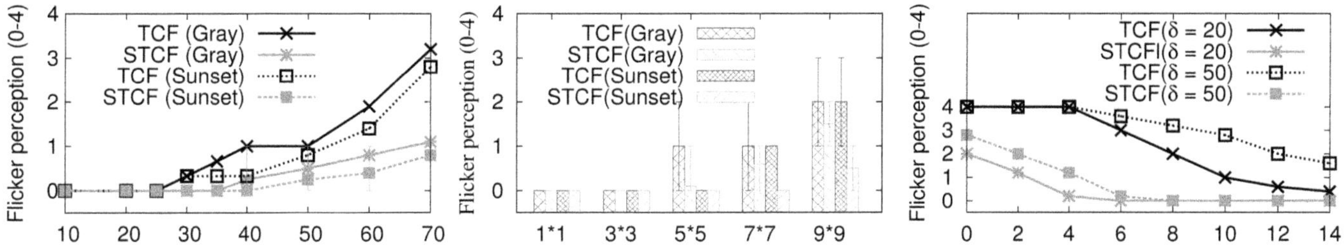


(a) Flicker vs. adjustment $\delta$ (b) Flicker vs. cell size $c$ (c) Flicker vs. transition count $\tau$

**Figure 14: Perception degradation (flickers) versus design options of adjustment range $\delta$, cell size $c$ and transitional frame count $\tau$.**

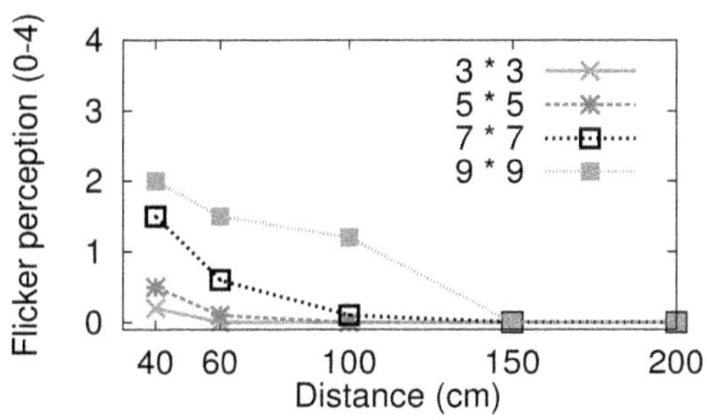


**Figure 15: Flicker vs. distance when STCF is used for a gray background video.**

| Factor | Invisibility | Data | Choice |
|---|---|---|---|
| contrast range $\delta \uparrow$ | $\downarrow (< 60)$ | $\uparrow$ | $20 - 40$ |
| cell size c $\uparrow$ | $\downarrow (< 7 * 7)$ | $\uparrow$ | $3 * 3$ |
| transition $\tau \uparrow$ | $\uparrow (< 4)$ | $\downarrow$ | 4 |
| distance $\uparrow$ | $\uparrow$ | $\downarrow$ | N/A |

**Table 3: Summary of factor impact and design choice for INFRAME++.**

tance of 60cm. Clearly, the smaller size, the fewer flickers. STCF allows up to $7 * 7$ without noticeable flickers, at a 60cm distance. In this case, the user is more sensitive to the pure color (gray) because the contrast is more obvious. We further test with different watching distance. It is prone to more flickers at a closer distance. When the distance is larger than 150cm, no flickers are noticed. All these match with our common understanding of spatial resolution. However, we want to point out, while it become harder for us to see it, so does the camera. This will be observed in the following evaluation of data communication.

**Transitional frame count $\tau$.** Figure 14c studies the impact of temporal smoothing cycle $\tau$. Longer cycles tend to reduce the perceived flickers. It is clearly seen that STCF has made significant improvement over TCF. INFRAME++ needs at most 4 transition frames (2 are OK) to handle dynamic data while INFRAME [31] needs at least 10 frames even when $\delta = 20$.

**Summary.** Our assessment validates that INFRAME++ is able to achieve our first goal of no impaired viewing experience. Table 3 summarizes the parameter impact. All match with our expectation. Basically, a smaller $\delta$, a smaller cell $c$, and a larger $\tau$ tend to hide changes. Considering the requirements for data communication and invisibility robustness, we select design parameters given in Table 3. Here, we set the cell size $3 * 3$ because the good choice for invisibility should be no larger than $7 * 7$ and CDMA-like modulation may need to concatenate $\eta$ same cells. When we set $\eta = 2$, it is safe to use a $3 * 3$ cell, though a larger cell is still allowed in some cases.

## 6.2 Data Communication

We run experiments to evaluate the performance of each design module and its factor impact. We divide INFRAME++ into three module sets: (1) *Basic*, which includes only visual modulation (§5.1) and block localization(§5.2). They are needed to satisfy the minimum requirements for data communication. With them, we are able to retrieve data bits directly from the captured patterns, but it may be prone to a high error rate, without any enhancement from the error protection measures (§5.3); (2) *Basic+Guard+Reference*, also marked as "*w/ GR*" , covers two more modules to handle errors caused by distortions over screen-to-camera channels. Both are used to manually erase the errors which occurs with known pattens (*e.g.*, at the border or at several rows). As a result, it likely reduce the error rate but also reduce the available throughput. (3) *Basic+Guard+Reference+Code*, short for "*w/ GRC*", is a full-version INFRAME++, including all other modules such as channel coding. We deliberately treat channel coding as an independent module because we just apply the well-established technique. Its function is well known to make an tradeoff between redundancy and reliability. We first use *Basic* INFRAME++ to test the performance of demodulation and block location. We then compare with *w/ GR* to assess the performance impact of virtual guard and channel reference block. Finally, we run comprehensive experiments. We run experiments using the following default setting unless explicitly specified. We use the pure gray color and sunset as our default video sources. In each test, we offline generate 120 multiplexed frames from 30FPS source video clips and 10FPS data frames (randomly generated), and play for 1 second on a 120FPS monitor. That is, each data frame has 12 replica (including its complements), where 4 out of them are transitional frames ($\tau = 4$). Other parameters learnt from the user study is $\delta = 40$ and $c = 3$. The smartphone captures the screen at a distance of 60cm, using ISO 200 at the rear camera. We run experiments 9 runs and show the median results.

**CDMA code design.** The visual modulation module has two key parameters: the code size (matrix size) and the size of the code block set, which determines the number of bits carried in one block. We choose the first 2, 4, 8 (if applicable) codes using a matrix of size $2\times2$, $4\times4$, or $8\times8$ in Table 1. Specifically, given a $3\times3$ Cell, each Block has $6\times6$, $12\times12$, $24\times24$ pixels, respectively. Figure 16 shows their BER and raw throughput. Note that raw throughput (throughput hereafter) is not the achievable one in practice, due to the overhead caused by errors. It counts all correctly received bits and it can be simply calculated as the product of the source rate and (1-BER) if no erasure happens. But it can be regarded as

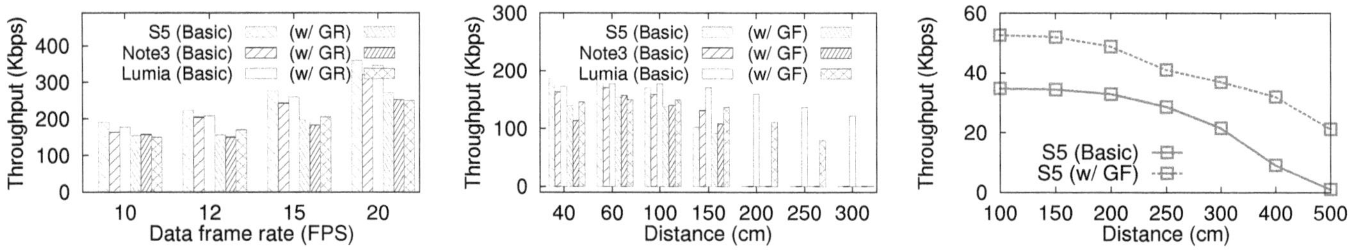


(a) Data frame rate (b) Watching distance (3 × 3 cell) (c) Watching distance (6 × 6 cell)

**Figure 18: Throughput w.r.t. different design parameters or settings: (a) data frame rate, (b) distance (a small $3 \times 3$ cell), (c) distance (using a larger size cell).**

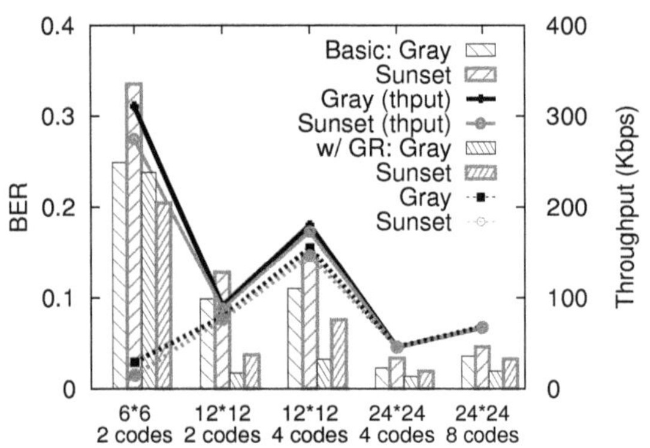


**Figure 16: Raw BER (bars) and throughput (lines) under various modulation designs in *Basic* mode and *w/ GR* mode where the modules of visual guard and channel reference are employed.**

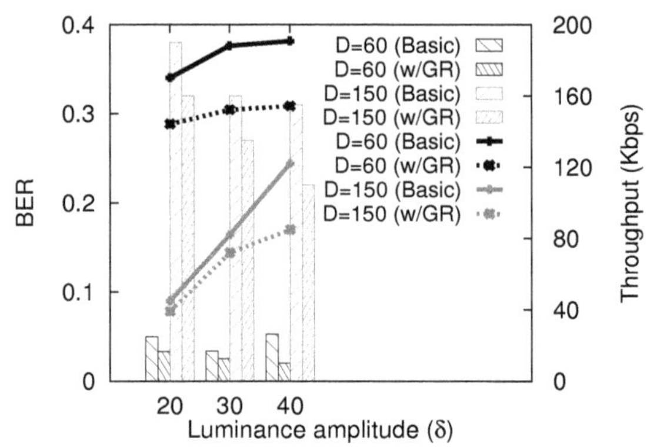


**Figure 17: BER and throughput vs. $\delta$.**

an indicator of the potential (upper bound) of achievable throughput, and is often used to evaluate screen-to-camera communication. We present the results using Lumia 1020 and the ones using other phones (S5 and Note3) are similar.

We have three observations. First, the larger block size can help to reduce BER when no measures of visual guard and channel reference are employed. The 6×6 block suffers from the highest error rate, as large as 30%. That is because only a 2 × 2 CDMA code is used and its correlation fails to reliably distinguish itself from the noise of primary video and inevitable distortions. As the block size grows, the orthogonal property is fully utilized. Its raw BER thus reduces to 10% (12×12 block) and 3–4% (24×24 block). Given the same block size, the one with fewer codes performs slightly better. This contributes to fewer block competitors. Second, with the error handling of visual guard and channel reference, the BER greatly reduces, especially when its raw error rate is slightly large. Especially, for a 12 × 12 Block, it reduces from 10-15% to 1-7%. It implies that many error happen at the border or are caused by rolling shutter effects. In fact, we also take a photo, not a video to capture the screen. We observe that the error rate is much lower, which also indicates that the rolling shutter effect is a major contributor to errors. Third, the impact on throughput is multi-facets. For 12 × 12 and 24×24 blocks, the throughput almost linearly increases w.r.t. the size of block set (*i.e.* the code number). It is easy to understand. CDMA codes are orthogonal and it can tolerate the existence with other codes. Though the 24×24 case has a lower error rate than the 12×12 one, its spatial efficiency (determining throughput) decreases due to more spaces to carry an unit bit. For instance, the 24×24 occupies 4x area but only doubles the throughput. As a consequence, the 12×12 outperforms 24×24 and other larger block design. The exception exhibits between 12×12 and 6×6 blocks. Ideally, the 6×6 has higher raw throughput but is hard to utilize due to a large error rate. So in the following experiments, we mainly use 12×12 Block with 4 codes (*i.e.*, 2 bit/block) as our default scheme. When we use the only one modulation scheme, the error rate and its throughput can be inferred. So we only plot the throughput due to space limit.

**Luminance adjustment range.** Figure 17 shows the results when $\delta$ varies from 20 to 40. We present only the sunset result because it is more challenging than the gray one. Basically, as $\delta$ increases, the throughput increases. At a near distance (60cm), no significant improvement is observed (about 20kbps gap). At a farther distance (150cm), a larger $\delta$ is of more help. Here we present the result for S5 because its performance degrades more at 150cm (see Figure 18b). This matches with our understanding. It also discloses that INFRAME++ offers a quite flexible room to fulfill its function. The gap between the basic and the w/GF implies a high erasure rate. We checked the captured videos and did observe strong rolling shutter effects. While INFRAME++ can detect the error through the reference block, it still requires extra mechanism to handle and recover from it. This can refer to recent work done by [14].

**Data frame rate.** Given a 120FPS fresh rate and a data frame rate $\mu$, each data frame will have $120/\mu$ replicas, out of which $\tau = 4$ frames are transitional frames. Figure 18a shows the throughput when the data frame rate increases from 10 to 20, that is, from

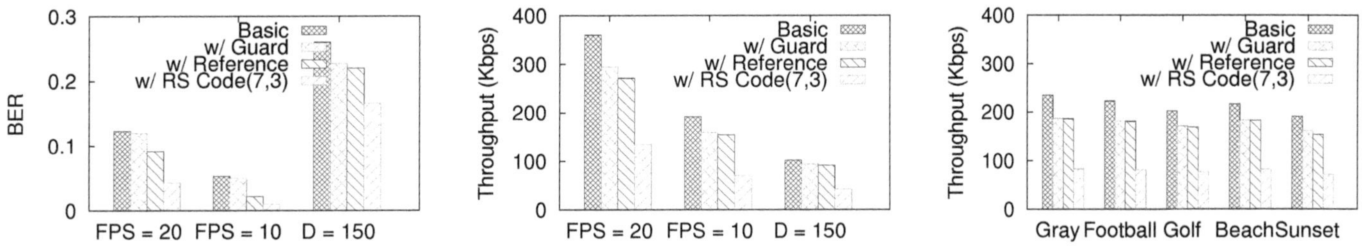


(a) BER under three settings (Sunset) (b) Throughput under three settings (Sunset) (c) Throughput for various sources

**Figure 19: BER and throughput after each module in INFRAME++.**

12 replicas to 6 replicas (minimum). Here, we only present the result for the sunset video, and the gray one has about 10–20Kbps improvement. We observe that the data rate steadily increases w.r.t $\mu$. It first implies that the camera is not a bottleneck, and it is able to capture data frames even it moves faster. Theoretically, it can support 360Kbps (*Basic*) and it still able to support as high as 270Kbps after the erasure made by visual guard and reference blocks. This demonstrates a significant improvement as high as 30–45x improvement than our prior work [31]. This is thanks to the adoption of STCF which allows a smaller number of transitional frame and a larger $\delta$. The CDMA design which carries more bits in one block, also contributes to the throughput improvement.

**Capture distance and phone models.** Figure 18b shows the throughput at different capturing distance. Basically, the nearer, the better. But we also notice there is an exception. For Note 3, when the capture distance reduces from 60cm to 40cm, more distortion occurs and thus hurts INFRAME++. We also notice that INFRAME++ fails when the distance is larger than one threshold (here, 2m for S5 and Note3, 3m for Lumia). We checked the captured videos and indeed observed that there were no patterns in the one captured by S5 and Note 3 and blurred patterns in Lumia. This matches with our expectation. Constrained by the requirement of unimpaired viewing even when being watched in vicinity, we configure the parameters, such as a $3 \times 3$ cell size; However, they can not work well at a far distance. In fact, a larger distance can allow a more flexible parameter choice (*e.g.* a larger $\delta$ and $c$), which can be leveraged to boost INFRAME++ without interfering video viewing. We further test with a larger cell size ($6 \times 6$, not $3 \times 3$). Figure 18c shows the throughput for S5 with the watching distance up to 5 meters. The results are similar for Lumia (better than S5) and Note 3 (worse than S5). The current setting can ensure unobstructive viewing experience between 1m and 5m. Clearly, the working distance is extended as the cell size increases. Note the overall throughput is decreased as a result of a smaller block density (declines by 4 fold). This is constrained by the physical size of the display. Under the current display and camera settings, when the distance goes beyond 3 meters, the error rate is pretty high, as large as 20-40%. This calls for a more robust scheme for communication.

**Design modules.** We now examine the role of each design modules. On top of the *basic* INFRAME++, we in turn enable the visual guard, channel reference blocks and channel coding. We use RS code (7,3) in this case. Figure 19a and Figure 19b show the BER as well as its throughput under three settings (1) default, (2) data frame rate $=$ 20 and the other same as default, and (3) distance is 150 cm and the other is the same as default. We only present the results for S5 when the sunset video is used. Figure 19b shows the throughput results for different video sources using $\delta = 40$, $D = 60cm$ and 10 FPS data frame. Clearly, the results are similar across video sources and the sunset video is slightly worse. We can see that all the error protection mechanisms are effective in reducing the error rate. However their cost is different. The channel coding depends on redundancy and thus decreases the throughput most. In most cases, Guard and reference block can efficiently reduce error rate while maintaining a graceful degrade on throughput. Under the default setting, all video sources can achieve about 200Kbps without any extra add-on feature (Basic) and eventually can achieve about 70-85kbps after all the error handling mechanisms are applied.

| | PC1 | PC2 | Mac Pro |
|---|---|---|---|
| Pure gray | 136FPS | 242 FPS | 250FPS |
| 720p video | 131FPS | 235 FPS | 185FPS |

**Table 4: The processing time for video/image encoding and rendering at three senders.**

| Threads | PC1 | PC2 | Requirement (10FPS) |
|---|---|---|---|
| single | 981ms | 908.7ms | 100ms |
| multiple | 269ms | 202.7 ms | |

**Table 5: The receiver's processing time for video decoding.**

**Encoding and Decoding Speed.** We finally examine the processing speed which is vital to real-time rendering and communication. We first measure the time to encode data frames, multiplex and render them in the screen. We use the default scheme: $12\times12$ block with 4 codecs, on the $1920\times1080$ resolution screen. We test with three machines: (1) PC1 with an Intel Core-i5 dual-core CPU, 8GB main memory and an AMD Radeon HD8490 video card; (2) PC2 with an Intel Xeon e5-1620 four-core CPU, 8GB main memory and an AMD FirePro V3900 video card; (3) Macbook Pro using an Intel Core-i5 dual-core CPU, 8GB main memory and Intel Iris integrated video card. Table 4 shows their processing speeds after they are stabilized. It is clear that the sender is able to support real-time operations since the processing speed is larger than 120FPS. This is attributed to the *DirectCompute* technique in GPU. However, the current processing time at the receiver is a little bit slower than the real-time requirement (Table 5). For 10FPS data frame rate (one new data frame is embedded every 100ms), it takes 200ms or 260ms to decode it, using multiple (4x) threads. The current receiver has not been optimized by GPU and thus it supports offline processing with a several seconds delay. We notice that similar GPU optimization is applicable. We are working on improving the decoding speed.

## 7. POTENTIAL APPLICATIONS

INFRAME++ is able to provide accompanying data communication without requiring any infrastructure (*e.g.*, Wireless, Mobile Networks). It offers a user-friendly approach to fetch information from an electronic display (*e.g.*, TV, ad board). We present two potential applications empowered by INFRAME++.

**Enhanced Video Ad (Ad++).** It offers an enhanced video advertising by providing metadata to the potential customers who are interested. The target scenario is to employ INFRAME++ on advertising electronic boards at the shopping malls or out of the buildings. It works as follows. At the screen corner, there is a small visible icon which indicates whether INFRAME++ is enabled or not. If so, the target user either use Google Glass or his phone camera to capture what he may be interested in, but not directly covered in the visible ad. Compare with the existing ad, it has several advantages. First of all, it still ensures the original, attractive video ad to most users. Data delivery is almost imperceptible to users and can be done on demand. For those who are really interested in the goods and want to know more, this offers a convenient channel to fetch extra information. Second, without being constrained by the screen size, it is able to carry on much richer information. The existing ad usually highlights several keywords (*e.g.*, price, phone number), while ad++ allows to carry several KB or more. Third, data dissemination adopts a digital form (bytes and texts) and thus it is ready for automatic processing, mining and archiving which are machine-friendly and user-friendly (no or litter human efforts). For instance, the user does not need to recognize and remember the seller's telephone number and manually type it into the phone. Instead, once the number is retrieved from the captured video, it can be automatically saved or prompted to the user for a call. Fourth, this scheme is infrastructure-free. This combats alternative solutions such as WiFi, Bluetooth, NFC which requires that the source (display) is equipped with extra hardware. Certainly, reliability of INFRAME++ should be greatly enhanced before its commercial adoption.

**Watching Authentication.** The co-channel delivery enforces a close association between human viewing activity and embedded data. Retrieving specific data from this video likely implies that the users indeed is watching this video. This intrinsic watching authentication provides one natural form to attract or allure real consumer attention, as well as a convenient and secure way to deliver some confidential or target information. For example, coupons or deals can be delivered through screen-to-camera links in INFRAME++. Many manufacturers hope to disseminate coupons to their customers only as a reward of watching their ads. If the coupon is embedded in the video, it will force the customers to watch the real videos. Otherwise, someone may play tricks to return to the ad page after the ad video ends, or through a simple click or a link after the video.

## 8. RELATED WORK

In this section, we compare INFRAME++ with the literature along three dimensions.

**Unobtrusive screen-to-camera communication.** Several recent studies seek to establish non-obtrusive screen-to-camera communications over static images, including VRCode [34], IVC [7], visual MIMO [36], and HiLight [19]. Specifically, VRCode delivers only static (tag) content using a hue-based barcode design [34]. [7, 36] hide data upon two consecutive frames (an original image and the one with embedded messages) where data is embedded in pyramid decomposition [36] and brightness change [7]. HiLight conveys data bits through the pixel transparency change within a time window [19]. Different from their work, we work on the dynamic video content with time-varying visual background, thus facing new challenges. In our solution, we leverage capability discrepancy between users and devices, as well as human vision characteristics when designing INFRAME++. Through the novel use of STCF, CDMA-like modulation and error protection, INFRAME++ has not only addressed more practical system issues, but also achieved higher data rate (360kbps with an 30-60x growth of our prior work [31]).

**Conventional screen-to-camera communications.** They focus on data communications while exclusively occupying the (entire or part of) the screen [11, 14, 15, 22, 30]. They thus differ from our primary goal of establishing dual-mode, concurrent visual channels for data communication and video viewing. Nevertheless, their proposed techniques, which address challenges inherent in screen-to-camera channels such as rolling shutter effect [14], dynamic capture quality [15], error handling [30], can be applicable to INFRAME++.

**Watermarking and Steganography.** Watermarking and steganography also embed data into signals (*e.g.*, images or videos) in a covert manner [8, 23, 37]. The main approach to data information hiding is to make the altered signals as close to the original ones as possible. For example, a common technique is to manipulate only the LSB (least significant bit) of pixels either in a deterministic fashion [5, 17, 20, 35] or in a randomized manner [9, 12, 26]. Watermarking is designed primarily for authenticity verification or integrity checking, whereas stealthiness is of less interest [37]. INFRAME++ differs from these two topics in both its goals and the target scenario. We seek to enable imperceptible data communications, rather than data hiding or authentication. Therefore, INFRAME++ must address real-world degradations over screen-camera channels while they do not.

## 9. CONCLUSION AND FUTURE WORK

In this paper, we describe INFRAME++, a system that enables simultaneous full-frame video-viewing experiences for users and screen-camera communications for devices, through multiplexing original video frames and data frames and rendering them on the same display. The proposed design exploits the flicker-fusion property of the human vision system and the superior capability of modern displays and cameras. Our prototype and evaluation have confirmed the viability of INFRAME++.

We believe that INFRAME++ explores a new paradigm for visual data communication. It retains the normal viewing quality for users while enabling high-rate visual communication to devices. From the comparative standpoint, it circumvents the distractive and hard-to-use downsides in the current barcode design. As the capability discrepancy between users and devices continues to expand, we envision the steady rise of opportunistic communications over the device-to-human visual channels. It offers a new venue for visual data communication to devices in the emerging cyber-physical world.

## ACKNOWLEDGMENTS

We greatly appreciate our shepherd, Dr. Prabal Dutta, and the anonymous reviewers for their insightful comments and constructive feedback. We also thank Jiaqi Xu, Ouyang Zhang and all other participants in the user study. This work is supported in part by the National Science Foundation under Grants No. CNS-1421933 and CNS-1421440.

# 10. REFERENCES


[1] Cisco Visual Networking Index: Forecast and Methodology, 2013–2018. http://tinyurl.com/mev32z8.

[2] Walsh function. http://en.wikipedia.org/wiki/Walsh_function.

[3] Wechat.

[4] D. A. Atchison, G. Smith, and G. Smith. *Optics of the human eye*. Butterworth-Heinemann Oxford, UK:, 2000.

[5] R. Balaji and G. Naveen. Secure data transmission using video steganography. In *IEEE International Conference on Electro/Information Technology (EIT)*, 2011.

[6] G. Brindley, J. Du Croz, and W. Rushton. The flicker fusion frequency of the blue-sensitive mechanism of colour vision. *The Journal of physiology*, 183(2):497–500, 1966.

[7] R. Carvalho, C.-H. Chu, and L.-J. Chen. IVC: Imperceptible video communication. 2014. Demo.

[8] A. Cheddad, J. Condell, K. Curran, and P. McKevitt. Digital image steganography: Survey and analysis of current methods. *Signal Processing*, 90(3):727–752, 2010.

[9] J. Fridrich and M. Goljan. Digital image steganography using stochastic modulation. In *Electronic Imaging*, pages 191–202, 2003.

[10] D. G. Green. Sinusoidal flicker characteristics of the color-sensitive mechanisms of the eye. *Vision research*, 9(5):591–601, 1969.

[11] T. Hao, R. Zhou, and G. Xing. Cobra: Color barcode streaming for smartphone systems. In *MobiSys*, 2012.

[12] J. He, J. Huang, and G. Qiu. A new approach to estimating hidden message length in stochastic modulation steganography. In *Digital Watermarking*, pages 1–14. Springer, 2005.

[13] W. A. Hershberger and J. S. Jordan. The phantom array: a perisaccadic illusion of visual direction. *The Psychological Record*, 48(1):2, 2012.

[14] W. Hu, H. Gu, and Q. Pu. Lightsync: Unsynchronized visual communication over screen-camera links. In *MobiCom*, 2013.

[15] W. Hu, J. Mao, Z. Huang, Y. Xue, J. She, K. Bian, and G. Shen. Strata: Layered Coding for Scalable Visual Communication. In *MobiCom*, 2014.

[16] I18004:2000. Automatic identification and data capture techniques - Bar code symbology - QR Code.

[17] R. Kavitha and A. Murugan. Lossless steganography on avi file using swapping algorithm. In *Conference on Computational Intelligence and Multimedia Applications*, volume 4, 2007.

[18] D. Kelly. Flicker. In *Visual psychophysics*, pages 273–302, 1972.

[19] T. Li, C. An, A. Campbell, and X. Zhoun. Hilight: Hiding bits in pixel translucency changes. In *ACM Workshop on Visible Light Communication Systems (VLCS)*, 2014.

[20] X. Liao, Q.-y. Wen, and J. Zhang. A steganographic method for digital images with four-pixel differencing and modified lsb substitution. *Journal of Visual Communication and Image Representation*, 22(1):1–8, 2011.

[21] NVIDIA. Directcompute. https://developer.nvidia.com/directcompute.

[22] S. D. Perli, N. Ahmed, and D. Katabi. Pixnet: interference-free wireless links using lcd-camera pairs. In *MobiCom*, 2010.

[23] F. A. P. Petitcolas, R. J. Anderson, and M. G. Kuhn. Information hiding – a survey. *Proceedings of the IEEE*, 87(7):1062 –1078, July 1999.

[24] N. Rajagopal, P. Lazik, and A. Rowe. Visual light landmarks for mobile devices. In *ISPN*, 2014.

[25] J. Roberts and A. Wilkins. Flicker can be perceived during saccades at frequencies in excess of 1 khz. *Lighting Research and Technology*, 45(1):124–132, 2013.

[26] T. Sharp. An implementation of key-based digital signal steganography. In *Information hiding*, pages 13–26. Springer, 2001.

[27] E. Simonson and J. Brožek. Flicker fusion frequency: background and applications. *Physiological reviews*, 1952.

[28] R. D. Valois and K. D. Valois. *Spatial Vision*. Oxford University Press, 1988.

[29] I. Vogels and I. Hernando. Effect of eye movements on perception of temporally modulated light. http://2012.experiencinglight.nl/doc/28.pdf.

[30] A. Wang, S. Ma, C. Hu, J. Huai, C. Peng, and G. Shen. Enhancing Reliability to Boost the Throughput over Screen-camera Links. In *MobiCom*, 2014.

[31] A. Wang, C. Peng, O. Zhang, G. Shen, and B. Zeng. InFrame: Multiflexing Full-Frame Visible Communication Channel for Humans and Devices. In *HotNets-XIII*, 2014.

[32] S. B. Wicker. *Reed-Solomon Codes and Their Applications*. 1994.

[33] wikipedia. Forward error correction.

[34] G. Woo, A. Lippman, and R. Raskar. Vrcodes: Unobtrusive and active visual codes for interaction by exploiting rolling shutter. In *IEEE International Symposium on Mixed and Augmented Reality (ISMAR)*, 2012.

[35] H.-C. Wu, N.-I. Wu, C.-S. Tsai, and M.-S. Hwang. Image steganographic scheme based on pixel-value differencing and lsb replacement methods. *IEE Proceedings-Vision, Image and Signal Processing*, 152(5):611–615, 2005.

[36] W. Yuan, K. Dana, A. Ashok, M. Gruteser, and N. Mandayam. Dynamic and invisible messaging for visual mimo. In *IEEE Workshop on Applications of Computer Vision (WACV)*, 2012.

[37] Y. Zhang. Digital watermarking technology: A review. In *Future Computer and Communication (FCC)*, 2009.

# Real-Time Screen-Camera Communication Behind Any Scene

Tianxing Li, Chuankai An, Xinran Xiao, Andrew T. Campbell, and Xia Zhou
Department of Computer Science, Dartmouth College, Hanover, NH
{tianxing, chuankai, campbell, xia}@cs.dartmouth.edu xinranxiao@gmail.com

## ABSTRACT

We present HiLight, a new form of real-time screen-camera communication without showing any coded images (e.g., barcodes) for off-the-shelf smart devices. HiLight encodes data into pixel translucency change atop *any* screen content, so that camera-equipped devices can fetch the data by turning their cameras to the screen. HiLight leverages the alpha channel, a well-known concept in computer graphics, to encode bits into the pixel translucency change. By removing the need to directly modify pixel RGB values, HiLight overcomes the key bottleneck of existing designs and enables real-time unobtrusive communication while supporting any screen content. We build a HiLight prototype using off-the-shelf smart devices and demonstrate its efficacy and robustness in practical settings. By offering an unobtrusive, flexible, and lightweight communication channel between screens and cameras, HiLight opens up opportunities for new HCI and context-aware applications, e.g., smart glasses communicating with screens to realize augmented reality.

## Categories and Subject Descriptors

C.2.1 [**Network Architecture and Design**]: Wireless communication

## Keywords

Screen-camera communication; visible light communication; alpha channel

## 1. INTRODUCTION

In a world of ever-increasing smart devices equipped with screens and cameras, enabling screens and cameras to communicate has been attracting growing interests. The idea is simple: information is encoded into a visual frame shown on a screen, and any camera-equipped device can turn to the screen and immediately fetch the information. Operating on the visible light spectrum band, screen-camera communication is free of electromagnetic interference, offering a promising out-of-band communication alternative for short-range information acquisition. The most popular example is QR code [6], where information (typically a URL) is encoded into a 2D barcode. Recent research endeavors have led to innovative barcode designs that boost the data rate [14, 26] or enhance the transmission reliability [15, 16, 28, 36].

These efforts are exciting; however, they commonly require displaying visible coded images, which interfere with the content the screen is playing and create unpleasant viewing experiences. In this paper, we seek approaches to enable unobtrusive screen-camera communication, which allows the screen to concurrently fulfill a dual role: displaying content and communication. Ultimately, we envision a screen-camera communication system that transmits and receives dynamic data in real time, while ensuring communication occurs unobtrusively regardless of the content the screen is displaying — let it be an image, a movie, a video clip, a web page, a game interface, or any other application window. As the user interacts with the screen and switches the content, the communication sustains. Hence, communication is truly realized as an additional functionality for the screen, without placing any constraints on the screen's original functionality (displaying content).

We are not alone in working towards this vision. Recent efforts have made valuable progress on designing unobtrusive screen-camera communication [10, 37, 39, 41, 42]. However, a fundamental gap to the vision remains, mainly because existing designs all require direct modifications of the pixel color (RGB) values of the screen content. This methodology cannot enable real-time unobtrusive communication atop arbitrary screen content that can be generated on the fly with user interactions. The reason is two-fold. First, modifying pixel RGB values in real time has to rely on the Graphics Processing Unit (GPU) by directly leveraging related GPU libraries. However, the operating system typically does not allow a third-party application to pre-fetch or modify the screen content of other applications or system interfaces (e.g., the home screen of a smartphone or tablet). Thus, to achieve real-time communication, existing designs are limited to screen content within a single application or standalone files (e.g., image, video). Second, although the main processor (CPU) can pre-fetch and modify arbitrary pixel RGB values, modifying RGB values at the CPU incurs a significant delay (hundreds of milliseconds), which makes these designs unable to support real-time communication atop dynamic content such as video.

To overcome this barrier, we propose a new design paradigm for unobtrusive screen-camera communication, which *decouples* communication and screen content image layers. Our key idea is to create a separate image layer (a black matte, fully transparent by default) dedicated to communication atop all existing content image layers. We encode data into the pixel translucency change at the separate image layer, so that the receiver (camera) can perceive the color intensity change in the composite image and decode data.


*MobiSys'15*, May 18–22, 2015, Florence, Italy.

http://dx.doi.org/10.1145/2742647.2742667.

To control pixel translucency, we leverage the alpha channel [27], a well-known concept in computer graphics. We control the level of pixel translucency change so that it is perceivable only to cameras but not human eyes. Furthermore, by controlling the translucency of each pixel independently, we enable multiple simultaneous transmitter elements on the screen. This creates a MIMO communication channel between screens and cameras [7], which can further boost data rate or improve transmission reliability.

Our methodology has two key benefits. *First*, operating on the alpha channel, the system no longer needs to directly modify pixel RGB values while achieving the same effect. Since alpha values are blended by the GPU, the encoding is almost instantaneous, which is critical to support real-time communication atop arbitrary dynamic content. More importantly, since alpha blending is a mature feature offered by the GPU, existing platforms (e.g., Android, iOS) provide application-layer functions that use related GPU APIs to modify pixel alpha values. Thus, the CPU can call these functions at the application layer without directly dealing with GPU APIs or modifying the OS or low-level drivers. *Second*, by realizing communication at a separate image layer, the system makes unobtrusive communication universally available and truly parallel to the content playing on the screen – no matter if it is a static, dynamic, or multi-layer content, and regardless of the frame rate it is playing at and the frame resolution. Users can use the screen as it is, while the communication between the screen and the camera occurs behind the scene in real time, unobtrusively.

Following our methodology, we design and build HiLight[1], the first system that supports real-time, unobtrusive screen-camera communication atop arbitrary screen content using off-the-shelf smart devices. We address the following specific design challenges. *First,* when determining the level of pixel translucency change, we face a tradeoff between user viewing experiences and transmission reliability. HiLight seeks the best tradeoff by adapting the translucency change based on the color distribution of screen content and the frame transition. It smooths the pixel translucency change across the screen while ensuring the change is reliably detectable by the receiver. *Second*, the whole encoding has to finish within a tight time limit (16 ms) to support video's normal playing speed and avoid the flicker effect [9]. We design lightweight encoding algorithms that require only sampled color information of sampled content frames. This reduces the overhead of pre-fetching content frames and ensures that data encoding and decoding can be finished within 8 ms. *Third*, the receiver perceives a mixture of color intensity change caused not only by encoded translucency change, but also by other interfering sources such as screen content change, ambient light, and camera noise. We design efficient algorithms to extract the desired color intensity change, and adapt our strategy to the scene type. This design ensures the system robustness under diverse practical settings.

We evaluate the HiLight prototype with an Samsung Tab S tablet as the transmitter and an iPhone 5s as the receiver. We test HiLight using 112 images, 60 video clips, and various web browsing and gaming scenarios. Our key findings are as follows:

- HiLight supports unobtrusive communication atop *arbitrary* screen content as the user is interacting with the screen, achieving 1.1 Kbps throughput with 84 – 91%+ accuracy for all scene types.

- HiLight realizes real-time data processing using off-the-shelf smart devices. Its encoding and decoding delays are both within 8.3 ms even for high-resolution video frames (1080p), sufficient to support video playing at 60 FPS and 120 FPS frame rates.

- HiLight is robust across diverse practical settings with hand motion and perspective distortion, supporting up to 1-meter viewing distance and 60° viewing angle for the 10.5-inch transmitter screen and maintaining stable performance once the ambient light is above 40 lux in indoor environments.

[1]We have made the demo video clips of HiLight available at `http://dartnets.cs.dartmouth.edu/hilight`.

**Contributions.** We summarize our key contributions as follows:

- We analyze existing unobtrusive screen-camera communication designs using detailed measurements and identify their limitations to enable real-time unobtrusive communication atop any screen content.

- We propose a new design paradigm for unobtrusive screen-camera communication, which decouples communication from the screen content and uses the alpha channel to encode data into pixel translucency change [21]. Since alpha values are blended by the GPU, data encoding is almost instantaneous, which is the key to enabling real-time communication atop arbitrary content.

- We design and build HiLight using off-the-shelf smart devices, the first system that realizes on-demand data transmissions in real time unobtrusively atop *arbitrary* screen content. We extensively evaluate our prototype under diverse practical settings, examine its potential performance on a wide range of devices (e.g., smartphones, tablets, laptops, and high-end cameras), and assess its user perception.

By offering an unobtrusive, flexible, and lightweight communication channel between screens and cameras, HiLight presents opportunities for new HCI and context-aware applications for smart devices. For example, a user wearing smart glasses can acquire additional personalized information from the screen (e.g., TV screen, smartphone, or tablet screen) without affecting the content users are currently viewing. HiLight also provides far-reaching implications for facilitating new security and graphics applications.

# 2. SCREEN-CAMERA COMMUNICATION: LIMITATIONS AND SOLUTION

In this section, we first present the design goals for a universal screen-camera communication system. We then analyze the inefficacy of existing designs to achieve these design goals. Finally we introduce our new methodology.

## 2.1 Design Goals

We bear in mind the following goals when designing a universal screen-camera communication system.

**Staying Unobtrusive to Users.** The screen-camera data communication is completely hidden from users and does not require showing any visible coded images on the screen. Hence, data communication does not interfere with any content that the user is viewing at the screen, and can be easily embedded into any existing screens (e.g., smartphone screens, laptop screens) without sacrificing their original functionality (i.e., displaying content).

**Supporting *Any* Scene.** The data communication can occur regardless of the screen content, let it be an image, a video clip, a movie, a gaming scene, a multi-layer application windows, or the home screen of a smartphone or tablet. Furthermore, the communication continues as the screen content changes on the fly (e.g., the user browses a web page, plays games, and watches a movie). To support all types of screen content, the communication needs to be independent of the screen content, which can be generated on the fly and vary over time as the user interacts with the screen.

**Processing Dynamic Data in Real Time.** The system can transmit and receive dynamic data on the fly, rather than pre-processing an image or a video file to embed data. This is necessary when the data comes on the fly or when the screen content is not known in advance (e.g., interactive gaming scene). The challenge is that when the screen is displaying video (e.g., movies, video clips), the frame rate is at least 24 frames per second (FPS). Thus, the system has to finish encoding data into a frame within 42 ms before the screen displays the next frame. When the video is played at 60 FPS or 120 FPS, the encoding has to finish within 16 ms or 8 ms.

**Operating on Off-the-Shelf Smart Devices.** The system can transmit and receive data in real time using existing smart devices (e.g., smartphones, tablets). These devices have limited computational power, and their cameras are not as sophisticated as high-end single-lens reflex (SLR) cameras. Hence the encoding and decoding designs have to be lightweight and robust, so that smart devices as transmitters and receivers can process data in time while supporting dynamic content such as video.

Next, we analyze existing proposals on unobtrusive screen-camera communication and examine whether they can achieve the above goals.

## 2.2 Current Limitations

Researchers have proposed designs [10, 37, 39, 41, 42] to remove the need of showing visible coded images while enabling screen-camera communication. Despite the tangible benefits of existing designs, they are unable to achieve all the design goals described in § 2.1, mainly because they directly deal with the color values of each pixel, specified as the color intensity values in red, green, and blue (RGB) diodes [34]. To ensure that RGB value changes are unnoticeable to users, they have to pre-fetch the RGB values of all content pixels to subtly modify RGB values and encode data. As a result, existing designs cannot serve as a unified solution that can achieve real-time data communication decoupled from the screen content (e.g., the home screen of a smartphone, the interface windows of other independent applications). Next, we analyze the two possible approaches to modifying pixel RGB values using existing designs and identify their limitations.

**GPU-Based RGB Modifications.** To enable real-time modifications of pixel RGB values, one has to rely on GPU's parallel processing power and leverage GPU-related libraries (e.g., OpenGL [1] on the Android and iOS). The key idea is to supply GPU with two programs, known as *shaders* or *kernels*, which are executed independently per pixel. Modern shaders are fast. Based on our experiments on a Google Nexus 6 (with Android 5.0 OS) phone, it takes only 0.13 ms to modify RGB values of all the pixels in a single video frame (1920 x 1080 pixels). This approach, however, has two limitations. *First*, it is limited to modifying screen content within a single application or a standalone file (e.g., a video or image file). Because of the system security model of existing platforms (e.g, Android), third-party applications cannot pre-fetch screen content from other applications or system interfaces (e.g., home screen). *Second*, by replacing the original screen content with an opaque, modified new content layer, the modifications can nullify the existing rendering optimization. For example, consider the user is browsing a web page in a browser. To enable data communication, we have to run an OpenGL application and display the modified page through this OpenGL app. This additional step can remove the rendering optimization made by the web browser. Therefore, although existing designs can leverage GPU programming to enable real-time unobtrusive communication, they are limited to the screen content within a single application or static standalone files and are unable to support all dynamic screen content.

**CPU-Based RGB Modifications.** Another approach to modifying pixel RGB values is to use the CPU to pre-fetch pixel RGB values of the current screen content. Although this approach allows the system to enable unobtrusive communication atop any scene, it entails long encoding delay and fails to support real-time data communication. We further quantify the processing time using off-the-shelf smart devices (Nexus 4, Nexus 5, Samsung Note 3, Samsung S5, Samsung Tab S, all with Android 4.4). To capture the screen content on an Android device, we read the frame buffer under the `/dev/graphics/` directory. We leverage the OpenCV library [2], a popular computer vision library, to calculate the complementary RGB values for each pixel. This calculation is a representative of the RGB modification step in all existing designs [10, 37, 39, 41, 42]. We then use the Simple Direct Layer (SDL) library to render an image on the screen. We choose SDL library because it is much more flexible than the rendering library [3] in the Android framework. For all smart devices we tested, the processing time of data encoding far exceeds 42 ms, the timing threshold (§ 2.1) required to support real-time screen-camera data transmission. Especially for high-resolution (1080p) video, CPU-based RGB modifications need 1–2 s to embed data into a frame. While the encoding time slightly drops as the frame resolution decreases, it never drops below 300–600 ms.[2] Note that these steps are the minimal for embedding data into the RGB values of the screen content frame. Some designs require additional steps (e.g., copying frames [37]), leading to even longer delays. To speed up encoding, one can modify only a subset of pixels. Yet this reduces the number of pixels used to transmit data, sacrificing either the data rate or the transmission reliability. More importantly, so far we have assumed a single image layer. For content with multiple image layers, the cost of pre-fetching and modifying pixel RGB values grows linearly with the number of image layers. Thus, CPU-based RGB modifications cannot achieve real-time data communication.

**Summary of Observations.** To sum up, existing unobtrusive screen-camera communication designs require direct modifications of content pixel color (RGB) values and fail to transmit dynamic data atop arbitrary dynamic content, where either data or screen content comes on the fly. Furthermore, by creating an opaque content layer with modified RGB values, these designs can nullify the existing rendering optimization. To mitigate the problem, current designs will have to give up whole-screen communication and sacrifice either the data rate or the transmission reliability. In addition, integrating communication with screen content greatly limits their applicable scenarios.

## 2.3 Solution: Decoupled Communication Using Alpha Channel

To overcome the above limitations, we propose a new design paradigm for unobtrusive screen-camera communication. Motivated by the fact that the tight integration of communication and screen content is problematic, we propose to decouple screen-camera communication from the image layers of screen content. Furthermore, we design lightweight data encoding that leverages the power

[2]We also test devices (e.g., Samsung S5, Nexus 5) with the recent Android 5.0, which provides a new screen capture API to speed up the process of pre-fetching screen content. Our results show that CPU-based RGB modifications still take more than 200 ms.

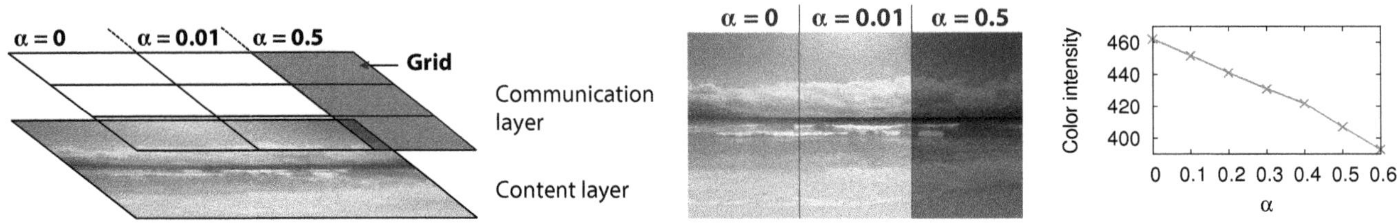


(a) Overview (b) Resulting composite image (c) Pixel color intensity perceived by a camera (receiver)

**Figure 1: Decoupling screen-camera communication from the content image layer on the screen. (a) Atop the content image layer, we create an additional image layer (a black matte, fully transparent by default) dedicated to data communication, referred to as the *communication layer*. To transmit data, we divide the communication layer into grids, and encode data into pixel translucency change of each grid without affecting users' viewing experiences. (b) shows the resulting composite image after modifying the pixel translucency of the communication layer. (c) Camera-equipped devices perceive color intensity change as $\alpha$ value increases.**

of GPU and does not require direct modifications of content RGB values. More importantly, since alpha blending is a mature feature offered by the GPU, alpha values can be modified by calling a system function at the application layer without any OS-level modifications (see more in § 5). At the high level, our design principle is two-fold:

- We create a separate image layer (a black matte, fully transparent by default) dedicated to communication, referred to as the *communication layer*, atop all content image layers (Figure 1(a)). By *decoupling* communication from screen content, we allow the screen to better fulfill its dual role (communication and displaying content).
- We encode data by changing the pixel transparency of the communication layer. This removes the need to directly modify pixel RGB values while achieving the same effect. In particular, we leverage *alpha channel*, a well-known concept in computer graphics, to control pixel transparency and encode data [21]. Since alpha values are blended by GPU (< 1 ms), our design significantly drives down the encoding delay, which is the key to support real-time, unobtrusive communication atop any screen content.

Next, we begin with the background on alpha channel and how we utilize it to transmit data. We then elaborate the key benefits of our methodology and design challenges.

**Communication Using Alpha Channel.** As a well-known concept in computer graphics, alpha channel is widely used to form a composite image with partial or full transparency [27]. It stores a value $\alpha$ between 0 and 1 to indicate the pixel translucency. 0 means that the pixel is fully transparent, and 1 means that it is fully opaque. By default, we set $\alpha = 0$ for all pixels in the communication layer to make it fully transparent and not interfere with the screen content. As we increase the $\alpha$ values of the communication layer (Figure 1(a)), we change how users perceive the color of the content layer. Specifically, when $\alpha = 1$, the pixel of the top communication layer is opaque, hence users perceive this pixel as black, the color of the communication layer. Thus we can essentially dim an area by increasing the $\alpha$ values of this area on the communication layer. As an example, Figure 1(b) shows the composite image on the screen, where we set pixel $\alpha$ values of the communication layer to 0 (left), 0.01 (middle), and 0.5 (right), illustrated in Figure 1(a). A higher $\alpha$ leads to a darker appearance in the composite image.

This dimming effect is perceived as color intensity (summation of RGB channel values) change by a camera. We further examine how cameras on existing smart devices perceive color intensity change. We set up a Samsung Note 3 phone as the transmitter, and a Samsung S5 phone 15 cm away as the receiver. We create a top black image layer in Note 3, adjust pixel $\alpha$ values of this top image layer uniformly, and measure the color intensity of each pixel captured by the S5's camera. Figure 1(c) shows the color intensity averaged over all pixels as $\alpha$ increases. It confirms that increasing $\alpha$ value on the top image layer linearly decreases the perceived color intensity. We also observe that even for the $\alpha$ change of 0.01, imperceptible to human eyes (Figure 1(b)), the S5's camera can still detect the difference.

Motivated by the above observations, we encode data into pixel translucency ($\alpha$) change on the top communication layer. For today's smart devices, the screen refresh rate is typically 60 Hz. Therefore, to ensure the change imperceptible to human eyes, we change $\alpha$ values by only 1%–8%, sufficient to avoid the flicker effect[3] [9]. Since the change can be perceived by cameras, camera-equipped devices can examine the perceived color intensity change in captured frames and decode data. Furthermore, we can divide the communication layer into grids and change the $\alpha$ values of the pixels in each grid independently. *Hence each grid functions as an independent transmitter element, resulting into a MIMO channel between screens and cameras.*

Note that the same principle holds when using a white matte as the communication layer, where increasing the $\alpha$ values of an area in the communication layer brightens this area in the composite image. However, black and white are the only two colors feasible for realizing alpha channel based communication. The reason is as follows. In general, assume the communication layer's color intensity in a color channel (i.e., red, green, or blue channel) is $C_1$ with the alpha value of $\alpha$. Based on the alpha blending principle, for a pixel in the content layer with color intensity $C_2$ in this color channel, this pixel's color intensity $C$ in this color channel in the final composite image is calculated as $C = \alpha \cdot C_1 + (1 - \alpha) \cdot C_2$, where $C_1, C_2 \in [0, 255]$ and $\alpha \in [0, 1]$. Hence setting $C_1$ to the minimal (0) or the maximal (255) in all color channels, which corresponds to the black or the white color, always dims or brightens a pixel in the composite image, regardless of the pixel's original color ($C_2$), the key for encoding data into the pixel translucency change atop any screen content. In contrast, setting $C_1$ to any value within (0, 255) in a color channel does not uniformly dim or brighten pixels in all colors and thus is unable to enable communication atop any pixel color of the content layer.

[3]The occurrence of the flicker effect depends on the screen refresh rate and the degree of change across frames.

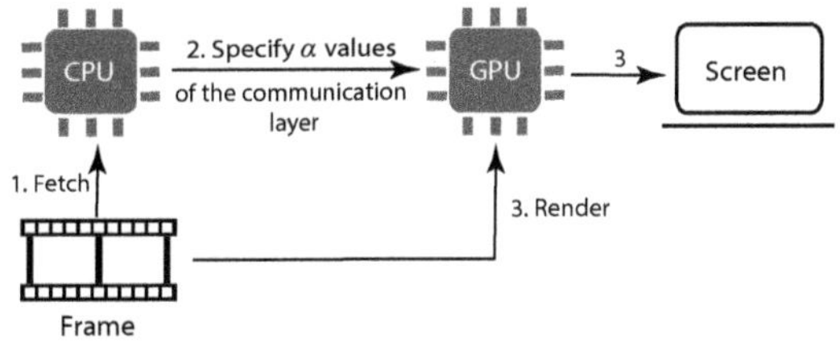


**Figure 2: Flowchart of modifying alpha values. The CPU passes specified $\alpha$ values to GPU using a system function at the application layer. The GPU then applies the alpha blending technique to combine $\alpha$ values with an image frame.**

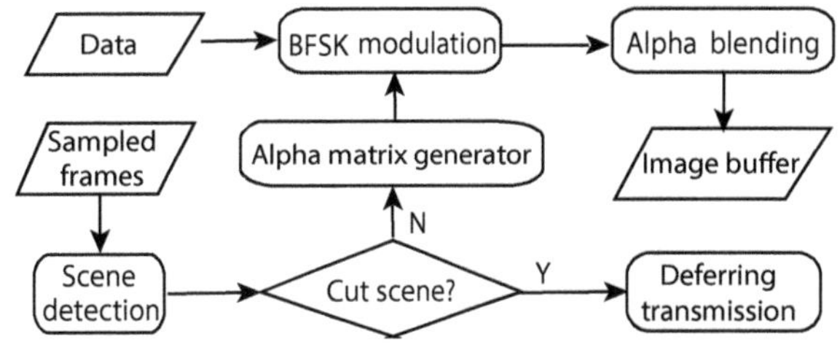


**Figure 3: The encoding procedure of the HiLight transmitter.**

**Benefits.** Our methodology offers three benefits. *First*, operating on the alpha channel significantly reduces the encoding time. Figure 2 shows the procedure for the system to process a frame using alpha-channel communication. The main processor passes specified $\alpha$ values of the communication layer to the GPU, which blends them with the content layer using the alpha blending technique [27]. The blending can be finished in 1 ms, several orders of magnitude faster than modifying pixel RGB values on CPU. *Second*, since we enable communication using a separate image layer (communication layer), communication can occur regardless of the screen content, its frame rate, and the number of content image layers. Thus our design allows the screen-camera communication channel to support arbitrary scene, including a multi-layer scene (e.g., Angry Birds) that needs to modify the $\alpha$ values of the content layer. Also, since data encoding is in the separate image layer, we can parallelize data encoding and content playing and further reduce encoding delay. *Third*, by adding a transparent communication layer and slightly adjusting its translucency, our design does not interfere with the GPU rendering optimization for the underlying image layers while achieving the same effect of directly modifying pixel RGB values.

**Challenges.** To implement our methodology, we face three key challenges. *First*, determining the level of translucency change is nontrivial. The change has to be unobtrusive to human eyes while reliably detectable by cameras. Also, $\alpha$ value changes RGB values by a percentage. Thus for darker colors, the absolute color intensity change is smaller and harder to detect. *Second*, when transmitting dynamic data atop a video, all encoding steps need to finish within 42 ms to support video's normal playing speed. Furthermore, to reduce the flicker effect [9], the frequency of the translucency change at the communication layer has to match the screen's refresh rate (60 Hz). Hence the encoding needs to be lightweight to finish within 16 ms, and can operate on smart devices. *Third*, for a dynamic scene, the screen content changes over time. The resulting color intensity change interferes with our encoded color intensity change. Even for static content, environmental factors such as ambient light and camera noise can affect decoding. All these interfering sources make it challenging to extract data from the perceived color intensity change.

We address the above challenges and design HiLight. In the next two sections, we describe in detail our design of HiLight on both the transmitter and the receiver.

# 3. HiLight TRANSMITTER

HiLight transmitter encodes data into the pixel translucency ($\alpha$ value) change at the communication layer. The translucency change is fixed at the screen's refresh rate (60 Hz), independent of the content frame rate that can change at any time. We face two design challenges. *First*, it is nontrivial to determine the $\alpha$ value change ($\Delta\alpha$) for each pixel. On one hand, $\Delta\alpha$ should stay minimal to be imperceptible to users. On the other hand, a larger $\Delta\alpha$ means a more detectable change in the perceived color intensity at the receiver. Hence we need to seek the best tradeoff between user experience and communication reliability. *Second*, the per-frame encoding needs to finish within 16 ms to support video's normal playing speed and avoid the flicker effect. While we remove the need to directly modify RGB values, the remaining steps for data encoding (fetching and rendering in Figure 2) can still take more than 16 ms. We need to further reduce the encoding delay.

We address the challenges as follows. *First*, we set the $\Delta\alpha$ small (1–8%) to keep the translucency change unobtrusive to users. To ensure that the change can be reliably detected, we configure the $\Delta\alpha$ of each pixel based on the color distribution of the content frame and the transition across frames. The configuration helps receivers deal with dark areas or frames with drastic content change. *Second*, to further reduce the data encoding delay, we fetch only one content frame per sampling window (0.1 s in our implementation) and sample a subset of pixels for their color values. This is not doable for existing designs to achieve whole-screen communication. Since existing designs rely on directly modifying content color values, they have to fetch every frame and obtain color values of all pixels in a frame.

Next, we first overview the overall encoding procedure, and then focus on two main design components in detail.

## 3.1 Overview

Figure 3 overviews the encoding procedure. We sample content image frames to configure $\Delta\alpha$ for each pixel at the communication layer. Note that the content frame information only helps optimize the $\Delta\alpha$ configuration and is not an enabler for the communication. Unlike current designs that require modifying content image frames, we only need to read (not write) coarse-grained information of content image frames. Given two adjacent sampled frames, the transmitter examines their color transition to adapt the encoding strategy. If the frame content changes drastically, the resulting color intensity change can overwhelm the intensity change encoded with data. We refer to these frames as *cut scene* frames, which typically occur rarely (1.3% in a test video stream in Figure 5(d)). We skip the cut-scene frames and defer encoding. Once detecting a non-cut scene frame, we determine the $\Delta\alpha$ based on the color brightness of the area in the content layer and the frame transition.

Given the $\Delta\alpha$ for each pixel, the transmitter modulates bits using Binary Frequency Shift Keying (BFSK). We choose BFSK because of its simplicity and its robustness to interference (e.g., ambient light). In our implementation, bit 0 and 1 are represented by translucency change at 20 Hz and 30 Hz respectively, over six frames (Figure 4). We set six frames as a frame window, because it is the minimal to achieve 20 Hz and 30 Hz change under the screen refresh rate of 60 Hz. By removing the low-frequency components

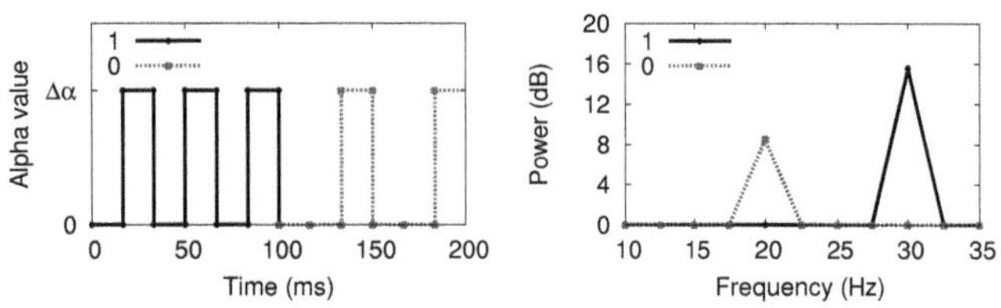


(a) Time domain (b) Frequency domain

**Figure 4: Encoding bits into pixel translucency ($\alpha$) change. (a) shows the sequence of $\alpha$ values for symbols '01'. (b) shows the translucency change in the frequency domain for bit 0 and 1 after applying FFT.**

($<$ 15Hz), the frequency power of the data bit is less affected by environmental noise (e.g., ambient light). In comparison, modulation schemes (e.g., Manchester code) that rely on phase transition in the time domain to extract data can suffer performance degradation caused by environmental noise. In addition, since FSK encodes data as relative color intensity changes, HiLight is robust against image quality degradation (e.g., block boundary effects caused by video compression).

After generating the sequence of $\alpha$ values for each pixel, the main processor passes these values to GPU. The GPU then applies the alpha blending technique [27, 34] to generate image layers (communication layer) with specified translucency, combines them with content image frames, forms composite images, and outputs them to the image buffer.

Next we describe two main design components (scene detection and determining $\alpha$ value changes $\Delta\alpha$) in detail.

## 3.2 Scene Detection

Scene detection is the key component for the system to support arbitrary screen scene. It runs continuously in the background, samples content frames, and identifies the screen scene type based on the frame transition. The scene type is crucial for deciding whether the encoding should be performed, and for determining the degree of pixel translucency change at the communication layer (§ 3.3).

Specifically, the transmitter periodically samples content frames every 0.1 s. We choose 0.1 s as the sampling window because it is sufficient for detecting frame transition accurately while missing a small number of frames. For each sampled frame, the thread further uniformly samples one-sixteenth of the pixels and obtains their color information.

Given the sampled pixels of two sampled frames, we aim to categorize the current frame into one of the following scene types: *the static, the gradual, and the cut scene*. These categories capture the degree of frame transition, and are widely used in computer vision [17]. Figure 5 shows example frame pairs for each scene type. While screen content can change drastically over a long time, the change between two adjacent frames is gradual and minor. Therefore, static and gradual scenes are the most common, while cut scene occurs rarely (Figure 5(d)). Because of the drastic color intensity change of the cut scene and its rare occurrence, we encode data only atop the other two types of scenes.

To determine the scene type, we measure the dissimilarity of two adjacent sampled frames using two existing metrics. The first metric [44], referred to as the *pixel-based* metric, calculates the difference of the pixel color intensity values of two frames. For frames $F$ and $F'$ each with $X \times Y$ pixels, the pixel-based metric $d_p(F, F')$ is calculated as:

$$d_p(F, F') = \frac{\sum_{\substack{1 \le i \le X \\ 1 \le j \le Y}} \mid C(p_{ij}) - C(p'_{ij}) \mid}{X \times Y}, \tag{1}$$

where $C(p_{ij})$ and $C(p'_{ij})$ are the color intensity values of pixels $p_{ij}$ and $p'_{ij}$ in frame $F$ and $F'$, respectively. The second metric [25, 31], referred to as the *histogram-based* metric, examines the difference in the color distribution of two frames. It partitions the whole color intensity range into bins, counts the number of pixels with color values within each bin, and calculates the difference as:

$$d_h(F, F') = \sum_{\substack{i \in [1,K] \\ \max(H(i), H'(i)) \neq 0}} \frac{(H(i) - H'(i))^2}{\max(H(i), H'(i))}, \tag{2}$$

where $H(i)$ and $H'(i)$ are the number of pixels in the $i$-th bin for frame $F$ and $F'$ respectively, and $K$ is the number of bins. We choose these two metrics because they are easy to compute, and complement each other. Pixel-based metric captures small local changes (e.g., a small moving object), while histogram-based metric captures the global change.

We combine these two metrics to classify a frame. For both metrics, a higher value indicates a more drastic frame transition. Hence we define two thresholds for each metric to signal a static and a cut scene. We denote the thresholds for the metric $d_p$ as $d_p^{static}$ and $d_p^{cut}$, and $d_h^{static}$ and $d_h^{cut}$ for the metric $d_h$. We classify a frame as a cut scene if the values of both metrics are above their cut scene thresholds, i.e., $d_p > d_p^{cut}$ and $d_h > d_h^{cut}$. We classify a frame as a static scene if both metric values are below the static scene thresholds, i.e., $d_p < d_p^{static}$ and $d_h < d_h^{static}$. A frame is a gradual scene if neither condition is satisfied. In our implementation, we empirically set $d_p^{static}$, $d_p^{cut}$, $d_h^{static}$, and $d_h^{cut}$ as 10, 100, 0.1, and 1, respectively. These values also align with the literature in computer vision [29, 30, 32].

## 3.3 Determining Alpha Value Change ($\Delta\alpha$)

Armed with the content frame information (scene type, and frame color distribution), the second key component determines the degree of pixel translucency change at the communication layer. The goal is to keep the resulting color intensity change unobtrusive while ensuring they are still reliably detectable by receivers.

To achieve the goal, we configure the $\Delta\alpha$ of each pixel based on the color distribution of the content frame and frame transition. Our configuration is driven by two observations. *First*, $\Delta\alpha$ changes the pixel color intensity by a percentage. Thus, for a fixed $\Delta\alpha$, the resulting absolute color intensity change of dark pixels is smaller and less detectable than that of bright pixels [21]. *Second*, frame content change also leads to color intensity change, which interferes with the intensity change encoded with data. Motivated by these observations, we increase the $\Delta\alpha$ for pixels atop dark content areas or upon a gradual scene frame. This enhances the coded intensity change in these two challenging scenarios, allowing the receiver to better extract data.

Specifically, we determine the $\alpha$ value change $\Delta\alpha$ for each pixel in two steps (Algorithm 1). The first step is to divide the screen into grids and decide the $\Delta\alpha$ at the grid level. For each grid $G_k$, we calculate its average color intensity value $C(G_k)$ over all sampled pixels in $G_k$. We configure the grid-level $\alpha$ change $\Delta\alpha_G$ within $[1\%, 8\%]$ based on the grid color intensity $C(G_k)$, and the scene type. A side effect of this step is that for adjacent grids with different $\alpha$ values, the grid border appears as a noticeable edge. To minimize this side effect, the second step is to fine-tune the $\Delta\alpha$ for each pixel within a grid and diminish the $\alpha$ value difference

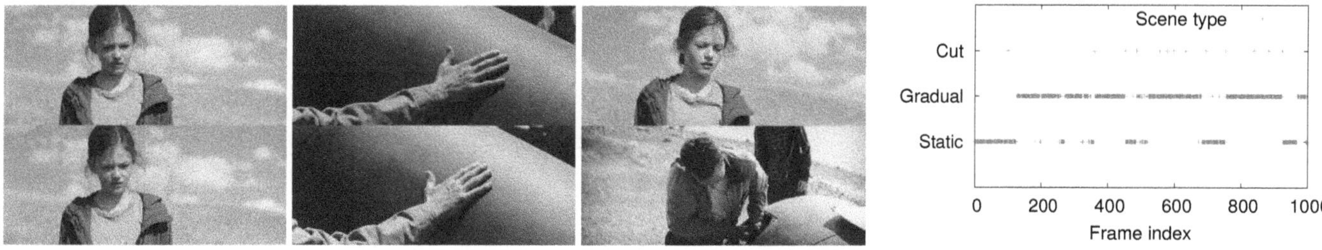


(a) Static scene ($d_p = 0.2$, $d_h = 0$) (b) Gradual scene ($d_p = 12.2$, $d_h = 0.2$) (c) Cut scene ($d_p = 216$, $d_h = 1.6$) (d) Frame scene type in a video stream

**Figure 5: (a)-(c) Example image pairs of three scene types (the static, the gradual, and the cut scene). We evaluate the difference of each pair of frames using both the pixel-based metric $d_p$ and the histogram-based metric $d_h$. (d) shows the scene type of each frame in a video stream.**

**Algorithm 1:** Determine alpha value change ($\Delta\alpha$).

**input** : 1) $F$, sampled content frame; 2) $S_T$, scene type.
**output**: $\alpha$ value change $\Delta\alpha$ for each pixel.

*Divide $F$ into X grids: $G_1, ..., G_X$*
**for** $k \leftarrow 1$ **to** $X$ **do**
  // Computing grid-level $\Delta\alpha$
  $C(G_k) = \texttt{Mean}\{C(p_{ij}) \mid p_{ij} \in G_k\}$
  **if** $C(G_k) \leq 50$ **then** $\Delta\alpha_G = 4\%$
  **else if** $C(G_k) \leq 100$ **then** $\Delta\alpha_G = 3\%$
  **else if** $C(G_k) \leq 150$ **then** $\Delta\alpha_G = 2\%$
  **else** $\Delta\alpha_G = 1\%$
  **if** $S_T =$ gradual **then** $\Delta\alpha_G = 2 \cdot \Delta\alpha_G$
  // Fine-tuning $\Delta\alpha$ within a grid
  $(x_c, y_c) \leftarrow \texttt{FetchCenter}(G_k)$
  **for** $p_{ij} \in G_k$ **do**
    $\Delta\alpha_{ij} = \frac{\Delta\alpha_G}{sqrt(2\pi)} \times e^{-\frac{(i-x_c)^2+(j-y_c)^2}{2}}$
  **end**
**end**

among pixels on the grid border. In particular, for pixels in the center of the grid $G_k$, their $\Delta\alpha$ is the same as the grid-level $\alpha$ change $\Delta\alpha_G$. This ensures that the receiver can still differentiate translucency changes of adjacent grids. For pixels further away from the grid center, we gradually decrease their $\Delta\alpha$ following a standard normal distribution $\mathcal{N}(0, 1)$ (Figure 6). The fine-tuning smooths the translucency change across grids. Finally the $\Delta\alpha$ values for all pixels are fed into the modulator, which modulates each bit into translucency ($\alpha$) change over time.

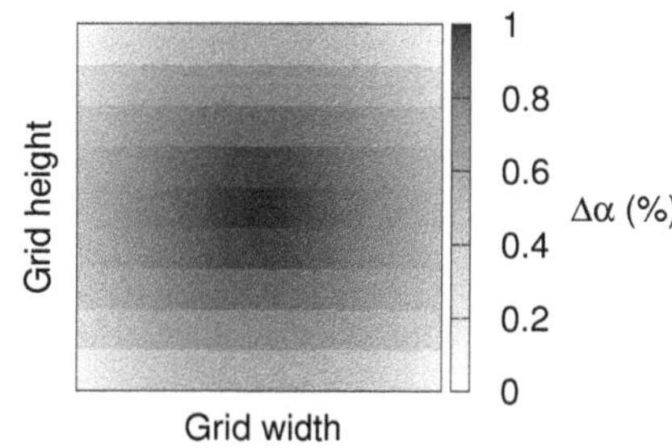


**Figure 6: Configuring $\Delta\alpha$ for each pixel within a grid, assuming the grid-level $\alpha$ change is 1%. Here the darkness indicates the $\Delta\alpha$ value, not the actual pixel appearance. We gradually decrease $\Delta\alpha$ as pixels become further away from the grid center. This diminishes the appearance of the grid border and optimizes the viewing experience.**

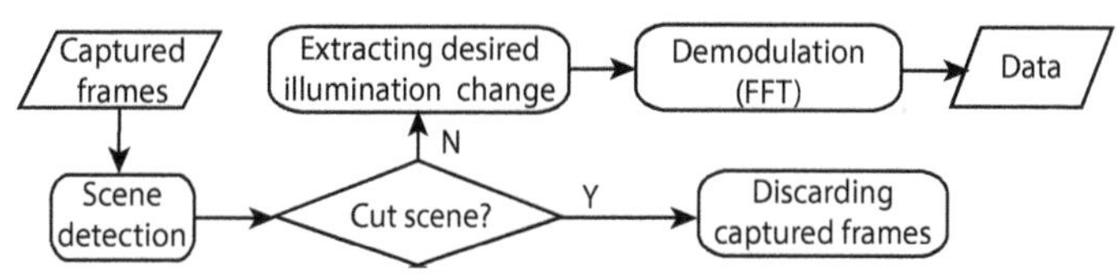


**Figure 7: An overview of the decoding procedure in HiLight.**

## 4. HiLight RECEIVER

HiLight receiver captures incoming frames, examines the perceived color intensity changes, and decodes data. The main design challenge is to extract the desired color intensity change out of the perceived change. This is challenging because the color intensity change perceived by the receiver comes from not only encoded $\alpha$ changes, but also changes in screen content, ambient light condition, as well as camera noises. The receiver needs to extract data from the perceived color intensity change given the presence of all these interfering factors.

To address the challenge, we design strategies to filter out color intensity change associated with interfering factors, and adapt our strategy to the current scene type. In particular, for the static scene, we leverage an audio beamforming algorithm [33, 35] to minimize the impact of interfering factors and extract the desired color intensity change encoded with data; for the dynamic scene, we identify patterns caused by the encoded change. These patterns help recover the bits hidden in the mixed intensity change. Note that we integrate these scene-dependent strategies into a single framework, which allows the system to support arbitrary scenes in a unified solution.

Next we first overview the decoding procedure, followed by a detailed description on extracting the desired color intensity change.

### 4.1 Overview

Figure 7 summarizes the main steps of decoding. The receiver keeps monitoring the incoming frames, and buffers frames in a frame window (six frames). It then samples a frame in this frame window, compares it to the last sampled frame, and applies the same scene detection algorithm as that in the transmitter (§ 3.2) to identify the scene type. If the scene type is the cut scene, the receiver discards this frame window since the transmitter does not encode data on these frames. For frames of other scene types (i.e., the gradual or static scene), the receiver divides the captured transmitter screen into grids, identifies and enhances the desired color intensity change in each grid (§ 4.2).

The extracted color intensity change is then passed to a BFSK demodulator, which applies Fast Fourier Transform (FFT) to project translucency change into the frequency domain. To reduce the impact of ambient light noise with frequency components close to 0, the receiver filters out frequency components below 15 Hz. Among the frequency components above 15 Hz, the receiver identifies the component with the highest power, maps it to the corresponding bit, and outputs the bit into a candidate pool. The receiver then slides the frame window by one frame, and repeats the above procedure to generate another candidate bit. The final bit for this frame window is the bit with the most occurrences in the pool.

## 4.2 Extracting Desired Color Intensity Change

The receiver perceives mixed color intensity change caused by encoded $\alpha$ values, screen content, ambient light, and camera noise. Among them, the color intensity change associated with encoded $\alpha$ values is the desired change that the receiver aims to extract, and the rest are interfering sources. To minimize the impact of these interfering sources, our design is driven by the fact that these interfering sources have nonuniform impact across the screen, depending on the brightness of the area. Therefore, we can further divide a grid into smaller regions, evaluate the impact of interfering sources on each region, and assign higher weight to regions less affected by interfering sources. This allows us to reduce the impact of the interfering factors, and enhance the desired change associated with data. The key question then is to determine the weight of each region within a grid. An effective weight assignment should leverage the scene type of the screen content. Next we describe our strategy for each scene type (the static and gradual scene) in detail.

**Static Scene.** For the static scene, we are inspired by an audio beamforming algorithm called Minimum Variance Distortionless Response (MVDR) [33, 35]. This algorithm was originally designed to enhance audio signals in a desired direction while canceling out noise signals. The key idea is to leverage the correlation (e.g., delay spread and energy distribution in the frequency domain) across noise signals and cancel the noise energy.

We develop a variant of this algorithm in our context, where the goal is to enhance the contribution of regions less affected by interfering sources. Specifically, for a grid with $N$ regions, we calculate the weight matrix for its regions as:

$$W = R^{-1}C \times R_{sum}, \tag{3}$$

where $R$ is a $N \times N$ noise correlation matrix capturing the correlation across regions of this grid, $C$ is a $N \times 1$ constant matrix with all elements equal to 1, and $R_{sum}$ is the summation of all elements in $R^{-1}$.

We obtain the noise correlation matrix $R$ via a training process for a static scene. In particular, once the receiver detects a static scene, it buffers frames for $M$ frame windows. It then applies FFT to compute the frequency components of each frame window, and estimates the correlation $R_{ij}$ between region $i$ and $j$ as:

$$R_{ij} = \frac{1}{M} \times \sum_{1 \le k \le M} X_{ik} X_{jk}^T,\ i, j \in [1, N], \tag{4}$$

where $X_{ik}$ and $X_{jk}$ are the vectors of frequency components of the $k$th frame window, for region $i$ and $j$ respectively. From our experiments, we find that $M = 5$ is sufficient to train the correlation matrix and cancel out the contributions of regions more affected by interfering sources. Thus the training takes 0.5 s overall.

**Gradual Scene.** When the screen content is dynamic, it is hard for training-based methods to catch up with the content change in real time. Thus we design a lightweight scheme without training to assign weights to regions within a grid.

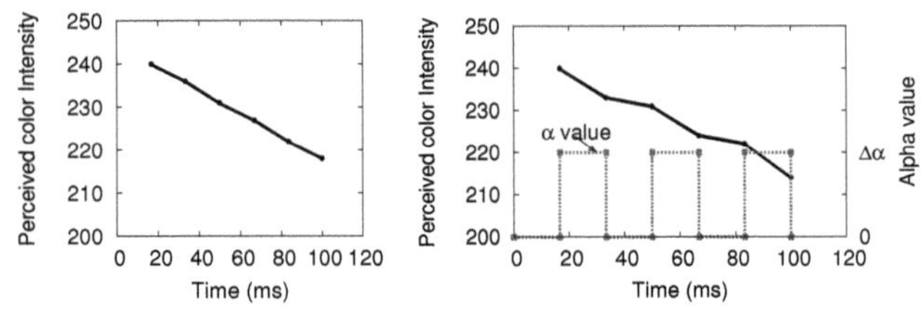


(a) w/o encoding bit 1 (b) w/ encoding bit 1

**Figure 8: Identifying patterns caused by encoded $\alpha$ values when examining the perceived color intensity changes over a frame window (0.1 s), assuming bit 1 is encoded.**

Our design is based on a simple observation: while frames can change drastically over a long time, when examining adjacent frames within a frame window (i.e., 0.1 s) and focusing on a tiny region, we observe that the color intensity change is often monotonic at a constant speed (Figure 8(a)). As a result, when it is mixed with the encoded $\alpha$ change, the $\alpha$ change creates variations in the speed of perceived color intensity change. As an example, Figure 8(b) shows the perceived color intensity of a region when mixed with $\alpha$ value change encode for bit 1. When the $\alpha$ value decreases (no dimming effect) at the second and fourth frames, it slows down the perceived color intensity change at both points. These speed variations are reflected by the sign of the second derivative of the color intensity change over time. Similarly, $\alpha$ value change for encoding bit 0 also leads to a pattern in the second derivative of color intensity change in a frame window. We leverage these patterns to infer the encoded bit.

Clearly, for regions less affected by interfering sources, these patterns resulting from encoded bits are less noticeable. Therefore, we can determine the weight of each region by examining whether these patterns in the second derivatives exist. In our implementation, for regions where these patterns do not exist, we set their weights as zero to minimize their impact. By focusing on regions that exhibit detectable patterns, we reduce the impact of interfering sources and make the system robust in diverse settings. Furthermore, the pattern detection only requires computing the second derivatives. Hence we can update the weight matrix on the fly based on current screen content.

# 5. SYSTEM IMPLEMENTATION

We implement HiLight at the application layer using off-the-shelf smart devices. We implement HiLight transmitter at the Android platform, and the receiver at the iOS framework using iPhone 5s. We choose iPhone 5s as the receiver because for the receiver to decode data, its camera needs to be able to capture at least 60 frames per second, and the iOS AVFoundation framework supports 120 FPS video recording on iPhone 5s. In contrast, the current Android framework (Android 4.4 or lower) does not support video recording at 60 FPS[4], and phone manufactures (e.g., Samsung, HTC) do not make their phone camera API/library public.

To implement the HiLight transmitter, we use `ImageView` (an Android UI container) to create the communication layer (Figure 1(a))

[4]The recent Android 5 framework [4] includes a new camera API, which supports 4K resolution video recording with 65 Mb/s bandwidth. It supports 60 FPS or a higher frame rate. We plan to implement HiLight on the new platform once the hardware support is available.

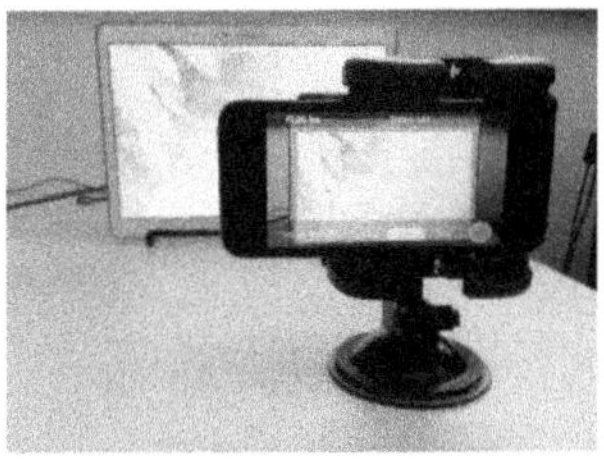

**Figure 9: Experimental setup with Samsung Tab S (left) as the transmitter and iPhone 5s as the receiver (right).**

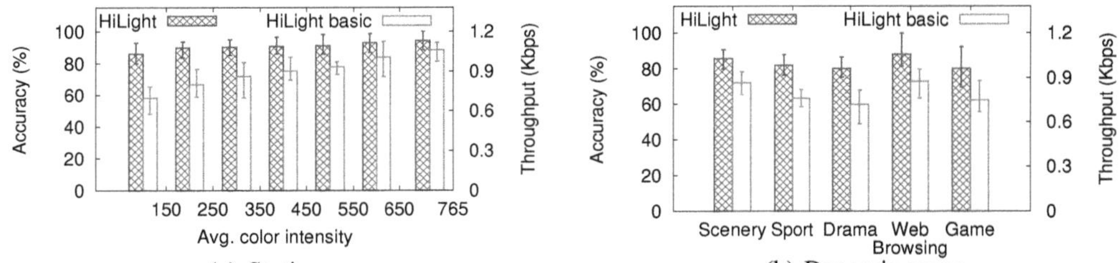


(a) Static scene

(b) Dynamic scene

**Figure 10: HiLight's performance atop arbitrary scene assuming 120 grids on the communication layer. We also plot the performance of HiLight basic [21] that excludes two design enhancements (§ 3.3 and § 4.2) to examine their contribution. Since the throughput is equal to the accuracy multiplied by the number of transmitted bits, we plot a single bar reflecting numbers in both accuracy and throughput.**

atop all image layers. We use the `setImageAlpha` method to specify $\alpha$ values at the application layer. This method passes the given $\alpha$ values down to the `SurfaceFlinger` layer of the Android framework, which further leverages the `glBlendFunc` API in the OpenGL ES library [24] to run the alpha blending on the GPU. Given the ubiquity of hardware accelerated compositing, a similar implementation can be realized on other mobile platforms (e.g., iOS, Windows). We implement scene detection and $\alpha$ value generation as two separate threads. In the first thread, we sample the frame buffer under `/dev/graphics/` to fetch the screen content every 0.1 s. We leverage the OpenCV library to implement the scene detection algorithm, which runs continuously to detect the scene type of the incoming sampled frames. The first thread passes the detection result and frame information to the second thread, which then generates $\alpha$ values and modulates each bit using BFSK. The transmitter signals the start of a transmission by sending 1 in all grids for 0.1 s. Finally, to avoid touch events being blocked by the communication layer, which is atop all content image layers, we register a `View.OnTouchListener` to return false so that the system ignores the communication layer and passes the touch event to the applications below the communication layer.

To implement the HiLight receiver, we use the AVCapture session in the iOS AVFoundation framework to capture frames. To reduce the camera noise in the dark environment, we leverage the built-in light sensor to detect the dark environment, and increase the camera ISO value to raise its sensitivity accordingly. We apply an existing screen detector [42] to locate the transmitter screen, extract the screen area from each captured frame, and divide the captured screen area into grids. To speed up the frame decoding, we fetch only a quarter of pixels in the screen area to decode bits. We implement the main components (scene detection, extracting desired color intensity change, and FFT decoding) in three separate threads. We display the decoding results in a pop-up window on the receiver's screen.

# 6. HiLight EXPERIMENTS

We perform detailed experiments to evaluate the HiLight prototype, focusing on its ability to support unobtrusive transmissions atop arbitrary scene in real time and its robustness in practical settings. We also seek to understand how hardware choice on screen and camera affects its performance, as well as user's perception on the unobtrusiveness of our system.

**Experimental Setup.** We use the Samsung Tab S as the default transmitter (we test other types of screens in § 6.4). We set up the transmitter and receiver (iPhone 5s) at their normal viewing distance (30 cm for the transmitter's 10.5-inch screen, see Figure 9).

**Table 1: Statistics of test images.**

| Avg. color intensity | <150 | [150, 250) | [250, 350) | [350, 450) | [450, 550) | [550, 650) | [650, 765) |
|---|---|---|---|---|---|---|---|
| # of images | 10 | 31 | 23 | 23 | 14 | 6 | 5 |

We increase the viewing distance when testing HiLight on transmitters with larger screens in § 6.4. While we fix them on two phone holders for most experiments, we also test the hand-held scenario in § 6.3. By default, we divide the transmitter screen into 120 grids, where each grid is 2.7 $cm^2$ in size (Table 2). We repeat each experiment for five rounds, and perform all experiments under a fluorescent lamp (100 lux) in an office environment. We focus on two performance metrics: 1) accuracy, the percentage of bits successfully received over all bits transmitted; and 2) throughput, the number of bits successfully received per second.

## 6.1 Supporting Arbitrary Scene

To evaluate HiLight's ability to support arbitrary scene, we randomly select 112 images with all levels of average color intensity (Table 1), 60 video clips, a 30-min web browsing scene, and 6 gaming apps[5]. We run HiLight to transmit random bits atop each screen content, and measure the throughput and accuracy at the receiver. In all of our graphs, we plot error bars covering the 90% confidence interval.

**Static Scene.** Figure 10(a) plots the average accuracy and throughput as the average pixel color intensity value varies, where a higher color intensity value indicates a brighter image. We divide the whole color intensity range into seven intervals, and average the results of images with color intensity values in the same interval. Intuition says that dark images lead to less detectable translucency changes and thus much lower throughput. Surprisingly, we observe that HiLight is not sensitive to image color intensity, maintaining 91%+ accuracy and 1.1 Kbps throughput for any images with average color intensity above 150. Even for dark images (color intensity values below 150), HiLight still achieves 85% accuracy and 1 Kbps throughput. This sets a notable improvement over our prior design, referred to as HiLight basic [21]. The improvement can be attributed to the effectiveness of two design components: the adaption of $\alpha$ value change (§ 3.3) and the strategy of extracting encoded color intensity change (§ 4.2). Our hypothesis is confirmed by the results of HiLight basic [21], which fixes the $\Delta\alpha$ to 1% and does not use weight matrix to extract desired color intensity

[5]All the test images and video clips are available at `http://dartnets.cs.dartmouth.edu/hilight-test`.

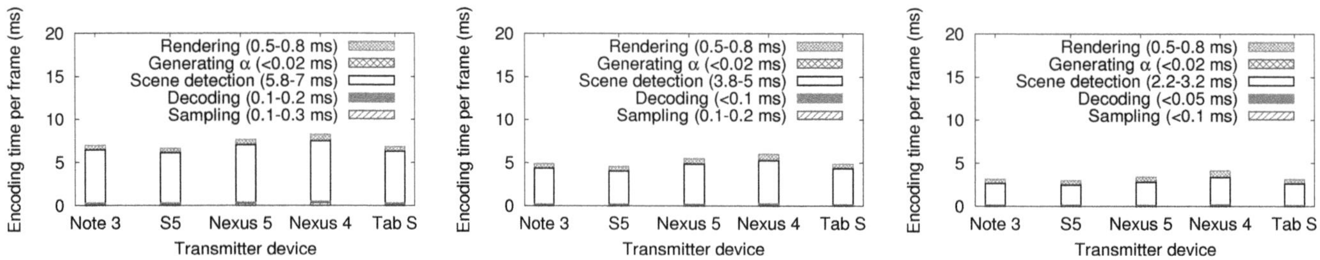


(a) High resolution (1080p) (b) Medium resolution (720p) (c) Low resolution (480p)

**Figure 11: HiLight's encoding time per frame under different frame resolution. Across all test devices, HiLight encodes a single frame within 8 ms, sufficient to support both 60 FPS and 120 FPS frame rates.**

changes. To future improve HiLight's performance on very dark scenes (color intensity below 150), we can set white as the grid color of the communication layer atop dark areas. We plan it for future work.

**Dynamic Scene.** For the dynamic scene, we test three types of video clips including scenery video (e.g., campus video), sports, and drama (e.g., TV shows, movie trailers). They represent video with minor, medium, and drastic frame transition, respectively. For each type, we test 20 video clips and each clip lasts 1–2 mins. We also test two example scenarios when the screen content is generated on the fly. These include 1) web browsing, where the user is reading and scrolling down a web page, refreshing the page, and switching to other web pages; and 2) gaming, where the user is playing games (e.g., Angry Bird, Super Mario).

Figure 10(b) plots the average throughput and accuracy under all types of dynamic scene. Our key observations are as follows. *First*, overall HiLight maintains 84% accuracy with 1 Kbps throughput across these scene types, even for drama video clips that contain drastic screen content change. By examining the performance of HiLight basic, we validate the efficacy of our two key design components, which lead to 18% improvement in general and 20% for drama video in particular. *Second*, dynamic scene leads to slightly lower throughput and accuracy than the static scene, mainly for two reasons. The first reason is that to configure $\alpha$ changes, the system uses sampled color information of sampled frames to estimate actual frames. The sampling leads to estimation errors as frames vary over time, making the adaptation of $\Delta\alpha$ sub-optimal. One solution is to sample more frequently upon more drastic frame transition. We plan it for future work. Another reason is that we defer transmissions upon cut scene. Yet since cut scene occurs rarely (only in sports and drama), the resulting throughput loss is less than 0.6% and 2.4% for sports and drama. *Third*, among different dynamic scenes, drama scene is the most challenging as it contains more drastic content changes that greatly interfere with encoded color intensity change. Web browsing scene achieves the best performance among all because it has a fair portion of static scene when the user reads web pages. Most games we test often change background images drastically, and thus the gaming scene is similar to drama.

**Varying the Grid Size.** We also examine how different grid size on the communication layer affects HiLight under the static or dynamic scene. We test seven grid sizes (Table 2) using 10 images and 10 video clips, and list HiLight's average throughput and accuracy in Table 2. Overall, as the number of grids increases, HiLight's throughput grows rapidly and its accuracy drops slowly. This is because more grids mean more concurrent transmitter elements, leading to more transmitted bits. Yet as each grid has fewer pixels, the

**Table 2: Impact of grid size on HiLight performance.**

| **# of grids** | 6 | 30 | 120 | 180 | 240 | 360 | 600 |
|---|---|---|---|---|---|---|---|
| **Size** (cm$^2$) | 54.2 | 10.8 | 2.7 | 1.8 | 1.4 | 0.9 | 0.5 |
| **# of pixels** | 683K | 137K | 34K | 23K | 17K | 11K | 6.8K |
| **Static scene** | | | | | | | |
| **Accuracy** (%) | 99.4 | 93.9 | 89.4 | 86.8 | 82.9 | 78.7 | 75.2 |
| **Throughput (Kbps)** | 0.06 | 0.3 | 1 | 1.6 | 2 | 2.8 | 4.5 |
| **Dynamic scene** | | | | | | | |
| **Accuracy** (%) | 91.0 | 87.1 | 85.4 | 80.3 | 78.3 | 73.2 | 67.2 |
| **Throughput (Kbps)** | 0.05 | 0.3 | 1 | 1.4 | 1.9 | 2.6 | 4 |

inter-symbol interference [26] kicks in, making it more challenging to differentiate pixel translucency changes across adjacent grids and causing more bit errors. However, the increase in the transmitted bits outweighs the accuracy drop, leading to the throughput growth. In particular, for the grid size of 0.5 mm$^2$ (600 grids), HiLight achieves 4 Kbps under both static and dynamic scene. The minimal grid size is ultimately limited by the resolution of the camera sensor and the distance between the transmitter and the receiver.

## 6.2 Processing Time

To evaluate HiLight's ability to support real-time communication, we measure its processing time of per-frame encoding and decoding. We measure the data encoding time as the duration starting from fetching a frame to the end of rendering. The decoding time is the time taken to process frames in a frame window (six frames) upon the arrival of a new frame.

**Encoding Time.** We measure HiLight's encoding time on five Android devices. Since the encoding time is not affected by the number of grids on the screen and heavily depends on the frame resolution, we test three resolution levels, each with 10 video clips. Figure 11 plots the total per-frame encoding time as well as the breakdown. We make three key observations. *First*, across all devices and frame resolution levels, HiLight's encoding delay is consistently below 8.3 ms. This is mainly because HiLight leverages GPU to process $\alpha$ values and removes the need to directly modify pixel RGB values. With the per-frame encoding time below 8.3 ms, HiLight can further support high-resolution video streaming at 120 FPS while transmitting data unobtrusively.

*Second*, among all encoding steps, scene detection occupies 78–87% of the encoding time and ranges from 2.5 ms to 7 ms. It is longer for the higher frame resolution, because there are more pixels for the algorithm to sample and process. *Third*, our sampling strategy significantly reduces the overhead of fetching and decoding a frame. Since we sample one frame per frame window (six frames) and sample one-sixteenth of pixels in the sampled frame,

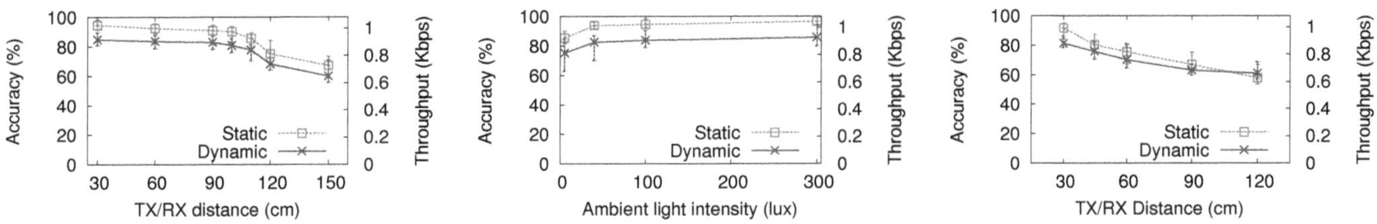


(a) Supporting distance (b) Ambient light (c) Hand motion

**Figure 12: Impact of practical factors on HiLight's performance.**

**Table 3: HiLight's decoding time over a frame window under different grid size, using iPhone 5s.**

| Decoding steps | Decoding time (ms) under varying # of grids | | | | | | |
|---|---|---|---|---|---|---|---|
| | 6 | 30 | 120 | 180 | 240 | 360 | 600 |
| Sampling | 2.95 | | | | | | |
| Scene detection | 1.22 | | | | | | |
| Extracting changes | 0.02 | | | | | | |
| Demodulation | 0.07 | 0.21 | 0.81 | 1.1 | 1.73 | 2.47 | 3.31 |
| **Overall** | 4.26 | 4.4 | 5 | 5.29 | 5.92 | 6.66 | 7.5 |

fetching pixel color values entails 0.35 ms, which is 1/96 of fetching every frame and obtaining the color values of all pixels.

**Decoding Time.** We further examine HiLight's data decoding time as the number of grids on the communication layer varies. Table 3 lists the time taken by each decoding step when processing frames in a frame window on iPhone 5s. Aiming to capture the decoding time upon each incoming frame on the fly, we do not include the MVDR training delay (§ 4.2) in the table, because we do not need to perform the training for each frame, but only in the beginning of the whole decoding process for a static scene[6]. From Table 3, our key observations are as follows. *First*, under all the grid sizes, HiLight is able to decode frames in a frame window within 8 ms. This demonstrates that even when the transmitter is sending data at 120 Hz (supported by higher screen refresh rate), the receiver is able to process all incoming data in real time. *Second*, for all decoding steps except BFSK demodulation, their running time is independent of the number of grids. This is because these steps are performed upon sampled pixels of each frame. Only the number of sampled pixels affects their running time. In comparison, BFSK demodulation performs FFT for each grid independently to decode each bit. More grids lead to more FFT computations and thus a longer processing time.

## 6.3 Practical Considerations

We now evaluate the impact of practical factors on HiLight's performance. We test 10 images and 10 video clips, and repeat all experiments for five rounds.

**Supporting Distance.** We start with examining the transmission distance HiLight supports. We increase the distance between the screen and the camera from 30 cm (the normal viewing distance) to 150 cm, and plot the resulting throughput and accuracy under both static and dynamic scene in Figure 12(a). Overall HiLight's performance is relatively stable when the distance is within 1 m, maintaining 90%+ accuracy for the static scene and 85%+ for the dynamic scene. This demonstrates the efficacy of HiLight design.

[6]Our measurements show that MVDR training takes 1 ms to 27 ms as the number grids increases from 6 to 600, respectively.

As the distance further increases, throughput and accuracy start to drop quickly. This is expected, because light attenuates over distance, leading to weaker illumination changes that are harder to detect. In addition, since the receiver camera does not have an optical zoom, as the receiver is further away, the transmitter screen becomes smaller in the captured frame. This reduces the captured pixels for decoding and lowers the decoding accuracy.

**Ambient Light.** Next, we examine HiLight's sensitivity to ambient light. We test four indoor ambient light conditions (1 lux, 40 lux, 100 lux, and 300 lux), and plot HiLight's performance in Figure 12(b). Intuitively, dark settings are challenging for HiLight, where pixel translucency changes are harder to detect and camera noise is also higher. Yet we observe that the HiLight's performance is fairly stable once the light illuminance is above 40 lux (far below the normal ambient light, which is around 100 lux). HiLight achieves the robustness because the system leverages the built-in light sensor on iPhone 5s to sense the ambient light and raises the camera sensitivity in dark settings. This allows the receiver to better sense the pixel translucency change. While increasing camera sensitivity also introduces camera noise, most camera noise is filtered out by our weight matrix used to extract the desired color intensity change (§ 4.2).

**Hand Motion.** We now move on to examining the impact of hand motion on HiLight. We hold the receiver in the air facing a fixed transmitter, and vary the distance between the transmitter and the receiver. Figure 12(c) plots the results when the transmitter screen is displaying static or dynamic content. As expected, hand motion causes misalignment between two devices, leading to image blur and thus lowering the accuracy. Yet at the normal viewing distance (30 cm), the accuracy drop is minor (<3–4% compared to the perfectly aligned scenario in Figure 12(a)). As the distance increases, the performance gap to the perfectly aligned scenario increases. This is because at longer distances, hand motion causes more significant screen misalignment, and the receiver is more likely to misidentify the grids on the screen. Comparing the two types of scene, we observe that the accuracy of the static scene drops more quickly. This is because the weight matrix for the static scene is calculated once during decoding, while for the dynamic scene, the weight matrix is updated for every frame window and thus can better deal with screen misalignment. To minimize the impact of hand motion, one can leverage image tracking and alignment algorithms in computer vision to track the transmitter screen. The challenge is to ensure that these algorithms can be performed in real time. We plan to study this as part of our future work.

**Viewing Angle.** Finally, we examine HiLight with varying horizontal and vertical viewing angles to assess the impact of the misalignment between the transmitter and the receiver. In the first two experiments, we fix the transmitter screen and rotate the receiver either horizontally or vertically by 0° to 60° while keeping their

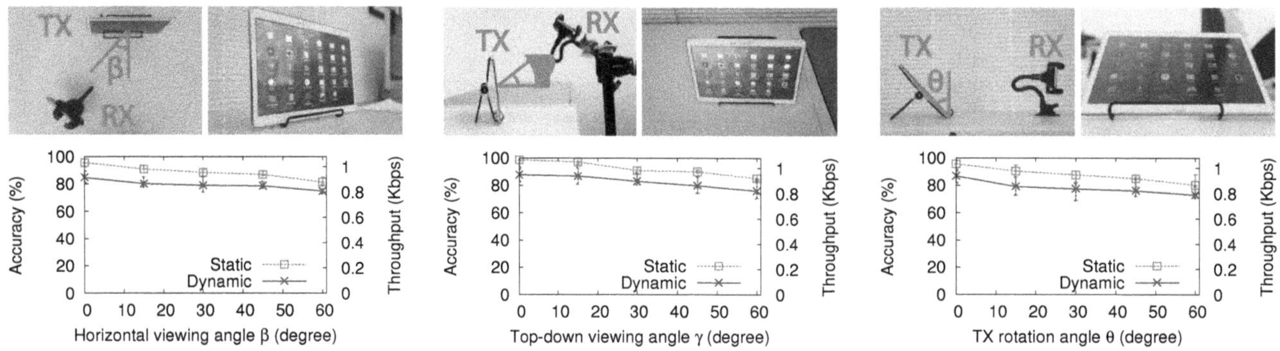


(a) Horizontal viewing angle $\beta$ (b) Top-down viewing angle $\gamma$ (c) TX rotation angle $\theta$

**Figure 13: Impact of the horizontal and vertical viewing angle on HiLight's performance.**

**Table 4: Impact of screens on HiLight's performance, using iPhone 5s as the receiver.**

| TX | Screen | Scene type | Through-put (Kbps) | # of grids | Accuracy (%) |
|---|---|---|---|---|---|
| Samsung Tab S | OLED 10.5" 2560 × 1600 | Static | 1.1 | 120 | 91 |
| | | Dynamic | 0.3 | 30 | 90 |
| Nexus 5 | LCD 5.0" 1920 × 1080 | Static | 0.6 | 60 | 91 |
| | | Dynamic | 0.2 | 20 | 91 |
| Mac Air | LED 13.3" 1440 × 900 | Static | 1.1 | 120 | 91 |
| | | Dynamic | 0.3 | 30 | 90 |
| iMac | LED 27" 2560 × 1440 | Static | 1.6 | 180 | 91 |
| | | Dynamic | 0.6 | 60 | 91 |

**Table 5: Impact of cameras on HiLight's performance, using Samsung Tab S as the transmitter.**

| Receiver | Cam-era | Scene type | Through-put (Kbps) | # of grids | Accuracy (%) |
|---|---|---|---|---|---|
| iPhone 5s | 8 MP | Static | 1.1 | 120 | 91 |
| | | Dynamic | 0.3 | 30 | 90 |
| Samsung Note 3 | 13 MP | Static | 4.9 | 540 | 90 |
| | | Dynamic | 4.9 | 540 | 90 |
| Samsung S5 | 16 MP | Static | 6.7 | 720 | 93 |
| | | Dynamic | 4.9 | 540 | 90 |
| Canon 60D (SLR camera) | 18 MP | Static | 6.6 | 720 | 92 |
| | | Dynamic | 5.0 | 540 | 92 |

distance the same (30 cm). In the third experiment, we fix the receiver and make the transmitter screen self-rotate from 0° to 60°. Figure 13 shows the three experimental setups, the observed perspective distortion in each setup[7], and HiLight's throughput and accuracy. Overall, HiLight supports up to 60° viewing angle in all directions for both types of scenes. Its performance gracefully degrades as the viewing angle increases, because the transmitter screen captured by the receiver distorts as a trapezoid, making it challenging for the receiver to identify grids. In addition, since different pixels on the screen have different depths to the receiver, some portion of the captured screen can be out of focus. However, the performance degradation is less than 7–8% for both scene types. This is because HiLight relies on the relative color intensity change to extract data and is insensitive to static noises such as the image quality degradation caused by being out of focus. To further enhance HiLight's robustness against perspective distortion, one can leverage image projection algorithms (e.g., affine transformation [8]) to avoid grid misidentification. Our experiments show that the current implementation of these algorithms requires 100 ms to process a frame, thus we need an optimized implementation to support real-time communication.

## 6.4 Impact of Screen/Camera Hardware

We next examine how the physical capability of screens and cameras affects HiLight's performance. We test HiLight on different screens and cameras and examine its highest throughput while maintaining accuracy above 90%. We adjust the distance for each pair of devices to ensure the captured screen size in the camera preview the same.

[7]Using the 10-inch OLED screen, we observe minor pixel brightness degradation caused by viewing angle change (<10% at 60° viewing angle). Its impact on HiLight's performance is negligible.

**Varying the Screen.** We first fix iPhone 5s as the receiver and test different types (LCD, LED, OLED) of screens in varying sizes (5–27 in) as transmitters. Since our current implementation of the HiLight transmitter is based on the Android framework, to test HiLight on devices such as Mac Air and iMac, we make video clips with data embedded into a static or dynamic scene, play these video clips on each screen, and measure the real-time accuracy and throughput at the receiver. Table 4 lists the results for 10 static and 10 dynamic scenes. Clearly screen resolution and size are the two key factors affecting the performance. iMac's screen works the best with the largest size and second-highest resolution. Among different screen types, OLED screens are the most preferable, because OLED screens do not have backlight and each pixel emits light independently. Therefore, colors on OLED screens are brighter with higher contrast, making color intensity change easier to detect. In comparison, both LCD and LED screens have backlight that reduces the color contrast. LED screens outperform LCD screens because the LED backlight renders color change more precisely.

**Varying the Camera.** Next, we fix the Samsung Tab S as the transmitter, use different cameras to capture frames, and process captured frames offline to examine the accuracy and throughput. We test four types of cameras including a high-end SLR camera with 18 MP resolution. Results in Table 5 demonstrate the significant performance gain brought by high-resolution cameras for both types of scene. Higher-resolution cameras capture more pixels on the transmitter screen, and thus they support smaller grids on the transmitter screen and achieve higher throughput. In particular, the high-end SLR camera supports 720 grids on the 10-in screen enabling 6.6 Kbps throughput, six times higher than that achieved by iPhone 5s in our prototype. Even the cameras on some existing smart devices (Note 3 and S5) are sufficient for HiLight to reach 5 – 6 Kbps, similar to that of the high-end camera. This demonstrates

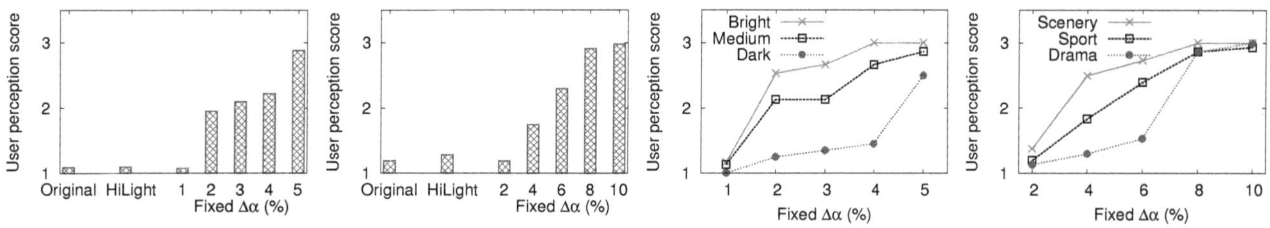

(a) Static scene


(b) Dynamic scene


(c) Static scene, fixed $\Delta\alpha$


(d) Dynamic scene, fixed $\Delta\alpha$

**Figure 14: User perception on HiLight's unobtrusive transmissions, where the perception scores are explained in Table 7. Achieving scores of 2 or below is acceptable. Comparing to changing pixel translucency uniformly with a fixed amount, HiLight adapts the pixel translucency changes ($\Delta\alpha$) non-uniformly across pixels, and thus diminishes the visual effects caused by data communication.**

**Table 6: Statistics of the 20 video clips used in our user study.**

| Scene type | Static scene | | | Dynamic scene | | |
|---|---|---|---|---|---|---|
| | Bright | Medium | Dark | Scenery | Sport | Drama |
| # of video clips | 3 | 3 | 4 | 3 | 3 | 4 |

**Table 7: User perception scores.**

| Score | User perception |
|---|---|
| 1 | Certainly no noticeable visual effects. Good viewing experience. |
| 2 | Uncertain about visual effects. Still good viewing experience. |
| 3 | Certainly noticeable visual effects. |

HiLight's robustness on diverse hardware platforms and its great potential on future smart devices with more sophisticated cameras.

## 6.5 User Perception

Finally, we conduct a user study to examine whether HiLight causes any noticeable visual artifacts on the original screen content. Our user study is conducted with 10 participants (5 male and 5 female) in the age range of 18 to 30. We select 20 original video clips (each lasts for 10 s) covering diverse scenes (Table 6). For each video clip, we create six modified versions by encoding data into pixel translucency ($\alpha$) changes. In one version, we use HiLight to encode data, which adapts $\Delta\alpha$ non-uniformly across pixels (Algorithm 1). In the other five versions, we change the $\alpha$ values of all pixels uniformly with a fixed amount, varying from 1% to 5% for the static scenes and 2% to 10% for the dynamic scenes. Among the total 140 video clips (20 original and 120 modified), we randomly assign 100 of them to each participant. To avoid participant response bias [12], we do not inform participants which video clips are modified and which are original. Before the study, each participant watches the original video clips on a Samsung Tab S screen to gain an initial sense of the video content. During the study, each participant watches the assigned 100 video clips (mixed with the original and modified versions) in a random order on the Tab S screen and rates from 1 to 3 to indicate the certainty of observing visual effects in each video clip[8]. Table 7 shows the perception scores. Achieving a score of 1 is ideal and 2 is acceptable.

We plot the average user perception scores in Figure 14(a) and (b). We make two key observations. *First*, by adapting the amount of translucency changes ($\Delta\alpha$) non-uniformly across the screen, HiLight significantly reduces the visual effects caused by the $\Delta\alpha$ in both static and dynamic scenes. User's perception level on HiLight is very close to that of watching the original video clips. In contrast, a fixed $\Delta\alpha$ across all pixels easily leads to noticeable visual effects even for small $\Delta\alpha$ values (4% for static scenes and 6% for the dynamic scenes). This result demonstrates the effectiveness of HiLight's adaptation of $\Delta\alpha$ based on sampled screen content pixels and its gradient smoothing of $\Delta\alpha$ within each grid (Figure 6).

*Second*, the maximal amount of translucency changes that users cannot perceive depends on the screen content. Between static and dynamic scenes, dynamic scenes allow larger pixel translucency changes that are unnoticeable by users. We hypothesize that this is because human eyes are less sensitive to subtle changes in pixel brightness when the screen content itself contains more drastic color intensity changes. We observe a similar pattern as we analyze different types of dynamic scenes. Figure 14(d) plots the average user perception score for three types of dynamic scenes, as the fixed $\Delta\alpha$ increases. For drama scenes that have the most drastic color intensity changes, 6% of fixed $\alpha$ changes are still almost unnoticeable by users. Among the static scenes, we observe that users can tolerate larger pixel translucency changes ($\Delta\alpha$) atop darker screen content (Figure 14(c)). This is because the absolute brightness changes of darker areas are smaller than that of brighter areas. These observations together justify the $\Delta\alpha$ configuration in HiLight (Algorithm 1), which increases the $\Delta\alpha$ for dark areas and dynamic scenes.

[8]A participant can replay a video clip multiple times to determine the score.

# 7. POTENTIAL APPLICATIONS

**Augmented Reality.** HiLight can enable innovative interaction designs for augmented reality (AR) apps. For AR glasses with heads-up displays and cameras, they can leverage HiLight to obtain additional information layers from any surrounding screens. Users wearing smart glasses can acquire personalized information from any screen, including the subtitles of a movie or TV program, customized coupon or URL link within an advertisement, and hints in gaming apps, without affecting the content shown on the screen.

**Continuous Authentication.** Operating on the visible light spectrum, HiLight communication occurs only when the camera is physically facing the screen. This allows us to continuously authenticate user's physical presence, highly valuable for many existing apps. Consider a user wearing smart glasses in front of a screen. Online banking or health-related apps can leverage HiLight to continuously authenticate user's presence and immediately log out the user when the user leaves the screen. In addition, online video streaming providers such as Amazon can leverage HiLight to monitor the exact portion of video a user has watched, and define accurate pricing scheme based on the information.

**Video Tagging.** When capturing a video, it is hard to add object tags on the fly. Using HiLight, we can embed information associated with the local object or location into all public screens. Thus, when a camera captures video, it also simultaneously fetches the additional information from surrounding screens and attaches it with the video. Social apps such as Facebook can then automatically extract the information in the captured video and add tags for the user.

# 8. RELATED WORK

We categorize existing research on screen-camera communication into two categories.

**Obtrusive Screen-Camera Communication.** Active research has examined screen-camera communication using visible coded images [6]. One class of work focuses on boosting data rate, by leveraging better modulation schemes [26] or innovative barcode designs [14, 43]. Another class of work aims to enhance link reliability, by tackling the frame synchronization problem [15, 22, 28], or enabling barcode detection at long distances [16, 23], or designing multi-layer error correction schemes [36]. A recent study [40] generates dynamic QR code to transmit sensor data on the fly. Our work leverages insights from these studies, but differs in that we aim to enable screen-camera communication without showing visible coded images.

**Unobtrusive Screen-Camera Communication.** Prior work has studied how to hide information in a given screen content while enabling screen-camera communication. Yuan *et al.* leverage watermarking to embed messages into an image [41, 42]. [10, 37, 39] enable unobtrusive communication by switching barcodes with complementary hue. PiCode and ViCode [19] integrate barcodes with existing images to enhance viewing experiences. All these methods have greatly reduced the visual artifacts of visible codes. Yet they all require direct modifications of content pixel RGB values, which prevents them from supporting arbitrary scene in real time. The unique contribution of HiLight is to broaden the applicable scenario of unobtrusive screen-camera communication. It removes the need to directly modify RGB values and decouples communication from screen content. HiLight is similar in spirit to prior efforts that modulate bits by changing the screen's backlight [13, 18, 20]. All these designs, however, require special hardware support (e.g., shutter plane). HiLight differs in that it works upon off-the-shelf smart devices.

# 9. CONCLUSION

We presented HiLight, the first system enabling real-time, unobtrusive screen-camera communication atop any screen scene (can be generated on the fly). We implemented HiLight on off-the-shelf smart devices and evaluated HiLight in diverse practical settings. By placing no constraint on the screen's original functionality (displaying content) while enabling communication, HiLight opens up opportunities for new HCI and context-aware applications.

Our current system has several limitations and possible extension that we plan to address in future work. *First*, the throughput of our system is currently limited by the screen refresh rate (60 Hz). For OLED screens, the physical response time of a pixel can be less than 0.01 ms [5], translating into the pixel change frequency higher than 100 KHz. We plan to seek methods to better approach this physical limit and boost the system throughput. *Second*, we plan to explore advanced modulation and coding schemes to improve the transmission reliability. We observe that most bit errors are randomly spread out. Since the current communication channel is one-way without any feedback from the receiver, error handling schemes such as low-density parity-check (LDPC) code [11] or Reed-Solomon code [38] are good candidates. *Third*, our current design sets a uniform color (black) for the communication layer. We plan to vary the color (between black and white) across different grids of the communication layer based on the content area color (e.g., use white color for dark areas and black for bright areas). This color adaptation can enhance the system reliability atop a wide range of screen content. *Forth*, to better support device mobility (e.g., a user wearing smart glasses as the receiver), we plan to integrate low-complexity object tracking algorithms into HiLight, so that the receiver can keep tracking the screen area and decode data even during constant hand or head movement. *Finally*, our system is still a one-way channel. To realize a two-way channel, we can place two devices with screens facing each other and each device uses its front-facing camera to receive data. Obtaining receiver feedback allows the transmitter to adapt its configuration (e.g., grid size, frame window). We plan to explore the associated systems and design challenges.

# 10. ACKNOWLEDGMENTS

The authors sincerely thank shepherd Chunyi Peng and the reviewers for their valuable feedback and Jiawen Chen at Google for his insights on GPU programming. We also thank DartNets Lab members Zhao Tian, Rui Wang, Fanglin Chen, and Xiaole An for their support on our study. This work is supported in part by the Dartmouth Burke Research Initiation Award and the National Science Foundation under grant CNS-1421528. Any opinions, findings, and conclusions or recommendations expressed in this material are those of the authors and do not necessarily reflect those of the funding agencies or others.

# 11. REFERENCES


[1] `https://www.opengl.org/`.

[2] `http://opencv.org/platforms/android.html`.

[3] `http://developer.android.com/guide/topics/resources/drawable-resource.html`.

[4] `https://developer.android.com/about/versions/android-5.0.html`.

[5] `http://en.wikipedia.org/wiki/OLED`.

[6] Automatic identification and data capture techniques - QR code 2005 bar code symbology specification. ISO/IEC 18004:2006.

[7] ASHOK, A., ET AL. Challenge: Mobile optical networks through visual MIMO. In *Proc. of MobiCom* (2010).

[8] BERGER, M. *Geometry I*. Springer Science & Business, 2009.

[9] BULLOUGH, J., ET AL. Effects of flicker characteristics from solid-state lighting on detection, acceptability and comfort. *Lighting Research and Technology 43*, 3 (2011), 337–348.

[10] CARVALHO, R., CHU, C.-H., AND CHEN, L.-J. IVC: Imperceptible video communication. In *Proc. of HotMobile (poster)* (2014).

[11] DAVEY, M. C., AND MACKAY, D. J. Low density parity check codes over gf (q). In *Information Theory Workshop, 1998* (1998), IEEE, pp. 70–71.

[12] DELL, N., VAIDYANATHAN, V., MEDHI, I., CUTRELL, E., AND THIES, W. "Yours is Better!": Participant Response Bias in HCI. In *Proc. of CHI* (2012).

[13] FATTAL, D., ET AL. A multi-directional backlight for a wide-angle, glasses-free three-dimensional display. *Nature 495*, 7441 (2013), 348–351.

[14] HAO, T., ZHOU, R., AND XING, G. COBRA: Color barcode streaming for smartphone systems. In *Proc. of MobiSys* (2012).

[15] HU, W., GU, H., AND PU, Q. LightSync: Unsynchronized visual communication over screen-camera links. In *Proc. of MobiCom* (2013).

[16] HU, W., MAO, J., HUANG, Z., XUE, Y., SHE, J., BIAN, K., AND SHEN, G. Strata: Layered coding for scalable visual communication. In *Proc. of MobiCom* (2014).

[17] HUANG, C.-L., AND LIAO, B.-Y. A robust scene-change detection method for video segmentation. *IEEE Transactions on Circuits and Systems for Video Technology 11*, 12 (2001), 1281–1288.

[18] HUANG, S. Backlight modulation circuit having rough and fine illumination signal processing circuit, Mar. 27 2012. US Patent 8,144,112.

[19] HUANG, W., AND MOW, W. H. PiCode: 2D barcode with embedded picture and ViCode: 3D barcode with embedded video (poster). In *Proc. of MobiCom* (2013).

[20] KIMURA, K., MASUDA, S., AND HAYASHI, M. Display apparatus and method for controlling a backlight with multiple light sources of a display unit, Sept. 11 2012. US Patent 8,264,447.

[21] LI, T., AN, C., CAMPBELL, A., AND ZHOU, X. HiLight: Hiding bits in pixel translucency changes. In *Proc. of the 1st ACM MobiCom Workshop on Visible Light Communication Systems (VLCS)* (2014).

[22] LIKAMWA, R., RAMIREZ, D., AND HOLLOWAY, J. Styrofoam: A tightly packed coding scheme for camera-based visible light communication. In *Proc. of the 1st ACM MobiCom Workshop on Visible Light Communication Systems (VLCS)* (2014).

[23] MOHAN, A., WOO, G., HIURA, S., SMITHWICK, Q., AND RASKAR, R. Bokode: Imperceptible visual tags for camera based interaction from a distance. In *Proc. of SIGGRAPH* (2009).

[24] MUNSHI, A., GINSBURG, D., AND SHREINER, D. *OpenGL ES 2.0 programming guide*. Pearson Education, 2008.

[25] NAGASAKA, A., AND TANAKA, Y. Automatic video indexing and full-video search for object appearances. In *Proc. of the IFIP TC2/WG 2.6 Second Working Conference on Visual Database Systems II* (1992).

[26] PERLI, S. D., AHMED, N., AND KATABI, D. PixNet: Interference-free wireless links using LCD-camera pairs. In *Proc. of MobiCom* (2010).

[27] PORTER, T., AND DUFF, T. Compositing digital images. In *ACM SIGGRAPH Computer Graphics* (1984).

[28] RAJAGOPAL, N., LAZIK, P., AND ROWE, A. Visual light landmarks for mobile devices. In *Proc. of IPSN* (2014).

[29] ROSIN, P. L. Thresholding for change detection. In *Computer Vision, 1998. Sixth International Conference on* (1998), IEEE, pp. 274–279.

[30] ROSIN, P. L., AND IOANNIDIS, E. Evaluation of global image thresholding for change detection. *Pattern Recognition Letters 24*, 14 (2003), 2345–2356.

[31] SETHI, I. K., AND PATEL, N. V. Statistical approach to scene change detection. In *IS&T/SPIE's Symposium on Electronic Imaging: Science & Technology* (1995), pp. 329–338.

[32] SMITS, P. C., AND ANNONI, A. Toward specification-driven change detection. *IEEE Transactions on Geoscience and Remote Sensing 38*, 3 (2000), 1484–1488.

[33] SUR, S., WEI, T., AND ZHANG, X. Autodirective audio capturing through a synchronized smartphone array. In *ACM Mobisys 2014*.

[34] TAN, K. W., ET AL. FOCUS: a usable & effective approach to OLED display power management. In *UbiComp* (2013).

[35] VAN DE SANDE, J., AND ASSIGNOR, T. Real-time beamforming and sound classification parameter generation in public environments. *TNO report TNO-DV* (2012), S007.

[36] WANG, A., MA, S., HU, C., HUAI, J., PENG, C., AND SHEN, G. Enhancing reliability to boost the throughput over screen-camera links. In *Proc. of MobiCom* (2014).

[37] WANG, A., PENG, C., ZHANG, O., SHEN, G., AND ZENG, B. InFrame: Multiflexing full-frame visible communication channel for humans and devices. In *Proc. of HotNets* (2014).

[38] WICKER, S. B., AND BHARGAVA, V. K. *Reed-Solomon codes and their applications*. John Wiley & Sons, 1999.

[39] WOO, G., LIPPMAN, A., AND RASKAR, R. VRCodes: Unobtrusive and active visual codes for interaction by exploiting rolling shutter. In *Proc. of ISMAR* (2012).

[40] YONEZAWA, T., OGAWA, M., KYONO, Y., NOZAKI, H., NAKAZAWA, J., NAKAMURA, O., AND TOKUDA, H. SENSeTREAM: Enhancing online live experience with sensor-federated video stream using animated two-dimensional code. In *Proc. of UbiComp* (2014).

[41] YUAN, W., DANA, K., VARGA, M., ASHOK, A., GRUTESER, M., AND MANDAYAM, N. Computer vision methods for visual mimo optical systems. *Proceedings of the IEEE International Workshop on Projector-Camera Systems (held with CVPR)* (2011), 37–43.

[42] YUAN, W., ET AL. Dynamic and invisible messaging for visual mimo. In *IEEE Workshop on Applications of Computer Vision (WACV)* (2012).

[43] ZHANG, B., ET AL. SBVLC: Secure barcode-based visible light communication for smartphones. In *Proc. of INFOCOM* (2014).

[44] ZHANG, H., KANKANHALLI, A., AND SMOLIAR, S. W. Automatic partitioning of full-motion video. *Multimedia Systems 1*, 1 (1993), 10–28.

# Starfish: Efficient Concurrency Support for Computer Vision Applications

Robert LiKamWa and Lin Zhong
Rice University, Houston, TX
roblkw@rice.edu, lzhong@rice.edu

## ABSTRACT

Emerging wearable devices promise a multitude of computer vision-based applications that serve users without active engagement. However, vision algorithms are known to be resource-hungry; and modern mobile systems do not support concurrent application use of the camera. Toward supporting efficient concurrency of vision applications, we report *Starfish*, a split-process execution system that supports concurrent vision applications by allowing them to share computation and memory objects in a secure and efficient manner. Starfish splits the vision library from an application into a separate process, called the Core, which centrally serves all vision applications. The Core shares library call results among applications, eliminating redundant computation and memory use. Starfish supports unmodified applications and unmodified libraries without needing their source code, and guarantees correctness to the applications. In doing so, Starfish improves both the performance and energy efficiency of concurrent vision applications. Using a prototype implementation on Google Glass, we experimentally demonstrate that Starfish reduces the time spent processing repeated vision library calls by 71% – 97%. When running two to ten concurrent face recognition applications at 0.3 frames per second, Starfish reduces CPU utilization by more than 42% – 80%. Notably, this keeps CPU utilization below 13%, even as the number of applications increases. This reduces system power consumption by 19% – 58%, as Starfish maintains a power consumption at approximately 1210 mW while running the concurrent application workloads.

## Categories and Subject Descriptors

I.4.m [**Image Processing and Computer Vision**]: Miscellaneous; D.0 [**Software**]: General

## Keywords

Computer vision; vision library; mobile computing; memoization

## 1. INTRODUCTION

In our envisioned future of *continuous mobile vision* [3], multiple vision applications continuously and concurrently run on mobile devices, analyzing camera frames to understand its environment without active user engagement, e.g., [12, 25]. A wearable device could simultaneously recognize faces to log social interactions, and detecting food items to record eating habits. The same device may also be tasked with remembering where a car is parked and detecting landmarks for rapid localization. We believe that it is highly likely that these applications will be developed by various parties each with their own specialization such as medical informatics, personal analytics, and social networking.

Unfortunately, modern mobile systems support only a single application's access to a camera, which is adequate for photo/video taking and interactive vision applications. Furthermore, camera devices and vision algorithms are known to be too power hungry for always-on operation [17, 18]. Thus, there is an urgent need to support concurrent vision applications efficiently. While hardware innovations are necessary [17, 20], this work approaches the above challenge in system software.

We hold two key insights. First, concurrent vision applications operate on the same root data: frames from the camera. Second, typical vision applications use a relatively small set of foundational algorithms, usually implemented with a standard library, e.g., OpenCV or FastCV. Thus, there is often significant redundancy in the library functions they execute and the objects they create. This presents an opportunity to share redundant library processing among multiple applications to perform simultaneous vision tasks with efficient system performance.

To exploit these insights, we design the *Starfish* software system that not only supports concurrent vision applications, but also allows them to share computation and memory objects securely and efficiently. Our design stems from two major decisions. (*i*) Starfish splits the vision library from an application into a separate process, called the Core, which centrally serves all applications. Essentially, Starfish converts a vision library call into a remote procedure call into the Core. (*ii*) The Core shares library call results among applications securely, eliminating redundant computation and memory use. Importantly, Starfish supports unmodified applications and unmodified vision libraries without their source code, and guarantees correctness to vision applications.

In doing so, Starfish improves the performance and energy efficiency of concurrent vision applications. Leveraging work in remote invocation [4, 21] and computation memoization [13, 19], Starfish contributes novel techniques that meet its unique constraints.

We also report an implementation of Starfish on Android KitKat. Our work intercepts calls to OpenCV by replacing its C++ linked library with our own, and forwards calls over an Android Binder with `MemoryHeapBase` shared memory regions. We support 22 OpenCV functions and 19 OpenCV objects and design interfaces to ease Starfish library development and reduce source code redun-


*MobiSys'15,* May 18–22, 2015, Florence, Italy.

http://dx.doi.org/10.1145/2742647.2742663.

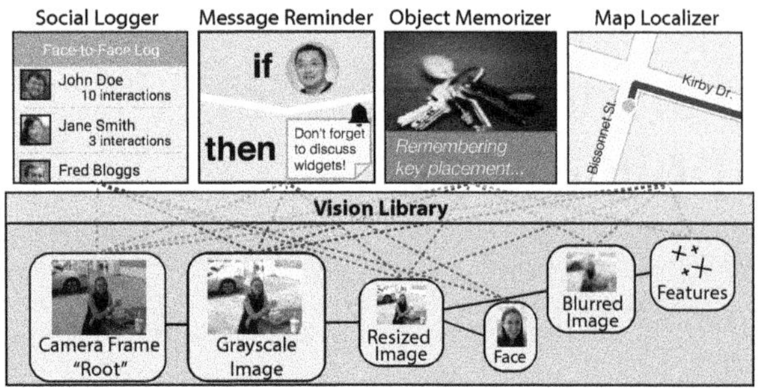


**Figure 1: Vision applications use a vision library to request computations on the root data to create derivative vision objects. Multiple vision applications often require the same vision objects.**

dancy. To fulfill the need to provide concurrent vision applications with camera frame access, we design a frame service that operates on top of the OpenCV camera framework mechanisms, allowing Starfish to send frames to foreground and background applications with no modification to application functionality.

We evaluate the Starfish design and implementation on a Google Glass. We use microbenchmarks to understand the per-call overhead of Starfish library call requests, validating the effectiveness of our split-process and function caching design choices. We measure that our optimizations reduce the per-call Starfish overhead from 20.9 ms to 5.9 ms. We then evaluate the effectiveness of Starfish on a combination of application benchmarks that share computations and do not share computations to explore the range of benefits that Starfish provides. We show that Starfish provides minimal negative impact to applications that do not share computations, while providing substantial benefits to applications that do share computations. While running multiple face recognition applications typically incurs significantly increasing CPU utilization, scaling up to 60% for ten concurrent vision applications running at 0.3 frames per second, Starfish maintains a CPU utilization, staying below 15%. Under Starfish, the system consumes 19% – 58% less power, as Starfish maintains a power consumption at approximately 1210 mW while running the concurrent application workloads. Starfish thus successfully provides system efficiency benefits to concurrent vision applications.

The rest of the paper is organized as follows. §2 provides a background of vision applications and libraries. §3 presents a high level overview of the Starfish design. §4 describes design strategies that reduce the overhead of the split-process execution. §5 details caching policies that allow reuse of previously computed library results. §6 offers details regarding our Android + OpenCV Starfish implementation, including a shared frame delivery service among multiple applications. §7 evaluates Starfish using a combination of application benchmarks, and §8 discusses related work.

# 2. COMPUTER VISION BACKGROUND

We derive our Starfish design through examining contemporary implementations of vision applications. Typical computer vision applications read frames from the camera service and use libraries of computer vision algorithms to extract important information about the content or geometry of a camera frame. In this section, we discuss various systems implications and opportunities of computer vision applications.

## 2.1 Resource usage

Vision applications are resource-intensive, consuming memory, memory bandwidth and CPU cycles. Sampling a full color image uses 0.5 MB for a 640×360 color frame. At 30 frames per second, this introduces 15 MB/s of data creation and usage. To maximize memory reuse, Android applications typically issue a pre-allocated multi-frame buffer to allow the Android camera service to write frames to pre-allocated memory with every new frame capture. In addition to removing the latency of allocating memory, this allows the camera service to record new frames while others are being processed or retained by the application.

Vision operations on received frames consume further CPU cycles; computing corners on the frame can take 2.2 seconds at 40% CPU utilization on a Google Glass. As such, applications typically operate on subsampled frames to reduce memory-handling and computation bottlenecks. Still, real-time vision operations need to maintain an acceptable frame rate while performing tasks that may be highly computationally expensive and memory intensive. This implies a necessity to optimize frame and feature processing.

## 2.2 Frame and feature redundancy

For continuous vision applications, the camera service streams frames from the camera to the application as they become available. This frame becomes the root data for repetitively computed vision processing operations within an application. First, frame-level image processing operations, such as resize and blur convolutions, create derivative frames from the root data. Other processing operations then generate successive derivatives when computing corners, edges, or other feature locations and descriptors, as illustrated in the bottom half of Figure 1.

These streams of root data and derivative objects form common first steps of many algorithms and applications. Many applications utilize the same camera resource, and therefore can share the same root data, as shown in the top half of Figure 1. Executing on the root data, many applications follow the same basic image processing steps. For example, for efficiency, many vision algorithms begin by downsampling a frame and converting it to grayscale. Our benchmarks for face recognition, scene geometry, and object recognition all perform both of those tasks as common first steps. Moreover, low-level vision features are commonly used across vision algorithms; an integral image serves as the basis for Viola-Jones object recognition for face detection and character recognition [2]. Our scene geometry and object recognition benchmarks both employ SURF features. Even the same high-level features, such as detected and recognized faces, can be utilized by diverse applications, including life-loggers [26], photography taggers [28], and alert notification services [14].

## 2.3 Computer vision libraries

To incorporate packaged vision algorithms, developers of vision applications harness libraries, such as the OpenCV Library for iOS, Android, and Windows Phone, or Qualcomm's FastCV Library for the latter two. While the libraries are useful for rapidly prototyping applications, the recent trend of implementations have become attractive for product-grade application performance and efficiency. OpenCV versions increasingly leverage hardware to optimize the processing, e.g., SIMD processing with Intel SSE and ARM NEON, GPGPU computing through CUDA and OpenCL, and vision hardware support through OpenVX. As the library implementations handle the hardware acceleration, vision libraries provide an easy pathway to efficient vision performance. Optimizing library use will multiply the benefits of the library processing acceleration.

An Android application incorporates OpenCV by linking to the OpenCV libraries and calling the appropriate functions. OpenCV Java functions call their associated native C++ functions to execute.

For further speed and control, many developers use the Java Native Interface to directly call the OpenCV C/C++ functions. At that level, an application invokes shared library functionality by using classes and functions prototyped in header files. As of March 2015, opencv.org reports a user base of 47,000 developers and 9 million downloads [15].

## 2.4 Motivational observations

To summarize, we have the following insights about vision applications:

- *Vision is memory-expensive and compute-intensive.* Vision uses heavy resource utilization to process frames and features. There is much need to alleviate memory bandwidth and CPU utilization.
- *Vision libraries are common-case utilities.* The code reuse of the shared library is valuable for a variety of applications. Optimizing vision library performance thus improves a widely-applicable developer tool.
- *Library calls are redundant across multiple applications.* Multiple applications call the same streams of library functions on the same data for both low-level and high-level computations. This redundancy provides an opportunity to collectively share computation results.
- *Library calls are repetitive within an application.* Vision applications compute frames and features on incoming streams of frame data; a single application calls the same set of library functions on incoming frames. Thus, the opportunity for sharing library execution occurs not just once, but repeatedly throughout an application's execution.

These observations motivate our Starfish design, which services concurrently running applications through memory and computation reuse through a split-process execution.

# 3. DESIGN OF STARFISH

We present a software system design called ***Starfish***. Starfish enables a system to concurrently run multiple vision applications with improved overall system efficiency, reducing computational overhead, memory pressure, and energy usage. Starfish employs two key techniques. First, it features split-process execution that uses a separate process to service vision library calls. Second, Starfish allows that process to serve all applications with function caching and shared memory distribution to reduce compute and memory redundancy.

We constrain our design to maintain *application transparency* for development: application developers use Starfish as though it is the original library, with no need to understand the Starfish system's underlying mechanisms. We also preserve *library transparency*: our design does not require modification of the library binaries, allowing Starfish to work with closed-source libraries and open-source libraries that can be rapidly-changing. Finally, we target application *performance preservation*: an application should perform as though it is a single application running without Starfish.

## 3.1 Split-process execution

Starfish splits a vision application's execution into a pair of processes, using the library call as the boundary. This allows Starfish to: (*i*) separate vision processing from the calling application; and (*ii*) use a single process to centrally service vision library calls across all applications. The library boundary provides transparent function indirection and allows Starfish to create a centralization point for shared computations.

### *3.1.1 Library Call Indirection*

Because Starfish splits the application execution at the library boundary, it supports legacy applications and legacy libraries without requiring their source code. The API documentation and headers of library structures and functions provide important information that guide a Starfish implementation. Specifically, we can glean the following understanding from the API:

- *Memoizable Library Calls:* The API documentation can reveal which library calls are deterministic, computationally intensive, and widely useful among many applications. Such functions will be targets for Starfish to optimize. Other functions will be passed through to the original library for computation.
- *Object Structure:* The library's header files reveal the structure of library objects, allowing the Starfish implementation to specify efficient methods for communicating marshalled structures between applications.

The library boundary allows Starfish to use the above insights to ensure correctness and improve efficiency. Using the library as the boundary has a caveat: Starfish functions must strictly follow the API specification, taking expected library input and returning expected library output. This requires that Starfish does not alter object structures defined by the original library, e.g., by adding a member.

### *3.1.2 Centralization point for shared computation*

By transferring library call computation out of the application process and into the central service process, Starfish creates opportunities to share common computations among multiple applications.

Starfish matches library calls with identical arguments, reusing computation results to reduce system-wide computational redundancy, as described in §5. Centralizing library calls also allows efficient library designs — such as hardware acceleration or offloading optimization described in §2.3 — to extend to all applications.

Furthermore, centralized service of library calls avoids possible security and privacy flaws introduced by sharing library call results among multiple untrusted applications. For example, a distributed computation scheme in which each application computes library calls and shares the output would require trust of all participating applications; an untrusted application could create accidentally or maliciously erroneous objects, which would then be propagated to other applications as putatively valid results. Instead, by using library calls themselves as the boundary and handling vision processing in the central process, Starfish provides tight security and control over library computation results.

Unfortunately, computing library calls on the central service introduces communication overhead, as input and output arguments need to be transferred between processes. We reduce this overhead by efficiently reusing arguments over shared memory regions, as discussed in §4.

## 3.2 Starfish overview

Using the vision library API as a boundary, we design Starfish, illustrated in Figure 2, as a split-process execution system to efficiently perform library computations.

The Starfish *Core* process centrally services a library call and caches its arguments (both input and output). The computer vision applications that use the library constitute the *Apps* of Starfish. Our execution model assumes that the Core and App processes run on an operating system that supports shared memory for inter-process communication.

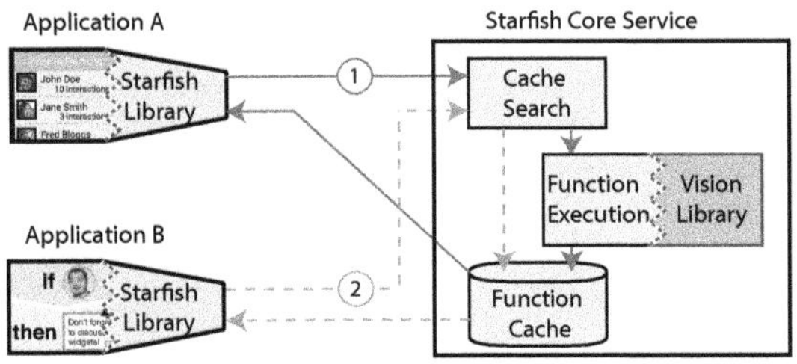


**Figure 2: Apps compile to original vision library headers, but link to Starfish Library, which communicates with the Core to execute library calls. For a first library call ①, the Core uses the original library to compute the result, which is stored in the function cache and returned to the caller. For subsequent identical calls ②, the Core retrieves the cached result, reducing the overhead of redundant operations.**

### *3.2.1 Starfish App*

At runtime, an application's binary dynamically links with our *Starfish Library* in place of the original computer vision library. This linked pair of application binary and Starfish Library becomes the Starfish App. Dynamic linking is supported by all major languages (C/C++/Java/Obj-C/C#) to efficiently distribute and reuse third-party codebases.

To redirect library calls, the Starfish Library replaces the original library in the filesystem, intercepting the dynamic linking. We move the original library elsewhere for use by the Starfish Library and Core. This theoretically allows Starfish to support unmodified applications. However, to enable our Android + OpenCV implementation to distribute camera frames, Starfish requires the developer to change a single SurfaceView object in the layout file, as described in §6.2.

To implement the function behavior, the Starfish Library makes a request to the Core process to service library calls. Starfish blocks the calling thread on the App while waiting for the library call request to return. This preserves the behavior of original library call execution, which also blocks execution on the thread. This also allows the operating system to schedule other threads while the Core is handling the library call request.

### *3.2.2 Starfish Core*

The Starfish Core is a central process that executes and tracks shared computations and objects among multiple Apps; it maintains a function cache of recently performed library calls, along with their input and output arguments. The Core links to the original vision library to execute the computations.

The Core is responsible for executing vision library calls. When an App makes a library call, the Starfish Library makes a library call request by passing input arguments to the Core. On the Core, library calls enter a queue of call requests. Multiple threads on the Core operate on requests, searching the function cache for an input argument match. If there is no match, the Core executes the function using the original vision library and marshals output arguments into the function cache, as ① in Figure 2. Otherwise, the Core retrieves output arguments from the cache, providing them to the calling App's Starfish Library to complete the library call, as ② in Figure 2.

### *3.2.3 Unsupported library calls*

Because Starfish relies on library call arguments to pass states between Core and App, it does not support *functions that modify program/system state beyond the arguments*, e.g., functions that modify global variables or write to the filesystem; Starfish does not maintain a unified namespace across Apps.

Moreover, because the Core reduces computation redundancy by reusing library calls among multiple Apps, Starfish cannot support *non-deterministic functions*, such as those that use random variables or data from a changing network resource; providing cached results would violate correctness for non-deterministic functions.

Finally, Starfish does not efficiently support all library calls. For *lightweight functions* that are quick to compute, the overhead of retrieving values from the Core outweighs the benefit of computation reuse in some cases, e.g., for single pixel value changes. A Starfish implementation should choose not to support lightweight functions.

The implementation of the Starfish Library links to the original vision library to execute all unsupported functions in the App, returning the resulting values (not shown in Figure 2 for clarity). This fully preserves original library functionality and correctness.

Nevertheless, we observe that Starfish supports a significant portion of OpenCV vision functions; none of the functions in our evaluation benchmarks exhibit system-modifying or non-deterministic behavior. Blur, SURF, and face detection operations are some of the many deterministic compute-heavy operations that Starfish supports.

## 4. SPLIT-PROCESS EXECUTION

The Starfish Core services library calls as a separate process. This design naturally invites the use of remote procedure calls (RPCs) over shared memory. On top of standard RPC mechanisms, we design zero-copy strategies for argument passing and shared memory management that reduce the overhead of passing calls.

## 4.1 Argument passing via shared memory

While RPC argument passing has been researched and optimized since its invention [29], Starfish is subject to a unique set of constraints that are not met by existing solutions such as those used in [4, 21] or in the recent mobile system literature [10, 8, 6]. In particular, supporting unmodified applications and libraries prohibits the use of shared pointer structures. Furthermore, as the Starfish Library must be transparent to the application, Starfish must work with virtual addresses prescribed by each application; we cannot forcibly maintain a common virtual address space across multiple applications.

Instead, we design Starfish argument passing strategies over a reusable pool of shared memory regions for all Starfish Apps, guaranteeing both efficient and correct object marshalling. Specifically, Starfish minimizes the number of *deep copies* during argument passing. A deep copy involves a full traversal of an object's structure and is thus particularly expensive: a $640 \times 360$ color image takes approximately 3.5 ms to copy using `memcpy` on a Google Glass. Typical RPC solutions on library calls incur four deep copies: two per input argument and two per output argument. Starfish avoids the inefficiency of these deep copies by: (1) reusing input and output arguments across multiple applications, and (2) guiding function execution output directly into memory shared by the Core and the Apps.

### *4.1.1 Starfish marshalling sequence*

Here we use a simple yet common code pattern in computer vision algorithms, `{b=foo(a); c=bar(b,a);}`, to explain how Starfish passes arguments efficiently. Both `foo()` and `bar()` are vision library functions. Figure 3 shows how the code works in six steps. When a Starfish App makes a library call request `b=foo(a)`, the Library and the Core follow a standard RPC sequence. First, the Library marshals a serialized representation of input argument `a`'s member fields into a shared memory region **(1)**. The Core un-

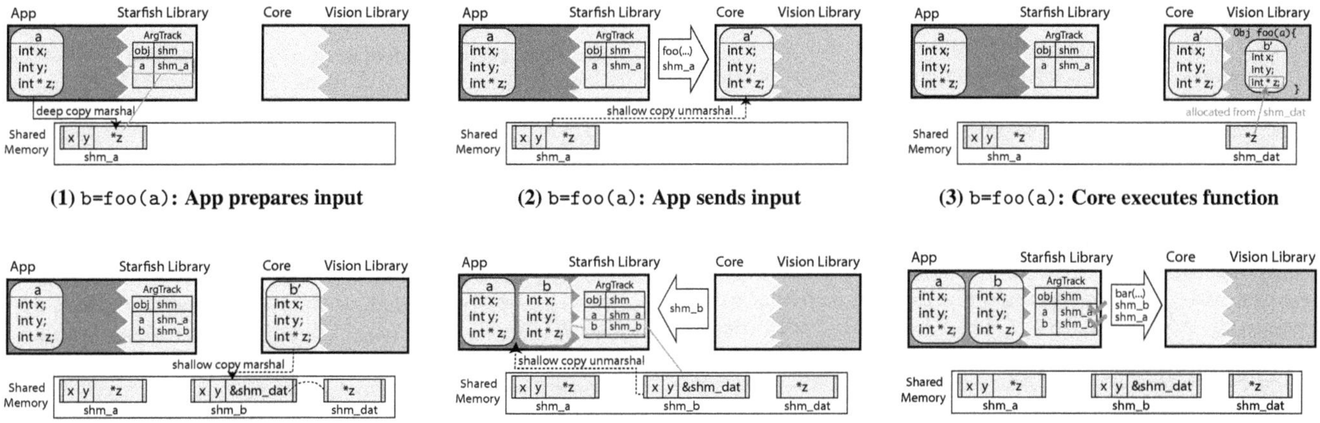


(1) `b=foo(a)`: **App prepares input**

(2) `b=foo(a)`: **App sends input**

(3) `b=foo(a)`: **Core executes function**

(4) `b=foo(a)`: **Core prepares output**

(5) `b=foo(a)`: **App receives output**

(6) `c=bar(b,a)`: **App reuses arguments**

**Figure 3: Example code: `{b=foo(a); c=bar(b,a);}`, where `foo()` and `bar()` are vision library functions. Starfish marshalling procedures minimize deep copies by tracking argument marshals and directly allocating library call output data into shared memory between the App and the Core.**

marshals `a`, creating an object from the member fields **(2)**, and then executes `foo` using the vision library **(3)**. The Core marshals the output argument `b` **(4)**. Finally, the Library unmarshals `b` and supplies it as the return of the function **(5)**. The App reuses `a` and `b` for a subsequent call `bar(b,a)` **(6)**.

During unmarshalling, Starfish will direct member pointers to the data in the shared memory region, i.e., Starfish unmarshals using shallow copies. The Core and the Starfish Library mark all unmarshalled object data with Copy-on-Write, such that object modifications will not affect the physical memory, which may be shared with other Apps.

However, marshalling object data typically requires deep copies to write into the shared memory regions. We design Starfish to guide data creation directly into the shared memory regions and reuse previously-marshalled arguments, limiting this deep copy overhead of the marshalling procedure.

### *4.1.2 Direct data marshalling of library output*

To reduce deep copying of library output. Starfish writes objects directly to shared memory regions during library execution, as shown in Figure 3:**(3)**. While the original library performs the library call, the Starfish Core intercepts calls to `malloc`. Starfish defines any memory allocation requested from the heap during a function execution to allocate memory from a shared memory region instead. While this may generate temporary intermediate shared memory allocations during execution, Starfish frees any non-output shared memory regions when the library call returns to minimize the shared memory footprint.

After the library function executes, the Core can marshal the specially-allocated output arguments by directing member pointers to addresses in the shared memory region, so no deep copying is required. This is illustrated in Figure 3:**(4)**.

### *4.1.3 Tracking arguments for shared memory reuse*

The Starfish Library tracks opportunities to reuse arguments already marshalled into shared memory. If a previously-marshalled object has not been modified, then it is consistent with its marshalled representation in shared memory and does not need to be marshalled again. The Starfish App performs this tracking by maintaining *ArgTrack*, a map between objects in the virtual address space of the App and their shared memory region ids. The Starfish Library places a library call's input arguments into ArgTrack after marshalling the objects into their shared memory region, as shown in Figure 3:**(1)**. The Library also places output arguments into ArgTrack after unmarshalling the objects from their shared memory regions, as shown in Figure 3:**(5)**.

Starfish tracks an object's consistency with the shared memory region by applying `mprotect` on the argument objects on the App, trapping write operations to the object. If the application attempts a write access to a protected region, the Starfish Library removes the arguments from ArgTrack, lifts the memory protection, and allows the write.

Starfish references ArgTrack when marshalling input arguments; if an object has already been marshalled, the Library simply sends the shared memory region ID, removing the need for a deep copy for reused arguments, as shown in Figure 3: **(6)**. Searching an ArgTrack of 100 elements induces minimal overhead, consuming less than 100 µs. Similarly, trapping a write operation incurs a negligible overhead of only 1 ms. By removing the deep copies, ArgTrack greatly minimizes the Starfish marshaling overhead.

Thus, Starfish completely eliminates all deep copies from each library call except: (*i*) to transmit previously unused input arguments, (*ii*) to record an output argument if it writes data to a specified pointer address, and (*iii*) to maintain shared memory immutability for application correctness.

At worst, each library call uses two deep copies per input argument and 1 deep copy per output argument. However, as an application derives most input arguments from previous Starfish calls, Starfish can reuse the arguments, eliminating all deep copies in many cases. Minimizing deep copies greatly reduces the shared memory pressure and communication overhead for performing remote procedural calls.

## 4.2 Shared memory region management

Operating on a pool of shared memory regions allows the Starfish Core to reuse input and output arguments among many Apps. However, allocating a new shared memory region for each passed argument would be expensive; a Google Glass takes approximately 0.6 ms to perform a `MemoryHeapBase` allocation of a 128 KB region. Starfish must also judiciously use the limited heap memory provisioned by the Dalvik VM; Google Glass processes may have at most 192 MB of heap memory. Hence, we conservatively limit the total size of all of the Starfish shared memory regions, e.g., to 128 MB. While the operating system handles heap management issues of memory allocation, e.g., physical memory fragmentation, the Starfish Core centrally manages the distribution of the shared memory regions for argument passing. Exploiting this central control, the Starfish Core adopts memory reuse techniques to reduce the cost of shared memory allocation, while maintaining a heap memory size limit.

To foster reuse of shared memory regions, the Core handles shared memory requests using free lists of reusable shared memory regions. Starfish designates a separate free list for a particular fixed memory size, e.g., 2 KB, 16 KB, 128 KB, 1 MB, 2 MB. Memory allocation requests pull empty regions from the free list of the smallest fixed size that would satisfy the request. Upon releasing the memory region, the Core returns the region to the free list for reuse. If the stack is depleted upon allocation request, the Core allocates a new shared memory region from the OS. Such fixed-size free lists, as used by the GCC standard library's multi-thread memory allocator [27] and by the classical buddy system memory management [16], allow for rapid reuse of memory regions, as applications recycle empty memory regions without redundantly allocating new physical memory or virtual memory regions. Fixed-size free lists come with the drawback of wasting space when rounding up to the next-largest free list region size. However, using a common fixed-size promotes the reusability of memory regions, which allows Starfish to reuse allocated shared memory.

To provision for dynamic region-size partitioning of the shared memory, Starfish does not fix the number of shared memory regions in each free list. Instead, Starfish handles each free list as a dynamically allocated stack, growing and shrinking as regions are added or removed.

If a shared memory region allocation would cause the Core to allocate more than the allotted total shared memory size (e.g., 128 MB), Starfish must free allocated memory regions. To maintain function reusability, the primary candidates for clearing are the empty regions in the free lists, regardless of size. However, if the free lists are vacant, Starfish then clears regions referenced only by the Core, ordered by least recent use. Starfish releases these least recently used regions until there is enough free memory to allocate a new region. These free list structures and policies allow Starfish to efficiently allocate and reuse shared memory regions within a fixed total memory size.

# 5. OPTIMIZING CENTRALIZED LIBRARY CALL EXECUTION

As library calls into the Starfish Core arrive from multiple applications, the Core tracks identical library calls and reuses computed results across multiple applications.

While exploiting this opportunity reduces computational redundancy and promotes memory reuse, it also introduces caching and concurrency challenges, including:

- Efficiently memoizing library calls across Starfish Apps;
- Enforcing consistent code behavior;
- Handling concurrent library call requests; and
- Promoting memoization through camera frame reuse.

We address these problems through thorough bookkeeping structures and policies, elaborated below.

## 5.1 Cached execution as function lookup table

The Core caches computed results to reuse library call outputs for identical library calls with identical arguments. We design *MemoCache*, a two-layer structure on the Core that tracks library call input and output arguments.

Because the search for a match must be efficient and accurate, we organize MemoCache as a function lookup table. At its top-level, MemoCache consists of a list of *function vectors*, each representing a library function symbol, e.g., **`resize`**. Each function vector contains a list of MemoCache entries, representing previous library calls to the library function. A MemoCache entry includes a list of pointers to its input argument shared memory regions and a list of pointers to its output argument shared memory regions.

Starfish consults the MemoCache to handle library call requests, as illustrated by Figure 4. The Core first retrieves the MemoCache function vector corresponding to the function symbol, creating the function vector if it does not exist ①. The Core then matches the request's input arguments against the contents of each entry in the function vector ②. Because each function vector maintains few entries (e.g., 100s), running a memory compare (`memcmp`) against entry arguments is significantly more efficient than performing a non-cryptographic hash on a library call's arguments. For example, on a Google Glass, we measure that computing a `fnv1` hash requires approximately 19 ms of processing on a $640 \times 360$ frame, whereas a `memcmp` requires only 6 µs.

If the request's arguments do not match any function vector entries, Starfish creates a new entry with the request's input arguments and inserts it into the function vector ③. It then executes the function and supplies the list of output arguments to the MemoCache entry ④. Starfish creates the entry prior to function execution to support concurrent library calls, as elaborated in §5.3. After the function execution, the Core returns the output to the App ⑥.

If instead the request's input arguments match those of a previous MemoCache entry, the Core retrieves the corresponding entry ⑤ and delivers its output arguments to the App ⑥.

As detailed in §4.2, Starfish clears shared memory segments to create room for free shared memory regions. If a freed segment serves as an input or output argument of the MemoCache entry, the Starfish Core clears the entry from its parent MemoCache function vector. This effectively serves as a Least-Recently-Used (LRU) cache eviction policy and limits the size of MemoCache.

## 5.2 Consistent computation return timing

The rationale behind caching is that executing a library function takes much longer than retrieving cached results. This also implies that when a Starfish App make a library call, it could take a very different amount of time to return. This opens a source code vulnerability due to code privacy timing attacks, similar to web privacy timing attacks from browser caching [9]. That is, if a library call returns immediately, a developer could determine that another application had recently requested the same library call with the same input arguments. These side channel timing attacks pose a threat to the security of the application' proprietary algorithms. Fortunately, attacks can be easily deterred by mimicking execution time across multiple library calls.

Thus, Starfish emulates library execution time for memoized functions. When executing a library call, ④ in Figure 4, Starfish monitors the time it takes to run the function, the *execution delay*, and stores it in the MemoCache entry. When another App is to receive memoized results, we only return the function after blocking execution for the same amount of time ⑤. By emulating execution delay, Starfish makes it indistinguishable whether the Starfish Library is

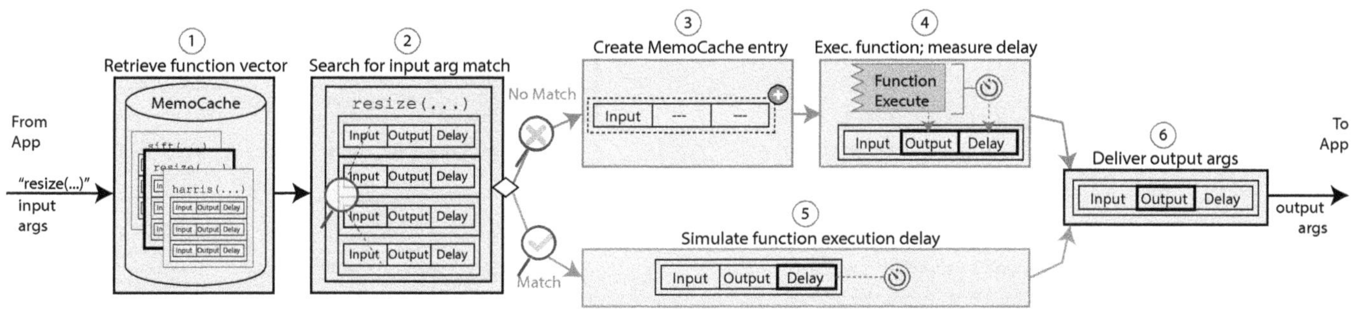


**Figure 4: Starfish Core library call request. When receiving a library call request, the Core retrieves the corresponding MemoCache function vector ① and compares library call input arguments against the entries of the function vector ②. If there is no match, the Core creates a new MemoCache entry ③. The core then executes the vision function with the vision library, measuring the execution delay ④, and delivers the output ⑥. If there is a match, the Core simulates the execution delay ⑤, before delivering the matched entry's output ⑥.**

returning a cached library call or performing the computation anew. As Starfish blocks an App's calling thread while waiting for the library call to return, the delay allows App threads to temporarily sleep, thus improving system efficiency.

## 5.3 Concurrent library call requests

The Starfish Core handles requests from multiple Starfish Apps, using multiple threads to operate on a queue of library calls in order of arrival. However, handling multiple asynchronous library call requests introduces two concurrency issues. First, multiple threads may wish to simultaneously read and write to a MemoCache function vector, introducing concurrency dependency conflicts. Second, a new library call request could arrive while another thread is computing the same function with identical arguments. Evaluating immediately would prohibit the use of memoized results, as they would not yet be ready.

Contention over a MemoCache function vector may be created by a thread accessing the function vector to search for an input argument match, while another thread alters the function vector by creating or deleting an entry. To solve this contention, the Starfish Core issues a readers-writer (RW) lock [7] on each function vector. RW locks allow simultaneous read operations, but require exclusive access for write operations. The Core issues a read-lock on a function vector while searching its input arguments, and obtains the write-lock when inserting new entries and deleting old entries. The RW lock thus allows concurrent searches over the function vector without contention, while only pausing to update the cache. To ensure timely updates, the Core issues write-preference on the RW lock; no new read locks are acquired while there are pending write locks. Using one RW lock per function vector is efficient; lock contention occurs only if there is a function symbol collision.

To handle concurrent library calls with identical arguments, the Core issues another lock on the delay element of the MemoCache entry – not the MemoCache entry itself – while the Core uses the original library to execute a function. This allows the Core to compare a library call request against any MemoCache entry's input arguments, but introduces a waiting period between concurrent requests; a library call request must wait for the completion of an earlier identical library call request. Starfish then can insert the execution delay from §5.2, subtracting the time spent waiting for the first library call to complete. After the delay, Starfish uses the output arguments as the results for the second library call.

Thus, we guarantee thread safety on the MemoCache structures, while allowing non-interfering concurrent execution to proceed. As our entry delay locks are independent, the system is deadlock-free.

## 5.4 Camera frame reuse

As camera frames are the root data of vision tasks, Starfish establishes *frame coalescing* to share frames between applications to maximize function and memory reuse. Because of the lenient timing allowance of computer vision applications, Starfish can relax the timing of frame requests, i.e., Starfish can supply a recently captured frame, or wait for the next frame to be captured.

Starfish does this by optionally allowing the application developer to annotate their frame capture with a *freshness* latency and a *patience* latency. When a App requests a frame, if Starfish has previously supplied a frame (to another App) within the freshness latency, we deliver it to the requesting App. Otherwise, the App waits for the patience latency. If Starfish captures a frame while the App is waiting, then it is delivered to the waiting App. If the patience latency expires and Starfish has not received a frame, Starfish initiates a capture to supply the frame immediately.

Depending on the App, different freshness and patience latency bounds may be justified. Developers of object recognition tasks may not be concerned with the real-time immediacy of the vision task, while motion estimation applications may have precise timing conditions. Without developer annotation, the Core measures the time between frame capture requests, and uses this as the freshness latency, and sets the patience latency to 0. This satisfies typical image request contracts, as the frame rate is usually processing bound.

Sharing the coalesced frame – and all its computed derivatives – significantly reduces the computation overhead, memory allocation, shared memory burden, and marshalling expense on the system.

# 6. IMPLEMENTATION

The Starfish system design described above is agnostic to vision library, device, operating system, and programming language, provided that there are inter-process communication and shared memory protocols, and that the vision library can be dynamically linked. We implement the Starfish System to retrofit OpenCV's C++ library on Android 4.4.2 "KitKat" to demonstrate its feasibility. As OpenCV Android Java calls operate using native JNI/C++ calls, our implementation naturally supports the OpenCV Android library. Although OpenCV is open-source, we treat its C++ library as closed-source, not altering any OpenCV code. However, we intercept Java support files to capture and distribute camera frames, explored in §6.2. Here, we discuss details specific to our Android implementation of Starfish. We evaluate this Starfish implementation performance on a Google Glass, explored in §7.

```
void resize(const Mat& src, Mat& dst, Size *
    dsize, double fx=0, double fy=0, int
    interp=INTER_LINEAR ){

  //Input Marshallers and Inputs
  vector<pair<IMarshaller*,void *> > mIn;
  mIn.push_back(make_pair(&MatM,&src));
  mIn.push_back(make_pair(&SizeM,(void*)dsize
      ));
  mIn.push_back(make_pair(&DoubleM,&fx));
  mIn.push_back(make_pair(&DoubleM,&fy));
  mIn.push_back(make_pair(&intM,&interp ));

  //Output Marshallers and Outputs
  vector<pair<IMarshaller*,void *> > mOut;
  mOut.push_back(make_pair(&MatM,&dst));

  //Function Request
  starfishCall(CV_RESIZE, mIns, mOut);
}
```

**Listing 1: Library hook function wrapper for `resize` library call. Library hooks simply involve forwarding the correct arguments along with their object marshallers.**

In our implementation, the base of the Core consists of 1099 lines of C++ code, while the Starfish Library 489. The Starfish-CameraView.java camera distribution framework consists of 396 lines of Java code. These sets of source code can be reused to support additional libraries with little to no modification.

On top of the base code, Starfish marshalling supports 19 OpenCV objects with 853 lines of source code and 22 OpenCV functions using 1748 lines of source code in C++. This code is shared for the Starfish Core and Library. While seemingly large, the marshalling codebase is simple to write, and adding new marshallable objects and functions is straightforward, as shown in §6.1. Many lines of code are spent defining repetitive object oriented prototypes.

We compile the Starfish Library into a `.so` file to replace the OpenCV library. The developer's application links to this file to become the Starfish App. Meanwhile, we compile and run the Starfish Core as an Android background service.

Android specifies `Binder` as their inter-process communication interface. We implement the Starfish Core as an Android Binder service to receive calls from the Starfish Library. Starfish uses Android's `MemoryHeapBase` to generate shared memory segments for use across the Binder. These standard Android protocols serve as the substrate for our inter-process communication.

## 6.1 OpenCV function hooks

The Starfish Library intercepts OpenCV calls through library hooks, providing implementations for the OpenCV function headers. To complete the call, each library hook must marshal objects into shared memory and transmit them over the `Binder` interface. We simplify the library hook code itself to ease the development of additional library hooks into the Starfish Library.

To do this, we standardize an object marshaller interface `IMarshaller`. Each object marshaller has three functions: (1) prescribe the required size of a shared memory region, (2) serialize an object into a region, and (3) deserialize an object from a region. We provide an `IMarshaller` implementation for each argument data type.

To reduce source code redundancy in our implementation, we also create a reusable function `starfishCall()` to handle the duties of allocating shared memory regions for the inputs, marshalling input arguments, structuring the `Binder` transactions to the Starfish Core to execute the function, and unmarshalling the output arguments. `starfishCall` requires a function handler, a list of input objects and their object marshallers, and a list of output objects and their object marshallers. Then, as it simply needs to cycle through the lists of arguments and their marshallers, the `starfishCall` is able to generically serve any Starfish library call.

The `starfishCall` and `IMarshaller` thus reduce the effort of developing additional OpenCV library hooks. The implementation of a library hook simply needs to form input and output argument lists with their object marshallers, and call the `starfishCall` function, as shown in Listing 5.4.

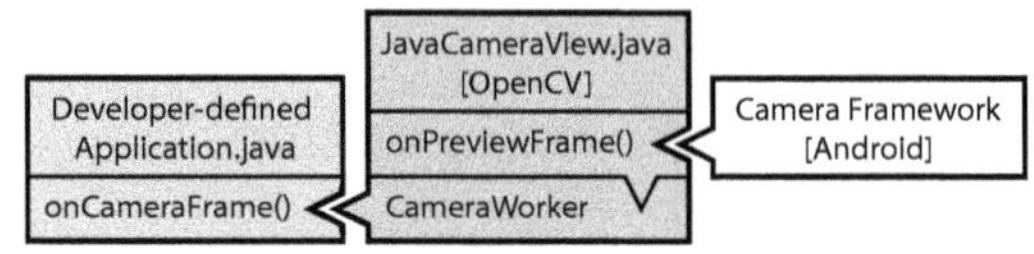


**(1) OpenCV-Android `JavaCameraView` Framework**

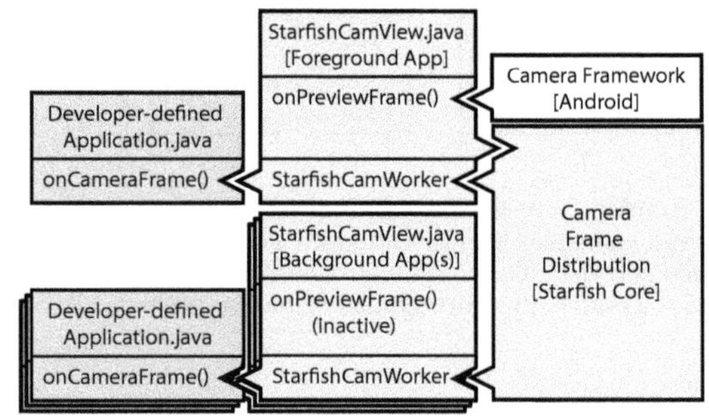


**(2) `StarfishCamView` Framework**

**Figure 5: `StarfishCamView` replaces OpenCV's `JavaCameraView` to multiplex the single-application frame delivery to all Starfish Apps. Starfish defines the `onPreviewFrame()` callback to transfer frames to the Starfish Core. The Core sends frames to `StarfishCamWorkers` on all foreground and background Apps. Each `StarfishCamWorker` calls its App's developer-defined `onCameraFrame()` callback.**

## 6.2 Android camera frame distribution

At the root of all vision algorithms is the camera frame, containing raw pixel scene data. Starfish employs a frame distribution system that supports multiple applications under the existing developer interface while increasing the opportunity for frame memory reuse.

The camera device service on Android binds to a single application running in the foreground. Fortunately, because the OpenCV framework manages frame captures, we are able to augment the existing framework to use Starfish to capture and supply camera frames, allowing for centralized distribution of captured frames.

### *6.2.1 Legacy Android + OpenCV Frame Capture*

OpenCV provides a camera framework for Android development that operates with minimal developer intervention, shown in Figure 5 **(1)**. The developer specifies code to run on incoming frames by providing an `onCameraFrame()` callback function with code to be run for each incoming frame. The developer also specifies an OpenCV `JavaCameraView` SurfaceView on which to draw results.

The OpenCV Java support files provide mechanisms to route camera frames to an application's callback. The `JavaCameraView` captures the frame by providing the `onPreviewFrame()` callback function and a foreground SurfaceView (itself) to the Android Camera Framework. From the callback, it writes incoming frames into an OpenCV `InputFrame` buffer. A separate `CameraWorker` thread continuously runs the developer-specified `onCameraFrame` callback function on any incoming frames. Frames are captured continuously to limit latency, but the `CameraWorker` only triggers `onCameraFrame` after a previous `onCameraFrame` has completed. When an application leaves the foreground, the camera service pauses, preventing `onPreviewFrame` and `onCameraFrame` callbacks from triggering.

### 6.2.2 *Starfish Camera Frame Distribution*

We design a frame distribution system, illustrated in Figure 5 **(2)**, to provide camera frames to all running Starfish Apps while maintaining the same simple OpenCV callback interface. We do this by overriding the `JavaCameraView` object with our `StarfishCameraView`, which forces the foreground App to pipe frame captures through the Starfish Core. In the `StarfishCameraView` file, we use shared memory regions as our frame buffers and declare `onPreviewFrame` to deliver frames to the Core. Changing the JavaCameraView to the StarfishCameraView requires developer intervention in the Android XML layout file of their application.

As with the legacy system, we launch a `CameraWorker` thread from the StarfishCameraView. The CameraWorker requests and receives frames from the Core and calls the developer's `onCameraFrame` callback on received frames. This maintains the frame processing operation expected by the developer.

Backgrounding an application halts the Android camera service, pausing all vision activity. However, when another application's StarfishCameraView is brought to the foreground, its onPreviewFrame will resume providing frames to the Core, allowing all Starfish activity to resume. Thus, Starfish frame distribution can transition seamlessly between applications as long as at least one Starfish application is in the foreground with control of the camera.

The Starfish Core marshals frames through the same split-process shared memory system discussed in §4. Starfish calls can thus reuse frames in the Core without further frame marshalling or allocation.

## 6.3 Single-App mode

As characterized in our evaluation in §7, passing arguments to the Core presents a computational overhead – 7.2 ms per library call on our Google Glass implementation. While this overhead is negligible compared to the efficiency of sharing vision computations across multiple applications, the overhead substantially degrades the performance when running a single Starfish App. Thus, if there is only one active Starfish App, the Core tells the Starfish Library to enter Single App Mode, simply using the original vision library to execute library calls on the App. This eliminates the overhead of Starfish communication to preserve the application performance of the single vision application.

During our characterization of Starfish in §7, we disable Single App Mode to understand the overhead of Starfish on the vision applications.

# 7. EVALUATION

We evaluate our Starfish implementation on a Google Glass, powered by a TI OMAP4430 with a dual-core Cortex-A9. Because dynamic frequency scaling can introduce uncontrollable factors in our measurements, we pin the CPU clock frequency of our evaluated Glass to a constant 600 MHz. Our evaluation seeks to answer the following pair of questions:

*How effective are major design decisions by Starfish in achieving their objectives?* We evaluate our design decisions by performing a per-call analysis of the computation time of Starfish library calls. We analyze the impact of our optimizations discussed in §4 and §5 to validate the effectiveness of the marshalling reuse, shared memory re-allocation, and cache search strategies.

*What is the computational benefit of Starfish with concurrent applications?* We quantitatively analyze the impact of Starfish on multiple sets of concurrent applications running vision tasks, employing metrics of CPU utilization (using `mpstat`) and processing time for each frame. We run benchmarks of concurrent applications that employ the same vision tasks and concurrent applications that do not. This displays the range of benefits possible with Starfish. We also test the scalability of Starfish, evaluating its performance ability on many simultaneous applications and its effect on the power draw of concurrent vision applications.

## 7.1 Starfish per-call overhead

We microbenchmark a SURF feature `detect()` library call on a $160 \times 90$ frame, producing a vector of keypoints. The computationally intensive detect library call takes 214.5 ms, exhibiting the benefits of caching expensive library calls.

We also microbenchmark a `resize()` library call, reducing a $640 \times 360$ color image to $160 \times 90$. The `resize()` library call uses an entire frame as an input argument and produces another frame as an output argument, challenging the Starfish memory allocation and marshalling overhead. Furthermore, the relatively quick processing time of the native `resize()` function execution, taking 20.9 ms, highlights the need to optimize Starfish overhead.

We do a per-call analysis on our microbenchmarks by averaging 15 instances of library calls. We execute benchmarks for library calls before and after optimizations, for the first library call and subsequent library calls. We list the benchmark results in Table 1 and chart the results in Figure 6. While unoptimized Starfish introduces a substantial overhead of as much as 20.89 ms per call, our design optimizations reduce Starfish overhead by 55% – 75%.

### 7.1.1 *Impact of argument and memory reuse*

The transfer of input and output arguments dominates the unoptimized Starfish overhead, occupying 84% of the processing time. This overhead can be almost entirely eliminated through our marshalling optimizations from §4.

Using ArgTrack allows Starfish Apps to track and reuse already-marshalled arguments. This includes input frames, which are received from the Core and are thus already in shared memory. By sending the shared memory id from ArgTrack to send to the Core, the App completely evades the 4.5 ms overhead of marshalling the input arguments. Searching ArgTrack creates negligible overhead, on the order of hundreds of microseconds, in marshalling inputs and receiving outputs.

Unoptimized output arguments also pose a large overhead, requiring 3.36 ms to allocate and another 1.60 ms to deep copy. However, our Starfish Core directly allocates library outputs into shared memory during function execution, eliminating the overhead to allocate the shared memory region and deep copy the argument objects. Furthermore, because Starfish re-allocates shared memory regions, objects are allocated quicker, reducing the function execution time as well.

The combination of these remote execution optimization designs reduces the per-call 16.4 ms argument-passing overhead to only 3.0 ms for each library call.

### 7.1.2 *Impact of cache search strategies*

The MemoCache reduces the overhead of computing multiple identical library calls with identical arguments. Even with an unoptimized cache search, this poses great benefits, as Starfish Apps

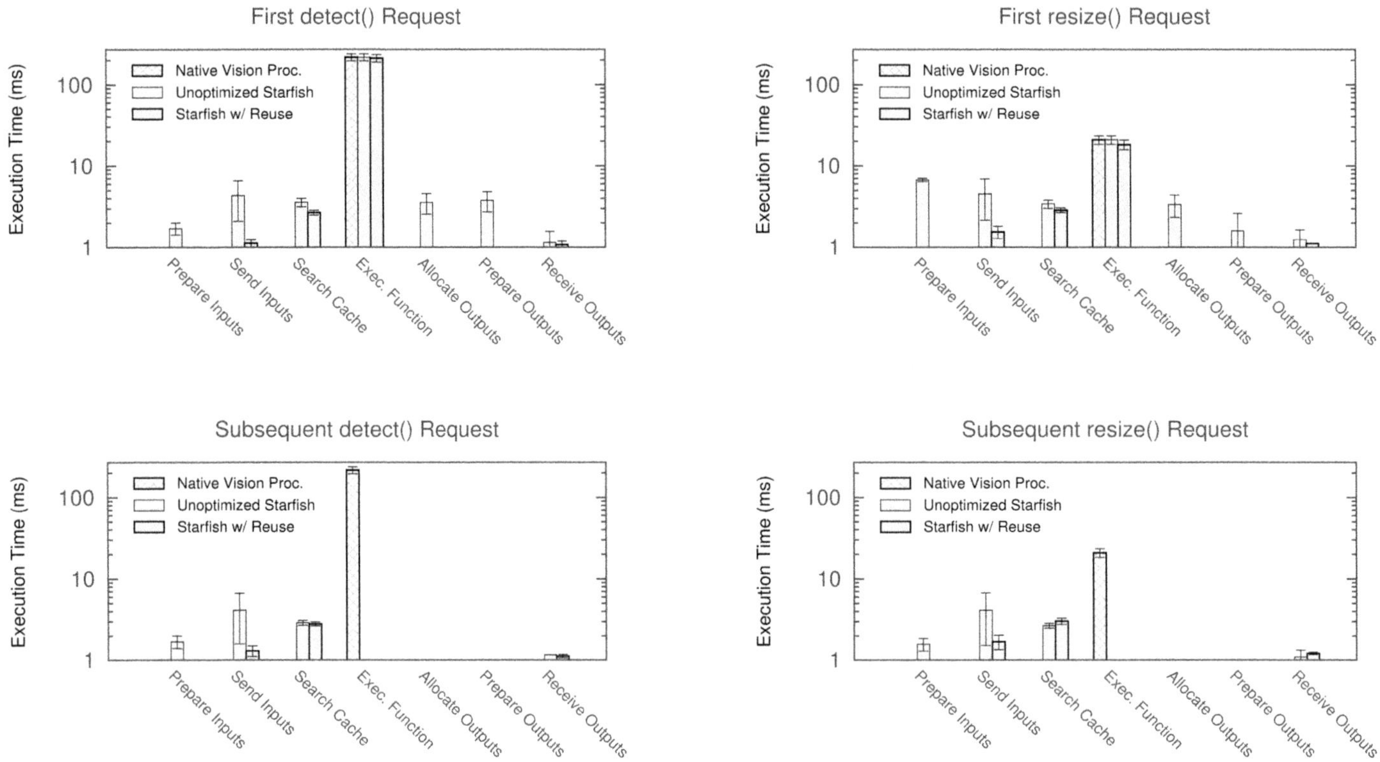


(a) SURF detect()    (b) resize()

**Figure 6: Execution time of `resize` and `detect` library call requests, with and without marshalling reuse and shared memory reuse optimizations. Subsequent requests made by a separate App showcase the low cache retrieval overhead compared to the intensive library call.**

avoid the large computational overhead of the function execution – 20 ms for `resize()`, and 215 ms for `detect()`. Starfish uses cache design described in §5 to further minimize the cache search overhead.

Our unoptimized Starfish MemoCache uses a lookup table structure with argument hash vectors to perform its searches. An `fnv1` hash operates on input arguments to organize the cache entries by hash value. This performs with a cache search time of 3.5 ms. By contrast, our decision to organize the lookup table by function vector only involves a direct lookup on the function symbol, without requiring any computation. We search the function vector by using `memcmp` on the entries. As the function vector size is fairly small, including only 10s to 100s of entries, this poses a smaller overhead than the `fnv1` hash computation. The result is a 16% reduction in cache search time to 2.9 ms.

In summary, using our design optimizations in argument reuse, shared memory reallocation, and cache structure, Starfish reduces the per-call overhead from 20.9 ms to only 4.2 ms. This lowers the computation time of repeated `resize()` calls by 71% and repeated `detect()` calls by 97%, reducing per-frame processing time by 15 ms and 210 ms respectively.

## 7.2 Multi-App performance

We next analyze the ability of Starfish to service concurrent Apps. We employ foundational vision tasks as benchmarks to examine the benefits and overhead of Starfish on Apps that do and do not use the same vision tasks.

### *7.2.1 Benchmark vision tasks*

We evaluate Starfish App performance using benchmark vision tasks of Face Recognition, Object Recognition, and Scene Geometry. Apps employ these vision tasks to perform a diverse set of duties, as described below. While these tasks do not comprehensively cover the expansive OpenCV library, these selected computations serve as a basis for many vision applications that can potentially run concurrently. In our evaluation, each of our Apps receives the camera stream through the Starfish frame distribution. The App sends the frame through each benchmark vision task, which begins by converting the frame to grayscale, and resizing it to $160 \times 90$. We include these pre-processing steps in our evaluation results.

*Face recognition* algorithms detect and identify individuals in an image, useful for applications such as social network taggers and alert notification services. Face recognition consists of two components: *detection* and *classification*. The Viola-Jones face detection algorithm compares a computed integral image against a cascade of pre-trained Haar-like classifiers. If a region passes all cascade layers, the algorithm determines it to be the region containing a face. Face classification identifies detected faces by matching against a tagged dataset of faces. The Local Binary Pattern-based algorithm compares a matrix of spatial histograms from the image with a database of pre-trained spatial histogram matrices. The nearest-neighbor is determined to be the identity. Under controlled lighting and well-posed images, the face classification operates with 97% accuracy [1]. On the Glass, running natively outside of Starfish, face recognition performs at 4.36 frames per second (FPS) with a memory footprint of 61.28 MB.

Table 1: Starfish execution time for first and subsequent calls to the same library functions. Reuse optimizations reduce Starfish overhead by 36%–71%

| | `detect()` | | | | `resize()` | | | |
|---|---|---|---|---|---|---|---|---|
| | Unoptimized Request | Starfish Reuse | Subsequent Request | Subsequent w/ Reuse | Unoptimized Request | Starfish Reuse | Subsequent request | Subsequent w/ Reuse |
| Prepare Inputs | 1.71 ± 0.29 | 0.10 ± 0.01 | 1.70 ± 0.30 | 0.09 ± 0.02 | 6.72 ± 0.31 | 0.11 ± 0.02 | 1.58 ± 0.29 | 0.15 ± 0.03 |
| Send Inputs | 4.33 ± 2.24 | 1.12 ± 0.12 | 4.13 ± 2.54 | 1.30 ± 0.20 | 4.54 ± 2.38 | 1.55 ± 0.27 | 4.13 ± 2.61 | 1.70 ± 0.35 |
| Search MemoCache | 3.57 ± 0.42 | 2.67 ± 0.18 | 2.90 ± 0.20 | 2.81 ± 0.15 | 3.43 ± 0.40 | 2.87 ± 0.19 | 2.67 ± 0.18 | 3.04 ± 0.27 |
| Execute Function | 216.46 ± 20.84 | 210.94 ± 22.07 | - | - | 20.85 ± 2.56 | 18.17 ± 2.43 | - | - |
| Allocate Out | 3.56 ± 1.00 | - | - | - | 3.36 ± 1.02 | - | - | - |
| Marshall Out | 3.77 ± 1.04 | 0.25 ± 0.03 | - | - | 1.60 ± 1.01 | 0.21 ± 0.05 | - | - |
| Transfer Out | 1.14 ± 0.43 | 1.08 ± 0.11 | 1.15 ± 0.11 | 1.11 ± 0.05 | 1.25 ± 0.39 | 1.11 ± 0.21 | 1.09 ± 0.24 | 1.21 ± 0.05 |
| **Total Exec. Time** | 234.55 ± 26.26 | 216.15 ± 14.00 | 9.88 ± 1.07 | 5.31 ± 0.12 | 41.74 ± 3.60 | 24.02 ± 4.20 | 9.47 ± 0.97 | 6.10 ± 0.41 |
| **Starfish Overhead** | 18.08 ± 3.19 | 5.21 ± 0.38 | 9.88 ± 1.07 | 5.31 ± 0.12 | 20.89 ± 2.08 | 5.85 ± 0.39 | 9.47 ± 0.97 | 6.10 ± 0.41 |

*Homography mapping* estimates a camera's relative motion is through plane-to-plane mappings, which can be useful for applications such as indoor map localization and obstacle awareness. To compute a homography, we compute SURF corner points and match them between two frames in a camera stream. On the matched pairs, we use the RANSAC algorithm and a least squares regression to generate a homography matrix, revealing the geometric transform between two camera frames. Running natively, scene homographies performs at 3.54 FPS with a memory footprint of 59.97 MB.

*Object detection* recognizes food items, brand logos, and office keys, enhancing applications such as life-loggers and reminder notifications. A popular algorithm for object recognition uses Bag-of-Words (BoW), which forms a collection of salient visual features and compares them to a pre-trained dataset. We used SURF to form the input vector of corners and feature descriptors. These feature descriptors are then compared against the BoW dataset using a Support Vector Machine. Running natively, object recognition performs at 1.17 FPS with a memory footprint of 59.7 MB.

### 7.2.2 Overhead and benefits on App combinations

When running the Starfish Apps at a fixed 600 MHz clock frequency on the Google Glass, `mpstat` indicated that the system maintained a CPU utilization average of approximately 60%, regardless of the number and type of applications running. This is likely due to thermal throttling. However, the application workloads significantly affect the time it takes to process each frame through vision computations, impacting the effective frame rate. We use the processing time as our metric to evaluate Starfish performance. We list the processing time performance in Table 2.

Our benchmarks consist of seven combinations of Apps running vision tasks. In a potential scenario, a mobile device would run simultaneous background applications running multiple vision tasks, e.g., logging social interactions with face recognition, memorize object placement with object recognition, observing scene changes with homography fitting. This combination is represented by the 7th row of Table 2.

Different combinations of vision tasks hold different potentials for library call sharing. Object recognition and homography fitting both utilize SURF computations on the input frame but utilize different library calls later in their stream (RANSAC and SVM). Face recognition uses a different set of features entirely, computing Viola Jones and LBPH algorithms to detect and classify faces. All of our benchmarks resize the input frame and convert it to grayscale. We also simultaneously run two instances of the benchmarks (column x2). This represents running multiple Apps using the same vision task, such as a photo tagger and a lifelogger both using face recognition.

Our benchmarks reveal the overhead of running Starfish. In isolation, Starfish adds at most 30 ms of processing time per frame. At this low overhead, the performance impact of running Starfish on a single vision task only increases frame processing time by 10% at most. (Although, as mentioned in §6.3, one should not activate Starfish for use with a single App.)

Starfish's efficiency benefits become apparent when running multiple identical vision tasks. While native processing time is doubled when running two tasks, Starfish maintains the performance within 22% of the original frame processing time. This reduces the per-frame processing time of running two identical vision task instances by 35%–41%. Non-identical combinations combinations of applications also benefited from Starfish efficiency. Through sharing the `resize()` library call on the input frame; Starfish decreased the processing time of Homog/Face and Face/Obj by 5.5% and 4.7% respectively. Starfish performed best when sharing SURF features for Homog/Obj, reducing processing time by 22%. The combination of Homog/Face/Obj fell inbetween these, reducing processing time by 9.7%.

Computational benefits continue to scale with additional vision tasks. As shown in Figure 7, natively running additional face recognition Apps significantly limits the frame rate, dropping to 0.3 frames per second when running 10 Apps. However, using Starfish, the frame rate degrades at a much reduced pace, sustaining 1.8 frames per second when running 10 Apps. Thus, Starfish provides App scalability, as many Apps can run with minimally impacted frame rate performance.

### 7.2.3 CPU utilization and system efficiency

Stemming from constant activity, high CPU utilization contributes to the high power draw of systems running vision applications. For tasks with relaxed frame rates, the Starfish reduction of processing time reduces the CPU utilization, and in turn, the energy consumption and heat generation of the system.

We characterize this by running face recognition vision tasks at a fixed frame rate of 0.3 FPS. At this rate, a single application's average CPU utilization is 5.3%, processing at 60% CPU utilization for 230 ms, then idling near 1% for the remainder of a frame period. Without Starfish, the CPU utilization will grow linearly with the number of application instances, as each App will need to perform its own 230 ms of processing. Starfish allows multiple applications to share the same processing; when running 10 simultaneous face recognition applications at 0.3 FPS, Starfish keeps the average CPU utilization below 13%, limiting the power draw to an average of about 1210 mW, as measured with a Monsoon Power

Table 2: **Average processing time per frame (seconds) on homography, face recognition, and object recognition benchmarks, running natively (NAT) and with Starfish (SF). x1 runs a single benchmark instance; x2 runs a pair of instances.**

| Benchmarks | NAT x1 | NAT x2 | SF x1 | SF x2 |
|---|---|---|---|---|
| Homog | 0.282 | 0.513 | 0.310 | 0.332 |
| Face | 0.230 | 0.438 | 0.239 | 0.271 |
| Obj | 0.855 | 1.692 | 0.864 | 1.001 |
| Homog/Face | 0.577 | 1.135 | 0.547 | 0.611 |
| Face/Obj | 0.496 | 1.014 | 0.472 | 0.525 |
| Homog/Obj | 1.185 | 2.202 | 0.918 | 1.012 |
| Homog/Obj/Face | 1.288 | 2.616 | 1.164 | 1.355 |

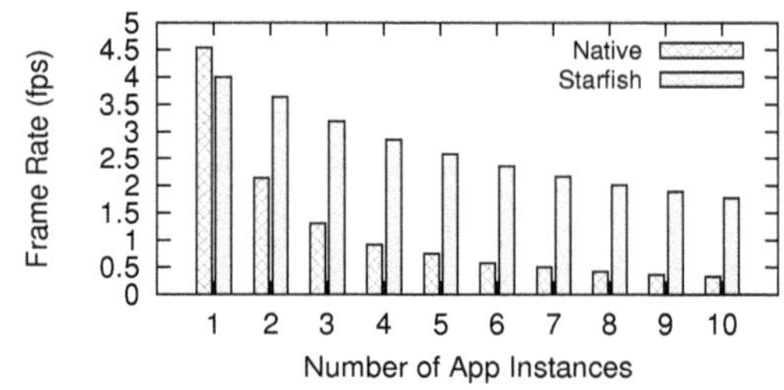


**Figure 7: Maximum frame rate of running simultaneous face recognition apps, with and without Starfish.**

Monitor. The same applications without Starfish natively draw an average of 2263 mW at 60% CPU utilization. The reduced power overhead also reduces the device heat generation. As reported in [18], each watt of average power consumption constitutes a 11 °C increase in surface temperature. Thus, Starfish provides more comfortable use and longer battery life to systems running concurrent vision applications with shared library calls.

In summary, we find that Starfish provides efficient, scalable support for multiple simultaneous vision Apps. The argument reuse, shared memory reallocation, and cache structure designs significantly reduce the per-call overhead of Starfish, which in turn allows for applications to transparently and efficiently share library computation results.

# 8. RELATED WORK

Three groups of research work are related to Starfish. First, *remote execution* or *offloading* partitions applications to run on disjoint resources, such as the cloud or cloudlet. Starfish has a different objective and faces different challenges. The goal of eliminating redundant computation by vision tasks across multiple applications dictates that Starfish use library calls as the boundary of splitting, instead of VMs, e.g., Gabriel [12], or threads, e.g., COMET [10] and CloneCloud [6]. Our need to support unmodified applications and libraries prevents the use of new programming models, e.g., Odessa [24]. MAUI [8] is related in its use of library call boundary and support of largely unmodified applications. Starfish, however, leverages that the Core and Apps run on the same system and optimizes RPC over shared memory, as shown in §4.

Second, *privilege separation* splits computations across processes to isolate data privileges to specific parts of an application for security purposes [5, 22, 30]. Some of these works actually split a program across the boundary of a library, like Starfish. For example, in [22], Murray and Hand use disaggregated libraries to run an application across multiple Xen hypervisor domains. This provides complete isolated protection between the host process and the disaggregated library. To share data, they use a shared memory area which only grants control to the library upon execution attempts. CodeJail [30] separates library calls into a separate process to isolate memory interactions. It can switch between trusted and untrusted library memory to ensure that library interactions only modify expected memory. Starfish, in contrast, does not place trust restrictions on the data provided to each App or the Core library processing. As vision algorithms only operate on the input and output arguments, all updates are provided through the library calls. Thus, as any state changes are encoded as output arguments of the function request, the Starfish Core does not alter existing App memory. Furthermore, each App has full privilege to read and write to its memory; Copy-on-Write preserves shared memory alterations from affecting other Apps. This allows Starfish to supply output arguments across many applications through our function cache, as described in §5.

Finally, reusing computation results, widely known as *memoization*, is an established computing methodology, as embodied by the dynamic programming paradigm. Indeed, advanced techniques exist for single applications, including automatic creation of memoization functions [13, 19] and dynamic analysis to determine the effectiveness of caching memoized results [11]. However, these techniques avoid complex objects and data structures in the input and output parameters of the functions. Additionally, the memoization takes place within a single application, whereas Starfish faces the challenge of maintaining consistent application performance and preventing developers from determining whether an object was cached or not, as shown in §5.2.

# 9. DISCUSSION

*Library modification:* We avoid modifying the vision library to preserve existing function behavior. To maintain backward compatibility, libraries rarely change APIs, even with iterative versioning. As of November 2014, OpenCV function headers have remained identical since OpenCV version 2.4.0, released April 2012 [23]. However, it is possible to fork OpenCV source code, and library integration would allow for further optimization. For example, data structures with shared pointers could be ordered for rapid marshalling.

*Developer annotation:* Starfish targets developer transparency, such that developers need not know the mechanisms underlying Starfish. However, developers may wish to publicize which vision library calls their applications use. By using annotation to relax developer privacy, this would allow for improved joint application performance as different developers share common library calls. Additionally, a slight difference in specific parameters of a library call will prevent an application from leveraging a previous computation. Developers could annotate a range of parameters that satisfies their function request. This would allow Starfish to select parameters that maximize computational sharing.

*Optimizing Core execution:* As mentioned in the related work, devices can offload execution to a network for efficiency. Devices can also use increasingly present vision hardware and heterogeneous units; the upcoming OpenVX API will increase the availability of vision hardware. The Starfish Core can act as the central hub for offloaded processing, aggregating decisions regarding tradeoffs in latency, efficiency, and workload across all library calls. The Core could also use centralized knowledge to improve system cache efficiency for the hardware resources, e.g., by ordering operations for optimal spatial reuse of the memory cache.

*Broader use of Starfish:* Beyond vision libraries, Starfish can enhance other libraries that are computationally intensive with frequent calls to deterministic functions, e.g., those processing sensor data such as speech and gesture recognition. We foresee that adoption of wearable devices will warrant more concurrent always-on tasks that are serviced by such sensor-processing libraries. In addition to efficiency benefits, Starfish also helps guard applications from untrusted libraries. With Starfish, an application can contain untrusted libraries in a separate process (the Core) and only needs to send the latter the data relevant to library computation.

## 10. CONCLUSION

Starfish employs split-process execution to reduce redundant vision computations across multiple applications. The Starfish design incorporates argument reuse, shared memory reallocation, and caching policies to minimize the overhead of operating on library call requests. We demonstrate Starfish's effectiveness through a Google Glass implementation, evaluating the system performance of running concurrent vision applications. We demonstrate that Starfish provides scalable benefits with additional applications; with a workload of two to ten concurrent face recognition applications that typically increases the computational burden from 10% to 60% CPU utilization, Starfish maintains a CPU utilization under 13%, which in turn reduces system power consumption by 19% – 58%, as Starfish maintains a power consumption at approximately 1210 mW. Starfish allows concurrent vision applications to run with efficient system performance, thus contributing an important step towards efficient wearable vision systems.

## Acknowledgments

The authors thank Edward Hickman for his assistance in developing OpenCV marshalling code and benchmark tasks for Starfish. The authors are grateful for comments made by anonymous reviewers and the paper shepherd Dr. Rajesh Balan. This work was supported in part by NSF Awards CNS #1054693, CNS #1218041, and CNS #1422312. Robert LiKamWa was supported in part by a Texas Instruments Graduate Fellowship.

## References

[1] Timo Ahonen, Abdenour Hadid, and Matti Pietikäinen. Face recognition with local binary patterns. In *Proc. European Conf. on Computer Vision (ECCV)*, 2004.

[2] Clemens Arth, Florian Limberger, and Horst Bischof. Real-time license plate recognition on an embedded DSP-platform. In *Proc. IEEE Conf. on Computer Vision and Pattern Recognition (CVPR)*, 2007.

[3] Paramvir Bahl, Matthai Philipose, and Lin Zhong. Vision: cloud-powered sight for all: showing the cloud what you see. In *Proc. ACM Workshop on Mobile Cloud Computing and Services (MCCS)*, 2012.

[4] Brian N. Bershad, Thomas E. Anderson, Edward D. Lazowska, and Henry M. Levy. Lightweight remote procedure call. *ACM Transactions on Computer Systems*, 8(1):37–55, 1990.

[5] David Brumley and Dawn Song. Privtrans: Automatically partitioning programs for privilege separation. In *Proc. USENIX Security Symp.*, 2004.

[6] Byung-Gon Chun, Sunghwan Ihm, Petros Maniatis, Mayur Naik, and Ashwin Patti. Clonecloud: Elastic execution between mobile device and cloud. In *Proc. European Conf. on Computer Systems (EuroSys)*, 2011.

[7] Pierre-Jacques Courtois, Frans Heymans, and David Lorge Parnas. Concurrent control with "readers" and "writers". *Communications of the ACM*, 14(10):667–668, 1971.

[8] Eduardo Cuervo, Aruna Balasubramanian, Dae-ki Cho, Alec Wolman, Stefan Saroiu, Ranveer Chandra, and Paramvir Bahl. MAUI: Making smartphones last longer with code offload. In *Proc. ACM Int'l. Conf. on Mobile Systems, Applications, & Services (MobiSys)*, 2010.

[9] Edward W. Felten and Michael A. Schneider. Timing attacks on web privacy. In *Proc. ACM Conf. on Computer and Communications Security (CCS)*, 2000.

[10] Mark S Gordon, Davoud Anoushe Jamshidi, Scott A Mahlke, Zhuoqing Morley Mao, and Xu Chen. Comet: Code offload by migrating execution transparently. In *Proc. USENIX Symp. on Operating Systems Design and Implementation (OSDI)*, 2012.

[11] Philip J. Guo and Dawson Engler. Using automatic persistent memoization to facilitate data analysis scripting. In *Proc. ACM Int'l. Symp. on Software Testing and Analysis*, 2011.

[12] Kiryong Ha, Zhuo Chen, Wenlu Hu, Wolfgang Richter, Padmanabhan Pillai, and Mahadev Satyanarayanan. Towards wearable cognitive assistance. In *Proc. ACM Int'l. Conf. on Mobile Systems, Applications, & Services (MobiSys)*, 2014.

[13] Marty Hall and J. Paul McNamee. Improving software performance with automatic memoization. *Johns Hopkins APL Technical Digest*, 18(2):255, 1997.

[14] Richard Hull, Philip Neaves, and James Bedford-Roberts. Towards situated computing. In *Proc. ACM Int'l. Symp. on Wearable Computers (ISWC)*, 1997.

[15] Itseez. OpenCV Computer Vision Library. `http://opencv.org`.

[16] Kenneth C. Knowlton. A fast storage allocator. *Communications of the ACM*, 8(10):623–624, 1965.

[17] Robert LiKamWa, Bodhi Priyantha, Matthai Philipose, Lin Zhong, and Paramvir Bahl. Energy characterization and optimization of image sensing toward continuous mobile vision. In *Proc. ACM Int'l. Conf. on Mobile Systems, Applications, & Services (MobiSys)*, 2013.

[18] Robert LiKamWa, Zhen Wang, Aaron Carroll, Felix Xiaozhu Lin, and Lin Zhong. Draining our glass: An energy and heat characterization of Google Glass. In *Proc. Asia-Pacific Work. on Systems (APSys)*, 2014.

[19] Paul McNamee and Marty Hall. Developing a tool for memoizing functions in C++. *ACM SIGPLAN Notices*, 33(8):17–22, 1998.

[20] David Moloney, Brendan Barry, Fergal Connor, Martin O'Riordan, Cormac Brick, David Donohoe, David Nicholls, Richard Richmond, and Vasile Toma. Always-on vision processing unit (VPU) for mobile applications. *IEEE Micro*, 2014.

[21] Gilles Muller, Renaud Marlet, E-N Volanschi, Charles Consel, Calton Pu, and Ashvin Goel. Fast, optimized Sun RPC using automatic program specialization. In *Proc. IEEE Int'l. Conf. on Distributed Computing Systems (ICDCS)*, 1998.

[22] Derek G. Murray and Steven Hand. Privilege separation made easy: trusting small libraries not big processes. In *Proc. European Work. on System Security*, 2008.

[23] Andrey Ponomarenko. API changes/compatibility report for the OpenCV library. `http://upstream.rosalinux.ru/versions/opencv.html`.

[24] Moo-Ryong Ra, Anmol Sheth, Lily Mummert, Padmanabhan Pillai, David Wetherall, and Ramesh Govindan. Odessa: Enabling interactive perception applications on mobile devices. In *Proc. ACM Int'l. Conf. on Mobile Systems, Applications, & Services (MobiSys)*, 2011.

[25] Swati Rallapalli, Aishwarya Ganesan, Krishna Chintalapudi, Venkat N. Padmanabhan, and Lili Qiu. Enabling physical analytics in retail stores using smart glasses. In *Proc. ACM Int'l. Conf. on Mobile Computing & Networking (MobiCom)*, 2014.

[26] Abigail J. Sellen, Andrew Fogg, Mike Aitken, Steve Hodges, Carsten Rother, and Ken Wood. Do life-logging technologies support memory for the past?: an experimental study using Sensecam. In *Proc. ACM SIGCHI Human Factors in Computing Systems*, 2007.

[27] Richard M. Stallman and GCC DeveloperCommunity. *Using The GNU Compiler Collection: A GNU Manual For GCC Version 4.3.3*. CreateSpace, Paramount, CA, 2009.

[28] Zak Stone, Todd Zickler, and Trevor Darrell. Autotagging Facebook: Social network context improves photo annotation. In *Proc. IEEE Computer Vision and Pattern Recognition Work. (CVPRW)*, 2008.

[29] James E White. A high-level framework for network-based resource sharing. In *Proc. National Computer Conf. and Exposition*, 1976.

[30] Yongzheng Wu, Sai Sathyanarayan, Roland HC Yap, and Zhenkai Liang. CodeJail: Application-transparent isolation of libraries with tight program interactions. In *Proc. European Symp. on Research in Computer Security (ESORICS)*, 2012.

# TypingRing: A Wearable Ring Platform for Text Input

Shahriar Nirjon, Jeremy Gummeson, Dan Gelb, Kyu-Han Kim
Hewlett-Packard Labs, CA, USA
{nirjon, jeremy.gummeson, dan.gelb, kyu-han.kim}@hp.com

## ABSTRACT

This paper presents *TypingRing*, a wearable ring platform that enables text input into computers of different forms, such as PCs, smartphones, tablets, or even wearables with tiny screens. The basic idea of TypingRing is to have a user wear a ring on his middle finger and let him type on a surface – such as a table, a wall, or his lap. The user types as if a standard QWERTY keyboard is lying underneath his hand but is invisible to him. By using the embedded sensors TypingRing determines what key is pressed by the user. Further, the platform provides visual feedback to the user and communicates with the computing device wirelessly. This paper describes the hardware and software prototype of TypingRing and provides an in-depth evaluation of the platform. Our evaluation shows that TypingRing is capable of detecting and sending key events in real-time with an average accuracy of $98.67\%$. In a field study, we let seven users type a paragraph with the ring, and we find that TypingRing yields a reasonable typing speed (e.g., $33 - 50$ keys per minute) and their typing speed improves over time.

## Categories and Subject Descriptors

C.3 [**Special-Purpose and Application-Based Systems**]: Real-time and embedded systems

## General Terms

Algorithm, Design, Experimentation

## Keywords

Wearable, Typing, Ring

## 1. INTRODUCTION

As computing systems evolve, so do their input methods. With advancements in computing technology, different forms of text input methods have been proposed and used in practice. These forms include the standard QWERTY keyboards for PCs, alphanumeric keypads and small keypads in earlier mobile phones, and on-screen soft keyboards in modern smartphones and tablets. Each of these input methodologies for text have been invented out of the need for a change, as the form factor and the mobility requirements of these devices have also changed. We are now at the forefront of technology where wearable computers, such as smart watches and smart bands, have entered the consumer market. These devices have even smaller screen sizes and none of the existing typing methods are viable for these devices. A quick fix to this problem has so far been in the form of speech-to-text or shared keypads. However, the core problem has still remained unsolved, i.e. *there is no typing accessory that is portable and usable with computers of all form factors and mobility requirements.*

To meet this need we have created TypingRing, which is a wearable keyboard in the form factor of a ring. A user wears the ring on his middle finger and types in text with three fingers (the index, middle and traditional ring finger) on a surface, such as – a table, his lap, or a wall. The user types and moves his hand as if there is an invisible standard keyboard underneath his hand. By moving the hand horizontally and vertically, TypingRing distinguishes one region from another on the imaginary keyboard. Further, by pressing one of his three fingers, the user types in the key. By using the embedded sensors surrounding the ring, TypingRing determines what key is pressed by the user completely inside the ring and then sends the key event to a remote computer over a Bluetooth Low Energy (BLE) communication link. TypingRing implements a standard BLE keyboard protocol so that it can be used with commercially available computing devices, such as – PCs, smartphones, tablets, or even wearables with tiny screens that support an external BLE keyboard. A piece of software running on the computing device intercepts key events and provides visual feedback to the user by highlighting a key or a portion of a custom on-screen keyboard, as the user moves his hand on the surface and types in keys.

Several salient features when combined together make TypingRing the first of its kind. First, TypingRing being a wearable device, is mobile and portable. The ring comes in handy in scenarios where a quick and on-the-go text input is needed or scenarios when an alternative input method is not convenient, e.g. devices with tiny screens. Second, TypingRing is fast and highly accurate in detecting keys, and it performs all its computations inside the ring – without requiring any computational support from a more capable device. Third, TypingRing is multi-platform. Because of its adoption of a standard BLE keyboard protocol, TypingRing is usable with any computing device that supports an external BLE keyboard. Fourth, typing with TypingRing is intuitive and it is easy to learn. TypingRing breaks down the task of typing on a standard keyboard into two intuitive tasks, i.e. moving a hand on a surface and then pressing a finger, which require little or no practice to get


*MobiSys'15,* May 18–22, 2015, Florence, Italy.

http://dx.doi.org/10.1145/2742647.2742665.

started with. Fifth, TypingRing is flexible and extensible. It is not tied to the English alphabet or any specific keyboard layout. By changing the mapping between a position and a key, TypingRing is usable with keyboards of different layouts and dimensions.

TypingRing brings both engineering and computational challenges in front of us. The hardware architecture of TypingRing is designed to obtain the relative movements of the finger, and horizontal and vertical motions of the hand on a surface, so that thus-obtained data can be used to infer the position of the hand and typing gestures from just a single finger. To realize this, we embed a tiny microcontroller, an accelerometer, multiple line sensors, an optical displacement sensor, and a BLE chip on the perimeter of a circular ring platform. These sensors are read by software running inside the ring, which detects and classifies typing gestures using an offline trained Hidden Markov Model (HMM) classifier. As an additional feature in TypingRing, we have implemented a simple Naï£¡ve Bayesian classifier to infer 3D gestures, such as - pitch, roll, and yaw, and map them to commonly used keys on a keyboard to offer shortcut keys to the user.

We have created a prototype of TypingRing using off-the-shelf sensors and an open source miniature hardware platform called TinyDuino [11]. In order to tune various parameters of the system and train the typing and gesture classifiers, we perform an empirical study involving 18 users who use the ring to type in letters, words, lines, and gestures while we store all the raw sensor readings. Based on this empirical data, we measure execution time, energy consumption, and the accuracy of typing and gesture classifiers. Our empirical evaluation shows that TypingRing is capable of detecting and generating key events in real-time with an average accuracy of 98.67%. Finally, we perform a field study, in which, we let seven users type a paragraph with TypingRing and we find that TypingRing yields a typing speed of $0.55 - 0.81$ keys per second, and their typing speed improves over time.

The contributions of this paper are the following –

- We introduce TypingRing, which is a wearable, portable accessory device that allows a user to input text into mobile and non-mobile computers of different forms.
- We describe a Hidden Markov Model (HMM) based typing gesture recognizer that uses acceleration, optical displacement and proximity sensors to infer the typing finger in real-time and with an average accuracy of 98.67%.
- We perform a field study where seven users type a paragraph with TypingRing and we find that TypingRing yields a typing speed of $33 - 50$ keys per minute, and their typing speed improves over time.

# 2. USING TYPING RING

This section describes the working principle of the TypingRing along with some potential use cases.

## 2.1 Working Principle

TypingRing is worn on the middle finger of a user. As the user rests his ring on a horizontal surface, three consecutive keys on the on-screen keyboard of the computing device are highlighted. By using embedded sensors surrounding the perimeter of the ring, the TypingRing detects typing gestures made by the user's three fingers – middle, index, and traditional ring fingers. To highlight a different set of keys, the user simply drags the ring up, down, left or right on the surface. As long as the user is seeking a key or typing it in, visual feedback is provided to him on the screen of the computing device.

TypingRing assumes that the standard keyboard layout is divided into multiple *zones*. A zone is defined as a sequence of consecutive 3 keys on the same row on a keyboard layout. With this definition of a zone, the task of locating a key becomes a two-step problem: first, to identify the zone of the intended key, and second, to identify the key within that zone.

By moving the ring horizontally and vertically on a surface, a user moves from one zone to another. The user is given visual feedback by either highlighting the 3 keys on the zone on a soft-keyboard or just showing 3 keys on the screen when the computing device has a limited screen space. Once a zone is selected, each of the three fingers is associated with one of the 3 keys in that zone. To type in a specific key, the user makes a typing gesture using the corresponding finger. The ring detects the finger and sends the key associated with it to the computing device over the wireless channel.

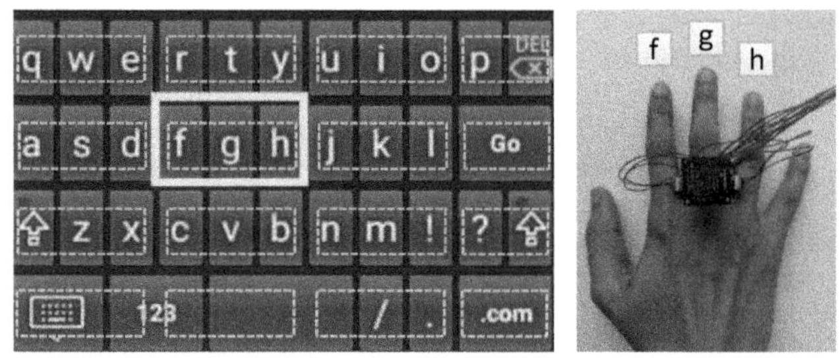


(a) 3-Letter Zones (b) Typing Ring

**Figure 1: Working principle of TypingRing.**

**Example.** In Figure 1(a), we show sixteen zones on an Android keyboard layout marked with dotted rectangles and the selected zone `fgh` with a solid rectangle. Only one zone is allowed to be active at a time. A large key (e.g. the space bar) may be a part of multiple zones and the last zone on a row may not have all three keys. To type in a letter, e.g. `W`, the user at first moves his ring up and left to select the `QWE` zone, and then makes a typing gesture with his middle finger to input the key.

## 2.2 Usage Scenarios

TypingRing may be used with a variety of computing devices that support standard external wireless keyboards. The list includes desktops, laptops, tablets, smartphones, and smart watches. However, below we list several compelling usage scenarios, where TypingRing is a more convenient choice than other input methods (e.g., on-screen keyboard).

- **Devices with Tiny Screens.** Some computing devices, such as smart watches and smart wristbands, have very small sized screens where a full scale touch enabled keyboard is not an option. TypingRing can be used with these devices as it physically separates the actual typing action from the visual feedback, and hence, the keyboard layout can be scaled down enough to just to show a tiny keyboard with highlighted keys, or a single row of keys, or just the 3 keys in a selected zone.
- **Saving Screen Space on a Mobile Display.** Typical on-screen soft keyboards on a mobile device block out more than 40% of the display. This is annoying to the user as the blocked out area may contain information that the user needs to see while typing in his inputs. With TypingRing, the size of the blocked area is reduced up to 10 times, and hence, the freed space can be utilized by the application to improve user experience.

- **Quick and On-the-Go Typing.** In some situations, e.g. self check-in at an airport kiosk, transactions at ATMs, or inputting pass codes into locks, we want to input text quickly and on-the-go. Health conscious people who may want to avoid touching the keypads on these public devices might want to use their personal mobile device for input. The TypingRing being a wearable device, is more convenient in these scenarios than pulling out a mobile phone from the pocket and interacting with the display.

Although TypingRing has its use cases and it is even possible to use the ring as a generic text input system, we admit that it is unlikely for TypingRing to become mainstream in the near future. Making a new input method popular, such as Twiddler [23] or Dvorak Keyboard [27], has been unsuccessful in the past, even if they were more efficient than standard QWERTY keyboards. While diffusion of innovation is unpredictable, we are hopeful that – in this age of mobility, TypingRing will find its way to become a strong competitor of existing text input systems.

# 3. SYSTEM OVERVIEW

This section overviews the system architecture of TypingRing. We defer the algorithms and implementation details to subsequent sections.

## 3.1 The Hardware Architecture

The TypingRing hardware platform is a redesign of a conventional ring that has sensors embedded in its perimeter and a tiny microcontroller unit that has wireless data communication capability. The platform enables continuous sensing of a user's hand and finger movements and processes the sensor data on-board to generate key events. Figure 2 is a schematic of the TypingRing– showing the components and their placements on the ring.

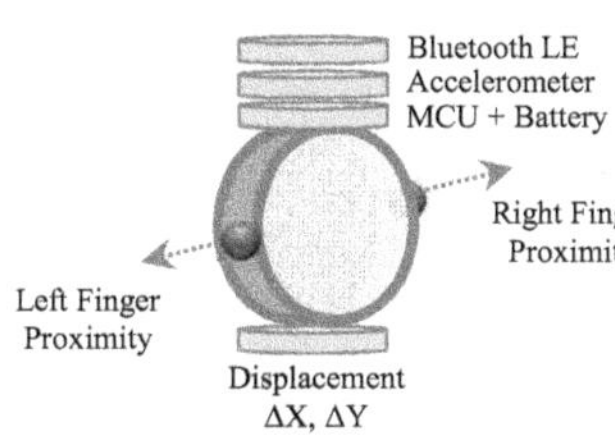


**Figure 2: Hardware architecture of TypingRing.**

- **Microcontroller.** The top of the ring, where usually a jewel is placed, consists of three boards stacked on top of each other. One of these is a micro-controller unit (MCU) that drives all the system components, processes sensing data to determine key events, and transmits the key information. The MCU is powered by a thin film battery.
- **Accelerometer.** A 3-axis accelerometer is placed on top the ring, and it primarily detects the movement of the middle finger and helps detect other fingers. This sensor is kept always on to detect the presence of motion and turn on and off other sensors as needed.
- **Proximity Sensors.** Two proximity sensors are placed on the sides of the ring facing the two fingers which are next to the middle finger. Their placement allows the ring to measure the proximity between the middle finger and the two fingers next to it. This is used to detect which finger is used for typing.
- **Displacement Sensor.** An optical displacement sensor, like the ones used in an optical mouse, is placed underneath the ring to detect the $X$ and $Y$ displacements of the ring. This is used to detect when the user changes his typing zone.
- **Bluetooth LE.** A BLE radio is integrated on top of the ring, which is used by the MCU to send key events wirelessly to the computing device using the standard BLE keyboard protocol.

Our current TypingRing prototype does not have an ON/OFF switch so that it can be turned ON and OFF before and after using the ring. While this can easily be added to our next prototype, an alternate way of doing this could be to allow tapping the ring to switch ON/OFF the device. We leave this design choice open for now and rely upon the presence or absence of the battery as an alternative to switching.

## 3.2 The Firmware Architecture

The TypingRing determines the key events completely inside the ring without relying on the computing device for any computational assistance. This makes it a self-sufficient input accessory just like a regular Bluetooth LE keyboard. An alternative to this would be to transmit raw or partially processed sensing data and let the device determine the key events. This, however, would require higher bandwidth communication, increase the data transmission cost, and make the ring a non-standard input accessory. The firmware running inside the TypingRing is responsible for controlling the sensors, determining the key strokes, and generating and sending key events to the computing device.

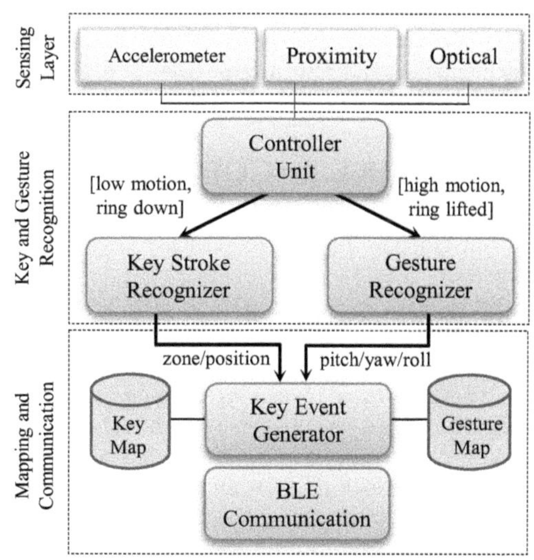


**Figure 3: Firmware architecture of TypingRing.**

Figure 3 shows the architecture of the firmware. Figure 3 shows the architecture of the firmware. As shown in the figure, the firmware is composed of three layers: sensing, recognition, and communication.

**Sensing Layer.** The top layer of the firmware contains sensor sampling modules, which are the accelerometer, the left and right proximity sensors, and the optical displacement sensor modules. These modules read and hold sensor values in bounded circular FIFO queues.

**Key and Gesture Recognition Layer.** The `Controller Unit` is responsible for turning on and off a particular type of sensor. Since sampling the accelerometer is relatively inexpensive, only the accelerometer is continuously monitored. If it detects a significant motion, it turns on the optical sensor to check if the ring is lifted up or is on a surface, and triggers either the key or the gesture detection module.

The `Key-Stroke Recognizer` kicks off when the user's hand movement is low to moderate and the ring is on a surface. It takes into account all three types of sensors to determine the zone or the finger using the algorithm in Section 4. The `Gesture Recognizer`, on the other hand, starts when the ring is lifted up and the user's hand movement is relatively higher. Using the algorithm described in Section 4.4, TypingRing detects simple 3D gestures (e.g. pitch, roll, and yaw) to enable short-cuts for commonly used keys.

**Mapping and Communication Layer.** The `Key Event Generator` translates the detected zone, finger, or the 3D gesture into appropriate key events according to a predefined mapping.

- A reported typing gesture by the `Key-Stroke Recognizer` is mapped into a real key event corresponding to the finger in the currently selected zone.
- A reported change of zone by the `Key-Stroke Recognizer` is mapped to a 'fake' key event, such as an unused `ALT` + a specific key, and is sent to the computing device to enable visual feedback to the user. Such a fake key event is ignored by the OS of the computing device, but is useful to the TypingRing system, as this is used to determine which zone to highlight (Section 5.3 describes this in detail).
- A reported 3D gesture by the `Gesture Recognizer` is mapped to a commonly used key. For example, pitch is mapped to space bar, double pitch to enter, yaw to delete, and roll to shift.

In our current design, we have made the two maps (key-stroke and gesture) separate from each other in order to simplify the design, implementation and also usage. However, these could be combined to introduce additional 3D gestures and key shortcuts.

# 4. KEY STROKE RECOGNITION

This section describes the typing finger recognition algorithm for key strokes along with a simple gesture recognition algorithm for shortcut keys.

## 4.1 The State Machine

As described earlier, typing with the ring involves two phases – seeking for a zone followed by making a typing gesture. To enable this, the ring maintains a state machine which is shown in Figure 4. The transitions between states occur after detecting specific events (shown in brackets), which are determined by processing the sensor streams. Below we describe the states, the events and transitions.

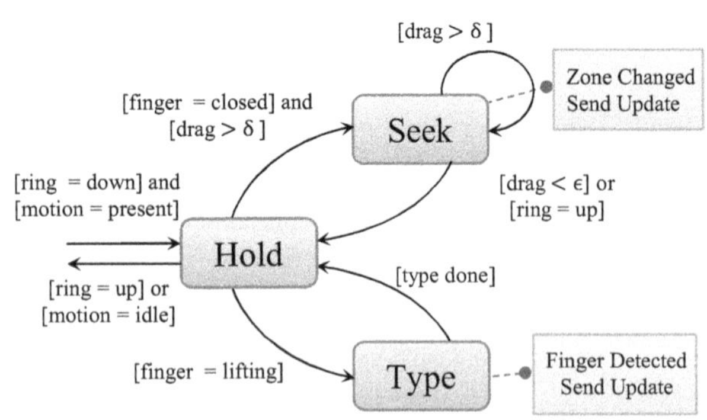


**Figure 4: The state machine for key stroke detection.**

Once the `Key-Stroke Recognizer` is activated, the ring stays in one of its three states: `hold`, `seek`, or `type`.

- **Hold.** This is both the start and the final state of the state machine. This state is entered when the ring is on a surface (`ring = down`) and motion is detected (`motion = present`). From then on, this acts as the intermediate state between the seeking and the typing phase. The ring leaves this state when it is lifted up (`ring = up`) or is idle (`motion = idle`).
- **Seek.** The `seek` state is entered when the user starts dragging the ring on the surface (`drag` $> \delta$) while keeping his fingers close to each other (`finger = closed`), i.e. the user is not making any typing gestures. Since a user may have to cross multiple zones until he reaches the desired one, the seek state repeats itself. Every time there is a change in zone, the information is sent to the key event generator. The ring leaves this state when it is lifted up (`ring = up`) or no significant movement is detected (`drag` $< \epsilon$).
- **Type.** The `type` state is entered when the user lifts up one or both of his fingers (`finger = lifting`) indicating an intention to type. This state runs the typing gesture detection algorithm (Section 4.3) to determine a valid typing gesture and the finger used, and then goes back to the hold state. In case of a valid gesture, it sends the detected finger to the key event generator.

## 4.2 Detecting Sensor Events

All the state transitions in the state machine depend on the values of four types of event variables: ring, motion, drag, and finger.

- **Drag Events.** The `drag` event relates to the dragging of the ring on a surface. These events are triggered whenever the displacement of the ring over a period crosses a certain threshold. A large drag results in a change of zone whereas the ring leaves the seek state when there is no significant drag. The value of a drag is calculated from the optical displacement sensor's readings. The optical sensor periodically sends updates on X- and Y- displacements of the ring as a vector, $\Delta d = (\Delta x, \Delta y)$. These values are too noisy and are hardware accelerated. To compute a drag, $\Delta d$ is first passed through a moving average filter and then integrated continuously. Transition from one zone to another happens when the integrated value exceeds an empirically obtained threshold $\delta_d$. Because this threshold is empirically obtained and is fixed for all users, it may require a new user of TypingRing some practice to get used to it. This is somewhat similar to a user who is using a mouse for the first time. Equations 1 and 2 show the filtering and drag computation steps.

$$\Delta d = \alpha\, \Delta d_k + (1-\alpha)\, \Delta d_{k-1} \quad (1)$$

$$\text{drag} = \left| \int \Delta d\, \mathrm{d}t \right| \quad (2)$$

- **Finger Events.** The `finger` events happen whenever the user lifts up one of his fingers or presses down both of his fingers. These events are determined by two identical detectors, one for each finger. Each of these detectors accumulate proximity values, $\{p_k\}$ over a period of $\tau_p$ and compute the range. The range is compared to two empirically obtained thresholds $\delta_p$ and $\epsilon_p$ to detect finger lifting and pressing events. In order to reduce false positives, we select conservative values for these thresholds, which is described in Section 6.2.3.

$$\text{range} = \max_{t-\tau_p \le k \le t} \{p_k\} - \min_{t-\tau_p \le k \le t} \{p_k\} \quad (3)$$

- **Motion Events.** The presence or absence of `motion` is determined from the 3-axis accelerometer sensor readings $(a_x, a_y, a_z)$. The ring keeps track of running variances of the magnitude of acceleration $\sqrt{a_x^2 + a_y^2 + a_z^2}$ over a period $\tau_a$, and based on a threshold, $\epsilon_a$, it determines the presence or absence of motion.
- **Ring Events.** The `ring` events, i.e. whether or not the bottom of the ring is touching the surface, are read directly from the optical sensor. The optical sensor has a built-in lift detector, which is programmed to detect up to 5 mm lifting.

### 4.3 Detecting the Typing Finger

A naive algorithm to detect the typing finger is to use thresholds to detect finger events similar to Section 4.2 and thereby identify the finger. However, we empirically found that such an algorithm does not work in practical cases and results in false positives (multiple detections of one or more fingers), false negatives (no detection), and does not provide any confidence on the inference. By employing conservative thresholds false positives may be eliminated, but this induces delays in typing gesture detection and frustrates the user as unlike zone seeking there is no visual feedback on how much additional effort is needed to exert to type in the key.

In order to enable a robust and accurate finger detection, we leverage an observation that – each finger's movement has an effect on the accelerometer readings obtained from the middle finger – either directly (for the middle finger) or indirectly (for the other two). With this observation, we design an algorithm that takes both the proximity sensors and the accelerometer into account. Hence, the problem of typing finger detection is stated as – *given periodic proximity and accelerometer sensor readings over an interval, what is the probability of making a typing gesture with one of the three fingers?*. If the highest probability for a finger is greater than a threshold, the finger is reported by the algorithm. Because the algorithm runs inside the ring, the solution has to meet some additional requirements. The algorithm needs to be simple enough for implementation inside the ring's microcontroller, and also has to be fast, accurate, and robust.

To achieve this, we use a $N$-state Hidden Markov Model (HMM). This satisfies our goals as HMMs are known to be robust classifiers for gesture recognition problems [28] and TypingRing's goal is to detect 'typing gestures' as the user types. The proximity sensor readings are analog values and a time series plot of proximity range values of a well-posed typing gesture has a different time dependent signature than casual finger movements. This is captured by an HMM, which is capable of learning a time series of events. Besides, HMMs provide a confidence value of the solution (i.e. a probability for each class), and a trained HMM is compact enough to store inside the ring and is fast enough to obtain the probabilities in real time. We experimentally show in Section 6.1.1 that our implemented HMM classifier inside the ring runs in real-time. The steps of the algorithm are as follows:

- **Quantization**. The left and right proximity sensor values, $p_i^L$ and $p_i^R$, and the accelerometer reading $\mathbf{a_i}$, are first quantized using $Q'$ and $Q''$ functions, respectively.

$$Q'(p_i) = \underset{1\leq k\leq L}{\text{argmin}}\left|q'_k - p_i\right| \quad (4)$$

$$Q''(\mathbf{a_i}) = \underset{1\leq k\leq L}{\text{argmin}}\left|q''_k - V(||\mathbf{a_i}||)\right| \quad (5)$$

  where, $V(||\mathbf{a_i}||)$ is the variance in acceleration over a second, $L$ is the number of quantization levels, and $q'_k$ and $q''_k$ are the quantization levels for proximity and acceleromoter sensors, respectively. To limit the number of possible states in the HMM, we use $L = 3$ level quantization, and the levels correspond to the quartiles of the empirical data.
- **Encoding.** At every sampling interval, the quantized values from the 3 sensor streams produce a 3-tuple, $(\rho_i^l, \rho_i^r, \alpha_i)$, $1 \leq \rho_i^l, \rho_i^r, \alpha_i \leq L$. Considering all possible combinations and 3-level quantization, there can be at most $L^3 = 27$ different tuples. Each of these tuples is considered as an observed event (called an *emmision*) in the HMM, resulting in a set of possible emissions, $\{Y_i\}$, $1 \leq i \leq 27$, at each state of HMM.
- **HMM Classification.** Assuming we have a precomputed HMM corresponding to sensor data obtained by typing with a specific finger, this step computes the likelihood of a given sequence of emissions, $y = (y_1, ..., y_T)$ being generated by the model. The length of the sequence $T$ depends on the sampling frequency $f_s$ and the duration of a typing event $W$. In TypingRing, we use a sliding window of $W = 1$ second (with 50% overlap) to capture a typing event. This bounds the value of $T$ to $\lceil W/f_s \rceil$. Using Viterbi [14] algorithm, we compute the maximum likelihood of $y$ given the precomputed HMM – having a state space $S$, initial probabilites of each state $\pi_i$, $1 < lei \leq |S|$, and transition probabilities $u_{i,j}$ of transitioning from state $i$ to $j$ – as follows:

$$v(1, i) = p(y_1|i).\, \pi_i \quad (6)$$

$$v(t, i) = p(y_t|i).\, \max_{s\in S}(u_{s,i}.\, v(t-1, s)) \quad (7)$$

  where, $v(t, i)$ is the probability that the most probable state sequence that could emit $y$ ends in state $i$. Now, to obtain the maximum likelihood of our HMM to generate $y$, we apply the following:

$$v_{ML} = \max_{1\leq i\leq|S|} v(T, i) \quad (8)$$

This step is performed once for each of the 3 HMMs corresponding to typing with 3 fingers and the model that has the maximum $v_{ML}$ is classified as the most likely finger. The complexity of this algorithm is $O(T * |S|^2)$.

In order to train the HMMs, we use our empirical data to estimate the parameters of these HMMs offline. At first, all labeled training examples – containing the proximity and accelerometer sensor readings for typing with one of the three fingers – are quantized and encoded to form a time series of emissions. We truncate each instance of typing data to 1 second by removing the leading and trailing no-motion values. This makes the length of each encoded training example exactly $1/f_s$ elements long, which is used in classification. Using the encoded training examples for each finger, we use the standard Baum-Welch [28, 32] algorithm to find the unknown parameters of the HMM. These models are stored inside the ring and the ring only runs the classification step in real-time.

### 4.4 Detecting Gesture Shortcuts

Gesture recognition from motion data is a well-studied problem and there are many efficient and highly accurate algorithms that detect a wide variety of gestures from accelerometer readings obtained from mobile and wearable devices. We have adopted one of the simplest of them in TypingRing that uses an offline trained Naïve Bayesian classifier to detect the gestures from 3-axis accelerometer readings from the middle finger. TypingRing recognizes three simple 3D gestures - pitch, roll, and yaw, and maps them to six commonly used non-alphabetic keys on a keyboard. In general, the mapping could be anything, but in our implementation, we have done it as shown in the Table 1. To support more than three keys, we consider repetitions of the same gesture within a small period of time (2 seconds) as two different keys.

| Gesture | Repetition | Key |
|---|---|---|
| Pitch | 1 | Space Bar |
| | 2 | Enter |
| Roll | 1 | Shift |
| | 2 | Caps Lock |
| Yaw | 1 | Delete (letter) |
| | 2 | Delete (word) |

**Table 1: Gesture shortcuts in TypingRing to enable faster entry of common keys.**

We use an offline-trained Gaussian Naïve Bayesian classifier that uses the variance in each of the three axes of acceleration as a feature. The steps that run inside the ring for real-time gesture classifications are the following-

- **Windowing.** The ring periodically samples the accelerometer and accumulates 1 second worth of 3-axis accelerometer readings, $a^i = (a^i_x, a^i_y, a^i_z)$. This window of 1 second is shifted by 0.5 second to form the window for the next iteration.
- **Feature Computation.** We compute a 3-element continuous valued feature vector, $f = (f_1, f_2, f_3)$, where the elements are the variances of $\{a^i_x\}$, $\{a^i_y\}$, and $\{a^i_z\}$, respectively.
- **Classification.** To determine the most likely class, $v_{NB}$ for the feature vector $f$ among the classes, $C = \{pitch, roll, yaw\}$, we use Equation 9:

$$v_{NB} = \operatorname*{argmax}_{c \in C} \prod_{i=1}^{3} \frac{1}{\sqrt{2\pi\sigma^i_c}} \exp\left\{-\left(\frac{f_i - \mu^i_c}{2\sigma^i_c}\right)^2\right\} \quad (9)$$

where, $\mu^i_c$ and $\sigma^i_c$ are the mean and standard deviation of the feature $f_i$ for the class $c \in C$ which are empirically determined in our system.

We use this model as our empirical observation reveals that, for each gesture, the features – i.e. the variance in acceleration along each axis – closely follow normal distributions. The algorithm is also highly efficient as these variances are calculated as part of motion detection, hence no extra computation is required for feature extraction. Given a fixed set of classes the classification step is also essentially a constant operation and runs very fast.

# 5. SYSTEM IMPLEMENTATION

This section describes the implementation details of our TypingRing prototype. We describe the hardware, communication between the ring and the computing device, and the software that enables visual feedback.

## 5.1 Hardware Implementation

The hardware is comprised of a total of seven sensor boards surrounding all four sides of a circular titanium ring. Figure 5 shows the top view, side view, and the bottom view of the TypingRing prototype.

The top of the ring consists of a stack of four TinyDuino [11] boards. TinyDuino is an open source platform that features the full capability of the popular Arduino platform but miniaturizes the board to make its size smaller than a quarter. Each board has dimensions of 20 mm × 20 mm, and the stack of four boards has a height < 15 mm. Of the four boards, the bottom one contains an

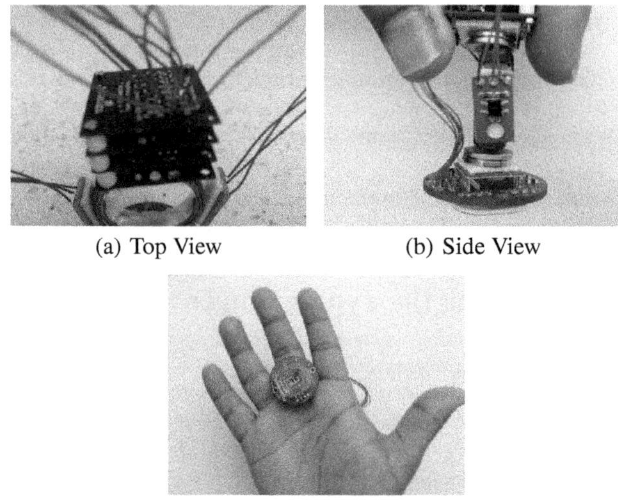

(a) Top View (b) Side View

(c) Bottom View

**Figure 5: The top view, side view, and bottom view of the TypingRing.**

Atmel ATmega328P MCU (8MHz, 32KB Flash, 2KB RAM, 1KB EEPROM) and is powered by a coin cell battery. The board on top of it is a Bosch BMA250 3-axis accelerometer shield, which connects to the MCU using the I2C bus. The third board contains a low energy Bluegiga BLE112 [1] Bluetooth module, which is used to send the key events over the air. The top is an extension board of the MCU, containing ten digital and four analog IO pins.

The two sides of the ring, facing the index finger and the traditional ring finger, have two identical QRE 1113 IR line sensor boards attached to them. Each of these boards contains an IR emitting LED and an IR sensitive photo transistor and has an optimal sensing distance of 3 mm. At the bottom of the ring, there is an ADNS 9800 optical motion sensor board. This sensor is used by the ring to measure the $X$ and $Y$ displacements when the user drags the ring on a surface. The motion sensor communicates to the MCU over the standard SPI interface.

Our current hardware prototype was constructed using components available off-the-shelf and currently has a somewhat bulky form factor. Including the circuitry, battery, and the circular frame, the total weight of our prototype is about 15.5 grams, which is about 4 times of a typical Tungsten ring (4.25 grams). Future versions of TypingRing will be constructed using a custom 3D printed enclosure which will allow sensors to be embedded within the ring's structure, rather than attached to the outside. While the open source Arduino platform is great for prototyping projects, the board stack is currently much larger than it needs to be – the next generation of TypingRing will use a single board BLE system-on-chip (SoC) solution. Finally, an alternative design may not require the use of an optical displacement sensor to further reduce size. While real-time displacement data provides a rich user experience, it may suffice to use several X/Y 'nudge' type gestures detected by the accelerometer to navigate between the different keyboard zones. With these modifications, the size and weight of the ring is expected to be $2 - 3$ times smaller and lighter than the current prototype.

## 5.2 Ring to Device Communication

The Bluegiga BLE112 Bluetooth low energy system on chip (SoC) is used for communications. A Tinyduino microcontroller communicates with the SoC using the BGLib API to configure the hosted radio stack. After the user presses a button, the SoC begins sending undirected, connectable advertisement beacon packets that contains the name "Typing Ring"; additionally, a field indicates the ring should have the appearance of a keyboard-based human interface device (HID).

After scanning for devices, a remote device will see "Typing Ring" appear in a list of available devices and has the option of connecting to it. During the connection process, Android's Bluetooth Low Energy stack scans the remote device's global attribute table (GATT) and determines that the device is implementing the HID over GATT profile [2]. Once this discovery process completes, the remote Android device can receive keystroke events generated by the ring.

In order to send a keystroke to the remote device, the ring encodes key presses as HID reports that each consist of 8 bytes. The first byte indicates a modifier value (i.e. Shift, Alt, Control), the second byte is reserved, and the remaining 6 bytes contain slots that indicate individual characters that are in the *key down* state. Communications between the ring and the remote device are achieved by sending a key down event, where a single slot in an HID report is populated by a character, and optionally the modifier field. After transmitting the key down event, a null report where all bytes are set to 0x00, indicate that the key(s) have been released from their down state.

Two types of HID reports are sent to the remote device. The first type indicates values that indicate the visual feedback a user receives should be updated. As the user moves their hand around on the surface, the position on the virtual keyboard changes in terms of the row/column position. These movements are encoded as non-visible keyboard values that make use of the identifier slot: ALT+1-4 indicate the column of the currently highlighted zone, and ALT+6-9 indicate the row of the currently highlighted zone. In total, 4 HID reports are used to indicate an update to the current row/column position – 2 key down reports and 2 key release reports.

Additionally, when a virtual key is pressed, the user uses one of their middle 3 fingers on the ring worn hand. The index finger is encoded as ALT+Q, the middle finger as ALT+W and the ring finger as ALT+R – this is used as additional feedback to highlight a particular key in the currently highlighted zone. The second type of HID report that is sent consists of the characters themselves. Each HID report contains a single key value in byte position 3, while the modifier is either set to 0x00 – no modification, or 0x02 – indicating capital letters with the left shift modifier.

## 5.3 Enabling Visual Feedback

We have created an Android keyboard application to run on the user's device and provide visual feedback for the ring. It functions similarly to a traditional Android software keyboard but has additional functionality to provide ring related feedback. It can be used as a traditional on-screen software keyboard when the ring is not connected. When the ring is in use with the app the ring transmits three types of messages. All the messages are sent as Bluetooth keyboard HID events. The first type of message is used to indicate the current zone. This is used to draw a box around the currently active zone to the user has visual feedback on what keys finger typing gestures will activate. The second message type is to indicate a finger press event and which finger was pressed. This is used to draw a circle around the pressed key to give visual feedback that a press was registered. These messages are based as ALT-key modifiers of keys that have no meaning in Android. The ALT-key messages are intercepted by the keyboard app and used to update the visual feedback as shown in Figure 6. The final message type is the actual key character event generated by a press event. This is sent as a standard key event so that the ring could be used for typing with any device that supports Bluetooth keyboards or if the keyboard app was not running. Figure 6 shows the appearance of the visual feedback for a normal sized Android keyboard when a key has been recently pressed. The circle around the pressed key serves as visual feedback that the key press event was detected.

**Figure 6: This full layout is enabled in mobile devices that have enough screen space to show all the keys in a keyboard.**

Our technique can be easily adapted for devices with very limited screen area, such as wearables including watches or eyeglass displays. In such devices displaying a full keyboard is undesirable since it can consume a significant portion of the display, hiding valuable visual information from the user. In these situations we can display only a very limited keyboard representation showing only the active region. This is illustrated in Figure 7. As the user moves their hand and changes the active zone the micro-keyboard is updated. The figure shows a region in a keyboard with the typical QWERTY layout, but other layouts including a simple alphabetically ordered keyboard can also be used if desired.

**Figure 7: This minimal layout is suitable for mobile devices whose screens have just enough space to show only 3 keys.**

# 6. EVALUATION

In this section, we describe three types of experiments. First, we measure the execution time and energy consumption of various components of TypingRing. Second, we perform an empirical study to select various parameters and to evaluate the performance of the key-stroke detection algorithm. Third, we perform a user study by letting 7 users type with the ring and summarize the findings.

## 6.1 System Measurement

The TypingRing is a self-contained system where all the computations – from sensing to key stroke detection and then sending the key events to the computing device – happen inside the firmware of the ring. Understanding the execution time and the energy consumption of its component is important to gauge its responsiveness and lifetime.

### 6.1.1 Execution Time

We measure the execution time of all major components of the system software. Since the timer provided by the Arduino platform is not precise, we use a more reliable approach to measure the execution time using a Saleae Logic16 high-sensitivity logic probe [8]. Prior to measuring the execution time, we instrument the code by enclosing it inside two instructions – one that writes a logic `HIGH` to an unused digital pin of Arduino and another that writes a logic `LOW` to high. The digital pin is monitored by the logic probe which samples the pin at 100 MHz – giving us a 10 ns resolution in time measurement. We cross-check measured execution times using Arduino's `micros()` API which has a $\mu s$ level resolution and have found that the measurements are close to each other when rounded to the nearest ms.

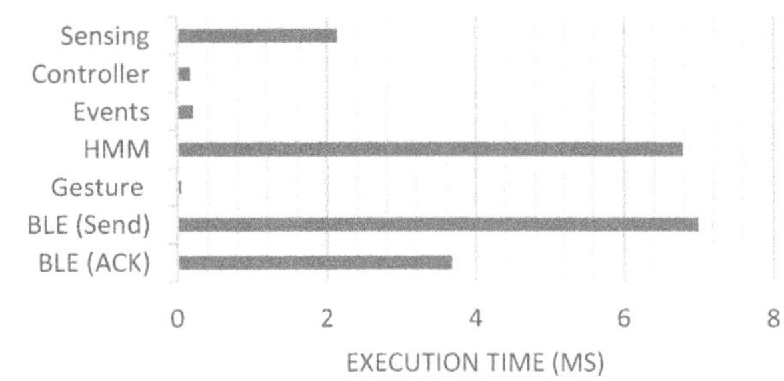


**Figure 8: Execution time of different components in TypingRing.**

Figure 8 shows the measured execution time of seven major components of the TypingRing system software which includes both computation and communication modules. Among all the computational modules, the HMM classification task takes the highest amount of execution time of 6.75 ms, while combining all other tasks the total computation time still remains < 10 ms. The BLE (Send) of 6.99 ms denotes the duration between time of issuing a send command and the instant when the key is actually transmitted by the Bluetooth LE chip. The BLE (ACK) of 3.67 ms denotes the time it takes to get an acknowledgment back from the computing device, after a key has been sent. Overall, the system has an end-to-end execution time of about 20 ms from making a typing gesture to getting back an acknowledgment. Considering the 100 ms sensor sampling interval of TypingRing, this indicates that the system is capable of detecting and sending a key in real-time.

### 6.1.2 Energy Profile

We create an energy profile of our prototype and estimate its lifetime. We identify the states of the system and the components (e.g. processor, sensors, and BLE) that consume power in each state. Using the estimated power of each component and the duration of each state from our empirical data, we obtain an energy profile that is shown in Figure9.

We show the energy consumption per key in this figure. The labels on the left show the hardware components and their power consumption when they are active. From our empirical data, we get the fraction of time each of these components are active when typing a key and by multiplying the power to an average key stroke length, we obtain the energy values. For example, BLE TX/RX power in general is about 80 mW. However, when we consider idle time and data exchanges separately, the average power to maintain connection and send one key becomes less than 0.3 mW. Similarly, not all sensors are active at all states - e.g. proximity sensors are not used during seeking, optical sensors are not using during typing, and accelerometer is used in hold and gesture states. With this energy profile and a coin cell battery of $125mAh$, TypingRing's life-time is about $13,650 - 15,500$ key events. Assuming approximately 1s per key stroke, the lifetime of TypingRing is about $3.8 - 4.3$ hours.

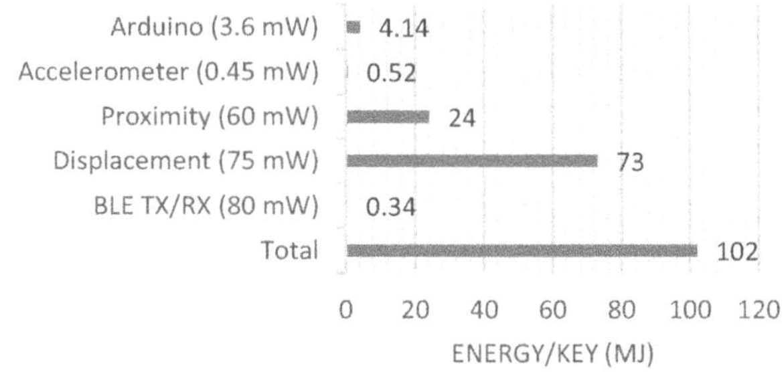


**Figure 9: Energy profile of TypingRing.**

## 6.2 Empirical Evaluation

In this section, we evaluate various aspects of the key stroke recognition algorithm. First, we determine the parameters of the sensor event detectors that have been introduced in section 4.2. Second, we evaluate the accuracy of the HMM based finger detector and compare its performance with two other baseline classifiers. Third, we evaluate the accuracy of the gesture recognition algorithm.

### 6.2.1 Empirical Dataset

We have created an empirical dataset that we obtained by letting 18 users (4 females, and 14 males) use the ring. The users were shown randomly generated characters and randomly selected text from a standard phrase set [24] on a mobile device. They typed the text – at first, using the TypingRing, then on the touch-based soft keyboard of a mobile device, and then by clicking on a Windows 7 on-screen keyboard. Each user typed in about 50 random characters, $5 - 15$ phrases, and about 30 gestures. The users were given visual feedback on the screen by showing the input text, the highlighted zone, and the typed text. In order to enable visual feedback, we used a bootstrap classifier that is trained on a singe user prior to the data collection. We programed the ring to sample and store accelerometer, proximity, and optical sensor readings at 100 ms interval. The collected data were analyzed offline in a desktop computer.

### 6.2.2 Drag Events

The drag event depends on two parameters – the smoothing factor ($\alpha$) and the drag threshold ($\delta_d$) which we determine in this experiment.

The smoothing factor is used to reduce the variance in optical sensor reading prior to integration. However, the required amount of smoothing depends on the surface material on which the sensor is being dragged. Hence, we conduct an experiment to understand the relationship between the quality of a surface and the amount of variance in displacement sensor reading on that surface. We leverage this relationship in TypingRing to tune in the smoothing factor ($\alpha$) based on the surface on which the user is typing.

The ADNS 9800 optical sensor comes with a register that contains the amount of high-quality optical features it used to compute the displacement. This gives us an indication of the quality of the surface underneath the sensor. In our experiment, we collect displacement sensor readings from various types of surfaces, such as

– wooden table, wall, plastic, white board, various types of fabrics, and paper. As read by the ADNS 9800, these materials have a surface quality value ranging from 15 to 75. On each surface, we drag the ring horizontally, vertically, and diagonally for about 3 feet, at a speed of approximately 4 inches per second, and then measure the variance in displacement.

From Figure 10 we see that there is a linear relationship between the surface quality and the variance in sensor readings. We leverage this information to obtain the smoothing factor $\alpha$ for a particular surface. We do the mapping by first computing $\alpha$ for a white paper surface so that the zone transitions are smooth. For other surfaces, we scale the value of $\alpha$ according to its relative surface quality with respect to white paper. This technique makes the zone transition consistent across different types of surface materials.

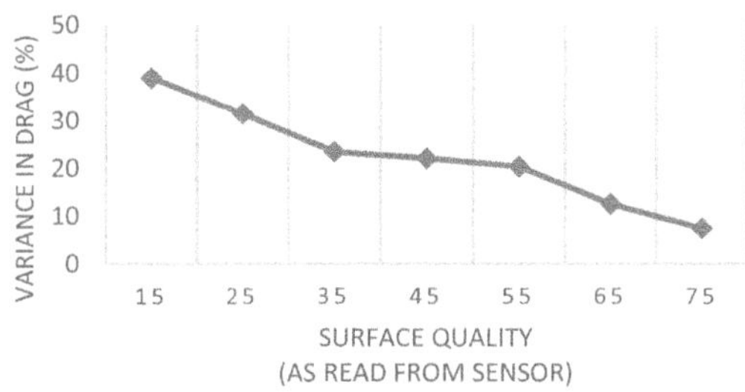


**Figure 10: Impact of surface quality on variance in data.**

The drag threshold ($\delta_d$) represents the total linear displacement reached when a zone transition happens. A smaller $\delta_d$ results in a quicker zone transition and vice versa. We perform an experiment to quantify this inverse relationship between the drag threshold and the zone transition rate. Figure 11 shows that as the total displacement (shown in units of optical sensor reading) increases from 60 to 270, the ring updates the zone at the rate of 200 to 50 times per minute.

In TypingRing, we adopt an adaptive thresholding scheme for $\delta_d$ depending on the state of typing. For an initial zone transition, we use a larger threshold to make certain that the user really wants to move and it is not just casual hand motion. For successive zone transitions, a smaller threshold is used so that the zone transitions are smoother.

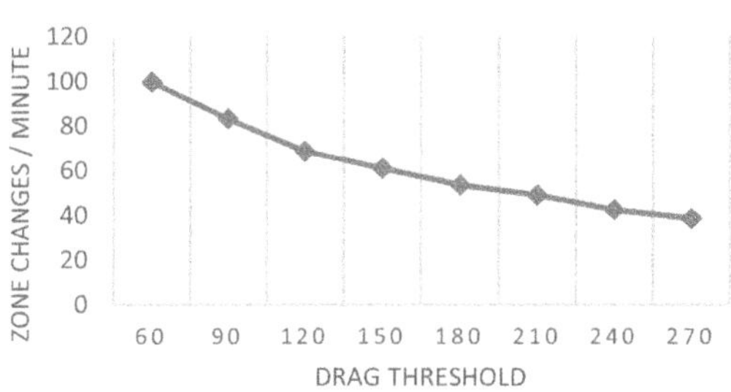


**Figure 11: Adaptive thresholding for smooth zone transitions.**

### 6.2.3 *Finger Events*

The finger lift and press events depend on the range of proximity sensor values. Two thresholds $\delta_p$ and $\epsilon_p$ are used to detect these two types of events. Both of these thresholds are chosen so that the false positives, false negatives, and the overall error in event detection are minimal. As an illustration of this, we describe how $\delta_p$ is determined.

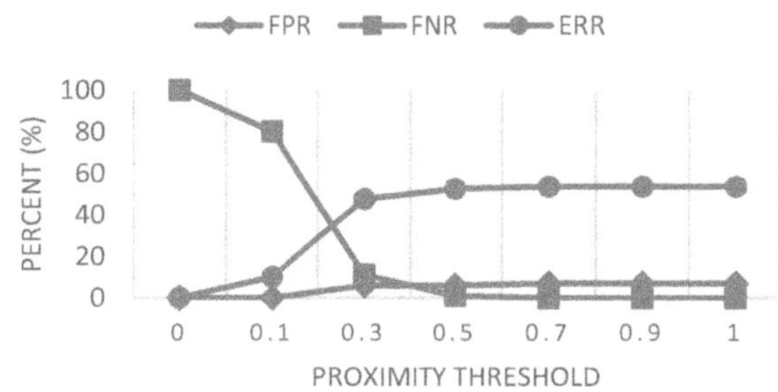


**Figure 12: Finger threshold to reduce false positive/negatives and overall error.**

Each typing gesture made by either the left or the right finger in our dataset contains exactly one finger lift event and one finger press event. For a given threshold, based on the type of finger and the number of times the time vs. proximity curve crosses the threshold, we determine whether it contributes to false positives or false negatives, or if it is accurate.

Figure 12 shows the false positive rates (FPR), false negative rates (FNR), and the error in detection (ERR) of the finger lift events, as the threshold $\delta_p$ is varied. A smaller $\delta_p$ increases the false positives and larger ones tend to increase both the false negative rate and the overall error. We choose $\delta_p = 0.25$ to ensure negligible false positives as this is more problematic than the other two.

### 6.2.4 *Motion Events*

The presence or absence of significant motion is detected from the variance in acceleration. To obtain a threshold to distinguish motion and non-motion, we divide our empirical data into two subsets – one containing examples that are collected when a user is typing or seeking a zone, and the other one containing examples when the user's hand is resting and idle. Figure 13 shows the box plot of variance in acceleration for these two cases. We see that the two classes are clearly separable with a small threshold between 20 – 50.

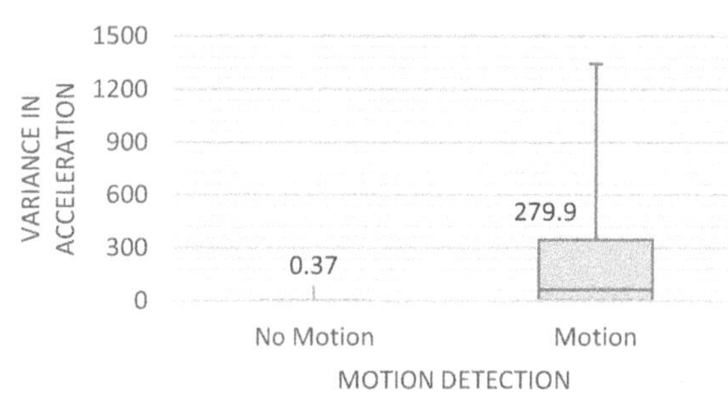


**Figure 13: Variance in acceleration for motion detection.**

### 6.2.5 *Typing Finger Detection*

The goal of this experiment is to evaluate the accuracy of the HMM based classifier that determines which of the three fingers a user used to make a typing gesture. The HMM is trained and tested on the empirical dataset that contains a total of over 2500 letters (including phrases). Each letter in the alphabet is typed in at least 75 times, and each of the three fingers has been used at least 650 times. Letters in a phrase are isolated by noting the duration in zones, and sensor values for each letter are stored separately. The training phase of HMM is run for 1000 iterations and the initial values of transition and emission matrices are randomized. Because there is randomness involved, the experiment is repeated 10 times to increase the confidence. On each run, 70% of the examples are used for training and the rest are used for testing. The accuracy is measured by calculating the percentage of correct predictions among all test cases. The accuracy of the algorithm is compared with the accuracy of two other baseline classifiers: a decision tree classifier and a Naïve Bayesian classifier. Both of these use the same set of features – which are the quantized proximity and accelerometer readings.

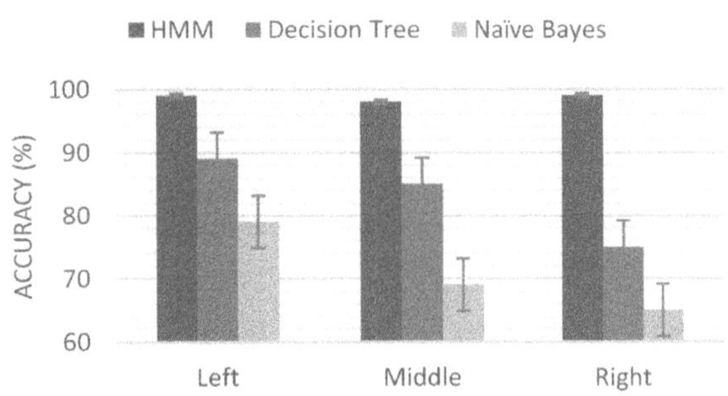


**Figure 14: Accuracy of typing finger detection.**

Figure 14 compares the accuracy of the three algorithms in detecting the typing finger. Of the three, HMM performs the best with an average accuracy of 98.67%, which is 15% – 27% higher compared to the other two. The main reason for HMM to perform better than the other two is that the HMM considers the sequence of states and each state is formed by taking all combinations of the three sensors into account. The other two classifiers are fundamentally extreme in this issue. The Naïve Bayesian classifier assumes independence of all three sensor types – which is not true in our problem. The decision tree classifier, on the other hand, assumes that all variables interact with each other – which is also not quite true in TypingRing, e.g. the left and the right proximity sensors are mostly independent of each other. The decision tree also suffers from over fitting the training data, which results in better training accuracy, but because of their poor generalization ability, the cross validation accuracy remains lower than the HMM.

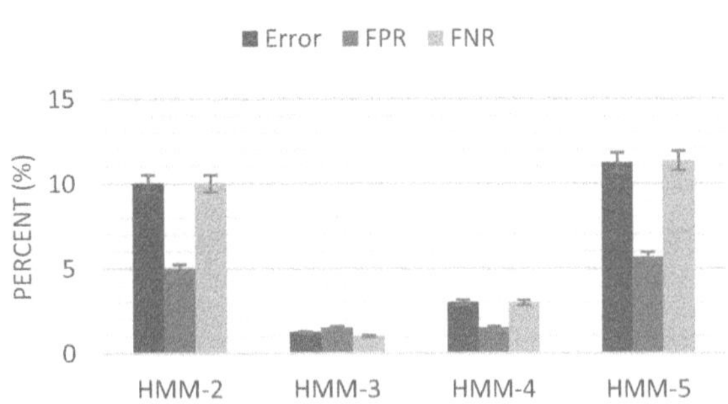


**Figure 15: Performance of different sizes of HMMs.**

One design decision in HMM is to select the number of hidden states. For our problem, we empirically determine this by varying the number of states from 2 to 5, and then comparing the accuracy. Figure 15 compares the classification error, false positive rate, and the false negative rate of four HMMs. The number after the HMM denotes the number of states. We observe that a 3 state HMM is the best among the four having the lowest error rate of 1.3% with less than the 1.5% false positive and false negative rates. Compared to other models, this is 2.4 – 9.13 times lower. HMM-3 is better than HMM-2 as it is more expressive and capable of encoding more information. HMM-4 and HMM-5 however is not better than HMM-3, because of their tendency to overfit the training data and then failing to recognize unknown examples from the test set.

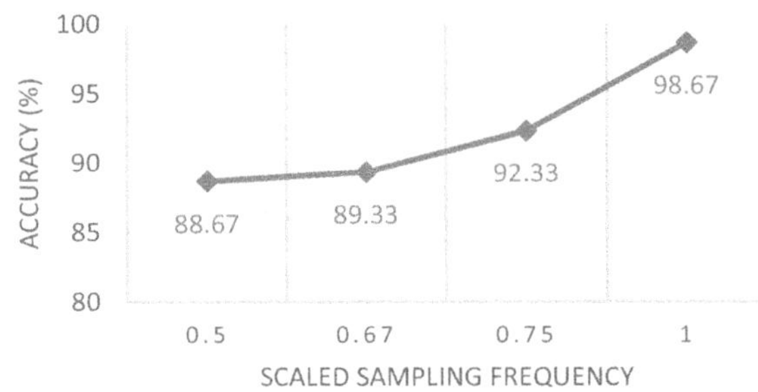


**Figure 16: Effect of sampling frequency.**

While detecting the typing finger, we use a sampling period of 100 ms for all three types of sensors. This results in a very high accuracy in finger detection of over 98%. A higher frequency does not have enough room for further improvement, but we wanted to determine the lowest sampling frequency for which our algorithm still performs reasonably well. To do this test, we down-sample the sensor streams to lower the sampling frequency to $\frac{3}{4}$, $\frac{2}{3}$, and $\frac{1}{2}$ of the original frequency and then evaluate the accuracy of HMM using these modified samples. Figure 16 plots the results. We see that we could potentially double the sampling interval, but in that case we have to sacrifice about 10% accuracy. Further investigation reveals that most of the misclassifications at the lower frequencies come from the right finger (the traditional ring finger when worn on the right hand) detection errors. This is due to the fact that humans have limitations in lifting up the traditional ring finger higher than other fingers. This results in higher false positives and false negatives unless the right proximity sensor is sampled at a higher rate. We leave this as a future work to enhance the efficiency of the ring by suitably choosing the sampling intervals for each sensor individually.

### *6.2.6 Gesture Detection*

We perform an experiment to determine the accuracy of the gesture recognizer. Our participants perform about 25 – 35 gestures of each type, i.e. pitch, roll, and yaw, which results in a sample size of over 500 gesture instances. This dataset is used to train the 3-class Gaussian Naïve Bayesian gesture recognizer in TypingRing. We use randomly chosen 70% examples for model training and use the rest for testing. The experiment is repeated 10 times.

Figure 17 shows the accuracy of gesture recognizer for various sampling intervals of the accelerometer. During data collection, we set the sampling interval to 100 ms. During our analysis, we down-sample the accelerometer readings to vary the sampling frequency and compute the accuracy of the classifier for different sampling intervals in the range 100 – 800 ms.

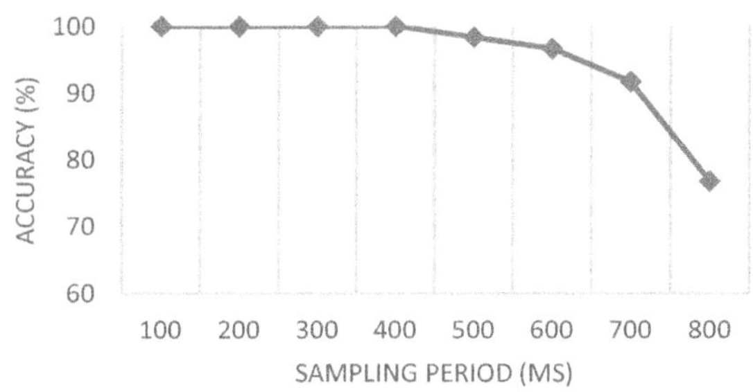


**Figure 17: Accuracy of gesture recognizer.**

We observe that up until 400 ms sampling interval, the classifier's accuracy remains 100%, and it starts to make mistakes afterward. This indicates that when the ring is lifted by the user to make a gesture we may use a larger sampling interval to save some CPU cycles. However, this does not help much in practice as gestures in TypingRing are for shortcut keys with long intervals and last for a short duration. In applications where short-cut keys may be used for a longer duration, e.g. pressing only the 'next', 'cancel' or 'okay' button at an interactive kiosk, this principle could be applied.

## 6.3 User Study

We performed a user study involving 7 users (2 females and 5 males). The differences between this experiment and our empirical data collection experiments were that during the user study the system was trained on empirical data and computations happened inside the ring. The users who participated in this user study are in the age range of $28 - 36$ and all of them are smartphone users. We gave each user a paragraph printed on a piece of paper to type using the TypingRing. The paragraph was created by concatenating all 500 phrases that we found in the MacKenzie phase set [24]. Users were asked to type the entire paragraph correctly – i.e. they were allowed to use the delete key in case of an error. Each user participated in the study in two sessions – each session lasting for $10 - 15$ minutes and there was at least a day gap between the two sessions for any user. The users were allowed to use gesture shortcuts in both sessions, however, only four users (U4-U7) have used them at least once during their second sessions. For visual feedbacks, users were shown a full keyboard layout – like the one in Figure 6.

In order to compare the performance of TypingRing, we used two baseline solutions. The first one is an on-screen soft keyboard of an Android smartphone, and the second one is a Windows 7 on-screen keyboard where a user types by clicking a mouse. While there are several alternate text entry methods [25], such as – shape and hand writing, speech, and eye tracking, we picked on-screen soft keyboard and typing by clicking as two of our baselines as these two methods have similarity with TypingRing. For example, TypingRing's visual feedback is essentially a soft keyboard, where instead of touch events to entry a key, we are using finger gestures. The zone seeking in TypingRing and then making a typing gesture is also very similar to typing by clicking, where a mouse pointer is used to locate a key and the click events are used to entry it.

### 6.3.1 *Typing Speed*

Figure 18 plots typing speed in terms of number of correctly typed keys per second (i.e. deleting and correcting a letter is counted as a single correct key) for each user, for each of the three key entry methods. We order the users according to their typing speed with TypingRing. We observe that, the typing speed on a soft keyboard (shown as Soft KB) is the highest with an average speed of 1.63 keys/sec or 97.8 keys/min. This is about 2.4 times higher than TypingRing. This is somewhat expected as our users are highly experienced with touch-screen keyboards on mobile devices. A major reason of this gap in speed is the amount of hand movements in each technique. In case of a soft keyboard, fingers can be directly targeted to a key, but in case of TypingRing, a user needs to seek a zone and then press the key. TypingRing's speed, however, is comparable to that of a mouse based on-screen keyboard. For some users, e.g. U1, U5, U6, and U7, TypingRing's speed is as close as $0.92 - 1.0$ times and on average the ratio is 0.88. Overall, TypingRing yields about 41 keys/minute, which is roughly about 8 words/minute.

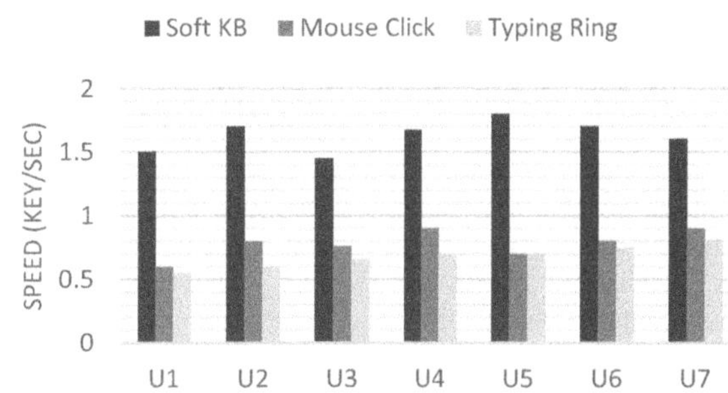


**Figure 18: Typing speed of our participants.**

### 6.3.2 *Learning Effect*

As TypingRing is a new input technique, it requires some practice to get used to it. This is evident when we compare a user's typing time in two separate sessions, which is shown in Figure 19. For the first 4 users, we see a dramatic reduction in typing time by $4.5 - 8.6$ times. Further investigation reveals that, for the most part, the improvement comes from the reduction in seek time. This is intuitive since zone seeking is more time consuming than making typing gestures and it also requires some practice to coordinate between ring movement and visual feedback. From our experience with end users we noticed that those who took time to practice before telling us that they are ready for the session were the ones who achieve the best results with TypingRing.

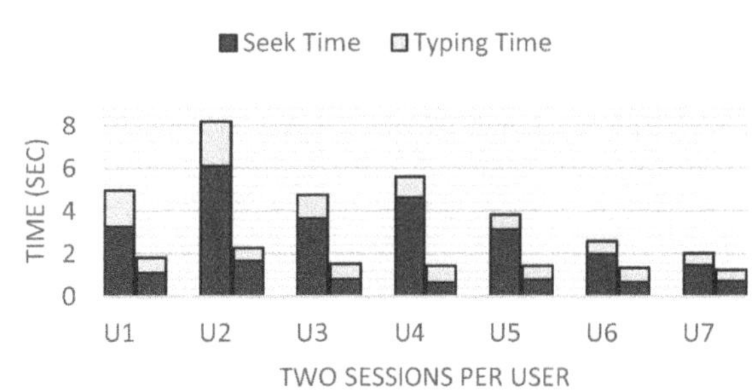


**Figure 19: Learning effect in TypingRing.**

### 6.3.3 *User Survey*

At the end of the sessions, we ask our participants some questionnaire to understand their satisfaction on various aspects of the system. We ask them how they feel about the size, weight, portability, usability, and visual feedback. We also ask them if they notice any difference in their own performance between two sessions, and their feeling about the ring to becoming a replacement for other text input methods on mobile computers. From their responses, some unanimous things are noticed, e.g. everybody seems to love the visual feedback, felt that the system is easy to use, and with practice they are doing better. For other issues, such as about the size, weight, and portability, we have got mixed responses. Several of them think that it is fine for typing, but they might not want to wear it all day long. Some of them complain about the size as it is larger than a typical ring. Others who have used a smart ring before, are somewhat neutral on this issue. Most of them would like to see this replace the on screen keyboard so that they get more screen space which is a limitation of current mobile devices.

The survey had an optional section for the users to write any comments or concerns that they had. One key concern raised by multiple users was about the flat placement of fingers and the palm on a surface to make TypingRing work. This required some practice for the users to get used to this new platform. One possible solution to this problem is to choose a different lens for the optical sensor having a larger focal length. This would allow the user to curl his fingers while typing with the ring. We note this feedback and plan to improve the usability of the ring in our next iteration of TypingRing.

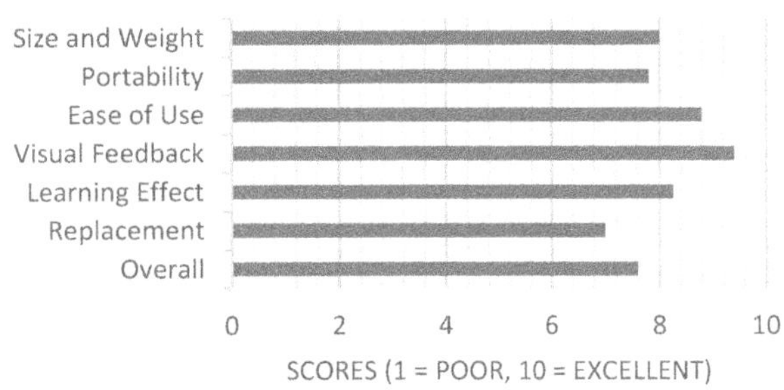


**Figure 20: Summary of user ratings.**

# 7. RELATED WORK

**Ring-based wearable devices.** Several ring-based wearable devices have been proposed for variety of purposes. [16] proposes an energy harvesting wearable ring platform for gesture input on surfaces. Ring [7] is proposed for text recognition, gesture detection, and payment. Fin [3] is another gesture detecting ring that a user wears on his thumb and then makes gestures by touching other fingers with his thumb. NFC Ring [5] uses passive near field communication to provide easy locking/unlocking of a door or a smartphone. Thumb-Track [10] is an ergonometric ring that performs the functions of a mouse. Similarly, a ring proposed in [21] uses a mouse optical sensor and an RGB camera to detect finger movements as well as surface types / textures. SmartyRing [9] pairs with a smartphone and shows useful information, such as notifications, triggers camera, tracks phone, and shows time. In contrast, TypingRing is designed specific for a text-input with all types of computer devices.

**Wearable input devices.** Other than the ring-form factor used in our work, there have been various wearable form-factors used for new input methods. Keyglove [4] is a wearable glove that places 37 touch sensors on the palm of a glove. Using the combination of these touch sensors, it is possible to input text on to a computer. [15] uses sensors worn on each finger as a PDA input device, while our system uses only one finger. Virtual keyboard [6] is another wearable keyboard with high detection accuracy achieved by using artificial neural networks. It requires a user to wear the device on both hands, while TypingRing requires only one finger.

**Gesture recognition with various sensors.** Gesture recognition as an input method has been extensively investigated. uWave in [21] uses dynamic time warping (DTW) techniques to classify movements of a hand in free space as 1 of 8 different gestures. Work in [29] is similar to uWave, but it uses a HMM approach to classify 5 different gestures. Authors in [12] use an accelerometer to detect characters and words drawn in the air. Recently, authors in [30] used a RF signal and NFC receiver to detect a gesture in air and translate it to characters. While these gesture recognition work is exciting, TypingRing is different in that it focuses on both key events and hand gestures.

**Keyboards for mobile devices and surfaces.** Various types of keyboards have been proposed for mobile devices and surface environments. Recently the use of acoustic sensors for keyboard has drawn significant attention. Ubik [31] is a portable text-entry method that allows a user to make keystrokes on conventional surfaces, e.g., wood desktop, by extracting location-dependent multipath fading features from the audio signals. This however relies upon the dual-microphone interface on a smartphone and not suitable for other devices or surfaces. Stane [26] is a synthesized surface that makes particular sounds and facilitates tactile interactions based on the sounds. [17] uses a microphone on a stethoscope attached to different surfaces to interpret gestures based on sound alone. In [20], identifiers are carved into a surface similar to a barcode. A microphone listens to a fingernail move through the notches to determine the identifier. [22, 18] use microphones inside the surface to distinguish between different types of finger strikes (e.g., Knuckle vs. pad of finger). [13, 19] combine acoustic sensors and sounds from the body (e.g., bone movement) to detect movement/gesture of finger or location of taps. TypingRing uses off-the-shelf motion and proximity sensors without requiring any external computing entity or synthesized surfaces.

# 8. CONCLUSION

This paper describes the design, implementation, and evaluation of a ring-based wearable platform, called TypingRing that enables text inputs into computers of different forms and mobile requirements. TypingRing employs embedded sensors to detect the position of a hand and typing gestures made by a finger, and infers the key using a HMM classifier. Evaluations on empirical data and field tests show that the ring detects and reports keys in real-time, achieves over 98% accuracy, yields a typing speed of up to 0.81 keys per second, the typing speed improves as a user uses it more. While TypingRing is capable of inputting text into any computer that supports a BLE keyboard, its typing speed is still not comparable to that of a regular keyboard or on-screen soft keyboards. However, in some scenarios where quick text input is needed or other methods are inconvenient, TypingRing presents a viable solution.

# 9. REFERENCES


[1] Bluegiga technologies. bluegiga.com/.
[2] Bluetooth Developer Portal. developer.bluetooth.org/.
[3] Fin. www.finrobotics.com.
[4] Keyglove. keyglove.net.
[5] NFC Ring. nfcring.com.
[6] Project Virtual Keyboard. www.senseboard.com/.

[7] Ring: Shortcut Everything. www.kickstarter.com/projects/1761670738/ring-shortcut-everything.

[8] Saleae Logic Probe. saleae.com/logic16.

[9] Smarty Ring. smartyring.com.

[10] ThumbTrack. mindstreaminc.com.

[11] Tiny Duino. tiny-circuits.com/.

[12] S. Agrawal, I. Constandache, S. Gaonkar, R. Roy Choudhury, K. Caves, and F. DeRuyter. Using mobile phones to write in air. In *Proceedings of the 9th international conference on Mobile systems, applications, and services*, pages 15–28. ACM, 2011.

[13] T. Deyle, S. Palinko, E. S. Poole, and T. Starner. Hambone: A bio-acoustic gesture interface. In *Wearable Computers, 2007 11th IEEE International Symposium on*, pages 3–10. IEEE, 2007.

[14] G. D. Forney Jr. The viterbi algorithm. *Proceedings of the IEEE*, 61(3):268–278, 1973.

[15] M. Fukumoto and Y. Tonomura. "body coupled fingerring": wireless wearable keyboard. In *Proceedings of the ACM SIGCHI Conference on Human factors in computing systems*, pages 147–154. ACM, 1997.

[16] J. Gummeson, B. Priyantha, and J. Liu. An energy harvesting wearable ring platform for gestureinput on surfaces. In *MobiSys*, pages 162–175. ACM, 2014.

[17] C. Harrison and S. E. Hudson. Scratch input: creating large, inexpensive, unpowered and mobile finger input surfaces. In *Proceedings of the 21st annual ACM symposium on User interface software and technology*, pages 205–208. ACM, 2008.

[18] C. Harrison, J. Schwarz, and S. E. Hudson. Tapsense: enhancing finger interaction on touch surfaces. In *Proceedings of the 24th annual ACM symposium on User interface software and technology*, pages 627–636. ACM, 2011.

[19] C. Harrison, D. Tan, and D. Morris. Skinput: appropriating the body as an input surface. In *Proceedings of the SIGCHI Conference on Human Factors in Computing Systems*, pages 453–462. ACM, 2010.

[20] C. Harrison, R. Xiao, and S. Hudson. Acoustic barcodes: passive, durable and inexpensive notched identification tags. In *Proceedings of the 25th annual ACM symposium on User interface software and technology*, pages 563–568. ACM, 2012.

[21] J. Liu, L. Zhong, J. Wickramasuriya, and V. Vasudevan. uwave: Accelerometer-based personalized gesture recognition and its applications. *Pervasive and Mobile Computing*, 5(6):657–675, 2009.

[22] P. Lopes, R. Jota, and J. A. Jorge. Augmenting touch interaction through acoustic sensing. In *Proceedings of the ACM International Conference on Interactive Tabletops and Surfaces*, pages 53–56. ACM, 2011.

[23] K. Lyons, T. Starner, D. Plaisted, J. Fusia, A. Lyons, A. Drew, and E. Looney. Twiddler Typing: one-handed chording text entry for mobile phones. In *Proceedings of the SIGCHI conference on Human factors in computing systems*, pages 671–678. ACM, 2004.

[24] I. S. MacKenzie and R. W. Soukoreff. Phrase sets for evaluating text entry techniques. In *CHI'03 extended abstracts on Human factors in computing systems*, pages 754–755. ACM, 2003.

[25] I. S. MacKenzie and K. Tanaka-Ishii. *Text entry systems: Mobility, accessibility, universality*. Morgan Kaufmann, 2010.

[26] R. Murray-Smith, J. Williamson, S. Hughes, and T. Quaade. Stane: synthesized surfaces for tactile input. In *Proceedings of the SIGCHI Conference on Human Factors in Computing Systems*, pages 1299–1302. ACM, 2008.

[27] E. M. Rogers. *Diffusion of innovations*. Simon and Schuster, 2010.

[28] S. M. Ross. *Introduction to probability models*. Academic press, 2014.

[29] T. Schlömer, B. Poppinga, N. Henze, and S. Boll. Gesture recognition with a wii controller. In *Proceedings of the 2nd international conference on Tangible and embedded interaction*, pages 11–14. ACM, 2008.

[30] J. Wang, D. Vasisht, and D. Katabi. Rf-idraw: virtual touch screen in the air using rf signals. In *Proceedings of the 2014 ACM conference on SIGCOMM*, pages 235–246. ACM, 2014.

[31] J. Wang, K. Zhao, X. Zhang, and C. Peng. Ubiquitous keyboard for small mobile devices: harnessing multipath fading for fine-grained keystroke localization. In *Proceedings of the 12th annual international conference on Mobile systems, applications, and services*, pages 14–27. ACM, 2014.

[32] L. R. Welch. Hidden markov models and the baum-welch algorithm. *IEEE Information Theory Society Newsletter*, 53(4):10–13, 2003.

# U-Wear: Software-Defined Ultrasonic Networking for Wearable Devices

G. Enrico Santagati and Tommaso Melodia
Wireless Networks and Embedded Systems Laboratory
Northeastern University, Boston, MA, U.S.A.
{santagati, melodia}@ece.neu.edu

## ABSTRACT

Wearable medical sensing devices with wireless capabilities have become the cornerstone of many revolutionary digital health applications that promise to predict and treat major diseases by acquiring and processing health information. Existing wireless wearable devices are connected through radio frequency (RF) electromagnetic wave carriers based on standards such as Bluetooth or WiFi. However, these solutions tend to almost-blindly scale down traditional wireless technologies to the body environment, with little or no attention to the peculiar characteristics of the human body and the severe privacy and security requirements of patients. We contend that this is not the only possible approach, and we present U-Wear, the first networking framework for wearable medical devices based on ultrasonic communications.

U-Wear encloses a set of physical, data link and network layer functionalities that can flexibly adapt to application and system requirements to efficiently distribute information between ultrasonic wearable devices. U-Wear also offers reconfiguration functionalities at the application layer to provide a flexible platform to develop medical applications. We design two prototypes that implement U-Wear and operate in the near-ultrasonic frequency range using commercial-off-the-shelf (COTS) speakers and microphones. Despite the limited bandwidth, i.e., about 2 kHz, and COTS hardware components not optimized for operating at high frequency, our prototypes (i) achieve data rates up to 2.76 kbit/s with bit-error-rate lower than $10^{-5}$ using a transmission power of 20 mW; (ii) enable multiple nodes to share the medium; and (iii) implement reconfigurable processing to extract medical parameters from sensors with high accuracy.

## Categories and Subject Descriptors

C.2.1 [**Computer-Communication Networks**]: Network Architecture and Design

## Keywords

Wearable Devices, Acoustic Communications, Digital Health, Body Area Networks


*MobiSys'15,* May 18–22, 2015, Florence, Italy.

http://dx.doi.org/10.1145/2742647.2742655 .

## 1. INTRODUCTION

Wearable medical sensing and actuating devices with wireless capabilities have become the cornerstone of many revolutionary digital health applications [1]. Wearable electrocardiography (ECG) devices and blood pressure sensors can enable remote cardiovascular monitoring for early diagnosis of cardiac arrhythmias and hypertension [2], and therefore prevent heart failures and strokes. Skin patches with wireless connectivity can be arranged in a closed-feedback-loop drug delivery system [3]. For instance, a sensor patch can measure the level of subcutaneous blood glucose, while a drug pump patch can adaptively deliver the required amount of insulin [4]. Motion sensors, e.g., accelerometers, can collect large amounts of data for fitness and medical applications. For example, wireless motion trackers can record athletes' step rate, speed, and acceleration for performance monitoring. Similar devices can also collect information for post-surgery telerehabilitation in case of lower-limb injuries or strokes [5], or measure the motor degradation of patients affected by *Parkinson* disease [6]. Likewise, by correlating motion with sleep activity, the same sensors can monitor the REM sleep duration of a patient and provide information on the development of *post-traumatic stress disorders* [7].

Existing wireless wearable medical devices are connected through radio frequency (RF) electromagnetic waves. Standards in use are often scaled down versions of wireless technologies (e.g., Bluetooth and WiFi), with little or no attention to the peculiar characteristics of the human body and to the severe privacy and security requirements of patients. For example, many commercial activity trackers [8], as well as smart glasses [9], smart watches [10] and smart clothing [11] connect to smartphones using Bluetooth or WiFi. Alternatively, other medical monitoring solutions [12, 13] use proprietary RF-based technologies to collect medical data in a centralized manner. We contend that this is not the only possible approach, and that RF-based technologies have several limitations that can negatively affect the patients' medical experience with wearable devices.

**Limitations of RF Technology.** First, the RF frequency spectrum is scarce and already crowded with many devices interfering with one another. At the same time, the number of wireless devices that compete to access the RF spectrum is growing exponentially. This includes wireless sensors, but also more largely and pervasively deployed RF devices such as WiFi and Bluetooth, and even microwave ovens. Quoting the FDA's recent guideline on wireless med-

This material is based upon work supported by the National Science Foundation under grant CAREER CNS-1253309.

ical devices, "an increasingly crowded RF environment could impact the performance of RF wireless medical devices" [14]. Therefore, RF-based technologies raise serious concerns about potential interference from existing RF communication systems that can unintentionally undermine the reliability and security of the wearable network, and ultimately the safety of the patient. Second, RF communications can be easily jammed, i.e., intentionally disrupted by artificially generated interference, or eavesdropped by malicious agents using cheap and off-the-shelf equipment, i.e., a simple radio device. Jamming may not even be illegal on ISM spectrum frequencies where devices are allowed to transmit with no need for special permissions. This raises major privacy and security red flags for wearable networks, and a risk for the patient. Third, the RF spectrum is strictly regulated. This clearly constrains the system in terms of flexibility in allocating spectrum resources. Fourth, the medical community is still divided on the risks caused by continuous exposure of human tissues to RF radiation - the World Health Organization classifies RF waves as "possibly carcinogenic to humans" [15]. Therefore, a massive deployment of RF wearable devices on the body may represent a potential risk for the patient. Finally, the dielectric nature of the human body also affects the coupling between on-body RF antennas and the body itself. In particular, the gain and the radiation pattern of the antenna deteriorate because of the contact or proximity with the human body [16], while the resonant frequency and the input impedance of the antenna may shift from their nominal values.

Based on these observations, in this paper, we propose to use ultrasonic waves to interconnect wearable devices, and present U-Wear, the first software-defined networking framework for wearable medical devices based on ultrasonic communications. Ultrasonic waves are acoustic waves with frequency higher than the upper threshold for human hearing (nominally 20 kHz). Acoustic waves have found application in underwater communications [17], in airborne applications [18] such as indoor localization [19, 20] and gesture recognition systems [21], and, massively, in ultrasonic medical imaging [22]. Finally, ultrasonic waves have been proven to be a viable alternative to RF waves for creating wireless networks of implantable medical devices [23, 24, 25, 26].

**Advantages of U-Wear.** U-Wear has several advantages over traditional networking frameworks based on RF communications.

i. U-Wear eliminates any potential conflict with existing RF systems and overcrowded RF environments.

ii. The ultrasonic frequency spectrum is (at least currently) unregulated and enables nodes to flexibly adapt the occupied frequency to specific requirements such as maximum level of tolerable co-channel interference, maximum tolerable channel multipath and Doppler spreading in the channel and minimum data rate needed at the application layer, among others.

iii. As compared to RF waves, ultrasonic waves do not easily penetrate through solid materials and do not propagate far in air; therefore, ultrasonic communication systems are inherently more secure with respect to eavesdropping and jamming attacks that would require close proximity between the attacker and the victim.

iv. The medical experience of the last decades has demonstrated that ultrasounds are fundamentally safe, as long as acoustic power dissipation in tissues is limited to predefined safety levels [27, 23].

v. By equipping wearable devices with ultrasonic transducers, U-Wear can implement ultrasonic power transmission schemes [28] that enable wireless battery charging functionalities.

vi. On-board ultrasonic transducers can be used to enable acoustic localization and tracking, which are known to have better accuracy than RF-based systems because of the low propagation speed of sound in air [29].

vii. U-Wear can easily be interfaced with ultrasonic intra-body networks [24], and can work as a bridge between implantable intra-body sensors and the external world.

viii. The U-Wear software-defined framework runs on general-purpose hardware; thus, it allows commercial devices, such as smartphones, laptops and smart-TVs, to communicate with wearable devices in the near-ultrasonic frequency range, i.e., $17 - 22$ kHz, using commercial-off-the-shelf (COTS) speakers and microphones [30].

ix. Finally, the U-Wear software-defined ultrasonic networking functionalities can be reconfigured to adapt to application requirements, offering more flexibility with respect to RF-based networking systems entirely implemented in hardware, e.g., Bluetooth or WiFi.

U-Wear consists of a set of software-defined cross-layer functionalities designed to network ultrasonic wearable devices that offer real-time reconfigurability at different layers of the protocol stack, i.e., the physical (PHY), data link, network and application layer. Specifically, U-Wear encloses a set of PHY, data link and network functionalities that can flexibly adapt to the application and system requirements to efficiently distribute information among wearable devices. U-Wear also offers real-time reconfigurability at the application layer to provide a flexible platform to develop medical applications. In particular, sensor data processing applications running in the nodes are decomposed into *primitive building blocks* that can be arbitrarily arranged to create new sensing applications that fit user requirements.

As a proof of concept, we design two prototypes that implement the U-Wear framework and operate in the near-ultrasonic frequency range, i.e., $17 - 22$ kHz, using COTS speakers and microphones. Specifically, we operate at 18kHz with a bandwidth of about 2 kHz. Despite the use of COTS audio components not optimized for operations at high frequency, our prototypes (i) can achieve data rates up to 2.76 kbit/s with bit-error-rate (BER) lower than $10^{-5}$ at a transmission power of 20 mW; (ii) enable multiple nodes to share the same medium, with tradeoffs between packet delivery delay and packet drop rate; and (iii) implement reconfigurable data processing to extract medical parameters from sensors with high accuracy. Moreover, U-Wear proposes for the first time the use of a Gaussian minimum-shift keying (GMSK) signaling scheme for the near-ultrasonic frequency range that allows our prototypes to achieve relatively high data rates when compared to previously proposed near-ultrasonic systems; more importantly, it ensures virtually inaudible[1] click-free transmission because of the GMSK phase-continuity as we will discuss in Section 3.1.1.

Note that we do not claim improved performance as compared to RF in terms of traditional performance metrics

[1]The upper threshold for human hearing is nominally 20kHz, however hearing starts degrading significantly above 15 kHz.

(e.g., data rate, bit error rate, energy consumption). Any such comparison would clearly be premature - current performance of RF systems is the result of many years of research and development in multiple fields and of a multi-billion dollar industry. Yet, we believe that, for the reasons discussed above, ultrasonic networking is a viable alternative, and in this paper we present a proof of concept and explore several system tradeoffs.

The paper also reports on the design principles and on the core challenges faced during the design and implementation of U-Wear. In Section 2, we discuss the fundamentals of ultrasonic communications along the body. This study highlights the core differences between ultrasonic propagation and RF propagation in air, including the relatively low speed of sound compared to RF, Doppler spreading, and the multipath effect caused by reflections and scattering. In Section 3, we introduce U-Wear, the first networking framework for wearable medical devices, and discuss its architecture. We highlight design choices at different layers of the protocol stack made to overcome limitations posed by the propagation characteristics of ultrasonic waves in air. For example, two signaling schemes (GMSK and orthogonal frequency-division multiplexing) are selected because of their high spectral efficiency and resilience to multipath. Two different synchronization modes can be alternatively used for channels strongly affected by multipath or by Doppler effect. Upper layer protocols and functionalities are designed to address challenges posed by the long propagation delays of ultrasounds in air that might prevent accurate timing. In Section 4, we present the design and implementation of two prototypes. Hardware components are selected with the objective of striking a reasonable balance between keeping the hardware design simple and inexpensive, and meeting the communication performance requirements of the family of applications we consider. The software architecture has also been carefully designed to enable reuse of existing code and to meet the constraints posed by the resource constrained devices in use. In Section 5, we thoroughly discuss the performance of U-Wear through experimental results. In Section 6, we discuss related work, and finally, in Section 7, we conclude the paper.

## 2. ULTRASONIC COMMUNICATIONS IN AIR

Ultrasounds are mechanical pressure waves that propagate through elastic media at frequencies above the upper limit for human hearing, i.e., 20 kHz.

**Attenuation.** Two mechanisms mainly contribute to acoustic attenuation in air, i.e., spreading loss and absorption loss [31]. The former includes spherical spreading, i.e., the acoustic pressure falls off proportionally to the surface area of a sphere. The latter is mainly related to atmospheric absorption caused by the interaction of the acoustic wave with the gas molecules of the atmosphere, and is frequency-, temperature-, and humidity-dependent.

For a signal at frequency $f$ [Hz] over a transmission distance $d$ [m], the attenuation can be expressed in [dB] as

$$A_{dB} = 20\log_{10}(d) + d\,\alpha(f), \qquad (1)$$

where $\alpha(f)$ [dB/m] is the absorption coefficient, which increases quadratically with the frequency, but also depends on the ambient atmospheric pressure, temperature, and the molar concentration of water vapor, i.e., humidity [32].

**Propagation Speed.** The propagation speed of acoustic waves in air is approximately 343 m/s at $20°C$ and at atmospheric pressure of 101.325 kPa, as compared to $3 \times 10^8$ m/s for RF waves. The speed of sound in air increases with temperature and humidity, going from 331 m/s at a temperature of $0°C$ and 10% relative humidity to 351 m/s at a temperature of $30°C$ and 90% relative humidity.

**Doppler Spreading.** Doppler spreading occurs as a result of Doppler shifts caused by relative motion between source and receiver, and is proportional to their relative velocity. Doppler spreading generates two different effects on signals: a frequency translation, and a continuous spreading of frequencies that generates intersymbol interference (ISI), thus causing degradation in the communication performance. Since the speed of sound is several orders of magnitude lower than the speed of electromagnetic waves, the resulting doppler effect is severe, even at relatively low speeds.

**Reflections and Scattering.** The on-body ultrasonic channel is composed of several interfaces between air and human body, and between air and on-body and near-body objects. Because of this inhomogeneous pattern, the on-body channel can be modeled as an environment with pervasive presence of *reflectors* and *scatterers*. The direction and magnitude of the reflected wave depend on the orientation of the boundary surface and on the acoustic impedance[2] of the different media involved. Scattered reflections occur when an acoustic wave encounters an object that is relatively small with respect to its wavelength. Consequently, the received signal is obtained as the sum of numerous attenuated, possibly distorted, and delayed versions of the transmitted signal.

**Air-coupled Ultrasonic Transducers.** An ultrasonic transducer is a device that converts electrical signals into ultrasonic signals and vice versa. Ultrasonic transducers can be categorized into two main classes based on the physical mechanism that enables the conversion, i.e., *piezoelectric* and *electrostatic* transducers. A piezoelectric transducer produces a mechanical vibration through a thin piezoelectric element under an external voltage variation, and produces a voltage variation under an external mechanical vibration. In *electrostatic* transducers the fundamental mechanism is the vibration of a thin plate under electrostatic forces.

When sound passes across an interface between two materials, it is in part transmitted and in part reflected. To maximize the acoustic energy radiated by the transducer, the acoustic impedance of the radiating surface should match the acoustic impedance of the propagation medium. Today, microelectro-mechanical (MEMS) technology has enabled the fabrication of microscopic piezoelectric and electrostatic transducers, so-called Micromachined Ultrasonic Transducers (MUTs). With MUTs, the acoustic impedance can be controlled to match the external medium by manipulating the device geometry, making them ideally suited for air-coupled applications [33].

When the operating frequency of the ultrasonic communications falls in the near-ultrasonic frequency range, i.e., $17 - 22$ kHz, acoustic waves can be recorded and generated using COTS components, such as microphones and speakers. Even though COTS components are often designed to op-

[2]The acoustic impedance is defined as the product between the density of a medium $\rho$ and the speed of sound in the medium $c$.

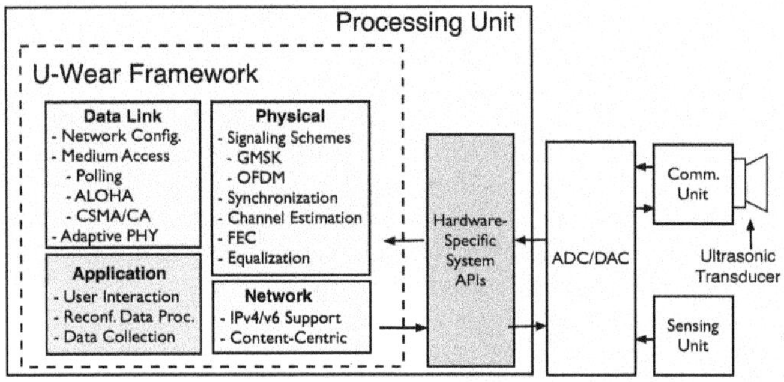


Figure 1: Overview of the U-Wear framework.

erate at lower frequencies, i.e., 0 − 17 kHz, they can still sense and generate, albeit less efficiently, near-ultrasonic frequency waves. Since many commercial devices such as smartphones, tablets and laptops among others, are equipped with audio interfaces, they can support near-ultrasonic communications with no additional hardware [30].

# 3. U-Wear ARCHITECTURE

U-Wear consists of a set of software-defined multi-layer functionalities that can be implemented on general-purpose processing units, e.g., microprocessors, microcontrollers or FPGAs, among others, to enable networked operations between wearable devices equipped with ultrasonic connectivity, i.e., air-coupled ultrasonic transducers, and sensing capabilities, i.e., sensors.

Figure 1 shows an overview of the U-Wear framework. U-Wear runs on a processing unit. It accesses an hardware analog-to-digital converter (ADC) and digital-to-analog converter (DAC) through hardware-specific system APIs. In the transmit (Tx) chain, the DAC collects and digital-to-analog converts U-Wear's outputs, i.e., the waveforms to be transmitted, before passing these to the communication unit. In the receive (Rx) chain, the ADC analog-to-digital converts and passes to U-Wear the received waveforms coming from the communication unit. The communication unit consists of an ultrasonic transducer and an amplification stage, i.e., preamplifier in Rx chain and power amplifier in Tx chain. U-Wear also collects the analog-to-digital converted data coming from the sensing unit. U-Wear consists of (i) PHY layer functionalities, e.g., modulation and synchronization, (ii) data link layer functionalities including forward error control and medium access control (MAC) protocols, (iii) network layer functionalities, e.g., IPv4 and IPv6 support and content-centric networking, and (iv) application layer functionalities, i.e., reconfigurable sensing data processing and user interface.

## 3.1 Physical Layer

U-Wear PHY layer libraries define the signaling scheme, channel estimation, equalization, synchronization and forward error correction (FEC) functionalities.

### *3.1.1 Signaling Schemes*

U-Wear offers two fully-functional signaling schemes, a narrowband scheme based on GMSK modulation, and a wideband scheme based on orthogonal frequency-division multiplexing (OFDM). Moreover, U-Wear includes a set of software-defined primitive blocks, e.g., programmable filters, and Fast Fourier Transform (FFT) modules, among others, that can be used to implement additional signaling schemes.

**Narrowband GMSK.** GMSK is a continuous-phase modulation (CPM) used worldwide in GSM cellular systems [34]. In frequency-shift keying (FSK) and phase-shift keying (PSK), information is encoded in the variations of the carrier frequency, or carrier phase, respectively. Since frequency and phase switches occur instantaneously, FSK and PSK signals do not have continuous phase. Phase discontinuity generates out-of-band power, leading to poor spectral efficiency. Moreover, in near-ultrasonic transmissions based on COTS speakers and microphones the out-of-band power introduces audible noise (clicks), which makes the communication perceptible to humans.

Differently, GMSK signals have phase continuity, and each symbol is represented by a phase variation, from a start value to a final value, over the symbol duration. Thus, the initial phase of each symbol is determined by the cumulative total phase variation of all previous symbols. A Gaussian filter is used to smooth the phase variation and improve the spectral efficiency. The product between the signal bandwidth $B$ and the symbol time $T$ is a measure of the scheme spectral efficiency. Lower $BT$ product leads to higher spectral efficiency, but increases the intersymbol interference (ISI). Based on these characteristics, GMSK is the signaling scheme of choice for U-Wear narrowband communications in the near-ultrasonic frequency range based on COTS speakers and microphones. Thanks to its phase-continuity, GMSK enables click-free transmissions, and therefore is to be preferred over non-continuous-phase modulations such as FSK and PSK.

**Wideband OFDM.** OFDM has been extensively used in underwater acoustic communications [35] because of its robustness against frequency-selective channels with long delay spreads. The idea behind OFDM is to use a large number of closely spaced orthogonal sub-carriers, such that for each sub-carrier the channel is subject to flat fading. In each sub-carrier a conventional modulation is used, e.g., M-PSK or M-Quadrature-Amplitude-Modulation (QAM). OFDM offers high spectral efficiency and robustness against narrowband co-channel interference, intersymbol interference (ISI) and multipath fading. Finally, OFDM can be efficiently implemented using FFT and inverse FFT (IFFT) algorithms. These characteristics make OFDM ideal for ultrasonic communications based on wideband transducers.

### *3.1.2 Synchronization*

Synchronization in U-Wear is achieved in two steps. First, an energy collection identifies any incoming packet, i.e., coarse synchronization. Once a packet is detected, the receiver performs a fine synchronization operation that identifies the exact starting point of the packet. Fine synchronization is achieved by correlating the received signal with a local copy of the preamble, i.e., a sequence that precedes each packet, which outputs a peak corresponding to the first sample of the packet. U-Wear offers two synchronization modes:

**PN-sequence mode.** The pseudo noise (PN)-sequence mode uses PN-sequences as a preamble, i.e., binary sequences with sharp autocorrelation peak and low cross-correlation peaks, that can be deterministically generated. Specifically, we consider maximum length sequences (MLSs), a family of PN-sequences that can be generated in software and hardware through linear feedback shift registers (LFSRs). Because of their desirable correlation characteristics, PN-sequences have been widely used to enable strong resilience to multipath [36]. Therefore, they are well suited for ultrasonic in-air communications, as discussed in Section 2.

**Chirp-based mode.** The chirp-based mode uses a chirp signal as preamble, i.e., a sinusoidal waveform whose frequency varies from an initial frequency $f_0$ to a final frequency $f_1$ within a certain time $T$. Chirp signals have been widely used in radars [37] due to their good autocorrelation and robustness against Doppler effect. In fact, a frequency-shifted chirp still correlates well with the original chirp, although with lower amplitude and time-shifted peak. This characteristic makes chirp synchronization desirable in ultrasonic in-air communications under severe Doppler effect conditions as experienced, for example, under fast movement conditions as in sensors worn by athletes for performance monitoring. The price we pay for the Doppler robustness is higher cross-correlation peaks compared to PN-sequences that result in lower resilience to multipath.

#### 3.1.3 Channel Estimation and Equalization

As discussed in Section 2, ultrasonic communications in air are strongly affected by multipath and Doppler spread, leading to frequency selectivity and ISI that compromise the bit recovery operations at the receiver. U-Wear implements channel estimation and equalization functionalities to estimate the channel impulse response (CIR) and mitigate the distortion produced by the channel.

**Channel Estimation.** U-Wear offers a training-based channel estimation approach that requires the presence of a training sequence known *a-priori* in the transmitted packet. In particular, U-Wear leverages the good autocorrelation property of the synchronization preamble sequence, discussed in Section 3.1.2, to estimate the CIR. By correlating the output of the channel, i.e., the received signal, with the input, i.e., the known preamble sequence, we obtain an estimate of the time-domain CIR [38].

**Zero-forcing Equalization.** U-Wear implements a linear equalization technique, zero-forcing (ZF) [39], that aims to minimize the ISI signal distortion produced by the channel. As the name suggests, a ZF equalizer is a finite-impulse-response (FIR) filter of order $N$ that, for each input symbol, "forces to zero" the ISI components introduced by the $2N$ adjacent symbols. The filter taps are numerically calculated starting from an estimate of the CIR, which also accounts for the ISI effect.

#### 3.1.4 Forward Error Correction

U-Wear offers a forward error correction (FEC) functionality based on Reed-Solomon (RS) codes. RS codes are linear block error-correcting codes widely used in data storage and data transmission systems. An RS encoder takes $k$ information symbols and adds $t$ *parity* symbols to make an $n$ symbol block. Therefore, there are $t = n - k$ overhead symbols. On the other hand, an RS decoder is able to decode the received $n$-symbol block, and can correct up to $\frac{t}{2}$ data symbols that may contain potential errors due to the channel fluctuation or collisions with interfering packets. The RS coding rate can be defined as the ratio between the message length and the block length, i.e., $k/n$.

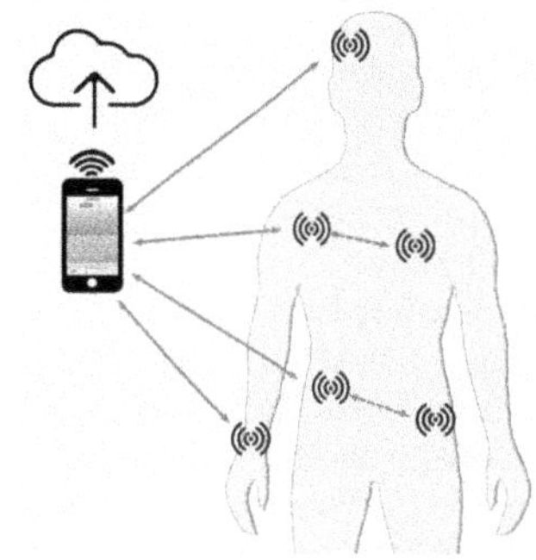

Figure 2: U-Wear scenario with both M/S (continuous line) and P2P (dashed line) network configurations.

## 3.2 Data Link Layer

The U-Wear data link layer provides a set of functionalities that allow multiple nodes to efficiently access the medium under the challenges posed by the ultrasonic in-air channel, e.g., long propagation delays, among others, as discussed in Section 2.

#### 3.2.1 Network Configuration

U-Wear is designed to internetwork wearable devices in master/slave (M/S) or peer-to-peer (P2P) configurations. Both configurations can coexist in the same network in what we refer to as hybrid configurations. Figure 2 shows a hybrid configuration system design.

**Master-Slave Configuration.** In the M/S configuration, one node takes the role of master, i.e., network coordinator, while the remaining nodes operate as slaves. In this scenario, the network control is concentrated on a master node, typically with higher resources available, e.g., processing, memory, power and connectivity. For example, M/S configurations may be used in continuous monitoring systems where a master node, e.g., a smartphone or a laptop, is used to fetch, analyze and display data collected by wearable sensors. Wireless or wired Internet connectivity may allow the master node to connect the wearable network with a medical center where the patient's data can be stored, and analyzed remotely.

**Peer-to-Peer Configuration.** In the P2P configuration, all the network wearable nodes are treated as peers. This scenario suits, among others, applications that require distributed coordination among nodes for closed-feedback-loop monitoring and actuating tasks. For example, this may include a skin patch drug-delivery system where a drug pump can trigger a sensor for measurement, or where a sensor may trigger the drug pump for drug injection after a measurement.

#### 3.2.2 Medium Access Control Protocols

U-Wear offers three fully-functional multiple access protocols, i.e., polling, ALOHA and carrier sense multiple access (CSMA) with collision avoidance (CA), as well as primitive functions to implement custom protocols, e.g., idle listening, random backoff, or checksum-based error control mechanisms.

**Polling Protocol.** Polling is a deterministic access protocol for the M/S network configuration. In a polling scheme, the master node has complete control over channel access, while each slave node is granted access to the medium in a round-robin fashion.

**ALOHA.** ALOHA is a random access protocol where nodes do not check whether the channel is busy or idle before transmitting [40]. Nodes that want to transmit data simply access the channel and transmit the data. When collisions occur, nodes attempt retransmissions after a random time interval, i.e., backoff time.

**Carrier Sense Multiple Access.** CSMA/CA is a multiple access technique based on carrier detection, which allows multiple nodes to share the channel by avoiding simultaneous transmissions, therefore avoiding collisions among transmitted packets [41]. When a node wants to transmit a data packet, it first listens to the channel. If the channel is sensed as idle during a fixed time interval, the node transmits, otherwise it waits for a backoff time before attempting a new transmission.

#### *3.2.3 PHY Layer Adaptation*

U-Wear defines a set of cross-layer functionalities that enable real-time reconfiguration of PHY layer parameters from upper layers of the protocol stack, e.g., data link or network layer. By leveraging the flexibility of the software-defined architecture, upper layer protocols can reconfigure on-the-fly PHY layer parameters such as modulation, signal bandwidth and FEC coding rate, among others. Reconfiguration functionalities allow to develop reactive or proactive control algorithms to adapt the underlying communication link to the channel variations or to upper layer protocol requirements [25, 35].

### 3.3 Network Layer

#### *3.3.1 IPv4 and IPv6 Support*

U-Wear provides interoperability with the Internet by defining an adaptation layer that integrates IPv4 and IPv6 protocol support [42]. The adaptation layer consists of a set of functionalities that interface the traditional IP network layer with the U-Wear data link layer, by offering IP header compression and IP packet fragmentation functions optimized for ultrasonic wearable networks with long propagation delays discussed in Section 2 that potentially prevent accurate timing of network protocols. For example, by leveraging cross-layer header information, the long IPv4 and IPv6 headers can be shortened to reduce network delay and energy consumption when exchanging small information packets.

#### *3.3.2 Content-centric Networking*

U-wear offers content-centric networking (CCN) functionalities that make the network content directly addressable and routable. Each sensor data or actuation command, i.e., each *content object*, is labeled with a name, and can be accessed through this name. Nodes can request content objects by broadcasting a *request message*. When a match is found, i.e., the content is found on a network node, a *response message* containing the requested content is sent back.

### 3.4 Application Layer

#### *3.4.1 Reconfigurable and Modular Data Processing*

U-Wear adopts the idea of decomposing the data processing applications running in the sensor nodes into *primitive blocks*, and offering real-time reconfigurability at the application layer. The sensing application consists of a sequence of basic operations that are executed on the sensed data to extract desired medical parameters. Real-time modular reconfiguration offers three main advantages. First, the network coordinator can wirelessly transmit and install new applications on sensor nodes at runtime, as needed. Based on this, resources are allocated only when the application is requested, thus reducing the processing and memory overhead due to static applications continuously running in background. Second, modular reconfiguration enables programmers to easily create new applications by arranging the primitive building blocks in the desired execution sequence. As a consequence, new medical parameters can be extracted from the raw data coming from a sensor, while maximizing code reusability. Finally, in case of template matching applications, e.g., ECG anomaly detection by matching traces with known templates [43], adding or updating templates becomes very easy with a reconfigurable application layer.

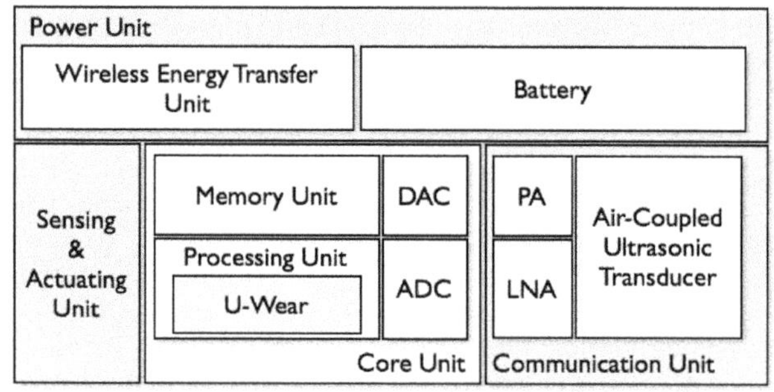


Figure 3: Proposed hardware design of a wuMote.

Defining new applications consists of specifying inputs, a chain of primitive blocks, and outputs. An input is the physical sensor that generates the data, e.g., accelerometer or electrocardiogram (ECG). An output can be either the local memory for storing a measured parameter, or a transmission for sending a measured parameter to another node. We divide the set of primitive blocks into three main classes, *filters*, *data operations*, and *detectors*. Filters enable filtering the raw data to remove offsets, drift of the sensors and any other noise components coming from external sources. Data operations include common signal processing operations performed on sensor data, e.g., correlation with templates, and FFT, among others. Finally, detectors allow measuring the desired parameters by detecting specific elements in the processed signal, e.g., peaks, patterns and time distances, among others.

#### *3.4.2 Data Collection*

The application layer can operate in two different modalities to exchange and collect data, *fetch* and *push* mode. Fetch mode is used when the application layer requires content from the network. Push mode is used when sensed data needs to be pushed to another node, e.g., high glucose level in the blood, or when a node requires another node to accomplish some actuating operation, e.g., inject insulin or trigger a neurostimulation. In case of actuating commands, the push packet may contain further information about the required action, e.g., the quantity of insulin to inject or the pattern of the neurostimulation.

## 4. U-Wear PROTOTYPES

We now present the design of two prototypes that implement the U-Wear framework discussed in Section 3. The first U-Wear prototype is a wearable ultrasonic sensor node

Figure 4: Circuit diagram of the wuMote prototype.

based on a custom hardware platform, which we refer to as *wuMote*. The second prototype is a wearable ultrasonic coordinator based on an iOS commercial smartphone device, which we refer to as *wuMaster*.

## 4.1 wuMote Prototype

### *4.1.1 Hardware Design*

In Fig. 3, we show the hardware architecture of the wuMote. The *core unit* includes a processing unit, e.g., microprocessor or microcontroller, a memory unit, e.g., RAM or flash memory, and digital-to-analog and analog-to-digital converters. The *processing unit* executes the U-Wear functionalities discussed in Section 3. The *communication unit* enables ultrasonic wireless connectivity by embedding power and low noise amplifiers, and air-coupled ultrasonic transducers. The *power unit* mainly consists of a battery to power the wuMote. An optional *wireless energy transfer unit* can be installed to leverage ultrasonic power transmission to wirelessly charge the node battery. Finally, the *sensing and actuating unit* can incorporate several sensors and actuators according to the specific application design.

We implemented a prototype of the architecture in Fig. 3 based on Teensy 3.1 [44]. The wuMote implementation offers near-ultrasonic capability, by using COTS audio speakers and microphones as air-coupled ultrasonic transducers. Figure 4 shows the basic circuit design of the wuMote prototype on a solderless breadboard. The prototype includes a Teensy 3.1, i.e., the core unit, a power amplifier, a microphone with low noise amplifier, and a small audio speaker, i.e., the communication unit. A lithium ion polymer battery, not shown in the figure, is connected to the bus strip of the breadboard to power the electronic components. A smaller, more compact, and more visually appealing prototype board can be designed by developing a customized PCB board that embeds the wuMote hardware components.

**Teensy 3.1.** Teensy 3.1 is a small-footprint, i.e., about $3.5 \times 1.8$ cm, inexpensive development board, based on a 32 bit ARM Cortex-M4. It comes with 64K of RAM, 256K of Flash, 12 bit DAC, dual ADC, and USB connectivity. Teensy 3.1 can be programmed in C and C++ using Teensyduino, a customized version of the Arduino integrated development environment (IDE), and supports many of the code libraries designed for Arduino and others specifically designed for Teensy, e.g., the audio library [45], among others. Teensy 3.1 can be powered via USB, or through external coin batteries connected to the $Vin$ and $GND$ pins.

We selected Teensy 3.1 over other available COTS platforms such as USRP N210, Raspberry Pi, or Arduino Uno, for the following reasons. Compared to USRP N210 and Raspberry Pi, where software operations are executed on top of an operating system running on external or internal microprocessors, Teensy 3.1 and Arduino Uno are designed around a low-power microcontroller that provides low-level control of the hardware peripherals. Microcontroller-based platforms offer higher hardware flexibility and computational efficiency that suit the design requirements of wireless wearable devices. Finally, we selected Teensy 3.1 over Arduino Uno because of the more powerful microcontroller and larger available memory that can support high audio sampling rates compatible with the near-ultrasonic communication range, e.g., 44.1 kHz for acoustic frequencies up to 22 kHz. Teensy 3.1 still supports the Arduino libraries that can significantly ease the prototyping process of the wuMote. Ideally, lower-power and smaller-packaged solutions would be desirable for a more stable product. In a final product, the Cortex M4 currently used in our prototype would be likely replaced by a Cortex M0 microcontroller such as the mm-size low-power Freescale KL03 microcontroller [46]. Even though development boards for Cortex M0 microcontrollers exist, none of these are comparable to the Teensy platform in terms of hardware and software capabilities, and they do not offer Arduino library support. Thus, at this stage we select the less energy efficient hardware platform Teensy 3.1 in exchange for shorter prototyping time.

**Power Amplifier.** The wuMote includes a small and efficient class D audio amplifier [47] able to deliver a maximum of 1 W into 4 ohm impedance speakers, with a voltage supply of 3.3 V DC, and efficiency up to 80%. The amplifier consumes less than 2 mA of current when quiescent and less than 2 $\mu$A in standby mode. In Fig. 4, the right channel of the power amplifier is connected to Teensy via the DAC pin, and to the speakers via the 3.5 mm screw-terminal blocks. The $Vcc$ and $GND$ pins are connected to the bus strip to power the device.

**Microphone.** The wuMote includes a tiny breakout board that embeds an ADMP401 MEMS microphone and a low-noise amplifier (LNA) [48]. The ADMP401 offers a mostly flat bandwidth, i.e., $-3$ dB roll off, between 100 Hz and 15 kHz, omnidirectional sensitivity pattern, and requires a supply voltage between 1.5 V and 3.3 V DC. Although a microphone with larger bandwidth would perform better [49], we selected ADMP401 because of the COTS breakout board package that eases prototyping. Moreover, even though with lower sensitivity, the ADMP401 can still detect higher frequency acoustic waves up to 22kHz. The microphone is connected to one of the analog pins (ADC) available in Teensy 3.1, and is powered by connecting the $Vcc$ and $GND$ pins to the bus strip.

**Audio Speaker.** The output of the wuMote is a small and compact COTS speaker, Dayton Audio CE28A-4R [50], with 4 ohm impedance, 4 W maximum output power supported, and flat frequency response between 100 Hz and 15 kHz. The speaker is connected to the power amplifier using 3.5 mm screw-terminal blocks.

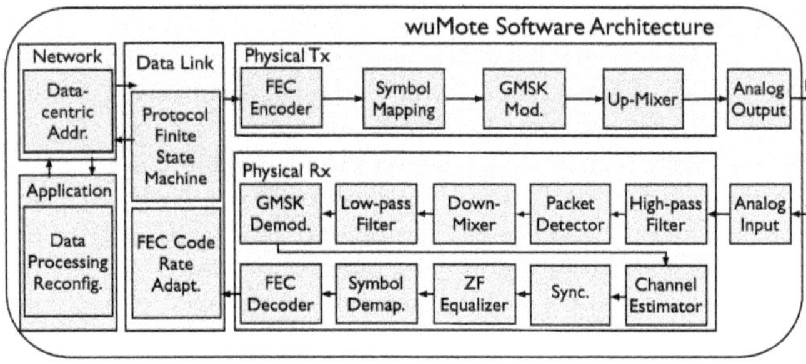


Figure 5: Software architecture of the wuMote prototype.

### *4.1.2 Software Architecture*

We implemented the U-Wear framework in Teensy 3.1 to enable ultrasonic wireless connectivity and networking on the wuMote hardware prototype. In Fig. 5, we show the block diagram of the wuMote software architecture that includes (i) narrowband GMSK transceiver with synchronization, channel estimation, equalization, and FEC functionalities at the PHY layer, (ii) polling and ALOHA multiple access protocol with FEC coding rate reactive adaptation at the data link layer, (iii) content-centric addressing at the network layer, and (iv) data processing reconfiguration with fetch and push support at the application layer.

We implemented the U-Wear functionalities using Teensyduino, an add-on for the Arduino IDE, leveraging many of the code libraries available for the Arduino platform. Since ultrasonic waves are nothing but sound at higher frequencies, we based the PHY layer signal processing on the audio library specifically designed for Teensy 3.1 [45]. The Teensy audio library consists of a set of objects that enable recording, processing, and playback of audio sampled at 44.1 kHz. Objects instantiate specific audio functionalities, e.g., a waveform synthesizer and finite-impulse-response (FIR) filters, while new functionalities can be enabled by creating new objects. A cascade of objects forms a processing chain that performs a set of operations on inputs to produce a desired output. Each object in the chain operates in pipeline on chunks of 128 audio samples, which correspond to 2.9ms of audio. To guarantee audio continuity, each block must execute its processing operation within 2.9 ms.

In the wuMote implementation we built custom-made objects that implement specific signal processing operations. Finally, since some computationally expensive operations exceed the audio library time constraints of 2.9 ms, we implemented these outside the audio library. We refer to these as *off-the-chain* objects.

**Physical Tx.** The first object of the PHY layer Tx chain is the `FEC Encoder`. Here, each data packet coming from the data link layer is coded, as discussed in Section 3.1.4, and overhead symbols are appended to the original packet. We select $n = 255$ symbols and parity symbols $t$ to achieve different coding rates. Because of the computation complexity of RS coding, the `FEC Encoder` is implemented as an *off-the-chain* object. The coded packet is then passed to the `Symbol Mapping` object that inputs the audio stream in the processing chain. Here, the coded packet is serialized, i.e., converted into a stream of bits, differentially encoded, and transformed into a non-return-to-zero (NRZ) signal. The NRZ signal is then GMSK modulated by the `GMSK Modulator` object and up-converted to the carrier frequency by the `Up-Mixer` object. The modulated and up-converted waveforms are passed to the `Audio Output` object, i.e., a system API that interfaces U-Wear with the DAC, digital-to-analog converted and transmitted through the audio speaker.

**Physical Rx.** The received acoustic signal is converted into an electrical signal by the MEMS microphone. The signal is amplified by the LNA, and analog-to-digital converted by the Teensy 3.1 ADC at 44.1 kHz. The `Audio Input` object is a system API that interfaces U-Wear with the embedded Teensy 3.1 ADC, and inputs the audio stream into the PHY layer Rx chain. The received digital signal is first high-pass filtered by the `High-pass Filter` object to eliminate low-frequency noise and interference, i.e., external human voice and ambient noise. The `Packet Detector` processes the input signal to detect incoming packets using an energy-based approach to check wether there is energy at the expected carrier frequency. The incoming packet is then down-converted by the `Down-Mixer`, i.e., converted into a complex in-phase/quadrature baseband signal, and low-pass filtered to eliminate undesired higher-frequency harmonics introduced by the nonlinearity of the down-conversion operation. Channel estimation, synchronization and equalization operations normally follow down-conversion and are applied to the complex baseband signal. However, these operations are computationally expensive, and their execution exceeds the audio library time constraints of 2.9 ms. To overcome this limitation, we first demodulate the complex baseband signal in the `GMSK Demodulator` object to extract the phase variation that carries the coded information bits. Then, we execute off-the-chain the computationally expensive operations. The `Channel Estimator` object estimates the CIR using the packet preamble as training sequence, as discussed in Section 3.1.3, while the `Synchronizer` object attempts to achieve fine synchronization through the PN-based mode discussed in Section 3.1.2. The `ZF Equalizer` object filters the input for ISI recovery, as discussed in Section 3.1.3. The equalized symbols are demapped into a bitstream, collected into a packet structure, and passed to the `FEC Decoder` object. Here, FEC decoding operations attempt to correct potential bit errors, as discussed in Section 3.1.4. Finally, the error-corrected packet is passed to the data link layer.

**Data Link Layer.** The wuMote data link layer is implemented in a Finite State Machine (FSM) block that currently includes two of the MAC protocols discussed in Section 3.2, i.e., polling and ALOHA. The wuMote data link layer also implements a PHY layer adaptation to optimally select the FEC coding rate that minimizes the number of retransmissions. During packet transmission, the MAC FSM collects data from upper layer protocols and creates the data-link-layer packet. The packet is then forwarded to the PHY layer Tx chain, where it is encoded in a digital waveform before being transmitted. At the receiver side, the MAC FSM detects the received packet based on information coming from the `Packet Detector` block and triggers the PHY layer to start processing the received waveform.

**Network Layer.** The wuMote network layer implements the content-centric addressing scheme discussed in Section 3.3. Although IPv4 and IPv6 support is an important aspect of the U-Wear framework, at this prototyping stage we left most IP-related aspects out of the scope of this work. Each *content object* is mapped into a binary mask, where it is represented by the bit position in the mask. In an M/S configuration, a node joining the network is first paired with the master. The master maps the content available in the

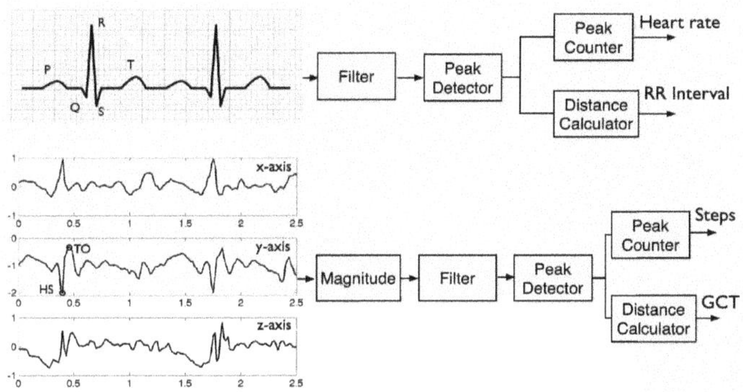


Figure 6: Primitive blocks of heart rate and RR interval monitor (top), and footstep and GCT monitor (bottom).

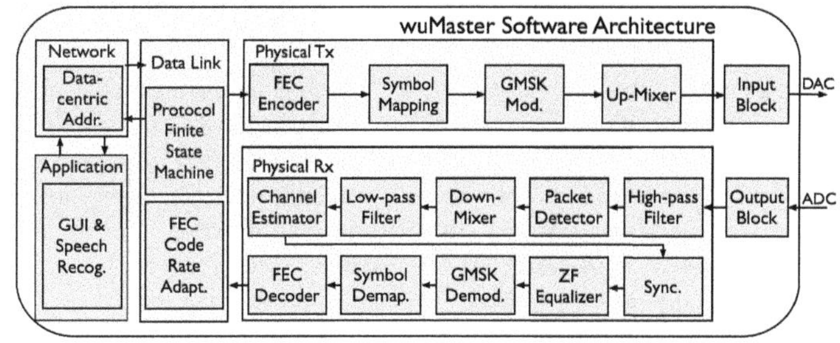


Figure 7: Software architecture of the wuMaster prototype.

new node into the binary mask, and broadcasts the updated mapping to all the nodes in the network. Each node builds a local mask based on the entities that it possesses. To request an entity, the master broadcasts a request message containing a *request mask* with '1' set in the position mapped to the desired content.

**Application Layer.** The wuMote application layer implements the real-time modular reconfiguration functionalities discussed in Section 3.4.

Based on this modular approach, applications can be represented by chains of binary sequences, i.e., keys. Each primitive function is mapped to a binary key. A concatenation of keys represents a concatenation of operations, and therefore represents an application. The application is encapsulated into reconfiguration packets and transmitted over-the-air. The receiving node extracts the binary keys, and feeds these into an FSM where each state represents a primitive block function. By parsing the consecutive function keys, the FSM transitions from state to state, processing inputs and producing outputs. Inputs and outputs of each function are mapped to binary keys as well, and are implemented in a C-struct `output_struct` that contains a pointer to an array, and a binary key variable. The input and output keys allow to parametrically pass data between functions.

As a proof of concept, we developed some applications based on the primitives discussed above.

**Electrocardiogram Processing.** We consider a single-electrode ECG signal. Fig. 6 shows a template signal with five labelled characteristic waveforms, $P$, $Q$, $R$, $S$ and $T$, that correspond to three electrical events during one heart beat, i.e., atrial contraction (P), ventricular contraction (QRS) and ventricular recovery (T). The first application measures the heart rate in beat-per-minute [bpm]. This is done following two different approaches. The first approach, here *R method*, counts the number of peaks, *R waves*, in a 6-second trace and multiplies the result by 10. The second approach, here *RR method*, finds the number of heartbeats per second by inverting the average of the *RR interval* duration, i.e., distance between two consecutive $R$ waveforms in the trace, and multiplies this by 60. This approach has higher complexity with respect to the R-method, but results in higher resolution, i.e., 1 bpm against 10 bpm of the R method. The second application measures average and standard deviations of temporal separation between electrical events in the ECG. For example, the distance between peaks, i.e., $R$ waves, gives the RR interval duration. The mean and standard deviation of the RR interval provide information about potential heart arrhythmias [51]. Figure 6 (top) shows the simplified primitive block sequences of the R method heart rate detector and the RR interval monitor applications.

**Accelerometer Processing.** The accelerometer trace in Fig. 6 shows the frontal acceleration on the x-axis, the vertical acceleration on the y-axis, and the lateral acceleration on the z-axis. We label in the y-axis two main events that occur during a single step, i.e., *heel strikes* (HSs) and *toe-off* (TO), that correspond to the instants at which the foot touches the ground, and the instants at which the foot leaves the ground, respectively. Based on this, the first application calculates the magnitude of the acceleration from the three-axis components, low-pass filters it to remove high frequency noise, and counts the number of peaks in the resulting signal, i.e., the number of HSs. The peaks within a time interval represent the number of footsteps performed by the patient. The second application measures average distances between events in the accelerometer trace. For example, the distance between non-consecutive peaks in the acceleration magnitude gives the *gait cycle time* (GCT), i.e., time between consecutive HSs on the same foot. GCT offers a measure of the motor degradation of patients affected by *Parkinson* disease [6]. Figure 6 (bottom) shows the simplified primitive block sequences of the footstep counter and the GCT monitor applications.

## 4.2 wuMaster Prototype

We implemented the wuMaster prototype on the iOS 8 platform for Apple iPhone smartphones. The prototype consists of an app running on an iPhone that implements the U-Wear multi-layer functionalities. In Fig. 7, we show the software architecture of the wuMaster prototype that includes (i) narrowband GMSK transceiver with synchronization, channel estimation, equalization, and FEC functionalities at the PHY layer, (ii) polling and ALOHA multiple access protocol with FEC coding rate reactive adaptation at the data link layer, (iii) content-centric networking at the network layer, and (iv) a graphic user interface (GUI) and speech recognition functionalities at the application layer that allow users to interact with the wearable network.

The iOS prototype wirelessly communicates with the wuMotes through an ultrasonic narrowband GMSK link, using the phone's embedded microphone and speaker. We developed the software prototype in Objective-C programming language using Xcode 6 integrated development environment (IDE) [52]. We use (i) the *vDSP library* [53] of the iOS Accelerate framework that implements digital signal processing operations (DSP), (ii) *Novocaine* [54], a high performance audio library that enables record/play audio functionalities, and (iii) *wit.ai* framework [55] that offers speech recognition services.

**vDSP Library.** The vDSP library is part of the Accelerate framework available in iOS, and provides several DSP functionalities including vector and matrix arithmetic, Fourier transforms, convolution and correlation operations between real or complex data types. We leverage the vDSP functionalities to perform arithmetic operations and correlations on real and complex vectors in the PHY layer.

**Novocaine.** Novocaine is a high performance audio processing library for iOS. Novocaine hides all the low-level audio implementation details, giving simple block-based callbacks that are called when audio comes in, and when audio needs to go out. Specifically, a Novocaine object, i.e., the Audio Manager, offers `InputBlock` and `OutputBlock` callbacks, inside which we can simply place the DSP code for processing input and output data.

**Wit.ai Framework.** Wit.ai provides natural language processing in the form of multi-platform APIs, which we use to integrate voice command in U-Wear. Wit.ai allows developers to create commands, and to match these commands with intents. A command is what the user would say to trigger an operation while the intent represents the operation itself. Voice commands are sent to the wit.ai server, and the intent with maximum confidence is returned as a response.

**PHY Layer Tx/Rx.** The PHY layer Tx and Rx are implemented in two classes named `PHYLayerTx` and `PHYLayerRx`, respectively. Here, the Novocaine Audio Manager triggers the `InputBlock` and `OutputBlock` callbacks to record and play audio, and the vDSP functions process the input and output data. At the transmitter, the `PHYLayerTx` class gets the data from the data link layer, generates the GMSK waveform, and then passes it to the Audio Manager. The latter transmits the GMSK waveform through the speaker. At the receiver, the operations in `PHYLayerRx` match those implemented in the wuMote PHY layer, discussed in Section 4.1.2. Because of the less stringent memory and processing constraints of the iOS platform, here channel estimation, synchronization and equalization follow the down-conversion, and are applied to the complex baseband signal.

**Data Link and Network Layer.** The wuMaster data link layer implements polling and ALOHA MAC protocols, as well as FEC coding rate adaptation. The MAC functionalities are implemented in a class named `MACLayer`, where a FSM implements the MAC protocol operations. The wuMaster network layer implements the same content-centric addressing scheme seen in the wuMote prototype, with the exception that here the centralized mapping functionalities are also implemented.

**Application Layer.** The wuMaster application layer consists of a GUI and a set of wit.ai commands that allow users to interact with the U-Wear multi-layer functionalities. The GUI's principal element is a three-tab `TabViewController` class. The first tab, shown in Fig. 8 (left), contains a `PHYViewController` object. It inherits from `UIViewController`, i.e., a basic view controller in iOS, and is implemented to test the PHY layer performance. The second tab contains a `MACViewController` object that inherits from `UIViewController` and allows the user to test the MAC Layer functionalities by requesting, receiving and visualizing sensed data coming from the deployed wuMotes. The `MACViewController` embeds a `UICollectionView`, a collection of objects that represent the sensed data. In Fig. 8 (center) we show six objects in the collection, which are associated with the number of footsteps, sleep hours, the heart rate, the breathing rate and the respiratory minute volume, the glucose level in the blood and the diastolic/systolic blood pressure. Finally, a `WITMicButton`, defined in the wit.ai framework, enables voice command processing. The third tab contains an `APPViewController` object that gives access to application layer reconfiguration functionalities discussed in Section 3.4. In the `APPViewController` we group the applications based on the sensing unit that provides the required input data, e.g., accelerometer and ECG. Each `UIButton` represents a group of applications, and it gives access to a `PopViewController` object that shows the available applications in that group. Users can select which application to run on the wuMote. For example, in Fig. 8 (right) we show how users can select to install heart rate or RR interval monitor on wuMotes equipped with ECG.

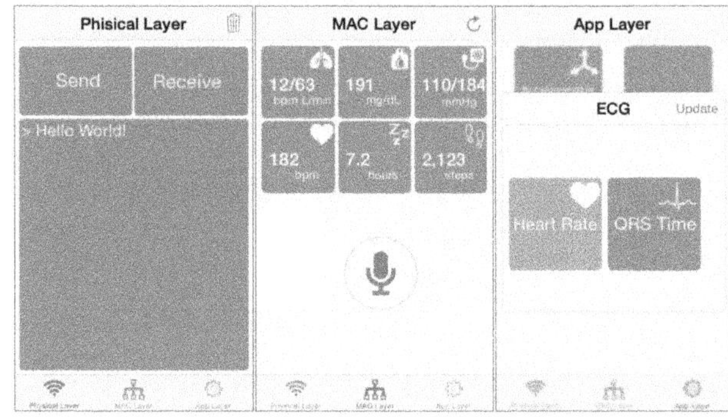


Figure 8: wuMaster GUI for PHY layer (left) and MAC layer (center) and application layer (right).

# 5. PERFORMANCE EVALUATION

In this Section, we demonstrate the feasibility of ultrasonic communications for wearable devices through testbed experiments, and we evaluate the performance of the U-Wear prototypes discussed in Section 4. We start by evaluating the physical layer performance of the prototypes in terms of BER as a function of (i) the signal-to-noise ratio (SNR) measured at the receiver, and of (ii) FEC coding rate. Then, we show how the U-Wear MAC protocols allow network nodes to coexist while enabling users to efficiently access the sensed medical parameters. Finally, we leverage the U-Wear reconfigurable data processing to install and run three applications built using the set of primitive blocks. We evaluate the three applications in terms of processing accuracy, i.e., the gap between the obtained outputs and a ground truth.

## 5.1 PHY Layer Performance

**Experiment Setup.** The experiment setup consists of a wuMote communicating bidirectionally with a wuMaster in two different scenarios, line-of-sight (LOS) and near-line-of-sight (nLOS). In the LOS scenario the two devices are aligned, 50 cm apart, without obstacles in between, so as to minimize reflections and scattering. In the nLOS scenario, we locate the wuMotes along the body of a user, on the chest and on the right leg, as shown in Fig. 9. The wuMaster, i.e., the smartphone, is held in the user's right hand. Under this setup, objects within the propagation area cause reflections and scattering that introduce ISI and degrade the communication performance. In Fig. 10, we show the uplink CIRs of

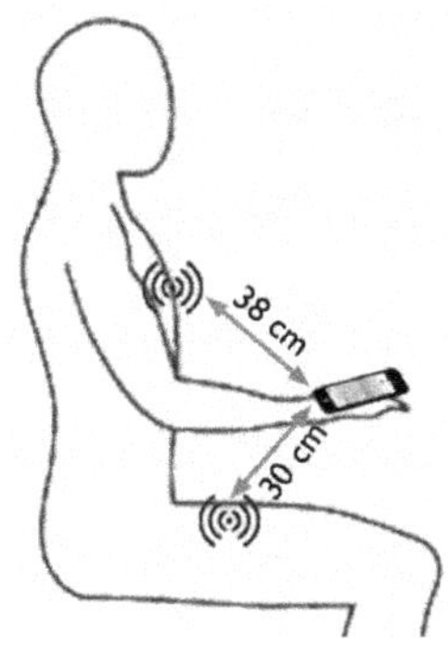


Figure 9: Near-line-of-sight (nLOS) experimental setup.

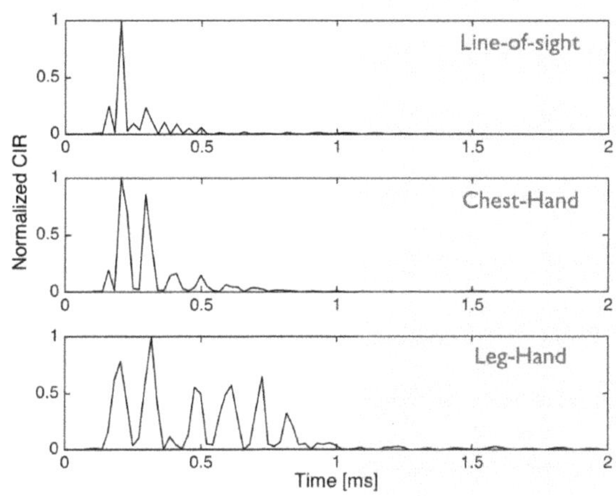


Figure 10: Ultrasonic in-air CIR for LOS (top), chest-hand nLOS (center) and leg-hand nLOS (bottom).

the three scenarios discussed above. We observe that, in the LOS scenario, the CIR contains a single dominant component. In the nLOS scenario, because of the multipath there are multiple components that contribute to ISI distortion at the receiver. In particular, in the chest-hand setup, the CIR clearly presents a second path, most likely because of a reflection from the user's hand, while in the leg-hand setup we can count up to 6 paths, most likely caused by multiple reflections from the user's trunk and hand. The coherence bandwidth in these three scenarios is approximately 21 kHz, 14 kHz and 6 kHz, respectively.

For each BER measurement we transmit up to 600 packets of 32 bytes, i.e., approximately 256 kilobits, containing pseudorandom-generated raw data. The experiment was performed indoor with a temperature of about 21° C and relative humidity around 30%. We configure the physical layer such that each GMSK symbol is represented by 16 samples. The sampling rate is set to 44.1 kHz as required by the audio hardware in use. Based on this, the raw physical layer data rate, obtained as the ratio between sample rate and sample per symbol, is approximately 2.76 kbit/s. We fix the GMSK BT product to 0.7, which represents a good tradeoff between ISI distortion and spectral efficiency. The resulting signal bandwidth is about 2 kHz, which is lower than the coherence bandwidth of the three experimental setups, thus complying with the definition of narrowband transmission scheme. The central frequency is set to 18 kHz, which,

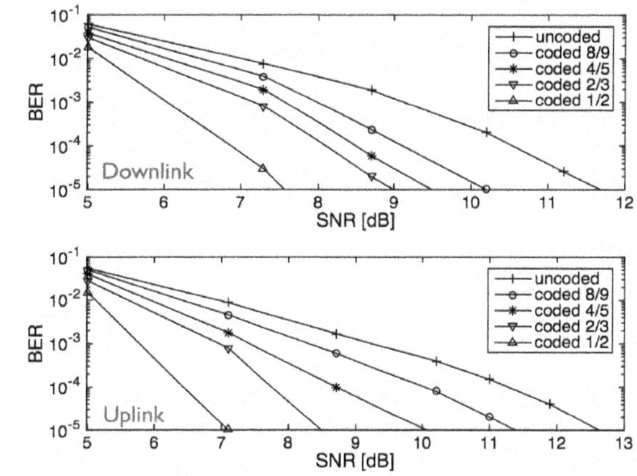


Figure 11: BER of the downlink (top) and uplink (bottom) in LOS as a function of the SNR for different coding rates.

while still in the audible frequency range, represents a good tradeoff between low audibility, fair propagation efficiency, and fair acoustic generation and detection with the COTS microphones and speakers in use. Specifically, we found that 18kHz is the highest frequency, given the spectral response of microphones and speakers in use, for which we could obtain highly reliable communications, i.e., relatively low BER, in the range of distances of interest, i.e., up to $1m$. At the same time, the signal transmission is almost inaudible by the user wearing the device. Finally, a 64-bit PN-sequence is used as preamble for synchronization and channel estimation.

**BER Performance in LOS.** In Fig. 11 (top), we show BER results for the downlink, i.e., from the wuMaster to the wuMote, and we compare the performance of an uncoded transmission scheme to four coded transmission schemes with coding rates in $\{8/9, 4/5, 2/3, 1/2\}$. The information rate for the five transmission schemes ranges from 2.76 kbit/s for the uncoded transmissions to 2.45kbit/s for coding rate 8/9, 2.20 kbit/s for coding rate 4/5, 1.84 kbit/s for coding rate 2/4, and 1.38 kbit/s for coding rate 1/2. Figure 11 (bottom) shows the same comparison for the uplink, i.e., from the wuMote to the wuMaster. The SNR is calculated at the receiver as the ratio between the received average signal power and the average noise power measured after amplification and high-pass filtering. We vary the measured SNR by reducing the signal power driving the transmitter speaker. In the downlink, we do so by reducing the volume of the smartphone speaker, while in the uplink, we reduce the signal full-scale at the input of the amplifier. The maximum power is selected such that the transmitted sound results inaudible to people in proximity of the transmitter.

From Fig. 11, we observe that the BER is a decreasing function of the SNR, and that the FEC scheme mitigates the channel distortion by recovering part of the channel errors. At 5 dB SNR the BER is too high for the FEC to have an impact on the communication performance. Over 5 dB SNR, higher coding rate transmissions have clearly better mitigation performances, thus lower BER.

By measuring the power at the output of the wuMote amplifier, we see how our prototypes achieve 2.76 kbit/s on an uncoded uplink transmission, with a $10^{-5}$ BER, using a transmission power of 20mW, i.e., 13dB SNR at the receiver. We can lower the transmission power by compensating with

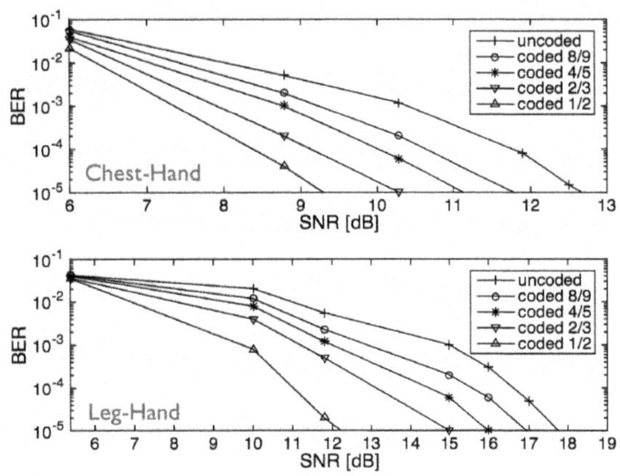


Figure 12: BER of the chest-hand (top) and of the leg-hand uplinks as a function of the SNR for different coding rates.

lower FEC coding rate, thus reducing the information rate. For example, in the current implementation, for a transmission power of 10 mW, i.e., 7 dB SNR, our prototypes achieve 1.38 kbit/s with a $10^{-5}$ BER using a coding rate of 1/2. Finally, by proposing for the first time a GMSK scheme for the near-ultrasonic frequencies our prototypes achieve relatively high data rates when compared to previously proposed near-ultrasonic systems; more importantly, it ensures virtually inaudible click-free transmission because of the GMSK phase-continuity as discussed in Section 3.1.1.

**BER Performance in nLOS.** Figure 11 shows the BER performance of uplink transmissions in nLOS scenario chest-hand setup (top) and leg-hand setup (bottom). We observe that, while the curves follow the same pattern as in the LOS scenario, the corresponding BER levels are higher because of the worse channel conditions. The BER in the chest-hand scenario is slightly higher than the LOS one, i.e., about 1 dB more of SNR is required for the same BER. Differently, in the leg-hand scenario we need an increase of 4dB SNR to achieve the same BER performance of the LOS scenario. In the chest-hand uplink, our prototypes achieve 2.76 kbit/s with a $10^{-5}$ BER using a transmission power of 45 mW, i.e., about 13 dB SNR at the receiver, while the same BER is obtained with 45 mW transmission power, i.e., approximately 9 dB SNR at the receiver, halving the data rate through FEC coding. In the leg-hand uplink, we obtain $10^{-5}$ BER with a transmission power of 250 mW, i.e., about 18 dB SNR at the receiver, for uncoded transmission at 2.76 kbit/s and, and 130 mW of transmission power, i.e., approximately 12 dB SNR at the receiver, for coded transmission at 1.78 kbit/s.

These results show how multipath effect and higher attenuation caused by the user's clothing require higher power transmission as compared to the LOS scenario. Even though ultrasonic signals are further attenuated by solid materials, they can still be used to communicate over short distances through clothing. In general, the transmission power can be reduced by using speakers and microphones with wider flat bandwidth or custom-made optimized ultrasonic transducers. In fact, a significant portion of the transmission power is lost during the electro-acoustic conversion in the COTS speaker and microphone in use, which are not designed to operate efficiently at near-ultrasonic frequencies.

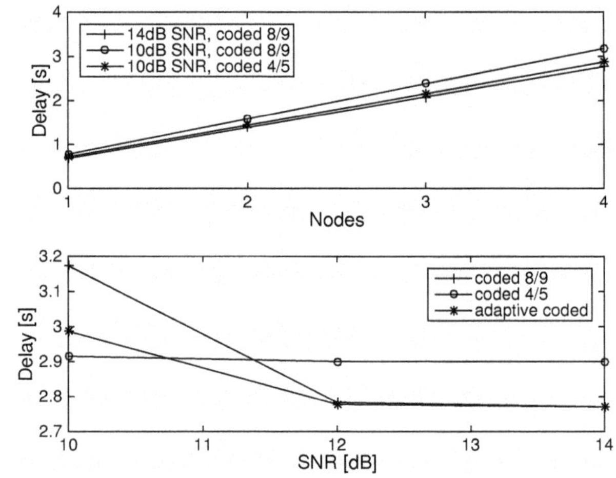


Figure 13: Polling data delivery delay as a function of number of nodes for different level of SNR and coding rates (top), and as a function of the SNR for non-adaptive and adaptive scenarios.

## 5.2 MAC Layer Performance

In this Section, we evaluate the performance of the MAC layer protocols implemented on the prototypes, i.e., polling and ALOHA, in terms of data delivery delay as a function of the number of nodes in the network.

**Experiment Setup.** We set up a M/S configuration where devices lay in nLOS on a 2-dimensional surface, and each wuMote is positioned 40 cm apart from the wuMaster. The experiment consists of collecting data at the wuMaster from up to four wuMotes using polling or ALHOA MAC protocols. We consider six different parameters than can be fetched, and we distribute these among four wuMotes.

**Adaptive Polling.** Using the polling protocol, the wuMaster fetches data from one node a time. The wuMotes are addressed through physical addresses, e.g., node ID. The PHY layer adaptation allows to reactively adapt the FEC coding rate based on the packet drop rate experienced at the wuMaster to minimize the number of consecutive retransmissions. Specifically, every time the wuMaster retransmits a fetching packet, a lower coding rate is used from the set {8/9, 4/5, 2/3, 1/2}. We fix the maximum number of retransmissions for each fetch command to four. We evaluate the protocol in terms of data delivery delay, which we define as the time between the instant when the first fetching packet is transmitted by the wuMaster and the instant when the last data packet is correctly received at the wuMaster. In Fig. 13 (top), we show the polling data delivery delay as a function of the number of nodes in the network for two levels of SNR measured at the wuMaster, i.e., 10 dB and 14 dB, and two coding rates, i.e., 8/9 and 4/5. As expected, since each node in average is granted the same time to transmit, we observe that the delivery delay increases linearly with the number of nodes in the network. Moreover, since retransmissions are only caused by the channel conditions, i.e., there are no collision among different users, the delivery delay decreases by increasing the SNR or the coding rate. Figure 13 (bottom) shows the delivery delay as a function of the SNR for two fixed coding rates, i.e., 8/9 and 4/5, and for the adaptive scenario. We observe that at lower SNR, a coding rate of 8/9 gives delivery delays higher than a coding rate of 4/5 because of the frequent retransmissions

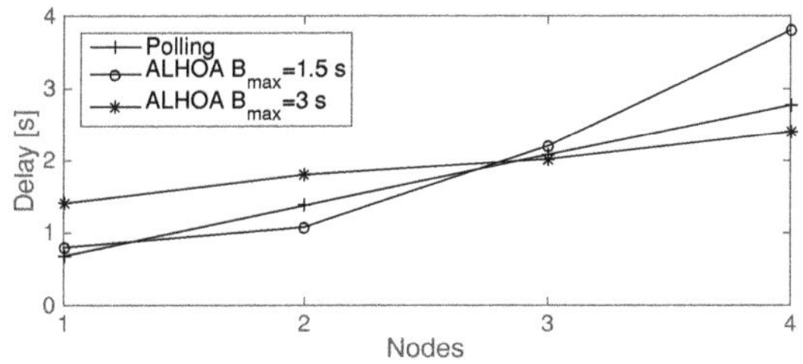

Figure 14: ALOHA data delivery delay as a function of number of nodes for different $B_{max}$, compared to polling.

due to higher BER at the PHY layer. On the contrary, at higher SNR a coding rate of 4/5 introduces more overhead than needed, giving higher delivery delays than coding rate 8/9. As expected, the adaptive scenario results in delivery delays in between the two fixed coding rate scenarios.

**ALOHA.** With ALOHA, we use the content-centric addressing scheme discussed in Section 4.1.2. Hence, the wuMaster broadcasts a request message to fetch data from multiple wuMotes. The wuMotes transmit the requested data, if available, by accessing the channel randomly. Finally, we select the backoff time between transmissions from 0 to a maximum backoff $B_{max}$, and we vary it during our experiments, while fixing the SNR to 14 dB and FEC coding rate to 8/9. Figure 14 shows the data delivery delay as a function of the number of nodes in the network for two different values of $B_{max}$, i.e., 1.5 s and 3 s. We compare the results with the data delivery delay experienced by the polling protocol for 14 dB SNR and 8/9 coding rate. When the number of nodes in the network is lower than three, we observe that $B_{max}$ = 1.5 s gives lower delay than $B_{max}$ = 3 s. Here, a higher $B_{max}$ increases the probability of selecting a higher backoff time, leading to channel underutilization. On the other hand, for number of nodes higher and equal to three, $B_{max}$ = 1.5 s gives high probability of collisions, thus higher delay due to retransmissions.

## 5.3 Data Processing Performance

To test the effectiveness of the application layer reconfiguration functionalities, we evaluate the data processing accuracy in terms of displacement between the obtained outputs, i.e., what the application reads on a given sensor trace, and the expected ones, i.e., what the application should read on that given sensor trace. We consider three applications, two running on ECG-equipped sensor nodes, i.e., heart rate monitor, ECG *RR interval* monitor, and one running on accelerometer-equipped sensor nodes, i.e., footstep counter.

**ECG Processing.** To show a fair comparison, we feed the application-layer processing with reference raw sensor data that are externally recorded and then loaded in the wuMote memory. For the ECG-based applications, we use traces from the MIT-BIH Normal Sinus Rhythm Database [56], which collects ECG recording from patients that were found to have no significant arrhythmias. The MIT-BIH database also specifies heart rate and RR interval of the traces. The traces are sampled at 128 Hz. We extract, and load to the wuMote, 10 one-minute long traces from the MIT-BIH recording. In Table 1, we show the heart rate estimation of the wuMote using the *R method*, second column, and *RR method*, third column, discussed in Section 4.1.2, and we compare these with the heart rate reference provided by the MIT-BIH database, fourth column. The first column shows the database trace ID. We observe that both *R method* and *RR method* give a good estimate of the reference heart rate, offering an average accuracy of 96.1% and 98.7%, respectively.

In Table 2, we show the *RR interval* mean $\mu$ and standard deviation $\sigma$ estimated by the wuMote, second and fourth columns, and we compare these with the *RR interval* reference statistics provided by the MIT-BIH database, third and fifth columns. We observe that the wuMote accurately estimates the *RR interval* mean, i.e., around 99.6% of accuracy. For the standard deviation $\sigma$ we obtain lower accuracy, i.e., 83.6%, for two reasons, (i) the relatively low sampling rate gives a sensibility of 8 ms, which can affect the measurement of small quantities such as the standard deviation, (ii) failures in the peak finding algorithm also affect the measurement. Higher sampling rate and outlier detection techniques could be used to further enhance the standard deviation measurement.

Table 1:
Results for heart-rate (HR) with R and RR method.

| Trace | 6s R [bpm] | 6s RR [bpm] | Ref HR [bpm] |
|---|---|---|---|
| 16265 | 100 | 97 | 96 |
| 16272 | 60 | 62 | 62 |
| 16273 | 100 | 97 | 95 |
| 16420 | 90 | 94 | 95 |
| 16483 | 100 | 97 | 97 |
| 16539 | 80 | 80 | 79 |
| 16773 | 70 | 74 | 75 |
| 16786 | 70 | 72 | 71 |
| 16795 | 70 | 67 | 65 |
| 17052 | 70 | 68 | 69 |

Table 2:
Results for RR interval mean $\mu$ and std. deviation $\sigma$.

| Trace | $\mu$ [s] | $\sigma$ [s] | Ref. $\mu$ [s] | Ref. $\sigma$ [s] |
|---|---|---|---|---|
| 16265 | 0.62 | 0.62 | 0.016 | 0.019 |
| 16272 | 0.96 | 0.96 | 0.109 | 0.115 |
| 16273 | 0.64 | 0.64 | 0.023 | 0.049 |
| 16420 | 0.63 | 0.63 | 0.015 | 0.018 |
| 16483 | 0.62 | 0.62 | 0.015 | 0.012 |
| 16539 | 0.74 | 0.75 | 0.062 | 0.054 |
| 16773 | 0.79 | 0.79 | 0.056 | 0.058 |
| 16786 | 0.85 | 0.84 | 0.046 | 0.036 |
| 16795 | 0.91 | 0.92 | 0.070 | 0.069 |
| 17052 | 0.85 | 0.85 | 0.047 | 0.047 |

**Accelerometer Processing.** We record ten 3-dimensional accelerometer traces with a sample rate of 60 Hz using Sensor Log [57], an iOS app that allows to read sensor data from the device, and export them in character-separated values (CSV) format. Sensor Log also provides information about the number of footsteps counted by the iOS device. We use this as a reference to evaluate the accuracy of the footstep counter application in the wuMote. In Table 3, we show the footstep count estimated by the wuMote, second column, and we compare this with the footstep estimate of the iOS device, third column, and real footstep number counted by the user while performing the steps, fourth column. The first column shows the trace name, where we list 3 walking traces, 3 running traces and 3 stair climbing traces, i.e., downward, upwards and down/upwards. We observe that, in average, the wuMote counts footsteps with the same accuracy of the iOS device, i.e., approximately 94% with respect to the number of steps counted by the user.

Table 3:
Evaluation results for footstep counter.

| Trace | wuMote | iOS | Real |
|---|---|---|---|
| walk_0 | 44 | 49 | 46 |
| walk_1 | 39 | 39 | 40 |
| walk_2 | 48 | 48 | 50 |
| run_0 | 32 | 33 | 34 |
| run_1 | 37 | 42 | 40 |
| run_2 | 32 | 33 | 32 |
| climb_up | 19 | 19 | 18 |
| climb_down | 17 | 18 | 18 |
| climb_do_up | 34 | 34 | 39 |

# 6. RELATED WORK

The idea of using ultrasonic waves for in-air communications has been proposed in the past, and several studies have successfully proven the viability of using ultrasonic waves as an alternative to RF waves for short-range and medium-range in-air communications. In [58], the authors discuss the possibility of using sounds for in-air communication purposes, and explore several different physical-layer approaches that can be used in a ubiquitous computing environment. In [59, 60], the authors studied the performance of ultrasonic in-air transmissions over directional short-range links of a few meters using custom-made transducers. The proposed solutions achieve data rates in the order of 100 kbit/s, on relatively large bandwidths, i.e., 80 kHz and 56 kHz, using QPSK and on-off-keying (OOK). In [61], medium-range communications, i.e., up to 20m, are achieved with data rates up to 100 bit/s, on a 4 kHz FSK-modulated bandwidth. While U-Wear is based on the same idea of using ultrasonic waves for in-air communications, the framework goes well beyond a simple point-to-point transmission scheme, such as those presented in the above works. In this paper, to the best of our knowledge, we propose for the first time the use of ultrasonic waves for interconnecting wearable devices in a network, and we present the first networking framework based on ultrasonic communications that offers multi-layer functionalities spanning the PHY, data link, network and application layer.

In the last few years, researchers have proposed to use acoustic waves in the audible and near-ultrasonic frequency ranges to enable in-air communications between devices equipped with COTS microphones and speakers. In [62, 63], the authors use audible sound around 8 kHz for near-field-communications between smartphones, using OFDM and FSK schemes, and achieving data rates in the order of a few kbit/s. In [64, 30], the authors propose in-air communication systems that operate in the near-ultrasonic frequency range, and achieve low data rates, i.e., up to 20 bit/s, over medium-range directional links, i.e., up to 20 m. While U-Wear can certainly operate in the near-ultrasonic frequency range to enable communications with commercial devices such as smartphones and laptops, among others, it has been primarily designed to provide connectivity between wearable devices at higher ultrasonic frequency ranges. In this paper, we implement near-ultrasonic communications to demonstrate interoperability of the wuMote with commercial smartphones, and also because of the availability of inexpensive COTS audio speakers and microphones that can be used as a proxy for air-coupled ultrasonic transducers. With this idea in mind, we proposed for the first time the use of a narrowband GMSK modulation for the near-ultrasonic frequency range, which enables relatively high data rates when compared to other existing works, i.e., up to 2.76 kbit/s on a 2 kHz bandwidth around 18 kHz, and ensures virtually inaudible click-free transmission because of the phase-continuity of the GMSK waveform. Higher data rates can be achieved by using microphones and speakers with wider bandwidth, or by developing custom-made air-coupled transducers. For example, by using OFDM signaling schemes with high-order modulations, e.g., 16-PSK or 32-QAM, on a 24 kHz bandwidth centered around 100 kHz, we could possibly achieve data rates in the order of hundreds of kbit/s.

Finally, other multilayer solutions have been specifically designed to network wearable devices. ANT+ [65], for example, is a wireless sensor network protocol operating in the 2.4 GHz ISM band that offers low-power and easy-to-use functionalities to network sensing devices. Although ANT+ and U-Wear share the same goals, i.e., networking wearable devices, the two solutions have significant differences. First, U-Wear is not just a networking solution as ANT+. U-Wear is a networking framework that can be used to build several networking solutions through software-defined functionalities. Secondly, U-Wear operates using ultrasonic waves, while ANT+ uses RF waves and offers a predefined PHY layer upon RF carriers in the 2.4 GHz ISM. Finally, ANT+ requires hardware add-ons to connect with commercial devices such as tablets or smartphones.

# 7. CONCLUSIONS

In this paper, we presented U-Wear, the first networking framework for wearable medical devices based on ultrasonic communications. U-Wear consists of a set of cross-layer functionalities to network ultrasonic wearable devices that offer real-time reconfigurability at the physical, data link, network and application layer. We designed two prototypes that implement the U-Wear framework and operate in the near-ultrasonic frequency range, using commercial-off-the-shelf (COTS) speakers and microphones. Despite the limited bandwidth, i.e., about 2 kHz, and the COTS audio hardware components not optimized for operating at high frequency, we showed how our prototypes (i) can operate at data rate up to 2.76 kbit/s with bit-error-rate (BER) lower than $10^{-5}$, using a transmission power of 20 mW; (ii) enable multiple nodes to share the same medium offering tradeoffs between packet delivery delay and packet drop rate; (iii) can implement reconfigurable data processing applications that can extract medical parameter from sensor traces with high accuracy. U-Wear can offer higher performance through specialized hardware components. Future smart devices, e.g., smartphones and laptops, with wider-bandwidth speakers and microphones (e.g., flat over a bandwidth of 100kHz) will enable higher data rates and lower energy consumption. Through custom-made ultrasonic air-coupled transducers that operate at higher frequency ranges and larger bandwidth, wuMotes may be able to achieve data rates in the order of hundreds of kbit/s with lower energy consumptions.

## 8. REFERENCES


[1] G-Z Yang. *Body Sensor Networks.* Springer-Verlag New York, Inc., Secaucus, NJ, USA, 2006.

[2] J.J. Oresko, Zhanpeng Jin, Jun Cheng, Shimeng Huang, Yuwen Sun, H. Duschl, and A.C. Cheng. A wearable smartphone-based platform for real-time cardiovascular disease detection via electrocardiogram processing. *IEEE Transactions on Information Technology in Biomedicine*, 14(3):734–740, May 2010.

[3] N. Roxhed, B. Samel, L. Nordquist, P. Griss, and G. Stemme. Painless drug delivery through microneedle-based transdermal patches featuring active infusion. *IEEE Transactions on Biomedical Engineering*, 55(3):1063–1071, March 2008.

[4] Heller A. Drug-delivering integrated therapeutic systems. In *Proc. of the Intl. Workshop on Wearable and Implantable Body Sensor Networks (BSN)*, London, UK, 2005.

[5] S. Patel, R. Hughes, T. Hester, J. Stein, M. Akay, J. Dy, and P. Bonato. Tracking motor recovery in stroke survivors undergoing rehabilitation using wearable technology. In *Prof of the IEEE Intl. Conf. of Engineering in Medicine and Biology Society (EMBC)*, Buenos Aires, Argentina, Aug 2010.

[6] A. Salarian, H. Russmann, F.J.G. Vingerhoets, C. Dehollaini, Y. Blanc, P.R. Burkhard, and K. Aminian. Gait assessment in parkinson's disease: toward an ambulatory system for long-term monitoring. *IEEE Transactions on Biomedical Engineering*, 51(8):1434–1443, Aug 2004.

[7] Maurice M. Ohayon and Colin M. Shapiro. Sleep disturbances and psychiatric disorders associated with posttraumatic stress disorder in the general population. *Comprehensive Psychiatry*, 41(6):469 – 478, 2000.

[8] Fitbit fitness trackers, `https://www.fitbit.com/`.

[9] Google Glass, `https://www.google.com/glass/`.

[10] Apple iWatch, `https://www.apple.com/watch/`.

[11] Hexoskin, wearable body metrics, `http://www.hexoskin.com/`.

[12] APDM, movement monitoring solutions, `http://www.apdm.com/`.

[13] Zephyr, measure life...anywhere! , `http://zephyranywhere.com/`.

[14] U.S. Food Drug Administration (FDA), Wireless Medical Devices, `http://goo.gl/8k3qZJ`.

[15] WHO/International Agency for Research on Cancer. IARC classifies radio frequency electromagnetic fields as possibly carcinogenic to humans. May 2011.

[16] K.Y. Yazdandoost and R. Kohno. UWB antenna for wireless body area network. In *Asia-Pacific Microwave Conference (APMC)*, Yokohama, Japan, 2006.

[17] T. Melodia, H. Kulhandjian, L. Kuo, and E. Demirors. Advances in Underwater Acoustic Networking. In S. Basagni, M. Conti, S. Giordano, and I. Stojmenovic, editors, *Mobile Ad Hoc Networking: Cutting Edge Directions*, pages 804–852. John Wiley and Sons, Inc., Hoboken, NJ, second edition edition, 2013.

[18] T. Dahl, J. L. Ealo, Hans J. Bang, Sverre Holm, and Pierre Khuri-Yakub. Applications of airborne ultrasound in human-computer interaction. *Ultrasonics*, 54(7):1912 – 1921, 2014.

[19] P. Lazik and A. Rowe. Indoor pseudo-ranging of mobile devices using ultrasonic chirps. In *Proc. of the ACM Conf. on Embedded Network Sensor Systems (SENSYS)*, 2012.

[20] G. Oberholzer, P. Sommer, and R. Wattenhofer. Spiderbat: Augmenting wireless sensor networks with distance and angle information. In *Proc. of Intl. Conf. on Information Processing in Sensor Networks (IPSN)*, Apr. 2011.

[21] R.J. Przybyla, Hao-Yen Tang, S.E. Shelton, D.A Horsley, and B.E. Boser. 3D ultrasonic gesture recognition. In *Proc of IEEE Intl. Solid-State Circuits Conference Digest of Technical Papers (ISSCC)*, Feb. 2014.

[22] F.L. Thurstone, H.E. Melton. Biomedical Ultrasonics. *IEEE Transaction on Industrial Electronics and Control Instrumentation*, 17(2), April 1970.

[23] G.E. Santagati, T. Melodia, L. Galluccio, and S. Palazzo. Ultrasonic networking for e-health applications. *IEEE Wireless Communications*, 20(4):74–81, 2013.

[24] G.E. Santagati, T. Melodia, L. Galluccio, and S. Palazzo. Medium access control and rate adaptation for ultrasonic intra-body sensor networks. *IEEE/ACM Transactions on Networking*, 2015.

[25] G. E. Santagati and T. Melodia. Sonar Inside Your Body: Prototyping Ultrasonic Intra-body Sensor Networks. In *Proc. of IEEE Conf. on Computer Communications (INFOCOM)*, Toronto, Canada, April 2014.

[26] Z. Guan, G. E. Santagati, and T. Melodia. Ultrasonic Intra-body Networking: Interference Modeling, Stochastic Channel Access and Rate Control. In *Proc. of IEEE Conference on Computer Communications (INFOCOM)*, Hong Kong S.A.R., PRC, April 2015.

[27] K. Kirk Shung. *Diagnostic ultrasound: imaging and blood flow measurements.* CRC Press, 2006.

[28] Yong Zhu, S. O R Moheimani, and M.R. Yuce. A 2-DOF MEMS ultrasonic energy harvester. *IEEE Sensors Journal*, 11(1):155–161, Jan 2011.

[29] M. Scherhaufl, R. Pfeil, M. Pichler, and A. Berger. A novel ultrasonic indoor localization system with simultaneous estimation of position and velocity. In *IEEE Topical Conference on Wireless Sensors and Sensor Networks (WiSNet)*, Santa Clara, CA, USA, Jan 2012.

[30] H. Lee, T. H. Kim, J. W. Choi, and S. Choi. Chirp Signal-Based Aerial Acoustic Communication for Smart Devices. In *Proc. of IEEE Conf. on Computer Communications (INFOCOM)*, Hong Kong S.A.R., PRC, April 2015.

[31] L. B. Evans, H. E. Bass, and L. C. Sutherland. Atmospheric absorption of sound: Theoretical predictions. *The Journal of the Acoustical Society of America*, 51(5B):1565–1575, 1972.

[32] Iso. ISO 9613-1, Acoustics - Attenuation of sound during propagation outdoors - Part 1: Calculation of the absorption of sound by the atmosphere, Dec 2010.

[33] M. Pappalardo, G. Caliano, A. S. Savoia, and A. Caronti. Micromachined ultrasonic transducers. In *Piezoelectric and Acoustic Materials for Transducer Applications*, pages 453–478. Springer US, 2008.

[34] K. Murota and K. Hirade. GMSK modulation for digital mobile radio telephony. *IEEE Transactions on Communications*, 29(7):1044–1050, Jul 1981.

[35] E. Demirors, G. Sklivanitis, G. E. Santagati, T. Melodia, and S. N. Batalama. Design of a software-defined underwater acoustic modem with real-time physical layer adaptation capabilities. In *Proc. of ACM Intl. Conf. on Underwater Networks & Systems (WUWNet)*, Rome, Italy, November 2014.

[36] F. Tufvesson, O. Edfors, and M. Faulkner. Time and frequency synchronization for OFDM using PN-sequence preambles. In *Proc. of the IEEE Vehicular Technology Conference*, Houston, TX, USA, 1999.

[37] M. Skolnik. *Radar Handbook, Third Edition.* Electronics electrical engineering. McGraw-Hill Education, 2008.

[38] Robert J. Polgember and E.M. Mitchell. Impulse response determination by cross correlation. *IEEE Transactions on Aerospace and Electronic Systems*, AES-6(1):91–97, Jan 1970.

[39] J. Proakis and M. Salehi. *Digital Communications.* McGraw-Hill higher education. McGraw-Hill Education, 2007.

[40] Norman Abramson. The ALOHA system: Another alternative for computer communications. In *Proc. of the Fall Joint Computer Conference (FJCC)*, AFIPS, Houston, Texas, Nov. 1970.

[41] L. Kleinrock and F.A. Tobagi. Packet switching in radio channels: Part i–carrier sense multiple-access modes and their throughput-delay characteristics. *IEEE Transactions on Communications*, 23(12):1400–1416, Dec. 1975.

[42] Y. Sun and T. Melodia. The Internet Underwater: An IP-compatible Protocol Stack for Commercial Undersea Modems. In *Proc. of ACM Intl. Conf. on UnderWater Networks and Systems (WUWNet)*, Kaohsiung, Taiwan, November 2013.

[43] Vessela Krasteva and Irena Jekova. QRS template matching for recognition of ventricular ectopic beats. *Annals of Biomedical Engineering*, 35(12):2065–2076, 2007.

[44] Teensy USB Development Board, `https://www.pjrc.com/teensy/`.

[45] Teensy Audio Library, `https://www.pjrc.com/teensy/td_libs_Audio.html`.

[46] Freescale, Kinetis KL03, `http://goo.gl/ckPkl0`.

[47] Stereo 2.8W Class D Audio Amplifier - TS2012, `http://www.adafruit.com/product/1712`.

[48] MEMS Microphone Breakout - INMP401 (ADMP401), `https://www.sparkfun.com/products/9868`.

[49] ST MEMS microphones, `http://goo.gl/9Eojhq`.

[50] Dayton Audio CE28A-4R , `http://goo.gl/u5VMRR`.

[51] C.L. Chang, K.P. Lin, T.H. Tao, T. Kao, and W.H. Chang. Validation of automated arrhythmia detection for holter ECG. In *Proc. of the IEEE Intl. Conf. of the Engineering in Medicine and Biology Society (EMBC)*, Oct 1998.

[52] Xcode 6, the complete toolset for building great apps, `https://developer.apple.com/xcode/`.

[53] vDSP Library, iOS Accelerate Framework, `http://goo.gl/6gvpFT`.

[54] Novocaine, An analgesic for high-performance audio on iOS and OSX, `https://github.com/alexbw/novocaine`.

[55] wit.ai, Natural Language for the Internet of Things, `https://wit.ai`.

[56] MIT-BIH Normal Sinus Rhythm Database, `http://physionet.org/physiobank/database/nsrdb/`.

[57] SensorLog by Bernd Thomas, `https://itunes.apple.com/us/app/sensorlog/id388014573`.

[58] C.V. Lopes and P.M.Q. Aguiar. Acoustic modems for ubiquitous computing. *IEEE Pervasive Computing, Mobile and Ubiquitous Systems*, 2(3):62–71, July 2003.

[59] Chuan Li, D.A. Hutchins, and R.J. Green. Short-range ultrasonic communications in air using quadrature modulation. *IEEE Transactions on Ultrasonics, Ferroelectrics, and Frequency Control*, 56(10):2060–2072, October 2009.

[60] W. Jiang and W. M.D. Wright. Ultrasonic wireless communication in air using OFDM-OOK modulation. In *Proc. of IEEE Intl. Ultrasonics Symposium (IUS)*, Chicago, IL, USA, Sept 2014.

[61] S. Holm, O.B. Hovind, S. Rostad, and R. Holm. Indoors data communications using airborne ultrasound. In *Proc of the IEEE Intl. Conf. of Acoustics, Speech, and Signal Processing (ICASSP)*, Philadelphia, PA, USA, March 2005.

[62] R. Nandakumar, K. K. Chintalapudi, V. Padmanabhan, and R. Venkatesan. Dhwani: Secure peer-to-peer acoustic NFC. In *Proc. of the ACM Conf. on SIGCOMM*, Hong Kong, China, 2013.

[63] B. Zhang, Q. Zhan, S. Chen, M. Li, K. Ren, C. Wang, and D. Ma. Priwhisper: Enabling keyless secure acoustic communication for smartphones. *IEEE Internet of Things Journal*, 1(1):33–45, Feb 2014.

[64] M. Hanspach and M. Goetz. On covert acoustical mesh networks in air. *Journal of Communications*, 8(11):758–767, 2013.

[65] ANT+ , `http://www.thisisant.com`.

# LookUp: Enabling Pedestrian Safety Services via Shoe Sensing

Shubham Jain†, Carlo Borgiattino§, Yanzhi Ren♯,
Marco Gruteser†, Yingying Chen♯, Carla-Fabiana Chiasserini§
†WINLAB, Rutgers University, North Brunswick, NJ, USA
†{shubhamj, gruteser}@winlab.rutgers.edu
§Politecnico di Torino, Torino, Italy
§{carlo.borgiattino, chiasserini}@polito.it
♯Stevens Institute of Technology, Hoboken, NJ, USA
♯{yren2, yingying.chen}@stevens.edu

## ABSTRACT

Motivated by safety challenges resulting from distracted pedestrians, this paper presents a sensing technology for fine-grained location classification in an urban environment. It seeks to detect the transitions from sidewalk locations to in-street locations, to enable applications such as alerting texting pedestrians when they step into the street. In this work, we use shoe-mounted inertial sensors for location classification based on surface gradient profile and step patterns. This approach is different from existing shoe sensing solutions that focus on dead reckoning and inertial navigation. The shoe sensors relay inertial sensor measurements to a smartphone, which extracts the step pattern and the inclination of the ground a pedestrian is walking on. This allows detecting transitions such as stepping over a curb or walking down sidewalk ramps that lead into the street. We carried out walking trials in metropolitan environments in United States (Manhattan) and Europe (Turin). The results from these experiments show that we can accurately determine transitions between sidewalk and street locations to identify pedestrian risk.

## Categories and Subject Descriptors

H.4 [**Information Systems Applications**]: Miscellaneous

## General Terms

Design, Experimentation, Algorithms, Performance

## Keywords

Pedestrian Safety; Smartphone; Localization; Inertial Sensing; GPS; Accelerometer; Gyroscope

## 1. INTRODUCTION

Evidence is mounting that technology distractions have a negative impact on pedestrian traffic safety. In the last decade, from 2003 to 2012, American streets have witnessed more than 676,000 pedestrians injured in traffic accidents, 47,025 of them fatally [1]. Pedestrians account for nearly 14% of all traffic fatalities in the US [2] and about 22% worldwide [3]. While motorist fatalities have declined, pedestrian fatalities have been rising at an annual rate of 4.9% from 2009-2012 [3, 4] (the 2013 estimates look more positive, fortunately). Econometric analysis has shown that at high densities of cell phone use, the life-taking effect due to distractions outweighs the life-saving effect of improved emergency medical response times [5]. According to a study, 26% of pedestrians text or email, 51% talk on the phone and 36% listen to music while crossing the street [6]. While the evidence is not yet fully conclusive, it is significant enough that municipalities have started stenciling "LOOK" signs at crosswalks in an attempt to alert pedestrians who text while crossing the street (see Figure 1).

**Figure 1: Signage at crosswalks in Delaware and New York City [7, 8].**

We believe that a technology solution would be more effective for the problem at hand. Smartphones and future wearable devices, which are part of the problem, can also be part of the solution by suppressing distractions or alerting pedestrians to dangers. Smartphones could also be integrated with the emerging wireless road traffic management and safety infrastructure (e.g., DSRC [9] [10]) to provide information about pedestrian behaviors and positions to vehicles and vice versa. If they could sense potentially dangerous situations, they could generate much more targeted and noticeable alerts. Achieving targeted notifications and accurate suppression of distractions, however, requires a sensing technique that can identify when more attention is required from the pedestrian.

In prior work, the Walksafe project has presented preliminary results on using cameras on pedestrians' smartphones for detecting oncoming vehicles [11]. Even if further significant improvements in accuracy will make this approach feasible, the energy consumption of continuous camera operation is likely to remain


*MobiSys'15*, May 18–22, 2015, Florence, Italy.

http://dx.doi.org/10.1145/2742647.2742669.

a challenge. Smartphones can also sense when they are being used while walking using existing activity recognition techniques [12], but this information is not sufficient to precisely target an alert. If pedestrians' smartphones and in-car devices can communicate (e.g. DSRC[9], [13]), they can determine when they are in close proximity. This can be useful for generating alerts in select scenarios but in busy urban areas pedestrians that are safe on a sidewalk are frequently very close to passing cars.

Pedestrian safety improvements, however, do not necessarily require such near-collision detection. Since the majority of pedestrian fatalities occur during road crossing at intersections or mid-block locations [14], safety improvements could also be achieved by supporting good crossing habits or by alerting distracted pedestrians who enter the roadway.[1] Phones can easily monitor when they are being used for texting and other potentially distracting purposes. The challenge, however, is to determine when pedestrians are crossing and to distinguish this from walking in relatively safe areas on a sidewalk. Existing localization technologies such as cellular, WiFi, and satellite positioning do not consistently achieve the accuracy necessary to discriminate sidewalks and roadways. The Global Positioning System may come close under ideal open-sky conditions but cannot achieve the same accuracy in many urban centers, where it would be most needed for pedestrian safety.

In this work, we address this challenge through a shoe-based step and terrain gradient profiling technique that can detect transitions between sidewalks and streets. This approach exploits the trends toward wearable sensing in shoes for health and fitness [16, 17]. While prior research and products have used sensors in shoes for tracking a person's movements (exercise tracking, posture analysis, and step counting), we show that similar inertial sensors can also sense properties of the ground. This allows constructing ground profiles which are useful in a pedestrian safety context and potential other applications such as localization. We note that sidewalks in urban environments (at least in more developed regions) follow relatively consistent design guidelines [18] with curbs separating roadways from sidewalks and increasingly ramps leading into dedicated crossings. These features are specifically designed to let even visually impaired pedestrians distinguish relatively safe sidewalk areas from street crossings.

We leverage these design features and develop a sensing system that can automatically detect transitions from a sidewalk into the road. This includes stepping over a curb, which often occurs when crossing a street. More importantly, however, our solution can track the inclination of the ground and detect the sloped transitions (ramps) that are installed at many dedicated crossing to improve accessibility. We focus on ramps because they are common in urban environments and we believe that the smoother transition makes it more likely that a distracted pedestrian fails to recognize the transition into the street. We have developed a prototype sensing system based on an inertial device affixed to a shoe to evaluate the effectiveness of this approach, both in laboratory experiments and in approximately 80 hours of walking, spread over the downtown area of a small city, the European city of Turin, and the midtown area of Manhattan.

In summary, the major contributions of this work are as follows:

- Proposing the use of shoe-mounted inertial sensors for step and ground profiling, and not just for step counting.

[1]Indeed, after a sharp 2012 uptick in traffic fatalities in New York City, the Transportation Commissioner blamed it in part on distracted walking and lamented: "I don't think that the iPhone has invented an app yet that will ping you when you hit a crosswalk." [15].

(a) Sidewalk-street transitions.

(b) LookUp screenshot.

**Figure 2: Virtual Look Up.**

- Designing step and slope profiling algorithms that identify when a pedestrian enters the street by sensing changes in the step and ground profile due to typical sidewalk design features such as ramps and curbs.
- Prototyping a LookUp safety feature to demonstrate the feasibility of alerting distracted pedestrians when entering the street.
- Experimentally analyzing the performance of the detection algorithms across pedestrian environments including major cities on two continents with different sidewalk designs (Manhattan, NY and Turin, Italy). The total distance walked during these experiments was 112.5 miles and this experimental dataset included 1670 street crossings.

## 2. APPLICATIONS

There are multiple applications that could benefit from a sensing technique to detect the transitions from sidewalks to streets. These applications impose different requirements based on the timeliness of detections, the need for online processing of gradient data, the target environment and the tolerance to false positives. We enumerate selected applications with their requirements in Table 1 and detail them in the remainder of this section.

***Virtual Look Up.*** Rather than relying on signs painted on the roadway, which may lead to warning fatigue, smartphones could issue a much more targeted electronic alert when an apparently distracted pedestrian is about to step into the street (illustrated in Figure 2).

The exact mode of alert or notification could range from visual (for texting users) to auditory, and might differ based on the robustness of detection. More intrusive alerts might be desirable when the system can attain high confidence that the user is at risk; more peripheral warnings may be suitable when there is lower confidence. We leave the exact design of such alert mechanisms to user experience designers and focus our discussion and effort on the robustness of the underlying sensing techniques. A sensing technique to support this application would need to be accurate in entrance detections and exhibit low false positives to be effective (and not cause warning fatigue). It will also need to determine detections online and with high timeliness requirement, since a distracted pedestrian should be alerted when entering the street. Note, however, that many accidents do not occur on the very first step into the street. They often occur after several steps, when emerging behind a parked car, for example. This means that short detection delays of 1-2 steps are often tolerable. This application is best suited to urban environments where car traffic is relatively dense and the likelihood of being struck when inattentive is higher.

| Application | Online Processing | Timeliness | Target Environment | Tolerance to False Positives |
|---|---|---|---|---|
| Virtual Look Up | Yes | High | Urban | Low |
| Driver Pedestrian Awareness | Yes | High | Urban/Suburban | Low-High |
| Reducing In-street Notifications | Yes | Medium | Urban | Medium |
| Feedback on Crossing Habits | No | – | Urban/Suburban/Rural | Low |

**Table 1: Applications of street entrance detection for safety services.**

***Driver Pedestrian Awareness.*** Government transportation departments are working with car makers towards a vehicle communication network that can be used to provide vehicles with better situational awareness [19]. To support safety applications and increasingly automated driving, over time all vehicles are expected to announce their current position and other vehicle dynamics information to vehicles in the vicinity. While this network was initially planned only for vehicles, prototype smartphones now exist that can participate in such an 802.11p based network [10]. Including smartphones would not just enable pedestrians' devices to learn about oncoming cars, but they could also potentially announce the presence of the pedestrian to nearby vehicles. These announcements would need to be generated on the go and processed online, while restricting timeliness requirement to be high for rendering usefulness. In suburban areas, where vehicles are rare, a pedestrian need not be warned at every crossing, but only if a vehicle is approaching; which makes this scenario resilient to false positives. However, owing to the high density of pedestrians and vehicles in urban areas, such announcements would have to be more selective, so that the system can distinguish pedestrians that are safely walking on the sidewalk from pedestrians that may be at risk. This system could be more forgiving to false positives if an additional layer of filtering is added to the vehicle, that can identify true alerts based on added information. Consequently, this application finds use over a wide range of target scenarios, which also alter its tolerance to false positives.

***Reducing In-street Notifications.*** Smartphones could silence distractions emanating from incoming calls, texts, or app notifications while the pedestrian is crossing a street. Since a crossing usually lasts no more than a few tens of seconds, the phone can simply delay the call/text (e.g. by disabling vibration or ringing) till the pedestrian exits the street. Such delays should be acceptable for most messages or notifications and if a call is missed, it can simply be returned when the pedestrian reaches the sidewalk. This application is more tolerant to false positives than the prior applications because even in case of a false detection the notification or call is delayed by only a small duration. The timeliness requirement is also slightly lower, since many distractions can still be suppressed even if the pedestrian is already several steps in the street when the system realizes this. This application could be an asset for urban environments where fatalities due to distracted walking are a rising concern.

***Feedback on Crossing Habits.*** Not all applications require distinguishing pedestrian walking locations in near real-time. Offline analysis of historical walking traces can also be useful to monitor and provide feedback on good crossing-habits. For example, our proposed technique can be a very useful component of a sensing system that could allow parents to monitor whether children that walk to school are stopping (to look) before an intersection or whether they dash into the street. While this system would work in all kinds of environment, it would still need to be precise in detections, with few false positives.

***Other Applications of Gradient Sensing.*** Besides these safety applications that benefit from a technique for detecting when pedestrians enter the street, we believe that a variety of other applications can also gain from this work. In particular, the shoe-based ground gradient sensing techniques are more generally applicable. By leveraging the slope traces and crowdsourcing them from a large number of people that walk the same path almost everyday, we can create a unique terrain profile for each sidewalk. Using the rough position estimate from the GPS and the sidewalk profile, we can improve localization in urban canyons by matching the terrain profile of the currently observed walking trace to this database of sidewalks. Additionally, we can also use these sidewalk profiles to monitor sidewalk status (surface health monitoring) as well as to identify the level of accessibility in an urban area to people with mobility impairments (e.g., surface smoothness, availability of ramps).

# 3. GPS LIMITATIONS FOR PEDESTRIAN SAFETY

Consider a straw-man approach that attempts to localize the pedestrian using existing methods and distinguish sidewalks and roadways by comparing the position coordinates with the location of known roadways on a map. The requirements and challenges for GPS-based crossing detection assume different meanings across scenarios.

In out-of-town environments such as rural roads or highways, walking along the roads, which typically do not have sidewalks, can be particularly hazardous. Since pedestrians are sparse and tend to walk along roads for extended periods, the accuracy requirements on a positioning system are relatively low, in the order of tens of meters. It thus suffices to know if a pedestrian is walking along a street and a GPS-based approach can be expected to work.

In suburban or residential areas, there may or may not be sidewalks, and one may expect occasional pedestrians, walking in the street (when no sidewalks are present) or on the sidewalk. For the latter case, solely detecting that there is a pedestrian walking along the street would result in generating alerts uselessly. It is thus beneficial to identify the events when this person may be stepping into the street, putting himself at a higher risk of being hit by car. This requires the ability to distinguish the pedestrian's location as street or sidewalk.

Most urban downtowns and cities are well developed and have sidewalks, with a large number of pedestrians walking along the street. Just knowing that a pedestrian is walking along a street would create far too many alerts and cause warning fatigue. In such a scenario, more fine-grained differentiation of pedestrians at risk is not only beneficial but necessary. Since a pedestrian is usually safe when walking on the sidewalk, our approach is to identify pedestrians that are in the roadway. Accurate detection of street entrance therefore becomes a key concern.

Typical GPS accuracies are in the order of a few meters under good conditions and the accuracy can quickly degrade to tens of meters in urban canyons. Through experiments conducted in environments ranging from suburban to small and metropolitan cities, it is evident that the performance of GPS-based detection of pedes-

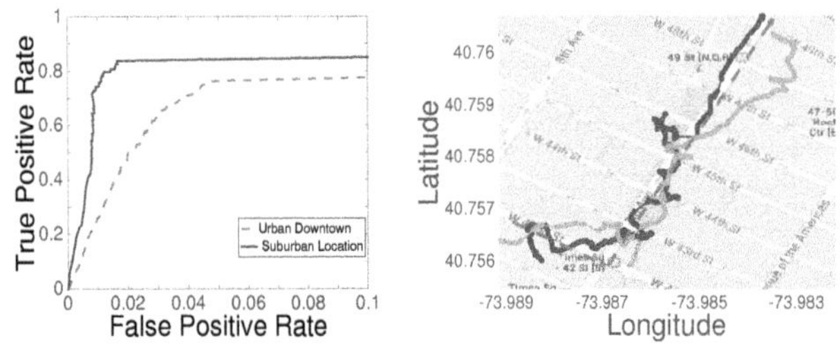


(a) In-street detection performance for urban and suburban testbeds.

(b) Sample GPS traces from Manhattan experiments and actual walk (dashed trace).

**Figure 3: GPS based approach.**

trian's transitions from sidewalk to street is limited even in a relatively benign suburban environment.

Using the location coordinates of the pedestrian and the heading, both obtained from the GPS, we can extrapolate a person's path of motion to approximate his position in the next $d$ meters. We can then check this extended path for intersection with a nearby street. Such an intersection of the pedestrian's predicted path and the street would indicate that the pedestrian might be purposed to cross the street. The distance $d$ is fixed to roughly half the width of the street. The underlying street network data can be accessed from OpenStreetMap [20], an open-source map database, which provides information about street orientations and locations. Figure 3(a) shows the performance of the GPS-based crossing detection in a suburban environment compared to an urban environment (e.g., downtown New Brunswick, NJ). The suburban environment exhibits a better performance with a detection rate of 85% than that of the urban environment (i.e., 78%). The maximum rate at which we can sample GPS is approximately once per second. It is evident from the performance curves that GPS does not suffice for applications with a stringent timing and fine grained localization requirement, such as pedestrian safety applications. More details on the limits of GPS-based pedestrian risk detection can be found in our earlier works [21, 22].

Figure 3(b) presents our best GPS traces collected in the urban environment of Manhattan, using a Nexus 5, held in hand. The green and blue lines are two separate GPS traces collected on different days. The red dashed line is the actual walked path. It is further evident from these results that GPS alone cannot serve the purpose for fine-grained localization such as detecting transitions from the sidewalk to street. Cellular and WiFi positioning could provide little help in such scenarios. Since sidewalks are often only a few meters wide, this level of accuracy makes it extremely challenging to distinguish a pedestrian on the sidewalk from one in the street, let alone determine the event when a person transitions from the sidewalk to the street.

***Other Challenges.*** Even with accurate positioning, the GPS-based system would have to compare the position coordinates with a map to distinguish sidewalks from streets. Unfortunately, road maps such as those available from OpenStreetMap [20] record only road centerlines. Whether a sidewalk is present along the roadway is not always stored. Even if it were, the boundary between street and sidewalk would need to be estimated based on assumptions of typical road width. This further limits accuracy or requires additional effort in constructing such a map.

To overcome these challenges, we explore a sensing-based approach that detects events in a local frame of reference for the pedestrian, instead of relying on absolute positioning.

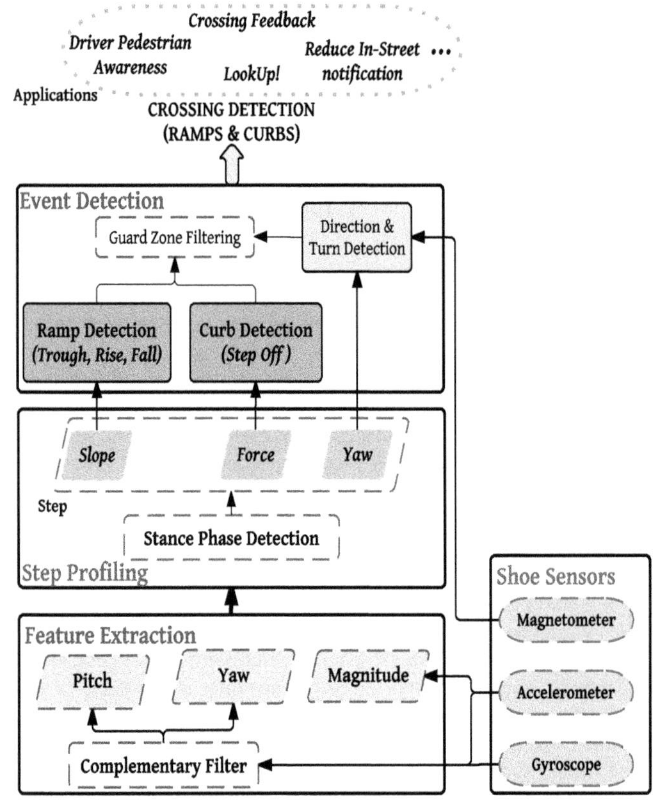


**Figure 4: System overview of crossing detection.**

# 4. STEP AND SLOPE PROFILING

Our primary idea is to distinguish street and sidewalk locations of the pedestrian through inertial sensing of ground features, particularly by sensing the sidewalk design features that demarcate roadways and sidewalks. In more developed regions, engineers are required to follow increasingly precise and consistent sidewalk design guidelines [18, 23] to improve accessibility. Typically, sidewalks and roadways are separated by curbs, which are lowered at designated crossings through a ramp. These features make sidewalk-roadway transitions and special crossings detectable by the visually impaired yet do not pose significant barriers for wheelchair users. We recognize that the same features can also be sensed for pedestrian safety services. The proposed approach therefore addresses the aforementioned challenges because it does not rely on absolute localization from GPS or maps and achieves robustness by taking advantage of unique sidewalk design features.

**Shoe-based Step and Slope Sensing.** More specifically, we propose a pedestrian safety system that acquires inertial data from a shoe-mounted sensor, to detect changes in step pattern and ground patterns caused by ramps and curbs. In particular, a salient feature of this work is that it senses small changes in the inclination of the ground, which are expected due to ramps and the sideways slope of roadways to facilitate water runoff. The shoe-mounted sensor has the capability to measure the foot inclination at any given point in time and reflects the slope of the ground when the foot is flat on the ground. We chose inertial sensors because they allow us to infer information about the ground with a very modest power budget, compared to GPS or camera-based approaches.

We selected a shoe placement of the sensors because they are closer to the ground than other wearable or smartphone sensors and move along with the foot. They can therefore trace the exact movement of the foot at each step and provide accurate information about ground features. Note that the trend towards wearable shoe sensors for fitness purposes [16, 17] has already made such sensors available in some shoes. With continuing technology advances, we envision that such shoe sensors will be increasingly available for other emerging tracking [24], fitness [16] and healthcare monitoring [25, 26] applications. They could first be embedded in shoes for especially vulnerable traffic participants (e.g., children) and eventually most shoes.

**System Overview.** The system comprises inertial sensor modules on both shoes that share their measurements with a smartphone over a wireless Bluetooth connection. While a sensor on one foot can also achieve most of the ramp detections, sensors on both feet substantially improve the detection of stepping over a curb. It allows us to detect foot movements over the curb, irrespective of the foot the pedestrian uses for the action. A smartphone can serve as a hub for processing the shoe sensor data and implementing any of the aforementioned applications. The key processing steps of our sensing system are depicted in Figure 4. The core components of our system are *Feature Extraction, Step Profiling* and *Event Detection*.

The *Feature Extraction* block processes raw accelerometer and gyroscope readings (sampled at 50 Hz in our implementation) through a complementary filter, and extracts traces of pitch, yaw, and acceleration magnitude features from these measurements (see Figure 5 for an illustration of key features). While it primarily relies on this inertial data, it also collects magnetometer readings to assist with the Guard Zone filtering step in the Event Detection component.

The *Step Profiling* component divides these traces into distinct steps and for each step cycle extracts the period when the foot is flat on the ground, which we refer to as *Stance Phase Detection.* It then estimates the slope of the ground from the pitch readings and the relative rotation of the foot from the yaw readings, during the stance phase. It also extracts peak acceleration magnitude over an entire step cycle as an indication of foot impact force.

Finally, *Event Detection* layer aims to detect stepping into the roadway through ramp and curb detection. Ramps manifest themselves through characteristic changes in slope, while steps over a curb usually show higher foot impact forces. These candidate detections can then be filtered through a guard zone mechanism. It helps to remove spurious events caused by uneven road surfaces. Since many cities feature somewhat regular intervals between road crossings (especially so for cities that are laid out in a grid shape), it is rare for a pedestrian that walks straight to encounter a crossing immediately after previous crossing. The guard zone mechanism tracks whether a pedestrian walks straight and then suppresses detections that come to soon.

# 5. CROSSING DETECTION

Below, we detail the feature extraction, step profiling, and event detection layers depicted in Figure 4 and outlined in the previous section.

## 5.1 Feature Extraction

This component extracts changes in pitch, yaw and acceleration magnitude for each sample from the tri-axis accelerometer and tri-axis gyroscope measurements. For simplicity, let us assume that the inertial sensor unit is oriented such that the $x$ axis points approximately forward in the direction of motion, the $y$ axis points sideways, and the $z$ axis points opposite to the direction of gravity, as shown in Figure 6. Note, that the sensor orientation does not need to be precisely calibrated; small discrepancies can be tolerated since we only track changes in pitch, yaw, and magnitude from step to step. For arbitrary mounting positions, the system can also be extended to include a complete coordinate system calibration step similar to [27].

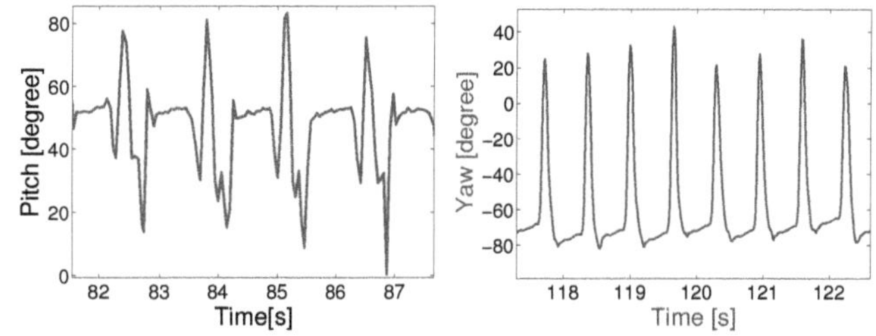


(a) Pitch vs. Time. (b) Yaw vs. Time.

**Figure 5: Pitch and Yaw traces.**

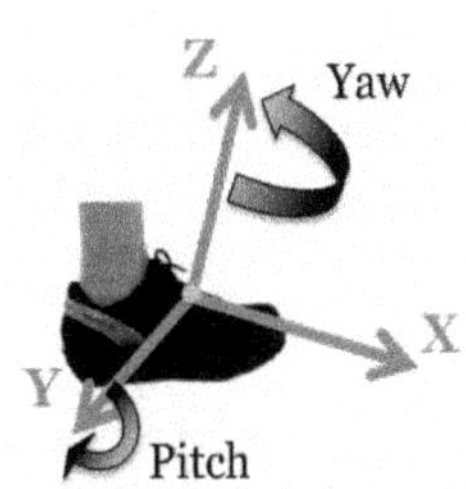


**Figure 6: Shoe mounted sensor with axis orientation.**

**Pitch.** Pitch is the rotation of the foot along the sideways $y$ axis (see Figure 6), which represents the inclination of the ground during the stance phase. We measure changes in pitch relative to the first step, to account for mounting offset. Changes in pitch can be determined from the accelerometer readings, since the change leads to a different projection of the gravity force on the accelerometer axes. These estimates can suffer from vibration errors, however. An alternative way of obtaining changes in pitch angle is by using the gyroscope data. Since the gyroscope directly measures angular velocity around all axes, integrating the angular velocity around the $y$ axis will yield the change in pitch. While the gyroscope allows tracking small changes more precisely, the integration process accumulates error over time, leading to significant errors for longer integration intervals. To overcome the drawbacks of the individual sensors, we borrow a popular technique from robotics, for accurate pitch measurement. This technique involves combining the accelerometer and gyroscope data using a complementary filter [28, 29]. To obtain the pitch from raw accelerometer and gyroscope readings, we use a second order complementary filter.

The second order complementary filter takes the following inputs: the accelerometer readings along $x$ and $z$ direction, $A_x$ and $A_z$, and the gyroscope rotations along the $y$ axis, $G_y$. The filter also needs two parameters, $k$ - the bandwidth of the filter and $T$ - the sampling rate. For our system, the sampling frequency is 50 Hz, i.e. $T$ is 0.02 and we empirically set $k$=13.5. The filter is given by the following set of equations, where $i$ is the generic sampling step and $\alpha(i) = atan(A_x(i)/A_z(i))$ represents the angle between the accelerometer readings along the $x$ and $z$ axis.

$$v(i) = Tk^2[\alpha(i) - pitch(i-1)] + v(i-1) \quad (1)$$

$$w(i) = v(i) + 2k[\alpha(i) - pitch(i-1)] + G_y(i) \quad (2)$$

$$pitch(i) = Tw(i) + pitch(i-1) \quad (3)$$

In (1), a low-pass filter is applied to the difference between the current angle and the previous pitch so as to only let long-term changes through, filtering out short-term fluctuations. The output of the filter is integrated over the sampling step $T$. Equation (2) sums the output of (1) to the output of a low-pass filter and gyroscope rotation $G_y$. Finally, (3) performs an integration over the sampling step and adds the result to the pitch. A typical pitch trace is shown in Figure 5(a).

**Yaw.** Yaw is the change in rotation of the foot around the vertical axis, the $z$ axis. We measure yaw relative to the previous step. We can obtain the yaw from the complementary filter in the same way as the pitch, by only changing the axis. Note, however, that the yaw information primarily stems from the gyroscope since the accelerometer tends to convey less information about yaw. In fact, if the accelerometer $z$ axis is aligned with the gravity axis, then a change in yaw will yield no measurable difference in the $x - y$ plane, since there is no gravity component on these axes. A typical yaw trace is shown in Figure 5(b). Yaw gives information on whether the pedestrian is walking straight or turning, which we use for turn detection and in the Guard Zone Filtering, as described later.

**Magnitude.** The magnitude of the acceleration helps us detect the event of stepping off a curb. We notice that during step off events, the accelerometer records a peak in acceleration along the axis on which the gravity is acting. Therefore we calculate the magnitude of acceleration along the $z$ axis and the $y$ axis, for every sample. We remove the $x$ axis from consideration to filter out significant acceleration in the walking direction.

## 5.2 Step Profiling

The foot mounted inertial sensors are used to obtain the slope of the ground at each step the walker takes, hence the measurement of the ramp inclination. This algorithm proceeds in three steps. First, it tracks the pitch angle 50 times a second. Second, it uses this pitch trace to extract the slope from the stance periods of a walking cycle, the period when the foot is flat on the ground. A sequence of these slope values corresponds to the slope profile of the ground that the pedestrian is walking on. Third, in addition to the slope, each step also has yaw and force attributes, that are derived from the yaw and magnitude features. Therefore, at the end of the profiling algorithm, we obtain a sequence of steps, where each step has a slope, yaw and force attribute. While the slope is acquired by sensing the terrain gradient, the yaw and the force attributes are particular to the walking style. Below, we provide further details on the stance phase detection algorithm.

**Stance Phase Detection.** We use the pitch trace to identify the different phases of a person's walk. Figure 7 shows one such trace and the corresponding phases of walking. We require the *stance* phase of the walk, which is when the foot is flat on the ground. The inclination measurement obtained in this phase results from the slope of the ground at that spot, in addition to the initial pitch due to mounting.

As a person walks, the inclination of the foot changes continuously, varying rapidly during the swing phase but maintaining a small amplitude during the stance phase. Thus, the stance phase detection algorithm identifies the large negative peaks in the trace and isolates the samples between consecutive peaks. This is one walking cycle. By tracking the variation of the pitch during each cycle, the stance phase is identified as the interval in which the foot is stationary implying very small or no changes at all to the pitch. The samples making up each stance phase are determined as the collection of at least *count* number of pitch values within a few degrees of each other. Here *count* depends on the sampling rate of the sensor and the duration for which the foot is in contact with the ground. For our analysis we assume that the foot remains in contact with the ground for at least one-third of a second, during normal walking. At a sampling rate of 50 Hz, this implies that the stance phase should have approximately 15 samples. The mean of

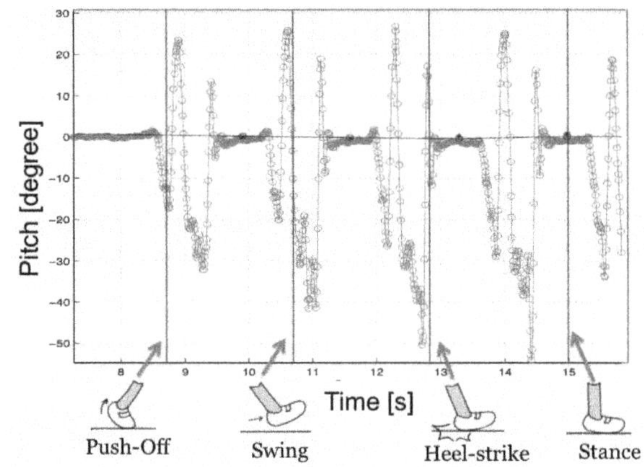


**Figure 7: A pitch trace identifying different phases of a walking cycle.**

the inclination values (pitch) during the stance phase provides us with the slope of the ground at that step.

By repeating this calculation for each stance phase, we acquire a sequence of slope values, the slope trace, where each slope corresponds to a step. From this slope trace, we obtain an estimate for the slope of the ground by subtracting the initial tilt of the accelerometer, caused by the shoe mounting.

We assume that pedestrians walk in the forward direction and not backwards. However, if a person halts and only stamps his feet without moving, the pitch trace does not record a complete walking cycle. The swing phase of the stamping activity is distinct from the swing phase of the walking activity and thus these spurious steps are easily filtered out.

## 5.3 Event Detection and Classification

The pitch computation and stance phase detection discussed above are performed independently for each foot. After these procedures, we obtain the slope measurement of the ground at each step from both feet. Each time a walking cycle is completed, we compare the slope of the current step to the slope acquired in the past 3 steps. We determine the 3-step window by observation. Events are detected by applying a threshold to the slope change in this window. This threshold reflects the typical ramp inclination and is determined empirically.

The force at each step is also evaluated against a step off threshold to detect steps with a force significantly higher than past 3 steps, likely implying stepping-off curbs. The events detection and classification details are provided in Algorithm 1. To ensure robust detection, not only do we identify events that exceed the threshold, but we further process them as explained below. First, we categorize the detected events as follows.

***Trough.*** A trough is typical of a street entrance via a ramp. As a pedestrian walks from the sidewalk to the street, there is a negative slope measured off the descending sidewalk ramp. As the person steps into the street, the sensors measure a positive slope, due to the street curvature. A combination of the negative slope of the sidewalk ramp and the positive incline of the street edge forms a trough, if the detected change in slope is significant (higher than a given threshold). Figure 8(a) shows an example *trough* event. While this is the ideal measurement case, we do not observe this ideal pattern at all crossings, due to measurement errors and surface invariations.

***Rise.*** A rise is an event detected due to a sharp increase in the measured slope of the ground, i.e. a positive incline. This occur-

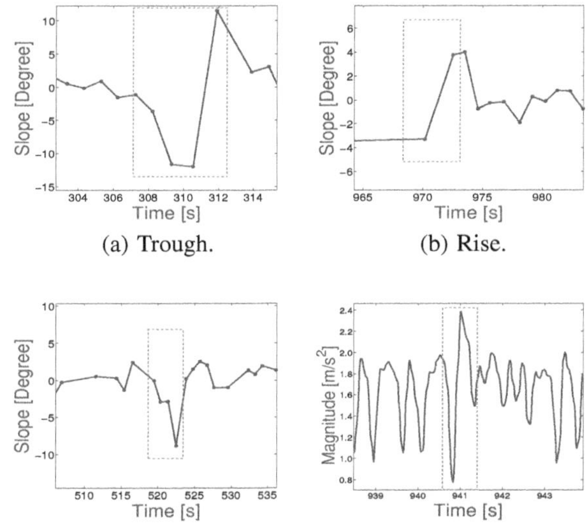


(a) Trough. (b) Rise.

(c) Fall. (d) Step Off.

**Figure 8: Event patterns.**

rence is most common when the pedestrian just steps into the street. This is due to the fact that streets have a convex curvature to facilitate water to drain off to the sides. When walking from sidewalk to street, this curve is measured as the positive incline. Figure 8(b) shows an example *rise* event.

***Fall.*** A fall is an event detected due to a sharp decrease in the measured slope of the ground. This event is most commonly detected when a pedestrian is walking down the sidewalk ramp, which shows up as a negative incline. Figure 8(c) shows an example *fall* event.

***Step Off.*** A step off event occurs as a sudden increase in the accelerometer magnitude along the vertical direction. This signifies the force associated with that step. If the force at a step is higher than the person's average force over the past 3 steps, we flag this event as a step off event. This event is very important for detecting street entrances where a person steps off the curb instead of walking down a ramp. Figure 8(d) shows an example *step off* event.

We then classify a combination of these events as *high confidence* and *low confidence* events. A pair of trough events, one from each foot, constitutes a high confidence event. Similarly, a pair of step off events is also classified as high confidence event occurrence. All other events are classified as low confidence events. A low confidence event could also be triggered by various obstacles on the sidewalk or unexpected discrepancies in the pedestrian's movement.

An example of low confidence event is a fall event, which can occur at both, entrances (when walking down a sidewalk ramp) and exits (at the edge of the road, when leaving). However, the algorithm can identify an entrance based on the spatial and temporal occurrence of the events. If the events occur close to each other, they denote an entrance and the following exit. Also, as detailed later, when a high confidence event allows the detection of an entrance, the guard zone is set and the exit event can be easily discarded.

We remark that, in addition to detecting actual events, the algorithm is also equipped to handle error cases. While thresholding the slope, only relative slope change is tracked over a small window of steps. Therefore, if the sidewalk has a gradual uphill or downhill incline, the algorithm does not detect it as a ramp, since the relative slope of the ground does not change considerably in a small window. Unfortunately, obstacles in the sidewalk, such as bumps are

**Data**: $pitch$ - Pitch trace
  $mag$ - Magnitude trace
  $W_{step}$ - Step Window for comparison
  $Th_r$ - Threshold for ramp detection
  $Th_c$ - Threshold for curb detection
**Result**: $\mathcal{S}$ - Event Type
**begin**
  **foreach** $pitch, mag$ **do**
    **if** *walkCycleComplete(pitch)* == *TRUE* **then**
      $[Slope(i), Force(i)]$ = getStancePhaseMean($pitch$, $mag$);
      **if** *(Slope(i)– Slope(i-1)* $> Th_r$*) and (Slope(i-1)– Slope(i-1-*$W_{step}$*))* $< -Th_r$*) and (range(Slope(i-1-*$W_{step}$*:i-1))* $> Th_r$*)* **then**
        $\mathcal{S} \leftarrow$ *Trough*;
      **else**
        **if** *range(Slope(i:i-*$W_{step}$*))* $> Th_r$ **then**
          diff=slope(i)-slope(i-$W_{step}$);
          **if** *diff* $> Th_r$ **then**
            $\mathcal{S} \leftarrow$ *Rise*;
          **else if** $diff < -Th_r$ **then**
            $\mathcal{S} \leftarrow$ *Fall*;
      **if** *Force(i)>*$Th_c$ **then**
        $\mathcal{S} \leftarrow$ *Step Off*;
      **if** *inGuardZone(*$\mathcal{S}$*)* == *FALSE* **then**
        **return** $\mathcal{S}$
      **else**
        Discard $\mathcal{S}$;

**Algorithm 1:** Event Detection Algorithm.

single step events and hard to filter by themselves, unless they fall in the guard zone.

## 5.4 Guard Zone Filtering

When a high confidence event is detected, such as a pair of *trough* events or a pair of *step off* events, the algorithm reckons this to be a definite entrance into the street and sets a *guard zone* following that entrance, until the next entrance can occur. We define *guard zone* as a stretch of the sidewalk on which true events of entering the street are unlikely to occur. Thus, any events detected within the guard zone are discarded because they can be caused by measurement noise or irregularities in the sidewalk (uneven road surfaces, potholes, bumps), and can trigger false positives. The guard zone is reset (i.e. set to zero) when a turn is detected. If a turn is made before crossing the street, the turn detection algorithm resets the guard zone. This implies that events after a turn will not be discarded, and the guard zone will be set again when a high confidence event is detected. This is done to account for pedestrians who cross a street, turn, and then cross again, shortly after the first crossing. Guard zone filtering has been primarily designed to discard false warnings due to the irregularities of the sidewalk.

Obtaining the length of the guard zone is important to reduce false positives and maintain a high rate of crossing detections. However, accurately determining this size poses several challenges. First, crossings occur not only at the ends of a street block, but pedestrians can also perform midblock crossings. Second, the complexity and varying characteristics of the road environments make it difficult to provide a generic length setting of guard zone. To overcome this issue, the guard zone algorithm takes the closeness of streets (block length) into account and sets the length of the guard zone to

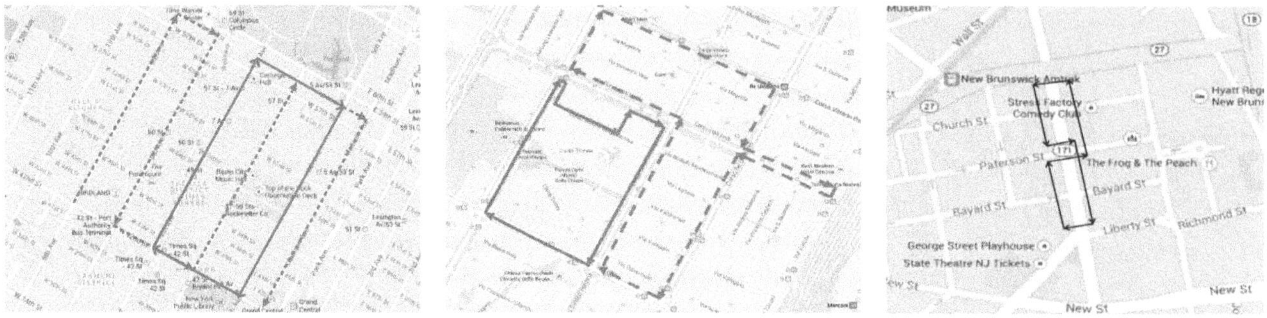


(a) Manhattan Testbed. (b) Turin Testbed. (c) New Brunswick Testbed.

**Figure 9: Test paths from Manhattan (New York), Turin (Italy) and New Brunswick (NJ).**

a fraction of the street block size. This setting also helps us recover in case the guard zone is incorrectly applied after a false detection. We seek to derive a sensing-based mechanism to estimate the length of the guard zone by using the pedestrian's walking direction and turning information. In this mechanism, the size of the guard zone continues to increase by accumulating the pedestrian's walking steps after the first street entrance (i.e., a high confidence event) is detected, and it resets to zero when the pedestrian makes a turn. We implement this mechanism by performing *walking direction determination* and *turn detection*, as described below.

**Walking Direction Determination.** This task is accomplished by leveraging magnetometer readings. Magnetometer measures the earth's magnetic field in $x$, $y$ and $z$ directions and its readings remain unique for certain direction. The magnetometer embedded in the shoe sensor can thus become a useful discriminator for the walking direction determination. Specifically, we assume $\vec{R} = (x_r, y_r, z_r)$ and $\vec{R}' = (x'_r, y'_r, z'_r)$ be the average of the real time magnetometer readings obtained from the current observation window and the previous non-overlapping observation window with a length of $n$ walking steps, respectively. The angle between $\vec{R}$ and $\vec{R}'$ can be found using the dot product: $\theta_{\vec{R},\vec{R}'} = \cos^{-1}\frac{\vec{R}\cdot\vec{R}'}{\|\vec{R}\|\|\vec{R}'\|}$. If $\theta_{\vec{R},\vec{R}'}$ is smaller than a pre-defined threshold, the system declares that the walking direction of the user remains the same and the guard zone size increases by $n$ walking steps.

**Turn Detection.** By analyzing the yaw values, we are able to detect turns made by pedestrians. A turn corresponds to a continuous change, along the same direction, of yaw readings over both feet. We develop a turn detection technique that takes the yaw value associated with each step and computes the difference between yaw at consecutive steps. Then, it sums these differences over a fixed number of steps so as to obtain the overall rotation angle. A turn is detected when such rotation exceeds an angle threshold for both feet. As mentioned before, turn detection is used to avoid discarding real entrances when guard zone filtering is applied. Indeed, we observed that most turns happen right before or after street entrance events, either at intersections or mid-block locations. Thus, if a detected event is preceded by a turn, it is likely to be a real street entrance, hence it is not discarded and the guard zone size is reset to zero. In addition to turn detection, considering both feet allows us to distinguish between actual turns and small heading variations due to the need to dodge people on a crowded sidewalk.

# 6. PROTOTYPE IMPLEMENTATION

Our prototype includes a shoe-mounted sensor, two Android applications for data collection and a LookUp safety feature to demonstrate the feasibility of our approach. The sensor mounted on the shoe is an Invensense MPU-9150 [30] 9-axis motion sensor, shown in Figure 10(a). It is a self-calibrating device, set to collect data at a sampling rate of 50 Hz. During our in-lab experiments we analyzed the system performance using different sampling frequencies. We chose 50 Hz considering that some people walk much faster, and this sampling frequency provided us with enough data points to extract the stance phase. The board we used comprises an accelerometer, gyroscope, magnetometer, a Bluetooth module and a battery. We chose this platform because it offers relatively high precision inertial sensing module. In order to capture all foot movements, we strapped a sensor on each of the walker's shoes, as shown in Figure 10(b). We chose a mounting position for the sensor after testing out four different positions in a controlled laboratory environment. As shown in the evaluation section (Figure 18(b)), the mounting position that was found to be consistent across separate experiments was on top of the foot. A sensor mounted on each foot ensured that stepping off the curb is detected, irrespective of the foot used

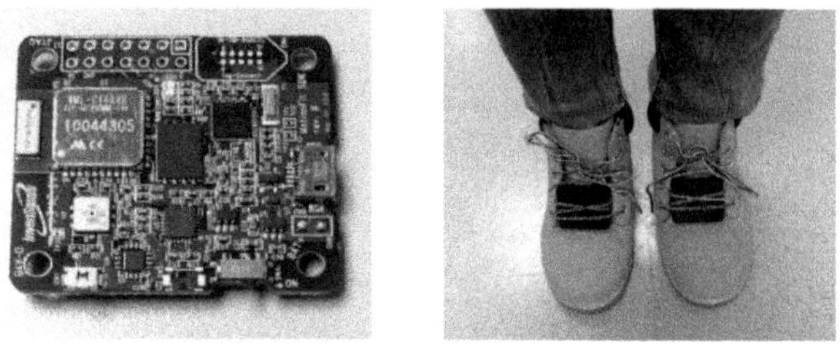

(a) MPU 9150 sensor. (b) Sensor mounting on shoes.

**Figure 10: Set up for shoe-mounted sensor.**

We implemented an Android application to collect sensor data on the user's smartphone via Bluetooth. The application logs the accelerometer, gyroscope and magnetometer data from the two sensors independently. Each reading is timestamped and contains raw data from the three axis. A second Android application was implemented to collect the ground truth for offline evaluation of the proposed system. This application has buttons to mark the exact time when the walker transitions between a sidewalk and a street, and whether this transition occurs via a ramp or a curb. To ensure that measurements are unbiased and the pedestrian is undistracted while crossing the street, the ground truth was entered by a second person walking with the pedestrian.

We also developed a prototype LookUp safety application on the Android platform, which alerts distracted pedestrians when entering the street. This is a shoe sensor-based crossing detection application that implements the algorithms described in Section 5. The

(a) A ramp in Manhattan. (b) A curb in Manhattan. (c) A cobblestone ramp in Turin. (d) A curb in Turin.

**Figure 11: Typical roadway features from Manhattan and Turin.**

screenshot from the application is shown in Figure 2(b). When a pedestrian approaches a street, a LookUp warning flashes on his mobile screen, alerting him to pay attention to traffic. This application runs in the background and does not alter the user's interaction with the smartphone.

# 7. EXPERIMENTAL SCENARIOS

To evaluate the performance of our system, 21 volunteers, 16 male and 5 female, walked along predefined routes in three locations with a sensor attached to each of their shoes. Most volunteers were students from our laboratories and about 20 - 40 years old. The only instruction provided was to walk as usual along the given route. An experimenter accompanied each walker to record, through a smartphone app, ground truth information (i.e., the time when transitions occurred and whether they occurred via a ramp or a curb). Most volunteers were not aware of the objective of the experiment other than it being related to pedestrian safety. We highlight that volunteers were free to use either a ramp or a curb to cross a street (the system collected both the ground slope data as well as acceleration events for street crossing detection at the same time). The experiments in Manhattan were conducted in the months of February and early March. There were a fair number of obstacles to deal with such as icy patches, accumulated snowpiles, and street/sidewalk potholes. The data includes the movements to avoid these and volunteers may have walked faster due to cold weather. Additionally, these walking trials were performed during different times, including rush hour and weekends. At times, the volunteers had to weave around people. None of our test areas, however, included stairs or unpaved surfaces.

***Midtown area of Manhattan.*** This location gave us the opportunity to evaluate our system in a challenging environment, with different kinds of ramps, crowded sidewalks and long paths. The experiments were performed near Times Square, which is one of the world's busiest pedestrian intersections. Five volunteers walked at different times, including rush hours and weekends. We selected two test paths. A short one that volunteers were able to cover several times (namely, 20) so as to analyze the variance of our results over the same path. Another, longer path was completed twice and allowed us to understand variations in the results depending on the different street and crossing layout. The first test path starts from Times Square (42nd Street, 7th Avenue) and goes through Central Park (58th Street, 5th Avenue) before returning to Times Square, as shown by the solid red lines in Figure 9(a). The entire path is about 2.1 miles. The average path travel time is about 60 mins, and it includes 32 street crossings. The dashed path in Figure 9(a) shows the second test path, which is about 4 mile-long. In this case, the average path travel time is approximately 120 mins, and it includes 60 street crossings. Thus, a total of nearly 25 hours of sensor data was collected. Figure 11(a) and (b) show a typical ramp and curb in Manhattan.

***Turin Metropolitan Area.*** In order to verify the performance of our system in a different urban street layout, we selected the European city of Turin, in Italy, which has a population of about one million people. While in Manhattan most of the sidewalks are made of concrete or tiles, in Turin almost all of them are made of either asphalt or bricks. Six volunteers walked over two different test paths in the city center, as shown in Figure 9(b). The shorter path is 1.6 mile-long, includes 20 crossings and is travelled in about 30 mins. The longer one is 2.5 mile-long, includes around 40 crossings and it takes about one hour to complete it. In total, volunteers completed 10 long and 20 short paths, thus collecting a total of 20 hours of sensory data. A typical cobblestoned ramp from Turin is displayed in Figure 11(c).

***New Brunswick Downtown.*** We conducted walking trials in the downtown area of the small city of New Brunswick. The selected area comprises only sidewalk ramps. Eleven volunteers walked over ten possible paths, each of which is 20 minute-long and covers about 800 meters. Figure 9(c) provides a map of this testing scenario and shows one of the ten possible paths, which includes 8 crossings. The number of crossings over the possible paths ranges between 8 and 12. The New Brunswick testing scenario has been used to evaluate the impact of people's walking style and speed on the performance of our system.

# 8. EVALUATION

We evaluate the robustness of our crossing detection system for the three testbeds discussed earlier.

## 8.1 Entrance Detection

First off, we evaluate the crossing detection algorithm for delay and detection performance. This evaluation is carried out for our two main testbeds, Manhattan and Turin. These results establish that our crossing detection algorithm has very low false positives for a high detection rate, even at locations that have completely different street designs. In the second part of the entrance detection evaluation, we test the robustness of the algorithm and analyze how it is affected by the pedestrian's walking style and sensor mounting. For this evaluation we use our smaller testbed, in New Brunswick, New Jersey as well as controlled indoor experiments. We show that the detection performance is not significantly influenced by walking style and that a shoestring mounting position as used in current exercise tracking products also works well for ground sensing and entrance detection.

We use steps as the evaluation metric, which provides a comprehension of both time and distance. Due to varying speeds of walking and the time spent in waiting in differently crowded environments, the metric of time alone is insufficient without a sense of

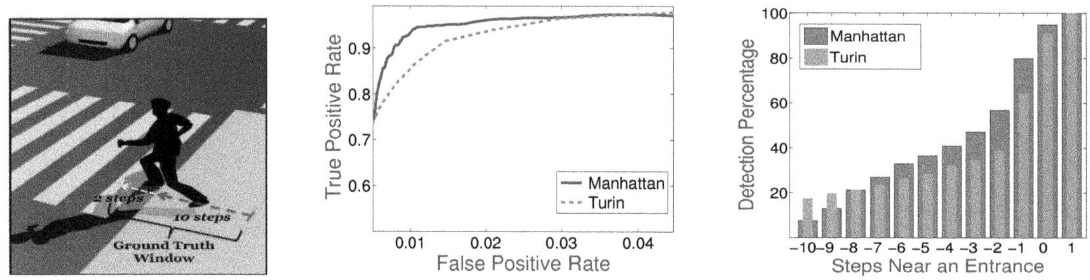


(a) A ground truth window of 12 steps at an entrance

(b) Entrance Detection Performance for Manhattan and Turin testbeds

(c) Cumulative entrance detection in ground truth window

**Figure 12: System performance evaluation.**

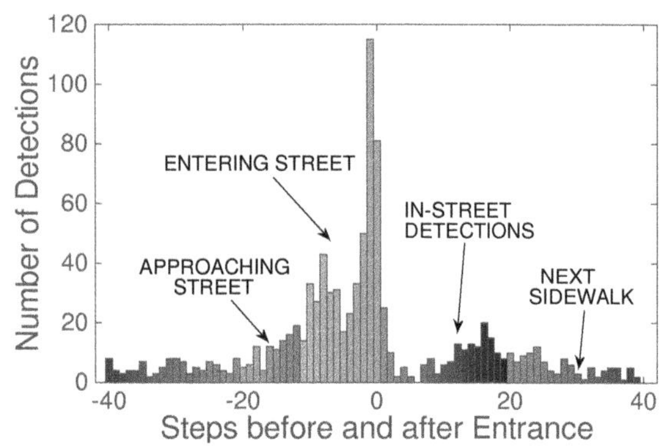


**Figure 13: Detection latency for Manhattan testbed.**

pedestrian motion. For example, when a person enters the street, a few seconds later we cannot tell how far the pedestrian is in the street without also tracking motion and speed. Steps help us estimate the risk to a pedestrian based on how far (how many steps) he is, into the street.

### *8.1.1 Detection Latency*

For safety applications, it is essential to understand the timeliness of event detections. To this end, we graph the delay distribution of the detections in number of steps from an actual entrance. Figure 13 shows a histogram that displays the number of detected events in a 40 step window before and after a real entrance. The negative and positive x-axis values correspond to steps before and after the entrance, respectively. Zero on the $x$ axis marks the step when the pedestrian enters the street. We observe that the maximum number of detections occur at the step right before the entrance, followed by the first step into the street. The highest density of detected events lies in the steps before the entrance, depicted in fading shades of green to the left of zero. On either side of this window, the detections fall rapidly. The bars from 2 - 20 steps after entrance denote the detections occurring while the pedestrian is crossing the street. While these detections are late for warning the pedestrian, they are very useful for a pedestrian-2-vehicle communication scenario, where we need to know when a pedestrian is in the street to relay that information to an approaching vehicle.

### *8.1.2 Detection Performance*

We next evaluate our system for the Lookup application, which has the most stringent timing requirement. We classify all event detections as true positives or false positives. We define a true positive as a detected event that falls in a window around the actual entrance. We refer to this window as the *ground truth window*. It is evident from Figure 13 that most detections occur in the steps very close to the entrance, therefore we selected a long ground truth window. We define the ground truth window as a sequence of 12 steps around an entrance. Figure 12(a) shows the ground truth window at an entrance in an urban scenario. Since sidewalk ramps can be of varying lengths and early detections are helpful for warning pedestrians, we use 10 steps before an actual entrance as an appropriate window for in-time warnings. The most worrisome pedestrian accident scenarios are when the pedestrian enters the traffic lane in front of standing or stopped traffic at intersections, and when a vehicle is turning left at an intersection [14, 2]. The first is very common when a pedestrian enters the street from in between parked cars, and an approaching vehicle has no line of sight to the person. These accidents occur a few steps away from the sidewalk bounds. A warning that is triggered up to a couple of steps into the street would be beneficial, since pedestrians do not immediately put themselves in the way of a moving vehicle when they enter the street. Bearing this in mind, we consider 2 steps into the street still in time to warn a pedestrian.

Figure 12(b) shows our entrance detection performance results from the Manhattan and Turin testbeds. We use the Receiver Operating Characteristic (ROC) curve to illustrate our entrance detection results by varying the slope detection threshold from 0.1 to 15 degrees in steps of 0.1. For a large testbed such as New York City, with one of world's busiest intersections, our system achieves 90% detection rate with only 0.7% false positives in midtown Manhattan. With a 1.1% false positive rate we can reach up to 95% of crossings being detected. Occasionally, the transitions from sidewalk to street are not sharp, and the sidewalk could be at the same level as the street with no subtle inclination. In such cases our algorithm has difficulty in detecting the transitions from sidewalk to street. For the Turin testbed, our algorithm provides a true detection rate of above 90% for less than 1.5% false positives. The proximity of the two curves in Figure 12(b) demonstrates that our algorithm performance is not affected by location or by differences in sidewalk designs. Even with several walking paths of varied lengths in both testbeds, the performance of the entrance detection stays unaffected, indicating that it is not affected by the length or duration of the pedestrian's walking.

Within the ground truth window, it is interesting to study the cumulative probability of detection as the person approaches the entrance point. For all true detections, we plot this cumulative detection rate in Figure 12(c). $-1$ denotes the last step on the sidewalk and 0 denotes the first step into the street. With each step in the ground truth window, the y-axis marks the true detections that occurred until that step. We see that 80% of the times, the entrance was detected before entering the street, while almost all the times it was detected right after entering the street.

(a) Manhattan Testbed

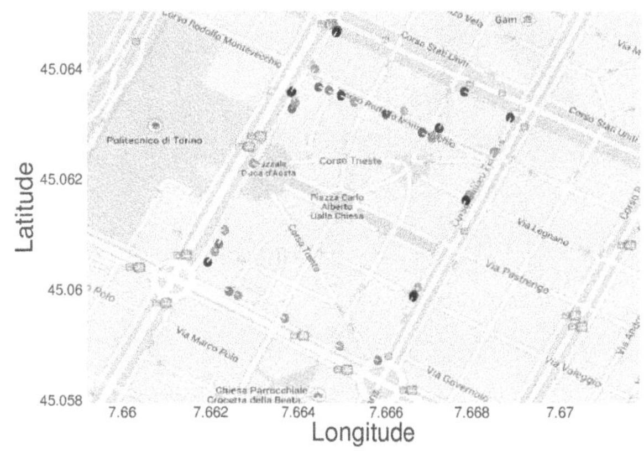


(b) Turin Testbed

**Figure 14: Locations of crossing detections for latency and performance analysis.**

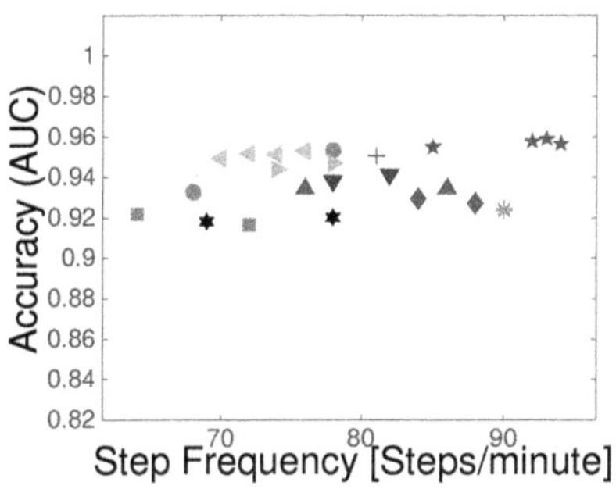


**Figure 15: Performance at different walking rates for New Brunswick testbed. Each symbol represents one loop. Each person is represented by a unique symbol.**

To obtain a finer perspective on where exactly these detections happen, we estimate the location for each step by interpolating location coordinates between consecutive crossings. We plot the locations of the detections from our system on maps for Manhattan and Turin testbeds as depicted in Figure 14(a) and (b). The yellow trace marks the interpolated location coordinates of each step of the path walked. The color scheme for detections on this map corresponds to the histogram in Figure 13. Fading shades of green mark the detections before an entrance, while shades of red mark detections on the sidewalk. It is evident that most detections occur close to intersections, indicating the utility for detecting pedestrian risk. The Turin map also shows few false detections. Some of these events are detected because of the guard zone being reset when a pedestrian turns, as they are likely to make another crossing.

### *8.1.3 Effect of Walking Style*

Next we analyze the effect of differences in walking styles on the crossing detection algorithm. For this analysis, we use our smaller testbed in New Brunswick and conduct walking trials at different speeds and with different experimenters carrying the device. Walking speed and stride length are important metrics that distinguish walking styles. We use step frequency as a combined metric for evaluation because it accounts for the changes in speed as well as stride length. Figure 15 shows the accuracy of the algorithm for different step frequencies. We measure this accuracy in terms of the area under the ROC curve, called AUC, a metric used in machine learning to describe the performance of a classifier. The average walking speed varied between 65 and 95 steps per minute. To obtain a fair comparison in the step frequency calculation, we discarded the time during which a walker was waiting to cross an intersection. This value depends on the traffic condition and not on the walking style. The figure shows the AUC values for different walkers. Each symbol in the figure represents a loop completed by a walker. Each color and marker style correspond to a different walker. All AUC values range between 0.9 and 0.98, indicating that our system has a high accuracy irrespective of the walking speed.

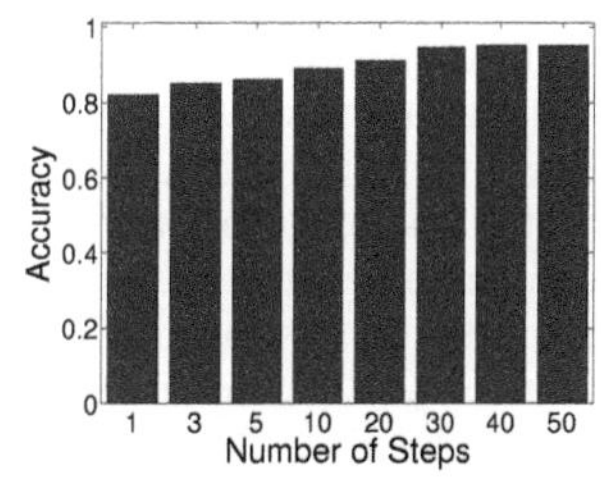


(a) Direction determination using magnetometer

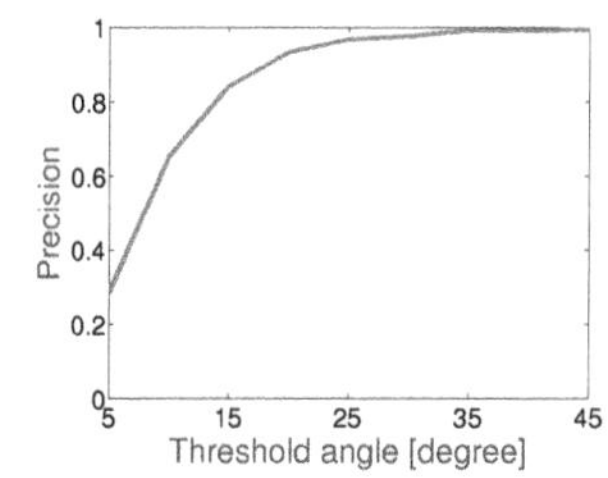


(b) Turn detection using yaw

**Figure 17: Direction determination and turn detection.**

## 8.2 Direction Determination and Turn Detection

Finally, we evaluate the effectiveness of walking direction determination using magnetometer for guard zone filtering. We use the magnetometer traces collected from the Manhattan testbed and treat the direction of the walking trajectory obtained from the map as the ground truth. We divide the whole trace into non-overlapping observation windows in terms of number of steps. An angle between each pair of consecutive observation windows is estimated using our proposed scheme in Section 5.4, based on the magnetometer readings within two windows, and then compared with a threshold to determine whether user's walking direction has changed. The accuracy is defined as the percentage of window pairs in which the determined direction matches the ground truth. Figure 17 (a) presents the accuracy of direction determination under varying lengths of observation window. We observe that the accuracy starts from 80% even with one step and exhibits an increasing trend as the number of steps increases. It is stabilized at about 95% when it

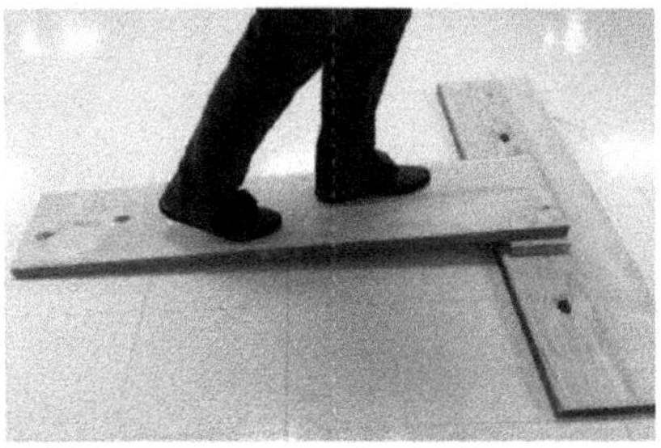

(a) Indoor ramp set up

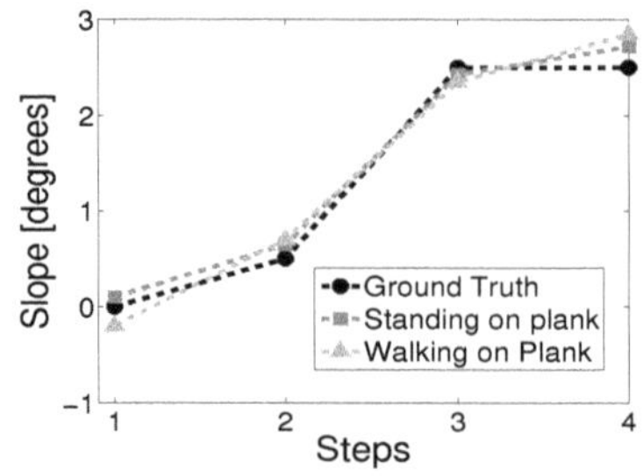

(b) Step vs. Slope at indoor ramp

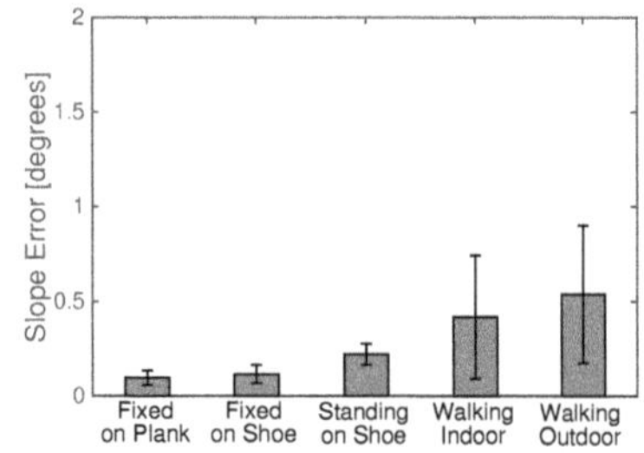

(c) Slope measurement error at different error placements

**Figure 16: Sensor accuracy analysis.**

reaches 30 walking steps. This is encouraging as it indicates that our magnetometer-based walking direction determination scheme is effective.

For the evaluation of the turn detection technique, we collected a new set of data in our laboratory. Different volunteers completed about 400 turns of various angles. During these tests, walkers marked the time instant at which they started turning, which is used as reference to evaluate the performance of the turn detection technique. Figure 17 (b) shows the turn detection precision for varying threshold angles. It is computed as the ratio between the number of true positives and the sum of true and false positives. We define a true positive as a detection event that falls within three steps after the actual turn (marked during data collection). All events detected outside this window are considered as false positives. For a threshold angle of 40 degrees we can achieve a 99% precision.

## 8.3 Sensor Position Comparison

One of the first challenges that we had to face was deciding the sensor mounting position on a shoe. We wanted to ensure that the performance of the gradient sensing technique is not affected by the mounting position and remains consistent over independent trials. Owing to its limited dimension, the sensor was easily mounted in different sites and setting on the shoe. As shown in Figure 18 (a), we selected four candidate positions: top, bottom, behind heel and side. The bottom location required us to dig the sole in order to avoid a direct contact between the sensor and the ground, which may damage the device and affect the data from the inertial sensors. No shoe modifications were needed for the other positions.

We conducted several walking trials in an indoor environment with a flat ground surface to determine the position that manifests consistent accuracy over time. At the start of each test, the sensors were firmly attached to the shoes and removed at the end to charge the battery. Figure 18(b) shows the cumulative distribution function of the step-to-step pitch (slope) variation for different sensor positions. The ground truth values were measured by placing an inclinometer on the floor at consecutive step positions. As expected, all sensor curves show a higher step-to-step variation compared to the ground curve, due to measurement noise. We remark that the sensor readings were collected while walking. Instead, the ground truth was collected by placing an inclinometer on the floor for few seconds. From Figure 18(b) we can infer that all sensor positions have similar performance. However the top position was found to be more consistent over independent mounting and walking trials.

## 8.4 Ground Slope Accuracy

To understand the accuracy of the underlying ground slope sensing technique and isolate different sources of error, we conducted the following controlled experiments. These experiments compare the sensed slope against ground truth established with a 0.2 degree accurate inclinometer.

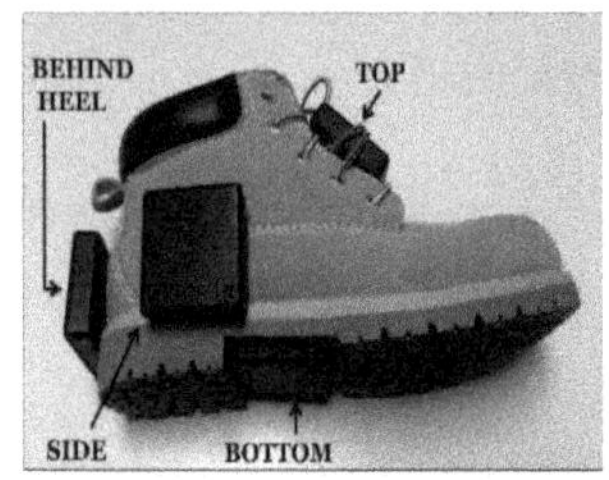

(a) Alternate sensor positions

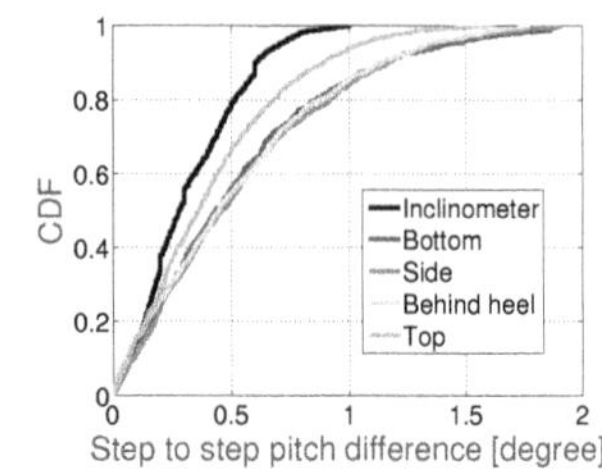

(b) Sensor position analysis

**Figure 18: Sensor position comparison.**

To remove errors from foot movement and walking, we first placed the unmounted sensor on a tilted plank and measured its slope. We then repeated this procedure with a shoe-mounted sensor. The process was further repeated for different plank inclinations. Figure 16(c) shows the mean error and standard deviation for these experiments, marked as fixed on plank and fixed on shoe, respectively. As can be seen, the errors are below the specified accuracy of our ground-truth inclinometer. We then continue the experiment with shoe that is actually worn, first by having an experimenter stand on the larger wooden plank shown in Figure 16(a), which had roughly the same length and inclination as a sidewalk ramp. In a second experiment, the experimenter walked over the plank. The results in the same figure are labeled standing on shoe and walking indoor. They show that standing results have slightly larger errors than the unworn shoe, likely due to some involuntary movements and that walking adds more noticeable but still small errors of about 0.4 degree. We further compare this with walking on an actual sidewalk ramp, where we measured the ground truth inclination at each footstep. The results show a slight increase in errors, presumably because the ground is not uniform, even within the area of a footstep. Overall, the errors are far below the expected slope variations at sidewalk ramps.

# 9. RELATED WORK

Pedestrian tracking using inertial sensors has been of interest to the research community for some time. Most inertial sensor- based applications use some form of dead reckoning for localization [24, 31]. They estimate the distance traveled from a known initial location, by using the stride length and implementing step count, as done by Cho et al. [32].

Robertson et al. [33] explore indoor localization for pedestrians using foot-mounted inertial sensors. Jimenez et al. [34] use ramp detection in indoor environments to provide drift correction in indoor locations. Woodman et al. [35] developed a tracking system that uses a foot-mounted inertial sensor, a model of a building, and a particle filter to track a pedestrian in an indoor environment. Skog et al. [36] developed a Kalman Filter-based zero-velocity detector for foot-mounted inertial navigation systems and evaluate their algorithm by errors in positioning. Madgwick et al. [37] develop an algorithm, which is compared to the Kalman Filter, for computing the orientation of foot mounted inertial sensors. Most of these navigation and orientation computation techniques are tested in controlled indoor environments and do not quite meet the requirements for any level of outdoor gradient sensing system.

In the pedestrian safety domain, Gandhi et al. [38] provide an overview of video, radar and laser distance measurement based approaches for active pedestrian safety. An RFID-based approach is discussed by Fackelmeier et al. [39]. Another approach that needs no line of sight and is based on 3G and WLAN is presented by Sugimoto et al. [40]. David et al. [41, 42, 43] present a radio based approach that assumes that the GPS location is precise up to 10 to 80 cm. They also add movement recognition to the radio-based solution [44]. Another pedestrian safety app by Wang et al. [11] uses the smartphone's camera to detect vehicles approaching the pedestrian when she is talking and walking. Camera-based approaches pose a challenge when it is dark and can easily drain the smartphone's battery. WiFi-honk by Dhondge et al. [13] could be a potential application for our system. They have developed a communication technique to transmit messages from pedestrian to approaching vehicles based on the pedestrian's risk level. Since our system can efficiently identify when pedestrians enter the street, their presence can be announced to approaching vehicles using this communication technique.

Pedestrian safety is now a high priority for car manufacturers. In AKTIV [45], a German road safety project launched in 2006, cameras and radar sensors installed on the vehicle are used to monitor its surrounding. Many car producers [46, 47, 48] are now integrating night vision, active breaking and automatic steering solutions in their new models to reduce pedestrian accidents. Honda is developing a Vehicle-to-Pedestrian technology that is able to detect a pedestrian with a DSRC enabled smartphone [10].

## 10. DISCUSSION

We have presented the design and experimental analysis of a shoe sensor-based technique, which, unlike previous work, aims at ground profiling rather than step counting. Our experiments show that foot mounted inertial sensors can be used to measure the slope of the ground and generate a corresponding slope profile, to detect when a pedestrian enters the street.

The approach does, of course, rely on instrumentation and power in shoes but it could potentially be an additional feature of existing shoe-mounted exercise tracking devices. It might also be suitable for special applications for some of the most vulnerable pedestrians (e.g., children, the elderly, people with disabilities). Furthermore, we observed that performance can be sensitive to the sensor mounting method and therefore believe that performance could be further improved with more robust mounting designs.

A convenient shoe sensing solution should also offer long battery lifetimes. Our current prototype is not optimized in this regard. To reduce the communication energy overhead, it would be desirable to move most of the sensor data processing from the smartphone into dedicated motion processor in the shoe itself. Wake-up mechanism should only activate the system when a pedestrian is walking in an urban area. Shoe sensing systems could also exploit energy harvested from walking movement. We expect that future careful circuit design with wake-up when walking and optimized low energy communications could achieve battery lifetimes of months to years, depending on the amount of walking activity.

Our current system primarily aims to reduce pedestrian-vehicle collisions that are due to the pedestrian being distracted by a smartphone. This is an increasing concern and we have focused our evaluation on a likely scenario: simply walking into the street without noticing. There are many other scenarios unrelated to smartphone distractions, such as running across a street, that put a pedestrian at risk. The shoe sensor approach may also be useful for such traditional pedestrian safety concerns, although we have not designed for or evaluated this case yet.

Similarly, we have not evaluated our framework for the elderly or children. We remark that although our user base was uniform in terms of age and walking style, our algorithm extracts the stance phase and compares users' steps to their past steps. Thus, this extraction can be adapted to various walking speed and style.

The transition detection approach also relies on consistent sidewalk designs. In the United States and the European Union, we are aware of conscious effort to follow consistent guidelines for improved accessibility, although regional customization of the algorithms may be necessary. In our experiments, we were able to detect street entrance events with high accuracy, whenever the sidewalk descends into the street either through a ramp or a curb. We encountered only one situation in which street entrances were hard to detect, i.e., the case where the sidewalk and the street are at the same level. However, the percentage of such crossing conditions was negligible in our experimental scenarios and is, in general, very low in urban environments [18, 23].

Besides safety applications such as Virtual Look Up or Driver Pedestrian Awareness, multiple applications could benefit from our approach. As an example, we have run some preliminary experiments which show that slope profiles can be matched to specific sidewalk locations, if a map of such profiles is available. While perhaps not yet robust enough on its own, the information could be combined with other positioning information to achieve more precise urban localization. Additionally, our approach could be used to create sidewalk profiles to monitor the status of the sidewalk surface and their accessibility.

## 11. CONCLUSION

Motivated by pedestrian safety applications, we explored how effectively shoe-mounted inertial sensors can profile ground gradients and step patterns to detect sidewalk-street transitions. We developed a sensing system to address this multifaceted problem ranging from sensory data acquisition on shoes to the development of a LookUp application. What also sets our approach apart is that we carried out walking trials in-the-wild and collected miles of data in complex metropolitan environments. Our results show a lot of promise achieving detection rates higher than 90% at 0.7% false positives, even in the intricate midtown Manhattan pedestrian environment. Not only did our approach work in the United States, we obtained similar performance from the Italian city of Turin. Overall, we hope that this work demonstrates the broader applicability of shoe-based sensing and inspires developments that go far beyond current exercise tracking applications.

## Acknowledgments

This material is based in part upon work supported by the National Science Foundation under Grant Nos. CNS-1329939, CNS-1409811, CNS-1409767, CNS-1217387, SES-1450091, and by Qualcomm University Relations, as well as by the LIMPID project (POR FESR 2007/2013) funded by Regione Piemonte (Italy).

## 12. REFERENCES


[1] Smart Growth America, Dangerous by Design 2014. http://www.smartgrowthamerica.org/documents/dangerous-by-design-2014/dangerous-by-design-2014.pdf, 2011.

[2] U.S. Department of Transportation, Traffic Safety Facts, August 2013.

[3] Reversal in Three-Year Uptick in Pedestrian Fatalities. http://goo.gl/I389KR.

[4] International Transport Forum, Road Safety Annual Report 2013.

[5] Peter D. Loeb and William A. Clarke. The cell phone effect on pedestrian fatalities. *Transportation Research Part E: Logistics and Transportation Review*, 45(1):284 – 290, 2009.

[6] Liberty Mutual Insurance, Study shows three out of five pedestrians prioritize smartphones over safety when crossing street. http://goo.gl/5z2DzQ, June 2013.

[7] Delaware Online, if you text and walk, remember to look up. http://goo.gl/ww5pRc, May 2012.

[8] The Big Story, NYC Crosswalks urge pedestrians to look! http://bigstory.ap.org/article/nyc-crosswalks-urge-pedestrians-look, September 2012.

[9] U.S. Department of Transportation, Dedicated Short Range Communication. http://www.its.dot.gov/factsheets/dsrc_factsheet.htm.

[10] Honda. Honda Demonstrates Advanced Vehicle-to-Pedestrian and Vehicle-to-Motorcycle Safety Technologies. http://www.honda.com/newsandviews/article.aspx?id=7352-en, August 2013.

[11] Tianyu Wang, Giuseppe Cardone, Antonio Corradi, Lorenzo Torresani, and Andrew T. Campbell. Walksafe: a pedestrian safety app for mobile phone users who walk and talk while crossing roads. In *Proceedings of the Twelfth Workshop on Mobile Computing Systems; Applications*, HotMobile '12, 2012.

[12] Kazushige Ouchi and Miwako Doi. Indoor-outdoor activity recognition by a smartphone. In *Proceedings of the 2012 ACM Conference on Ubiquitous Computing*, UbiComp '12, pages 537–537, New York, NY, USA, 2012. ACM.

[13] Kaustubh Dhondge, Sejun Song, Younghwan Jang, Hyungbae Park, Sunae Shin, and Baek-Young Choi. Video: Wifi-honk: Smartphone-based beacon stuffed wifi car2x-communication system for vulnerable road user safety. In *Proceedings of the 12th Annual International Conference on Mobile Systems, Applications, and Services*, MobiSys '14, pages 387–387, New York, NY, USA, 2014. ACM.

[14] Federal Highway Administration, Crash-Type manual for pedestrians, April 1997.

[15] New York Times, Deaths Rise for Drivers, Bikers and Walkers on City Streets. http://goo.gl/DFhqP, 2012.

[16] Nike+ Sensor. http://www.apple.com/ipod/nike/, 2012.

[17] Adidas Speed Cell. http://goo.gl/Xs9CXK.

[18] Federal Highway Administration, Sidewalk Design Guidelines, July 1999.

[19] U.S. Department of Transportation announces decision to move forward with vehicle-to-vehicle communication technology for light vehicles. http://goo.gl/UlrBzx, February 2014.

[20] Openstreetmap. http://www.openstreetmap.org/.

[21] Shubham Jain, Carlo Borgiattino, Yanzhi Ren, Marco Gruteser, and Yingying Chen. On the limits of positioning-based pedestrian risk awareness. In *Proceedings of the 2014 Workshop on Mobile Augmented Reality and Robotic Technology-based Systems*, MARS '14, 2014.

[22] Trisha Datta, Shubham Jain, and Marco Gruteser. Towards city-scale smartphone sensing of potentially unsafe pedestrian movements. In *Proceedings of the 2014 IEEE 11th International Conference on Mobile Ad Hoc and Sensor Systems*, MASS '14. IEEE Computer Society, 2014.

[23] European Union Pedestrian Planning. http://goo.gl/r2QNsT.

[24] E. Foxlin. Pedestrian tracking with shoe-mounted inertial sensors. *Computer Graphics and Applications, IEEE*, 25(6):38–46, Nov 2005.

[25] C. Mariotti, V. Lakafosis, M.M. Tentzeris, and L. Roselli. An ipv6-enabled wireless shoe-mounted platform for health-monitoring. In *Wireless Sensors and Sensor Networks (WiSNet), 2013 IEEE Topical Conference on*, Jan 2013.

[26] E.S. Sazonov, G. Fulk, J. Hill, Y. Schutz, and R. Browning. Monitoring of posture allocations and activities by a shoe-based wearable sensor. *Biomedical Engineering, IEEE Transactions on*, 58(4), April 2011.

[27] Yan Wang, Jie Yang, Hongbo Liu, Yingying Chen, Marco Gruteser, and Richard P. Martin. Sensing vehicle dynamics for determining driver phone use. In *Proceeding of the 11th Annual International Conference on Mobile Systems, Applications, and Services*, MobiSys '13, pages 41–54, New York, NY, USA, 2013. ACM.

[28] Shane Colton. The balance filter. http://goo.gl/WR8e6m, 2007.

[29] Eun Tae Jeung Hyung Gi Min. Complementary filter design for angle estimation using mems accelerometer and gyroscope. http://goo.gl/F2PeSX.

[30] Invensense. Invensense MPU-9150 product specification. http://www.invensense.com/mems/gyro/documents/PS-MPU-9150A-00v4_3.pdf.

[31] John-Olof Nilsson, Amit K Gupta, and Peter Händel. Foot-mounted inertial navigation made easy. In *International Conference on Indoor Positioning and Indoor Navigation*, volume 27, page 30th, 2014.

[32] Seong Yun Cho and Chan Gook Park. Mems based pedestrian navigation system. *Journal of Navigation*, 59(01):135–153, 2006.

[33] Patrick Robertson, Michael Angermann, and Bernhard Krach. Simultaneous localization and mapping for pedestrians using only foot-mounted inertial sensors. In *Proceedings of the 11th International Conference on Ubiquitous Computing*, Ubicomp '09, pages 93–96, New York, NY, USA, 2009. ACM.

[34] A Jimenez, F Seco, F Zampella, J Prieto, and J Guevara. Pdr with a foot-mounted imu and ramp detection. *Sensors*, 11(10):9393–9410, Oct 2011.

[35] Oliver Woodman and Robert Harle. Pedestrian localisation for indoor environments. In *Proceedings of the 10th International Conference on Ubiquitous Computing*, UbiComp '08, pages 114–123, New York, NY, USA, 2008. ACM.

[36] I. Skog, J.-O. Nilsson, and P. Handel. Evaluation of zero-velocity detectors for foot-mounted inertial navigation systems. In *Indoor Positioning and Indoor Navigation*

*(IPIN), 2010 International Conference on*, pages 1–6, Sept 2010.

[37] S.O.H. Madgwick, A.J.L. Harrison, and R. Vaidyanathan. Estimation of imu and marg orientation using a gradient descent algorithm. In *Rehabilitation Robotics (ICORR), 2011 IEEE International Conference on*, June 2011.

[38] T. Gandhi and M.M. Trivedi. Pedestrian protection systems: Issues, survey, and challenges. *Intelligent Transportation Systems, IEEE Transactions on*, 8(3), 2007.

[39] Andreas Fackelmeier, Christian Morhart, and Erwin Biebl. Dual frequency methods for identifying hidden targets in road traffic. In *Advanced Microsystems for Automotive Applications 2008*, pages 11–20. Springer, 2008.

[40] C. Sugimoto, Y. Nakamura, and T. Hashimoto. Prototype of pedestrian-to-vehicle communication system for the prevention of pedestrian accidents using both 3g wireless and wlan communication. In *Wireless Pervasive Computing, 2008. ISWPC 2008. 3rd International Symposium on*, 2008.

[41] K. David and A. Flach. Car-2-x and pedestrian safety. *Vehicular Technology Magazine, IEEE*, 5(1), 2010.

[42] A. Flach and K. David. Combining radio transmission with filters for pedestrian safety: Experiments and simulations. In *Vehicular Technology Conference Fall (VTC 2010-Fall), 2010 IEEE 72nd*, 2010.

[43] C. Voigtmann, Sian Lun Lau, and K. David. Evaluation of a collaborative-based filter technique to proactively detect pedestrians at risk. In *Vehicular Technology Conference (VTC Fall), 2012 IEEE*, 2012.

[44] A. Flach, A.Q. Memon, Sian Lun Lau, and K. David. Pedestrian movement recognition for radio based collision avoidance: A performance analysis. In *Vehicular Technology Conference (VTC Spring), 2011 IEEE 73rd*, 2011.

[45] Aktiv project. `http://www.aktiv-online.org/english/aktiv-as.html#KAS`.

[46] Audi. Audi: Night vision assistant with highlighting of detected pedestrians. `http://goo.gl/21GD2g`.

[47] Volvo. Volvo car corporation's emergency brake assist. `http://www.volvocars.com/intl/top/corporate/volvo-sustainability/pages/sustainability-news.aspx?itemid=280`, 2011.

[48] Toyota. Toyota develops new pedestrian safety technology. `http://www.toyota.com/esq/safety/active-safety/toyota-develops-new-pedestrian-safety-technology.html`, 2013.

# ZOE: A Cloud-less Dialog-enabled Continuous Sensing Wearable Exploiting Heterogeneous Computation

Nicholas D. Lane[†], Petko Georgiev[§], Cecilia Mascolo[§], Ying Gao[‡]
[†]Bell Labs, [§]University of Cambridge, [‡]Intel Research

## ABSTRACT

The wearable revolution, as a mass-market phenomenon, has finally arrived. As a result, the question of how wearables should evolve over the next 5 to 10 years is assuming an increasing level of societal and commercial importance. A range of open design and system questions are emerging, for instance: How can wearables shift from being largely health and fitness focused to *tracking a wider range of life events*? What will become the *dominant methods through which users interact with wearables* and consume the data collected? Are wearables *destined to be cloud and/or smartphone dependent* for their operation?

Towards building the critical mass of understanding and experience necessary to tackle such questions, we have designed and implemented ZOE – a match-box sized (49g) collar- or lapel-worn sensor that pushes the boundary of wearables in an important set of new directions. First, ZOE aims to perform multiple deep sensor inferences that span key aspects of everyday life (viz. personal, social and place information) on *continuously sensed data*; while also offering this data not only within conventional analytics but also through a speech dialog system that is able to answer impromptu casual questions from users. *(Am I more stressed this week than normal?)* Crucially, and unlike other rich-sensing or dialog supporting wearables, ZOE achieves this *without* cloud or smartphone support – this has important side-effects for privacy since all user information can remain on the device. Second, ZOE incorporates the latest innovations in system-on-a-chip technology together with a custom daughter-board to realize a three-tier low-power processor hierarchy. We pair this hardware design with software techniques that manage system latency while still allowing ZOE to remain energy efficient (with a typical lifespan of 30 hours), despite its high sensing workload, small form-factor, and need to remain responsive to user dialog requests.

## Categories and Subject Descriptors

H.1.2 [**User/Machine Systems**]: Human information processing

## General Terms

Design, Experimentation, Performance

## Keywords

mobile sensing, wearable, dialog system, continuous sensing


*MobiSys'15,* May 18–22, 2015, Florence, Italy.

http://dx.doi.org/10.1145/2742647.2742672.

## 1. INTRODUCTION

The wearable market is rapidly advancing both in terms of raw technology and user adoption rates. As is often the case during periods of considerable innovation, wearable technology continues to prompt questions at a faster rate than we are able to answer them. In this paper, we start to examine a series of wearable system design questions that we believe will be important for the evolution of this category of mobile sensing devices moving forward. Specifically, we investigate in the context of wearables:

*1. Continuous Sensing of a Diverse Range of User Behaviors and Environments.* Most wearables today largely focus on health and fitness. What is missing is a more comprehensive awareness of the lives of users because real people have existences outside of the gym. Increasingly sophisticated sensing algorithms are being developed on more powerful platforms, such as smartphones, that can gather deep insights into areas like our conversation patterns [46], incidents of stress [50], the places we live and work [33]. An understanding needs to be developed about how such sensing techniques can be integrated together into wearable-class hardware and run simultaneously on continuous sensor streams.

*2. Cloud-free Operation by exploiting Heterogeneous Local Computation.* The capabilities and sophistication of mobile energy-efficient processors progress at a relentless rate. For example, an iPhone 6 represents a 10-fold increase in computation over a 5-year old iPhone 3GS. Extensive research has given us a solid set of techniques and an understanding of cloud-offloading and cyber-foraging [18] – with recent work even exploring within the context of wearable specifically [30]. But benefits exist for privacy (as data never leaves the device) and energy with purely device-only solutions. Consumers are growing ever more wary of the remote processing of sensor data, that contains potentially sensitive personal information [16]. An important gap in our understanding is precisely how far we can push emerging wearable hardware to execute sensing and related algorithms without the assistance of remote computation. Options within mobile architectures continue to diversify (e.g., big.LITTLE technology, availability of FPGAs and DSPs, CPUs interacting with sensor-attached MCUs). To maximize these advances, we need to study how to best architect the sensor inference and user interaction workloads for wearables cross such heterogeneous hardware.

*3. In-situ User Sensor Data Analysis with Near Real-time Responsiveness.* Detailed analysis of user data from wearables is largely only computed and offered to the user in off-line fashion for post event consumption. For many activities which involve the "now", near real-time reporting can become pivotal: examples include the calculation of current levels of stress with respect to other days, simple queries for memory assistance – when did I last visit this place? Or the reporting on past sporting activity performance compared to the current activity. Supporting such forms of user experience requires investigation of how inference, analysis and user interaction methods can be provided on-demand. It also provokes questions: could any seldom used natural user interface methods, such as speech dialog systems, be made responsive and resource efficient enough for wearables?

We investigate these questions through the design and implementation of a novel wearable sensor – ZOE. The goal of ZOE is to continuously sense a comprehensive set of user behaviors and contexts that span three key areas of everyday life (specifically personal-, social- and place-oriented sensing); while also providing natural impromptu access to collected information with an interactive speech dialog subsystem (complemented with more conventional user interaction methods). Towards this goal, we have developed an integrated sensing module that incorporates a range of state-of-the-art sensing algorithms designed for devices more powerful than typical wearable hardware – critically, almost all of these algorithms have previously been studied in isolation. Together, with the demands of the dialog system, this forms a highly demanding sensing and interaction workload, parts of which require near real-time responsiveness.

We demonstrate this workload can be serviced with a wearable device – without cloud assistance – and still provide acceptable energy and responsiveness performance. This is possible through a custom wearable hardware prototype and a combination of workload optimizations and resource management algorithms. The prototype for ZOE is designed around the recently released Intel Edison SoC [5] that includes a dual-core 500 MHz CPU and 100 MHz MCU. In our design, Edison is coupled with another MCU present on a custom designed daughter-board to form a 3-tier computational hierarchy. Each tier in the hierarchy offers a different computation and energy trade-off that, when managed efficiently, enables ZOE to meet user experience needs.

The contributions of our work include:

- The study of a collection of diverse, complex sensing algorithms that are integrated together and performed simultaneously within the computation and energy constraints of wearable-class hardware.
- The proposal of a new, spontaneous way for wearable users to interact with their data through a verbal dialog. We demonstrate this is feasible even without cloud assistance while offering near real-time responsiveness.
- The design and prototyping of new wearable hardware that offers the heterogeneous computation necessary to meet the workload demands of ZOE. Through proposed performance techniques, we show the hardware capabilities of our prototype are efficiently used in support of sensing and interaction workloads.
- The systematic evaluation of the end-to-end design of ZOE using a variety of large-scale datasets and fine-grain energy and responsiveness measurements. Our results indicate ZOE can provide acceptable levels of inference accuracy, battery life and responsiveness.

## 2. ZOE DESIGN OVERVIEW

We begin our description of ZOE, with a comprehensive overview. After describing how this wearable can impact the everyday life of its users, we proceed to discuss the design goals that are natural extensions of such scenarios. We close with a comparison of ZOE to existing wearables of commercial, academic or industry lab origins.

**Figure 1:** ZOE Prototype

### 2.1 Targeted User Experiences

ZOE offers many new capabilities not seen in today's wearables. By sketching usage scenarios for these capabilities we also highlight the technical challenges that must be solved.

**Life with ZOE.** As shown in Figure 1, ZOE is designed to be worn on a collar or lapel. At just 49g and with a typical lifetime of 30 hours, it is designed to be worn constantly during everyday activities. As such, ZOE aims to capture a broad set of user actions and ambient conditions, not just a single domain such as health and wellbeing. Shown in Table 1, the current prototype captures a diverse set of inferences from three main areas of life (viz. personal sensing, social sensing, place sensing). Because ZOE has built-in WiFi-host support any nearby computer or the user's own smartphone can be used to browse collected user information by simply connecting to the wearable (and being able to successfully authenticate), with ZOE acting as a local web-server (technique first proposed in [69]). Beyond such conventional interaction methods, users are also able to spontaneously ask spoken questions regarding their data and perform basic control operations (see Table 3). By providing both interaction methods users have conventional access to comprehensive analytics about their behavior, while still being able to informally gather short personal factoids whenever a question occurs to them. Significantly, ZOE can provide all of this functionality without the support of the cloud or off-loading computation to the user's smartphone. This addresses some aspects of user privacy concerns by allowing all data to remain on the device rather than data leaking to the cloud for analysis.

We envision many scenarios of potential use for ZOE. Within the sphere of personal use there are a number of natural application domains related to mHealth, life-logging, cognitive assistance, persuasive systems and the quantified-self movement. In more emerging fields there are applications of productivity, "life-hacking" and time accounting in which users want to optimize their activities by maximizing what they can accomplish each day. For example, with minor changes to the design presented in this paper, users would be able to understand which behavioral patterns lead to their most productive days or more simply track precisely how they spend their days in the office. When multiple ZOE devices are used in organizational and company settings, we expect they will be able to highlight, for instance, which teams work more closely together and how such co-operation relates to intra- and inter-team social interactions. Finally, ZOE can be a powerful tool in the hands of social scientists providing unobtrusively captured fine-grain behavioral data from which they can understand fundamental characteristics and relationships that shape our actions.

**Technical Challenges.** For ZOE to function as described above, the following challenges must be addressed.

*1. Multi-domain User Sensing.* To capture a broad understanding of a user's life will require multiple inference algorithms operating

| Category | Subtype | Inferences |
|---|---|---|
| Personal | Transportation | {*motorized, non-motorized*} |
| | Phy. Activities | {*walk, stationary, run, other*} |
| | Stress Detection | {*stressed, neutral*} |
| Social | Social Interaction | {*conversation, other*} |
| | Conversation Analysis | estimators: *dominance, turns* |
| Place | Place Recognition | {*home, work, other*} |
| | Place Context | occupancy estimation |
| | | estimators: *music, noise, chatter* |

**Table 1:** Sensor inference capabilities of ZOE

in concert, often even simultaneously as they examine differing elements of the same event. Broadening the scope of user monitoring also requires more complex algorithms capable of mining deeper types of inferences.

*2. Energy Efficiency.* Wearables like ZOE work best when worn continuously day-after-day. This becomes impractical if they must be frequently recharged by users. Therefore wearables must be highly energy efficient and remain active for multiple days on a single charge. The design tension here, however, is that for similar reasons they also need to be small and light – which promotes small batteries. Furthermore, the need for additional sensing algorithms (see above) only applies more pressure to battery reserves.

*3. Near Real-time Processing.* The user experience of dialog interactions are highly time sensitive; for example, a typical pause before responding in normal conversations is around 500 ms [27]. The benefit of offering casual and impromptu questions or instructions disappears if user wait times are either excessive or even just inconsistent (leading to uncertainty – e.g., did it understand me?). Similarly, because ZOE provides not only longitudinal information but also the ability to query recent events or make comparisons (e.g., Am I being interrupted more today than normal?), sensor inferences must complete in a timely fashion, likely over time-scales of an hour or two.

## 2.2 Prototype Design

We will now describe in detail how ZOE overcomes the challenges just described. However, before diving into such details we briefly outline key aspects of our hardware design and software dataflow.

**Hardware Prototype.** As shown in Figure 2, the current hardware is only 49mm by 10mm with a depth of 57mm. Figure 1 shows ZOE within its 3D-printed case. These dimensions and device weight measurement (49g) assume the use of a 1500 mAh battery – as shown in all figures. Further details of our hardware design are discussed in §5.1.

The heart of our prototype is the Intel Edison [5] SoC that is paired with a custom daughter-board containing a programmable micro-controller, wireless charger, speaker and sensors (viz. gyroscope, accelerometer and microphone). The Edison itself has a further two processing units, the primary one being a dual-core 500 MHz Atom processor which is supported by a 100 MHz Quark processor. WiFi is also built-in directly to the Edison SoC which is required for both sensing and user interaction tasks. Essentially they form a three-tier processing hierarchy. Collectively, different configurations of these tiers offer a variety of energy usage and computational trade-offs that we leverage towards high levels of responsiveness and energy efficiency in ZOE.

**Software Operation.** ZOE is comprised of three core components illustrated in Figure 3. Specifically these are: Sensing Algorithms (§3), Dialog Subsystem (§4) and Performance Controller (§5). Each component relies on a secondary set of shared auxiliary modules (§6) – the most prominent of these is the User Knowledge

**Figure 2:** ZOE hardware showing the heterogeneous MCUs and CPU. (Inset image: Underneath prototype, showing recharging coil.)

Store. We now describe the operation of ZOE in terms of each of these core components.

*Sensing Algorithms.* We integrate into a single sensing module a broad set of accelerometer-, gyroscope-, WiFi- and microphone-based based algorithms that infer user behaviors and ambient contexts. Table 1 summarizes the specific inferences made by ZOE continuously throughout the day. Inferences are selected to provide well-rounded sensing coverage across key areas of the user's life. In our current prototype these domains include: *Personal Sensing* – which spans the actions, behaviors and the status of the user themselves; *Social Sensing* – that monitors and quantifies the interactions the user has with other people; and finally, *Place Sensing* – aiming to track locations of importance to users (home, work etc.) and characterize their conditions.

The stream of inferences generated by this component are organized into a local user knowledge store designed to support dialog queries. Using a few relatively simple inference processing mechanisms even single inferences generate multiple knowledge base entries. For example, as the user is detected to arrive home by ZOE, many behavioral data points are created, including: the duration of the commute, the distance, and a simple carbon footprint estimate. By storing this information in structured storage, supporting a diverse set of user inquires is simplified. Additional details are presented later in §6.

*Dialog Subsystem.* The purpose of this component is to recognize and respond to user queries for information and device commands (e.g., privacy settings) they issue. In many respects, the Sensing Algorithms component previously described shares many characteristics with the Dialog Subsystem. Both components track sensor data (only the microphone in this case) and react by performing different actions based on the content of observed data. For example, when a special activation keyword is spoken (e.g., the name of the system) then the complete sentence is analyzed so that the system can understand and respond. Our implementation includes optimizations based on fixed point math and fast methods for processing Gaussian Mixture Models (GMMs) on embedded hardware. However,

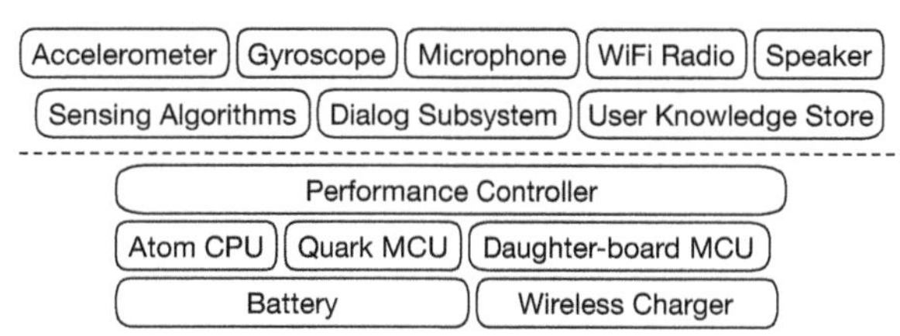


**Figure 3:** ZOE Architecture

| Mobile Device | Dimensions | Weight | Lifetime | Battery | Cloud? | Inferences Made |
|---|---|---|---|---|---|---|
| ZOE | 47 x 10 x 57mm | 49g | 30 hours | 1500mAh | No | Physical Activity (Walking, Stationary, Running, Other); Stress; Transportation; Place; Place Context; Voicing; Conversation Analysis |
| MSP [23] | 51mm x 36mm x NA | 115g | 10/20 hr | 1800 mAH | No | Physical Activity (Walking, Running, Cycling, Stairs); Cooking; TV; Voicing; Eating; Working on a Computer; Elliptical Trainer; Elevator |
| Gabriel [30] | Glasss-sized | 42g | 1 hr | 2.1Wh | Yes | Face Recognition; OCR; Object Recognition; AR; Motion/Activity |
| Microsoft Band [9] | 19mm x 8.7 mm x NA | 60g | 48 hr | 200mAh | Partial | Heart Rate; Sleep; Exercise Routine; Jogging; Hiking; Cycling |
| Jawbone Up3 [7] | 220 x 12.2 x 3.0-9.3mm | 29g | 168 hr | 38 mAh | No | Heart Rate; Sleep; Running; Steps; Calories; Automated Fitness Activity Recognition |
| Opo [35] | $14cm^2$ | 11.4g | 93 hr | 40mAh | No | Physical Proximity; Face-to-Face Interaction |
| LG G Watch R [8] | 46.4 x 53.6 x 9.7mm | 62g | 23 hr [2] | 410 mAh | Partial | Heart Rate; Sleep, Physical Activity; Voice Commands; Running; Steps; Calories |

**Table 2:** Comparison of ZOE with recent and/or popular wearables from the literature and available commercially

| |
|---|
| How much time did I spend driving over the last week? |
| How many different places did I visit in the last four days? |
| Give me the number of times I was here this month? |
| Compared to the previous time I was here am I more stressed? |
| How does the amount of my cycling this week compare to last week? |
| How long did I talk to people this morning? |
| What fraction of my time do I spend listening to music? |
| On which day do I travel in a vehicle most? |
| Where do I spend more time chatting with people than usual? |
| Am I more stressed than normal on weekdays? |
| How many times was I feeling stressed this month? |
| If I leave for home now how long does it normally take me to get there? |
| When did I finish jogging? |

**Table 3:** Representative sentences supported by Dialog Subsystem

we find that the most critical factor in determining the accuracy and latency of the Dialog Subsystem is the design of the language model and the composition of the vocabulary. Table 3 provides representative examples of our design decisions, under which interactions remain quasi-natural but limited in scope to device inferences and control. Responses are determined by the template-matching technique, each template is tied to handlers in code that dictates how to respond.

*Performance Controller.* This component collectively refers to the key design decisions that largely enable ZOE to operate for more than a day with a single battery charge and be responsive while still performing a rich set of sensing inferences. Our control plane leverages the built-in inter-processor communication mechanisms for synchronizing the operation of the three processor units (2 MCUs and Atom CPU). Critically, the MCUs offload the sensor sampling from the Atom and execute sensor data pre-filtering to control the workload generated for the CPU. The Quark MCU, for instance, filters silent samples and approaches the CPU for computation only when noise is detected in the user surroundings. This allows the CPU to remain in low-power sleep state for a large fraction of the day. Other functions falling under the umbrella term of performance control include speech activation (to spawn speech-related pipelines only when the context is human voice), owner triggered keyword spotting (to detect the commands issued by the owner), as well as dialog command prioritization over sensor processing to promote system responsiveness.

## 2.3 Comparisons to Existing Wearables

Table 2 surveys a range of wearables both from the literature and those commercially available. Devices in this table capture a number of wearable sub-categories. First, the very popular, but health-focused offerings from Jawbone and Microsoft. Second, examples of systems built on Google Glass (or glass-like) devices that primarily rely on vision techniques for inference. Third, very small single purpose devices like Opo [35] that have excellent battery life – in the case of Opo specializing in tracking face-to-face user interactions. Fourth, devices such as the Mobile Sensing Platform (MSP) [23] and the watch-style wearables represented in the table by the LG G Watch R [8]. Because these final two device classes are both multi-sensor and computationally capable, they therefore can support a variety of user inferences. However, watch wearable apps are still in their infancy and so the MSP is the closest wearable to ZOE in terms of breadth of *user-focused* activity recognition supported.

**Inference Depth.** One clear message from Table 2 is that *ZOE distances itself from other wearables due to the range of inferences it can support.* Commercial wearables, for example, only partially support the personal sensing inferences of ZOE and miss advanced microphone features such as stress detection – although ZOE is unable to track sleep, something that all of these health-targeting wearables can perform. Gabriel [30] is the closest comparison in shear inference depth because it leverages the vision capabilities of Google Glass to offer a number of deep context inferences. However, this device has much worse battery-life as well as being larger and heavier. The MSP is the nearest single device in terms of size and weight – supporting a few high-level user inferences similar to those of ZOE. But even acknowledging mobile technology advancements since 2008 (when the MSP v2, with which we compare, was developed), unlike ZOE this system does not include the performance control mechanisms needed to the maximize benefits of such hardware.

In fact, some of the best comparisons of inference breadth available are not designed for wearables but rather phones. For example, apps like PEIR [56] and CenceMe [54] support multiple inferences (such as activity, voicing, and transportation in the case of CenceMe) during their operation. Essentially ZOE provides levels of inference depth that exceeds even sensing apps for smartphones, and brings this experience to a different, miniaturized class of device: wearables.

**Battery-Life and Form-Factor.** ZOE has a high ratio of inference breadth to energy efficiency. It has a battery life comparable to the Microsoft Band [9] (30 hours vs 48 hours) but with a larger set of inferences; other devices, like Gabriel, that also support a number of inferences have lifespans of just 1 or 2 hours. Yet, ZOE does not approach the lifespans of the Jawbone Up3. In terms of form-factor, its size and weight are similar again to commercial devices like the Band. Although ZOE has a collar form factor and most devices in Table 2 are wrist-worn, the volumes of these devices are still comparable.

**Interaction Model.** None of the wearables we survey offer the same set of interaction modes as ZOE. All rely on cloud-based services to present wearable data to either the user's smartphone or desktop. None support the direct serving of data from the wearable to the user's devices like ZOE. Only one device (the Microsoft Band [9]) includes dialog support, but this was supported via a smartphone interacting with the cloud rather than the wearable operating in isolation. However, many devices do include screens for

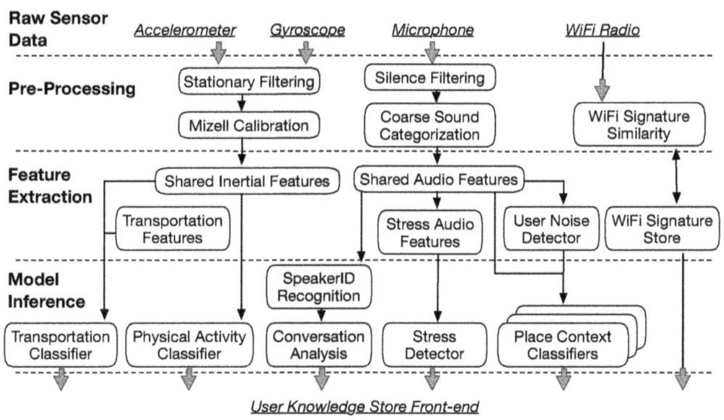


**Figure 4:** Sensing Algorithm Module

presenting data – although the lapel position of ZOE likely makes reading a screen difficult.

**Leveraging Heterogeneous Computation.** The general approach of MCU offloading of tasks from a CPU is not new for wearables. The recent MotoActv smartwatch [10] from Motorola, to name just one wearable, performs step counting on an MCU rather than the more energy consuming CPU. ZOE however relies on dual MCUs, with the Quark MCU itself having similar computational capacity as the MCU used by the Microsoft Band (ARM Cortex M4 MCU processor). Due to this design, and a number of performance controller optimizations (see §5), this architecture affords ZOE previously unseen features such as always-on audio sensing and user dialog support, all without cloud involvement. Other wearables include similarly rich computational options (the LG G Watch R, for example, incorporates a Qualcomm Snapdragon 400 SoC [11] complete with 4-core CPU and Hexagon DSP). But, such hardware is not yet being used to its full potential (in the case of the LG G Watch R its software only exploits 1 CPU core, and not the DSP [2]).

# 3. SENSING ALGORITHMS

In this section, we describe the sensing algorithms adopted in the current design of ZOE that span the categories of personal-, social- and place-related inference. Each form of sensing incorporated has already been validated in previously published work. The focus in ZOE is to combine these techniques into a single integrated sensing module that operates within hardware (and energy) constraints.

**Overview.** Figure 4 details the interaction between each signal processing and machine learning component needed to implement the collection of sensing algorithms in ZOE. A high degree of component sharing can be seen in the figure, especially between those components operating on data from the same sensor. Overall, the data-flow of each individual algorithm within the module is, at a high-level, very similar. *All sensors are continuously sampled* with this data feeding into pre-processing stages that perform operations like applying a low-pass filter or estimating the direction of gravity (see §6 for more details). Domain specific features are then extracted that project raw data into representations designed to accentuate patterns of similarity between features from the same logical class (intra-class distance); while doing the opposite (i.e., emphasizing the differences) between features of different logical classes (inter-class distance). Finally classification models determine which class the data belongs to (e.g., does the collected data correspond to the user driving or not driving).

Accelerometer and gyroscope processing algorithms (transportation mode and activity inferences) share pre-processing techniques and have a number of overlapping common features. Furthermore, both utilize the same classifier design and combine a static classifier with simple temporal smoothing. WiFi-radio processing is very simple in comparison and is not shared with any other algorithm. By far the most complex is audio processing. Two pipeline branches are encoded, one for human speech and one for background ambient sound. Shared pre-processing includes silence detection and coarse category classification {music, voicing, other}. Deep processing occurs along the voicing branch with stages including binary user-oriented speakerID and stress detection, while ambient audio is mined for various characteristics of the place (e.g., number nearby people). Sharing features is common in the voicing branch as are models in some cases (such as GMMs). Furthermore, social interaction metrics (that are somewhat distinct from the other classifiers included in the module) reuse whole components together – for example, conversation is detected using coarse classification, the presence of silence periods along with speaker ID to recognize that a user is actually involved in the conversation and simply not just nearby.

As previously mentioned, raw inferences from this module are expanded upon while being stored in the User Knowledge Store (§6). For example: frequency counts, durations, start and end-times. This explicitly captures multiple pieces of information each inference can hold about a person.

## 3.1 Personal Sensing

ZOE supports 3 forms of personal sensing; namely the detection of physical activities and transportation mode along with a recognizer of periods when the user is under stress.

**Physical Activities.** By extracting a series of 24 time- and frequency-domain features (adopted from [52]) from the accelerometer and gyroscope, the common user actions of {walk, stationary, run, other} are tracked. A 7-layer deep J.48 decision tree is trained that is then coupled to a 4-state Markov Model which smooths class transitions based on typical activity sequences. This classifier combination is common practice in many mobile sensing systems such as in [47]. Although relatively simple, this design has been shown to be sufficient for this combination of activities (e.g., [57]).

**Transportation Mode.** Most proposed transportation mode recognition techniques require data from either the GPS [63] or a WiFi-radio [41]. Instead ZOE incorporates less common accelerometer- and gyroscope-based approaches (e.g., [52, 32]) that can achieve similar levels of accuracy with a significantly lower energy overhead (as inertial sensors require much less power than GPS or a WiFi radio). In its current design this classifier only makes a binary decision {motorized, non-motorized}; although [32] indicates with further refinement finer-grain distinctions (trains, buses, cars) are possible. Again, we use a 4-second frame of 128 accelerometer samples and a superset of the features used for physical activity tracking are taken (adopted from [32]) with additional adopted features proposed first in [32]. To perform classification, we settle on an Adaboost ensemble learner with decision stumps acting as the weak learner (essentially two-level decision trees) – empirically we find that an ensemble of 20 stumps maximizes accuracy. The final inference is made after (again) smoothing with a two-state Markov model. In [32], this technique was found to outperform other candidate designs and, historically, it has been popular in many activity recognition settings (e.g., [47]).

**Stress Periods.** ZOE applies the findings of [50], and more loosely [61], towards detecting periods when the user is under stress. Whenever the user is detected to be speaking the voicing sample is analyzed and assigned into one of two categories: {*stressed*, *neutral*}. In addition to shared acoustic features that are also used by all audio classifiers in ZOE, stress detection uses additional features that focus on: pitch, speaking rate and a 17-dimension feature (TEO-CB-AutoEnv) that captures distinctive variations, especially in high-level talking styles ("anger", "loud"). For classification, as in [50], we use 16-component GMMs for both classes with a decision made by applying a likelihood function assuming equal priors. A single universal model is applied under all conditions and for all users, we leave albeit useful extensions to the [50] method involving model adaptation for future exploration.

## 3.2 Social Sensing

ZOE leverages two microphone pipelines, namely speech detection and speaker identification, as the basis for gathering a set of conversation-related metadata and inferences. The speech detection component is based on a simple decision tree and enables the detection of when and for how long a user socializes/interacts with other nearby people. The algorithm borrows elements from [51] and extracts features from 32ms sound frames every 1.28s when noise is detected. It has the dual role of both providing social inferences and acting as a trigger for other speech-related analysis.

The speaker identification module is used to detect whether the currently talking speaker is the owner of the wearable. This enables the monitoring of a wide set of additional conversation patterns including dominance (i.e. the fraction of time the owner is talking), turn taking periods, and even interactiveness (whether the user takes short turns frequently with other people) [37]. The speaker identification algorithm is adopted from [61] and relies on two Gaussian Mixture Models, one representing the targeted speaker and the other acting as a sink for other people. Similarly to the original pipeline, Perceptual Linear Predictive (PLP) coefficients are extracted every 30ms and accumulated over a window of 3s. We use a shorter window to capture the onset of turns.

## 3.3 Place Sensing

The final category of sensing performed by ZOE is based on significant places – i.e., locations that users frequently visit and spend the majority of their time. We utilize two types of place sensing: one that performs place recognition and another that analyzes the ambient conditions of a place.

**Place Recognition.** The most common method to recognize places is by comparing the signatures of WiFi scans (e.g., [40, 33]). A signature is simply a vector of WiFi access point SSIDs. If the signatures of two scans differ enough then they are assumed to be two distinct places; similarly, a user returning to the same places again (such as their home) is detected when the current signature matches prior visits. We perform WiFi scans periodically on a 15-minute duty-cycle, and use the Tanimoto coefficient to compute signature similarity. Because this approach is unable to determine place semantics (e.g., the meaning of the place) ZOE adopts a heuristic derived from [42] to identify the two most important user locations – their home and work locations. This is done based on the times and days of arrival and departure, along with visit frequency.

**Place Context Analysis.** To characterize the user's environment in different places, ZOE adopts a series of audio-based sensing techniques originally proposed in [70] and [67]. By combining the techniques of these two respective systems we are able to coarsely monitor: the number of people close to the user, and the intensity of background chatter, music and overall noise level. Three categories of place context (viz. music, noise, chatter) are recognized with category specific 4-class GMMs, each class corresponding to the level of intensity of the particular characteristic. Relatively common audio classification features are used, and these overlap with features already required for already described audio classifiers; the

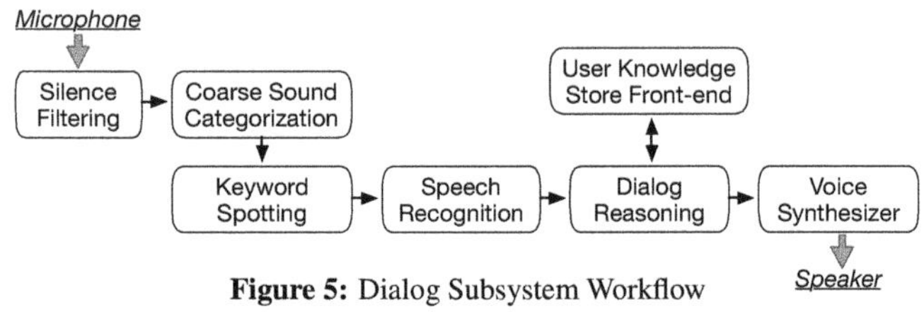


**Figure 5:** Dialog Subsystem Workflow

exception being a binary indicator that signals when the user is engaged in conversation that must be accounted for as it can skew the assessment of the ambient environment. In contrast, the estimation of occupancy is performed in a distinctly different manner, using an unsupervised counting algorithm from [70]. The features that feed into this counting algorithm include a 19-dimension MFCC feature vector along with pitch features that are used for gender disambiguation. A final occupancy estimate is produced by a clustering like process designed for this specific task.

# 4. DIALOG SUBSYSTEM

ZOE understands user instructions and requests through a purpose-built dialog system designed to operate within a series of hardware- and energy-based constraints.

**Overview.** Figure 5 illustrates the components that comprise the dialog subsystem, along with the dataflow between them. Operation begins with a continuous stream of microphone data from which audio frames containing non-silence and spoken words are extracted. This front-end is shared with the sensing algorithms detailed in §3. When voicing frames are identified then Keyword Spotting (KWS) is performed to recognize any sentences that begin with the dialog activation phrase (in the case of our prototype: "*ZOE*"). Any sentences beginning with the phrase are escalated to the Speech Recognition unit. At this stage, all words are attempted to be recognized through by a constrained vocabulary and language model that describes the boundaries of what ZOE is expected to understand. A template-based dialog reasoning phase occurs next that maps the sequence of inferred words for each sentence to a response or action from ZOE. Most responses are synthesized sentences spoken aloud by ZOE, the specific user information provided is determined by the keywords recognized in the dialog template. Alternatively, user instructions simply just alter a device setting, such as temporarily disabling sensing for reasons of user privacy.

**Keyword Spotting.** Robust recognition of the activation phrase (e.g., the name of the device) is critical to successful dialog support. False positive results will cause needless processing of irrelevant sentences. False negative results cause ZOE to ignore user speech input. To minimize this, we implement a state-of-the-art deep learning-based recognizer modeled on recent advances [21] in low-memory and low-complexity Deep Neural Networks (DNNs).

Within the KWS stage, and a continuous stream of sampled audio, certain frames that are identified as containing voicing are first represented as 40-dimension filter-bank energies (FBE) [20]. This variety of features is closely related to the MFCC and PLP features used in a number of the audio-related sensing described in §3. However, within the context of speech recognition FBE has been shown to be much more robust than its MFCC and PLP counterparts. Features are extracted from 30 ms audio frames that slide by 10 msec at a time. A 3-hidden-layer DNN is used that begins with 128 nodes corresponding closely to values of features that are ultimately linked to 2 output states in the final layer – one for each possible outcome – {keyword, no keyword}. The value of each node in the DNN is based on the values of all nodes in the prior

| Processor | Operation |
|---|---|
| Quark MCU | Silence Filtering |
| Daughter-board MCU | Stationary Filtering, Mizell Calibration<br>Physical Activities Classifier<br>Transportation Classifier<br>Shared Inertial Features<br>Transportation Features |
| Edison CPU | Shared Audio Features, Stress Detector<br>User Noise Detector, WiFi Similarity<br>Conversation Analysis, SpeakerID<br>Stress Features |

**Table 4:** Allocation of ZOE workload to hardware components

layer and computed with activation functions uniquely parameterized on a node by node basis. As is standard practice, the final (2-state) layer uses softmax activation functions to result in a binary outcome given earlier inputs. Similarly, the proceeding layers have activation functions trained by a rectifier linear unit [24] (ReLU) selected for their performance in other related KWS systems.

**Speech Recognition.** To understand even a relatively limited vocabulary and constrained language model using a DNN-style solution similar to the one just described is not yet possible given the local computation available to ZOE. The length of processing delays – to name just one problem – would be unacceptable to users. Instead, we adopt proven speech recognition methods that target memory and computation constrained devices (e.g., [29]). We also carefully assemble our vocabulary and language model to sharply lower runtime evaluation (reported in §7.3) while still supporting ≈300 words and thousands of supported unique sentences.

Once KWS confirms the presence of the activation word within voicing speech audio segments, the beginning of that frame are passed to the Speech Recognition stage. We train an acoustic model using a 5-state HMM coupled to 39-dim. GMMs at each state corresponding to sub-word utterances. Multiple groups of candidate words for each sentence can be computed using the acoustic model. These candidates are further assessed with a bi-gram language model to judge the likelihood that particular word collections are correct given their sequential usage with an entire sentence.

**Dialog Reasoning.** We adopt the popular template-based approach to dialog interactions. Based on the probability of words in the recognized sentence it is matched to one of a fixed set of query templates by a fitness score. Below a fixed threshold the user is asked for clarification. For each template a query handler exists to generate requests to the User Knowledge Store (see §6). Parameters are determined by spoken keywords in the sentence; if one of them has an accuracy below a threshold, the user is asked to clarify. The logic in each query handler might dictate other processing to resolve certain keywords such as "normal" which will enact a separate query to determine the average for the user within some bound. As has been found in dialog system research, for close-world domains template matching can be highly effective but difficult to scale to general purpose usage – often due to its dependence on hand crafting of templates and template handlers.

**Voice Synthesizer.** ZOE replies to user dialog through a lightweight text-to-speech (TTS) synthesizer that incorporates the *formant synthesis* [26] technique. This approach can support a variety of languages and pronunciations without resorting to recordings of actual human voices; a critical factor in maintaining a low computational requirements along with a small memory footprint. Input to this component is simply plain text responses generated during Dialog Reasoning. Like most TTS systems words are then broken into the phonemes that describe how the letters in words should sound when spoken aloud. As a result, the generated speech is stilted and less natural (i.e., robotic sounding) than synthesizers with more onerous runtime resource requirements (based on real recordings). eSpeak uses a "formant synthesis" method. This allows many languages to be provided in a small size. The speech is clear, and can be used at high speeds, but is not as natural or smooth as larger synthesizers which are based on human speech recordings.

# 5. PERFORMANCE CONTROLLER

In this section, we outline the hardware and optimization design choices that heavily determine ZOE's energy profile.

## 5.1 Hardware Prototype

To provide context for the optimization control plane, we begin with a component-level description of the hardware. We briefly provide specifications of two primary modules (viz. Edison and daughter-board); additionally we describe how the 3-tier inter-processor communication functions.

**Intel Edison SoC.** The SoC and mount board is only 3.55 x 2.5 x 0.39 cm in size. Within the SoC are two programmable units. First, a dual-core Atom 22nm "Tangier" CPU that runs at 500 MHz and has access to 1GB of RAM. Second, a Quark processor operating at 100 MHz is currently configured as an MCU; both code and memory must occupy less than 192KB.

**Custom Daughter-board.** Designed to be roughly the same width of Edison, our daughter-board is around twice the height. All necessary sensors are either mounted or connected to this device. It also contains the power regulator components necessary to connect both a battery and the wireless recharging coil. Importantly, it also contains the 3rd processor (that acts as a 2nd MCU): an IT 8350 processor (from ITE) running at 48 MHz with 64KB of RAM.

**Inter-Processor Communication.** The operation of both MCUs (Quark and Daughter-board processor) is similar with respect to the signaling and message facilities enabling the communication with the primary CPU. Within the respective OSs of each MCU, a controller arbitrates incoming and outgoing messages transfered via IPC calls and shared memory. Within the MCU, code communication takes the forms of function calls. In the CPU, control nodes exist within the kernel that are also wrapped by libraries supporting interaction from within CPU-based source code.

## 5.2 Optimizations

We now elaborate on several design choices that are aimed at maximizing the power and performance benefits of the hardware components listed in the previous subsection. Table 4 summarizes the placement of primary ZOE components (shown in Figure 3) between computational tiers.

**Sensor Pre-Processing.** All microphone and accelerometer algorithms rely on a front-end of shared pre-processing routines residing partly in the MCUs or the Atom CPU. In the case of accelerometer-based ones (activities and transportation mode) these routines are placed on the daughter-board MCU and concern admission control and calibration. The admission control pre-processing is simple: by applying low-pass filter along with a threshold it seeks to recognize when the device is completely stationary; perhaps when a user leaves the device on a table. By filtering out these events the remainder of the accelerometer stages are only exercised when there is actually data to be processed. Calibration orients accelerometer values into gravitational units using parameters learned by applying the Mizell technique [55]. For the microphone, the front-end of shared stages are only comprised of two processes. The design for these two processes are adopted from [51]. First, an admission control separates silence from actual sound – a threshold-based decision is made based on the Root Mean Square (RMS) [64]. Second, for those microphone samples that contain non-silence, a coarse-grain category classifier is used to recognize frames containing voicing, music and other.

**MCU Utilization.** The proper use of the additional low-power processors is critical to maintaining acceptable levels of energy consumption. The MCUs excel at continuous sensor sampling at a low power cost and we take advantage of this by allocating to these units key filter-type computations conforming with the memory and run-time constraints. The daughter-board MCU samples the accelerometer without interruption at 50 Hz, whereas the Quark monitors the microphone continuously at 8KHz. The processing units liberate the Atom CPU from performing sensor sampling allowing it to go into a low-power standby state when the MCUs can handle the sensor events from the stream of incoming data.

The daughter-board MCU performs the full physical activity and transportation mode pipelines without assistance from the Atom CPU. The MCU needs to periodically communicate its accumulated inferences with the Atom CPU which is responsible for transferring the labeled data to the knowledge base. There is a communication overhead involving the transition of the CPU from sleep to high-power active state. To minimize the interactions between the two processing units we set the synchronization period to 20 minutes which is when the main CPU needs to be woken up to merge the inferences in the database.

Strategically, the simple silence filter is performed on the Quark so that whenever the environment is silent the energy hungry CPU is kept at bay. The performance limitations of the pre-release Quark MCU preclude us from deploying more complex pipelines such as speech detection; yet, the silence filter proves immensely useful given that a large proportion of the time users are in a silent context, e.g. a night's sleep. In the presence of noise, i.e. a non-silent frame is detected, the Atom CPU is approached with the next 1.28 secs of raw microphone data which is when the second-order speech/music/ambiance filter is applied.

# 6. IMPLEMENTATION

We conclude our description of ZOE by discussing implementation specific details.

**Source and Binaries**. The source tree of ZOE spans ≈18,000 lines-of-code written in C++ and Python – excluding large trunks of source code imported and modified for the components within the Dialog Subsystem (primarily for Speech Recognition) or for any model training toolkits utilized. The majority of the implementation runs on the Atom CPU of the Edison. Three separate cross-compilers are used – two for each respective MCU which build complete binary images and include MCU-specific OSs; with the last being the Atom where software is more conventionally compiled and installed (within a Linux-like OS, Yocto [15]). Complete binaries for each MCU are 48KB (daughter-board MCU) and 122KB (Quark MCU), respectively. In terms of workflow, the Atom CPU acts as the primary orchestrator within ZOE, but will sleep periodically (governed by the Performance Controller – §5) only to be woken by interrupts from either MCUs based on sampled data.

**Sensor Algorithms.** For many of the more standard algorithms such as GMM classification, Markov Models (MMs), Fast Fourier Transforms (FFTs) and a few common feature extractors, we port implementations from the HTK Speech Recognition Toolkit [4]. Others such as Decision Trees and Adaboost are ported from the Weka [31] toolkit. Lastly, for more domain specific features (MFCC, Teo-Auto-CB, WiFi Place signatures etc.) we have custom implementations based on algorithm descriptions. Off-line training steps utilize previously mentioned toolkits (HTK, Weka), along with the scikit-learn Python library [13].

**User Knowledge Store and Front-end.** Primarily to service dialog queries – but also to maximize the information readily available from inferences – ZOE maintains a User Knowledge Store. Instead of only storing the raw timestamped output of inferences, the front-end of the knowledge store generates information that is implied by individual or combinations of inferences; often, a single inference can generate dozens of new knowledge store records. Examples include estimating the calories burned during various forms of activities or the carbon footprint of transportation activity – both of which can be coarsely estimated based on commonly used reference material that maps calories to the time spent on certain activities [17], with similar references available for pollution and transport choices. Simple estimators are also built into the Knowledge Store for predicting, for example, the duration of events like commuting home at certain times of day. Finally, the Knowledge Store is encoded with simple common sense information such as: How many calories should a user burn everyday? This information is sourced from reference material.

Currently, effort has not been put into using the best predictors or estimators. It is simply a framework to collect and organize information. As a result, the Dialog Reasoning is made easier with essentially every dialog template being linked to code that understands how to generate a query to the Knowledge Store. Queries are parameterized by keywords spoken by the user. For example, when a user asks: "How many conversations did I have today?". The word "today" is a keyword that defines the timespan. Dialog Reasoning understands a limited number of such keywords. This component is implemented currently as a local Sqlite database with the front-end written in Python.

**Dialog System.** Our dialog system is a composite of code adapted from three open-source projects. First, the inference runtime of KWS that resides on ZOE hardware is a C++ DNN library implementation including many of the techniques described in [21]. To train this DNN we use Kaldi [59] and build the necessary glue to format the models generated. Second, we make extensive use of Pocketsphinx [36] for both the training of acoustic and language models, in addition to inference-time execution. Any necessary optimizations to speed up execution, were performed to the standard open source code-base. Third, to realize our TTS the implementation of eSpeak [3] was adopted and modified to support the audio driver of the Edison. Finally, template generation and links to the User Knowledge Base were built with Python as required.

# 7. EVALUATION

In this section, we provide key insights with respect to the system energy profile, the sensing algorithm accuracy and the dialog subsystem performance characteristics. The main findings can be summarized as follows:

- ZOE lasts 30 hours with a typical sensing/dialog load. A key enabler for this is the 3-tier design which offers a more than 30% relative improvement in the battery lifetime to alternatives.
- The dialog subsystem is 87% accurate and is able to respond within a second of finishing a 4-second long voice command.
- The oldest inferences a user may get are at most 20 minutes old which equals the accelerometer personal sensing synchronization period between the MCU and the Atom CPU. The sound-related inferences performed by the sensing algorithms are obtained largely in real-time on the Atom CPU.

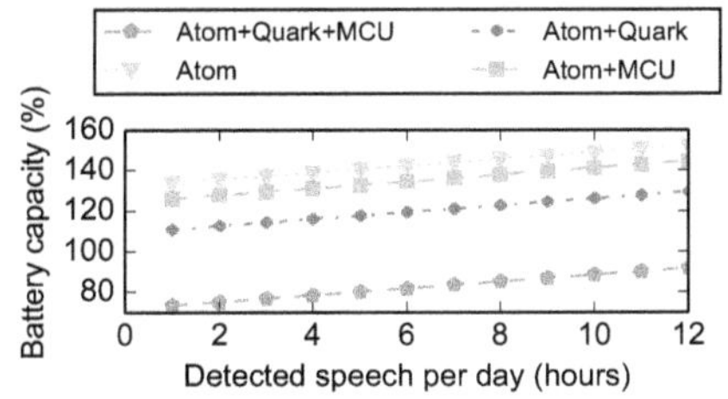


**Figure 6:** Percentage of the battery needed to handle the sensor processing of a daily workload (8h of silence, 1h to 12h of speech, 20 questions per day). Values higher than 100% indicate the battery needs to be recharged at least one more time during the day to sustain the workload.

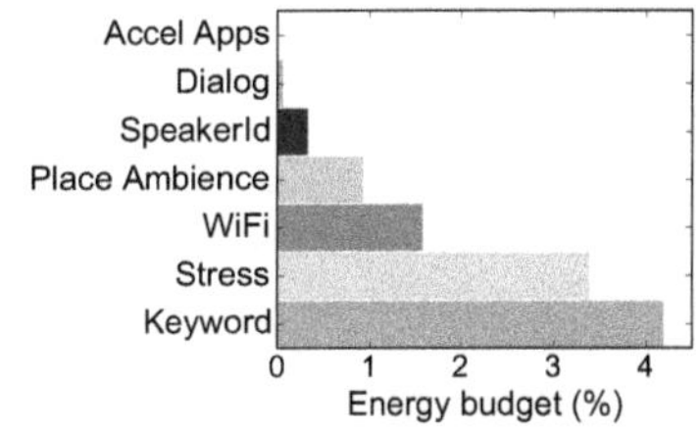


**Figure 7:** Breakdown of the energy consumed by the various system component computations for the workload scenario of 4.5h of speech, 11.5h of ambient context, 15min WiFi duty cycle and 20 dialog commands per day. The reported energy budget reflects the additional energy of the raw processing on top of what the Atom CPU consumes in an active state.

## 7.1 Energy Consumption

Here we detail the energy consumed by ZOE assuming a variety of workload conditions and different mobile device costs. The most notable results are 1) *our design is practical* as it allows the user to wear the device for well over a day with a single battery charge; and 2) compared to other off-the-shelf mobile devices, a *dedicated wearable* proves to be the only solution to have a reasonable energy drain and sustain common sensing workloads for at least a day.

**System Lifetime.** In this part of the analysis we show the total system energy consumption and the benefits of incorporating additional sensor processing units (Intel Quark and an MCU). We compare our heterogeneous design (Atom CPU + Quark co-processor + MCU) against three baseline models that exclude either the Quark, the MCU or both of the additional processing chips. In this experiment we generate synthetic sensing workloads by varying the amount of encountered speech. This is a prime determiner of the sensing workload because the heavier sensor pipelines are triggered by the presence of human voice: dialog subsystem interactions, stress detection, as well as device owner recognition and conversation analysis. We fix the time users are in a silent environment to 8 hours which roughly amounts to a night's sleep. We also assume 20 questions per day on average submitted to the dialog system as life logging inquiries. The battery used for the reported measurements is a typical 1500mAh Lithium-ion model with 3.7 volts.

In Figure 6 we plot the percentage of the battery capacity required by ZOE to process a day worth of sensing as a function of the number of hours users spend in conversations. The first critical observation is that our system design is the only among the alternatives that is able to make the battery last at least one day with a single charge. With 4.5 hours of speech, which is found to be an average amount of time users spend in conversations throughout the day [45], the system needs 78% of the battery capacity to handle a 24-hour processing load. This leaves us with *a system lifetime of* 30 *hours*. In contrast, the 2-tier solutions as well as the bare bones Atom-only deployment require 109% or more of the battery to handle the same workload which means that the Edison wearable needs to be recharged before the day expires. Overall, *the* 3*-tier design offers more than* 30% *improvement in the system longevity* and this is largely attributed to the fact that part of the sensor processing is offloaded to the dedicated low-power co-processors.

When either of the two additional chips (Quark or MCU) is left out, the sensor sampling that would otherwise be performed there will need to be delegated to the general-purpose Atom CPU. This prevents the CPU from going to low-power standby mode and instead keeps the processor active with an average current draw of 63mA. When the MCU is removed, the accelerometer sampling keeps the CPU busy, whereas when the Quark is not used, the microphone sampling maintains the CPU awake. Both of the 2-tier designs do not offer significant energy improvement over the Atom-only deployment because 1) their limited memory and performance capabilities allow them to run only simple pipelines such as silence filtering that on the Atom run in less than 2ms, and 2) in both cases the Atom CPU is burdened with sampling one or both of the sensors where the energy hog is maintaining a high-power active state. As shown in Figure 7, the energy budget for the additional processing of the system components remains cumulatively below 12%, meaning that the majority of the system energy is spent in keeping the CPU active to do the processing in the non-silent periods.

**Effect of False Atom Wake-Ups.** As discussed in the previous paragraph, keeping the Atom CPU awake is a major source of energy consumption which is why it is vital that the times the CPU is unnecessarily woken up to do processing are minimized. Such false wake-ups may occur when the silence filter running on the Quark co-processor errs and flags a silent frame as non-silent, i.e. the filter introduces a false negative with respect to silence. To evaluate the likelihood of such false wake-ups given our implementation of the RMS threshold-based silence filter, we assemble a dataset with 10 minutes of noise, including speech, and 10 minutes of silence. The silent samples are collected from smartphone recordings, whereas the noise samples reuse part of the ambient context dataset [68].

In Table 5 we list the confusion matrix for the silence filter applied on the prepared 20-minute dataset. The main result is that the false wake-up rate remains relatively low at 2.76% which ensures that the energy overhead of unnecessarily waking up the Atom is kept acceptably low. Depending on the chosen silence filter threshold, the false wake-up rate can be further reduced at the expense of decreasing the 92.74% accuracy with which noise is detected. We believe the current set-up provides a reasonable trade-off between accuracy and false wake-up energy overhead.

| Actual/Predicted | **Silence** | **Noise** |
|---|---|---|
| **Silence** | 97.23 % | 2.76% |
| **Noise** | 7.26% | 92.74 % |

**Table 5:** Confusion matrix for the silence filter running on the Intel Quark.

**Projected Lifetime for Other Mobile Devices.** In this next subsection we investigate the following research question: *can we deploy ZOE on another mobile device such as a smartphone and achieve similar or better battery life*? We perform back-of-the-envelope energy analysis for several other mobile devices including a smartphone and Google Glass. The smartphone and Edison energy measurements are performed with a Monsoon Power Monitor attached to the corresponding device. For the smartphone case, we port the sensing algorithms through the Android Native Development Kit to a Qualcomm Snapdragon 800 Mobile Development Platform (MDP) [12], a dedicated device for testing and debugging Android applications. It features the popular Snapdragon 800 SoC available in many high-end smartphone models (e.g., Google Nexus 5, Samsung Galaxy Note 3). We used energy estimates for Google Glass provided by [49] and without loss of generality assumed the pipeline processing runtimes to be similar to what is measured on the smartphone MDP. Given this set-up we report the projected energy budget required by the system to sustain a daily workload with 4.5 hours of speech in Table 6.

Out of the mobile devices, the custom-built Intel Edison wearable with the larger 1500mAh battery is the only one to be able to not fully drain the battery in a day. The second best alternative, a smartphone with a sizable 3200mAh, battery needs 151% of the capacity to process the sensing workload presented in the previous subsection. The massive energy drain can again be attributed to keeping the CPU active during the continuous sensor sampling. This energy profile is unacceptable given that the smartphone can and will be used for other tasks throughout the day such as phone calls, text messages, camera photos, web browsing, games and social networking applications. Last on the energy efficiency list is Google Glass, which according to our coarse projected measurements will need multiple recharges in a day (more than 7) to meet ZOE's sensing demands. This can be explained by both the relatively smaller battery and higher power consumption needed by a powerful CPU that supports augmented reality applications. To summarize, *among the evaluated options, the only feasible solution for supporting the application scenarios induced by ZOE proves to be a dedicated wearable with the lower power characteristics of an Intel Edison board.*

| Mobile Device | Battery Specs | Energy Budget (%) |
|---|---|---|
| Intel Edison | 1500mAh | 78% |
| Smartphone (MDP) | 3200mAh | 151% |
| Intel Edison | 400mAh | 295% |
| Smartphone (MDP) | 1500mAh | 321% |
| Google Glass | 2.1Wh (568mAh) | 744% |

**Table 6:** Energy expenditure required by ZOE to meet a daily workload if it was running on alternative devices. Table entries are sorted by energy budget. Measurements for the MDP and Edison are made with a Monsoon Power Monitor, and power estimates for Google Glass are from [49].

## 7.2 Sensing Algorithm Accuracy

In this subsection we discuss the accuracy of the adopted sensing pipelines that underlie the activity inferences performed by ZOE. The basic components of the personal and place sensing pipelines are largely unchanged from their original versions and here we briefly summarize their accuracy on the datasets we have access to while also detailing any differences. In addition, we provide preliminary results about the effectiveness with which the social sensing subsystem infers conversation patterns: device owner identification, dominance and turn taking.

Most of the algorithms accuracies are in line with previously published results: these include physical activity recognition [52], motorized vs. non-motorized vehicle detection [32], stress detection with a universal model [50], place recognition [40] and place ambient context analysis [68]. For correctness, we report results on the listed datasets but detailed evaluation of how the algorithms fare in more challenging conditions can be found in the original publications. One of the differences we find is the speaker identification [61] accuracy which on our dataset reaches 95% (94%) when 5 (3) seconds of audio data is used for the speech feature extraction. This is likely attributed to two factors: 1) we use up to 9 minutes of training data for each user (and 1 minute is held out for testing); and 2) the recordings are made in a clean environment.

| Sensing Pipeline | Sensor | Dataset | Accuracy |
|---|---|---|---|
| Physical Activity | Accel | 10 mins of activities | 82% |
| Transportation Mode | Accel | 150h transportation data [32] | 85% |
| Stress Periods | Mic | Emotional Prosody [48] | 71% |
| Place Recognition | WiFi | LifeMap [22] | 90% |
| Place Context | Mic | local business ambience [68] | 74% |
| Speaker Id (5s) | Mic | 23 people, 230 mins of speech | 95% |
| Speaker Id (3s) | Mic | 23 people, 230 mins of speech | 94% |

**Table 7:** Accuracy of the pipelines.

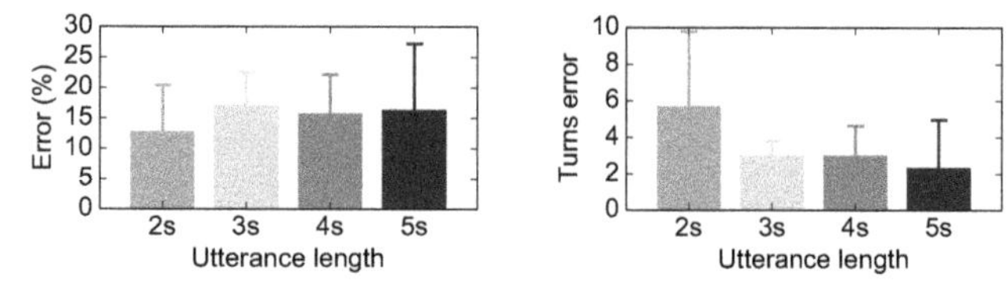


(a) Dominance (b) Turn taking

**Figure 8:** Conversation pattern errors as a function of the utterance length used to identify the wearable owner.

**Social Sensing Accuracy**. We recall that we adopt the speakerID pipeline as a tool to monitor conversation patterns. Examples are inferring the percentage of time a person is talking (dominance levels) or the periods and durations of their turns. Here we shed light on how effective speaker recognition is in deriving such inferences. We perform a preliminary evaluation on a dataset of several conversations each lasting between 4 and 5 minutes. In all of the conversations one of the speakers is designated as a device owner with a personalized speaker identification model. The rest of the participants are unknown and their speech data is not used in the training of the sink GMMs representing other people. Given this setup, we replay the conversations and perform owner identification once every few seconds.

We repeat the above mentioned experiment for utterance lengths ranging from 2 to 5 seconds inclusive and in Figure 8 report the observed errors when speaker identification is adopted to estimate two conversation patterns: the speaker dominance levels and turn taking. An interesting result is that *using shorter periods of audio data for user recognition appears to reduce the dominance errors but significantly increases the turn taking uncertainty*. This phenomenon can be explained by the fact that shorter audio segments increase the temporal precision of understanding when someone is talking even when some errors are introduced, hence the higher dominance accuracy. However, those same errors tend to largely overestimate the number of turns.

Overall, *the algorithm for detecting dominance is off by 12% to 16% depending on the utterance length which is sufficient for coarse estimations of total speaking time*. On the other hand, the mean turn taking errors of 2 to 3 missed or additionally detected turns per conversation are comparatively large given that the average number of turns the target speaker takes is 7. That speaker identification algorithm on 3 to 5 second long utterances does not prevent us from roughly inferring conversation dynamics but may not be suitable for finer grained turn monitoring as has also been highlighted by the authors of SocioPhone [46]. Their proposed multi-device volume topography analysis for the same inference task has limited applicability in our setting, however, because the Edison wearable is supposed to be a self-contained personal sensing assistant and in general we cannot rely on other people owning the same device or having the same set of applications installed on their smartphone/mobile device.

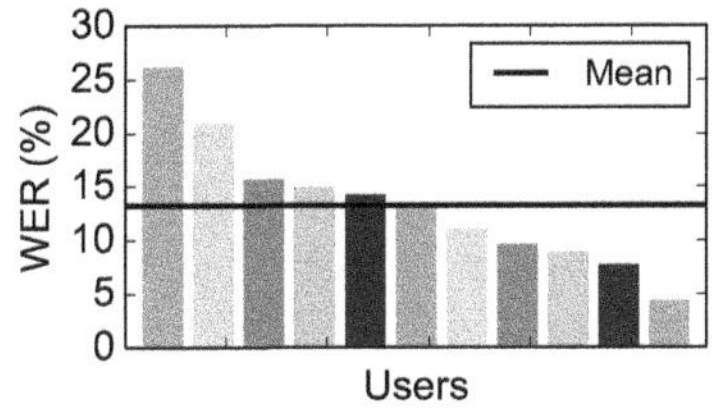


**Figure 9:** Word error rate (WER) of the 11 users on whom the speech recognition subsystem was tested.

| Sensing Pipeline | Runtime (s) | Inference Window (s) |
|---|---|---|
| Physical Activity | 0.002 | 4.000 |
| Transportation Mode | 0.002 | 4.000 |
| Stress Periods | 0.353 | 1.280 |
| Place Context | 0.025 | 1.280 |
| Speaker Identification | 0.105 | 5.000 |
| Keyword Spotting | 0.236 | 1.000 |

**Table 9:** Runtime of the sensing pipelines as measured on the Intel Atom 500 MHz CPU and the MCU for the accelerometer ones. The inference window shows the amount of time raw data is accumulated before the pipeline is run on the sensor samples.

## 7.3 Dialog Accuracy and Responsiveness

In this subsection we elaborate on the accuracy with which the dialog system interprets the commands issued by users as well as the level of system responsiveness to those commands. The latter is measured along two dimensions which we evaluate separately: the time required to decode a voice command and the staleness of the inferences when presenting aggregate results to users.

**Dialog Accuracy.** We begin by discussing the word-level accuracy of the custom-built dialog language model as a preliminary indication to how well ZOE interprets commands. To evaluate this we performed a controlled experiment on 11 speakers, 3 of which were female and 7 of which were non-native English speakers. The participants were required to read aloud a set of 25 command sentences spanning the type of questions supported by ZOE, e.g. *"What fraction of my time do I spend listening to music?"*. We recorded the audio files in an office environment with a sampling rate of 8kHz and fed them as input to the CMU Pocket Sphinx batch analysis tool. The word error rate (WER) is reported in Figure 9. Overall, we observe a mean WER of 13.24% across users which corresponds to an accuracy approaching 87%. We note that although the reported numbers are showing the word-level error rate, the majority of confused words are non-keywords which suggests the command-level accuracy is not critically impacted. A key component enabling these reasonably high figures is the custom-built language model that targets a domain-specific restricted vocabulary of a few hundred words related to daily activities. We find that the accuracy may drop by as much as 30% or 40% when a generic language model with a large dictionary is used.

| Language Model | Dictionary Size | Real-time Factor |
|---|---|---|
| ZOE's custom | 300 words | 0.23x |
| CMU Sphinx HUB4 | 6000 words | 1.98x |
| CMU Sphinx HUB4 | 133000 words | 2.15x |

**Table 8:** Dialog system runtime responsiveness as a function of the language model and dictionary size. The real-time factor shows how much time on average it takes ZOE to decode an utterance relative to its length.

**Dialog Responsiveness.** A major factor determining the real-time responsiveness of ZOE is the time it takes the speech recognition subsystem to decode the words in the voice commands. In Table 8 we show the real-time delay of the decoding process running on the Edison's Atom CPU as a function of the language model and number of words in the vocabulary. The key result is that *using a custom-built model with a domain-specific dictionary is necessary to reach the real-time performance of the system.* The real-time factor of 0.23x means that an utterance of length 4 seconds, for example, is transcribed in 0.92s so that a result can be delivered to the user within a second of completing the voice inquiry. In contrast, using larger general-purpose dictionaries significantly increases the transcription time so that with 6K words, for instance, the same 4-second command will be decoded in almost 8 seconds after issuing it, hardly a practical outcome.

**Freshness of Inferences.** A critical aspect shaping the life logging experience is what the amount of time is between the arrival of a sensor event and obtaining an inference. In general, sensor events trigger data processing requests which are queued in a FIFO manner and the actual time of the processing may not be immediate. Depending on how busy the system is the accumulated requests may be temporarily ignored. In our case, this scenario arises when the user initiates a voice command and the Keyword Spotting application detects the system name. ZOE servers the user with priority in which case sensor tasks accumulate in the queue. However, as shown in Table 9, *all of the sensing pipelines run with sub-second latency for a small fraction (up to 25%) of the time sensor data is gathered.* In effect, even in the busiest scenario for the system when speech is detected, the keyword spotting, speaker identification and stress detection can run all together and in real time. This property allows *inferences on the data to be obtained immediately in the absence of dialog commands.* The worst case is when the user initiates a series of commands, one after another without pauses in between, which is when the sensor data will be queued. Since long command sequences are highly unlikely, the sub real-time nature of the pipelines allows for the system to catch up with the sound inferences within a minute of successively issuing a few commands. Finally, the freshness of the WiFi localization and accelerometer inferences are determined by the WiFi scan duty cycle (15 min) and the update period when the MCU synchronizes accelerometer inferences with the Atom (once every 20 min).

# 8. DISCUSSION AND LIMITATIONS

We briefly survey a variety of issues related to the design and evaluation of ZOE.

**Absence of End-to-End User Study.** ZOE currently uses features of the Edison SoC (such as, MCU access) not publicly available. Because of this we had access to only two pre-release versions of this SoC, this precluded any meaningful user study. We plan to build a number of ZOE devices in the coming months as soon as this situation changes. Instead, the focus and contribution of this work is the systematic study of the hardware capabilities under the workload ZOE presents, along with series of proposed techniques that allows this workload to achieve acceptable levels of energy efficiency and responsiveness.

Of particular interest in future user studies will be user reaction to wearable-based dialog as a means of interaction. Dialog systems are generally gaining popularity and user acceptance in more powerful form factors, such as smartphones; along with always-on home targeted appliances like Amazon's Echo [1]. But clearly there will be times such interaction will not be appropriate, such as in public or within social groups (e.g., a meeting). While certainly the responses of ZOE may not be suitable for others to hear, users may also be uncomfortable with what the questions they ask indicate about themselves and their interests.

**Is Custom Hardware Warranted?** It is likely that a ZOE-like software system could have been designed for a number of mobile platforms. However, overall it would have failed to meet key technical challenges described in §2.1. For example, as we discussed in §7.1 the energy efficiency on alternative platforms like a smartwatch is significantly worse than ZOE's due to lack of low-power MCUs. More broadly, the mobile industry is shifting to increase use of specialized computation; for example, Apple's A7 motion co-processor [6] for interpreting primarily inertial sensors, and more complex speech [14] and vision algorithms appearing in Integrated Circuits providing leaps in performance that software advances alone struggle to match.

**Battery Lifetime.** Currently, ZOE has a lifetime comparable to the more sensor-rich wearables already on the market (such as the Microsoft Band). It is also likely that the energy efficiency of ZOE will improve dramatically as soon as two key available, but still inaccessible, Edison features are opened. First, the Edison CPU can operate at a range of higher and lower clock speeds, yet currently this is fixed at 500 MHz. This speed is unnecessary for some ZOE operations (and wasteful) while others would benefit from a temporary increase; because the CPU consumes most of the device energy, clock speed control will likely offer significant gains. Second, the Edison-located MCU is based on a processor that is much more capable than the tasks it currently performs. Due to limitations in early Edison compiler support, we are only able to perform a few basic inference stages on it, a situation that will be changed subsequently.

**Size and Form-factor.** As shown in Table 2, ZOE achieves an impressive ratio of inference capabilities to size/weight relative to comparison devices. We also expect to be able to decrease the footprint of ZOE by half in the next version by relatively simple layout optimizations to the daughter-board, allowing it to match the dimensions of the Edison. The more challenging issue in doing this will be to cope with a similar reduction in battery capacity that such changes would entail.

# 9. RELATED WORK

ZOE touches upon a wide range of topics, here we discuss the most salient prior work in each area.

**Smartphone Sensing and Activity Recognition.** The design of ZOE contributes to the area of human activity inference by investigating how a diverse set of existing techniques can be combined into a single integrated sensing module; in turn this module can run on a platform and form-factor where few have been previously seen individually (and certainly not being all supported simultaneously). Along with the recent explosion of techniques targeting smartphones (e.g., [58, 46, 66]), there is a long history of platform agnostic algorithms from activity recognition (e.g., [19]). However, even though many share building block components (features, related classes) few studies exist that investigate their usage together (e.g., [39]). Towards wearables with a more complete understanding of the life of users, ZOE incorporates more than 10 distinct inferences from three different sensors that have previously been often studied in isolation.

The few mobile systems that seek a more complete monitoring of user behavior and environment often focus on health (e.g., [25, 57]). Other systems that have targeted a diverse set of inferences have focused on a single sensor – the microphone being a popular one [51, 28]. DSP.Ear [28], for example, also supports sensing algorithms that cover a variety of activities but lacks the place- and social- inferences of ZOE, and ignores modalities other than audio.

**Wearables and Personal Sensing Hardware.** As surveyed in §2.3, ZOE distinguishes itself, particularly from commercial systems, largely because of the depth and range of its user inferences and exploration of features like dialog systems, heterogeneous computation and constraints like operating without a cloud. Wearable systems that seek the type of breadth as ZOE are almost always based on vision or audio data because of the richness of the two modalities. ZOE relies on multiple sensors but makes strong use of the microphone which sets itself apart in terms of sensing algorithms with wearables like [30][53][34]. Examples of microphone-based wearables include [62] but this system has a specific narrow focus on internal body sounds captured with a specially designed microphone. Instead, ZOE has a number of commonalities with the MSP [23] that was also a heavy user of the microphone. However, as described in §2.3 while ZOE monitors general user activities, as the MSP does, it also provides: detailed measurements of user state and social interactions; in addition to providing a dialog system through which to offer the user this information.

**Heterogeneity and Mobile Resource Bottlenecks.** Energy has been a considerable focus of a variety of mobile sensing systems [44, 43, 38]. Towards such challenges, low-power processors and multiple-tiers of computational units are commonly used approaches [18, 65]. ZOE adds to this knowledge by exploring the use of dual-MCUs to allow a comparatively very heavy sensing and interaction workload to remain feasible, especially in terms of energy. Architecturally similar approaches include [58, 60] that combine high- and low-power processors for energy efficient sensing. Even commercially, many smartphones today use DSPs and other processors to continuously sense and wait for one specific keyword to be spoken (a keyword) before initiating a dialog. Although the core of the techniques we use have appeared in such systems, it is the first time they have been applied to many of the more complex sensing algorithms (e.g., seen in our social sensing monitoring) and especially when they are integrated into a single system.

# 10. CONCLUSION

In this paper, we have presented the design, implementation and evaluation of ZOE – a prototype wearable that leverages the type of heterogeneous high-performance computation increasingly available to this class of mobile device. Through a mixture of hardware- and software-based approaches, ZOE offers a first-of-its-kind user experience by enabling the continuous sensing of a range of deep inferences along with a near real-time dialog system through which users can access captured information. All of this is provided without cloud assistance, which provides significant privacy assurances to the user by removing the need for third-party remote computation. We hope ZOE acts as an important reference example for future investigations into the design of wearables, and also provokes further study of: heterogeneous computation in wearables; in-situ dialog-based access to information for users; and, the limits of cloud-free wearable functionality.

## Acknowledgments

This work was supported by Microsoft Research through its PhD Scholarship Program. We would also like to thank the anonymous reviewers and our shepherd, Jeremy Gummeson, for helping us improve the paper.

# 11. REFERENCES


[1] Amazon Echo. http://www.amazon.com/oc/echo.

[2] Android Wear hardware review: Sometimes promising, often frustrating. http://tinyurl.com/m9zb3yz.

[3] eSpeak. http://espeak.sourceforge.net.

[4] HTK Speech Recognition Toolkit. http://htk.eng.cam.ac.uk/.

[5] Intel Edison. http://www.intel.com/content/www/us/en/do-it-yourself/edison.html.

[6] iPhone 5s M7 Motion Coprocessor. https://www.apple.com/iphone-5s/specs/.

[7] Jawbone Up 3. http://jawbone.com/store/buy/up3.

[8] LG G Watch R. https://www.qualcomm.com/products/snapdragon/wearables/lg-g-watch-r.

[9] Microsoft Band. http://www.microsoft.com/Microsoft-Band/.

[10] Motorola MotoActv. https://www.motoactv.com.

[11] Qualcomm Snapdragon 400. https://www.qualcomm.com/products/snapdragon/processors/400.

[12] Qualcomm Snapdragon 800 MDP. https://developer.qualcomm.com/mobile-development/development-devices/snapdragon-mobile-development-platform-mdp.

[13] Scikit-Learn Python Library. http://scikit-learn.org/stable/.

[14] Sensory. http://www.sensory.com/products/integrated-circuits/.

[15] Yocto Project. https://www.yoctoproject.org/.

[16] Your Samsung SmartTV Is Spying on You, Basically. http://www.thedailybeast.com/articles/2015/02/05/your-samsung-smarttv-is-spying-on-you-basically.html.

[17] B. E. Ainsworth, W. L. Haskell, M. C. Whitt, M. L. Irwin, A. M. Swartz, S. J. Strath, W. L. O'Brien, D. R. Bassett, K. H. Schmitz, P. O. Emplaincourt, D. R. Jacobs, and A. S. Leon. Compendium of Physical Activities: an update of activity codes and MET intensities. *Medicine & Science in Sports & Exercise*, 32(9):498–516, Sept. 2000.

[18] R. K. Balan, D. Gergle, M. Satyanarayanan, and J. Herbsleb. Simplifying cyber foraging for mobile devices. In *Proceedings of the 5th International Conference on Mobile Systems, Applications and Services*, MobiSys '07, pages 272–285, New York, NY, USA, 2007. ACM.

[19] L. Bao and S. S. Intille. Activity recognition from user-annotated acceleration data. In *Pervasive computing*, pages 1–17. Springer, 2004.

[20] A. Biem, E. Mcdermott, and S. Katagiri. A discriminative filter bank model for speech recognition. In *Proceedings of the IEEE, ICASSP-96*, pages 545–548, 1995.

[21] G. Chen, C. Parada, and G. Heigold. Small-footprint keyword spotting using deep neural networks. In *IEEE International Conference on Acoustics, Speech, and Signal Processing*, ICASSP'14, 2014.

[22] J. Chon and H. Cha. Lifemap: A smartphone-based context provider for location-based services. *IEEE Pervasive Computing*, 10(2):58–67, Apr. 2011.

[23] T. Choudhury, G. Borriello, S. Consolvo, D. Haehnel, B. Harrison, B. Hemingway, J. Hightower, P. P. Klasnja, K. Koscher, A. LaMarca, J. A. Landay, L. LeGrand, J. Lester, A. Rahimi, A. Rea, and D. Wyatt. The mobile sensing platform: An embedded activity recognition system. *IEEE Pervasive Computing*, 7(2):32–41, Apr. 2008.

[24] L. Deng and D. Yu. Deep learning: Methods and applications. Technical Report MSR-TR-2014-21, January 2014.

[25] T. Denning, A. Andrew, R. Chaudhri, C. Hartung, J. Lester, G. Borriello, and G. Duncan. Balance: towards a usable pervasive wellness application with accurate activity inference. In *Proceedings of the 10th workshop on Mobile Computing Systems and Applications*, page 5. ACM, 2009.

[26] T. Dutoit. *An introduction to text-to-speech synthesis*, volume 3. Springer, 1997.

[27] J. Edlund, M. Heldner, and J. Hirschberg. Pause and gap length in face-to-face interaction. In *INTERSPEECH 2009, 10th Annual Conference of the International Speech Communication Association, Brighton, United Kingdom, September 6-10, 2009*, pages 2779–2782, 2009.

[28] P. Georgiev, N. D. Lane, K. K. Rachuri, and C. Mascolo. Dsp.ear: Leveraging co-processor support for continuous audio sensing on smartphones. In *Proceedings of the 12th ACM Conference on Embedded Network Sensor Systems*, SenSys '14, pages 295–309, New York, NY, USA, 2014. ACM.

[29] K. Gupta and J. D. Owens. Three-layer optimizations for fast gmm computations on gpu-like parallel processors. In *ASRU*, pages 146–151. IEEE, 2009.

[30] K. Ha, Z. Chen, W. Hu, W. Richter, P. Pillai, and M. Satyanarayanan. Towards wearable cognitive assistance. In *Proceedings of the 12th Annual International Conference on Mobile Systems, Applications, and Services*, MobiSys '14, pages 68–81, New York, NY, USA, 2014. ACM.

[31] M. Hall, E. Frank, G. Holmes, B. Pfahringer, P. Reutemann, and I. H. Witten. The weka data mining software: An update. *SIGKDD Explor. Newsl.*, 11(1):10–18, Nov. 2009.

[32] S. Hemminki, P. Nurmi, and S. Tarkoma. Accelerometer-based transportation mode detection on smartphones. In *Proceedings of the 11th ACM Conference on Embedded Networked Sensor Systems*, SenSys '13, pages 13:1–13:14, New York, NY, USA, 2013. ACM.

[33] J. Hightower, S. Consolvo, A. LaMarca, I. Smith, and J. Hughes. Learning and recognizing the places we go. In *Proceedings of the 7th International Conference on Ubiquitous Computing*, UbiComp'05, pages 159–176, Berlin, Heidelberg, 2005. Springer-Verlag.

[34] S. Hodges, L. Williams, E. Berry, S. Izadi, J. Srinivasan, A. Butler, G. Smyth, N. Kapur, and K. Wood. Sensecam: A retrospective memory aid. In *UbiComp 2006*, pages 177–193. Springer, 2006.

[35] W. Huang, Y.-S. Kuo, P. Pannuto, and P. Dutta. Opo: A wearable sensor for capturing high-fidelity face-to-face interactions. In *Proceedings of the 12th ACM Conference on Embedded Network Sensor Systems*, SenSys '14, pages 61–75, New York, NY, USA, 2014. ACM.

[36] D. Huggins-Daines, M. Kumar, A. Chan, A. W. Black, M. Ravishankar, and A. I. Rudnicky. Pocketsphinx: A free, real-time continuous speech recognition system for hand-held devices. In *Acoustics, Speech and Signal Processing, 2006. ICASSP 2006 Proceedings. 2006 IEEE International Conference on*, volume 1, pages I–I. IEEE, 2006.

[37] D. Gatica-Perez, and D. K. Heylen. Multi-modal analysis of small-group conversational dynamics. *Multimodal Signal Processing*, 2012.

[38] N. D. Lane, Y. Chon, L. Zhou, Y. Zhang, F. Li, D. Kim, G. Ding, F. Zhao, and H. Cha. Piggyback CrowdSensing (PCS): energy efficient crowdsourcing of mobile sensor data by exploiting smartphone app opportunities. In *Proceedings of the 11th ACM Conference on Embedded Network Sensor Systems*, SenSys '13, pages 1–14, New York, NY, USA, 2013. ACM.

[39] Y. Ju, Y. Lee, J. Yu, C. Min, I. Shin, and J. Song. Symphoney: A coordinated sensing flow execution engine for concurrent mobile sensing applications. In *Proceedings of the 10th ACM Conference on Embedded Network Sensor Systems*, SenSys '12, pages 211–224, New York, NY, USA, 2012. ACM.

[40] D. H. Kim, Y. Kim, D. Estrin, and M. B. Srivastava. Sensloc: Sensing everyday places and paths using less energy. In *Proceedings of the 8th ACM Conference on Embedded Networked Sensor Systems*, SenSys '10, pages 43–56, New York, NY, USA, 2010. ACM.

[41] J. Krumm and E. Horvitz. Locadio: Inferring motion and location from wi-fi signal strengths. In *MobiQuitous*, pages 4–13. IEEE Computer Society, 2004.

[42] J. Krumm and D. Rouhana. Placer: Semantic place labels from diary data. In *Proceedings of the 2013 ACM International Joint Conference on Pervasive and Ubiquitous Computing*, UbiComp '13, pages 163–172, New York, NY, USA, 2013. ACM.

[43] K. Lin, A. Kansal, D. Lymberopoulos, and F. Zhao. Energy-accuracy trade-off for continuous mobile device location. In *Proceeding of the 8th Annual International Conference on Mobile Systems, Applications, and Services*, MobiSys '10, pages 285–298 ACM, 2010.

[44] S. Nath. ACE: exploiting correlation for energy-efficient and continuous context sensing. In *Proceeding of the 10th Annual International Conference on Mobile Systems, Applications, and Services*, MobiSys '12, pages 29–42 ACM, 2012.

[45] Y. Lee, C. Min, C. Hwang, J. L. 0001, I. Hwang, Y. Ju, C. Yoo, M. Moon, U. Lee, and J. Song. Sociophone: everyday face-to-face interaction monitoring platform using multi-phone sensor fusion. In *Proceeding of the 11th Annual International Conference on Mobile Systems, Applications, and Services*, MobiSys '13, pages 499–500. ACM, 2013.

[46] Y. Lee, C. Min, C. Hwang, J. Lee, I. Hwang, Y. Ju, C. Yoo, M. Moon, U. Lee, and J. Song. Sociophone: Everyday face-to-face interaction monitoring platform using multi-phone sensor fusion. In *Proceeding of the 11th Annual International Conference on Mobile Systems, Applications, and Services*, MobiSys '13, pages 375–388, New York, NY, USA, 2013. ACM.

[47] J. Lester, T. Choudhury, N. Kern, G. Borriello, and B. Hannaford. A hybrid discriminative/generative approach for modeling human activities. In *Proceedings of the 19th International Joint Conference on Artificial Intelligence*, IJCAI'05, pages 766–772, San Francisco, CA, USA, 2005. Morgan Kaufmann Publishers Inc.

[48] M. Liberman, K. Davis, M. Grossman, N. Martey, and J. Bell. Emotional prosody speech and transcripts. 2002.

[49] R. LiKamWa, Z. Wang, A. Carroll, F. X. Lin, and L. Zhong. Draining our glass: An energy and heat characterization of google glass. In *Proceedings of 5th Asia-Pacific Workshop on Systems*, APSys '14, pages 10:1–10:7, New York, NY, USA, 2014. ACM.

[50] H. Lu, D. Frauendorfer, M. Rabbi, M. S. Mast, G. T. Chittaranjan, A. T. Campbell, D. Gatica-Perez, and T. Choudhury. Stresssense: Detecting stress in unconstrained acoustic environments using smartphones. In *Proceedings of the 2012 ACM Conference on Ubiquitous Computing*, UbiComp '12, pages 351–360, New York, NY, USA, 2012. ACM.

[51] H. Lu, W. Pan, N. D. Lane, T. Choudhury, and A. T. Campbell. Soundsense: Scalable sound sensing for people-centric applications on mobile phones. In *Proceedings of the 7th International Conference on Mobile Systems, Applications, and Services*, MobiSys '09, pages 165–178, New York, NY, USA, 2009. ACM.

[52] H. Lu, J. Yang, Z. Liu, N. D. Lane, T. Choudhury, and A. T. Campbell. The jigsaw continuous sensing engine for mobile phone applications. In *Proceedings of the 8th ACM Conference on Embedded Networked Sensor Systems*, SenSys '10, pages 71–84, New York, NY, USA, 2010. ACM.

[53] A. Mayberry, P. Hu, B. Marlin, C. Salthouse, and D. Ganesan. ishadow: Design of a wearable, real-time mobile gaze tracker. In *Proceedings of the 12th Annual International Conference on Mobile Systems, Applications, and Services*, MobiSys '14, pages 82–94, New York, NY, USA, 2014. ACM.

[54] E. Miluzzo, N. D. Lane, K. Fodor, R. Peterson, H. Lu, M. Musolesi, S. B. Eisenman, X. Zheng, and A. T. Campbell. Sensing meets mobile social networks: The design, implementation and evaluation of the cenceme application. In *Proceedings of the 6th ACM Conference on Embedded Network Sensor Systems*, SenSys '08, pages 337–350, New York, NY, USA, 2008. ACM.

[55] D. Mizell. Using gravity to estimate accelerometer orientation. In *Proceedings of the 7th IEEE International Symposium on Wearable Computers*, ISWC '03, pages 252–, Washington, DC, USA, 2003. IEEE Computer Society.

[56] M. Mun, S. Reddy, K. Shilton, N. Yau, J. Burke, D. Estrin, M. Hansen, E. Howard, R. West, and P. Boda. Peir, the personal environmental impact report, as a platform for participatory sensing systems research. In *Proceedings of the 7th International Conference on Mobile Systems, Applications, and Services*, MobiSys '09, pages 55–68, New York, NY, USA, 2009. ACM.

[57] Nicholas Lane, M. Lin, M. Rabi, X. Yang, A. Doryab, H. Lu, S. Ali, T. Choudhury, A. Campbell, and E. Berke. *Bewell: A smartphone application to monitor, model and promote wellbeing*. IEEE Press, 2011.

[58] S. Nirjon, R. Dickerson, J. Stankovic, G. Shen, and X. Jiang. smfcc: Exploiting sparseness in speech for fast acoustic feature extraction on mobile devices – a feasibility study. In *Proceedings of the 14th Workshop on Mobile Computing Systems and Applications*, HotMobile '13, pages 8:1–8:6, New York, NY, USA, 2013. ACM.

[59] D. Povey, A. Ghoshal, G. Boulianne, L. Burget, O. Glembek, N. Goel, M. Hannemann, P. Motlicek, Y. Qian, P. Schwarz, J. Silovsky, G. Stemmer, and K. Vesely. The kaldi speech recognition toolkit. In *IEEE 2011 Workshop on Automatic Speech Recognition and Understanding*. IEEE Signal Processing Society, Dec. 2011. IEEE Catalog No.: CFP11SRW-USB.

[60] B. Priyantha, D. Lymberopoulos, and J. Liu. Littlerock: Enabling energy-efficient continuous sensing on mobile phones. *IEEE Pervasive Computing*, 10(2):12–15, 2011.

[61] K. K. Rachuri, M. Musolesi, C. Mascolo, P. J. Rentfrow, C. Longworth, and A. Aucinas. Emotionsense: A mobile phones based adaptive platform for experimental social psychology research. In *Proceedings of the 12th ACM International Conference on Ubiquitous Computing*, Ubicomp '10, pages 281–290, New York, NY, USA, 2010. ACM.

[62] T. Rahman, A. T. Adams, M. Zhang, E. Cherry, B. Zhou, H. Peng, and T. Choudhury. Bodybeat: A mobile system for sensing non-speech body sounds. In *Proceedings of the 12th Annual International Conference on Mobile Systems, Applications, and Services*, MobiSys '14, pages 2–13, New York, NY, USA, 2014. ACM.

[63] S. Reddy, M. Mun, J. Burke, D. Estrin, M. Hansen, and M. Srivastava. Using mobile phones to determine transportation modes. *ACM Trans. Sen. Netw.*, 6(2):13:1–13:27, Mar. 2010.

[64] E. Scheirer and M. Slaney. Construction and evaluation of a robust multifeature speech/music discriminator. In *Proceedings of the 1997 IEEE International Conference on Acoustics, Speech, and Signal Processing (ICASSP '97)-Volume 2 - Volume 2*, ICASSP '97, pages 1331–, Washington, DC, USA, 1997. IEEE Computer Society.

[65] J. Sorber, N. Banerjee, M. D. Corner, and S. Rollins. Turducken: Hierarchical power management for mobile devices. In *Proceedings of the 3rd International Conference on Mobile Systems, Applications, and Services*, MobiSys '05, pages 261–274, New York, NY, USA, 2005. ACM.

[66] W.-T. Tan, M. Baker, B. Lee, and R. Samadani. The sound of silence. In *Proceedings of the 11th ACM Conference on Embedded Networked Sensor Systems*, SenSys '13, pages 19:1–19:14, New York, NY, USA, 2013. ACM.

[67] H. Wang, D. Lymberopoulos, and J. Liu. Local business ambience characterization through mobile audio sensing. In *23rd International World Wide Web Conference (WWW)*, 2014.

[68] H. Wang, D. Lymberopoulos, and J. Liu. Local business ambience characterization through mobile audio sensing. In *Proceedings of the 23rd International Conference on World Wide Web*, WWW '14, pages 293–304, New York, NY, USA, 2014. ACM.

[69] R. Want, T. Pering, G. Danneels, M. Kumar, M. Sundar, and J. Light. The personal server: Changing the way we think about ubiquitous computing. In *Proceedings of the 4th International Conference on Ubiquitous Computing*, UbiComp '02, pages 194–209, London, UK, UK, 2002. Springer-Verlag.

[70] C. Xu, S. Li, G. Liu, Y. Zhang, E. Miluzzo, Y.-F. Chen, J. Li, and B. Firner. Crowd++: Unsupervised speaker count with smartphones. In *Proceedings of the 2013 ACM International Joint Conference on Pervasive and Ubiquitous Computing*, UbiComp '13, pages 43–52, New York, NY, USA, 2013. ACM.

# Reducing Smartphone Application Delay through Read/Write Isolation

David T. Nguyen*, Gang Zhou*, Guoliang Xing†, Xin Qi*, Zijiang Hao*, Ge Peng*, Qing Yang*
*College of William and Mary
McGlothlin-Street Hall 126
Williamsburg, VA 23185, USA
{dnguyen, gzhou, xqi, hebo, gpeng, qyang}@cs.wm.edu
†Michigan State University
3115 Engineering Building
East Lansing, MI 48824-1226, USA
glxing@cse.msu.edu

## ABSTRACT

The smartphone has become an important part of our daily lives. However, the user experience is still far from being optimal. In particular, despite the rapid hardware upgrades, current smartphones often suffer various unpredictable delays during operation, e.g., when launching an app, leading to poor user experience. In this paper, we investigate the behavior of reads and writes in smartphones. We conduct the first large-scale measurement study on the Android I/O delay using the data collected from our Android application running on 2611 devices within nine months. Among other factors, we observe that reads experience up to 626% slowdown when blocked by concurrent writes for certain workloads. Additionally, we show the asymmetry of the slowdown of one I/O type due to another, and elaborate the speedup of concurrent I/Os over serial ones. We use this obtained knowledge to design and implement a system prototype called SmartIO that reduces the application delay by prioritizing reads over writes, and grouping them based on assigned priorities. SmartIO issues I/Os with optimized concurrency parameters. The system is implemented on the Android platform and evaluated extensively on several groups of popular applications. The results show that our system reduces launch delays by up to 37.8%, and run-time delays by up to 29.6%.

## Categories and Subject Descriptors

C.4 [**Performance of Systems**]: Design studies; C.5.3 [**Computer System Implementation**]: Microcomputers-Portable devices

## General Terms

Design, Experimentation, Measurement, Performance

## Keywords

Smartphone Application Performance; Flash Disk I/O Optimizations; Application Response Time; Application Launch


*MobiSys'15,* May 18–22, 2015, Florence, Italy.

http://dx.doi.org/10.1145/2742647.2742661.

## 1. INTRODUCTION

The number of smartphones used worldwide increases each year. According to International Data Corporation, smartphone vendors shipped a total of 918.6 million smartphones in 2013, up 27.2% from the 722.4 million units shipped in 2012 [15]. With their increasing use, smartphone users tend to demand better performance. Moreover, smartphone users are increasingly using phones for work-related activities such as processing emails, reading documents, etc. A study by Forrester Research [9] found that one quarter of work devices were smartphones and tablets. Therefore, it is crucial to study application performance in smartphones. In particular, reducing the application delay can greatly improve user productivity. In addition, a recent analysis [43] indicates that most user interactions with smartphones are short. Specifically, 80% of the applications are used for less than two minutes. With such brief interactions, applications should be rapid and responsive. However, the same study reports that many apps incur significant delays (up to 10 seconds) during launch and run-time.

Our study reveals that Android devices spend a significant portion of their CPU active time (up to 58%) waiting for storage I/Os to complete. This negatively affects the smartphone's overall application performance, and results in slow response time. Therefore, in order to improve the application performance, it is essential to investigate possible reasons of such waits. This paper addresses two key research questions towards achieving rapid application response. (1) *How does disk I/O performance affect smartphone application response time?* (2) *How can we improve application performance with I/O optimization techniques?*

In order to address the first research question, we study the behavior of read and write I/Os. First, the slowdown of reads in the presence of writes is investigated. This slowdown can be one of the main reasons causing the slow launch of applications due to the dominance of reads while launching. Next, the difference in the slowdown of one I/O type due to another may require better I/O scheduling and prioritizing. Therefore, this slowdown asymmetry is researched. Finally, we look at the speedup of concurrent I/Os over serial ones. This provides insights into what type of I/Os benefit more from concurrency.

To address the second research question, we design and implement a system prototype called SmartIO on the Android platform. SmartIO measures optimal concurrency parameters for each type of I/O, and issues I/Os with the use of the obtained concurrency parameters. The system reduces the application delay by applying a set of I/O optimizations. Specifically, it assigns higher priority to reads, lower priority to writes, and groups the I/Os based on these priorities. The approach proves to have smaller performance improvement on launch delays of applications currently running in the background (warm launch). This is expected, since once an app is already in memory, its launch is much faster (on average by 65% based on our experiments). Because there is little I/O traffic going to the flash disk during warm launch, SmartIO reduces warm launch delays on average only by 6.8%. Our work focuses on reducing launch delays of applications currently *not* running in the background (cold launch).

Little work in the research community directly relates to ours. Kim et al. [29] present an analysis of storage performance on Android smartphones and external storage devices. Their discovery of a strong correlation between storage and application performance degradation serves as motivation for our work. Yan et al. [43] propose a system predicting application launch using context such as user location and temporal access patterns. Their system reduces perceived delay through application prelaunching. However, the proposed system does not address the issue of slow application launch from the root, but instead lessens its impact.

In summary, the contributions of our paper are as follows:

- First, through a large-scale measurement study based on the data collected from 2611 devices using an app we developed, we find that Android devices spend a significant portion of their CPU active time (up to 58%) waiting for storage I/Os to complete. This negatively affects the smartphone's overall application performance, and results in slow response time. Further investigation reveals that a read experiences up to 626% slowdown when blocked by a concurrent write. Additionally, the results indicate significant asymmetry in the slowdown of one I/O type due to another. While the slowdown ratio of a read is up to 6.15, the slowdown ratio of a write is only up to 1.6. Finally, we study the speedup of concurrent I/Os, and the results suggest that reads benefit more from concurrency.
- Second, we design and implement a system prototype called SmartIO that shortens the application delay by prioritizing reads over writes, and grouping them based on assigned priorities. SmartIO issues I/Os with optimized concurrency parameters.
- Third, we evaluate our system using 40 popular applications from four groups (games, streaming, miscellaneous, and sensing) and we show that SmartIO reduces launch delays by up to 37.8%, and run-time delays by up to 29.6%. Moreover, SmartIO also reduces power consumption by 6%.

The remainder of this paper is organized as follows. Section 2 presents the related work. In Section 3, we introduce the background of our work. Section 4 provides preliminary measurements and motivation. In Section 5, we present the system architecture of our solution to improve smartphone application performance, and Section 6 elaborates implementation details. Section 7 evaluates our implementation, and Section 8 provides discussion with future work. We conclude our work in Section 9.

## 2. RELATED WORK

The previous work can be classified into four categories: smartphone storage, smartphone application delay, Linux I/O schedulers, and enterprise solutions.

**Smartphone Storage.** Kim et al. [29] present an analysis of storage performance on Android smartphones and external flash storage devices. Their discovery of a strong correlation between storage and application performance degradation serves as motivation for our work. We take one step further and investigate possible reasons of such performance degradation, and propose a system to reduce application response using smart I/O optimizations. Nguyen et al. [33] study the impact of the flash storage on smartphone energy efficiency, while the main focus of our paper is the application performance. Finally, Jeong et al. [28] propose novel journaling methods that, however, are not our focus. We use obtained knowledge from the study of I/O behaviors to design and implement a system that improves the response time by prioritizing reads over writes, and grouping them based on assigned priorities.

**Smartphone Application Delay.** Yan et al. [43] propose a system that predicts which apps are to be launched using the context such as user location and temporal access patterns. Their system then provides effective application prelaunching that reduces perceived delay. Parate et al. [36] propose another prediction algorithm to reduce the launch delay. Compared to the previous work, their approach does not require prior training or additional sensor context. However, mis-predictions of the proposed approaches will lead to significant memory and energy overhead. We address the problem of slow application launch by analyzing possible reasons of the slowdowns in the granularity of read and write I/Os. With this knowledge, we design a system that improves the response time by prioritizing reads over writes. This has a positive impact on the application performance beyond delay.

**Linux I/O Schedulers.** The default I/O scheduler since Linux kernel version 2.6 is the Complete Fair Queuing scheduler (CFQ) [17]. This scheduler has also been adopted as the default one in most Android smartphones, including the ones used in our experiments. However, not optimized for smartphone environments, CFQ may cause long application response time that is the main focus of our work. Other available I/O schedulers (Noop and Deadline [2]) are only used for specialized workloads.

**Enterprise Solutions.** Flash technology has been recognized in enterprise systems. This is mainly due to its technical merits highlighted in [16, 25], including low power consumption, compact size, and fast random access. This motivated researchers to propose I/O schedulers for flash memory based Solid State Drives in computer storage systems [26, 30, 31]. Inspired by these works, we study I/O characteristics of smartphones that have some differences, and require careful design considerations for optimal performance. For instance, while large block sizes dominate in conventional systems, small 4KB I/Os account for up to 65% of smartphone operations [32]. Our proposed solution is simple, and reduces application delays by up to 37.8%, while still being power efficient. Other enterprise solutions focus on fairness policies [37, 40]. SmartIO builds upon the default Linux I/O scheduler, and adds an additional priority level that preserves the original priorities. Further fairness optimization is beyond the scope of this work.

## 3. BACKGROUND

First, we introduce the background of our work. In particular, the kernel components on the I/O path are discussed, with the emphasis on the block layer and the flash disk that are directly related to our work. We illustrate the main kernel components affected by a block device operation on the I/O path in Figure 1. The figure is adapted from the literature [21].

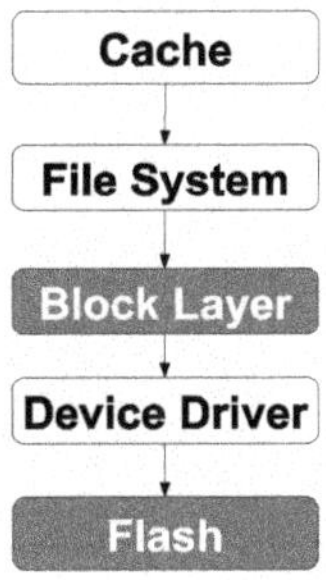


**Figure 1: Kernel Components on the I/O Path.**

## 3.1 Block Layer

At the block layer [8], the main work is scheduling I/O requests from above and sending them down to the device driver. The Linux kernels on recent Android smartphones offer 3 scheduling algorithms: Complete Fair Queuing (CFQ), Deadline, and Noop.

CFQ scheduler presented in [17] is the default I/O scheduler in Android smartphones. It attempts to distribute available I/O bandwidth equally among all I/O requests. There are two priority levels: one is the class, and the other is the priority within the class. There are three classes: real-time, best effort, and idle. Real-time class requests have the highest priority, followed by the best effort class whose disk access requests are granted only when there is no real-time request left. The idle class is given a disk access only when the disk is idle. Within the real-time and best effort classes, there are eight additional priorities [0(highest) to 7(lowest)]. Requests are placed into queues where each of the queues gets a time slice allocated. There are 8 queues in the real-time class, 8 queues in the best effort class, and 1 queue in the idle class.

## 3.2 Flash Disk

The last level to be reached by the I/Os is the storage subsystem that contains an internal NAND flash memory, an external SD card (optional), and a limited amount of RAM. The subsystem contains different numbers of partitions, depending on the manufacturer. The partitions can be found in the /dev/block directory.

Flash disk differs significantly from the conventional rotating storage. While rotating disks suffer from the seek time bottleneck, flash disks do not. Although providing superior performance compared to conventional storage, flash does have its own limitations. For instance, the erase-before-write limitation requires erase before overwriting a location. This leads to a substantial read/write speed discrepancy, which, among other issues, is discussed in the following subsections as a motivation for our work.

# 4. MEASUREMENT STUDY

In order to understand how disk I/O performance affects smartphone application response time, we conduct a measurement study. First, we investigate what portion of the CPU active time is spent in storage waiting for I/Os to complete. When the time the CPUs spend in the storage subsystem is significant, this will negatively affect the smartphone's overall application performance, and result in slow response time. To identify what may be causing such waits, we learn more about I/O activities and their properties. The first property that may be a reason of such waits is I/O slowdown, which quantifies how one I/O type is slowed down due to presence of another. If one I/O activity (e.g., read) is slowed down by another (e.g., write), there will be certain cases in the application life cycle that will suffer from such slowdown (e.g., launch, since reads dominate during launch). The impact of such slowdown on the application delay may vary depending on its ratio. This is studied in the slowdown asymmetry subsection. Another property to be researched is concurrency. Depending on hardware characteristics, different devices may benefit differently from concurrency. Therefore, in the last subsection we study the speedup of concurrent I/Os over serial ones. Finally, we discuss the measurement results and their implications.

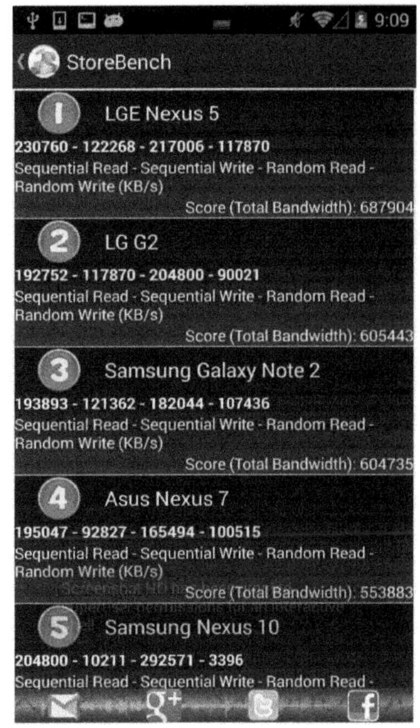


**Figure 2: StoreBench Storage Benchmark.**

## 4.1 Measurement Setup

In a small-scale study, a Samsung S5 phone with Android 4.4.2 is utilized. The phone is normally used daily by the first author. During measurements, our Samsung S5 has all radio communication disabled, and the screen is off. Additionally, no app is in the foreground or background, and the cache is cleared before each measurement. To verify small-scale key observations, we design and implement a storage benchmarking tool called StoreBench [12] as an Android app, and make it available for free download on Google Play [11]. StoreBench is utilized to collect data for a large-scale study.

In the large-scale study, through StoreBench we obtain data from 2611 Android devices (complete list at [13]) that installed our benchmark from Google Play (97% of the devices run Android 4.0 or higher) in the period of nine months (November, 2013 - July, 2014). StoreBench tests the I/O performance of the internal flash storage and external SD card. Specifically, the tool measures the I/O bandwidth, response time, and CPU active time spent waiting for disk I/Os to complete (*iowait*). Additionally, it measures the launch and run-time delay of 20 popular apps. With the permission of users, results are submitted to our online database for further analysis and performance ranking. Our app anonymizes all data to maintain users' privacy. Note that we do not collect or derive any data from human subjects. Instead, we only collect technical information of the devices. Therefore, no IRB approval is required in our case. The dataset of the large-scale storage performance study will

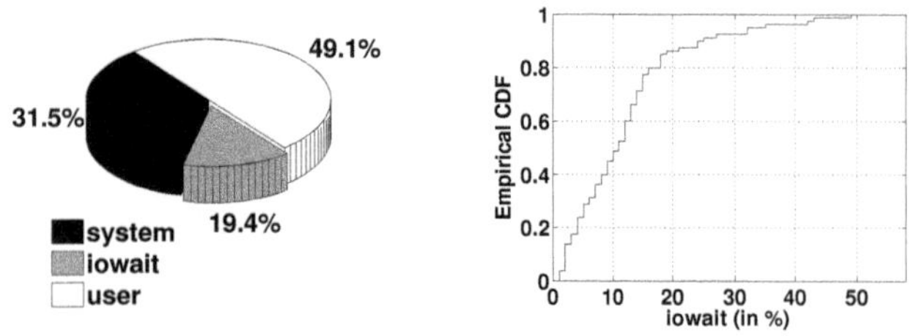


(a) Samsung S5 CPU Breakdown

(b) Iowait of 2611 Devices

**Figure 3: Iowait Values.**

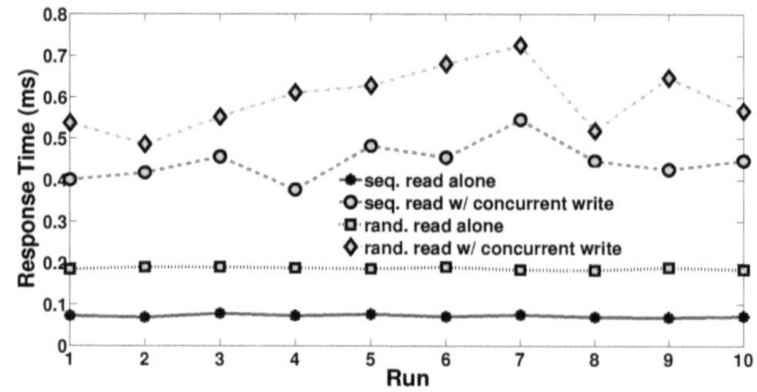


(a) Samsung S5 I/O Slowdown

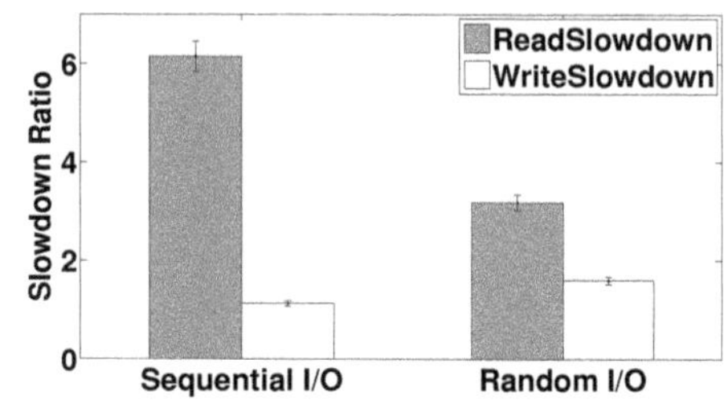


(b) Samsung S5 Slowdown Asymmetry

**Figure 4: I/O Slowdown.**

be made available at [12]. StoreBench requires a rooted [10] device with Android 3.0 or higher, and installed BusyBox [1] on the device. The app's screenshot is in Figure 2.

## 4.2 Storage Contribution

To investigate what portion of the CPU active time is spent in storage, we use the *iostat* [4] shell command to output the I/O statistics of our Samsung S5 phone. The statistics from 30 days of use include detailed numbers of reads/writes of each block device in the flash disk. More importantly, the information includes the breakdown of the CPU active time spent in three domains:

- *iowait* - the percentage of time that the CPUs were idle during which the system had an outstanding disk I/O request, which simply means the time spent waiting for *disk I/Os* to complete. This does not include the wait for network I/Os.
- *user* - the percentage of CPU utilization that occurred while executing at the user level (application).
- *system* - the percentage of CPU utilization that occurred while executing at the system level (kernel).

The output of *iostat* for each domain is illustrated in Figure 3(a). The results show that a decent portion of time is spent in storage (19.4% of total active time), corresponding to 61.6% of system level time and 39.5% of user time. The output values observed are stable, and the standard deviation is as little as 0.1%. Note that the numbers are from the total use of all apps through the whole time period. Hence, some more I/O intensive apps can spend considerably longer than 19.4% waiting for disk I/Os to complete.

Since the measurements may be different from device to device, we also extract the *iowait* results from our large-scale study obtained through StoreBench to verify the pattern. The *iowait* empirical cumulative distribution function across 2611 Android devices is plotted in Figure 3(b). 40 percent of the devices have *iowait* values between 13% and 58%, which represents a significant portion of CPU active time. The averaged standard deviation is 0.1%. These results are also consistent with those of the Samsung S5.

Although the statistics vary for different devices and usage patterns, it is safe to say that CPUs in Android devices spend a significant amount of time waiting for disk I/Os. Then a following question is, what may be the main causes of such I/O waits? To answer this question, we study several important properties of Android I/O activities, including I/O slowdown, slowdown asymmetry, and concurrency.

## 4.3 I/O Slowdown

In the following experiment, the goal is to understand how one I/O type is slowed down due to another, in particular, how reads are slowed down by concurrent writes. For this purpose, we utilize the Linux flexible I/O tester named *fio* [18] to issue read and write I/Os from/to the Samsung S5 phone's internal flash disk. We port *fio* to Android OS, patch the modifications to the original *fio* code, and cross-compile it. We make *fio*'s binary available for interested readers at [3].

First, we want to measure the response times of reads when they are running *alone*. We start by sequentially reading a 128MB file (32768 read I/Os, each I/O size of 4KB), and calculating the average response time of a read I/O as the total response time divided by the number of I/Os. This is repeated for 10 runs. The average response time of a sequential *read when running alone is 0.072ms*, and standard variation is 2.3%. The choice of a 128MB file is to ensure that this workload is large enough to provide statistically significant measurements but at the same time does not overwhelm the phone's storage capacity. We use this size throughout the paper unless otherwise stated. The choice of the 4KB block size in our workloads is due to the fact that the default file system (Ext4) employed in recent Android devices utilizes this block size. Therefore, only 4KB is considered throughout this paper, even though it has been reported that large block sizes can improve performance [20]. Smartphone manufacturers use this small block size, since 4KB I/Os account for up to 65% of smartphone operations [32].

Next, we record the response times of reads in the presence of concurrent writes. We start by sequentially reading a 128MB file and concurrently writing a 256MB file (larger write size to assure there is concurrent write running when we read), and calculate the average response time of a read I/O. This is repeated for 10 runs. The average response time of a sequential *read in the presence of*

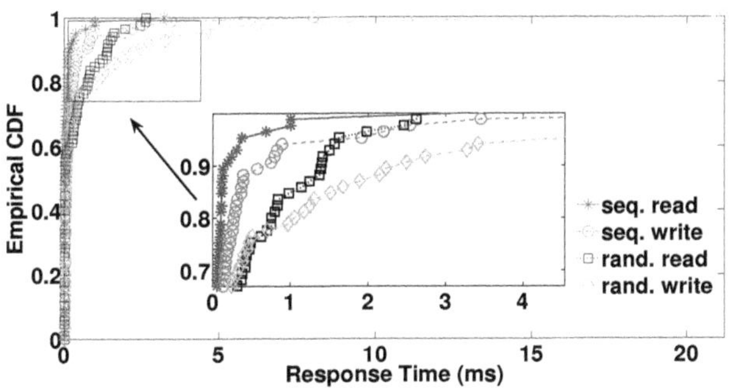


**Figure 5: Response Time ECDF of 2611 Devices.**

*a concurrent write is 0.445ms*, and standard variation is 3.1%. The two concurrent workloads are issued via *fio* as two separate processes. Buffers and caches are bypassed to obtain native properties. The above experiment is repeated for random I/Os. The average response time of a random *read when running alone is 0.187ms*, and standard variation is 3.3%. The average response time of a random *read in the presence of a concurrent write is 0.595ms*, and standard variation is 3.7%. The results of the two experiments are illustrated in Figure 4(a). There are a few observations from the figure. A sequential read experiences on average 515% slowdown (6.15 times slowdown) and up to 626% slowdown when blocked by a concurrent write. Similarly, a random read experiences on average 218% (3.18 times slowdown) and up to 293% slowdown when blocked by a concurrent write. This is important since it can be one of the main sources of slow application launch, when loading data is being blocked by a concurrent write. The root cause of the slowdowns is the flash read/write speed discrepancy (reads take much faster to complete). Additionally, reads become less predictable and the response times vary significantly over runs in the presence of a concurrent write.

Finally, we can observe that random reads are about 2.6 times slower than sequential reads. Although there is no seek time as in conventional rotating storage, random I/Os still suffer from processing overhead. When random I/O requests are issued, the CPUs have to coalesce the requests, and the storage controller has to interpret and pass them down to the correct block device, where a proper ordering is determined. Moreover, random file operations often involve file table access, which adds additional delay.

## 4.4 Slowdown Asymmetry

The next property that may affect I/O performance (and *iowait* as a result) is slowdown asymmetry. In the following we compare the average slowdown ratio of a read and a write. The slowdown ratios are calculated as follows:

- *ReadSlowdown = Response time of a read in the presence of a concurrent write / Response time of a read when running alone*
- *WriteSlowdown = Response time of a write in the presence of a concurrent read / Response time of a write when running alone*

The Samsung S5 results for both sequential and random I/Os with standard deviations are displayed in Figure 4(b). For sequential I/Os, while the slowdown ratio of a read is 6.15, the slowdown ratio of a write is only 1.13. For random I/Os, while the slowdown ratio of a read is 3.18, the slowdown ratio of a write is only 1.6.

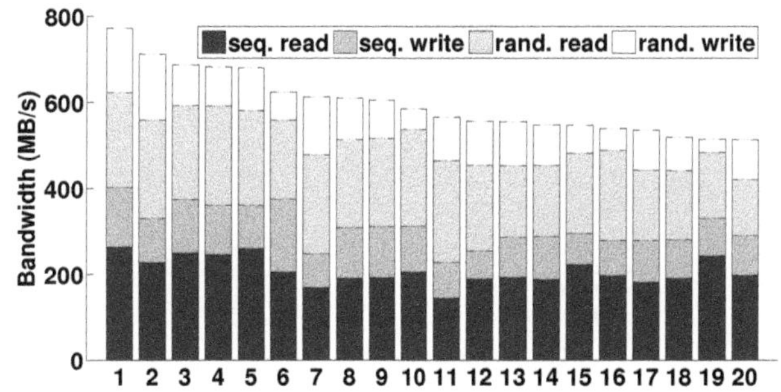


**Figure 6: Storage Performance of Top 20 Models. 1:**LG Nexus 5; **2:**OnePlus One (A0001); **3:**Motorola Nexus 6; **4:**Bq Aquaris E10; **5:**Motorola Moto G; **6:**Samsung Galaxy Note 2 (GT-N7100); **7:**Sony Xperia Z Ultra (XL39h); **8:**Samsung Galaxy S3 (GT-I9300); **9:**LG G2 (LG-D800); **10:**Nubia Z7 Max (NX505J); **11:**Sony Xperia Z1 (C6903); **12:**Samsung Galaxy Note 3 (SM-N9002); **13:**Asus Nexus 7; **14:**Sony Xperia Z2 (D6503); **15:**LG L70 (LG-D321); **16:**Lenovo A328; **17:**Hisilicon Hi3798CV100; **18:**LG Optimus F6 (LGMS500); **19:**HTC One M8; **20:**LG G3 (LG-D850).

This large asymmetry in the slowdowns has a following reason. Writes in the flash storage take already significantly longer than reads, hence, there is a smaller impact of the slowdown. While the response time of a sequential write running alone is on average 0.19ms, a sequential read running alone takes only 0.072ms. While the response time of a random write running alone is on average 0.41ms, a random read running alone takes only 0.187ms.

To understand the trend in the large scale, we plot the response time distributions obtained via StoreBench benchmark in Figure 5. In general, writes take longer than reads, and random I/Os take longer than sequential ones. This is consistent with the small-scale study using Samsung S5.

We also add Figure 6 with storage performance ranking obtained from the devices submitted by our users. Specifically, the figure includes the total bandwidth of the top 20 devices in MB/s. If a model has more devices in the ranking, then it is represented by its top device. An interesting observation is that a more recent model does not necessary mean higher ranking. For instance, while Nexus 5 (2013) tops the whole chart, Nexus 6 (2014) only occupies the 3rd place. Nexus 5 manufactured by LG mainly dominates thanks to its strong random write performance.

## 4.5 Concurrency

The next property that may affect I/O performance (and *iowait* as a result) is concurrency. An obvious approach to speeding up the application response is to issue I/Os concurrently. However, a large number of concurrent I/Os may overwhelm the processing capacity, and thus cause performance degradation. Therefore, it is necessary to find a sweet spot in concurrency to achieve maximal speedup. The last experiment's goal is to study the speedup of the concurrent I/Os over serial ones in the Samsung S5 phone. This is done for reads and writes separately. First, we issue two serial reads, each of size 32MB, and record the total response time. Then we issue two concurrent reads, each of size 32MB, and record the response time (use the larger result of the two reads if they differ). The speedup is calculated as the ratio of the two response times (serial / concurrent). This is repeated with four reads, eight reads, 16 reads,

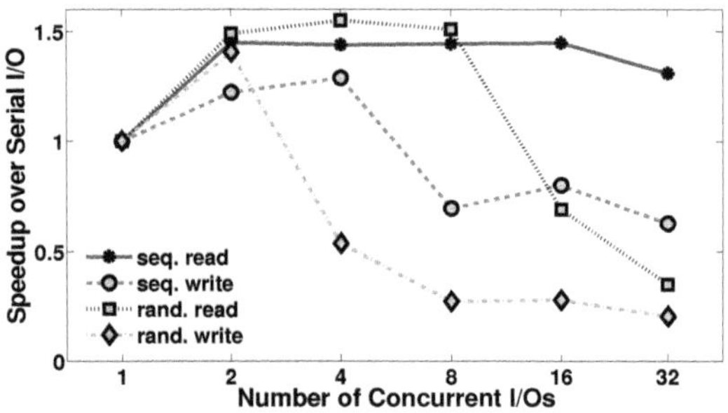


**Figure 7: Samsung S5 Speedup over Serial I/O.**

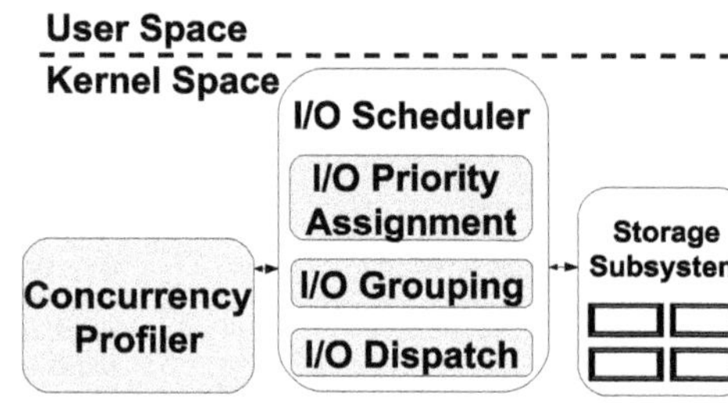


**Figure 8: SmartIO.**

and 32 reads, respectively. The choice of smaller workloads in this section (32MB) is because we issue up to 32 of such workloads concurrently, and do not want to overwhelm the phone's storage capacity.

To see how writes benefit from concurrency, we repeat the above with writes. First, two serial writes are issued, each of size 32MB, and the total response time is recorded. Then we issue two concurrent writes, each of size 32MB, and record the response time (use the larger result of the two writes if they differ). The speedup is calculated as the ratio of the two response times. This is again repeated with four writes, eight writes, 16 writes, and 32 writes, respectively. The speedup of concurrent I/Os over serial I/Os is illustrated in Figure 7.

We obtain four concurrency parameters from the figure. The number of concurrent sequential reads with maximal speedup (1.45) is 2, and the number of concurrent sequential writes with maximal speedup (1.29) is 4. The number of concurrent random reads with maximal speedup (1.55) is 4, and the number of concurrent random writes with maximal speedup (1.41) is 2. The speedup of reads is higher than the one of writes for both cases, which implies that reads benefit more from concurrency. This is expected. Intuitively, with growing processing time, the wait time also increases. Moreover, if the processing needs exceed the processing capacity, then there is no well-defined average waiting time because the queue can grow without bound. Since writes take longer to process than reads, it is expected that writes would overwhelm the processing capacity sooner, and thus benefit less from increased concurrency. In addition, different devices may benefit differently from concurrency, since they may have different speedup represented by concurrency parameters. Since these concurrency parameters may differ for various devices, a solution with the maximum benefits from concurrency requires a design that is capable of adapting to each phone's concurrency characteristics.

## 4.6 Summary

The above experiments lead to several important observations that shed light on how to improve smartphone application performance, and we summarize them below.

First, Android devices spend a significant portion of their CPU active time waiting for storage I/Os to complete. Specifically, 40% of the devices have *iowait* values between 13% and 58%. This negatively affects the smartphone's overall application performance, and results in slow response time. Therefore, in order to improve the application performance, it is essential to investigate possible causes of such waits.

One of the reasons causing such waits is I/O slowdown. Our first experiment studies slowdown of one I/O type due to presence of another, and reveals significant slowdown of reads in the presence of writes. Specifically, a sequential read experiences on average 515% slowdown and up to 626% slowdown when blocked by a concurrent write. Similarly, a random read experiences on average 218% and up to 293% slowdown when blocked by a concurrent write. This significant read slowdown may negatively impact the application performance during the life cycles when the number of reads dominates. A good example is application launch.

Next, the impact of such slowdown on the application delay may vary depending on the slowdown ratio of a read and a write. As demonstrated earlier, there is a significant asymmetry in read and write I/O slowdown. Specifically, for sequential I/Os, while the read slowdown ratio is 6.15, the write slowdown ratio is only 1.13. For random I/Os, while the read slowdown ratio is 3.18, the write slowdown ratio is only 1.6.

Finally, the last property researched is concurrency. Our experimental study reveals that different devices may benefit differently from concurrency. The above results also suggest that reads benefit more from concurrency. However, in order to optimize the application performance, we need to be able to adapt to the concurrency characteristics of each device. Such characteristics include four concurrency parameters of the maximal speedup: the number of concurrent sequential reads, the number of concurrent sequential writes, the number of concurrent random reads, and the number of concurrent random writes.

# 5. SYSTEM ARCHITECTURE

In order to improve the application delay performance in smartphones, we present SmartIO [35, 34], a system that reduces the application response time by prioritizing reads over writes, and grouping them based on assigned priorities. SmartIO issues I/Os with optimized concurrency parameters. The architecture of SmartIO is illustrated in Figure 8. It is fully located in the kernel space, and consists of two main modules: the I/O Scheduler and the Concurrency Profiler. The I/O Scheduler encapsulates 3 submodules: I/O Priority Assignment, I/O Grouping, and I/O Dispatch. We elaborate each module and its functionalities below.

**I/O Priority Assignment.** Our system prototype follows the implications from the previous experimental study. First, since a read suffers a large slowdown in the presence of a concurrent write, the goal is to allow reads to be completed before writes, and delay writes as long as there are reads, while avoiding write starvation. In order to achieve this, a third level of I/O priority is added into the current block layer, assigning higher priority to reads and lower to writes. This third priority level has a lower priority than the first two priority levels (class priority, and priority within each class) from the block layer explained earlier in the Background section. Write starvation is avoided by applying a time slice, which is a

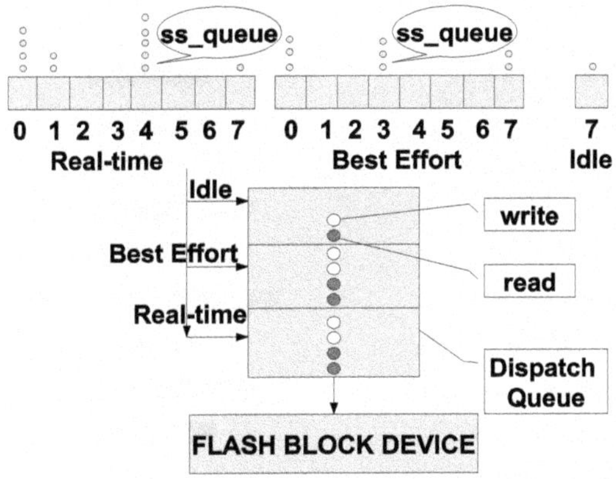


**Figure 9: Dispatch Example.**

maximal period of time assigned to a process, and is by default 100ms as used in the Linux scheduler time slice concept.

**I/O Grouping.** The dispatch queue further groups reads and groups writes based on the three levels of priority. Reads are ordered in front of writes, and reads are then dispatched before writes. Due to the read/write discrepancy nature of the flash storage (reads take much faster to complete), the read-preference reordering does not introduce a major delay to write I/Os.

This reordering enforced by SmartIO does not affect correctness and semantics of write barriers. It is common knowledge that write barriers [38] are essential for consistency of many file systems. That is, however, maintained at the file system layer, which is above the I/O scheduler. Therefore, requests issued to an I/O scheduler can be reordered without affecting correctness. In fact, reordering is a common practice to minimize the seek costs in mechanical disks.

**I/O Dispatch.** A sample dispatch is illustrated in Figure 9. In the current CFQ implementation, each block device has 17 queues (ss_queue) of I/O requests (8 Real-time, 8 Best Effort, and 1 Idle). The existing system selects a queue based on the priorities, takes a request in the queue, and inserts it in the dispatch queue. The queue selection process accounts for two priority levels: the class priority (Real-time, Best Effort, Idle), and the priority within the class (0-7).

Our system does not change the above dispatch process but uses a third priority level to organize the dispatch queue in favor of the read I/Os. The dispatch queue is then divided into three sections, from the bottom up real-time, best effort, and idle requests. Each section is organized such that reads precede writes.

**Concurrency Profiler.** The system uses the knowledge of the phone's four concurrency parameters to issue the I/Os to the block device. The parameters include the optimal number of sequential or random reads (writes) that benefit most from concurrency, as discussed earlier in the Concurrency subsection. Based on the parameters, the system issues the appropriate number of reads (writes) concurrently from the dispatch queue. To achieve this, SmartIO measures the concurrency parameters during installation by invoking the *fio* tool to benchmark the phone. *fio* issues reads and writes, and calculates the speedup of concurrent I/Os over serial ones, as performed in the measurement study. The concurrency parameters with optimal speedup are then used to complete the I/O requests. This assures robustness of our system to different characteristics of the flash storage in the phones. With the use of *fio*, SmartIO can adapt to different devices without prior knowledge of their concurrency parameters.

# 6. IMPLEMENTATION

In this section, we elaborate implementation details of the SmartIO system. In particular, we explain the algorithm of the scheduler's dispatch process. Next, we highlight important implementation challenges of the SmartIO system. Specifically, we discuss the I/O testing tool integration in the Concurrency Profiler module. The module utilizes the tool to obtain optimized concurrency parameters that allow SmartIO issue optimal number of I/Os concurrently to block devices.

**SmartIO.** First, we discuss implementation details of our solution. We implement the SmartIO system on the rooted Samsung S5 smartphone with Android 4.4.2 (KitKat), kernel 3.10, and Ext4 file system. The phone is equipped with a 2.5 GHz quad-core Krait 400 CPU, 2 GB of RAM, and 16 GB of internal flash storage. The implementation consists of 2 main modules, the I/O Scheduler and the Concurrency Profiler, both of which are in the kernel space.

The I/O Scheduler is implemented as a kernel patch of the default CFQ Linux scheduler. Users can switch to our scheduler with a simple shell command that changes the scheduler file. For instance, the scheduler is set on all block devices on-the-fly as follows:
*echo* $ss > /sys/block/mmcblk0/queue/scheduler$. Similarly, the users can go back to the default scheduler by:
*echo* $cfq > /sys/block/mmcblk0/queue/scheduler$.

Details of the dispatch are explained below. First, the system selects a queue from the 17 priority queues, then chooses a request in the selected queue, and inserts the request into the dispatch queue. If the time slice of the current queue is not expired (default 100ms as in CFQ), and the queue is not empty, the dispatch continues with the current queue. Otherwise, it chooses a different queue based on the priorities. The time slice serves as an ultimate mechanism to avoid starvation. When a queue $q$ is chosen, the algorithm dispatches a request from it. If it may dispatch, it picks a request from the queue in the FIFO fashion, and inserts the request into the dispatch queue. The *dispatch* is elaborated in Algorithm 6.1.

**Algorithm 6.1:** DISPATCH($queue * q$)

//choose a queue
**if** current queue $q$ *empty* or *its time slice expired*
**then** choose another queue and assign it to $q$

//if queue $q$ may dispatch
**if** $may\_dispatch(q)$
**then** { pick a request in FIFO fashion; insert request to dispatch queue }

To find out if we can dispatch from a queue $q$, *may_dispatch* is envoked. First, it checks whether the queue has more I/Os in flight than allowed. If not, it allows the dispatch. If the queue has already reached the dispatch limit, the system checks how many queues are waiting for dispatch. In case when there is another queue waiting, the dispatch is not allowed. If the queue is the only one, SmartIO sets no limit for it. The number of in-flight I/Os of a queue from the Linux default settings is 8. *may_dispatch* is elaborated in Algorithm 6.2.

**Obtaining Concurrency Parameters.** As discussed earlier, based on the concurrency parameters, SmartIO issues the appropriate num-

**Algorithm 6.2:** MAY_DISPATCH($queue * q$)

```
//does this q already have too many I/Os in-flight?
if (q.dispatched >= max_dispatch)
  then
    if (busy_queues > 1)
      then
        //we have other queues,don't allow more
        //I/Os from this one
        return (false)
    else if (busy_queues == 1)
      then
        //sole queue user, no limit
        max_dispatch ← ∞
    else
        max_dispatch ← quantum
        //default init quantum is 8

//if we're below the current max, allow dispatch
return (q.dispatched < max_dispatch)
```

ber of reads (writes) concurrently from the dispatch queue. To achieve this, SmartIO measures the concurrency parameters during installation by invoking the *fio* tool to benchmark the phone. *fio* issues reads and writes, and calculates the speedup of concurrent I/Os over serial ones, as performed in the measurement study. *fio* [18] is a Linux I/O testing tool that directs different types of I/Os to block devices, and returns information on the delay performance. The first step to get *fio* issue a desired workload is to write a job file. The typical contents of the job file is a global section defining shared parameters, and one or more job sections describing the jobs involved. For instance, the following code tests the sequential read and write performance of the /data partition on a phone:

```
[global]
directory=/data
bs=4k
size=32m

[sequential-read]
rw=read
numjobs=1
stonewall

[sequential-write]
rw=write
numjobs=1
stonewall
```

*Stonewall* allows a job to start only when a previous one has finished. Without the two *stonewall*s above, the tool issues two jobs running concurrently. The *directory* defines the destination for the workload, *bs* stands for block size, and *size* defines the size of the workload to be issued.

To integrate *fio* in SmartIO, we patch the *fio* code with Android compiling adjustment, and cross-compile it to get its binary. We make the binary and job files available at [3]. The binary then is imported into the Concurrency Profiler module, and in run-time transferred to the /data partition directory in the internal flash disk.

# 7. PERFORMANCE EVALUATION

This section evaluates SmartIO, and answers the following questions. *(1) How does SmartIO reduce iowait?* We output *iostat* values of five smartphones with SmartIO. *(2) How does SmartIO improve the benchmark performance?* We address this by investigating the I/O slowdown and asymmetry of the synthetic benchmarks. The experiments are conducted with SmartIO disabled, and enabled. Additionally, SmartIO is compared with other existing I/O schedulers. *(3) How does SmartIO improve the application performance?* This is addressed by recording the launch and run-time delay of the 40 popular apps from Google Play with and without SmartIO. In addition, we conduct an experiment on the Facebook application to determine the user-perceived performance improvement of our solution.

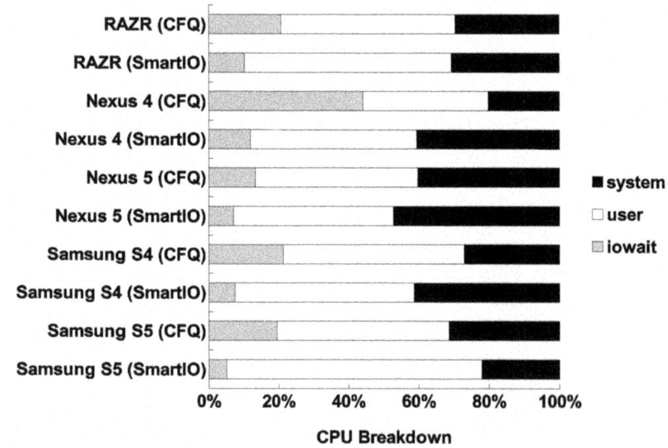


**Figure 10: Iowait Before and After.**

## 7.1 Iowait

As in the measurement study, we utilize the *iostat* [4] shell command to output the I/O statistics of five devices: Samsung S5, Samsung S4, Nexus 5, Nexus 4, and Motorola RAZR Maxx. The devices are normally used daily by the authors, and are running Android 4.4, 4.3, 4.4, 4.2, and 4.0, respectively. The statistics from the use of SmartIO within 30 days and the use of CFQ within 30 days are illustrated in Figure 10. The results indicate a significant iowait reduction on Samsung S5 (74.2%) and Nexus 4 (73.2%). These numbers highly depend on the individual I/O traffic resulted from usage patterns of each smartphone user. In particular, Samsung S5 and Nexus 4 have both the total amount of blocks read almost an order of magnitude larger than the amount of blocks written (10,122,938 vs. 1,017,864; 250,005,743 vs. 26,042,265; each block of 4KB). This read intensive traffic benefits from our solution that favors reads over writes, which contributes to the reduction of the CPU time the devices spend waiting for I/Os to complete. The other devices also show a decent reduction in iowait: 65.1% (Samsung S4), RAZR (50.5%), and Nexus 5 (47%).

## 7.2 Benchmark Performance

To determine SmartIO's performance gain and cost, we investigate the I/O slowdown and asymmetry of benchmarks. Since the proposed system is designed to serve in favor of reads over writes, writes are expected to perform slightly worse. We run two benchmarks, first with SmartIO disabled, and the second time with SmartIO enabled. When SmartIO is disabled, the default I/O scheduler (CFQ) is utilized. The first benchmark consists of an 1-reader (128MB) and an 1-writer (128MB) process. The second benchmark consists of a 4-reader (4 x 128MB) and a 4-writer (4 x 128MB)

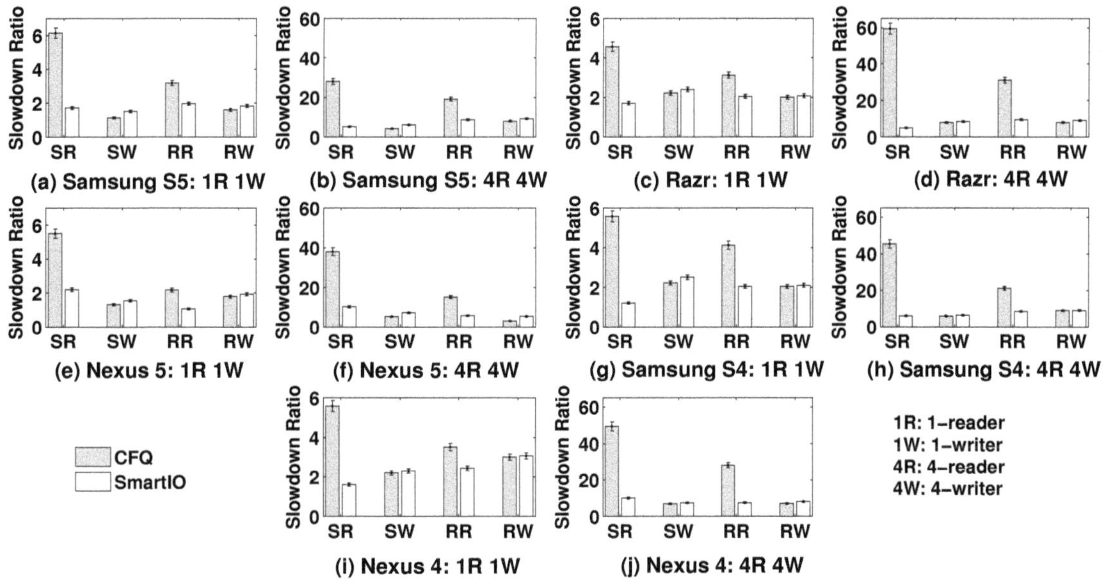


**Figure 11: I/O Slowdown.** SR=sequential read; SW=sequential write; RR=random read; RW=random write.

process. We consider both sequential and random I/Os. First, the experiment is done on the Samsung S5 phone. The I/Os are issued by the *fio* tool.

**Gain vs. Cost.** The I/O slowdown of the 1-reader and 1-writer with standard deviations is illustrated in Figure 11(a). For sequential I/Os, the read slowdown improves from 6.15 (CFQ) to 1.72 (SmartIO). Since our system delays writes in favor of reads, it is important to make sure that writes do not suffer a large performance degradation. As observed, this read performance improvement comes with only little cost due to the read/write discrepancy nature of the flash storage (reads take much faster to complete). Specifically, the write slowdown ratio worsens from 1.13 to 1.51. Similar behavior is observed for the random I/Os. While the read slowdown ratio improves significantly from 3.18 to 1.97, the write slowdown worsens slightly from 1.6 to 1.83. However, the random reads achieve smaller performance gain than the sequential ones. This is consistent with the results from the Measurement Study (Section 4), which show the random reads having lower slowdowns in the presence of the concurrent writes, hence, the benefit from the SmartIO read-preference scheduling is smaller.

The I/O slowdown of the 4-reader and 4-writer is illustrated in Figure 11(b). For sequential I/Os, the read slowdown ratio improves dramatically from 28.03 to 5.12. This large performance gain comes from the read-preference of SmartIO, together with the speedup from improved concurrency. The write slowdown ratio worsens from 4.21 to 6.12, which is the cost of SmartIO's lower write's priority. The random read slowdown improves from 19.22 to 8.75, while the write slowdown worsens from 8.01 to 9.32. Again, the random I/Os benefit from SmartIO slightly less than the sequential I/Os, which agrees with the theory.

**Adaptation to Different Phones.** As for validation, we also deploy our solution on other phones. First, we look at the Motorola Razr smartphone with the Android OS 4.0 (ICS), kernel 3.0, Ext4 file system, and duo-core. The Razr's default I/O scheduler is also CFQ, and its four concurrency parameters with maximal speedup found by SmartIO are: 2 concurrent seq. reads, 2 concurrent seq. writes (different from Samsung S5), 2 concurrent random reads (different from Samsung S5), and 2 concurrent random writes. The I/O slowdown of the 1-reader and 1-writer is illustrated in Figure 11(c). The I/O slowdown of the 4-reader and 4-writer is illustrated in Figure 11(d). Both figures are plotted with standard deviations. The 1-reader and 1-writer shows a similar behavior as on the Samsung S5 phone. The 4-reader and 4-writer indicates even larger read performance improvement compared to the Samsung S5 phone. The sequential read slowdown ratio improves from 59.4 to 4.98, while its write slowdown only worsens from 7.92 to 8.41. The random I/Os also show great improvement, the read slowdown improves from 31.12 to 9.5, while the write worsens from 8.01 to 9.08. This large performance boost is due to higher gains from concurrency, and demonstrates that SmartIO with its concurrency parameters measurement can adapt to different flash characteristics. The Samsung S5's smaller performance gain is due to the fact that the phone is more recent, and its four cores already offer great baseline performance. While the Razr's duo-core architecture shows even larger read performance improvement due to the lower baseline performance of the smaller number of cores. For comparison, we also display further results on the rest of the devices: Nexus 5 in Figure 11(e)(f), Samsung S4 in Figure 11(g)(h), and Nexus 4 in Figure 11(i)(j). They all demonstrate significant reductions in the read slowdown, while the write slowdown only worsens little. From these three devices, Samsung S4 has the largest read slowdown reduction (7.6 times in (h)), while Nexus 5 has the largest write slowdown increment (1.77 times in (f)). In summary, the above benchmarking experiments show different performance gains for a diverse set of devices. This is reasonable, since each device is equipped with different hardware components, and hence different results are expected. However, the experiments also confirm that SmartIO is able to adapt to different phones.

## 7.3 Scheduler Comparison

This section aims to compare SmartIO with other existing I/O schedulers: Complete Fair Queuing (CFQ), Deadline, and Noop. These are the only three schedulers available on recent Android de-

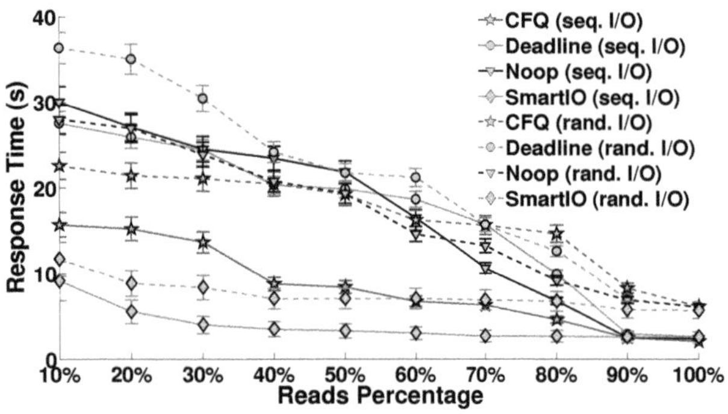


**Figure 12: Scheduler Comparison.** Solid lines are sequential I/Os; dashed lines are random I/Os.

vices. CFQ attempts to distribute available I/O bandwidth equally among all I/O requests. The requests are placed into per-process queues where each of the queues gets a time slice allocated. Further details on CFQ are explained earlier in the Background section. Deadline algorithm attempts to guarantee a start time for a process. The queues are sorted by expiration time of processes. Noop inserts incoming I/Os into a FIFO fashion queue and implements request merging.

To compare the schedulers, we utilize *fio* to issue mixed workloads of both reads and writes to the Samsung S5 phone's internal flash disk, and measure the time delay that takes to complete the workloads (response time). This is repeated on all mentioned schedulers, and the comparison is done for both sequential and random I/Os.

**Sequential I/O.** For each scheduler we issue a 128MB mixed workload with 10% of sequential reads (90% of sequential writes), and record the response time. Next, we issue a 128MB mixed workload with 20% of reads (80% of writes), and record the response time. We continue issuing a workload with 30% reads, 40% reads, etc. Until the workload with 100% reads. The block size is set to 4KB, the queue depth to 128, and the cache is cleared after each measurement.

The resulting response times are plotted in Figure 12 *(solid lines)*. In general, for all four schedulers, with the increased percentage of reads, the response time decreases. For instance, with a workload consisting 10% reads, the response time for SmartIO is 9 seconds, CFQ 16 seconds, Deadline 28 seconds, and Noop 30 seconds. With 50% of reads, the response time is faster, SmartIO needs 3 seconds, CFQ 8 seconds, Deadline 20 seconds, and Noop 22 seconds. This is consistent with our measurement study, since reads are faster to complete, and less writes also means smaller I/O slowdown. For most workloads, SmartIO provides the fastest response time, while the current I/O scheduler in Samsung S5 (CFQ) is second best. Deadline and Noop perform poorly, and one beats another depending on the workload. Consequently, by changing the scheduler from the default CFQ to the proposed SmartIO, we achieve on average 42% faster response times (max of 64%).

**Random I/O.** The above experiment is reiterated for random I/Os. The resulting response times are plotted in Figure 12 *(dashed lines)*. Again, it is safe to say that with the increased percentage of reads, the response time decreases for all schedulers. This is consistent with our experimental study, since reads are faster to complete, and less writes also means smaller I/O slowdown. For all random I/O workloads, SmartIO has fastest response times. As a result, by changing the scheduler from the default CFQ to the proposed SmartIO, we may achieve on average 49% faster response times (max of 66%). Compared to sequential I/Os, random I/Os take longer to complete. This is also consistent with our findings in the measurement study, which identifies that random activities generally take longer to complete.

## 7.4 Application Performance

To address the third question on how SmartIO improves the application performance, we measure the launch and run-time delay of 40 popular apps (10 games, 10 streaming, 10 miscellaneous, and 10 sensing) from Google Play, with and without SmartIO. Among others, the miscellaneous group also includes two file processing applications (File Commander and File Manager) and two write-intensive applications (ZArchiver and RAR for Android). During the experiment, our Samsung S5 has all radio communication disabled except for WiFi that is necessary to provide stable Internet connections required on most apps. The screen is set to stay-awake mode with constant brightness, and the screen auto-rotation is disabled. Only one app runs at a time, and no other app is in the background. This is to achieve a fair comparison between the two cases: with SmartIO, and without SmartIO. The cache is cleared before each measurement in order to evaluate real performance improvement caused by SmartIO.

**Launch Delay.** The Android Monkey tool [6] is utilized to trigger the launch process of each app. The application *launch delay* starts when the launch process is triggered, and ends when the process completes. The launch delay includes three components. We use the *time* command [14] to output the three time components: the time taken by the app in the user mode (*user*), the time taken by the app in the kernel mode (*system*), and the time the app spends waiting for the disk and network I/Os to complete (*totalIO*). The storage I/O delay is obtained by dividing the total number of I/Os completed *(kBread + kBwrtn)* over the total rate of I/Os completed *(kBreadRate + kBwrtnRate)* in a flash block device. The network I/O delay is then calculated as the total I/O delay *(totalIO)* subtracted by the storage I/O delay *(storageIOdelay)*.

Formally,

$$storageIOdelay = \frac{kBread + kBwrtn}{kBreadRate + kBwrtnRate}, \quad (1)$$

where *kBread* is the amount of data read from a flash block device, *kBwrtn* is the amount of data written to a flash block device, *kBreadRate* is the data rate read per second from a flash block device, and *kBwrtnRate* is the data rate written per second to a flash block device. All four variables are obtained from the output of the *iostat* Linux command.

$$networkIOdelay = totalIO - storageIOdelay, \quad (2)$$

where *totalIO* is the time an app spends waiting for both disk and network I/Os to complete. The variable is obtained from the *time* command during application launch.

The *cold launch delay* is a launch delay required to launch an application not currently running in the background. Such application also has its cache cleared before each measurement. The cold launch delay of the 40 apps with and without SmartIO is illustrated in Figure 13(a). The figure includes 10 games (1-5, 21-25), 10 streaming apps (6-10, 26-30), 10 miscellaneous apps (11-15, 31-35), and 10 sensing apps (16-20, 36-40). Applications running with

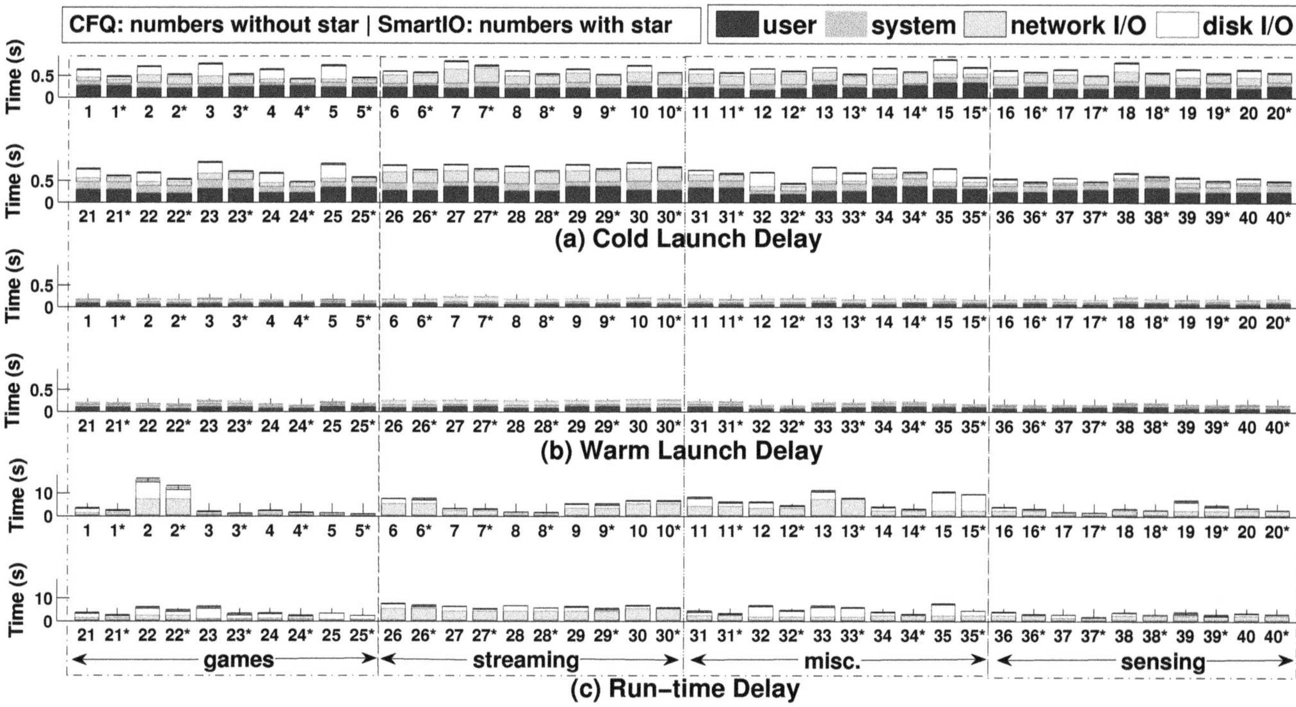


**Figure 13: Launch and Run-time Delay.** **1:**Angry Birds; **2:**GTA; **3:**Need for Speed; **4:**Temple Run; **5:**The Simpsons; **6:**CNN; **7:**Nightly News; **8:**ABC News; **9:**YouTube; **10:**Pandora; **11:**Facebook; **12:**Twitter; **13:**Gmail; **14:**Google Maps; **15:**ZArchiver; **16:**Accelerometer M.; **17:**Gyroscope Log; **18:**Proximity Sensor; **19:**Compass; **20:**Barometer; **21:**2048 Puzzle; **22:**Pet Rescue Saga; **23:**Pou; **24:**Solitaire; **25:**Words; **26:**CT 24; **27:**Live Extra; **28:**VEVO; **29:**VOYO.cz; **30:**WATCH ABC; **31:**Instagram; **32:**File Commander; **33:**RAR for Android; **34:**Dropbox; **35:**File Manager; **36:**Physics Toolbox; **37:**Sensor Kinetics; **38:**Android Sensor Box; **39:**Sensor Music Player; **40:**Sensor Mouse.

SmartIO are denoted with a star (*). The figure is plotted with standard deviations. The reduction in cold launch delays with SmartIO ranges from 6.3% (Accelerometer Monitor) to 37.8% (The Simpsons) as compared to delays without SmartIO. The cold launch delay with SmartIO enabled for all the 40 apps is on average 20.5% faster than with SmartIO disabled. These results are expected. The app launch is I/O intensive, and includes a lot of read activities. The average number of reads observed for the 40 apps is 5 times higher than writes. Some apps even go to the extremes, for instance, the Temple Run game has reads exceeding writes by 58 times. Therefore, the read-preference nature of SmartIO contributes to reducing disk I/O delay during the launch. Specifically, the disk I/O delay portion itself is reduced on average by 69%. Slight difference in the user and system time of several apps suggests that SmartIO also affects other time components. We reserve further investigation for future work.

The *warm launch delay* is a launch delay required to launch an application currently running in the background. The cache of such application is not cleared before the measurement. The warm launch delay of the 40 apps with and without SmartIO is illustrated in Figure 13(b). The absolute values of warm launch delays are on average 65% smaller than those of cold launch delays. This is reasonable, since once an app is already in memory, its launch is much faster. In addition, since there is little I/O traffic going to the flash disk (81% less than during cold launch), the reduction in delays for all 40 apps with SmartIO is on average only 6.8%. The disk I/O delay portion itself is reduced on average by 13%.

**Run-time Delay.** In order to test delays of apps running on the phone with SmartIO, we utilize again the Android Monkey tool to generate streams of 500 user events such as clicks, touches, or gestures. The *run-time delay* is defined as the time needed to complete the 500 user events in a running app. We run the experiments with the same 40 Android apps mentioned previously. Each app has a predefined set of user activities triggered through the Monkey tool. The run-time delay for both cases is measured with the *time* command, once with SmartIO enabled, and once with SmartIO disabled. Monkey is a command-line tool that can send a stream of events into the phone's system in a repeatable manner. We apply a constant seed value (10) to generate the same sequence of events. The events are individually adjusted for each app to represent a typical usage, for instance, in Gmail we read and write an email, add a contact, change a label, etc.

The run-time delay of the 40 apps with and without SmartIO is illustrated in Figure 13(c). The figure is plotted with standard deviations. The reduction in run-time delay with SmartIO ranges from 2% (Pandora) to 29.6% (Angry Birds) as compared to run-time delay without SmartIO. The run-time delay with SmartIO enabled for all the 40 apps is on average 16.9% smaller than with SmartIO disabled. Clearly, the run-time delays do not benefit from using SmartIO as much as the application launch. This is reasonable, since the application launch is more I/O intensive than the application run-time. For the 40 apps, the average number of I/Os during launch is 2 times higher than during run-time. While the run-time delay of the games with SmartIO is on average 23% smaller, the streaming apps have on average only 4% smaller run-time delay. This is

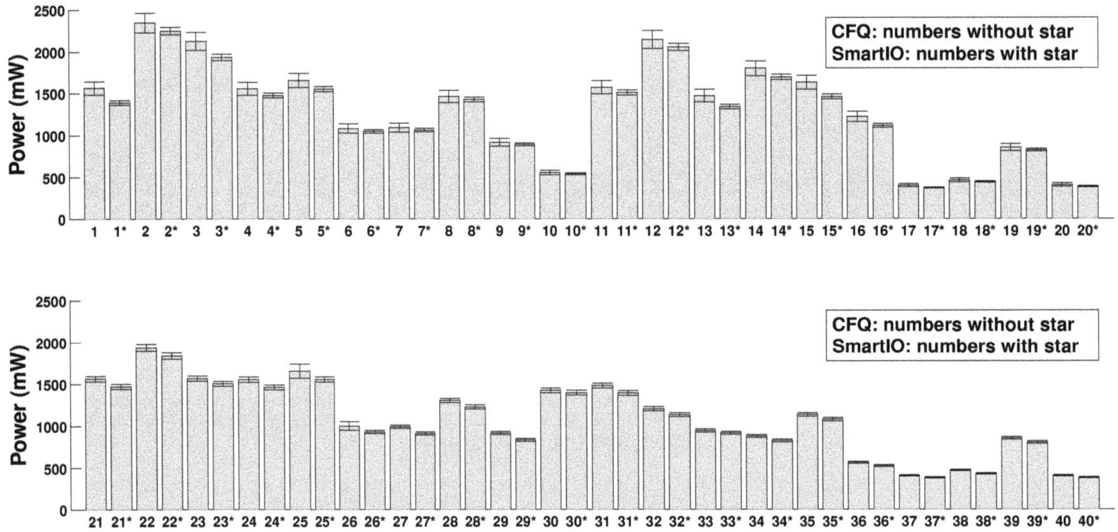


**Figure 14: Power Consumption.** **1:**Angry Birds; **2:**GTA; **3:**Need for Speed; **4:**Temple Run; **5:**The Simpsons; **6:**CNN; **7:**Nightly News; **8:**ABC News; **9:**YouTube; **10:**Pandora; **11:**Facebook; **12:**Twitter; **13:**Gmail; **14:**Google Maps; **15:**ZArchiver; **16:**Accelerometer M.; **17:**Gyroscope Log; **18:**Proximity Sensor; **19:**Compass; **20:**Barometer; **21:**2048 Puzzle; **22:**Pet Rescue Saga; **23:**Pou; **24:**Solitaire; **25:**Words; **26:**CT 24; **27:**Live Extra; **28:**VEVO; **29:**VOYO.cz; **30:**WATCH ABC; **31:**Instagram; **32:**File Commander; **33:**RAR for Android; **34:**Dropbox; **35:**File Manager; **36:**Physics Toolbox; **37:**Sensor Kinetics; **38:**Android Sensor Box; **39:**Sensor Music Player; **40:**Sensor Mouse.

expected, since the games have decent disk I/O activity during the run-time, whereas the streaming apps are mainly network-bounded. For example, 56% of Angry Birds's run-time delay stems from disk I/Os, and the disk I/O delay portion itself is reduced by 49%. While 64.7% of CNN's run-time delay originates from network I/Os, and the disk I/O delay portion itself is only reduced by 8%. Finally, the average gains of the sensing and miscellaneous category are 18% and 20%, respectively. The improvement in the disk I/O portion of the time spent during run-time is on average by 54%.

**Power Consumption.** While improving the application performance is important, having solid power efficiency is equally important. To measure power consumption, the Monsoon Power Monitor [7] is utilized. Each of the 40 apps is run with SmartIO disabled, and then enabled. The Android Monkey tool triggers the launch process of each app, and then generates the same stream of 500 user events as previously. The results with standard deviations are presented in Figure 14. The average power consumption with SmartIO enabled is lower than the consumption with SmartIO disabled by 6%. Hence, our solution does not have energy overhead, and even contributes to lower power levels. We attribute this to the read-preference approach of the system that essentially allows shorter jobs to be completed first, which contributes to smaller application delay and consequently also lower power consumption.

## 7.5 User-Perceived Performance: Facebook

In this subsection we conduct an experiment on the Facebook application to determine the user-perceived performance improvement of our solution. Since the delays in Figure 13 are obtained in the OS layer, the values are precise but significantly smaller than if obtained in the application layer. In order to acquire measurements in the application layer, we may use a stop watch, which is however inaccurate. Instead, we choose to slightly modify the Facebook source code[1] to record timestamps of several performance parameters. Specifically, we focus on three metrics that are critical to Facebook users: cold launch, warm launch, and timeline loading. A short demo of a modified Facebook version is available at [5]. The app uses test accounts and automates 150 measurements per metric without necessity of any user interaction. The experiment is conducted on the five phones listed above.

**Cold Launch.** Cold launch in Facebook is defined as the time required to complete loading all components of the start activity and rendering of the News Feed. All cache data is cleared except the login information. The ultimate goal of Facebook Inc. for the following years is to have cold launch of less than 5 seconds on devices released in 2012 or newer, and less than 10 seconds on older devices. The results in Figure 15(a) show that cold launch on our oldest device RAZR (2012) takes 9.9 seconds with CFQ and 6.2 seconds with SmartIO. The newest phone Samsung S5 (2014) spends 3.7 seconds on cold launch with CFQ, and 2.3 seconds with SmartIO. Finally, cold launch with CFQ on Nexus 5 (2013), Nexus 4 (2012), and Samsung S4 (2013) requires 4 seconds, 9.5 seconds, and 7.8 seconds, respectively. While with SmartIO, the three devices need 2.5 seconds, 6 seconds, and 5.1 seconds, respectively. Since the shortest human perceivable delay is 100ms [22], we can conclude that SmartIO can contribute significantly to reducing the user-perceivable cold launch delay.

**Warm Launch.** Warm launch is defined similarly as cold launch, except the cache is not cleared before each measurement. Figure 15(b) indicates that RAZR has the most noticeable reduction in the delay. Specifically, warm launch with CFQ takes 5.6 seconds, while with SmartIO it takes 3.5 seconds. Nexus 4's warm launch delay is reduced from 4.1 seconds to 2.6 seconds. Samsung S4 shows a reduction from 3.8 seconds to 2.4 seconds. Finally, the

[1]The first author interned with Facebook Inc.

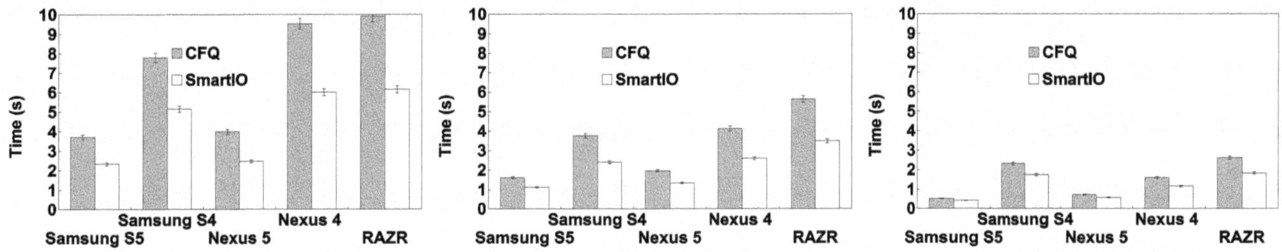


(a) Cold Launch (b) Warm Launch (c) Timeline Loading

**Figure 15: User-Perceived Performance of Facebook**

newest devices Samsung S5 and Nexus 5 get their delays reduced from 1.6 second to 1.1 second, and from 2 seconds to 1.3 second, respectively.

**Timeline Loading.** Timeline is a user profile page. Its loading is defined as the time required to complete loading and rendering of all components in the profile activity, where the origin activity is the News Feed. This can be seen as switching from the News Feed to the Timeline page. The results in Figure 15(c) show less noticeable reductions in the delay. This is reasonable, since this timeline loading corresponds to run-time delays in Figure 13, where the I/O traffic is usually less intensive. RAZR and Samsung S4 show most significant delay reductions: from 2.6 seconds to 1.8 second, and from 2.3 seconds to 1.7 second, respectively.

# 8. DISCUSSION AND FUTURE WORK

Launch and run-time delays are critical to user experience, since one launches and runs apps repeatedly throughout the day. Therefore, we focus on launch and run-time delays. However, in future work we plan to evaluate the impact of other stages of the life cycle on application performance such as install, update, switch, and uninstall, and quantify their effects on everyday phone usage. We intend to extend this study by researching how other common usage patterns are impacted. For instance, taking photos, recording movies, messaging, calling, email sync (recently studied in [41]), etc.

As discussed earlier, one of the main reasons causing longer launch delay is the disk I/O performance, specifically read I/O performance. This is due to the read-intensive nature of application launch. The average number of reads observed during launch on the 40 popular apps in our experiment is five times higher than writes. Other factors may also play a role in the high variation of launch delays. In particular, the launch delay also depends on the app's physical location, i.e., whether on the internal flash or external SD card. According to our analysis, the application size is not a big contributor to the launch delay. While the three largest apps Angry Birds (42.4MB), The Simpsons (41.7MB), and Temple Run 2 (36.7MB) have the launch delay around 0.65s, the smallest app Proximity Sensor (0.02MB) has the fifth largest launch delay (0.8s). Finally, we plan to analyze the impact of network I/O based on existing results [42, 19, 23, 24, 27, 39, 44].

Our work only focuses on reducing the application delay with respect to the internal flash storage. It may be also interesting to study how different applications use SD cards. Kim et al. [29] already performed a series of benchmarking experiments on SD cards from multiple speed classes. However, it will be useful to go beyond benchmarking and investigate I/O access patterns on these devices. This especially can benefit multimedia applications that store data on the external storage.

The major overhead of SmartIO is the additional delay in writes because it is designed to serve in favor of reads. As demonstrated in the evaluation, the write slowdown ratio worsens from 1.13 to 1.51 for sequential I/Os, while for random I/Os it worsens from 1.6 to 1.83. In another experiment, we install the 40 apps researched, and the results reveal that writes are on average 4.7% slower with SmartIO. However, at the same time, many other processes in the background may benefit from SmartIO. Based on our large-scale study, there are on average 255 processes running on each device at any point of time, from which 98 have some I/O activity and generate a workload. These processes are expected to have faster response time with SmartIO.

Our system keeps most of the dispatch process from the current Linux I/O scheduler unchanged. In particular, it only adds a third priority level to organize the dispatch queue in favor of reads. This third priority level preserves the original Linux scheduler design because it has a lower priority than the first two priority levels from the block layer. Therefore, the fairness between processes is still maintained, and a read from a process with lower priority may not incur unfair performance penalty on a service process with higher priority.

Finally, the observations made in our measurement study are based on data obtained in the Samsung S5 phone and 2611 Android devices through StoreBench. I/O slowdown and concurrency measurements were excluded from StoreBench, since these tests take too long (around 1 hour) to complete, and would discourage users from using this benchmark tool.

# 9. CONCLUSION

This paper presents a measurement study on the behavior of reads and writes in smartphones. Among others, we observe that reads experience up to a 626% slowdown in the presence of concurrent writes. The obtained insights are used to design and implement a system that reduces the application delay by prioritizing reads over writes, and grouping them based on assigned priorities. The evaluation on 40 apps demonstrates that SmartIO reduces launch delays by up to 37.8%, and run-time delays by up to 29.6%.

# 10. ACKNOWLEDGMENTS

We extend our thanks to Prof. Mahadev Satyanarayanan (CMU) for shepherding this work. We would also like to thank Aaron Carroll (NICTA), Dr. Duy Le (EMC), and Tommy Nguyen (RPI) for helpful discussions. Many thanks also go to Mai Anh Do (CNU) for helping with measurements, and Daniel Graham for recruiting StoreBench users. Finally, we thank anonymous reviewers for their comments. This work was supported in part by U.S. National Science Foundation under grants CNS-1250180 and CNS-1253506 (CAREER).

# 11. REFERENCES


[1] Busybox. `http://goo.gl/CF6vJ`, 2014.

[2] Deadline io scheduler tunables. `http://goo.gl/mB9alK`, 2014.

[3] fio: Flexible io tester ported for android. `http://storebench.com/fio.html`, 2014.

[4] Iostat. `http://goo.gl/OtZ33`, 2014.

[5] Modified facebook application demo. `http://goo.gl/b1AxQ2`, 2014.

[6] Monkey. `http://goo.gl/F14hW`, 2014.

[7] Monsoon monitor. `http://www.msoon.com`, 2014.

[8] Notes on the generic block layer rewrite in linux 2.5. `http://goo.gl/SwdLZ5`, 2014.

[9] One quarter of work devices are smartphones and tablets, forrester finds. `http://goo.gl/K23yGu`, 2014.

[10] Rooting your android. `http://www.androidcentral.com/root`, 2014.

[11] Storebench download. `http://goo.gl/ava9eV`, 2014.

[12] Storebench web. `http://StoreBench.com`, 2014.

[13] Storebench's list of devices. `http://StoreBench.com/list.html`, 2014.

[14] Time man page. `http://goo.gl/dEKuxs`, 2014.

[15] Worldwide smartphone 2013-2017 forecast and analysis. `http://goo.gl/v5vg2b`, 2014.

[16] N. Agrawal, V. Prabhakaran, T. Wobber, J. D. Davis, M. Manasse, and R. Panigrahy. Design tradeoffs for ssd performance. In *USENIX ATC 2008*.

[17] J. Axboe. Linux block io-present and future. In *Ottawa Linux Symp 2004*.

[18] J. Axboe. fio: Flexible io tester. `http://linux.die.net/man/1/fio`, 2014.

[19] A. Balasubramanian, R. Mahajan, and A. Venkataramani. Augmenting mobile 3g using wifi. In *ACM MobiSys 2010*.

[20] S. Boboila and P. Desnoyers. Performance models of flash-based solid-state drives for real workloads. In *IEEE MSST 2011*.

[21] D. Bovet and M. Cesati. *Understanding the Linux Kernel*. O'Reilly & Associates, Inc., 2005.

[22] S. K. Card, G. G. Robertson, and J. D. Mackinlay. The information visualizer, an information workspace. In *ACM SIGCHI 1991*.

[23] R. Chakravorty, S. Banerjee, P. Rodriguez, J. Chesterfield, and I. Pratt. Performance optimizations for wireless wide-area networks: Comparative study and experimental evaluation. In *ACM MobiCom 2004*.

[24] M. C. Chan and R. Ramjee. Tcp/ip performance over 3g wireless links with rate and delay variation. In *ACM MobiCom 2002*.

[25] F. Chen, D. A. Koufaty, and X. Zhang. Understanding intrinsic characteristics and system implications of flash memory based solid state drives. In *ACM SIGMETRICS 2009*.

[26] M. P. Dunn. *A new I/O scheduler for solid state devices*. PhD thesis, Texas A&M University, 2009.

[27] J. Huang, Q. Xu, B. Tiwana, Z. M. Mao, M. Zhang, and P. Bahl. Anatomizing application performance differences on smartphones. In *ACM MobiSys 2010*.

[28] S. Jeong, K. Lee, S. Lee, S. Son, and Y. Won. I/o stack optimization for smartphones. In *USENIX ATC 2013*.

[29] H. Kim, N. Agrawal, and C. Ungureanu. Revisiting storage for smartphones. In *USENIX FAST 2012*.

[30] J. Kim, Y. Oh, E. Kim, J. Choi, D. Lee, and S. H. Noh. Disk schedulers for solid state drivers. In *ACM EMSOFT 2009*.

[31] J. Kim, S. Seo, D. Jung, J.-S. Kim, and J. Huh. Parameter-aware i/o management for solid state disks (ssds). In *IEEE Transactions on Computing 2012*.

[32] K. Lee and Y. Won. Smart layers and dumb result: Io characterization of an android-based smartphone. In *ACM EMSOFT 2012*.

[33] D. T. Nguyen, G. Zhou, X. Qi, G. Peng, J. Zhao, T. Nguyen, and D. Le. Storage-aware smartphone energy savings. In *ACM UbiComp 2013*.

[34] D. T. Nguyen, G. Zhou, and G. Xing. Poster: Towards reducing smartphone application delay through read/write isolation. In *Proc. of ACM MobiSys*, 2014.

[35] D. T. Nguyen, G. Zhou, and G. Xing. Video: Study of storage impact on smartphone application delay. In *Proc. of ACM MobiSys*, 2014.

[36] A. Parate, M. Böhmer, D. Chu, D. Ganesan, and B. M. Marlin. Practical prediction and prefetch for faster access to applications on mobile phones. In *ACM UbiComp 2013*.

[37] S. Park and K. Shen. Fios: A fair, efficient flash i/o scheduler. In *USENIX FAST 2012*.

[38] P. Reisner and L. Ellenberg. Replicated storage with shared disk semantics. In *Linux System Technology 2005*.

[39] S. Sen, N. K. Madabhushi, and S. Banerjee. Scalable wifi media delivery through adaptive broadcasts. In *USENIX NSDI 2010*.

[40] K. Shen and S. Park. Flashfq: A fair queueing i/o scheduler for flash-based ssds. In *USENIX ATC 2013*.

[41] F. Xu, Y. Liu, T. Moscibroda, R. Chandra, L. Jin, Y. Zhang, and Q. Li. Optimizing background email sync on smartphones. In *ACM MobiSys 2013*.

[42] Q. Xu, S. Mehrotra, Z. Mao, and J. Li. Proteus: Network performance forecast for real-time, interactive mobile applications. In *ACM MobiSys 2013*.

[43] T. Yan, D. Chu, D. Ganesan, A. Kansal, and J. Liu. Fast app launching for mobile devices using predictive user context. In *ACM MobiSys 2012*.

[44] Z. Zhuang, T.-Y. Chang, R. Sivakumar, and A. Velayutham. A 3: Application-aware acceleration for wireless data networks. In *ACM MobiCom 2006*.

# AccelWord: Energy Efficient Hotword Detection through Accelerometer

Li Zhang, Parth H. Pathak, Muchen Wu, Yixin Zhao and Prasant Mohapatra
Computer Science Department, University of California, Davis, CA, 95616, USA
Email: {jxzhang, phpathak, muwu, yxzhao, pmohapatra}@ucdavis.edu

## ABSTRACT

Voice control has emerged as a popular method for interacting with smart-devices such as smartphones, smartwatches etc. Popular voice control applications like Siri and Google Now are already used by a large number of smartphone and tablet users. A major challenge in designing a voice control application is that it requires continuous monitoring of user's voice input through the microphone. Such applications utilize *hotwords* such as "Okay Google" or "Hi Galaxy" allowing them to distinguish user's voice command and her other conversations. A voice control application has to continuously listen for hotwords which significantly increases the energy consumption of the smart-devices.

To address this energy efficiency problem of voice control, we present AccelWord in this paper. AccelWord is based on the empirical evidence that accelerometer sensors found in today's mobile devices are sensitive to user's voice. We also demonstrate that the effect of user's voice on accelerometer data is rich enough so that it can be used to detect the hotwords spoken by the user. To achieve the goal of low energy cost but high detection accuracy, we combat multiple challenges, e.g. how to extract unique signatures of user's speaking hotwords only from accelerometer data and how to reduce the interference caused by user's mobility.

We finally implement AccelWord as a standalone application running on Android devices. Comprehensive tests show AccelWord has hotword detection accuracy of 85% in static scenarios and 80% in mobile scenarios. Compared to the microphone based hotword detection applications such as Google Now and Samsung S Voice, AccelWord is 2 times more energy efficient while achieving the accuracy of 98% and 92% in static and mobile scenarios respectively.

## Categories and Subject Descriptors

H.5.2 [**User Interfaces**]: Voice I/O; I.5.4 [**Pattern recognition**]: Applications—*Signal processing*


*MobiSys'15,* May 18–22, 2015, Florence, Italy.

http://dx.doi.org/10.1145/2742647.2742658.

## General Terms

Mobile, System, Energy, Efficiency

## Keywords

AccelWord, hotword detection, accelerometer, energy, measurement

## 1. INTRODUCTION

With remarkable advancement in smartphone technology and increasing popularity of upcoming wearable devices, voice control is emerging as an attractive method of interaction with smart-devices. Voice control applications like Siri [1] on iOS devices and Google Now [2] on Android devices are already used by many smartphone and tablet users. Voice control is especially an attractive choice for wearable devices like smartglass and smartwatch. Such devices have a very small touch-enabled screen which restricts the applicability of touch-based control beyond a few primitive touch gestures. For this reason, voice control is commonly used in current commercial smartwatches [3] and smartglasses [4]. It also holds tremendous potential as objects surrounding us (in homes, offices and elsewhere) become more and more intelligent, and can provide various capabilities like electronic assistance. Such devices are already becoming commercially available (e.g. voice controlled intelligent speaker [5] that also acts as electronic assistant).

Although voice control enables an intuitive way for users to interact, one major challenge is that it requires continuous sensing of audio signals. This means that a device should turn on the microphone to continuously monitor user's voice commands. This results in significant energy consumption which is a major challenge for battery-powered mobile devices such as smartphones, smartwatches and smartglasses. Voice controlled devices implement *hotwords* (e.g. "Okay Google", "Hi Galaxy") in order to distinguish between user's voice commands to the device and her other conversations. This requires the device to continuously perform hotword detection by recording audio through microphone and checking whether the spoken words are the hotwords. Reducing the energy consumption of the hotword detection is an extremely challenging problem. To reduce the energy consumption, some devices utilize other low power sensors like accelerometer. Here, voice control applications monitor certain movements or gestures performed by the user (like double tap on screen [3] or tilting head up [4]) before turning on the microphone to listen for voice commands. However, such solutions are often not user-friendly (only work when user can touch/wear the device) and require user to get accustomed to different wake-up patterns for different devices. In some latest smartphones (e.g. Nexus 6 [6]), a dedicated low-power processor is used for audio sensing. However, this incurs additional cost which is not suitable for low-cost devices for pervasive Internet-Of-Things (IoT) applications. Moreover, there are a number of new smart devices (such as fitness bands and smartwatches) that do not have a microphone embedded in them. Enabling voice commands on such devices still remains a difficult challenge to solve.

In this paper, we propose AccelWord - an energy efficient solution for hotword detection using the accelerometer sensor. AccelWord is based on the observation that the MEMS (MicroElectroMechanic System) accelerometer sensors available in smartphones, smartwatches and nearly all smart devices are sensitive to user's spoken voice. When the user speaks, the generated audio signal causes variations in the observed acceleration in the accelerometer sensor. In fact, we show that these variations represent user's spoken words surprisingly well, and it is possible to extract unique signatures of user's speaking the hotwords simply from accelerometer data. Based on this, we build the AccelWord system which performs the hotword detection purely using the acceleromter data and turns on the microphone once the accelerometer data matches the extracted signature of the hotword. We show that AccelWord has the hotword detection accuracy of 85% in static scenarios with less than 5% of false positive rate. Compared to the microphone-based hotword detection, AccelWord is 2 times more energy efficient while achieving the accuracy of 98%. Since low-power low-cost accelerometer sensor is available in majority of the devices for motion recognition, we think AccelWord will enable accurate yet low-energy and low-cost implementation of voice control.

In recent research such as [7], [8], it has been observed that MEMS accelerometer/gyroscope sensors are sensitive to user's speech and nearby keystrokes, posing severe privacy risks of information leakage. However, in this paper, we are primarily concerned with how this sensitivity can be exploited for energy-efficient hotword detection. AccelWord addresses multiple challenges towards creating an accurate and energy-efficient hotword detection. First, since the impact on accelerometer due to user's voice can be considered as user's voice signals modulated at a lower frequency (200 Hz in case of current accelerometers), it is not clear which features can be used to extract hotword signatures. For higher energy efficiency, it is essential that the computational cost of calculating features is not very high. To address this challenge, AccelWord utilizes low complexity features that are often used in activity recognition (e.g. walking, running etc.) through accelerometer. Our study reveals that these features can accurately distinguish hotwords from other spoken words of the user.

The other important challenge in using accelerometer for hotword detection is to separate the accelerometer variations due to user's movement from that due to user's voice. This is especially important because mobile devices like smartphones and smartwatches consistently move when carried or worn by the user. In such cases, the accuracy of hotword detection should be still high even in the presence of mobility. By applying a suitable high-pass filter on the accelerometer data, AccelWord can achieve a similar level (94.5%) of accuracy as in static cases.

The contribution of this paper breaks down into the following aspects:

- We provide measurement-based evidence that accelerometers used in today's mobile devices are sensitive to user's voice. It is also demonstrated that the variations in accelerometer data when user speaks different words are sufficiently different which allows us to extract unique signatures of hotwords.
- We design and implement AccelWord framework which detects user's speaking of hotword purely by monitoring the accelerometer sensor data. It utilizes statistical pattern and frequency analysis to create signatures of the hotwords using the accelerometer readings. The extracted signatures are then used to train a classifier that can detect the hotword in real-time. We show that AccelWord can perform accurate hotword detection even in the presence of user mobility and high audio noise.
- We implement AccelWord on Android smartphone and evaluate it using experiments with 10 users. It is shown that AccelWord can detect the hotword with an average accuracy of 85% in static scenarios and average false-positive rate of 4.7%. When the user is mobile, the accuracy and false positive rate are observed to be 80% and 5.6% respectively. Compared to microphone-based hotword detection applications - Google Now and Samsung S Voice - AccelWord can achieve 98%, 92% and 93% of accuracy in static, mobile and noisy scenarios respectively.
- We show that AccelWord performs accurate hotword detection while consuming comparatively very low energy. Measurement results on two different phones show that AccelWord consumes 50% and 57% less power than Google Now and Samsung S Voice respectively.

The rest of the paper is organized as follows. We give a brief overview of AccelWord in Section 2. The feasibility of AccelWord is verified in Section 3. In Section 4, we present how the voice signature is extracted and how the training is performed. The implementation and the performance evaluation of AccelWord are presented in Section 5 and Section 6. We discuss the future explorations and the related work in Section 7 and Section 8 respectively. Section 9 concludes the paper.

# 2. OVERVIEW OF ACCELWORD

## 2.1 Motivation: Energy Expensive Voice Control

In this section, we first take a look at how current voice control applications operate and their energy efficiency. Most current voice control applications use "hotwords" detection to enable complete speech recognition. This is shown in Fig. 1. When a voice control application is running, it constantly listens for the hotwords spoken by the user. Examples of such hotwords include "Okay Google" or "Hi Galaxy" for Google Now [2] and Samsung S Voice [9] applications respectively. When the hotwords are detected, any following spoken words by the user are recognized using speech recognition. The purpose of using hotword detection instead of

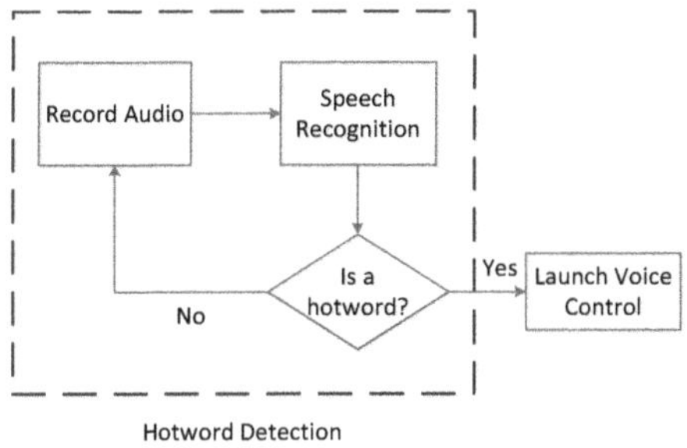


Figure 1: Flow chart of microphone based hotword detection

continuously recognizing every word user speaks is that it is more computationally efficient. This is because hotword detection merely classifies the spoken words into two classes - the hotwords and the other words - with light-weight speech signature matching.

Although hotword detection requires lesser computation than complete speech recognition, both of them require the device microphone to be on all the time. Constantly listening on the microphone makes the current voice control applications very energy inefficient. To demonstrate this, we measure and compare the power consumption of 2 voice control applications - Google Now and Samsung S Voice. We use the Monsoon Power Monitor [10] to record power consumption on two smartphones - Samsung Galaxy S4 and Google Nexus S. For understanding the baseline power consumption, we create an android app (called "Microphone") that simply turns on the microphone but does not perform any speech recognition. The example traces of power consumption for all three apps are presented in Fig. 2. In order to isolate the power consumption of the apps, we disable all network interfaces using airplane mode (except for Samsung S Voice which requires active Internet connection to operate) and restrict the number of background processes to 0. After ensuring that only the desired app is running, we measure the power consumption of app's Graphical User Interface (GUI) before starting the hotword detection. This power consumption is deducted from the total power consumption of the app when it is running to obtain the power consumption of listening, hotword detection and speech recognition. The average values of 30 minutes are reported in Fig. 3. Since Samsung S Voice is exclusive for Samsung phones and is not available in Android app store, the power consumption of S Voice on Nexus is not applicable.

It is observed from Fig. 3 that the power consumption of the 2 voice control apps is higher than the Microphone app due to their additional computational requirement of hotword detection and speech recognition. Depending on the hotword detection and speech recognition algorithms, the power consumption increases slightly when the user is speaking. However, in any case, the major factor on average power consumption in all the apps is when the app is listening for the hotword. Because such apps are designed to listen for user's commands at all times, keeping the microphone on and detecting hotword consumes substantial energy.

Continuous listening using the microphone and hotword detection in current voice control apps are energy inefficient. This motivates us to investigate an alternative way of continuous voice sensing that is both accurate and energy efficient.

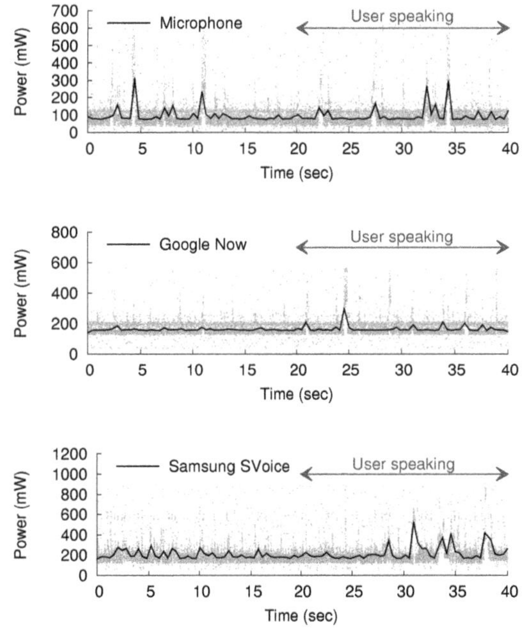


Figure 2: Example: the power trace of three apps

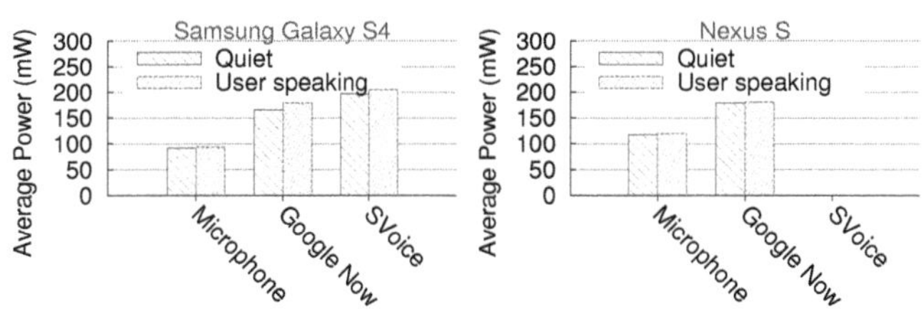


Figure 3: The Power Consumption of Current Hotwords Detection Apps.

## 2.2 Design Goals and Challenges

A hotword detection scheme should meet the following design goals in order to be truly pervasive.

**Accuracy:** We define the accuracy of a hotword detection scheme to be the ratio of the number of times user spoken hotwords are correctly detected to the total number of times the user speaks the hotword. Accurately detecting the hotword is essential to any voice control application. Even though recent voice control applications such as Google Now have shown to achieve high accuracy in hotword detection, frequent failures to detect the hotword is one of the dominant factors preventing pervasive use of voice control in smartphones and wearable devices. Note that the other dominant factor in slow adaptation of voice control application is inaccuracy in speech recognition after the hotword is detected. However, since there is plethora of research [11–15] already done on this topic, we do not consider complete speech recognition in this work and simply focus on the hotword detection.

**Robustness:** Another important design goal is that a voice control application should be robust to its dynamic operating environment. This means that it should be robust in hotword detection in the following three scenarios:

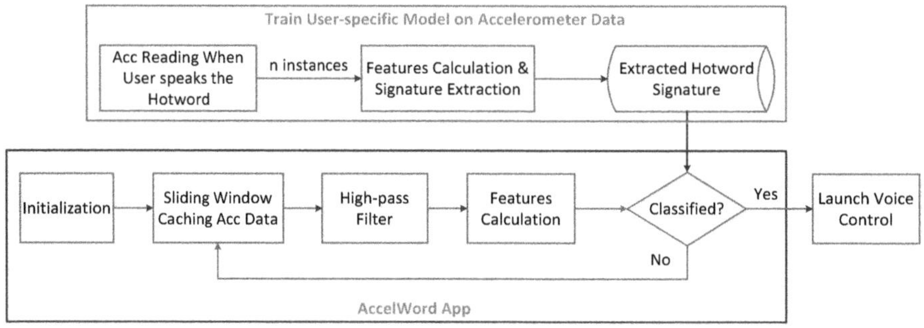


Figure 4: The System Architecture of AccelWord

(1) User mobility: It is necessary that the hotword detection accuracy is high even when the device is in constant motion. For example it is necessary that a smartwatch detects user's hotword even when the user is walking.

(2) Different voice frequency (female or male): It is essential that the voice control application detects the hotwords for both female and male users. Because female voice exhibits higher frequency [16] than the male voice, accuracy should be least affected by the input voice frequency.

(3) Noisy surroundings: The noise of the surrounding environment can affect the voice input recognition especially when the user is in noisy outdoor places such as malls, cafes, etc. The hotword detection accuracy should not be affected by the surrounding noise.

**Energy Efficiency:** As we showed in the previous section, the current voice control applications are expensive in terms of their energy consumption. For ubiquitous deployment of voice control in all battery-operated smart devices, it is necessary that it operates with a smaller energy footprint. This requires that both - sensing of voice input and hotword detection using signature matching - are energy efficient.

## 2.3 System Architecture

To this end, we design and implement *AccelWord* which achieves high accuracy and energy efficient hotword detection. AccelWord utilizes accelerometer instead of microphone to listen the sound signal of the input voice. Specific signatures are then extracted from the accelerometer data and inserted into the AccelWord app for hotword detection. Fig. 4 illustrates the architecture of the system.

- **Hotword signature extraction:** Due to the low power consumption property of accelerometer, we try to extract the signatures of hotwords from the accelerometer readings instead of microphone samples. The signature is constructed by comparing the set of accelerometer readings of hearing of hotwords and the set of accelerometer readings of hearing other random sentences. For energy efficiency purpose, the training is done offline.

- **AccelWord app:** AccelWord is a standalone app running on Android devices. During the initialization stage, AccelWord will load the extracted signature of the hotword. AccelWord dynamically buffers a certain number of accelerometer samples and periodically calculates the features of the samples. The calculated features are compared with the extracted signature loaded in the initialization stage. If a hotword is detected, AccelWord will send an intent to the Android OS to launch the voice control, otherwise the process will be repeated.

# 3. FEASIBILITY OF ACCELWORD

## 3.1 Accelerometer Design

Current accelerometer sensors found in smartphones and other smart devices like smartwatches and smartglasses are Micro Electro Mechanical Systems (MEMS). Such MEMS accelerometers have three main components - an inertial mass, spring legs and stationary fingers. This is shown in Fig. 5. The inertial mass is anchored to the substrate using two pairs of flexible spring legs. When an acceleration is applied, the inertial mass moves which causes a change in the capacitance between the stationary fingers. This change is recorded to accurately measure the acceleration. In a 3-axis accelerometer, 3 separate sets of components are employed to measure the accelerations separately.

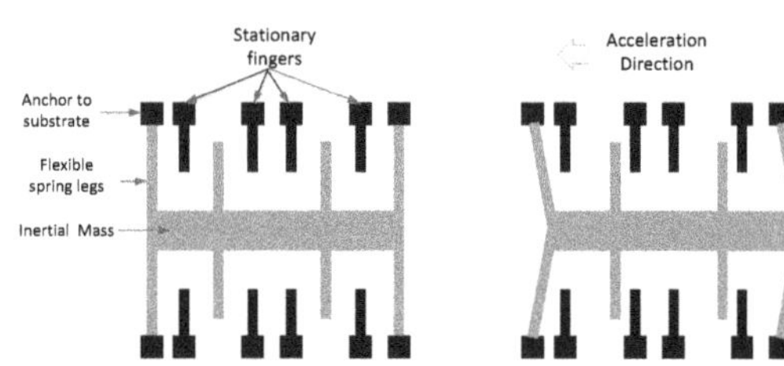


Figure 5: A sketch of a MEMS accelerometer

## 3.2 Impact of Voice Signal on Accelerometer

When a user speaks, the resultant acoustic signals strike the inertial mass of the accelerometer, causing it to move and report very small changes in acceleration. From the perspective of the accelerometer, such variations are considered undesirable noise, and [17–19] have studied its effects and proposed ways to combat the noise. Depending on the sampling frequency of the accelerometer, the acceleration changes can reflect a part of the characteristics of the user's voice and the spoken words. The typical maximum sampling frequency of today's MEMS accelerometers is in the range of a few thousand Hz. For example, Invensense MPU-65xx accelerometer found in Apple iPhone 6, Google Nexus 5 and Samsung Galaxy S5 has the highest sampling frequency of 4000 Hz (referred as "output data rate" in [20]). However, our experiments with Android 4.4 OS shows that the operating system restricts the maximum sampling frequency of an accelerometer to 200 Hz in order to reduce power consumption (similar restriction was also observed for gyroscope [7]). This sampling frequency has important implications on how voice signal affects the accelerometer readings.

A human ear can perceive any sound that is within the range of 20 Hz to 20 KHz [21]. This is why a typical microphone has a sampling frequency over 40 KHz since Nyquist sampling theorem states that the sampling frequency should be at least twice ($\geq$ 40 Hz) the highest frequency in the signal (20 Hz) for reconstruction. This implies that with 200 Hz of sampling frequency of the accelerometer, we can not perfectly reconstruct the sound. In this work, we are not interested in the complete reconstruction of the voice using accelerometer. Such reconstruction requires a very high sampling rate which can result in very high energy cost. Instead, we are interested in generating signatures of different hotwords spoken by the user through the analysis of accelerometer readings available at a lower sampling frequency.

AccelWord is feasible because of the fact that typical fundamental frequency of a male's speaking voice is between 85 Hz and 155 Hz, and female's speaking voice is between 165 Hz and 255 Hz [22]. This means that accelerometer data even at the sampling frequency of 200 Hz, can reflect some parts of human voice. We first demonstrate using an experiment that human voice has a measurable effect on accelerometer data even when sampled at 200 Hz.

**Experiment Setup:** To validate the impact of voice on smartphone's accelerometer, we use the experiment setup as shown in Fig. 6. The goal of the setup is to emulate a scenario where a user is speaking to her smartphone in her hand or on a desk, or to a smartwatch on her wrist. For repeatability, user's voice is recorded by a professional sound recording software (Audacity) at sampling frequency of 384000 Hz and played on a phone (iPhone 4S) repeatedly as needed. Another smartphone (Samsung Galaxy S4 running Android 4.4.2) acts as a receiver of the voice. The receiver phone collects the accelerometer data at the highest sampling rate (measured to be 199 Hz). The speaker and receiver phones are fixed at a distance of 12 inch (typical distance between user's mouth and her phone or watch). To avoid any effects of direct surface vibrations, we place both the phones on separate desks that are not in contact with each other. This first set of experiments were carried out in a silent room inside a university building. To avoid the acoustic interference from human presence, we remotely control the speaker iPhone wirelessly from a different room using a MacBook Air.

The speaker phone's output volume is varied to generate different Sound Pressure Levels (SPL) at the receiver. The SPL is measured using an Android app (Sound Meter [23]) on the receiver phone (Samsung Galaxy S4). Table 1 show the measured SPL at the receiver and example scenarios where the SPL is observed [16, 24].

**Impact on Accelerometer:** Fig. 7 shows the variation of accelerometer reading when the speaker is playing vowel "A" spoken by two of the authors. The spectrum analysis of the two users and the background noise are shown in Fig. 7a. The average SPL of the background noise measured on the receiver is 25 dB. The receiver's accelerometer readings under different SPLs are shown in Fig. 7b and Fig. 7c. Since the voice comes from right above side of the receiver,

Figure 6: Experiment Setup

| Measured SPL (dB) | Typical Scenario [16, 24] |
|---|---|
| 70 | Human to phone conversation. (distance: 12 inch) |
| 60 | Human to human conversation. (distance: 1 meter) |
| 50 | Gentle keystroke. |
| 40 | Quiet university libraries. |
| 30 | Quiet bedroom at night. |
| 20 | Calm breathing. |

Table 1: Example Scenarios of SPL Levels

the accelerometer reading on the Y axis does not vary much ($< 0.02m/s^2$). However, on the X axis and Z axis, we can observe considerable amount ($0.06m/s^2$ - $0.15m/s^2$) of difference on the accelerometer reading when the male SPL is increased from 25dB to 70dB. The similar phenomenon is also observed on the female voice input. Although the variations on X axis and Z axis caused by the female voice is slightly lesser than the male voice, they are still significantly higher than the variation on the Y axis. This indicates that the human voice at high enough SPLs will have a detectable amount of impact on the smartphone accelerometers.

## 3.3 Accelerometer vs. Gyroscope - Energy Comparison

Accelerometer is sensitive to acoustic signals mainly because it is an MEMS sensor. Another MEMS sensor - gyroscope - is also widely used in smartphones and other smart devices. The gyro sensor is also shown to be affected by the voice signals in [7]. Since our objective is to use the acoustic sensitivity of accelerometer to perform energy-efficient hotword detection and not to reconstruct the complete sound, it is necessary to compare the energy efficiency of accelerometer and gyroscope. Due to the design differences in MEMS, it is known that gyroscope sensors consume more energy than the accelerometer sensors even at the same sampling frequency [17, 20]. Comparing the specifications of accelerometer and gyroscope sensors used in all major smartphones, it is found that normal operating current of only operating gyroscope is on an average 6 times higher than the that of operating only accelerometer [17, 20]. However, the actual power consumption when collecting these sensors' data depends on many other factors such as data collection application, OS, other hardware components like CPU and memory. We measure this total power consumption on Nexus S and Samsung Galaxy S4. Here the sensor data is collected by our Android app at 200 Hz, and the power is measured

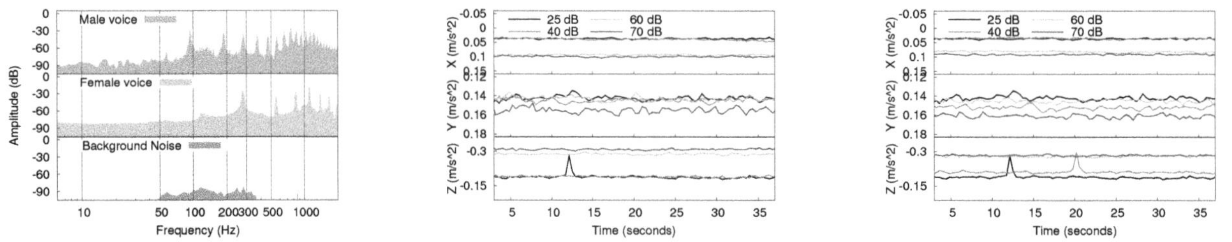


(a) The Normalized FFT of The Input Voice (b) Accelerometer Readings When User Speaks Vowel "A" (Male) (c) Accelerometer Readings When User Speaks Vowel "A" (Female)

Figure 7: The Impact of Speaking Vowel "A" on Accelerometer

using the Monsoon power monitor. We use the exact same implementation for collecting the data from both sensors in our app. The power consumption results are shown in Fig. 8. It is observed that collecting gyroscope data consumes 55.8% more power than the accelerometer, and as expected, both acclerometer and gyroscope consume significantly lower energy compared to the microphone (as shown in Fig. 8d).

Based on the observations, it can be concluded that (i) accelerometer is sensitive to the human voice, and (ii) it is also energy efficient. Therefore, we make use of the accelerometer sensor to implement AccelWord, an app using accelerometer to detect specific voice signals (hotwords).

# 4. HOTWORD DETECTION USING ACCELWORD

From the previous section, we know that accelerometer sensor is affected by user's voice. In this section, we demonstrate that the effect on the accelerometer data due to the user's voice is rich enough so that it can also be used to detect the hotwords spoken by the user. For this, we first show what features of accelerometer data can be used to create signatures of the hotword. Based on the signature, we build a machine learning classifier that performs the hotword detection.

While creating the signature of hotwords using the accelerometer data, we focus on two goals:

(1) We are only interested in *distinguishing* the hotword from other spoken words of users. This way, our hotword detection is a binary classification problem in terms of machine learning and not a speech recognition problem where all spoken words are reconstructed. Once the hotword is detected, the microphone can be turned on to record user's voice and existing methods of speech recognition can be applied.

(2) Such hotword detection should be online and energy efficient. This means that the process of accelerometer data collection, analysis and matching with hotword signatures should be computationally efficient in order for the hotword detection to be energy efficient. We already know from Fig. 8 that accelerometer data collection consumes less power than recording via microphone. However, it is necessary to design efficient ways of analyzing and matching the accelerometer data.

One of the most difficult challenges in accurate hotword detection is that user's mobility causes significant changes in accelerometer data. It is necessary that the hotwords are detected even when user is mobile. For this, we need to filter the mobility *interference* from the accelerometer signals to distill the effect of user's voice before performing the hotword classification. We first show how to extract hotword signature from the accelerometer data in a stationary case and then extend our analysis to user's mobility.

## 4.1 Extracting Hotword Signature

One possible approach of identifying hotword is to upsample the accelerometer data collected at 200 Hz to 40 KHz, and then reproduce some parts of user's spoken words from the resultant audio file. However, this can incur huge energy cost due to the computational complexity of upsampling as well as analyzing the additionally generated data. Also, since we are not interested in reproducing the voice, such additional processing is unsuitable for our application. Instead, we take a different approach in analyzing the accelerometer data as described next.

**Candidate Features:** We propose to use activity recognition related features to analyze the accelerometer data. Table 2 lists a set of features that are found to be highly correlated [25] to physical activity of humans such as walking, running, sitting, standing, etc. The main advantage of using these features over the audio analysis related features (used in speech recognition [26,27]) is their lower computational complexity. Majority of features in Table 2 are time series analysis of data which can be efficiently calculated for fast online processing.

**Feature Selection:** Because the candidate set of features we want to use are primarily studied in terms of activity recognition, it is not clear how well they can be used for hotword detection. To evaluate their usefulness, we calculate the values of the features when user speaks the hotword and other sentences or randomly chosen text. We use the experiment setup discussed in Section 3. Two separate recordings of user's spoken words are played through the speaker phone at 100% volume level (70 dB SPL at the receiver phone). In the first recording, the user speaks the hotword "Okay Google" once which is repeated 200 times. In the second recording, the user speaks commonly used sentences ("Good morning", "How are you", "Fine, thank you" etc.) which are then repeated 400 times in random order. After playing the recordings through the speaker phone, the accelerometer data from the receiver device is used to calculate the candidate set of features. We set the time window for feature calculation to be 2 seconds based on the observation that most user could complete speaking the hotword within that time. Note that an online hotword detection would require considering many practical issues such as using a sliding window for continuous evaluation, and we have addressed these

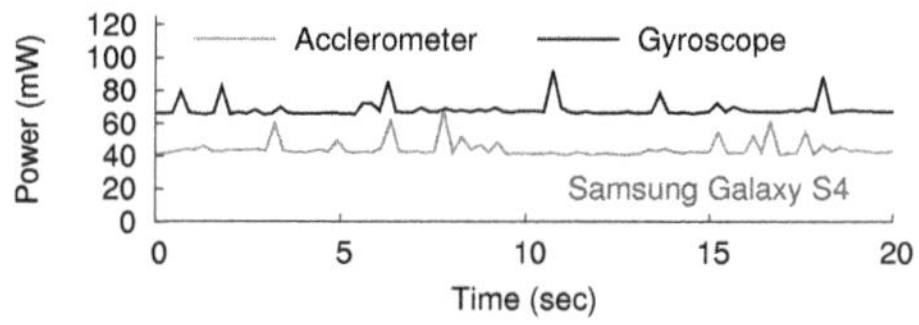


(a) Example: The Power Monitor Trace of Galaxy S4

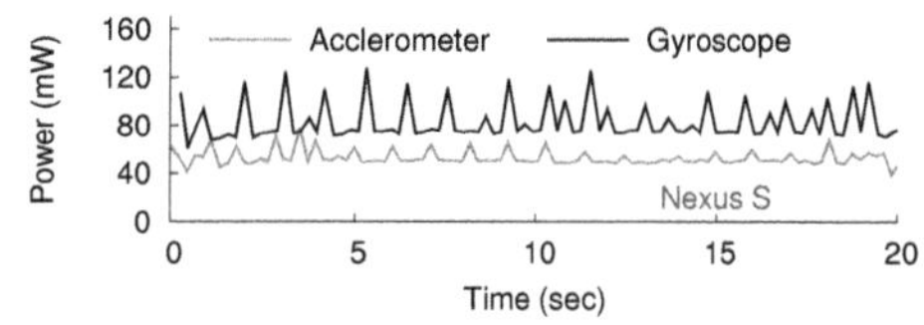


(b) Example: The Power Monitor Trace of Nexus S

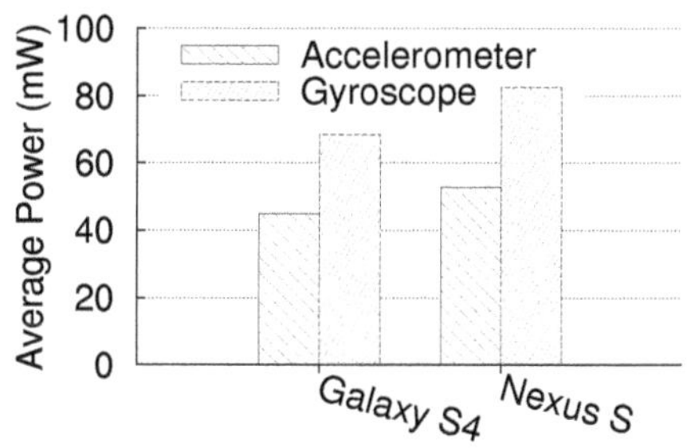


(c) The Average Energy Consumption of a 30 minutes Trace

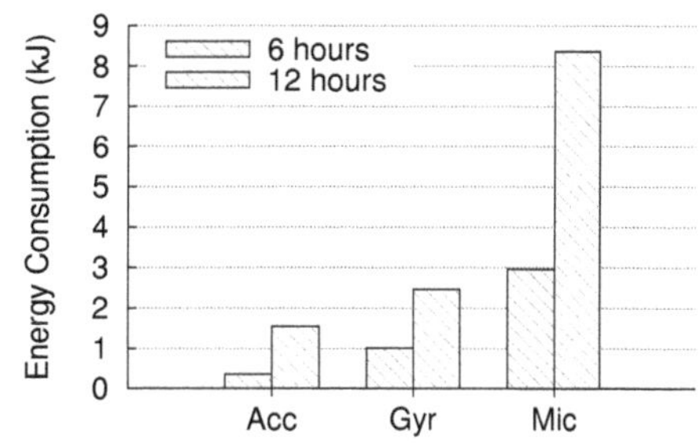


(d) The Long Term Total Energy Consumption of Three Sensors

Figure 8: The Energy Consumption of Accelerometer, Gyroscope and Microphone

issues in our AccelWord app design in Section 5. Here, we first seek to understand how the presented features can be used to distinguish the hotword from the other words.

To determine how well a given feature can distinguish the hotword from other spoken words, we use Information Gain based feature selection. Information gain [28] is a commonly used feature evaluation method where entropy of classification is compared in the presence and the absence of a given feature. Let $G$ be the set of instances in which $H$ are hotword instances and $N$ are instances of other spoken words. Let $E(G)$ be the entropy of $G$. If $p(H)$ and $p(N)$ are the fraction of hotword and non-hotword instances then $E(G)$ can be calculated as

$$E(G) = -p_H \cdot \log_2 p_H - p_N \cdot \log_2 p_N \quad (6)$$

Let $I(F)$ be the information gain of the feature $F$. $I(F)$ can be calculated as

$$I(F) = E(G) - \sum_{f \in V(F)} \frac{|G_f|}{|G|} E(G_f) \quad (7)$$

where $V(F)$ is the set of values the feature $F$ can take and $G_f$ is the subset of $G$ where the feature $F = f$. This way, $I(F)$ can be considered as a measure of additional information available due to the presence of feature $F$ in classifying the hotword and other words. The information gain values are between 0 and 1 where a higher value indicates a feature being more useful in classification.

Fig. 9 shows the information gain of candidate features with respect to two classes - hotword and not hotword. It is observed that most features in the candidate set exhibit high information gain which shows that they can be used for hotword classification. Some features (Kurtosis, Skewness and MCR) have zero information gain which means that they do not have any useful value in classifying the hotword. We use the rest of the features to build the AccelWord classifier.

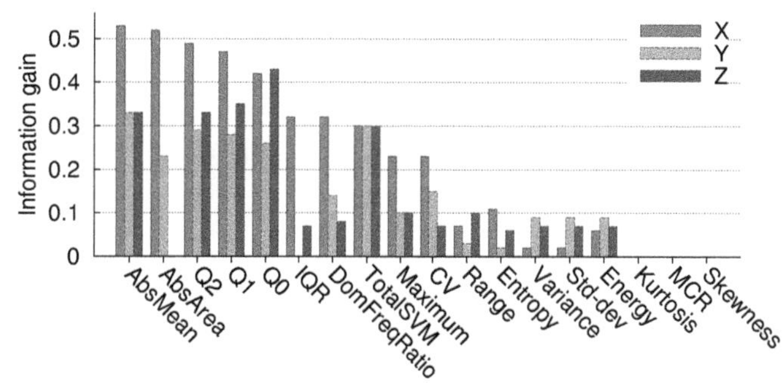


Figure 9: Information gain of candidate features

## 4.2 Combating Mobility Interference

To combat the noise caused by user's mobility, we first conduct a series of mobility experiments to understand the interference of user's mobility to our problem. Based on the observations and analyzing the numerical results of the mobile scenarios, we are able to design proper techniques to detect hotwords even when the users are moving.

**Mobility Experiment Setup:** For the mobility experiments, we use the same phones as in the static experiments (Section 3.2). As shown in Fig. 10, the receiver phone is wrapped to the left wrist of the user, while the speaker is held closely to the user's mouth. The volume of the speaker is adjusted to ensure that the SPL at the receiver is 70 dB when the distance is 12 inch. The user walks in approximately 1 m/s speed in a $4m \times 9m$ room along an elliptic trajectory. For repeatability of the experiments, we will only focus on the walking and speaking mobility pattern, since the other mobility patterns, e.g. running and speaking, jumping and speaking, are quite hard for our experimenters and volunteers to repeat for a large number of times. Therefore,

**The following features are calculated for accelerometer signal of X, Y and Z axis over time window of $t$ seconds**

• Time domain:
**Calculated separately for each X, Y and Z axis:**
- Minimum, maximum, median, variance, standard deviation
- Range: difference between maximum and minimum, measure of extreme changes in acceleration
- Absolute Mean (AbsMean): average of absolute values of acceleration
- CV: ratio of standard deviation and mean times 100; measure of signal dispersion
- Skewness (3rd moment): measure of asymmetry in distribution of signal samples
- Kurtosis (4th moment): measure of peakedness in distribution of signal samples
- Q1, Q2, Q3: first, second and third quartiles; measures the overall distribution of accelerometer magnitude over the window
- Inter Quartile Range (ICR): difference between the Q3 and Q1; also measures the dispersion of the signal
- Mean Crossing Rate (MCR): measures the number of times the signal crosses the mean value; captures how often the signal varies during the time window
- Absolute Area (AbsArea): the area under the absolute values of accelerometer signal. It is the sum of absolute values of accelerometer samples in the window. Let $a_{s_i}$ denote the $i^{th}$ sample of accelerometer's $s \in \{X, Y, Z\}$ axis, then

$$AbsArea_s = \sum_{i=1}^{window\ length} |a_{s_i}| \quad (1)$$

**Calculated across X, Y and Z axis:**
- TotalAbsArea: sum of AbsArea of all three axis.

$$AbsArea = \sum_{i=1}^{window\ length} |a_{x_i}| + |a_{y_i}| + |a_{z_i}| \quad (2)$$

- TotalSVM: the signal magnitude of all accelerometer signal of three axis averaged over the time window.

$$TotalSVM = \frac{\left[\sum_{i=1}^{window\ length} \sqrt{\sum_{s \in \{X,Y,Z\}} {a_{s_i}}^2}\right]}{window\ length} \quad (3)$$

• Frequency domain:
**Calculated separately for each X, Y and Z axis:**
- Energy: it is a measure of total energy in all frequencies. Let $m_i$ be the magnitude of FFT coefficients.

$$Energy = \sum_{i=1}^{window\ length/2} m_i^2 \quad (4)$$

- Entropy: captures the inpurity in the measured accelerometer data. Let $n_i$ be the normalized value of FFT coefficient magnitude.

$$Entropy = - \sum_{i=1}^{window\ length} n_i\ log_s(n_i) \quad (5)$$

- DomFreqRatio: it is calculated as the ratio of highest magnitude FFT coefficient to sum of magnitude of all FFT coefficients.

Table 2: Candidate features

we will leave the study of other mobility patterns for future exploration.

Figure 10: Mobility Experiment Setup

**Impact of Mobility Interference:** The results of mobile experiments are shown in Figs. 11 and 12. Fig.11 shows an example 1 second window of the accelerometer readings when the user is walking and speaking. Comparing Fig. 11 with Fig. 7, we can observe that the readings of the accelerometer in mobile scenarios are at least one order of magnitude higher than the readings in static scenarios, which indicates extremely low signal-to-interference ratio. In other words, the data collected on accelerometer must be pre-processed before being used to generate the signatures of hotwords.

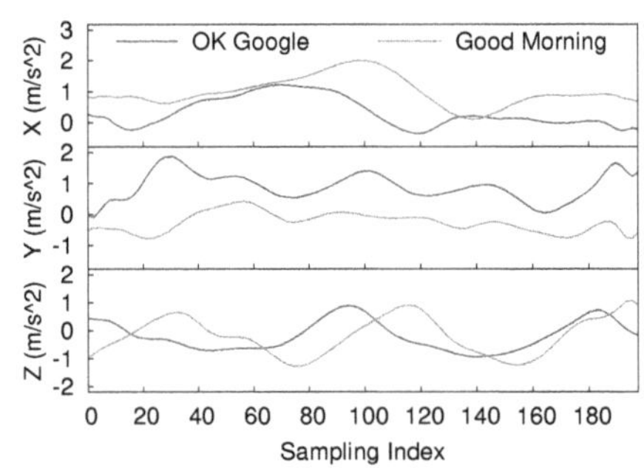


Figure 11: Example: Accelerometer Readings when User Moves and Speaks Short Sentenses

There has been a considerable amount of research in recognizing human activities through accelerometer data. From previous works [25,29,30], it is known that the most human activities (such as walking, changing postures etc.) exhibit lower frequency (0.1-2 Hz). Fig. 12 compares the frequency domain of the accelerometer reading of the static and the mobile scenario. It is observed that even when user is mobile and performs high intensity activities, the energy is mainly concentrated in the lower frequency band (<= 30 Hz). This is confirmed in Fig. 12 which compares the FFT coefficients of the accelerometer signals for static and mobile scenarios. It is observed that the energy in frequency band lower than 30 Hz is much higher for the mobile case. We also analyze another mobility scenario where user is sitting on a chair performing routine activities at workplace. Compared to walking, such an activity is of lower intensity, however, it forms an important use-case for AccelWord where user sitting at home or workplace provides voice commands to her phone. Fig. 13 shows the FFT coefficients of such sitting activity and compares it with a typical waking activity. In

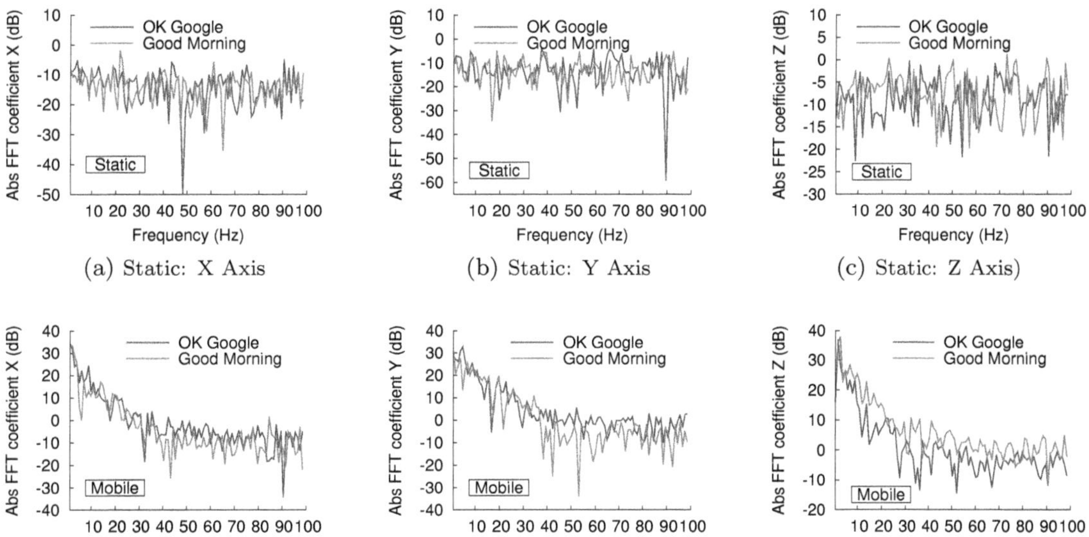


(a) Static: X Axis (b) Static: Y Axis (c) Static: Z Axis)

(d) Mobile: X Axis (e) Mobile: Y Axis (f) Mobile: Z Axis

Figure 12: The FFT of the Static and Mobile Scenarios

both cases, the user is assumed to be not speaking anything. We observe that sitting results in even less energy at lower frequencies (<=20 Hz) compared to walking activities.

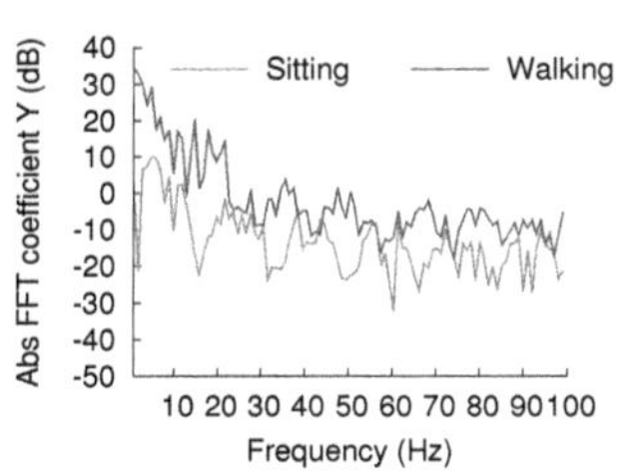


Figure 13: FFT of User's Sitting and Walking Activity

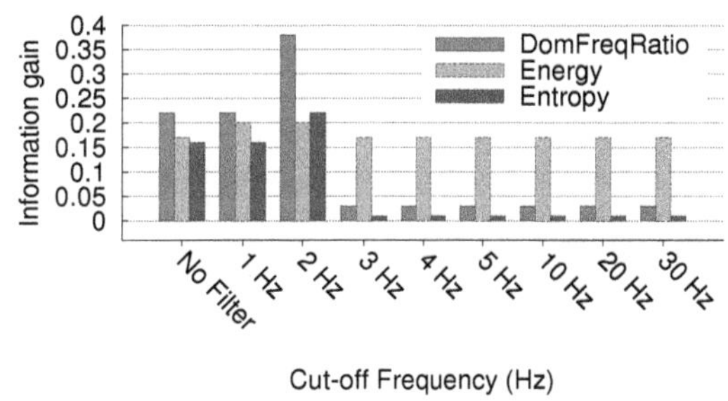


Figure 14: Impact on information gain with varying values of cut-off frequency of high-pass filter; For each feature, we report the information gain value which is the maximum across all three axis

This means that a high-pass filter can be used to filter out the mobility interference from the accelerometer signal before calculating the features we discussed in Section 4.1.

The problem, however, is to choose the correct cut-off frequency for the high-pass filter since attenuating signals more than necessary at the lower frequencies may also remove the effect of user's voice. Since in our case, the human voice is "received" by the accelerometer, high-pass filtering with 30 Hz can cause severe reduction in the accuracy of hotword detection. We rely on the empirical data to find the suitable cut-off frequency that can accurately remove mobility interference while preserving the effect of user's voice on accelerometer signal. We observed in Fig. 9 that in stationary case, all three frequency domain features - DomFreqRatio, Entropy and Energy - have high information gain. This means that they are useful in classifying the hotwords from the other spoken words. We evaluate the information gain of these three features while applying a high-pass filter with different cut-off frequency. Fig. 14 shows the change in information gain as the cut-off frequency increases from 1 Hz to 30 Hz. When the information gain reduces, it can be inferred that the frequency domain features which were previously important in classification are no longer useful and the overall classification accuracy will also reduce. We observe that the information gain for the three features first increases until the cut-off frequency of 2 Hz. This means that until this point, the high-pass filter works well in removing the mobility interference and improving the classification. However, the information gain values drop sharply (for DomFreqRatio and Entropy) after 2 Hz which indicates that filtering beyond 2 Hz removes information that is useful in classification. Based on this empirical observation, we choose the cut-off frequency of 2 Hz for the high-pass filter.

## 4.3 Training AccelWord Classifier

For training the AccelWord classifier, a user is required to speak the hotword a certain number of times while the accelerometer data is collected. The user is also required to utter any other randomly chosen words or sentences. Once the accelerometer data is collected, the AccelWord classifier can be trained. Additional details of how many times the hotword is spoken etc. are provided in Section 5. Once the training instances are provided, the features are calculated and the machine learning classifier is built. This process of calculating features and building the classifier can be done on the smartphone or it can be offloaded to a cloud for energy savings. Note the this process is only performed once and is not required to be repeated after the training. Also, we do not build separate classifiers for stationary and mobile cases as doing so would require to first detect if the user is mobile or stationary. In all cases, we simply use one classifier where any mobility in training instances is filtered using the high-pass filter. Once the classifier is built, it can perform the hotword detection in real time by monitoring the accelerometer data.

**Decision Tree Classifier:** For real-time classification, we propose to use a simple sliding window based approach where at any time instance, last $t$ seconds of accelerometer signals are buffered. After every certain period, the features are calculated for the buffered data and signature matching is performed using the classifier to check if the hotword was spoken in the last $t$ seconds or not. Because both the feature calculation and model checking need to be performed periodically, it is necessary to choose a computationally efficient machine learning classifier. We use simple decision tree to build our AccelWord classifier. Because a decision-tree based classifier can be implemented using simple if-else conditions, it can perform the classification with very low computational complexity. This is crucial to meet our low energy consumption goal of AccelWord.

We note that using more complex machine learning methods (such as decision trees with bagging or boosting [31]) can improve the hotword detection accuracy, they might also increase the computational cost and energy for hotword detection. We leave this exploration of optimizing accuracy and energy of AccelWord to future work.

## 5. IMPLEMENTATION

We implemented *AccelWord* as a standalone app running on Android 4.4.2 (API Level 19) devices. To avoid any GUI related power consumption variations, we design the AccelWord's front-end to be simple, as shown in Fig. 15. For efficient calculation of the features, we rely on the data structures defined in widely used Java library "commons math". Since typical hotwords are usually quite short in length and most users can speak them in less than 2 seconds, AccelWord buffers 2 seconds of accelerometer data (400 samples) in a FIFO queue. Note that this can be adjusted based on the typical time taken to speak the hotword. In each run of the feature calculation, AccelWord first filters the data using a high-pass filter with cut-off frequency of 2 Hz. Then the calculated features are compared with the extracted hotword signature. We set the time interval between each feature calculation to be a variable and test with different interval lengths.

We train the AccelWord classifier off-line on a workstation and import the model to the app. This is similar to other voice control applications like Google Now where pre-trained model of user speaking the hotword is incorporated in the app. This allows a fair comparison in terms of the energy consumption since there is no extra energy consumed for training during the run-time.

Once the hotword is detected by the AccelWord app, it initiates the "Google Voice Search" using "SEARCH_ACTION" Android intent. Here, the microphone is turned on and user's voice commands are recognized by Google voice search engine. For better repeatability, we implement two modes in the app. In the first mode (referred as AccelWord Energy mode), we simply log the result of hotword detection algorithm and do not initiate a Google search even when the hotword is detected. This allows us to measure the energy in a more controlled way where there is no additional energy consumed for Android intent access and other relevant processes. In the second mode (referred as AccelWord Performance mode), the app will not only perform hotword detection, but will also switch to Google Voice Search GUI if the hotword is detected.

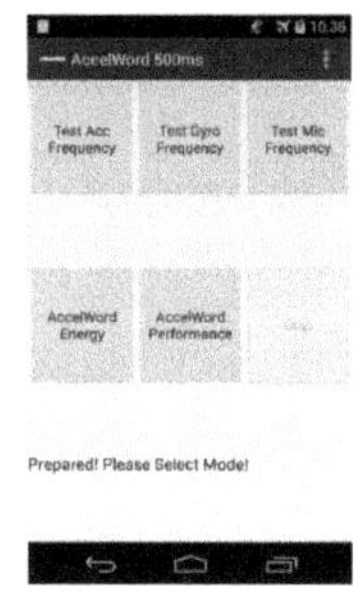


Figure 15: AccelWord Android App

## 6. PERFORMANCE EVALUATION

To evaluate the performance of AccelWord, we conduct hotword detection tests with 10 volunteers (5 females and 5 males). Two other voice control applications (Google Now and Samsung S Voice) are used to provide the performance comparison. The experiments are conducted on two phones: Samsung Galaxy S4 and Google Nexus S. Since the Samsung S Voice is exclusive to Galaxy phones, its data is not reported (marked N/A) in a few (less than two) scenarios.

In the experiments, we choose "Okay Google" to be our hotword - the same as Google Now. The Samsung S Voice uses "Hi Galaxy" to be its hotword. For training the AccelWord classifier, each volunteer speaks the hotword 10 *vaild* times. Here, *valid* means that the hotword speaking instance is used in the training only if it can be successfully recognized by Google Now or Samsung S Voice. Each volunteer also speaks 20 other randomly chosen short sentences (<= 2 seconds) of their liking to generate non-hotword test instances. Once the hotwords and random sentences are recorded, each sentence is repeatedly played 10 times (5 static and 5 mobile) in the experiments (100 times "Okay Google", 100 times "Hi Galaxy" and 200 times other random sentences) to evaluate in presence of other randomness (background noise etc.).

The performance of AccelWord is evaluated in two aspects - accuracy and energy consumption.

**Accuracy:** Accuracy is evaluated with two metrics:

- **True Positive (TP) Rate:** It is defined as the percentage of instances where speaking of the hotword is correctly recognized as speaking of the hotword.
- **False Positive (FP) Rate:** It is defined as the percentage of instances where speaking of other sentences is recognized as speaking of the hotword.

It is worth noting that AccelWord is a user-specific classifier which means that a separate classifier is built for each user. This is because the accelerometer-based hotword detection has an added advantage that it can distinguish the user for which the classifier was trained from the other users. This loose form of user authentication is especially beneficial for voice control applications since it is not only possible to detect the hotword but it is also possible to recognize if it was the owner user who spoke the hotword. We will evaluate this claims of speaker recognition in Section 6.3. Because the frequency of male and female voice is different, we present the accuracy results for both male and female users separately. The results with label "female" are the average values of the 5 female volunteers, and the same for the results of the 5 male volunteers.

**Energy:** For comparing the energy consumption, we first measure the GUI power consumption of each of the AccelWord, Google Now and Samsung S Voice applications when the app is in the foreground (screen on) but it is not running the hotword detection. This GUI power consumption is then removed from the subsequent measurements when the app is performing the hotword detection. This allows a fair comparison since the GUI power consumption can be significantly different depending on the front-end design. The energy comparison is provided for both the devices separately.

Our experimental results show AccelWord can achieve similar accuracy of hotword detection as Google Now and Samsung S Voice applications while consuming only 50% of the energy compared to both the apps. Sections 6.1, 6.2 and 6.3 show the hotword detection accuracy, energy efficiency and speaker recognition results respectively. For better presentation, we show all the TP rate in figures and all the FP rate in tables consistently.

## 6.1 Accuracy

We study the hotword detection accuracy in terms of three factors: (1) SPL at the receiver phone, (2) background noise and (3) user's mobility.

**Sound Pressure Level (SPL):** Intuitively, higher value of SPL on the receiving phone should result in better detection of hotword. We evaluate this using two cases - one where both training and testing instances have the same SPL and the other where they have multiple different SPLs. To achieve a desired SPL on the receiving phone, we play the recorded audio of hotword and non-hotword sentences on the iPhone 4S used in Fig. 6 and Fig. 10 and adjust the iPhone's volume without changing the distance between the iPhone and the receiving phone.

*Trained and Tested with the Same SPL:* We use 5 different values of SPL (70, 65, 60, 55, 50 dB) and train and test separate classifiers for each. In each case, all the instances of training and testing are of the same SPL value. 10-fold cross-validation is used to evaluate the TP and FP rates. Fig. 16 shows the TP and FP rate values. It is observed that the TP rate decreases monotonically as the SPL decreases while the FP rate increases. This indicates that the signatures generated at higher SPLs are better which allows improved classification. We can also observe both the TP rate and the FP rate drop to almost 0 when the SPL becomes 50 dB. The reason is that very low sound input at 50 dB SPL fails to cause any noticeable variation in the accelerometer data. As we will show next while comparing with other applications, at 50 dB SPL, both Google Now and S Voice also fail to recognize any human voice.

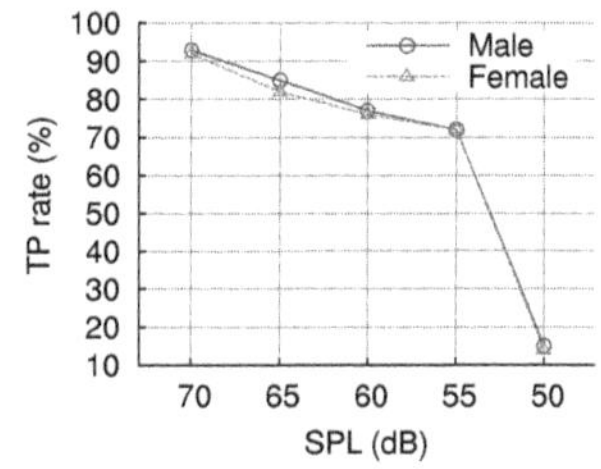


| SPL (dB) | FP Rate (%) Male | FP Rate (%) Female |
|---|---|---|
| 70 | 4.8 | 4.1 |
| 65 | 5.5 | 5.1 |
| 60 | 7.8 | 7.5 |
| 55 | 8.5 | 8.0 |
| 50 | 1.8 | 2.1 |

Figure 16: TP and FP rates when AccelWord is trained and tested with instances of the same SPL

*Trained and Tested with Multiple SPL:* In reality, when user speaks the hotword, the reported SPL at the receiving phone is likely to be different at different times. To test this realistic case, we train the classifier using instances of multiple different SPLs and then test it with instances of a given SPL. For example, the classifier can be trained with instances of 60, 65 and 70 dB SPLs, and tested with instances of 60 dB SPL. The results are presented in Fig. 17 and Table. 3. It is observed that when the classifier is trained with instances of SPL >= x, the TP rate is high for all cases when testing instances have the SPL >= x. For example, for training with SPL >= 60 dB, the TP rates of 60, 65 and 70 dB testing instances are above 80% in male users. Compared to training and testing with the same SPL, we observe that the accuracy drops a little when trained with multiple SPLs. This is expected since training and testing with the same SPL instances is likely to produce a model that fits better. However, since training with instances of multiple SPLs is more realistic, we will use the model trained with instances of SPL >= 55 dB in the rest of the paper for comparing with other apps and evaluation in noisy environments.

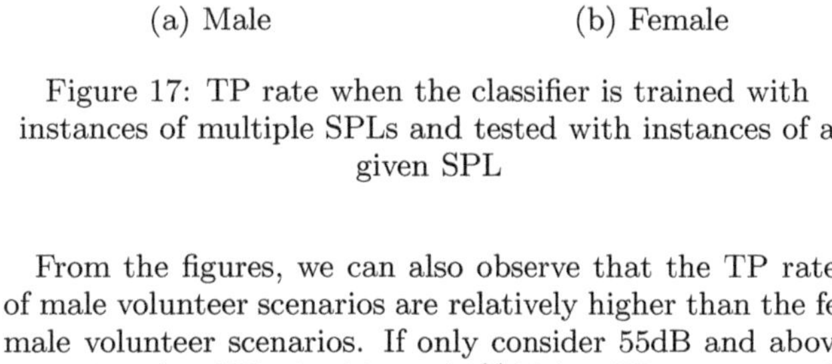


(a) Male (b) Female

Figure 17: TP rate when the classifier is trained with instances of multiple SPLs and tested with instances of a given SPL

From the figures, we can also observe that the TP rates of male volunteer scenarios are relatively higher than the female volunteer scenarios. If only consider 55dB and above scenarios, AccelWord achieves 4.1% higher TP rates on male volunteers than on female volunteers on average. This is because the female vocal range is slightly higher than males, while the sampling frequency of the accelerometer is limited at 200Hz. Therefore signature generated by male voice

| SPL Tested (dB) | FP Rate (%) SPL Trained (dB) | | |
|---|---|---|---|
| | >=55 | >=60 | >=65 |
| 70 | 4.8 | 3.3 | 1.3 |
| 65 | 6.5 | 5.8 | 2.0 |
| 60 | 6.9 | 8.3 | 1.3 |
| 55 | 7.4 | 4.3 | 0.3 |
| 50 | 2.0 | 2.1 | 1.5 |

(a) Male

| SPL Tested (dB) | FP Rate (%) SPL Trained (dB) | | |
|---|---|---|---|
| | >=55 | >=60 | >=65 |
| 70 | 5.7 | 3.5 | 0.3 |
| 65 | 3.0 | 5.1 | 0.8 |
| 60 | 4.3 | 1.8 | 0.5 |
| 55 | 2.7 | 0.0 | 0.0 |
| 50 | 3.0 | 0.0 | 1.5 |

(b) Female

Table 3: FP rates when classifier trained and tested with multiple SPLs

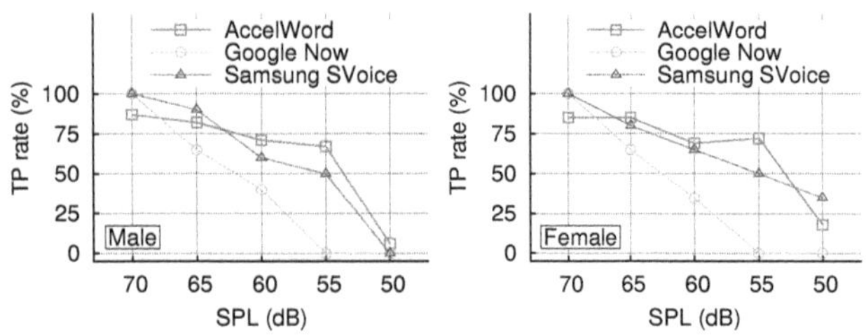


(a) Male (b) Female

Figure 18: Accuracy Comparison with Google Now and Samsung S Voice

instances is relatively more significant than the signature generated by female voice instances.

**AccelWord vs. Other Apps:** We now compare the hotword detection accuracy of AccelWord with Google Now and S Voice with varying SPL. The results are presented in Fig. 18. Since all the instances we consider for AccelWord training are the ones which are *valid* in Google Now and S Voice, both the apps achieve 100% of TP rate at 70 dB. In comparison, AccelWord achieves an accuracy of 86% at 70 dB SPL. For 65 and 60 dB, AccelWord achieves higher TP rate than Google Now and comparable TP rate to S Voice. Starting from 60 dB, we observe that Google Now does not react to majority of the hotwords. Since its internal implementation details are unknown, it is unclear why the hotword detection drops sharply after 60 dB. One possible reason is that the FP rate increases significantly at lower SPL. The same phenomenon is also observed with Samsung S Voice starting from 55 dB. Therefore, we only compare the TP rates in 65dB and above. On average, the TP rate of AccelWord is 99.1% and 97.6% of the TP rates of Google Now and S Voice in 65dB and above SPLs.

**Accuracy in Noisy Environment:** Another important aspect to study is the impact of audio noise on AccelWord. When a user is in a noisy environment (such as public places, malls, cafes, etc.), the surrounding audio noise can be sufficiently high to cause variations in accelerometer. To evaluate how AccelWord works in presence of the audio noise, we generate two kinds of background noise - white noise using Audacity and the background noise recorded at a local cafeteria. We vary the audio noise level from 30 to 70 dB. Note that 70 dB of audio noise is already considered upper limit of acceptable noise pollution by most countries e.g. USA (65 dBA) [32], China (70 dB) [33], Japan (65 dB) [34]. Fig. 19 and Table 4 show the TP rates and the FP rates in different background noise SPLs. The presented results are average

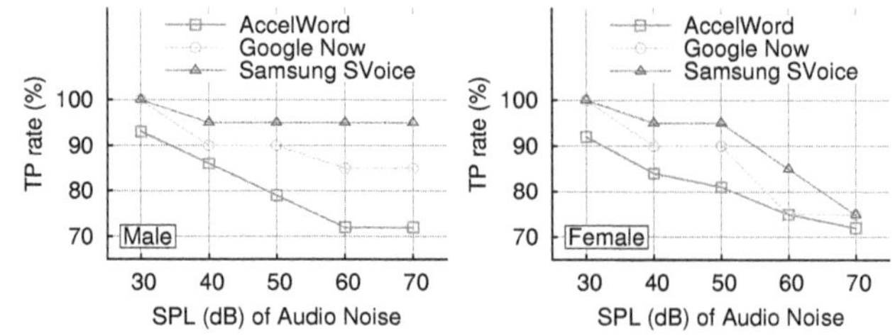


(a) Male (b) Female

Figure 19: True Positive Rate vs. Audio Noise SPL

values when two kinds of noise are applied separately. The hotword SPL is fixed to 70dB for all the three apps in the noisy environment experiments.

| Noise SPL (dB) | FP Rate (%) Male | Female |
|---|---|---|
| 30 | 4.8 | 4.1 |
| 40 | 6.9 | 5.4 |
| 50 | 6.8 | 4.2 |
| 60 | 6.3 | 7.8 |
| 70 | 7.9 | 8.3 |

Table 4: False Positive Rate vs. Audio Noise SPL

From the figure, we can observe AccelWord can achieve comparatively lower TP rate than Google Now and S Voice in noisy environment. On average, the TP rate of AccelWord is only 9% and 13% percent less than Google Now and S Voice respectively. From Table. 4, we can observe the FP rate of the AccelWord increases as the noise SPL increases. However, the FP rate of AccelWord is still less than 10% in environment as noisy as 70 dB SPL. We consider this as one of the limitations of AccelWord in its current form. Today's microphones employ advanced techniques for noise canceling that can filter out the background noise. However, in its current form, AccelWord does not have any mechanism to cancel the effect on accelerometer caused by the audio noise. This is further discussed in Section 7.

**Accuracy in Mobile Scenarios:** We also tested the performance of AccelWord in mobile scenarios. The setup described in Fig. 10 is used for the experiments. Here, each volunteer walks in circle for 5 minutes and this is repeated 3 times. We fix the distance between the speaker phone and the receiving phone to be 30 inches, and the speaker phone volume is adjusted such that received SPL is 70 dB.

As discussed in Section 4.2, the mobility causes interference to the AccelWord hotword detection and it can be removed using a high-pass filter. It was shown that a high-pass filter with 2 Hz cut-off frequency can be used as it allows us to remove the mobility interference without removing the effect of audio signal. We verify this by varying the cut-off frequency of the high-pass filter and observing the resultant TP rate of AccelWord. The results are shown in Fig. 20. Same as Fig. 14, we observe that hotword detection TP rate first increases from applying no filter to cut-off frequency of 2 Hz. This is because the high-pass filter removes the low-frequency noise of user's walking movement which improves the extracted hotword signatures and in turn increases the classification accuracy. Further increasing the cut-off fre-

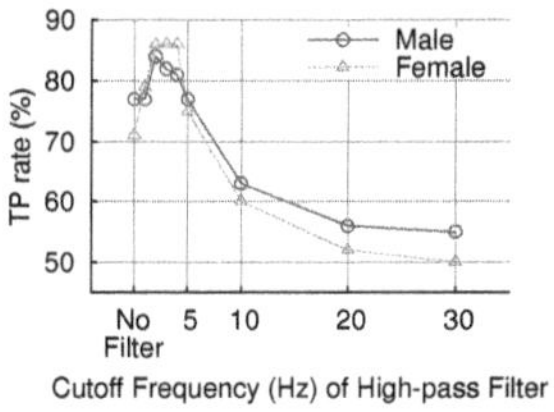


| Cutoff Frequency (Hz) | FP Rate (%) Male | FP Rate (%) Female |
|---|---|---|
| 0 | 1.5 | 2.1 |
| 1 | 5.3 | 6.2 |
| 2 | 5.3 | 6.2 |
| 3 | 7 | 6.8 |
| 4 | 7 | 6.8 |
| 5 | 7 | 6.8 |
| 10 | 8 | 7.2 |
| 20 | 7.5 | 6.8 |
| 30 | 6.9 | 7.1 |

Figure 20: Change in TP and FP Rates for Different Cutoff Frequency

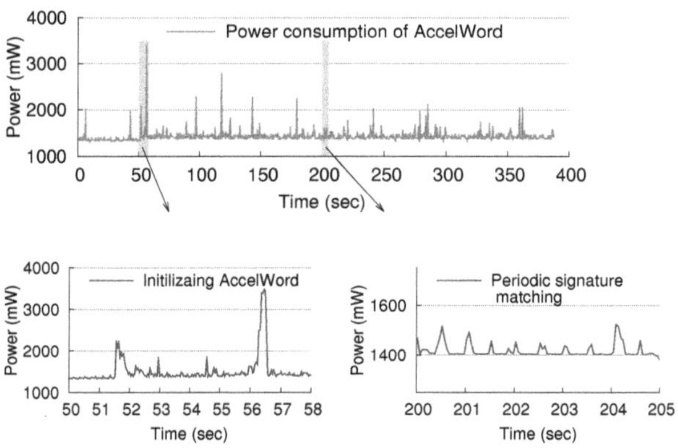


(b) (c)

Figure 21: Example: Energy Trace of AccelWord

quency causes a drop in TP rate because more and more "useful" signal is filtered out while removing mobility interference, generating weaker signatures of hotword.

Although the accuracy of AccelWord is slightly lower than in the static scenarios, the TP rate (84% with 2Hz high-pass filter) is still high enough for accurate hotword detection. Further improvements can be achieved by designing more advanced methods of mobility interference cancellation.

## 6.2 Energy Efficiency

In this section, we will compare the power consumption of the three apps: AccelWord, Google Now and S Voice. The power consumption is measured using the Monsoon Power Monitor at sampling frequency 5 kHz. An example of the power trace of AccelWord running on Galaxy S4 is shown in Fig. 21. Between 0s and 51s, the AccelWord app is in the foreground but not running. This shows the GUI power consumption of the AccelWord app. The AccelWord app is started at 51s and it finishes its initialization at 57s, as shown in Fig. 21b. The initialization process includes: initialize the queue cache, register the accelerometer listener to the OS and load the pre-trained classifier model. After 57 seconds, AccelWord begins to monitor the hotwords. In this example, we set the interval between each feature calculation to be 500 ms, and hence, we can observe approximately 10 pulses each 5 second, as shown in the enlarged Fig. 21c.

The power consumption of AccelWord is measured on a Galaxy S4 and a Nexus S. We vary the time interval between each feature calculation from 500ms to 1500ms. For each time interval setting, 5 runs of measurements are conducted on each phone, where each run lasts for 30 minutes. The average values are shown in Fig. 22.

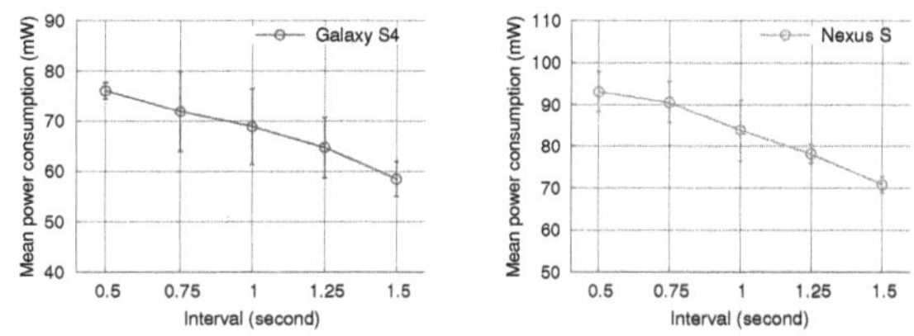


(a) Galaxy S4 (b) Nexus S

Figure 22: The Power Consumption of AccelWord

From the figure, we observe the expected that the computation energy can be reduced if the interval between each feature calculation is longer. However, the energy consumption of accelerator sampling will not be affected. Comparing the power consumption at 500ms interval (the highest) with the power consumption of Google Now and S Voice shown in Fig. 3, we can observe that AccelWord only consumes half of the power consumed by Google Now and Samsung S Voice, as shown in Table. 5. It is worth noting that current speech recognition employs much more sophisticated machine learning techniques such as early rejection (compute low-cost features first to quickly reject the non-hotwords and calculate the high-cost features only if necessary). It also worth noting that in terms of processing and implementation, AccelWord may be less efficient compared with its counterparts with large development and maintenance teams, e.g. Google and Samsung. It is necessary to point out that the energy savings of AccelWord is primarily due to energy-inexpensive sensing via accelerometer instead of using the microphone. Given that our current implementation of AccelWord is not optimized (compared to well-designed solutions like Google Now), even more energy savings are likely with AccelWord when more sophisticated machine learning methods are used along with better implementation.

| | **Energy Saving (%)** | |
|---|---|---|
| | Galaxy S4 | Nexus S |
| Google Now | 46.19% | 53.85% |
| Samsung S Voice | 57.14% | N/A |

Table 5: The percentage of energy saved

## 6.3 Speaker Identification

Although our objective of designing AccelWord is to enable energy-efficient hotword detection, we observe that it can also distinguish a user's voice from other users. We claim that the AccelWord hotword signatures are user-specific. Because every user's voice frequency is different, the extracted hotword signature of accelerometer also reflects the user who speaks the hotword. Such speaker recognition can be especially useful in scenarios where there are multiple users and each of them wants to only interact with their own smart-device without any cross-talk.

To evaluate that AccelWord users can be distinguished from each other, we perform a multi-class classification. Here, we use all the instances of the 10 users speaking the hotword for training and testing with 10-fold cross-validation. The classification results are presented in the form of a confusion matrix in Fig. 23.

Classified As

| Actual User | M1 | M 2 | M 3 | M 4 | M 5 | F 1 | F 2 | F 3 | F 4 | F 5 |
|---|---|---|---|---|---|---|---|---|---|---|
| M 1 | 100 | 0 | 0 | 0 | 0 | 0 | 0 | 0 | 0 | 0 |
| M 2 | 0 | 87 | 13 | 0 | 0 | 0 | 0 | 0 | 0 | 0 |
| M 3 | 0 | 12 | 76 | 9 | 3 | 0 | 0 | 0 | 0 | 0 |
| M 4 | 0 | 0 | 8 | 89 | 3 | 0 | 0 | 0 | 0 | 0 |
| M 5 | 0 | 2 | 2 | 7 | 89 | 0 | 0 | 0 | 0 | 0 |
| F 1 | 0 | 0 | 0 | 0 | 0 | 95 | 3 | 2 | 0 | 0 |
| F 2 | 0 | 0 | 0 | 0 | 0 | 2 | 65 | 26 | 0 | 7 |
| F 3 | 0 | 0 | 0 | 0 | 0 | 0 | 24 | 75 | 0 | 1 |
| F 4 | 0 | 0 | 0 | 0 | 0 | 0 | 0 | 0 | 95 | 5 |
| F 5 | 0 | 0 | 0 | 0 | 0 | 0 | 7 | 1 | 10 | 82 |

Figure 23: Confusion Matrix of Speaker Identification (M: Male F: Female)

It is observed from Fig. 23 that AccelWord can identify the speakers with very high accuracy (female - 82% and male - 88%). It is interesting to observe that none of the female users are ever classified as male users (and vice versa). This means that classifying whether user is male or female using accelerometer data can be done with very high accuracy. The feasibility of speaker and its gender identification can be leveraged to provide user authentication along with hotword detection using AccelWord.

# 7. DISCUSSION

In this section, we discuss the limitations of AccelWord and suggest directions for further exploitation of using accelerometer for specific word detection.

**Higher Sampling Rate:** One possible strategy to improve the accuracy of AccelWord is to increase the sampling frequency of accelerometer. On the other hand, increasing sampling frequency may increase the energy spent on sampling. So there is an optimization problem in the trade-off of accuracy and energy efficiency.

**Low-power Processor:** Latest smartphones such as Moto X [35] and Nexus 6 [6] use a dedicated low-power processor for continuous sensing related tasks (e.g. audio sensing). When AccelWord is executed via such a processor, the energy savings are still likely to be proportionally lower than audio sensing on such a processor.

**Audio Noise Cancellation:** In microphone based speech recognition research area, there exists many high performance and efficient noise cancellation techniques, e.g. Least Mean Squares (LMS), Normalized Least Mean Squares (NLMS) and Affine Projection (AP) [36]. However, the noise cancellation in the accelerometer based hotword detection scenario is more complex, since the noise comes from two aspects: background audio noise and the mobility inference. Deeper exploration on how the voice is modulated on accelerometer will help to design noise cancellation algorithms for accelerometer based hotword detection mechanisms.

**Other Mobility Patterns:** In this work, we only considered the walking and speaking mobility pattern. In reality, the mobility of the users may be more complex, e.g. running, driving or taking flights, which will result in more severe interference. To resolve these possible problems, new methods should be developed to remove or reduce the interference cased by different mobility patterns.

**Privacy Implications.** The confusion matrix shown in Fig. 23 reveals the potential risk of using AccelWord to identify some of the user's privacy information, e.g. user's gender. Worse still, if the attacker is able to apply a patch to the Android system to tune up the sampling frequency of accelerometer, it is also possible to use accelerometer readings to reconstruct portions of the human speech. If this is possible, applications with access permissions to accelerometer can also hear user's speech creating a huge privacy risk. In our ongoing work, we are exploring the feasibility and severity of such privacy leakage, and possible protection mechanisms.

# 8. RELATED WORK

**Speech Recognition by Microphones:** In [11], the authors introduced *JustSpeak*, a universal voice control solution which enables Google speech recognition on any screen of the Android system. In [12], Ignacio*et al.* used Deep Neural Networks (DNN), a state-of-art machine learning technique, to identify the language spoken by smartphone users. There are also a number of theoretical papers focusing on improve the computation efficiency of the training process of speech recognition [13–15]. These works are quite different from ours, since AccelWord relies on accelerometer to monitor voice signals and targets only on hotword detection.

**Identify User Activities by Accelerometer:** There are a number of works focusing on identify or detect user actives by analyzing the accelerometer data. [25,29,30,37,38] talk about general machine learning algorithms on identifying mobility actives, e.g. speaking, walking, running, dancing, stairs-up, stairs down. In [39], the authors designed a wearable ring platform to detect user's gestures up to 2Hz frequency. In [8], the authors presented (sp)iPhone which uses the accelerometer on a smartphone to detect human keystrokes through the vibration disseminated by the desk surface. This is different from Accelword where the accelerometer variations are due to sound instead of direct vibrations of a physical surface. Accelword does not require the speaker and the receiver to be placed on the surface of the same solid object.

**Audio Reconstruction:** Davis *et al.* presented the *Visual Microphone* system which can passively reconstruct the sound in a room by camcording the vibration of a potato chip bag in the room [40]. In [41], the authors presented *AVASR* which reconstructs human speech by processing the speaker's lip motion captured by Microsoft Kinect. *Gyrophone* [7] is a system which upsamples the gyroscope samples received at 4000 Hz to reconstruct the audio. The upsampling and reconstruction procedure is computationally expensive and unsuitable for our objective of energy efficient hotword detection. We have demonstrated that the accelerometer variations sampled at 200 Hz is enough for hotword detection at low energy cost.

# 9. CONCLUSION

In this paper, we introduced AccelWord, an accelerometer based hotword detection system for smart devices. AccelWord proves the feasibility of using accelerometer to detect the signatures of voice signals. Comprehensive experiments show AccelWord performs accurate hotword detection while consuming comparatively very low energy. Future exploration directions are also provided to further improve the performance of AccelWord.

## 10. REFERENCES


[1] "Apple siri, https://www.apple.com/ios/siri/."

[2] "Google now, http://www.google.com/landing/now."

[3] "Android wear." http://www.android.com/wear/.

[4] "Google glass." https://www.google.com/glass/start/.

[5] "Amazon echo." http://www.amazon.com/oc/echo.

[6] "Nexus 6, https://www.google.com/nexus/6/."

[7] Y. Michalevsky, D. Boneh, and G. Nakibly, "Gyrophone: Recognizing speech from gyroscope signals," in *USENIX'2014*.

[8] P. Marquardt, A. Verma, H. Carter, and P. Traynor, "(sp)iphone: Decoding vibrations from nearby keyboards using mobile phone accelerometers," in *Proceedings of the 18th ACM Conference on Computer and Communications Security*, CCS'2011.

[9] "Samsung s voice." http://www.samsung.com/global/galaxys3/svoice.html.

[10] "Monsoon power monitor." https://www.msoon.com/LabEquipment/PowerMonitor/.

[11] Y. Zhong, T. V. Raman, C. Burkhardt, F. Biadsy, and J. P. Bigham, "Justspeak: Enabling universal voice control on android," in *W4A 2014*, 2014.

[12] I. Lopez-Moreno, J. Gonzalez-Dominguez, and O. Plchot, "Automatic language identification using deep neural networks," in *ICASSP'2014*.

[13] W. Zhang and P. Fung, "Discriminatively trained sparse inverse covariance matrices for speech recognition," *IEEE/ACM Trans. Audio, Speech and Lang. Proc.*, vol. 22, pp. 873–882, May 2014.

[14] C. Chelba, P. Xu, F. Pereira, and T. Richardson, "Distributed acoustic modeling with back-off n-grams," in *ICASSP'2012*.

[15] O. Abdel-Hamid, A.-R. Mohamed, H. Jiang, L. Deng, G. Penn, and D. Yu, "Convolutional neural networks for speech recognition," *IEEE/ACM Trans. Audio, Speech and Lang. Proc.*, vol. 22, no. 10, 2014.

[16] Wikipedia. Examples of Sound Pressure, `http://en.wikipedia.org/wiki/Sound_pressure#Examples_of_sound_pressure`.

[17] STMicroelectronics. Everything about STMicroelectronics 3-axis digital MEMS andoscopes, `http://www.st.com/web/en/resource/technical/document/technical_article/DM00034730.pdf`.

[18] Ceramic capacitors feature reduced acoustic noise, `http://www.electronics-eetimes.com/en/ceramic-capacitors-feature-reduced\-acoustic-noise.html`.

[19] G. Roth, "Simulation of the effects of acoustic noise on mems gyroscopes," *Thesis, Auburn Univeristy*, 2009.

[20] "Inven sense inc. mpu-6000 and mpu 6050 product speficication." http://www.invensense.com/mems/gyro/documents/PS-MPU-6000A-00v3.4.pdf.

[21] Wikipedia. Human Hearing Range, `http://en.wikipedia.org/wiki/Hearing_range`.

[22] Wikipedia. Voice Frequency, `http://en.wikipedia.org/wiki/Voice_frequency`.

[23] S. Meter. Google Play Store, `https://play.google.com/store/apps/details?id=kr.sira.sound`.

[24] EngineeringToolnbox. Sound Pressure Levels of Common Sources, `http://www.engineeringtoolbox.com/sound-pressure-d_711.html`.

[25] E. Munguia Tapia, *Using machine learning for real-time activity recognition and estimation of energy expenditure*. PhD thesis, Massachusetts Institute of Technology, 2008.

[26] X. Huang, F. Alleva, H.-W. Hon, M.-Y. Hwang, K.-F. Lee, and R. Rosenfeld, "The sphinx-ii speech recognition system: an overview," *Computer Speech & Language*, vol. 7, no. 2, pp. 137–148, 1993.

[27] H. Hermansky, D. P. Ellis, and S. Sharma, "Tandem connectionist feature extraction for conventional hmm systems," in *IEEE ICASSP'2000*.

[28] I. H. Witten, E. Frank, and M. A. Hall, *Data Mining: Practical Machine Learning Tools and Techniques*. San Francisco, CA, USA: Morgan Kaufmann Publishers Inc., 3rd ed., 2011.

[29] J. R. Kwapisz, G. M. Weiss, and S. A. Moore, "Activity recognition using cell phone accelerometers," in *SIGKDD'2010*.

[30] A. Bayat, M. Pomplun, and D. A. Tran, "A study on human activity recognition using accelerometer data from smartphones," *Procedia Computer Science*, vol. 34, pp. 450–457, August 2014.

[31] T. K. Ho, "The random subspace method for constructing decision forests," *Pattern Analysis and Machine Intelligence, IEEE Transactions on*, vol. 20, no. 8, pp. 832–844, 1998.

[32] United States Environmental Protection Agency, Summary of the Noise Control Act, 1972.

[33] Enviroment Projection Agency of the State Council of China, The quality standared of noisy enviroment, 2008.

[34] Ministry of the Environment of Japan, Current Framework of Vehicle Noise Regulation in Japan, September 2012.

[35] "Moto x (2rd generation), https://www.motorola.com/us/motomaker?pid=flexr2."

[36] S. A. Hadei and M. Lotfizad, "A family of adapative filter algorithms in noise cancellation for speech enhancement," *International Journal of Computer and Electrical Engineering*, vol. 2, April 2010.

[37] A. Matic, V. Osmani, and O. Mayora, "Speech activity detection using accelerometer," in *IEEE EMBC'2012*.

[38] S. V. Dusan, E. B. Andersen, A. Lindahl, and A. P. Bright, "System and method of detecting a user's voice activity using an acceleromter." US Patent No. 20140093093 A1.

[39] J. Wang, K. Zhao, X. Zhang, and C. Peng, "Ubiquitous keyboard for small mobile devices: Harnessing multipath fading for fine-grained keystroke localization," MobiSys'14.

[40] A. Davis, M. Rubinstein, N. Wadhwa, G. J. Mysore, F. Durand, and W. T. Freeman, "The visual microphone: Passive recovery of sound from video," *ACM Trans. Graph.*, July 2014.

[41] G. Galatas, G. Potamianos, and F. Makedon, "Audio-visual speech recognition incorporating facial depth information captured by the kinect," in *EUSIPCO'2012*.

# Wearables Can Afford: Light-weight Indoor Positioning with Visible Light


Zhice Yang[1†] zyangab@connect.ust.hk
Zeyu Wang[1†] zwangas@ust.hk
Jiansong Zhang[2] jiazhang@microsoft.com
Chenyu Huang[3] hcyray@gmail.com
Qian Zhang[1] qianzh@cse.ust.hk

[1]CSE, Hong Kong University of Science and Technology [2]Microsoft Research Asia [3]Wuhan University
[†]Co-primary Authors



## ABSTRACT

Visible Light Positioning (VLP) provides a promising means to achieve indoor localization with sub-meter accuracy. We observe that the Visible Light Communication (VLC) methods in existing VLP systems rely on intensity-based modulation, and thus they require a high pulse rate to prevent flickering. However, the high pulse rate adds an unnecessary and heavy burden to receiving devices. To eliminate this burden, we propose the polarization-based modulation, which is flicker-free, to enable a low pulse rate VLC. In this way, we make VLP light-weight enough even for resource-constrained wearable devices, *e.g.* smart glasses. Moreover, the polarization-based VLC can be applied to any illuminating light sources, thereby eliminating the dependency on LED.

This paper presents the VLP system PIXEL, which realizes our idea. In PIXEL, we develop three techniques, each of which addresses a design challenge: 1) a novel color-based modulation scheme to handle users' mobility, 2) an adaptive downsampling algorithm to tackle the uneven sampling problem of wearables' low-cost camera and 3) a computational optimization method for the positioning algorithm to enable real-time processing. We implement PIXEL's hardware using commodity components and develop a software program for both smartphone and Google glass. Our experiments based on the prototype show that PIXEL can provide accurate real-time VLP for wearables and smartphones with camera resolution as coarse as 60 pixel $\times$ 80 pixel and CPU frequency as low as 300MHz.



## Categories and Subject Descriptors

C.3 [**Special-Purpose and Application-Based Systems**]: ; C.2.1 [**Computer-Communication Networks**]: Network Architecture and Design—*Wireless communication*

## General Terms

Algorithms, Design, Experimentation, Measurement




*MobiSys'15,* May 18–22, 2015, Florence, Italy.



ACM 978-1-4503-3494-5/15/05 ...$15.00.
http://dx.doi.org/10.1145/2742647.2745924.

## Keywords

Indoor Localization; Visible Light Communication; Polarization; Mobile Devices; Wearables


## 1. INTRODUCTION

We envision indoor positioning as being an indispensable feature of smartphones and wearables (*e.g.*, smart glasses) in the near future to support indoor navigation as well as plenty of location based services in shopping malls, supermarkets, office buildings, *etc.* To realize this goal, we need technologies that can provide high positioning accuracy as well as being light-weight enough to run in resource-constrained mobile devices, as these devices (especially wearables) are normally equipped with CPU, memory and camera that are optimized more for power-efficiency than performance.

*Visible Light Positioning* (VLP) [25, 26] is an emerging positioning technique that broadcasts anchor locations through *Visible Light Communication* (VLC). Benefited by densely deployed indoor lamps, VLP can easily achieve sub-meter accuracy in indoor localization. Compared with Wi-Fi and other RF based approaches which normally provide accuracy in meters, VLP holds the promise for beneficial applications such as retail navigation and shelf-level advertising in supermarkets and shopping malls.

However, we observe that in existing VLP systems, receiving devices are heavily burdened in VLC to avoid light flickering, which is caused by their intensity-based modulation method. As human eyes are sensitive to low rate changes in light intensity, the lamps have to transmit pulses at a high rate (over 1 kHz) to prevent flickering. Since the pulse rate far exceeds the camera's sampling capability (30fps), the design of the receiving side has to incorporate hardware modification to mobile devices – an additional customized light sensor is required and it relies on cumbersome calibration for the received signal strength to work properly [26] . A recent interesting idea is to leverage the rolling shutter effect of the CMOS image sensor to decode high-rate pulses from the high-resolution image [25,32,36]. Although its effectiveness has been shown in high-end smartphones with high-resolution (40 megapixel) cameras, the decodable distance is very limited in middle-end smartphones with 10 megapixel cameras or smart glasses with 5 megapixel cameras. Moreover, the high-resolution image incurs huge computation which requires a long processing time or cloud off-loading, therefore it lengthens response time, increases energy cost and sacrifices reliability.

The heavy burden on receiving devices motivated us to try to eradicate the light flickering. Our idea is to modulate the light's polarization instead of its intensity for communication. This paper presents our VLP system PIXEL, which realizes this idea. PIXEL enables a light-weight VLP that is even affordable by wearables (Google glass), without incurring hardware modifications or computational off-loading. PIXEL also makes other types of illuminating light beyond LED light (even sun light, §3) usable for transmitting location anchors, therefore eliminating the potential barriers to its deployment.

The design of PIXEL's polarization-based VLC is inspired by the *Liquid Crystal Display* (LCD). We borrow *polarizer* (§2.2.1) and *liquid crystal* (§2.2.2) from LCD as PIXEL's major components. A challenge in PIXEL's design is that the SNR in the channel of the polarization-based VLC differs dramatically in different receiving orientations. To address this problem, we propose to add a *dispersor* to PIXEL's VLC transmitter and employ a novel modulation scheme, called *Binary Color Shift Keying* (BCSK) (§3.1). With the help of these two modulation techniques, PIXEL is able to achieve reliable channel quality despite the user's mobility. Moreover, on the receiving side, PIXEL also incorporates novel system designs to combat the uneven sampling in low-cost cameras (§3.2). The idea is to exploit the operating system's clock to obtain more accurate timing for video frames. Finally, in order to make the system as light-weight as possible, we optimize all the algorithms and their implementations. Particularly, we optimize the implementation of the camera-based localization algorithm and achieve orders of magnitude performance gain (§3.3).

We prototype PIXEL's transmitters with commodity components and develop a communication and localization program for both Android smartphone and Google glass. Our experiments based on the prototype system show:

- We enable polarization-based VLC between PIXEL's transmitters and camera-equipped smart devices. Reliable communication over a long distance of 10-meters only requires an image/video capturing resolution of 120 pixel×160 pixel.
- We enable a fast positioning algorithm in mobile devices. Our optimization reduces the processing time of the camera-based positioning algorithm by three orders, from seconds to milliseconds.
- We enable realtime visible light positioning in resource-constrained devices and the average positioning time is less than 3 seconds. Even when the CPU frequency is as low as 300MHz, PIXEL's light-weight design works properly.

In this paper, with the design of the PIXEL system, we make following contributions:

- We identify the problem in existing VLP systems - the heavy burden on receiving devices, and propose a polarization-based VLC to address it. As far as we know, we propose the first system design that leverages polarization-based VLC in open space.
- We propose to add a dispersor to the VLC transmitter and develop a novel VLC modulation scheme called BCSK. These two techniques make it possible for the system to provide reliable communication despite the device's mobility.
- We develop a novel OS-clock based downsampling scheme to handle the uneven sampling problem of cameras.
- We optimize the implementation of the VLC receiving program and the positioning algorithm, thereby making the system light-weight enough for smartphones and wearables.
- We implement a prototype of PIXEL and conduct a systematic evaluation on it. Experimental results validate our design.

# 2. OVERVIEW

This section provides an overview of PIXEL. We first introduce the background of VLP and the flickering problem which motivates our work. Then we introduce the basics of polarization-based VLC, including techniques for generating/detecting polarized light and modulating light's polarization. Finally, we introduce the idea of PIXEL' system which is inspired by the design of one pixel in LCD screen.

## 2.1 VLP and the Flickering Problem

*Visible Light Positioning* (VLP) relies on *Visible Light Communication* (VLC) to broadcast location information through modulated light beams. The receivers, which are usually mobile devices carried by humans, use the light sensor [26] or the camera [25] to receive the location information as well as measuring their relative position to the lamps to perform fine-grained positioning. The mechanism is very similar to Wi-Fi positioning except that the visible light is used as the carrier to carry beacon messages instead of the microwave signal. Benefiting from the high density of the indoor lamps, visible light positioning can achieve much better (submeter level) accuracy than Wi-Fi positioning.

A major headache in VLP is the flickering problem. In current VLP designs, communication is based on modulating the light's intensity. Optical pulses are generated and data bits are encoded using pulse rate or pulse width. The varying light intensity causes flickering which can make people uncomfortable or even nauseous [19, 34]. In order to avoid the negative impact of flickering, a high pulse rate has to be used to make the pulses unnoticeable, though the message size required for localization is small. For example, the existing designs use over-1kHz pulse rates to transmit 7-bit beacons [25] or over-10kHz pulse rates to transmit 16-byte beacons [26].

The forced high pulse rate indeed adds a heavy burden to receiving devices. Considering the camera as the most common visible light sensor, the normal frame rate of 30 frames per second (fps) [22] is much lower than the pulse rate, which means it is far from sufficient to recover the transmitted pulses if we take one light intensity sample from every frame[1]. An interesting idea to tackle this problem is to leverage the rolling shutter effect of CMOS image sensor [25, 36]. The effect means rather than scanning a scene all at once, the image sensor scans one line at a time. Rolling shutter increases the sampling rate by up to thousands of times (from tens of fps to tens of thousands of lines per second), therefore making it possible to cover the pulse rate. However, according to our experience, the usefulness of rolling shutter is limited for two reasons. First, the camera must have very high resolution if it is not close enough to the lamp. This is because the lamp is only a small portion of the image, but a certain number of occupied lines/pixels are required to carry a message. In other words, if the receiving device does not contain a high-resolution camera, the communication distance will be short. For example, on a Samsung Galaxy 4 with a 13-megapixel camera, we can reach up to 1.6 meters, and with Google glass's 5-megapixel camera, we can reach up to 0.9 meters. Second, processing high-resolution image requires very high computational power. As a consequence, the existing design [25] relies on a cloud/cloudlet server to process the image and decode the message. Besides camera and rolling shutter, another solution [26] leverages a customized light sensor which is capable of taking high-rate samples on light intensity. Different from camera-based solu-

[1]Even cameras specially designed for capturing slow-motion video, for example, the 240-fps camera in the latest iphone6, the frame rate is still not sufficient to cover the over-1kHz or higher pulse rate. We also do not expect this slow-motion capable camera to be widely equipped into low-end phones and wearables.

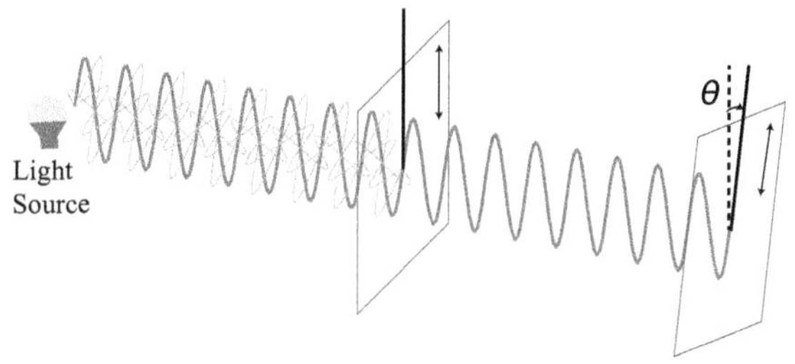


**Figure 1: Generating and detecting polarized light.**

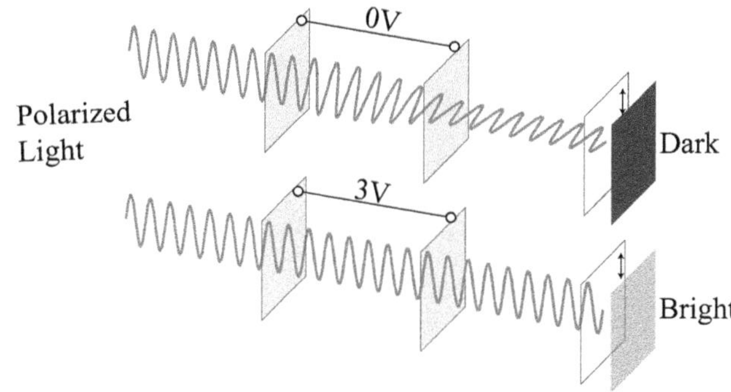


**Figure 2: Modulating polarization to encode bits.**

tions which use the angle-of-arrival based positioning algorithm, the light sensor based solution relies on *received signal strength* (RSS) technique to estimate the distance, this however are difficult to calibrate. Both hardware customization and RSS calibration are heavy burdens for VLP clients.

Finally, high-pulse-rate VLC also requires the transmitter to be a Light-Emitting Diode (LED), therefore, lamp replacement is needed if the existing lamps are not LED.

In this paper, we propose to exploit light polarization to realize low-pulse-rate VLC, so as to avoid the heavy burdens mentioned above and enable a light-weight VLP design that is affordable on wearable devices.

## 2.2 Basics of Polarization Based VLC

Polarization is a property of light waves that they can oscillate with more than one orientation. Similar to oscillating frequency which is another property of light, polarization preserves during light propagation in the air. However, different from oscillating frequency which determines color and thus can be perceived by human eyes, light's polarization is not perceptible [21]. This human-imperceptible nature has been proved very useful in that the polarization has led to the invention of Liquid Crystal Display (LCD) techniques, in which screens indeed always emit polarized light [39].

In the following subsections, we introduce two basic techniques in polarization-based VLC which solve the problems of generating/detecting polarized light and modulating light's polarization.

### 2.2.1 *Generating/Detecting Polarized Light*

Most of the common light sources, including sun light and man-made lighting systems, *e.g.* fluorescent light, incandescent light, *etc.*, produce unpolarized light which contains light of mixed polarization. The technique to convert unpolarized light into polarized light, called *polarizer*, is mature and very inexpensive. For example, the polarizer we use in this paper is a thin film, which costs roughly \$0.01 per lamp. Polarizer is also widely used to detect polarized light and filter out certain unwanted light[2]. The theory behind polarizer is the Malus' law. That is, if the polarized light incident to a polarizer has intensity $I_0$, the passed light will have intensity $I_\theta$, which is determined by the bearing angle $\theta$ between the polarization of the light and the polarizing direction of the polarizer:

$$I_\theta = I_0 \cos^2 \theta \tag{1}$$

Therefore, if the incident light has polarization in a direction parallel to the polarizer, *i.e.* $\theta = 0$, the light will pass through the polarizer without being attenuated. Otherwise, if their directions are perpendicular, *i.e.* $\theta = 90°$, the incident light will be entirely blocked by the polarizer. Malus' law can be applied to the case of converting unpolarized light into polarized light by considering unpolarized light to be a mix of polarized light with all possible polarizations. Figure 1 illustrates the process of generating and detecting polarized light according to Malus' law.

[2]For example, both polarized sunglasses and photographic polarizing filter are used to eliminate unwanted reflections.

### 2.2.2 *Modulating light's Polarization*

Modulating polarization of visible light using *liquid crystal* (LC) is also a mature and inexpensive technique. In this paper, we use Twisted Nematic (TN) liquid crystal which is very popular in the LCD screens of personal computers, digital watches, *etc.* TN liquid crystal costs only \$0.03 per $cm^2$ or \$1.5 per lamp in our design.

We explain how to modulate polarization to encode bits using Figure 2. The two surfaces, between which a variable voltage is applied, are the surfaces of a TN liquid crystal layer. TN liquid crystal has the characteristic that when a voltage is applied, its molecules will be realigned – twisted/untwisted at varying degrees depending on the voltage. Most commodity TN liquid crystal components are manufactured to have a 90° twist when no voltage is applied. Therefore a beam of polarized light will be rotated by 90° while passing through the liquid crystal, as shown in the upper sub-figure. If we use a polarizer parallel to the incident light to detect the light, as shown in the figure, the light will be entirely blocked by the polarizer. Then when we increase the voltage, the liquid crystal will untwist and the polarizer will become brighter. Once a certain voltage level is reached, *e.g.* $3V$ as in the figure, the liquid crystal will become totally untwisted and the polarizer will show the brightest state. In this way, we can tune the applied voltage to modulate the polarization and encode '0' and '1' using dark and bright states[3].

## 2.3 PIXEL – A Pixel of LCD

Our system, PIXEL, is inspired by the design of the pixels in LCD. As shown in the upper sub-figure of Figure 3, a pixel of LCD consists of two polarizer layers and a liquid crystal layer in between. The backlight generates unpolarized light which is converted into polarized light by polarizer 1. The liquid crystal layer twists/untwists the light's polarization according to the applied voltage. Polarizer 2 has a fixed angle of 90° in the polarizing direction with polarizer 1. Therefore, the strength of the emitted light is controlled solely by the voltage applied on the liquid crystal layer. Finally, a lot of pixels each of which has an independent control voltage constitute an LCD screen.

The lower sub-figure illustrates the VLC design of PIXEL. We convert a lamp into PIXEL's VLC transmitter by adding a polarizer and a liquid crystal layer. The transmitter thus emits polarized

[3]In theory, we can encode more bits using multiple levels of brightness. However, in this paper we only encode 1 bit to get rid of complicated calibration.

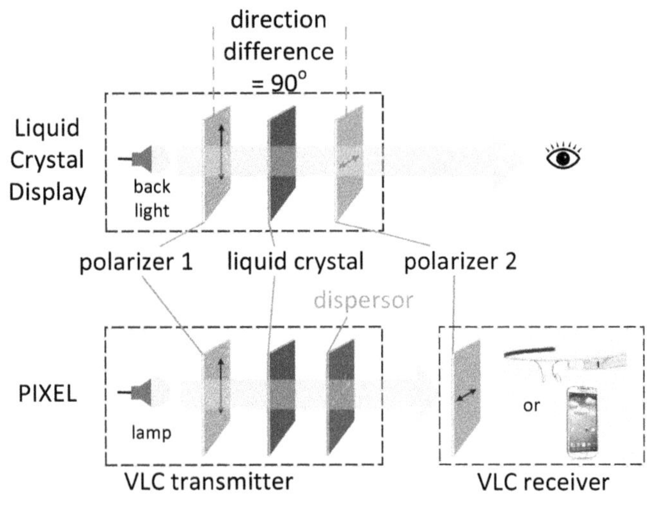


**Figure 3: PIXEL is inspired by the design of LCD.**

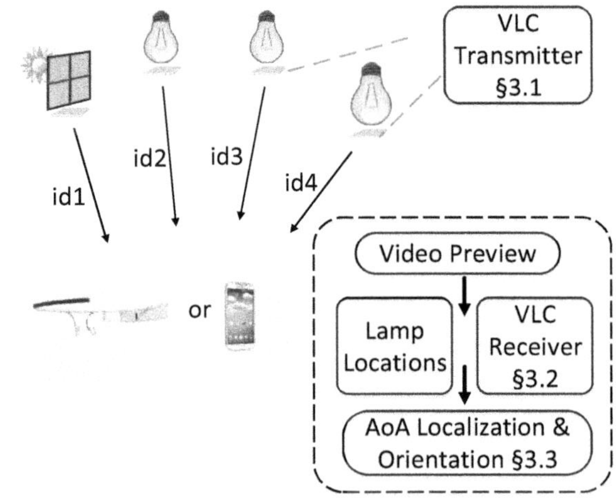


**Figure 4: PIXEL Architecture.**

light. Light's polarization can be changed by the voltage applied to the liquid crystal layer. The change of light's polarization cannot be perceived by human eyes[4] or directly captured by cameras. PIXEL's VLC receiver is a mobile device which equips a camera, *e.g.* smart glasses and smartphones. We add another polarizer to the camera for the purpose of detecting the changes of light polarization. As discussed in §2.2.2, the polarizer converts polarization changes into brightness changes that can be captured by the camera. We notice that the effect of adding polarizer to the camera, considering normal photo taking and video recording, is very similar to the use of polarizing filter in photography [28], *i.e.*, the polarizer does not bring noticeable changes except a slightly reduction in the strength of the ambient light.

However, from Figure 3, we can observe an important difference between PIXEL and LCD. In PIXEL, the polarizing direction between polarizer 1 and polarizer 2 does not always remain constant, because the receiving device may move and rotate with the person who holds it. This varying angle is one of the major challenges in our design. In the worst case the receiving camera will capture almost the same light intensity in the two polarization states. To tackle this problem, we leverage the camera's ability of capturing chromatic images and add a dispersor to disperse light of different colors to different polarizations. The details as well as other challenges and solutions are elaborated on in the next section.

# 3. PIXEL DESIGN

PIXEL presents a system design which makes visible-light based accurate indoor positioning affordable in wearables and low-end smartphones. As shown in Figure 4, every location beacon periodically sends out its identity through visible light communication. A wearable device or smartphone captures multiple beacons using the camera's video preview. Relative locations of beacons are obtained directly from the video. The identities of beacons are decoded by PIXEL's VLC receiver. Finally, with the help of a location database indexed by beacon identities, both location and orientation of the receiving device are determined using *angle-of-arrival* (AoA) based algorithms.

In PIXEL, it is possible to make use of any type of visible light source to construct a location beacon. As illustrated in Figure 4, a location beacon may consist of a lamp (not just the LED lamp, but any lamp) and a PIXEL's VLC transmitter. A location beacon may also consist of a window with incident sun light and a PIXEL's VLC transmitter.

In the following of this section, we elaborate on three main components of PIXEL, *i.e.* VLC transmitter, VLC receiver and the AoA based localization/orientation algorithm, to explain the challenges as well as our solutions in the design.

## 3.1 VLC Transmitter

The VLC design in PIXEL is borrowed from LCD, as has been described in §2.3. The VLC transmitter contains a polarizer and a liquid crystal layer that can convert the unpolarized illuminating light into polarized light and modulate the light's polarization using a control voltage. Then when the light propagates to receiving devices, polarization changes will be converted into intensity changes by another polarizer and identified by the receiving camera. Finally, the VLC transmitter also contains a simple electronic module to encode information, which translates the beacon's location identity into a series of control voltages.

A big challenge to PIXEL's VLC comes from the receiver's mobility, as has been briefly mentioned in §2.3. Unlike the two fixed polarizers in LCD, in PIXEL, though the polarizer in VLC transmitter is fixed (attached to the lamp), the polarizer in the receiver is mobile. Therefore, the two polarizers could end up with arbitrary angles in their polarizing directions. Since this angle determines the intensity of light, which is finally captured by the receiving camera, angle ambiguity will lead to a varying *intensity difference* (intensity-diff) between '1' and '0' states, meaning varying *signal-to-noise-ratio* (SNR) for communication. In the worst case, the intensity-diff will approach zero, therefore the encoded states will be totally undecidable. In order to quantify the relation between the intensity-diff and the polarizing angle between two polarizers, we build a mathematical model using Malus' law. Theoretical results based on this model are shown in the rightmost side of Figure 5. We can see when the angle is roughly in a 20° range around 45°(or 20% possibility), the intensity-diff drops quickly towards zero and can hardly fulfill the SNR requirement for communica-

[4]The change of light's polarization can be perceived if a person wears polarized sunglasses. However, we believe the case that someone wears polarized sunglasses in indoor environments is very unusual.

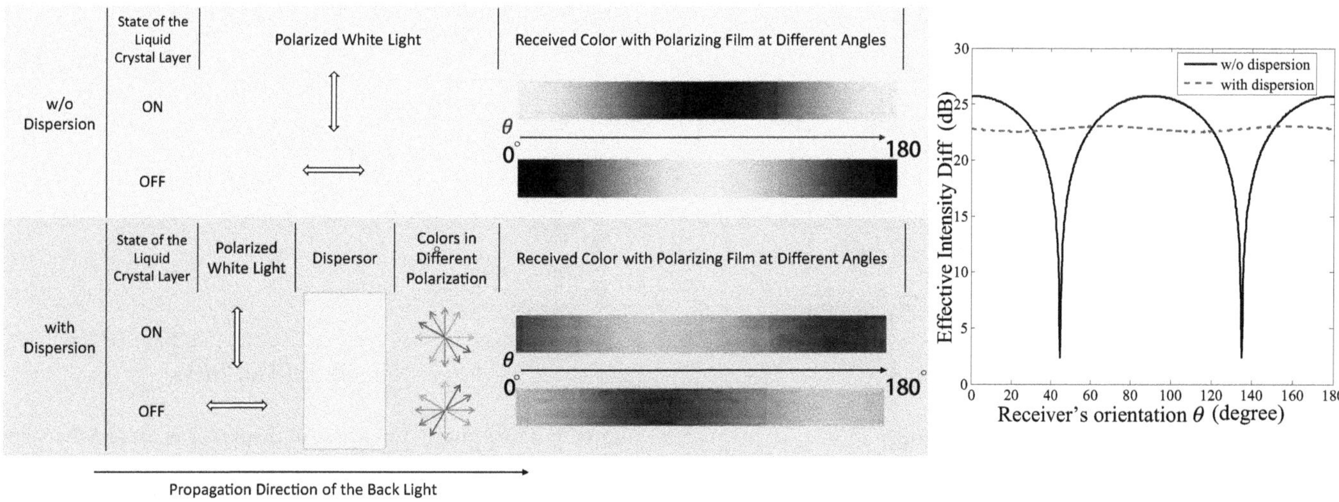


**Figure 5: Comparison between BCSK (w/ dispersion) and BISK (w/o dispersion). In BISK as in the upper sub-figure, the captured white light in receiving camera can only be quantified using light intensity. In BCSK as in the lower sub-figure, a dispersor is added in the VLC transmitter, the captured chromatic light can be quantified using a vector in RGB domain (*i.e.* color). The right sub-figure shows in BISK, intensity-diff of two encoded states largely fluctuates with receiver's orientation, whereas in BCSK, the effective intensity-diff is stable.**

tion. We also verified the result using experiments, in the angle of 45°, the intensity-diff is indeed very low.

A possible solution is to ask users to rotate the receiving devices. However, we believe it would be a cumbersome task. Since the polarizing angle is not perceivable by eyes, there is hardly any information to guide users on how to rotate. Also, rotating wearable devices could require big weird gestures.

To tackle this problem, we exploit the camera's capability of taking chromatic video. Recall the rainbow, the white light consists of multiple colors of light. The basic idea is to disperse the polarized light emitted from the liquid crystal layer into different colors, so that the receiving camera can capture different colors in different orientations after the filtering of the receiving polarizer. We fine tune the color dispersion to guarantee that, in any orientation, the captured colors in two encoded states will be largely different. We term this color-based modulation as *Binary Color Shift Keying* (BCSK). Next, we describe the dispersor and BCSK in details.

### 3.1.1 Dispersor and BCSK

Some materials have a property called *optical rotatory dispersion* (ORD), *i.e.* they can rotate the light's polarization differently with different frequencies (colors) of light [10]. These substances may be solid such as quartz, liquid such as alcohol or gas such as Hexadiene. This property has been studied for decades and widely used in industry, chemistry and optical mineralogy. For example, the method for measuring the blood sugar concentration in diabetic people is based on the ORD property of the sugar. In this paper, we use a liquid substance called Cholest [13] as our dispersor for the ease of fine-tuning the thickness and dispersion.

We use Figure 5 to illustrate BCSK by comparing it with *Binary Intensity Shift Keying* (BISK). We can see the beam of the polarized white light emitted from the liquid crystal is dispersed into multiple beams of polarized light with each having a unique color and polarization. The receiving polarizer passes through one beam of light according to its polarizing direction and filters out other beams. Therefore, only a certain color is captured by the receiving camera. When the encoded state is changed by the control voltage on the liquid crystal layer, the color of the captured light changes as well. Although the captured color still differs with the orientation of the receiving device, with proper dispersion we can guarantee the received colors largely differ between two encoded states in any orientation.

Next, we describe how to tune the dispersion for the purpose of guaranteeing a reliable SNR in all orientations.

### 3.1.2 Tuning Dispersion and Optimizing SNR

Dispersion tuning is performed by choosing the best thickness for disperor. The best thickness is mainly determined by the substance of dispersor. The spectrum of the illuminating light may slightly affect the best thickness, but this effect is very small because most illuminating light sources emit white light which represents a similar flat spectrum. When the substance of dispersor and the type of light is determined, the best thickness is also determined.

The target we optimize for is a metric called *effective intensity-diff.* It quantifies the color difference between two encoded states which is measured by camera. Therefore, it represents the received signal strength of the communication channel. Specifically, as shown in Figure 6, the colors captured by camera are mapped into a *{Red, Green, Blue}* (RGB) space. Given certain receiver orientation, the two colors in two encoded states can be indicated using two vectors $\vec{s_1}$ and $\vec{s_2}$. The difference between two colors is therefore $\vec{\delta} = \vec{s_1} - \vec{s_2}$. Then, effective intensity-diff is defined as $|\vec{\delta}|$.

We formulize the optimization problem and solve the best thickness $L_{best}$ as follows.

When a beam of polarized light passes through a dispersor, it is dispersed into multiple beams of polarized light in which each has a unique frequency (color). The polarization of a beam with frequency $f$ is rotated by an angle $\Delta\phi_f$, which is determined by:

$$\Delta\phi_f = n(f)L, \tag{2}$$

where $L$ is the thickness of dispersor, $n(f)$ is a function of $f$ which describes the rotation of light polarization in a unit thickness. $n(f)$ describes the property of a substance.

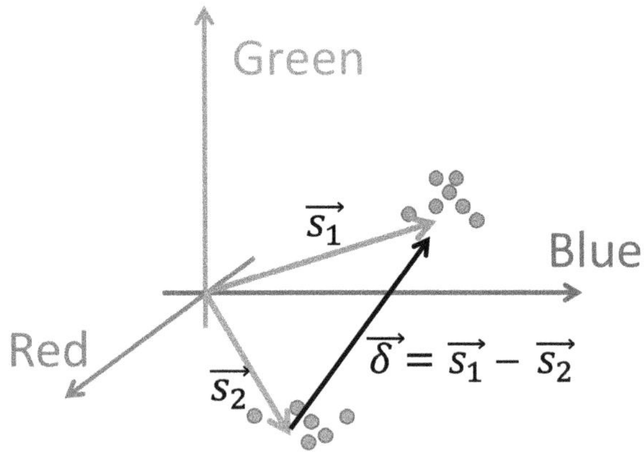


**Figure 6: Effective Intensity-diff $|\vec{\delta}|$.**

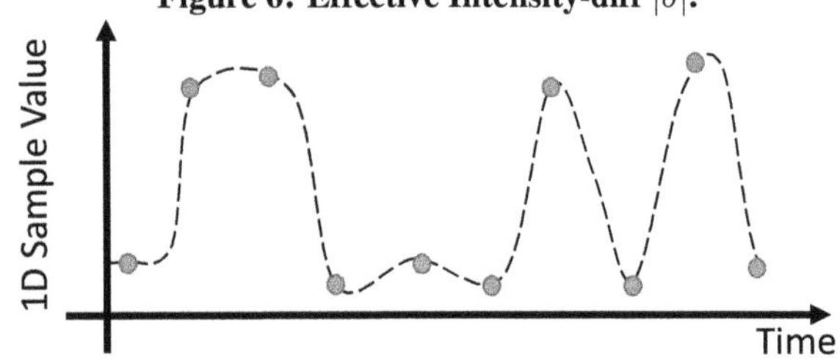


**Figure 7: Result of dimension reduction. These 1D samples reduced from 3D samples in Figure 6 constitute the received waveform.**

After the filtering by the receiving polarizer, the light captured by camera is described with a vector $\{I_R, I_G, I_B\}$ in RGB space. $\{I_R, I_G, I_B\}$ can be derived using the Malus' law:

$$I_N(\theta, L) = \int_{f_{min}}^{f_{max}} p_N(f)\cos^2(n(f)L - \theta)\,df, N \in \{R, G, B\}$$

where $\theta$ is the polarizing angle between transmitter's polarizer and receiver's polarizer. $f_{min}$ and $f_{max}$ are the upper/lower frequency bounds of the light's spectrum. $p_N(f)$ describes the light spectrum projected on the dimention $N$ of RGB space. $p_N(f)$ is determined by the camera's chromatic sensor. From this formula, we can observe that the light captured by camera is determined by both optical rotatory dispersion $(n(f)L)$ of the substance and the light spectrum $(p_N(f))$, as mentioned above.

The final goal of the optimization problem is to maximize the minimal effective intensity-diff in all receiving orientations. Considering the two encoded states between which the polarizing angle is rotated by 90°, we can formulize the optimization problem as follows:

$$\arg\max_{L}\min_{\theta}\sqrt{\sum_{N\in\{R,G,B\}}(I_N(\theta, L) - I_N(\theta + 90°, L))^2}$$

To solve this problem and get $L_{best}$, we need to know $n(f)$ and $p_N(f)$ in advance. $n(f)$ and $p_N(f)$ can be obtained from specification or calibration. In our work, we calibrate the $n(f)$ of our dispersor by ourselves and derive $p_N(f)$ from specification [8] and calibration results in literature [2]. We found $p_N(f)$ almost does not affect the vlaue of $L_{best}$, as shown in Figure 8[5]. We believe that

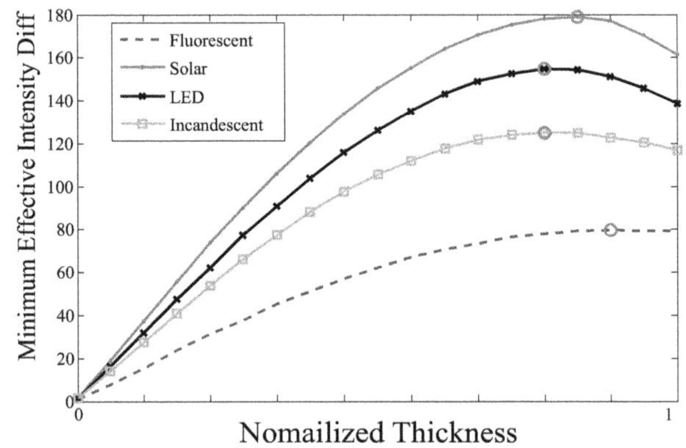


**Figure 8: The optimal thickness of dispersor is almost the same with various types of illuminating light, as most illuminating light is white light.**

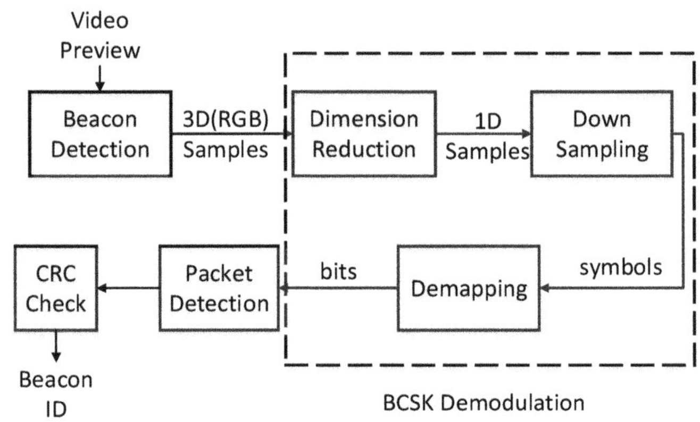


**Figure 9: Structure of PIXEL's VLC receiver.**

it is because most illuminating light sources emit white light which has a similar flat spectrum.

To compare BCSK with BICK, we calculate the effective intensity-diff under $L_{best}$ in all possible receiver orientation (represented by $\theta$). Results are shown in the rightmost of Figure 5. We can see the effective intensity-diff is quite stable in all the receiver orientations.

To conclude, the dispersor in PIXEL's VLC transmitter and the color-based modulation scheme BCSK well solve the problem of varying SNR caused by users' mobility.

## 3.2 VLC Receiver

PIXEL's VLC receiver decodes beacon's identity from camera's video preview. Figure 9 shows the structure of the VLC receiver.

The first step is beacon detection. In order to save computation, we first downsample the video to contain less pixels. According to our experience, 100 × 100 pixels will be sufficient for decoding in a distance within 10 meters. Then we calculate the difference between every two consecutive frames to detect the VLP beacons. In order to make the detection reliable, we add up the differences from 10 consecutive frames. Usually a detected beacon contains 10 or more pixels which contain its color value. We finally average these pixels to generate a 3-dimensional ($\{R, G, B\}$) color sample

[5]We use the normalized thickness to plot the trend for dispersors with different materials. Given the condition that the $n(f)$ is approximately linearly related to $f$, the trend of the Figure holds. Length "1" means the the difference of the rotated angles between $f_{min}$ and $f_{max}$ is 180°: $|\Delta_{f_{max}} - \Delta_{f_{min}}| = 180°$ and length "0" means no difference in rotation, *i.e.* L=0.

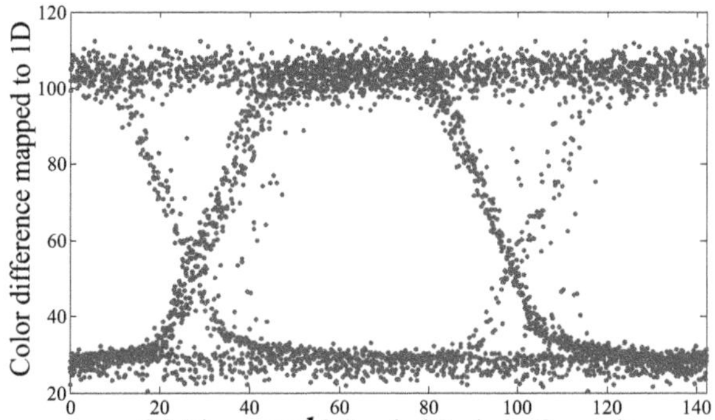


**Figure 10: 3000 video samples overlay with their sampling timestamp mod two symbol periods. The eye patten indicates the clock drift between the OS clock and VLC transmitter is negligible.**

from every video frame. Once a beacon is detected, one frame without downsampling is buffered for calculating its image location for the localization algorithm in §3.3.

As illustrated in Figure 6, these 3D samples in $\{R, G, B\}$ space are mainly distributed around two points, which represent the two encoded states. Since there are only two points/states, for the ease of further processing, we perform dimension reduction to convert 3D samples into 1-dimensional samples as the first step of BCSK demodulation. The requirement of dimension reduction is to preserve the distance between samples of the two encoded states. Therefore, we perform reduction by projecting these 3D samples to the difference vector between the two states, *i.e.* $\vec{\delta}$ in Figure 6. The projection from a 3D sample $\vec{s}$ to 1D sample $s$ is calculated by:

$$s = \frac{\vec{s} \cdot \vec{\delta}}{|\vec{\delta}|}, \tag{3}$$

Figure 7 shows the 1D sample waveform reduced from 3D samples in Figure 6. To determine $\vec{\delta}$, we calculate difference vectors between every two consecutive 3D samples, then take the average of those difference vectors with large norm and right direction as $\vec{\delta}$.

In PIXEL's transmitter, we set the symbol rate roughly the half of the camera's sampling rate for the purpose of meeting the sampling theorem. As the low cost cameras in wearables are not stable in the sampling interval, the downsampling process is non-trivial and we will elaborate on it in §3.2.1.

The output of the downsampling module is symbols. Since the symbols are in 1 dimension (scalar), demapping is equivalent to bit arbitration which determines '1' or '0' from every symbol. Similar to classic 1-bit arbitrator designs, we set the average of all symbols as the threshold.

The final step is to recover packets from the bit stream. In PIXEL, we use a 5-bit header for packet detection and synchronization. Since the packet is short, we use a 4-bit CRC for error detection and do not perform channel coding or forward error correction. More details about the packet design is shown in §4.

### *3.2.1 Combating the uneven camera sampling*

The downsampling (decimation) algorithm in classic digital signal processing [30] cannot be applied to PIXEL's VLC receiver. A basic assumption behind these algorithms is that digital samples are taken with a constant interval from the analog signal. However, this assumption does not hold in the low-cost cameras. As [22] pointed out, cameras in mobile devices do not offer fixed sampling rate (frames per second). Specifically, the sampling rate differs on different cameras, and also differs under different levels of ambient light. Moreover, the sampling rate may even vary during a single video recording.

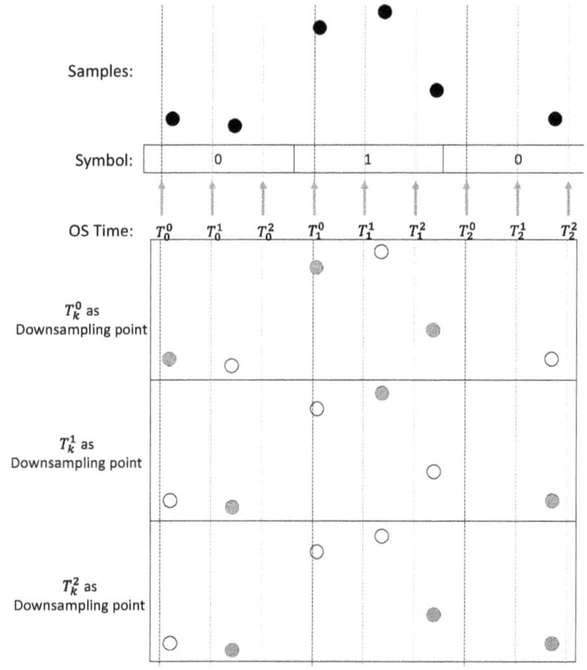


**Figure 11: Downsampling example on real samples. Each $T_0^j$ determines a sampling sequence, PIXEL chooses $T_0^1$ since it has the best decoding SNR.**

In PIXEL, we leverage the device's OS clock to perform downsampling. The core observation is that the clock drift between the receivers' operating system and the transmitter is negligible in the time scale of several packet durations (seconds). This can be proven by Figure 11, where every sample is timestamped by the OS clock and plotted with the time modulo of two symbol intervals. The cross lines between the upper line and the lower line in the figure are the boundary of the symbols. When there is a clock drift between two clocks, the boundary will keeps moving. However, as we can see from the figure, the clock drift can hardly be observed.

We downsample the uneven samples according to the OS clock. Although the sampling interval is changing, the relative optimal sampling time in one symbol period is stable. In Figure 10, samples around 60 can achieve higher SNR than those close the symbol boundary. In order to find the optimal sampling time, we use a method similar as searching. Several candidates of the sampling time are used to downsample the incoming wave simultaneously, and the best candidate in SNR gains weight in being the final choice. We choose the candidate which has the largest cumulative weight as our sampling time for this symbol period. Note that the algorithm can automatically adapt to different start conditions and bootstrap the sampling time to the optimal choice. Once the sampling time is determined, we choose the nearest input point as the downsampling result.

We explain the detailed downsampling method through Figure 11. PIXEL maintains sampling candidates $T_k^j$ with same time interval: $T_k^j = T_0 + kC + jC/N, k \in \mathbb{N}, j \in \{1, .., N\}$, where $k$ represents different symbol period and $j$ represents the incremental searching step within one symbol period. $C$ is the time for one symbol period. Once $T_0^0$, for example, in the figure is selected as the first sampling time, then $T_k^0 = T_0^0 + kC$ is the corresponding sampling sequence. According to the nearest rule, the selected samples for each $T_0^j$ is shown in the bottom half of Figure 11. Ap-

**Algorithm 1** Adaptive Downsampling

**Input:**

$N$: The number of the sampling time candidates.
$L$: The length of historical samples used to calculate SNR.
$k$: The symbol period $k$.
$T_k^1 \sim T_k^N$: Sampling time candidates at symbol period $k$.
$t_i^s \sim t_j^s$: Timestamp of samples, $t_i^s <= T_k^1 < T_k^N <= t_j^s$.
$x_i^s \sim x_j^s$: The corresponding samples at $t_i^s \sim t_j^s$.
$Y_{k-L}^i \sim Y_{k-1}^i$: The historical downsampled samples by $T_k^i$.
$S_k^i$: The SNR of the samples sequence $\{Y_{k-L}^i \sim Y_{k-1}^i\}$
$E_{k-1}$: The index $i$ of the best $T_{k-1}^i$.

**Output:**

$E_k$: The index $i$ of best $T_k^i$.

```
for each i ∈ {1, ..., N} do
    Find the nearest t_j^s so that t_j^s <= T_k^i <= t_{j+1}^s.
    Let Y_k^i = x_j^s.
end for
for each i ∈ {1, ..., N} do
    Calculate the S_k^i.
end for
E'_k = i where S_k^i = max_{i∈[1,N]}(S_k^i).
Calculate E_k by averaging E_{k-1} with E'_k.
return E_k
```

parently, the choice of the $T_0^j$ affects the decoding quality. PIXEL selects them according to the decoding SNR. We define the SNR of a sequence of $L$ samples $\{x_i\}, i \in \{0, ..., L-1\}$ as:

$$SNR = \frac{\left((mean(X_1) - mean(X_0)\right)^2/4}{(var(X_1)|X_1| + var(X_0)|X_0|)/L} \quad (4)$$

where $X_1 = \{x_i : decode(x_i) = 1\}$ and $X_0 = \{x_i : decode(x_i) = 0\}$. PIXEL keeps tracking and updating its choice of the sampling sequence to maintain the highest decoding SNR. The detailed algorithm is shown in Algorithm 1.

## 3.3 Positioning Algorithm

As a benefit of using a camera as the light sensor, comparing with other light sensors [26], PIXEL is able to derive both location and orientation from a captured video containing three or more location beacons. The positioning algorithm used is the same as Luxapose [25]. In this subsection, we describe our effort to optimize the implementation of the algorithm for the purpose of accelerating its execution, especially for wearables which equip low-frequency CPU.

We briefly describe the algorithm. The algorithm is a camera-based *angle-of-arrival* (AoA) localization method. Similar to other AoA based algorithms, a big advantage is that it does not require the difficult distance estimation between the receiver and location beacons. Instead, it leverages the properties of optical imaging that the mutual distance relations of beacons are distorted in the image according to the camera's location. Based on this knowledge, it takes two steps to localize the camera. First, the algorithm extracts the mutual distance relation of beacons in the image and searches for the optimal scaling factors $K_i$ to match the real mutual distance relation. $K_i$ describes how much the beacon $i$ is zoomed in the image. Second, the real location $[T_x, T_y, T_z]$ of the camera is calculated according to $K_i$ and each beacon's real location.

The camera-based AoA algorithm requires a large searching space to optimize the location value. When using normal searching methods, *e.g.* evaluating the optimization function at each point of a multidimensional grid of points, the localization process could bring

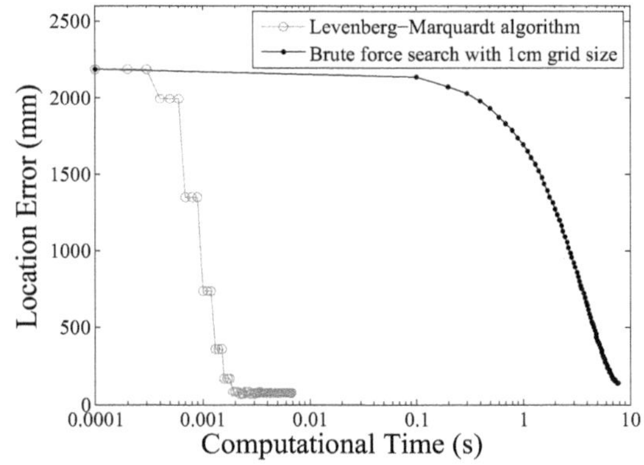


**Figure 12: Time cost for different optimization methods.**

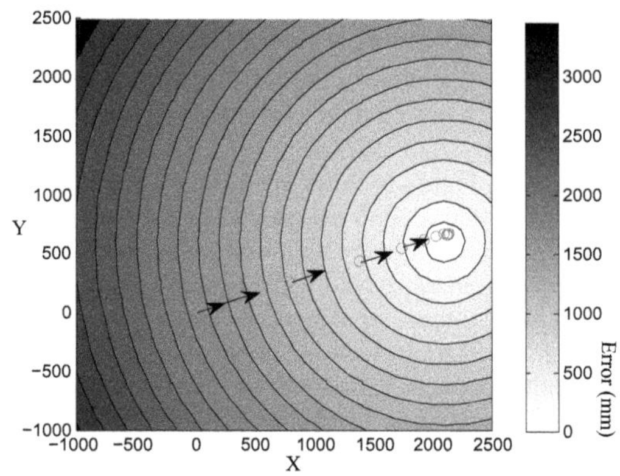


**Figure 13: Optimizing the searching speed with gradient. This 2D map illustrates the searching space of the localization problem in the horizontal dimension. The value of the object function, *i.e.* localization error, is represented in brightness. The real location with minimum error is the brightest area. Initial searching starts from $[0, 0]$ and arrows plot the optimal direction for finding the real location.**

significant calculation overhead to the mobile device, and thus the processing delay would be unacceptable. Dotted line in Figure 12 shows the time consumed in our smartphone when the normal searching is used. In order to find the location within 10cm accuracy, the processing time exceeds seconds, which is harmful for the user experience.

PIXEL reduces the searching space by leveraging the gradient of the optimization function to guide searching. Notice that the two optimization problems in AoA estimation are both non-linear least square problem, as they both have the following optimization object function:

$$\vec{x}_{opt} = \arg\min_{x} \sum_i f_i(\vec{x})^2$$

Optimization for the above function can be accelerated by searching along the direction of the gradient, which towards the minimum value(Figure 13). PIXEL adopts the widely-used Levenberg-Marquardt algorithm [29] which has a similar intuition. Circled line in Figure 12 shows significant acceleration of three orders in optimizing camera's location.

# 4. IMPLEMENTATION

Our implementation includes hardware part and software part. We prototype PIXEL's VLC transmitter using commodity compo-

| Preamble | Payload(Location ID) | CRC |
|---|---|---|
| 5bit | 8bit | 4bit |

**Figure 14: Message format of the location beacon.**

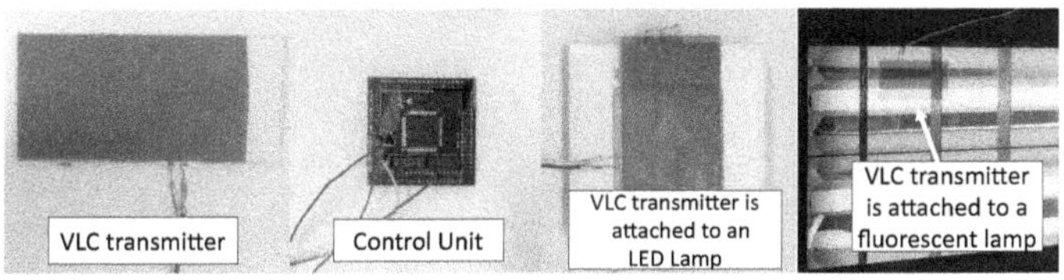


**Figure 15: Photos of PIXEL's components. From left to right: (1) VLC transmitter including a polarizing film, a liquid crystal layer and a dispersor. (2) The control unit with Altera Cyclon 2 FPGA. (3) VLC transmitter attached to a LED lamp. (4) VLC transmitter attached to a florescent lamp.**

nents except the dispersor which are constructed using liquid and transparent container. On the other side, we implement the VLC receiver and the positioning algorithm in a software program for both Android phones and Google glass.

## 4.1 PIXEL's Hardware

One VLC transmitter consists of three transparent optical layers and one control unit. The first layer is a linear polarized film [6], which functions as a polarizer to polarize the illuminating light. The second layer consists of two pieces of glasses with liquid crystal in between. We add electrodes on both glasses to control the applied voltage. This layer is a kind of simplified LCD with only one pixel, and many LCD manufacturers have the service for costuming LCD [4]. The third layer is a dispersor. We prototype this layer by filling the optical rotation material (Cholest) into a glass box. We choose the liquid material because it is easy to tune the thickness, but solid materials [7] with appropriate thickness could be a good choice for the real deployment. We adopt Altera's Cyclone II FPGA to control the voltage of the liquid crystal layer. Its clock rate is 40MHz and the output voltage is 0V/3.3V. The two electrodes of the liquid crystal layer are directly connected to two output ports of the FPGA to modulate the light's polarization.

Each PIXEL's transmitter works independently by facing to normal light sources such as solar light, LED light, fluorescent light and so on. As Figure 15 shows, normal light sources can thus be easily upgraded to have VLC ability with PIXEL's transmitter design.

The hardware of PIXEL's client devices requires no modification or customized accessories. The only requirement is a small piece of off-the-shelf linear polarizing film, and it is placed in front of the camera to detect and receive VLC signals.

## 4.2 PIXEL's Software

The packet format of VLC is designed for the indoor localization purpose. PIXEL's transmitter continuously broadcasts its location identity to receivers. The beacon packet contains a 5-bit preamble, an 8-bit data payload and a 4-bit CRC. The preamble is used for packet synchronization. Once the receiver detects a preamble from cross-correlation, it will start to decode the following packet payload which contains the identity of the beacon. We choose 8-bit as the length of an identity by considering the lamp density of the real world deployment. For the 4-bit CRC, the probability of false-positive detection is only $1.7 \times 10^{-8}$ [24] in our scenario, which is small enough.

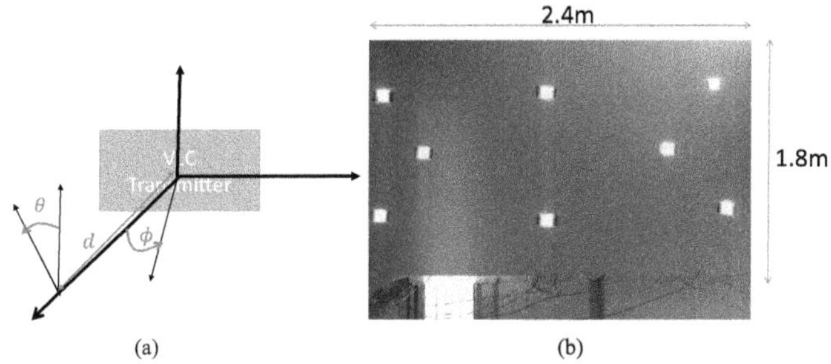


**Figure 16: Evaluation Setting. (a) is the settings for single VLC pair. $d$ is the distance from the receiver to the transmitter. $\theta$ is the orientation of the camera. $\phi$ is the viewing angle of the transmitter. (b) is the testbed for the VLP evaluation.**

We implement the VLC decoding and the positioning algorithm in both Android system and an offline simulator[6]. The code can be easily ported to other platforms since it does not depend on specific APIs. In Android 4.1.4, it takes 1200 lines of codes and the size of the executable file (apk) is about 320kb. We use the preview data from the camera to process decoding in realtime. As the system will automatically adjust camera's exposure time according to the intensity of the received light, which may affect the BCSK decoding. We walk around this issue by manually locking the exposure time in the software. This is not an issue in new Android release [1], since more flexible control of exposure time is provided. Once enough beacon packets are received, we use the buffered video frame to calculate the locations of lamps in the image for the localization algorithm. Other required parameters (*i.e.* the focal length of the lens and the size of the image sensor) can either be read from the EXIF stamp of the camera or obtained from online specifications.

# 5. EVALUATION

In this section, we evaluate PIXEL's design based our prototype implementation. We first describe the evaluation setup, then we conduct experiments to verify the component design in PIXEL. After that, we thoroughly evaluate different impact factors on PIXEL's VLC subsystem and the computational cost of each part of the client application. Lastly, we present the overall performance of our VLP system.

## 5.1 Experiment Setting

Evaluation involving one single pair of transmitter and receiver is performed in controlled conditions. Figure 16 (a) shows controlled parameters related to user's mobility. $d$ is the distance between the transmitter and the receiver. $\theta$ is the receiver's orientation whose rotation plane is parallel to the receiver's plane. $\phi$ is the viewing angle whose rotation plane is vertical to the transmitter's plane. Other impact parameters such as the downsampled resolution[7] and the exposure time are also controlled in the evaluation. If not mentioned, we take $d = 3m$, $\theta = 0°$, $\phi = 0°$, downsampled resolution = $120 \times 160$ and exposure time = $1/100s$ as default settings.

Evaluation involving multiple pairs of transmitter and receiver is performed with the testbed in Figure 16 (b). We fix eight PIXEL's

[6]We extract Presentation Time Stamp (PTS) from `ffmpeg` [3] to simulate timestamps of frames in recoded videos.

[7]The downsampling is used to reduce processing overhead as we mentioned §3.2, we fix the downsampled resolution to certain values, such as $120 \times 160$. The reason is to normalize different resolutions across cameras.

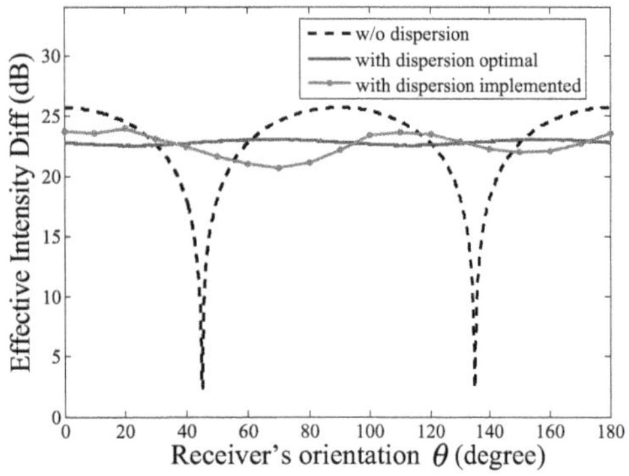


**Figure 17: Evaluation of the dispersor design**

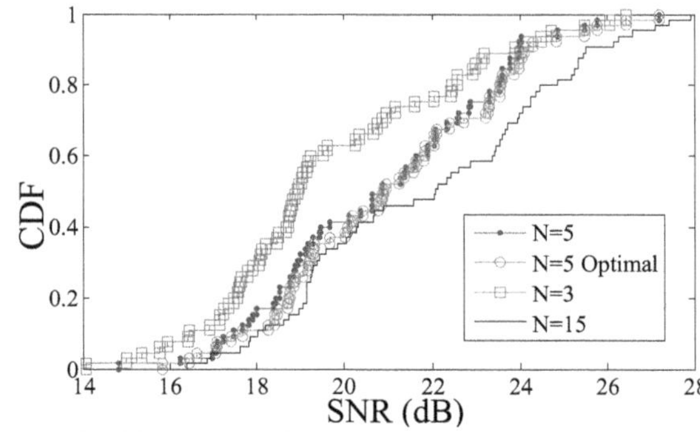


**Figure 18: SNR of adaptive downsampling. We choose the appropriate number of searching candidates $N = 5$ in our design to balance the accuracy and computational cost. Moreover, our adaptive downsampling algorithm almost has the same performance with the optimal downsampling choice.**

transmitters into a board which is elevated to the ceiling. The location of each transmitter is measured and mapped to the location ID in client's database. When the testbed is used for positioning evaluation, transmitters transmit their location ID through frame defined in §14. Under the testbed, we grid another board to serve as ground truth reference for client's location.

We use controlled random bit stream for transmission to measure BER and SNR. In these experiments, the transmitter repeatedly transmits a random pattern with a length of 100 bits, while the receiver keeps logging the received color values and the decoded bits. Since the length of the random pattern is long enough, we determine the start of the transmitted pattern through correlation. Therefore, the decoded bits can be used to calculate BER by comparing with the known random pattern. With the known random pattern as ground truth, the received color values can be used to calculate SNR according to formula (4).

All the experiments are done without a fixed ambient light source. In the morning, the ambient light is solar light and becomes fluorescent light in the evening. We adopt the 5W 10cm×10cm LED lamp as the light source of the transmitter for convenient setup. We also have performed similar evaluation experiments for fluorescent light and solar light, but we found little difference from LED.

## 5.2 Visible Light Communication

### 5.2.1 *Dispersor and BCSK*

**Experiment**: We study the effectiveness of the dispersor design in PIXEL. The evaluation is taken in a static situation, *i.e.* the transmitter stops transmitting and is either in on or off stage. At each stage, we take pictures of the light in different orientations from 0° to 360° in step of 10°. From the two pictures at the same angle but different stages, we compute the effective intensity diff according to the extract color of the light.

**Results**: The lined dot in Figure 17 shows the effective intensity diff of our dispersor prototype. Results from 180° to 360° are symmetrical to 180° to 0° and omitted. Compared with the dash line, which is the results without the dispersor, the dispersor design significantly increases the detectable difference for the on/off stages in degrees around 45°. Compared to the solid line, which is the situation with theoretical optimal dispersor design, our current prototype can be improved. The reason is not the hardness for manufacturing the dispersor, but lies in the fact that we can only purchase glass boxes with fixed thickness in the market. We choose the best existing thickness to prototype and we believe its performance is enough to illustrate our design.

### 5.2.2 *Adaptive Downsampling*

**Experiment**: We evaluate the adaptive downsampling algorithm through real data and the offline processing. 65 logged cases are collected by receiving VLC data from different locations and orientations. Each log lasts for 30s. According to the logged color sequence and timestamps, we use offline simulator to adjust the number $N$ of the potential choices of the sampling time. In each choice of $N$, we calculate SNR for the whole sequence.

**Results**: Figure 18 shows the results. First, we compare the adaptive downsampling with the fixed downsampling, where a fixed sampling time is chosen during the whole decoding. According to our previous description for Figure 10, the optimal choice of the fixed sampling time is fixed but unknown. Adaptive downsampling bootstraps and approximates such optimal choice. Figure 18 shows that when $N = 5$ the adaptive downsampling has little difference from the optimal choice of fixed sampling. We note that the same conclusion holds for different $N$, but we omit the curves for clarity.

Second, we study the trend of the decoding SNR when $N$ increases. Reasonably, the SNR curve of larger $N$ is better. This is simply because the choice for sampling time is more fine-grained and flexible with larger $N$. However, the gain is bounded by the intrinsic noise in the sampling timestamp and the communication channel. Therefore, the SNR gain from $N = 3$ to $N = 5$ is more significant than the gain from $N = 5$ to $N = 15$, and the gain is even smaller when $N$ is increased to larger values. According to the measurement of our receivers, the standard derivation of the sampling time is in $6ms$ level. So we choose $N = 5$, *i.e.* $1s/14/5 = 14ms$, to bound the random timing error. Other devices can easily obtain appropriate $N$ according to their local measurement.

### 5.2.3 *End-to-End Communication*

**Experiment**: We study PIXEL's VLC subsystem against five impacting factors caused by user mobility and device diversity: the distance $d$, the receiver's orientation $\theta$, the viewing angle $\phi$, the downsampled resolution and the exposure time of the camera. The experiment for certain factor varies that factor to all the reasonable values, and fixes other factors.

**Results**: Figure 19 (a) shows the SNR against the distance and the downsampled resolution. The downsampled resolution and the distance determine the number of pixels of the transmitter in the received image, and thus affect the SNR in a similar way. Therefore, we list them in the same figure for better illustration. From the results, our system achieves the SNR higher than 15dB under $120 \times 160$ resolution within $13m$, which is sufficient for most in-

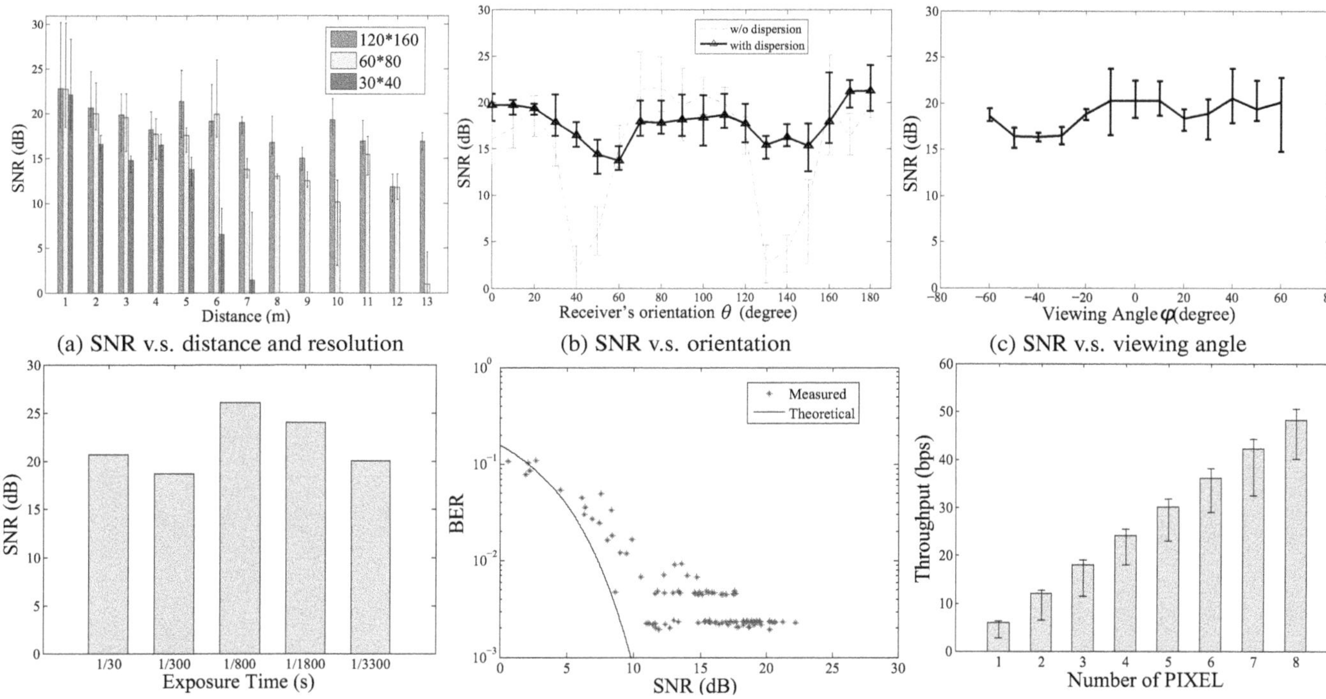


(a) SNR v.s. distance and resolution (b) SNR v.s. orientation (c) SNR v.s. viewing angle

(d) SNR v.s. exposure time (e) BER v.s. SNR (f) Rate v.s. number of PIXEL

**Figure 19: PIXEL communication evaluation**

door localization scenarios. In addition to that, the VLC system works even when the downsampled resolution is as low as $30 \times 40$. Notice that the SNR of the downsampled resolution of $60 \times 80$ and $30 \times 40$ drops to 0 at $13m$ and $7m$ respectively. The reason is that our decoding algorithm needs enough pixels to extract color. However, when the distance from the transmitter increases, the transmitter's pixels in the image decrease. This is not a problem since even $13m$ is enough for VLP in a normal building. Moreover, the size of the transmitter or the intensity of the background light can easily be increased to satisfy the possible requirement.

Figure 19(b) shows the VLC performance under different orientations. Without the dispersor, the SNR becomes undecodable when the view angle between the transmitter and receiver is around $40°$ or $130°$. This result is in accord with our previous analysis about effective intensity diff in §5.2.1. On the other hand, the result is improved a lot when the dispersor is deployed. The SNR of the received data is around 16dB in all the orientations, implying that the VLC quality is stable despite different orientations.

Figure 19(c) implies that the performance of VLC is stable under different viewing angles from $-60°$ to $60°$, which is sufficient for normal localization scenarios. From the results, we also observe that the variance of the SNR in the positive and negative sides are asymmetric. This is caused by the viewing angle limitation of the prototyping TN LCD, and can be solved by using better TN LCD or other LCD such as In-Plane Switching LCD.

Figure 19(d) shows the SNR against different exposure time settings of the camera. The result implies that there is no obvious relationship between exposure time and SNR. The reason is that our decoding algorithm will use different areas for decoding according to the exposure time. When under short exposure time, the amount of the received light from the transmitter is small and the decoding algorithm uses the center part of transmitter to extract color. When under long exposure time, the center of the transmitter is overexposed and displays white. However, the color can be extracted from the glow of the transmitter's image. Therefore, our VLC is robust under different exposure settings.

Figure 19(e) summarizes the data from all the experiments and get the relationship between BER and SNR. The theoretical curve for BCSK is calculated according to BPSK. However, since the camera of our smartphone is not stable enough and may occasionally drop frames during the capturing, the bit error rate is slightly higher than the theoretical result. Another reason is the number of samples for statistics is not enough. It can be observed from the two "horizontal lines" in the bottom of the Figure 19(e). Since each logged data only contains hundreds of bits on average, the upper "line" is plotted by cases with 2 error bits and the other "line" is formed by cases with 1 error bit.

Figure 19(f) shows the VLC throughput versus the number of transmitters. The rate is counted by the received payload, which does not contain the preamble and CRC. The result shows that the throughput increases linearly with the number of transmitters. It implies that concurrent transmissions don't affect the performance of our VLC. This is reasonable, since each transmitter is independent and the decoding process for each transmitter is also independent.

## 5.3 Visible Light Based Positioning

### *5.3.1 Computational Cost*

**Experiment**: We study the computational cost of PIXEL's client application in detail. The evaluation is performed with Samsung Galaxy SII. Its CPU has dual cores with maximum frequency of 1200 MHz. We fix the frequency to 1200 MHz though an app `SetCPU`. It has two cameras and we use the back one with 8 Megapixel for this evaluation. The smartphone is fixed in one location to perform VLP and its distance to the testbed in Figure 16(b) is $3m$. We log the start and end time exclude the sleep period in each part of our program to calculate the processing time. This method may be affected by the CPU scheduling, so we close all the other applica-

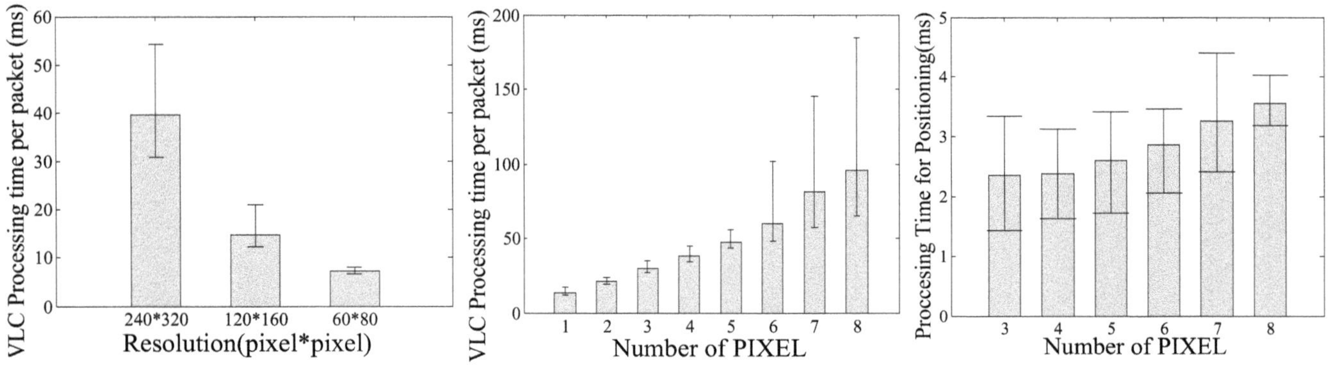


(a) Processing time for VLC v.s. resolution (b) Processing time for VLC v.s. number of PIXEL (c) Processing time for localization algorithm v.s. number of PIXEL

**Figure 20: Computational cost of each component**

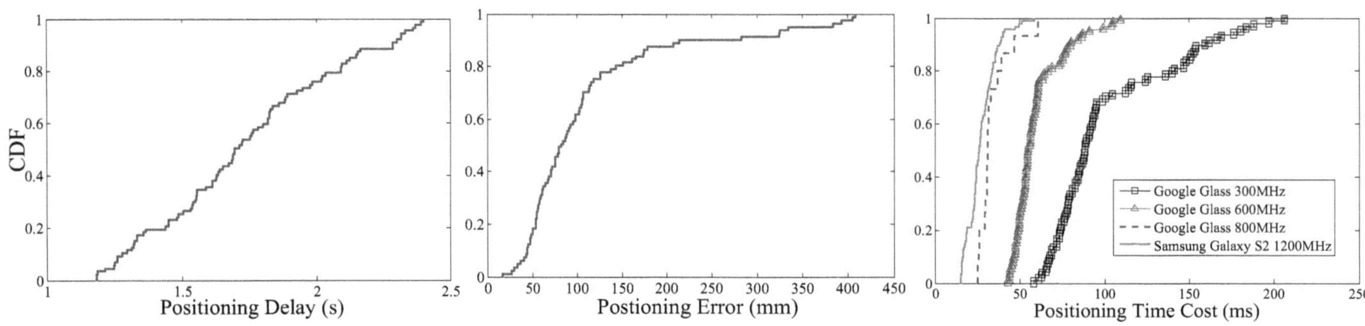


(a) Positioning Delay (b) Positioning Error (c) Processing time of VLP

**Figure 21: VLP overall performance**

tions and unnecessary services in the smartphone to keep the results as accurate as possible.

**Results**: Figure 20(a) shows the computational cost under different resolutions with single transmitter. Each packet is 17 bits and takes $1200ms$ air time for transmitting, but our decoding algorithm costs less than $50ms$ even when the resolution is $240 \times 320$. The result indicates our decoding algorithm performs fast enough. The figure also shows that it takes less time for processing when the downsampled resolution is lower. This is intuitive, because it takes less pixels for processing color extraction.

Figure 20(b) shows the time cost when the client is receiving from multiple transmitters. It shows that the total time of decoding 8 concurrent packets is less than $200ms$, which is still far less than the packet air time $1200ms$. The trend shows the decoding time increases linearly with the number of transmitters. This is because the decoding process for each transmitter is independent and scalable. We also note that the 8 cases share a small portion of basic processing cost, which is actually contributed by the shared downsampling process.

Figure 20(c) shows the time cost of the localization algorithm. Since it requires at least 3 anchors, the number of transmitters starts from 3. The result demonstrates that the localization can be finished within $5ms$ after the client receives enough beacons. The processing time slightly increases with the number of anchors, this is caused by the increased dimension in the object function.

### *5.3.2 VLP Performance*

**Experiment**: We study the overall VLP performance of PIXEL in three aspects: positioning delay, positioning error and positioning overhead. We use Samsung Galaxy SII and Google Glass as client devices while the transmitters in Figure 16(b) serve as VLP anchors. We place client devices to 100 random locations with arbitrary orientations and ensure that at least 3 transmitters can be captured by the camera. The start time and the end time of each test are logged for delay analysis. The localization results and the corresponding ground truth are recorded to estimate localization error. Like previous subsection, we log the processing time of the application to analyze the overhead. Since Google Glass has different frequency settings, we traversal all the configurations in our tests.

**Results**: Figure 21(a) shows that the average time from the launch of the application to a successful positioning is about $1.8s$. It is reasonable, because the time from the launch of the application to the earliest arrival of the beacon packet is uniformly distributed between 0 and 1200ms. Figure 21(b) shows the localization error is less than 300mm in 90% test cases. The accuracy is in accord with existing results [25]. Figure 21(c) shows the CDF of the computational cost under different CPU settings. As mentioned above, the computational cost includes the VLC decoding and the localization algorithm. Even with a limited processing ability such as 300MHz, our design can finish all the calculation within 150ms on average, which is still far less than the transmission time of one location beacon (1200ms). Therefore, the results validate that PIXEL can provide smart devices with light-weight and accurate localization ability.

## 6. RELATED WORK

**Visible Light Communication.** VLC has been studied with different context and design goals. Comparing with radio communication using microwave or mmwave, VLC uses visible light which has much higher frequency and much wider bandwidth. Typical VLC research aims to provide very high link throughput communication [23] for the purpose of wireless access [33]. Normally the receiver requires a photodiode to receive the modulated light. Different from this goal, our design focuses on providing a light-weight

VLC solution for camera-equipped and resource-constrained mobile devices.

In recent literatures [17,25,32,36] it has been proposed to leverage rolling shutter effect of CMOS camera to conduct VLC. It makes use of the fact that LED light with different pulse rates can generate different line patterns in the images captured by camera. However, according to our experience, the rolling shutter based VLC requires high camera resolution and high computational power. In contrast, the VLC in PIXEL allows very low camera resolution and only requires light computation.

Using camera to decode static or dynamic bar-code [20,22,31,37] is a special case of VLC. It has enabled a lot of interesting applications. Comparing to bar-code, PIXEL's VLC transmitter allows longer communication distance and is human imperceptible.

**Visible Light Based Indoor Positioning.** Indoor positioning has been studied for decades [9,38]. Recent literature [25,26,32] shows that receiving location beacons from lighting infrastructure provides a promising means for accurate indoor localization. Comparing to existing designs, PIXEL aims for a more ambitious goal of enabling light-weight visible light positioning that is even afforable in wearables. Comparing to existing LED-based VLC transmitter, PIXEL leverages light polarization to avoid the flickering problem, therefore significantly reduces the requirement on transmitting pulse rate. As a result, the requirement on the VLC receiver is largely reduced that only low resolution camera is needed.

PIXEL shares the same AoA-based positioning algorithm with other camera based solutions [25,32]. However, we spent a lot of effort to optimize the implementation of the algorithm, therefore make it possible to conduct realtime indoor positioning in wearables.

**Polarization Based Modulation.** VLC has been widely studied in the context of fiber communication and space communication. In the large body of the literature, some [11,18,35] has mentioned polarization based modulation. However, most of them do not contain a system design. Moreover, as far as we know, none of them has addressed the problem caused by the varying angle between transmitter and receiver because usually a fixed angle is assumed.

# 7. DISCUSSION

In this section, we discuss some limitations of our current system and potential directions for future work.

**Bit Rate.** In our current implementation, the baud rate of the VLC transmitter is set to 14Hz to allow most camera-equipped devices reliably decode. As a result, the bit rate of our implementation is 14bps. Though it is already sufficient for positioning purpose, the bit rate still can be increased in two ways. First, since the VLC transmitter is not the bottleneck (off-the-shelf LCD screens can achieve 1000Hz [5] refreshing rate), increasing the sampling rate of camera will make higher baud rate possible. For example, if Apple iPhone 6 that contains a 240-fps slow-motion camera is used as the receiver, the baud rate can be increased to 120Hz. Second, if we define more states of the polarizing direction, *i.e.* using higher modulation density, we can encode multiple bits into one symbol thereby increasing the bit rate. However, higher modulation density can make the color-based demodulator much more complicated. Moreover, it may also require calibration for the relation between polarizing direction and the captured vector in RGB space. We leave this study as our future work.

**Effect to Illuminating.** In our current design, the polarized light is generated by attaching a polarizing film to the illuminating light sources. Although the polarizing film blocks half of the incident light, we found that it does not incur noticeable effect to illuminating because the whole VLC transmitter is small and only covers a small portion of the light source. Alternatively, we can totally avoid the effect to illuminating by leveraging some special light sources (LED [16] or OLED [14]) which directly emit polarized light.

**Deployment Issues.** Our VLP design has the merit that it is compatible with most of the existing lighting infrastructures because it does not require the light source to be LED. To further facilitate the deployment, we can add a solar-based energy harvesting module into the system to solve the power supply problem. We leave this study as our future work. On the receiver side, the polarizing film can be integrated with the screen protection film, *i.e.* the material around the front camera is made by the polarizing film. Moreover, since the polarizing film is very inexpensive (0.001$ per camera), it can be used in an one-time use manner, *e.g.* the positioning service provider provides the polarizing film for free.

**Beacon Message Size.** The beacon message size in our current design is 8-bit. Therefore, we can support up to 256 unique IDs. The message size is similar to existing design [25] and sufficient to cover one floor of normal buildings, *e.g.* shopping malls. In certain cases that require more/less unique IDs, the message size can be increased/decreased. As a consequence, the positioning delay will increase/decrease accordingly.

**Viewing Angle.** In our current design, we take TN Liquid Crystal as the liquid crystal layer. A limitation of TN LCD is the view angle, *i.e.* when viewing from a very large angle ($|\phi| > 80^\circ$), the light will be blocked by the liquid crystal layer. However, we note that this is not a fundamental problem, because advanced LCD techniques, *e.g. In Phase Switching* (IPS) LCD, has well solved this problem. The same technique can be applied to our design as well.

**Power Consumption of Camera.** Our VLC receiver relies on camera's video preview, therefore, we need to keep the camera on during the positioning process. A normal camera consumes around 300mW [27] power, which is comparable to the screen [12, 15]. However, since the overall positioning process is less than three seconds, the consumed power by the camera is limited.

**Interference to Polarization Based Devices.** PIXEL does not interfere with the existing polarization based devices, such as LCD and polarized sunglasses. However, the polarization change of PIXEL's VLC transmitter may be observed through these devices because they also contain polarizer like PIXEL's receiver. As an interesting observation, when an LCD is off, the modulated light by PIXEL's VLC transmitter can be observed when it is reflected by the LCD. However, since the reflected light is weak, we believe it does not bring any big issue. Moreover, when the LCD is on, the polarization change will be totally invisible through reflection. This is because the polarization of the incident light (to LCD) is changed by the crystal layer and eventually be blocked by the second polarizer layer. Finally, people who wearing polarized sunglasses can observe the polarization change of PIXEL's VLC transmitter. However, we do not think it is common that people wear sunglasses in indoor environment.

# 8. CONCLUSION

This paper presents the system design of PIXEL, which provides a light-weight visible light positioning solution for resource constrained mobile devices. Our idea is to use polarization-based visible light communication which does not have the the light flickering problem as intensity-based visible light communication. In this way, we successfully eliminate the heavy burden on receiving devices caused by high pulse rate. We also enable other illuminating light sources beyond LED lamps to be used for visible light positioning.

To address the design challenges, PIXEL incorporates a noval color-based modulation scheme, an adaptive downsampling algorithm and computational optimization methods to handle the problems of user mobility, uneven camera sampling and limited computational resource. We implemented a prototype of PIXEL, in which the hardware was constructed using commodity components and the software program was built for both Android phones and Google glass. We conducted systematic evaluation based on this prototype. Experiment results validated our idea as well as the system design.

## Acknowledgement

We would like to thank our shepherd, Dr. Anthony LaMarca for his help with the final version. We also thank our group members and all the anonymous reviewers for their insightful comments. We are grateful to Su Pan for helping us with LCD and Hang Wu for helping us with the deployment on Google Glass. This work was supported by grants from 973 project 2013CB329006, RGC under the contracts CERG 622613, 16212714, HKUST6/CRF/12R, and M-HKUST609/13, ITS/194/12, and the grant from Huawei-HKUST joint lab.

## 9. REFERENCES

[1] Android 5.0. https://developer.android.com/about/versions/android-5.0.html, Mar 2015.

[2] Colour rendering of spectra. http://www.fourmilab.ch/documents/specrend/, Mar 2015.

[3] ffmpeg/ffprobe. http://www.ffmpeg.org/ffprobe.html, Mar 2015.

[4] Lcd. http://www.alibaba.com/product-detail/3D-Shutter-glasses-lcd-with-90_1909619852.html?s=p, Mar 2015.

[5] Pi cell. http://www.liquidcrystaltechnologies.com/tech_support/Pi_Cell.htm, Mar 2015.

[6] Polarizing film. http://www.alibaba.com/product-detail/Polarizer-film_458324790.html?s=p, Mar 2015.

[7] Quartz glass. http://www.alibaba.com/product-detail/clear-optical-quartz-plate-glass_846087937.html, Mar 2015.

[8] Spectrum data. https://plot.ly/~arducordermini, Mar 2015.

[9] P. Bahl and V. N. Padmanabhan. Radar: An in-building rf-based user location and tracking system. In *INFOCOM 2000. Nineteenth Annual Joint Conference of the IEEE Computer and Communications Societies. Proceedings. IEEE*, volume 2, pages 775–784. Ieee, 2000.

[10] N. Berova, K. Nakanishi, and R. Woody. *Circular dichroism: principles and applications*. John Wiley & Sons, 2000.

[11] R. Calvani, R. Caponi, and F. Cisternino. Polarisation phase-shift keying: a coherent transmission technique with differential heterodyne detection. *Electronics Letters*, 24(10):642–643, 1988.

[12] A. Carroll and G. Heiser. An analysis of power consumption in a smartphone. In *USENIX annual technical conference*, pages 1–14, 2010.

[13] S. Chandrasekhar. Optical rotatory dispersion of crystals. *Proceedings of the Royal Society of London. Series A. Mathematical and Physical Sciences*, 259(1299):531–553, 1961.

[14] A. C. Chen, S. W. Culligan, Y. Geng, S. H. Chen, K. P. Klubek, K. M. Vaeth, and C. W. Tang. Organic polarized light-emitting diodes via förster energy transfer using monodisperse conjugated oligomers. *Advanced Materials*, 16(9-10):783–788, 2004.

[15] X. Chen, Y. Chen, Z. Ma, and F. C. Fernandes. How is energy consumed in smartphone display applications? In *Proceedings of the 14th Workshop on Mobile Computing Systems and Applications*, page 3. ACM, 2013.

[16] V. Cimrova, M. Remmers, D. Neher, and G. Wegner. Polarized light emission from leds prepared by the langmuir-blodgett technique. *Advanced Materials*, 8(2):146–149, 1996.

[17] C. Danakis, M. Afgani, G. Povey, I. Underwood, and H. Haas. Using a cmos camera sensor for visible light communication. In *Globecom Workshops (GC Wkshps), 2012 IEEE*, pages 1244–1248. IEEE, 2012.

[18] E. Dietrich, B. Enning, R. Gross, and H. Knupke. Heterodyne transmission of a 560 mbit/s optical signal by means of polarisation shift keying. *Electronics Letters*, 23(8):421–422, 1987.

[19] D. Giustiniano, N. Tippenhauer, and S. Mangold. Low-complexity visible light networking with led-to-led communication. In *Wireless Days (WD), 2012 IFIP*, pages 1–8, Nov 2012.

[20] T. Hao, R. Zhou, and G. Xing. Cobra: color barcode streaming for smartphone systems. In *Proceedings of the 10th international conference on Mobile systems, applications, and services*, pages 85–98. ACM, 2012.

[21] G. Horváth and D. Varjú. *Polarized light in animal vision: polarization patterns in nature*. Springer, 2004.

[22] W. Hu, H. Gu, and Q. Pu. Lightsync: Unsynchronized visual communication over screen-camera links. MobiCom '13, pages 15–26, New York, NY, USA, 2013. ACM.

[23] T. Komine and M. Nakagawa. Fundamental analysis for visible-light communication system using led lights. *Consumer Electronics, IEEE Transactions on*, 50(1):100–107, 2004.

[24] P. Koopman and T. Chakravarty. Cyclic redundancy code (crc) polynomial selection for embedded networks. In *Dependable Systems and Networks, 2004 International Conference on*, pages 145–154. IEEE, 2004.

[25] Y.-S. Kuo, P. Pannuto, K.-J. Hsiao, and P. Dutta. Luxapose: Indoor positioning with mobile phones and visible light. MobiCom '14, pages 447–458, New York, NY, USA, 2014. ACM.

[26] L. Li, P. Hu, C. Peng, G. Shen, and F. Zhao. Epsilon: A visible light based positioning system. In *11th USENIX Symposium on Networked Systems Design and Implementation (NSDI 14)*, pages 331–343, Seattle, WA, Apr. 2014. USENIX Association.

[27] R. LiKamWa, B. Priyantha, M. Philipose, L. Zhong, and P. Bahl. Energy characterization and optimization of image sensing toward continuous mobile vision. Mobisys '13, pages 69–82. ACM, 2013.

[28] M. MacKay. Camera lens and filter adapter assembly, May 4 1993. US Patent 5,208,624.

[29] D. W. Marquardt. An algorithm for least-squares estimation of nonlinear parameters. *Journal of the Society for Industrial & Applied Mathematics*, 11(2):431–441, 1963.

[30] A. V. Oppenheim, R. W. Schafer, J. R. Buck, et al. *Discrete-time signal processing*, volume 2. Prentice-hall Englewood Cliffs, 1989.

[31] S. D. Perli, N. Ahmed, and D. Katabi. Pixnet: interference-free wireless links using lcd-camera pairs. MobiCom'10, pages 137–148. ACM, 2010.

[32] N. Rajagopal, P. Lazik, and A. Rowe. Visual light landmarks for mobile devices. In *Proceedings of the 13th international symposium on Information processing in sensor networks*, pages 249–260. IEEE Press, 2014.

[33] S. Schmid, G. Corbellini, S. Mangold, and T. R. Gross. Led-to-led visible light communication networks. MobiHoc '13, pages 1–10. ACM, 2013.

[34] E. Star. *ENERGY STARÂő Program Requirements for Residential Light Fixtures*. 2010.

[35] X. Tang, Z. Ghassemlooy, S. Rajbhandari, W. Popoola, C. Lee, E. Leitgeb, and V. Ahmadi. Free-space optical communication employing polarization shift keying coherent modulation in atmospheric turbulence channel. In *Communication Systems Networks and Digital Signal Processing (CSNDSP), 2010 7th International Symposium on*, pages 615–620, July 2010.

[36] H.-M. Tsai, H.-M. Lin, and H.-Y. Lee. Demo: Rollinglight - universal camera communications for single led. MobiCom '14, pages 317–320, New York, NY, USA, 2014. ACM.

[37] A. Wang, S. Ma, C. Hu, J. Huai, C. Peng, and G. Shen. Enhancing reliability to boost the throughput over screen-camera links. MobiCom'14, pages 41–52. ACM, 2014.

[38] Z. Yang, X. Feng, and Q. Zhang. Adometer: Push the limit of pedestrian indoor localization through cooperation. *Mobile Computing, IEEE Transactions on*, 13(11):2473–2483, Nov 2014.

[39] P. Yeh and C. Gu. *Optics of Liquid Crystal Displays*. Wiley Publishing, 2nd edition, 2009.

# OverLay: Practical Mobile Augmented Reality

Puneet Jain
Duke University
Durham, NC, USA
puneet.jain@duke.edu

Justin Manweiler
IBM Research
Yorktown Heights, NY, USA
jmanweiler@us.ibm.com

Romit Roy Choudhury
University of Illinois
Urbana-Champaign, IL, USA
croy@illinois.edu

## ABSTRACT

The idea of augmented reality – the ability to look at a physical object through a camera and view annotations about the object – is certainly not new. Yet, this apparently feasible vision has not yet materialized into a precise, fast, and comprehensively usable system. This paper asks: *What does it take to enable augmented reality (AR) on smartphones today?* To build a ready-to-use mobile AR system, we adopt a top-down approach cutting across smartphone sensing, computer vision, cloud offloading, and linear optimization. Our core contribution is in a novel *location-free* geometric representation of the environment – from smartphone sensors – and using this geometry to prune down the visual search space. Metrics of success include both accuracy and latency of object identification, coupled with the ease of use and scalability in uncontrolled environments. Our converged system, *OverLay*, is currently deployed in the engineering building and open for use to regular public; ongoing work is focussed on campus-wide deployment to serve as a "historical tour guide" of UIUC. Performance results and user responses thus far have been promising, to say the least.

## Categories and Subject Descriptors

H.3.4 [**Information Storage and Retrieval**]: Systems and Software

## General Terms

Algorithms, Design, Experimentation, Performance

## Keywords

Augmented Reality, Gyroscope, Localization, Mobile, Tagging

## 1. INTRODUCTION

The concept of mobile augmented reality is tantalizing. Researchers, designers, and the authors of science fiction have converged on the vision of using a hand-held camera as a sort of "magnifying glass" to browse the physical world. Digital annotations may seamlessly appear when the camera is pointed at an object. Looking at spaghetti in a grocery store may trigger recipes and product reviews; pointing the camera at a sculpture in a museum may pop up the artist's bio data; viewing a corridor in an airport can display restaurants located downstream in that path. Despite such exciting potential applications, a generic and usable solution remains elusive. The core challenge lies in carefully mitigating the tradeoff between accuracy and latency, i.e., the ability to precisely recognize an object and pop-up its annotation without perceivable time-lag. Given that hundreds of objects may be annotated in the same vicinity, slight inaccuracies or delays can degrade the quality of human experience. Moreover, authoring and retrieving annotations should be simple, and on the spot. If Alice is the first to annotate a painting in a museum, Bob should be able to view her annotation in the very next moment.

It is natural to wonder *why this is not a solved problem despite substantial research in augmented reality.* We began this project with the same question and realized that while several prototypes have been built in isolation – each making technical contributions in vision, sensing, and even information fusion – to the best of our knowledge, no system has made a holistic effort end to end [11, 13, 20, 35, 41].

Pure sensor based approaches such as Wikitude [9] rely on the smartphone GPS to position the camera, the compass to infer direction, and the accelerometer to identify the tilt. By computing the camera's 3D line of sight (LoS) from these data, Wikitude estimates the object that should be within the camera's viewfinder, and pops up the corresponding annotation. Unfortunately, sensory data has proven largely insufficient. Compass error measurable in tens of degrees severely derails the LoS accuracy; GPS errors of $5m$ or more exacerbates the condition. The application works when large objects are located near the camera, such as a user looking at the White House while standing at its fenced perimeter. For less favorable cases, especially when the annotation density is high, results are far from acceptable. Indoor environments lacking precise localization are of course out of scope.

In contrast to sensory approaches, computer vision enables a tradeoff of latency for better accuracy. Latency arises from matching the image in the camera's view against various images in the annotated database. When the match occurs, the results are precise – the annotation perfectly pops up on the screen atop the object. However, in uncontrolled environments, users view an object from different angles, under dif-


*MobiSys'15,* May 18–22, 2015, Florence, Italy.

http://dx.doi.org/10.1145/2742647.2742666.

ferent lighting conditions, and from different distances – all adding to the complexity of the problem. If the database contains many images of the same object (e.g., Alice and many others have annotated the same painting), image matching exploits this diversity to gain robustness. However, it takes longer. With only one or few images in the database per object, the operation is faster, but at the cost of accuracy.

Recent years have witnessed hybrid approaches that fuse sensor data and computer vision [24, 28, 33]. By utilizing the location of the user and orientation of the phone, authors in [38] prune the search space for image matching. This certainly offers improvement, however, the lack of precise location and large compass fluctuations make them unreliable indoors. The latency is also in the order of several seconds, requiring users to take a picture and wait for the annotation. Real-time object browsing – like a magnifying lens – really warrants sub-second latency.

Based on extensive literature search, we conclude that despite meaningful technical advances, and many released apps and media articles, no single effort has fully delivered on the complete vision. There are holes in the end to end processing pipeline – achieving the strict latency and accuracy targets would warrant a holistic look at the system. The system also needs to relax any assumptions on location to be deployable universally in the near future. Finally, sheer engineering is necessary to cope with corner cases in uncontrolled environments, including hand vibrations in some users, some objects being identical, weak network connections, etc.

We aim to complete and test the vision – to deliver, from a top-down design, a viable mobile AR framework that enables a useable and rewarding experience. While many of the challenges that must be addressed are not fundamental, they are "hard" and previously undemonstrated. It needed many design iterations to get the pipeline sufficiently optimized so that a viable solution could even be within grasp. Initially, we expected our efforts to be primarily engineering. *However, we also found ripe opportunity for novel heuristics to improve accuracy, responsiveness, and ultimately, the human user experience.* Especially, we developed an optimization framework that underpins computer vision with a geometric representation of objects in the surroundings. We are able to learn that geometry from the natural human movements across space and time, bringing the system to a desirable level of robustness.

Finally, we evaluate our approach not only through micro benchmarks, but also live, through the natural usage of independent and unbiased volunteers. For the first time, we were able to observe real human behaviors when interacting with a viable mobile AR solution.

In developing our solution, we learned the key contribution of this paper: *Mobile AR is best addressed not through sensing, computer vision, or any modality in isolation. Instead, each may be most advantageously combined within a stateful model, underpinned by the geometry and time of motion. With this spatiotemporal awareness, its possible to deliver content to the human user, at consistent precision and sub-second latency.*

For a sense of the accuracy and realtime responsiveness of the prototype, we invite the reader to watch the following video demonstration of our live system. **http://synrg.csl.illinois.edu/projects/MobileAR**

# 2. MEASUREMENTS AND GUIDELINES

OverLay aims to enable real time augmented reality on today's smartphone platforms. This section develops basic design guidelines through measurements and observations.

## Location and Orientation Sensors Inadequate

We believe that sensor-only approaches are inadequate to realize OverLay in any generalized settings. Even in outdoor settings, where GPS locations are precise to around $5m$, sensor based approaches fall short. Figure 1 shows measurements performed with Wikitude [9], a popular app on the app store that uses the phone's location, compass, and accelerometer to display annotations. The graph plots Wikitude's error in line of sights (LoS) measured by computing the perpendicular distance from the true object to the LoS. The median separation is around $12m$, implying that an object has to be at least $12m$ wide for the annotation to still be correct. Clearly, this offers limited applicability.

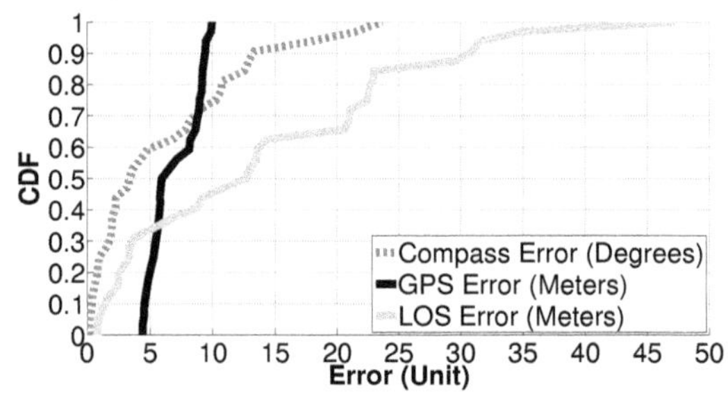


**Figure 1: Difference in estimated LoS vs. ground truth when measured through the Wikitude app.**

Indoor environments are far worse. Figure 2 measures compass errors due to ferromagnetic material in the ambience – as a user walks through a straight corridor, compass angle deviations are measured against ground truth. The median deviation is more than $15°$ with a heavy tail of up to $180°$. Finally, indoor location is still not universally available, and some that are starting to roll out in a few places are limited to $5m$ accuracies, at best. Such accuracies easily derail a augmented reality approach. Thus, to make OverLay robust and immediately deployable in all environments, we must desensitize the solution to localization and orientation estimates.

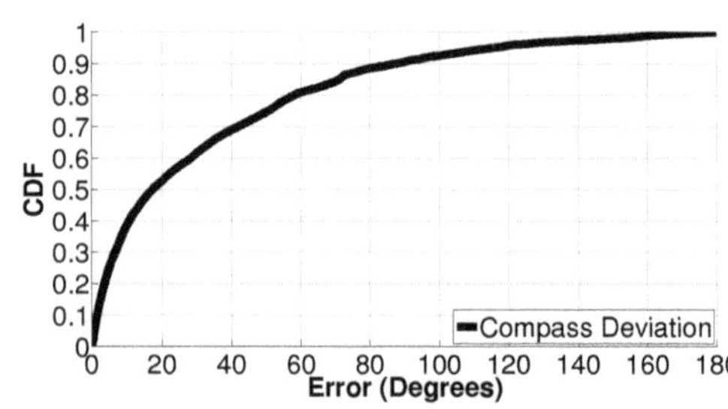


**Figure 2: Distribution of compass deviation in various indoor environments.**

## Computer Vision and Cloud Offload Essential

The reality we intend to (digitally) augment is visual. In light of this, it seems most intuitive to take advantage of the camera, a sensor that "sees" the world similar to humans[1]. Of

[1]We assume current generation cameras in smartphones. While 3D cameras would open further opportunities, we wish to ensure the widest generalizability across devices today.

course, computer vision algorithms (needed to "perceive" objects and display annotations) warrant non-trivial computational support. The way in which this computation is to be delivered presents a fundamental design decision.

Google's Project Tango [6] convincingly presents the premise that tomorrow's hardware might have computational and (therefore) visual sensory powers far beyond anything on the marketplace today: a laptop-grade GPU able to perform heavyweight computer vision on-device, such as simultaneous localization and modeling (SLAM) through bundle adjustment. While the concept is fascinating, today's reality is quite different, and we target a nearer-term solution. It is also worth noting upfront that as we are without access to this hardware, we will not be able to compare our techniques against it.

Excluding such forward-looking hardware prototypes, we establish our second design guideline. Mobile devices do not have sufficient computational capability, even with embedded GPUs, to perform suitable computer vision for immersive (and thus compelling) Mobile AR. Contrastingly, today's cloud environments afford on-demand provisioning of vast computational resources, to include dedicated GPUs (especially, Amazon EC2 and IBM SoftLayer). As evidence of the performance contrast, Figure 3 shows CDFs of computational latency in extracting local image features from a 1080p video frame (using the state-of-the-art SURF heuristic) on a desktop CPU, GPU, and a current-generation mobile CPU. Mobile CPU performance is a factor of 1000 – *three orders of magnitude* – slower than desktop GPU. Any hope to attain real time AR today will probably be infeasible without cloud offloading.

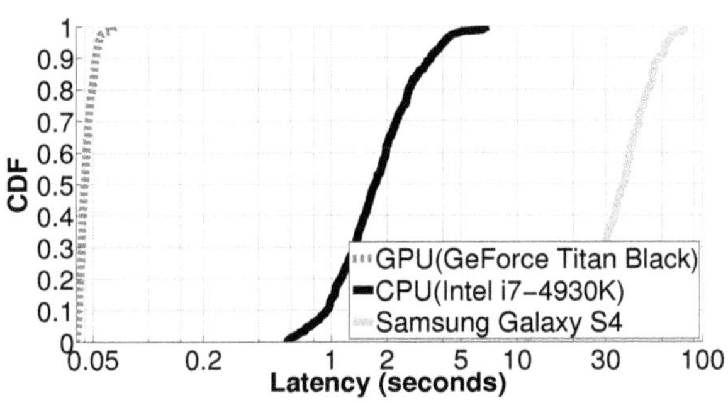


**Figure 3: Compute latency: extracting SURF local features on GPU vs CPU (single thread) vs mobile CPU (single thread) for 1 HD-quality video frame.**

## Network Latency Dictates Lower Bound

The latency gain from cloud offloading is obviously offset by the network latency in moving images to the cloud. Figure 4 shows a CDF of latency for moving a single HD video frame from a mobile device, over Wi-Fi, to a local server for processing. Even with a low-latency connection, limited throughput makes realtime operation untenable. While reduced image resolution will reduce the data burden (and hasten transmission times), a commensurate reduction in computer vision efficacy is an undesirable penalty. In response, OverLay must be highly selective in *which* imagery it uploads. Selected portions of selected frames will need to be transmitted to reduce data transfer by orders of magnitude.

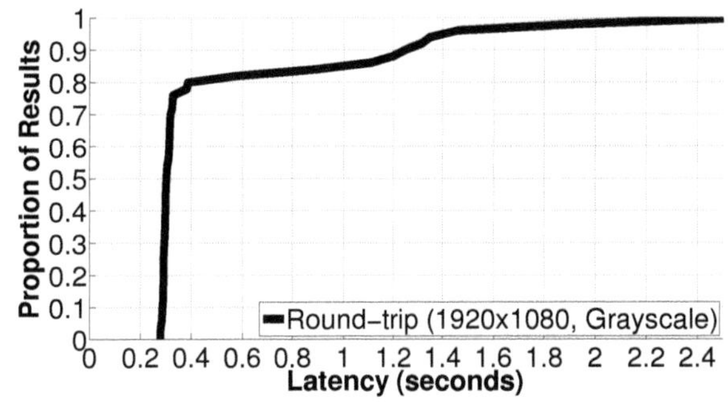


**Figure 4: Network latency: upload time for a single HD-quality video frame (1920 x 1080).**

## Computer Vision: Still Too Slow

Cloud offloading only alleviates the resource crunch. Even when running on the cloud, the accurate computer vision techniques are still heavyweight (hence slow and perhaps unscalable to many users), while the lighter and quicker ones are less accurate. The choice of the suitable technique is a matter of engineering. Figures 5(a) and (b) plot image matching accuracy and computational latency of a range of well-established feature extraction and matching techniques. Unsurprisingly, there is a tradeoff. Our intuition is that accuracy must not be overly sacrificed – false positive and negative pop-ups will simply "break" the user's sense of immersion. The latency penalty has to be mitigated some other way, suggesting that computer vision is necessary but insufficient for delivering the end to end experience.

As a side note, its possible to bring down the latencies by parallelizing the image matching computation on many CPU/GPUs in the cloud. However, that would not scale to real-world many-user deployments. With an eye towards scalability, we perform our experiments on a single consumer-grade desktop GPU (resembling a cloudlet [36]), and support tens of users. The same techniques should hold with real-world user densities on a real-world cloud.

## Opportunities for Geometric Optimization

The computational latency in Figure 5(b) is dominated by image matching, which is in turn a function of the number of candidates in the image database. Pruning the candidate set can aid in bringing down the latency to sub-second. To this end, it may be useful to develop a spatial understanding of the objects in the physical surrounding. If objects A, B, C, and D are known to be in spatial proximity, it may be possible to "prefetch" objects B, C, and D when the user is currently viewing object A. If among these four, A and B are known to be in angular proximity, only B can be prefetched. In the absence of location information, spatial proximity may be statistically inferred from the temporal separation observed between various pairs of objects. Angular proximity can be deduced from gyroscope rotation as users scan across objects.

By synthesizing sensor data through a geometric optimization framework, it may be possible to infer a spatio-angular representation of objects in a non-absolute coordinate system. In other words, anchoring any given object at the origin of such a coordinate system, it may be feasible to understand how other objects are relatively located. This allows for prediction and prefetching, offering opportunities to attain our real-time goals. Humans use such multi-sensor anchoring to

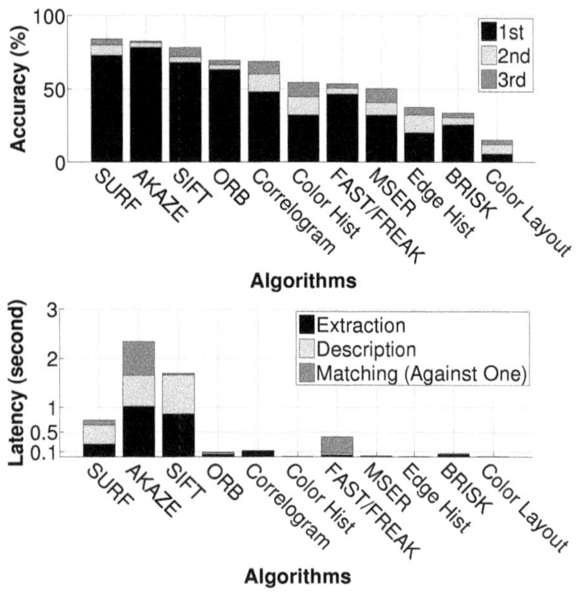


**Figure 5: (a) Accuracy/latency of image matching based on local or global features. Accuracy for 1st, 2nd, or 3rd-best match plotted from an 100-image database. (b) Latency bars reflect stages of the matching process (all numbers for server CPU)**

reason about their movement through environments; OverLay makes an attempt to mimic some of these abilities.

# 3. SYSTEM OVERVIEW

## Desired User Experience

Our ideal end goal is as follows. As a user Alice points her mobile camera at an object in the physical world, an appropriate annotation pops up immediately atop the corresponding object. Alice moves her hand to browse other objects, and tags keep popping up with non-perceivable lag. If Alice wishes to annotate a particular object, she simply brings the object in the center of her viewfinder and enters the annotation (which could be text, multimedia, or even software code). Bob passing by that object soon after can look at the same object and see Alice's annotation pop-up on his screen. When multiple annotated objects are in the viewfinder, all the annotations are overlaid atop the respective object.

We have not been able to achieve this "seamless" goal – the current system requires a median of $480ms$ (includes $302ms$ network latency) to pop-up annotations, along with more than 95% image matching accuracy. Thus, when using OverLay, Alice must pause her camera at an object of interest, and the annotation pops up within a second (except in rare occasions). Figure 6 presents a screenshot of our prototype running on an Android smartphone. Even this relaxed goal was non-trivial.

## Main Technical Modules

OverLay's end to end design firmed up after multiple iterations – in retrospect, we see three logical phases in the development process. (1) As an initial target, we focused on laying the groundwork with computer vision techniques, characterizing the best possible tradeoff between accuracy and latency. This phase included building the complete processing

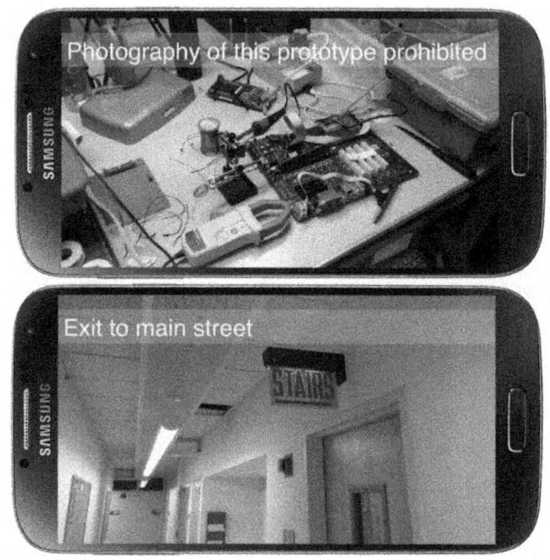


**Figure 6: Live object retrieval using OverLay.**

pipeline, evaluating a wide range of vision techniques, understanding their assumptions and possible modifications for our application, and finally reducing latency to the extent possible, through GPU parallelization, code optimizations, and sheer engineering. We do not make novel contributions here, nonetheless, the exercise was "hard" and time consuming to attain a desired degree of robustness and predictability. (2) With this framework in place, we heavily leveraged sensing (especially gyroscope) to reduce the amount of imagery that would be uploaded from device to server. This alleviated load on the GPU cutting the response time in half. (3) Finally, using sensor data from users, we developed an optimization framework to create the geometric representation of annotated objects. This pruned down the search space, translating to $4x$ load reduction in image matching and ultimately translating to sub-second response latency.

## Terminology

**Tag or Annotation:** Used interchangeably, they refer to content associated to physical objects. The user may tag or annotate an object, and these tags/annotations pop up when a OverLay–enabled camera is pointed at it. Tags and annotations can be text, multimedia, or a trigger for more actions (e.g., purchase of an item).

**Constant Scan:** The ability to continuously browse the physical environment with the camera, even when the user is moving. Tags expected to pop up when camera pauses on an object.

**Search Space:** Set of candidate objects against which a given object is being matched. Our search space is a spatial/angular region surrounding the most recently matched objects (better explained later).

**Micro/Macro Trajectory:** Observed or predicted human path through physical space, exploited to refine the search space. A macro trajectory is substantial movement with translational and rotational components, such as walking and taking turns. A micro trajectory is minor hand movement, likely while standing in a fixed position – common when entering a room and rotating the camera to scan objects on the wall.

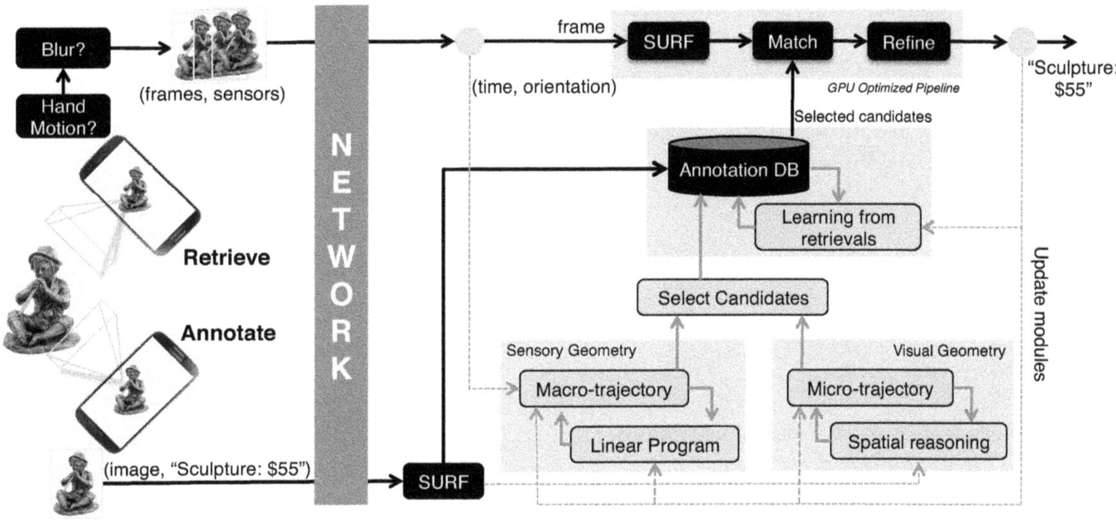


**Figure 7: System Overview. Left: client-side. Right: offloaded compute, database on server (cloud).**

# 4. SYSTEM DESIGN

Figure 7 illustrates our simplified system architecture. In the basic execution flow, an annotated object (bottom left) is uploaded to the OverLay server, where SURF features are extracted and systematically indexed in an annotated (image) database. When objects are retrieved later (top left), the phone uses vision and sensing data to filter out unusable frames caused by hand vibration and blur. The uploaded frames are processed through a GPU optimized pipeline – the operation includes SURF feature extraction, matching with selected candidate sets, and refining the match. If a confident match is found, the server returns the corresponding "annotation" to the smartphone for on-screen display.

OverLay underpins this basic execution pipeline with optimizations that prune the search space during retrieval. To this end, 3 modules are invoked at different places in the overall system. (1) Sensor data received during the retrieval process (i.e., time and gyroscope orientation) is fed into a "Sensory Geometry" module responsible for inferring the the spatiotemporal relationships between objects. Two objects retrieved in a corridor can be "connected" in terms of their relative time and angular separation. As new retrievals arrive, and as images get correctly matched (top right), all these information are fed back into a *linear program* to ultimately converge on a geometric representation of annotated objects in the environment. (2) Such inter-object relationships are also extracted in the visual domain – if object $A$ and $B$ are viewed in the same image, OverLay infers relationships such as "A is on the left of B". The "Visual Geometry" module uses data from annotated images to develop this understanding. (3) Finally, correctly matched images are fed back into the annotated database to improve/complete the visual models of an object – this allows for accurate recognition even when users are viewing objects from different locations, angles, lighting conditions. The details of these modules are described next.

## 4.1 Object Geometry (Sensory and Visual)

When Alice's camera points at an object, the video frames are uploaded to the OverLay server, which matches the frame against annotated images in its database. Matching against all database objects will be prohibitively slow. For maximized performance, both in terms of accuracy and speed, it is important to prune the matching search space to only the likely candidate objects. GPS location, erroneous to $30m$ or more in indoor environments, prunes the candidate set to the order of a building or a wing in a shopping mall. A real-world deployment could easily present more than 100 annotations in such areas – far more pruning is necessary to attain our accuracy and latency targets.

Towards this goal, we prune across *spatial* and *temporal* dimensions by learning a spatiotemporal relationship among annotated objects. At a high level, this results in a graph of objects where the shape of the graph essentially reflects how humans observe the (angular and temporal) separation between objects, as they walk through them. As a simplistic example, imagine we have three tagged objects $A$, $B$, and $C$ in sequence on along a hallway (Figure 8). Unsurprisingly, if we observe $A$ then $B$, it is quite likely we will soon observe $C$. Further imagine a fourth object, $D$, located on the left in a perpendicular hallway as shown in Figure 8. To make a left turn, we would expect a rotation $\approx 90^\circ$ counterclockwise. If instead, a clockwise rotation is observed, the user has likely turned away, and the possibility of observing $D$ is dramatically reduced. As a result, once OverLay recognizes an object $X$, it is able to infer the user's location in the object graph. Only objects near $X$ are now candidates for the next recognition task, resulting in substantial pruning. Once the next object $Y$ is recognized, OverLay knows that the user is now close to $Y$ and selects objects near $Y$ as the new candidate set. This operation carries on and the user's motion path is tracked through this spatiotemporal object graph. Of course, the first object recognition must rely on computer vision alone and crude GPS location.

We limit our understanding of this natural human trajectory to time and rotation only (note that no form of localization is necessary). The gyroscope is accurate enough to capture a high-fidelity awareness of user rotation. Further, we learn and leverage these trajectories at both *macro* (long-lived with

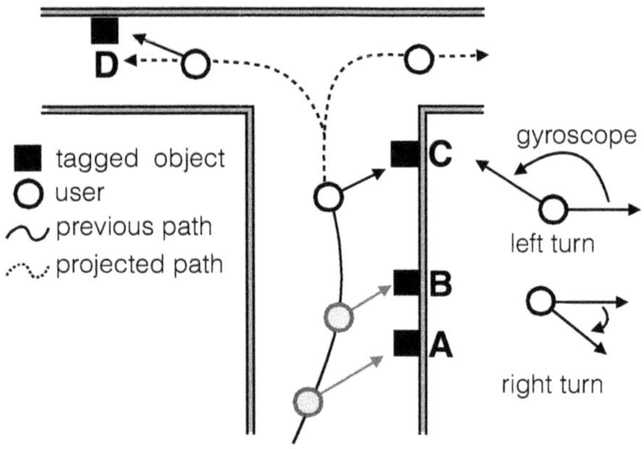


**Figure 8: Example macro trajectory. Counterclockwise rotation observed after $C$ is predictive of $D$.**

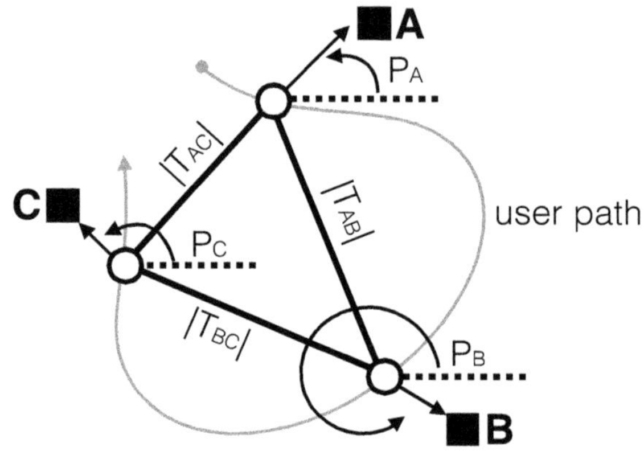


**Figure 9: User macro trajectory as it relates to rotational and temporal optimizations. $P$ values reflect rotation of the user as she views multiple tagged objects. $T$ values reflect time elapsed walking.**

substantial motion) and *micro* scales (small movements of the device in hand). The details follow.

## Learning Macro Trajectories

As the server matches images to its object database, it tracks which objects the user has observed in the recent past (across minutes of walking motion). When observing object $i$ followed by object $j$, the server records an event $k$ represented by a net rotation $R_k$ (normalized between $0 \leq R < 2\pi$) and by measured time $M_k$ (in arbitrary units). Of course, not all users will view $i$ and $j$ from the same location, and hence $R_k$ will vary. Let $E_k^R$ denote some unknown "error" by which $R_k$ will deviate from the mean rotation from $i$ to $j$ (computed across all users). Similarly, let $E_k^M$ denote some unknown "error" by which $M_k$ will deviate from the mean time taken between the observations of $i$ and $j$.

With $K$ observation pairs, we may construct a pair of optimizations for $N$ tags, independently solving for rotation and time. In addition to the known values $R_k, M_k$ and unknown values $E_k^R, E_k^M$, we further introduce unknowns for each annotation $i$, $P_i$ and $\forall j > i | T_{ij}$. Values of $P_i$ may be understood as the "rotation" of annotation $i$ relative to an arbitrary frame of reference (consistent across all annotations). Thus, $|P_i - P_j|$ may be understood as the the mean observed rotation between annotations $i$ and $j$. $T_{ij}$ may be understood as the mean time to observe annotation $j$ after observing $i$.

Values of $P_i$ and $T_{ij}$ do not represent absolute properties of the annotated object. Instead, they reflect *where the object is typically observed*, relative to others – how much rotation is typical from annotation $A$ to $B$ to $C$, and how much time typically elapses in between – illustrated in Figure 9.
Tables 1 and 2 provide optimizations for rotation and time. To ensure computational tractability in dense areas with many annotations, it was important to formulate each as a linear program (LP). An earlier attempt using a mixed integer linear program (MILP) was unsolvable in days of compute time – these solve in seconds using CPLEX. Given low latency, the server re-solves both LPs for each new annotation, immediately as it is added to the database.

These optimizations explicitly track error attributed to each observation recorded in the annotation database. The solutions to these error terms yield "confidence" estimates for the solved rotation and time estimates, per annotation. For annotation $i$, median error per observation is computed as:

$$E_*^R(i) := \forall j,k : \text{median}\{E_k^R | \exists R_k^{i \to j} \vee \exists R_k^{j \to i}\}$$
$$E_*^M(i) := \forall j,k : \text{median}\{E_k^M | \exists M_k^{i \to j} \vee \exists M_k^{j \to i}\}$$

OverLay combines rotational ($P$) and temporal ($T$) values with these error terms ($E_*^R, E_*^M$) to score which annotations should be prioritized as the best *candidate set* for a user.

## Learning Micro Trajectories

*Macro trajectories* reflect the general, typical behavior of users as they move from annotation to annotation. This is quite useful for users who also move in this typical fashion. For others, the value degrades. For example, if most users walk down the center of a hallway, the angles at which various annotations are observed will reflect observation from this typical trajectory. If a user walks atypically against the wall, the angles she observes will be shifted, and the spatial optimization will become less correct *for her*. Equivalently, a user walking exceptionally quickly will incur faster timings than the typical walking pace. To accommodate these atypical motion patterns, OverLay builds a simple model of *invariant spatial relationships* that hold true even for the atypical user. Simply, these relationships characterize if an annotation $A$ is observed, some annotation $B$ may be known to appear to the *left*, *right*, *above*, or *below* $A$. Especially as the user makes *micro* (rotational) motions (e.g., scanning around a room looking for annotations), these pairwise spatial relationships enable OverLay to shortlist those annotations the user is most likely to encounter next.

Smartphone cameras have a substantial field of view at their widest setting (zoom is not used in our prototype). In environments with dense annotations, often multiple annotations will be in view simultaneously – detected when a camera frame matches to two or more annotations concurrently. Figure 11 provides pseudocode for inferring *micro trajectories* when two annotations appear simultaneously in view. When a visual match is made we can compute the 2D centroid of the match in the image. Centroids are compared to infer the general direction from one to the other (e.g., right). Figure 10(a) shows the centroid for $B$ appearing right of $A$ (the circle in the figure denoting the camera).

$$
\begin{array}{rcl}
\textbf{Minimize} & & \sum_{\forall k \in 1 \ldots K} E_k^R \\
\textbf{Subject to} & & \\
\forall R_k^{i \to j} | i < j & : & P_i - P_j \leq R_k^{i \to j} + E_k^R \\
 & & P_i - P_j > R_k^{i \to j} - E_k^R \\
\forall R_k^{i \to j} | j < i & : & P_i - P_j \leq -R_k^{j \to i} + E_k^R \\
 & & P_i - P_j > -R_k^{j \to i} - E_k^R \\
\forall i \in 1 \ldots N & : & 0 \leq P_i < 2\pi(N-1) \\
\forall k \in 1 \ldots K & : & 0 \leq E_k^R < 2\pi \\
\textbf{Solving for} & & \\
\forall i \in 1 \ldots N & : & P_i \\
\forall k \in 1 \ldots K & : & E_k^R \\
\textbf{With parameters} & & \\
\forall k \in 1 \ldots K | \exists i, j & : & 0 \leq R_k^{i \to j} < 2\pi
\end{array}
$$

| Name | Parameter / Variable Interpretation |
|---|---|
| $R_k^{i \to j}$ | Observation $k$; rotation from anno. $i$ to $j$ |
| $P_i$ | Rotational position of a anno. $i$ |
| $E_k^R$ | Rotational error for observation $k$ |

**Table 1: LP, relative angular (rotational) position.**

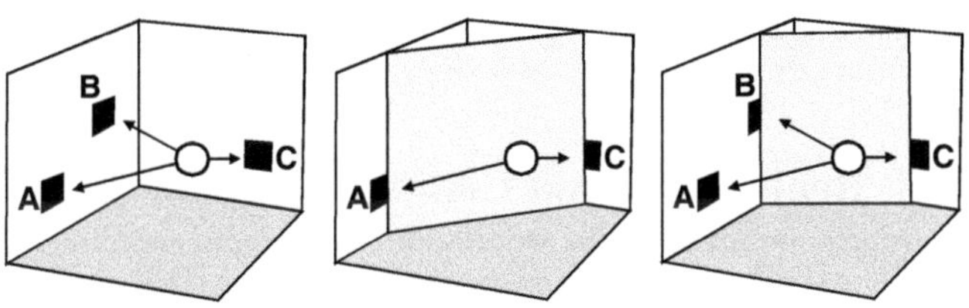


**Figure 10: Micro trajectories for annotations $A, B, C$ on walls of a room. (a) $A \leftrightarrow B$ invariant. (b) $A \leftrightarrow C$ *conditionally invariant* – effectively invariant, so long as the observer remains outside the shaded boundary. (c) $B \leftrightarrow C$ also conditionally invariant.**

Under certain conditions, *these micro trajectory relationships will hold invariant, regardless of where in the room $A$ and $B$ are observed.* $A \leftrightarrow B$ is *spatially invariant* when $A$ and $B$ are coplanar with a room's wall (e.g., mounted). OverLay assumes $A \leftrightarrow B$ *could* be spatially invariant, if they have been found simultaneously in view by one or more observers. Assume w.l.o.g. $A$ is positioned left of $B$. At the time of retrieval, once $A$ is observed, we may immediately shortlist $B$ as a potential candidate. If the user rotates right (tracked by gyroscope), we increase our confidence: $B$ should shortly appear in view.

Shortlisting is most productive when $A, B$ are truly spatially invariant, the condition does not have to hold universally to be useful. Often, a *conditional invariance* occurs. That is, a region in which the observer may view $A, B$ such that the condition holds. In Figure 10, $A \leftrightarrow B$ reflects true spatial invariance. $A \leftrightarrow C$ are invariant under the condition that the observer remains outside the illustrated shaded "barrier." Similarly, $B \leftrightarrow C$ are also conditionally invariant.

$$
\begin{array}{rcl}
\textbf{Minimize} & & \sum_{\forall k \in 1 \ldots K} E_k^M \\
\textbf{Subject to} & & \\
\forall M_k^{i \to j} | i \leq j & : & T_{ij} \leq M_k^{i \to j} + E_k^M \\
 & & T_{ij} > M_k^{i \to j} - E_k^M \\
\forall M_k^{i \to j} | i > j & : & T_{ji} \leq -M_k^{j \to i} + E_k^M \\
 & & T_{ji} > -M_k^{j \to i} - E_k^M \\
\forall i < j \in 1 \ldots N & : & 0 \leq T_{ij} \\
\forall k \in 1 \ldots K & : & 0 \leq E_k < \max\{\forall k | M_k\} \\
\textbf{Solving for} & & \\
\forall i < j \in 1 \ldots N & : & T_{ij} \\
\forall k \in 1 \ldots K & : & E_k^M \\
\textbf{With parameters} & & \\
\forall k \in 1 \ldots K | \exists i, j & : & 0 \leq M_k^{i \to j}
\end{array}
$$

| Name | Parameter / Variable Interpretation |
|---|---|
| $M_k^{i \to j}$ | Observation $k$; time from anno. $i$ to $j$ |
| $T_{ij}$ | Time separation between anno. $i$ and $j$ |
| $E_k^M$ | Temporal error for observation $k$ |

**Table 2: LP, relative temporal spacing.**

**Prioritizing Candidate Tags**

At the *macro* and *micro* scales, OverLay develops an understanding of which annotation a user is most likely to encounter next, given a current observation. OverLay prioritizes candidate annotations according to this understanding before matching against the user's live camera imagery. The prioritization is applied as follows.

Consider Figure 12. OverLay considers time then rotation. First, we construct a spatiotemporal radius $M_U$ around the user, reflecting the set of annotations it would have been *possible* for the user to visit since the last match (illustrated as $A$) in $M_U$ time. For each annotation $i$, we expand the radius to $M_U + E_*^M(i)$, to account for the computed temporal uncertainty. Annotation $i$ is accepted to step two only if $T_{Ai} < M_U + E_*^M(i)$, otherwise it is immediately rejected.
Next, we are able to impose an ordering based on rotation. Given a user's rotation $R_U$ since tag $A$, we find orientation $P_U := (P_A + R_U) \bmod 2\pi$, the user's current orientation. We consider the rotational distance from any tag $i$ as $|P_i - P_U| \bmod 2\pi + E_*^R(i)/2$. We include only half of the error term to reflect the 50-50 probability that the error should work in favor or against accepting tag $i$.

Since micro trajectory is rotation, we may factor it into the (macro) rotational distance scores. If a micro trajectory relationship {ABOVE, BELOW, LEFT, RIGHT} is inferred with annotation $i$ and the user's gyroscope reflects motion in the corresponding direction (i.e., clockwise for right, counterclockwise for left, up for above, and down for below) from $i$, we subtract a value $w\pi$ from the rotational score. $w$ is a weight which lets us (de)emphasize micro trajectory context.

**Regionalized Analysis**

When the OverLay application is first launched, the user has no history of recent matches – OverLay has no notion yet of the user's macro/micro trajectory. To limit the search space, OverLay leverages the user's rough GPS location. The user's

Input : $t_i$ = Descriptors of image $i$
    $t_j$ = Descriptors of image $j$
Output: Spatial relationships $\in$ {A, B, L, R, NONE}
$match_{ij} = descriptorMatch(t_i, t_j)$
**if** $|match_{ij}| \geq threshold$ **then**
  $centroid_i = computeCentroid(t_i \in match_{ij})$
  $centroid_j = computeCentroid(t_j \in match_{ij})$
  $W_i = Width_i; H_i = Height_i;$
  `/** inferRelation example **/`
  **if** $centroid_i \in [(W_i/3, 2W_i/3), (0, H_i/3)]$ and $centroid_j \in [(W_j/3, 2W_j/3), (2H_j/3, H_j)]$ **then**
    `relationship is above-below`
  **end if**
  `/** inferRelation example end **/`
  **return** $inferRelation(centroid_i, centroid_j)$
**end if**
**return** *none*

**Figure 11: Pseudocode: micro trajectory inference.**

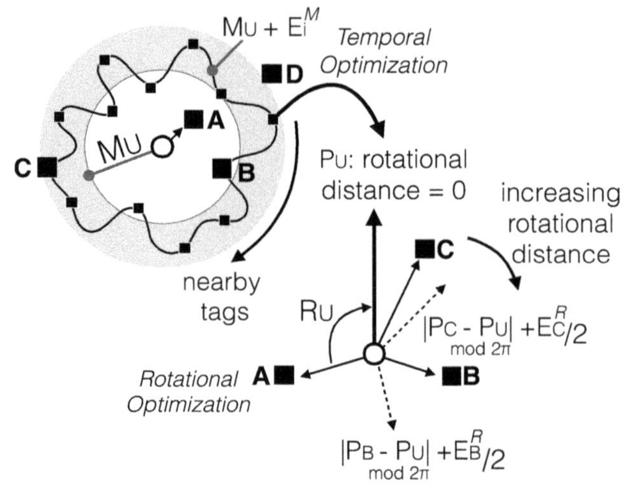


**Figure 12: Prioritizing the annotation candidate set. We compare the user's last matched tag $A$ with all other tags. Elapsed time $T_U$ defines a radius (containing $B$), expanded by error term $E_*^M(i)$ for each annotation (containing $C$, $D$ excluded.) $B, C$, and others in this expanded radius proceed to step 2 (rest rejected). They are prioritized by rotational deviance from the user, including error terms $E_*^R(i)$.**

location and the location of every annotation in the database is discretized using the "Geohash" algorithm. OverLay attempts matches only against annotations in the user's square Geohash "cell" or in any of the eight neighboring cells.

## 4.2 Learning from Retrieval

Initially, an annotated object is only represented by a single image in the database. Intuitively, the crowdsourced effect of many users viewing the same annotated object (over time) might be useful: more views → more visual context → a refined database → higher precision for later users. OverLay exploits this potential for *learning from retrieval*.

Learning from retrieval is a periodic four step process, run as a background server daemon. (1) All past retrievals and the original annotation images are used to reconstruct a 3D model of the object and surroundings (a process known as *structure from motion*, or specifically, *bundle adjustment*). The 3D model provides a geometric representation of both the object and each *camera pose*, the 3D position and orientation of the user during retrieval. (2) Due to false positive matches ($\approx$ 5% in our tests), 3D reconstruction [10] can yield erroneous camera poses. Fortunately, these retrievals are outliers in the resultant 3D *point cloud*. We remove these false camera poses by performing outlier removal based on the point cloud centroid and variance of the model points. (3) All remaining retrievals contain the same object, but often contain redundant visual information. Including all retrieval imagery in the annotation database would create bloat and increase matching latency. Instead, OverLay identifies the most diverse retrievals (i.e., angles from which the object appears sufficiently different). For this, we use KMEANS clustering on 3D camera pose angles to cluster similar retrieval poses together. (4) We select one representative view from each of the retrieval clusters to construct a secondary matching database for each annotation, to be invoked only when primary matching with the original fails.

Since learning from retrieval creates a secondary database, it imposes zero latency for image frames which match the primary database. When the primary database is insufficient, the secondary database provides valuable matches. The overall experience is thus improved as users who would otherwise see no annotation content are presented with results from the secondary database, albeit at a slight delay.

## 4.3 Real-time Cloud Computer Vision

A primary requirement for Mobile AR is that annotations must quickly appear as the user scans around a room. This section describes necessary engineering refinements to ensure that OverLay can surpass a tight usability bound.

### Sub-selecting Frame Regions from Gyroscope

Often the user will hold the device reasonably steady while reading on-screen annotations. Frames generated during this time are near duplicate of the previous frames and need not be uploaded. We leverage accelerometer and gyroscope to cheaply identify such frames. No further processing steps are invoked; simply the previously-identified annotation remains on screen.

Even when the user makes nontrivial movements, there is still often partial overlap between the prior and current frames. This overlap can be inferred by (1) monitoring accelerometer and gyroscope to deduce that a user's movements are primarily rotational (and not from walking); and (2) inferring the angular difference from gyroscope to see which portions of the view are new. The gyroscope measures the relative three-axis angular movement of device from a previous position (a point in time), and infers the percentage of new content that should have appeared in the field of view. Specifically, for a lens projecting a rectilinear image, angle of view may be computed in radians as $\alpha = 2\arctan(d/2f)$ where $d$ is the sensor size and $f$ is the focal length. Assume w.l.o.g. that the gyroscope records a clockwise rotation $0 < \beta < \alpha$ radians. Only $100\beta/\alpha\%$ of the screen contains new content, and only that portion should be shipped to the server for analysis.

#### Managing Frame Motion Blur

User hand movements from "scanning" the physical environment result in blurred camera frames (motion blur and active adjustment from the autofocus system), causing computer vision underperformance. By applying a Canny edge detector for blur detection, we score frames to select only those most likely to contain usable imagery. As Canny is relatively robust to image resolution, we can apply it at low computational latency to a down-sampled preview image – the first step of the algorithm is to apply Gaussian blur to remove image speckle, roughly equivalent to resolution downsampling. By throwing away useless frames without further processing, we achieve a higher effective frame rate of useful image data, both improving accuracy and latency.

#### Extracting, Matching, and Refining Image Features

Once a crisp frame (or frame region) has been uploaded to the server and a prioritized candidate set of annotated images has been identified, we must then match the frame imagery to these annotations. Each annotation is represented in the database as a collection of local image features, computed using the SURF [14] feature extractor and descriptor. Each feature is represented as a keypoint, an $x$, $y$ position in the image at which the feature has been detected and a descriptor vector of 64 floating point values. Two features are considered similar as an inverse function of the Euclidean distance ($l^2$-norm) between their respective descriptor vectors.

We find $M_{AB}$, the minimum distance bipartite matching between feature vectors for a pair of images $I_A$ and $I_B$. Each descriptor value $d_i^A$ of $I_A$ may be compared with each descriptor value $d_j^B$ of $I_B$. Let $m_i^{AB}$ be the feature descriptor of $I_B$ which has the lowest Euclidean distance from feature $i$ in $I_A$. Formally, $m_i^{AB} := \forall d_j^B$, argmin $l^2(d_i^A, d_j^B)$. Let $M_{AB} := \{\forall i, m_i^{AB}\}$, the set of all such best matches from image $I_A$ into image $I_B$.

Although optimal, $M_{AB}$ likely has many false positive, poor image descriptor matches. We may now refine to $M_{AB}^* \subseteq M_{AB}$, the subset of high quality matches from $I_A$ into image $I_B$. From common practice, we apply the following tests to construct $M_{AB}^*$ from $M_{AB}$:

**Distance Ratio** Ratio of the Euclidean distance of the best match value ($m_i^{AB}$) to the distance of the second best match value. Typically, threshold $\geq 0.8$.

**Cross Check** Ensures the inverse match $I_B \rightarrow I_A$ would result in the same pairs; $m_i^{AB} = j \Leftrightarrow m_j^{BA} = i$. Thus, $M_{AB}^* = M_{BA}^*$.

**Homography** Runs RANSAC (random sample consensus) to find an approximate projective transformation from $I_A$ to $I_B$. A match $m_i^{AB}$ is rejected if it is an outlier to this transformation.

Early testing revealed an excess number of false positive or negative matches, depending on the thresholds given to homography. So, we add a final binary test for the entire image.

**Slope Variance** Imagine $I_A$ and $I_B$ composited into a single image, $I_A$ on left and $I_B$ on right. For each match $m_i^{AB} = j$, we draw a line from $I_A$ to $I_B$ between the corresponding feature keypoints. We compute the slope for each line. If the variance of slope is low, all remaining values $m_i^{AB}$ are accepted. Otherwise we reject all matches and set $M_{AB}^* := \emptyset$.

OverLay performs all computer vision (SURF feature extraction, feature matching, and feature filtering) on GPU.

#### Asynchronous GPU Pipeline

To exact the value of mobile-to-cloud computer vision computational offloading, we must leverage the extreme parallelism available on a modern GPU. The cost of that GPU is only acceptable if we can amortize across multiple concurrent users. However, we found that available implementations of feature extraction and matching assume a single thread of execution (i.e., a single CPU core controlling the entire GPU for each synchronous operation).

When multiple CPU threads attempt concurrent access, conflicts arise. While it is possible to use a CPU semaphore to isolate access to the GPU, this approach leads to intolerably poor GPU utilization. Instead, we heavily modify the CUDA (NVIDIA architecture GPU programming language) implementations of SURF, feature matching, and feature filtering to utilize CUDA Streams. CUDA Streams provides an asynchronous GPU processing pipeline based on a series of micro operations (e.g., copying data into or out of the GPU memory, memory allocation, and kernel execution).

## 5. EVALUATION

From the onset, we were keen on a real-time evaluation of OverLay with a live fully-functional prototype in the hands of unbiased volunteers. However, we did not want to burden these volunteers with tasks of identifying correct versus incorrect annotations, or other feedback on ground-truth. This could slow them down or distract them from the seamless (environment scanning) experience that OverLay should offer. Thus, for purposes of evaluation, we added instrumentation to the server side of our system. All uploaded imagery and sensory data were recorded to disk. Later we were able to replay the image and sensing data, and exactly observe the ground truth – what the users saw in each video frame, their camera pose, their camera motion, the time between viewing, etc. We labeled $\approx 10K$ video frames based on whether the annotations displayed on screen were correct or not. Note that in some frames, one or many annotations should appear (if multiple objects are present). In others, "NO ANNOTATION" is expected. Importantly, this form of "offline" control allowed us to improve the system even after the live user studies, and test the results through accurate data playback and emulation.

### 5.1 Experiment Methodology

We annotated $\approx$ 100 objects on the $2^{nd}$ floor of the coordinated science lab (CSL) – the floor is around $50m$ long and $10m$ wide, as shown in Figure 13. Objects are annotated just once, and selected arbitrarily – they include printers, exit signs, posters, research prototypes, water fountains, objects on display, etc. Now, with a completely functional prototype, we invited volunteers[2] to use it live. With limited guidance, volunteers were free to explore the building, scan whatever interested them, and they would see the matching annotations live on their phone screen – all without our interference. In this way, their walking and scanning with the device reflects their natural behavior. If they found the experience unenjoyable, they were free to give up at any point. Thankfully, our volunteers were universally curious and excited by

[2] In compliance with our institutions' policies for IRB.

the experience, each spending far longer exploring the space than we asked or anticipated (table below)

| | |
|---|---|
| Number of tagged objects | 100 |
| Volunteers, Men / Woman / Total | 6 / 3 / 9 |
| Images captured, Min / Mean / Max | 700 / 1188 / 1800 |
| Volunteer time, Min / Mean / Max | 12 / 18 / 27 min |

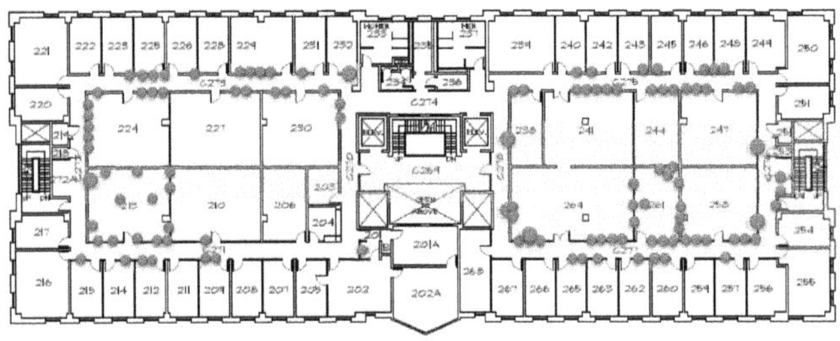

**Figure 13: $2^{nd}$ floor CSL: dots denote annotations.**

Our volunteers were only asked to use a single version of our system, CONSERVATIVE. The CONSERVATIVE version includes our complete solution except for optimizations to prune the search space of candidate annotations. From the CONSERVATIVE test data, we emulate (offline) results for our ROTATION and TIME macro trajectory optimizations as well as with micro Trajectory identification. In all subsequent versions, the processed client imagery and sensory data are identical (e.g., gyroscope-based frame sub-selection is used in all). As CONSERVATIVE performs worse in terms of latency, the end user experience can be assumed to be the lower bound of what OverLay can achieve.

## 5.2 Metrics

Across all volunteers, we evaluate accuracy and latency *per frame* and *per annotation*. Each frame uploaded from the device app to the server is considered in isolation. It may be blurred or crisp; it may capture an annotated object or not; it may be captured intentionally (while the user is actively looking at an object) or incidentally (as the user moves about the space). Similarly, each annotation has unique performance characteristics – it may be easy or hard to identify; the search space optimizations may characterize its location well or poorly. Therefore, each graph presents a CDF (empirical distribution) of accuracy or latency with 100 points, one for each annotated object, generated from $\approx 10K$ samples, one for each frame.

Let $Y$ be the set of all processed frames. Let $V \subset Y$ be the set of frames containing annotated object $k$. Let $P \subset Y$ be the set of frames identified by our system as having $k$. Then, $V \setminus P$ denotes our system's false negative predictions, $P \setminus V$ denotes false positive predictions, and $Y \setminus V$ denotes the set of frames which do not contain object $k$. *We evaluate OverLay's prediction efficacy by the following standard metrics of information retrieval:*

**Precision**$_k$ $= |V \cap P|/|P|$
: i.e., among all frames that OverLay believes has object $k$, what fraction truly has $k$.

**Recall**$_k$ $|V \cap P|/|V|$
: i.e., among all frames that truly have object $k$, what fraction was identified by OverLay.

**Fallout**$_k$ $|(Y \setminus V) \cap P|/|Y \setminus V|$
: i.e., among all frames that truly do not have object $k$, what fraction was believed to have $k$.

## 5.3 Comparison with Approximate Matching

Our image-to-database matching process employs brute force (on GPU) to find the optimal match. As an alternative, a number of heuristics exist for approximate matching [30]. By design, these approximate schemes are computationally inexpensive (i.e., runs faster), at the cost of greater error. To understand this tradeoff, we compare all proposed schemes against APPROXIMATE. Briefly, APPROXIMATE matching computes a set of FLANN indices and loads them into CPU memory – a one-time operation. Later, each incoming image descriptors are matched in real time against these indices (using schemes like KDTREE, KMEANS). The best matched descriptor is up-voted, ultimately resulting in a best match image. To be favorable to APPROXIMATE, we pick the $top-5$ images, and perform a brute-force search on it – as long as the correct candidate is in this set of 5, brute force should output the correct match. This reflects an optimistic view of APPROXIMATE, and we will plot its results alongside ours.

## 5.4 Overall Results: Accuracy and Latency

Figure 14 presents CDFs of overall accuracy as (a) precision, (b) recall, and (c) fallout. Graphs compare the accuracy of our CONSERVATIVE scheme against optimizations ROTATION, TIME, and FULL, as well as APPROXIMATE. Figure 15 presents a CDF of end-to-end latency (system responsiveness). Each curve reflects 100% of volunteer data, every frame captured by the system. None of the volunteers had any prior exposure to the system nor were given any special knowledge of its technical approach.

We would expect, and confirm here, that the strongest accuracy performance is achieved by the CONSERVATIVE version of our system. Precision is consistently high indicating that when an annotation is shown, it is almost always accurate. ROTATION, TIME, and FULL reflect optimizations aimed to improve system responsiveness (not accuracy). ROTATION is found to be comparatively unreliable in isolation. TIME is highly accurate, and to our surprise, often outperforms even the FULL version of the system (which jointly optimizes across time and rotation, along with micro trajectory context). Upon deeper inspection of the data (the $\approx 10K$ camera frames recording by our volunteers), we find our volunteers were more consistent in time taken to move between objects than they were for angular separation. All these schemes consistently outperform APPROXIMATE, implying how latency reduction indeed incurs a strong penalty in vision-only schemes.

Of course, recall is not impressive, implying that some annotations are not captured/displayed in time. We partly expected this since – if a user's hand shakes, if lighting is poor, if the person views the object from a corner, they will all affect recall. This clearly motivates the need to learn from new retrievals made by users over time – Figure 17 will later demonstrate the efficacy of retrieval.

Latency results also align well with intuition (Figure 15). The sensor optimizations (ROTATION, TIME, and FULL) heavily outperform CONSERVATIVE. APPROXIMATE performs slightly worse than sensor optimizations. Since GPU implementation of APPROXIMATE is unavailable, we estimate latency numbers using 3-dimension implementation of KDTREE and scale

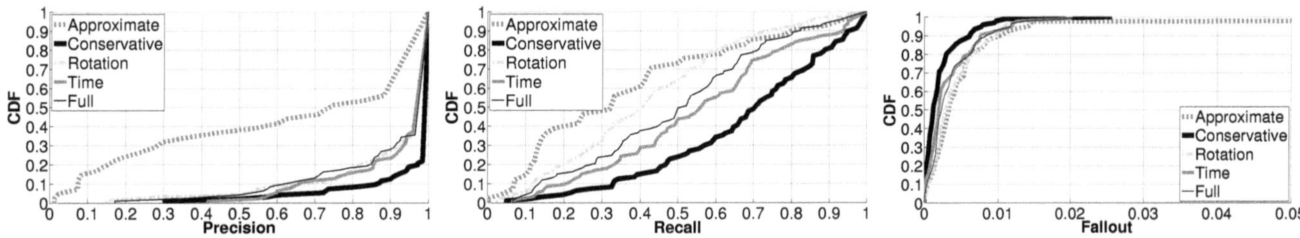


**Figure 14: Main accuracy results: (a) Precision; (b) Recall; and (c) Fallout. Graphs compare accuracy of our CONSERVATIVE system against enhancements through optimizations, ROTATION, TIME, and FULL.**

accordingly for 64-dimension SURF descriptors. For each of the optimization-based approaches (ROTATION, TIME, and FULL), our budgeted candidate set size is 10 annotations, one tenth of the total 100 annotated objects. As shown in Figure 16, matching is the primary latency component in the CONSERVATIVE system version, reduced here by 90%. Overall speedup from the added optimizations is around $4x$.

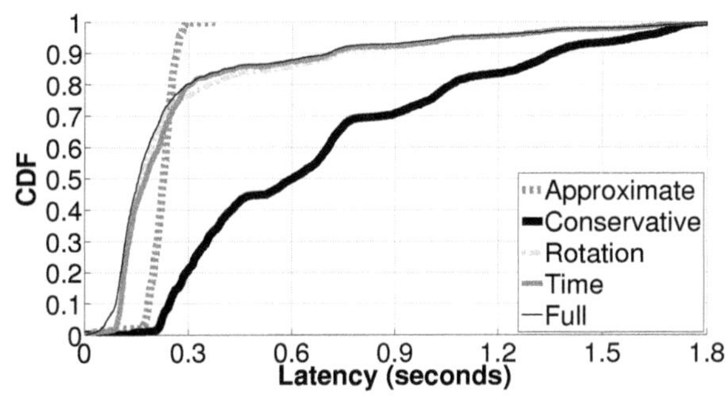


**Figure 15: Latency: Optimizations reduce candidate set from 100 to 10, decreasing median end-to-end latency by more than a factor of 4, to 180ms.**

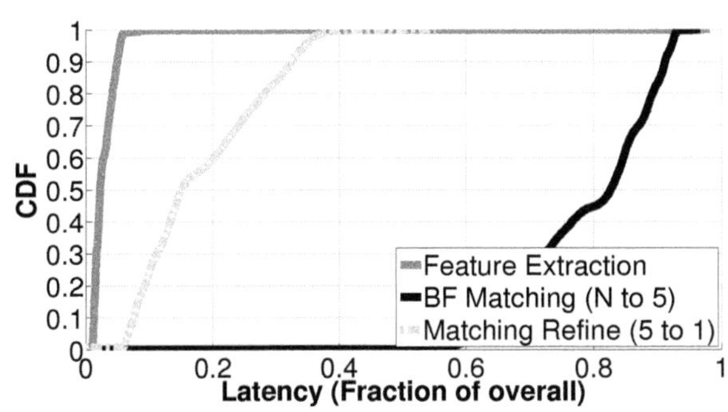


**Figure 16: Computer vision latency by component, CONSERVATIVE system version. Optimized versions eliminate 90% of the primary component, matching.**

## 5.5 Learning from Retrievals

OverLay only requires users to annotate objects once, with a single image. While this places minimal burden on an end user, diverse perspectives of the object cannot be captured. Thus, when another user retrieves from a sufficiently different location/angle/lighting condition, the object is sometimes not recognized, diminishing recall (as noted earlier). The issues can get pronounced over time, with minor changes in object's appearance and background. Robust multi-view feature matching is still an unsolved problem in computer vision [37], so its mandatory that features of a stored object are updated periodically. Figure 17 shows the efficacy of such learning from retrievals. Consistent improvements are evident in both precision and recall. Some objects were still unrecognized – delving into the data, we recognized cases of poor network connection (even transient disconnection), heavily delaying the frames from reaching the server. Such cases are entirely out of our control for OverLay.

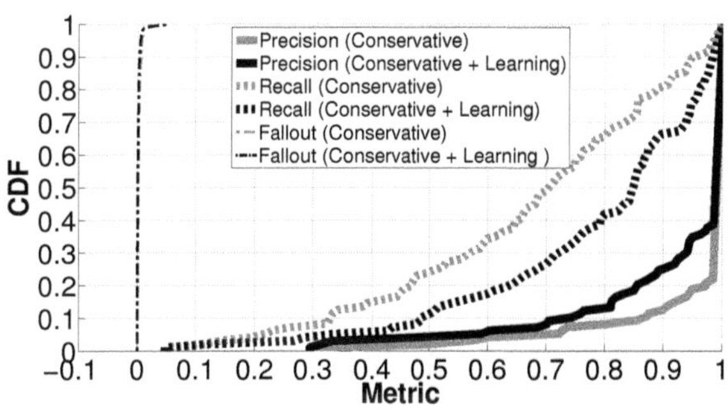


**Figure 17: Enhanced accuracy results based on learning from past three retrievals chosen based on diversity in the camera pose in the 3D reconstruction when compared against CONSERVATIVE system.**

## 5.6 Micro Benchmarks

We evaluate some details of OverLay's performance through micro-benchmarks. Figure 18 shows decrease in responsiveness with multiple simultaneous clients on the same server, under (a) the CONSERVATIVE (most GPU intensive) version of the system and (b) the optimized FULL version. The CONSERVATIVE version cannot support more than three concurrent clients; FULL supports six at equal user latency.

Figure 19 shows energy consumed (Samsung Galaxy S4 Android). System power measured using Monsoon Solutions hardware monitor through the battery contacts. Figure 20 shows app UI performance in display frames per second (FPS). Running the complete system, the app maintains 8 FPS (median) on a Samsung Galaxy S4.
Figure 21 shows the percentage of blurred frames rejected without upload to the server, per volunteer. Overall, 46% of frames are rejected without upload, saving substantial upload bandwidth and server processing.

# 6. LIMITATIONS AND DISCUSSION

We consider several limitations of the OverLay prototype as implemented today, and avenues for future enhancement.

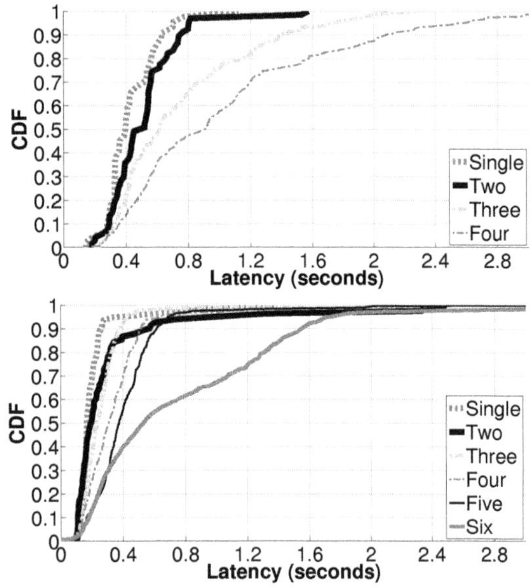


**Figure 18: Responsiveness, simultaneous clients, (a) CONSERVATIVE and (b) FULL optimized version.**

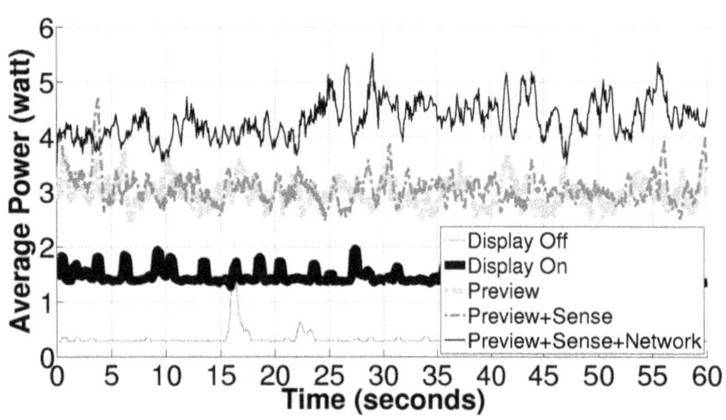


**Figure 19: Energy consumption. DISPLAY + PREVIEW (camera enabled) + SENSE (GPS, gyroscope, accelerometer, and compass) + NETWORK TRANSFER reflects the complete system (average $\approx 4.5$ watts).**

### Exact placement of the annotations on screen

OverLay displays object annotations at a fixed screen location. An enhanced user interface might display the annotation directly atop or adjacent to the corresponding object. Our rationale for this this simplification is twofold: (1) when the annotation is authored, the user does not explicitly mark which part of the image corresponds to the object of interest – *multiple objects* might be in view, and (2) during retrieval, the annotation would need to remain aligned to the object, even as the user makes fine hand movements.

The "multiple objects" issue may be addressed in varied ways: (A) requiring the user to draw a rectangle or denote the intended object; (B) marking *candidate objects* on screen and allowing the user to make a simple multiple-choice selection; or (C) assuming the center of the user's screen most likely corresponds to the intended object, and tolerating errors when this assumption does not hold. The "annotation alignment" issue can be roughly accommodated by tracking fine hand movements and shifting the annotations on screen in the opposite direction. Optical flow and gyroscope based techniques are both possible for such motion compensation;

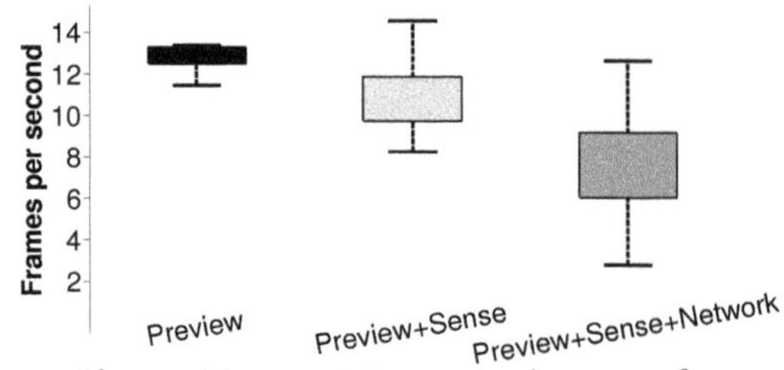


**Figure 20: App UI responsiveness, frames/second.**

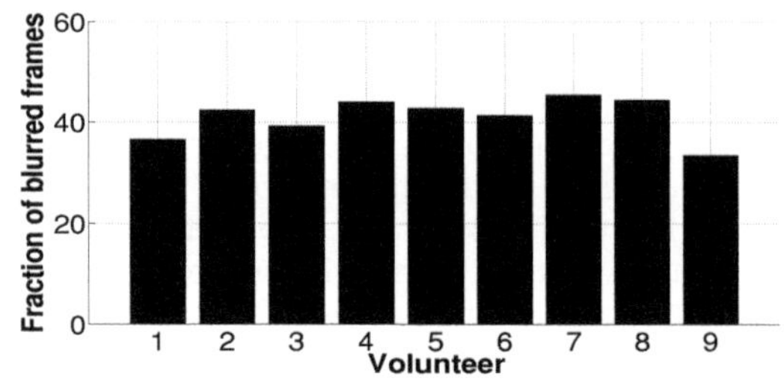


**Figure 21: Percentage of frames rejected due to blur.**

recent work has even combined the two for enhanced precision and speed [22].

### Searching for annotations

OverLay is most compelling when annotations are dense – when many objects around are annotated. Value decreases with sparsity: the user must "hunt" more between annotated objects. One possibility is to use rough location estimates passively to alert the user when annotations are nearby, for example, through a signature vibration. Once the user opens the app, on-screen arrows might indicate which direction the user should rotate until a nearby annotation appears in view. OverLay is being readied for the *Illinois Distributed Museum* project on the UIUC campus [3], and such "on-screen arrows" will be added in the next release.

### Handling appearance changes

OverLay records image data to identify the physical location of an annotation. However, OverLay must cope with environmental dynamism, including changes to the object's appearance. One of our users annotated his office desk, and its appearance changed every day. While we cannot expect to address extreme changes, micro-movement of objects or minor appearance changes could be accommodated through continuous database enhancement, discarding older visual data to be replaced with that from later retrievals. OverLay does not apply to objects such as digital displays — whose appearance changes continuously. Similarly, OverLay does not immediately apply if a retrieval is made from a significantly different angle to that of annotation. However, some of these limitations are addressable using techniques discussed in 5.5.

### Distinguishing objects in close proximity

OverLay cannot distinguish visually-similar objects in close proximity. This might be problematic in environments with repetitive design features, such as different name tags on adjacent doors in a corridor. False positives will undoubtably result, although our geometric linear optimizations will partly help (Section 4.1).

# 7. RELATED WORK

Mobile augmented reality has been studied for more than a decade. [21, 31] outline a broad vision and discuss various possible applications. [42] considers the challenges, strategies, and limitations one needs to overcome in building mobile AR systems. [27] and [16] address two important aspects of Mobile AR – low-power continuous vision and code offloading to cloud. Several works establish sensing-based primitives for Mobile AR: GPS-compass triangulation [17, 19, 32]; camera-pose estimation using Kinect depth sensors [23]; and gyroscope based camera-pose tracking [44]. Some have leveraged physical markers deployed in the environment such as: QR codes [34], color markers [29], and RFID tags [39]. Others have applied 3D camera pose estimation, finding a correspondence between 2D image features and a 3D world coordinate system [25, 40, 45]. [38] is the closest research prototype to our work, using SURF feature extraction and location based pruning to enable mobile AR in outdoor environments. Our primary advantage beyond this effort is in applicability of our search space optimizations to indoor environments, *with zero reliance on location information*.

While prior art has often considered computer vision and mobile sensing in isolation, there has been some recent success in hybridization. Smartphone inertial sensors can be used to imitate or enhance the computation of various vision algorithms (e.g., bundle adjustment, optical flow) [24, 28]. [4, 26] fuse vision and sensing to create hyperlapse video summaries (a form of offline augmented reality). [26] takes a vision-oriented approach, strongly relaxing any latency requirement. [4] priorities lightweight computation, emphasizing gyroscope. [43] proposes energy efficient design of a distributed image search engine. Most of these research are bottom-up and do not deliver an end-to-end application – the challenges of very little training, physical indoor space, and human authoring of content, combined with opportunities of geometric optimizations, makes this paper's design constraints unique.

Object recognition (OR) for mobile devices is a overlapping research effort to Mobile AR, such as Amazon's Fire phone or Google Goggles [1, 2, 15]. Visual MIMO [12], communication between LED screens and a camera, can be used for Mobile AR but the approach is not generalizable. In contrast to mobile AR, OR systems: (1) typically operate on a trained model of multiple images of the same object [1, 2, 18, 20]; (2) are typically invariant to the user's context; and (3) typically do not allow dynamic insertions to the content database as retraining costs are often high. Qualcomm Vuforia [7] is a commercial Mobile AR SDK for object recognition and 3D object tracking. Videoguide [8] is a Vuforia app used to animate architecture work in Barcelona museum. Contrary to Vuforia which requires deployment in advance, OverLay is an anywhere, anytime system for everyone.

# 8. CONCLUSION

Mobile AR has been an exciting, yet unrealized, vision. This paper attempts to complete the vision within the constraints of today's smartphones. We combine cloud-offloaded computer vision with an optimization framework on space and time – capturing typical human behavior and pruning the computer vision search space. In conjunction with a suite of engineered systems optimizations, these techniques enable a practical system for mobile AR. We demonstrate a response time well within tolerable bounds yet while preserving strong accuracy. Our approach provides a ready-to-use platform for enabling a broad spectrum of compelling mobile AR applications, and is currently deployed in our building and being readied for a campus wide roll-out.

# 9. ACKNOWLEDGMENTS

We sincerely thank our many volunteers, Professor Peter Druschel our shepherd, as well the anonymous reviewers for their invaluable feedback. We are also grateful to Intel, Google, and NSF for partially funding this research through the grant NSF 1430064.

# 10. REFERENCES

[1] Amazon fire phone. `https://developer.amazon.com/public/solutions/devices/fire-phone`.

[2] Google goggles. `https://play.google.com/store/apps/details?id=com.google.android.apps.unveil&hl=en`.

[3] Illinois distributed museum. `http://distributedmuseum.blogspot.com/`.

[4] Instagram hyperlapse. `http://hyperlapse.instagram.com/`.

[5] Mobile augmented reality, video demonstration. `http://synrg.csl.illinois.edu/projects/MobileAR/`.

[6] Project tango. `https://www.google.com/atap/projecttango/`.

[7] Qualcomm vuforia. `https://www.qualcomm.com/products/vuforia`.

[8] Videoguide, antoni gaudi modernist museum in barcelona. `http://www.casabatllo.es/en/visit/videoguide`.

[9] Wikitude. `http://www.wikitude.com/`.

[10] S. Agarwal, Y. Furukawa, N. Snavely, I. Simon, B. Curless, S. M. Seitz, and R. Szeliski. Building rome in a day. *Communications of the ACM*, 54(10):105–112, 2011.

[11] C. Arth and D. Schmalstieg. Challenges of large-scale augmented reality on smartphones. *Graz University of Technology, Graz*, pages 1–4, 2011.

[12] A. Ashok, M. Gruteser, N. Mandayam, J. Silva, M. Varga, and K. Dana. Challenge: mobile optical networks through visual mimo. In *MobiCom*, pages 105–112. ACM, 2010.

[13] R. Azuma, Y. Baillot, R. Behringer, S. Feiner, S. Julier, and B. MacIntyre. Recent advances in augmented reality. *Computer Graphics and Applications, IEEE*, 21(6):34–47, 2001.

[14] H. Bay, T. Tuytelaars, and L. Van Gool. Surf: Speeded up robust features. In *ECCV*, pages 404–417. Springer, 2006.

[15] D. M. Chen, S. S. Tsai, R. Vedantham, R. Grzeszczuk, and B. Girod. Streaming mobile augmented reality on mobile phones. In *ISMAR*, pages 181–182. IEEE, 2009.

[16] E. Cuervo, A. Balasubramanian, D.-k. Cho, A. Wolman, S. Saroiu, R. Chandra, and P. Bahl. Maui: making smartphones last longer with code offload. In *MobiSys*, pages 49–62. ACM, 2010.

[17] S. Feiner, B. MacIntyre, T. Höllerer, and A. Webster. A touring machine: Prototyping 3d mobile augmented

reality systems for exploring the urban environment. *Personal Technologies*, 1(4):208–217, 1997.

[18] P. Föckler, T. Zeidler, B. Brombach, E. Bruns, and O. Bimber. Phoneguide: museum guidance supported by on-device object recognition on mobile phones. In *Proceedings of the 4th international conference on Mobile and ubiquitous multimedia*, pages 3–10. ACM, 2005.

[19] S. Gammeter, A. Gassmann, L. Bossard, T. Quack, and L. Van Gool. Server-side object recognition and client-side object tracking for mobile augmented reality. In *CVPR Workshops*, pages 1–8. IEEE, 2010.

[20] B. Girod and C. et al. Mobile visual search. *Signal Processing Magazine, IEEE*, 28(4):61–76, 2011.

[21] A. Henrysson and M. Ollila. Umar: Ubiquitous mobile augmented reality. In *Proceedings of the 3rd international conference on Mobile and ubiquitous multimedia*, pages 41–45. ACM, 2004.

[22] M. Hwangbo, J.-S. Kim, and T. Kanade. Inertial-aided klt feature tracking for a moving camera. In *Intelligent Robots and Systems, 2009. IROS 2009. IEEE/RSJ International Conference on*, pages 1909–1916. IEEE, 2009.

[23] S. Izadi et al. Kinectfusion: real-time 3d reconstruction and interaction using a moving depth camera. In *UIST*. ACM, 2011.

[24] P. Jain, J. Manweiler, A. Acharya, and K. Beaty. Focus: clustering crowdsourced videos by line-of-sight. In *SenSys*, page 8. ACM, 2013.

[25] G. Klein and D. Murray. Parallel tracking and mapping on a camera phone. In *ISMAR*, pages 83–86. IEEE, 2009.

[26] J. Kopf, M. F. Cohen, and R. Szeliski. First-person hyper-lapse videos. *TOG*, 33(4):78, 2014.

[27] R. LiKamWa, B. Priyantha, M. Philipose, L. Zhong, and P. Bahl. Energy characterization and optimization of image sensing toward continuous mobile vision. In *MobiSys*, pages 69–82. ACM, 2013.

[28] J. G. Manweiler, P. Jain, and R. Roy Choudhury. Satellites in our pockets: an object positioning system using smartphones. In *MobiSys*, pages 211–224. ACM, 2012.

[29] P. Mistry and P. Maes. Sixthsense: a wearable gestural interface. In *ACM SIGGRAPH ASIA 2009 Sketches*, page 11. ACM, 2009.

[30] M. Muja and D. G. Lowe. Fast approximate nearest neighbors with automatic algorithm configuration. In *VISAPP (1)*, pages 331–340, 2009.

[31] H. E. Pence. Smartphones, smart objects, and augmented reality. *The Reference Librarian*, 52(1-2):136–145, 2010.

[32] W. Piekarski and B. Thomas. Arquake: the outdoor augmented reality gaming system. *Communications of the ACM*, 45(1):36–38, 2002.

[33] C. Qin, X. Bao, R. Roy Choudhury, and S. Nelakuditi. Tagsense: a smartphone-based approach to automatic image tagging. In *MobiSys*, pages 1–14. ACM, 2011.

[34] J. Rekimoto and Y. Ayatsuka. Cybercode: designing augmented reality environments with visual tags. In *Proceedings of DARE 2000 on Designing augmented reality environments*, pages 1–10. ACM, 2000.

[35] J. P. Rolland, L. Davis, and Y. Baillot. A survey of tracking technology for virtual environments. *Fundamentals of wearable computers and augmented reality*, 1:67–112, 2001.

[36] M. Satyanarayanan, P. Bahl, R. Caceres, and N. Davies. The case for vm-based cloudlets in mobile computing. *Pervasive Computing, IEEE*, 8(4):14–23, 2009.

[37] F. Schaffalitzky and A. Zisserman. Multi-view matching for unordered image sets, or âĂIJhow do i organize my holiday snaps?âĂİ. In *Computer VisionâĂŤECCV 2002*, pages 414–431. Springer, 2002.

[38] G. Takacs and C. et al. Outdoors augmented reality on mobile phone using loxel-based visual feature organization. In *Proceedings of the 1st ACM international conference on Multimedia information retrieval*, pages 427–434. ACM, 2008.

[39] R. Tenmoku, M. Kanbara, and N. Yokoya. A wearable augmented reality system using positioning infrastructures and a pedometer. In *ISWC*, pages 110–110. IEEE Computer Society, 2003.

[40] D. Wagner, G. Reitmayr, A. Mulloni, T. Drummond, and D. Schmalstieg. Pose tracking from natural features on mobile phones. In *ISMAR*, pages 125–134. IEEE Computer Society, 2008.

[41] D. Wagner and D. Schmalstieg. First steps towards handheld augmented reality. In *ISWC*, pages 127–127. IEEE Computer Society, 2003.

[42] D. Wagner and D. Schmalstieg. Making augmented reality practical on mobile phones, part 1. *Computer Graphics and Applications, IEEE*, 29(3):12–15, 2009.

[43] T. Yan, D. Ganesan, and R. Manmatha. Distributed image search in camera sensor networks. In *SenSys*, pages 155–168. ACM, 2008.

[44] S. You, U. Neumann, and R. Azuma. Hybrid inertial and vision tracking for augmented reality registration. In *Virtual Reality, 1999. Proceedings., IEEE*, pages 260–267. IEEE, 1999.

[45] F. Zhou, H. B.-L. Duh, and M. Billinghurst. Trends in augmented reality tracking, interaction and display: A review of ten years of ismar. In *ISMAR*, pages 193–202. IEEE Computer Society, 2008.

# Visually Fingerprinting Humans without Face Recognition

He Wang
University of Illinois at Urbana-Champaign

Xuan Bao
Samsung Research America

Romit Roy Choudhury
University of Illinois at Urbana-Champaign

Srihari Nelakuditi
University of South Carolina

## ABSTRACT

This paper develops techniques using which humans can be visually recognized. While face recognition would be one approach to this problem, we believe that it may not be always possible to see a person's face. Our technique is complementary to face recognition, and exploits the intuition that human motion patterns and clothing colors can together encode several bits of information. Treating this information as a "temporary fingerprint", it may be feasible to recognize an individual with reasonable consistency, while allowing her to *turn off* the fingerprint at will.

One application of visual fingerprints relates to augmented reality, in which an individual looks at other people through her camera-enabled glass (e.g., Google Glass) and views information about them. Another application is in privacy-preserving pictures – Alice should be able to broadcast her "temporary fingerprint" to all cameras in the vicinity along with a privacy preference, saying "remove me". If a stranger's video happens to include Alice, the device can recognize her fingerprint in the video and erase her completely. This paper develops the core visual fingerprinting engine – *InSight* – on the platform of Android smartphones and a backend server running MATLAB and OpenCV. Results from real world experiments show that 12 individuals can be discriminated with 90% accuracy using 6 seconds of video/motion observations. Video based emulation confirms scalability up to 40 users.

## Categories and Subject Descriptors

H.3.4 [**Information Storage and Retrieval**]: Systems and Software; C.2.4 [**Computer-Communication Networks**]: Distributed Systems

## Keywords

Visual fingerprinting; smartphones; augmented reality; matching


*MobiSys'15*, May 18–22, 2015, Florence, Italy.

http://dx.doi.org/10.1145/2742647.2742671.

**Figure 1: Example social event: Alice views people's posts displayed in her Google Glass. The whole operation orchestrated by the *InSight* server running in the cloud.**

## 1. INTRODUCTION

Imagine a near future where humans are carrying smartphones and wearing camera-embedded glasses, such as the Google Glass. This paper intends to recognize a human by looking at him from any angle, even when his face is not visible. For instance, Alice may look at people around her in a social gathering and see the names of each individual – like a virtual name tag – suitably overlaid on her Google Glass display. Where revealing names is undesirable, only a short message could be posted. People at the airport could post "looking to share a cab ", students in a startup event could post "seeking a co-founder", and Alice could view each individual's posts above their heads (Figure 1). In general, the ability to differentiate individuals visually could enable human-centric augmented reality [21, 30].

Face recognition [29, 34] is a possible approach to the above problem. However, faces are not always visible. Moreover, many people express discomfort releasing their profile pictures to the cloud, given that it can become a permanent identifier for de-anonymizing other content in the web [7]. Ideally, what is necessary is a *temporary* visual identifier, that can be activated at will, and will identify the individual momentarily but not later.

This paper pursues the intuition that human motion patterns and visual appearance (e.g., clothing colors) can together serve as a temporary visual fingerprint. The key idea is simple. Consider Alice looking at an individual $X$ through her Google Glass (or smartphone camera). The *InSight* server could request Alice to upload a short video snippet of that individual, and use the frame sequence in this video to extract a motion fingerprint of $X$, denoted by $V_X^{Alice}$. This motion fingerprint is essentially a string of micro-activities such as walking direction, stepping frequency, stopping, turning, etc., extracted from the video. The server can simultaneously request sensor data (e.g., accelerometer, gyroscope, compass) from people around Alice, and extract a similar motion fingerprint from it. Let $M_i$ denote this sensor-based motion fingerprint for user $i$. By matching $V_X^{Alice}$ against $M_i$ of each user $i$, the server can find the strongest match, say for $i = Bob$. The server can convey to Alice that she is looking at Bob and display Bob's message (e.g., "looking for interns") on her glass.

Generalizing, visual fingerprints may not only be from motion patterns, but also from clothing colors, body structure, etc. If Alice recognizes Bob through motion fingerprints, she can extract Bob's clothing features and update a database inside the *InSight* server. In the steady state, the database would cache clothing fingerprints for different individuals. When John looks at Bob later, his Glass only needs to send an image of Bob. The server can extract the clothing fingerprint from the image sent by John and match against pre-computed clothing fingerprints, ultimately notifying John that he is looking at Bob. In summary, we believe that a person's non-facial visual appearance can serve as an identifier. There is evidence of this opportunity given that humans can often recognize other humans without looking at their faces. This paper demonstrates that (wearable) cameras and smartphones can together achieve the same.

Realizing the above idea presents a number of challenges. Extracting fingerprints from sensors and videos can be non-trivial, even though a variety of tools are available in the signal processing and computer vision literature. The fingerprints need to be general for scalability across individuals, while being adequately discriminating for identification. Moreover, fingerprint matching must be done across incompatible dimensions (sensor and vision) requiring the system to cope with normalization issues, dynamic ranges, depth, perspectives, etc. Even for matching clothing fingerprints, challenges emerge due to lighting conditions, wrinkles, and various view angles – the front and back of a dress may have different colors and patterns. Finally, the system needs to support incremental deployment (i.e., not everyone may run *InSight*) while bandwidth and energy overheads should be minimal.

While developing a robust system is challenging, we find that the rich diversity in human behavior offers hope. People walk/turn/pause at different time instants, even when they are walking in groups – observed long enough, their motion sequence should begin to become unique. Encouraged by this opportunity of uniqueness, we adopt a "digital" approach to processing the information. Put differently, we express fingerprints as *strings* defined on a pre-specified motion alphabet. An example fingerprint could be *EEEOOR*..., where *E*, *O*, and *R* correspond to the actions of *walkEast*, *noMotion*, and *turnAround*, respectively. Such motion alphabets are extracted from both sensors and videos, allowing *InSight* to employ string matching algorithms for comparing fingerprints.

*InSight* translates these ideas into a functional system using Android Galaxy phones and videos taken from Google Glasses. We have not attained real-time operations yet – the server runs on MATLAB with links to OpenCV and machine learning libraries, and returns the result within ten seconds. Evaluations from real world demonstrate the ability to discriminate 12 individuals with 90% accuracy, using 6 seconds of video/motion observations. Video based emulation shows the ability to scale the technique to the order of 40 people. The main contributions may be summarized below.

- *Identifying the possibility that human clothing colors and motion patterns could serve as temporary fingerprints, complementing face recognition.* Using these fingerprints as new degrees of freedom for human-centric visual applications.
- *Quantifying the viability and accuracy of fingerprinting with real-world human behavior.* Building a fully functional prototype and demonstrating promise through micro-benchmarks, real-user evaluation, and larger scale video simulation.

The subsequent sections will expand on these contributions beginning with an overview of *InSight*, followed by detailed system design. However, we first discuss a few potential applications.

## 2. APPLICATIONS

The goal of this paper is to develop the core visual fingerprinting primitives, with the hope that they will enable new use-cases or aid known applications. We briefly discuss a few possibilities here different from the augmented reality application described above.

### (1) Privacy Preserving Pictures/Videos (PPP)

The proliferation of cameras, and wearables cameras in recent years, has raised various discussions on privacy. Many citizens have expressed discomfort at the thought of being included in a video or a picture taken by a stranger, even if it was legally done in a public place. Today's solution is to hastily move out of the camera's field of view when it is clear that a picture is being taken. Of course, this is not always possible because people are often unaware that videos or pictures are being taken around them. Sensitized by this, many privacy conscious users have wished for a capability to express their privacy preferences, such as "please remove me from the video".

Now, assume Alice is taking a video, and Bob, present in the field of view, intends to be removed from Alice's video. Bob can share his motion fingerprint with the server. When Alice takes the video and sends it to the server, visual fingerprints can be computed for every individual in the video, and compared against Bob's. A match suggests Bob is indeed in the video – *InSight* can then remove Bob by replacing him with background imagery in the video. Authors in [6] recently proposed using QR codes on clothing as a means of expressing privacy preferences – we believe *InSight* is a more usable solution.

### (2) Visual Addressing and Communication

A grocery store is in conversation with us regarding the applicability of *InSight* for customer localization and communication. The idea is to use wide-angle surveillance cameras mounted on high ceilings to observe the top view of moving customers (each customer visible to the camera as a small blob). Consider the case where Alice is shopping in the store and her smartphone records her motion fingerprint, $M_{Alice}$. The surveillance camera could also compute her motion fingerprint from the video frames, $V_{Alice}$. Of course, it might take longer since the motion alphabet (from a top view) will be limited — the camera would only detect `moving`, `paused`, and `moving direction`. However, even these few bits of information should be adequate to disambiguate customers in the scale of a minute (no two customers move/pause in lock step for that long).

Now, it should be possible for the camera to send a message to Alice, by including $V_{Alice}$ as an address inside the message (like a virtual MAC address). When Alice's device receives the message, a comparison between $M_{Alice}$ and $V_{Alice}$ would indicate that the message is meant for her. Thus, the grocery store can now establish a communication channel with Alice, sending her location-based product information (since the camera exactly knows Alice's location). Even Alice can ask questions such as "where can I find brown rice" and the store can respond with "ahead on your right, at the bottom shelf". Observe that this *visual address-based communication* offers privacy since Alice need not reveal her (permanent) MAC/device IDs. Moreover, she can turn off her motion sensors at will, terminating all interaction with the store.

While the above applications may not be the best, they define the design landscape reasonably well for us to build a generic visual fingerprinting system. The most suitable applications, we hope, will emerge in time.

# 3. SYSTEM OVERVIEW

This section presents a functional overview of *InSight*; the technical components will follow in Section 4. For preserving context, we use the augmented reality application as the central theme in the rest of the paper, although the techniques extend (with minor modifications) to the other applications.

Consider a university-organized matchmaking event for startups, where variety of students and faculty come with the goal of forming teams. Upon entering, users check-in with the *InSight* server and specify their rough locations. Later, say Alice looks at an individual $X$ through her Google Glass (or smartphone camera) and requests to identify the individual. During the initial bootstrap phase, the *InSight* server running in the cloud asks Alice's glass to record and upload a video snippet of that individual. The server also requests sensor data (accelerometer, gyroscope, and compass) from smartphones of all people around Alice (Figure 2). Once the data arrives, the server processes these sensor data and extracts motion fingerprints, $M_i$, for each user $i$. This motion fingerprint is essentially a feature vector, where features include `isStanding`, `isWalking`, `walking-direction`, `step-duration`, `phase`, `isRotating`, `pause-timings`, etc. The server also analyzes the video snippet from Alice and computes a similar motion fingerprint, but from the consecutive frames of the video. Let $V_X^{Alice}$ denote this video-based motion fingerprint. By matching $V_X^{Alice}$ against all values of $M_i$, *InSight* finds the strongest match, say for $i = Bob$. If this matching score is greater than a confidence threshold, the server conveys to Alice that she is looking at Bob, and displays the message Bob intends to share with others, e.g., "PhD student in CS, looking for CEO for mobile analytics startup".

Now, once *InSight* recognizes Bob in the video snippet, it extracts Bob's color fingerprint, $C_{Bob}$, and updates a fingerprint database. This fingerprint essentially captures color features and patterns from Bob's clothing. Thus, in the steady state, when everyone's color fingerprint is registered in the database, users no longer need to update videos or sensor readings. If John looks at Bob

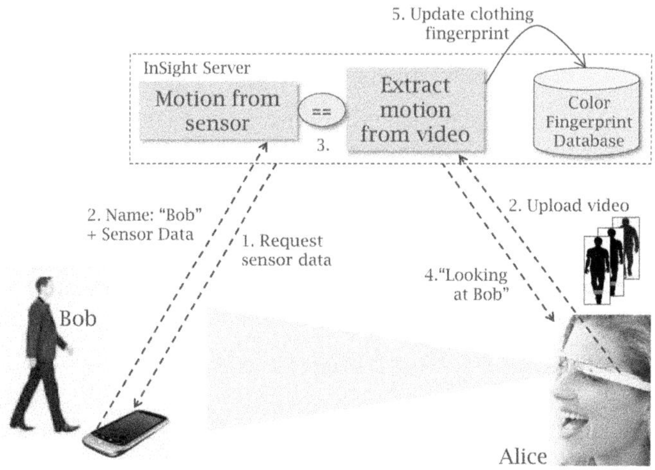


**Figure 2: Motion fingerprint based matching during initialization and for new *InSight* users.**

later (see Figure 3), his Glass only needs to send to the server an image of Bob. The server extracts the color fingerprint from John's image, $C_X^{John}$ and matches against all $C_i$ in the database (the candidate set can be trimmed using John's rough location). Assuming $C_X^{John}$ matches best with $C_{i=Bob}$, and the matching score is above a threshold, the server informs John that he is looking at Bob. Of course, these color fingerprints are valid in the time scale of events – for another event next day, people will be wearing different clothes, and the color database will have to be re-populated.

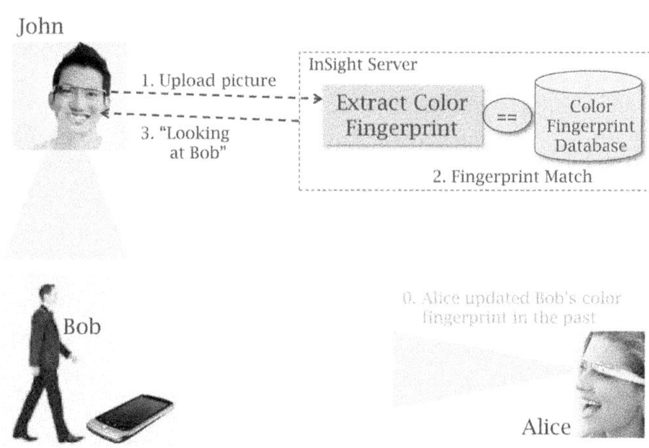


**Figure 3: Color fingerprint matching in steady state.**

We make two observations about the properties of motion and color fingerprinting.

1. A short window of sensor data is mostly adequate to compute a discriminating motion fingerprint for an individual. This is due to the inherent diversity of human motion, i.e., people's micro-motions are not likely to be synchronous for long durations, and the first instance of "asynchrony" can be used to tell them apart.

2. As mentioned earlier, once Alice identifies Bob using motion fingerprints, Bob's color fingerprint, $C_{Bob}^{Alice}$, is added to the fingerprint database ($C_{Bob} = C_{Bob}^{Alice}$). When John

identifies Bob later, perhaps from a different angle, Bob's fingerprint is further refined ($C_{Bob} = C_{Bob} \cup C_{Bob}^{John}$).

In general, people's color fingerprints increasingly become complete over time, which improves the accuracy of recognition, which further completes the fingerprint. Thus, *motion fingerprints are only necessary to "register" a person for the first time. Once* InSight *has bootstrapped, color profiles become effective, and motion fingerprints are used only to boost matching confidence, if necessary.* The details on what constitutes color and motion fingerprints are presented in Section 4.

## Matching Motion Fingerprints

Motion–fingerprint matching at the *InSight* server is non-trivial because the fingerprints are in different domains – $M_{Bob}$ is obtained from accelerometer/gyroscope/compass readings, while $V_X^{Alice}$ is extracted from video frames. To bring compatibility, we propose to translate all motion fingerprints into a common *semantic alphabet*, where example alphabets are "walking north", "rotating", "pausing" (see example alphabets in Table 1). Thus, both $M_{Bob}$ and $V_X^{Alice}$ are represented as strings on this alphabet, and fingerprint matching boils down to string matching. As an example, say Bob and Neil walk northward for 3 time units, and then Bob pauses while Neil continues walking for one more unit, and then Neil pauses too. Their respective strings will then be $M_{Bob} = NNNOO...$ and $M_{Neil} = NNNNO...$, and it would be possible to tell them apart at the fourth time unit. Specifically, if Alice is looking at Bob, then *InSight* will compute $V_X^{Alice} = NNNOO...$, which is expected to match better with $M_{Bob}$. In our actual implementation, the motion alphabet is far more sophisticated, including different directions of walking, duration and phase of walking steps, rotations, etc. In fact, for the above case, *InSight* will analyze the duration and phase of walking steps, and unless Bob and Neil are well synchronized in their footsteps, they will be separated within 4 time units.

**Table 1: A few examples of motion alphabet. *InSight* uses much more fine grained alphabets.**

| | |
|---|---|
| $O$ | stationary, paused |
| $N$ | walking north |
| $S$ | walking south |
| $E$ | walking east |
| $W$ | waling west |
| $R$ | rotating |
| $U$ | undetermined motion |

# 4. SYSTEM DESIGN

This section describes the extraction of motion and color fingerprints from sensor and video data, followed by fingerprint matching schemes. The techniques borrow from literature where suitable, with appropriate adaptions to this specific cross-sensor application.

## 4.1 Extracting motion from sensor data

We begin with a description of how sensor readings from Bob's smartphone are translated into a motion string. The key motion alphabets that make up this string are derived from: (1) rotation, (2) walking, (3) walking step duration, (4) walking step phase, and (5) walking direction.

• **Rotation Detection**: Since the phone can be in an unknown orientation, we cannot rely on any single axis of the gyroscope (x, y, or z) to properly detect rotation. Therefore, we first project the rotation rate vector $r = (r_x, r_y, r_z)$ on to gravity vector $g = (g_x, g_y, g_z)$ in the phone's coordinate system, i.e., $r_{gravity} = (r_x g_x + r_y g_y + r_z g_z)/\sqrt{g_x^2 + g_y^2 + g_z^2}$. Then, the rotation angle around gravity is $\alpha_{gravity} = \int r_{gravity} dt$. If $\alpha_{gravity}$ exceeds a certain threshold, the user's motion is labeled as rotating (denoted by $R$ in the motion alphabet). The alphabet $R$ is essentially a binary indicator and its natural to ask: *why not extract more bits of information from rotation?* This is because detecting various degrees of human rotation from videos is a difficult problem.

• **Walking Detection**: The act of human walking manifests on the accelerometer with periodic high/low impulses as well as some rotation around the gravity axis. However, due to movements of the phone inside the pocket, and certain unusual gait patterns, simple threshold based schemes were inadequate to recognize walking patterns. Instead, we employ a bagged decision tree model and train it with two features, namely (1) standard deviation on the magnitude of accelerometers, and (2) rotation around gravity. We omit details in the interest of space, but found this to offer high consistency (as evident in Section 5.1).

• **Walking Step Duration**: Given that people walk with varying speeds, the duration of walking steps can be a useful discriminator. To this end, we first detect if the user is walking; if so, we apply a standard Kalman filter on the accelerometer data to first smooth out the reading and accurately identify the local maxima. These local peaks – shown in Figure 4 – are actually the time points when the human feet land on the ground. The peaks closer to the taller raw impulses correspond to the leg that carries the phone. The step duration, denoted $T_{step}$, may be computed as half of the time window between two consecutive peaks. Note that $T_{step}$ can be computed without prior knowledge of which pocket the phone is in. Even if the phone is in the shirt pocket, or held in the hand, such peaks are visible, and $T_{step}$ can be computed. We have not evaluated the case of backpacks and jacket pockets.

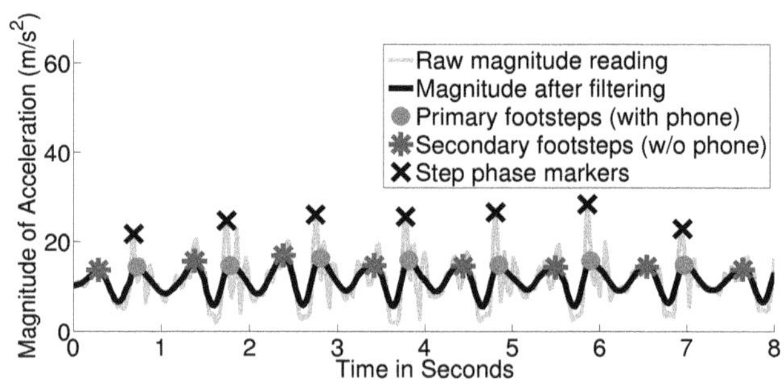


**Figure 4: Walking: magnitude of accelerometer readings (smoothed) with step marker while user is walking.**

• **Walking Phase**: Even when two users are walking at the same speed, i.e., $T_{step}$ is identical, their exact step timings may be out of phase. Thus, the phase of walking can also be a component of the motion fingerprint of a person. To this end, we use the peak around the bigger jerk as the step phase marker, shown in Figure 4. If different users exhibit these peaks at different times, they may be separated so long as time is appropriately synchronized among devices. If the accuracy of synchronization is upper bounded by, say $\delta$, then the phase differences can be measured in that granularity. We show later that our synchronization is in the order of $\frac{T_{step}}{3}$, permitting us to create 3 buckets of users with respect to their walking phases.

• **Walking direction**: *InSight* intends to leverage the user's walking direction, with some granularity, as an attribute of her motion. However, walking direction estimation is challenging given that the phone is in an unknown orientation on the user's body. The problem is difficult because the act of walking imposes various kinds of vertical, horizontal, and sideward forces on the smartphone (to stabilize the body), and there is a narrow window during which the acceleration on the phone is most dominantly along the user's heading direction. This narrow time window is actually when the user's leg swings (or rotates) forward, captured by the cross product of rotation axis, $\mathscr{R}_{axis}$ and gravity $g$. More precisely, the user's heading vector, $H = \mathscr{R}_{axis} \times g$, illustrated in Figure 5. Given the rotation matrix $\mathscr{R}$ from gyroscope, $\mathscr{R}_{axis}$ is the null space of $(\mathscr{R} - I)$ ($I$ is the identity matrix) and rotation angle $\mathscr{R}_\theta = arccos(\frac{trace(\mathscr{R}) - 1}{2})$. In our system, we make $\mathscr{R}_\theta$ always positive and the sign of $\mathscr{R}_{axis}$ is determined by the right-hand rule. When the leg carrying the phone (called the primary leg) swings, the $\mathscr{R}_{axis} \times g$ points to user's heading direction; the same cross product points in the opposite direction when the secondary leg swings.

**Figure 5: Heading vector = cross product of rotation axis and gravity.**

Importantly, this cross product must be computed when the leg is in full swing, otherwise, the sensor data can be polluted with noise (especially when the leg slows down and strikes the ground). To avoid such noise, *InSight* chooses a period of 30% of $T_{step}$ starting from the time when the secondary leg strikes the ground (i.e., when the primary leg is about to swing). $\mathscr{R}_{axis}$ is derived from this time window. Figure 6(b) shows the $H(t) = \mathscr{R}_{axis}(t) \times g(t)$, where $\mathscr{R}_{axis}(t)$ is the rotation axis during $[t, t+30\%T_{step}]$. Clearly, $H(t)$ alternates its direction as the user swings its primary and secondary legs alternately.

The heading vector is in the phone's coordinate system and needs to be interpreted in the global magnetic reference frame (i.e., with respect to North). For this, we project the magnetometer reading to the horizontal plane [32], and record the angle between this projected vector and the heading vector. Figure 6 shows the results. Vertical dotted lines are the moments when the heading vector is recorded. As expected, heading direction alternates roughly 180° between primary and secondary steps. At the moments of heading vector recordings, the direction matches the ground truth as it corresponds to the window when the primary leg swings. Upon close scrutiny, we find that the estimated walking directions are always slightly higher than

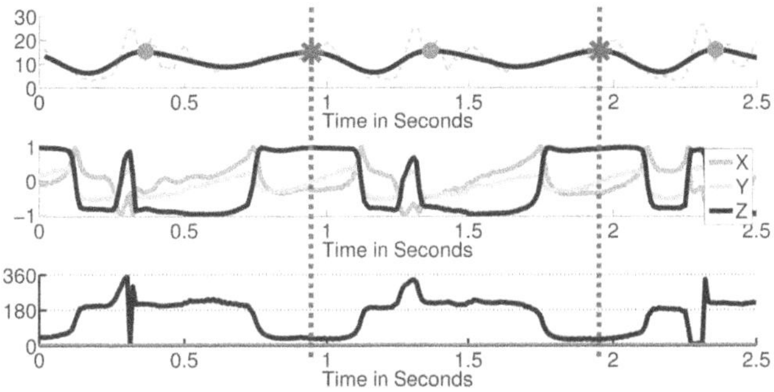


**Figure 6: Walking direction: (top) Magnitude of acceleration while user is walking. (middle) Heading direction. Dotted lines are the moments when heading vector is calculated; (bottom) Estimated walking direction (ground truth of 0° in red). As expected, they match at the primary steps and differ by 180° at the secondary steps (with heading direction opposite of the primary).**

the ground truth. This is because human leg motions are often slightly diagonal, and the actual walking direction is an average of two diagonals from two steps, resulting in forward locomotion. We use a calibration factor of 35° to compensate for this effect. The final walking direction is divided into 8 directions, in the granularity of 45°, which creates 8 motion alphabets. The following subsection describes how the same motion alphabets are also derived from videos (of Bob) captured from (Alice's) Google Glass camera.

## 4.2 Extracting motion from video

Given that a video can contain multiple moving individuals, *InSight*'s first step is to mark and track every person in the video. This calls for enveloping each individual with a bounding box. Of course, for motion related insights (such as walking period, phase, etc.) lower regions of the bounding box needs to be processed to extract alphabets. This section describes each of these steps systematically.

• **Detection and Tracking**: To detect and track humans in the video, we borrow existing techniques from computer vision [11, 12] and modify it per *InSight*'s needs. Using the borrowed techniques, Figures 7 (a)-(e) show the accuracy of placing a bounding box around each person, along with a confidence score. To cope with false positives, we only consider the boxes with a confidence score above 50. Now, to track people across the video frames, we again employ a Kalman filter [19]. Formally, the state of each *tracker* is denoted by $\mathbf{s}_k = [x_k, y_k, v_{x_k}, v_{y_k}]^T$, where $\{x_k, y_k\}$ and $\{v_{x_k}, v_{y_k}\}$ are the position and speed of the person in the 2D frame $k$. Observation $z$ is the center of the bounding box obtained from the pedestrian detector. We use the following state and observation equations.

$$s_{k+1} = Fs_k + \omega_k \quad (1)$$

$$z_k = Hs_k + u_k \quad (2)$$

where

$$F = \begin{pmatrix} 1 & 0 & dt & 0 \\ 0 & 1 & 0 & dt \\ 0 & 0 & 1 & 0 \\ 0 & 0 & 0 & 1 \end{pmatrix} \qquad H = \begin{pmatrix} 1 & 0 & 0 & 0 \\ 0 & 1 & 0 & 0 \end{pmatrix}$$

$dt$ in F is the duration between adjacent frames. $\omega_k \sim N(0, Q_k)$ and $u_k \sim N(0, R_k)$ are state model noise and measurement noise

Figure 7: Pedestrian detection and tracking: (a)~(e) are with pedestrian detection; (f)~(j) are with tracking. (b) shows a temporal miss. (c) shows a temporally wrong detection. (d) shows a miss caused by occlusion. As we can see from (f) ~ (j), these errors are fixed by tracking. (f) ~ (j) also show people can be tracked properly after temporal encounters.

respectively. $Q_k$ and $R_k$ are proportional to the person's size. $Q_k$ is also inversely proportional to the number of tracked frames.

When processing a new video frame, we employ the method in [8] to associate each bounding box with a tracker. In the association process, we leverage the observation that position, direction of speed, and size, are not likely to change significantly in adjacent frames; in fact, the higher the speed of the user, the larger the chance that the direction of speed remains the same. Thus, after association, each target's Kalman filter goes one iteration further. Unlike [8], where a single particle filter is used to track the center of the target, we enrich each tracker with four corners of the bounding box. Each corner is also passed through a Kalman filter as described above. The bounding box thus filtered is later utilized for estimating walking direction and step phase detection.

Figures 7(a)-(e) show the results from pedestrian detection. Although reasonable, it fails to detect a person in Figure 7(b), falsely detects one in Figure 7(c), and suffers from occlusion in Figure 7(d). However, Figures 7(f)-(j) show the efficacy of applying tracking. Also, Figures 7(f) and 7(j) show that people can be tracked properly even after temporal encounters.

• **IsWalking and Walking Direction**: To detect whether the target person is walking, we use the speed of the bounding box. Since speed is one of the states in the Kalman filter, we obtain it from the tracking process described earlier. Figure 8 shows 2D speed of the center of the bounding box – higher speeds denoted with a longer arrow. People in Figures 8(a)-(e) are walking and the person in Figure 8(f) is standing in place. If a person's movement has significant speed, then we can detect walking by the mean of 2D speed, $s_{xy}$, normalized by that person's height, during a predefined period as given by Equation 3.

$$s_{xy} = \frac{1}{L_P} \sum_{i \in P} \frac{\sqrt{(c_x^i)^2 + (c_y^i)^2}}{h^i} \tag{3}$$

where P is a collection of frames in the period; $L_P$ is the cardinality of $P$; $c_x^i$ and $c_y^i$ are the horizontal and vertical components of the target's center speed at frame $i$; and $h^i$ is the target's height at frame i. However, if the person is walking mainly along the line perpendicular to the camera's plane (Figures 8(d) and (e)), $s_{xy}$ can be as small as the case where the person is just standing. To cope with this scenario, we use a term $s_z$ to estimate the target's motion along the z axis.

$$s_z = \alpha_z \frac{h^{L_P} - h^1}{mean\{h^i : i \in P\}} \tag{4}$$

where $\alpha_z$ is a calibration factor such that $|s_z|$ and $s_{xy}$ are roughly similar if the target's speed is the same whether moving in 2D plane or along the z axis. When the combined value of $s_{xy} + |s_z|$ of a target is above a certain threshold, we mark that person as walking.

We calculate the user's walking direction with respect to the camera's facing direction. The relative direction is quantized to 8 bins with centers at 0°, 45°, 90°,..., 315°. To classify the direction, we train a model with bagged decision tree with features $s_x$ (Equation 5), $s_z$, and $d_z$, where $d_z$ is the slope of linear regression of heights. Intuitively, the bounding box's speed and increase/decrease of its height together help in determining the user's relative direction.

$$s_x = \frac{1}{L_P} \sum_{i \in P} \frac{c_x^i}{h^i} \tag{5}$$

• **Step Duration and Phase**: To detect the duration and phase of walking steps, we choose the lower region of the bounding box obtained from the tracker. We represent the motion in this region through Space-Time Interest Points, which essentially captures fast changes in video pixels. This technique is borrowed from [13] and we omit the details in the interest of space. As an abstraction, the technique marks the fast-changing spots on the video (Figures 9(a)-(c)) with brighter spots indicating faster movements. Clearly, the distribution of spots and their brightness vary while the user is walking. We define a feature, $F_{center}$, which captures the rhythm of this alteration. Figure 9(d) shows a typical path of $F_{center}$ – the peaks are essentially the step phase, while the time separation between the peaks is the step duration. The technique becomes unreliable when the user is walking towards or away from the camera, in which case, we refrain from extracting step duration and phase.

• **Rotation**: The technique of Space-Time Interest points can be applied for detecting rotation as well. The key observation is that

**Figure 8: Center speed in 2D plane: (a)-(c) have significant speed, and (d)-(f) have insignificant speed.**

rotation causes fast changing spots to be scattered over the entire bounding box, while other activities cause the spots to be confined to a relatively smaller region. Figure 10 shows an example where the spots are confined to the hands when the user is moving them; in contrast, rotation causes the spots to cover the entire body. Formally, we define $X = \{x_i\}$ and $Y = \{y_i\}, (i = 1, 2, .., N)$ as the X and Y coordinates of the centroid of the spots. We define the following four features – $f_1 = max\{X\} - min\{X\}$, $f_2 = max\{Y\} - min\{Y\}$, $f_3 = var\{X\}$, and $f_4 = var\{Y\}$ – and train a bagged decision tree to classify the spot distribution. The output is a binary answer: rotation or not.

• **Unknown**: *InSight* extracts a motion alphabet from each time unit (one second). However, confusions arise when the user transitions from one action to another within that second (e.g., stationary user starts walking). We conservatively deem these time units as an "unknown". The motion string thus contains motion alphabets and unknowns interspersed with each other.

## 4.3 Matching Motion Strings

We now describe how motion strings obtained from sensors are matched with motion strings extracted from videos. First, since the walking direction estimated from sensors is with respect to global north, we map it to one of the 8 quantized directions relative to our camera-facing direction. Then, *InSight* computes the "distance" between the two strings, similar in spirit to *edit distance.*

Specifically, denote the motion strings based on the video and sensor data as $V$ and $M$ respectively, and their length $L$ (note that the string lengths are same). For each position $i$ in the strings, we compare $V(i)$ and $M(i)$. The difference between them is 0 only if: (1) $V(i)$ and $M(i)$ are identical or (2) $V(i)$ and $M(i)$ both correspond to walking in identical or adjacent directions, their step durations are within a threshold ratio, and their step phase marker of $M(i)$ falls into a range calculated from step phase makers of $V(i)$. Otherwise, their difference is recorded as 1. Let $D$ be the total difference across the length of the strings. Then we define string similarity as $(1 - \frac{D}{L})$. When comparing a video string of

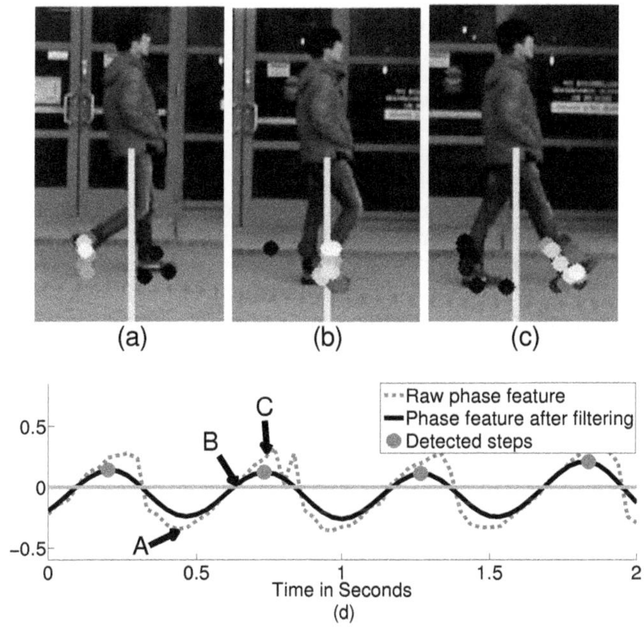


**Figure 9: Walking phase and duration: (a)~(c) Centers of detected cuboids; (d) Walking phase feature changes over time and detected steps. Points A, B and C in (d) correspond to the instances in (a), (b) and (c) respectively.**

a person $X$ against multiple people's sensor strings, we pick the one (say Bob's) with the single highest similarity (if any). Only if this highest similarity is above a certain threshold, then $X$ is identified as Bob, otherwise we declare the recognition as "unsure".

## 4.4 Extracting color fingerprint

Once Bob is identified based on his motion, the server extracts and adds his color fingerprint to its repository. Thereafter, server may be able to recognize Bob from an image without seeking video and sensor data, saving both latency and bandwidth. While various visual features of Bob can be considered to form his color fingerprint, clothing is an obvious choice as a temporary fingerprint. Therefore, in this paper, we extract the features of Bob's clothing and use them as Bob's color fingerprint. As a first step in getting the fingerprint, we detect the clothing area in the per-

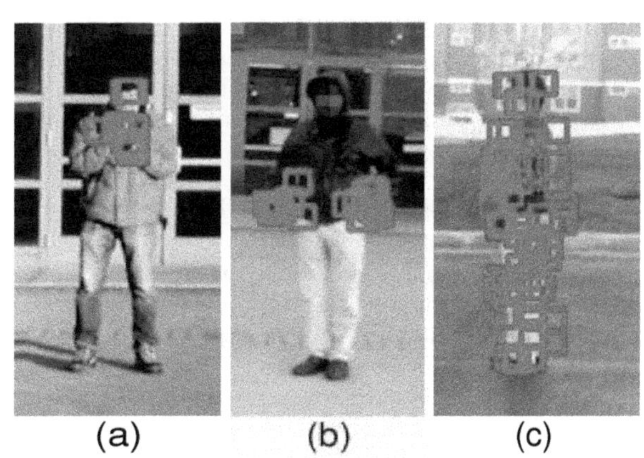


**Figure 10: Scattering of motion spots: (a) rubbing hands, (b) putting hands into pocket, (c) rotating**

son's image. Then, we use a well known technique, namely spatiograms, to extract a color fingerprint.

**Clothing area detection**: We extract color fingerprints when target is in near-front or near-back view. Calvin Upper-body Detector [14] model is trained to return bounding-boxes fitting the head and upper half of the torso. Figures 11(a) and 11(b) show the detected upper-body; Figure 11(c) shows that the detector doesn't fire in other views. We then use a pose estimation model [33] trained on Buffy dataset [15], which returns with joints such as neck, shoulder, etc. The neck and shoulder joints (red lines in Figure 11) help crop the upper-torso area as the clothing area. Then, we apply spatiograms on the cropped image to extract the target's color fingerprint.

(a) (b) (c)

**Figure 11: View detection and shoulder estimation. Green dashed boxes show the detected upper-body. The upper-body detector can detect upper-bodies in either near-front view (a) or near-back view (b), but it cannot detect upper-bodies in other views (c). Red solid lines are shoulder extracted by pose estimation.**

**Spatiograms:** Spatiograms are essentially color histograms with spatial distributions encoded in its structure. Put differently, while basic color histograms only capture the relative frequency of each color, spatiograms capture how these colors are distributed in 2D space. The second order of spatiogram can be represented as [5]:

$$h_I(b) = < n_b, \mu_b, \sigma_b >, \quad b = 1,2,3,\cdots,B,$$

where $B$ is the number of color bins, $n_b$ is the number of pixels whose value falls in the $b^{th}$ bin, and $\mu_b$ and $\sigma_b$ are the mean vector and covariance matrices of the coordinates of those pixels respectively. Through such a representation, a white over red stripe can be distinguished from a red over white stripe, even if the number of red and white pixels are identical in both. Also, to cope with various viewing distances, we normalize the spatial information with respect to the *shoulder width* so that all the spatial representation is relative to the captured body size in each photo. Finally, to decouple lighting conditions from the colors, we convert the pixels from $RGB$ to $HSV$, and quantize them into $B = 5x1x2$ bins.

## 4.5 Color Fingerprint Matching

When John views Bob through his glass – either from the front or the back – *InSight* again crops out a region around Bob's upper body, and applies the same fingerprinting operations on this image. These fingerprints – one in the repository and another from John – are now ready for matching. Our matching algorithm first computes the spatiogram similarity between each person in John's view with Bob's fingerprint in the repository. Denote the spatiograms to be compared as $S = \{n,\mu,\sigma\}$ and $S' = \{n',\mu',\sigma'\}$, both having $B$ color bins. We define the similarity measure as in [9]:

$$\rho = \sum_{b=1}^{B} \sqrt{n_b n'_b}\, 8\pi |\Sigma_b \Sigma'_b|^{1/4} \mathcal{N}(\mu_b; \mu'_b, 2(\Sigma_b + \Sigma'_b))$$

Essentially, the similarity decreases (following a Gaussian function) with increasing difference between the colors and their spatial locations. Fingerprints are considered to match if $\rho$ is greater than a certain threshold.

When motion information (video and sensor data) is available in addition to clothing fingerprints, *InSight* server utilizes them both to make the recognition more robust. First, it computes the $\rho$ value for each video frame that captures target's near-front or near-back view, and calculates the mean $\bar{\rho}$. It deems clothing similarity as 1, if $\bar{\rho}$ is above a certain threshold and 0 otherwise. Next, it will compute the overall similarity as the average of motion similarity and color similarity. Then, it will pick a person with the single highest overall similarity. If this person's overall similarity is above a certain threshold, then *InSight* returns the person's name, and unsure otherwise.

# 5. EVALUATION

This section is organized in 3 parts: **(1) Micro-benchmarks** to evaluate the accuracy with which motion alphabets can be detected from each second of video and sensor data. **(2) Scenario with real users** to evaluate *InSight*'s ability to discriminate individuals through motion/visual fingerprint comparison. **(3) Video simulation** to evaluate scalability across large number of users. The experiment design and details are presented under each of the 3 sub-sections.

## 5.1 Micro-benchmark (for Motion Alphabets) Experiment Design:

Motion alphabets define the atomic operation in *InSight* – this section evaluates whether each second in videos and sensor data can be reliably converted to motion alphabets. For this, we recruited 12 volunteers, gave each of them a Samsung Android phone running an *InSight* client, and asked each of them to cover various actions, such as walking, rotations, taking turns, standing still, etc., as well as some upper body movements like checking emails, stretching, etc in an area of $20mx15m$ outside our building. During the entire experiment, a designated observer video recorded each volunteer's motion patterns separately. The experiment was performed in 4 sessions and in total 80 minutes of sensor and video data were collected (and each frame manually labeled for ground truth). These videos were then examined frame by frame and manually labeled with ground truth (i.e., each second of the video tagged with one of the motion alphabets, such as walking or not, walking direction, starting and ending frame of each step, rotating or not, etc.).

## Results

**Walking detection**: We use a 3-fold cross-validation to evaluate the accuracy of walk-detection. Recall that walking detection with sensors is based on bagged decision trees, while for videos, we used a calibration factor $\alpha_z$ and a motion threshold. We set $\alpha_z = 4$ and motion threshold of 0.5. Figure 12 shows the confusion matrix – evidently, the detector is highly accurate for both sensors and videos, with mis-detection not above 0.6% and 1.5% respectively.

**Step duration**: We painstakingly computed the ground truth for step duration, i.e., the start and end time of each step. This enables comparison with estimates made from video and sensor

| (a) | No | Yes |
|---|---|---|
| No | 99.9% | 0.1% |
| Yes | 0.6% | 99.4% |

| (b) | No | Yes |
|---|---|---|
| No | 98.9% | 1.1% |
| Yes | 1.5% | 98.5% |

**Figure 12: Detecting walking vs. not-walking: (a) from sensors; (b) from vision.**

data. Figure 13 plots the CDF of the relative error for both dimensions of information. The error distribution with videos exhibits a staircase function since the ground truth was marked in the units of video frames. Overall, the relative error is less than 8% in more than 85% instances for both video and sensor data.

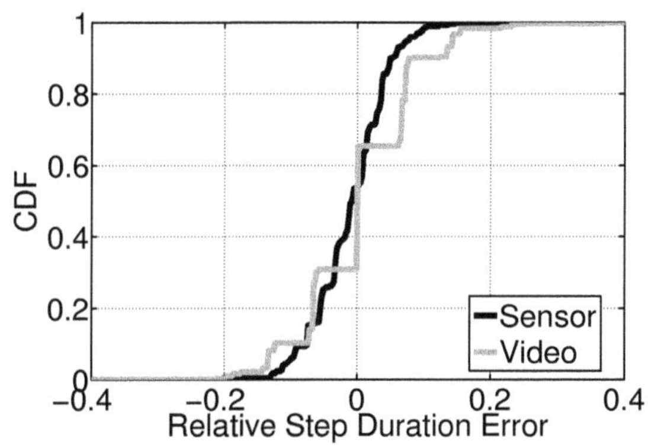


**Figure 13: Step duration estimation error compared to ground truth.**

**Walking direction**: Using sensor data, we compute the walking direction w.r.t. global north and plot the relative error in Figure 14. Evidently, the error is not high and confined mostly to ±45° around the true value. We also estimate the walking direction from the videos and classify them into one of 8 classes – Figure 15 reports the confusion matrix. Classification accuracy (at 45° granularity) is consistently high, and the slight confusion is mostly with adjacent angular directions.

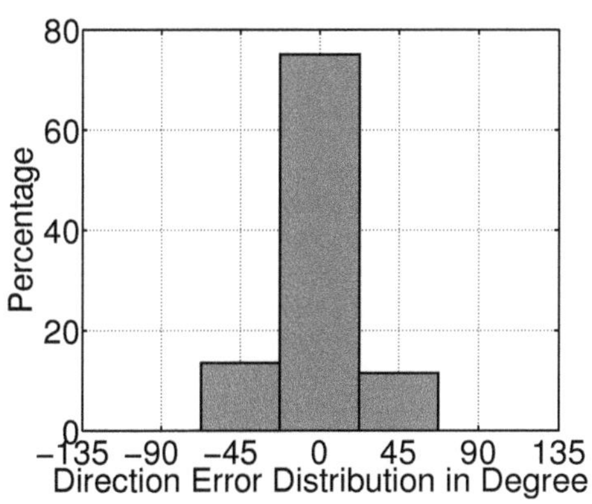


**Figure 14: Walking direction estimation: relative error with sensors.**

**Step Phase**: Recall that step phase of two individuals is the difference between the time points at which their respective feet strike the ground. Figure 16(a) shows the histogram of the difference in the phase (normalized by $T_{step}$), estimated from the sensor data

| | 0 | 45 | 90 | 135 | 180 | 225 | 270 | 315 |
|---|---|---|---|---|---|---|---|---|
| 0 | 99.6% | 0.4% | 0.0% | 0.0% | 0.0% | 0.0% | 0.0% | 0.0% |
| 45 | 1.0% | 99.0% | 0.0% | 0.0% | 0.0% | 0.0% | 0.0% | 0.0% |
| 90 | 0.0% | 0.9% | 97.4% | 1.7% | 0.0% | 0.0% | 0.0% | 0.0% |
| 135 | 0.0% | 0.0% | 0.0% | 99.0% | 1.0% | 0.0% | 0.0% | 0.0% |
| 180 | 0.0% | 0.0% | 0.0% | 1.7% | 98.3% | 0.0% | 0.0% | 0.0% |
| 225 | 0.0% | 0.0% | 0.0% | 0.0% | 0.4% | 99.2% | 0.4% | 0.0% |
| 270 | 0.0% | 0.0% | 0.0% | 0.0% | 0.0% | 2.5% | 93.4% | 4.1% |
| 315 | 0.5% | 0.0% | 0.0% | 0.0% | 0.0% | 0.0% | 0.5% | 99.0% |

**Figure 15: Walking direction estimation: confusion matrix for quantized directions based on video.**

and compared against ground truth. Figure 16(b) shows the same histogram but computed from video data. However, for recognizing individuals in *InSight*, what matters is the video-sensor phase offset (i.e., the difference in phase computed between video and sensor data). Figure 16(c) shows this difference. The graph suggests that the resolution at which step phases can be discriminated is around $0.3 \times T_{step}$ ($T_{step}$ is the step duration) – two individuals that are different by less than this value will appear to be in lock-step.

**Rotation**: Recall that, rotation is detected from videos by training a bagged decision tree and classifying the identified spot distribution (Figure 10). For extracting rotation from sensor data, we compute the rotation angle around gravity, $\alpha_{gravity}$, and apply a threshold of 15°. Figure 17 reports the a confusion matrix – the high accuracy confirms reliable rotation detection.

| (a) | No | Yes |
|---|---|---|
| No | 97.8% | 2.2% |
| Yes | 1.3% | 98.7% |

| (b) | No | Yes |
|---|---|---|
| No | 98.9% | 1.1% |
| Yes | 1.2% | 98.8% |

**Figure 17: Rotating or not: (a) by sensors; (b) by vision.**

## 5.2 Real User Scenario

The above evaluation shows the consistent accuracy of detecting motion alphabets from both video and sensor data. This subsection extracts motion strings from individuals and examines the discriminative abilities in them. The overall performance depends on 2 factors: (1) the inherent diversity in human motion patterns, and (2) effectiveness of *InSight*'s fingerprint design and matching schemes.

### Experiment Design

We again conduct experiments with the help of the same 12 volunteers as before. But, unlike the micro-benchmark setting, in this set of experiments, the volunteers' motion and behavior were completely natural. They were allowed to naturally move around or pause, and do as they pleased. They were also not

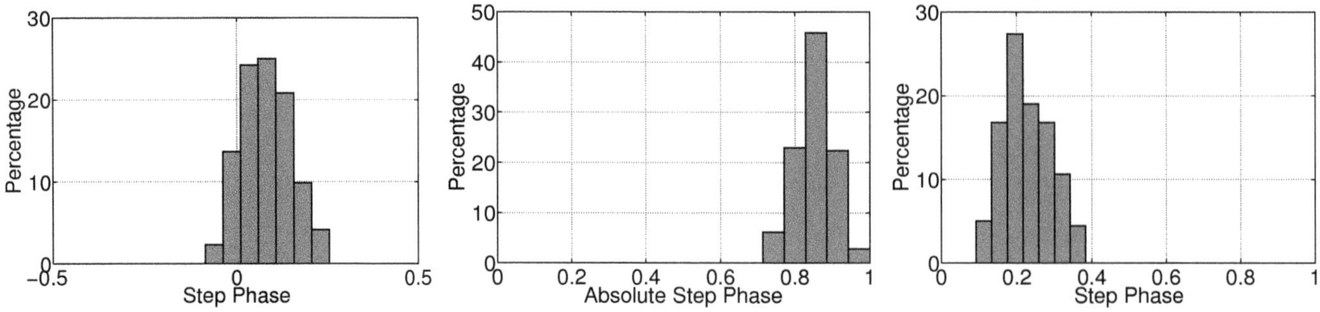


**Figure 16: Step phase marker distribution: (a) sensor phase markers with respect to ground truth; (b) video phase markers with respect to ground truth; (c) sensor phase markers with respect to video phase markers.**

instructed about clothing – they came to the experiment wearing the same clothes that they wore to school that morning.

We have not developed a real-time version of *InSight* – our current evaluation is offline and structured as follows. We pretend that the observer requests to recognize one of the volunteers at a random time $t$. Starting at time $t$ in our data set, we crop out a 10 second video of that volunteer, as well as a 10 second sensor stream from all 12 smartphones. A motion string derived from this video is then matched against all the motion strings derived from the sensors. The string matching algorithm either returns a matching smartphone (or volunteer), or returns *unsure* if there is no single highest score or the score is below a threshold (set to 0.95). We repeat this experiment 100 times with different request times.

## Results

Figure 18 shows the recognition accuracy. To understand the contribution of different motion alphabets towards overall human recognition, we evaluate various combinations of alphabets. Figure 18(a) starts with the simplest one – walking or not. In other words, for each second of the video and sensor data, a volunteer's motion is categorized as walking or not walking. Then, for increasing string lengths, we plot the performance of the matching scheme. For increasing time durations (on the x-axis), we show the fraction of people correctly recognized, incorrectly recognized, and unsure. For instance, from the first 7 seconds of video and sensor data, we could correctly recognize 2% of the cases and the rest were unsure (none incorrectly recognized). As we consider longer durations of motion, recognition performance improves, reaching 7% with 10 seconds of motion. This improvement is expected since motion of two individuals diverges over time making them more distinguishable. Of course, the distinguishability is not high in this case, since *walking* alone, is hardly a strong discriminator.

To improve over a binary walking indicator, we include *walking direction* in the motion alphabet (quantized to 8 classes) and present its performance in Figure 18(b). Understandably, walking direction helps improve the recognition, up to 30%. Similarly, Figure 18(c) and Figure 18(d) indicate that considering step phase and duration together along with walking direction can recognize individuals correctly in 50% of the cases. Figure 18(e) shows that when rotating or not is further added to the alphabet (in addition to walking direction/phase/duration), a person can be recognized in close to 72% cases with 10 seconds of observations.

Finally, clothing fingerprints can also be used in combination with motion based alphabets for recognizing humans. Figure 18(f) shows that when clothing fingerprint is used in conjunction with motion, 6 seconds of observation are sufficient to recognize a person with 90% probability. Overall, these results demonstrate that motion and clothing together help recognize individuals accurately, and recognition performance improves over time.

# 5.3 Video Simulation (for Scale)

## Experiment Design

Recruiting large number of volunteers and bringing them for multiple social experiments proved more difficult than we imagined. Still, to gain insights on *InSight*'s scalability to higher user density and different settings, we resort to an approximation. Our key idea is to record video of people in public places, and even though we do not have sensor data from them, we will *synthesize sensor data by injecting statistical error into ground truth observations.* For this we execute the following steps:

- record videos of people in public places, such as university cafes, grocery stores, busy street intersections.
- extract the video-based motion fingerprints for each user in the video, denoted $V_i$,
- also manually extract ground truth for each user from the video, denoted $T_i$,
- inject errors into the ground truth based on past error distributions, observed when extracting motion alphabets from sensors (i.e., $M_i = T_i + Error$),
- compare the video based motion strings to the synthetic sensor based strings (i.e., $V_x == M_i$?).

Our earlier evaluation in Section 5.1 demonstrated that sensor based strings achieve high accuracy, so this synthetic sensor strings should well mimmic reality. The results should be a faithful approximation of *InSight*'s performance at scale.

The motion alphabets are synthesized as follows. To determine whether a person is walking or not, we use the confusion matrix shown in Figure 12(a). Specifically, if a person is walking as per the ground truth, then she is marked as walking with 99.4% probability and as not-walking with 0.6% probability; when she is not walking, her motion is marked as walking and not-walking with 0.1% and 99.9% probability respectively. We follow the same for deciding rotating or not, using the rotation confusion matrix in

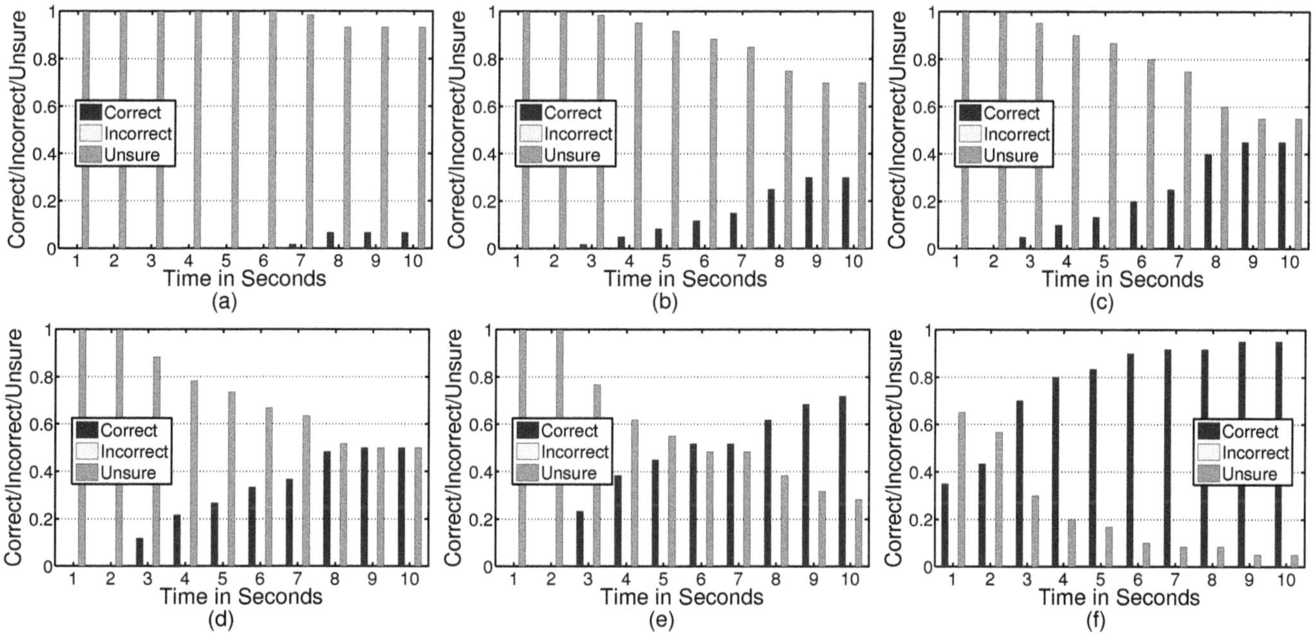


**Figure 18: Recognition performance with motion alphabets and color fingerprints: (a) Walking or not only; (b) Walking direction only; (c) Walking direction with walking phase; (d) Walking direction with step phase and duration; (e) All motion alphabets including rotation; (f) All motion alphabets along with color fingerprints.**

Figure 17(a). To obtain the step duration, we add a random error to the ground truth, following the distribution in Figure 13. For step direction, we do the same using the distribution from Figure 14. For determining the step phase, we add a random shift according to the step phase distribution in Figure 16 (a). The random shift varies from −9.1% of $T_{step}$ to 25.3% of $T_{step}$. Now, since the error distributions were from a 12 member evaluation, the variance is likely to be smaller compared to a larger population. To account for such situations, we added additional errors to ensure the data is not optimistic.

The public videos were recorded under 3 different scenarios – near a busy area outside the student union during summer (referred to as the "union" video later), at the CS department cafe in the winter (referred to as "cafe" video) and at the entrance of a Target store in the winter (referred as "store" video). Figure 19 show example video frames. People moved in and out of the videos – so at any typical time instant, we observed between 3 to 10 in the view finder. However, for each of the videos, we computed motion fingerprints of all the people across time, and then compare against each other. For instance, the union video included 40 distinct individuals in 5 minutes, and we pretend as if all the 40 people were present at the same time. *InSight* is expected to be able to discriminate each individual accurately from these 40 individuals. The cafe and store had 15 people each due to less churn.

## Results

Figure 20 reports results from the "union" video simulations. As a high level summary, *InSight* was able to recognize most of the user by combining motion and clothing. Specifically, since the recording was in summer, people wore colorful clothing, which by itself achieved 50% accuracy among 40 people. Expectedly, motion aided this discrimination, however, given that many users walked often, walking-or-not was not a major discriminator. Walking direction and step duration were helpful, but still not sufficient due to the high density of users (users mostly walked in two dominant direction, one towards the restaurants, and another towards dorms). However, when including walking phase, results improved significantly.

We zoom into the results here. Figure 20(a) shows the clothing confusion matrix across 40 people. Figures 20(b) and (c) plot the recognition performance over time, using motion alone followed by motion+clothing. Figure 20(d) shows the confusion matrix after combining motion and clothing and the similarity threshold set to 0.95. Using clothing alone, *InSight* recognizes 50% of individuals. Using motion alone, *InSight* recognizes 40% of individuals within 10 seconds; with combination of clothing and motion, the recognition performance rises up to 88% within 5 seconds and 90% within 8 seconds.

Figure 21 and 22 report on the results from the "cafe" and "store" video simulations. Since both scenarios were recorded in winter, a majority of the people were wearing dark shades (dominantly black and gray). Thus, in both cases, clothing offered fewer bits of information. However, motion compensated well, especially in the cafe where people walked, paused, turned, etc. With combined clothing and motion, *InSight* achieves 80% accuracy in 6 seconds, 93% in 8 seconds at the cafe, and 87% in 5 seconds, 93% in 10 seconds at the store.

The results above suggest that humans inherently exhibit diversity in their motion and clothing patterns that even low resolution feature vectors offer promise of identification. Where faces are permanent and high entropy fingerprints, these motion strings could serve as a useful alternative, when temporary "visual identification" is of interest, without revealing persistent identities.

# 6. POINTS OF DISCUSSION

We discuss a number of limitations and untapped opportunities with *InSight*.

**Figure 19: Example frames from (a) outside student union, (b) university cafe and (c) Target store.**

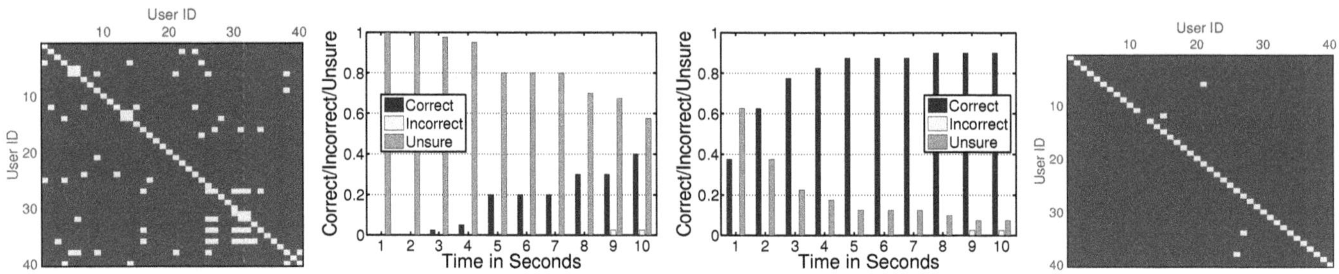


**Figure 20: Union video Performance: (a) clothing only confusion matrix; Recognition over time using (b) motion only (c) motion + clothing (d) motion + clothing confusion matrix (after applying a threshold of 0.95 on similarity score).**

**Coping with Practical Hurdles**. While we believe *InSight* is amenable to deployment in the real-world, it needs to be engineered, tested, and fine-tuned for various practical scenarios. Occlusions is perhaps the key limitation at this point. In a crowded environment, an individual is likely to be occluded by others, preventing the computer vision algorithm from carving out a precise bounding box for each person. This can inject confusion in the system, especially if the bounding boxes erroneously include different parts of two or more individuals. Coping with these complications is left to future work. Also, low lighting intensity in certain environments may affect visual clarity and fingerprinting. Further, people may change clothing – put on a scarf or take off their jackets – after their fingerprints have been registered in the database. Of course, motion fingerprints are a dependable fallback to cope with some of these situations, however, their efficacy in the wild remains to be seen.

**Real Time Operation**. In its current form, *InSight* is an offline system. Running this online will require substantial "heavy lifting" likely to be executed in the cloud [10] or cloudlets [27]. This paper's focus is towards demonstrating the core opportunity – the necessary engineering for an end to end system will depend on the application in question, and is a separate work altogether. Innovative research is yielding intelligent cloud-offloading techniques [10,27], designed explicitly for applications like *InSight*. In view of this, we believe real-time operation will be feasible over time, perhaps requiring porting *InSight* on MAUI-like programming frameworks [10].

**Energy**. The energy footprint of *InSight* may not be excessive. Motion sensors on smartphones need not consume much energy even after prolonged continuous sensing. The camera on the other hand can be activated only when the user desires to view annotations of the environment (e.g., when Alice wants to learn who a particular person is). This is true even for other applications such as privacy preserving pictures – the camera is again used only during the recording of a video or for taking a picture.

**Incremental Deployment**. If some users do not run *InSight* on their phones, the fingerprint matching process faces additional challenges. For instance, Alice may be looking at Bob in reality, and even though Bob is not running *InSight*, Bob's clothing fingerprint may match best with Chris (a registered user). To avoid such errors, *InSight* requires that the fingerprint matching threshold be very high, with the hope that motion-based matching would be triggered. Nonetheless, certain scenarios (such as weddings, funerals, uniformed school children) may still derail *InSight*. Perhaps an adaptive process is needed, where the *InSight* server identifies large similarities in clothing patterns and triggers motion based matching more aggressively.

**Utilizing all bits of information**. Upon receiving a video clip, *InSight* can extract clothing fingerprints for multiple people even if it is unable to map them to their identities. Over time, the repository of unnamed clothing fingerprints increase. Now, as individuals get identified through motion, it may be possible to resolve some of the other clothing fingerprints via the process of elimination. We envisage that such a form of inferencing would be possible due to the global view on the fingerprint data, available at the *InSight* server. We have not tapped this opportunity in this paper.

**Peer-to-peer version of *InSight*.** While we describe *InSight* as a cloud-based system, it is also possible to realize it over a peer-to-peer model. The sequence of operations, somewhat different from Figure 2, can be as follows. (1) Alice's glass takes a picture of $X$ and broadcasts it, asking "who is the person in the picture"; simultaneously it starts recoding a video snippet. (2) Smartphones in the vicinity receive the image (over Bluetooth or WiFi Direct), extract the color fingerprint, and match it with their self color fingerprint (if they have one); simultaneously each of them activate their motion sensors. (3) These smartphones send their color fingerprint matching score along with their sensor data to Alice's glass. (4) Alice's phone computes the motion matching score, combines with the color score, and ultimately identifies $X$ as Bob. (5) Alice's glass extracts Bob's color fingerprint from the video snippet and unicasts it to Bob's smartphone, which updates its own fingerprint. Of course, such a system assumes that smartphones are capable of executing the compute-heavy algorithms locally, perhaps difficult in today's platforms.

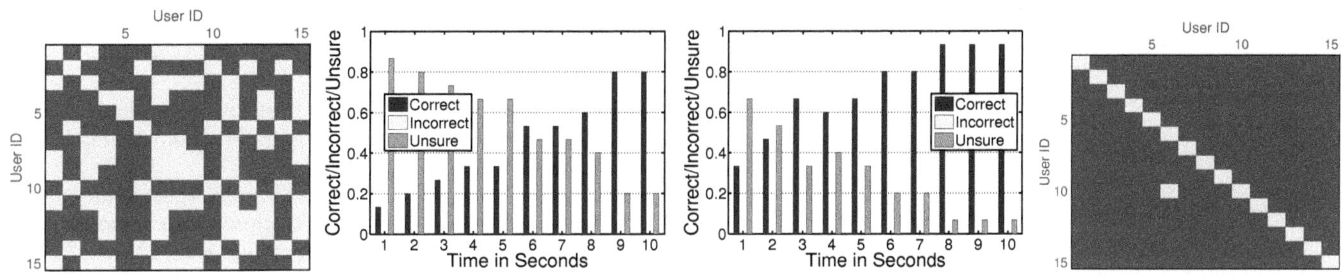


**Figure 21: Cafe video simulation: (a) clothing only confusion matrix; Recognition over time using (b) motion only (c) motion + clothing (d) motion + clothing confusion matrix (after applying a threshold of 0.95 on similarity score).**

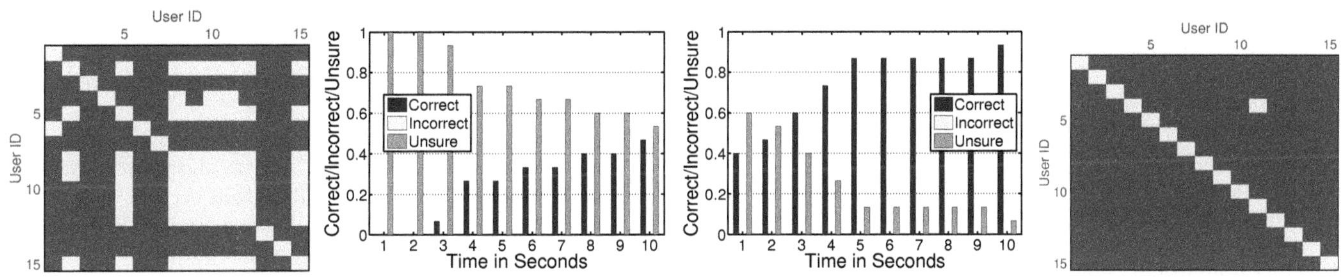


**Figure 22: Store video simulation: (a) clothing only confusion matrix; Recognition over time using (b) motion only (c) motion + clothing (d) motion + clothing confusion matrix (after applying a threshold of 0.95 on similarity score).**

# 7. RELATED WORK

There exist several works on activity recognition based on video [13, 26] and sensors [4]. TagSense [23] uses motion as an indication of whether a person is in the picture, but does not need to actually identify each individual. Face recognition and other visual bio-metrics are of course possible alternatives [16, 18, 34], but need the face to be visible (in addition to practical concerns on revealing a permanent identifier). *InSight*, on the other hand, temporarily fingerprints individuals, exposing only soft-biometrics of the user that cannot identify them later. We observe that *InSight* is different from gait analysis [16], used to "fingerprint" individuals. While gait analysis zooms into the intricacies of walking patterns (i.e., how one walks), we use far higher level motion alphabets capturing duration of walks, turns, pauses (none of which is permanent).

The specific applications we have discussed have received research attention in the recent past [3, 17, 20, 22, 25, 28]. Researchers have explored the possibility of looking at objects in a store, using wearable devices and radio-optical beacons [3] and/or RFID based techniques [28]. Such modes of communication are innovative and complementary to *InSight*. Qualcomm Vuforia [1] is a commercial Mobile AR SDK for object recognition and 3D object tracking. Videoguide [2] is a Vuforia app used to animate architecture work in Barcelona museum. Contrary to Vuforia which requires deployment in advance, *InSight* is a training-free system intended for humans.

Privacy preservation in the age of wearable cameras is also witnessing considerable research attention. Authors in [6] suggest a QR code pasted on people's clothing, as an expression of privacy preferences to surrounding cameras. Of course, the QR code may not necessarily be in view of the camera; reading from longer ranges is difficult; with human motion, reading QR codes is hard. PrivateEye [24] proposes to avoid recording objects by drawing a signature shape around it. *InSight*, on the other hand, does not require any form of instrumentation, except that the smartphone should run the app. Natural behavior of humans should exhibit adequate diversity for recognition, in turn useful for for inclusion, exclusion, or communication.

Our workshop paper on *InSight* [31] was an initial exploration into the possibility of using clothing colors as a temporary visual identifier. This paper builds on the workshop version in multiple fronts, including (1) the significant addition of motion information to the notion of visual fingerprinting, (2) a range of techniques to correlate motion from vision and device sensors, (3) the idea of expressing fingerprints as activity–strings and applying string matching algorithms on them, (4) a more complete evaluation through micro-benchmarks and offline evaluation, and finally (5) isolating the notion of visual fingerprinting and discussing its various applications in augmented reality, privacy preserving pictures, and indoor localization.

# 8. CONCLUSION

This paper pursues a hypothesis that motion patterns and clothing colors may pose as a human fingerprint, adequate to discriminate one individual from others. If successful, such a fingerprint could be effectively used towards human recognition or content announcement in the visual vicinity, and more broadly towards enabling human-centric augmented reality. Pivoted on this vision, we develop a proof of concept – InSight – which correlates motion fingerprint extracted from the video with those extracted from smartphone sensors. Clothing colors offer additional dimensions of correlation, boosting the confidence in recognition. We find promise in this direction, and are committed to building a fuller, real-time, system.

# 9. ACKNOWLEDGMENTS

We sincerely thank our shepherd Dr. Tam Vu and the anonymous reviewers for their valuable feedback. We are grateful to Google and to NSF for partially funding this research through grant CNS-1430064.

## 10. REFERENCES


[1] Qualcomm Vuforia. https://www.qualcomm.com/products/vuforia.

[2] Videoguide, Antoni Gaudi Modernist Museum in Barcelona. http://www.casabatllo.es/en/visit/videoguide.

[3] A. Ashok, M. Gruteser, N. Mandayam, J. Silva, M. Varga, and K. Dana. Challenge: mobile optical networks through visual MIMO. In *ACM MobiCom*, pages 105–112, 2010.

[4] L. Bao and S. S. Intille. Activity recognition from user-annotated acceleration data. In *Pervasive Computing*, pages 1–17, 2004.

[5] S. T. Birchfield and S. Rangarajan. Spatiograms versus histograms for region-based tracking. *IEEE CVPR*, 2:1158 – 1163, 2005.

[6] C. Bo, G. Shen, J. Liu, X. Li, Y. Zhang, and F. Zhao. Privacy.tag: Privacy concern expressed and respected. In *ACM SenSys*, pages 163–176, 2014.

[7] K. W. Bowyer. Face recognition technology: security versus privacy. *IEEE Technology and Society Magazine*, 23(1):9–19, 2004.

[8] M. D. Breitenstein, F. Reichlin, B. Leibe, E. Koller-Meier, and L. Van Gool. Online multiperson tracking-by-detection from a single, uncalibrated camera. *Pattern Analysis and Machine Intelligence, IEEE Transactions on*, 33(9):1820–1833, 2011.

[9] C. O. Conaire, N. E. O'Connor, and A. F. Smeaton. An improved spatiogram similarity measure for robust object localisation. *IEEE ICASSP*, 1:1069–1072, 2007.

[10] E. Cuervo, A. Balasubramanian, D.-k. Cho, A. Wolman, S. Saroiu, R. Chandra, and P. Bahl. MAUI: making smartphones last longer with code offload. In *MobiSys*, pages 49–62, 2010.

[11] P. Dollár. Piotr's Image and Video Matlab Toolbox (PMT). http://vision.ucsd.edu/~pdollar/toolbox/doc/index.html.

[12] P. Dollár, R. Appel, and W. Kienzle. Crosstalk cascades for frame-rate pedestrian detection. In *ECCV*, pages 645–659, 2012.

[13] P. Dollár, V. Rabaud, G. Cottrell, and S. Belongie. Behavior recognition via sparse spatio-temporal features. In *IEEE VS-PETS*, pages 65–72, 2005.

[14] M. Eichner and V. Ferrari. Calvin upper-body detector. http://groups.inf.ed.ac.uk/calvin/calvin_upperbody_detector/.

[15] V. Ferrari, M. Marin-Jimenez, and A. Zisserman. Progressive search space reduction for human pose estimation. In *IEEE CVPR*, pages 1–8, 2008.

[16] J. Han and B. Bhanu. Individual recognition using gait energy image. *Pattern Analysis and Machine Intelligence, IEEE Transactions on*, 28(2):316–322, 2006.

[17] A. Henrysson and M. Ollila. UMAR: Ubiquitous mobile augmented reality. In *ACM MUM*, pages 41–45, 2004.

[18] A. K. Jain, A. Ross, and S. Prabhakar. An introduction to biometric recognition. *Circuits and Systems for Video Technology, IEEE Transactions on*, 14(1):4–20, 2004.

[19] R. E. Kalman. A new approach to linear filtering and prediction problems. *Journal of Fluids Engineering*, 82(1):35–45, 1960.

[20] A. Mayberry, P. Hu, B. Marlin, C. Salthouse, and D. Ganesan. iShadow: Design of a wearable, real-time mobile gaze tracker. In *MobiSys*, pages 82–94, 2014.

[21] P. Mistry and P. Maes. SixthSense: A wearable gestural interface. In *ACM SIGGRAPH ASIA 2009 Sketches*, number 11, 2009.

[22] W. Piekarski and B. Thomas. ARQuake: the outdoor augmented reality gaming system. *Communications of the ACM*, 45(1):36–38, 2002.

[23] C. Qin, X. Bao, R. Roy Choudhury, and S. Nelakuditi. TagSense: A smartphone-based approach to automatic image tagging. In *ACM MobiSys*, pages 1–14, 2011.

[24] N. Raval, A. Srivastava, K. Lebeck, L. Cox, and A. Machanavajjhala. MarkIt: Privacy markers for protecting visual secrets. In *ACM UbiComp Adjunct*, pages 1289–1295, 2014.

[25] J. Rekimoto and Y. Ayatsuka. CyberCode: designing augmented reality environments with visual tags. In *ACM DARE*, pages 1–10, 2000.

[26] N. Robertson and I. Reid. A general method for human activity recognition in video. *Computer Vision and Image Understanding*, 104(2-3):232–248, 2006.

[27] M. Satyanarayanan, P. Bahl, R. Caceres, and N. Davies. The case for VM-based cloudlets in mobile computing. 8(4):14–23, 2009.

[28] R. Tenmoku, M. Kanbara, and N. Yokoya. A wearable augmented reality system using positioning infrastructures and a pedometer. In *IEEE ISWC*, page 110, 2003.

[29] M. A. Turk and A. P. Pentland. Face recognition using eigenfaces. In *IEEE CVPR*, pages 586–591, 1991.

[30] D. Wagner, G. Reitmayr, A. Mulloni, T. Drummond, and D. Schmalstieg. Real-time detection and tracking for augmented reality on mobile phones. *Visualization and Computer Graphics, IEEE Transactions on*, 16(3):355–368, 2010.

[31] H. Wang, X. Bao, R. Roy Choudhury, and S. Nelakuditi. Recognizing humans without face recognition. In *ACM HotMobile*, number 7, 2013.

[32] H. Wang, Z. Wang, G. Shen, F. Li, S. Han, and F. Zhao. Wheelloc: Enabling continuous location service on mobile phone for outdoor scenarios. In *IEEE INFOCOM*, pages 2733–2741, 2013.

[33] Y. Yang and D. Ramanan. Articulated pose estimation with flexible mixtures-of-parts. In *IEEE CVPR*, pages 1385–1392, 2011.

[34] W. Zhao, R. Chellappa, P. J. Phillips, and A. Rosenfeld. Face recognition: A literature survey. *ACM Computing Surveys*, 35(4):399–458, 2003.

# Analyzing the Use of Quick Response Codes in the Wild


Adam Lerner
University of Washington
lerner@cs.washington.edu

Alisha Saxena
Massachusetts Institute of Technology
alishais@mit.edu

Kirk Ouimet
Scan, Inc.
kirk@kirkouimet.com

Ben Turley
Scan, Inc.
ben@scan.me

Anthony Vance
Brigham Young University
anthony@vance.name

Tadayoshi Kohno
University of Washington
yoshi@cs.washington.edu

Franziska Roesner
University of Washington
franzi@cs.washington.edu



## ABSTRACT

One- and two-dimensional barcodes, including Quick Response (QR) codes, have become a convenient way to communicate small amounts of information from physical objects to mobile devices. While there is much discussion, awareness, and proposed use of such barcodes, both in academia and in industry, to our knowledge there has not been a systematic and in-depth analysis of the actual ecosystem surrounding these codes. To fill this gap, we analyze a log of all scans performed by users of a popular QR and barcode scanning app available for Android, iPhone, and Windows Phone. Our dataset includes over 87 million scans performed over a 10-month period from May 2013 to March 2014. We examine general use patterns of QR and barcodes in the wild and identify common and uncommon uses and misuses. We see the presence of both conventional (e.g., web) and emerging (e.g., Bitcoin) uses of QR codes, and develop an informed understanding of the types of QR codes being created and how users interact with QR and barcodes in the wild.



## Categories and Subject Descriptors

[**Human-centered computing**]: Empirical studies in ubiquitous and mobile computing

## Keywords

QR codes; barcodes; empirical studies; mobile computing; ubiquitous computing; mobile malware


## 1. INTRODUCTION

With the growing prevalence of smartphones and other mobile devices, Quick Response (QR) codes have become a convenient way to quickly communicate a small amount of information, such as a URL, to a user's device. Figure 1 shows a sample QR code; Figures 2 and 3 show examples in real-world contexts. To read these codes, users typically install third-party QR code scanning applications onto their mobile devices. The number and popularity of such applications speaks to the popularity of QR codes themselves. For example, the most popular QR and barcode scanning application for Android boasts over 100 million downloads (as of November 2014, according to `http://appbrain.com`).

**Figure 1: Sample QR code.**

QR codes are among the most prevalent technologies *bridging the physical and digital worlds*, raising unique opportunities and challenges. QR codes are often associated with physical objects. When a user scans a QR code with a mobile device, that mobile device may perform some follow-on digital action, such as visiting a website (Figure 2) or pairing accounts (Figure 3). Anecdotally, QR codes are used for marketing purposes or to provide pointers to additional information about a physical location or object (e.g., in a museum). QR codes are also used for a growing number of security-sensitive operations, such as authentication, device pairing, and connecting to password-protected WiFi networks. The prevalence and utility of QR codes is likely to increase with the growing adoption of wearable devices such as Google Glass, where text or other traditional forms of input may be cumbersome. For example, Google Glass already utilizes QR codes to connect to password-protected WiFi networks [11]. The research community has also turned to QR codes as a mechanism for linking physical spaces with digital information or computation (e.g., [1, 2, 8, 9, 13, 15, 18, 21, 27–30] — see Section 2 for a discussion).

Though QR and barcode scanning applications and anecdotes about their uses abound, to our knowledge there has been no systematic, in-depth study of their use in the wild. Designers of QR code-based systems are thus forced to rely on speculation, or their own measurements, of the QR code



*MobiSys'15*, May 18–22, 2015, Florence, Italy.
ACM 978-1-4503-3494-5/15/05.
http://dx.doi.org/10.1145/2742647.2742650.

**Figure 2: A QR code in a museum, encoding the URL for a video related to the exhibit. Image source:** `https://www.flickr.com/photos/balboaparkonline/`

**Figure 3: A QR code used to pair a user's YouTube account with the YouTube app on their Xbox. Image source:** `http://instagram.com/p/icywcsKZbo/`

ecosystem. To fill this gap, we study the use of QR codes in the wild. We leverage a unique and powerful data set: approximately 87 million scans of QR and barcodes made using Scan (`https://scan.me/`), a popular scanning application with an install base of over 10 million devices.[1] This dataset allows us to examine both the types of QR codes that exist in the wild, and the frequency with which individuals users interact with these codes. We find, for example, that approximately 75% of QR and barcode scans in our dataset lead to web URLs, and that the set of popular websites found in QR codes differs significantly from the set of websites popular on the web in general. We also find that 25% of scans represent other use cases, and we investigate these varied applications (e.g., phone numbers, Bitcoin payments, and two-factor authentication). We also observe examples of malicious uses of QR codes, including links to Android applications containing malware. These cases of misuse are rare, but their presence in our dataset suggests that users may encounter them in the wild.

In this paper, we analyze the use and misuse of QR codes, and we develop an informed understanding of the types of codes that are created and that are encountered by users in practice. Our contributions include:

- We conduct the first (to our knowledge) large-scale academic analysis of QR and barcode use in the wild, using a dataset of 87 million scans. We present general trends about the scans, codes, and devices present in our data.
- We investigate specific use cases for QR codes, including a deep dive into the content of popular codes in our dataset, a comparison between frequently and infrequently scanned codes, and an exploration of the varied use cases present in our data (e.g., cryptographic currencies, device pairing, one-time passwords). We also investigate several potential vectors for malicious QR codes, including malware or phishing URLs and links to malicious Android applications.
- From these findings, we distill a set of lessons and recommendations for QR and barcode scanning application designers as well as for future systems that rely on QR codes or similar techniques to communicate between objects.

We now provide additional background and discuss related work in Section 2 before describing our dataset in more detail in Section 3. We then present general analyses of the dataset (Section 4), and then an analysis of different use cases that manifest in the dataset (Section 5). We discuss the implications of our findings and avenues for future work in Section 6 and then conclude in Section 7.

## 2. BACKGROUND AND RELATED WORK

One- and two-dimensional barcodes have become popular as a convenient way to quickly communicate a small amount of information, such as a URL, to a user's device. Figures 2 and 3 show examples of Quick Response (QR) codes, a common type of two-dimensional barcode. The prevalence of QR codes has risen alongside the popularity of smartphones [20], with one study showing that European usage of QR codes doubled between 2011 and 2012 [6]. To read these codes, users can install on their devices a variety of third-party QR and/or barcode reading applications, such as the popular ZXing Barcode Scanner, which boasts over 100 million downloads on Android, or Scan (`https://scan.me/`), which has been downloaded over 10 million times for Android.[2]

**Research applications.** QR and barcodes have been applied in a variety of research contexts. Several efforts leverage the ability of these codes to bridge the physical and digital worlds [2, 29], such as for indoor navigation [27], grocery bargain hunting [8], accessibility [1], and to aid augmented reality applications [15]. Additionally, many security and privacy related uses of QR and barcodes have been proposed, including for communicating privacy policies [4, 28], device-to-device authentication [21], web authentication [13], encryption or verification of real-world paper content [18, 30], and as tattoos of medical device passwords [9].

**Security issues.** Other researchers have explored the security challenges raised by QR and barcodes, including attacks enabled by ambiguous decoding protocols [7], a study of people's susceptibility to QR code based phishing attacks [32], the potential use of QR codes to spread malware and phishing URLs [35], and other attacks [16]. While these attacks are all technically possible, how prevalent are they in practice? We investigate several types of potentially malicious QR codes in this work, including malicious URLs.

[1]These scans were logged in accordance with Scan's terms of service and privacy policy, and our use of the dataset was approved by our institutions' IRB boards.

[2]Download numbers for Android, according to `http://appbrain.com` in November 2014. The total number of downloads for all platforms is higher.

Table 1: **The schema of our dataset. Device UUIDs are random and each corresponds to a single device which has installed the Scan app.**

| *Column* | *Example* |
|---|---|
| Barcode Type | e.g., QR, UPC, etc. |
| Contents | URI or other data |
| Location | Lat/lon coordinates |
| City | City |
| Region | e.g., state, province, etc. |
| Country | Country |
| Platform/Version | Mobile OS and version |
| Device Type | Phone make and model |
| Device ID | UUID |
| Timestamp | Date and time |
| Scan Source | Camera/History/Gallery |

**Commercial use.** Commercially, QR codes are frequently used for marketing purposes [5, 14], but they have also been applied in various security-sensitive contexts, such as authentication or device pairing. For example, Google experimented with QR codes for passwordless login [25], and Google Glass uses QR codes to connect to password-protected WiFi networks [11]. Indeed, the prevalence and utility of QR codes is likely to increase with the growing adoption of wearable, camera-enabled devices like Google Glass.

**Missing knowledge about real-world use.** Though QR and barcodes have been frequently applied in a diversity of research and commercial applications, to the best of our knowledge no large-scale academic study has been conducted of the use of such codes in the wild. Thus, we have little concrete knowledge about the prevalence of the various applications and attacks described above. We also have little concrete knowledge about the behavior of real users who may encounter QR codes. We aim to close that gap in this paper, leveraging our unique dataset of 87 million scans from a popular QR and barcode scanning application. In the next section, we detail our dataset.

# 3. THE DATASET

**Origin and Scope.** We obtained a log of scans performed by users of Scan (`https://scan.me`), a popular barcode and QR code scanning application for Android, iOS, and Windows Phone. The log includes scans made by real users using the software over a 10 month period from May 2013 to March 2014, including 87,647,504 scans of 18,763,779 distinct barcodes by 15,484,921 distinct devices in 241 countries.

**Schema.** Table 1 describes the full schema of the dataset. It includes the location and time of each scan as well as an anonymized UUID distinguishing devices which have installed the app. We note that devices are not one-to-one with users, since a user may have multiple devices at once or over time, and a single device may have multiple users. Hence, for expository purposes, when we refer to "users" in this paper, we are often referring to devices.

**Human Subjects.** The dataset was collected for academic research purposes in accordance with Scan's terms of service and privacy policy (e.g., for Android: `http://scan.me/mobile/apps/scan/android/legal/eula`). We also received IRB approval for this study from the IRBs of the University of Washington and Brigham Young University.

When not stored at Scan according to Scan's policies, we store the data in an encrypted form and performed all of our analyses on machines that we physically control. Though the dataset contains some personally identifiable information (e.g., names and phone numbers in QR codes encoding business cards), we report only aggregate or anonymized data in this paper.

**Definitions.** Throughout the paper we refer to a "code" as a distinct piece of data contained in a barcode or QR code. For example, Alice and Bob might both embed the url `http://example.com` in a QR code. If a user scans Alice's code and another user scans Bob's code, we consider the *code* `http://example.com` to be scanned twice.

A scan is the act of a user scanning a code with the app, corresponding to one row in the dataset, with all the fields described in the schema (Table 1).

# 4. GENERAL ANALYSES

We begin by presenting an overview of the barcode and QR code scans in our dataset. We analyze the relative popularity of different types of codes, and examine variations over time and geographical region.

## 4.1 Basic Distributions

**Devices.** Our dataset includes 15,484,921 distinct devices, each of which corresponds to a user's mobile device such as a phone or tablet. These devices serve as proxies for users of the app, though we note that devices may not correspond directly to users (e.g., a user may have multiple devices).

We find that a minority of devices account for the majority of scans in our dataset. Specifically, the most prolific 10% of devices performed approximately half of the scans, while just over 30% (4,667,012) performed only one scan over the 10 months covered by our study. Since the dataset is naturally truncated, users who installed the app near the end of our study period will appear to have very few scans. Thus the proportion of infrequent users is slightly exaggerated.

Figure 4 shows the distribution of scans across devices. That figure presents the data over all scans, as well as for only QR code scans and only non-QR code (product barcode) scans. We note that the distribution remains very similar in each of these cases. We speculate that this suggests that the tendency to use a mobile device to scan barcodes is influenced not only by the location and context of barcodes in the environment but also significantly by the individual person's experience and skills — perhaps based upon their affinity to technology. If true, this has implications for adoption of these types of technologies: it may suggest that the uptake of technologies like mobile barcode scanners may depend more on user familiarity or skill than on the ways barcodes are deployed in the environment.

Our results confirm that one- and two-dimensional barcodes can be an effective mechanism for having a physical device influence a digital device for *some* users. For example, 10% of users (accounting for over 1.5 million devices) performed more than 43 million scans in our dataset. The existence of these users supports the use of QR codes in emerging technologies and research projects. On the other hand, QR codes do not currently seem to have sufficient

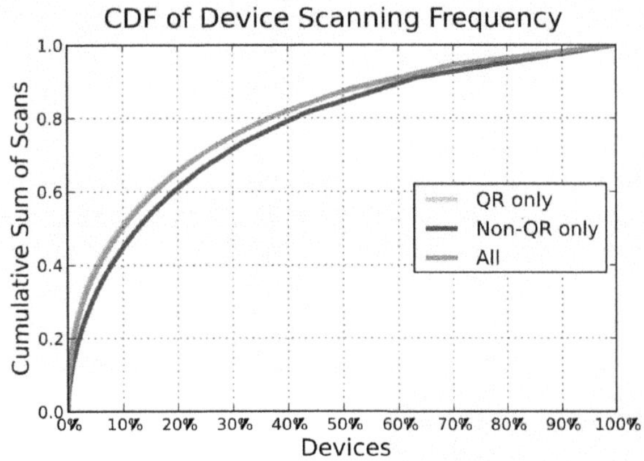


**Figure 4: The distribution of scans across devices. Devices had nearly identical distributions of scanning for QR codes and all codes combined — the yellow (QR only) and orange (All) lines overlap almost entirely. The right hand side of the figure shows 30% of devices which contributed only one scan each. Heavy hitters on the left: 10% of devices performed half the total scans in the dataset.**

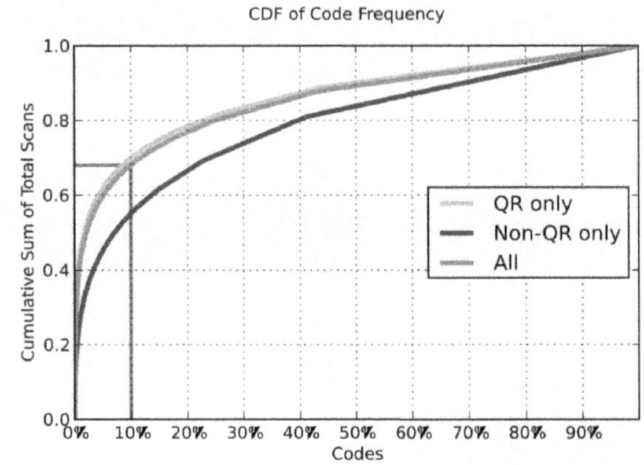


**Figure 5: The distribution of code popularity. The top 1% of codes were extremely popular: they made up over 42% of total scans. 10% of codes accounted for over 65% of the total scans that occurred, while in the tail, just over half of codes were only ever scanned once. We see similar trends among all codes, QR codes, and non-QR codes.**

appeal for all users (e.g., the 30% of devices with only one scan), thus suggesting that applications that involve a QR-code-based path may not (yet) see much adoption.

**Codes.** The 18.7 million distinct codes seen in the dataset also followed a typical heavy-hitter vs. long-tail distribution, with a small number of codes scanned many times and many codes scanned only once or a few times. Figure 5 shows the distribution of popularity amongst codes. The most popular code in the dataset had 244,660 scans (0.28% of all scans) while the top 11 individual codes accounted by themselves for 1% of all scans. (We note that the proportion of unpopular codes is artificially inflated by the fact that codes introduced near the end of our time period will necessarily show a low scan count, even if they were subsequently scanned many times.)

Counter to our initial hypotheses, about half of all codes were only ever scanned once, and only a small fraction of codes reach a large number of people. These popular codes speak to a particular set of uses and user experiences of mobile barcode scanning; we explore these popular codes in detail in Section 5.1. For example, we observe that many of the most popular codes are web links to sites of corporations, suggesting that heavy-hitters may be primarily scanned due to their presence in successful marketing efforts.

In addition, we find that less popular codes are more likely to correspond to a different set of applications, including interesting emerging applications such as cryptographic coins, business cards or WiFi pairing. These results thus suggest that QR codes are an attractive tool for designers of emerging mobile technologies. We explore these less popular codes in Sections 5.2 and 5.3.

**Code Types and URI Schemes.** Scan supports scanning both ordinary barcodes as well as QR codes. QR codes dominate usage of the app: about 87% of all 87 million scans were of QR codes, with the remaining 13% divided between different types of one-dimensional EAN and UPC product barcodes. Table 2 shows this breakdown.

**Table 2: Distribution of barcode types appearing in all scans in our dataset. Note that this table counts the appearance of code types in scans, i.e., codes that were scanned more than once are counted once per scan.**

| *Barcode Type* | *Count* |
|---|---|
| QR | 76,304,319 (87.06%) |
| EAN-13 | 6,554,534 (7.48%) |
| UPC-A | 3,701,269 (4.22%) |
| EAN-8 | 687,889 (0.78%) |
| UPC-E | 399,493 (0.46%) |
| *Total* | 87,647,504 (100%) |

While one-dimensional product barcodes encode only numbers, QR codes can contain arbitrary text. When this arbitrary text contains something more than a direct web URL, it is often made more useful by structuring it to contain a URI scheme, such as `tel:` for telephone numbers or `mecard:` for business cards. Table 3 describes the distribution of URI scheme among the scans in our dataset.

In our dataset, we find that the use of QR codes to encode web URLs dominates: as reflected in Table 3, about 86% of QR code scans (about 75% of all scans, including non-QR code scans) contained a web URL. This suggests that quickly connecting a mobile device to a website is by far the most common use case for QR codes. Of these web URLs, we find that only about 10% specified SSL through the `https:` URI scheme.

Though web URLs dominate the QR code scans in our dataset, we nevertheless observe that 14% of QR code scans (about 25% of all scans, including non-QR code scans) contain something other than a web URL. These 10,175,509 scans represent a non-trivial engagement with a variety of other use cases. For example, we did not initially anticipate the prevalence of some URI schemes, such as `wifi:` and `bitcoin:`. We return to discussing such use cases in

**Table 3: Distribution of URI schemes appearing in all QR code scans in our dataset. This table shows the number of scans of codes encoding actions in various protocols. Percentages are reported out of the 76 million QR code scans, not the total 87 million scans (that include barcode scans).**

| *URI Scheme* | *Note* | *Count* |
|---|---|---|
| `http://` | | 58,488,390 (76%) |
| `https://` | | 7,640,420 (10%) |
| `mecard:/vcard:` | Business cards | 1,759,773 (2.3%) |
| `market:` | Android app store | 197,407 (0.25%) |
| `smsto:` | Send SMS | 180,752 (0.23%) |
| `otpauth:` | Two-factor auth | 172,091 (0.22%) |
| `wifi:` | Connect to Wifi | 133,963 (0.17%) |
| `tel:` | Phone number | 123,150 (0.16%) |
| `bitcoin:` | Crypto currency | 39,073 (0.05%) |
| `itms-services:` | iOS app store | 30,663 (0.04%) |
| `litecoin:` | Crypto currency | 11,796 (0.01%) |
| `dogecoin:` | Crypto currency | 317 (<0.01%) |
| Other | | 7,526,524 (9.9%) |
| *Total* | | 76,304,319 (100%) |

**Table 4: Data density of codes of varying frequency of scanning.**

| | Bytes/code | |
|---|---|---|
| *Popularity* | *Mean* | *Median* |
| Infrequent (1-5 scans) | 58.7 | 43 |
| Moderate (6-100 scans) | 49.9 | 32 |
| Frequent (>100 scans) | 40.9 | 30 |

Section 5. A key takeaway from this general analysis, however, is that our dataset provides strong evidence that QR codes are used for many things besides websites.

**Data Density.** QR codes that encode less information are less visually dense. We investigate the distribution of densities among QR codes in our dataset. We find that on average, more popular codes encode about 18 fewer bytes of information than unpopular codes. The difference is smaller in the median, with a difference of 13 bytes between popular and unpopular codes.

This information suggests that successful, widely scanned QR codes tend to be shorter. We cannot tease apart from this fact whether people who create popular codes tend to make shorter codes (e.g., they tend to include nothing but a URL or explicitly optimized) or whether shorter codes are more likely to be scanned (e.g., a shorter code is processed by scanning applications more quickly, and therefore is more likely to be scanned before the user gives up in frustration).

## 4.2 Analyses over Time

**Usage Trends.** Our above analyses suggest that one- and two-dimensional barcodes are effective means to reach some users. We now ask: how do users engage with QR codes over time? For example, once a user installs the app, do they steadily scan codes over time, or does their usage peak initially due to factors like the novelty of the technology?

To investigate this question, we first examined user adoption rate throughout the time period of the data, looking at the first time each device was seen. Adoption rate remained relatively constant throughout the 10 month span — 

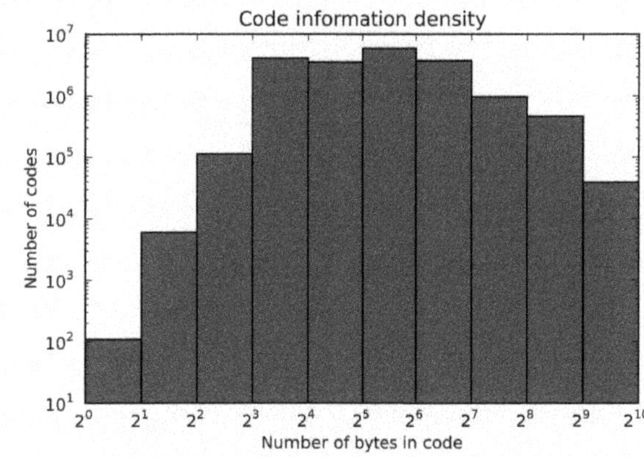


**Figure 6: Histogram of data density in codes, on a log scale. Codes of length 8-128 are most common.**

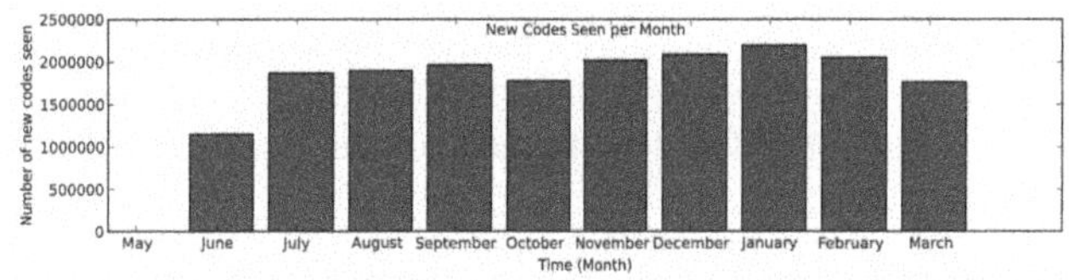


**Figure 8: Number of new codes seen per month.**

Figure 7 shows the weekly adoption rate by new devices, which hovers below 500,000.

We then examined the number of scans that took place in each week of the studied 10-month time period. The results are also shown in Figure 7. The rate fluctuated from about 1.3 million at the start to about 2.67 million in February of 2014, increasing initially and then leveling off around 1.5 million scans per week.

Comparing the two lines in Figure 7, we observe that although new users appear in the dataset at a regular rate, the number of scans does not increase at the same rate. There are several possible factors that may contribute to this trend besides users whose usage decreases after initial installation and exploration. For example, when a user replaces one device with another, that new device will contribute to the adoption rate but not cause an increased number of scans. Overall, however, this trend suggests that not all users continue to use the app at the same rate after initial installation.

**Codes.** We also explore the appearance of new codes over time. Figure 8 shows the rate of the appearance of new codes. Each bar shows the number of codes with unique text content, never seen up to that point in time, that were first scanned during that month. The high rate of appearance of new codes suggests that the ecosystem of QR and barcodes present in the physical world is constantly changing.

Note that the rate of new code appearance is quite similar to the rate of new user adoption. This trend suggests an active interest in the QR code ecosystem for both creating new codes and experimenting with the scanning of codes.

## 4.3 Variations by Geographic Region

Finally, we consider variations by geographic region in our dataset. We use location data reported by devices themselves when they perform a scan.

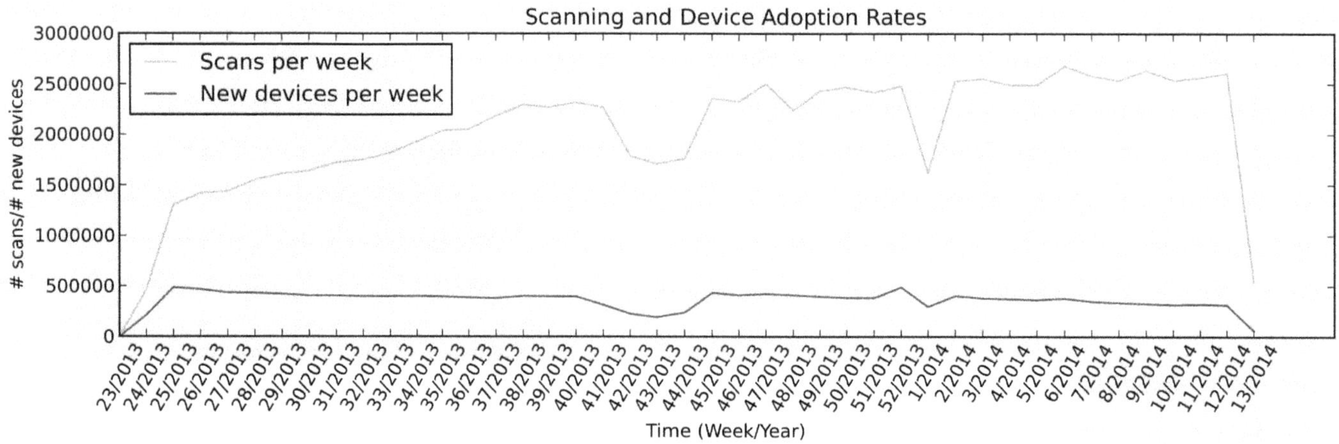


**Figure 7: Comparisons between scans per week and new devices appearing in the data per week, which is a proxy for user adoption of the app. These two properties are significantly correlated ($R^2 = 0.295$), suggesting that new users of these types of technologies may be a significant driver of the technology's usage in general. Note that the first and last data points are low because our data for those weeks is incomplete; similarly, the last week of 2013 is low because it is not a full seven days.**

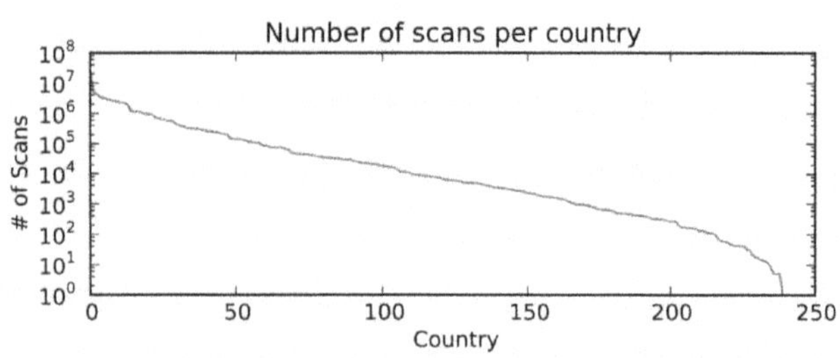


**Figure 9: The distribution of scans across the 241 countries seen in the dataset. The United States is at the top with an order of magnitude more scans than its nearest competitor, Germany. Note, however, that the United States has a much larger population than Germany.**

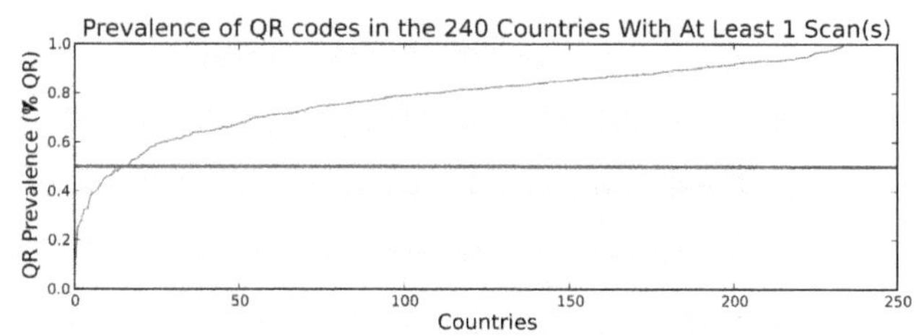


**Figure 10: Percentage of scans which were of QR codes (as opposed to 1D barcodes) per country for all countries. The blue line indicates the 50% QR mark — countries below the line performed more 1D barcode scans than QR code scans, whereas countries above the line performed predominantly QR code scans. 6 out of 15 of these 1D dominated countries had fewer than 1000 total scans in the database, and none of the 15 had more than 51,000 scans.**

**Scans.** Our data includes occurring in 241 countries. Of those countries, 19 had at least 1,000,000 scans and 60 had at least 100,000. We note that geographical diversity in scanning might be explained by the popularity of different QR and barcode scanning apps rather than the popularity of QR codes themselves. Our vantage with this dataset cannot distinguish such a difference.

Figure 9 shows the distribution of scans across countries worldwide, and Table 5 shows the number of scans in the most popular 32 cities in the dataset. We find that the top-scanning cities are quite geographically diverse, including cities in the United States, Europe, and Asia. These results suggest that QR codes are a global phenomenon, and not something restricted to a particular region of the world.

**Codes.** Looking across geography, we find that countries vary dramatically in the patterns of their usage of barcodes. Figure 10 shows the ratio of QR code scans to 1D barcode scans in each country as a PDF. Only a small number of countries have more one-dimensional barcode scans than QR scans, but there is notable variance even between those countries which are dominated by QR code scans. For example, QR code scans in one country (Bosnia and Herzegovina) make up about 99% of its 631,812 scans, while scans in Russia (4,482,254 total scans) were split 60%/40% between QR codes and one-dimensional QR codes barcodes.

Figure 11 shows the same data limited to the countries in which at least 100,000 scans were performed over the studied period. None of these 59 most scanning countries scanned more one-dimensional barcodes than QR codes, suggesting that QR code based use cases dominate among frequent users of the application. We emphasize that our geographical findings may not be representative of the entire QR code usage ecosystem because our results are only from a single application, and the popularity of this application compared to other applications may vary by geographic region.

Thus far, we have analyzed our dataset as a whole, considering distributions of the frequency of scans and types of codes, analyses over time, and geographic variations. In the next sections, we dive more deeply into specific popular and

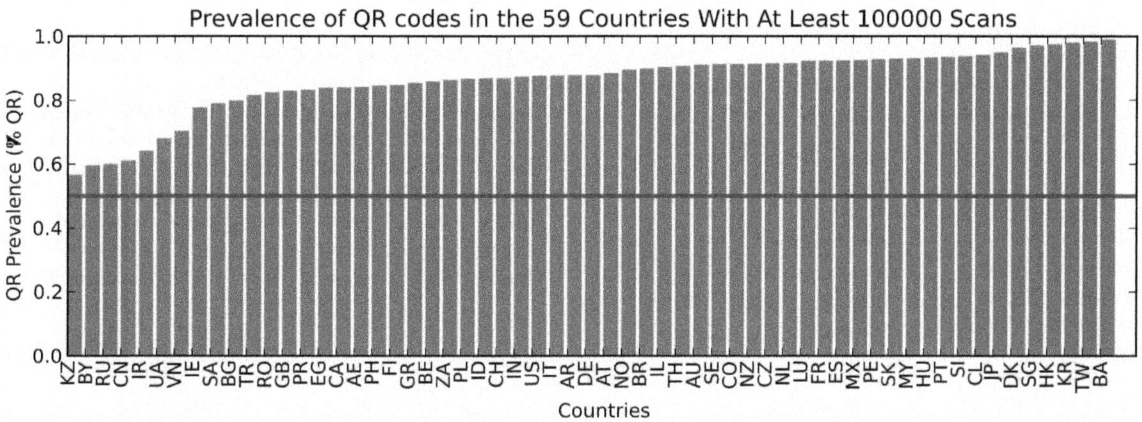


**Figure 11: Percentage of scans which were of QR codes (as opposed to 1D barcodes) per country for the most scanning countries. The blue line indicates the y-coordinate for 50% QR codes — all countries with at least** 100,000 **scans are above the line and performed predominantly QR code scans.**

unpopular codes as well as investigate specific use cases of QR codes.

## 5. USE CASE ANALYSES

Having analyzed the overall properties of the dataset, we now turn to analyzing specific use cases of QR codes and barcodes. Our analysis is three-fold. First, we consider the most popular codes (Section 5.1). These codes reflect the most common uses of QR codes in our dataset, and hence our analysis of them gives insight into a sizeable and important fraction of the one- and two-dimensional barcode ecosystem. However, our dataset contains many codes that are scanned infrequently (half of all codes in the dataset appear only once). Thus, we also conduct an analysis of infrequently scanned codes, which we define as codes that appear 5 or fewer times in our dataset (Section 5.2). Given the diversity of the unpopular codes, our analysis of unpopular codes in Section 5.2 is by necessity different than our analysis of popular codes in Section 5.1. We cannot, for example, simply pick the 100 least popular codes and analyze each of them (indeed, there are 16,792,603 codes scanned 5 or fewer times). Instead, in Section 5.3, we turn to analyzing in more detail specific use cases of QR codes (which span both popular and unpopular codes).

### 5.1 Popular Codes

#### 5.1.1 Contents of Popular Codes

We first investigate the contents of the 100 most popular (i.e., most frequently scanned) codes. The number of scans of the 100 most popular codes range from 244,660 for the most popular code to 11,925 for the 100th most popular code. The fact that even the most popular codes in the dataset are scanned a relatively modest number of times compared to the total number of scans suggests that users encounter a huge diversity of codes in practice.

We observe that the QR codes real users encounter often contain web links, and that many of the most popular of these links lead to corporate websites. Even among the most popular, however, corporate marketing links do not stand alone, with religious organizations and non-profits like Wikipedia appearing. We also observe a few niche but very popular uses of QR codes, including a code which appears *inside* a video game and a Bitcoin transfer code.

**Web Codes.** The most frequently scanned codes in the dataset are dominated by links to the web: 95 of the top 100 codes are web links. Most are explicit `http://` links, with a few exceptions: 5 are SSL (`https://`), while 2 are web links that don't specify HTTP or HTTPS explicitly. 40 of the links are to `.com` domains; 8 to `.org`; 3 to `.com.hk` or `.hk`; 4 to `.de`; 5 to `.jp`. At least 15 are shortened links from shortener services and/or QR-code generation services such as `goo.gl`, `bit.ly`, `j.mp`, and `tinyurl.com`, `qrs.ly`, `qr2.it`, and `qrstuff.com`.

The most popular web domains found in the top 100 codes were `jw.org` (Jehovah's Witnesses, 5 of the top 100 codes), `mcd.com`, `mcdonalds.com`, and `happystudio.com` (McDonalds Corporation, including their Happy Studio game, a total of 10/100), and `costco.ms` (3/100). We discuss popular domain in our dataset further below.

**Plain Text Codes.** Three of the most popular 100 codes are plain text, including the following texts: "**", "tpl_not_defined", and a multi-lingual free text message congratulating the person who scans it for having "successfully identified and scanned a QR code! Great job!" which was included in the video game *Guacamelee! Gold Edition* and was scanned 14,558 times by 8098 different devices. The popularity of QR codes displayed in the game speaks to the viability of mobile system applications that use QR codes as an exchange medium between two devices.

The meanings of "**" and "tpl_not_defined" are unclear to the authors of this study. We hypothesize that the latter may come from the QR code at `http://myopenapps.blogspot.com/2014/04/twilight-war-apk-for-android-free.html`, which appears that it intends to be a QR code that links to the associated application. The resulting QR code may have been created in error and published online before testing.

**Other.** The only non-QR code in the top 100 codes (#73) is an EAN-8 code for a bottle of a Coca-Cola product, 54491472. The 90th most popular code, with 13,177 scans, is a `bitcoin:`

**Table 5: Number of scans in the cities where we observe the most scans.**

| *Count* | *Country* | *City* |
|---|---|---|
| 1458830 | TW | Taipei |
| 756964 | HK | Central District |
| 436141 | RU | Moscow |
| 362383 | JP | Tokyo |
| 288478 | US | New York |
| 287529 | MX | Mexico |
| 235983 | CA | Toronto |
| 233458 | US | Chicago |
| 223886 | US | Austin |
| 223373 | US | Houston |
| 220564 | US | Minneapolis |
| 194981 | SG | Singapore |
| 187634 | FR | Paris |
| 180562 | GB | London |
| 179355 | CA | Montreal |
| 171356 | US | San Antonio |
| 170302 | US | Las Vegas |
| 164443 | DE | Berlin |
| 161584 | US | Los Angeles |
| 159301 | US | Virginia Beach |
| 153074 | KR | Seoul |
| 151308 | TW | Nankang |
| 150853 | US | Brooklyn |
| 149544 | US | Charlotte |
| 143165 | DK | Copenhagen |
| 140164 | US | Dallas |
| 137590 | RU | Saint Petersburg |
| 136527 | CH | Full |
| 135315 | US | Arlington |
| 134301 | US | Washington |
| 133922 | DE | Hamburg |
| 130249 | US | San Diego |

link specifying a Bitcoin transfer to a wallet belonging to `thepiratebay.sx`. We discuss the use of QR codes for Bitcoin and other cryptocurrencies in Section 5.3 below.

### 5.1.2 Popular Domains

As discussed above, a majority of QR codes contain web URLs. We break these URLs down by domain: Table 6 shows the top 50 domains in codes, ordered by the number of times each domain appeared in a code. Table 6 also shows the Alexa global rank of each domain for comparison.[3]

Counter to our initial expectation, we find little correspondence between domains that are popular on Alexa and domains that are popular in our dataset. While we do see some of the expected popular sites, including `google.com` and `facebook.com`, we also see a large presence of sites that are unpopular on the web in general. Indeed, 15 of the top 50 domains in our dataset do not even appear in the top 1 million sites on Alexa; an additional 7 domains do not appear in the Alexa top 100,000.

Instead of the conventionally popular websites, we observe increased prevalence of URL shorteners (such as `goo.gl` and `bit.ly`), domains that appear to be specific to QR codes

[3]Domain rank data acquired from `http://www.alexa.com` in November 2014. The domain ranks may have differed at the time the codes containing the domains were scanned.

**Table 6: The most popular domains found in URLs in codes scanned. These counts are of distinct codes which included one of these domains — multiple scans of a code are not counted here. Note that the count for `google.com` includes subdomains such as `play.google.com` and `docs.google.com`. The right-hand column shows the global Alexa rank for each domain as of November 2014 (values of N/A mean that Alexa does not have data for this domain).**

| *Domain* | *Unique Codes* | *Alexa Rank* |
|---|---|---|
| goo.gl | 2732005 | 462 |
| youtube.com | 2474840 | 3 |
| google.com | 1685677 | 1 |
| bit.ly | 1453335 | 4406 |
| facebook.com | 1436226 | 2 |
| apple.com | 1266273 | 35 |
| qrs.ly | 1063665 | 2789080 |
| kaywa.me | 689613 | 3124084 |
| delivr.com | 566530 | 243915 |
| premier-kladionica.com | 527672 | 133052 |
| scn.by | 507066 | N/A |
| 645lotto.net | 374325 | 288448 |
| youtu.be | 369834 | 10515 |
| mcd.com | 347196 | 152098 |
| jw.org | 341542 | 1415 |
| qq.com | 316432 | 10 |
| naver.com | 311335 | 112 |
| bitly.com | 309755 | 388 |
| mta.info | 293387 | 6151 |
| scan.me | 277870 | 140254 |
| nlotto.co.kr | 269148 | 57408 |
| vqr.mx | 266588 | 3349845 |
| tagr.com | 256771 | 13590936 |
| naver.jp | 250224 | 187 |
| towerofsaviors.com | 249296 | 98650 |
| mon-gain.fr | 239418 | 5561369 |
| dropbox.com | 237684 | 85 |
| metrohk.com.hk | 187164 | 81666 |
| bby.us | 181854 | 11907472 |
| tinyurl.com | 165680 | 591 |
| 2d-co.de | 163990 | 17873277 |
| augme.com | 160901 | N/A |
| safeshare.tv | 160412 | 17952 |
| windowsphone.com | 158093 | 1245 |
| phonegap.com | 150780 | 6809 |
| q-r.to | 137553 | 2758289 |
| happystudio.com | 137437 | 98193 |
| tipico.com | 133337 | 10734 |
| wikipedia.org | 126085 | 6 |
| mcdonalds.de | 122256 | 30767 |
| azon.biz | 109331 | N/A |
| j.mp | 106171 | 159932 |
| vk.com | 105176 | 22 |
| opn.to | 104969 | 8613897 |
| notifii.com | 104804 | 2065475 |
| padlet.com | 101033 | 6232 |
| qr2.it | 99324 | 16832364 |
| costco.ms | 98246 | N/A |
| paninifootballleague.com | 95096 | 137979 |
| bokgwon.or.kr | 93588 | N/A |

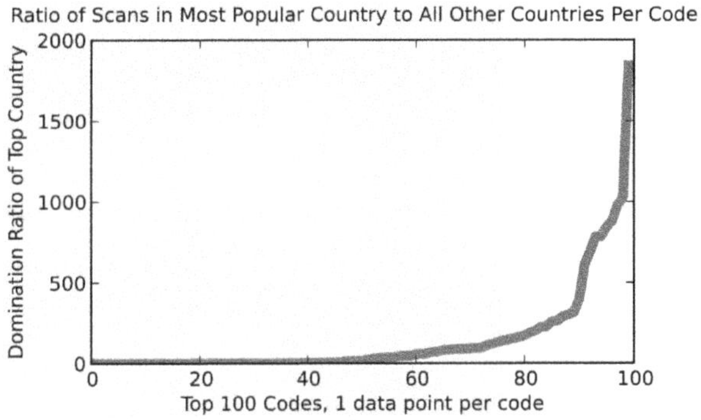


**Figure 12: The degree of geographic diversity in scans of the top 100 codes. The y-axis represents the degree to which the most scanning country dominates scans from all other countries, represented as a ratio of scans from that country to scans from all other countries.**

(such as `qrs.ly` and `kaywa.me`), domains related to lotteries (such as `645lotto.net` and `nlotto.co.kr`), and more. These results suggest that the QR code-based web ecosystem is different than the traditional browser based web, with some of the major QR code-based web sites not having a proportionately large presence on the browser-based web.

### *5.1.3 Geography of Popular Codes*

The most popular codes in the dataset are quite diverse in terms of geographic diversity. On the one hand, some codes show very high geographic diversity, with the most popular country for one of these popular codes responsible only for about 9% of scans. On the other hand, some codes show almost no geographic diversity. 37 codes are dominated by scans from a single country by a factor of 100: the most popular country for each of these codes has scanned the code 100 times more often than all other countries combined. In the most extreme case, the most popular country for a particular code (Japan) has over 1800 times the number of scans (12900 scans) as all other countries combined (12907 combined scans total).

Figure 12 shows the ratio of top-country scans to all scans for the 100 most popular codes. For a third of the most popular 100 codes, this ratio is under 1, indicating that no single country was responsible for more than half the scans of these codes. The content of these high-diversity codes are quite diverse, including the link to donate bitcoins to The Pirate Bay, the code from the Guacamelee video game, English language Wikipedia, and a link to a personal blog. 11 of these 33 high-diversity codes lead to pages which are primarily offering the download of mobile apps or which include calls to action to download mobile apps. This suggests that codes with high geographical diversity are more likely to be used in at least two particular cases: more unusual/less corporate uses (religious and non-profits), and to encourage installation of mobile applications.

The most popular code in the dataset (244,660 scans) links to a landing page for a mobile game for iOS and Android. Its scans are dominated by scans from Taiwan (243,450 scans in Taiwan), with a ratio of 200 Taiwanese scans to each scan from any other country (443 scans in the next-closest country, Malaysia). Digging deeper, those scans in Taiwan are dominated by scans in Taipai, but the code retains significant geographic diversity of scans within Taiwan.

## 5.2 Unpopular Codes

Having considered popular codes, we now turn to unpopular codes. In particular, we consider infrequently scanned codes, which we define to be those that appear 5 or fewer times in our dataset. Note that while the vast majority of codes are infrequently scanned (89% of codes), the scans of those codes account for only 31% of all scans in the dataset, since the frequently scanned codes are often scanned hundreds or thousands of times (see Figure 5).

Given the large number of infrequent codes (16,792,603) and their diversity, we cannot simply pick the 100 least frequently scanned codes (as we did for popular codes) and analyze each of them. Rather, we explore now the quantitative differences between frequently scanned, moderately scanned, and infrequently scanned codes.

Specifically, we compare trends of content and usage among codes of differing scanning frequency. For this analysis, we defined "frequently" scanned codes to be those scanned more than 100 times in our dataset, "moderately" scanned codes to be those scanned 6-100 times, and "infrequently" scanned codes to be those scanned 5 or fewer times. This division into bins of 1-5, 6-100 and over 100 scans serves to divide the codes into groups each accounting for approximately one third of all scans in the dataset.

Table 7 lists the fraction of codes for each content type (e.g., web, telephone, etc.) that were infrequently, moderately, or frequently scanned. The important comparisons in this table are not across columns — since most codes are scanned infrequently, a given code is most likely to be an infrequent code. Instead, this table allows us to compare across content types in a column: is one content type more or less likely than another content type to be in that frequency category? For example, Android `market:` QR codes are more likely to be scanned moderately than business cards.

## 5.3 Specific Use Cases

We now turn to our analysis of specific uses — and *mis*uses — of QR codes present in our dataset. These use cases, which span both popular and unpopular codes, present a snapshot of different actual uses of QR codes in the wild.

We organize this section into subsections corresponding to five themes: web-related use cases, codes including private data, emerging uses, errors, and malicious uses. A single use case may in fact span multiple themes, but we have organized the section this way to highlight these themes.

### *5.3.1 Specific Web-Related Uses*

We dive more deeply into two specific web-related use cases: shortened URLs and links to adult websites.

**Shortened URLs.** Many of the web URLs scanned by users were shortened by one of several URL shortening services (e.g., `bit.ly` or `goo.gl`). 984,447 of 11,763,834, or about 8% of URLs seen in the dataset were shortened. To find shortened URLs we checked them against a list of about 40 shortening services that we compiled from sources on the Internet and manually checking URLs which looked like they might be shorteners. A small number of URL shortening services dominated the shorteners seen: 88% of shortened URLs were shortened by Google's URL shortener (`goo.gl`) or by Bitly (`bit.ly`, `bitly.com`). `qr.net`, a service which

**Table 7: Comparison of QR code contents for three categories of code: frequent, moderate and infrequent codes. We defined infrequent codes to be those with 1-5 scans, moderate codes those with 6-100, and frequent codes those with over 100 scans. The table lists the fraction of codes for each content type that were infrequently, moderately, or frequently scanned. For example, 18.15% of codes leading to Android apps on the market (last row, `market:`) had 6-100 scans (moderate), while a business card is only 1.78% likely to be scanned that many times. The dominance of infrequent codes in general is due to the fact that most codes in the dataset are infrequently scanned — 89% of all codes had 5 or fewer scans (see Figure 5).**

| Scheme | Total Codes | Frequent % | Moderate % | Infrequent % |
|---|---|---|---|---|
| Business cards (vcard + mecard) | 670359 | 0.01% | 1.78% | 98.20% |
| Dogecoin | 184 | 0.00% | 3.26% | 96.74% |
| BBM (Blackberry Message) | 71985 | 0.01% | 3.45% | 96.54% |
| Litecoin | 525 | 0.19% | 4.38% | 95.43% |
| otpauth (2-factor auth) | 79000 | 0.00% | 4.87% | 95.13% |
| Bitcoin | 10199 | 0.16% | 4.98% | 94.86% |
| Wifi | 55741 | 0.03% | 6.58% | 93.40% |
| iOS apps (`itms-services:` ) | 10179 | 0.14% | 7.51% | 92.36% |
| Barcode | 3647582 | 0.00% | 8.14% | 91.86% |
| Telephone # | 38849 | 0.13% | 8.62% | 91.26% |
| HTTPS | 1507300 | 0.43% | 9.88% | 89.69% |
| SMS | 839 | 0.12% | 10.73% | 89.15% |
| HTTP | 12254403 | 0.53% | 11.13% | 88.33% |
| Android Market (`market:`) | 18544 | 1.15% | 18.15% | 80.70% |
| All (mean over all contents) | 18763779 | 0.4% | 10.2% | 89.4% |

simultaneously shortens a URL and generates a QR code linking to that shortened URL, appeared as the 7th most popular shortener with 4224 shortened URLs.

We can hypothesize a few purposes for shortening URLs in QR codes. While it may seem odd to shorten URLs in a format which is already only machine readable, we note that URL shorteners are often used for analytics purposes (e.g., to track clicks). Additionally, QR codes with shorter URLs will have less data density, and hence may be easier to scan by some QR code scanners.

**Adult Websites.** We observed a number of scans of URLs leading to websites which serve adult content. We manually identified 4 domains in the Alexa top 100 whose names clearly indicate that they are adult sites (we may have missed adult sites with less obvious names). We found 7736 scans of 1929 distinct links to these 4 domains.

The human-opaque nature of QR codes makes them a vector for displaying or referencing age- or context-inappropriate material in plain view. We note that for many popular barcode scanners, including the most popular one in the Android Marketplace, the scanner app automatically fetches and displays the title of the specified website. Thus, even if the app doesn't automatically take the user to the site, and even if the site asks visitors for their age (the most popular site in the dataset does not), users will be shown the title of the video or page linked to, which may be inappropriate for them or their context. Further, automatically fetching the website's title will cause the user's device to connect to the site in question without the user's explicit intention.

Our dataset shows that QR codes with links to adult content do exist and are scanned by real users with some regularity. We thus suggest that the designers of QR code scanning applications consider these concerns, perhaps using a list of known adult websites to mask website titles, avoid automatically fetching titles at all, or show additional warnings before redirecting users to such sites.

### *5.3.2 Private Data*

We observe a number of use cases that involve encoding private information into a QR code.

**Wifi Setup Codes.** QR codes can be used to encode the information needed to connect a device to a Wifi network. We found 55,809 unique such codes, which were scanned a total of 134,121 times.

For private Wifi networks, these codes contain the plaintext password used to authenticate with the network, exposing that password to anyone with a QR code reader in range of the QR code. As always-on devices with the capability to read QR codes become more prevalent (e.g., Google Glass), we might expect that the threat of (intentional or unintentional) shoulder surfing to read QR codes containing such sensitive information will increase. Another lesson from these results is that designers of applications that emit QR codes should consider the implications of putting private information in the QR codes — an untrustworthy QR code scanner would be able to extract that information. The makers of QR code scanners must also take precautions to protect the privacy of data contained in scanned QR codes.

**Two-Factor Authentication.** We found 79,017 distinct codes using the `otpauth://` scheme, which is used to set up two-factor authenticators (e.g., Google Authenticator). This suggests that two-factor authentication is used by a significant number of people. The URIs included codes to set up authenticators for Microsoft-related accounts (25,753), as well as accounts for Facebook (15,977), Gmail (10,108), Dropbox (2360), Zoho (766), WordPress (741), GitHub (524 codes), DigitalOcean (427), and a large number of others, some of which appeared to be malformed. Most of these codes (78,680) used the standard time-based (TOTP) version of the protocol; the remaining well-formed URIs specify the HMAC-based (HOTP) version of the protocol.

Of the `otpauth://` codes we found, the vast majority (about 99.5%) were only ever scanned by a single device, indicating that only one device was set up to authenticate for that account. Note that unlike Wifi setup codes containing passwords (discussed above), viewing another user's two-factor authentication setup code is not as dangerous, as they do not allow the attacker to compromise the user's account without the primary authentication password. However, they would allow someone to compromise the user's second factor by obtaining the secret used to initiate it.

**PGP Keys.** A QR code containing a public key such as a PGP key is a natural way to convey cryptographic credentials. For example, a person might include their public key as a QR code on their business card to make it easy for acquaintances to import the key and support subsequent communications. Key distribution has long been a topic of interest and study for making cryptographic systems of trust usable and used. Physical artifacts such as QR codes represent an interesting point in the space of these solutions.

The dataset contains 30 codes representing PGP public keys and 4 codes representing private keys. One of these PGP keys is found embedded in a business card format, while the others stand alone, with the entire QR code representing a full PGP public key block. The public keys were scanned only a total of 56 times, representing a tiny percentage of the scans in the data. The 4 private keys were scanned only 7 times altogether. While we cannot conclude anything in particular from these examples, we note that sharing a private key instead of a public key could be a serious breach of cryptographic security, and that code creator error could result in the inclusion of private keys in scenarios like QR code generation. While these inclusions of private keys could be intentional, the danger of human error in QR code creation is illustrated here. As with Wifi and two-factor setup codes, this finding suggests that QR code creators and consumers should exercise care with private data.

### *5.3.3 Emerging and Niche Uses*

**Bitcoin and Other Crypto Currencies.** Our dataset provides us with a glimpse into the use of Bitcoin [24] and other crypto currencies, such as Dogecoin [10] and Litecoin [26]. The `bitcoin:` URI scheme is used for directing a device to make a Bitcoin payment and includes the wallet to pay to and the number of bitcoins to transfer. We found 10,199 codes containing Bitcoin URIs, specifying payments to 8541 distinct Bitcoin wallets. The most popular Bitcoin URI in our data points to `thepiratebay.se`'s Bitcoin address, suggesting that many people made (or considered making) donations to that site. This URI was popular enough to be one of the 100 most scanned codes. Note, however, that the presence of a Bitcoin transaction scan in our dataset does not necessarily mean that the transaction was confirmed by the user and committed to the Bitcoin network.

Bitcoin is significantly more prevalent in our dataset than other cryptocurrencies; we found only 186 Dogecoin URIs and 525 Litecoin URIs.

We also found codes which appear to represent Bitcoin private keys in Wallet Import Format (WIF) [3]. Keys in WIF are 51 characters long and begin with 5 for private keys. We found 2483 codes in the format of a bitcoin private key, according to the above definition, and verified that 1260 of them are well formatted, i.e., that they can be decoded into private keys which could be used to import the corresponding wallet. We did not import any of them.

**Boarding Passes and Event E-Tickets.** We found electronic tickets, both for transportation as well as for events such as concerts, among the codes scanned in the dataset.

For boarding passes, we found 2416 codes which appear to be in a standardized format for airline boarding passes containing confirmation codes, flight departure and arrival times, airport codes, and names of passengers. These boarding passes were scanned a total of 5396, with 1101 of them scanned only once, 668 scanned twice, and the remaining 647 were scanned more than twice. One boarding pass was scanned 25 times by the same device.

We also found a variety of URLs and eTicket formats for event tickets. We note significant diversity in the formats and strategies used by eTicketing systems. For example, some codes included an `https://` link to a backend ticket processing system which doesn't seem to host public content , while others lead to sites on the public web. These systems seemed not to follow a common standard or format.

There is greater standardization in airline boarding passes than in other eTicketing systems. We attribute this naturally to the need for interoperability between different airlines, security agencies and airports. The contrast between these two systems with similar purposes (admission of a person to a restricted location or event) but differing levels of standardization speaks to the different ways that technologies like QR codes can be used depending on usage context.

**Never Gonna Give You Up.** A popular joke on the Internet is to link unexpectedly to a video of the Rick Astley song "Never Going to Give You Up" (referred to as "rickrolling") [34]. Because QR codes are not human-readable, they may be an appealing mechanism for delivering this URL to an unsuspecting victim. Indeed, we found 1614 scans of 40 un-shortened codes and 24 shortened codes containing the URL of the video (`https://www.youtube.com/watch?v=dQw4w9WgXcQ`) by devices in 63 countries. The simplest code for a rickroll (with only the URL presented above) was scanned over a thousand times and was likely created by many different people who all chose to create identical codes which were scanned in a diversity of places and at differing times. The most popular country for rickrolling was the United States (with 589 scans), followed by Great Britain and France (with 194 and 154 scans respectively). This suggests that while a few dozen people may have thought to use QR codes in such a joke, each individual creator is unlikely to have spread their code far. While these numbers are small, it suggests that people are using QR codes for innovative, homebrew purposes.

Similar in spirit to rickrolling, we find 993 scans, over 711 different devices and 597 different cities, of the following quote from the movie *Fight Club*: "It could be worse. A female could cut off your Dick while your sleeping and throw it out a moving vehicle." (sic) This QR code, which consisted entirely of text and not a link, also demonstrates that QR codes can be used as a vehicle for communicating directly with humans, rather than first to a mobile device for processing (e.g., rather provide a URI or a PGP key).

**TagMeNot.** Our dataset gives us a unique opportunity to measure the prevalence of emerging uses of QR codes.

For example, `TagMeNot.info` is a "pre-emptive, anticipatory, vendor independent, and free opt-out technology for pictures taken in public places" [4]. TagMeNot is an early example of cyber-physical interactions in which aspects of the physical world can be interpreted in digital context. QR codes from TagMeNot indicate that the wearer of the code wishes to opt-out of certain sharing or usage of their likeness or property by the takers of photographs. We found that the code `TagMeNot.info` was scanned only 7 times by 5 different devices in Mexico, Italy, Great Britain, and the United States, suggesting that such opt-out QR codes have not been widely adopted for privacy in the face of ubiquitous cameras.

### *5.3.4 Erroneous Uses*

Throughout our analysis of our dataset, we observed a variety of malformed QR codes. In this section, we consider one potentially erroneous use in detail.

**JavaScript.** To our surprise, we observed a number of QR codes containing JavaScript or HTML content. For example, 154 codes, which were scanned a collective 303 times, contained JavaScript code under the URI scheme `javascript:`. Most of these codes are treated merely as plaintext by most QR code readers (i.e., the readers do not attempt to execute the JavaScript, or even offer the opportunity to do so).

We hypothesize that most of these codes suggest a lack of understanding of how to use these code snippets or of the purpose and usage model of QR codes on the part of QR code creators. For example, one of the JavaScript snippets is code for a browser bookmarklet that creates a QR code [17]. Its presence in our dataset suggests that the creator misunderstood how to use this code, which should be pasted into a browser bookmark rather than into a QR code.

### *5.3.5 Malicious Uses*

Finally, we consider a number of potential malicious uses of QR codes and investigate their prevalence in our dataset.

**Premium Telephone Numbers.** In the United States and Canada, certain telephone number area codes designate sets of numbers as toll-free or premium numbers [31]. One might hypothesize that QR codes are a vector for tricking people into calling expensive premium numbers. However, we did not find any numbers that we believe to be premium numbers from the US/Canadian system. We did find 667 numbers which appear to be toll free numbers (for example, 1-800 numbers). These numbers were overwhelmingly scanned in the US (91% of scans), suggesting that our guess that these numbers are US toll free numbers is correct.

**Special Phone Numbers.** Phones often respond with special actions, such as displaying statistics or factory resetting, when special codes are dialed. For example, some Samsung phones display their IMEI number when "*#06#" is typed into the dialer. We find 126 scans of Samsung special codes in our dataset. One such code factory resets certain Samsung devices (*2767*3855#) [22]. Putting such a code into a QR code may be dangerous, since the code must only be displayed in the dialer (i.e., the user must not press the call button) and the device does not ask for confirmation. Indeed, we find 17 scans of this code, suggesting that someone may have attempted to test or actually carry out an attack. Fortunately, none of the scans come from devices of the make and model that treats this code as a factory reset.

**Malicious URLs.** Prior work [32, 35] has suggested that QR codes are a promising vector for distributing malicious URLs. Intuitively, QR codes seem like a natural conduit for phishing attacks or the distribution of malware (e.g., sending users to drive-by-download sites). QR codes are opaque, machine readable pointers, which might make it harder for a user to check that a link is trustworthy. Some QR code apps (including Scan) can be configured to automatically load the URL in a browser without user confirmation. Additionally, the real-world context surrounding a QR code (e.g., its placement on a marketing poster for a trusted brand) might cause the user to trust the code. Our dataset gives us the unique opportunity to study whether users encounter malicious QR code links in the wild.

We investigate this question using Google's Safe Browsing API[4], which provides classifications of a URL as *malware* and/or *phishing*, or *ok*. We randomly sampled URLs in our dataset and queried them against this API (unshortening any URLs shortened by `bit.ly` in the process, using `bit.ly`'s API). Note that the malware/phishing status of a website may change over time (e.g., as a malicious site is taken down or a legitimate site is compromised), but the Safe Browsing API does not provide us with historical data, so our results are necessarily limited.

Of the 1,017,955 unique URLs that we tested, we found 209 URLs flagged as *malware* (0.02%) and zero URLs flagged as *phishing*. We were surprised by the latter result, which may suggest that QR codes are presently not a common way to distribute phishing websites. The 209 malicious URLs represent 106 unique domains. Though the fraction of malicious URLs in our dataset is low, the fact that we observe some instances of potentially dangerous URLs suggests that QR code scanning applications should integrate the Safe Browsing API or similar to check URLs before automatically visiting them or allowing the user to visit them.

Note that like QR codes, shortened URLs hide the destination URL and thus might serve as convenient vectors for distributing malware and phishing links. However, similar to our findings, prior work has found that users rarely encounter malicious shortened URLs [19].

**Malicious Android Applications.** Digging deeper into the many web URLs in the dataset, we find that a non-trivial number point to Android applications (i.e., `apk` files). Of QR codes containing web URLs, 49,282 (0.07%) contain such links. Whereas the `market:` URI scheme points to Android applications on the official Google Play app store, `apk` files referenced by web URLs do not come from the official store. Users who have enabled the setting on their Android device allowing application installs from untrusted sources may be prompted to install apps they download through a link.

Since QR codes visually obfuscate links, an attacker may be able to trick an unsuspecting user into installing an Android application in this way. Thus, a natural question to ask is whether any of the `apk` links in our dataset point to malicious Android applications. To investigate this question, we first downloaded each of these `apk` files that was still accessible on the web, and then submitted it to the VirusTotal API for scanning. VirusTotal[5] is a subsidiary of Google that scans files and URLs using multiple antivirus scanners and website engines.

[4] `https://developers.google.com/safe-browsing/`
[5] `https://www.virustotal.com/`

Indeed, we do find instances of known Android malware among the `apk` links in our dataset. We attempted to download the `apk` files from a random sample of 4000 scans containing `apk` links. Of these, 2591 downloads were successful, with the rest failing due to 404 (not found) errors or connection timeouts. We submitted each of these applications to VirusTotal, receiving a result specifying the number of third-party virus scanners checked (generally 40-60) and the number of these that flagged the file. We investigate the VirusTotal report for each application that triggered more than 5 warnings. We find that 26 applications (1.0% of the 2591 apps we downloaded and scanned) are classified as explicit malware (e.g., Trojans). Another 45 applications (1.7%) are classified as Adware, and another 26 (1.0%) are classified as otherwise suspicious. None of these flagged applications appeared twice in the 4000 scans we considered.

We were surprised at the relatively high percentage of `apk` files flagged as malicious or suspicious. Possibly, some users scan QR codes with the intent of downloading applications to help them root their phones (such apps are considered malware by VirusTotal). For example, this video walks a user through the process of rooting their phone and shows a QR code that, when scanned, will download the rooting application: `https://www.youtube.com/watch?v=np18BC6BOOY` (at 1:35). This use case may account for the relatively high number of malicious `apk` files in our dataset.

We spot-checked some of the URLs pointing to malicious `apk` files against the Google Safe Browsing API. The API does not necessarily flag these URLs as malicious. This suggests that it may not be sufficient for a scanning app to check URLs against the Safe Browsing API or similar.

# 6. DISCUSSION AND FUTURE WORK

We conducted a systematic, in-depth analysis of barcode and QR code usage in the wild. Our results show that barcodes and QR codes, which can enable a physical object to communicate information to a mobile device via a visual channel, are widely used. We analyze that usage in depth. Overall, we believe that our results should be encouraging the researchers and industry practitioners developing new ways of leveraging barcodes and QR codes with mobile devices. We see strong evidence of emerging use cases in our dataset. Our results do, however, provide a cautionary note: while some users seem to frequently scan codes, other users seem to use their code scanner more as a novelty (with some users only scanning a single code).

We now turn to several lessons from our study, as well as recommendations to the designers of QR and barcode scanning applications.

**Key Lessons.** Stepping back, we summarize the key lessons our analyses reveal about the use cases for QR codes and the frequency with which real users encounter these use cases in practice. These lessons include:

- *QR codes are an effective way to reach some users, but many users are infrequent.* QR codes are still an active technology. However, their use is not universal or uniform: the top users in our dataset performed a stunning number of scans. Half of scans were performed by only 10% of devices, suggesting that this set of users is easily reached by QR codes (e.g., in marketing campaigns). However, many users scan only infrequently: almost one third of devices in our dataset scanned only once. Indeed, we find that despite a steady adoption rate by new devices, the rate of total scans levels out.
- *Web use cases dominate QR codes.* The majority (75%) of scans are of QR codes containing web URLs, suggesting that QR code use is dominated by the use case of quickly connecting users to websites. The popular domains appearing in QR codes do not correspond with domains that are popular on the web in general, with higher popularity of domains specific to QR codes (e.g., `qrs.ly`) and certain use cases (e.g., lottery).
- *Nevertheless, non-web uses are prevalent and varied.* Though non-web codes accounts for only about 25% of all scans (14% of QR code scans), the raw numbers of such scans are still significant. Moreover, the non-web use cases are distributed across a variety of different uses, including Wifi and one-time password setup codes, Bitcoin transactions, and other more niche uses cases. Thus, QR codes appear to be commonly used for a variety of emerging uses.
- *Some codes are intended for broadcast, while others are more limited use.* In comparing frequently and infrequently scanned QR codes, we observe that unique instances of some types of codes (e.g., Android app store URLs) are scanned more frequently than unique instances of other types (e.g., device pairing codes).
- *Scans and codes show no predictable geographic trends.* We observed no consistent geographic distributions of top codes: some are scanned only in one country, others are widely distributed. The cities where we observe the most scans are also geographically diverse. Our caveat about perspective of a single app still applies.
- *QR codes are not commonly used for malicious purposes, but users do encounter some malicious codes in practice.* Though we find that users in our dataset rarely encounter malicious QR codes, our dataset does several examples of malicious QR codes appearing in the wild, including URLs flagged as malicious by Google, links to Android applications containing malware, and a (possibly malicious) factory reset telephone code. Though these cases are rare, users may still encounter them, which informs our recommendations to creators of QR codes and scanning applications below.
- *Some code creators struggle to create correct QR codes.* We observed evidence of malformed QR codes of various types, including QR codes that containing JavaScript intended for a browser bookmarklet. In fact, we hypothesize that one of the top 100 most frequently scanned QR codes was created in error. System designers should not trust code creators to always create correct codes, and researchers should consider code creation as a possible point of failure.

**Recommendations.** Based on our findings, we make the following recommendations to the designers of QR and barcode scanning applications. Scan plans to take these recommendations into account in future version of the application.

*Check for malicious or questionable URLs before automatically opening the link found in a QR code.* Although we find that malicious URLs are uncommon, we nevertheless find some examples of malicious links in our dataset, including links to malicious Android applications, URLs marked as malware by the Google Safe Browsing API, and telephone codes that can factory reset some devices. We also find a significant number of links to adult sites, which, while not malicious, may not be appropriate for all users and in all contexts. Since users are unable to evaluate the content of a QR code visually, QR code scanning applications should be careful not to automatically load content, including a website's title, for potentially questionable links without first obtaining explicit user consent. We note that checking whether a link is malicious may not always be straightforward — for example, we observed that not all URLs leading to malicious `apk` files are flagged by the Safe Browsing API.

As wearable devices with the capability to quickly and automatically read QR codes, such as Google Glass, become more common, this recommendation will become even more critical. There have already been attacks against Google Glass that take advantage of automatic QR code reading, tricking Glass devices into joining unsafe Wifi networks [12].

*Take steps to protect private information.* Some codes contain private information, such as secrets used to authenticate to Wifi networks, initialize one-time passwords, or access Bitcoin private keys. These codes expose secrets to bystanders, who may be able to intentionally or unintentionally shoulder surf (especially if the bystander has a wearable devices such as Google Glass). Thus, designers of systems that use QR codes should consider the privacy needs of the data in the codes. They also need to consider the set of all potential scanning apps as part of the system's trusted computing base since, if the scanning applications are not trustworthy, the system's privacy properties may not be met. On the scanning side, perhaps the results of a scan of a QR code that contains certain classes of private information (such as private keys) should not be shown to users unless the user (rather than the device) has explicitly initiated the scan; this design would eliminate accidental shoulder surfing.

Users may face significant security risks if the ways in which scanning tools and system designers use QR codes don't match up well with users' expectations of the sensitivity of code data. While system designers should take steps behind the scenes, communicating a better model to users of which actions may be risky and which data may need to be protected could improve security significantly.

As a result of these findings, Scan plans for future releases to (1) add a user-friendly option to opt-out of data collection and to (2) emphasize their data collection policies directly in the user interface of the app.

**Future work.** We briefly outline directions for future work. First, an additional investigation of QR code misuse that we may be able to conduct with our dataset is an exploration of QR code based attacks attempting to exploit QR and barcode scanning applications themselves (e.g., via input validation vulnerabilities and other attacks described in related work [7, 16]) or the website linked to in the QR code (e.g., via malicious query parameters). We did not study these exploit attempts in this paper because, for example, we do not know of a public repository of exploits against different scanning app + operating system configurations. A rigorous analysis might involve running each QR code through different combinations of scanning apps and operating systems, e.g., as was done for web browsers [23, 33].

We would also like to explore how much of the web linked from QR codes is not reachable by crawling the general web. The answer to this question has implications for any application that relies on the reachability of sites via a web crawl. For example, an application like Google Safe Browsing may find webpages to scan based on a crawl and might therefore miss websites linked only in the QR code based web. This gap would in turn pose challenges to QR code scanning applications attempting to test scanned URLs for safety.

This study focused on what we can learn about QR code use from our dataset of real-world scans. It would be valuable to extend our knowledge with a user study that more directly investigated both code creators' and scanners' motivations and experiences with creating and scanning QR codes — e.g., building on [32] to understand how frequently users scan codes in specific physical locations. A user study would also allow us to learn about non-users of QR and barcode scanning applications, a population that is inaccessible in our current dataset by definition.

**Limitations.** Finally, we mention several limitations of our dataset. First, while our dataset is large and and diverse enough that we believe it provides us with general information about the use of QR and barcodes, we are nevertheless limited to this single vantage point of one QR and barcode scanning application. Other applications may be popular among different user groups or in different regions with different behaviors. Similarly, because our dataset ends at a particular date, we expect that devices and codes appearing late in the dataset may be underrepresented; they may become more popular after the end of our dataset. As discussed above, while we use the term "user", we do not strictly have information about users but about devices, which may not map one-to-one onto the set of users.

## 7. CONCLUSION

One- and two-dimensional barcodes, including QR codes, present a convenient way to link physical objects to digital actions and have been widely adopted in both commercial and academic settings. In this paper, we have presented (to the best of our knowledge) the first in-depth study of QR and barcodes in the wild, leveraging a unique dataset of 87 million scans from users of Scan, a popular QR code scanning application.

In our analysis, we examined general use patterns of QR and barcodes in the wild, finding that QR codes dominate barcodes and that some users interact frequently with QR codes in the wild whereas other users scan only a single code. We find that a majority of scans contain web URLs, but we also identify a wide range of varied and emerging uses of QR codes, including device pairing and crypto currencies (e.g., Bitcoin). We also identify misuses of QR codes, both by code creators who create malformed codes, as well as potentially intentional malicious behaviors, including links to malware.

Our findings allow us to develop an informed understanding about the types of QR codes being created and how users interact with them in the wild. From these findings, we distill concrete recommendations for QR and barcode scanning applications (e.g., to protect private data and check for malicious URLs). The sheer number of users, scans, and use cases represented in our dataset should be encouraging to researchers and industry practitioners developing new ways of leveraging QR and barcodes with mobile devices.

## Acknowledgements

We thank our shepherd, Mary Baker, and our anonymous reviewers for valuable feedback on an earlier version. We thank VirusTotal for providing access to premium services for the scanning of APK files. We also thank Adam Shostack for the idea of looking for rickrolls and Alexei Czeskis for earlier discussions. This work was supported in part by NSF Award CNS-0846065, by the Short-Dooley Endowed Career Development Professorship, and by the University of Washington Tech Policy Lab, which was founded with a gift from Microsoft in 2013.

## References

[1] C. M. Baker, L. R. Milne, J. Scofield, C. L. Bennett, and R. E. Ladner. Tactile graphics with a voice: Using QR codes to access text in tactile graphics. In *Proceedings of the 16th International ACM SIGACCESS Conference on Computers & Accessibility*, 2014.

[2] A. J. Bernheim Brush, T. Combs Turner, M. A. Smith, and N. Gupta. Scanning objects in the wild: Assessing an object triggered information system. In *Proceedings of the 7th International Conference on Ubiquitous Computing (UbiComp)*, 2005.

[3] Bitcoin community. Wallet import format, 2014. `https://en.bitcoin.it/wiki/Wallet_import_format`.

[4] A. Cammozzo. TagMeNot, 2011. `http://tagmenot.info/`.

[5] D. Chaffey. The Who, Why and Where of using QR or action codes for marketing. Smart Insights, sep 2012. `http://www.smartinsights.com/mobile-marketing/qr-code-marketing/qr-codes-location-demographic-statistics/`.

[6] Comscore. QR Code Usage Among European Smartphone Owners Doubles Over Past Year, Sept. 2012. `http://www.comscore.com/Insights/Press-Releases/2012/9/QR-Code-Usage-Among-European-Smartphone-Owners-Doubles-Over-Past-Year`.

[7] A. Dabrowski, K. Krombholz, J. Ullrich, and E. R. Weippl. QR inception: Barcode-in-barcode attacks. In *Proceedings of the 4th ACM Workshop on Security and Privacy in Smartphones & Mobile Devices*, 2014.

[8] L. Deng and L. P. Cox. LiveCompare: Grocery bargain hunting through participatory sensing. In *Proceedings of the 10th Workshop on Mobile Computing Systems and Applications*, HotMobile '09, 2009.

[9] T. Denning, A. Borning, B. Friedman, B. T. Gill, T. Kohno, and W. H. Maisel. Patients, pacemakers, and implantable defibrillators: Human values and security for wireless implantable medical devices. In *Proceedings of the SIGCHI Conference on Human Factors in Computing Systems*, 2010.

[10] Dogecoin Project. Dogecoin, 2014. `https://dogecoin.org/`.

[11] Google. Google Glass: Setting up Wi-Fi. `https://support.google.com/glass/answer/2725950?hl=en`.

[12] A. Greenberg. Google Glass Hacked With QR Code Photobombs. Forbes, July 2013. `http://www.forbes.com/sites/andygreenberg/2013/07/17/google-glass-hacked-with-qr-code-photobombs/`.

[13] E. Hayashi, B. Pendleton, F. Ozenc, and J. Hong. WebTicket: Account management using printable tokens. In *Proceedings of the SIGCHI Conference on Human Factors in Computing Systems*, 2012.

[14] O. Israeli. 2013 QR Market Summary: Are QR Codes Dead or Alive? Visualead, dec 2013. `http://www.visualead.com/blog/2013-qr-market-summary-are-qr-codes-dead-or-alive/`.

[15] T.-W. Kan, C.-H. Teng, and W.-S. Chou. Applying qr code in augmented reality applications. In *Proceedings of the 8th International Conference on Virtual Reality Continuum and its Applications in Industry*, 2009.

[16] P. Kieseberg, M. Leithner, M. Mulazzani, L. Munroe, S. Schrittwieser, M. Sinha, and E. Weippl. QR code security. In *Proceedings of the International Conference on Advances in Mobile Computing and Multimedia*, 2010.

[17] Kirkmc. Create a QR code bookmarklet. Mac OS X Hints, Dec. 2012. `http://hints.macworld.com/article.php?story=20121121054934966&mode=print`.

[18] C. M. Li, P. Hu, and W. C. Lau. Demo: Authpaper - protecting paper-based documents/credentials using authenticated 2d barcodes. In *Proceedings of the 12th Annual International Conference on Mobile Systems, Applications, and Services*, 2014.

[19] F. Maggi, A. Frossi, S. Zanero, G. Stringhini, B. Stone-Gross, C. Kruegel, and G. Vigna. Two years of short urls internet measurement: Security threats and countermeasures. In *Proceedings of the 22nd International Conference on World Wide Web*, 2013.

[20] MarketingCharts. Data dive: QR codes, July 2013. `http://www.marketingcharts.com/online/data-dive-qr-codes-29525/`.

[21] J. McCune, A. Perrig, and M. Reiter. Seeing-is-believing: using camera phones for human-verifiable authentication. In *IEEE Symposium on Security and Privacy*, 2005.

[22] Misterjunky. Samsung S4 Dial pad Phone Codes Discussion. XDA Developers, Dec. 2013. `http://forum.xda-developers.com/showthread.php?t=2558791`.

[23] A. Moshchuk, T. Bragin, S. D. Gribble, and H. M. Levy. A crawler-based study of spyware on the web. In *Proceedings of the 13th Annual Network and Distributed Systems Security Symposium (NDSS 2006)*, 2006.

[24] S. Nakamoto. Bitcoin: A Peer-to-Peer Electronic Cash System, 2008. `https://bitcoin.org/bitcoin.pdf`.

[25] R. Naraine. Google testing login authentication via QR codes. ZDNet, 2012. `http://www.zdnet.com/blog/security/google-testing-login-authentication-via-qr-codes/10105`.

[26] L. Project. What is litecoin?, 2014. https://litecoin.org/.

[27] S. Robinson, J. S. Pearson, and M. Jones. A billion signposts: Repurposing barcodes for indoor navigation. In *Proceedings of the SIGCHI Conference on Human Factors in Computing Systems*, 2014.

[28] F. Roesner, D. Molnar, A. Moshchuk, T. Kohno, and H. J. Wang. World-Driven Access Control for Continuous Sensing Applications. In *ACM Conference on Computer and Communications Security*, 2014.

[29] J. Rouillard. Contextual qr codes. In *The Third International Multi-Conference on Computing in the Global Information Technology*, 2008.

[30] M. Simkin, A. Bulling, M. Fritz, and D. Schroeder. Ubic: Bridging the gap between digital cryptography and the physical world. In *ESORICS*, 2014.

[31] US Federal Communications Commission. What is a toll-free number and how does it work?, 2014. https://www.fcc.gov/guides/toll-free-numbers-and-how-they-work.

[32] T. Vidas, E. Owusu, S. Wang, C. Zeng, L. Cranor, and N. Christin. QRishing: The susceptibility of smartphone users to QR code phishing attacks. In *Proceedings of the 2013 Workshop on Usable Security (USEC)*, 2013.

[33] Y.-M. Wang, D. Beck, X. Jiang, R. Roussev, C. Verbowski, S. Chen, and S. King. Automated web patrol with Strider HoneyMonkeys: Finding web sites that exploit browser vulnerabilities. In *Proceedings of the 13th Annual Network and Distributed Systems Security Symposium (NDSS 2006)*, 2006.

[34] Wikipedia. Rickrolling. http://en.wikipedia.org/wiki/Rickrolling.

[35] H. Yao and D. Shin. Towards preventing QR code based attacks on android phone using security warnings. In *AsiaCCS*, 2013.

# Beyond the Radio: Illuminating the Higher Layers of Mobile Networks

Narseo Vallina-Rodriguez*, Srikanth Sundaresan*, Christian Kreibich*†, Nicholas Weaver*‡, Vern Paxson*‡
*ICSI, †Lastline, ‡UC Berkeley
{narseo,srikanth,nweaver}@icsi.berkeley.edu, {christian,vern}@icir.org

## ABSTRACT

Cellular network performance is often viewed as primarily dominated by the radio technology. However, reality proves more complex: mobile operators deploy and configure their networks in different ways, and sometimes establish network sharing agreements with other mobile carriers. Moreover, regulators have encouraged newer operational models such as Mobile Virtual Network Operators (MVNOs) to promote competition. In this paper we draw upon data collected by the ICSI Netalyzr app for Android to characterize how operational decisions, such as network configurations, business models, and relationships between operators introduce diversity in service quality and affect user security and privacy. We delve in detail beyond the radio link and into network configuration and business relationships in six countries. We identify the widespread use of transparent middleboxes such as HTTP and DNS proxies, analyzing how they actively modify user traffic, compromise user privacy, and potentially undermine user security. In addition, we identify network sharing agreements between operators, highlighting the implications of roaming and characterizing the properties of MVNOs, including that a majority are simply rebranded versions of major operators. More broadly, our findings highlight the importance of considering higher-layer relationships when seeking to analyze mobile traffic in a sound fashion.

## Categories and Subject Descriptors

C.2.1 [**Computer-communication networks**]: Network Architecture and Design; C.2.3 [**Computer-communication networks**]: Network Operations

## General Terms

Design, Measurement, Performance

## Keywords

Mobile Networks; Cellular Networks; Middleboxes; HTTP Proxy; DNS; PEP; Mobile Traffic; HTTP Header Injection; Privacy; Android; Measurement


*MobiSys'15,* May 18–22, 2015, Florence, Italy.

http://dx.doi.org/10.1145/2742647.2742675.

## 1. INTRODUCTION

Cellular networks are complex, and this complexity extends across multiple layers: from the radio link, where a host of different access technologies compete, to the application layer, which reflects influences such as the effectiveness of DNS lookups and their interaction with Carrier-Grade NATs, and beyond, where regulatory agencies control spectrum allocations that determine carrier coverage. Economic factors, such as roaming agreements between operators, operators trying to monetize user traffic, and the rise of new business models such as Mobile Virtual Network Operators (MVNOs), further muddy the waters. While a large body of work has focused on different aspects of cellular networks, we still lack a holistic understanding of the factors that affect performance, and thus users and to some extent regulators remain in the dark regarding fully understanding user performance, privacy, and security.

Mobile operators deploy and configure their networks in multiple ways: they deploy middleboxes to alter traffic, enhance performance [32], or monetize user traffic using targeted advertising [47]. Operators also establish network sharing agreements with other operators, which leads to their users traversing other networks at least part-way when they reside outside "home" coverage area. All of this typically occurs without user intervention and awareness; indeed, the user has little say in how the operator handles their traffic. Only a small fraction of users take advantage of trusted VPN clients and servers to avoid middlebox interference. At the other end of the spectrum, even aspects technically within the user's control—in particular the APN settings that define how the user connects to the network—potentially affect performance and service quality without their knowledge.

In this work we present a characterization of middlebox behavior and business relationships in cellular networks. In doing so we aim to develop perspectives beyond the substantial body of work that has analyzed network performance using fine-grained metrics such as latency and throughput [36], characterized Carrier-Grade NATs [43], and evaluated DNS performance [33]. We analyze 70 mobile operators in the USA, Canada, Australia, France, Germany, and the UK. We collected our crowd-sourced dataset from Android users running Netalyzr, our comprehensive network troubleshooting tool that gathers a host of measurements regarding cellular networks beyond radio performance. Drawing upon this dataset, we characterize the behavior of network middleboxes such as HTTP proxies and DNS resolvers, and identify business relationships and operational models, including how they affect user traffic, service quality and privacy. We make the following contributions:

1. We demonstrate the widespread use in cellular networks of middleboxes such as HTTP and DNS proxies, many of which are imposed in a manner invisible to users. These middleboxes can potentially modify user traffic, compromise user

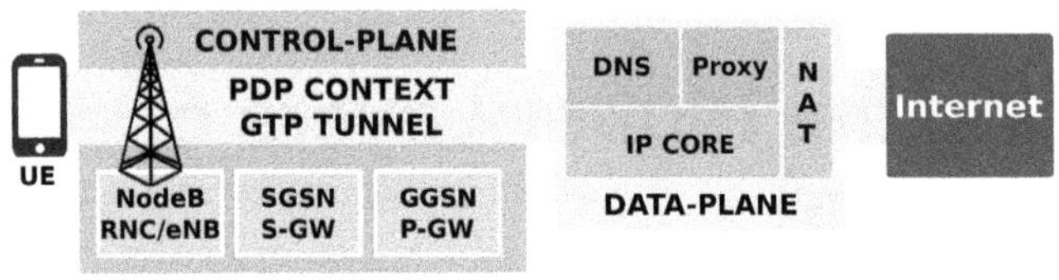


Figure 1: Schematic representation of an MNO's network deployment connected to the Internet, including control- and data-plane. The GTP tunnel hides the control-plane elements.

privacy by injecting HTTP headers that uniquely identify users or reveal their location, and in some cases appear to expose users to security threats by running unpatched software. We show how APN diversity within the same network complicates mobile networks analysis and causes service variability for customers.

2. We identify network sharing agreements between operators, highlighting the implications of roaming and characterizing MVNOs based on their relationship with the parent Mobile Network Operator (MNO). The nature of this relationship has significant implications for analyzing observed network properties and the quality of service delivered to the end user. We show that a majority of MVNOs are simply rebranded versions of major operators; as a result, MVNO subscribers can be vulnerable to inefficiencies and security and privacy issues present in the host MNO network.

This paper describes the implications of middlebox deployment in mobile networks, and business relationships between mobile operators impose on mobile users, researchers, developers, and content providers alike. Our broader theme is that efforts to measure and analyze mobile traffic need to take these dynamics into account to avoid misidentifying the root causes or over-generalizing from limited measurements in an unsound fashion.

# 2. MODERN MOBILE NETWORKS

Modern cellular networks differ from other access technologies in fundamental ways. In this section, we provide an overview of the technical and economic aspects of the current mobile network ecosystem. We provide a brief introduction of how cellular networks operate and then sketch the popular business models that underpin the mobile market, and how these two combine. Table 1 lists the notations we use in the paper.

## 2.1 Cellular Network Infrastructure

A primary distinguishing factor for cellular networks is the presence of a clearly delineated control plane. For security and management reasons, this control plane typically remains transparent to the user, and is difficult to monitor and probe directly. While our earlier work has demonstrated how to monitor certain control-plane elements, this requires privileged access to the network or hardware [37]. The data plane tunnels directly to the IP core. We describe both planes in detail.

### *2.1.1 The Control Plane:*

The control plane consists of two logical components:

- *Radio Access Network (RAN).* The handset connects to the base station (Node B in 3G networks), which in turn is controlled by the Radio Network Controller (RNC). In 4G LTE networks, the RNC and Node Bs combine into an enhanced Node B (eNB); this has the advantage of reducing latency to the handset. The RNC is primarily responsible for managing spectrum and battery usage of handsets.

- *Support Nodes.* The Serving GPRS Support Node, or SGSN (S-GW in LTE), is responsible for billing, authentication, mobility management, and relaying packets between the base stations under its control and the gateway (Gateway GSN, or GGSN, in 3G; Packet Gateway, or P-GW, in LTE). It also interconnects decoupled 2G, 3G, and 4G deployments for a given mobile operator. The GGSN serves as the gateway for handsets to the Internet.

| | |
|---|---|
| **APN** | Access point name |
| **CG-NAT** | Carrier-Grade NAT |
| **GGSN** | Gateway GPRS support node (3G) |
| **GPRS** | General packet radio service |
| **GTP** | GPRS tunneling protocol |
| **MMS** | Multimedia Messaging Service |
| **MNC/MCC** | Mobile network/country code |
| **MNO** | Mobile network operator |
| **MVNO** | Mobile virtual network operator |
| **Node B / eNB** | Base station (3G) / enhanced Node B (4G) |
| **P-GW** | PDN gateway (4G) |
| **PDN** | Packet data network |
| **RNC** | Radio Network Controller |
| **S-GW** | Serving gateway (4G) |
| **SGSN** | Serving GPRS support node (3G) |
| **SIM** | Subscriber Identifier Module |
| **SUPL** | Secure User Plane Location protocol |
| **UE** | User equipment, or handset |

Table 1: Summary of the most common 3GPP terms and acronyms used throughout the paper.

### *2.1.2 The Data Plane:*

The data plane, represented by the yellow pipe in Figure 1, consists of a direct IP tunnel created by the GPRS Tunneling Protocol (GTP) [13] between the handset and a gateway specified in the APN settings on the device. To connect to the Internet, a mobile device must possess an APN configuration provided by its operator. It determines various parameters of the network connection, including the services the gateway offers (e.g., Internet access and multimedia messaging), or SUPL for assisting location sensors [38]), and IP addressing (IP version, static or dynamic IP address use). However, most mobile platforms like Android allow users to edit the APN settings in case they are not pre-installed in the OS.

Beyond the GGSN resides the IP core, oftentimes behind a Carrier-Grade NAT (CG-NAT). Many mobile operators deploy their own IP core, including middleboxes such as DNS resolvers, HTTP and DNS proxies, NATs, and firewalls. These elements have functional reasons to exist: they accommodate address space depletion (NATs), improve security (firewalls), enhance performance (TCP splitters), or reduce latency (proxies). However, these middleboxes generally remain hidden from the user and operators unilaterally impose their use via in-path deployment or settings locked down in the handset.

## 2.2 Business Relationships—the $8^{th}$ Layer

Business relationships form a vital part of the mobile ecosystem. In fact, two classes of mobile operators exist: those who own spectrum (MNOs), and those who do not (MVNOs). This section describes in detail the two business models and network sharing agreements between operators (i.e., roaming), as well as the role played by regulatory bodies in the market emergence of MVNOs.

### 2.2.1 Mobile Network Operators and Roaming

Mobile Network Operators, or MNOs, are the "traditional" mobile operators. MNOs provide mobile voice and data services after acquiring a radio spectrum license from a government body. They also deploy their own network and support infrastructure.

Due to financial or spectrum availability constraints an MNO might not offer service in parts of the region it operates in. In such cases, the MNO typically enters into a business relationship with another MNO that does have service in that region. This allows the first MNO to provide coverage to its subscribers in the region through "roaming". Roaming is the ability of a cellular customer to automatically use any mobile service when traveling outside the geographical coverage area of the home network, by using a partnering visited network. Roaming agreements, particularly domestic ones, provide a cost-efficient way for MNOs to increase their coverage area without deploying actual infrastructure on the ground; they are thus a cost-saving technique for sparsely populated areas within a "liberalized" (open) mobile market [20]. In the US, such agreements have frequently emerged after the FCC eased restrictions on carriers to obtain automatic roaming agreements in areas where they owned spectrum but do not have infrastructure.

Network sharing agreements increase the complexity of network analysis due to the fact that two ways exist to realize the interconnection between the visited network and the home network. The first one, called *home-routed*, tunnels a user's traffic to their home network by inter-connecting this network with local SGSNs. This option increases the length of the path required by the handset to access the Internet and thus the network latency, but it provides a more homogeneous service as the customers always connect to their home network (i.e., the customer is effectively using its home data-plane, including performance enhancing proxies and DNS resolvers). The second option, *local breakout*, allows a roaming device to connect to the Internet as if it were a local device. As a result, the roaming device uses the data plane of the host network. This solution shortens the data path to the Internet, but it makes the user vulnerable to possible inefficiencies, bugs, and poor practices of the host network.

### 2.2.2 Mobile Virtual Network Operators (MVNOs)

An MVNO does not have a licensed mobile spectrum; it therefore enters into a business agreement with an MNO to lease spectrum to provide service. This time- and cost-effective approach, sometimes encouraged by regulatory agencies, allows new operators to enter the market and increase competition for the benefit of the consumer. MNOs also promote the creation of MVNOs in order to monetize network capacity that may otherwise remain unused.

MVNOs span a wide range of deployment types and business practices such as branding, marketing, and billing. In this paper we classify MVNOs by the type of service they provide as well as their network infrastructure. The most basic model is known as "light MVNO" or "resellers". In this case, the MVNO acts as a rebranded version of the host MNO, thus fully using its infrastructure. MNOs sometimes promote this model, creating and operating their own light MVNOs as low-cost versions of their own brand (e.g., by not providing customer support to their subscribers, as in the case of GiffGaff in the UK). The other model is known as "full MVNO". Here, the host MNO only provides radio network access; the MVNO deploys their own IP core and customized services. Full MVNOs therefore have more operational freedom from their parent MNO than light MVNOs; however this comes at the cost of making a larger initial investment. As a result, full MVNOs can better tailor their services to target specific communities or demographics, or monetize their user base with alternative business models. Consequently, a large variety of MVNO realizations has emerged.

## 3. RELATED WORK

Previous cellular network studies focused mainly on performance, rather than feature and behavior characterization. In 2004, Rodriguez *et al.* identified DNS operations as one of the root causes for poor performance on early UMTS networks [32]. To overcome such limitations, they proposed performance-enhancing proxies using techniques such as TCP tuning, aggregating TCP connections, content compression, and DNS optimizations [14,31]. Other studies about web performance focused on client-side optimizations [41,42], and cache behavior optimization [16,18]. The work by Rula *et al.*, and the study by Xu *et al.* used active DNS probing from mobile handsets to evaluate the performance of DNS resolvers [33,48].

More recently, Zarifis *et al.* measured the length of the path between the GGSN and the end of the IP core [49], highlighting the reduced number of ingress points for 3G networks present even in a country as large as the USA. Wang *et al.* identified and characterize carrier-grade NATs present on cellular networks [43]. Their study focused on the security vulnerabilities of such NATs and their impact on the battery life of handsets due to short connection timeouts. Leong *et al.* analyzed the other side of the coin: non-NATed users. In their work, they observed that a malicious user can perform attacks such as data quota drain, DoS flooding, and battery drain to users with routable IP addresses [25]. None of these studies analyzed the deployment of middleboxes such as HTTP and DNS proxies in commercial networks and their impact on users' network connectivity, security, and privacy.

The research community has studied MVNOs mainly from an economic and regulatory perspective. Specifically, there has been considerable interest in understanding how they penetrate a market traditionally dominated by MNOs [15, 23, 35], stressing aspects such as branding and user behavior [34]. From a technical angle the only work comparing MNO–MVNO performance (i.e., TCP throughput and HTTP download time) is the recent study performed by Zarinni *et al.* for two undisclosed MNOs and three associated MVNOs for each in the USA [50]. Our analysis extends and complements this study by analyzing proxy behavior and privacy leaks in terms of operators, cellular technologies, and APN configurations, as well as characterizing business relationships and operational modes. Finally, Mulliner characterized privacy leaks on WAP proxies based on HTTP headers collected by a web server [29]. Our analysis confirms that many of these issues still remain 5 years later.

## 4. NETALYZR FOR ANDROID

Netalyzr is a free, user-driven network troubleshooting platform we have developed and maintained since 2009. Originally built as a browser-based client, Netalyzr analyzes a broad spectrum of network properties as observed from the edge of the network; it interacts with a suite of custom-built test and measurement servers, looking for a wide range of behavioral anomalies such as DNS transport limitations, hidden proxies, HTTP proxy behavior, network path anomalies, DNS manipulations and performance, outbound port filtering, bufferbloat, and UPnP-enabled gateways. We refer the reader to our earlier work [24, 44–46] for a full description of the tests and for architectural and operational details of the Netalyzr platform.

Due to the growth and continuous evolution of cellular networks, we have adapted and extended Netalyzr as an Android app. Numerous iOS API restrictions make it difficult to port our full test suite to iOS. The mobile app implements the set of tests run by the browser and additionally leverages Android's APIs to extend the test suite and obtain the device's contextual information such as signal-to-noise ratio, the mobile carrier, TLS root certificates, and APN settings. We launched Netalyzr as a free app on Google Play [7] and the Amazon App Store [6] in November 2013. The app has since been installed by 28,000 users in some 120 countries.

## 4.1 Test description

We next describe the tests relevant for characterizing business relationships and their effect on user experience. We have two broad classes of tests: to characterize the radio and IP network that the user is on, and to characterize the effect of middleboxes, particularly HTTP and DNS proxies, in the network.

### *4.1.1 Network Identification and IP Core characterization*

Due to the complexities inherent in cellular access to the Internet it becomes necessary to identify and decouple the mobile service provider at the radio level, SIM card level, and IP level. For example, a roaming user might be using the radio network of the visited network and the IP core of the home network. As stated earlier, full MVNOs have their own IP core while light MVNOs do not, but both always use an MNO's radio network. We collect three kinds of data with these tests.

**IP Addressing.** Netalyzr identifies the client's local IP address via Android's APIs and system properties, and uses TCP connections and UDP flows to our echo servers to identify the public IP address of the device. We use the `whois` tool to identify the organization owning the IP address.

**Cellular Network Provider Identification.** To identify the network service operator we use Android's `TelephonyManager` and `ConnectivityManager` APIs, and extract the APN settings as reported by the handset. This allows us to identify the name of the mobile operator, the name of the operator as reported by the SIM card, the APN providing the service, the cell ID (if permitted by the user), the 3GPP standard providing the service, as well as the MNC and MCC parameters (integer numbers allocated by the ITU that, in combination, uniquely identify the mobile operator at the radio level and the country it operates in—e.g., MCC=310, MNC=410 identify AT&T in the USA [2]).

**Location.** Android allows us to extract city-level device location if the user allows it. This information helps identify roaming between mobile operators and lets us identify locations with poor network performance.

### *4.1.2 Proxy Detection*

Netalyzr studies HTTP and DNS behavior, including proxy implementation technologies, implementation artifacts, and limitations. The app employs Java's APIs as well as our own customized HTTP and DNS engines in order to analyze these protocols.

In principle we can detect the presence of a proxy any time it permutes a connection's properties. Our basic detection approach is to employ a client and server under our control that exchange precisely known messages; we then look for deviations from the expected. For the present study the most relevant tests for proxy identification and characterization include tests for HTTP and DNS.

#### *HTTP proxies.*

**Non-responsive server test.** TCP-terminating proxies may be deployed in cellular networks for performance improvement [14, 32]. Such proxies are likely to respond with a `SYN-ACK` to a client's connection request before connecting to the intended origin server. We test for this behavior by attempting a connection to a server that replies with a `RST`. If the Netalyzr client's attempt to connect to this server on port 80 initially succeeds, this indicates the presence of a TCP-terminating proxy.

**Header modification test.** RFC 2616 [17] specifies that systems should treat HTTP header names as case-insensitive, and, with few exceptions, free of ordering requirements. Furthermore, RFC 2615 indicates that any proxy *must* add the `Via` header to indicate its presence to intermediate protocols and recipients [17]. Netalyzr fetches custom content from our server using mixed-cased request and response headers in a known order. Any changes indicate the presence a proxy. This method also allows identifying additional headers added by the HTTP proxy, as in the case of tracking headers [27], and whether intermediate proxies modify traffic using techniques such as image transcoding, which can affect the fidelity of content delivered to mobile clients through CDNs and other cloud infrastructure.

**HTTP enforcement test.** In addition to standard HTTP, Netalyzr attempts to fetch an entity using the protocol declaration `ICSI/1.1` instead of `HTTP/1.1`. If this request is rejected, we know that the network has a protocol-parsing proxy.

**Invalid `Host` header value test.** CERT VU 435052 [19] describes how some in-path proxies would interpret the `Host` request header and attempt to contact the listed host rather than forward the request to the intended address. We check for this vulnerability by fetching from our server with an alternate `Host` header of `www.google.com`. The presence of this vulnerability in commercial proxies is alarming as it suggests that operators may not have their middlebox software upgraded, thus potentially having other vulnerabilities not covered by our test suite.

#### *DNS proxies.*

Netalyzr checks for DNS awareness and proxying by using custom DNS messages. Our DNS server answers requests for `entropy.netalyzr.edu` with a CNAME encoding the response parameters, including the public address of the device, UDP port, DNS transaction ID, and presence of `0x20` encoding. The client sends such DNS requests directly to the back-end server, bypassing the configured resolver. If the client observes any change in the response (e.g., a different transaction ID or public address), then we have found in-path DNS proxying. After that, Netalyzr makes another direct request, this time with deliberately invalid formatting, to which our servers generate a similarly broken reply. If the request is blocked, we have detected a DNS-aware middleboxes that prohibit non-DNS traffic on UDP port 53.

## 4.2 Usability Considerations

Besides serving as a crowd-sourced data collector for our study, Netalyzr offers a comprehensive troubleshooting service for mobile device users. We aim to appeal to a broad audience with varying technical sophistication. As a result, we put significant effort (still with potential for improvement) into presenting technical results to the user in an accessible fashion.

Figure 2 shows three screenshots of the application, including a real results summary for an Optus (Australia) subscriber. Users can share their results, seeking help through social media or via email. Indeed, we have received more than 700 emails from Netalyzr users, and have seen users reporting problems to their mobile providers through Twitter.

The tests execute largely sequentially in order to minimize the risk of test-induced connectivity problems. As a result, the execu-

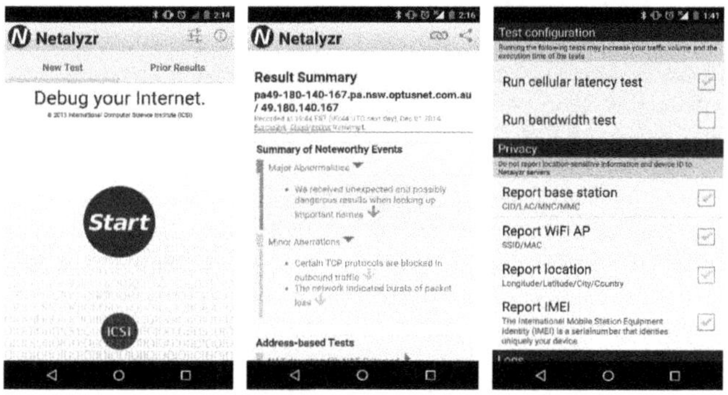


Figure 2: Netalyzr for Android screenshots. Start button activity (left), part of a result summary for a cellular session (center), and app settings and privacy panel (right).

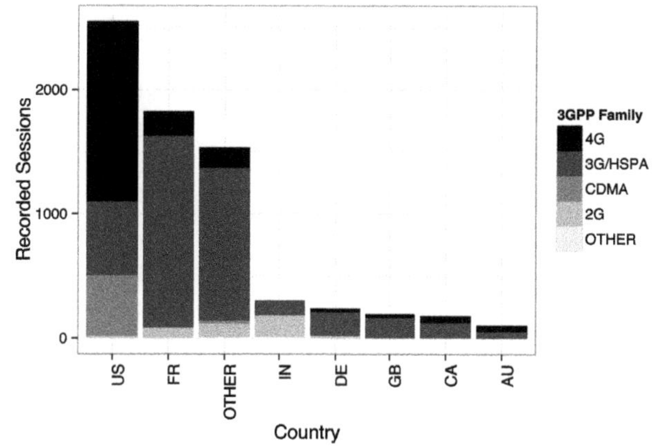


Figure 3: Number of sessions per country per 3GPP technology.

tion time depends on link latency and speed, ranging from 3 minutes in WiFi to 10 minutes in GPRS.

## 4.3 Privacy considerations

We stress that this research strives to understand the interplay of provider infrastructure and mobile devices, and does not focus on human subjects (confirmed by our institute's IRB). Accordingly, while we collect data on a wide range of network and device properties, little of the data collected has any bearing on the user's privacy. The users may nevertheless control specific aspects of the data collection (e.g., turn off location reporting) if they so desire.

# 5. DATASET AND METHODOLOGY

Between November 2013, when we released Netalyzr for Android, and September 2014 we recorded 39,110 sessions. In this paper we focus on studying properties of cellular networks, thus we exclude sessions generated over WiFi and WiMax links. We also remove sessions where the handset was tethering, leaving us with 6,918 sessions covering 371 operators in 128 countries. As a result of its crowd-source nature, our dataset has biases in terms of countries, demographics, and technologies from which the sessions originated. We received most of our sessions from the USA and France due to media coverage in those countries.

We potentially have a "geek bias", with 34% sessions coming from rooted phones. Furthermore, CDMA, HSPA variants, and LTE dominate in our datasets. We also observe a long tail in the distribution of sessions run per operator.

We focus our analysis on 6 countries with more than 100 sessions recorded, as shown in Figure 3. We exclude India from our analysis even though we have numerous sessions from it due to the complexity of India's spectrum allocation at a state level—still dominated by 2G standards—and regulatory legislation [22]. Even with the reduced set of countries, we faced significant challenges both in annotating the data and in sanitizing it. We now turn to our approaches for doing so.

## 5.1 Mobile Operator Identification

Identifying the mobile operator providing the service to a customer is a daunting task. One may think that the operator name reported by the native APIs and the MCC/MNC tuple suffice to associate a session to a mobile operator. However, with the rise of MVNOs relying on such fields can prove misleading: many MVNOs do not necessarily have an MNC value and in some cases they buy access from multiple MNOs to increase their coverage. While some MVNOs, particularly full MVNOs which have their own IP core, have an MNC, the values reported by Android's `TelephonyManager` only identifies the current registered operator (i.e., the MNO providing the radio link).

We developed a technique to identify and classify both flavors of MVNOs by correlating public IP addresses with existing MNOs, `whois` information, DNS resolvers, APN settings, proxy properties, operator name, and the MNC/MCC as reported by Android APIs, along with manual trawling of MVNO Directory databases [4]. For example, this technique allows us to characterize sessions reporting the mobile carrier `HOME` as TracFone Wireless sessions, an MVNO in the USA that allows their subscribers to use either T-Mobile or AT&T's network. By correlating sessions with these two operator names, we observed that they both have two different APNs: `tfdata` and `wap.tracfone`, and their public IP address is owned by Syniverse Technologies. Moreover, the MCC and MNC values report two different MNOs providing the radio link: AT&T (310/410), and T-Mobile (310/260).

This method furthermore allows us to correct errors in the data reported by Android APIs, and also to characterize MVNOs as either light or full MVNOs (§ 2.2.2) based on IP core characteristics. We identified 43 different MVNOs in the countries of interest; this is a small fraction of the total number of existing MVNOs. According to the MVNO Dynamics website [5] 138 MVNOs operated in the first quarter of 2014 in the USA alone, some with marginal market penetration and a short lifespan. Unfortunately, due to Netalyzr's crowd-sourcing approach, we were not able to penetrate and collect traces from all of them.

## 5.2 Data Sanitization

As a consequence of the crowd-sourced nature of the Netalyzr dataset and the difficulty of controlling the circumstances under which users launch Netalyzr, our dataset presents inaccuracies and corner cases that can potentially bias the results. Consequently, we take into account a variety of factors when vetting our dataset and exclude the following sessions:

1. Sessions collected in testing or engineering mode by network engineers: the MCC code for such sessions is 1 as defined by ITU [2], and the operator name in many cases is "DEFACE".

2. Pre-3G standards such as GPRS, EDGE, and 1xRTT.

3. Sessions in which we could not identify the global IP address of the handset. In a small number of sessions, Netalyzr could

| Total number of cellular sessions | 6,918 |
|---|---|
| **Sessions from selected countries** | **5,083** |
| Testing networks | 7 |
| Pre-3G standards | 207 |
| Erroneous local IP address | 21 |
| Static IP addresses | 77 |
| User-customized DNS | 84 |
| VPNs | 84 |
| AdBlock app | 51 |
| Femtocells | 36 |
| Erroneous operator name | 32 |
| International roaming | 11 |
| **Remaining valid sessions** | **4,512** |

Table 2: Dataset pruning due to data impurities and unusual cases. Note that sessions may have more than one problem.

not identify the global IP address of the device, possibly as a result of app crashes. Because such sessions considerably limit the fidelity of our analysis, we remove them.

4. Sessions that report static IP addresses. Such sessions are quite rare; mobile networks generally deploy carrier-grade NATs [43].

5. Sessions indicating network customization by users. Android supports traffic tunneling through VPNs (including users with proxy-based TOR clients such as Orbot [8]), and savvy users with rooted devices can configure Google or OpenDNS as their default DNS resolvers. Furthermore, applications such as AdBlock behave as local proxies to block mobile advertising. Such customization modifies the network path and hides properties of the mobile network we are trying to measure.

6. Sessions executed through femtocells, which we identify based on the operator name. Femtocells route traffic directly to the Internet using wired or satellite links rather than the cellular infrastructure.

7. Sessions that exhibit inconsistencies in the mobile operator name as reported by Android's `TelephonyManager` API. This could arise due to APN misconfigurations, erroneous sessions due to app crashes, or re-branding by MVNOs. For instance, some clients still report Orange and T-Mobile in the UK, which merged to form a new MNO known as Everything-Everywhere (EE). Despite our efforts to correct such anomalies by correlating different sources of information (as explained in the following sections), we could not identify the operator providing the service for 32 sessions.

8. Sessions from international roaming users.

Table 2 lists the number of sessions cleaned using the process listed above. After applying our filtering, 4,512 sessions from 70 operators in 6 countries remain that we consider valid for further analysis (49% of the total cellular sessions). Although this provides only a relatively low number of sessions per carrier, it still suffices for identifying structural problems in cellular networks, MNO and MVNOs relationships, domestic roaming agreements, misconfigurations, traffic manipulations, and privacy leaks. Our analyses characterize discrete properties of the provider infrastructure that are unlikely to vary significantly over time from the same provider (unlike metrics such as latency or throughput).

## 5.3 Dataset Release

We have released the relevant data used for this paper through CRAWDAD [39] after performing the dataset sanitization process explained in § 5.2. We have also made available a larger Netalyzr dataset through PREDICT [21]. We do not include sessions generated by smartphones through VPN tunnels, and remove sensitive information which could identify our users. This includes geographical location, HTTP header modifications—as in the case of HTTP headers injected by HTTP proxies—and some APN fields such as username and passwords. We have anonymized additional sensitive values, such as public IP addresses.

# 6. CHARACTERIZING MNOs

It is well known that operators commonly deploy proxies in cellular networks for performance enhancement [14, 31]. However, the architecture of MNO networks—particularly the deployment, configuration, and behavior of middleboxes—and network sharing agreements between MNOs can similarly affect performance, data fidelity, as well as user security and privacy. Such design and operational decisions generally remain unknown and unapparent to users, developers and researchers alike. In this section, we analyze these aspects of MNOs. To determine whether a given operator constitutes an MNO or an MVNO, we use documentation from the ITU and national regulatory bodies such as the FCC in the USA, and OFCOM in the UK. MNOs dominate the market [30] and also dominate our dataset, with 86% of our sessions from MNO subscribers.

## 6.1 Proxy Deployment and Behavior

We focus our analysis on two predominant kinds of middleboxes deployed in cellular networks: HTTP and DNS proxies. While our data also indicate occasional presence of proxies for SMTP, POP3, or IMAP we do not consider these further in this paper.

### *6.1.1 HTTP Proxies*

HTTP proxies intercept and relay HTTP traffic. They are typically used for enhancing performance, and are widely deployed on cellular networks for adapting content, saving bandwidth using caches, compression and transcoding, and for traffic filtering [14, 32].

We confirm substantial presence of HTTP proxies in cellular networks: Netalyzr detected proxies in 59% of sessions. In comparison, our previous analysis revealed that only 14% of clients in wired networks were proxied [44]. Figure 4 shows the percentage of sessions for a given MNO enforcing various flavors of proxies. The color map indicates the percentage of penetration using a gradient from 0% (white) to 100% (red). Where we do not possess sessions conducted using a given cellular technology, we report it in gray, as in the case of Wind (Canada), O2 (GB), and E-Plus (Germany) on 4G LTE.

Our analysis shows that most MNOs generally deploy in-path proxies performing HTTP header re-ordering, HTTP header injection, and header modification. § 6.2.2 discusses HTTP header injection in upstream traffic and their privacy implications in detail. The US operator C Spire modifies non-HTTP traffic going through their proxies. Other MNOs, such as Vodafone and Optus in Australia, Vodafone and T-Mobile in Germany, SFR in France, and T-Mobile in the USA transcode images to reduce data volume. Most proxies remain transparent to the user. RFC 2616 stipulates that proxies *must* indicate their presence using the `Via` general-header field [17]. Despite the fact that proxies are widely present, the `Via` field proves rare: Netalyzr detected its presence in only one ISP (SFR, France) and then only in sessions going through

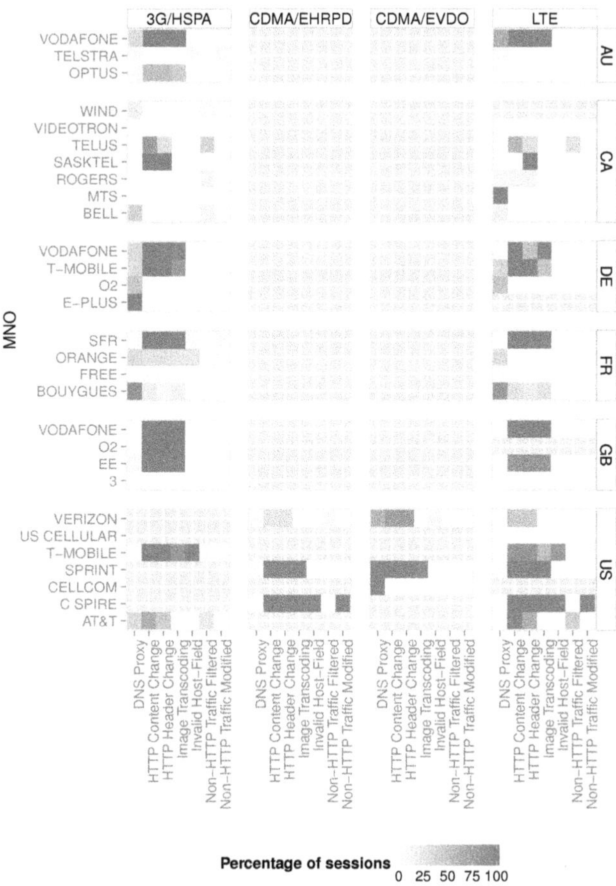


Figure 4: Map showing the deployment and behavior of DNS and HTTP proxies for the MNOs in the considered countries. Each box represents a given property. The color reflects the percentage of sessions with it on a gradient from 0% (white) to 100% (red). Gray indicates we did not identify any session from a MNO for a given technology.

a legacy WAP gateway, `proxy.cwg.net`. Only 2.3% of SFR sessions pass through these gateways. Unfortunately, since these proxies are generally transparent to the user, this behavior affects the fidelity of the data delivered to the customer without their (or the content providers') knowledge or consent. For example, users will not be able to download high-resolution images, even if they explicitly desire to do so.

### *6.1.2 DNS Proxies*

Netalyzr sends custom DNS queries directly to our DNS resolver to identify whether the mobile network is proxying DNS traffic, and whether they modify these queries. Netalyzr also sends non-DNS messages over DNS to test if a proxy enforces (its idea of) the DNS protocol, blocking non-DNS traffic on port 53. From our data, we see that a significant number of mobile operators proxy DNS queries. In total, 18% of DNS queries were proxied, of which 70% changed the sender IP address or DNS request ID in queries sent directly to our name servers. The remainder enforced DNS semantics on UDP port 53, blocking non-DNS traffic on this port.

Figure 4 also shows the penetration of DNS proxies among MNOs. We see DNS proxies more commonly in resource-constrained standards such as 3G and CDMA/EVDO, with exceptions such as Bouygues in France, MTS in Canada, and Vodafone in Australia. We speculate that operators rely on such proxies to keep control over the network, particularly relatively resource-constrained ones. For example, AT&T proxies DNS only for a small subset of subscribers that go through their legacy APNs, as explained in § 6.3. Verizon, Cellcom, and Sprint deploy DNS proxies only on their CDMA networks.

Operators also have the ability to interfere with DNS name lookups. Our records indicate that Free mangled and blocked Google Ads (in particular the domains `partner.googleadservices.com` and `ad.doubleclick.net`) due to a peering dispute between Free and Google [12]. Queries for both of these domains resolved to an IP address owned by Free (212.27.40.246, or `white.proxad.net`), serving a blank web page.

## 6.2 Security and Privacy

As we show in the previous section, a great deal of diversity exists among operators regarding how they manage their networks: some ISPs proxy DNS and HTTP, some do not, while others actively modify user traffic. We next examine the effects of these actions on user security and privacy.

### *6.2.1 Security implications*

Proxies in cellular networks are generally enforced without any choice on behalf of the user. This means that any security vulnerability or performance degradation affecting them afflicts all users of that network. Our tests show that middleboxes in T-Mobile and C Spire in the USA as well as Orange in France still remain vulnerable to CERT VU435052 [19], a vulnerability dating back to 2009. While the impact might prove minor in the case of an ISP proxy (the attack primarily enables same-origin bypass within corporate network proxies), the presence of a five-year-old vulnerability naturally raises questions about what other, potentially more serious, vulnerabilities affect these proxies.

### *6.2.2 Privacy implications*

Proxies that modify user traffic may not only affect service quality but also violate the users' privacy. We have observed that many operators inject additional headers into every HTTP request generated by their users. The type of headers varies, but the more insidious cases uniquely identify the subscriber, their location, or their IP address. Table 3 summarizes injected HTTP headers containing sensitive information about the users and the operators that add them, as evident in our dataset. Some of these headers, particularly `X-ACR` (by AT&T) and `X-UIDH` (by Verizon), uniquely identify the mobile subscriber.

Tracking-enablers (or "perma-cookies" [27]) are associated with advertisement programs deployed by mobile operators such as Verizon Selects [40, 47]. They allow partner companies to identify the user so they can deliver targeted advertisements more effectively. However, such headers also allow malicious tracking of visiting web users. These privacy leaks violate the trust relationship between mobile operators and their users, and have recently attracted significant press attention [26, 27]. The "perma-cookie" practice prompted us to call out these headers' presence in the Netalyzr session results, and one article recommends using Netalyzr to identify such privacy leaks. While AT&T stopped adding these headers soon after the media exposure, we note that Verizon still continues the practice at the time of this writing. Looking beyond the countries we focus on in this study, we identified a similar "perma-cookie" header in sessions from Vodafone Netherlands (X-VF-ACR). Other operators such as T-Mobile in Germany, EE and O2 in the UK, and SFR in France also leak private information about their users in other forms.

Proxies widely use headers such as X-Forwarded-For, X-EE-Client-IP, and X-Gateway to identify the client's provider-internal IP address as well as its location. Finally, we have also observed proxies explicitly defining the maximum uplink and downlink speed for a given device, a unique ID of the gateway, as well as the gateway vendor. While these headers might not necessarily compromise user security, they can augment and complement classic HTTP cookies to facilitate user tracking and enable price/search discrimination [28].

## 6.3 Service Variability Within Providers

A given ISP's middlebox behavior can change depending on the wireless technology used. For example, in the USA Sprint proxies DNS on CDMA/EVDO, but not on LTE. This does not surprise much because the 2G, 3G, and 4G networks often operate independently. However, one would expect that the behavior of such networks to remain uniform within the same ISP and technology. In Figure 4 this should translate to white or red boxes. However, we see that in many cases, the boxes have varying shades or red, indicating that users within the same ISP and using the same technology could experience differing properties for their networks. We did not, however, observe any difference between IPv4 and IPv6 for Verizon, T-Mobile, or Telstra.

Again turning to Figure 4, we observe variability in caching and content modification even within the same ISP and technology. We identify and explain two such cases. For a small fraction of sessions originating from AT&T, the public IP address is owned by WDSPCo, a consortium of some of the major wireless providers in the USA [10]. We also noticed that these sessions correspond to the APN wap.cingular, which supports legacy WAP services. These sessions were markedly different in their proxy properties: while their HTTP traffic was not proxied (and the X-ACR header not added), DNS lookups were proxied. This clearly suggests this network is different from the network that serves other AT&T customers. Another interesting case study is Orange in France. We see that the properties of the network change depending on the public IP address of the session. For example, sessions that had public IP addresses in the 90.84.144/24 and 90.84.146/24 subnets had an HTTP proxy that does header reordering (92% of sessions), while the other Orange subnets do not (1.0% of sessions). We could not identify any specific APN defining such behavior; we speculate that in Orange's case, service diversity could arise due to a heterogeneous proxy deployment in certain geographical areas.

The ISP controls the network that users traverse; however, APN settings for ISPs are freely available online (via the ISP's website or forums such as xda-developers [11]) and users can easily misconfigure their phones by experimenting with such settings, negatively affecting their own service quality. For example, we have received numerous emails from users reporting app crashes when connecting to the Internet, as a result of using APNs that enforce compression by default while using apps that lack compression support.

## 6.4 Business Relationships

As described in § 2.2, roaming agreements between MNOs frequently serve the purpose of providing higher network coverage to their customers while incurring minimal deployment costs. In this section we demonstrate that this practice is common in certain countries and happens transparently to the user.

### *6.4.1 Method*

We identify roaming sessions by comparing the IP core provider, the provider of the radio link, and APN information when available. This allows us to identify home-routed roaming implementations (cf. § 2.2.1) easily, but not local breakout, as in this case the devices are fully connected to the host network at both the radio and IP level. To differentiate devices doing local breakout from other host network subscribers, we require access to the issuer of the SIM card. Unfortunately, Netalyzr only began collecting this information in September 2014. Furthermore, VPN tunnels to IP addresses of ISPs providing both wired and wireless access can be easily confused with roaming sessions. APN and network interface configuration information sometimes provide an alternative way to identify such cases.

### *6.4.2 Home Routing*

Our analysis identified 91 roaming sessions between MNOs in our database, with 92% seen in France between Free and Orange (only for their 3G network), and between other MNOs as reported in Table 4. Android's TelephonyManager API flags none of these roaming cases. Free's agreement with Orange is particularly interesting as they account for 81% of all national roaming sessions identified, and for 10% of the total mobile sessions recorded from Free subscribers.

Free subscribers can access Orange's network in locations where Free has no network infrastructure deployed (Free was the last MNO entering the French market, and is still deploying its infrastructure). We can see roaming happening all over France, even in large metropolitan areas such as Paris and Bordeaux. When roaming, the operator name reported by Android is Orange, whereas the APN settings and the IP core belong to Free (their public IP address is in the 37.160.0.0/12 subnet). Moreover, middlebox behavior matches that of customers under Free coverage, as a result of home routing. Consequently, if we based our characterization solely on the operator name, we would have incorrectly mapped Free's Google ad services blocking (described in § 6.1.2) to Orange France.

While users roaming on local breakout implementations are potentially susceptible to inefficiencies and vulnerabilities present in the home network, they can experience significantly higher network latency (e.g., due to increased path-lengths, see § 2.2.1) and performance inefficiencies (e.g., due to the masking of user locations which can impair CDN replica selection) in home routing scenarios. Netalyzr can measure the effect of the different roaming implementations, but we do not currently possess enough data to reach statistically significant conclusions.

We have also identified a reduced number of sessions of MNOs roaming in the US, as listed in Table 4. Cricket has roaming agreements with other MNOs for their CDMA deployment. 4 sessions report "Extended Network" or "Preferred System" as the operator name, while the IP core is Verizon's. We verified that these sessions are actually generated by Verizon subscribers roaming in other MNOs from USA or Canada, in which home airtime rates still apply [9]. We have seen such sessions for CDMA, and in this case, all sessions present Verizon's HTTP "perma-cookies" (even when roaming abroad as in the case of some Verizon subscribers roaming in Canada on Roger), and DNS traffic is proxied and modified.

## 6.5 Discussion

Middleboxes are not just pervasive in cellular networks, but also transparent to the user. We identify HTTP and DNS proxies in 59% and 18% of our sessions, respectively. Aside from proxying, some middleboxes also actively modify user traffic by modifying HTTP

| HTTP Header | Operator | First time seen | Last time seen | Notes |
|---|---|---|---|---|
| X-ACR | AT&T (US) | 2014-05-17 | 2014-08-26 | Unique perma-cookie. |
| X-EE-Client-IP | EE (GB) | 2014-06-11 | 2014-06-11 | Private IP address of the subscriber. |
| X-Forwarded-For | BOUYGUES (FR) | 2014-02-01 | 2014-02-01 | Private IP address of the subscriber. |
| X-Forwarded-For | O2 (GB) | 2013-12-27 | 2014-07-17 | Private IP address of the subscriber. |
| X-Forwarded-For | SASKTEL (CA) | 2014-03-02 | 2014-08-16 | Private IP address of the subscriber. |
| X-Forwarded-For | SFR (FR) | 2013-11-07 | 2013-12-08 | Private IP address of the subscriber. |
| X-Forwarded-For | T-MOBILE (DE) | 2013-11-07 | 2014-08-28 | Private IP address of the subscriber. |
| X-Gateway | O2 (GB) | 2013-12-27 | 2014-07-17 | Network gateway and its location. |
| X-UIDH | VERIZON (US) | 2013-10-23 | 2014-08-25 | Unique perma-cookie. |
| X-VFPROVIDER | SFR (FR) | 2013-11-07 | 2013-12-08 | Operator name. |

Table 3: HTTP header identifiers added by different operators.

| Country | MNO | Host MNO |
|---|---|---|
| France | FREE | ORANGE |
| | FREE | BOUYGUES |
| | ORANGE | SFR |
| USA | AT&T | T-MOBILE |
| | CRICKET | US CELLULAR |

Table 4: List of observed network sharing agreements between MNOs.

headers, HTTP content, transcoding images, or leaking sensitive information about the subscribers. Furthermore, business relationships between MNOs can result in users experiencing middlebox manipulations originating from another operator's network.

Our results highlight the general opacity that shrouds cellular networks. Users have little say in (or, indeed, knowledge about) how their ISP treats or manipulates their traffic. This results in users experiencing differing service quality depending on how in-path middleboxes are configured (often caused by APN misconfigurations), and also leaves users vulnerable to potential security problems or privacy leaks. Transparent roaming agreements between MNOs mean that users do not know which network carries their traffic at any given time. Depending on the actual business relationship, users could either face potential performance hits if their operator uses home routing, or vulnerabilities or tracking of the host network if it does local breakout.

Variability in middlebox performance, often within the same ISP, also complicates research into cellular network performance. It does not suffice simply to obtain the provider name from the operating system; not only can the radio provider and coverage differ, but the path the traffic takes can affect measured service quality. The consequences affect developers, content providers (e.g., ad networks), and researchers. Middleboxes intercept, modify and block traffic, affecting data fidelity. Moreover, they also invalidate server-side performance measurement as a result of the connection-decoupling done by connection-terminating proxies, requiring the control of both endpoints to effectively characterize mobile network performance.

# 7. CHARACTERIZING MVNOs

In this section we delve into how MVNOs deploy their networks and the potential resulting impact on customers. In § 2.2.2 we developed a basic taxonomy of MVNOs, classifying them as either full or light MVNOs. We first develop these notions further, then classify the MVNOs we see in our dataset according to this taxonomy, and characterize their properties.

## 7.1 Classifying MVNOs

Figure 5 shows the MVNOs in the six countries we analyze using the method described in § 5.1. For each MVNO we show the MNO providing radio access as well as the provider of the IP core infrastructure (according to `whois`). The line style represents the type of MVNO: we show full MVNOs with solid gray lines and light MVNOs with dotted ones. We validated our findings with information from official MVNO websites (when available) and industry forums [5]. As in § 6 we also describe the network behavior for each of the identified MVNOs, per Figure 6.

### *7.1.1 Light MVNOs*

Light MVNOs are globally most common. We have identified light MVNOs in each country under study, and they are the only type of MVNO we find in Australia, Canada, Germany, and Great Britain. Our results indicate that most light MVNOs provide Internet access through only one parent MNO, per Figure 5, though we also find NRJ in France using both Orange's and SFR's networks.

MVNO sessions generally come from users connected via 3G/HSPA standards. We have not recorded any MVNO session in France over 4G, even when parent MNOs have 4G infrastructure deployed. This suggests that MNOs can block access to their most advanced 3GPP technology. Only 22% of MVNO sessions happened over LTE, as opposed to 40% of LTE sessions generated by MNO subscribers. Furthermore, 88% of the MVNO sessions we recorded over LTE originated from the USA.

We observe that light MVNOs exhibit behavior identical to that of their parent MNOs. In fact, MVNOs such as Fido, Metro PCS, and GiffGaff are owned by Rogers, T-Mobile, and O2 respectively. However, as in the case of MNOs, APN settings can affect behavior. For example, Virgin Australia users can choose between the APNs `VirginInternet` (that proxies DNS traffic and only provides 3G coverage), and `YESINTERNET` (which grants access to the 4G network). The price for these two APN settings varies [1]. Legacy APN settings also propagate through MVNO subscribers. We have identified sessions with the `Via` header `proxy.cwg.net` coming from Leclerc and Prixtel subscribers. Consequently, MVNO users are susceptible to the vulnerabilities of the parent MNO: MetroPCS proxies also present the CERT VU435052 vulnerability [19] found in T-Mobile networks. It remains an open question to what degree MVNO network performance differs from that offered by their host MNOs. A preliminary study for some US operators suggests that MVNO quality of experience proves sub-par compared to the MNO one, for popular applications [50].

### *7.1.2 Full MVNOs*

We have identified four full MVNOs in our dataset: Virgin and Numericable in France, and TracFone and Cricket in the USA.

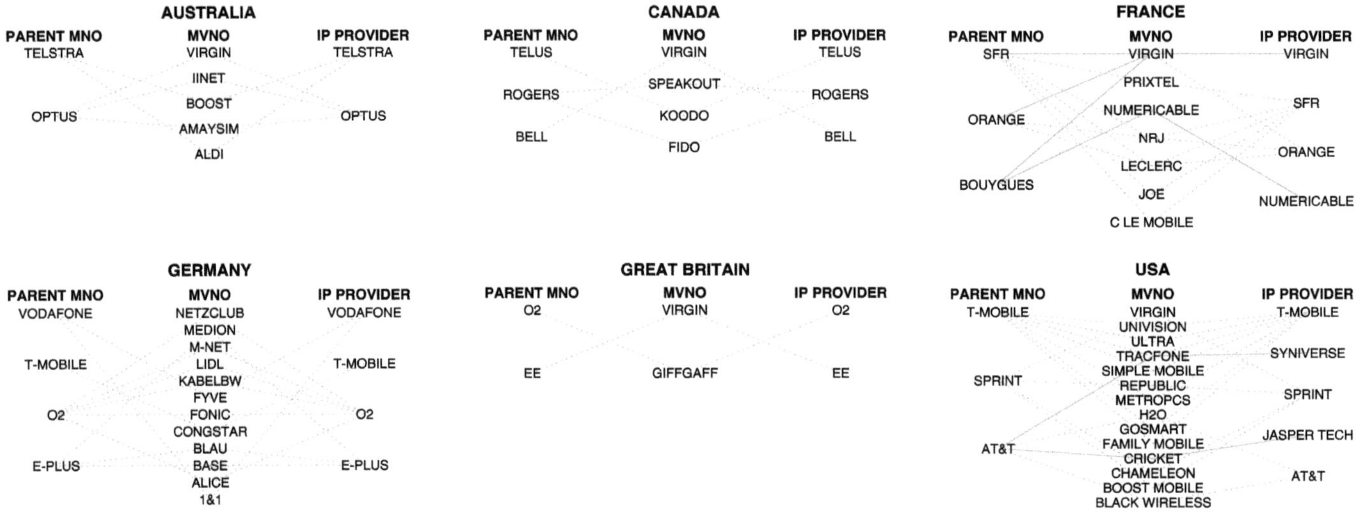


Figure 5: MVNO relationship with parent MNOs and cloud providers for each one of the MVNOs. Solid lines represent full MVNOs, dotted lines light ones.

We represent them in Figure 5 using solid gray lines. Since full MVNOs need to invest larger sums of money to deploy their own IP infrastructure, the fact that we find fewer full MVNOs than light ones does not surprise. Cable and DSL providers such as Numericable can enter the mobile business as MVNOs, forwarding mobile subscribers' data to their IP core.

Full MVNOs differ from light MVNOs in two ways. First, since they have their own IP core, the behavior of such networks can deviate from that observed in their parent MNOs. For instance, when TracFone customers connect through T-Mobile they still use TracFone proxies and thus are not vulnerable to CERT VU435052, unlike other MVNOs who run on T-Mobile. TracFone also performs image transcoding, as opposed to other full MVNOs like Numericable in France. Second, full MVNOs generally use more than one host MNO and IP provider, as shown in Figure 5. Doing so allows full MVNOs to provide coverage to a wider population without being constrained to the network deployment of a single mobile operator, with more competitive prices (due to buying in bulk) than MNOs. TracFone subscribers have the freedom to decide which network they want to use (by entering the APN settings accordingly) while seeing the the same IP core behavior. Nonetheless, most sessions come from a single MNO, AT&T (56 % of sessions), with the rest using Sprint and T-Mobile.

Finally, some MNOs are MVNOs for certain radio frequencies. Both MetroPCS and Cricket have their own CDMA legacy infrastructure, but become MVNOs for their 3G/4G network. While MetroPCS behaves as a light MVNO on T-Mobile's 3G/4G network, Cricket is a full MVNO on AT&T. Interestingly, Cricket partners with Jasper Wireless for their 4G IP infrastructure rather than using AT&T's or their own. Jasper Wireless is a cloud provider partner with a large number of MNOs and MVNOs all over the world [3]. Consequently, the behavior of their CDMA middleboxes differs from the ones they use for their LTE/HSPA networks.

## 7.2 User Security and Privacy

Light MVNOs' subscribers are susceptible to problems introduced by their host MNO. This holds for GiffGaff in the UK as well as Prixtel and Leclerc subscribers in France, all vulnerable to PII leaks caused by their host MNO proxies provided by O2 and SFR. Table 5 provides a summary. The `X-VFPROVIDER` header added by SFR proxies identifies the name of the mobile operator, even if it is an affiliated MVNO as Prixtel and Leclerc. Full MVNO subscribers can suffer from other network problems, but we have not observed any PII leaks. We cannot verify whether they monetize subscribers' data in other ways.

| MVNO | HTTP Header |
|---|---|
| CONGSTAR (DE) | `X-Forwarded-For` |
| GIFFGAFF (GB) | `X-Forwarded-For` |
| GIFFGAFF (GB) | `X-Gateway` |
| LECLERC (FR) | `X-Forwarded-For` |
| LECLERC (FR) | `X-VFPROVIDER` |
| PRIXTEL (FR) | `X-Forwarded-For` |
| PRIXTEL (FR) | `X-VFPROVIDER` |

Table 5: Permanent identifiers found on MVNOs which are inherited from the MNO providing their access.

## 7.3 Discussion

MVNOs represent an emerging business model that allows providers to offer service without buying spectrum. The MVNO model has several advantages: it lowers the bar for entry for providers, increases competition, and offers the opportunity for MNOs to sell unused capacity. Light MVNOs, which use the host MNO for both radio and IP infrastructure, are more common than full MVNOs, which have their own IP core.

The general problem of opacity extends to MVNOs as well. Light MVNOs are typically little more than rebranded versions of the parent MNO, which renders them susceptible to the problems associated with the parent MNO, including privacy leaks. Full MVNOs do not face this problem as they control their user traffic. However, they are either limited to the coverage area of the host MNO, or, if they have relationships with multiple MNOs, susceptible to differing service quality depending on which MNO currently provides the radio connectivity.

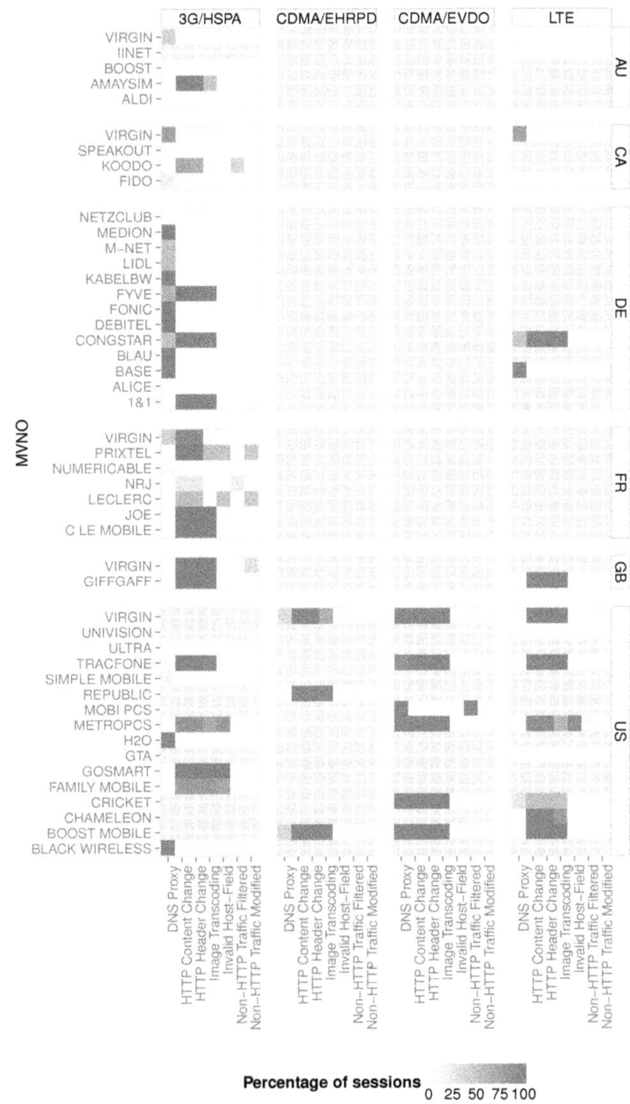


Figure 6: Deployment and behavior of DNS and HTTP proxies for the MVNOs in the considered countries. Only TracFone and Cricket in the USA, and Virgin and Numericable in France, are full MVNOs. The remaining light MVNOs exhibit the same behavior as their parent MNO. (See Figure 5 for details about the MVNO–MNO relationships.)

It proves difficult to identify the mobile operator using information provided by Android's APIs; we combine several features, including IP core behavior, to achieve this (§ 5.1). It is vital to do so in order to correctly attribute network behavior.

Middleboxes commonly occur in cellular networks: 59% of sessions have an HTTP proxy, while 18% of sessions have a DNS proxy. These proxies usually remain unapparent to the user, and, even if they reveal themselves, are difficult to avoid. (§ 6.1)

Middleboxes may have security vulnerabilities, modify user traffic (§ 6.2.1), and leak private information (sometimes intentionally) about the user (§ 6.2.2). Savvy users take advantage of trusted and commercial VPN clients and servers to avoid middlebox manipulation and tracking.

Middleboxes may possess heterogeneous configurations within a single ISP, particularly with differing APN settings. This can lead to middleboxes treating similar traffic differently. (§ 6.3)

Roaming agreements are common, particularly in France. However, in many cases such agreements remain transparent to the user, meaning that the device may not flag the fact that roaming on another operator's network occurs. (§ 6.4)

MVNOs reside in every country we study; they mostly constitute rebranded versions of the parent MNO. (§ 7.1.1)

Light MVNOs' subscribers remain vulnerable to the same inefficiencies, security holes, and privacy leaks as subscribers of the parent MNO, as a result of sharing the same IP core. (§ 7.1.1 and § 7.2)

Full MVNOs, which we observe only in France and the USA, deploy their own IP core and thus have great control over their user traffic. Consequently, the treatment of their subscribers' traffic may differ from that of the parent MNO's subscribers. (§ 7.1.2)

Table 6: Highlights of our work.

# 8. SUMMARY

In this paper, we have provided perspectives on the state of the art of mobile network characterization and middlebox behavior. Looking beyond the predominant radio-centric angle of analysis, we have used Netalyzr's rich test suite to shed light on key properties of HTTP and DNS proxies in provider networks, business relationships, and their implications for users, developers, and mobile researchers alike.

Using data collected by Netalyzr for Android, we evaluated mobile operators from the USA, Canada, Australia, France, Germany, and the UK. We summarize our results in Table 6. We first highlight the difficulty in identifying the mobile operator; simply using the operator name or the MCC/MNC value as reported by Android often does not suffice. We supplement the above with a host of features, including the IP core and APN settings, to identify the operator. Doing so helps us accurately attribute network features and behavior to operators (e.g., attributing to a full MVNO rather than the host MNO). Netalyzr's rich proxy detection suite identified the presence of transparent HTTP proxies in 59% of cellular sessions. We show how proxies can modify or block DNS and HTTP traffic; in some cases affecting data fidelity with techniques such as image transcoding. We report proxies with five-year-old vulnerabilities, indicating a lack of upgrading or patching that suggests the likely presence of other non-identified vulnerabilities. We also find proxies that facilitate tracking of customers by adding new header fields to HTTP requests, as in the case of "perma-cookies". We have identified fundamental differences in proxy behavior even for subscribers from a given operator as a result of supporting different middlebox and APN configurations. Our results underscore the importance of considering proxy behavior to avoid biases while evaluating mobile performance.

In addition to proxy behavior, we identified roaming agreements between operators and different MVNO–MNO relationships by combining radio information, handset settings, and IP-layer information. Each one of the mobile markets in this study has its own peculiarities, but in most of the cases, MVNOs are simple rebranded versions of the actual mobile provider, so the service quality delivered to the customer potentially remains constant. Unfortunately, we could not evaluate whether link performance is degraded (e.g., link capacity, or latencies for DNS lookups or HTTP fetches) due to the high variability of the radio links and their best-effort nature. We refer the reader to the work by Zarinni *et al.* for a first performance evaluation in the USA [50].

*The Need for Operational Transparency.*

As we highlight throughout the paper, most mobile users, developers, and researchers lack visibility into network behavior, due to both middlebox configuration and business relationships, and its impact on performance, service quality, data fidelity, security, and privacy. Practices such as image transcoding can affect data fidelity, and HTTP header injection can compromise privacy without the user's knowledge. The vast majority of HTTP proxies deployed in today's commercial cellular networks do not comply with the HTTP standards, which indicate that any proxy *must* advertise its presence both to the client and the server with the `VIA` general-header [17]. Unfortunately, users and online services have limited power to avoid middleboxes due to their direct imposition on the user's path communication. Only a small fraction of savvy users take advantage of "trusted" VPN clients and servers to avoid middlebox interference in their traffic.

Mobile users also do not generally understand the role of APN settings and how these can affect their service quality. Some users find APN settings via web searches, which can lead to baffling configuration problems due to mismatches with the user's mobile environment. Moreover, mobile users also lack a clear picture of what MVNOs are and how they operate on top of an MNO either as a light or as a full MVNO. In fact, it generally proves difficult to identify the MNO providing the service or determine the operational mode employed by the MVNO. Similarly, most mobile operators notify users with visual notifications or text messages about the possibility of experiencing differing service quality when roaming on a different provider as a result of network sharing agreements. However, as we have seen in this work, a large number of roaming cases happen inapparently to the user.

*Conclusion.*

Our work has highlighted the challenge of attempting to characterize the behavior of mobile networks based only on fine-grained network measurements. While the presence of proxies in cellular networks may be expected by users, developers and researchers with a good technical background, these middleboxes' purpose, effect on quality of service, and impact on data fidelity are generally not well-defined and difficult to determine empirically. Without an understanding of the broader ecosystem from which the measurements come—including the technical implications of different business relationships—any mobile network analysis risks misattributing network performance, as well as security and privacy issues, to parties other than those actually responsible.

The key implication of our work is that the traditional notion of "the mobile provider" as perceived by users, developers, researchers, and regulators needs rethinking. Providing mobile network connectivity is not a task fulfilled by a monolithic, immutable entity, but rather the result of a complex and dynamic interplay of a set of service providers.

## Acknowledgments

As always, we are deeply grateful to our Netalyzr users for enabling this study. This work was partially supported by funding provided to ICSI through National Science Foundation grants CNS-1111672 ("Measuring and Modeling the Dynamics of IPv4 Address Exhaustion"), CNS-1213157 ("User-Centric Network Measurement"), and CNS-1237265 ("Beyond Technical Security: Developing an Empirical Basis for Socio-Economic Perspectives") and by the DHS Directorate of Science and Technology under grant N66001-12-C-0128. Any opinions, findings, and conclusions or recommendations expressed in this material are those of the authors or originators and do not necessarily reflect the views of the NSF or of the DHS. The authors would like to thank the anonymous reviewers and our shepherd Ramon Caceres (Google) for constructive feedback on preparation of the final version of this paper. We also wish to thank Amazon, Comcast, and Google for their generous support, as well as Moritz Steiner (Akamai), Andrius Auçinas (University of Cambridge), and Jon Crowcroft (University of Cambridge) for their valuable feedback.

# 9. REFERENCES

[1] APN Settings Virgin Mobile AU. https://community.virginmobile.com.au/t5/Phones-knowledge-base/What-are-the-generic-APN-settings-for-Internet-MMS-and-tethering/ta-p/76.

[2] ITU Operational Bulletin. http://www.itu.int/dms_pub/itu-t/opb/sp/T-SP-OB.1056-2014-OAS-PDF-E.pdf.

[3] Jasper Wireless. http://www.jasper.com/operators.

[4] MVNO Directory. http://www.mvnodirectory.com/overview.html.

[5] MVNODynamics. http://www.mvnodynamics.com.

[6] Netalyzr for Android. Amazon App Store. http://www.amazon.com/International-Computer-Science-Institute-Netalyzr/dp/B00IM1TXMA.

[7] Netalyzr for Android. Google Play. https://play.google.com/store/apps/details?id=edu.berkeley.icsi.netalyzr.android.

[8] Orbot: Proxy with Tor. https://play.google.com/store/apps/details?id=org.torproject.android.

[9] Verizon coverage locator. http://www.verizonwireless.com/b2c/coveragelocator/mapInformation.jsp.

[10] WDSPCo. http://www.wdspco.org.

[11] Xda-Developers. http://www.xda-developers.com/.

[12] France v Google. http://www.economist.com/news/business/21569414-xavier-niel-playing-rough-internet-giant-france-v-google, 2013.

[13] 3GPP. General Packet Radio Service (GPRS); GPRS Tunneling Protocol (GTP) across the Gn and Gp interface. http://www.3gpp.org/DynaReport/29060.htm.

[14] R. Chakravorty, S. Banerjee, P. Rodriguez, J. Chesterfield, and I. Pratt. Performance Optimizations for Wireless Wide-area Networks: Comparative Study and Experimental Evaluation. In *Proc. ACM MobiCom*, 2004.

[15] L. Cricelli, M. Grimaldi, and N. L. Ghiron. The Competition Among Mobile Network Operators in the Telecommunication Supply Chain. *International Journal of Production Economics*, 2011.

[16] L. Fan, P. Cao, W. Lin, and Q. Jacobson. Web Prefetching Between Low-bandwidth Clients and Proxies: Potential and Performance. In *Proc. ACM SIGMETRICS*, 1999.

[17] R. Fielding, J. Gettys, J. Mogul, H. Frystyk, L. Masinter, P. Leach, and T. Berners-Lee. Hypertext Transfer Protocol – HTTP/1.1. RFC 2616, IETF, June 1999.

[18] A. Finamore, M. Mellia, Z. Gilani, K. Papagiannaki, V. Erramilli, and Y. Grunenberger. Is There a Case for Mobile Phone Content Pre-staging? In *Proc. ACM CoNEXT*, 2013.

[19] R. Giobbi. CERT Vulnerability Note VU 435052: Intercepting proxy servers may incorrectly rely on HTTP headers to make connections, February 2009.

[20] International Chamber of Commerce. Telecoms Liberalization. 2004.

[21] International Computer Science Institute. Netalyzr dataset. PREDICT. `https://www.predict.org/Default.aspx?tabid=104`.

[22] R.S. Jain. Spectrum auctions in India: lessons from experience. *Telecommunications Policy*, 25, 2001.

[23] A. Kiiski. Impacts of MVNOs on mobile data service market. In *17th European regional ITS conference*, 2006.

[24] C. Kreibich, N. Weaver, B. Nechaev, and V. Paxson. Netalyzr: Illuminating The Edge Network . In *Proc. ACM IMC* , 2010.

[25] W. K. Leong, A. Kulkarni, Y. Xu, and B. Leong. Unveiling the Hidden Dangers of Public IP Addresses in 4G/LTE Cellular Data Networks. In *Proc. ACM HotMobile*, 2014.

[26] R. McMillan. Verizon and AT&T are the only wireless carriers using Perma-cookies. `http://http://www.wired.com/2014/11/permacookie-free/`.

[27] R. McMillan. Verizon's perma-cookie is a privacy-killing machine. `http://www.wired.com/2014/10/verizons-perma-cookie/`.

[28] J. Mikians, L. Gyarmati, V. Erramilli, and N. Laoutaris. Detecting price and search discrimination on the internet. In *Proc. ACM HotNets*, 2012.

[29] C. Mulliner. Privacy leaks in mobile phone internet access. In *Proc. IEEE ICIN*, 2010.

[30] Piran Partners. MVNO Observatory. `http://www2.piranpartners.com/component/joomdoc/doc_download/24-piran-partners-mvno-observatory-spring-2014.html`, 2014.

[31] P. Rodriguez and V. Friedman. Performance of PEPs in Cellular Wireless Networks, 2003.

[32] P. Rodriguez, S. Mukherjee, and S. Ramgarajan. Session Level Techniques for Improving Web Browsing Performance on Wireless Links. In *Proc. WWW*, 2004.

[33] J. P. Rula and F. Bustamante. Behind the Curtain: Cellular DNS and Content Replica Selection. In *Proc. ACM IMC*, 2014.

[34] D. Shin. Overlay Networks in the West and the East: a Techno-Economic Analysis of Mobile Virtual Network Operators. *Telecommunication Systems*, 2008.

[35] D. H. Shin and M. Bartolacci. A Study of MVNO Diffusion and Market Structure in the EU, US, Hong Kong, and Singapore. *Telematics and Informatics*, 2007.

[36] J. Sommers and P. Barford. Cell vs. WiFi: On the Performance of Metro Area Mobile Connections. In *Proc. ACM IMC*, 2012.

[37] N. Vallina-Rodriguez, A. Aucinas, M. Almeida, Y. Grunenberger, K. Papagiannaki, and J. Crowcroft. RILAnalyzer: A Comprehensive 3G Monitor on Your Phone. In *Proc. ACM IMC*, 2013.

[38] N. Vallina-Rodriguez, J. Crowcroft, A. Finamore, Y. Grunenberger, and K. Papagiannaki. When assistance becomes dependence: Characterizing the costs and inefficiencies of a-gps. *ACM SIGMOBILE Mob. Comput. Commun. Rev.*, 2013.

[39] Narseo Vallina-Rodriguez, Srikanth Sundaresan, Christian Kreibich, Nicholas Weaver, and Vern Paxson. CRAWDAD data set icsi/netalyzr-android (v. 2015-03-24). Downloaded from http://crawdad.org/icsi/netalyzr-android/, March 2015.

[40] Verizon. Verizon Selects Participation Agreement. `http://www.verizonwireless.com/support/terms/products/verizon-selects.html?MID=810452&RID=178021460&CMP=EMC-C-S-RWDS-Announcement1-T1-JulyAug2014-RD&EMHID=E007D0ABF359C5E4BC3832F3C2B204B6&CUHID=E1583E4C8FA54F0CB9FA01EC656DBD5F`.

[41] Z. Wang, F. X. Lin, L. Zhong, and M. Chishtie. Why Are Web Browsers Slow on Smartphones? In *Proc. ACM HotMobile*, 2011.

[42] Z. Wang, F. X. Lin, L. Zhong, and M. Chishtie. How Far Can Client-only Solutions Go for Mobile Browser Speed? In *Proc. WWW*, 2012.

[43] Z. Wang, Z. Qian, Q. Xu, Z. M. Mao, and M. Zhang. An Untold Story of Middleboxes in Cellular Networks. *SIGCOMM Computer Communication Review*, 2011.

[44] N. Weaver, C. Kreibich, M. Dam, and V. Paxson. Here Be Web Proxies. In *Proc. PAM*, 2014.

[45] N. Weaver, C. Kreibich, B. Nechaev, and V. Paxson. Implications of Netalyzr's DNS Measurements . In *Proc. SATIN*, 2011.

[46] N. Weaver, C. Kreibich, and V. Paxson. Redirecting DNS for Ads and Profit. In *USENIX FOCI Workshop*, 2011.

[47] WebPolicy.org. How Verizon's Avertising Header Works. `http://webpolicy.org/2014/10/24/how-verizons-advertising-header-works/`.

[48] Q. Xu, J. Huang, Z. Wang, F. Qian, A. Gerber, and Z. Mao. Cellular Data Network Infrastructure Characterization and Implication on Mobile Content Placement. In *Proc. ACM SIGMETRICS*, 2011.

[49] K. Zarifis, T. Flach, S. Nori, D. Choffnes, R. Govindan, E. Katz-Bassett, Z. Mao, and M. Welsh. Diagnosing Path Inflation of Mobile Client Traffic. In *Proc. PAM*, 2014.

[50] F. Zarinni, A. Chakraborty, V. Sekar, S. Das, and P. Gill. A first look at performance in mobile virtual network operators. In *Proc. ACM IMC*, 2014.

# Mobilyzer: An Open Platform for Controllable Mobile Network Measurements

Ashkan Nikravesh* Hongyi Yao* Shichang Xu* David Choffnes† Z. Morley Mao*
*University of Michigan †Northeastern University
{ashnik,hyyao,xsc,zmao}@umich.edu choffnes@ccs.neu.edu

## ABSTRACT

Mobile Internet availability, performance and reliability have remained stubbornly opaque since the rise of cellular data access. Conducting network measurements can give us insight into user-perceived network conditions, but doing so requires careful consideration of device state and efficient use of scarce resources. Existing approaches address these concerns in ad-hoc ways.

In this work we propose *Mobilyzer*, a platform for conducting mobile network measurement experiments in a principled manner. Our system is designed around three key principles: network measurements from mobile devices require tightly controlled access to the network interface to provide isolation; these measurements can be performed efficiently using a global view of available device resources and experiments; and distributing the platform as a library to existing apps provides the incentives and low barrier to adoption necessary for large-scale deployments. We describe our current design and implementation, and illustrate how it provides measurement isolation for applications, efficiently manages measurement experiments and enables a new class of experiments for the mobile environment.

## Categories and Subject Descriptors

C.4 [**Performance of Systems**]: [Measurement techniques, Performance attributes]; C.2.1 [**Computer-Communication Networks**]: Network Architecture and Design—*Wireless communication*

## General Terms

Design, Measurement, Performance

## Keywords

Measurement Tool; Cellular Networks; Network Performance; Video; Mobile Web

## 1. INTRODUCTION

Given the tremendous growth in cellular data traffic, it is increasingly important to improve the availability, performance and reliability of the mobile Internet. To adequately address these challenges, we ideally would be able to collect network measurement data from any mobile device on any network at any time. With this information, users could evaluate the service they are paying for, carriers could study the factors impacting performance and detect problems causing degradation, and application developers could tune and improve their service. Many of these optimizations can be performed dynamically when data are available in real time.

Despite a need for performance improvement and policy transparency in this space [27, 45], researchers currently still struggle to measure, analyze and optimize mobile networks. Mobile Internet performance characterization is a challenging problem due to a wide variety of factors that interact and jointly affect user experience. For example, the performance that a user receives from an application can depend on the device's available hardware resources, radio's network state, the network access technology used, contention for the wireless medium, distance from cell towers, session initiation overhead, congestion at various gateways and the overhead of executing code at the communicating endpoints. Further, this performance can change over time and as the user moves with the mobile device. Other challenges include resource constraints (data and power) on mobile platforms in addition to interference affecting measurements.

This problem has not gone unnoticed by researchers, operators and providers. A number of small testbeds and user studies have enabled progress in the face of these challenges [13, 16, 22, 35, 60], but with limited scope, duration, coverage and generality. We argue that previous work suffers from three key limitations that hamper their success. First, these individual solutions do not *scale*: each individual app or measurement platform is inherently limited to the population of participating users running a single piece of software. Second, each solution is *inconsistent* and *inflexible* in the set of network measurements it supports and the contextual information describing the experimental environment, making it difficult to ensure scientific rigor and to merge disparate datasets. Third, these solutions are *uncoordinated* in how they conduct network measurements: multiple apps can wastefully measure the same property independently or, worse, interfere with each other by running measurements at the same time from the same device.

Instead of proliferating apps that conduct independent network measurements in inconsistent ways, we argue that there should be a common measurement service that apps include in their code. Toward this goal, we designed and built *Mobilyzer*, a unified platform for conducting network measurements in the mobile environment. Our system is designed around three key principles:

1. **Measurement isolation:** Network measurements from mobile devices require tightly controlled access to the network


*MobiSys'15,* May 18–22, 2015, Florence, Italy.

http://dx.doi.org/10.1145/2742647.2742670.

interface to provide isolation from competing flows that impact measurement results.

2. **Global coordination:** Uncoordinated measurements from individual devices have limited scalability and effectiveness, so we provide a global view of available devices and their resources as a first-class service to support efficient and flexible measurements without overloading any device or network.

3. **Incentives for researchers and developers:** Instead of focusing on a single "killer app" to obtain a large user base, we distribute the platform as a library to include in any new or existing app. Developers and researchers who write apps needing network measurement benefit from reduced operational cost and coding/debugging effort when using our library, and are given network measurement resources across *all Mobilyzer* devices in proportion to the number of users they convince to install their *Mobilyzer*-enabled apps.

This paper answers key questions of how to (1) design a system that efficiently provides controllable and accurate network measurements in the mobile environment, and (2) leverage crowdsourcing to enable measurement studies previously infeasible in mobile networks.

*Mobilyzer* provides an API for issuing network measurements using a standard suite of tools, and manages measurement deployment and data collection from participating devices. Each device runs a measurement scheduler that receives measurement requests and gives experiments explicit control over the context in which a measurement runs. A cloud-based global manager dynamically deploys measurement experiments to devices according to available resources, device properties and prior measurement results.

*Mobilyzer* is currently deployed as a library that can be included in Android apps, and a cloud-based Google App Engine service for managing measurements across participating devices. *Mobilyzer* supports standard implementations of useful measurement primitives such as ping, traceroute, DNS lookups, HTTP GET, TCP throughput, and the like. These rich set of measurement primitives support experiments traditionally popular in fixed-line networks, such as mapping Internet paths (via traceroute), measuring and comparing performance for different destinations, and understanding broadband availability. We also support advanced application-layer and cellular-specific measurements, such as inferring RRC timers, measuring Video QoE, and breaking down Web page load time into its constituent dominant components.

Our design supports a constrained form of programmable measurements: an experiment may consist of sequential and/or concurrent measurements, where the execution of subsequent measurements can depend on the results of prior results and contextual information (*e.g.,* signal strength or location). We demonstrate the flexibility of these *compound measurements* using several experiments as case studies. For instance, we use this feature to trigger diagnosis measurements when anomalies in network performance are detected, or when we predict that a handover might occur.

We evaluate our deployed system in terms of our design goals. We demonstrate that it effectively provides measurement isolation, and failure to do so can lead to unpredictable and large measurement errors. Further, we show that *Mobilyzer* manages measurement scheduling efficiently, adapts to available resources in the system, is easy to use, and reduces development effort for measurement tasks.

We further evaluate our system in terms of new measurement studies that it enables, using *Mobilyzer*'s support for coordinated measurements among large numbers of vantage points to evaluate the performance of Internet-scale systems. We use *Mobilyzer* to identify and diagnose cases of CDN inefficiency, characterize and decompose page load time delays for Web browsing, and evaluate alternative video bitrate adaptation schemes in the mobile environment. For example, we find that (1) poor CDN replica selection adds 100 ms or more latency in 10% of our measurements, (2) limited mobile CPU power is a critical bottleneck in Web page load times (typically between 40-50% of load times) and doubling CPU speed can reduce load times by half, and (3) buffer-based adaptive video streaming improves the average delivered bitrate by 50% compared to commonly used capacity-based adaptation for low bandwidth clients.

## 2. BACKGROUND AND RELATED WORK

A variety of existing approaches attempt to shed light on mobile networks, but each exhibits limitations that we address with our work.

**Existing research platforms.** Our work shares many of the same goals of successful testbeds such as PlanetLab [47], RIPE Atlas [52], and BISMark [63], and our work uses M-Lab [38] servers as targets for many measurement tests. These are general-purpose experimentation platforms that require deployment of infrastructure and do not operate in the mobile environment. These systems are insufficient alone for understanding mobile networks because mobile networks generally use firewall/NATs [66]. We also share goals with Dasu [55], but differ fundamentally in that properly characterizing network performance in mobile environment requires different strategies than in the wired/broadband environment due to scarce resources and measurement interference. Seattle [20] is a general-purpose platform that supports deploying code on Android devices, and it shares many goals with *Mobilyzer*. It does not provide network measurement isolation, but many of its device management and security features can be integrated into *Mobilyzer*.

**View from operators.** Operators and manufacturers such as AT&T and Alcatel-Lucent have deployed in-network monitoring devices that passively capture a detailed view of network flows traversing their mobile infrastructure [18, 24]. Several studies use these passive measurements to understand network traffic generated by subscriber devices, with important applications to traffic engineering, performance characterization and security [18, 28, 37, 49, 53, 64, 68]. However, this approach does not allow the carrier to understand the performance experienced at the mobile device. For example, when the throughput for a network flow suddenly changes, it is difficult to infer from passive measurements alone whether it is due to wireless congestion, signal strength, and/or simply normal application behavior.

Further, most interesting behavior occurs at or near the edge of mobile networks, making an infrastructure-based deployment costly. For example, Xu et al. point out that monitors located near a cellular provider's core cannot account for detailed user mobility, and adding the infrastructure to support these measurements would require a deployment at least two orders of magnitude larger [67].

**Existing measurement apps.** Motivating the need for a mobile measurement library, several academic, governmental and commercial mobile performance measurement tools have been released recently. The FCC released a network measurement app [27] to characterize mobile broadband in the US but the system is closed and data is not publicly available. Several commercial apps measure mobile Internet performance by collecting measurements such as ping latency and throughput [21, 44, 61]. However, because the source code is closed, the methodology is under-specified, and the datasets tightly controlled, it is difficult for the research community and end-users to draw sound conclusions. Further, these tests are generated on-demand by end-users, creating a strong selection bias in the data, as users may be more likely to run tests when they experience problems.

A number of research projects use apps to gather network measurements from hundreds or thousands of mobile devices [31, 36, 40, 41, 48, 57–59]. Such measurements reveal information not visible from passive in-network measurements, such as radio state, signal strength and the interaction between content providers and network infrastructure [34,59,67,69]. Further, these measurements reveal information across carriers, allowing researchers to understand different ISP network policies and performance [66]. Such one-off studies provide a useful snapshot of mobile networks, but they do not support longitudinal studies that inform how mobile network performance, reliability and policy changes over time, nor do they support targeted measurements that are required to understand the underlying reasons for observed network behavior.

Each of the above projects uses a separate codebase, a different set of collected contextual information and different privacy/data sharing policies. As such, experiments are conducted in an ad-hoc manner, with limited or no ability to compare and combine measurements from each limited deployment. As an example pitfall from the current approach, consider the case of interpreting the result of a simple ping measurement. Because mobile device radios enter a low power state during idle periods, a ping measurement that wakes the radio (and experiences additional delay during the wakeup period) can affect a subsequent ping measurement that occurs while the radio is in full power mode. Without contextual information, a researcher might falsely attribute network delays to the carrier instead of the device. Worse, if there are two measurement apps running on the same device, one app's measurements can interfere with the other's.

Our work is also motivated by other efforts in building measurement libraries, especially on mobile platforms. For example, Insight [46] and AppInsight [51] offer platforms for instrumenting and measuring application performance, rather than network measurements.

# 3. GOALS

The goal of *Mobilyzer* is to provide a scalable platform for conducting meaningful network measurements in the mobile environment. This is the first open-source platform[1] to support mobile measurements in the form of a library. It is designed to achieve:

## 3.1 Standard, Easy-to-use Measurements

There is a tension between arbitrary flexibility and standardization in a platform for network measurements. While allowing experimenters to execute arbitrary code within a sandbox provides flexibility, a lack of standards means that these experiments are difficult to incorporate into existing and future datasets. In *Mobilyzer*, we opt for standard measurements, facilitating comparative and longitudinal studies atop our platform (see §4.2).

## 3.2 Measurement Isolation

The mobile environment poses unique challenges for controlling how network measurements are isolated from each other, and from network traffic generated by other apps and services. *Mobilyzer* accounts for these properties and gives experimenters explicit control over device state and concurrent network activity

[1] *Mobilyzer* source code is publicly available at http://mobilyzer-project.mobi/

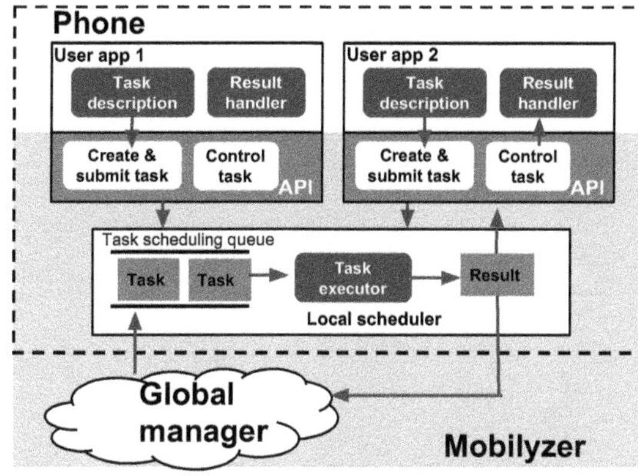


Figure 1: *Mobilyzer* architecture (shaded region). Apps (top) include the *Mobilyzer* library, which provides an API to issue network measurements, and a scheduler service (middle) that provides measurement management and isolation. The scheduler communicates with a global manager (bottom) to fetch measurement requests and report measurement results.

during measurement. *Mobilyzer* achieves the goal of measurement isolation via a local measurement scheduler (see §4.3).

## 3.3 Global Coordination

Data quota and power are scarce resources for mobile networks, requiring that researchers use more principled approaches than "shotgun" measurement. With a global view of available network resources and the ability to coordinate measurements from multiple devices, we can coalesce redundant measurements and allow researchers to specify targeted experiments that use device resources efficiently (see §4.4). For instance, coordination among the *Mobilyzer*'s clients provides opportunities to (1) evaluate the performance of Internet-scale services and (2) schedule measurements in an interactive fashion, where a set of measurements scheduled on one device may depend on the results *Mobilyzer* receives from other devices.

## 3.4 Incentives for Adoption

As a crowdsourcing approach, *Mobilyzer* requires a crowd of mobile users to adopt our platform. We argue that no single app will provide the necessary crowd. Instead, we opt for a "bring your own app" deployment model, where researchers/developers develop *Mobilyzer*-enabled apps with user incentives.

We propose the following incentives for researchers and developers to use our library.

- *Incentive for researchers.* The incentive for researchers to develop *Mobilyzer*-enabled apps is that they can conduct measurements on *any* of the devices in the system (including those not running their app), with measurement quota proportional to the number of devices their app(s) bring to the system. This is analogous to the PlanetLab and RIPE Atlas models, except using a software (instead of hardware) deployment.
- *Incentive for developers.* One incentive for adopting *Mobilyzer* is reduced operational costs. As an example, an app that provides "speed tests" of peak transfer rates can incur significant bandwidth charges for the servers hosting transferred content. Our system uses resources donated by M-Lab, and this was the main reason that MySpeedTest adopted our tool.

  A second incentive is reduced coding/debugging effort. Supporting any app that requires network measurement (and pos-

| Measurement Type | Supported Measurements | Usage |
|---|---|---|
| Basic | DNS lookups, ping, traceroute, HTTP GET, TCP throughput, and UDP burst | Supports experiments traditionally popular in fixed-line networks, such as mapping Internet paths, measuring and comparing performance for different destinations and carriers, and understanding broadband availability |
| Composed | Sequential and parallel | Combines multiple measurements programmatically to support new measurements, such as diagnosis measurements |
| Complex | RRC timer inference, Video QoE, and Page load time measurements | Supports application-layer and cellular-specific active measurements |

Table 1: Measurement types supported by *Mobilyzer*.

sibly access to measurements from multiple devices) entails writing and maintaining software for measurement and data storage/retrieval. Our experience is that correct implementations of such functionality can take man-months to man-years of work. We provide this functionality out-of-the-box with *Mobilyzer*.

We also consider altruism and relationships with developers as incentives. For example, the Insight [46] project successfully convinced developers of a popular app to instrument and share data with researchers. Similarly, altruism has attracted users to support platforms such as RIPE Atlas and DIMES.

**Comparison with ad libraries.** Our library-based deployment model is inspired in part from the successful adoption of advertising (ad) libraries in mobile apps. We believe that ad libraries are successful in large part because they have direct incentives for developers (payment for click-throughs) and a limited impact on apps. Our direct incentive for developers is that they "earn" measurement resources proportional to the size of the *Mobilyzer*-enabled app deployment. This is analogous to the RIPE Atlas credit model, which has helped grow a hardware-based platform to more than 7,000 active hosts. Like ad libraries, which periodically pull advertisements for display, *Mobilyzer* primarily uses a pull-based model to fetch measurements.

However, ad libraries and *Mobilyzer* differ from the perspective of privacy and resource usage. Ad libraries can be used to track arbitrary information about users, often without any explicit privacy policy or user awareness. *Mobilyzer* is explicit about the data it collects, was designed with privacy concerns in mind, and requires explicit user consent. Further, it is unclear if or how ad libraries limit the resources consumed by their service. *Mobilyzer* provides controllable, limited impact on apps by enforcing hard limits on resource consumption (in terms of energy and data quota) and avoiding interference with network traffic from other apps. While *Mobilyzer* provides direct incentives for developers in terms of measurement resources, unlike ad libraries it will not directly subsidize app development costs.

## 3.5 Nongoals

First, we do not provide a "PlanetLab for mobile"; i.e., we do not provide a platform for deploying arbitrary distributed system code on mobile devices. Instead, we focus on the more constrained problem of providing a platform for principled network measurements in lieu of one-off, nonstandard measurement studies. Second, we do not provide a service for arbitrary data-collection from mobile devices; rather, we focus on active and passive network measurements annotated with anonymized contextual information. Collecting arbitrary data from users is a potential privacy risk that we avoid in *Mobilyzer*. Third, we do not propose any specific incentives for device owners to adopt *Mobilyzer*-enabled apps. Rather, we urge experimenters to either develop apps with user incentives in mind, or convince maintainers of existing popular app codebases to include our library. Currently, there are hundreds of apps [6] that simply do network measurements (e.g., speed tests) or network diagnosis (signal strength/coverage maps) and have large user bases. We believe this is strong evidence that users will install a *Mobilyzer*-enabled tool as long as it is useful. We also believe that *Mobilyzer*'s limited data collection is not a strong impediment to user adoption, as ad libraries are known to collect more intrusive information with no known effect on adoption.

# 4. DESIGN AND IMPLEMENTATION

## 4.1 Overview

Figure 1 provides a high-level view of the Mobilyzer platform. It consists of an app library, a local measurement scheduler, and a cloud-based global manager.

**Measurement Library.** *Mobilyzer* is designed to be easy to use and integrate into existing apps, while providing incentives for doing so. It is deployed to apps as a library with a well-defined API for issuing/controlling measurements and gathering results locally. This facilitates development of new apps that use network measurements. For example, an app that includes our library can issue a measurement and retrieve results with under 10 lines of code. Existing apps can incorporate our library to take advantage of our validated measurement tools and server-side infrastructure.

**Local measurement scheduler.** *Mobilyzer* achieves the goal of measurement isolation via the local measurement scheduler. The scheduler listens for measurement requests and ensures that any submitted measurements are conducted in the intended environment (*e.g.,* radio state, state of other apps using the network, and contextual information such as location, signal strength and carrier). Regardless of how many apps on a device use it, *Mobilyzer* ensures that there is exactly one scheduler running. If apps with multiple versions of the scheduler are present, the latest version is guaranteed to be used. The scheduler enforces user-specified limits on resource (data/power) consumption.

**Global manager.** The *Mobilyzer* global manager provides coordination for the following services: dynamic measurement deployment, resource cap enforcement, and data collection. This support is quite unique to our platform, as global centralized coordination improves the design of mobile experiments despite limited resources. Experimenters use the global manager to deploy measurement experiments to devices. For example, an experiment may contain a number of network measurements that should be conditionally deployed and executed according to device properties. The global manager deploys these measurements to devices based on device information reported periodically, and ensures that measurements are not deployed to devices that have exceeded user-specified resource caps. The manager maintains a datastore of anonymized data collected from all devices and

| API Function | Description |
|---|---|
| `MeasurementTask` **`createTask`**`(TaskType type, Date startTime, Date endTime, double intervalSec, long count, long priority, Map<String,String> params)` | Create a task with the specified input parameters including task execution frequency task priority, etc. |
| `String` **`submitTask`**`( MeasurementTask task )` | Submit the task to the scheduler and return `taskId`. |
| `void` **`cancelTask`**`(String taskId)` | Cancel the submitted task, only allowed by the application that created this task. |
| `void` **`setBatteryThreshold`**`(int threshold)` | Set the battery threshold for check-in and running the global manager scheduled tasks. |
| `void` **`setCheckinInterval`**`(long interval)` | Set how frequently the scheduler checks in. |
| `void` **`setDataUsage`**`(DataUsageProfile profile)` | Set a limit for *Mobilyzer*'s cellular data usage. |

Table 2: *Mobilyzer* key API functions to support issuing and controlling measurement tasks.

makes this available for interactive measurement experiments and for offline analysis. The data collection and scheduling support at the global manager enable dynamically triggered measurements based on observed network behavior, achieving a feedback loop of measurement, analysis, and updated measurements.

## 4.2 Measurement Library and API

**Design.** A key design principle for *Mobilyzer* is that the platform should remove barriers to widespread adoption so that it facilitates a large-scale deployment. We chose to implement *Mobilyzer* as a network measurement library that app developers include in their code. This code provides an API for issuing measurements using a standard suite of tools (Table 2), and a device-wide measurement scheduler.

The measurement model supported by *Mobilyzer* represents a trade-off between complete flexibility to run arbitrary code and complete safety in that all resources consumed by a measurement can be predicted in advance. Specifically, *Mobilyzer* supports a small set of commonly used *measurement primitives*, e.g., ping, traceroute, DNS lookup, HTTP get and throughput tests. These measurements can be performed independently in isolation, or they can be chained (do a DNS lookup for google.com, then ping the IP address) or executed in parallel (e.g., ping google.com during a TCP throughput test) in arbitrary ways.

Using this model, the amount of data and power consumed by each task (simple or complex) is predictable with few exceptions (e.g., downloading an arbitrary Web page) that can be mitigated via scheduler-enforced constraints on the data and power consumption of a task. Like Dasu, this approach avoids concerns from running arbitrary code; however, unlike Dasu this allows us to strictly control resource consumption (which is not a primary goal of Dasu).

**Implementation.** The *Mobilyzer* measurement library is implemented as Android code that is added by reference to an existing app's source code. *Mobilyzer* supports three types of measurements: *Basic*, *Composed*, and *Complex Measurements (Table 1).*

*Basic Measurements Supported.* *Mobilyzer* supports both passive, contextual measurements and active network measurements. Currently, the active measurements supported are DNS lookups, ping, traceroute, HTTP GET, and a TCP throughput and UDP burst test. For each measurement task, users can specify general task parameters (*e.g.,* the time at which to run) and task specific parameters (*e.g.,* TTL value for ping measurement). Further, each task can specify a *pre-condition* which must evaluate to true before a task can be executed (*e.g.,* location is Boston, signal strength is greater than 50, network type is cellular).

*Mobilyzer* also collects passive measurements on both network performance and device state, and associates a set of passive measurements with every active test run. It collects the signal strength (RSSI values) and the device's battery level, battery charging state, coarse-grained location, the network technology, the total number of bytes and packets sent and received by the device, as well as static context information such as the carrier, OS, and support for IPv6. Our set of measurements and monitored device properties do not require special privileges; however, we can support measurements that require rooted phones (if available).

*Measurement composition.* *Mobilyzer* supports combining multiple measurements into a single experiment, where sets of measurement tasks can run sequentially and/or in parallel. Further, the result of each sequential task can be used as a pre-condition for executing a subsequent task. This feature improves experiment flexibility—we use this feature to trigger diagnosis measurements in response to detecting anomalies in network performance. Figure 2 shows how this feature can help in building a simple diagnosis task, where the client will run traceroute, if latency and signal strength is above a threshold.

*Supporting complex measurements.* *Mobilyzer* is designed to provide extensible support for application-layer and cellular-specific measurements. These include inferring RRC timers, measuring Video QoE, and breaking down Web page load time into its constituent dominant components. Further, our system can incorporate new complex measurements as they become available. Each new task must have predictable power consumption, data usage, and duration, so that *Mobilyzer* can ensure that the measurement task will not exceed a device's battery and data usage limits.

We now describe how long-running, complex tasks motivate the need for additional scheduler features to ensure measurements complete successfully. Mobile devices change between different power states, called RRC states, in response to network traffic [26, 33]. The device's RRC state is not exposed to the OS due to a lack of an open API, so identifying how long devices stay in each power state entails sending a large number of individual packets with long gaps between them, and inferring power states based on observed packet delivery delays.

This type of measurement poses two key challenges. First, it is a long-running, low-rate measurement that should run only when connected to a cellular network. With no other tasks running on the device, the test can easily take half an hour. Given our pre-emptive priority scheduler (described in the next section), the RRC inference task will either block other tasks for long durations or will be constantly interrupted by higher priority tasks. The latter situation can lead to a large volume of wasted measurement bandwidth (as interrupted measurements must be discarded and restarted), and with sufficient interruptions the RRC task may not have a chance to complete.

Second, this task requires complete isolation from other network activity. Any concurrent traffic will alter the results of this test by changing the radio power state. To detect whether the network isolation property holds, *Mobilyzer* collects information about device-wide background traffic through the *proc* file system and discards results taken when there is background traffic.

These challenges motivate the following approach for the RRC state task. First, it runs with low priority so it does not block other measurements for unreasonable periods. Second, because it may be frequently pre-empted or unable to run due to the device using WiFi, we support suspending and resuming this task. Third, we upload partial measurement results when the task fails to complete, so the data collected is not wasted. We used this measurement to understand the impact of RRC states on latency and packet loss for various network protocols and applications, and found the presence of unexpected application-layer delays [54].

More generally, we include these features for any task that logically supports suspend, resume and partial measurements. For example, traceroute includes these features but atomic measurements such as ping do not.

## 4.3 Local Measurement Scheduler

**Design.** The local measurement scheduler is a service running on a device that manages the execution of measurement tasks. It can be implemented in the operating system or run as a user-level background service. The scheduler provides a measurement execution environment that can enforce network isolation from other measurements and apps running on the device. It also enforces resource-usage, priority, and fairness constraints.

*Task priorities.* The scheduler supports measurement task priorities with pre-emption. It executes tasks with the highest priority first and will pre-empt ongoing measurements if they are of lower priority. Certain measurement tasks cannot produce correct results if pre-empted (*e.g.,* a ping task pre-empted between sending an echo request and receiving a response), so pre-emption will lead to wasted measurement. To balance the trade-off between this waste and scheduler responsiveness to high-priority tasks, the scheduler waits for a short time (*e.g.,* one second) before pre-empting a measurement.

This is sufficient time for a ping measurement to complete, but not necessarily for other tasks (*e.g.,* traceroute). To minimize wasted measurement resources for pre-empted tasks, we define a `pause()` method that signals to measurement tasks that they should save their state due to an imminent pre-emption. For traceroute, this means that the traceroute measurement can save its current progress and continue to measure a path once it is rescheduled.

Not all measurements can (or should) be pre-emptible. In addition to the traceroute task mentioned above, we have also implemented a pre-emptible long-running task for inferring RRC state timers on mobile devices [26, 33]. Measurements like DNS lookup and ping are not pre-emptible (i.e., they are killed at pre-emption time) because they are short-lived tasks with minimal (or no) state to cache. In general, network measurement tasks (e.g., throughput measurement) to characterize time-varying properties of the network cannot benefit from saved state when pre-empted; this is in contrast to measurements of more stable properties (e.g., RRC state machine and NAT policies).

*Traffic Interference.* To avoid inference from (and with) traffic from other apps, *Mobilyzer* monitors traffic generated by other apps (using the TrafficStats API in Android) and pauses/kills measurement tasks that are subject to interference. For example, the TCP throughput task, which attempts to saturate bandwidth to measure throughput, will be stopped if scheduler detects any concurrent network traffic; failing to do so may adversely affect other applications' performance and lead to inconclusive measurement results.

*Resource constraints and fairness.* The scheduler accounts for how much data and power is consumed by network measurements and ensures that they stay within user-specified limits. Users specify hard limits on how much data *Mobilyzer* consume, and at what battery level the library should stop conducting measurements.

We enforce limits as follows.

- The scheduler does not execute a task if its data or energy consumption estimates exceed available resources. Such tasks are suspended until the constrained resource(s) is replenished. For energy, this happens when a device is recharged; for data plans, this is typically done according to the billing cycle.
- The scheduler monitors data and power consumption for ongoing measurements, and terminates a task if it consumes more data than expected, and/or exceeds a device's data/power quota. Because measurement tasks cannot execute arbitrary code, we can always predict in advance the maximum resources they may consume, and use that as a conservative estimate for scheduling purposes.
- To ensure liveness and fair access to resources, the scheduler enforces an upper bound on task duration by terminating execution of a measurement task exceeding that limit. This limit must be specified in the task description.

All measurement tasks generated by apps running on a device are assigned the same high priority value. To ensure fairness among multiple apps on the same device competing for resources, we ensure that each app receives an equal share of the constrained resource.

**Implementation.** The scheduler is currently implemented using an Android service, which guarantees that at most one scheduler is present regardless of the number of *Mobilyzer*-enabled apps running on a device. The library communicates with the scheduler service via IPC calls.

*Forward compatibility.* Our library-based deployment model means that different *Mobilyzer*-enabled apps running on the same device may use different versions of the measurement library and scheduler. We want to ensure that all apps on the device bind to the *newest* version of the scheduler service as soon as it is installed by an app. A key challenge for providing this functionality is that by default on Android, apps will bind only to the scheduler of the app that is first installed, which is unlikely to be the latest version.

We address this as follows. First, we exploit the Android priority tag in the *bind* Intent when declaring the scheduler in the manifest file. The scheduler with the highest priority is bound if there is no other bound scheduler, so we increment the priority value with each new *Mobilyzer* version. However, if an older scheduler has already been bound, apps bound to an older version do not switch until the device is rebooted. To address this, we deliver the scheduler version information via the *start* Intent. When the scheduler receives a *start* Intent, it compares its version with the one in the intent and terminates if it sees a newer scheduler version.

## 4.4 Global Manager

**Design.** The *Mobilyzer* manager maintains a global view of measurement resources, efficiently dispatches experiment tasks to available devices and coordinates measurements from multiple devices to meet various experiment dependencies. Atop the manager is a Web interface that allows experimenters to specify measurement experiments that are deployed to devices.

Specifically, researchers can submit a measurement schedule, along with information about the properties of devices that should participate in the experiment (e.g., location, device type, mobile provider). Devices periodically check in with the manager and

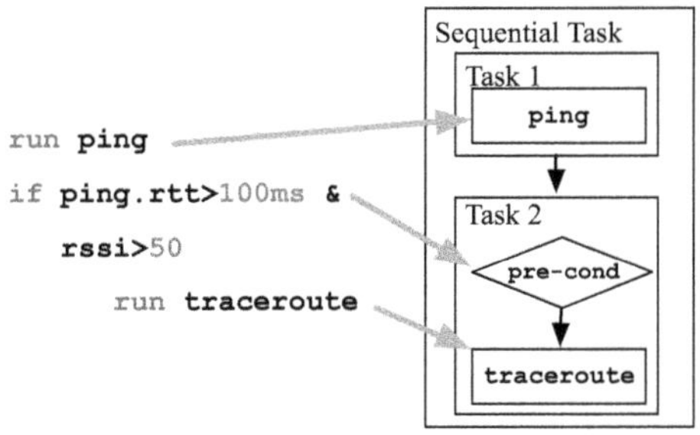


```
params = new HashMap<String, String>();
params.put("target", "www.google.com");
MeasurementTask pingTask = api.createTask(PingTask.TYPE,
    params);
MeasurementTask tracerouteTask =
    api.createTask(TracerouteTask.TYPE, params);
tracerouteTask.setPreCondition(AndCriteria(
      Criteria(Criteria.RESULT, 0 ,"mean_rtt_ms",">",100),
      //0 is index of prior task
      Criteria(Criteria.RSSI,">",50)));
MeasurementTask seqTask = api.createTask(SequentialTask.TYPE,
    Config.DEFAULT_MEASUREMENT_COUNT,
    Config.DEFAULT_MEASUREMENT_INTERVAL_SEC,
    API.USER_PRIORITY);
seqTask.setSubTasks([pingTask,tracerouteTask])
api.submitTask(seqTask);
```

Figure 2: Using sequential tasks to build a simple diagnosis task.

receive a list of experiments to run. When complete, devices report the results of the measurements to the manager.

The manager ensures: (i) no experiment uses more than its fair share of available measurement capacity across *Mobilyzer* devices; (ii) experiments are scheduled in a way that maximizes the likelihood that the targeted devices will complete their measurements during the period of interest; and (iii) it enforces limits that prevent harm to the network or hosts (*e.g.,* via a DDoS).

*Fairness under contention.* In a successful *Mobilyzer* deployment, there are likely to be cases where measurement requests exceed available measurement resources. In periods of contention, we must dispatch measurement tasks according to some fairness metric.

We assign measurement tasks to devices such that the fraction of assigned tasks for an experimenter is proportional to the number of measurement-enabled devices that the experimenter has contributed to *Mobilyzer*. When measurement demand from an experimenter is lower than their fair share, we backfill available resources from remaining pending tasks to ensure that our system is work conserving. Similar to previous work [19, 42], we can use an auction-based approach as a building block to provide such fairness.

*Availability prediction.* Available devices in *Mobilyzer* are subject to high churn and mobility, meaning that simply deploying an experiment to some random fraction of devices may lead to a low rate of successful measurements. To improve this, the global manager incorporates knowledge of experiment dependencies, prediction for resource availability and accounting for failures due to issues such as disconnections and loss of power. For example, we use prediction to prevent wasted measurement resources by preventing experiments from being dispatched if they are likely to fail (*e.g.,* due to unavailable measurement quota or due to measurement preconditions not being met on the device).

*Other features.* *Mobilyzer* supports a variety of other features, described in detail in the technical report [43]. Briefly, we support live measurement experiments, which allows researchers to specify measurement experiments that are driven by results from ongoing measurements; i.e., experiments that cannot be specified a priori (demonstrated in §5.4.1). The global manager can prevent harm to the network and to other hosts by accounting for all measurement activity in the system and ensure that no host or network is overloaded by measurement traffic. Last, users can access their data by logging into our dashboard [7], and collected data is anonymized and publicly accessible online [8].

**Implementation.** The *Mobilyzer* manager is currently implemented using a Google App Engine (GAE) instance, providing a highly scalable platform for managing thousands or millions of devices. The manager currently uses a pull model for experiment deployment, where devices check in with the manager periodically to retrieve updated experiments and to update their contextual information (coarse location, remaining battery, access technology). We also support Google Cloud Messaging (GCM) services to provide a push-based model for experiments with tighter timing constraints, which is subject to the same resource constraints as pull-based measurements.

Experimenters currently can specify simple measurement schedules using an interface that permits control over measurement parameters, experiment durations and periodicity. We have also developed several dynamic measurement experiments as described in Section 5.4, where the measurements issued to a device depend on the results of prior measurements (from potentially many other devices).

The manager deploys measurements based on contextual information gathered from devices. For example, the manager will reduce the measurement rate for periodic tasks that would otherwise exceed device quota. Similarly, measurement tasks for devices in a specific geographic region are not deployed to devices outside that region.

## 4.5 Security

Security is paramount in any large, controllable distributed system. Our design addresses the following threat model: an attacker who subverts the system by taking over our control channel, hacking our global manager, participating in the system to launch as DDoS, or control/drain resources on devices. We address these attacks as follows:

- **Subverting the control channel:** We use Google App Engine (GAE) to control our devices, which relies on HTTPS to communicate with the trusted GAE hosts. Subverting the control channel requires subverting the PKI for Google certificates, which is difficult.
- **Subverting the GAE controller:** We use Google account authentication to control access to our global manager and limit access only to authorized users. This does not address account compromise, which we cannot rule out. However, we monitor system usage, which should allow us to react quickly should this occur.
- **Insider attack:** A malicious developer could try to use our system to launch "measurements" that actually consist of a DDoS attack or resource drain. To prevent the former, we account for all measurement requests scheduled either by check-in or push-

| Measurement App | Measurement LoC |
|---|---|
| FCC SpeedTest [27] | 12550 |
| MySpeedTest [40] | 9545 |
| Mobiperf | 8976 |

Table 3: Lines of code (LoC) for open-source measurement apps. By integrating *Mobilyzer* into existing apps, developers can save thousands of lines of code.

based mechanism and conducted by all participating devices, and place limits on how many measurements can target a given domain or network. To prevent the latter, we use the hard limits on resource constraints mentioned above.

- **App compromise:** An attacker may wish to take control of apps/devices by executing code that compromises the app/device OS. We support executing only measurements we validate, limiting the attack surface for compromise. We further rely on the Android/Java sandboxes to prevent OS compromise.

# 5. EVALUATION

We now evaluate *Mobilyzer* in terms of deployment experience, performance, and applications.

## 5.1 Deployment Experience

One key advantage of *Mobilyzer* is that apps requiring network measurements are easier to write and maintain. Our platform provides validated measurement code, prevents interference from other *Mobilyzer*-enabled apps, collects and stores measurement data and utilizes existing infrastructure (via M-Lab) for bandwidth testing. We believe that by separating measurement management and data collection code from app development, *Mobilyzer* helps researchers focus on interesting measurement experiments and compelling incentives for user adoption.

Table 3 lists the lines of code (LoC) used for network measurements in three popular measurement apps. In Mobiperf, 80% of the code was for measurement. Using a library-based model, we simplify the app codebase, making it easier to focus on UI and other elements to encourage user adoption. With *Mobilyzer* one can issue a measurement task and retrieve the results with fewer than 10 LoC.

*Mobilyzer* has been adopted by the developers of MySpeedTest, a throughput-testing app. The experience from the main developer was overall quite positive, and identified cases where instructions for use were unclear. While it took several e-mail exchanges to clarify these issues, the developer reported that writing the code to port MySpeedTest to *Mobilyzer* took "about an hour or less" and they have used our library since May, 2014. We are currently in discussions with other researchers about integrating *Mobilyzer* into their apps.

## 5.2 Measurement Isolation

An important feature of *Mobilyzer* is that it schedules measurements to provide applications with control over if and when measurements are run in isolation. We now use this feature to demonstrate the value that isolation brings. In particular, we use a compound measurement task that consists of a TCP throughput test run in parallel with a ping measurement. We vary the start time for the ping measurement such that it occurs before, during, and after the throughput test and plot the results. We also control whether the cellular radio is in a low-power state before measurement. Each experiment is repeated 40 times; we plot a CDF of ping latencies for each configuration. We omit throughput results because they are unaffected by ping measurement cross traffic.

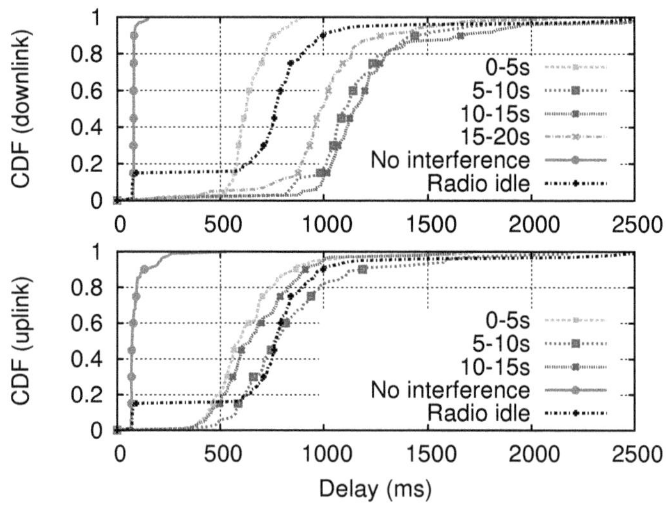


Figure 3: Impact of throughput measurements (grouped into time periods) and radio state on measured RTT. Results vary with radio state, and upstream or downstream cross-traffic with varying throughput. *Mobilyzer* provides strict control over these kinds of dependencies.

Figure 3 shows that ping measurements are significantly affected by cross traffic, and the difference in latency compared to the case with no interference can be hundreds of milliseconds or seconds. The additional delay, presumably from queuing behind the TCP flow from the throughput test, also varies depending on how much cross traffic occurs. As a result, interference from cross traffic essentially renders the latency measurement meaningless. Note that the downlink interference is more severe likely due to higher throughput (2.5 Mbps down vs. 0.35 Mbps uplink), which leads to more queuing inside the network and on the device.

The figures also show differences in measured latencies when the radio is active compared to when it is idle before measurement. Similar to the above scenario, not accounting for this effect can cause misleading or incorrect conclusions. With *Mobilyzer*, experimenters can tightly control the impact of these sources of noise in measurement experiments.

## 5.3 Microbenchmarks

This section presents results from controlled experiments evaluating *Mobilyzer* overhead in terms of measurement-scheduling delay, power usage, and data consumption.

### *5.3.1 Scheduling Delays*

The scheduling delay introduced by *Mobilyzer* consists of the delay from using IPC (interprocess communication) between an app and the scheduler, and the delay introduced by the scheduler. As we show, these delays are reasonably low for all measurements and under significant load.

The IPC delay (Fig. 4) is the sum of (i) the delay between when the client submits a task and when the server receives it (IPC part I in the figure), and (ii) the delay between when the scheduler sends the result to the client, and the client receives it (IPC part II).

We use an HTC One (Android 4.1.1, using LTE) to run measurement tasks for characterizing the IPC overhead. Each task is run 100 times. Fig. 6 presents a CDF of the delay; for all tasks, the maximum delay is below 100ms, while most delays are within 20ms. These values match the performance analysis for IPC latency using Intents [30]. Note that this delay affects the time until a measurement runs but does not interfere with measurement execution.

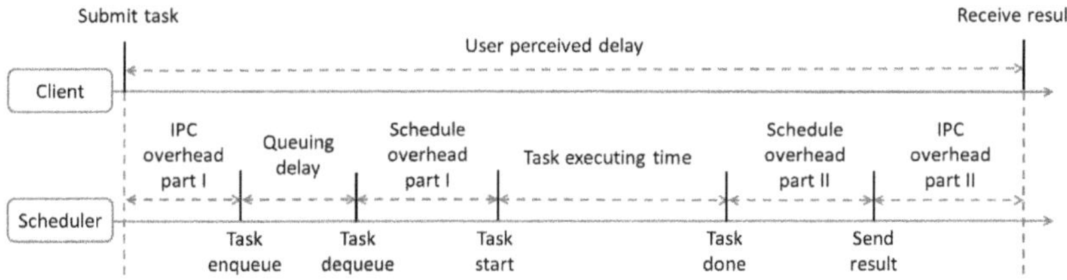


Figure 4: Scheduling overhead for a *Mobilyzer* measurement task.

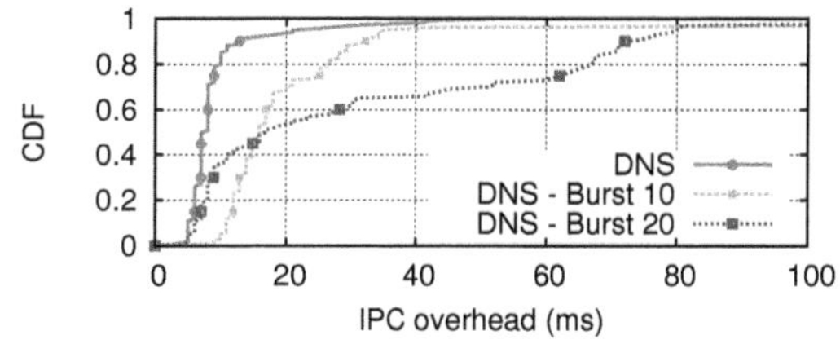


Figure 5: IPC overhead for DNS burst sizes.

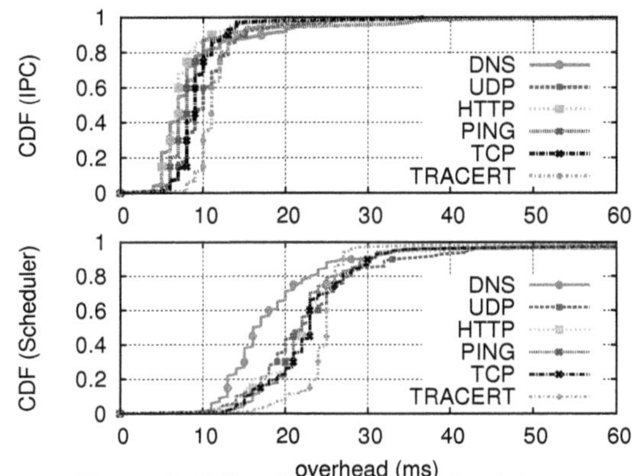


Figure 6: IPC and schedule overhead, 1 app.

| Task | Power consumption under WiFi (mAh) | Power consumption under LTE (mAh) |
|---|---|---|
| DNS | 0.03 (0.01) | 0.09 (0.01) |
| HTTP | 0.05 (0.01) | 0.12 (0.01) |
| UDP (Down) | 0.06 (0.02) | 0.17 (0.02) |
| UDP (Up) | 0.08 (0.03) | 0.17 (0.04) |
| PING | 0.21 (0.01) | 0.52 (0.02) |
| TCP (Down) | 0.11 (0.28) | 2.88 (0.24) |
| TCP (Up) | 1.33 (0.04) | 2.36 (0.20) |
| Traceroute | 0.75 (0.25) | 2.34 (0.02) |
| Sum(unbatched) | 3.51 (0.38) | 8.66 (0.32) |
| Sum(batched) | 3.75 (0.61) | 5.06 (0.25) |

Table 4: Power consumption of *Mobilyzer*: each cell lists the average, then the standard deviation in parentheses.

Note that the IPC overhead increases when many tasks are submitted back to back, due to the way Android implements Intent-based IPC. Specifically, there are two IPCs for each Intent-based IPC – one from sender to the Intent manager, and then one from the manager to the receiver [30].

To test the impact of this, we submit bursts of 1, 10 and 20 tasks with 15 ms between each burst. If several IPCs are sent to the Intent manager at once, there may be a delay in redirecting them to the receiving app. Fig. 5 shows the IPC overhead under high load for the DNS task (other tasks exhibit a similar pattern). Although larger burst sizes lead to longer delays, with a burst of 10 the delay is mostly within 50 ms. For a burst of 20, over 90% are below 100 ms, which we believe is acceptable for scheduling measurement tasks. It is unlikely that user-generated activity will create such a large burst of measurements, so we do not expect these delays to affect user-perceived responsiveness.

We similarly measure the scheduling delay introduced by *Mobilyzer*, *i.e.,* the delays in starting the measurement and sending the result (schedule overhead part I and II in Fig. 4). The scheduling delay distribution for a single client is shown in Fig. 6. It is slightly higher than the IPC overhead, but still on the order of tens of milliseconds. Again, we believe this is acceptable for scheduling and reporting results from measurement tasks.

### 5.3.2 Power Usage

We now estimate the power consumed by *Mobilyzer*. In general, it is difficult to distinguish power consumption of our library from the application that runs it. To address this, we measure the power consumption of an app using the *Mobilyzer* service as it runs in the background executing server scheduled measurement tasks and compare it to power consumed by the same app before integrating *Mobilyzer*, with the overall functionality kept the same.

We measure the power consumption of measurement tasks using a Samsung Galaxy Note 3 as the test device, and a Monsoon power monitor [9] to measure the device power usage.We run each task 5 times with a 15-second delay between tasks to determine the power drain in isolation (unbatched). All experiments are repeated 3 times to identify possible outliers, and we record the average power consumption. Additionally, we run a batched task consisting of all 8 tasks 5 times, and measure the power consumption during the entire measurement period to better reflect that most tasks in *Mobilyzer* run in batches. For comparison, we also sum the average power consumption for all 8 tasks, denoted as Sum(unbatched) based on individual experiments. Table 4 shows the results for WiFi and LTE.

Of the unbatched experiments, we can see that the TCP throughput test has the highest power consumption. This is consistent with prior results showing that power drain is roughly linear with the throughput and duration that the network interface is in a high power state [33]. The power drain from remaining tasks is proportional to the measurement duration because their throughput is low. Note that traceroute has higher power consumption under LTE than under WiFi, since it sends a large number of ICMP packets with an interval of roughly 0.5s. While on LTE, the device will stay in the high power state between these packets.

For batched tasks, we found that on WiFi the power consumption for batched and unbatched tasks are similar. However, on LTE the total power consumption of the batched measurements is much smaller than that of the sum of the individual measurements, by 41.5%. This is because of the tail energy effect on LTE, where the device remains in a high power radio state for several seconds after a network transmission. In each individual task, there is a contribution from the tail time of an average of 48.2% to the total energy consumed [33]. When the tasks are batched, there is only one tail time, demonstrating the effect of batching in saving energy in cellular networks.

These microbenchmarks identify the energy for individual measurements, but not the relative cost compared to other services running on devices. We evaluate this using the built-in Android battery consumption interface on a Samsung Galaxy S4 device actively running a *Mobilyzer*-enabled app with a 250 MB monthly measurement quota. We find that the power consumed by *Mobilyzer* in this scenario is nearly identical to the Android OS itself, with each comprising about 5% of the total energy drain. We believe this power consumption to be reasonably low for most users, and emphasize that *Mobilyzer* allows users to specify limits on the maximum energy our measurements consume.

#### 5.3.3 Data Usage

We now evaluate adaptive measurement scheduling in response to per-device caps of *Mobilyzer* data consumption. Our system consumes data quota from (i) fetching measurement requests from the global manager, (ii) uploading measurement results, and (iii) running the measurement tasks. The last category constitutes the vast majority of data consumption, so we set the frequency of periodic measurements according to each device's data cap. We now demonstrate how well this works in practice.

For this experiment, we monitor the data consumption on a HTC One device by reading the proc files under `/proc/uid_stat/<app uid>` once per minute to monitor the app-specific data usage for *Mobilyzer*. Figure 7 shows *Mobilyzer*'s data usage on a cellular network during 14 hours for a 250 MB and 50 MB data cap, along with the corresponding ideal data consumption. The server adjusts the measurement frequency for tasks based on estimates of the data consumed by each task and the device's data cap. Data is consumed at a slightly higher rate than expected, as the server estimates are not precise. For more precise data consumption control, a client-side data monitor measures all data consumed by *Mobilyzer* and stops running server-scheduled tasks as soon as the limit is reached.

### 5.4 Server Scheduling

The *Mobilyzer* global scheduler enables dynamic, interactive measurement experiments where tasks assigned to devices vary in response to results reported from prior measurements. We present two applications of this feature: measuring the *CDN redirection effectiveness* of major CDNs, and *network diagnosis with adaptive scheduling*, which dynamically schedules diagnosis measurements in response to observed performance issues.

#### 5.4.1 CDN Redirection Effectiveness

In previous work [62], Su et al. used PlanetLab-based experiments to show that CDNs typically send clients to replica servers on low latency paths, instead of optimizing for factors such as load balancing. This requires measuring paths not only to replica servers returned by a DNS redirection, but also testing the latency to other replica servers that could have been selected. Using a dynamic measurement experiment, we repeat this study for the mobile environment to test the extent to which this holds true.

Specifically, we select DNS names served by five large CDNs (Akamai, LimeLight, Google, Amazon CloudFront, and EdgeCast) and measure the latency to the servers that mobile clients are directed toward via DNS lookups. In addition, we measure the latency to servers (5 servers with lowest latency from the recent device measurements and 5 randomly selected servers in distinct /24 prefixes) that *other* devices are directed toward.

For each round of measurement, we find the delay difference between the lowest-latency server and the one returned by the DNS lookup to determine the quality of the mapping. In addition, we sort the latencies to determine the *rank* of the server. For example, if the server returned by the CDN is the second-fastest of ten, its rank is 2.

We summarize our rank results in Figure 8 for 476 devices which used either WiFi (860K measurements) or cellular (393K measurements). Each data point represents the ranking result for one round of measurement.

The figures show that CDNs do not pick the best server half of the time, and as we show below, a this leads to a significant performance penalty for many of our measurements. We calculate the latency difference between the lowest-latency CDN replica and the CDN-selected replica for the same devices in each round of ping measurements. In more than 40% of cases, the latency to the CDN-selected server is optimal. Figure 9 plots the latency difference for cases where the CDN-selected replica is not optimal. We find that for cellular users, 20% of the cases lead to a latency difference of higher than 100ms, which is particularly bad for small downloads common in Web pages. In the worst 10% of cases, there is a noticeable difference between WiFi and cellular; for some CDNs (*e.g.,* Akamai and EdgeCast), the latency difference for WiFi is 50 ms, compared to 500 ms for cellular. While we do not identify the reason for each of these cases, previous work identifies a variety of cases caused by path inflation [69]. Importantly, in contrast to previous work in 2011 showing little opportunity for CDN optimization in mobile networks [68], our study indicates that mobile carriers have more egress points today and CDNs have multiple options for serving clients, but they do not always make optimal decisions for mapping clients to CDN replicas, which can have a significant impact on performance.

#### 5.4.2 Network Diagnosis with Adaptive Scheduling

Dynamic scheduling not only enables new measurements in the mobile environment, it also provides an opportunity to improve measurement efficiency. For example, consider a measurement experiment that measures performance periodically and issues diagnosis measurements in response to anomalous conditions, *e.g.,* to isolate whether there is a problem with a specific server, endpoint or network. Without a priori knowledge about when and where network problems will manifest, the only way to ensure diagnosis information is always available is to issue diagnosis measurements even when there is no problem detected. We now use two examples to show how *Mobilyzer* allows us to issue diagnosis measurements on demand in response to observed problems. For both cases, the global manager scheduled a diagnosis traceroute task only after observing an increase in ping round trip time.

**Data Roaming.** When roaming, a subscriber's IP traffic may egress into the public Internet directly from the roaming carrier, or it can be forwarded to the home carrier [15], to facilitate data-usage accounting and provide access to services located only in the home carrier. Our diagnosis measurements identified the cost of the latter approach. When a Verizon (US) user roamed on five Europe carriers, the that latency to google.com (server in US) increased from 198±46ms to 613±34ms for the same cellular access technology. Our traceroutes reveal that the first hop of the path belongs to Verizon network for all the measurements from five roaming carriers and the first hop round trip time increased from 159±47ms (non-roaming) to 469±26ms (roaming), indicating that *traffic from Europe was tunneled to the US and back for this user, incurring hundreds of additional milliseconds of delay.*

**Path Dynamics.** In this example, the path measurement revealed that 100 ms increase in latency for a Vinaphone user was due to a transient path change (perhaps due to a failure and/or BGP update): latency and hop counts increased by a factor of 3 and 1.5, respectively.

## 6. NEW MEASUREMENTS ENABLED

*Mobilyzer* enables us to crowdsource and measure[2] the performance of two popular Internet services on mobile devices: Web

[2]This study is IRB-approved and participating users are consented before participating via an in-app dialog. Users may report data via a Google account, which allows them to view and delete their data at any time, or they may report data anonymously. We strip all user information and IDs from the data we gather; further, we coarsen the location granularity to one square kilometer.

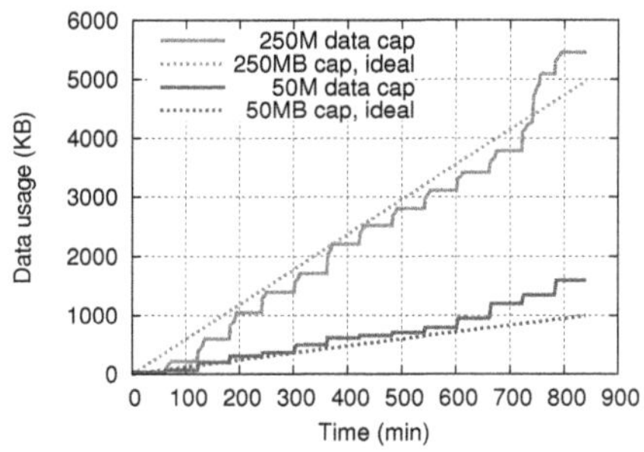


Figure 7: Data usage under different data caps.

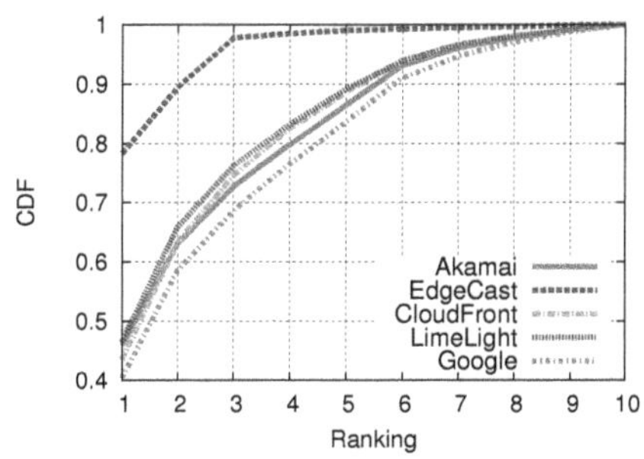


Figure 8: CDF of CDN-selected server rank (in terms of latency) compared to ten other CDN servers. WiFi and cellular redirections have similar distributions, so we show only the aggregated result here.

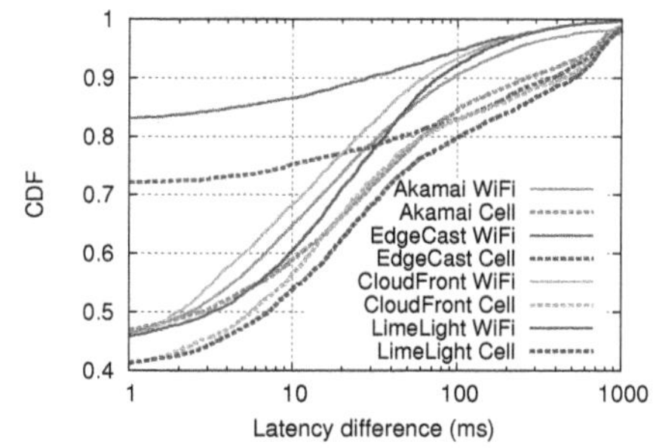


Figure 9: CDF of ping latency difference between the CDN-selected server and the CDN IP with lowest latency.

page load time (PLT) and Video QoE. We use the PLT measurement to show that mobile CPUs can be a significant bottleneck in browser performance, and simple optimizations can improve it. With our video QoE testing, we compare the performance of different bit-rate adaptation schemes in the mobile environment.

## 6.1 Page Load Time Measurement

Recent studies show that a significant fraction of mobile Internet traffic uses HTTP [56], and many of those flows come from Web browsing. The wait time between requesting a Web page and the page being rendered by the browser has a significant impact on users' quality of experience (QoE). This is often measured using the PLT metric, defined to be the delay to fetch all the resources for a page. In addition to measuring PLT for mobile devices, our work is the first to characterize and compare it with page interactive time (PIT), which is the delay to first render the page by the browser so that a user can interact with it.

PLT and PIT are important performance metrics, useful for predicting user experiences. Large PLT and PIT values can lead to users abandoning the pages. As a result, there are several efforts to improve PLT measurements. Browsers collect and report fine-grained page performance and usage info using the Telemetry API [1, 14], without identifying the reasons for the measured performance. Systems such as WebPageTest [17] and others [39] provide similar information from a small set of dedicated hosts in multiple locations. The Wprof [65] approach helps explain the resource dependencies that affect page load times, but it requires a custom browser and has been used primarily in a lab environment.

Importantly, there is a poor understanding of PLTs in the *mobile environment*. The key challenge is that it is difficult to instrument existing mobile browsers (*e.g.,* because they do not support extensions). Huang et al. [31] studied and measured mobile Web browsing performance using controlled experiments and inferred PLT from packet traces. However, we still have a limited understanding of the key factors that affect PLT behavior in the mobile environment.

In this section, we use *Mobilyzer* to conduct the first crowd-sourced measurements of mobile Web page performance. We use a novel methodology that combines empirical data from resource download timings with Wprof dependency graphs generated outside the mobile environment. This allows us not only to measure summary statistics like PLT and PIT, but also understand bottlenecks such as network and computation.

### *6.1.1 Methodology*

We use a PLT measurement task to investigate page load times on mobile devices. Previous methods to measure PLT either instrument the browser to report resource load timings [65], or rely on packet traces to infer the page load time [31,50]. Some also used the change in layout to infer PLT [23]. Using crowdsourcing, we cannot modify a browser or infer from network traces. Instead, we use the Navigation Timing (NT) API as described below, which is arguably one of the most accurate ways of measuring PLT, as uses system clock time and measured by the browser itself.

**Metrics.** Our implementation loads a URL in a `WebView`, a browser commonly embedded in mobile apps. We measure the time for a `WebView` to load a particular page using the NT API [10], a W3C standard implemented in all browsers. This allows us to measure timings for DNS lookup, TCP handshake, transfer of the main HTML file, parsing and constructing the Document Object Model (DOM), render time, and the completion of the page load. After loading a URL using `WebView`, we use JavaScript to read these timings and report them in the measurement result.

A key limitation of the NT API is that it reports timings only for the main HTML page, not any other referenced resources. To get resource timings, we intercept resource requests from the `WebView` using an Android API that notifies our PLT task when each resource is requested, allowing us to capture all of a page's resources and their timings.

When parsing completes and the DOM is constructed, the browser can start rendering and painting the initial view of the page. At this time, called *above-the-fold render time*, page becomes interactive. In this paper, we refer to this as the *page interactive time* (PIT). Developers argue that PIT is a better metric to quantify the user perceived performance of the page than the total PLT, as it can reflect how quickly the user can begin interacting with the page [29].

**Pages measured.** To study the PLT of webpages on mobile devices, we selected ten popular webpages, one from each of the following categories in the top 100 Alexa pages: social networking, image and video hosting services, forums, wikis, shopping, and banking Web sites. For sites with a landing page that only shows a login screen or redirects the client to an Android app, we selected a custom profile page for testing to obtain a more meaningful result.

### *6.1.2 Summary results*

We collected measurements from 80 mobile devices worldwide, providing resource timings for 2,000 measurements per page on average. We present summary results in Fig. 10, which separates page load time into TCP handshake, SSL handshake, time to first byte, parsing, PIT, and total PLT.

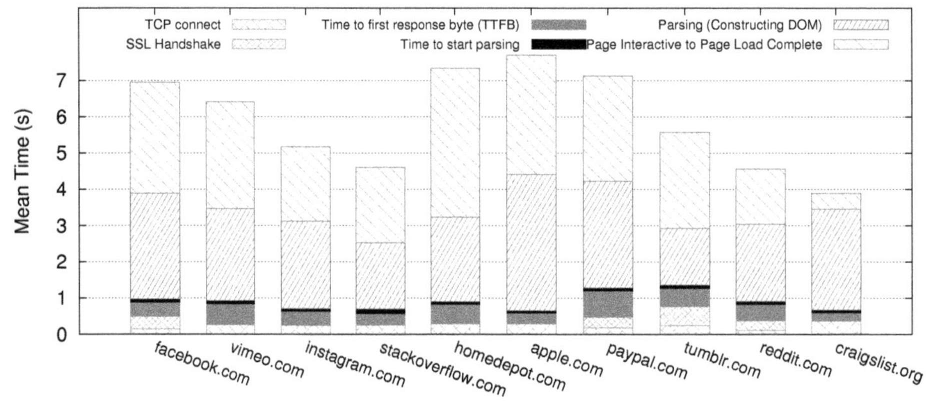


Figure 10: Navigation timing data from crowdsourced PLT measurements, comprising 80 users during six weeks (2000 measurements per page on average).

A key result is that total PLTs range from 4 (craiglist) to 7 (apple.com) seconds, which is substantially larger than reported in desktop environments (*e.g.,* most PLTs were less than 2 seconds in a previous study [65]). As expected, the pages with higher total PLTs tend to be more resource-rich (images, JavaScript). Fig. 10 shows that the initial network costs (TCP and SSL handshake, time to first byte) are a small fraction of total page load time. That said, the SSL handshake can add up to hundreds of milliseconds of delay in the PLT [25]. Importantly, the network delays for loading pages are nearly identical for all pages and quite small, suggesting that *improving network latencies alone is unlikely to significantly reduce PLTs in the mobile environment.*

The figure also shows that most of the page load time comes from rendering and resource loading. It is important to note the large gap between PIT (when the DOM construction is complete) and total PLT. This typically occurs due to network delays for downloading resources and processing delays for parsing them. In the next section, we disentangle these two factors to identify the bottlenecks for page rendering on mobile devices.

Based on the gap between PIT and PLT, the proportion of page interactive time to total page load time ranges from 45% for homedepot to 90% for craigslist, and the mean ratio of PIT to PLT is 0.62 (median 0.63) for the top 200 Alexa pages. This is in contrast to findings in previous work [50], which reported that for 60% of the pages, page render time is equal to page load time. Our results indicate that *it is important to consider both PIT and PLT because of their high variability across sites.*

### 6.1.3 Is the bottleneck computation or network?

The previous analysis describes that most of the user delays for loading Web pages result from parsing and resource loading, without further separating the time spent downloading objects from that processing them. We now disentangle these factors and demonstrate that processing delays are by far the largest bottleneck.

**Inferring processing time.** This requires understanding when a browser spends time downloading objects versus processing them — the NT API reports only the start the the end of the resource download, without detailing the processing time. The Wprof project provides this missing information, but requires running a custom browser that we could not distribute to our users. We propose a new methodology consisting of running Wprof analysis on a Web page loaded in our lab environment, followed by using the resulting dependency graph to infer processing times based on empirical resource timing gathered using *Mobilyzer*.

We argue that the dependency graph generated by Wprof for Chrome is likely identical to the one for the Android WebView, because of these reasons: (1) most of the dependencies in the pages are flow dependencies, which are imposed by all browsers [65], and (2) both Android WebView and Chrome use WebKit as their rendering engine. To help validate this assumption, we compared the download order of resources in Chrome (dependency graph) and Android WebView (resource timing), and found them to be consistent.

**Results.** To determine the amount of computation time, we exclude the network transfer time; *i.e.,* we emulate the case where all resources are cached. Figure 13 presents the average and standard deviation for PLT, PIT and computation time. The results show that for most of the pages in our study, computation is responsible for about half of the PLT and an even larger fraction of PIT. Note that for pages such as Tumblr with fewer scripts or more static content (*e.g.,* images), the network is responsible for approximately 80% of total PLT. To compare, the Wprof study reported the median portion of computation time for the top 200 Alexa pages in the desktop environment to be 35%, higher than the computation time of our five pages (Fig. 13). This difference results from using the mobile version of pages in our experiments, which are simpler than the full version used in previous work.

We further used our crowdsourced measurements to understand the impact of mobile-device CPU speed on loading Web pages. We grouped the devices in our dataset into two clock frequency ranges of their processor: 1-1.5 GHz (17 distinct models) and 1.9-2.5 GHz (13 distinct models). We also loaded the pages on a desktop computer with a 2.6GHz CPU to compare the computation time in a device with a powerful processor. Figure 12 demonstrates that PLT in mobile devices can significantly benefit from faster CPUs. Specifically, the computation time of smartphones with 1.9-2.5GHz processor is around half of the smartphones with 1-1.5GHz processors on average. *Thus, Web site load times can significantly benefit from faster processors.*

Importantly, desktop load times are significantly faster than mobile devices. A potential pitfall of using desktops to simulate the mobile environment is clear: while Wprof finds that increasing the CPU frequency from 2GHz to 3GHz will decrease the computation time by only 5%, we find in the mobile environment that the benefit of using faster processors is significantly higher. Figure 13 indicates that, compared to a desktop computer with a 3 Mbps downlink (*i.e.,* similar to 3G's 2-3 Mbps), the CPU resources in smartphones is a bottleneck for Web page rendering, as it accounts for half of the total PLT.

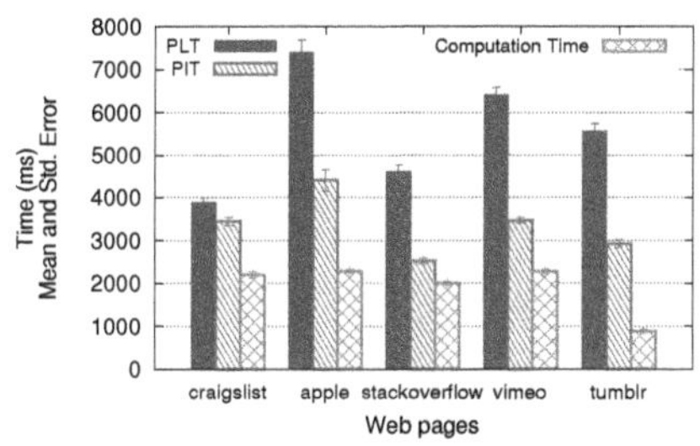


Figure 11: Browser computation time versus PLT and PIT. The fraction of load time due to computation is variable, but often a significant portion.

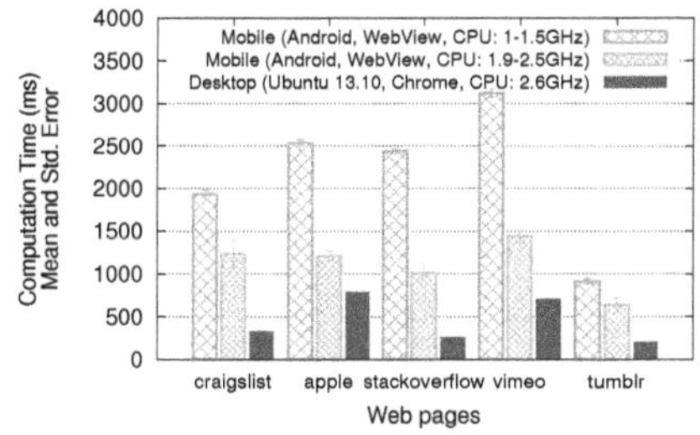


Figure 12: Computation time of different mobile processors (30 distinct device models) compared with desktop.

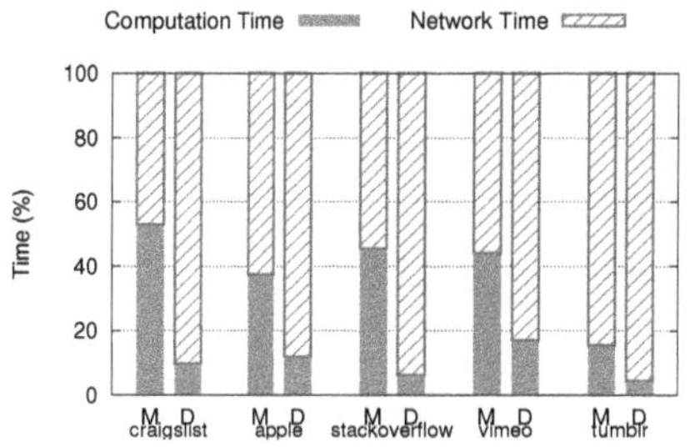


Figure 13: Computation time in mobile devices can account for more than half of the PLT. (Desktop was connected to a 3Mbps broadband internet service.)

### *6.1.4 Critical Rendering Path and Render Time*

To shorten the PIT, developers attempt to optimize the critical rendering path (CRP) [4] — the sequence of steps the browser uses to construct the DOM and render the initial view of a Web page. During parsing, some network and computation processes can occur in parallel, but certain blocking resources prevent parallelism and are the main factors for the CRP time. Importantly, optimizing resources not on the CRP (*non-blocking* resources) cannot shorten the render time. We now use our Wprof-generated dependency graphs and empirical page load times to diagnose cases where the CRP is unduly long.

We compare the total parsing time and total computation time in Figures 10 and 11, and find that for some of the pages, total computation time differs from the total parsing time, implying that the parser is blocked by the network. For example, for craigslist and tumblr, the blocking time due to network in the CRP comprises 27% and 24% of total parsing time, respectively. By investigating the dependency graphs for tumblr and craigslist, we find that large blocking JavaScript files (150-260KB) are the culprit, since these resources may not have been downloaded yet when the parser needs to process them. In some cases, these problems can easily be remediated: for craiglist the 255 KB JavaScript file would require only 77 KB if the server supported gzip compression.

## 6.2 Video QoE Measurement

Video streaming over mobile devices is gaining popularity: YouTube [5] reorted recently that about 50% of views come from a mobile phone or tablet. Further, the average bandwidth achievable in cellular networks in 2014 is 11 Mbps [11], sufficient for high resolution content (1440p).

Despite the higher capacities in today's mobile networks, a key challenge for streaming video providers is how to ensure reliable and high quality video delivery in the face of variable network conditions common in the mobile environment. This requires avoiding stalls and rebuffering events, and adapting the video bitrate to available network bandwidth. This is commonly done via Dynamic Adaptive Streaming over HTTP (DASH), which tries to seamlessly adapt the requested video quality based on available bandwidth, device capability and other factors. In this section, we evaluate the relative performance of two alternative schemes for DASH, using crowdsourced measurements over mobile networks experiencing a diversity of network conditions.

**Methodology.** We use the ExoPlayer library [2], which provides a pre-built customizable video player for Android with DASH. ExoPlayer is currently used by YouTube and Google Play Movies [3], thus allowing us to directly apply our findings to these popular video services. This library allows us to record throughput, bitrates and rebuffering events over time during video playback.

Using ExoPlayer, we implement a recently proposed buffer-based adaptive (BBA) streaming algorithm [32], and compare it with capacity-based adaptive (CBA) streaming, implemented by YouTube. Both CBA and BBA attempt to minimize rebuffering during playback. BBA [32] dynamically adapts the video bitrate by monitoring the buffer occupancy. To avoid rebuffering, it downloads chunks with a lower bitrate when the buffer starts draining. During the startup phase, it uses the estimated bandwidth to select the appropriate bitrate. On the other hand, CBA only considers estimated bandwidth when selecting the proper bitrate. It always chooses a bitrate that is less than or equal to the estimated bandwidth.

We use a two-minute YouTube video[3] with 5 bitrates (144p to 720p) for our measurements, and streamed it using BBA and CBA on *Mobilyzer* clients. We collected 10K video measurements from 40 users during two weeks.

**Results.** We considered two QoE metrics to evaluate the performance of these algorithms: (1) Average bitrate of the video that is shown to user, which shows the average quality of video, and (2) rebuffering events, which reports if the video gets interrupted during the playback.

*Average Bitrate.* To investigate the performance of BBA and CBA under different conditions, we group the measurements based on their average bandwidth[4] into two groups: larger than highest video bitrate ($2193 Kbps$) and smaller than the highest bitrate. In the former case, there should be no need for rate adaptation, and in the latter, the streaming algorithm must pick a bitrate lower than the highest quality.

Figure 14 shows the average throughput and bitrates achieved by the two algorithms in crowdsourced measurements. In the low bandwidth scenario, BBA displays videos with a higher average bitrate. To understand why, we focus on two BBA and CBA experiments with the same throughput during the measurement (Fig. 15). The figure shows that BBA switches to a higher bitrate when the buffer occupancy is high, while CBA does not adapt its rate because it considers only the instantaneous estimated throughput. Therefore, when available bandwidth falls between available bitrates (or switches between them), BBA will provide a higher bitrate than CBA on average. On the other hand, we observe that CBA adapts more quickly to sudden changes in throughput by switching to higher or lower bitrates, while BBA maintains its current bitrate based on its current buffer occupancy.

For devices with larger bandwidth, CBA provides a slightly higher average bitrate than BBA. This occurs because BBA is

[3]We pick this value to limit data consumption; further, a recent study indicates that most video views are less than 3 minutes [12].
[4]Bandwidth is estimated from the chunk download times.

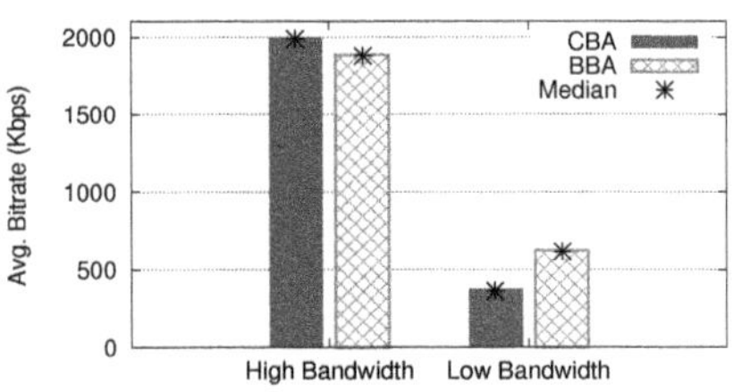


Figure 14: Comparing BBA with CBA bitrates and throughput for users with throughputs that are higher and lower than the maximum bitrate.

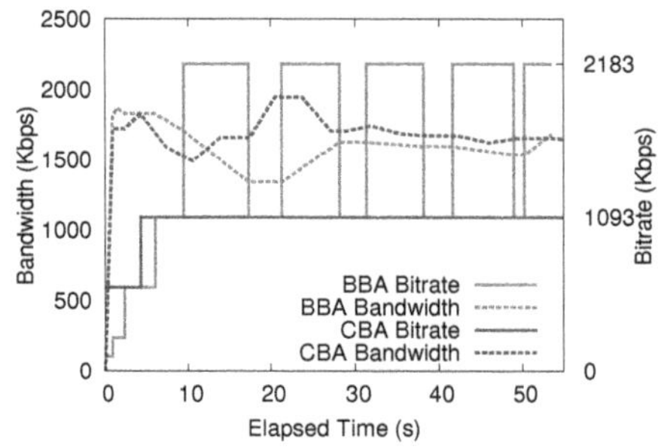


Figure 15: Timeline plots of typical throughputs and bitrate adaptations for BBA and CBA. BBA tends to achieve higher average bitrates than CBA with minimal impact on rebuffering.

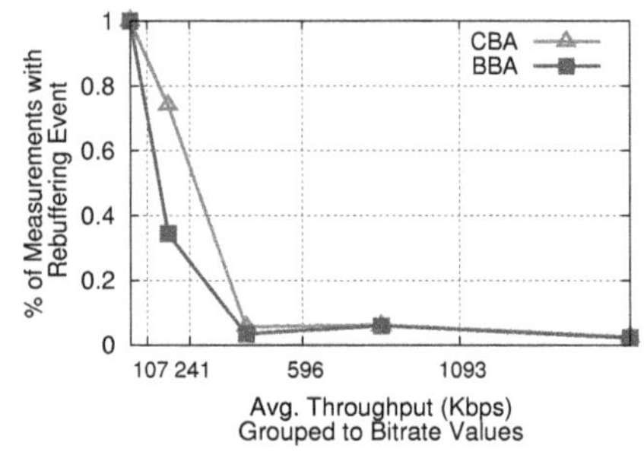


Figure 16: BBA leads to lower rebuffering rates compared with CBA, particularly for users with lower throughput.

more conservative and increases its bitrate incrementally during the startup phase.

*Rebuffering.* A significant additional component of video QoE is the rate of rebuffering events — the lower, the better. We investigate the performance of BBA and CBA using this metric in Figure 16, which shows the percentage of measurements with rebuffering events. We group our results into five bandwidth buckets based on the video bitrates. The figure shows that when the average bandwidth is lower than the smallest throughput, all the measurements experience at least some rebuffering. However, with higher bandwidths, BBA experiences fewer rebuffering events. This occurs because it avoids rebuffering by switching to the lowest bitrate when the buffer is nearly drained.

*Competition under limited bandwidth.* To understand how BBA and CBA behave when they compete for a limited bandwidth, we stream videos using a smartphone connected to an AP with constrained bandwidth. We played a BBA and CBA stream at the same time using a *Mobilyzer* parallel task. When using the *load control* ExoPlayer feature, streaming pauses when the playback buffer reaches a threshold; in this case, CBA will pauses for 22.9s on average, while BBA pauses only for 2.9s. This lower pause time occurs because BBA switches to higher bitrates when the buffer is nearly full. Thus, while the throughput is lower than the highest bitrate, BBA will not pause. In contrast, playback buffer size for CBA will grow continuously, due to choosing a bitrate lower than the estimated throughput.

These behaviors have a significant impact on energy and performance. In terms of energy, CBA improves efficiency by letting the radio go idle during pauses. However, when CBA pauses, BBA consumes the remaining bandwidth and achieves higher average throughput. In our experiments, BBA achieved 63% higher throughput and 57% higher bitrate than CBA, meaning that BBA will provide higher QoE.

In summary, our evaluation shows that the BBA algorithm performs better than CBA in the mobile environment based on common QoE metrics. Further investigation is needed to determine how frequent rate adaptation affects the user experience, and to understand the broader network impact of large numbers of clients using BBA instead of CBA.

## 7. CONCLUSION

This paper makes the case for network measurement as a service in the mobile environment, and demonstrates how we addressed several challenges toward making this service practical and efficient. *Mobilyzer* provides (i) network isolation to ensure valid measurement results, (ii) contextual information to ensure proper scheduling of measurements and interpretation of results, (iii) a global view of available resources to facilitate dynamic, distributed experiments and (iv) a deployment model with incentives for experimenters and app developers. We showed that our system is efficient, easy to use and supports new measurement experiments in the mobile environment. As part of our future work, we are designing an interface to facilitate new measurement experiments and testing new ideas for predicting resource availability and optimizing measurement deployment.

## Acknowledgements

We thank the anonymous reviewers and our shepherd, Rajesh Balan, for their helpful feedback. This work was supported in part by NSF under CNS-1059372, CNS-1345226, and CNS-1318396, a Google Faculty Research Award, and Measurement Lab.

## 8. REFERENCES

[1] Chrome's Telemetry performance testing framework. http://www.chromium.org/developers/telemetry.

[2] ExoPlayer. http://developer.android.com/guide/topics/media/exoplayer.html.

[3] ExoPlayer: Adaptive video streaming on Android - YouTube. https://www.youtube.com/watch?v=6VjF638VObA.

[4] Google Developers, Critical Rendering Path. https://developers.google.com/web/fundamentals/performance/critical-rendering-path/.

[5] Half of YouTube's traffic is now from mobile - CNBC.com. http://www.cnbc.com/id/102128640.

[6] Internet Speed - Android Apps on Google Play. https://play.google.com/store/search?q=network%20tools&c=apps&hl=en.

[7] Mobilyzer dashboard. https://openmobiledata.appspot.com.

[8] Mobilyzer data repository. https://console.developers.google.com/storage/openmobiledata_public/.

[9] Monsoon Power Monitor. http://www.msoon.com/LabEquipment/PowerMonitor/.

[10] Navigation Timing. https://dvcs.w3.org/hg/webperf/raw-file/tip/specs/NavigationTiming/Overview.html.
[11] Ookla NET INDEX EXPLORER. http://explorer.netindex.com/maps.
[12] Ooyala Global Video Index Q2 2014. http://go.ooyala.com/rs/OOYALA/images/Ooyala-Global-Video-Index-Q2-2014.pdf.
[13] Phonelab testbed. http://www.phone-lab.org.
[14] Telemetry. https://wiki.mozilla.org/Telemetry.
[15] The LTE Network Architecture, A comprehensive tutorial. Alcatel-Lucent.
[16] University of Notre Dame NetSense Project: A study into the formation and evolution of social networks using mobile technology. http://netsense.nd.edu/.
[17] WebPagetest - Website Performance and Optimization Test. http://www.webpagetest.org/.
[18] Alcatel-Lucent. 9900 wireless network guardian, 2013. http://www.alcatel-lucent.com/products/9900-wireless-network-guardian.
[19] A. Auyoung, P. Buonadonna, B. N. Chun, C. Ng, D. C. Parkes, J. Shneidman, A. C. Snoeren, and A. Vahdat. *Two Auction-Based Resource Allocation Environments: Design and Experience*. John Wiley & Sons, Inc., 2009.
[20] J. Cappos, I. Beschastnikh, A. Krishnamurthy, and T. Anderson. Seattle: A platform for educational cloud computing. In *SIGCSE*, 2009.
[21] Carrier Compare. Compare speed across networks. https://itunes.apple.com/us/app/carriercompare-compare-speed/id516075262?mt=8.
[22] Carrier IQ. Carrier IQ: What it is, what it isn't, and what you need to know. http://www.engadget.com/2011/12/01/carrier-iq-what-it-is-what-it-isnt-and-what-you-need-to/.
[23] Q. A. Chen, H. Luo, S. Rosen, Z. M. Mao, K. Iyer, J. Hui, K. Sontineni, and K. Lau. QoE Doctor: Diagnosing Mobile App QoE with Automated UI Control and Cross-layer Analysis. In *Proc. of IMC*, 2014.
[24] C. Cranor, T. Johnson, O. Spataschek, and V. Shkapenyuk. Gigascope: a stream database for network applications. In *SIGMOD*, 2003.
[25] D. Naylor, A. Finamore, I. Leontiadis, Y. Grunenberger, M. Mellia, M. Munafoo, K. Papagiannaki, and P. Steenkiste. The Cost of the "S" in HTTPS. In *Proc. of ACM CoNEXT*, 2014.
[26] F. Qian, Z. Wang, A. Gerber, Z. M. Mao, S. Sen, and O. Spatscheck. Characterizing Radio Resource Allocation for 3G Networks. In *Proc. of IMC*, 2010.
[27] FCC Announces "Measuring Mobile America" Program. http://www.fcc.gov/document/fcc-announces-measuring-mobile-america-program.
[28] A. Gerber, J. Pang, O. Spatscheck, and S. Venkataraman. Speed testing without speed tests: estimating achievable download speed from passive measurements. In *Proc. of IMC*, 2010.
[29] I. Grigorik. Deciphering the Critical Rendering Path. http://calendar.perfplanet.com/2012/deciphering-the-critical-rendering-path/.
[30] C.-K. Hsieh, H. Falaki, N. Ramanathan, H. Tangmunarunkit, and D. Estrin. Performance evaluation of android ipc for continuous sensing applications. *SIGMOBILE Mob. Comput. Commun. Rev.*, 2012.
[31] J. Huang, Q. Xu, B. Tiwana, Z. M. Mao, M. Zhang, and P. Bahl. Anatomizing application performance differences on smartphones. In *Proc. of MobiSys*, 2010.
[32] T.-Y. Huang, R. Johari, N. McKeown, M. Trunnell, and M. Watson. A Buffer-based Approach to Rate Adaptation: Evidence from a Large Video Streaming Service. In *Proc. of ACM SIGCOMM*, 2014.
[33] J. Huang, F. Qian, A. Gerber, Z. M. Mao, S. Sen, and O. Spatscheck. A Close Examination of Perfomance and Power Characteristics of 4G LTE Networks. In *Proc. of MobiSys*, 2012.
[34] K. Jang, M. Han, S. Cho, H. Ryu, J. Lee, Y. Lee, and S. Moon. 3G and 3.5 G Wireless Network Performance Measured from Moving Cars and High-Speed Trains. In *Proc. of Workshop on Mobile Internet through Cellular Networks*, 2009.
[35] P. Kortum, A. Rahmati, C. Shepard, C. Tossell, and L. Zhong. LiveLab: Measuring wireless networks and smartphone users in the field. http://livelab.recg.rice.edu/traces.html.
[36] C. Kreibich, N. Weaver, B. Nechaev, and V. Paxson. Netalyzr: Illuminating the edge network. In *IMC*, 2010.
[37] M. Laner, P. Svoboda, E. Hasenleithner, and M. Rupp. Dissecting 3G Uplink Delay by Measuring in an Operational HSPA Network. In *Proc. PAM*, 2011.
[38] Measurement Lab website. http://www.measurementlab.net/.
[39] V. S. Michael Butkiewicz, Harsha Madhyastha. Understanding Website Complexity: Measurements, Metrics, and Implications. In *Proc. of IMC*, 2011.
[40] MySpeedTest App. https://play.google.com/store/apps/details?id=com.num.
[41] NetRadar. https://www.netradar.org/en/about.
[42] C. Ng, P. Buonadonna, B. N. Chun, A. C. Snoeren, and A. Vahdat. Addressing strategic behavior in a deployed microeconomic resource allocator. In *Workshop on Economics of Peer-to-Peer Systems*, 2005.
[43] A. Nikravesh, H. Yao, S. Xu, D. Choffnes, and Z. M. Mao. Mobilyzer: An Open Platform for Principled Mobile Network Measurements. Technical report, University of Michigan, 2014. http://www.eecs.umich.edu/~zmao/Papers/Mobilyzer.pdf.
[44] Ookla. Ookla speedtest mobile apps. http://www.speedtest.net/mobile/.
[45] P802.16.3 - standard for mobile broadband network performance measurements. http://standards.ieee.org/develop/project/802.16.3.html.
[46] A. Patro, S. Rayanchu, M. Griepentrog, Y. Ma, and S. Banerjee. The anatomy of a large mobile massively multiplayer online game. In *Proc. of MobiGames*, 2012.
[47] PlanetLab website. http://www.planet-lab.org.
[48] Portolan. The portolan network sensing architecture. http://portolan.iet.unipi.it/.
[49] F. Qian, Z. Wang, A. Gerber, Z. M. Mao, S. Sen, and O. Spatscheck. Profiling Resource Usage for Mobile Applications: a Cross-layer Approach. In *Proc. of MobiSys*, 2010.

[50] Qian, Feng and Sen, Subhabrata and Spatscheck, Oliver. Characterizing Resource Usage for Mobile Web Browsing. In *Proc. of MobiSys*, 2014.

[51] L. Ravindranath, J. Padhye, S. Agarwal, R. Mahajan, I. Obermiller, and S. Shayandeh. AppInsight: Mobile app performance monitoring in the wild. In *Proc. of USENIX OSDI*, 2012.

[52] RIPE NCC. Ripe atlas. `https://atlas.ripe.net/`.

[53] P. Romirer-Maierhofer, F. Ricciato, A. D'Alconzo, R. Franzan, and W. Karner. Network-Wide Measurements of TCP RTT in 3G. In *Proc. of TMA*, 2009.

[54] S. Rosen, H. Luo, Q. A. Chen, Z. M. Mao, J. Hui, A. Drake, and K. Lau. Discovering Fine-grained RRC State Dynamics and Performance Impacts in Cellular Networks. In *Proc. of MobiCom*, 2014.

[55] M. A. Sánchez, J. S. Otto, Z. S. Bischof, D. R. Choffnes, F. E. Bustamante, B. Krishnamurthy, and W. Willinger. Dasu: pushing experiments to the internet's edge. In *NSDI*, 2013.

[56] Sandvine. Global Internet Phenomena Report 1H 2014. `https://www.sandvine.com/downloads/general/global-internet-phenomena/2014/1h-2014-global-internet-phenomena-report.pdf`, 2014.

[57] J. Sclamp and G. Carle. Measrdroid. `http://media.net.in.tum.de/videoarchive/SS13/ilab2/2013+05+02_1000+MeasrDroid/pub/slides.pdf`.

[58] S. Sen, J. Yoon, J. Hare, J. Ormont, and S. Banerjee. Can They Hear Me Now?: A Case for a Client-assisted Approach to Monitoring Wide-area Wireless Networks. In *Proc. ACM IMC*, 2011.

[59] J. Sommers and P. Barford. Cell vs. WiFi: on the performance of metro area mobile connections. In *Proc. of IMC*, 2012.

[60] Speedometer project source. `https://github.com/Mobiperf/Speedometer`.

[61] Speedtest.net. `http://www.speedtest.net/`.

[62] A.-J. Su, D. Choffnes, A. Kuzmanovic, and F. Bustamante. Drafting behind Akamai: Travelocity-based detouring. In *Proc. of ACM SIGCOMM*, Pisa, Italy, September 2006.

[63] S. Sundaresan, S. Burnett, N. Feamster, and W. De Donato. BISmark: A testbed for deploying measurements and applications in broadband access networks. In *Proc. of USENIX ATC*, 2014.

[64] F. Vacirca, F. Ricciato, and R. Pilz. Large-Scale RTT Measurements from an Operational UMTS/GPRS Network. In *Proc. of WICON*, 2005.

[65] X. S. Wang, A. Balasubramanian, A. Krishnamurthy, and D. Wetherall. Demystifying Page Load Performance with WProf. In *Proc. of USENIX NSDI*, 2013.

[66] Z. Wang, Z. Qian, Q. Xu, Z. Mao, and M. Zhang. An untold story of middleboxes in cellular networks. In *Proc. of ACM SIGCOMM*, 2011.

[67] Q. Xu, A. Gerber, Z. M. Mao, and J. Pang. Acculoc: practical localization of performance measurements in 3g networks. In *Proc. of MobiSys*, 2011.

[68] Q. Xu, J. Huang, Z. Wang, F. Qian, A. Gerber, and Z. M. Mao. Cellular data network infrastructure characterization and implication on mobile content placement. In *Proceedings of SIGMETRICS*, 2011.

[69] K. Zarifis, T. Flach, S. Nori, D. Choffnes, R. Govindan, E. Katz-Bassett, Z. M. Mao, and M. Welsh. Diagnosing path inflation of mobile client traffic. In *Proc. PAM*, 2014.

# Energy Efficient WiFi Display

Chi Zhang and Xinyu Zhang
University of Wisconsin-Madison

Ranveer Chandra
Microsoft Research

## ABSTRACT

WiFi Display, also called Miracast, is an emerging technology that allows a mobile device (source) to duplicate its screen content to an external display (sink) via a peer-to-peer WiFi link. Despite its diverse application scenarios and growing popularity, Miracast consumes substantial power due to a combination of video encoding/decoding and transmission. In this paper, we first conduct a measurement study to quantify and model key parameters that scale Miracast's power consumption. We then propose a set of optimization mechanisms to bypass redundant codec operations, reduce video tail traffic, and relocate the Miracast channel dynamically to maximize transmission efficiency. We have implemented this energy-efficient Miracast framework on an Android smartphone. Experimental results show that the legacy Miracast system costs 1.3 to 2.4 Watts. Our framework reduces the power consumption by 29% to 61%, depending on the Miracast application's video traffic patterns. Our optimization mechanisms do not affect the video quality, and can even reduce the latency of certain Miracast applications.

## Categories and Subject Descriptors

C.2.1 [**Computer-Communication Networks**]: Network Architecture and Design—*Wireless communication*

## Keywords

WiFi Direct; WiFi Display; Miracast; energy efficiency; mobile phones

## 1. INTRODUCTION

Contemporary mobile devices feature a one-to-one binding with small display units. Amid the insufficient display real-estate, many application scenarios (*e.g.*, gallery sharing, collaborative editing, presentation) call for a dynamic binding towards extraneous, large displays, such as PC monitors, TV screens and wall-projectors. Urged by such demands for screencasting, the Miracast standard (also referred to as *WiFi Display*) was recently developed by the WiFi Alliance. Acting like a wireless HDMI cable, Miracast allows a user to, for example, echo display plus audio from a smartphone onto an external screen in real-time. Unlike proprietary video-cast solutions such as Apple Airplay or Google Chromecast, once Miracast is enabled, every UI component – from the general interface to videos – will be duplicated on the screen. Thus, no modification is required for applications.


*MobiSys'15,* May 18–22, 2015, Florence, Italy.

ACM 978-1-4503-3494-5/15/05 ...$15.00.
http://dx.doi.org/10.1145/2742647.2742654.

WiFi-Direct, also referred to as WiFi P2P, serves as an enabling networking technology for Miracast. The Miracast source can mirror its local content via a peer-to-peer link with the sink, *e.g.*, a WiFi-enabled HDMI dongle connected to a TV screen. Meanwhile, it allows *tethered streaming*, *i.e.*, downloading content from an access point (AP) while streaming it to the sink. Such features offer easy compatibility with existing WiFi devices. In fact, latest mobile operating systems like Android [1] and Windows Phone [2] already have built-in support for Miracast. Corresponding sink adapters from Microsoft [3], Amazon [4], *etc.*, have recently witnessed a large consumer market.

However, for a battery-operated Miracast source like a smartphone, maintaining a wireless external display can be very costly. The source has to stream video frames through WiFi with high bit-rate towards the external display. Prior to sending, it has to encode (compress) the video stream so that the WiFi link is capable of handling the bit-rate. During tethered streaming, it also has to decode the downloaded content before compression and transmission. These activities together make Miracast power-hungry even when the mobile device is idle. The Miracast standard devised an optional energy-saving feature called *video frame skip*, which allows the source to stop generating/transmitting video frames if its screen content is static and not updating. However, this mechanism alone barely helps taming the energy cost, especially during continuous video streaming.

From a high level perspective, Miracast's power consumption involves many parts of the mobile device, including processing and networking, none of which can be trivially ignored. Despite a rich literature on mobile energy efficiency, Miracast necessitates new mechanisms to jointly optimize two aspects. First, existing work on mobile multimedia delivery (see [5] and the references therein) focused on curtailing the *receiver- or client-side* power consumption by reshaping the video server's traffic, thereby creating sleeping opportunities that can be harnessed by WiFi's Power Saving Mode (PSM). In contrast, Miracast's dominating operations reside on the source or *transmitter side*. Second, Miracast incurs substantial codec power consumption, especially in tethered streaming that requires real-time decoding and reencoding. It is the intersection between video-dominated application content generation and transmitter-centric network optimization that calls for a new, holistic approach towards energy-efficient Miracast.

This paper marks a first step towards systematic understanding and optimization of Miracast power consumption. We conduct a measurement of Miracast-compatible smartphones to obtain application-specific and component-wise power profile. The measurement results pinpoint key parameters such as screen resolution, video bit-rate, channel selection, which help establishing a power consumption model, later used in devising power-reduction strategies.

Grounded on the measurement insights, we explore a set of system optimizations to tame processing and networking related energy cost at the *Miracast source node*. First, for bursty screencast applications like slide show, we identify a video tail phenomenon that reflects a tradeoff between video quality and the source's traffic load that in turn affects its power consumption. We design an adaptive tail-cutting algorithm that reduces the power cost without noticeably impairing video quality.

Second, we explore a video pass-through mechanism that allows the source to circumvent decoding/reencoding of video frames, thus evading the power-hungry codec operations. For both encoded local content and network content downloaded via the AP (in tethered streaming mode), the source directly passes the video frames, and offloads the decoding tasks to the sink. This mechanism also enables batching and speculative transmission of video frames to the sink, without incurring the latency that used to appear when waiting for the codec to output frames at a slow, constant pace.

Third, observing that network contention affects the idle listening time and hence power efficiency of the source, we propose an off-channel Miracast scheme that opportunistically migrates the source-sink link to an energy-efficient channel. This so-called *off-channel* may differ from the AP-source channel in tethered streaming mode. Selection of the most energy-efficient channel is guided by the model that we have developed through measurement and calibration.

Besides, we have identified and curtailed background Miracast traffic due to silent audio generation and hidden image layers, which account for substantial energy wastage in certain applications with bursty video traffic patterns.

We have implemented the above power optimization mechanisms on Galaxy Nexus, a Miracast-compatible Android phone. The implementation is application transparent. Our experimental evaluation uses the Vanilla Android Miracast framework as a benchmark. The results demonstrate that the total system power savings range from 29% to 61% depending on application use cases and Miracast operation mode. Adaptive tail-cutting alone saves 2.3% to 19.6% for bursty applications. Video pass-through, combined with batching/prefetching, can save 52% to 61% for continuous video streaming. Off-channel miracasting can further add up to 8% for tethered streaming case under intensive contending traffic.

The main contribution of this work lies in a framework to optimize the *overall system-level power consumption* of a mobile device serving as Miracast source. This is feasible because when it is running, Miracast tends to dominate a mobile device's activities and computation/networking resources. Our specific contributions can be summarized as follows:

- Characterize Miracast power consumption in a component-wise manner, and develop a model to profile the impact of computation/network factors.
- Explore a set of power-optimization principles, including video tail cutting, video-frame pass-through, and energy-aware off-channel selection/switching. These principles also make it possible to execute conventional system-design principles, such as batching and prefetching, without hurting latency performance.
- Implement and evaluate the optimization mechanisms on top of Android's Miracast framework, in an application-transparent manner. Promising performance gains justify the proposed mechanisms, and demonstrate their potential as general guidelines for an energy-efficient Miracast system.

The remainder of this paper exposits each of the above contributions. Following background information about Miracast (Section 2), Section 3 describes our measurement and modeling of Miracast power consumption. Section 4 presents the power-optimization mechanisms with implementation, followed by Section 5 where we evaluate the energy savings. We discuss certain unexplored directions in Section 6, related works in Section 7, and finally conclude the paper in Section 8.

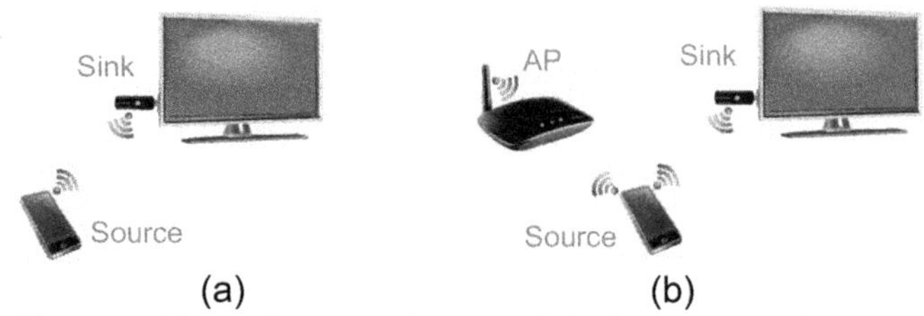

**Figure 1: Network topologies for WiFi Display: (a) P2P topology for source's *local content streaming*; (b) Two-hop topology for *tethered streaming*.**

# 2. BACKGROUND

## 2.1 WiFi Direct

WiFi Direct is a standard from the WiFi Alliance [6]. It enables devices to communicate by establishing P2P groups. Within the group, the device implementing AP functionality is called the *Group Owner (GO)*, whereas others are P2P *clients*. Group members negotiate roles during initial setup through a handshake with randomized ranking.

Two new power saving mechanisms are introduced for the GO. *Opportunistic power saving* mode allows the GO to sleep once all clients are asleep. Another mechanism, called the *Notice of Absence*, allows a GO to proactively announce time intervals where it powers down to save energy. In contrast to the GO, a WiFi Direct client is allowed to use legacy 802.11 Power Saving Mode (PSM).

## 2.2 Miracast: Wireless Display Over WiFi Direct

### 2.2.1 General Architecture

WiFi Display or Miracast [7] is another standard from the WiFi Alliance. It mirrors the screen of a device by streaming it as a live video over WiFi Direct to an external screen. Miracast enables a diverse set of use cases, such as: *(i)* Presentation slide or picture gallery show. *(ii)* Projecting GPS application in vehicles [8]. *(iii)* Mirroring videos to a TV screen or monitor. *(iv)* Multi-user gaming.

WiFi Direct's logical GO/client role assignment eases the deployment of two Miracast network topologies, as shown in Figure 1. In the *local streaming* topology, a mobile source node can mirror locally generated screen content, *e.g.*, general UI, game scenes, pictures and videos, towards the sink via a peer-to-peer connection. In the *tethered streaming* topology, the source downloads Internet content via the WiFi AP, renders it on the screen and casts it towards the sink. For compressed online video, the source needs to decode before rendering and casting. In both topologies, the source can act as either a GO or client *w.r.t.* the sink, but must be a client *w.r.t.* the infrastructure WiFi AP.

Miracast consists of multimedia protocols on top of the WiFi network stack as shown in Figure 2. The architecture is the same for the Miracast source and sink. The screen content is compressed into video frames and, along with audio frames, encapsulated in an MPEG2-TS container, and sent using UDP-based RTP. The TCP-based RTSP protocol provides session and playback control.

Figure 3 illustrates the source's workflow during a Miracast session on Android. Applications can generate screen content, which is composed with GPU and displayed on the UI. We emphasize that Miracast itself does not directly "capture" the screen. Instead, it leverages a media routing module to acquire the screen pixels directly, encodes them, and delivers them through the WiFi NIC. Whenever the screen rendering stops (*e.g.*, due to user turning off the screen), Miracast is also suspended.

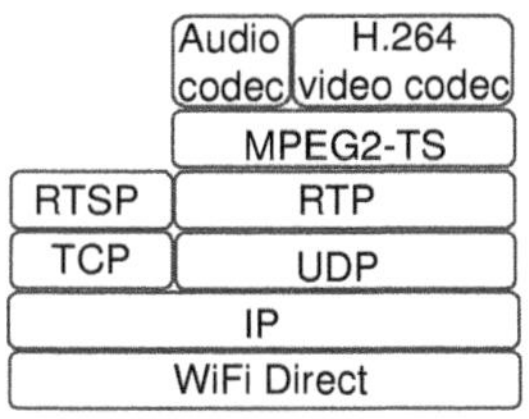


**Figure 2: System architecture of Wi-Fi Display.**

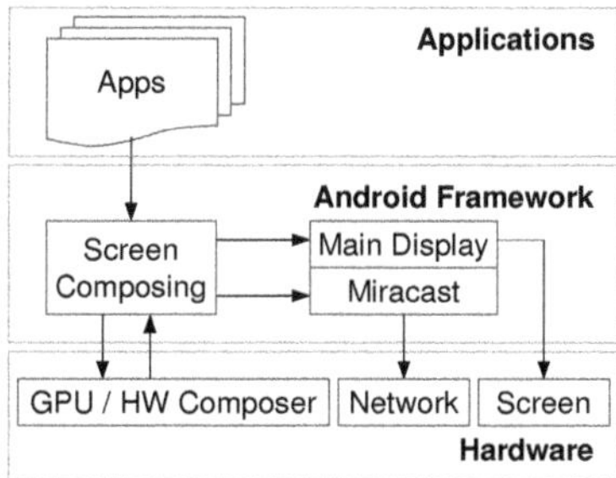


**Figure 3: WiFi Display work flow on Android.**

### 2.2.2 Media Codec

Screen mirroring can produce a huge traffic load. For example, the raw video stream of a screen with 1280x720 resolution, 16-bit color depth and 30fps refresh rate has a bit-rate of over 400Mbps, which is barely sustainable on current WiFi Direct. Thus the data must be compressed before casting over the P2P link.

**Video encoding.** Currently, H.264 is the only option for video encoding in the *Miracast* standard [7]. It is very efficient but also computationally intensive, and the CPUs on mobile devices usually lack the computational power to do the encoding in real-time. As a result, a dedicated hardware encoder is usually used, which can provide reasonable performance and relatively good energy-efficiency.

**Audio encoding.** Since audio data has a relatively low bitrate, compression of audio stream is optional [7]. There are 3 available formats: uncompressed LPCM, AAC and Dolby AC-3. Audio encoding needs to rely on CPU if the device does not have a corresponding hardware encoder. However, the CPU time consumption is usually only a small fraction of the total CPU time.

### 2.2.3 Power Saving Mechanisms in Miracast

Miracast proposes a new technique called Video Frame Skipping (VFS) [7] to save power. This is useful when the source's screen is temporarily static, in which case capturing the screen and casting it continuously will waste substantial channel time, and hence energy. VFS avoids such wastage by allowing the source to stop casting if it detects a static screen. The decision of how to detect and invoke VFS is left to the device vendor. Note that even when VFS is triggered, the RTSP still needs to send heart-beat messages (once per 25 seconds in Android 4.2) to keep the TCP control session alive.

# 3. UNDERSTANDING THE POWER CONSUMPTION OF WIFI DISPLAY

In this section, we present a measurement study that quantifies the energy overhead of Miracast. We then build simple models to pinpoint key variables that can be optimized.

## 3.1 A Breakdown of Power Consumption

**Measurement setup.** We use the Samsung Galaxy Nexus (GT-I9250) phone as our main testbed. It runs the Android Open Source Project (AOSP) 4.2.2 and can act as either a Miracast source or sink. Its hardware codec provides 30fps HD video encoding, and around 100fps of playback rate in H.264 format. In its default Miracast setting, the codec encodes videos with 720p resolution and a target video bit-rate of 5 Mbps. The Miracast implementation of AOSP 4.2.2 comes with the VFS mechanism and is enabled by default, and we use it as the baseline.

We use the Monsoon Power Monitor [9] to measure power consumption in real time when the Galaxy Nexus acts as a Miracast

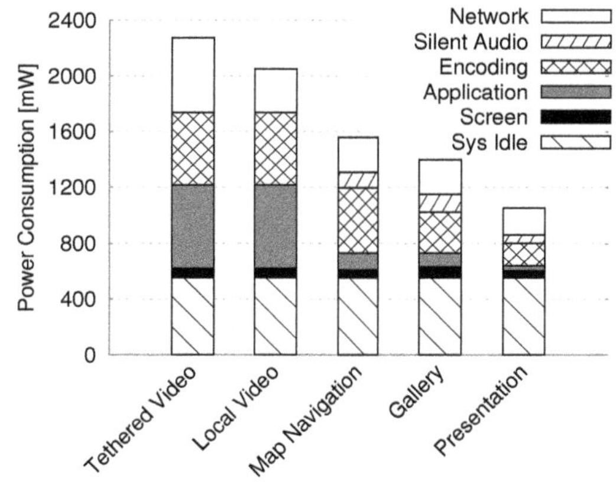


**Figure 4: A breakdown of Miracast's power consumption. Application workload decreases from left to right.**

source. For accuracy and consistency, we strive to eliminate irrelevant factors that may lead to random results. We always keep the phone in airplane mode to prevent the cellular modem from interfering with our measurements. We also turn off Bluetooth and GPS and screen auto-rotation unless they are required by the specific test. Screen brightness is set to the minimum by default. This mimics real scenarios – when a user is watching the mirrored screen, the phone tends to be left untouched, and thus can be switched to a low brightness state.

To obtain a component-wise breakdown of power consumption, ideally an instrumented phone is needed. Due to limited access to the Galaxy Nexus hardware, we approximate the breakdown by incrementally enabling system components. This enables measurement of 6 modules constituting Miracast: sys idle, screen, application, encoding, network, and silent audio.

We measure the *sys idle power* by blacking out the screen while keeping the phone awake in an idle state. To isolate irrelevant background applications, we install a clean AOSP on the phone without the Google services and also disable the dynamic wallpaper. To obtain *screen power*, we built an application that lights up all pixels from black state to the default brightness level. We measure the corresponding power increment. Galaxy Nexus has an AMOLED screen, whose power consumption depends on contents and may vary across different applications. To obtain the *application power*, we run the application but without Miracast, and then measure the power consumption increment to the sys idle and screen. To measure the *encoding power*, we put the network interface in sleep state, run the Miracast application, intercept and drop all video frames it generates to prevent them from triggering network operations. Again, the power increment is used to approximate the encoding power.

Besides, Miracast continuously delivers background audio even though the application is silent (details in Section 4.5.2). Correspondingly, it induces additional *silent audio power*. Finally, we isolate the *network power* consumption by enabling the source-sink miracasting and measuring the additional power on top of the prior 5 components.

**Measured Miracast applications.** We profile the following 5 typical Miracast applications.

*(i) Tethered video*: a popular video clip on YouTube is streamed to the source in real-time while being cast to the sink. *(ii) Local video*: a downloaded version of the YouTube video is used by the source for local playback and direct miracasting to the sink. *(iii) Gallery*: a random set of images from the Bing gallery, updated every 2 seconds. *(iv) Presentation*: 25 black-on-white slides, some with figures, updated every 15 seconds. *(v) Map navigation*: We use the OpenStreetMap data to design a route that fits on to a few

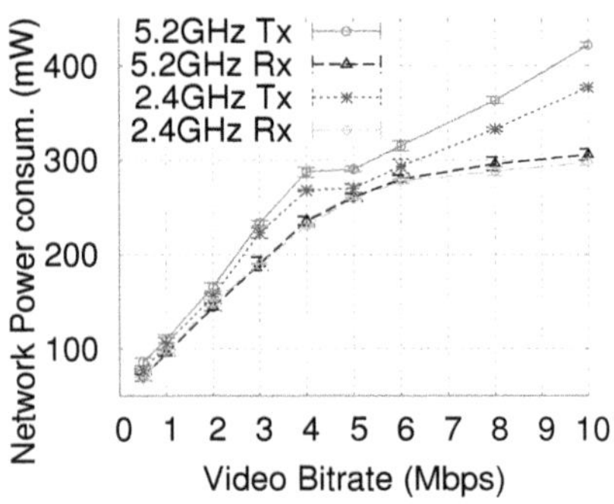


**Figure 5: Measured dynamic power from Miracast network interface.**

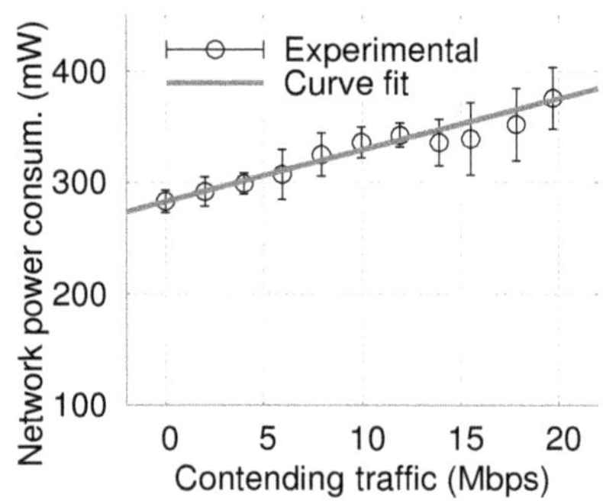


**Figure 6: Measured network power consumption vs. contention intensity.**

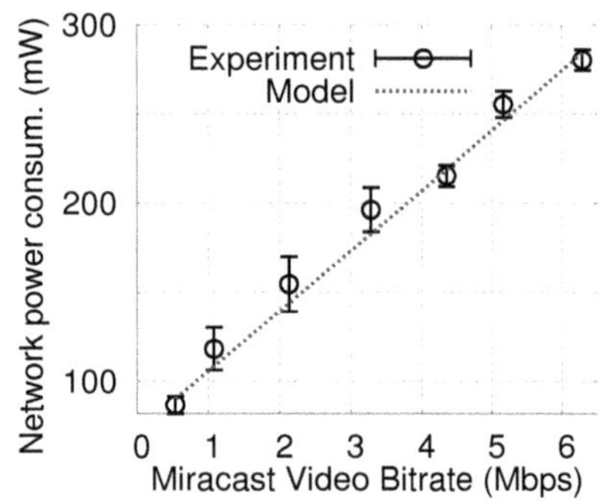


**Figure 7: Measured network power consumption vs. Miracast video traffic load.**

roads with at least 2 turns, covering middle to west part of the UW-Madison campus. We built an app that stitches, pans and renders the map tiles in real-time with 1Hz update rate, typical for GPS applications. Each tile has a resolution of $256 \times 256$ pixels and the route covers 100 tiles.

**Breakdown of Miracast power consumption.** Figure 4 presents the averaged power numbers. System idling consumes approximately $557 \pm 10$ mW, which accounts for a nontrivial fraction in the 3 applications with intermittent, bursty Miracast traffic (map, gallery and presentation). The screen power consumption falls in the range of 40 - 100mW, a relatively small fraction in all test scenes[1].

The application power consumption is negligible (35 mW or 3.2%) in the Presentation, but increases with the application's workload. Between the bursty application and continuous video application that involves a hardware codec, there is a drastic increase of application power (from below 120 mW to around 600 mW). This trend implies that the majority of the application power may be attributed to the codec's decoding operations, since other hardware components (*e.g.*, CPU and memory) are only handling lightweight tasks (*e.g.*, audio encoding and occasional user interaction).

The encoding power shows a similar increasing trend, accounting for 162 mW, 291 mW, 465 mW, 519 mW and 519 mW in the 5 applications with increasing work load. Accordingly, the Miracast video traffic becomes more intensive, resulting in increasing network power consumption (192 to 315 mW). Also note that the silent audio accounts for a non-negligible fraction in the 3 bursty video applications.

Overall, aside from the sys idle and screen power that is independent of Miracast, other modules together account for 450 mW to 1656 mW, or 43% to 73% depending on applications – thereby providing sufficient opportunities for power optimization.

## 3.2 Modeling WiFi Display Power Consumption

We aim to build a coarse model to highlight the key factors that dominate Miracast's asymptotic power consumption at the source. We focus on the local streaming mode. The tethered streaming differs only by adding a legacy (AP-source) WiFi link. Our model accounts for two major power consumers: network and codec.

### 3.2.1 Network Factors

Our network model estimates the energy overhead when performing Miracast on different channels (with different contention levels and hardware profile). This estimation will later facilitate our off-channel miracasting scheme. In contrast to prior analytical work that focused on 802.11 MAC layer [10, 11] or cognitive radios [12, 13], our model is measurement-driven and explicitly accounts for the impact of channel selection on power consumption.

**Model.** For a given channel and traffic load on the source-sink link, mean power consumption of the source can be dissected into 2 parts: $P_{\text{static}}$, the average *static power* or idle power to keep the network interface ready for transmission/receiving, and $P_{\text{dynamic}}$, the dynamic power, or *power increment* on top of $P_{\text{static}}$ when the source is actively transmitting/receiving. The total network power is the sum of $P_{\text{static}}$ and $P_{\text{dynamic}}$:

$$P_{\text{network}}(Ch, B_i) = P_{\text{static}}(Ch, B_i) + P_{\text{dynamic}}(Ch, B_i) \qquad (1)$$

where $B_i\,(i = t, r)$ denotes the traffic load in bps, for transmitting and receiving, respectively. For simplicity, we represent the total traffic load as $B = \sum_{i=t,r} B_i = B_t + B_r$.

The static part can be further decomposed as follows:

$$\begin{aligned} P_{\text{static}}(Ch, B) &= P_{\text{bs}}(Ch) \cdot R_{\text{active}}(Ch, B) \\ &= P_{\text{bs}}(Ch) \cdot \left( R_{\text{wait}}(Ch) + \frac{B}{B_{\text{PHY}} \cdot \eta_{\text{MAC}}} \right) \end{aligned} \qquad (2)$$

where $R_{\text{active}}$ denotes duty-cycle, or the fraction of time the NIC is not sleeping. $P_{bs}(Ch)$ is the base power, which only depends on WiFi hardware and may vary as it is tuned to different channels. The duty-cycle consists of the fraction of idle time $R_{\text{wait}}(Ch)$ plus the fraction in transmission/receiving. The former mainly depends on contention intensity on a given channel $Ch$. The latter depends on traffic load $B$, WiFi bit-rate $B_{\text{PHY}}$, as well as MAC efficiency $\eta_{\text{MAC}}$ (*i.e.*, ratio between MAC throughput and PHY bit-rate). In practice, since the source-sink distance tend to be short, and both tend to be relatively stationary, $B_{\text{PHY}}$ usually remains stable. Thus, the fraction of time in transmission/reception only depends on traffic load $B$.

For the dynamic component, suppose $E_i(Ch)$ is the additional energy per bit needed on top of static power for channel $Ch$, then,

$$P_{\text{dynamic}}(Ch, B_i) = \sum_{i=t,r} [E_i(Ch) \times B_i] \qquad (3)$$

This component also accounts for related CPU power budget. $E_i(Ch)$ $(i = t, r)$ can be obtained by running a constant-bit-rate UDP session with PSM disabled, and subtracting measured $P_{\text{bs}}(\text{Ch})$ from aggregate power.

Combining Eq. (2) and (3), we can pinpoint 4 factors to determine the network power consumption: $B$, $P_{\text{bs}}(Ch)$, $R_{\text{wait}}(Ch)$ and $E_i(Ch)$. For the 3 channel-dependent factors, only $R_{\text{wait}}(Ch)$ depends on contention intensity in the radio environment. $P_{\text{bs}}(Ch)$ and $E_i(Ch)$ can be measured and tabulated for each device model during factory calibration. Note that this model ignores the sleeping power. In

[1]However, at full brightness with all pixels being white, the AMOLED screen can consume $765.9 \pm 1.3$mW.

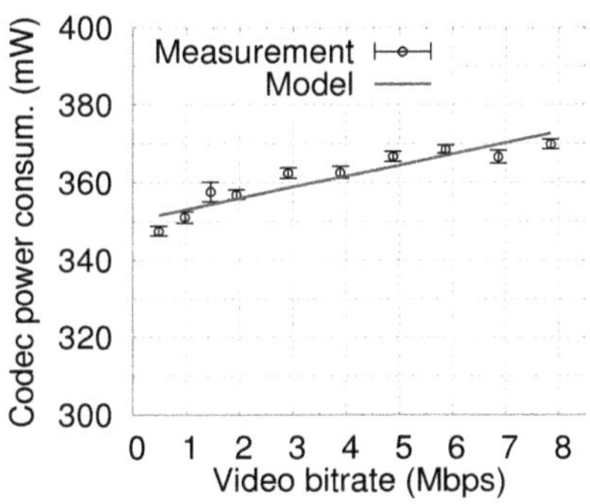


**Figure 8: Measured decoding power vs. video bit-rate.**

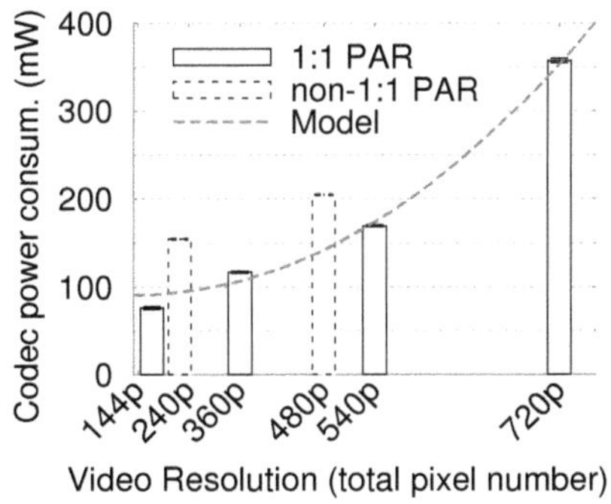


**Figure 9: Decoding power vs. video resolution. Video bit-rate is 1.5 Mbps.**

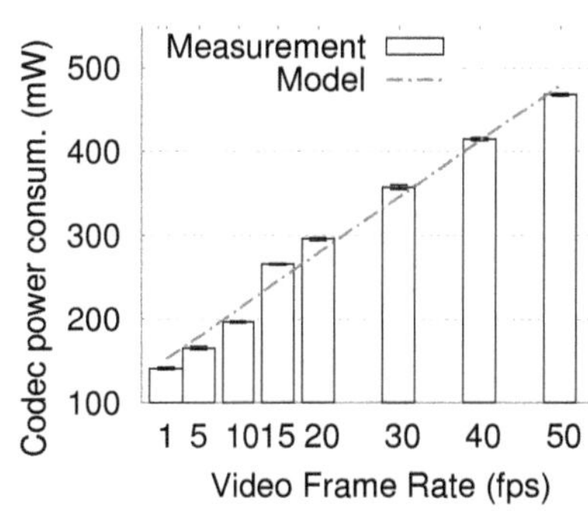


**Figure 10: Measured decoding power vs. frame-rate.**

addition, it does not explicitly model PSM, but the impact of PSM is to reduce idle listening power, which is indirectly reflected in $R_{\text{wait}}(Ch)$.

**Validation and observations.** We validate the above modeling approach on Galaxy Nexus. We first calibrate the $P_{\text{bs}}(Ch)$ and $E_i(Ch)$ parameters for this hardware model. $P_{\text{bs}}(Ch)$ is obtained by measuring the power difference between the case when the NIC is sleeping and when it is idle. Idle mode is created by disabling PSM while no packet transmission is going on. To obtain $E_i(Ch)$, we set up a WiFi Direct link between two phones on channel $Ch$, and run the *iperf* utility to generate a specific traffic load $B$. We then obtain $P_{\text{dynamic}}(Ch, B_i)$ by measuring the power increment on top of the $P_{\text{bs}}(Ch)$. $E_i(Ch)$ is taken as the first-order derivative of $P_{\text{dynamic}}$ with respect to $B_i$. Our experiments are done in late night to minimize the impact from ambient traffic.

The *dynamic power model* assumes a linear relation between $E_i(Ch)$ and $P_{\text{dynamic}}$, which we verify through measurement (Figure 5). We observe that $P_{\text{bs}}(Ch, B_t)$ is roughly linear *w.r.t.* $B_t$, except when $B_t$ falls between 4 and 5 Mbps, likely because of boundary effects caused by frame fragmentation. $P_{\text{bs}}(Ch, B_r)$ is close to linear when $B_r < 5$ Mbps, but levels off afterwards, likely because of interrupt aggregation for the network I/O. However, for a Miracast source, transmission traffic dominates and $B_r$ typically falls well below 5 Mbps. From Figure 5, we also note that 5.2GHz band consumes more dynamic power than 2.4GHz, which is attributed to radio hardware. We also observe that different channels within the 5 GHz band or 2.4 GHz band show similar dynamic power (curve omitted here). Thus, $E_i(Ch)$ only needs to be calibrated for one channel on each band.

To verify the *static power model*, we measure the network power under different contention intensity and hence $R_{\text{wait}}$ values, generated by varying the traffic load of an external link on the same channel. The traffic of Miracast is held constant at 5Mbps, such that the dynamic power remains constant and the power increase only comes from the static part. From the measurement results (Figure 6), we see contention intensity and $P_{\text{static}}$ fit a linear relation, consistent with the model in Eq. (2). In Section 4.4.1, we will develop a channel surveying mechanism that enables a Miracast source to estimate $R_{\text{wait}}$ directly.

Finally, Figure 7 depicts the Miracast source's *total network power* consumption $P_{\text{network}}$ as video transmission traffic $B_t$ increases (the source's receiving traffic $B_r$ is negligible). Due to linear relation between $B_t$ and static/dynamic power, the total power fits a linear relation as well.

Since $P_{\text{dynamic}}(Ch, B_t)$ is already measured, we can subtract it from $P_{\text{network}}(Ch, B_t)$ to obtain $P_{\text{static}}(Ch, B_t)$. Based on Eq. (2), we know the slope of the measured curve in Figure 7 equals $P_{bs}(Ch)/(B_{\text{PHY}}\eta_{\text{MAC}})$. Since $P_{bs}(Ch)$ and $B_{\text{PHY}}$ are known, we can also obtain $\eta_{\text{MAC}}$. By now, all stationary parameters have been calibrated and the model (1) can be used to compare the relative power consumption when the Miracast source runs a different $Ch$ and video bit-rate $B_t$.

### 3.2.2 Codec Factors

**Model.** We model the codec power consumption as:

$$P_{\text{codec}}(R_i, B_i) = \sum_{i=e,d} \left(E_{fi}(W \times H) \cdot R_i + E_{bi} \cdot B_i\right) \quad (4)$$

where $R_i$, $B_i$ and $W \times H$ represent the video frame-rate, bit-rate, and resolution, respectively. When VFS is enabled, we take the time-averaged values for $R_i$ and $B_i$. Also, $E_{fi}$ $(i = e, d)$ is the energy per frame that the codec consumes for encoding and decoding, respectively. $E_{bi}$ $(i = e, d)$ is the overhead energy per bit, mainly associated with memory movements and extra CPU computations. Note that audio codec is omitted by this model considering the relatively small power consumption.

**Validation and observations.** By playing a set of video clips encoded with different $W \times H$, $R_i$ and $B_i$ from the same lossless video source, we can measure the decoding power and thereby calibrating $E_{fi}$ and $E_{bi}$ $(i = d)$. The measurement methodology follows Section 3.1.

Figure 8 shows that the decoding power consumption indeed follows a *linear relation* with $B_i$ as modeled in Eq. 4, but the slope $E_{bi}$ is less than 3mW/Mbps. For a typical 720p video stream, corresponding bit-rate ranges from 2 to 8 Mbps. Within this range of bit-rate, $E_{bi}$ only contributes to a small fraction of the energy cost.

In contrast, the video resolution $W \times H$ affects the power consumption much, as shown in Figure 9. This is because the amount of computation scales non-linearly with number of pixels. In effect, the $E_{fi}$ fits a *square function* with resolution. Notably, the additional processing power is needed for videos with a pixel aspect ratio (PAR) other than 1:1. For example, 480p video with a 16:9 display aspect ratio can not have a square pixel shape since $(480/9) \times 16$ is not an integer. Thus, it consumes even more power than 540p.

Consistent with our model, measurement results in Figure 10 verify that decoding power grows *linearly* with frame rate, since the codec needs to sustain more workload per unit time. The base power component caused by the playback (CPU, GPU, screen, *etc.*) is estimated to be about 145.1mW.

We have observed similar trend in encoding power *w.r.t.* $B_i$, $R_i$ and $W \times H$, albeit with different model parameters. We omit the measurement details due to space constraint. Notably, the Miracast encoder on Android defaults to a fixed resolution of 720p, target bit-rate 5 Mbps and frame rate 30fps. Time-averaged $B_i$ and $R_i$ differ across applications and corresponding encoding power has been discussed in Section 3.1.

# 4. ENERGY EFFICIENT MIRACAST SYSTEM

## 4.1 Overview of Solution Set

We follow a set of simple principles to optimize the Miracast source's power consumption: when idle, maximize sleeping time; when busy, work in the most efficient way and cut unnecessary transmissions; amortize the cost of other states and offload tasks to the energy-insensitive sink node. Table 1 summarizes our specific designs and the applications, categorized according to network topology as local/tethered streaming, and according to traffic pattern as continuous/bursty video.

Our first solution mechanism, adaptive video tail cutting, reduces redundant transmissions that follow each traffic burst in intermittent screen-update applications (*e.g.*, map, gallery or slide show). Such redundancy is used to refine the quality of video frames, but at the cost of substantial traffic load and hence power consumption.

The second mechanism, video pass-through, applies to continuous video traffic. It allows the source to bypass the H.264 encoding and offload the decoding task as well to the sink node. Rather than waiting for the codec, the source can also batch a group of already coded frames and send them to the sink in a speculative manner.

In addition, we explore an off-channel Miracast mechanism, that executes an energy-aware channel selection scheme for the source-sink WiFi Direct link, based on the model in Section 3.2. In tethered streaming scenario, the source can alternate between the channel with AP (which may not be controllable), and the energy-efficient channel it selects. With this measure, it also avoids self-contention between the AP-source link and source-sink link, allowing for more efficient video data transportation.

In our system, the Miracast source acts as a client *w.r.t.* the sink and/or the AP. Thus, all the above mechanisms need to work coherently with the PSM protocol. Yet PSM itself is unaware of Miracast traffic patterns. We design a *PSMlock* mechanism, to manage PSM in a fine-grained manner following the typical clustered patterns of Miracast video traffic, thus creating more sleeping opportunities. Besides, background audio/video frames, invisible but presented to the Miracast source due to oblivious screen rendering driver, can be suppressed to save substantial power.

## 4.2 Cutting Video Tails

### 4.2.1 *Video Tail: Quality and Power Tradeoff*

The VFS allows a Miracast source to pause encoding and casting video frames when there are no updates on the screen. However, it is left to the vendor to decide when to pause. A trivial way is to encode one video frame for a still screen, and stop immediately afterwards. However, this may significantly impair video quality. For a sophisticated scene, the H.264 codec is unable to compress all the details into a single frame. Thus, the "encode-and-stop" approach may result in an incomplete or low-quality image delivered to the sink.

To deal with the problem, the Miracast source needs to add a "tail" after each sudden scene transition to gracefully refine the image quality. It keeps the encoder running and generating new frames until there are enough details in the image for human observation. In Android's Miracast framework, the tail is fixed to 30 frames per screen, lasting 1 second after each screen transition.

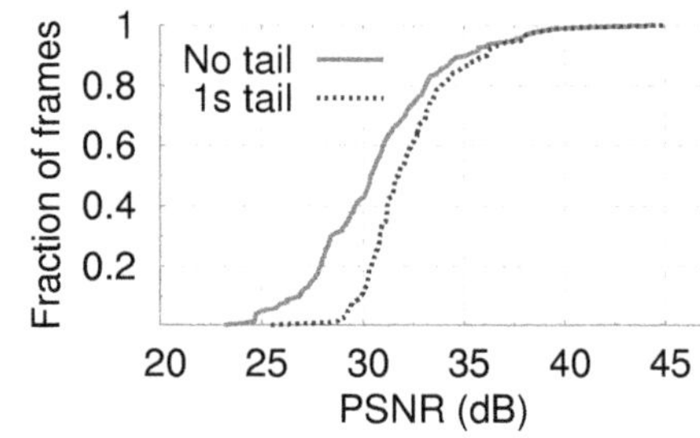


**Figure 11: PSNR distribution with and without inserting video tail.**

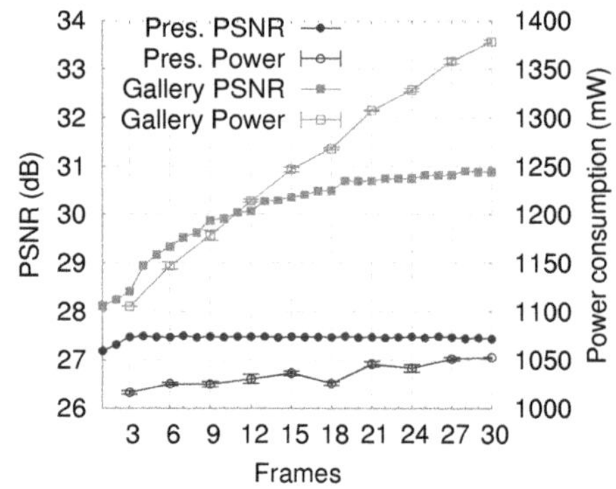


**Figure 12: Additional power consumption due to video tail, and the resulting PSNR increase.**

To gain a quantitative understanding of impact of tail on video quality, we rerun the gallery application with 0.5 Hz picture transition rate, using another Galaxy Nexus as sink node. We dump the sink's screen image data when each screen is encoded by one frame ("no tail" case) or 30 frames ("1s tail" case). Then we compute the PSNR by comparing with the original image at source side. Figure 11 plots the CDF of PSNR across all pictures. We see a median PSNR improvement of 1.1 dB and best case 5 dB, which upgrades the corresponding perceived picture quality at the sink.

On the other hand, a video tail generates additional frames that translate into energy cost. Figure 12 plots the average power consumption and PSNR as a function of tail length. For the gallery application, whereas PSNR increases by up to 3 dB, power consumption increases quickly – by 280 mW as tail length grows from 1 to 30 frames. For the presentation slide show, the power consumption increase is less obvious due to long idle period between 2 slides, within which network management overhead (*e.g.*, beacons and idle waiting) dominates the additional tail energy.

Note that for fast-changing scenes, like a 30fps continuous video casting, tails are not needed, as human eyes can not capture fine details before each next scene is displayed. However, for bursty video casting like slide show, we can identify much more details since each scene will be displayed for an extended amount of time to become discernible.

### 4.2.2 *Adaptive Tail Cutting*

Given the tradeoff between video quality and power consumption for certain bursty miracasting traffic, an adaptive algorithm is preferred that cuts the video tail but without hampering PSNR. A straightforward solution is to compute PSNR on-the-fly for each tail frame output by the codec, and stop encoding once PSNR plateaus. However, the computational cost is formidable. Alternatively, we can monitor the codec's output frame size to gauge how much information is included in the frame and whether more details need to be added to the picture. However, the relationship of encoded

| | Adaptive video tail cutting | Video pass-through | batching & prefetching | off-channel miracast | PSMlock | background suppression |
|---|---|---|---|---|---|---|
| Local streaming | ✓ | ✓ | ✓ | ✓ | ✓ | ✓ |
| Tethered streaming | ✓ | ✓ | - | ✓ | ✓ | ✓ |
| Continuous video | - | ✓ | ✓ | ✓ | ✓ | ✓ |
| Bursty video | ✓ | - | - | ✓ | ✓ | ✓ |

**Table 1: Solution space for energy efficient Miracast.**

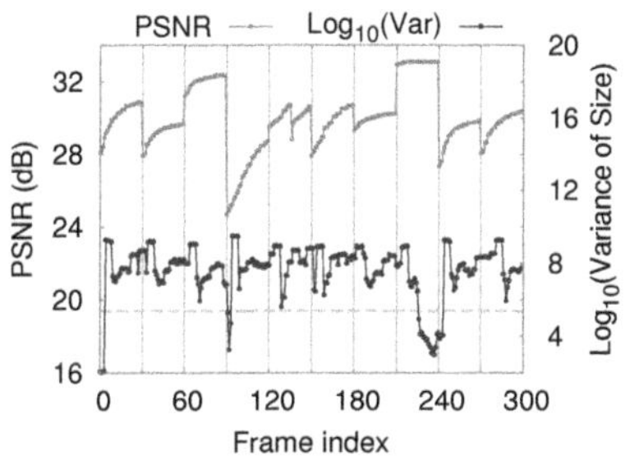


**Figure 13: PSNR and variance of tail frame size, across 10 example video scenes with 30 tail frames each, lasting 1 sec. The dash line indicates the threshold for cutting tail.**

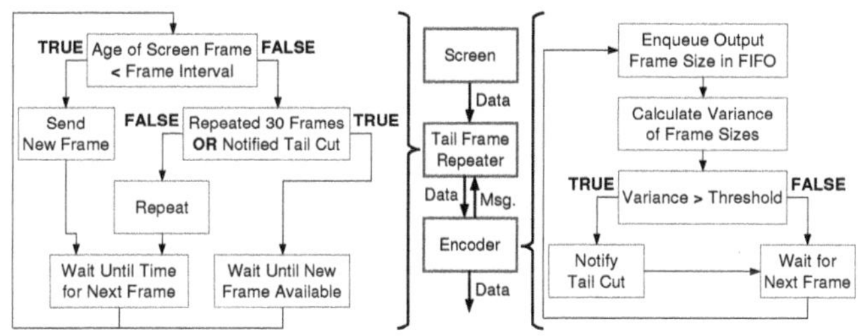


**Figure 14: Work flow of the adaptive tail cutting implementation.**

frame data size with the room of PSNR improvement is not straightforward – we found that absolute frame size is not monotonically decreasing as more tail frames are added.

Fortunately, we empirically observed that the *variance* of the output frame sizes will drop when PSNR stops growing. Figure 13 plots the PSNR growth with the tail length, in contrast to how variance of frame sizes changes over time, which testifies our observation. We suspect the phenomenon is caused by the interaction between the codec's bit-rate control and quantization. The H.264 encoder works to meet a fixed target video bit-rate constraint in Miracast (default to 5 Mbps in Android 4.2). Under this constraint, immediately after a scene change, the encoder oscillates between low/high quantization level and large/small frame size. The oscillation stops after PSNR saturates, because there is insufficient difference to encode to generate a large frame, and thus the frame size remains roughly consistent.

Our adaptive tail cutting algorithm uses the variance of tail frame size as a decision metric. We keep a moving window to calculate the size variance of 5 most recent frames, and cut the tail once the variance drops below a threshold. We found an empirical threshold of 250000 (corresponding to standard deviation 500 bits) works across a wide range of tested applications, although online tuning may yield even better quality/power tradeoff. Also, we upper-bound the tail length to 30 frames, corresponding to the 1 second tail in Android's Miracast framework. Figure 14 illustrates the integration between our algorithm and modules inside Android's Miracast framework, where a repeater keeps feeding the encoder with frames until tail ends. Decision of tail cutting in our algorithm is made by the encoder which notifies the repeater via a message interface.

## 4.3 Video Pass-Through

In this section, we describe the video pass-through mechanism that opportunistically offloads the source's codec tasks to the sink, while allowing batching and speculative transmission of videos as raw data.

### *4.3.1 Workflow and Implementation*

Our pass-through design is application-transparent: it detects H.264 coded video data from application, intercepts the frames, and passes them directly to the Miracast module without involving the codec. We note that this scheme precludes the casting of screen elements other than the video.

To understand how video pass-through works, we first introduce the source's default way of mirroring local/online video (Figure 15(a)). An application typically calls a multimedia player framework to read coded video data from either local file or network I/O. The player further leverages a codec interface to invoke the hardware codec which *decodes* the video data. The video frames are rendered on the source's screen and mixed with other UI elements, if any, through a composer module. The composite frames are passed to the Miracast module as screen content. Then, Miracast follows its standard procedure to *encode* the content using the hardware codec, and eventually deliver the coded data to the sink.

In the pass-through design, we add a format checker on the codec interface, and pause the hardware codec whenever an H.264 video is played (Figure 15(b)). Then, the video data are packetized directly and fast-tracked to the network interface, as if they are the codec output under the command of Miracast. However, before that, we need two manipulations over the video frames on behalf of the legacy Miracast module, so as to hide the pass-through operation from the sink, allowing it to play video as usual.

First, the passed-through video frames have their native timestamps relative to the video start point. To cast the video in a Miracast session, we need to replace the native timestamps with the Miracast timestamp, such that the video can be played in the correct order together with other screen-generated frames before/after the video.

Second, the passed-through frames also have their native sequence numbers. Ideally, these should be modified as well to match the Miracast video sequence. However, we found the sequence number can have variable length, from 4 bits used in Internet videos to 16 bits in Galaxy Nexus. Worse still, the offset of the sequence number within each video frame is unknown, because H.264 uses Golomb coding to encode the parameters field prior to the sequence number in a video frame's header.

We overcome this hurdle by forcing the source to execute certain reset operations. Specifically, when pass-through starts, the source composes an *end-of-sequence frame* to tell the sink to reset the sequence number, and a *parameter frame* to inform it of a new sequence number length. Both frames are standard configuration frames in H.264. When the pass-through video ends and the Miracast session switches back to the screen UI, we execute the same

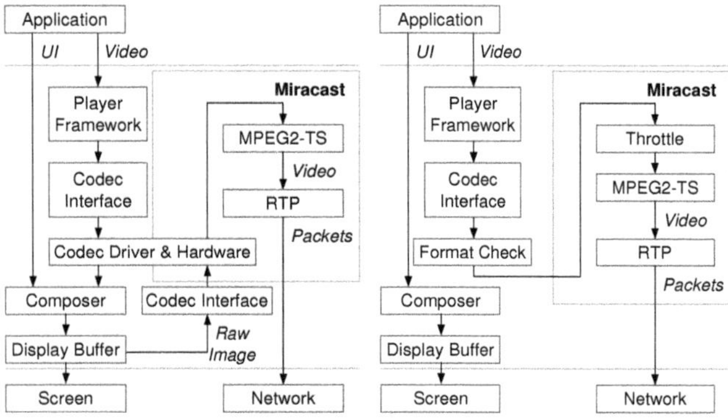


**Figure 15: Work flow of video pass-through (b) in contrast to the default Miracast (a).**

operation and request the codec to generate an I-frame[2] to start a new sequence of stream, without wrongly referring to frames in the pass-through stream. The overhead in delay caused by the resetting operation is minimal since most of the frames involved are without video data and are generated instantly, and the sink only needs very little extra time to process these frames.

#### *4.3.2 Enabling Batching and Prefetching in Local Video Miracast*

Video pass-through enables locally coded video data to be cast more efficiently, following two classical schemes: *(i)* Batched transmission; *(ii)* Prefetching of batched frames to the sink well before playback. Although we can enforce such schemes without video pass-through, the resulting playback latency will grow proportionally with batch size, because the codec outputs video frames at a constant pace (*e.g.*, 30fps) commensurate with the sink's playback frame-rate. For instance, our experiments show that aggregating merely 12 frames entails 1.2 seconds of waiting time (Section 5.1), apparently undesirable in practice.

To enable batching, we add a throttling function in the codec interface (Figure 15(b)), such that video frames are passed to the MPEG2-TS only if their number exceeds a batch size threshold. Meanwhile, we run a simple prefetching scheme: an entire batch of frames is sent once the due time of the first among them comes. To configure the batch size properly, we first need to understand the impact of batching/prefetching on power consumption and relevant tradeoffs.

**Impact of batching on power consumption.** We first cast a local video with pass-through and measure the power consumption under different batch sizes. Figure 16 plots the results. We evaluate a 2.4 GHz, 5.2 GHz channel, with and without our optimized PSM management scheme (Section 4.5.1). For all 4 settings, we observe the power consumption drop fits an exponential relation with batch size $S_{\text{batch}}$:

$$P_{\text{total}} = Ae^{-B\times S_{\text{batch}}} + P_0 \tag{5}$$

where the first term is the overhead and $P_0$ the energy truly spent on data processing/transmission. $S_{\text{batch}}$ denotes batch size as in number of aggregated video frames. $A$ and $B$ are empirical parameters defining how large the initial overhead is and how quickly it dies out with frame aggregation.

With the vanilla WiFi Direct PSM, substantial overhead still exists due to a tail effect: the Miracast source keeps the network interface alive after each batch of transmission [14]. Such overhead is consistently amortized as batch size increases, leading to consistent power consumption drop. In contrast, PSMlock cuts the PSM tail, so marginal power saving is observed (< 10 mW beyond a batch size of 10).

It might seem that latency will still grow with batch size (albeit more slowly than the case without video pass-through), due to the growth in batch download time, and thus it will depend on the output video bit-rate and WiFi Direct link throughput. However, in practice the player will always buffer substantial video data before the playback starts, in order to counteract the jitter effects. So the additional latency from batching may be merged with the initial buffering delay. We will quantify such latency effects in Section 5.1.

**Impact of prefetching.** An inherent tradeoff exists when the sink prefetches batches of video frames: if the user interrupts and stops the video, the prefetched but undisplayed frames will be wasted. Thus, the actual power saving from prefetching depends on not only batch size, but also frequency of user intervention.

Figure 17 shows this tradeoff quantitatively. We used the prior model from Figure 16 to compute power saving, and then subtract the cost from wasted transmitting, assuming user interrupts the playback periodically. The results verify that power consumption drops to a valley with batch size, but increases afterwards. The less frequently user interrupts the video display, the larger the "sweet spot" batch size is. Although user behavior is hard to predict, less than 5 seconds of holding time is not common in practice. Also, the power saving trend is similar among all user holding period larger than 5 s, as long as the batch size is not excessively large (below 20).

Based on observations from the above experiments, we can see that a batch size of 10 to 20 is sufficient to harvest the majority power saving from batching/prefetching. We thus adopt a fixed batch size of 20 in our implementation. For different devices, the suitable range of batch size may be calibrated separately following the above approach.

### 4.4 Energy-Aware Off-channel Miracast

WiFi-Direct allows a Miracast source to freely select wireless channels independent of any infrastructure. Our off-channel Miracast leverages this property, incorporating a model-driven, energy-aware channel selection/switching scheme.

#### *4.4.1 Energy-Aware Off-Channel Selection*

Considering the strong dependency of power consumption on network contention, the Miracast source can pick the least congested channel. Real-world wireless environment is highly dynamic and exact traffic intensity is hard to predict. However, it is feasible to distinguish two channels based on their long-term (*e.g.*, second or minute-scale) contention intensity and static power. Our off-channel selection scheme follows this principle – we require the source to quickly survey available channels, and then use a model-driven approach to rank them according to their potential for saving energy.

The power consumption model in Section 3.2.1 indicates that the only contention-dependent parameter is $R_{\text{wait}}$, whereas others can be obtained through factory calibration. We approximate $R_{\text{wait}}$ in a linear relation with $B_{ct}$, an intermediate parameter indicating intensity of contending traffic on the same channel, *i.e.*, $R_{\text{wait}} = \alpha_1 B_{\text{ct}} + \beta_1$. The linear model is calibrated in a controlled environment, where we generate different levels of contention traffic $B_{ct}$, follow the approach in Section 3.2.1 to measure all parameters in Eq. (2) except $R_{\text{wait}}$ which can be easily extrapolated. Given $B_{ct}$ and $R_{\text{wait}}$, $\alpha_1$ and $\beta_1$ can be easily calibrated.

In an uncontrolled environment, $B_{ct}$ may be obtained if the source can monitor and average the ambient traffic, yet the monitoring

[2]In H.264, an I-frame is a self-contained frame whose encoding does not depend on other frames.

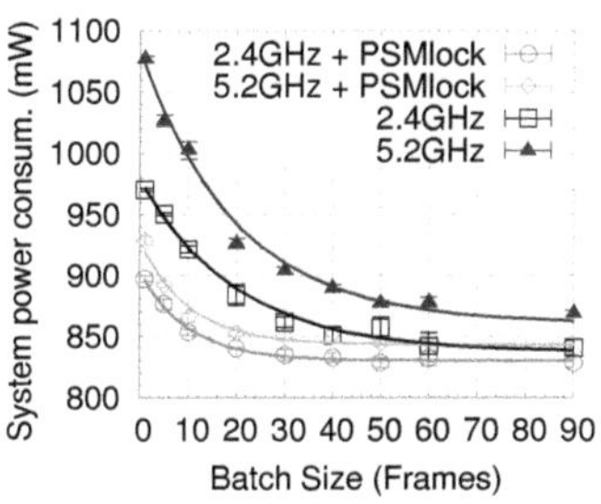


**Figure 16: Power consumption vs. batch size in local video miracast.**

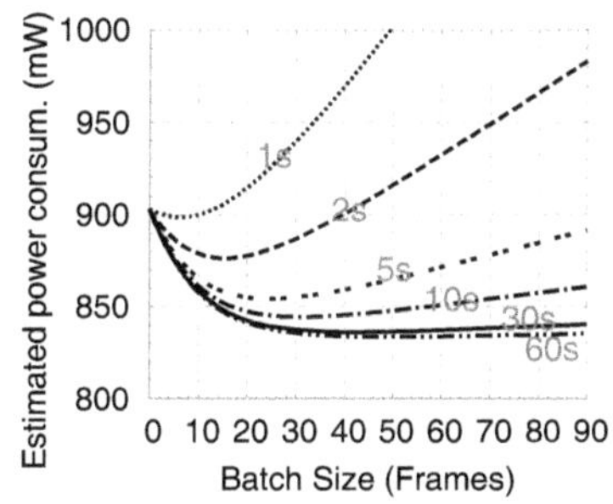


**Figure 17: Power consumption vs. batch size under user interruption.**

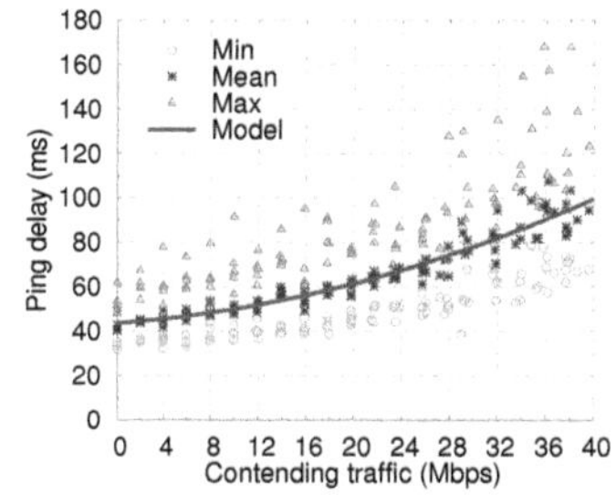


**Figure 18: Ping delay vs. contention intensity $B_{ct}$.**

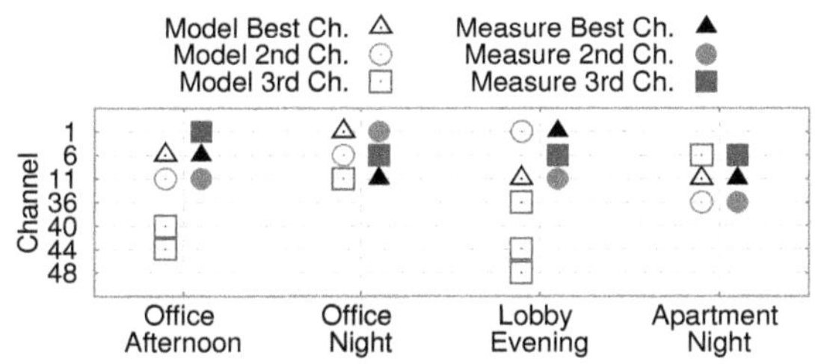


**Figure 19: Effectiveness of the model-based Miracast channel ranking based on energy efficiency.**

mode is unavailable on most smartphones. Instead, we require the source to send a ping message to the sink, and use a model to infer $B_{ct}$ based on its ping delay.

To corroborate this approach, Figure 18 plots ping delay as a function of intentionally generated contending traffic. For each contending traffic setting, we repeat the measurement for 5 times, each lasting 1 second. The scattered dots depict the max, min, and mean ping delay within each 1 second interval. Despite the unpredictable variation (partly due to interfering traffic), we see that the mean ping delay is densely concentrated and fits a polynomial model $T_{\text{ping}} \approx \gamma_2 B_{\text{ct}}^2 + \alpha_2 B_{\text{ct}} + \beta_2$. The model parameters depend on the WiFi protocol version, bit-rate, and processing capability of the device, and thus can be calibrated in advance.

To summarize, the source needs to survey available channels to obtain $T_{\text{ping}}$, from which it obtains $B_{ct}$ and consequently $R_{\text{wait}}$. Finally, it feeds $R_{\text{wait}}$ in Eq. (2) and selects the channel with the minimum $P_{\text{static}}$. The dynamic power is channel independent and thus ignored.

To test the energy-aware channel selection, we place the source-sink link to multiple locations and at different time of the day. In each setting, the source pings over each channel for 1 second, obtains the $T_{ping}$ and ranks the channels with the model. The ranking is compared with that from actual measurement, where we run a 30-second Miracast session for 3 times and then take the average power consumption. Figure 19 shows that, the model can select the top channels with high confidence. In case it errs, it only confuses the order of the top 2 channels out of a total of 7 channels, which we found to have similar power consumption. We emphasize that although the model parameters are only *calibrated once* in a controlled setting, it shows high channel selection confidence in random test environment.

Many WiFi devices support contention-based automatic channel selection (ACS) [15], which may resemble our Ping-based channel ranking approach. However, the ACS mechanism is not energy-aware and it only ranks the contention intensity. Although the current Ping-based approach is more costly than ideal, production level implementation can integrate more closely with the firmware to provide better energy-aware channel selection with less overhead.

### *4.4.2 Channel Flipping for Tethered Streaming*

For the tethered streaming, the AP-source and source-sink link can operate over two orthogonal channels. The source first selects an energy efficient channel for the source-sink link using the aforementioned channel selection method, and then switches (flips) between these two channels per beacon period, for video downloading and mirroring, respectively, making itself a virtual multi-channel device. Besides the flexibility of selecting an energy efficient Miracast link, this can isolate the two links, reduce their self-contention, thereby further improving the efficiency of video delivery. Such dual-channel operation is already supported by the WiFi Direct standard and does not require any hardware modification.

However, we found such fine-grained per-beacon-period switching is disabled by the WiFi firmware on Galaxy Nexus. We thus resort to a coarse-grained emulation to approximate the benefit from channel flipping. Specifically, we found that the NIC enforces the same channel for the infrastructure and P2P interface, and is willing to change only during a reassociation. Thus, whenever channel flipping is needed, we force a reassociation on the target channel. To isolate the artifact from emulation, we ignore the reassociation cost, and replace its time/power consumption value with that of a bare channel switching in actual measurement.

## 4.5 Other Optimizations

Besides the above principle approaches, we enforce two other schemes that refine WiFi Direct's PSM and reduces unnecessary traffic during a Miracast session.

### *4.5.1 PSMlock: Fine-grained PSM Management*

Although Wi-Fi Direct has a few built-in power management mechanisms [16], such as Notice of Absence (NoA), Opportunistic Power Saving (OppPS) and legacy PSM, there exist obstacles preventing us from utilizing them effectively. NoA and OppPS are not supported by any of the Miracast devices we are aware of. Also, together with PSM, these low-level mechanisms can not cooperate with upper level applications very efficiently. Thus, we design a PSMlock scheme to tighten the PSM schedule by leveraging the unique traffic pattern of Miracast. In a continuous video streaming application, video frames are generated following a periodic pattern (*e.g.*, 33.3ms per frame or 30fps), each frame wrapped by MPEG2-TS and converted into multiple WiFi packets. In a bursty video application (*e.g.*, slide show), such periodic pattern will remain for a few video frames after each scene change until the video tail ends (Section 4.2). Both cases end up with clusters of traffic demands followed by long/short idle period.

The WiFi PSM module is oblivious of such patterns. Modern smartphone clients widely adopt an adaptive-PSM (A-PSM) [14] protocol, that keeps the wireless interface active for extra time immediately after each burst of transmission, so as to avoid frequent mode switching [5]. As a byproduct, a PSM "tail" is introduced.

Our PSMlock scheme cuts the PSM tail after each burst of Miracast traffic, as we know deterministically when the next burst will come. PSMlock is application-transparent. It establishes a signaling channel between the MPEG2-TS module and WiFi Direct interface. Whenever a new video frame is generated, MPEG2-TS informs the network module that it will packetize a new cluster of RTP/UDP packets. Afterwards, the network module polls the packet transmission queue in the kernel associated with the Wi-Fi Direct interface at 1 ms interval, and switches the NIC into sleep mode immediately once the queue is empty (implying the transmission is finished). The switching operation requires the PSM client (Miracast source) to send a null frame containing a "PM=1" flag to inform the GO (Miracast sink) that it will sleep. The NIC is turned on again upon a new signal from MPEG2-TS.

### *4.5.2 Reducing Invisible Background Traffic*

We have also identified two redundant background traffic sources in Android, likely caused by lack of interaction between application and the Miracast framework.

**Silent background audio.** First, during Miracast, the audio codec is being fed audio data constantly, no matter whether the audio is silent or not. While local speakers will be put into standby by the system during absence of useful audio, Miracast code is not notified. The additional computational power and network traffic load in casting such audio data can be substantial in bursty video casting (*e.g.*, slide show) that is not associated with any audio track. We have modified the MPEG2-TS module such that it can skip silent audio. This has not affected the non-silent audio playback at the sink side.

**Background image layers.** Many mobile devices' screens have a status bar indicating time, WiFi download/upload activities, battery status, as well as cellular link quality. In Android, the screen composer treats the status bar as a separate layer of pixels even if it is hidden by a full-screen video. Such behavior is desired for certain applications that need both layers. In a full-screen Miracast, the status bar is invisible, but it keeps triggering new frames and traffic periodically. We found that when displaying a still image, such hidden traffic can escalate the power consumption by multiple folds.

# 5. EVALUATION

In this section, we present an experimental evaluation of the energy-efficient Miracast framework. The evaluation starts with a micro-benchmark profiling of the effectiveness and cost of each individual power-optimization mechanism in Table 1, followed by a summary accounting of the contribution of each mechanism across the 5 typical Miracast applications (Section 3.1).

## 5.1 Micro-benchmarks

Our micro-benchmark experiments are conducted in a student office during day time. Around 5 WiFi APs coexist on our experiment channel. The Miracast system on Galaxy Nexus (Android 4.2) is used as a *baseline system*. We disable the background image layer as its artifact unnecessarily magnifies the baseline power cost (Section 4.5.2). Since Galaxy Nexus is a single-stream 802.11n device, and in our test setup the source and the sink is just a few meters apart and without blockage in between, the PHY rate remains 65Mbps most of the time.

**PSMlock.** We first verify the PSMlock as other mechanisms are implemented on top of it. Figure 20 plots the power saving from PSMlock. Continuous video applications leave little chance for finer-grained PSM control (Section 4.5.1), and hence only 17.6 mW and 16.8 mW of saving on average, for local and tethered streaming, respectively. For bursty video applications, Map benefits most in terms of absolute (80 mW) power saving values, followed by Gallery and Presentation. This is consistent with the relative video traffic intensity they generate. Overall, the relative saving is 3% to 5.2%.

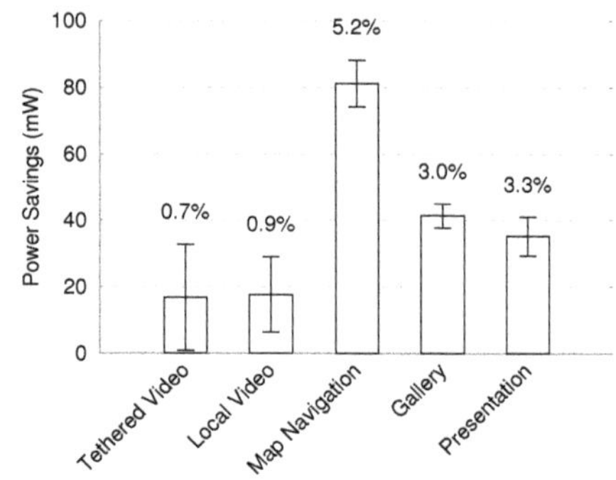


**Figure 20: Power saving from PSMlock.**

All our follow-on micro-benchmarks run on top of the PSMlock-optimized system.

**Video Tail Cutting.** We focus on the power saving from adaptive tail cutting in the local-streaming case. Tethered streaming differs only in base power. Figure 21 plots measurement results across 3 applications with bursty video traffic. Saving for presentation is only 2.3%, since the interval between video scenes is long and static system idle power dominates. Due to shorter interval, saving for the gallery application is more noticeable (5.6%). Map benefits most (19.6%) because of its short display interval and simple images that lead to more space for tail cutting.

We now evaluate the impact on video quality, focusing on the map application that experienced the most aggressive tail cutting. Figure 22 shows that PSNR is almost unaffected compared with the baseline 1-second fixed tail in Android. Thus, our adaptive tail cutting algorithm can effectively reduce video tail traffic without hurting user experience.

**Video Pass-through, batching and prefetching.** Since batching/prefetching needs to be enabled together with pass-through, we evaluate their joint impact on power consumption. In this experiment, the source plays a 1-minute video clip locally while miracasting. To quantify the power saving across different video configurations, the video clip has multiple versions with resolution from 144p to 720p, corresponding to bit-rate of 100 Kbps to 3 Mbps. We first measure the power saving from pass-through. Batching/prefetching's saving is measured as the additional power reduction after enabling them.

Figure 24 shows that pass-through saves 48% to 54% of power compared with the baseline system, and batching/prefetching saves additional 3% to 7% atop. It might seem counter-intuitive that the saving is insensitive to video resolution and bit-rate configurations, considering the codec power increases proportionally with video traffic load (Section 3.2). Note however that this measurement involves both codec and network power consumption. For a low resolution video, whereas pass-through saves less codec power, it saves more network power since much less video traffic is passed to the NIC. Without pass-through, the Miracast codec outputs at a constant bit-rate irrespective of the input video resolution.

To quantify the latency due to batching, we run a stopwatch application on the source and cast its UI on the sink. The timer on the sink's screen always lags behind the sources', and the difference equals Miracast's end-to-end latency. This measurement approach

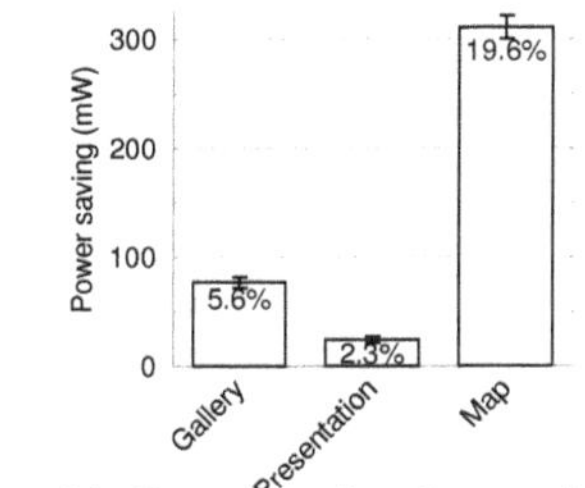

Figure 21: Power saving from adaptive tail cutting.

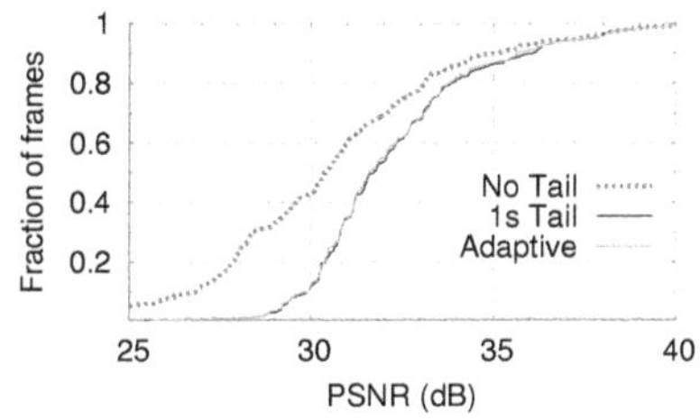

Figure 22: Distribution of PSNR across tiles in the Map application.

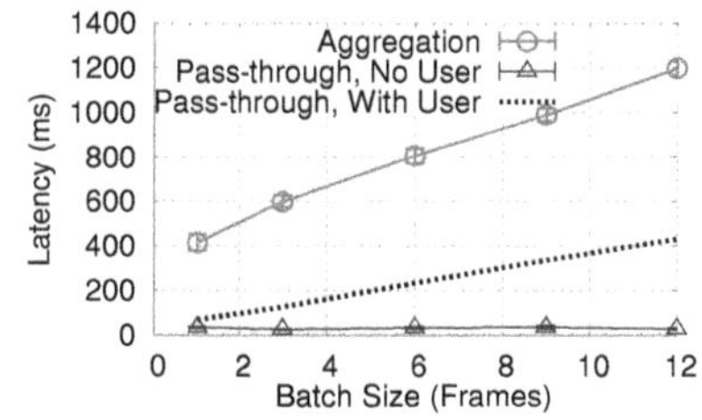

Figure 23: Impact of batching/aggregation on latency.

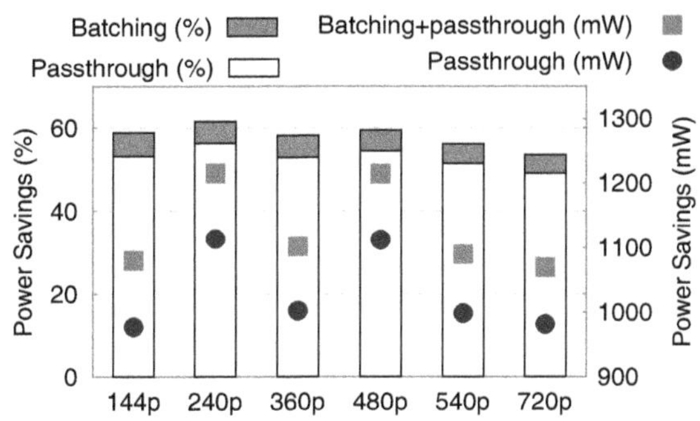

Figure 24: Power saving from pass-through and batching/prefetching (batch size 20) for local video Miracast.

|  | Energy-aware | Worst-case | Random |
|---|---|---|---|
| Local (mW) | 1955.5 | 2004.6 | 1991.1 |
| Tethered (mW) | 2424.4 | 2440.5 | 2427.9 |

Table 2: Effectiveness of energy-aware channel selection. Tests done in an office environment during day time.

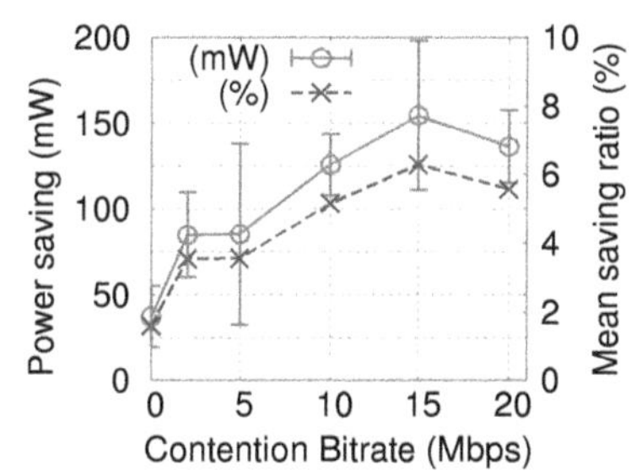

Figure 25: Power saving from off-channel Miracast for tethered video.

does not work when pass-through is enabled, since the source does not display the video. We thus synchronize the source and sink by synchronizing them to the same NTP server prior to the start of each test, and then measure the time it takes from user's playback command to the time when the sink starts playback. Similarly, when user intervention occurs, the latency equals the time it takes from the user's stop command to the time the sink stops playback. The error introduced by NTP is measured to be less than 10ms, and keeps consistent over a period of 10 minutes, which is long enough for each test to be done.

Using a similar measurement approach as in batching, we can quantify the latency of the straightforward *aggregation* approach (Sec. 4.3.2), which waits for the codec output and aggregates video frames together. Figure 23 shows that, without pass-through, straightforward aggregation increases latency linearly. Even an aggregation of 3 video frames results in an unacceptable latency of 1 second. Note that even without aggregation (aggregation size = 1) the baseline system experiences 400 ms latency, due to the codec's processing overhead and associated queuing delay.

Remarkably, with pass-through, the latency is reduced from 400 ms to around 26 ms with a batching/prefetching size of 1 frame. As the batch size increases, the increase of air-time cost is negligible, and further absorbed by the buffering at the sink side. Even with user intervention, we observe only 400 ms of latency when 12 frames are batched.

**Off-channel Miracast.** We verify the model-based channel selection (Section 4.4.1) directly in the office environment with natural contending traffic. Our energy-aware approach is compared with the most power consuming channel, and a random selection that picks 3 channels arbitrarily and take the average power consumption. The Miracast link setup is the same as in Section 4.4.1. Table 2 lists the measured power consumption. For local video, our approach further saves 49 mW (2.3%) and 36 mW (1.8%), compared with worst and random case, respectively. The small percentage is mainly attributed to the low contending traffic during the test period (below 1 Mbps). Since power consumption increases linearly with contention traffic, the saving will increase in environment where the worst-case channel is heavily congested. For tethered video, the saving is smaller due to self-contention between the AP-source and source-sink links.

We further evaluate the coarse-grained channel flipping protocol by injecting different levels of contention traffic on the AP-source channel, and allowing the source-sink link to flexibly select/switch channels. Experimental results in Figure 25 show that the saving from channel flipping increases with contention intensity, and plateaus at 8% when the AP-source channel becomes saturated by contention. Even if no external contention exists, channel flipping can still save 37 mW (1.3%) owing to reduction of self-contention.

## 5.2 System-Level Evaluation

We present a comprehensive evaluation of our energy-efficient Miracast system in two different contention environment: (i) severe contention, where we try to saturate the wireless channel by generating 42 Mbps of UDP traffic from a separate link, which makes the coexisting Miracast link extremely laggy. (ii) no contention, an environment with a completely idle 5 GHz channel. All other Miracast parameter settings are configured to the default in the baseline system (Section 3.1). We break down the power saving by incrementally enabling each optimization mechanism, in the following order: PSMlock, tail-cutting, pass-through, batching/prefetching/aggregation and background suppression. Contribution of each mechanism is the power saving incremental on top of previous ones. Since the experiment fixes on one channel, we disable the off-channel Miracast.

The results in Figure 26 show that, compared to the baseline system, the *overall power saving* ranges from 29% to 61% depending on application traffic patterns. Notably, contention intensity plays a

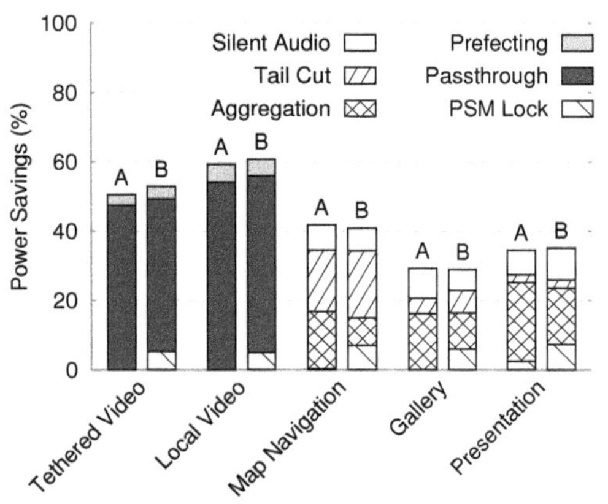


**Figure 26: Power saving breakdown for different applications, in two contention environment. A: under severe contention. B: without contention.**

marginal role on the overall percentage of power saving, although it affects the absolute value of power consumption by up to 100 mW (Section 3.2). However, contention does vary the relative contribution of different optimization mechanisms.

For continuous video applications, power saving comes predominantly from pass-through (42-54%), followed by batching/prefetching (3-7%). PSMlock barely helps in severe contention as each cluster of traffic is broken by contending transmissions, yet still offers 5% of saving when the channel is idle.

For bursty video applications, PSMlock exhibits similar behavior. The main contribution comes from tail cutting, frame aggregation, and background audio suppression. Tail cutting shows consistent savings as in our microbenchmark evaluation. By reducing redundant background traffic, silent audio suppression can save 5% to 9% of power. For frame aggregation, we configure the batch size to 3 video frames, which adds 200 ms of latency on top of the baseline (Section 5.1), and saves 17-21% in an idle environment, and 7% to 16% under severe contention.

We emphasize that the power saving evaluation involves an entire smartphone system, instead of the Miracast application power alone. Among all contributing factors, only the off-channel miracasting mechanism adopts a model-driven approach, and is evaluated separately in Section 5.1.

# 6. DISCUSSION AND FUTURE WORK

Our implementation and experiments have been conducted on the Galaxy Nexus Android phone. However, the Miracast power optimization mechanisms are not restricted to any hardware model. They do require modifications to the Miracast software inside the source node and may result in different power savings across different models.

Although Miracast is envisioned to support highly interactive applications like mobile gaming, we have not found any of such applications tailored to Miracast. Due to the 400 ms of end-to-end latency (Figure 23), we contend that the current Miracast framework is unsuitable for mobile gaming. Though pass-through and prefetching can reduce latency by an order of magnitude, they only help applications that provide encoded video frames. Improving the responsiveness/energy of interactive Miracast requires a joint optimization of codec and queuing operations between system models, which is left as our future work.

Due to limitation of the available firmware, we have not explored alternative WiFi Direct power saving protocols (*e.g.*, NoA) which, compared with PSMlock, enables more fine-grained control of the source's sleeping schedule. Similarly, the off-channel WiFi Direct, once enabled in firmware, will provide more power saving than the coarse-grained emulation approach that we evaluated. With new generation of WiFi, transmission cost may decrease. However, we note that the main power cost in Miracast lies in codec processing, plus the idle listening power caused by redundant traffic that keeps the NIC alive. Thus, we expect video pass-through, prefetching/batching and tail cutting to be useful even if WiFi evolves to much higher rate.

There are also some practical concerns for production level implementation of the video pass-through mechanism. For example, some users or applications may wish to pass-through full screen videos only, thus it is possible for other elements on the screen to be displayed together with the video side by side on the sink. We should allow users and applications to control their preferences about the behavior. Also, it is possible that multiple video elements can be present simultaneously while Miracast is in use. In this case, it might be favorable to disable video pass-through temporarily, or to employ extra algorithm to determine which video is the "main" one and should enforce pass-through.

# 7. RELATED WORK

**Quality-aware mobile video streaming.** Echoing the fast penetration of mobile devices in the past decade, substantial research work has focused optimizing video *quality* over wireless networks. The overarching goals involve minimizing startup latency, containing jitter under bandwidth fluctuation, *etc.* [17]. To date, commercial deployment has adopted many solution mechanisms [18], *e.g.*, video bit-rate adaptation, caching [19], and Dynamic Streaming over HTTP (DASH). The same server may enforce different mechanisms over different mobile devices or applications to balance between a matrix of practical factors such as video traffic profile and network condition.

**Energy-aware mobile video streaming.** Apart from performance optimization, energy cost reduction has been a parallel theme. Most solutions shape the downlink video traffic to create intermittent sleeping opportunities for the mobile client, while respecting video quality constraints. Depending on the vantage point of execution, the solutions can be classified as follows. *(i) Client-side protocols* allow a mobile video receiver to proactively pull contents from the streaming server based on playback buffer status [20] or prediction of demand [21]. *(ii) Proxy-based protocols* act on behalf of the server to reshape video traffic into bursts, and harnesses WiFi's PSM for clients' sleep scheduling [22]. *(iii) Server-assisted protocols* customize the traffic scheduler at streaming servers. For instance, it has been observed that YouTube, Vimeo and DailyMotion servers trigger a chunk-mode strategy [18] to create periodic bursts. Ultimately, the power saving depends on how aggressive the client's PSM decides to harnesses the sleeping opportunities.

At the application layer, content adaptation offers a flexible means of trading video quality for energy saving. The H.264 scalable video coding standard [23] compresses video data into a low-rate base-layer plus enhancement layers that can be gracefully added. It allows a client to inform the server of its video quality choice according to decoding capability and power budget [24]. The server is ready for such customized requests when running DASH [25].

**System-level power optimization for mobile video.** From a mobile system perspective, a variety of strategies exist to optimize the power consumption, some applicable beyond mobile video playback. For software codecs, dynamic voltage/frequency scaling can be executed based on observation of video workload [26]. For ASIC codecs, power consumption is closely related with the computational cost in compression. By modeling the relation between computational cost and rate-distortion (quality reduction), and leveraging extraneous information (*e.g.*, motion prediction from sensors [27]), it is possible to customize a set of codec parameters to optimize the power-quality tradeoff [28]. Yet to our knowledge, such customization is not supported by commercial smartphone video codecs. In addition, adaptive algorithms have been proposed that change backlight level or image brightness [29,30], to curtail the huge display power cost during video playback. On the other hand, caution has been posed *w.r.t.* fidelity loss due to aggressive screen content-aware optimization [31].

**Network interface power optimization.** Many energy saving protocols that are application-independent have been proposed to address the inherent limitations of the WiFi PSM. For example, NAPman [32] and SleepWell [33] isolate the traffic bursts of different APs/clients, to reduce the idle listening power due to contention. Many COTS smartphones use A-PSM (Section 4.5.1), but it is shown to nullify the energy saving of PSM during video streaming, as it tends to keep the client in active mode [34]. Further improvement to has been proposed that cuts A-PSM's keep-alive or tail time [14]. In cellular networks, the mobile network interface also bears a keep-alive period after each transmission, which incurs substantial *tail energy* when traffic is bursty [35]. The video tail problem that we have identified bears similar spirit, but a different tradeoff – between energy saving and video quality rather than network performance.

New protocols have also been designed to optimize the power consumption of mobile hotspots. DozyAP [36], for example, introduces a coarse sleep scheduling mechanism to 802.11 softAP. Cool-Tether [37] aggregates the cellular connections from multiple smartphones as a single backhaul, and employs a reverse-tethering architecture, requesting the smartphones to act as clients of a mobile host, thus enabling their PSM. The latest WiFi-direct power-saving schemes may fundamentally simplify such protocols.

**Optimizing screen sharing applications.** Screen sharing is a relatively new mobile application that garnered little attention in the research literature. Most recent work [38,39] focused on maintaining video quality. Ha *et al.* [40] simulated a frame-rate adaptation scheme that reduces Miracast traffic load by analyzing the dynamism of screen content. This approach involves substantial computational overhead and the practical power saving remains unknown.

Unlike Miracast, Chromecast [41] allows the sink side to directly download videos from the Internet, at the cost that each App must be modified accordingly, whereas Miracast provides a application-transparent solution. Also, in some situations the sink might not have Internet access, or the source has access to a private network while the sink does not, making it impossible for the Chromecast approach to work properly. Thus, the Miracast approach is more universal.

# 8. CONCLUSION

In this paper, we have conducted the first systematic measurement study on the power consumption of Miracast. The measurement enables a modeling framework that associates network/codec power with the Miracast channel selection as well as video traffic load. Insights from the measurement lead to a set of optimization mechanisms which uncover and remove redundant Miracast traffic, curtail unnecessary computations, and improve transmission efficiency via batching/prefetching. Our implementation on a Miracast-compatible smartphone consolidates these mechanisms and demonstrates substantial power savings.


# Acknowledgement

We appreciate insightful comments and feedback from the shepherd, Romit Roy Choudhury, and the anonymous reviewers. The work reported in this paper was supported in part by the NSF under Grant CNS-1318292, CNS-1343363, CNS-1350039 and CNS-1404613.


# 9. REFERENCES


[1] Android Nexus Device, "Project Your Android Device's Screen," 2014. [Online]. Available: https://support.google.com/nexus/answer/2865484

[2] Microsoft, "Project to a wireless display with Miracast," http://windows.microsoft.com/en-us/windows-8/project-wireless-screen-miracast, 2014.

[3] ——, "Microsoft Wireless Display Adapter," http://www.microsoft.com/hardware/en-us/p/wireless-display-adapter, 2014.

[4] Amazon.com, Inc., "Use Amazon Fire TV as a Display Mirroring Destination," 2014. [Online]. Available: http://www.amazon.com/gp/help/customer/display.html?nodeId=201453020

[5] M. Kennedy, A. Ksentini, Y. Hadjadj-Aoul, and G. Muntean, "Adaptive Energy Optimization in Multimedia-Centric Wireless Devices: A Survey," *IEEE Communications Surveys & Tutorials*, vol. 15, no. 2, 2013.

[6] D. Camps-Mur, X. Pérez-Costa, and S. Sallent-Ribes, "Designing Energy Efficient Access Points with Wi-Fi Direct," *Computer Networks*, vol. 55, no. 13, 2011.

[7] Wi-Fi Alliance, "Wi-Fi Display Technical Specification v1.2," 2011.

[8] Richard Lai, "CarKarPlay Display Mirrors Your Smartphone on Your Dashboard," 2014. [Online]. Available: http://www.engadget.com/2014/08/22/ipazzport-carkarplay-wireless-display/

[9] Monsoon Solutions, Inc., "Monsoon Power Monitor," http://www.msoon.com/LabEquipment/PowerMonitor/.

[10] A. Garcia-Saavedra, P. Serrano, A. Banchs, and G. Bianchi, "Energy Consumption Anatomy of 802.11 Devices and Its Implication on Modeling and Design," in *Proc. of CoNEXT*, 2012.

[11] M. Carvalho, C. Margi, K. Obraczka, and J. Garcia-Luna-Aceves, "Modeling Energy Consumption in Single-hop IEEE 802.11 Ad Hoc Networks," in *Proc. of IEEE ICCCN*, 2004.

[12] L. Zappaterra and H.-A. Choi, "Efficient Power-aware Multi-Channel Selection for Dynamic Cognitive Radio Networks," in *Proc. of IEE WCNC*.

[13] B. Yang, Y. Shen, X. Guan, and W. Wang, "Energy-aware Opportunistic Channel Access With Decentralized Channel State Information," in *Proc. of IEEE CDC*, 2011.

[14] A. J. Pyles, X. Qi, G. Zhou, M. Keally, and X. Liu, "SAPSM: Smart Adaptive 802.11 PSM for Smartphones," in *Proc. of ACM UbiComp*, 2012.

[15] Linux Wireless, "Automatic Channel Selection," 2014. [Online]. Available: http://wireless.wiki.kernel.org/en/users/documentation/acs

[16] D. Camps-Mur, A. Garcia-Saavedra, and P. Serrano, "Device-to-Device Communications With Wi-Fi Direct: Overview and Experimentation," *IEEE Wireless Communications*, vol. 20, no. 3, 2013.

[17] L. Guo, E. Tan, S. Chen, Z. Xiao, O. Spatscheck, and X. Zhang, "Delving into Internet Streaming Media Delivery: A Quality and Resource Utilization Perspective," in *Proc. of ACM IMC*, 2006.

[18] M. Hoque, M. Siekkinen, J. Nurminen, and M. Aalto, "Dissecting Mobile Video Services: An Energy Consumption Perspective," in *Proc. of IEEE WoWMoM*, 2013.

[19] S.-H. Shen and A. Akella, "An Information-aware QoE-centric Mobile Video Cache," in *Proc. of ACM MobiCom*, 2013.

[20] D. Bertozzi, L. Benini, and B. Ricco, "Power Aware Network Interface Management for Streaming Multimedia," in *Proc. of IEEE WCNC*, 2002.

[21] Y. Wei, S. M. Bhandarkar, and S. Chandra, "A Client-side Statistical Prediction Scheme for Energy Aware Multimedia Data Streaming," *IEEE Trans. on Multimedia*, vol. 8, no. 4, 2006.

[22] S. Chandra and A. Vahdat, "Application-Specific Network Management for Energy-Aware Streaming of Popular Multimedia Formats," in *Proc. of USENIX ATC*, 2002.

[23] H. Schwarz, D. Marpe, and T. Wiegand, "Overview of the Scalable Video Coding Extension of the H.264/AVC Standard," *IEEE Transactions on Circuits and Systems for Video Technology*, vol. 17, no. 9, 2007.

[24] K. Choi, K. Kim, and M. Pedram, "Energy-Aware MPEG-4 FGS Streaming," in *Proc. of Design Automation Conference (DAC)*, 2003.

[25] S. Akhshabi, A. C. Begen, and C. Dovrolis, "An Experimental Evaluation of Rate-adaptation Algorithms in Adaptive Streaming over HTTP," in *Proc. of ACM Multimedia*, 2011.

[26] Z. Cao, B. Foo, L. He, and M. van der Schaar, "Optimality and Improvement of Dynamic Voltage Scaling Algorithms for Multimedia Applications," *IEEE Transactions on Circuits and Systems*, vol. 57, no. 3, 2010.

[27] X. Chen, Z. Zhao, A. Rahmati, Y. Wang, and L. Zhong, "SaVE: Sensor-assisted Motion Estimation for Efficient H.264/AVC Video Encoding," in *Proc. of ACM Multimedia*, 2009.

[28] E. Akyol and M. van der Schaar, "Compression-Aware Energy Optimization for Video Decoding Systems With Passive Power," *IEEE Transactions on Circuits and Systems for Video Technology*, vol. 18, no. 9, 2008.

[29] P.-C. Hsiu, C.-H. Lin, and C.-K. Hsieh, "Dynamic Backlight Scaling Optimization for Mobile Streaming Applications," in *Proc. of IEEE ISLPED*, 2011.

[30] B. Anand, K. Thirugnanam, J. Sebastian, P. G. Kannan, A. L. Ananda, M. C. Chan, and R. K. Balan, "Adaptive Display Power Management for Mobile Games," in *Proc. of ACM MobiSys*, 2011.

[31] S. Chandra, J. T. Biehl, J. Boreczky, S. Carter, and L. A. Rowe, "Understanding Screen Contents for Building a High Performance, Real Time Screen Sharing System," in *Proc. of ACM Multimedia*, 2012.

[32] E. Rozner, V. Navda, R. Ramjee, and S. Rayanchu, "NAPman: Network-assisted Power Management for WiFi Devices," in *Proc. of ACM MobiSys*, 2010.

[33] J. Manweiler and R. Roy Choudhury, "Avoiding the Rush Hours: WiFi Energy Management via Traffic Isolation," in *Proc. of ACM MobiSys*, 2011.

[34] E. Tan, L. Guo, S. Chen, and X. Zhang, "PSM-throttling: Minimizing Energy Consumption for Bulk Data Communications in WLANs," in *IEEE International Conference on Network Protocols*, 2007.

[35] F. Qian, Z. Wang, A. Gerber, Z. M. Mao, S. Sen, and O. Spatscheck, "Characterizing Radio Resource Allocation for 3G Networks," in *Proc. of ACM IMC*, 2010.

[36] H. Han, Y. Liu, G. Shen, Y. Zhang, and Q. Li, "DozyAP: Power-efficient Wi-Fi Tethering," in *Proc. of ACM MobiSys*, 2012.

[37] A. Sharma, V. Navda, R. Ramjee, V. N. Padmanabhan, and E. M. Belding, "Cool-Tether: Energy Efficient On-the-Fly WiFi Hot-spots Using Mobile Phones," in *Proc. of ACM CoNEXT*, 2009.

[38] C.-F. Hsu, D.-Y. Chen, C.-Y. Huang, C.-H. Hsu, and K.-T. Chen, "Screencast in the Wild: Performance and Limitations," in *Proc. of ACM Multimedia*, 2014.

[39] S. Chandra, J. Boreczky, and L. A. Rowe, "High Performance Many-to-many Intranet Screen Sharing with DisplayCast," *ACM Trans. Multimedia Comput. Commun. Appl.*, vol. 10, no. 2, 2014.

[40] J. Ha, P. Bae, K.-W. Lim, J. Ko, and Y.-B. Ko, "Poster abstract: Mobile contents on the big screen: Adaptive frame filtering for mobile device screen sharing," in *Proc. of ACM SenSys*, 2014.

[41] B. Johnson, "How Chromecast Works," 2014. [Online]. Available: http://electronics.howstuffworks.com/chromecast.htm

# Practicalizing Delay-Tolerant Mobile Apps with Cedos

YoungGyoun Moon, Donghwi Kim, Younghwan Go, Yeongjin Kim,
Yung Yi, Song Chong, and KyoungSoo Park
Department of Electrical Engineering, KAIST
Daejeon, Republic of Korea
{ygmoon, dhkim, yhwan}@ndsl.kaist.edu, yj.kim@netsys.kaist.ac.kr,
{yiyung, songchong}@kaist.edu, kyoungsoo@ee.kaist.ac.kr

## ABSTRACT

Delay-tolerant Wi-Fi offloading is known to improve overall mobile network bandwidth at low delay and low cost. Yet, in reality, we rarely find mobile apps that fully support opportunistic Wi-Fi access. This is mainly because it is still challenging to develop delay-tolerant mobile apps due to the complexity of handling network disruptions and delays.

In this work, we present Cedos, a practical delay-tolerant mobile network access architecture in which one can easily build a mobile app. Cedos consists of three components. First, it provides a familiar socket API whose semantics conforms to TCP while the underlying protocol, $D^2TP$, transparently handles network disruptions and delays in mobility. Second, Cedos allows the developers to explicitly exploit delays in mobile apps. App developers can express maximum user-specified delays in content download or use the API for real-time buffer management at opportunistic Wi-Fi usage. Third, for backward compatibility to existing TCP-based servers, Cedos provides $D^2$Prox, a protocol-translation Web proxy. $D^2$Prox allows intermittent connections on the mobile device side, but correctly translates Web transactions with traditional TCP servers. We demonstrate the practicality of Cedos by porting mobile Firefox and VLC video streaming client to using the API. We also implement delay/disruption-tolerant podcast client and run a field study with 50 people for eight weeks. We find that up to 92.4% of the podcast traffic is offloaded to Wi-Fi, and one can watch a streaming video in a moving train while offloading 48% of the content to Wi-Fi without a single pause.

## Categories and Subject Descriptors

C.2.1 [**Computer-Communication Networks**]: Network Architecture and Design—*Wireless communication*

## General Terms

Algorithms, Design, Experimentation, Performance

## Keywords

Delay-Tolerant Networking; Mobility; Wi-Fi Offloading


*MobiSys'15,* May 18–22, 2015, Florence, Italy.
Copyright 2015 ACM 978-1-4503-3494-5/15/05 ...$15.00.
http://dx.doi.org/10.1145/2742647.2742664.

## 1. INTRODUCTION

Wi-Fi has become the most popular secondary network interface for high-speed mobile Internet access on mobile devices. Many mobile apps support the "Wi-Fi only" mode that allows the users to shun expensive cellular communication while enjoying high bandwidth and low delay. In addition, cellular ISPs are actively deploying Wi-Fi access points (APs) to further increase the mobile Internet access coverage [1, 2, 3].

However, current Wi-Fi usage is often statically bound to the location of mobile devices. While this "on-the-spot" Wi-Fi offloading is still effective, recent studies suggest that one can further extend the benefit of Wi-Fi access if we allow delay tolerance between network connections [4, 5]. The basic idea is to hold off using cellular networks in the absence of Wi-Fi service and to resume the data transfer when the device meets the next Wi-Fi AP. For example, [5] reveals that Wi-Fi offloading ratio, the fraction of data offloaded to Wi-Fi from cellular networks, could be increased to 93.7% if we allow only one hour of delay between Wi-Fi connections.

Despite the great potential of delay-tolerant Wi-Fi offloading, existing mobile apps rarely support disrupted network operations. This is mainly because the burden of handling network disruption or delay is placed solely on app developers. In reality, it is challenging to build delay-tolerant mobile apps. Existing network stacks are clumsy at addressing network disruptions/delays since they are designed to work in real-time environments. Moreover, popular servers are unfriendly to delay-tolerant apps that intermittently download the content in multiple networks. We find that many popular mobile apps do not properly address network switchings and few apps correctly handle a few minutes of delay between network connections.

Delay tolerance in mobile Internet access requires addressing two mobility events: network disruption and delay between network connections. We refer to network disruption as an event that a mobile device switches from one network to another due to user mobility. Network disruption often results in IP address change, which forces the termination of on-going TCP connections. To recover from a network disruption event, mobile apps should be programmed to resume from the last downloaded offset or to download the content from the start in a separate connection. Unfortunately, download resumption cannot be a general option since the content could be dynamically generated or the application layer protocol may not support it. Re-downloading from the start is also undesirable since it wastes network bandwidth and power consumption. Exploiting a long delay (*e.g.,* a few hours) between preferred network connections is another major issue. To maximize the Wi-Fi usage opportunity, a mobile app may want to resume network transfer only when the mobile device is within the Wi-Fi coverage. But at the same time, it may want to avoid an indefinite delay but to

| Type | App | Disruption Test | | Delay Test | | Opportunistic Wi-Fi Offloading |
|---|---|---|---|---|---|---|
| | | Task | Result | Task | Result | |
| SNS | Twitter [6] | Upload a photo | ✓ Resume | Upload a photo | ✓ Resume | ✗ No consideration |
| | Facebook [7] | | | | ✗ Fail if $D > 5$ min | |
| Podcast | Podcast Addict [8] | Download 5MB or larger podcast file | ✓ Resume | Download 5MB or larger podcast file | ✓ Resume | ✗ "Wi-Fi only" (W1, W3) |
| | BeyondPod [9] | | | | ✗ Fail if $D > 2$ min | ✗ "Wi-Fi only" (W2) |
| | Podcast Republic [10] | | | | ✗ Fail if $D > 1$ min | ✗ "Wi-Fi only" (W3) |
| Media streaming | YouTube [11] | Stream video<br>Post comment | ✓ Resume<br>✗ Fail | Stream video | ✗ Playback interrupts | ✗ No consideration for non-HD movies |
| | TuneIn Radio [12] | Stream audio<br>Tune into channel | ✓ Resume<br>✗ Fail | Stream audio | ✗ Playback interrupts | ✗ No consideration |
| | MXPlayer [13] | Stream video | ✓ Resume | Stream video | ✗ Playback interrupts | |
| | Google Play Movie [14] | | ✗ Fail | | | |
| | VLC [15] | | | | | |
| Web browsing | Chrome [16] | Download 100MB file<br>Load static web page | ✗ Fail<br>✗ Fail | Download 100MB file | ✗ Fail if $D > 5$ min | ✗ No consideration |
| | OperaMini [17] | Download 100MB file<br>Load static web page | ✓ Resume<br>✗ Fail | | ✗ Fail if $D > 1$ min | |
| Online shopping | eBay [18] | Load page | ✗ Fail | Load page | ✗ Fail if $D > 1$ min | ✗ No consideration |
| | Amazon [19] | Load page<br>Play demo song | ✗ Fail<br>✗ Fail | Load page<br>Play demo song | ✗ Fail if $D > 30$ sec<br>✗ Fail | |
| | Google Play Book [20] | Load ebook | ✗ Fail | Load ebook | ✗ Fail if $D > 1$ min | ✗ "Wi-Fi only" (W1, W3) |

* 'Fail' means no download resumption nor re-downloading. $D$ refers to delay.

**Table 1: Behavior of popular mobile apps at mobility events**

continue the transfer with a cellular network if the delay exceeds a certain threshold. To the best of our knowledge, no existing solutions support a long delay of network unavailability in the same TCP connection.

In this work, we bridge the gap between theory and practice in delay-tolerant Wi-Fi offloading. We propose Cedos, a practical delay-tolerant mobile network architecture for mobile apps. Cedos eases the development of a mobile Internet app with three salient features. First, it provides a familiar socket-like API whose semantics conforms to TCP in stationary environments. Developers write the code just like they do with the Berkeley socket API, but the underlying protocol below the API, $D^2$TP, transparently handles mobility events such as network disruptions or delays. Second, Cedos network API explicitly exposes how to handle delays between network connections. Developers may express a deadline and a content size with the API, and $D^2$TP completes the content download in time while exploiting the Wi-Fi network as much as possible. Also, the API provides real-time buffer management such that the transport layer automatically switches between cellular and Wi-Fi networks depending on the buffer availability. This allows to build a streaming application that maximizes opportunistic Wi-Fi usage without risk of being interrupted in the middle of streaming. Third, for backward compatibility, Cedos provides a protocol translation Web proxy, $D^2$Prox. $D^2$Prox manages the delay-tolerant HTTP connections with mobile clients while it downloads the content from the origin Web server using TCP. It also caches popular content to reduce the bandwidth consumption on the server side.

This paper makes two key contributions. First, while many previous works address challenges in delay-tolerant networking and Wi-Fi offloading, Cedos provides the first comprehensive solution to delay-tolerant mobile app development and deployment. There are many works that separate the host identity from its location [21, 22, 23, 24, 25, 26], but they do not provide network stack abstraction. TCP migrate [27] and Serval [28] support host mobility in a TCP connection, but they neither allow long delays nor expose an API to maximize opportunistic network access. Wiffler [4] exploits the delay in Wi-Fi offloading, but their network API does not conform to the TCP semantics. The goal of Cedos is to popularize delay-tolerant Wi-Fi offloading while significantly reducing the complexity of app development and deployment.

Second, we demonstrate the practicality of Cedos by porting existing mobile apps, VLC streaming client [29] and Mobile Firefox [30], with different network usage patterns. Not surprisingly, we find that large, non-interactive file downloads benefit the most from Cedos, but our real-time buffer management helps maximize Wi-Fi offloading opportunities even for real-time video streaming. In our evaluation with Cedos-vlc, we find that almost half (48%) of the streaming video is delivered via opportunistic Wi-Fi access without a single playback pause on a moving train. The benefit for short, interactive Web flows with Cedos-firefox is modest due to noticeable delay in network switching (*e.g.,* seconds), but we find that porting process is straightforward since the Cedos network API is similar to Berkeley socket API.

Along with porting existing apps, we build our first delay-tolerant podcast app, ReadyCast [31], to demonstrate the utility of delay-tolerance in real world. Unlike real-time podcast apps, ReadyCast allows "download reservation" with a user-specified deadline, and the content is made ready by the time the user wants. We have conducted a field study with 50 ReadyCast users for 8 weeks, and we find that Cedos does help download most of the podcast contents (92.4%) via opportunistic Wi-Fi access. Moreover, $D^2$TP successfully saves 38% of the data that would have to be re-downloaded due to natural network disruptions from user mobility.

## 2. MOBILE APP BEHAVIOR AT MOBILITY

In this section, we examine how existing mobile apps react to mobility events. We select 15 popular mobile apps [1] from Google Play [32] that might benefit from delay-tolerant Wi-Fi access. We report their behaviors on network disruption and during the delay at network unavailability.

**Methodology:** We install each app on a Nexus 5 smartphone [33], running Android v4.4. The device is connected to the Internet either via a Wi-Fi AP in our lab or through an LTE connection to a local cellular ISP. To simulate a network disruption event, we had the device use the Wi-Fi AP initially, but forced it to turn off the Wi-Fi interface to use the LTE interface. This event simulates moving the device from a Wi-Fi network to a cellular network, which results in IP address change. For a delay test, we had the device use

[1] We use the latest version of each app as of November 2014.

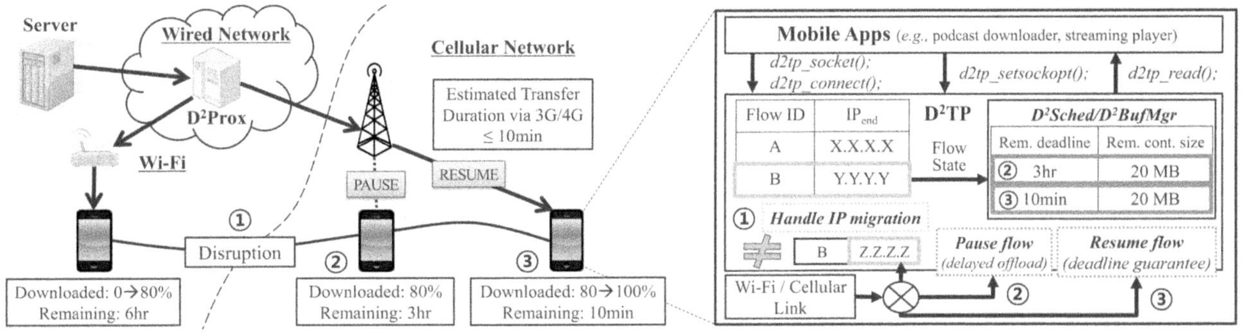


**Figure 1: Cedos delayed data offloading architecture. D$^2$TP handles both disruption and long delay. D$^2$Sched schedules the flows for delayed Wi-Fi offloading (e.g., downloads a file as much as possible via a Wi-Fi connection, and the remaining 20% via LTE to finish within the deadline).**

the Wi-Fi AP, but unplugged the cable of the AP to simulate network unavailability. We replugged the cable after 10, 30, 60, 120, 300, 3600 seconds of delay. This process does not change the IP address of the device, but injects a period of Wi-Fi network unavailability. Finally, we examine the apps that support Wi-Fi offloading via "Wi-Fi only" mode by toggling the option during data transfer. Since we do not have access to source code for majority of the mobile apps, we report only qualitative behavior of each app. During each test, we had the device download or upload data whose size is large enough to be interrupted by the mobility event.

**Findings:** Table 1 summarizes the results of our experiments. We find that many mobile apps do not handle network disruptions properly while notable exceptions are social networking service (SNS) apps, some media streaming apps, and podcast apps. All apps use standard TCP/IP protocols, so we notice that their TCP connection terminates when the host IP address changes. For graceful operation at network disruption, the developers have to write code to re-initiate a TCP connection to resume the data transfer, but that seems to be often neglected in mobile apps. What is surprising is that some mobile Web browser does not support download resumption even if HTTP supports range queries. In media streaming, app behavior varies - MXPlayer [13] and YouTube apps [11] resume video streaming even after IP address change, but VLC [15] and Google Play Movie [14] get stuck. Interestingly, posting comments in the YouTube app is not disruption-tolerant while its video streaming is. The disparity comes from the fact that the developers have to handle each case differently without the support from the transport layer. In contrast, all three podcast apps handle short network disruptions well. We think that podcast app developers are better-prepared for frequent network disruptions at large file download, and handle this case well.

The behavior for the delay test, however, is more disappointing. Except Twitter [6] and Podcast Addict [8], all apps fail to resume data transfer in a few minutes of network unavailability. We also find that all media streaming apps pause the playback during the delay. Since none of them support the "Wi-Fi only" mode, a desirable action would be to automatically switch to the cellular interface and to resume streaming if Wi-Fi access becomes unavailable. Twitter and Podcast Addict handle both network disruptions and delays well, but they do not support download deadline as discussed shortly.

Lastly, we have investigated if the apps support opportunistic Wi-Fi offloading. We find that some apps allow the "Wi-Fi only" mode, but none of them support any notion of download deadline. Without a deadline, a download in the "Wi-fi only" mode would wait indefinitely when there is no Wi-Fi connectivity. We further analyze how the apps behave with the "Wi-Fi only" option. We try turning on the option while downloading through an LTE interface and try turning it off while downloading via LTE network. No apps that support the "Wi-Fi only" mode handle these two cases correctly. They either continue with the cellular interface (W1) or end up with a download failure in the former case (W2). Or they do not resume the transfer by switching to the cellular interface in the latter case (W3).

In summary, we find that many popular mobile apps neither properly handle mobility events nor their behavior is consistent across app types. This is because the current network API assumes real-time operation and app developers have to write the action on their own. The goal of our work is to ease their burden by transparently handling the mobility events in the transport layer while providing the flexible knob to control the behavior with a familiar API.

# 3. DESIGN

In this section, we present the design of Cedos, a practical delay-tolerant networking architecture for mobile apps. Cedos transparently addresses mobility events in a new transport layer while it allows flexible control between opportunistic Wi-Fi and cellular network usage.

## 3.1 Overall Architecture

Figure 1 shows the overall architecture of Cedos. Cedos-based mobile app initiates a D$^2$TP connection to D$^2$Prox which relays downloading content from the TCP server to the app. D$^2$TP is a TCP-like transport layer protocol, but it transparently masks network disruptions and delays. D$^2$Prox works as a protocol translator, allowing client-side mobility while it supports backward compatibility to TCP-based servers. We assume that a mobile device can move around, and transfer data intermittently in multiple networks while the server is at a fixed location. Each D$^2$TP connection is characterized by a maximum-allowed delay, deadline, and a preferred network interface (*e.g.*, Wi-Fi). Until the deadline, D$^2$TP strives to transfer as much data as possible through the preferred network, even by intentionally delaying the transmission if the preferred network is unavailable.

For connections without a deadline or near deadline expiration, D$^2$TP uses any available interface to complete the data transfer. D$^2$Sched analyzes the current network status (available bandwidth and interfaces) together with a deadline and a content size, and decides if a flow should transfer data, wait for the preferred interface, or switch to a faster network. For dynamic content whose size is unknown (*e.g.*, video stream), D$^2$BufMgr calculates an appropriate deadline and size by analyzing the minimum throughput required

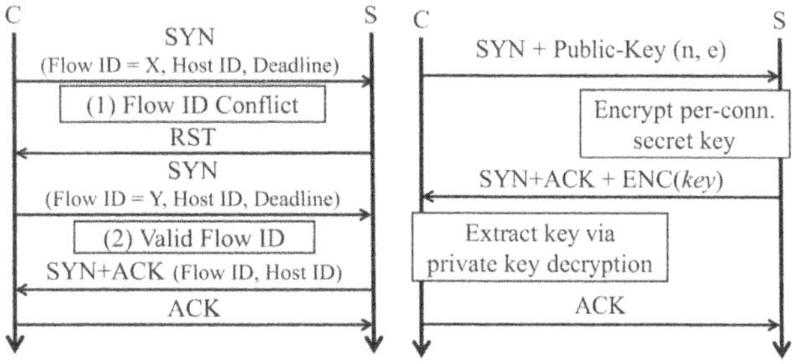


(a) Flow creation (b) Secret key sharing

**Figure 2: Initialization of $D^2$TP connection**

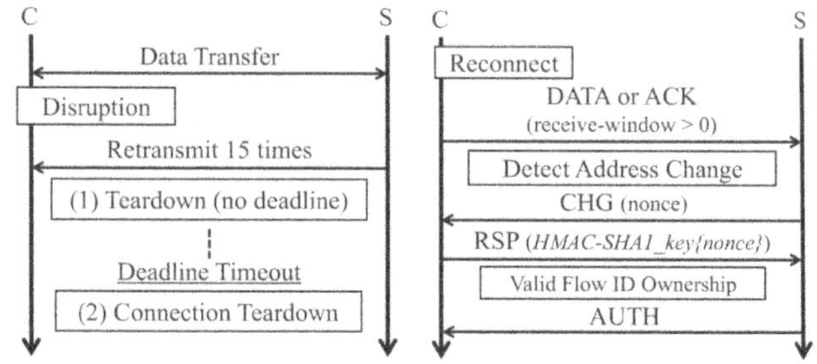


(a) Teardown at disruption (b) Challenge-and-response

**Figure 3: Flow handling in mobile environments**

to maintain the app's QoE (*e.g.*, bitrate), and chooses how a flow should transfer data similar to $D^2$Sched.

## 3.2 $D^2$TP: Transport Layer for Mobile Apps

$D^2$TP is a transport layer protocol for mobile apps, providing TCP-like, reliable data transfer in stationary environments but it hides network disruptions and allows delays when a mobile device is on the move. We choose to take the transport layer approach, hiding the mobility events from the application layer. This decision presents two advantages. First, it frees the mobile app developers from directly dealing with network disruptions or delays while providing a flexible knob to control the deadline. The rationale is that the developers need to focus on the core program logic rather than to keep track of the latest offset of an interrupted content or whether a network interface is on or off. Second, having this mechanism inside the transport layer allows providing more information as to delay-induced transmission with $D^2$Sched and $D^2$BufMgr, explained later. Maintaining the amount of data that has been transferred through Wi-Fi and cellular interfaces allows a more informed decision whether to transmit or not at any given time.

The key enabler for $D^2$TP disruption tolerance is in the separation of a connection from its network attachment as in [21, 23, 26]. Our contribution here is to implement the mechanism in a purely end-to-end fashion and to make it easy to use in real mobile networks. Specifically, each $D^2$TP connection is identified by a persistent flow id and a host id that do not change in the course of mobility. When a mobile device moves to another network, it resumes the connection with the flow and host ids from where it left off. One downside may be the overhead of keeping track of many idle connections at the $D^2$TP server, but we keep the connection metadata small enough to maintain as many as one million concurrent flows for less than 1 GB memory.

### 3.2.1 Connection setup and teardown

$D^2$TP is similar to TCP except it requires an explicit connection resumption process when the network is available again after disruption. Connection teardown may occur explicitly or implicitly depending on the user-defined deadline.

**Connection setup:** Figure 2(a) shows how a mobile client establishes a $D^2$TP connection with a server. The client first sends a SYN packet, but unlike TCP, the SYN packet must include a flow id and a client-side host id as its option fields. The host id is defined as a 20-byte SHA-1 hash of the MAC address of the cellular interface. The flow id is the least significant 4 bytes of the SHA-1 hash of the host id and a microsecond-granularity timestamp at connection setup. Since the purpose of the id pair is to identify the connection between the client and the server, the pair needs to be unique only on the two machines during connection lifetime. The SYN packet may include a deadline specified in seconds, as a 4-byte option field. When it is missing, the connection falls back to a normal TCP connection.

If the server already holds a $D^2$TP connection with the same flow id, it responds with a RST to ask for retrying with a new flow id. Or, the server replies with a SYN+ACK packet containing the server-side flow and host ids, and the client establishes the connection with an ACK. Besides a regular three-way handshake, the $D^2$TP server and client need to agree on a per-connection secret key to authenticate each other when the connection is disrupted and resumed later. Figure 2(b) shows the key exchange process. We employ an asymmetric key cryptographic algorithm (*e.g.*, RSA) and have the client send its public key (n, e) in the payload of the SYN packet. The server then generates a secret key, encrypts it with the client's public key, and sends it in the payload of the SYN+ACK packet. The client finally decrypts the message with its private key and stores the extracted secret key into the flow's state table for future use.

**Connection teardown:** A $D^2$TP connection is closed in two ways. First, when both hosts complete the data transfer, they explicitly close the connection by exchanging a FIN. Second, if an application closes the connection during network unavailability, the $D^2$TP layer waits until the network becomes available again, and does a normal closure. If the deadline expires before the device meets an available network, the $D^2$TP connection terminates itself without notifying the other. This should not be a problem since the other party would close the connection as well. The deadline can be updated by the application at any time during the connection to reflect the effective network bandwidth and actual transferred data size.

### 3.2.2 Data transfer in mobile environments

Once a connection is established, the client and the server exchange data as in a normal TCP connection. On network disruption, connection is resumed with a new IP address after verifying the ownership of the connection.

**Connection resumption:** If a client-side IP address changes due to network switching, the client can resume the connection by authenticating itself to the server to prevent connection hijacking. It first piggybacks flow and host ids as options to a normal data or ACK packet. Then, the server detects the client-side IP address change, and verifies the connection ownership through a challenge-and-response protocol shown in Figure 3(b). For this protocol, we define three special bit flags (CHG, RSP, and AUTH) in $D^2$TP packet header. The server first sends a challenge packet by setting the CHG bit flag on with an 8-byte random nonce in the payload. Then, the client calculates $HMAC - SHA1_{key}(nonce)$, using the shared key at connection setup, and sends it back with the RSP bit flag on. Once the hash is verified, the server responds with an authentication packet with the AUTH flag on, which gives an OK sign that the client can resume the data transfer. On verification failure, the server sends an RST packet to notify the client to start a new connection.

## 3.3 D²TP Flow Management

Cedos achieves efficient mobile network usage by avoiding the cellular data transfer whenever an app allows a delay. We describe how a $D^2$TP flow is managed to determine the scheduling action: wait, transfer data, or switch interface for minimum QoE guarantee.

### *3.3.1 Deadline-based flow management*

The core enabler for managing an efficient $D^2$TP flow data transfer is the deadline, set explicitly by Cedos socket API. Basically, the deadline is examined to decide whether the $D^2$TP flow should transfer data through the attached network for efficiency (Wi-Fi offloading), or should change the interface for reliability (deadline guarantee). For this, we collect information of currently attached interface, bandwidth for both networks (last measured for unconnected network), flow deadline and content size. When the mobile client moves out of Wi-Fi, the remaining deadline and time duration to transfer remaining content through a cellular network are calculated for flow scheduling. Additionally, the remaining deadline is periodically monitored to determine whether the current network throughput is large enough to transfer the content in time. Detailed algorithm on how a $D^2$TP flow is scheduled will be explained in Section 3.4.

### *3.3.2 Exploiting buffer for flow management*

Unfortunately, it is difficult to directly apply deadline-based flow management for dynamic content apps (*e.g.,* streaming) as there is no deterministic way to identify when the data transfer would end. A straightforward solution would be to periodically adjust the deadline and content size to match the minimal bitrate required. However, this can frequently interrupt streaming as the flow will not begin data transfer until the deadline is close. Reversely, setting too small deadlines would result in frequent CPU wakeups for deadline calculation, consuming much of mobile device's limited battery resources. Therefore, we propose an alternate method to calculate an appropriate deadline and content size, to be later used for flow scheduling.

*$D^2$BufMgr* is a flow manager for dynamic content that exploits a popular design semantics that many streaming apps follow for efficient playback: buffer that maintains to-be-played content. The goal of $D^2$BufMgr is to delay data transfer in a cellular network by consuming already buffered data only until the point that would result in interruption. For this, we introduce a low threshold, which represents the remaining buffer point where $D^2$TP flow should begin transferring data through a cellular network, assuming that either Wi-Fi is unavailable or its signal strength is too weak for continuous streaming. The deadline is thus determined by the estimated time that it takes to actually download the data via cellular network (= hardware interface switching time + $D^2$TP's challenge-and-response message exchange time + first data packet arrival time) while the content size is minimum data required to be transferred during that time according to its bitrate.

To minimize cellular traffic usage for efficiency, the device must return to a Wi-Fi network when it has buffered enough data with a cellular network. To this end, $D^2$BufMgr introduces a high threshold, that determines when the device stops using a cellular network by either switching to Wi-Fi if it is available or simply pausing the data transfer. The high threshold can be calculated similarly, which should be set large enough to begin downloading the data via Wi-Fi before reaching the low threshold. During cellular traffic usage, $D^2$BufMgr resets the deadline and content size to match the high threshold. Reversely, when the buffer reaches the high threshold, $D^2$BufMgr swaps the values back to guarantee the low threshold.

At each scheduling epoch,
**Input:** $(f_i, T_i : i = 1, \ldots, m)$, $r^c$, and $r^w$
**Output:** $I$ (the interface to use) and $i^\star$ (the flow to schedule)

*1.* For each flow $i$, let $\tau_i = \sum_{j=1}^{i} \lceil f_j / r^c \rceil$.
*2.* **if** $\tau_i \leq T_i$, for all flows $i = 1, \ldots, m$,
*3.* **if** Wi-Fi is unavailable
*4.* $I =$ `none`, $i^\star = 0$,
*5.* **else** $I =$ `Wi-Fi`, $i^\star = 1$.
*6.* **end if**
*7.* **else**
*8.* $I = \arg\max_{n=\{c,w\}} r^n$, $i^\star = 1$.
*9.* **end if**

**Figure 4: $D^2$Sched algorithm**

## 3.4 D²TP Flow Scheduling

When a mobile device opens a $D^2$TP flow, a flow scheduler, called *$D^2$Sched*, uses the values set from flow management to schedule the flow such that the flow should be idle or active in transmission and which interface it should use if it is active. In case of multiple flows, $D^2$Sched schedules flows by considering the contention between shared mobile resources (*e.g.,* bandwidth).

**Scheduling algorithm:** The scheduling algorithm of $D^2$Sched is described in Figure 4. Before explanation, we introduce several notations for ease of exposition. At each scheduling epoch with $m$ $D^2$TP flows, each $D^2$TP flow has remaining deadline of $T_i$, and content size of $f_i$ where $i \in \{1, \ldots, m\}$ respectively. We assume that $T_i$ is indexed in the increasing order of flow index $i$, *i.e.,* $T_1 \leq T_2 \leq \ldots \leq T_m$. We also let $r^c$ and $r^w$ be the estimated throughput (at this scheduling epoch) of cellular and Wi-Fi, respectively ($r^w = 0$ if the device has no Wi-Fi connection), for which we will explain how to measure them shortly.

In *line 1*, we first compute $\tau_i$ for each flow $i$, which corresponds to the time to finish flow $i$'s data delivery, if the flows were served in the increasing order of their remaining deadlines. We call $\tau_i$ as flow $i$'s *potential completion time*. Then, we check whether all flows' potential completion times are smaller than their deadlines (*line 2*), which means that the system is not in the "urgent" situation, *i.e.,* all flows have sufficient time until their deadlines expire. In this case, if the device has no Wi-Fi connection, it just waits and no flow is scheduled (*line 4*), but schedules the flow with the shortest remaining deadline to use Wi-Fi (*line 5*) otherwise. However, if we are in the urgent situation, where there exists a flow whose remaining deadline is less than its estimated completion time, we perform the Earliest Deadline First (EDF) scheduling by serving it via the network interface that would result in a larger expected throughput (*line 8*).

**Scheduling epochs and throughput estimation:** Scheduling in Figure 4 is periodically carried out every $N$ seconds with no environmental change (*e.g.,* Wi-Fi availability, flow configuration). In each scheduling epoch, $r^c$ or $r^w$ is updated by the average throughput over the past $N$ seconds. Clearly, $N$ should be appropriately chosen, such that it reacts to time-varying network conditions fast as well as it avoids too frequent switchings between Wi-Fi and cellular networks. In our real-world experiment, we choose it to be 1 second, considering both interface switching time and energy consumption. A smarter alternative is to keep a history of Wi-Fi access and to adjust $N$ according to the access pattern [34, 35], but we choose simplicity and fast adaptation at the cost of a slight overhead. Scheduling is also launched in an asynchronous manner to the change of flow configuration and Wi-Fi availability. In particular, in case a mobile device acquires a new Wi-Fi connection, it first spends $N$ seconds without active transmission to estimate $r^w$.

**Design rationales:** We design D$^2$Sched by the following rationales. First, D$^2$Sched naturally enables a single D$^2$TP flow to be assigned a low priority over other real-time TCP flows. This is because a *sequential* scheduling of serving only a single D$^2$TP flow inside D$^2$Sched leads our estimated data rate $r^c$ or $r^w$, which approximately corresponds to the throughput of a normal TCP flow, to be divided over $m$ D$^2$TP flows. This design comes from the rationale that D$^2$TP flows are less interactive large flows (*e.g.,* backup of data in smartphones or buffering of streaming movie) which should be served with lower priority than other real-time TCP flows. Second, a sequential scheduling of a single flow in an EDF manner is motivated by the following rationales that *(i)* an urgent flow has less opportunities of data transfer than others, and *(ii)* serving multiple flows concurrently generates frequent switching between flows with active transmission, causing overheads such as switching delay and small data rates due to the need of TCP's ramping-up time (*i.e.,* slow-start). We note that the sequential flow scheduling does not hurt the performance of offloading efficiency when the scheduling interval is short enough and the achievable sum throughput is independent of the number of activated flows; D$^2$Sched is an optimal scheduling policy in terms of offloading ratio for a fixed Wi-Fi and cellular throughputs [36]. In spite of time-varying nature of wireless connections, D$^2$Sched is expected to work in an highly efficient way, because Cedos's efficient Wi-Fi offloading targets at long flows, and mobile users are typically in indoor Wi-Fi networks, where data rate variations are reasonably small [37]. Third, D$^2$Sched tries to increase the offloading ratio by delaying flows as much as possible, *i.e.,* data transfer is even paused when Wi-Fi is unavailable and remaining deadlines are large.

## 3.5 Power Efficient CPU/Wi-Fi Wakeup

One practical concern when enabling flow scheduling in mobile devices is detecting environmental changes at idle device states. Current mobile OS platforms such as Android minimize battery consumption when a mobile device becomes idle by entering the CPU sleep or Wi-Fi "no-attach" mode. In this mode, the CPU is completely switched off until any external input event arrives, and all D$^2$TP flows in the background would stop even if Wi-Fi networks are available for offloading. What is worse is that the device will not retry scanning Wi-Fi APs during the sleep mode, and it would miss potential Wi-Fi opportunities. We thus require a mechanism to transparently wake up CPU and scan for Wi-Fi without user intervention.

One naïve workaround is to prevent the CPU and Wi-Fi interface from turning off by acquiring locks on them in the sleep mode, but it is impractical since it would quickly drain the battery. Instead, we decide to implement a D$^2$TP flow aware lock, called *D-Lock* that periodically locks CPU and Wi-Fi resources. If a preferred network is available, and there are D$^2$TP flows that want to use the network, D-Lock keeps the CPU on even if the device becomes idle. When the Wi-Fi network becomes unavailable, it allows the device to go to the sleep mode, but it periodically wakes up the CPU to probe the availability of Wi-Fi APs. The developers only need to hold a D-Lock during the D$^2$TP connection, and it automatically handles periodic scanning of APs at minimal power usage. Through real-world experiments, we find that locking with a period of 2 minutes is enough to detect most environmental changes with minimal power, shown in Section 5.2.2.

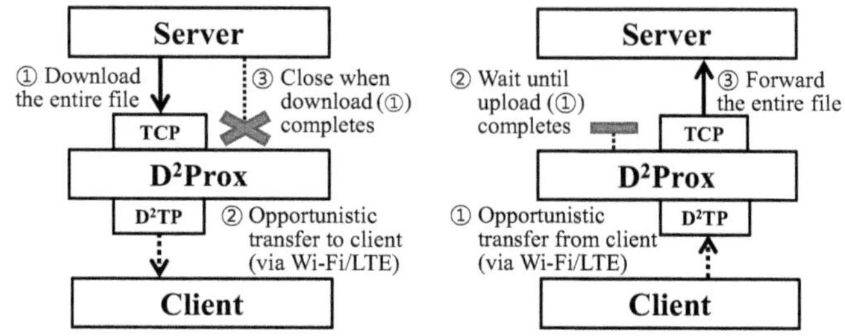


(a) D$^2$Prox on download case (b) D$^2$Prox on upload case

**Figure 5: Architecture of D$^2$Prox**

## 3.6 D$^2$Prox: Protocol Translation Proxy

Upgrading the existing infrastructure (*e.g.,* servers, middleboxes) to support D$^2$TP is costly and time-consuming. Instead, we propose placing a network-embedded Web caching proxy, D$^2$Prox, which enables D$^2$TP data transfers between a mobile client and an unmodified server. It basically hides the client-side mobility from the server by communicating with the client in D$^2$TP, but connects to the server using TCP. Note that D$^2$Prox operates as a non-transparent proxy that app developers or users can choose, depending on the characteristics of the apps. Although D$^2$Prox can sit anywhere in the Internet, we envision that it is located near a cellular ISP's core network to curb the latency stretch between an origin server and a client on a cellular interface.

Figure 5 shows the overall architecture of D$^2$Prox. When a new D$^2$TP connection is requested, D$^2$Prox creates an entry in the flow metadata table mapped by the flow id. Each entry consists of client/server IP addresses, a requested URL, and a connection deadline. Since TCP does not allow delay or network disruptions, D$^2$Prox only connects to the server when a full data transfer is possible in a single TCP connection. For downlink, D$^2$Prox simply downloads the entire content from the server, caches it in memory or disk, and forwards it to the client if the client is attached to a network. For uplink transfer (*e.g.,* HTTP POST), D$^2$Prox merges all of client's partial data from multiple physical connections, and forwards it to the server. D$^2$Prox removes the flow entry when the connection is explicitly closed or when the deadline expires but the client is out of reach.

Since D$^2$Prox maintains the flow metadata table in memory, a large number of connections with long deadlines could lead to memory pressure. We mitigate this problem by periodically flushing idle flow entries with long deadlines to disk. We believe this approach is reasonable in normal situations since such idle connections will be likely to stay paused to minimize the cellular traffic usage. However, we understand this is not a solution to a Denial-of-Service (DoS) attack on D$^2$Prox, which would require more careful thoughts. One mitigation approach would be to limit the number of concurrent D$^2$Prox flows per mobile device. If a cellular ISP employs D$^2$Prox, it could further require client authentication before using D$^2$Prox.

# 4. IMPLEMENTATION

We describe the implementation of Cedos components. We show the practicality of Cedos by porting two existing mobile apps (Mobile Firefox, VLC) to run on Cedos, and implement a delay-tolerant podcast client, ReadyCast, for real-world deployment.

**Socket operations *(Server/Client)***

```
int d2tp_socket(void);
int d2tp_bind(int fd,
              const struct sockaddr *addr,
              socklen_t addrlen);
int d2tp_connect(int fd,
                 const struct sockaddr *addr,
                 socklen_t addrlen);
int d2tp_listen(int fd, int backlog);
int d2tp_accept(int fd, struct sockaddr *addr,
               socklen_t *addrlen);
int d2tp_close(int fd);
```

**Data transfer and event notification**

```
ssize_t d2tp_read(int fd, void *buf, size_t count);
ssize_t d2tp_write(int fd, const void *buf,
                   size_t count);
int d2tp_select(int nfds, fd_set *readfds,
               fd_set *writefds, fd_set *exceptfds,
               struct timeval *timeout);
```

**Special socket options**

```
int d2tp_fcntl(int fd, int cmd, ...  /*arg*/);
int d2tp_getsockopt(int fd, int level,
                    int optname, void *optval,
                    socklen_t *optlen);
int d2tp_setsockopt(int sockfd, int level,
                    int optname, void *optval,
                    socklen_t *optlen);
```

**Figure 6: D$^2$TP socket API**

## 4.1 D$^2$TP

We implement D$^2$TP in the user level on top of UDP for easy portability and programming convenience. We implement all TCP core features such as slow start, flow and congestion control, fast retransmit and recovery, timeout and retransmission, delayed ACKs, selective ACKs and so on. These are implemented as a separate thread for each D$^2$TP application.

### *4.1.1 D$^2$TP Socket API*

D$^2$TP supports ease of portability by providing a socket API where each function maps to a BSD socket function by attaching the D$^2$TP prefix, `d2tp_` (see Figure 6). For example, `d2tp_socket()` returns a UDP socket while its associated context information is maintained in the D$^2$TP thread. Applications use this socket to bind, connect, listen on a port, and send or receive data with D$^2$Prox or any D$^2$TP-based applications. For event-driven programming, we support `d2tp_select()` and have it handle events for both D$^2$TP and TCP sockets. Since D$^2$TP socket is implemented as a UDP socket, `d2tp_select()` can simply use `select()` for event notification. Besides regular socket functions, we have special socket option support with `d2tp_setsockopt()` that allows setting a flow deadline (`D2TP_SO_DEADLINE`), a flow size (`D2TP_SO_ESIZE`), and high and low buffer thresholds for flow scheduling (`D2TP_SO_RCVBUFTH`). We show example code snippet of D$^2$TP-based client and D$^2$Prox in Figure 7.

### *4.1.2 Detecting Network Interface Availability*

To pause or resume the data transfer, the D$^2$TP layer must detect the change in the network availability. At start, the D$^2$TP layer reads the current status of network interfaces in the routing table at */proc/net/route*. Then, it monitors a netlink socket to be notified of any status change events of the network interfaces. If D$^2$Sched detects any D$^2$TP flows whose deadlines are about to expire but the quality of a Wi-Fi network is suspected too poor to meet their deadlines, the D$^2$TP layer switches to using the cellular network interface by modifying the routing table entry.

**D$^2$TP-based client**

```
fd = d2tp_socket();
if (non-interactive app) {
   // set deadline (10min) and flow size (1MB)
   int deadline = 10*60;
   int flowSize = 1000*1024;
   d2tp_setsockopt(fd, D2TP_SO_DEADLINE,
                   &deadline, sizeof(deadline));
   d2tp_setsockopt(fd, D2TP_SO_ESIZE,
                   &flowSize, sizeof(flowSize));
} else if (streaming app) {
   // set low/high buffer thresholds (20KB/1MB)
   struct d2tp_rcvbufth thr;
   thr.low = 20*1024;
   thr.high = 1000*1024;
   d2tp_setsockopt(fd, D2TP_SO_RCVBUFTH, &thr,
                   sizeof(thr));
}
d2tp_connect(fd, &sAddr, sizeof(sAddr));
d2tp_write(fd, buf, BUFSIZE);
d2tp_read(fd, buf, BUFSIZE);
d2tp_close(fd);
```

**D$^2$Prox as D$^2$TP-TCP protocol translation Web proxy**

```
sfd = d2tp_socket();
d2tp_bind(sfd, &sAddr, sizeof(sAddr));
d2tp_listen(sfd, 10);
cfd = d2tp_accept(sfd, &cAddr, &cSize);
d2tp_fcntl(cfd, D2TP_F_SETFL, D2TP_O_NONBLOCK);
FD_SET(cfd, rSet);
while (1) {
   d2tp_select(fdmax, &rSet, &wSet, NULL, NULL);
   // event notification from D2TP client
   if (FD_ISSET(cfd, &rSet) {
      d2tp_read(cfd, buf, BUFSIZE);
      // create tcp connection to server
      tcpfd = d2tp_socket();
      connect(tcpfd, &addr, sizeof(addr));
      // forward client message to server
      d2tp_write(tcpfd, message, BUFSIZE);
      FD_SET(tcpfd, rSet);
   }
   // event notification from TCP server
   if (FD_ISSET(tcpfd, &rSet) {
      read(tcpfd, buf, BUFSIZE);
      // forward server data to client
      d2tp_write(cfd, buf, BUFSIZE);
   }
}
```

**Figure 7: Sample code with D$^2$TP API (error processing is omitted)**

### *4.1.3 D-Lock*

We implement D-Lock by extending Android WakeLock [38] using AlarmClock [39]. If there is any active flow, D-Lock acquires WakeLock to prevent CPU from entering sleep mode. If there is no active flow, D-lock releases WakeLock and sets AlarmClock to wake up CPU for periodic Wi-Fi scanning. For every scanning period, D-Lock checks if D$^2$TP has any flow that needs to start before the next scan. If so, D-Lock sets another AlarmClock to trigger the D$^2$TP layer to continue the data transfer to meet the deadline.

## 4.2 D$^2$Prox

We base our D$^2$Prox implementation on a popular open-source Web server, nginx (v1.2.6), by porting it to use D$^2$TP socket functions. D$^2$Prox supports memory and disk caching, and transfers data to/from a server with normal TCP socket functions when it is able to send/receive a full content in a single connection. Porting is

| Implementation | Total (LoC) | Modified (LoC) |
|---|---|---|
| $D^2$TP thread and API | 11,166 | all |
| $D^2$Prox (nginx) | 129,340 | 55 |
| Mobile Firefox | 8,851,611 | 123 |
| VLC | 3,733,651 | 61 |
| ReadyCast | 9,868 | all |

**Table 2: Total implemented/modified lines of code**

mostly straightforward by replacing existing socket functions with $D^2$TP API, and the total number of modified lines is only 55 out of 129K lines of code as shown in Table 2. We have stress tested it to confirm correct delay-tolerant operation as well as Web caching.

## 4.3 Real-world Applications

To show the applicability of Cedos to real-world applications, we port two existing applications and implement a delay-tolerant podcast downloader. The number of modified lines of code is shown in Table 2.

**Mobile Firefox:** Since a Web browser is one of the most popular applications, we port mobile Firefox (Fennec [30]) to use $D^2$TP and retrieve web pages via $D^2$Prox. Original Fennec is built on top of NetScape Portable Runtime (NSPR) [40], which provides a platform-independent abstraction through a unified library API. We thus identify all network-related functions in Fennec and NSPR, and change them to use $D^2$TP API. With only 123 lines of code modification, Mobile Firefox enjoys seamless web browsing even after network disruptions. While it works well with large file download, we notice a few seconds of network interface switching delay at network disruptions when we browse regular Web sites; due to this reason, we do not evaluate it further in the next section.

**VLC:** To demonstrate that streaming media players could also benefit from Cedos, we port VLC [29] (v0.2.0), a popular open-source video player. We modify only 61 lines out of 3.7M lines of code to download streaming video via $D^2$Prox. VLC exploits $D^2$BufMgr in $D^2$TP by setting an appropriate deadline, and delays cellular data transfer if possible to offload to Wi-Fi. We find that by maintaining $D^2$BufMgr's buffer thresholds large enough to buffer drainage during network switching, VLC enjoys a constant video streaming without a single interruption (or buffer underrun) even in a moving train, further explained in next section.

**Podcast client:** Since there exists no deadline-based mobile app in the market, we have built our own delay-tolerant publish-and-subscribe podcast downloader, ReadyCast [31], and have registered it with Google Play [32]. ReadyCast supports subscription to any podcast feed published in the Internet. It allows the user to set the deadline of a podcast content download, benefiting from the $D^2$TP layer for transparent delay management. ReadyCast also uses D-Lock to minimize the power consumption at idle states while maximizing the offloading opportunities.

# 5. EVALUATION

We evaluate Cedos in two ways. First, we evaluate the basic functionalities of Cedos by measuring the data transfer throughput and bandwidth fairness, network switching delay, effect of flow scheduling, power consumption at idle states, and $D^2$Prox scalability. Second, we test if Cedos-based systems effectively offload cellular traffic to Wi-Fi networks in real-world applications.

## 5.1 Microbenchmark

We first measure the basic performance of Cedos components. We use Galaxy S3 (Android 4.1.2 and Linux kernel 3.0.31) with an 1.4 GHz quadcore CPU and 2 GB RAM or Nexus 5 (Android 4.4.2 with Linux kernel 3.4.0) with a 2.3 GHz quadcore CPU and 2 GB RAM as a client, and use a machine with an Intel Xeon E5-2650v2 octacore CPU with 32 GB RAM for $D^2$Prox and an origin server. For LTE access, we use SKT as our cellular ISP.

| Device | Galaxy S3 | | Nexus 5 | |
|---|---|---|---|---|
| Protocol | Throughput | CPU | Throughput | CPU |
| $D^2$TP | 89.1 Mbps | 16% | 90.6 Mbps | 11% |
| UDT | 89.3 Mbps | 25% | 90.5 Mbps | 14% |
| TCP | 49.2 Mbps | 7% | 91.3 Mbps | 8% |
| IBR-DTN | 45.1 Mbps | 15% | 87.0 Mbps | 18% |

**Table 3: Throughput/CPU usage during wireless data transfer**

| Protocol (# Connections) | Aggregate Throughput | JFI |
|---|---|---|
| TCP (100) | 95.1 Mbps | 0.99 |
| $D^2$TP (100) | 96.3 Mbps | 0.99 |
| TCP (50) + $D^2$TP (50) | 95.0 Mbps | 0.98 |

**Table 4: Concurrent connection performance via Wi-Fi**

**Throughput and CPU usage:** Table 3 compares the performances of downloading a 250 MB file using $D^2$TP, TCP, UDT (UDP-based reliable data transfer protocol [41]) and IBR-DTN (one of the delay-tolerant network group's disruption-tolerant data transfer implementations [42]) employing TCP as the underlying transport protocol. Both the client and the server run the same transport-layer protocol and a single connection is made between them via an 802.11n Wi-Fi AP. Overall, we find that $D^2$TP's performance is comparable to those of other protocols except for a slight increase in the CPU cycles due to user-level protocol implementation atop UDP. Interestingly, we observe much lower TCP performance on Galaxy S3, which we suspect is due to a kernel implementation bug (after code review) since we do not see the same problem on Nexus 5.

**Fairness:** We check if $D^2$TP provides a fair bandwidth share among competing flows by measuring Jain's Fairness Index (JFI) [43]. We compare following three cases: *(i)* 100 TCP connections, *(ii)* 100 $D^2$TP connections, *(iii)* 50 TCP and 50 $D^2$TP connections. We have each connection download a 1 GB file on a Nexus 5 device, and show the aggregate throughputs and JFIs in Table 4. We observe that $D^2$TP provides comparable per-flow bandwidth fairness to that of TCP both for $D^2$TP-only flows and for $D^2$TP flows mixed with TCP flows.

**Network switching delay:** We next measure the network switching delays to migrate a $D^2$TP flow between Wi-Fi and cellular networks. We measure the time between the last data packet from the previous network and the first data packet in the new network on a Galaxy S3 device. We measure it for 100 times and show the averages. The switching time includes the CHG-RSP-AUTH process for source authentication besides hardware interface switching.

We find that it takes 27 to 141 ms to switch from an LTE to a Wi-Fi network with an average of 45 ms. Switching from LTE to Wi-Fi is fast since the device can use LTE until the Wi-Fi access is fully ready. So, the network switching delay is the same as the $D^2$TP source authentication latency. However, in the reverse direction from Wi-Fi to LTE, we see 440 to 856 ms of delay with an average of 581 ms. This is because Android enforces a higher priority level on the Wi-Fi access, which requires the Wi-Fi interface to be turned off before the LTE interface is initialized. We note that it takes 88 ms on average for $D^2$TP source authentication in Wi-Fi-to-LTE switching.

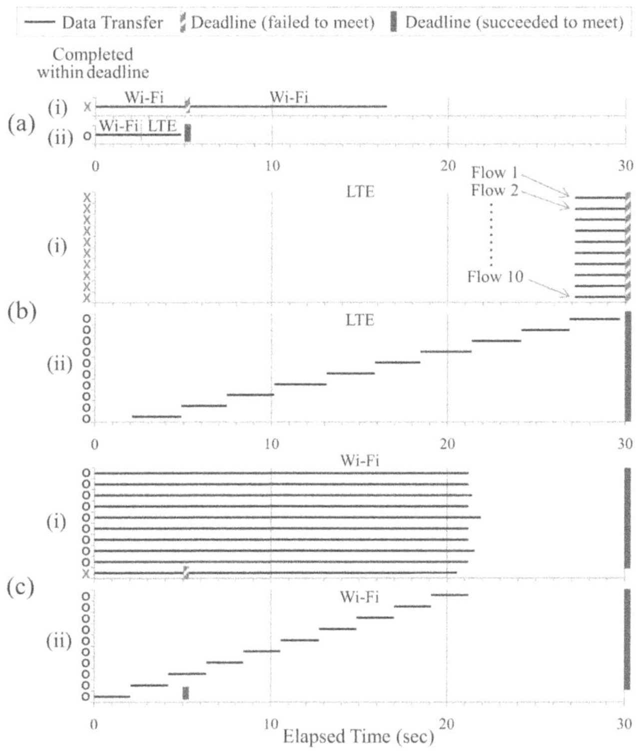


**Figure 8: Timecharts for flow scheduling experiments. Deadlines are shown as vertical bars.**

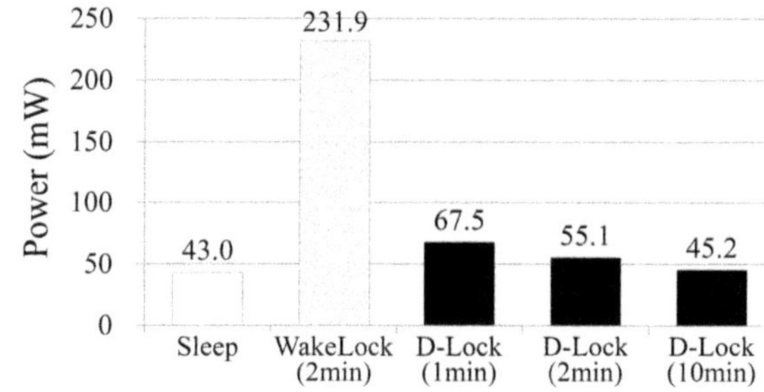


**Figure 9: Idle power usage for WakeLock and D-Lock at various scanning periods**

**Flow scheduling with D$^2$Sched:** We now evaluate whether D$^2$Sched can guarantee complete data transfer within user's delay tolerance when experiencing poor Wi-Fi connections (Figure 8(a)) or resource contention between multiple flows (Figure 8(b, c)). For these experiments, we use Galaxy S3 and have each flow download a 100 MB file from our server. For each graph, (i) represents a strawman scheduling method (*e.g.,* stick with Wi-Fi if available, schedule each flow independently) while (ii) represents D$^2$Sched's result.

For poor Wi-Fi connection experiment, we run one flow with a short deadline (5 min) in a Wi-Fi network whose bandwidth happens to be lower (0.8 Mbps) than that of a cellular network (4.7 Mbps). This is a valid scenario as it is often the case that a Wi-Fi bandwidth is lower than that of cellular access if the APs are congested or the signal strength is weak [4]. As shown in Figure 8(a)(i), blindly transferring data through Wi-Fi only fails to meet the deadline. On the other hand in (ii), we see that D$^2$Sched automatically switches to LTE to finish the download within flow's deadline. We note that D$^2$Sched still tries to maximize the Wi-Fi offloading ratio, receiving 16% of the data via Wi-Fi, which is close to optimal (17%).

For multiple flow experiment, we first run 10 flows with the same deadline (30 min) in a cellular network (LTE) without any Wi-Fi availability. The measured bandwidth of the cellular network is 4.7 Mbps on our client. Figure 8(b) compares the behavior of (i) scheduling each flow independently vs. (ii) D$^2$Sched. Under (i), we find that all flows miss their deadlines since they end up waiting for Wi-Fi too long. When they start using LTE, the bandwidth is divided into 10 flows, which delays the flow beyond its independently estimated finish time. In contrast, in (ii), all flows under D$^2$Sched finish in time since it schedules some flows earlier, operating with a minimum required time for meeting the deadlines of all flows. Next, we run 9 flows with a long deadline (30 min) along with one urgent flow with a much shorter deadline (5 min) in a Wi-Fi network. The measured bandwidth of the network is 6.3 Mbps. Figure 8(c) shows that the urgent flow misses its deadline under (i) since the other 9 flows compete for the bandwidth at the same time even if they have longer deadlines. However, in (ii), D$^2$Sched schedules the urgent flow first while holding off remaining 9 flows, eventually meeting the deadlines of all flows.

**Power usage at idle states:** We show the effectiveness of our D-Lock in reducing power consumption at idle states. Specifically, we compare the power usage of a Galaxy S3 device when we use *(i)* Android WakeLock (with WifiLock) vs. *(ii)* D-Lock. We set the device to use an LTE network during the experiment, and turn on the Wi-Fi module for periodic scanning. For accurate measurement, we turn off all the other user apps but the built-in apps, which cannot be killed by a user. We use Power Monitor by Monsoon [44] for power usage measurement, and show the results for various scanning periods in Figure 9.

We first see that at least 43 mW is needed to keep the device in a sleep state. If Android WakeLock is acquired, the CPU stays awake for the entire duration of the idle states while the device would scan for a Wi-Fi AP every 2 minute (default scanning policy in Galaxy S3). As a result, the power usage surges up to 231.9 mW, 5.4 times that of sleep state. Given that the battery capacity of Galaxy S3 is 7,980 mWh (3.7V with 2,100 mAh [45]), almost 70% of its total battery would be consumed per day even if no other activity is going on. In contrast, D-Lock with 2 minutes as the scanning period would curb the average power consumption at 55.1 mW, which outperforms WakeLock by a factor of 4.2. This is because the CPU is mostly turned off with D-Lock except when scanning a Wi-Fi AP. Even with a 1-minute period, the power usage reduction is significant (3.4x better than WakeLock), and increasing it to 10 minutes produces the power consumption close to that of sleep states.

**Power usage at transfer states:** We next examine the power usage of D$^2$TP during data transfer in comparison to that of TCP. We measure the power consumption on a Nexus 5 device while downloading a 1 GB file through Wi-Fi using *(i)* TCP vs. *(ii)* D$^2$TP. We find that for 825 seconds of the data transfer (bandwidth = 9.7 Mbps), TCP uses 1043 mW while D$^2$TP spends 1096 mW. This extra 5% of power consumption comes from increased CPU usage from user-level D$^2$TP implementation as is also shown in Table 3. However, we believe D$^2$TP will be more power-efficient in the mobility events as it avoids re-downloading the content from the start at network disruptions, also shown in our previous work [46]. Besides, it strives to use power-efficient Wi-Fi as much as possible over power-hungry cellular radio.

**D$^2$Prox scalability:** Finally, we evaluate the performance scalability of D$^2$Prox by having it handle a large number of concur-

| Wi-Fi | Cellular | Power (mW) | |
|---|---|---|---|
| | | 1 Mbps | 5 Mbps |
| off | transfer | 1,282 | 1,410 |
| idle | transfer | 1,301 | 1,420 |
| transfer | off | 568 | 686 |
| transfer | idle | 576 | 689 |

**Table 5: Power consumption with average bandwidth of 1 & 5 Mbps**

rent flows. For this experiment, we employ a client machine of the same specification as the server since it is difficult to create tens of thousands of connections from a single smartphone. We have the client initiate 64K concurrent connections to a D$^2$Prox server, and have each connection download a 1 GB file via a 10 Gbps interface (through a NetGear XSM7224S switch). We make 10% of the active connections go idle to simulate a network disruption for each minute, and when all connections become idle, we make 10% of the idle connections go active again for each minute. We observe that D$^2$Prox achieves almost 10 Gbps throughout the experiment while the bandwidth is evenly distributed among the active flows, producing a JFI above 0.9. Lastly, D$^2$Prox scales linearly as we introduce more D$^2$Prox nodes to the network.

## 5.2 Experience with Real-world Applications

We gauge the practicality of Cedos in real-world mobile applications. First, we evaluate if Cedos ensures automatic switching between Wi-Fi and cellular networks even for real-time video streaming with VLC. Second, we carry out a user study with ReadyCast for 8 weeks. We measure Wi-Fi offloading opportunities with delays in real environments, and observe how the users react to delayed data transfers.

### *5.2.1 Opportunistic data offloading with VLC*

**Experiment setup:** We watch a long streaming video of constant bit rate of 640 Kbps with Cedos-enabled VLC on a Nexus 5 device while riding a subway train in Daejeon, South Korea. The subway line consists of 22 stations, and we take a round trip to go from one end to the other end, and then come back to the starting station. Each subway station is equipped with publicly-accessible Wi-Fi APs but the train itself does not provide Wi-Fi access. So, the Wi-Fi service is available only when the train is staying at a station. Our goal is to opportunistically use the Wi-Fi access to buffer the streaming video but to automatically switch to the cellular network (LTE) if Wi-Fi access is unavailable and the buffered data is too small to be played back. We place D$^2$Prox and an origin server in our lab, which is 2 to 10 Km away from the client with an average RTT of 42.9 ms via LTE and 13.7 ms via Wi-Fi. We set D$^2$BufMgr's low and high receive socket buffer thresholds to 200 KB and 3 MB, respectively. We set the low threshold large enough to cover 0.3 seconds of LTE-to-Wi-Fi interface switching time during video playback. We set the high threshold conservatively large since we observe that many public Wi-Fi APs that advertise themselves as accessible actually do not function properly.

**Wi-Fi offloading ratio:** The experiment result shows that as much as 48.7% of the video data is being fetched through public Wi-Fi APs at the stations. For the entire period of video watching, the Wi-Fi data transfer is possible only for 310 seconds with an average of 6.29 Mbps while the device uses LTE for much longer, 2,447 seconds. However, D$^2$BufMgr's buffering mechanism ensures to limit the LTE usage by curbing the content download rate to the video bit rate (640 Kbps). Overall, the result is inspiring since it shows that almost a half of the large streaming data is delivered

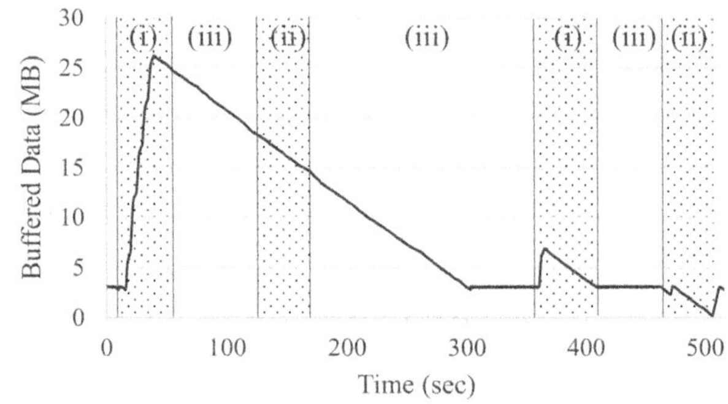


**Figure 10: Buffered data size over time for subway experiment. (i) Wi-Fi data transfer, (ii) Wi-Fi no data transfer, (iii) no Wi-Fi**

through Wi-Fi even if Wi-Fi access is available intermittently at a fraction of the stations. We confirm that Cedos effectively offloads the data to Wi-Fi without a single pause in the playback.

**Buffer size at network disruptions:** We next analyze how a D$^2$TP connection reacts to network disruptions during device mobility. Figure 10 shows the trace of the buffered data size during the time the train passes four subway stations. The shaded portions represent the availability of APs where (i) denotes that the APs are working properly while (ii) marks the period of malfunctioning APs that disallow data transfer. At the 20th second, the client starts buffering the video content through Wi-Fi as much as 26 MB. The device moves out of the Wi-Fi network at the 60th second, but it uses the buffered data for playback until the remaining size hits the high threshold at the 300th second. Then, it downloads the video content through LTE, but it keeps the buffer size at the high threshold (=3 MB) until it meets a Wi-Fi AP at the next station at the 360th second. The device attempts to buffer the data through the Wi-Fi AP, but the AP seems to be unstable and transfers the data for only about 5 seconds. At the 410th second, the device uses LTE again and when the device meets a malfunctioning AP at the 450th second, it tries to use Wi-Fi only to switch back to LTE at 500th second since the remaining buffer size hits the low threshold.

**Optimizing Wi-Fi offloading:** We now share our experience in optimizing the Wi-Fi offloading process. In our earlier experiments, we found that only 14.9% of the data was offloaded to Wi-Fi, which appeared lower than expected given the average Wi-Fi attachment time per station is 56.4 seconds while the period of Wi-Fi unavailability between two stations is 60.3 seconds on average. We later found out that once a device is attached to a Wi-Fi AP, it would not rescan for a better AP even if the available bandwidth of the AP is very low or even if it is not working. Actually, Wi-Fi data transfer worked at only 3 out of 44 train stops (round trip of 22-station line) in our earlier experiments.

We fix this problem by rescanning for a better AP every five seconds when a streaming application is running in the foreground. This allows the device to download 3.3 times more data through Wi-Fi at the cost of 8.5% of extra power consumption. With this fix, the number of stations that do transfer the data through Wi-Fi increases to 9 from 3, and the transfer time per station lasts for 34.4 seconds on average. We find that each Wi-Fi transfer at a station downloads 27.1 MB of the data, which is enough for watching the video for more than 5 minutes. Unfortunately, while the other 35 train stops report Wi-Fi availability, we could not transfer any data through their APs. We plan to investigate the reasons in the future.

Another problem we found is that it often takes as much as 3 seconds to turn on the 3G cellular interface when we switch from the

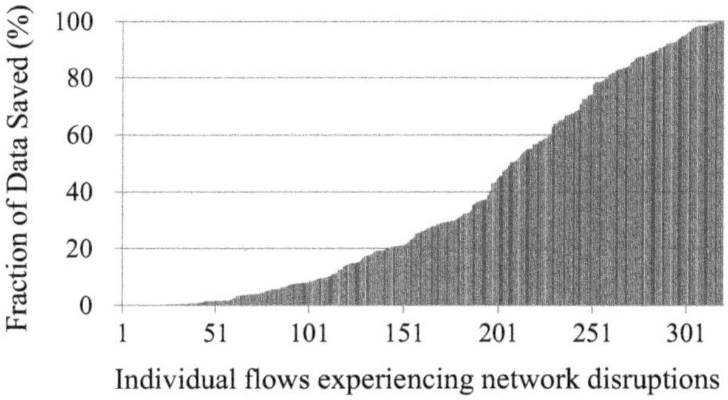


**Figure 11: Data portion saved by D²TP connection resumption**

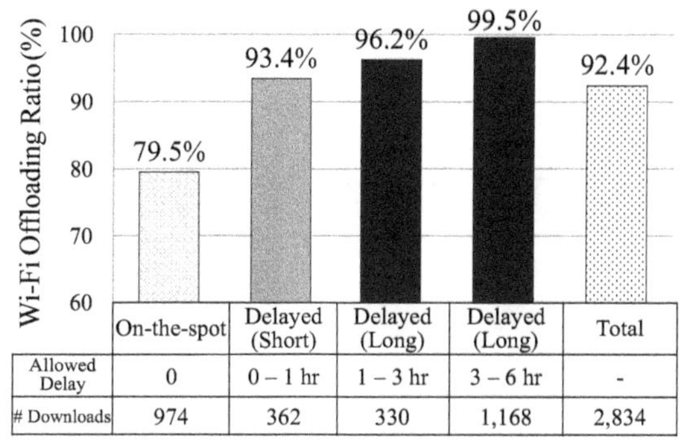


**Figure 12: Offloading ratios by user-configured delays**

| User Group with Monthly Limit (x) | Delayed Download | Average Allowed Delay | Offloading Ratio |
|---|---|---|---|
| $0 < x \leq 1$ GB | 62.7% | 186.1 min | 92.6% |
| 1 GB $< x \leq 5$ GB | 52.2% | 101.7 min | 90.7% |
| $x \geq 5$ GB | 47.6% | 100.9 min | 88.5% |

**Table 6: User study statistics based on monthly data cap**

Wi-Fi interface. Switching to LTE is not a big problem, but if LTE is not available, the device can fall back to the 3G interface. This implies that we need to have a larger low buffer threshold to reliably switch from Wi-Fi to cellular interfaces. But having a large low buffer threshold could lead to unnecessarily frequent switchings to cellular networks even if Wi-Fi is available (but its available bandwidth is temporarily fluctuating), which would reduce the Wi-Fi offloading opportunities.

One workaround is to keep the cellular interface on even if the device is attached to a Wi-Fi network so that the device could switch to the cellular interface at any time. One concern with the approach is that it would consume more power, which is obviously undesirable. Fortunately, we find that the extra power consumption is reasonable, ranging from only 0.7 to 1.5% as shown in Table 5 when it is compared with having only the Wi-Fi interface on. So, we decide to keep the cellular interface on even if the device is attached to a Wi-Fi AP.

### *5.2.2 Delayed data offloading with ReadyCast*

**Experiment setup:** We conduct a user study with ReadyCast by having 50 KAIST students use it for 8 weeks [2]. The students subscribe to any of 3,853 Podcast channels populated in ReadyCast links, and download the contents by setting an allowed delay between 0 to 6 hours. To simulate ISP-embedded D²Prox, we place two D²Prox servers in Korea Advanced Research Network (KOREN) PoPs in Seoul and in Daejeon, respectively. KOREN is a government-funded research network testbed in South Korea, offering high-speed linkage to Japan, China, U.S., and Europe as well [47]. We have ReadyCast choose the nearest D²Prox server by resolving a D²Prox domain name (*e.g.,* `dprox.net`) with our custom DNS server. For each download, the client leaves a per-flow log, which includes a deadline, play timestamps, network disruption/switching records, and data volume transferred via Wi-Fi and cellular connections. Overall, we have collected a total of 2,834 unique connections that complete the downloads, which is 71.2 GB in volume. While the users are mostly staying on campus during weekdays, many of them tend to travel outside the campus during weekends and holidays. So, the dataset covers remote mobility events beyond the campus networks to some extent.

**Network characteristics:** We describe the overall mobile network characteristics logged by ReadyCast. First, we observe that the users are well-exposed to Wi-Fi networks. We find that the user devices are attached to Wi-Fi for 62.9% of the download time. Data transfers via Wi-Fi show a higher average throughput (2.68 Mbps) than that of cellular access (0.82 Mbps), which matches the trend in previous experiments [5]. 336 downloads (11.9%) experience network switchings between Wi-Fi and cellular networks during the download. The average number of network switchings is 2.8 times per download. This means that a network switching is bimodal. The majority of downloads finish within a network, and if there is a network switching (user mobility), the users switch the networks almost 3 times per download before completion. Figure 11 shows the fraction of the data that are transferred before network disruptions, which amount to 38% of the entire downloaded data. This is the savings by D²TP while it would have been wasted on TCP without application-level resumption. We find that 80% of the downloads have non-zero user-allowed delays, which implies that the users are willing to benefit from Wi-Fi access even with delays when they expect network switchings while downloading the content.

**Wi-Fi offloading ratio:** We next look at how much data is offloaded to Wi-Fi by ReadyCast. Figure 12 shows the breakdown of Wi-Fi offloading ratios by the delays allowed by the users. Interestingly, even the downloads without any delay ("on-the-spot") deliver 79.5% of the data through Wi-Fi. We suspect that this is because the users choose "no delay" when they already know that they are in the Wi-Fi service area. We find that 70% of the on-the-spot flows download the data completely without cellular access, and only 24% of them receive the content solely from 3G/LTE access. In case a user allows some delays, the offloading ratio increases rapidly. We observe that almost 93% of the data is offloaded to Wi-Fi even for a few tens of minutes of delays. This implies that one does not need to wait very long to meet available Wi-Fi APs, and delayed offloading is a practical solution that could significantly reduce the traffic to cellular networks. If the allowed delay is larger than three hours, almost all traffic (99.5%) is offloaded to Wi-Fi. Overall, 92.4% of the total data is delivered through Wi-Fi without any wasted data transfer with ReadyCast.

**User reaction to delays:** We analyze how users react to delayed data transfers by looking at their deadline selection behavior. We first surveyed users' cellular data plans, and found the tendency that the users allow more delays as the monthly data cap is smaller, as shown in Table 6. The actual offloading ratios are in line with the deadline selection where more data is offloaded to Wi-Fi with longer delays.

[2] We anonymize all usage records for privacy.

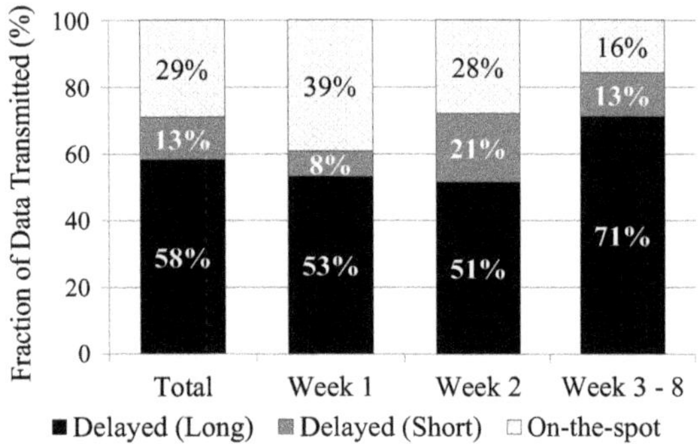


**Figure 13: Delay selection by users (short: $<$ 1hr, long: $\geq$ 1hr)**

We next analyze how users' delay selection changes during the experiment period. Figure 13 compares the fractions of user-selected delays for the first two weeks and the remaining six weeks. We see that almost 40% of the bytes are downloaded with no delay for the first week. However, once the users get used to delayed downloads, their delay tolerance grows accordingly, showing as much as 84% of the downloaded volume is tagged with a positive delay and more than 70% of the total bytes allow a delay of one hour or more. This suggests that the users are willing to allow delays as long as the application supports delayed downloads.

**User experience:** We conducted a user survey before and after the field study. Before the experiment, almost half of the users responded that they usually keep the Wi-Fi interface off to avoid abrupt connection closures during network disruptions. After the experiment, 94% of the users responded that ReadyCast was very useful since it automatically completed the downloads regardless of network disruptions, and 85% have felt almost no increase in battery consumption, implying that D-Lock with the 2-minute polling period works well in practice. Many wanted to extend the service to movies or TV shows, so delay-tolerant Netflix-like service could be promising.

# 6. DISCUSSION

In this section, we discuss other issues in developing and deploying delay-tolerant mobile applications.

**Leveraging delay tolerance:** Our work reconfirms that allowing even a slight delay in download offloads a significant fraction of cellular data to Wi-Fi. We believe there are many ways to encourage delayed downloads different from what we have presented in this paper. One simple example is automatic synchronization of periodically-generated contents (e.g., newspapers, TV shows, or even movies) by a daily deadline. Another way is to develop an app that automatically learns the user's acceptable delay and suggests the user a default value per each download. The app can analyze the content types or the download history and can calculate the time between the download and playback (or usage). Also, if an app can predict the next content to download (e.g., if it can access a playlist in on-line music streaming), it can opportunistically fetch the content through Wi-Fi as we have showed with VLC streaming.

**Concurrent multiple network interfaces:** In this work, we have not explored using both Wi-Fi and cellular interfaces at the same time, but it could be beneficial if the Wi-Fi bandwidth happens to be too small to finish downloading within a deadline. Allowing to use both networks is in line with adopting multipath TCP in Apple iOS 7 [48] and using a download booster [49] for fast download. To support concurrent multiple network interfaces, we should adjust D$^2$TP to conform to multipath TCP, and fix our flow scheduling algorithm to reflect concurrent data transfers.

**Operator-scale deployment cost:** We discuss the applicability of D$^2$Prox on a cellular ISP scale. A cellular ISP can decide to deploy D$^2$Prox in a number of vantage points close to the subscribers and allow mobile apps to use D$^2$Prox after authentication. This would efficiently distribute delay-tolerant contents to Wi-Fi with Cedos apps while the remaining interactive, real-time contents are delivered through cellular networks in case Wi-Fi is unavailable. We note the cost of the increasing end-to-end latency due to routing through D$^2$Prox, but we believe most of delay-tolerant flows that benefit from Cedos will be long-lived, large-data transfers that are less affected by it. Moreover, D$^2$Prox could reduce the latency by servicing popular content from its cache without contacting the origin server. By veering a large volume of cellular data traffic to cheap, widely-deployed Wi-Fi APs, Cedos would allow cellular ISPs to reduce the cost of expanding and maintaining the expensive cellular infrastructure.

**Handling hard failures:** We have focused mainly on how to transparently handle soft failures such as network disruptions and delay. However, maintaining delay-tolerant, long-lived flows in the face of hard failures such as app crash or device power outage is another challenge that needs to be addressed. For example, our ReadyCast could resume the data transfer after a hard failure by keeping all flow metadata such as URL, content length, file path and deadline persistent in its flash storage. We plan to support reliable crash recovery in D$^2$TP by using persistently storing flow metadata at minimum overhead [50].

**Security:** We discuss a few security issues in the operation of Cedos applications. First, D$^2$TP servers (or proxies) could be more vulnerable to state explosion attacks. For example, attackers may issue a large number of D$^2$TP connections with D$^2$Prox, but never download the content from it. Since D$^2$Prox keeps track of many concurrent D$^2$TP sessions, too many idle connections could exhaust the computing resources of D$^2$Prox. Second, attackers may intentionally issue repeated connection or connection resumption requests. Since the connection or connection resumption procedure requires more CPU cycles than regular TCP connection setup, attackers may attempt to use up CPU cycles to deny other requests. However, these attacks are not fundamentally different from other resource exhaustion attacks on regular TCP-based (or TLS-based) servers. One approach to mitigating these problems is to authenticate each app user, and to limit the number of concurrent requests or to enforce a rate on bandwidth consumption per client [51].

# 7. RELATED WORKS

There are many related works that address network disruptions or exploit the delay in Wi-Fi offloading. Due to the sheer number, comprehensive treatment is hard here, so we highlight the difference of our approach from other works.

## 7.1 Handling network disruptions/delays

There are various ways to handle network disruptions at content download. A popular approach is to resume the download using an application layer protocol (*e.g.,* HTTP range queries). One practical downside, however, is that it requires the modification of each application, which we find is often neglected in mobile apps. Mosh [52] and ATOM [53] provide seamless data transfer at network disruption by synchronizing to the latest state or by querying for the latest download offset. However, their applicability is limited as they base on UDP, or it requires mobile apps to support resumption. 3GPP's I-WLAN [54] specifies a way to integrate the cellular operator's LTE and user-owned Wi-Fi APs. More recently, IFOM [55] was proposed to support seamless flow-level offloading within I-WLAN architecture. However, implementations of I-WLAN and IFOM require tight integration of the two networks, and may result in heavy burden on the backhaul network (*e.g.,* anchoring on P-GW).

Another workaround is to eliminate the network address binding altogether and to use a unique identifier that persists between network disruptions. Locator/ID Separation Protocol (LISP) [23], i3 [26], and HIP [21] bring in a separate id for the location and use the IP address as an endpoint identifier. However, these protocols require upgrading the existing infrastructure (*e.g.,* routers) or adding a separate entity (*e.g.,* DNS support), which may be challenging for immediate deployment. Mobile IP [56] uses a fixed home address to hide a moving device, which is similar to $D^2$Prox in relaying the packets. But Cedos supports delayed offloading with a flexible network API that directly controls the mobility events.

TCP Migrate [27] and MPTCP [57, 58] remove separate entity requirement by extending TCP to include transport-level flow identifying token. Serval [28] introduces a new service access layer, which demultiplexes packets based on flow identifiers and migrates a flow from one address to another. Auspice [59] is a massively scalable global name service which resolves network location identities under high mobility. msocket [60] is a BSD socket-like API which provides mid-connection mobility for mobile-to-mobile and multipath cases by relying on Auspice. However, they all assume a short reconnection and are unable to handle hours of delay as they are based on default TCP teardown after 15 retransmissions [61].

Bundle protocol (BP) [62] is the standard communication protocol for Delay Tolerant Networks (DTN), which enables end-to-end reliable delivery through intermittent connectivity in the challenged networks (e.g., interplanetary [63] or rural Internet access [64]). Notable BP implementations include DTN2 [65], IBR-DTN [66], and ION [67]. Since these protocols are originally designed as transport protocols in multi-hop opportunistic networks, we find that they do not fit well into our system environments. First, BP requires bundling the data before sending it, which makes it unsuitable to deliver dynamically generated data (e.g., media streaming). Second, their programming API is largely different from the BSD socket API (e.g., requiring endpoint ID starting with "dtn://"), so that it would be difficult to port the existing mobile applications. Cedos adopts $D^2$TP, a transport layer protocol tailored to Wi-Fi offloading in mobile apps. $D^2$TP extends our early work, DTP [46], a disruption-tolerant transport protocol, by completing the API that allows delay and buffer management with multi-flow scheduling and by supporting $D^2$Prox for easy deployment with realistic mobile apps.

## 7.2 Wi-Fi offloading with delay

A large number of works have shown the potential of Wi-Fi offloading through mobility studies. A recent study on mobility estimates that over 60% of the cellular traffic can be offloaded to Wi-Fi [5, 4]. Lee et. al. [5] report that the offloading ratio would further improve up to 93.7% if the data transfer could be delayed by one hour. User surveys [68, 69], incentive mechanism [70], and economic analysis [71] also support the feasibility of Wi-Fi offloading with delay. These results may change depending on the experimental conditions, but they show that a slight delay helps a lot in increasing Wi-Fi contact chances for most mobile data transfers.

Wiffler [4] implements a Wi-Fi offloading system that leverages user delay tolerance to reduce cellular data traffic. However, Wiffler focuses on exploiting delay only in fixed-sized file transfers, and shifts the burden of handling mobility events to mobile apps. In contrast, Cedos provides transport-layer handling of the mobility events, which allows easy development of mobile apps. Also, since Wiffler does not provide multi-flow scheduling, it could make some flows miss the deadlines when there is resource contention. TUBE [69] builds an app that allows a user to set a delay on mobile apps. However, its application-level implementation requires to jailbreak the device (for autopilot) and to set a deadline per app (not per each flow), which limits flexibility. Like Wiffler, it does not provide transport-layer API nor network disruption handling. In Cedos, we aim to provide flexibility to app developers with minimal migration effort by providing the BSD socket-like API that supports a broad spectrum of apps, ranging from interactive, streaming to non-interactive file transfer apps.

We note that recent smartphones introduce advanced Wi-Fi network switching algorithms (e.g., "Smart Network Switch" from Samsung Android phones) to improve the QoE by automatically switching the Wi-Fi interface when the signal drops too low or the network is too slow. These features would help $D^2$TP to improve the QoE of the users, but blind switchings agnostic to the need of application workloads (e.g., delay tolerance) could result in increased cellular data usage. In contrast, our solution derives network switching decisions based on the deadline or the amount of data in the buffer to exploit the Wi-Fi network.

# 8. CONCLUSION

While delay-tolerant Wi-Fi offloading is known to be a great idea, there has been little systems support for it. In this paper, we have presented Cedos, which enables easy development of delay-tolerant mobile apps by hiding the complexity of handling mobility events in a new transport layer, $D^2$TP. $D^2$TP is designed to transparently handle network disruptions and delays, while it schedules multiple flows to meet deadlines for maximal Wi-Fi usage. $D^2$TP also allows real-time buffer management for video streaming through opportunistic Wi-Fi connections. Finally, we provide $D^2$Prox, which enables Cedos apps to coexist with TCP-based servers. We have demonstrated that it is easy to port existing apps to Cedos, and confirmed that the benefit is realized in the real-world usage scenarios. We hope that Cedos further encourages delay-tolerant app development and practicalizes the concept of delay-tolerant Wi-Fi offloading.

# 9. ACKNOWLEDGMENTS

We would like to thank the anonymous reviewers and our shepherd, Margaret Martonosi, for their insightful comments and suggestions to improve the paper. This work was supported in part by the ICT R&D program of MSIP/IITP, Republic of Korea [14-911-05-001, Development of an NFV-inspired networked switch and an operating system for multi-middlebox services] and [14-000-04-001, Development of 5G Mobile Communication Technologies for Hyper-connected smart devices], National Research Foundation of Korea (NRF) grant funded by the Korea government (MSIP) (NRF-2013R1A2A2A01067633), and KCA-2011-11913-05004.

# 10. REFERENCES

[1] ITBusinessEdge. Five Reasons Wi-Fi Will Overtake Traditional Telecoms, 2013. `http://www.itbusinessedge.com/slideshows/five-reasons-wi-fi-will-overtake-traditional-telecoms.html`.

[2] Wireless Broadband Alliance. Wireless Broadband Alliance Industry Resport 2013: Global Trends in Public Wi-Fi, 2013.

[3] ABC News. New York City Pay Phone Booths Noew Free WiFi Hotspots, 2012. http://abcnews.go.com/Technology/york-city-pay-phone-booths-now-free-wifi/story?id=16756016.

[4] A. Balasubramanian, R. Mahajan, and A. Venkataramani. Augmenting Mobile 3G Using WiFi. In *Proceedings of the International Conference on Mobile Systems, Applications, and Services (MobiSys)*, 2010.

[5] K. Lee, I. Rhee, J. Lee, S. Chong, and Y. Yi. Mobile Data Offloading: How Much Can WiFi Deliver? In *Proceedings of the ACM International Conference on Emerging Networking EXperiments and Technologies (CoNEXT)*, 2010.

[6] Twitter (Android application, v5.35.0). https://play.google.com/store/apps/details?id=com.twitter.android.

[7] Facebook (Android application, v22.0.0.15.13). https://play.google.com/store/apps/details?id=com.facebook.katana.

[8] Podcast Addict (Android application, v2.23.2). https://play.google.com/store/apps/details?id=com.bambuna.podcastaddict.

[9] BeyondPod (Android application, v4.0.32). https://play.google.com/store/apps/details?id=mobi.beyondpod.

[10] Podcast Republic (Android application, v2.5.7). https://play.google.com/store/apps/details?id=com.itunestoppodcastplayer.app.

[11] YouTube (Android application, v5.17.6). https://play.google.com/store/apps/details?id=com.google.android.youtube.

[12] TuneIn Radio (Android application, v12.9). https://play.google.com/store/apps/details?id=tunein.player.

[13] MXPlayer (Android application, v1.7.33). https://play.google.com/store/apps/details?id=com.mxtech.videoplayer.ad.

[14] Google Play Movie (Android application, v3.5.14). https://play.google.com/store/apps/details?id=com.google.android.videos.

[15] VLC (Android application, v0.9.10). https://play.google.com/store/apps/details?id=org.videolan.vlc.betav7neon.

[16] Chrome (Android application, v39.0.2171.59). https://play.google.com/store/apps/details?id=com.android.chrome.

[17] OperaMini (Android application, v7.6.2). https://play.google.com/store/apps/details?id=com.android.chrome.

[18] eBay (Android application, v2.8.2.1). https://play.google.com/store/apps/details?id=com.ebay.mobile.

[19] Amazon (Android application, v5.2.0). https://play.google.com/store/apps/details?id=com.amazon.mShop.android.

[20] Google Play Book (Android application, v3.2.61). https://play.google.com/store/apps/details?id=com.google.android.apps.books.

[21] R. Moskowitz and P. Nikander. Host Identity Protocol Architecture. RFC 4423, IETF, 2006.

[22] M. Walfish, J. Stribling, M. Krohn, H. Balakrishnan, and R. Morris. Middleboxes no longer considered harmful. In *Proceedings of the USENIX Symposium on Operating Systems Design and Implementation (OSDI)*, 2004.

[23] D. Farinacci, V. Fuller, D. Meyer, and D. Lewis. The Locator/ID Separation Protocol (LISP). RFC 6830, IETF, 2013.

[24] H. Balakrishnan, K. Lakshminarayanan, S. Ratnasamy, S. Shenker, I. Stoica, and M. Walfish. A layered naming architecture for the Internet. In *Proceedings of the ACM Special Interest Group on Data Communication (SIGCOMM)*, 2004.

[25] A. Feldmann, L. Cittadini, W. Muhlbauer, R. Bush, and O. Maennel. HAIR: Hierarchical architecture for Internet routing. In *In Proceedings of the ACM workshop on Re-architecting the internet (ReArch)*, 2009.

[26] I. Stoica, D. Adkins, S. Zhuang, S. Shenker, and S. Surana. Internet Indirection Infrastructure. In *Proceedings of the ACM Special Interest Group on Data Communication (SIGCOMM)*, 2002.

[27] F. Sultan, K. Srinivasan, D. Iyer, and L. Iftode. Migratory TCP: Connection Migration for Service Continuity in the Internet. In *Proceedings of the IEEE International Conference on Distributed Computing Systems (ICDCS)*, 2002.

[28] E. Nordstrom, D. Shue, P. Gopalan, R. Kiefer, M. Arye, S. Y. Ko, J. Rexford, and M. J. Freedman. Serval: An End-Host Stack for Service-Centric Networking. In *Proceedings of the USENIX Symposium on Networked Systems Design and Implementation (NSDI)*, 2012.

[29] VideoLAN Organization. VLC media player. http://www.videolan.org/vlc/index.html.

[30] MozillaWiki. Mobile/Fennec. https://wiki.mozilla.org/Mobile/Fennec.

[31] ReadyCast. https://play.google.com/store/apps/details?id=dtn.readycast.

[32] Google play. http://play.google.com/store.

[33] Google Nexus 5. http://www.google.com/nexus/5/.

[34] A. J. Nicholson and B. D. Noble. BreadCrumbs: Forecasting Mobile Connectivity. In *Proceedings of the Annual International Conference on Mobile Computing and Networking (MobiCom)*, 2008.

[35] O. B. Yetim and M. Martonosi. Adaptive Delay-Tolerant Scheduling for Efficient Cellular and WiFi Usage. In *Proceedings of the IEEE International Symposium on a World of Wireless, Mobile and Multimedia Networks (WowMoM)*, 2014.

[36] Y. Kim, J. Lee, J. Jeong, and S. Chong. Optimal multi-flow scheduling in delayed Wi-Fi offloading. In *Technical Report*, 2014. *available at* http://netsys.kaist.ac.kr/publication/multi-flow.pdf.

[37] A. Aguiar and J. Klaue. Bi-directional WLAN channel measurements in different mobility scenarios. In *Proceedings of the IEEE Vehicular Technology Conference (VTC)*, 2004.

[38] Android PowerManager.WakeLock. http://developer.android.com/reference/android/os/PowerManager.WakeLock.html.

[39] Android Alarm Clock. http://developer.android.com/reference/android/provider/AlarmClock.html.

[40] Mozilla Developer Network. NetScape Portable Runtime.

https://developer.mozilla.org/en-US/docs/Mozilla/Projects/NSPR.

[41] UDP-based Data Transfer. http://udt.sourceforge.net/.

[42] IBR-DTN. http://trac.ibr.cs.tu-bs.de/project-cm-2012-ibrdtn.

[43] R. Jain, A. Durresi and G. Babic. Throughput Fairness Index: An Explanation. http://www.cse.wustl.edu/~jain/atmf/ftp/af_fair.pdf.

[44] Monsoon Power Monitor. http://www.msoon.com/LabEquipment/PowerMonitor/.

[45] Samsung Galaxy S3 Specifications. http://www.samsung.com/global/galaxys3/specifications.html.

[46] Y. Go, Y. Moon, G. Nam, and K. Park. A Disruption-tolerant Transmission Protocol for Practical Mobile Data Offloading. In *Proceedings of the ACM International Workshop on Mobile Opportunistic Networks (MobiOpp)*, 2012.

[47] KOREN (Korea Advanced Research Network). http://www.koren.kr/koren/eng/.

[48] iOS: Multipath TCP Support in iOS 7. http://support.apple.com/kb/HT5977.

[49] Samsung Galaxy S5 Download Booster. http://galaxys5guide.com/samsung-galaxy-s5-features-explained/galaxy-s5-download-booster/.

[50] Y. Go, N. Agrawal, A. Aranya, and C. Ungureanu. Reliable, Consistent, and Efficient Data Sync for Mobile Apps. In *Proceedings of the USENIX Conference on File and Storage Technologies (FAST)*, 2015.

[51] X. Qie, R. Pang, and L. Peterson. Defensive Programming: Using an Annotation Toolkit to Build DOS-Resistant Software. In *Proceedings of USENIX Symposium on Operating Systems Design and Implementation (OSDI)*, 2002.

[52] K. Winstein and H. Balakrishnan. Mosh: An Interactive Remote Shell for Mobile Clients. In *Proceedings of the USENIX Annual Technical Conference (ATC)*, 2012.

[53] R. Mahindra, H. Viswanathan, K. Sundaresan, M. Y. Arslan, and S. Rangarajan. A Practical Traffic Management System for Integrated LTE-WiFi Networks. In *Proceedings of the Annual International Conference on Mobile Computing and Networking (MobiCom)*, 2014.

[54] 3GPP TS 24.327, Mobility between 3GPP Wireless Local Area Network (WLAN) interworking (I-WLAN) and 3GPP systems. http://www.3gpp.org/DynaReport/24327.htm.

[55] 3GPP TS 23.261, IP flow mobility and seamless Wireless Local Area Network (WLAN) offload. http://www.3gpp.org/DynaReport/23261.htm.

[56] C. Perkins. IP Mobility Support. RFC 2002, IETF, 1996.

[57] A. Ford, C. Raiciu, M. Handley, S. Barre, and J. Iyengar. Architectural Guidelines for Multipath TCP Development. RFC 6182, IETF, 2011.

[58] D. Wischik, C. Raiciu, A. Greenhalgh, and M. Handley. Design, implementation and evaluation of congestion control for multipath TCP. In *Proceedings of the USENIX Symposium on Networked Systems Design and Implementation (NSDI)*, 2011.

[59] A. Sharma, X. Tie, H. Uppal, A. Venkataramani, D. Westbrook, and A. Yadav. A global name service for a highly mobile internetwork. In *Proceedings of the ACM Special Interest Group on Data Communication (SIGCOMM)*, 2014.

[60] A. Yadav, A. Sharma, A. Venkataramani, and E. Cecchet. msocket: System support for developing seamlessly mobile, multipath, and middlebox-agnostic applications. In *Proceedings of the UMass SCS Technical Report*, 2014.

[61] J. Postel. Transmission Control Protocol. RFC 793, IETF, 1981.

[62] K. Scott and S. Burleigh. Bundle Protocol Specification. RFC 5050, IETF, 2007.

[63] S. Burleigh, A. Hooke, L. Torgerson, K. Fall, V. Cerf, B. Durst, K. Scott, and H. Weiss. Delay-Tolerant Networking: An Approach to Interplanetary Internet. In *IEEE Communications Magazine*, volume 41(6), pp. 128-136, 2003.

[64] S. Guo, M.H. Falaki, E.A. Oliver, S. Ur Rahman, A. Seth, M.A. Zaharia, and S. Keshav. Very Low-Cost Internet Access Using KioskNet. In *ACM SIGCOMM Computer Communication Review*, volume 37(5), pp. 95-100, 2007.

[65] M. Demmer, E. Brewer, K. Fall, S. Jain, M. Ho, and R. Patra. Implementing Delay Tolerant Networking. In *Technical Report, IRB-TR-04-020*, 2004.

[66] M. Doering, S. Lahde, J. Morgenroth, and L. Wolf. IBR-DTN: An Efficient Implementation for Embedded Systems. In *Proceedings of the ACM workshop on Challenged networks (CHANTS)*, 2008.

[67] S. Burleigh. Interplanetary Overlay Network: An Implementation of the DTN Bundle Protocol. In *IEEE Consumer Communications and Networking Conference (CCNC)*, pages 222–226, 2007.

[68] TUBE Survey, 2011. http://scenic.princeton.edu/tube/tdpsurvey.html.

[69] S. Ha, S. Sen, J. Carlee, Y. Im, and M. Chiang. Tube: time-dependent pricing for mobile data. In *Proceedings of the ACM Special Interest Group on Data Communication (SIGCOMM)*, 2012.

[70] X. Zhuo, W. Gao, G. Cao, and Y. Dai. Win-Coupon: An Incentive Framework for 3G Traffic Offloading. In *Proceedings of the IEEE International Conference on Network Protocols (ICNP)*, 2011.

[71] J. Lee, Y. Yi, S. Chong, and Y. Jin. Economics of WiFi Offloading: Trading Delay for Cellular Capacity. In *Proceedings of the IEEE International Workshop on Smart Data Pricing (INFOCOM SDP)*, 2013.

# Video: LookUp!: Enabling Pedestrian Safety Services via Shoe Sensing

Shubham Jain[†], Carlo Borgiattino[§], Yanzhi Ren[♯],
Marco Gruteser[†], Yingying Chen[♯], Carla-Fabiana Chiasserini[§]

[†]WINLAB, Rutgers University, North Brunswick, NJ, USA
[§]Politecnico di Torino, Torino, Italy
[♯]Stevens Institute of Technology, Hoboken, NJ, USA

## ABSTRACT

This video is a demonstration of the work discussed in our full paper available in the MobiSys'15 proceedings [1]. The video illustrates a sensing technology for fine-grained location classification in an urban environment, for enhancing pedestrian safety. Our system seeks to detect the transitions from sidewalk locations to in-street locations, to enable applications such as alerting texting pedestrians when they step into the street. Existing positioning technologies are not sufficiently precise to allow distinguishing a position on the sidewalk from a position in the street, as explored in our previous work [2]. To this end, we use shoe-mounted inertial sensors for location classification based on surface gradient profile and step patterns. This approach is different from existing shoe sensing solutions that focus on dead reckoning and inertial navigation. The shoe sensors relay inertial sensor measurements to a smartphone, which extracts the step pattern and the inclination of the ground a pedestrian is walking on. This allows detecting transitions such as stepping over a curb or walking down sidewalk ramps that lead into the street. We carried out walking trials in metropolitan environments in United States (Manhattan) and Europe (Turin). The results from these experiments show that we can accurately determine transitions between sidewalk and street locations to identify pedestrian risk.

## Categories and Subject Descriptors

H.4 [**Information Systems Applications**]: Miscellaneous

## General Terms

Design, Experimentation, Algorithms, Performance

## Keywords

Pedestrian Safety; Smartphone; Localization; Inertial Sensing; GPS; Accelerometer; Gyroscope


*MobiSys'15,* May 18–22, 2015, Florence, Italy.
ACM 978-1-4503-3494-5/15/05.
http://dx.doi.org/10.1145/2742647.2749242.

## Acknowledgments

This material is based in part upon work supported by the National Science Foundation under Grant Nos. CNS-1329939, CNS-1409811, CNS-1409767, CNS-1217387, SES-1450091, and by Qualcomm University Relations, as well as by the LIMPID project (POR FESR 2007/2013) funded by Regione Piemonte (Italy).

## 1. REFERENCES

[1] Shubham Jain, Carlo Borgiattino, Yanzhi Ren, Marco Gruteser, Yingying Chen, and Carla-Fabiana Chiasserini. Lookup: Enabling pedestrian safety services via shoe sensing. In *Proceedings of MobiSys*, 2015.

[2] Shubham Jain, Carlo Borgiattino, Yanzhi Ren, Marco Gruteser, and Yingying Chen. On the limits of positioning-based pedestrian risk awareness. In *Proceedings of the Workshop on Mobile Augmented Reality and Robotic Technology-based Systems*, 2014.

# Video: Lightweight Visible Light Communication for Indoor Positioning

Zeyu Wang[1†], Zhice Yang[1†], Jiansong Zhang[2], Chenyu Huang[3], Qian Zhang[1]
[†]Co-primary Authors [1]CSE, HKUST [2]Microsoft Research Asia, [3]Wuhan University

## ABSTRACT

Visible light positioning (VLP) is an emerging positioning technique that utilizes indoor light sources to broadcast archer locations through visible light communication (VLC). Benefited by the densely deployed light lamps, VLP holds the promise for more accurate positioning accuracy than RF based approaches, and thus enables interesting applications such as retail navigation and shelf-level advertising in supermarkets and shopping malls.

However, we observe that in existing VLP systems, receiving devices are heavily burdened in handling light flickering for VLC. In order to prevent human from being disturbed, the VLC transmitter lamps have to transmit pulses in a high rate (over 1kHz). Since the pulse rate far exceeds the cameras' sampling capability (30fps), receiver design either requires customized light sensor with cumbersome calibration on receiving signal strength [2] or processing high resolution images to leverage rolling shutter effect of the CMOS camera to decode message [1].

The heavy burden on receiving devices motivated us to try getting rid of light flickers. Since human eyes normally can not perceive changes in polarization, the idea is to modulate polarization instead of intensity for communication. In this demo, we demonstrate the VLC system in our VLP design [3] which realizes this idea. It enables lightweight VLC that is even affordable in wearables (Google Glass), without incurring hardware modification or computation off-loading. Moreover, it also makes other types of illuminating light beyond LED light (even sun light) possible to construct communication, therefore eliminates the barrier for deploying future VLC-based applications.

As detailed in the full paper [3], our design was inspired by the liquid crystal display (LCD), from which we borrowed polarizer and liquid crystal. Liquid crystal has the property to change the polarization of bypassing polarized light according to the applied voltage. We use polarizer to polarize illuminating light and leverage liquid crystal to modulate bits through changing the light's polarization. The receiver can thus detect changes in polarization with a polarizing film, through which different polarizations result in different intensities. Since the SNR of such communication channel may significantly vary with the mobility of receiving device, we propose to add a dispersion filter to the transmitter. The dispersion filter can cast different frequency of lights into different polarization directions so that SNR in different receiving directions are evened. With the above techniques, VLC transmitter generates signal in low baud rate and mobile devices can perform VLC through camera directly. The communication is long in distance and lightweight enough for resource-constrained devices since the information is carried in intensity changes rather than certain image patterns in rolling shutter approaches.

In this demo, we will illustrate the prototype implementation of the VLC communication system. We use incandescent lamps as illuminating light sources. The transmitter consists of a polarizing film, a liquid crystal layer, a dispersor and a control board. The receiver is demonstrated in Android smartphone with polarizing film in front of the camera. The following demo scenarios are planed to show our design (the demo space higher than 2.4m is preferred):

(1) Polarization based VLC modulation can solve the flickering problem. The modulated light provides normal illumination. When viewing the modulated light through a polarizing film, people can feel strong intensity changes.

(2) End-to-end VLC communication system. Smartphones with a polarizing film in front of the camera can receive and show transmitted messages from VLC transmitters.

(3) The VLC method enables accurate indoor positioning. After successfully receiving location beacons from VLC transmitters, smartphone performs location estimation.


*MobiSys'15,* May 18–22, 2015, Florence, Italy.
ACM 978-1-4503-3494-5/15/05.
http://dx.doi.org/10.1145/2742647.2745924.

## Categories and Subject Descriptors

C.3 [**Special-Purpose and Application-Based Systems**]; C.2.1 [**Computer-Communication Networks**]: Network Architecture and Design—*Wireless communication*

## Keywords

Polarization; Visible Light Communication; Pixel; Wearables

## 1. REFERENCES

[1] Y.-S. Kuo, P. Pannuto, K.-J. Hsiao, and P. Dutta. Luxapose: Indoor positioning with mobile phones and visible light. MobiCom '14. ACM, 2014.

[2] L. Li, P. Hu, C. Peng, G. Shen, and F. Zhao. Epsilon: A visible light based positioning system. NSDI '14, 2014.

[3] Z. Yang, Z. Wang, J. Zhang, C. Huang, and Q. Zhang. Wearables can afford: Light-weight indoor positioning with visible light. MobiSys '15. ACM, 2015.

# Demo: Mobile Crowdsensing of Road Surface Roughness

Giacomo Alessandroni, Alessandro Bogliolo, Alberto Carini, Saverio Delpriori
Valerio Freschi, Lorenz Klopfenstein, Emanuele Lattanzi
Gioele Luchetti, Brendan Paolini, Andrea Seraghiti
DiSBeF - University of Urbino
info@smartroadsense.it

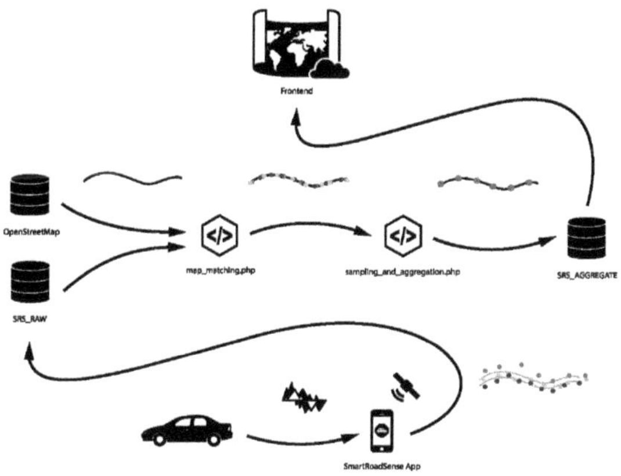


**Figure 1: System overview.**

**Figure 2: Road roughness map.**

The roughness of the road surface affects driving safety and comfort. Having complete and up to date information on the state of the road network is essential for maintenance planning, but it entails time consuming and costly monitoring activities. As a matter of fact, maintenance interventions are mainly based on the results of case by case inspections prompted by drivers' reports. Moreover, qualitative observations are seldom supported by objective measures, making it difficult for administrators to collect data providing a clear perception of the actual priorities.

Recent studies have shown that it is possible to exploit the triaxial accelerometers with which smartphones are equipped to obtain a sound indicator of road surface roughness [1, 2]. A crowdsensing system, called SmartRoadSense [3], has been developed to allow any driver to contribute with his/her smartphone in monitoring the status of the roads he/she travels by car.

As shown in Fig. 1, Smartroadsense is composed of: a mobile application, a cloud-based backend, and a web portal. The application runs in background on any car-mounted Android smartphone, reads the accelerometer data at a frequency of 100Hz, and computes roughness values once per second. All the values are associated with GPS coordinates and opportunistically sent to the server as soon as a suitable data connection is available. Traces are processed in cloud to compensate GPS inaccuracy and to aggregate data provided by different users. OpenStreetMap is used for map matching and aggregation, performed every 6 hours. Aggregated roughness estimates are then made publicly available online and displayed in color-scale on interactive maps (Fig. 2).

The demo shows the entire system at work, allowing the audience to directly install and test the app on their smartphones and to follow the processing steps by looking inside databases and software components. The main purpose of the demo is to highlight the distributed and collaborative nature of SmartRoadSense, which handles a large quantity of data in real time exploiting mobile terminals and cloud-based resources.

Demo trailer at http://smartroadsense.it/demo/.


*MobiSys'15*, May 18–22, 2015, Florence, Italy.
ACM 978-1-4503-3494-5/15/05.
http://dx.doi.org/10.1145/2742647.2745925.

## 1. REFERENCES

[1] G. Alessandroni et al. SmartRoadSense: Collaborative Road Surface Condition Monitoring. In *Proc. of UBICOMM-2014*. IARIA, 2014.

[2] V. Freschi et al. Geospatial Data Aggregation and Reduction in Vehicular Sensing Applications: the Case of Road Surface Monitoring. In *Proc. of ICCVE-2014*. IEEE, 2014.

[3] SmartRoadSense. http://smartroadsense.it/. 2015.

# Demo: D2D Rescue of Overloaded Cellular Channels

Farid Benbadis*, Filippo Rebecchi*†, Florian Cosnier*, Matteo Sammarco†,
Marcelo Dias de Amorim†, and Vania Conan*

*Thales Communications and Security, †LIP6/CNRS – UPMC Sorbonne Universités

## 1. CONTEXT AND MOTIVATION

Mobile data traffic is set to triple in three years from now according to Cisco. This trend is a real challenge for operators since wireless capacity is bounded.

To boost network capacity further, operators think about paradigm-shifting solutions to relieve their infrastructures. Recently, *data offloading* received increasing attention from the research community. Operators may leverage unused bandwidth across different technologies to shift part of the traffic onto less critical infrastructure (e.g., through Wi-Fi access points). In a further evolution, they can also benefit from the widespread diffusion of smart mobile devices with multiple communication interfaces. Users become the heart of the offloading strategy by employing multi-hop opportunistic communications to improve content dissemination, while reducing the load on the wireless infrastructure.

We propose an architecture that takes advantage of the latest advances in opportunistic networking to achieve efficient traffic offloading. In this approach, terminals are under continuous control of the operator – the cellular infrastructure serves as a control channel to track data dissemination. The demonstration builds on DROiD [2] as injection strategy, and Epics [1] to distribute data opportunistically.

## 2. DEMONSTRATION SETUP

In the demonstration, we want to distribute multimedia content (e.g., photos, videos, or podcasts) to a multitude of subscribers, saving the maximum amount of cellular data. We employ a laptop, hosting the main offloading blocks and the administration interface (Fig.1(a)). Each subscriber is equipped with Android-based terminal capable of both HSPA and ad hoc communications (Fig.1(b)). Initially, only a few *seed* users receive the content on the cellular channel. Seeds are in charge of propagating the content opportunistically. Whenever a subscriber receives the content, on either the ad hoc or the cellular interface, it acknowledges the reception to the offloading manager via the cellular network. Periodical estimation of the infection ratio may trigger the offloading manager to re-inject additional copies of the content so to boost the diffusion. When the maximum delay allowed for content dissemination is about to expire, the system pushes content to all the uninfected subscribers through the cellular infrastructure, assuring reception delays.



*MobiSys'15,* May 18–22, 2015, Florence, Italy.
ACM 978-1-4503-3494-5/15/05.
http://dx.doi.org/10.1145/2742647.2745920.

(a) Management UI (b) Mobile UI

**Figure 1: Offloading demo.**

## 3. OFFLOADING ARCHITECTURE

The offloading architecture should be integrated by operators inside their access network (e.g., at eNB or EPC level). In the demonstration, these functionalities are implemented on commodity hardware (laptop) that interfaces with the cellular network. We assume that the operator has the content to be distributed, the list of requesters, and their respective SLA (delay-tolerance, billing). The system is composed of the following blocks:

**Content tracker:** The dissemination evolution is constantly monitored using the acknowledgments from UEs.

**Dissemination strategy:** It determines which injection strategy to apply. It works in conjunction with the *content tracker*, adapting the injection strategy to the dissemination evolution. DROiD may decide to re-inject additional copies if content distribution evolves below expectations.

**User equipment (UE):** Opportunistic dissemination relies on Epics [1]. Epics splits large content into smaller chunks that are independently exchanged upon encounter with other nodes following a prevalence schema. Epics exploits two additional subcomponents: (i) a connectivity layer that manages the ad hoc interface; (ii) a neighborhood manager that regularly broadcasts UDP beacons to announce its presence to neighbors.

**Acknowledgments.** This work is supported by the FP7-MOTO project under grant no. 317959.

## 4. REFERENCES

[1] N. Belblidia, M. Sammarco, L. Costa, and M. Dias de Amorim. Epics: Fair opportunistic multi-content dissemination. *IEEE Trans. on Mob. Comp.*

[2] F. Rebecchi, M. D. de Amorim, and V. Conan. DROiD: Adapting to individual mobility pays off in mobile data offloading. In *IFIP Networking*, 2014.

# Demo: Irides: Attaining Quality, Responsiveness and Mobility for Virtual Reality Head-mounted Displays

Yury Degtyarev
St. Petersburg Polytechnic University
St. Petersburg, Russia

Eduardo Cuervo
Microsoft Research
Redmond, WA, USA

David Chu
Microsoft Research
Redmond, WA, USA

## 1. INTRODUCTION

Immersive virtual reality has long been an aspiration of many. Recent advances in wearable high resolution *head-mounted displays* (HMDs) — as embodied by Facebook's *Oculus Rift*, Sony's *Morpheus*, Samsung's *Gear VR*, Google's *Cardboard* and others — have stoked the imaginations of a new generation of VR users.

For a truly immersive VR experience, three properties are essential: *quality*, *responsiveness* and *mobility*. By quality, we mean that realistic and life-like visual portrayals in a virtual environment heighten our sense of immersion. By responsiveness, we mean that any motion, especially of the head, must be reflected as quickly as possible in visual feedback because ocular proprioception is tightly synchronized. By mobility, we mean that we ought to be able to move untethered in physical space, free to explore our virtual world. However, HMDs face a fundamental challenge in seeking to simultaneously provide quality, responsiveness and mobility; choosing any two rules out the third.

In this work, we present *Irides*, a stereo HMD system that simultaneously attains quality, responsiveness and mobility. Irides achieves this by offloading rendering work to a (possibly WAN) high-end GPU. The HMD client is mobile and only requires a wireless network connection, yet receives high quality and responsive visuals. Irides leverages prior work to overcome WAN latencies [2]. It employs speculative execution on the server, and compensates for misspeculation on the client.

However, a straightforward application of speculative execution for stereo HMDs is prohibitive because of the 2× increase in server, client and network bandwidth costs. Therefore, we introduce two techniques to reduce these costs as shown in Figure 1. The first technique, *interleaved stereo*, generates a stereo video stream with only a mono video stream's worth of work. Interleaved stereo uses image-based rendering (IBR), a way to warp a 2D image with depth information to a novel view. Synthesizing a stereo video from a mono source can introduce severe artifacts. We introduce novel "hole-filling" mechanisms that eliminate artifacts.

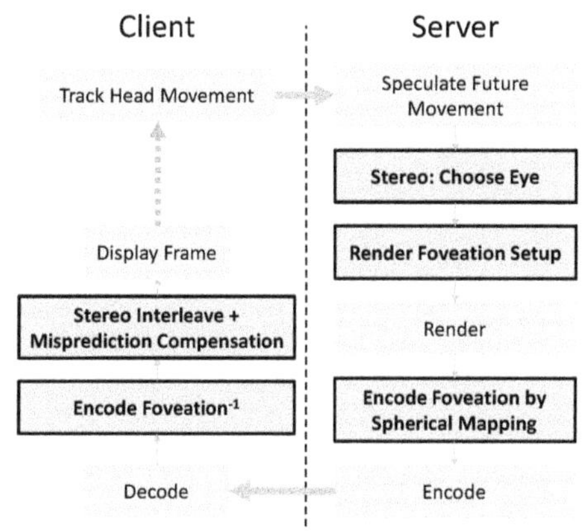


Figure 1: The Irides Architecture

The second technique, *likelihood-based foveation*, reallocates speculative pixels to areas where the user is likely to look. Specifically, we derive a novel sphere-based representation which not only is able to provide the desired client resolution for the maximum likelihood view and views near it, but is also able to gracefully degrade resolution for less likely views. As a result, we achieve high quality in the common case, and save server, client and bandwidth costs.

The Irides prototype is built atop Doom 3 [1], a commercially successful twitch-based first person video game. We demonstrate the benefits of Irides through a series of quantitative performance benchmarks and qualitative visual comparisons. Our demo asks participants to play Doom 3 with the Rift on Irides. There they can experience how Irides can offer significant rendering performance benefits and bandwidth savings to virtual reality applications. Our demo shows: (1) interleaving, increasing the rendering throughput by up to 30%; (2) and likelihood-based foveation, Irides improving framerate by 10% while improving the visual quality of the image shown to the user; (3) both techniques together reducing the bandwidth consumption by up to 40% by only requiring the information of one interleaved eye to be encoded per frame sent.


*MobiSys'15,* May 18–22, 2015, Florence, Italy.
ACM 978-1-4503-3494-5/15/05.
http://dx.doi.org/10.1145/2742647.2745923 .

## 2. REFERENCES

[1] IDSoftware. Doom 3, 2004. `http://www.idsoftware.com/games/doom`.

[2] K. Lee, D. Chu, E. Cuervo, J. Kopf, Y. Degtyarev, S. Grizan, A. Wolman, and J. Flinn. Outatime: Using speculation to enable low-latency continuous interaction for cloud gaming. In *MobiSys*, 2015.

# Demo: Using Wearables to Learn from Human Dynamics

Sébastien Faye, Raphael Frank
Interdisciplinary Centre for Security, Reliability and Trust; University of Luxembourg
4 rue Alphonse Weicker, L-2721 Luxembourg
sebastien.faye@uni.lu, raphael.frank@uni.lu

## Abstract

Recent technological advances have allowed the development of miniaturized sensors and the emergence of a wide range of connected objects. Whether it's smartphones or in the broader sense wearables, the diversity of these devices and their accessibility opens up new fields for applications in the computer sciences [2,3]. Smartwatches, which are experiencing a boom on the market, will be integral to the research that will shape the Internet in the years to come, namely big data, sensing systems and human behavior. Our demonstration falls within this context and aims to demonstrate the potential of these emerging technologies to respond to problems and to way of thinking introduced by industry and the scientific community, which are generally limited to smartphone sensing frameworks [1]. Further, we plan to present our research platform, SWIPE, which is dedicated to collecting, studying and learning about human dynamics by means of an ecosystem of wearables. A short presentation video is available online at `http://swipe.sfaye.com/mobisys15/`.

## SWIPE architecture

In summary, the SWIPE architecture is based on three fundamental elements described below.

(1) Firstly, the sensing system itself. On the one hand, a smartwatch worn on the user's wrist tracks his direct activity and health indicators, which are mainly provided by a built-in heart rate sensor and a 9-axis accelerometer. On the other hand, a smartphone in the user's pocket determines the context in which he is located by recording, for example, sound data or GPS localisation. Social interaction is determined via technologies such as Bluetooth Low Energy, which normally connect these two devices.

(2) Subsequently, the smartphone serves as a link to a pool of servers responsible for data storage and access management to protect the users' privacy. This Big Data aspect introduces issues related to code offloading and data management, finding a compromise between sample rate, rate of transmission and the consumption of energy.

(3) Finally, when correlated, data collected from a user can turn up some surprising findings. For example, apart from recording the user's heart rate, motion recognition can also lead to conclusions about his lifestyle or even his personality. Image 1 gives an example of data collected on our platform from one of the volunteers.


*MobiSys'15*, May 18–22, 2015, Florence, Italy.
ACM 978-1-4503-3494-5/15/05.
http://dx.doi.org/10.1145/2742647.2745932.

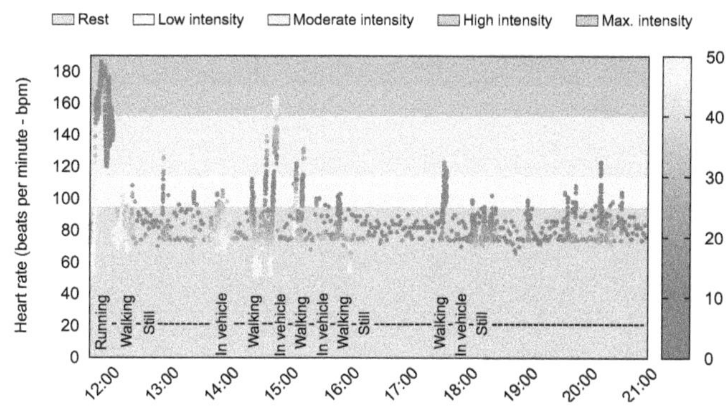


**Figure 1: Heart rate profile and detected activities (the color gradient indicates the difference in bpm between the heart rate measured with the smartwatch and the one measured with a heart rate belt).**

## Demonstration

Our demonstration is divided in two parts.

In the first, we will present the platform to the audience. By the means of a web interface we will visualize aggregated data that we have collected through our experiments on a few dozen users with whom we have an agreement, and derive non-obvious correlations. By presenting the platform architecture and the dataset, we want to demonstrate that the potential of these devices is not limited to specific applications (e.g., sport or health). We also want to highlight issues of energy, reliability and data management that we encountered during our experiments.

In the second part, we will equip a volunteer from the audience with a smartphone (LG Nexus 5) and a smartwatch (Samsung Gear Live) and show how our platform is able to retrieve and visualize data in real time. Further, we will ask the volunteer to perform several basic activities in order to calculate and present a quick assessment of his profile, broken down into several objectives presented as a score. Among them, a stress indicator based on the sensors built into the watch, and on the environmental sensors in the phone.

## References

[1] N. D. Lane, E. Miluzzo, H. Lu, D. Peebles, T. Choudhury, and A. T. Campbell. A survey of mobile phone sensing. *Communications Magazine, IEEE*, 48(9):140–150, 2010.

[2] J. Ranck. The wearable computing market: a global analysis, 2014.

[3] S. Tilenius. Will an app a day keep the doctor away? the coming health revolution cio central guest, 2013.

# Demo: Breathing-Based Text Input for Mobile Phones

Jackson Feijó Filho
Nokia Technology Institute
Av. Torquato Tapajós, 7200 - Col. Terra Nova. Manaus-AM Brasil
69093-415
+55 92 8134 0134
jackson.feijo@indt.org.br

Thiago Valle
Nokia Technology Institute
Av. Torquato Tapajós, 7200 - Col. Terra Nova. Manaus-AM Brasil
69093-415
+55 92 8109 0999
thiago.valle@indt.org.br

Wilson Prata
PUC - RJ
Av. Torquato Tapajós, 7200 - Col. Terra Nova. Manaus-AM Brasil
69093-415
+55 92 8805 1071
wilson.prata@indt.org.br

Assistive solutions have been investigated and established as an important field in human–computer interaction. Several forms of assistance have been produced for technology consumers with particular disabilities that lessen their capabilities to achieve inputting text on some devices. Several alternative interfaces for users with motor disabilities have been developed and reported. Frequently, these solutions include procedures that implement speech recognition methods, eye-trackers and sip-and-puff controllers. Speech recognition software is well accepted to be useful as textual input aid, while additional devices are usually employed as pointing devices, allowing the control of e.g. the mouse pointer [1].

A functional prototype application was built to perform user research in order to support the argument of this work. The mobile application hereby presented is able to provide a way for users to perform text input in a hands-free, speech-free manner. This substitute approach is software based, meaning it will not require extra hardware to function. It stands for a discreet and private solution, as it implies minimum representation of whatever is being written, to the periphery auditory.

This paper emphasizes the progress of exploring a puffing activated keyboard, compared to the work in [3] which proposes the use of a software-based, dynamically structured keyboard, with a cursor that highlight one letter at a time, enabling the user to "puff" when the desired letter is highlighted.

Several usability and performance tests were conducted after the implementation of [3]. The experiments were reproduced with the new software, proving the enhancements to be efficient and more user-friendly.

Usability studies were conducted in the context of a usability laboratory, capturing reactions of the test subjects using the present solution. The experiment described in detail in [3] was performed in eight rounds, over the period of four months. Each round consisted in recruiting at least six distinct subjects, being three disabled and three able-bodied. The disability on the test subjects made them unable to handle a mobile device manually. Two environments were setup in each round. One was consistently silent and the other had loud music and a playback of a large crowd having conversations.

Some of the subjects reported having difficulties when using the linear keyboard in [3]. They reported to frequently miss the cursor when it was positioned in the chosen letter, causing them the need to wait for it to go around the whole keyboard to have another chance of selecting the right character.

Ambient noise and microphone gain visual feedback also lacked in [3]. Subjects reported to be difficult to remember the strength they should puff – reducing memorability and learnability of the interface. Subjects have informed that it was difficult to avoid false-positives in noisy spaces and declared that a better visual feedback of sound levels would improve overall usability.

To enhance keyboard sequence understanding and provide visual feedback from the sound level of ambient noise and puff strength, we implemented a different user interface, in a form a grid (instead of the linear structure) over the amplified audio wave form. The cursor begins moving horizontally. When the system detects one puff, the cursor starts to move vertically, reaching the selected letters considerably faster.

Another very significant advance from [3] is the audio signal processing of the 'puffs'. As in [3] only sound level is being measured, using Fourier Transform has improved the "false position puff" scenario, frequently observed in loud/noisy spaces. The occurrence of false positives where near zero in several rounds of tests. Even under these favorable circumstances, additional background noise handling algorithm adapts sound level peak threshold and microphone gain to reduce false positives and increase overall performance.

The final average typing rates for the current solution with this study group and given text was 8.2 words per minute. Compare to [3] making 5.8, [2] where a Morse code typist makes 12.6 and a Mouth stick (hardware based) input solution gives 7.88 words per minute. The WPM was measured through logging character/timestamp in a text file on the phone and performing post-test calculation.


*MobiSys'15,* May 18–22, 2015, Florence, Italy.
ACM 978-1-4503-3494-5/15/05.
http://dx.doi.org/10.1145/2742647.2745917

## 1. REFERENCES

[1] Sibert L.E., Jacob R.J.K., Evaluation of eye gaze interaction. Proceedings of CHI 2000 Conference on Human Factors in Computing Systems. ACM Press (2000), The Hague, pp 281–288.

[2] Simon Levine, John Gauger, Lisa Bowersand Karen Khan,comparison of Mouthstick and Morse code text inputs. Augmentative and Alternative Communication 1986, Vol. 2, No. 2 , Pages 51-55 (1986)

[3] Feijó Filho, J., Valle, Thiago, and Wilson Prata. "Explorations on breathing based text input for mobile devices." In Proceedings of the 16th international ACM SIGACCESS conference on Computers & accessibility, pp. 345-346. ACM, 2014.

# Demo: Continuous Emotional Status in Mobile-Mediated Communications


Jackson Feijó Filho
Nokia Technology Institute
Rod. Torquato Tapajós, 7200,
Manaus, Brazil
jackson.feijo@indt.org.br

Wilson Prata
Nokia Technology Institute
Rod. Torquato Tapajós, 7200,
Manaus, Brazil
wilson.prata@indt.org.br

Thiago Valle
Nokia Technology Institute
Rod. Torquato Tapajós, 7200,
Manaus, Brazil
thiago.valle@indt.org.br


In everyday social interactions, humans depend on visual cues to fully communicate, and in an online text chatting scenario, the lack of sight interferes with the quality of such interactions. Since crucial nonverbal communication is comprised of facial gestures and expressions, text chat users are at a disadvantage when engaging in interpersonal communication.

Our research attempts to intervene in mobile online text chat by detecting and displaying users' emotional reactions during conversations. As an evolution of [2], we enhance the conveying of emotions in online text chat not only by inserting emotional reaction statements (e.g. "John smiles") to the conversation thread, but also continuously informing the emotional status of the chat partner. This novel feature is a result of tests and interviews in the context of a usability laboratory.

Primarily, we implemented the chat application itself to be integrated with the emotion detection feature. It was developed using the XMPP protocol [1] as not only it is defined in open standards but also widely deployed across the Internet.

In our system, the user chats from the mobile, using a mobile application. As soon as a conversation starts, the face images start being collected and sent to a server, which performs the image processing. The server sends back a JSON feed, which is parsed to retrieve two categories of emotional status. The first is the facial instant reaction, which can be a smile or the user looking away from the screen. The second is a more continuous representation of five different emotions: happiness, anger, confusion, calm and surprised.

For the relaying of the first category, a text phrase is inserted to the conversation thread, as shown in Figure 1. For the continuous emotion representation, the software compares the status of the five different emotions and display the one with the higher percentage.

Throughout the experiments and interviews we observed that people perceived their partners' reactions as an accomplishment or a reward to what they just posted. This has included some sort of pressure in the engagement of the conversation, in comparison to plain text chat. In some cases, subjects have mentioned that their partners inserted more humorous messages then usual to the dialogue, in order to receive the automatically detected smiles.



*MobiSys'15,* May 18–22, 2015, Florence, Italy.
ACM 978-1-4503-3494-5/15/05.
http://dx.doi.org/10.1145/2742647.2745919

**Figure 1. Screenshot of the application**

From the interviews, which were conducted individually and in groups, we were able to observe an overall rise of the sense of connection that chat partners experienced with one another.

## REFERENCES


[1] XMPP Standards Foundation, http://www.xmpp.org

[2] Feijó Filho, Jackson, Thiago Valle, and Wilson Prata. "Non-verbal communications in text chat: emotion-enhanced chat." Proceedings of the 16th international conference on Human-computer interaction with mobile devices & services. ACM, 2014.

# Demo: Mobile Software Emotions Logging: Towards an Automatic Usability Evaluation

Jackson Feijó Filho
Nokia Technology Institute
Rod. Torquato Tapajós, 7200,
Manaus, Brazil
jackson.feijo@indt.org.br

Wilson Prata
Nokia Technology Institute
Rod. Torquato Tapajós, 7200,
Manaus, Brazil
wilson.prata@indt.org.br

Thiago Valle
Nokia Technology Institute
Rod. Torquato Tapajós, 7200,
Manaus, Brazil
thiago.valle@indt.org.br

The evaluation of usability in mobile software provides valuable measures about the quality of these applications, which assists designers and developers in identifying opportunities of improvement. But analyzing the usability of mobile user interfaces can be a tiresome assignment. It might be extensive and require expert evaluation techniques such as cognitive walkthroughs or heuristic evaluations, not to mention often expensive usability lab equipment.

Emotional feedback is a significant aspect in user experience that chronically goes unmeasured in several user-centered design projects. [1] Human emotions are indispensable to understanding users, as these can enable the increase of persistence and strengthen interest in a subject or task. The examination of this affective aspect through well-known empirical user-centered design methods supports software creators in motivating users while using their systems. The gathering of emotional cues will provide an additional layer of analysis for collecting user data, augmenting common evaluation methods and resulting in a more accurate understanding of the user's experience.

Additionally, it is important to mention the value of automated tests, while being performed through and for mobile devices. In contrast to desktop, mobile applications have to compete with external stimuli, as users might not be sitting in front of a screen for considerable amounts of time. Due to the nature of mobility, in a real-world context, users might be walking on the street or sitting on a bus when interacting with mobile software [2].

Some methodologies have been reported about gathering affective data without asking the users what and how they feel. Physiological and behavioral signals such as body worn accelerometers, rubber and fabric electrodes can be measured in a controlled environment [3]. It is also feasible to evaluate users' eye gaze and collect electrophysiological signals, blood volume, pulse, heart rate, respiration and even, facial expressions detection software [1]. Most of these methods face the limitations of being intrusive, expensive, require specific expertise and additional evaluation time.


*MobiSys'15,* May 18–22, 2015, Florence, Italy.
ACM 978-1-4503-3494-5/15/05.
http://dx.doi.org/10.1145/2742647.2745926

Our proposal supplements the traditional methods of software usability evaluation by monitoring users' spontaneous facial expressions automatically as a method to identify the moment of occurrence of adverse and positive events. Identifying those moments and systematically linking them to the context of interaction, is clearly an advance towards overcoming design flaws and enhancing interfaces' strengths.

This work will efficiently, easily and cost-effectively assess the users' affective state by evaluating their expressive reactions during an interface evaluation process. These reactions are collected using the front camera on mobile devices and the analysis of five different emotions - happiness, surprise, anger, confusion and calmness – and two "emotional events" – spontaneous smile and gazing away from screen – are performed through server software. The validation of our approach include post-test questionnaires with test subjects. This automated test generates a graphical log report, timing a) user events e.g. tap, drag; b) emotions levels e.g. level of happiness, confusion and finally c) emotional events e.g. smiling or looking away from screen.

## REFERENCES

[1] de Lera, Eva, and Muriel Garreta-Domingo. "Ten emotion heuristics: guidelines for assessing the user's affective dimension easily and cost-effectively." 21st British HCI Group Annual pp. 163-166. British Computer Society, 2007.

[2] Oztoprak, A., and Erbug, C. Field versus laboratory usability testing: A first comparison. Tech. rep., Department of Industrial Design, Faculty of Architecture, 2008.

[3] Picard, R. W., and Daily, S.B. Evaluating affective interactions: Alternatives to asking what users feel. Presented at CHI 2005 (Portland, OR, April 2-7, 2005).

# Demo: TouchCom - Creating Real Excalibur Experience with Body Touch Communication

Yawhuei Lam[2], Virag Varga[1,2], Lito Kriara[1], Thomas Gross[2], Stefan Mangold[1]
[1]Disney Research Zurich, Switzerland [2]ETH Zurich, Switzerland
virag@disneyresearch.com

## 1. INTRODUCTION

Body Touch Communication (BTC) has been a research topic for the last two decades. However, certain challenges make it still an unsolved problem. The IEEE 802.15.6-2012 standard describes the physical and link layers of BTC, but important details on how the electrical signal should be transmitted, or how to realize the transmitter and receiver devices are not specified in detail.

Zimmerman et al. [1] use the human body as communication channel in the propagation of an electrical signal. Mazloum [2] reviews the different approaches in the field - including trade offs in data rate, transmission power, operation frequency and transmission distance, and proposes a new prototype and physical layer design.

Our TouchCom project aims to gain thorough understanding of the transmission channel for implementing protocols to support entertainment applications with haptics, human-computer interaction, and networked multihop body-to-body communication. A prototype of one transmitter and one receiver device is used to demonstrate our technology together with a story telling related to a well-known ancient legend.

## 2. DESIGN AND IMPLEMENTATION

The communication model consists of a transmitter device as source, a receiver device as target, and a human body as medium. Our prototype uses capacitive coupling at the human-device interfaces. The transmitter device generates a modulated signal containing arbitrary data. The signal is directed to an insulated signal electrode. Together with an insulated floating ground electrode, they generate a small electric field. If the human body is in close proximity (touch event), the electric field in induced onto it, and the signal passes through the body. The changes in the electric field can be observed by a similarly structured receiver device touched by the body.

For the physical layer design (frequency, filters, amplifiers, modulation) the characteristics of the human body should be considered. We use a 80 kHz baseband signal with differential quadratic phase modulation technique (DQPSK), multiplied by a carrier signal of above 1 MHz. Due to noise induced by the body tissues and neural activity, an amplifier and a band pass filter need to be used.


*MobiSys'15,* May 18–22, 2015, Florence, Italy.
ACM 978-1-4503-3494-5/15/05.
http://dx.doi.org/10.1145/2742647.2745930.

**Figure 1: Concept art © Disney: According to the legend of Excalibur, only *The Chosen One* is able to pull the sword out of the stone.**

## 3. DEMONSTRATION SETUP

In this paper, we introduce an Excalibur application using TouchCom for the entertainment industry. Our setup is the sword in the stone scenario, with a person trying to pull out the sword from the stone. The BTC transmitter device is embedded in a wristband and holds a unique ID. When the transmitter is activated, it generates an appropriate electrical signal containing that ID. The signal is induced into the body and propagates through the metallic sword touched by the person. The BTC receiver device is embedded in the stone. After the signal is received and processed, the ID is extracted. If the ID matches to a predefined value, the controller inside the stone gets a free signal, and activates a mechanical element to release the sword.

## 4. REFERENCES

[1] T. G. Zimmerman, J. R. Smith, J. A. Paradise, D. Allport, and N. Gershenfeld, "Applying Electric Field Sensing to Human-Computer Interfaces," *CHI Human Factors in Computing Systems*, 1995.
[2] N. S. Mazloum, "Body-Coupled Communications - Experimental characterization, channel modeling and physical layer design," *Master Thesis at Chalmers University of Technology and Philips Research*, 2008.

# Demo: Real-Time Screen-Camera Communication Behind Any Scene

Tianxing Li, Chuankai An, Xinran Xiao, Andrew T. Campbell, and Xia Zhou
Department of Computer Science, Dartmouth College, Hanover, NH
{tianxing, chuankai, campbell, xia}@cs.dartmouth.edu xinranxiao@gmail.com

## Categories and Subject Descriptors

C.2.1 [**Network Architecture and Design**]: Wireless communication

## Keywords

Screen-camera link; Visible light communication

## 1. EXTENDED ABSTRACT

Enabling screens and cameras to communicate has been attracting growing interests. The idea is simple: information is encoded into a visual frame shown on a screen, and any camera-equipped device can turn to the screen and immediately fetch the information. Operating on the visible light spectrum band, screen-camera communication is free of electromagnetic interference, offering a promising out-of-band communication alternative for short-range information acquiring. The most popular example is QR code [1], where information (typically a URL) is encoded into a 2D barcode. Recent research endeavors have led to innovative barcode designs to boost data rate or to enhance reliability.

These efforts are exciting, however they commonly require displaying visible coded images, which interfere with the content the screen is playing and create unpleasant viewing experiences. In this work, we seek approaches to enabling unobtrusive screen-camera communication, which allows the screen to concurrently fulfill a dual role: displaying content and communication. Ultimately, we envision a screen-camera communication system that transmits and receives dynamic data in real time, while ensuring communication occurs unobtrusively regardless of the content the screen is displaying — let it be an image, a movie, a video clip, a web page, a game interface, or any other app window. As the user interacts with the screen and switches the content, the communication sustains. Hence, communication is truly realized as an additional functionality for the screen, without placing any constraints on the screen's original functionality (displaying content). Existing designs on unobtrusive screen-camera communication, however, are limited to screen content in a standalone file (e.g., image, video) and fail to support arbitrary content on the screen, which can be generated on the fly with user interactions.


*MobiSys'15,* May 18–22, 2015, Florence, Italy.
ACM 978-1-4503-3494-5/15/05.
http://dx.doi.org/10.1145/2742647.2745929.

In this demo, we demonstrate HiLight [3], the first system that supports real-time, unobtrusive screen-camera communication atop arbitrary screen content using off-the-shelf smart devices. HiLight is built upon a new design paradigm that *decouples* communication and screen content image layers. Our key idea is to create a separate image layer (a black matte, fully transparent by default) dedicated to communication atop all existing content image layers. We encode data into the pixel translucency change at the separate image layer, so that the receiver (camera) can perceive the color intensity change in the composite image and decode data. To control pixel translucency, we leverage the alpha channel [4], a well-known concept in computer graphics. We control the level of pixel translucency change so that it is perceivable only to cameras but not human eyes. Furthermore, by controlling the translucency of each pixel independently, we enable multiple simultaneous transmitter elements on the screen. This creates a MIMO communication channel between screens and cameras, which can further boost data rate or improve transmission reliability.

Our methodology has two key benefits. *First*, since alpha values are blended by GPU, the encoding can be done with 1 ms, critical to support real-time communication atop arbitrary dynamic content. *Second*, by realizing communication at a separate image layer, the system makes unobtrusive communication universally available and truly parallel to the content playing on the screen — no matter it is a static, dynamic, or multi-layer content, and regardless of the frame rate it is playing and the frame resolution. Users can use the screen as it is, while the communication between screen and camera occurs behind the scene in real time, unobtrusively.

We have made a collection of HiLight demo video clips available at [2]. By offering an unobtrusive, flexible, and lightweight communication channel between screens and cameras, HiLight presents opportunities for new HCI and context-aware applications for smart devices. For example, a user wearing smart glasses can acquire additional personalized information from the screen (*e.g.*, TV screen, smartphone, or tablet screen) without affecting the content users are currently viewing. HiLight also provides far-reaching implications for facilitating new security and graphics applications.

## 2. REFERENCES

[1] Automatic identification and data capture techniques - QR code 2005 bar code symbology specification. ISO/IEC 18004:2006.

[2] HiLight demo. `http://dartnets.cs.dartmouth.edu/hilight.`

[3] LI, T., ET AL. Real-time screen-camera communication behind any scene. In *Proc. of MobiSys* (2015).

[4] PORTER, T., AND DUFF, T. Compositing digital images. In *ACM SIGGRAPH Computer Graphics* (1984).

# Demo: Energy Harvesting Using Everyday Objects

Adiyan Mujibiya[1] and Junji Torii[2]
Rakuten Institute of Technology, Rakuten Inc.
4-13-9 Higashi-shinagawa, Shinagawa-ku, Tokyo. Japan
[1]adiyan@acm.org, [2]ts-junji.torii@rakuten.com

## ABSTRACT AND INTRODUCTION

We present an energy harvesting technique that leverages readily available time-varying ambient electric field (EF) as source, and explore the utilization of surrounding everyday objects that are constructed from conductive materials. General concept of our approach is described in Figure 1, and the circuit model is depicted in Figure 2. We showed that by incorporating energy store and release circuitry, we were able to deliver power to a usable level. To thoroughly test the technique, we developed Wireless Logger hardware module and conduct extensive one week-long power harvesting experiment. The result is depicted in Figure 3. We show our ambient electric field profiler tool that checks the electrical properties of an environment. This tool is useful to obtain parameters to know whether our technique is feasible for a given environment. We highlight limitations that encourage us to refine our design, explore other grounding strategies, and implement techniques to extract the maximum harvestable energy in the future iterations of this strategy. We believe that the perpetual issue in Internet-of-Things is electrical power, and this research contributes as a simple, lightweight, thus usability-wise, a powerful solution for this issue.

## Categories and Subject Descriptors

B.m. Hardware: Miscellaneous

## Keywords

Power harvesting; electric field; capacitive reactance; electromagnetic inductance; wireless sensor network; IoT.

## 1. IMPLEMENTATION INSIGHTS

In this demo, we highlight principle of operation and report our prototype's input and output characteristics, showing that our proposed energy harvesting strategy can deliver up to 4.32mJ of energy in average of: 377 seconds when using the metal frame of a cabinet in typical house, 24.25 seconds when using the metal frame of a typical office work desk, and 53.34 seconds when using the same office work desk but with floating ground.

Figure 3 clearly depicts temporal fluctuations in energy harvesting module's capacitor charging time, which was generally faster (i.e., more energy harvested) in office working hours, especially weekdays (Monday to Friday). This was mainly caused by the increasing amount of electric field emitted by electrical appliances such as PCs, monitors, etc. that were turned on during these hours. In contrast, data for non-working hours and weekends (Saturday and Sunday) depict less temporal fluctuations but longer capacitor charging time. Mujibiya proposed a method to detect and classify body motion, gesture, and activity sensing using ambient electric field [1]. While not directly connected with energy harvesting form ambient electric fields, this previous work noted the correlation between human actions and ambient electric fields.


*MobiSys'15,* May 18–22, 2015, Florence, Italy.
ACM 978-1-4503-3494-5/15/05.
*http://dx.doi.org/10.1145/2742647.2745921*

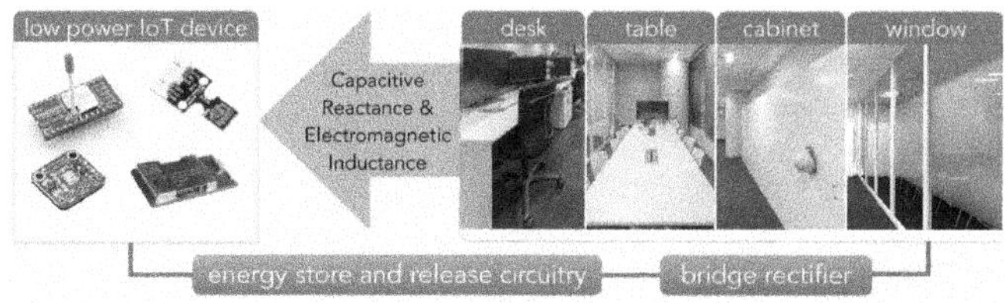


**Figure 1. Concept of energy harvesting strategy for powering low-power Internet-of-Things (IoT) devices, using everyday objects which are configured from conductive material.**

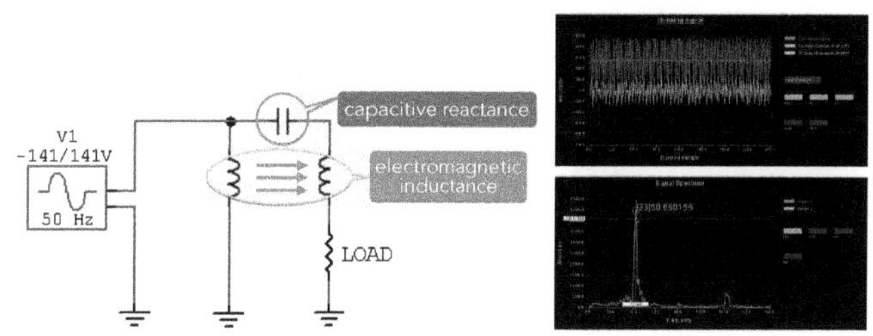


**Figure 2. Left: Circuit model of capacitive and inductive coupling between the everyday objects and the environment. Right: Our ambient electric field profiling platform**

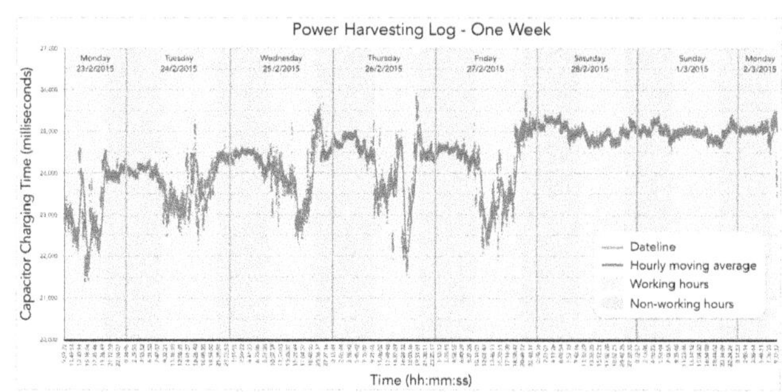


**Figure 3. Power harvesting log for a week-long experiment.**

## 2. DEMO OVERVIEW

In the demo, we show our Wireless Logger device and energy harvesting module in live action: sending sensor data using IEEE802.15.4, which is powered by energy scavenged from the ambient electric field. We also show our EF profiler platform (Figure 2 right) for visualizing real-time ambient electric field parameters. We also conduct poster presentation for discussion.

## 3. REFERENCES

[1] Adiyan Mujibiya and Jun Rekimoto. 2013. Mirage: exploring interaction modalities using off-body static electric field sensing. In *Proc. of UIST'13*. 211-220.

# Demo: NOMAD: An Edge Cloud Platform for Hyper-Responsive Mobile Apps

Andreas Pamboris
ap5309@doc.ic.ac.uk
Imperial College London

Miguel Báguena
mibaal@upvnet.upv.es
Universitat Politècnica de València

Alexander L. Wolf
a.wolf@imperial.ac.uk
Imperial College London

Pietro Manzoni
pmanzoni@disca.upv.es
Universitat Politècnica de València

Peter Pietzuch
prp@doc.ic.ac.uk
Imperial College London

## Categories and Subject Descriptors

C.2.4 [**Distributed Systems**]: Client/server

## Keywords

Edge cloud platform; Low-latency backend services

Fast access to backend services is crucial for many mobile apps. For example, emerging augmented-reality devices such as Google Glass require fast access to powerful servers to achieve seamless interactivity with the real world; and online gaming clients need to communicate in real-time through centralised game services. A major obstacle to achieving this *hyper responsiveness* is the performance of the underlying network that interconnects mobile clients and services. Network effects cannot be anticipated, let alone controlled, due to the unpredictability of wide-area networks and the fact that users roam between different networks.

Over time, organisations have gone to great lengths to reduce access latency to backend services by moving them "closer" to end users. In 2010, Google spent $1.9 billion on a data centre in New York, despite real estate prices being amongst the highest in the world, to gain direct access to local and global networks [5]. Similarly, cloud service providers such as Amazon AWS have rolled out new infrastructure in edge locations. Proactive measures against high network latencies, however, are limited by the fact that network proximity in a mobile setting is unknown a priori.

To enable hyper-responsive mobile apps, Balan et al. [1] first proposed *cyber-foraging*, i.e. the use of remote resources to augment smartphone capabilities. This led to proposals such as Cloudlets [7], which treat smartphones as thin clients served by virtual device clones, and systems such as MAUI [4] and CloneCloud [2], which apply a more fine-grained app partitioning to reduce response times.

In general, the above approaches can only improve application responsiveness to the extent that computation delays dominate performance. It remains a challenge to control the impact of high *network latencies*, especially when users roam between wireless networks of different operators.


*MobiSys'15,* May 18–22, 2015, Florence, Italy.
ACM 978-1-4503-3494-5/15/05.
http://dx.doi.org/10.1145/2742647.2745928.

We propose **NOMAD**, a **distributed edge cloud platform** that decouples services from fixed hosting locations. It enables services to migrate seamlessly between edge locations, thus adapting to changes in network conditions and user roaming on-the-fly. Its main features are:

**1. Network profiling.** Mobile clients continuously profile network latency to all service locations in their environment. The active service site periodically collects all profiling information and decides to migrate a service if it benefits clients collectively by minimising the maximum perceived latency.

**2. Transparent service migration.** NOMAD snapshots the state of the backend service without requiring application modifications [3]. A snapshot includes application memory page files and raw data images that capture IP addresses and routing tables.

**3. Caching mechanism.** To minimise service disruption during migration, NOMAD uses a caching approach in which migration occurs via the clients, and previous state snapshots are cached to avoid retransmitting unchanged backend state.

*Demo:* We demonstrate a NOMAD prototype over an emulated network using the CORE network emulator [6]. The demo shows how NOMAD can support *Cube 2: Sauerbraten*, a first-person shooter game with stringent low latency requirements. A major concern for this game is to provide fair performance amongst multiple clients. NOMAD improves the overall game experience by keeping the lag between clients low, despite changes in network conditions due to user roaming. Due to NOMAD's caching mechanism, the time to migrate a service is also kept low, i.e. in the order of seconds.

**Acknowledgements.** This work was partially supported by EIT ICT Labs as part of the 13130 Multi-Cloud Data Management (MC-Data) activity under the Future Cloud action line.

## References

[1] R. Balan, J. Flinn, et al. The Case for Cyber Foraging. In *SIGOPS*, 2002.

[2] B. Chun, S. Ihm, et al. CloneCloud: Elastic Execution Between Mobile Device and Cloud. In *EuroSys*, 2011.

[3] CRIU. *Checkpoint Restore in Userspace (CRIU)*, 2015. `http://www.criu.org/Main_Page`.

[4] E. Cuervo, A. Balasubramanian, et al. MAUI: Making Smartphones Last Longer with Code Offload. In *MobiSys*, 2010.

[5] Data Center Knowledge. *Google is Buying 111 8th Avenue*, 2013. `http://goo.gl/CRqBEC`.

[6] Networks and Communications Systems Branch. *CORE*, 2015. `http://goo.gl/pXIZsV`.

[7] M. Satyanarayanan, P. Bahl, et al. The Case for VM-based Cloudlets in Mobile Computing. In *PerCom*, 2009.

# Demo: Bringing the Internet of Toys to Life

Virag Varga[1,2], Lito Kriara[1], Vladimir Vukadinovic[1], Thomas Gross[2], Stefan Mangold[1]
[1]Disney Research Zurich, Switzerland [2]ETH Zurich, Switzerland
virag | lito | stefan @disneyresearch.com

The Internet of Things (IoT) will connect not only Zigbee-enabled devices but also Wi-Fi-enabled consumer electronics, given the recent rise of IPv6. We developed a power saving communication protocol for low-complexity IPv6-connected devices that can support multiple applications. We demonstrate here in an entertainment-related application scenario how to use that protocol to bring what we refer to as the Internet of Toys to life (Fig. 1).

We demonstrate a real-time Internet of Toys system using the Multi-Hop Power Saving Mode (MH-PSM) protocol developed for Wi-Fi enabled IPv6-connected devices on the Contiki OS embedded open source platform [1]. MH-PSM enables low-latency ad hoc communication using 802.11 over multiple hops [2]. The software system includes the RRPL dynamic routing [3] and Constrained Application Protocol (CoAP). The hardware platform is based on low-complexity Arduino Due boards.

The system setup includes a gateway, which is an Internet-connected laptop running a CoAP border-router. The toys and gateway create an 802.11 IBSS (ad hoc) network using IPv6. We have implemented an application that enables toys to speak together in coordination (i.e., to engage in a dialog according to a scripted story). The coordination requires signaling between toys. The gateway runs a web server allowing some features of the application to be controlled by a web browser on a phone. The web application creates signaling traffic between the phone and toy(s) which traverses the gateway. The toys can also be monitored and controlled remotely from anywhere in the Internet using CoAP.

Fig. 2 shows experimental results when ten toys are active simultaneously transmitting one packet per second to all the other nodes. Such a setup creates a congested environment, with the topology including up to five-hop routes. Comparing the demo setup with an earlier testbed that used MH-PSM [2] with static routes, we note an increase of the delay due to the routing overhead of RRPL. For similar reasons, the packet delivery ratio is also on average 5% lower in the real-time system compared to an earlier evaluation in a testbed. The real-time application clearly introduces new

**Figure 1: The IoT connectivity enables seamless connectivity between toys and wireless devices such as smartphones.**

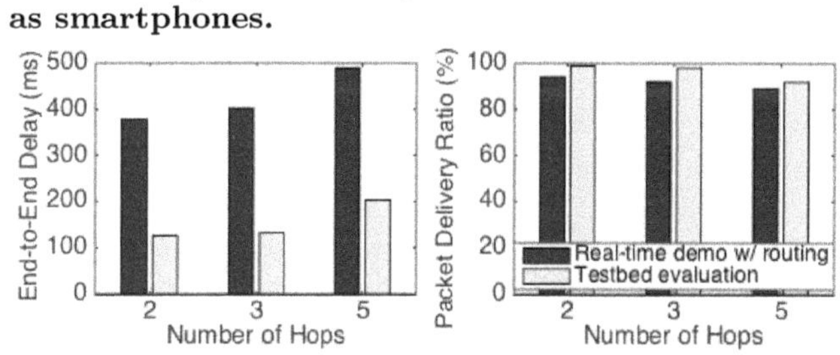


**Figure 2: End-to-end delay and packet delivery ratio for different number of hops.**

challenges that must be addressed compared to an evaluation in a testbed with predetermined routing tables. However, this application scenario can handle the extra work and the real-time system demonstrates that MH-PSM with RRPL and CoAP can efficiently support a wide range of IoT applications, with packet delivery ratio over 90%. Currently, we are working on moving this platform to support more powerful OpenWrt-enabled devices.

In our demonstration, participants can experience the Internet of Toys and use an iPhone (provided) to select a story for the toys to narrate.


*MobiSys'15,* May 18–22, 2015, Florence, Italy.
ACM 978-1-4503-3494-5/15/05.
http://dx.doi.org/10.1145/2742647.2745918.

## 1. REFERENCES

[1] Contiki OS. http://www.contiki-os.org/.
[2] V. Vukadinovic et al. Enhanced Power Saving Mode for Low-latency Communication in Multi-hop 802.11 Networks. *Elsevier Ad Hoc Networks*, Dec. 2014.
[3] C.A. La et al. Link reversal and reactive routing in Low Power and Lossy Networks. In *IEEE PIMRC*, 2013.

# Demo: Achieving Simultaneous Screen-Human Viewing and Hidden Screen-Camera Communication


Anran Wang[1], Zhuoran Li[2], Gan Fang[2], Chunyi Peng[2], Guobin Shen[3], Bing Zeng[4]

[1]Beihang University, [2] The Ohio State University, [3]Microsoft Research, China;
[4]University of Electronic Science and Technology of China

wangar@act.buaa.edu.cn; {li.5233, fang.254}@osu.edu; chunyi@cse.ohio-state.edu;
jackysh@microsoft.com; eezeng@uestc.edu.cn



## ABSTRACT

We present and demonstrate INFRAME++, a novel system that enables concurrent, dual-mode, full-frame communication for both users and devices. It achieves unobtrusive screen-camera data communication without affecting the primary video-viewing experience for human users. It leverages the capability discrepancy and distinctive features of the human vision system and devices (modern display and camera). We have implemented INFRAME++ as a PC-phone application. Both communication will be realized through multiplexed videos frames which will be displayed on a modern monitor (120FPS) and captured by a smartphone camera for data decoding. In this demonstration (Figure 1), we will show that INFRAME++ can yield normal video-viewing experience for humans, and high-rate data communication for devices (up to 300 kbps). User participation will be welcome in this live demo.


## Categories and Subject Descriptors

C.2.0 [**Computer-Communication Networks**]: General—*Data communications*; H.5.1 [**Information Interface and Presentation**]: Multimedia Information Systems—*Video*; H.5.2 [**Information Interface and Presentation**]: User Interfaces—*Screen design*


## Keywords

Screen-camera communication; Hidden visible communication; Dual-mode visible communication; Full-frame video; InFrame++


## 1. INTRODUCTION

Recent efforts in screen-camera visible communication has exploited the display for data communication. Such practices, albeit convenient, have led to contention between space allocated for user-friendly content (*e.g.*, video, image) and content reserved for devices (*e.g.*, barcodes). This also causes unpleasant visual anti-aesthetics and distractedness. We propose INFRAME++, a novel system that enables concurrent, dual-mode, full-frame communication for both users and devices.

In essence, INFRAME++ leverages the capability discrepancy and distinctive features of the human vision system and devices

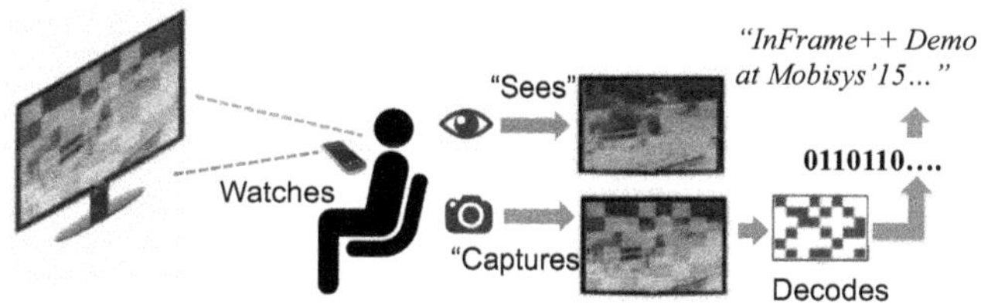


**Figure 1: A typical use scenario of INFRAME++.**

(display and camera), *e.g.*, screens can display content faster than human eyes perceive; cameras have shutter but human eyes do not, etc.. The key idea in INFRAME++ is to employ *Spatio-temporal complementary frame (STCF)*. Data are embedded into STCFs which consist of complementary pixels over consecutive frames and adopts spatially complementary patterns. When the resulting data frames are multiplexed with the original video frames under the superior display frame rate, human eyes can only perceive the average pixel values (thus data imperceptible) while the camera captures the artifacts to retrieve information bits. To further enhance unobtrusive viewing experience and data communication throughput, we propose and develop the following techniques in INFRAME++. We adopt *smoothing transitional frames* to alleviate flickers caused by STCF transitions and propose a novel *CDMA-like modulation* to boost the throughput. To handle the impact of primary video on screen-to-camera communication, we propose a hierarchical data frame structure and fast and accurate border localization. More technical details can be found in our paper [1].

## 2. DEMONSTRATION

In this demo, we will show the rationale, operations and performance of INFRAME++ (Figure 1). We will place a 23-inch LCD display which supports 120FPS frame rate as our sender. It is connected to a laptop, on which a user can select the video source and data source respectively. The video source can be a pure color, a static image, or an arbitrary video. The data source can be an a text file, or a randomly generated data stream. In the other side, we use a smartphone to capture the displayed multiplexed video and then decode the embedded data. We will show two settings. First, we show side-by-side comparison of original videos and multiplexed videos to illustrate that INFRAME++ ensures normal video-viewing experience. We then use one full-screen mode to play the multiplexed frames and decode the data bits embedded by INFRAME++.



*MobiSys'15*, May 18–22, 2015, Florence, Italy.
ACM 978-1-4503-3494-5/15/05.
http://dx.doi.org/10.1145/2742647.2745916.


## 3. REFERENCES


[1] W. Anran, L. Zhuoran, P. Chunyi, F. Gan, S. Guobin, and Z. Bing. Inframe++: Achieving simultaneous screen-human viewing and hidden screen-camera communication. In *MobiSys*, 2015.

# DEMO: Lightweight Visible Light Communication for Indoor Positioning

Zeyu Wang[1†], Zhice Yang[1†], Jiansong Zhang[2], Chenyu Huang[3], Qian Zhang[1]
[†]Co-primary Authors [1]CSE, HKUST [2]Microsoft Research Asia, [3]Wuhan University

## ABSTRACT

Visible light positioning (VLP) is an emerging positioning technique that utilizes indoor light sources to broadcast archer locations through visible light communication (VLC). Benefited by the densely deployed light lamps, VLP holds the promise for more accurate positioning accuracy than RF based approaches, and thus enables interesting applications such as retail navigation and shelf-level advertising in supermarkets and shopping malls.

However, we observe that in existing VLP systems, receiving devices are heavily burdened in handling light flickering for VLC. In order to prevent human from being disturbed, the VLC transmitter lamps have to transmit pulses in a high rate (over 1kHz). Since the pulse rate far exceeds the cameras' sampling capability (30fps), receiver design either requires customized light sensor with cumbersome calibration on receiving signal strength [2] or processing high resolution images to leverage rolling shutter effect of the CMOS camera to decode message [1].

The heavy burden on receiving devices motivated us to try getting rid of light flickers. Since human eyes normally can not perceive changes in polarization, the idea is to modulate polarization instead of intensity for communication. In this demo, we demonstrate the VLC system in our VLP design [3] which realizes this idea. It enables lightweight VLC that is even affordable in wearables (Google Glass), without incurring hardware modification or computation off-loading. Moreover, it also makes other types of illuminating light beyond LED light (even sun light) possible to construct communication, therefore eliminates the barrier for deploying future VLC-based applications.

As detailed in the full paper [3], our design was inspired by the liquid crystal display (LCD), from which we borrowed polarizer and liquid crystal. Liquid crystal has the property to change the polarization of bypassing polarized light according to the applied voltage. We use polarizer to polarize illuminating light and leverage liquid crystal to modulate bits through changing the light's polarization. The receiver can thus detect changes in polarization with a polarizing film, through which different polarizations result in different intensities. Since the SNR of such communication channel may significantly vary with the mobility of receiving device, we propose to add a dispersion filter to the transmitter. The dispersion filter can cast different frequency of lights into different polarization directions so that SNR in different receiving directions are evened. With the above techniques, VLC transmitter generates signal in low baud rate and mobile devices can perform VLC through camera directly. The communication is long in distance and lightweight enough for resource-constrained devices since the information is carried in intensity changes rather than certain image patterns in rolling shutter approaches.

In this demo, we will illustrate the prototype implementation of the VLC communication system. We use incandescent lamps as illuminating light sources. The transmitter consists of a polarizing film, a liquid crystal layer, a dispersor and a control board. The receiver is demonstrated in Android smartphone with polarizing film in front of the camera. The following demo scenarios are planed to show our design (the demo space higher than 2.4m is preferred):

(1) Polarization based VLC modulation can solve the flickering problem. The modulated light provides normal illumination. When viewing the modulated light through a polarizing film, people can feel strong intensity changes.

(2) Dispersor and binary color shift keying (BCSK). Transmitter without dispersor results in bad SNR in certain receiving angles. For normal transmitters, color changes can always be observed in different angles.

(3) End-to-end VLC communication system. Smartphones with a polarizing film in front of the camera can receive and show transmitted messages from VLC transmitters.

(4) The VLC method enables accurate indoor positioning. After successfully receiving location beacons from VLC transmitters, smartphone performs location estimation.


*MobiSys'15,* May 18–22, 2015, Florence, Italy.
ACM 978-1-4503-3494-5/15/05.
http://dx.doi.org/10.1145/2742647.2745924.

## Categories and Subject Descriptors

C.3 [**Special-Purpose and Application-Based Systems**]; C.2.1 [**Computer-Communication Networks**]: Network Architecture and Design—*Wireless communication*

## Keywords

Polarization; Visible Light Communication; Pixel; Wearables

## 1. REFERENCES

[1] Y.-S. Kuo, P. Pannuto, K.-J. Hsiao, and P. Dutta. Luxapose: Indoor positioning with mobile phones and visible light. MobiCom '14. ACM, 2014.

[2] L. Li, P. Hu, C. Peng, G. Shen, and F. Zhao. Epsilon: A visible light based positioning system. NSDI '14, 2014.

[3] Z. Yang, Z. Wang, J. Zhang, C. Huang, and Q. Zhang. Wearables can afford: Light-weight indoor positioning with visible light. MobiSys '15. ACM, 2015.

# Demo: Mobilyzer: Mobile Network Measurement Made Easy

Shichang Xu* Ashkan Nikravesh* Hongyi Yao* David R. Choffnes† Z. Morley Mao*
*University of Michigan †Northeastern University

## 1. INTRODUCTION

Mobilyzer [2] is a unified platform for conducting network measurements in mobile environment. It is implemented as an open-source network measurement library for Android to provide a low barrier to adoption for large-scale deployments. It provides app developers with a flexible and easy-to-use suite of standard measurement tools, including ping, traceroute, DNS lookups, HTTP GET, TCP throughput, and UDP burst, as well as application layer and cellular-specific measurements, such as inferring RRC timers [3], measuring Video QoE, and breaking down Web Page Load Time into its constituent dominant components. To the best of our knowledge, we are the first to support crowdsourcing of video streaming QoE and page load time measurements on mobile devices. Measurements can be scheduled either directly from applications using an API provided as a library, or from a cloud-based management service called the *global manager*.

We will demonstrate how it is simple to integrate Mobilyzer into user-developed apps and also illustrate the MobiPerf app as an example of a network measurement app built using Mobilyzer. In addition, we will demonstrate the interface for the global manager, which allows users to schedule measurement tasks on selected devices satisfying specific criteria, using push and pull mechanisms. The front-end also provides users with a real-time map of performance data collected from mobile devices world-wide.

## 2. DEMONSTRATION

In this demo, we will show how app developers and researchers can benefit from using Mobilyzer for better understanding cellular network performance. We will demonstrate how to use the platform and interact with it through the API via an app and our Web interface for the global manager.

- **Development effort:** To demonstrate how easy it is to include library into the apps, we will show how to develop and build a simple Mobilyzer-enabled toy app, where issuing a measurement and retrieving results takes less than 10 lines of code.
- **On-demand measurement:** Audience members will be able to schedule measurements from both the app and our Web interface. We will set up audiences with their own accounts for scheduling measurements on their device using either pull-based or push based mechanisms. In the pull-based approach, devices poll the global manager periodically to report measuerment results and receive a set (possibly empty) of measurement tasks. In the push-based approach, users can push measurement experiments to their device (using the Google Cloud Messaging service) and view the results in real time.
- **Real time map:** We will demonstrate how platform users can push measurements to a subset of active devices displayed on a real-time map, and observe the performance results immediately. This is a useful feature for network operators and developers to understand the current state of their network and their user-perceived network conditions.

Figure 1: Screenshot of the MobiPerf application, and real-time map.

Figure 1 shows an example screenshot from a device running MobiPerf [1], as well as our real-time map showing recent performance measurement data.

## 3. REFERENCES

[1] Mobiperf. http://www.mobiperf.com/.
[2] A. Nikravesh, H. Yao, S. Xu, D. Choffnes, and Z. M. Mao. Mobilyzer: An open platform for controllable mobile network measurements. MobiSys '15.
[3] S. Rosen, H. Luo, Q. A. Chen, Z. M. Mao, J. Hui, A. Drake, and K. Lau. Discovering fine-grained rrc state dynamics and performance impacts in cellular networks. MobiCom '14.


*MobiSys'15*, May 18–22, 2015, Florence, Italy.
ACM 978-1-4503-3494-5/15/05.
http://dx.doi.org/10.1145/2742647.2745927.

# Demo: Turning a Mobile Device into a Mouse in the Air

Sangki Yun, Yi-Chao Chen, Wenguang Mao, Lili Qiu
The University of Texas at Austin
{sangki,yichao,wmao,lili}@cs.utexas.edu

**Motivation:** A mouse is widely popular for controlling the graphic user interface due to its ease of use. Its attraction will soon penetrate well beyond just computers. There already have been mice designed for game consoles and smart TVs. A smart TV allows a user to run popular computer programs and smartphone applications. More and more devices in the future, such as Google Glasses, baby monitors, and new generation of home appliances, will all desire mouse functionalities, which allow users to choose from a wide variety of options and easily click on different parts of the view.

However, a traditional mouse, which requires a flat and smooth surface to operate, cannot satisfy many new usage scenarios. A user wants to interact with the remote device on the move. For example, a speaker wants to freely move around and click on different objects in his slide; a smart TV user wants to watch TV in any part of a room; a Google Glass user wants to query about objects while touring around. Wouldn't it be nice if a user can simply turn his smartphone or smart watch into a mouse by moving it in the air?

**Challenges:** To enable the air mouse capability, device movement should be tracked accurately, within a few centimeters. Existing indoor localization that provides meter-level accuracy cannot achieve this goal. Some smart TV and set-top box manufacturers provide motion control and gesture recognition using inertial sensors, such as accelerometers and gyroscopes. Accelerometers are well known for their significant measurement errors and cannot provide accurate tracking. We also confirm this using our measurement. Gyrosopes achieve better accuracy in tracking rotation. However, a user has to learn to how to rotate in order to control the displacement in a 2-D space. This is not intuitive, and is especially hard for moving in a diagonal direction, which degrades user experience and speed of control. A few recent works track RFID tags in centimeter-level [1, 2], but they require multiple special RFID readers, each with 4 antennas. Using external devices, such as depth sensor (*e.g.*, Kinect) and IR sensor (*e.g.*, Wii), incurs significant additional cost and limits the types of devices that can be controlled.

**Our approach:** In this demo, we will show Accurate Air Mouse (AAMouse) that accurately tracks device movement in real time. It enables any mobile device with a microphone, such as a smart phone and smart watch, to serve as a mouse to control an electronic device with speakers. A unique feature of our approach is that it uses existing hardware in mobile and electronic devices. Figure 1 shows an example of our system, where a mobile device with a microphone serves as a mouse for a smart TV with two speakers. The smart TV emits inaudible acoustic signals, and the mobile device records and feeds it back to the smart TV, which estimates the device position based on the Doppler shift.

**Figure 1: Enabling accurate device tracking using the Doppler effect of the acoustic signal.**

There are some existing work that leverages the Doppler shift for gesture recognition, but tracking is more challenging since gesture recognition only requires matching against one of the training patterns whereas tracking requires accurate positioning of the device. This not only requires accurate estimation of frequency shift, but also translating the frequency shift into a position involves significant additional research issues, such as how to estimate the distance between the speakers, the device's initial device position, and its new position based on the frequency shift.

We address these challenging issues as follow. We first estimate frequency shift and use it to position the device assuming that the distance between the speakers and the device's initial position are both known. Then we develop techniques to quickly calibrate the distance between the speakers using the Doppler shift. To address the device's unknown initial position, we employ particle filter, which generates many particles corresponding to the device's possible positions and filters the particles whose locations are inconsistent with the measured frequency shifts. The device's position is estimated as the centroid of the remaining particles. To further enhance robustness, we transmit signals at multiple frequencies, perform outlier removal, and combine the remaining estimations.

This demo will show our prototype on a smart phone and a laptop. We will let users hold our smart phone to control a cursor on the laptop screen. We will also ask users to trace simple shapes on the screen using the smart phone. Tracking is performed using either our approach or Gyroscope based approach for users to compare the accuracy and ease of use between these two schemes.


*MobiSys'15*, May 18–22, 2015, Florence, Italy.
ACM 978-1-4503-3494-5/15/05.
http://dx.doi.org/10.1145/2742647.2745931.

## 1. REFERENCES

[1] J. Wang, D. Vasisht, and D. Katabi. RF-IDraw: virtual touch screen in the air using RF signals. In *Proc. of ACM SIGCOMM*, 2014.
[2] L. Yang, Y. Chen, X.-Y. Li, C. Xiao, M. Li, and Y. Liu. Tagoram: Real-time tracking of mobile RFID tags to high precision using cots devices. In *Proc. of ACM MobiCom*, 2014.

# Demo: Finger and Hand Gesture Recognition using Smartwatch

Yixin Zhao, Parth H. Pathak, Chao Xu, Prasant Mohapatra
Computer Science Department, University of California, Davis, CA, 95616, USA
Email: {yxzhao, phpathak, haxu, pmohapatra}@ucdavis.edu

**Categories and Subject Descriptors:** C.5.3 [Computer System Implementation]: Microcomputers – portable devices

**Keywords:** Wearables; Gesture Recognition

## 1. INTRODUCTION

There has been a sharp increase in the popularity of smartwatches in last 2-3 years. Apart from the fitness applications, the smartwatch provides rich graphical interface to users that has enabled applications like email, messaging and navigation using the smartwatch. Since most current smartwatches come equipped with accelerometer and gyroscope sensors, they provide a unique opportunity for gesture recognition. It is expected that user's arm movements can be identified using the smartwatch easily, however it is not clear how much of user's hand and finger gestures can be recognized. For example, when user performs a hand gesture such as volume up by rotating hand right, the amount of motion registered with the smartwatch is likely to be very small. Even worse, when the user performs a finger gesture such as zoom-in or zoom-out using fingers and thumb, the movement recorded at the wrist area can be even smaller than hand gestures. If the hand and finger gestures can be recognized using smartwatch, a plethora of applications can be enabled using gesture recognition. For example, user wearing a smartwatch can remotely control nearby television, computer or smartphone, or user can write different characters on a surface to input the text to the smartwatch.

In this work, we will demonstrate the feasibility of finger and hand gesture recognition using a smartwatch. In our recent work [3], we showed that the motion energy recorded in the wrist while doing finger or hand gestures is enough to uniquely identify the gestures. We have identified that different tendons passing through the wrist create a unique signature of wrist movement while doing different gestures. In our implementation, we use various features [2] of motion energy, posture and motion shape to learn and recognize different gestures in real-time. Our gesture recognition system uses both - accelerometer and gyroscope - sensors in the smartwatch for hand and finger gesture recognition. With the use of machine learning classifier (based on Logistic Regression or Decision Tree), our gesture recognition system can classify 27 gestures (13 finger and 14 hand) with overall accuracy of 96%.


*MobiSys'15*, May 18–22, 2015, Florence, Italy.
ACM 978-1-4503-3494-5/15/05.
http://dx.doi.org/10.1145/2742647.2745922 .

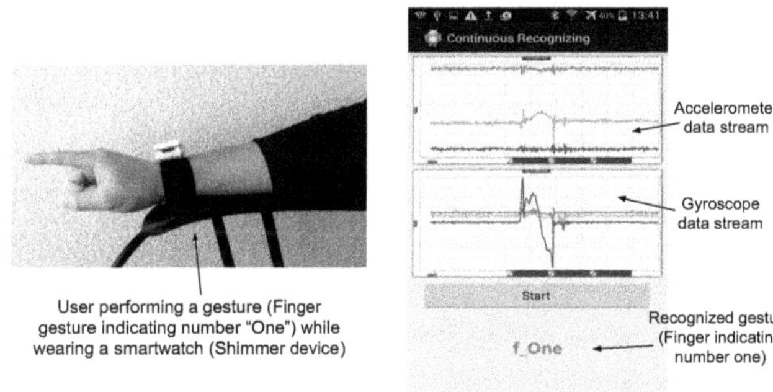


(a) User performing a gesture (b) Real-time gesture recognition on Smartphone

Figure 1: Gesture recognition using smartwatch

## 2. DEMONSTRATION

Our demonstration uses a Shimmer [1] device as the smartwatch as shown in Fig. 1a. The Shimmer device contains 3-axis accelerometer and gyroscope sensors which are sampled at 128 Hz in our implementation. In the demo, when the user performs a hand/finger gesture, the sensor data is transferred to an Android smartphone via Bluetooth. The android smartphone implements the learning and identification modules that can recognize the gesture in real-time as shown in Fig. 1b. The presenter will use a pre-trained model of 27 gestures to demonstrate the real-time gesture recognition performance. These gestures (complete list in [3]) include hand gestures like RotateRight (Volume up), RightOnce (Next) etc. and finger gestures like MouseClick and ThumbsUp. We will allow users to perform their own gestures while wearing the smartwatch and train their own machine learning classifier. They will be then able to perform the same gestures again and observe the gestures being recognized in real-time. The demonstration will also be accompanied with a short video that will show how a trained user performs different gestures and other related working mechanisms of the system.

## 3. REFERENCES

[1] `http://www.shimmersensing.com`.

[2] M. T. Emmanuel. *Using machine learning for real-time activity recognition and estimation of energy expenditure.* PhD thesis, Massachusetts Institute of Technology, 2008.

[3] C. Xu, P. H. Pathak, and P. Mohapatra. Finger-writing with smartwatch: A case for finger and hand gesture recognition using smartwatch. In *Proceedings of the 16th International Workshop on Mobile Computing Systems and Applications*, HotMobile '15, pages 9–14, New York, NY, USA, 2015. ACM.

# Poster: bPart - A Small and Versatile Bluetooth Low Energy Sensor Platform for Mobile Sensing

Matthias Berning, Matthias Budde, Till Riedel, Michael Beigl
Karlsruhe Institute of Technology, TECO
{berning, budde, riedel, beigl}@teco.edu

## 1. BLE FOR MOBILE COMPUTING

This work presents the bPart, a highly integrated autonomous sensor platform for use with mobile phones and devices. It consists of a Bluetooth Low Energy (BLE) radio and several MEMS sensors, all integrated in a volume of less than 1cm³, including the battery. Aside from the wireless transceiver, the bPart features sensors for ambient illumination, 3D-acceleration, temperature and relative humidity. In addition, there is a button and a magnetic switch for binary input and a RGB-LED for user feedback. A secondary LED in the infrared spectrum enables camera-assisted identification and tracking of the node. Runtimes of several years are possible on the included CR2023 lithium coin cell, through the low energy radio, onboard power-conversion and low-power sleep modes. The latter is rated below 2$\mu$W and a single data packet consumes about 75$\mu$Ws. Its low energy consumption makes the bPart suitable for operation with energy harvesting, which we have validated with a 33cm² solar cell in indoor lighting conditions.

Bluetooth Low Energy is an emerging standard for low power communication, which is quickly gaining a widespread adoption due to its close connection to the already familiar Bluetooth protocol. Released as an integral part in version 4.0 of the core specification [1], it uses a second protocol stack in parallel to the classical Bluetooth BR/EDR mode. Both options share the same physical interface and use the same hardware, but instead of high throughput for audio transmission, the BLE stack was optimized thoroughly for very low power consumption [2]. Single mode devices like the bPart only implement this part of the specification, usually embedded in a System-on-Chip. Dual mode devices in contrast, are usually less resource constrained and provide both protocol flavors, like smartphones or tablets. In fact, all major mobile and desktop operating systems support BLE by now and the number of capable device will soon reach billions [3]. This fact distinguishes the technology from other protocols with similar performance characteristics, like ZigBee, and enables the large-scale evaluation of several applications in the mobile computing domain. In the following, we describe some examples that we have already implemented using the bPart platform.

*Tangible interaction* – Due to its compact size, it is easy to integrate the node into small objects as tangible user interfaces. The embedded sensors and actuators provide different opportunities for interaction design. In this way, we were able to create physical controls for applications on the phone.


*MobiSys '15*, May 18–22, 2015, Florence, Italy.
ACM 978-1-4503-3494-5/15/05.
http://dx.doi.org/10.1145/2742647.2745903

**Figure 1. bPart sensor node (2.1cm x 2.1cm x 0.4cm) next to an industrial grade sensor housing.**

*Indoor localization and physical web* – A promising alternative to the connection oriented data transfer is the use of advertisement mode, where the bPart sends periodic radio beacons, encoding either geographical location or semantic information. A nearby mobile client can decode this information and approximate its distance, based on the received signal strength.

*Activity tracking* – The limited processing capabilities of the embedded CPU are complemeted by event-detection subsystems in the onboard sensors. The high-level APIs of BLE provide a persistent key-value store for easy and efficient data transfer.

*Participatory sensing* – The bPart supports easy configuration of both sampling and transmission intervals. In addition, it can store a limited number of sensor values on the board. A mobile user and his phone can fetch these values opportunistically, when he is in range, enabling data-collection and -analysis on the phone, as well as forwarding and aggregation of sensor-data to the backend.

*Condition monitoring* – The size, energy consumption and flexibility allow different industrial applications, where existing equipment is retrofitted with unobtrusive sensors. These are ranging from long-term monitoring, over logistics tracking, to live data acquisition and visualization for maintenance (Fig. 1).

While the bPart itself is a fully integrated solution, the concepts and architecture are easily adaptable to other sets of sensors. Code and schematics are available as open source. We plan to deploy and evaluate the node in long-term indoor and outdoor installations.

## 2. REFERENCES

[1] *Specification of the Bluetooth System, Version: 4.0.* (2010). The Bluetooth SIG. Kirkland, WA, USA

[2] Gomez, C., Oller, J., & Paradells, J. (2012). *Overview and evaluation of Bluetooth Low Energy: An emerging low-power wireless technology*. Sensors, 12(9), 11734-11753.

[3] West, A. *Smartphone, the key for Bluetooth low energy technology*. (accessed on 28 February 2015). http://www.bluetooth.com/Pages/Smartphones.aspx

# Poster: Detecting if a Smartphone is Indoors or Outdoors with Ultrasounds

Igor Bisio, Alessandro Delfino and Fabio Lavagetto
DITEN Dept., University of Genoa, Via Opera Pia 13, 16145, Genoa, Italy
igor.bisio@unige.it, alessandro.delfino@unige.it, fabio.lavagetto@unige.it

## 1. SYSTEM DESCRIPTION

Context information is fundamental for mobile application. A system able to detect if a smartphone is indoors or outdoors can give useful information to upper-level applications, permitting to improve their performance or reduce the computational load and consequently the lifetime of the smartphone battery. For example, GPS provides an accurate location reference in the outdoor environment while it performs poorly inside buildings. The proposed Indoor/Outdoor (IO) detector can provide a useful essential information to a localization application that can check whether the user is outdoors before turning on the GPS interface and decide not to turn it on and use other localization methods if the user is detected indoors. In mobile data services, mobile phones normally observe more WiFi access points (APs) with strong signals inside buildings, whereas it is unlikely to have good WiFi connections in outdoor environments. Therefore, knowing whether the smartphone is indoors or outdoors can help to make smarter decisions regarding whether to perform or not AP scans. Although it is clear that various applications may benefit from accurate and prompt indoor/outdoor information, the research work on indoor/outdoor detection of mobile devices is still lacking. There are mainly two techniques to perform such detection. One is to use GPS and its signal quality as a cue to infer if the user is indoor. This technique is proven to be highly power consuming. Another technique is to leverage the sensors which the smartphone is equipped with. IO detection can be done by exploiting lightweight sensors such as the light sensor, the radio interface and the magnetism sensor [1]. The proposed IO detector is an active system. The phone periodically emits an ultrasonic ping using its in-built speakers and continuously listens for the echoes through its microphone. It is impossible to identify the direction of the echoes being the microphone (as well as the phone speakers) non-directional. The idea is that indoors the number and the intensity of the echoes should be higher than outdoors due to the higher number of obstacles. Translating such an idea into a practical Indoor/Outdoor detector means finding those features that model such behaviour. The proposed method, rather than trying to exactly locate the position of the obstacles, extracts features that are statistically related to number and the amplitude of the echoes. Averaging consecutive pings' echoes we can achieve better accuracy at the expense of longer latency.


*MobiSys'15,* May 18–22, 2015, Florence, Italy.
ACM 978-1-4503-3494-5/15/05.
http://dx.doi.org/10.1145/2742647.2745907.

Table 1: Performance comparison of the IO detectors in [1] and the **proposed ultrasonic detector**.

| Detector | Accuracy | Latency |
|---|---|---|
| Light [1] | 91% | Fast |
| Cellular [1] | 87% | Slow |
| Magnetism [1] | 78% | Slow |
| **Ultrasonic** | **88.9%** | **Fast** |
| **Ultrasonic** | **92.7%** | **Slow** |

## 2. RESULTS AND CONCLUSIONS

A Nexus 5 Android phone has been employed for the tests. Approximately 90 minutes (more than 17600 pings) of ultrasonic recordings have been collected equally divided in two classes: "Indoor" and "Outdoor". The recordings have been collected either in the case the phone was laying on a table and in the case the phone was held by a walking or stationary user. A Naive Bayes classifier is used because of its simplicity and intuitiveness. It is very unlikely to overfit and represents a fair baseline. In [1] three different IO detectors, leveraging three different sensors, are presented. The first uses the light sensor exploiting the differences in indoor and outdoor light patterns; the second detects the attenuation on the cellular signal strength due to obstacles such as buildings walls; the third exploits the disturbance of the magnetic field inside or in the vicinity of buildings. Table 1 shows a performance comparison of IO detectors: it reports the accuracy and the latency of the detectors presented in [1] and of the proposed ultrasonic IO detector. In [1] the time required by the Cellular- and Magnetism-based detectors to retrieve an answer is slow (up to 10 s), while the Light-based detector is faster (less than 1 s). Under low latency constraints the proposed ultrasonic detector has an accuracy a little lower than the light detector which is the detector that gives the best performance in [1]. It is important to notice that light sensor performances depend on the time of the day and on the weather while the ultrasonic detector does not have such limitation. Without the low latency constraint the ultrasonic detector has better accuracy with respect to the others.

## 3. REFERENCES

[1] M. Li, P. Zhou, Y. Zheng, Z. Li, and G. Shen. Iodetector: A generic service for indoor/outdoor detection. *ACM Trans. Sen. Netw.*, 11(2):28:1–28:29, Dec. 2014.

# Poster: Swarming Drones Can Connect You to the Network

Albert Y. Chung, Jongtack Jung, Kangho Kim, Hyung Kyu Lee, Jiyeon Lee,
Suk Kyu Lee, Seungho Yoo, and Hwangnam Kim
School of Electrical Engineering, Korea University
Seoul, Rep. of Korea
{aychung, skylover89, mybalam2k, schk00, jiyeon524, sklee25, pen0423, hnkim}@korea.ac.kr

## Categories and Subject Descriptors

C.2.1 [**Network Architecture and Design**]: Wireless communication; C.5 [**Computer System Implementation**]: Miscellaneous; H.4 [**Information Systems Applications**]: Miscellaneous

## General Terms

Design, Implementation, Experimentation, Performance

## Keywords

Aerial network infrastructure; UAV; Multirotor

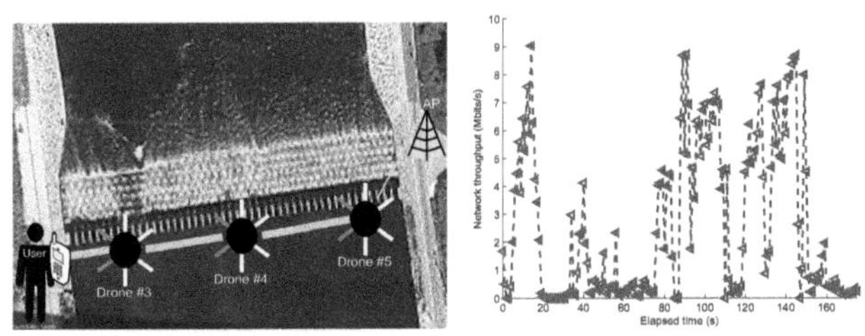


(a) Experimental setting (b) Network throughput

**Figure 1: Experimental setting and a preliminary result.**

## 1. INTRODUCTION

With the rise of the mobile device and the Internet of Things (IoT), establishing network connections is crucial nowadays. Although the demand for network connections and more bandwidth is continuously increasing, there are still areas where the network infrastructure is not deployed and the network bandwidth is not sufficient to fulfill the users' demands. In this paper, we propose a mobile network infrastructure based on swarming drones[1] to utilize the unused wireless medium of the sky and provide high mobility free from the ground obstacles. We believe that it is the first paper of utilizing a swarm of drones to provide a network infrastructure. The core objective of our proposed system is to provision network services to a designated area where the original network infrastructure is disabled or malfunctioning. Proposed system will be used to construct a network infrastructure on demand. Throughout this paper, we primarily focus on introducing our prototype and provide a preliminary result of the user using a swarm of drones to connect to the Internet.

## 2. DESIGN OF THE PROPOSED SYSTEM

We designed the proposed system based on the three main modules: drone module, network module, and ground station module. The drone module is designed to control the mobility of the drone while it is flying to the area where the network service is needed. We utilized the legacy flight controller and extended its technical features so that the drones can exchange their information through the network module and fly as a swarm of drones. Furthermore, the network module is built on a computing device that enables the connectivity among the drones within the swarm and the user. In specific, we utilized two communication interfaces where one is for enabling network connection for the user and the other is to maintain communication among the drones. Instead of relying on the legacy networking devices, we have implemented the networking infrastructure software within the computing device and we control communications based on our designed network protocol. Lastly, our ground control station manages the proposed system by commanding the swarm of drones to deploy at the designated location. The service provider can utilize our ground control station to command the swarm of drones.

[1]In this paper, we refer a multirotor as a drone.


*MobiSys'15,* May 18–22, 2015, Florence, Italy.
ACM 978-1-4503-3494-5/15/05.
http://dx.doi.org/10.1145/2742647.2745914.

## 3. PERFORMANCE EVALUATION

In this section, we briefly describe the preliminary result. Figure 1(a) illustrates the experimental setting of our preliminary experiment and Figure 1(b) is the result of a network throughput when a mobile device is connected to a swarm of drones. The video of the preliminary experiment is available at [1]. All of the communications are done through the TCP/IP protocol. The $y$-axis illustrates the network throughput in megabits per second (*Mbits/s*) and $x$-axis is the elapsed time. In this figure, we can see that the average throughput is 2.58 $Mbits/s$. Further, the highest network throughput that we were able to achieve was 9.05 $Mbits/s$. However, we observed that at certain interval of time, the network throughput was degraded. Based on this study, we learned that further research on stabilizing network throughput is needed.

## 4. ACKNOWLEDGMENTS

Authors of this paper contributed equally. This work was supported by Samsung Research Funding Center of Samsung Electronics under Project Number SRFC-IT1401-09.

## 5. REFERENCES

[1] S. Yoo. Swarming drones can connect you to the network. [Video] Retrieved from `http://youtu.be/zqRQ9W-76oM`, 2015.

# Poster: Constructing a Unique Profile for Mobile User Identification in Location Recommendation Systems

Muawya H. Sarnoub Eldaw
Dept. of Computer Science
Birkbeck, University of London
eldaw@dcs.bbk.ac.uk

Mark Levene
Dept. of Computer Science
Birkbeck, University of London
mark@dcs.bbk.ac.uk

George Roussos
Dept. of Computer Science
Birkbeck, University of London
g.roussos@dcs.bbk.ac.uk

## Categories and Subject Descriptors

H.1.1 [**Systems and Information Theory**]: Information Theory.

## Keywords

Mobility Traces; Fingerprint; Location Recommendation

## 1. INTRODUCTION

It has been established in previous research that only a small number of spatio-temporal points are enough to uniquely identify an individual [1]. This means, if a user $u$ visited the set of locations $\{a,b,\ldots,z\}$ then only a small number of these locations would be enough to prove the uniqueness of the mobility traces of $u$. In this research however, we argue that a profile constructed from such a small set of spatio-temporal points would not be very useful in the context of location prediction and recommendation. Indeed in such context, finding a distinct set of data that makes the individual unique is not the key point. It is much more useful to have a rich profile that, in addition to being unique also reflects the individual's interest in terms of the places that they visit and the activities that they undertake. Such a profile clearly offers a distinct advantage where it allows grouping together individuals with similar interest and taste. The ability to create such grouping is the foundation upon which collaborative prediction and recommendation systems are developed. Setting aside the sensitive privacy issues, we have been investigating the possibility of constructing a dynamic method of identification using mobility data which, for each individual user possesses measurable variations that make it suitable for *'mobility fingerprinting'*.

## 2. MOBILITY FINGERPRINT

We define a *Mobility Fingerprint* as a profile constructed from the user's historical mobility traces. To build such a profile, we propose a method that is a principled and scalable implementation of a variable length Markov model based on *n-grams*[1] [2]. Each trail is a sequence of spatio-temporal points that the user follows in a day. A user's *Mobility Fingerprint* contains all the *n-grams* generated from his trails.

We collect a sample of fingerprints from the publicly available Nokia Mobile Data Collection Campaign data set [3], which is relatively small but sufficient for proof of concept. We find that users have unique mobility fingerprints. Furthermore, we find that an observed mobility trail can be associated with the fingerprint of the user to whom the trail belongs, i.e. a user can be identified by his movements. Figure 1, shows the result of the experiment in which we identify the correct user from an observed trail of five spatio-temporal points. The Jaccard and Kullback-Leibler measures were used to compute the similarity between the fingerprints and the observed trail. The precision and recall were achieved within a given similarity threshold.

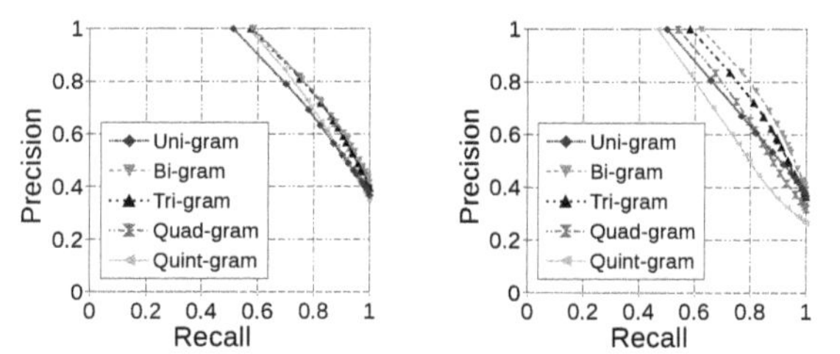


*Jaccard* *Kullback-Leibler Divergence*

**Figure 1: Identifying the user from his movements.**

## 3. REFERENCES

[1] Y.-A. de Montjoye, C. A. Hidalgo, M. Verleysen, and V. D. Blondel. Unique in the crowd: The privacy bounds of human mobility. *Scientific reports*, 3, 2013.

[2] M. H. S. Eldaw, M. Levene, and G. Roussos. Collective suffix tree-based models for location prediction. In *Proceedings of the 2013 ACM conference on Pervasive and ubiquitous computing adjunct publication*, pages 441–450. ACM, 2013.

[3] J. K. Laurila, D. Gatica-Perez, I. Aad, J. Blom, O. Bornet, T. M. T. Do, O. Dousse, J. Eberle, and M. Miettinen. The mobile data challenge: Big data for mobile computing research. In *Mobile Data Challenge by Nokia Workshop, in conjunction with Int. Conf. on Pervasive Computing, Newcastle, UK*, 2012.

[1] an *n-gram* is a contiguous sequence of $n$ spatio-temporal points in a given mobility trail.


*MobiSys'15,* May 18–22, 2015, Florence, Italy.
ACM 978-1-4503-3494-5/15/05.
http://dx.doi.org/10.1145/2742647.2745904.

# Poster: Detection of Cyberbullying in a Mobile Social Network: Systems Issues

Homa Hosseinmardi, Sabrina Arredondo Mattson, Rahat Ibn Rafiq, Richard Han, Qin Lv, Shivakant Mishra
Department of Computer Science, University of Colorado Boulder, Boulder, CO, USA
{homa.hosseinmardi,Sabrina.Mattson,rahat.rafiq}@colorado.edu

## ABSTRACT

Cyberbullying is a major problem affecting more than half of all American teens, and has been attributed to suicidal behavior among teens. Instagram, a media-based mobile social network, is one of the most popular social networks used for cyberbullying. In this paper, we describe the development of classifiers to detect cyberbullying in Instagram. We identify systems issues that need to be considered in the design of a cyberbullying detection system.

## 1. INTRODUCTION

Cyberbullying has been defined as intentionally aggressive behavior that is *repeatedly carried out* in an online context against a person *who cannot easily defend him or herself* [1]. It is important to this definition of cyberbullying that both the frequency of negativity and the imbalance of power between the victim and perpetrator be taken into account. Prior work has either largely ignored this proper definition, labeling data according to a looser definition of cyberaggression that ignores frequency and imbalance of power, or simply analyzed negative word usage without labeling [2].

We applied this stricter definition of cyberbullying to labeling of Instagram data collected from 25K Instagram users. These public profiles were collected using a snowball sampling method, resulting in 697K media sessions (images plus associated comments). We chose a subset of the media sessions with the highest percentage of negativity, i.e. those with more than 40% of comments with at least one negative word (and a minimum of 15 comments total), since such highly negative media sessions should give us a higher likelihood of identifying cyberbullying. This gave us about 1000 media sessions, which were labeled by workers on CrowdFlower according to our stricter definition of cyberbullying.

To design and train the classifier, our ground truth criterion was that if a media session was labeled by three out of five workers as cyberbullying, then the media session was seen as cyberbullying. This resulted in 52% of media sessions being labeled as cyberbullying. Three types of features were evaluated, namely those features obtained from the content of comments, images and graph properties based on the profile owner. Unigrams and lower case 3-grams were used as input features for SVM while image features and the number of followers, followed by's and likes were inputs for the Naïve Bayes classifier. *The Table shows that the SVM classifier achieves high accuracy, precision and recall above 80%.*

| classifier | accuracy | precision | recall |
|---|---|---|---|
| Linear SVM | 0.85 | 0.88 | 0.84 |
| Naïve Bayes | 0.74 | 0.74 | 0.78 |

**Table 1: Cyberbullying detection's classifiers performance by 5-Fold cross validation**

Our performance evaluation of the classifiers found that Naïve Bayes is about 32K times faster than SVM in the training phase, and is about 4K times faster than SVM in the prediction phase, the latter of which is what would be experienced when running the classifiers online. However, these values don't consider feature extraction time. Naïve Bayes is currently trained on images manually labeled as people, car, tattoo, etc. We would need to develop automated image processing algorithms that can extract these image categories, which is compute-intensive. A typical N-gram is also compute-intensive, with dimensionality of ˜300K.

To build a scalable system for cyberbullying detection in Instagram, which has over 300 million active users, we propose a distributed mobile cloud architecture that enables scaling while avoiding overloading of cloud servers with too much classification. First, users' mobile devices will prefilter all user media sessions that have insufficient negativity, e.g. in our sample, this drastically cuts the number of media sessions to be processed by the cloud server from 700K down to the 1000 most negative media sessions. Next, for these sessions, image and/or text feature extraction is also performed on the mobile. Finally, only these features are sent to the cloud server for classification. This hybrid mobile+cloud architecture better enables the server to scale to meet the demands of near real-time cyberbullying detection.


*MobiSys'15*, May 18–22, 2015, Florence, Italy.
ACM 978-1-4503-3494-5/15/05.
http://dx.doi.org/10.1145/2742647.2745908.

## References

[1] Kowalski, R. M.; Limber, S.; Limber, S. P.; and Agatston, P. W. 2012. Cyberbullying: Bullying in the digital age. John Wiley and Sons.

[2] H. Hosseinmardi, R. Rafiq, S. Li, Z. Yang, R. Han, Q. Lv and S. Mishra, "A Comparison of Common Users across Instagram and Ask.fm to Better Understand Cyberbullying". The 7th IEEE Intl. Conf. on Social Computing and Networking (SocialCom), Dec. 2014.

# Poster: A Hybrid Indoor Audio Localization System

Lito Kriara[1], Giorgio Corbellini[1], Vladimir Vukadinovic[1], Ruben Kaelin[1,2], Roman Frigg[1,2], Stefan Mangold[1]
[1]Disney Research Zurich, 8006 Zurich, Switzerland
[2]ETH Zurich, 8092 Zurich, Switzerland
lito|giorgio|stefan@disneyresearch.com

User localization with mobile devices remains a challenging research problem if the environment or required accuracy prevent the use of satellite navigation (GPS). In this paper, we present a hybrid system that performs real time localization on a mobile device, using the audio signals emitted by nearby loudspeakers. Such an approach is useful in controlled environments with background music and sound, such as shopping centers, malls, or entertainment theme parks (Fig. 1). Two known audio identification methods are used in combination: (1) watermarking [1] with hidden location markers and (2) fingerprinting [2] with sound matches in a database. Based on the performance of the two methods in terms of accuracy and energy consumption, a particle filter-based hybrid combination [3] of CRC-based watermarking and fingerprinting is proposed. Our localization scheme runs as stand-alone mobile application and enables a user to identify the current location. It also respects the user's privacy as it runs locally on a mobile device. We present the testbed implementation and experimental evaluation in an indoor environment with respect to the presence of noise, interference, user mobility, and power consumption. This implementation is the first step towards fine-grained localization using sound in the future.

**Figure 1: Concept art (© Disney): Theme park guests use park's sound system for localization in an attraction.**

| | Open area | Obstacle area | Power | Freq. |
|---|---|---|---|---|
| Idle | – | – | 753 mW | – |
| GPS | – | – | 2263 mW | – |
| Watermarking | 84.6% | 95.8% | 1379 mW | 112 |
| Fingerprinting | 92.5% | 97.6% | 960 mW | 233 |
| Naive combination | 92.4% | 97.1% | 1906 mW | 287 |
| Hybrid | 100% | 100% | 1069 mW | 21 |

**Table 1: Accuracy, power consumption and average frequency of responses of our hybrid system compared to fingerprinting, watermarking and their naive combination. GPS could not provide location results for our indoor testbed.**

Table 1 shows the percentage of times that the mobile device is able to correctly recognize its location using different localization methods. In the worst case, the accuracy of audio localization is close to 85% using watermarking in an open and interference prone space, whereas in the best case the accuracy is 97.6% in an obstacles setup employing the audio fingerprinting. As expected, the naive combination of the two methods (i.e., when both the audio watermarking and fingerprinting run in parallel) performs similarly to the best single mechanism without improving it. CRC-based watermarking is used for the Hybrid and it is able to eliminate mismatches, due to the particle filter mechanism, which only reports locations with the high confidence. Therefore, there are fewer responses compared to the other schemes (Table 1). Clearly, the Hybrid is the method providing location estimates less frequently, but still within acceptable limits for a location-based application.

Finally, Table 1 also shows the average power consumption of the smartphone application for the various methods. We see that our proposed Hybrid not only provides high accuracy but also consumes 53% less power than the commonly used GPS, which fails to provide location estimates indoors.


*MobiSys'15,* May 18–22, 2015, Florence, Italy.
ACM 978-1-4503-3494-5/15/05.
http://dx.doi.org/10.1145/2742647.2745910.

## 1. REFERENCES

[1] R. Frigg et al. Multi-Channel Acoustic Data Transmission to Ad-hoc Mobile Phone Arrays. In *ACM SIGGRAPH Mobile*, 2013.

[2] S. Baluja and M. Covell. Waveprint: Efficient Wavelet-based Audio Fingerprinting. *Elsevier Pattern Recognition*, 41(11), 2008.

[3] J. Hightower and G. Borriello. Particle Filters for Location Estimation in Ubiquitous Computing : A Case Study. In *ACM UbiComp*, 2004.

# Poster:TVisor — A Practical and Lightweight Mobile Red-Green Dual-OS Architecture

Wenhao Li, Liang Liang, Mingyang Ma, Yubin Xia, Haibo Chen
Institute of Parallel and Distributed Systems
Shanghai Jiao Tong University

## 1. INTRODUCTION

Mobile and embedded system software designer are often torn between choosing security and functionality. In particular, the security of out-of-band execution environment is sensitive to rich functionality. ARM TrustZone has been used to develop a Trusted Execution Environment (TEE), which runs in parallel with rich functionality commodity OS and provides an isolated execution context for trusted applications. TrustZone splits access of the processor, memory and peripherals into two different worlds, namely normal world and secure world. The secure world is more privileged and it's the recommended context to implement TEE. However, despite its security, the functionality is very limited.

Hardware virtualization could balance the tradeoff between security and functionality by creating two VMes atop of the hardware. However, most of embedded and mobile devices lack hardware virtualization support, which makes it hard to deploy.

Red-green dual-OS design, which provides a highly-protected and constrained trusted environment ("green" OS) to perform secure sensitive tasks and a general purpose environment ("red" OS) for all other tasks and applications, is an attractive design to achieve both security and functionality. Red-green dual-OS architecture uses resources partition instead of virtualization to achieve its goal and has been deployed in many mobile devices by running the red OS in normal world and the green OS in secure world of ARM TrustZone. However, even red-green dual-OS provides an isolated environment and rich functionality, the two OSes are not created equally: a compromise of the green OS would also result in the compromise of the red OS since secure world is more privileged.

We show that how TVisor, a lightweight dual-OS architecture that creates two born-equal OS and each of them could still use the secure services of TEE in secure world, balances security and functionality for mobile devices. TVisor could be deployed to many low-cost embedded and mobile devices which are equipped with ARM TrustZone but without hardware virtualization support.

## 2. DESIGN AND IMPLEMENTATION

Figure 1 shows the overall software architecture when deploying TVisor. In secure world, a secure OS and TEE are deployed, which

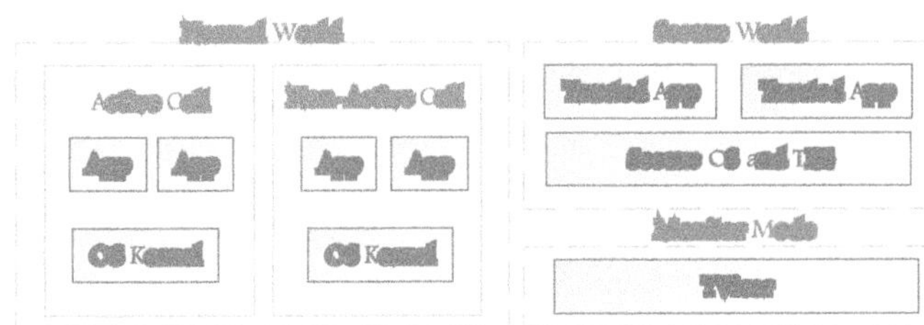

Figure 1: Mobile software architecture with TVisor

provide trusted execution environment for trusted applications and APIs for normal world applications. A Cell is introduced in normal world, which is a wrapper of a commodity OS. There are two Cells running in normal world, corresponding to red and green OS, and at most one Cell is active at the same time. When a Cell is active, its memory is set to be non-secure while the rest memory is set to secure memory so as to prevent the active Cell from tampering with the other Cell and software running in secure world. An active Cell could communicate with the TEE services running in secure world. TVisor runs in monitor mode and is responsible for managing states of the two Cells, including devices partition and management, Cell switching and scheduling. TVisor provides APIs for a Cell to register some real-time tasks notification so that the Cell could handle these critical tasks (i.e., phone call) when it is non-active.

**Comparison with hypervisor:** TVisor tries to minimize the abstraction layer as much as possible. For memory management, TVisor simply guarantees the isolation between Cells and let the Cell itself do the management. Consider CPU virtualization, hypervisor provides a virtual CPU to a VM while TVisor gives the real CPU view to Cells and manages the external unmarkable interrupts (i.e., secure timer, Cell notification) to schedule Cells. For IO devices sharing, hypervisor virtualizes the devices in a multiplex manner while TVisor takes the dynamic device partitioning way.

The beauty of TVisor is that it is a practical, lightweight and secure solution to meet dual-OS requirement for mobile and embedded devices. We implement a prototype of TVisor in ARM Cortex-A9 processor using Fast Model, which runs two vanilla Linux in Cells and T6 [1] secure OS in secure world. The OS runs at native speed and the switch time between Cells is negligible (3.32 $\mu$s).

## 3. REFERENCES

[1] T6: an arm trustzone based secure os for mobile devices. http://www.trustkernel.org, 2015.


*MobiSys'15,* May 18–22, 2015, Florence, Italy.
ACM 978-1-4503-3494-5/15/05.
http://dx.doi.org/10.1145/2742647.2745915.

# Poster: A Continuous and Noninvasive User Authentication System for Google Glass

Ge Peng*, David T. Nguyen*, Gang Zhou*, Shuangquan Wang†
*College of William and Mary, USA, †Institute of Computing Technology, Chinese Academy of Sciences, China
{gpeng, dnguyen, gzhou}@cs.wm.edu, wangshuangquan@ict.ac.cn

## Categories and Subject Descriptors

D.4 [**Security and Protection**]: Authentication

## Keywords

Continuous authentication; Google Glass

## 1. INTRODUCTION

Google Glass stores many kinds of user data, including contacts information, messages and emails, photos and videos, and much more. This brings privacy risks to the owner. To protect user privacy, Google Glass uses four touch gestures selected by the owner from eight pre-defined gestures to authenticate users. This is invasive and also susceptible to peeking. In this work, we propose a continuous and noninvasive authentication system for Google Glass, named GlassGuard. GlassGuard discriminates the owner and an imposter with touch behavioral biometrics and voice features, which are available during a user's normal daily usage. Touch behavioral biometrics have been studied on smartphones. However, due to user interaction differences between Google Glass and smartphones (e.g. holding smartphones with hand(s) but wearing Google Glass on head, different gestures), systems proposed for smartphones cannot be applied directly on Google Glass.

## 2. DESIGN AND EVALUATION

Figure 1 shows the system architecture. Event Monitor continuously monitors user input events when the screen is on. The event data is then forwarded for feature extraction. For a touch event, a set of features are extracted from both touch data and sensor data. For a voice command, MFCC vectors are extracted. After features are extracted from a user event, they are passed to one of the classifiers depending on the event type. There are 7 classifiers in the system, each for a specific type of user event (T-Classifier for single tap, SF-Classifier for swipe forward, SB-Classifier for swipe backward, SD-Classifier for swipe down, TFSF-Classifier for two-finger swipe forward, TFSB-Classifier for two-finger swipe forward, and VC-Classifier for voice command). All classifiers are trained with one-class SVM model and they make predictions independently. The Aggregator employs a mechanism adapted from Threshold Random Walking [1] to combine multiple classification results and make the final decision when and only when it is confident. The Power Control module decides when to pause or restart data processing (feature extraction and classification) and sensor sampling according to the current privacy risk level.


*MobiSys'15*, May 18–22, 2015, Florence, Italy.
ACM 978-1-4503-3494-5/15/05.
http://dx.doi.org/10.1145/2742647.2745906..

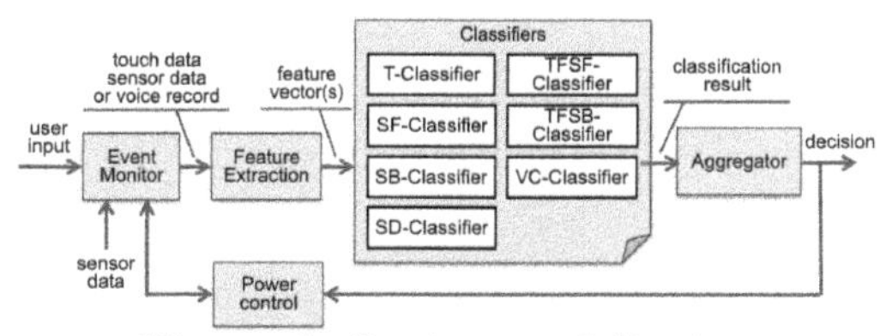


**Figure 1: System architecture**

We carry out a user study and collect real user interaction data from 32 subjects. With the data collected, we evaluate the performance of the classifiers as well as the whole system. Figure 2 shows the mean and standard deviation of Equal Error Rate for each classifiers in the system. Two-finger touch gestures provide lower EERs than one-finger touch gestures and VC-Classifier has the lowest EER 4.88%.

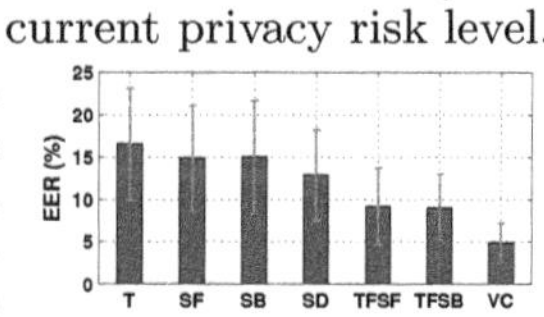


**Figure 2: Classifiers**

Table 1 shows the average performance of the system under five typical usage scenarios: 1) skim through the timeline. 2) delete a picture in the timeline. 3) take a picture and share it using voice commands. 4) take a picture and share it using touch gestures. 5) Google search. The decision delay is the number of events needed for the system to make a decision. Scenario 1 has the worst performance because it only consists of swipe forward gestures. Scenario 3 has voice commands. So, it has the best performance. Under all scenarios, the system has detection rate >93% and false alarm rate <3% after less than 5 user events.

**Table 1: system performance**

| No. | detection rate | false alarm rate | decision delay |
|---|---|---|---|
| (1) | 93.3% | 2.84% | 4.27 |
| (2) | 96.7% | 1.42% | 4.66 |
| (3) | 99.6% | 0.24% | 2.25 |
| (4) | 97.4% | 0.87% | 4.73 |
| (5) | 98.1% | 1.08% | 4.63 |

This work was supported in part by U.S. National Science Foundation under grant CNS-1250180 and CNS-1253506 (CAREER).

## 3. REFERENCES

[1] J. Jung, V. Paxson, A. W. Berger, and H. Balakrishnan. Fast portscan detection using sequential hypothesis testing. In *Security and Privacy*. IEEE, 2004.

# Poster: A Context Simulation Harness for Realistic Mobile App Testing

Manoj R. Rege, Vlado Handziski, and Adam Wolisz
Telecommunication Networks Group, Technische Universität Berlin, Germany
{rege,handzisk,wolisz}@tkn.tu-berlin.de

## 1. CONTEXT SIMULATION

Accurate performance testing of mobile apps require comprehensive simulation of real world context in a mobile emulator viz. location, sensor values, network conditions etc. Existing mobile emulators support such simulation, however they lack the capability for automated generation of **realistic, correlated, and dependent** context traces. As a result, the burden of their generation and injection is left to the developers who have to create their own traces. This is not straightforward: there are heterogenous remote databases of traces, mathematical models and trace files can be used as well, but the trace values should be correlated, and traces have to be converted to a common format. We are developing *ContextMonkey* - a framework that addresses these concerns by leveraging context traces from databases such as FourSquare [1], OpenSignal [2], Google Street View [3]. It acts as a harness to mobile emulators, and aims at improving the efficiency of mobile app performance tests.

## 2. DESIGN AND IMPLEMENTATION

The *ContextMonkey* design is data-source and emulator independent, modular, and is easily extensible to new context simulation scenarios. Its architecture (shown in figure 1a) is organized into three layers:

1) ***Trace Layer*** orchestrates extraction of correlated traces from various data-sources. In case of external databases, this includes: handling authorization and authentication for using database APIs, configuring correct parameters for API calls to obtain correlated context trace values, and modifying received trace value units and attributes if necessary. For example, an image trace might need modification of resolution, and file format attributes. It also handles failures due to trace unavailability by interpolating or extrapolating their values, and from exceeded API usage limits of the databases by signaling them to the higher layer. Finally, it converts traces from database specific formats to an internal representation format and forwards it to the layer above.

2) ***Context Layer*** specifies the context modality definitions: physical sensor sampling rates, their correlations, virtual sensor functions over different physical sensor values etc. It generates trace requests using these definitions and forwards them to the Trace layer. It computes virtual sensor functions based on the received trace values. Accordingly, it temporarily stores each received trace value copy in a queue to account for delay variations in fetching them. Finally, it forwards all context trace values to the higher layer.

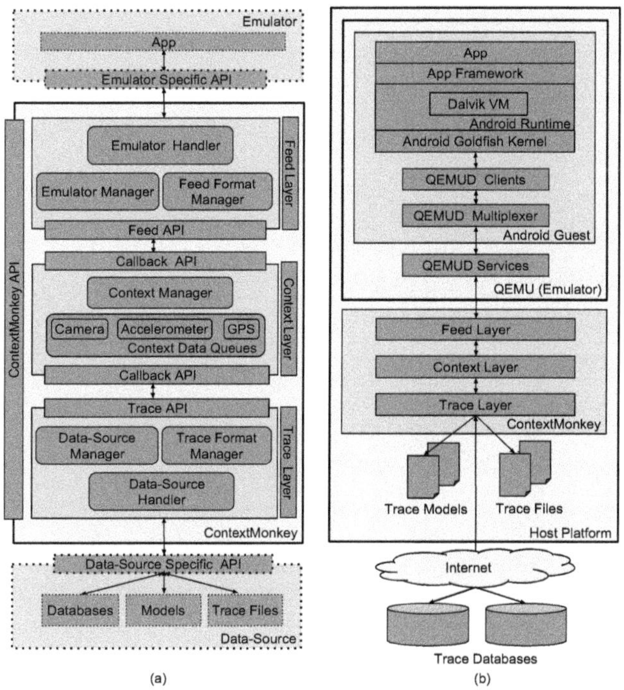


**Figure 1: *ContextMonkey* Architecture**

3) ***Feed Layer*** provides the glue to bind the framework to the specific emulator. It converts the received context trace values to the emulator specific format, and makes API calls to the emulator to feed these values.

The *ContextMonkey* prototype integration with Android emulator using the emulator Telnet service is shown in Figure 1b. The emulator implements a QEMU Daemon service, and clients that send the context trace values to the Android Goldfish Kernel which makes them available to the app. We have integrated the Google Street View database with the prototype to fetch location dependent images, and feed them to the emulator camera. We are currently in process of evaluating the prototype performance.

## 3. REFERENCES

[1] Foursquare. `https://developer.foursquare.com/`.
[2] Opensignal maps. `http://opensignal.com`.
[3] Google street view. `https://www.google.com/maps/views/streetview`.


*MobiSys'15,* May 19-22, 2015, Florence, Italy.
ACM 978-1-4503-3494-5/15/05.
http://dx.doi.org/10.1145/2742647.2745913.

# Poster: Localized Content for Village Schools


Morgan Vigil
Dept. of Computer Science
UC Santa Barbara
Santa Barbara, CA
mvigil@cs.ucsb.edu

David Johnson
Center for Industrial and Scientific Research
Cape Town, South Africa
djohnson@csir.co.za

Elizabeth Belding
Dept. of Computer Science
UC Santa Barbara
Santa Barbara, CA
ebelding@cs.ucsb.edu


## 1. INTRODUCTION

Studies on global Internet connectivity report that only 40% of the world population has access to the Internet [1]. While Internet connectivity has the potential to provide numerous educational opportunities, there is often a lack of educational content that is relevant with respect to the culture and language of those attending schools in largely disconnected communities. Inspired by the problem of sharing relevant educational content within and between schools, we extend VillageShare to facilitate content sharing between village schools that are networked together via low-bandwidth wireless links. Originally designed to localize social media content in a single community [2], the extended version of VillageShare operates across multiple sites to ensure that relevant educational content is 1) highly available to local users and 2) made globally available using a robust synchronization protocol. This design enables village teachers and students to create regional repositories of relevant digital curricula that are accessible even during network failures and outages.

## 2. SYSTEM OVERVIEW

The VillageShare system consists of a logical core (ownCloud Server), a social networking layer (Friends Application), a multi-server support layer (MultiInstance Application), synchronization directories, and a MySQL database that stores user information and user content information. VillageShare servers act as local content repositories that are fully functional during times of disconnection. VillageShare servers are networked together by long-distance wireless links or over the Internet. When VillageShare servers are connected, servers located near a high-bandwidth Internet link act as coordinators between VillageShare servers placed in resource-poor environments. A subset of the VillageShare database tables are synchronized between remote VillageShare servers and a central server. There is a trade-off between robustness to equipment failure and minimizing bandwidth requirements. Equipment failure is a documented challenge of deploying technical systems in rural developing contexts [3]. Likewise, limited bandwidth capacity is another significant challenge for these systems. Thus, creating full backups of all content and all database tables




*MobiSys'15,* May 18–22, 2015, Florence, Italy.
ACM 978-1-4503-3494-5/15/05.
http://dx.doi.org/10.1145/2742647.2745911.


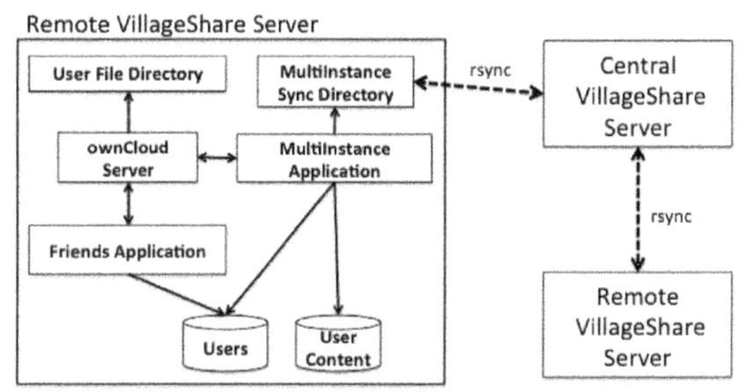


**Figure 1: Overview of VillageShare components.**

hosted by a rural VillageShare server would be inconceivable due to the bandwidth requirements. We address this trade-off by providing a backup of database tables required for content maintenance and sharing. Even though ownCloud provides database tables for maintaining app configuration, file versioning, deleted files, and system preferences, only user profiles, friendships, file metadata, and file contents are backed up at the central VillageShare server. This is done by storing data for remote backup in queued database tables. When it is time for synchronization, files are synchronized between remote synchronization directories using the Unix rsync utility[1]. Remote servers only maintain a single directory that corresponds with the central server through which they coordinate. Central servers maintain synchronization directories for each remote server they coordinate. Feasibility tests with laboratory evaluations of this synchronization process demonstrate that the latency of file synchronization for a single gigabyte file is less than 22 minutes for a link experiencing a bursty loss rate of 10% and a link latency of 3 seconds. Synchronization of a single gigabyte file scales linearly for link latencies up to 2 seconds. We are currently working with CSIR to deploy VillageShare in local South African schools.

## 3. REFERENCES


[1] International Telecommunications Union, "The World in 2014," `http://www.itu.int/en/ITU-D/Statistics/Documents/facts/ICTFactsFigures2014-e.pdf`, November 2014.

[2] David L Johnson, Veljko Pejovic, Elizabeth M Belding, and Gertjan van Stam, "VillageShare: Facilitating Content Generation and Sharing in Rural Networks," in *Proceedings of the 2nd ACM Symposium on Computing for Development*, Atlanta, Georgia, USA, March 2012, pp. 61–70.

[3] E. Brewer, M. Demmer, M. Ho, R.J. Honicky, J. Pal, M. Plauche, and S. Surana, "The Challenges of Technology Research for Developing Regions," *Pervasive Computing, IEEE*, vol. 5, no. 2, pp. 15–23, April 2006.


[1]http://linux.die.net/man/1/rsync

# Poster: Context-Triggered Mobile Network Measurement


Shichang Xu* Ashkan Nikravesh* Hongyi Yao* David R. Choffnes† Z. Morley Mao*

*University of Michigan †Northeastern University



## ABSTRACT

While the availability and accessibility of cellular network connectivity have improved in recent years, our ability to diagnose and debug network problems in this environment has not. One key challenge is that many of the network problems occur near the edge of the network where only mobile devices can perceive them, but network and battery resources to conduct measurements from these mobile devices are scarce. Traditional network measurement approaches that use continuous, periodic, or random measurements are either infeasible or ineffective in this environment.

In this work, we propose an alternative approach: triggering measurements based on relevant device context such as signal strength and historical performance data, which can inform decisions for when to measure current network performance. This context can be collected locally on the device as well as aggregated at a global scale to schedule measurement based on data collected from multiple devices. By carefully selecting when to conduct a measurement, and using prediction to improve the likelihood that triggered measurements will succeed, we can more reliably measure important network phenomena with less overhead. Using Mobilyzer [3] as a platform for evaluation, we propose an architecture that is sufficiently general to support a wide range of triggered measurement experiments. We demonstrate the use of this framework for measurements on mobile platforms that are traditionally difficult to capture, e.g., handoff measurement. Further, we can use the global scheduler to predict which devices will likely satisfy the preconditions for the triggered measurement to improve the measurement success rate.

Compared to previous work [2, 1, 4], ours is the first to propose a general framework to enable context-triggered mobile measurement, leveraging both local and global visibility into context while ensuring low overhead.


## 1. DESIGN

We design a framework that supports triggered measurement based on device context, including location, signal strength, movement and historical performance data collected from previous active measurements and passive monitoring. Figure 1 shows how the global scheduler can trigger measurements based on global context, including data from multiple devices and events from external sources, such as outage reports. After receiving measurement tasks from the server, clients will listen for corresponding context-based events and trigger measurements once the precondition is satisfied.

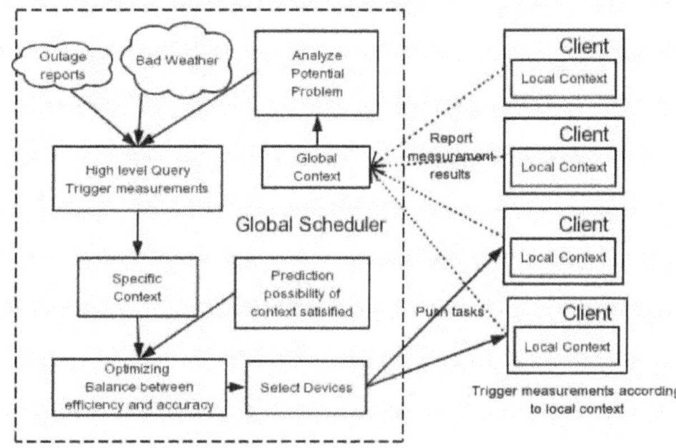


Figure 1: Framework for context-triggered measurement.

## 2. USE CASE

Context-triggered measurements facilitate efficient capture of transient events. For example, handoff between different cell sectors or different access technology can have non-negligible impact on network performance metrics such as throughput and delay. Since handoffs are determined by the signal strength received by the device from each cell, we can predict the handoff by monitoring the signal strength context and trigger measurements only just before the handoff occurs to understand its impact.


## 3. REFERENCES

[1] M. Allman and V. Paxson. A reactive measurement framework. In *PAM*. 2008.

[2] A. Gember, A. Akella, J. Pang, A. Varshavsky, and R. Caceres. Obtaining in-context measurements of cellular network performance. In *IMC*, 2012.

[3] A. Nikravesh, H. Yao, S. Xu, D. Choffnes, and Z. M. Mao. Mobilyzer: An open platform for controllable mobile network measurements. In *Mobisys*, 2015.

[4] M. A. Sánchez, J. S. Otto, Z. S. Bischof, D. R. Choffnes, F. E. Bustamante, B. Krishnamurthy, and W. Willinger. Dasu: Pushing experiments to the internet's edge. In *NSDI*, 2013.





*MobiSys'15,* May 18–22, 2015, Florence, Italy.
ACM 978-1-4503-3494-5/15/05.
http://dx.doi.org/10.1145/2742647.2745905.

# Poster: Emergency Management Using SHERLOCK

Roberto Yus and Eduardo Mena
University of Zaragoza, Spain
{ryus,emena}@unizar.es

## 1. INTRODUCTION

Emergency management has attracted the focus of mobile computing research in the last years due to the flexibility that it provides in critical scenarios. The lack of a pre-existing infrastructure or even a communication breakdown are important issues that mobile computing can deal with. In addition, Semantic Web techniques to handle the data in these scenarios, such as knowledge representation and reasoning, have been proven useful.

In the SHERLOCK project [1] we are developing a general system to provide users with interesting Location-Based Services (LBSs) that can help in emergency management. SHERLOCK executes on mobile devices and leverages their communication mechanisms to exchange information among them. The system uses: 1) ontologies and semantic reasoners to handle knowledge about LBSs and interesting objects, and 2) mobile agents to balance CPU consumption and communication load.

## 2. APPROACH

Thanks to its flexibility, SHERLOCK can handle emergency scenarios when provided with knowledge about them. For example, let us imagine that there has been a traffic accident in a secondary road (see Figure 1):

1. An emergency call is issued by drivers of cars involved or cars themselves. SHERLOCK's ontology defines that emergency calls trigger a request for assistance to emergency units in the area (defined in the ontology as police units, medical units, etc.). If the accident occurs in an area without 3G coverage, then SHERLOCK creates a network of agents that try to find any emergency unit nearby. The mobile agents jump from car to car and they find a police station nearby.

2. The police station receives the call with information about the accident (cars involved and their locations). The corresponding authority executes the service to manage an emergency that is defined in its local ontology as asking hospitals and fire stations near the accident to send units to a specific location and obtaining the real-time location of emergency units assigned to the accident (i.e., ambulances, firetrucks, etc.).

3. Coordinators of the hospital and fire station nearest to the accident receive the request for assistance through SHERLOCK and send ambulances and firetrucks. The ontology defines that obtaining pictures/videos of the accident would help coordinators to estimate the magnitude of such an event (i.e., number of cars involved, smoke, fire) and the kind of resources needed.

4. SHERLOCK triggers a request for pictures/videos to devices near the accident. A network of agents move to devices with cameras near that location and ask them to take pictures/videos which are sent to incoming emergency units to be prepared in advance and to coordinators to evaluate if more units are needed.

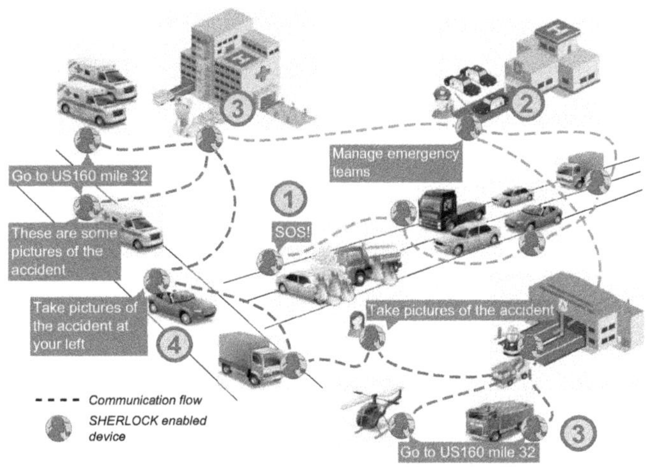


**Figure 1: Emergency management scenario.**

Therefore, SHERLOCK's flexibility in terms of the services offered (ontologies defining new services can be incorporated on the fly) and the execution of these services (wireless ad hoc communications are used when 3G is not available) are useful for emergency management. A prototype of the system and more information are available at [2].

## Acknowledgments

Work supported by TIN2013-46238-C4-4-R and DGA-FSE.

## 3. REFERENCES

[1] R. Yus, E. Mena, S. Ilarri, and A. Illarramendi, *SHERLOCK: Semantic Management of Location-Based Services in Wireless Environments*, Pervasive and Mobile Computing, 2014.

[2] SHERLOCK. `http://sid.cps.unizar.es/SHERLOCK`.


*MobiSys'15*, May 18–22, 2015, Florence, Italy.
ACM 978-1-4503-3494-5/15/05.
http://dx.doi.org/10.1145/2742647.2745909.

# Poster: Location Verification and Recovery for Mobile In-Vehicle Applications

Kexiong (Curtis) Zeng[1], Yanzhi Dou[1], Yaling Yang[1], Ranveer Chandra[2]
[1]Dept. of Electrical and Computer Engineering, Virginia Tech; [2]Microsoft Research
[1]{kexiong6, yzdou, yyang8}@vt.edu; [2]ranveer@microsoft.com

## 1. INTRODUCTION

Location information of vehicles has started to have high value in various mobile applications (valuable shipment tracking, intelligent transportation systems, Waze, Uber etc.). However, current widely-used localization systems are essentially based on wireless signals, which are inherently vulnerable to signal spoofing attacks due to their openness. Attackers have strong incentives to launch location spoofing attacks on these applications to gain benefits and cause chaos, such as surreptitious valuable shipment hijacking, life-threatening intelligent collisions and database manipulation attacks[1].

Existing location verification systems do not work for above scenarios. Because they either require trusted third party, or software and hardware modifications on devices, signals or infrastructure, which are too expensive to implement. Furthermore, some approaches, such as software abstractions for trusted GPS and location crosscheck between multiple wireless localization sources, are also vulnerable to signal spoofing attacks.

This work proposes a novel system, which leverages the correlation between mobile device sensor hints (move, stop, turn, camera image) and location physical features (intersection, stop sign, traffic light, street view etc.), to deliver accurate and timely location verification and recovery for mobile in-vehicle applications. Particularly, our system employs a novel location recovery scheme only using local wireless-independent sensors. Our system is attack-resistant and low-cost, since it is completely wireless-independent, modification-free and infrastructure-independent. The preliminary results indicate impressive performance.

## 2. DESIGN AND IMPLEMENTATION

In this work, we consider an external attacker who does not have physical access to the victim's device but launches location spoofing attacks remotely. We assume that the victim's device is mounted on the windshield of the vehicle. As shown in Figure 1, our system is composed of an offline module executed on a remote server and an online module deployed in a mobile device. (1) **Offline module**: At first, we collect location physical features from online sources (Google Map) to build up a database. We define

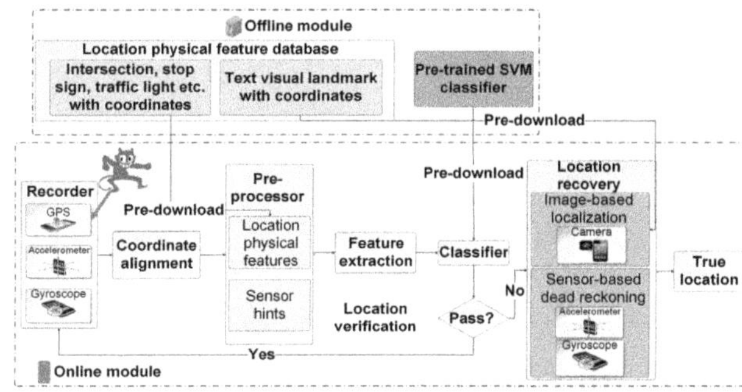


**Figure 1: System architecture.**

textual information appearing in shop signs, road signs, billboards, building walls etc. as text visual landmarks, which are used for image-based localization. Text visual landmarks with coordinates are extracted by applying OCR (Optical Character Recognition) to online geo-tagged images (Google Street View images). Then, we collect each user's normal driving sensor data and generate anomalous data by replacing real GPS data with falsified GPS data to simulate location spoofing attacks. SVM classifiers with different time window sizes are trained and saved in the user's profile. Finally, the user can download his pre-trained classifiers and location physical features as needed. (2) **Online module**: There are two processes – location verification and location recovery. The location verification process records raw sensor data during a configurable time window, aligns the coordinates of the device and the vehicle, detects sensor hints and compares them with pre-downloaded location physical features. Then, a feature vector is established and fed into the classifier, which returns a result of pass or fail. If it fails location verification, the location recovery process is activated. Image-based localization and sensor-based dead reckoning are combined to recover the true location. Specifically, the device automatically takes pictures of the street view and use OCR to extract textual information, which is compared with the pre-downloaded text visual landmarks for location estimation . Between text visual landmarks, a refined sensor-based dead reckoning is employed.

We implement our system on Android platform and evaluate it with different users in Blacksburg, VA. For location verification, we adopt an adaptive-size time window which grows from 1-min to 5-min with a 1-min step size. The average false negative rates are 51.97%, 35.18%, 18.34%, 2.58%, 4.09% and the average false positive rates are always close to zero. The average detection latency is 134s. For location recovery, the average accumulated localization error is 22m.

## 3. REFERENCES

[1] N. O. Tippenhauer, K. B. Rasmussen, C. Pöpper, and S. Čapkun. Attacks on public wlan-based positioning systems. In *Proceedings of the 7th international conference on Mobile systems, applications, and services*, pages 29–40. ACM, 2009.


*MobiSys'15*, May 18–22, 2015, Florence, Italy.
ACM 978-1-4503-3494-5/15/05.
http://dx.doi.org/10.1145/2742647.2745912.

# Author Index


Alessandroni, Giacomo ............ 439
An, Chuankai .................. 197, 455
Báguena, Miguel ...................... 459
Balan, Rajesh Krishna ............... 105
Bao, Xuan ................................ 345
Beigl, Michael .......................... 473
Belding, Elizabeth .................... 491
Benbadis, Farid ........................ 441
Berning, Matthias .................... 473
Bisio, Igor ................................ 475
Bogliolo, Alessandro ............... 439
Borgiattino, Carlo ............ 257, 435
Budde, Matthias ....................... 473
Campbell, Andrew T. ........ 197, 455
Carini, Alberto ......................... 439
Chandra, Ranveer ............ 405, 497
Chen, Bo .................................... 31
Chen, Dongyao ............................ 1
Chen, Haibo ....................... 75, 485
Chen, Peter M. .......................... 137
Chen, Yi-Chao ................... 15, 469
Chen, Yingying ................ 257, 435
Chiasserini, Carla Fabiana ... 435, 257
Cho, Kyong-Tak ........................... 1
Choffnes, David R. .... 493, 389, 467
Chong, Song ............................ 419
Chu, David ...................... 151, 443
Chung, Albert Y. ....................... 477
Conana, Vania .......................... 441
Corbellini, Giorgio ................... 483
Cosnier, Florian ....................... 441
Cox, Landon P. ......................... 121
Cuervo, Eduardo ...... 121, 151, 443
Degtyarev, Yury .............. 151, 443
Delfino, Alessandro ................. 475
Delpriori, Saverio .................... 439
Dias de Amorim, Marcelo ........ 441
Dou, Yanzhi ............................. 497
Eldaw, Muawya H. Sarnoub ..... 479
Fang, Gan ......................... 181, 463
Faye, Sébastien ........................ 445
Feijó Filho, Jackson .. 447, 449, 451
Flinn, Jason ...................... 137, 151
Frank, Raphael ........................ 445
Freschi, Valerio ....................... 439
Frigg, Roman ........................... 483
Gao, Ying ................................ 273
Gelb, Dan ................................ 227
Georgiev, Petko ....................... 273
Go, Younghwan ....................... 419
Gollakota, Shyamnath ................ 45
Gordon, Mark S. ........................137
Govindan, Ramesh .................... 89
Grizan, Sergey ..........................151
Gross, Thomas ..................453, 461
Gruteser, Marco ................257, 435
Gummeson, Jeremy ..................227
Han, Richard .............................481
Han, Sihui ..................................... 1
Handziski, Vlado ......................489
Hao, Zijiang ..............................287
Hong, David Ke .........................137
Hosseinmardi, Homa ................481
Huang, Chenyu ..........317, 437, 465
Jain, Puneet ...............................331
Jain, Shubham ..................257, 435
Jin, Hongxia ............................. 89
Jin, Zhizhuo ................................ 1
Johnson, David .........................491
Jung, Jongtack ..........................477
Kaelin, Ruben ...........................483
Kim, Donghwi ..........................419
Kim, Hwangnam ......................477
Kim, Kangho ............................477
Kim, Kyu-Han ..........................227
Kim, Yeongjin ..........................419
Klopfenstein, Lorenz ................439
Kohno, Tadayoshi ....................359
Kopf, Johannes .........................151
Kreibich, Christian ...................375
Kriara, Lito ...............453, 461, 483
Lam, Yawhuei ..........................453
Lane, Nicholas D. .....................273
Lattanzi, Emanuele ...................439
Lavagetto, Fabio .......................475
Lebeck, Kiron ...........................121
Lee, Hui-Yu .............................167
Lee, Hyung Kyu .......................477
Lee, Jiyeon ...............................477
Lee, Kyungmin .........................151
Lee, Suk Kyu ............................477
Lee, Youngki ............................105
Lerner, Adam ...........................359
Levene, Mark ...........................479
Li, Haibo ................................... 75
Li, Tianxing ......................197, 455
Li, Wenhao .........................75, 485
Li, Zhuoran .......................181, 463
Liang, Liang .............................485
LiKamWa, Robert ....................213
Lin, Hao-Min ........................... 167
Lin, Kate Ching-Ju ................... 167
Liu, Bin ..................................... 89
Liu, Bin ..................................... 89
Luchetti, Gioele ....................... 439
Lv, Qin .................................... 481
Ma, Mingyang ......................... 485
Mahlke, Scott ........................... 137
Mangold, Stefan ....... 453, 461, 483
Manweiler, Justin .................... 331
Manzoni, Pietro ....................... 459
Mao, Wenguang ....................... 469
Mao, Z. Morley ......... 467, 493, 389
Mao, Zhuoqing Morley ............ 137
Mascolo, Cecilia ...................... 273
Mattson, Sabrina Arredondo ...... 481
Melodia, Tommaso .................. 241
Mena, Eduardo ........................ 495
Mishra, Shivakant .................... 481
Mohapatra, Prasant .......... 301, 471
Moon, YoungGyoun ................ 419
Mujibiya, Adiyan .................... 457
Musuvathi, Madanlal ............... 121
Nandakumar, Rajalakshmi ......... 45
Nath, Suman ............................... 59
Nelakuditi, Srihari .................... 345
Nguyen, David T. ............. 487, 287
Nikravesh, Ashkan .... 389, 467, 493
Nirjon, Shahriar ....................... 227
Ouimet, Kirk ............................ 359
Pamboris, Andreas ................... 459
Paolini, Brendan ...................... 439
Park, KyoungSoo ..................... 419
Pathak, Parth H. ............... 301, 471
Paxson, Vern ........................... 375
Peng, Chunyi ................... 181, 463
Peng, Ge ......................... 287, 487
Pietzuch, Peter ........................ 459
Prata, Wilson ............ 447, 449, 451
Qi, Xin .................................... 287
Qiu, Lili ............................ 15, 469
Radhakrishnan, Meera ............. 105
Rafiq, Rahat Ibn ...................... 481
Razeen, Ali ............................. 121
Rebecchi, Filippo .................... 441
Rege, Manoj R. ....................... 489
Ren, Yanzhi ..................... 257, 435
Riedel, Till .............................. 473
Roesner, Franziska .................. 359
Roussos, George ..................... 479

Roy Choudhury, Romit ..... 331, 345
Sammarco, Matteo .................... 441
Santagati, G. Enrico .................. 241
Saroiu, Stefan ............................ 121
Saxena, Alisha ........................... 359
Seraghiti, Andrea ...................... 439
Shen, Guobin .................... 181, 463
Shin, Kang G. ............................... 1
Srinivasan, Kannan ..................... 31
Sundaresan, Srikanth ................ 375
Torii, Junji ................................ 457
Tsai, Hsin-Mu ........................... 167
Turley, Ben ............................... 359
Valle, Thiago ........... 447, 449, 451
Vallina-Rodriguez, Narseo ....... 375
Vance, Anthony ........................ 359
Varga, Virag ..................... 453, 461
Vigil, Morgan ........................... 491
Vukadinovic, Vladimir ..... 461, 483
Wang, Anran .....................181, 463
Wang, He ..................................345
Wang, Shuangquan ...................487
Wang, Zeyu ..............317, 437, 465
Watson, Nathaniel ...................... 45
Weaver, Nicholas .....................375
Wei, Yu-Lin ..............................167
Wolf, Alexander L. ....................459
Wolisz, Adam ............................489
Wolman, Alec ...................121, 151
Wu, Hsin-I ................................167
Wu, Muchen .............................301
Xia, Yubin ..........................75, 485
Xiao, Xinran .....................197, 455
Xing, Guoliang ..........................287
Xu, Chao ...................................471
Xu, Shichang ............389, 467, 493
Yang, Qing ...............................287
Yang, Yaling .............................497
Yang, Zhice ............... 317, 437, 465
Yao, Hongyi ............. 389, 467, 493
Yenamandra, Vivek .................... 31
Yi, Yung ...................................419
Yoo, Seungho ...........................477
Yun, Sangki ........................ 15, 469
Yus, Roberto .............................495
Zeng, Bing ........................ 181, 463
Zeng, Kexiong (Curtis) ............. 497
Zhang, Chi ...............................405
Zhang, Jiansong ........ 317, 437, 465
Zhang, Li ..................................301
Zhang, Nairan .......................... 105
Zhang, Qian ............... 317, 437, 465
Zhang, Xinyu ...........................405
Zhao, Yixin ....................... 301, 471
Zhong, Lin ...............................213
Zhou, Gang ....................... 287, 487
Zhou, Xia ......................... 197, 455

www.ingramcontent.com/pod-product-compliance
Ingram Content Group UK Ltd.
Pitfield, Milton Keynes, MK11 3LW, UK
UKHW051415290926
15471UKWH00009B/1611

9 781450 334433